Dover Memorial Library
Gardner-Webb University
P.O. Box 836
Boiling Springs, N.C. 28017

HANDBOOK
OF
TEST DEVELOPMENT

HANDBOOK OF TEST DEVELOPMENT

Edited by

Steven M. Downing
University of Illinois at Chicago

Thomas M. Haladyna
Arizona State University

LAWRENCE ERLBAUM ASSOCIATES, PUBLISHERS
2006   Mahwah, New Jersey   London

Editorial Director:	Lane Akers
Editorial Assistant:	Karen Willig-Bates
Cover Design:	Tomai Maridou
Full-Service Compositor:	TechBooks
Text and Cover Printer:	Hamilton Printing Company

This book was typeset in 10/12 pt. Times Roman, Italic, Bold, and Bold Italic.
The heads were typeset in Helvetica, Helvetica Italic, Helvetica Bold, Helvetica Bold Italic.

Copyright © 2006 by Lawrence Erlbaum Associates, Inc.
All rights reserved. No part of this book may be reproduced in
any form, by photostat, microform, retrieval system, or any
other means, without prior written permission of the publisher.

Lawrence Erlbaum Associates, Inc., Publishers
10 Industrial Avenue
Mahwah, New Jersey 07430
www.erlbaum.com

Library of Congress Cataloging-in-Publication Data

Handbook of test development / edited by Steven M. Downing, Thomas M. Haladyna.
   p. cm.
  Includes bibliographical references and index.
  ISBN 0-8058-5264-6 (casebound : alk. paper)—ISBN 0-8058-5265-4 (pbk. : alk. paper)
  1. Educational tests and measurements—Design and construction—Handbooks, manuals, etc.
  2. Psychological tests—Design and construction—Handbooks, manual, etc.
  I. Downing, Steven M.   II. Haladyna, Thomas M.
LB3051.H31987   2006
371.26′1—dc22   2005030881

Books published by Lawrence Erlbaum Associates are printed on
acid-free paper, and their bindings are chosen for strength and durability.

Printed in the United States of America
10 9 8 7 6 5 4 3 2 1

Contents

Preface ix
Steven M. Downing and Thomas M. Haladyna

I. FOUNDATIONS

1. Twelve Steps for Effective Test Development 3
   Steven M. Downing
2. The Standards for Educational and Psychological Testing: Guidance in Test Development 27
   Robert L. Linn
3. Contracting for Testing Services 39
   E. Roger Trent and Edward Roeber
4. Evidence-Centered Assessment Design 61
   Robert J. Mislevy and Michelle M. Riconscente
5. Item and Test Development Strategies to Minimize Test Fraud 91
   James C. Impara and David Foster
6. Preparing Examinees for Test Taking: Guidelines for Test Developers and Test Users 115
   Linda Crocker

II. CONTENT

7. Content-Related Validity Evidence in Test Development 131
   Michael Kane
8. Identifying Content for Student Achievement Tests 155
   Norman L. Webb
9. Determining the Content of Credentialing Examinations 181
   Mark Raymond and Sandra Neustel
10. Standard Setting 225
    Gregory J. Cizek

III. ITEM DEVELOPMENT

11. Computerized Item Banking — 261
C. David Vale

12. Selected-Response Item Formats in Test Development — 287
Steven M. Downing

13. Item and Prompt Development in Performance Testing — 303
Catherine Welch

14. Innovative Item Formats in Computer-Based Testing: In Pursuit of Improved Construct Representation — 329
Stephen G. Sireci and April L. Zenisky

15. Item Editing and Editorial Review — 349
Rebecca A. Baranowski

16. Fairness Reviews in Assessment — 359
Michael Zieky

17. Language Issues in Item Development — 377
Jamal Abedi

18. Anchor-Based Methods for Judgmentally Estimating Item Statistics — 399
Ronald K. Hambleton and Stephen J. Jirka

19. Item Analysis — 421
Samuel A. Livingston

IV. TEST DESIGN

20. Practical Issues in Designing and Maintaining Multiple Test Forms for Large-Scale Programs — 445
Cathy LW Wendler and Michael E. Walker

21. Vertical Scales — 469
Michael J. Young

22. Developing Test Forms for Small-Scale Achievement Testing Systems — 487
Paul Jones, Russell W. Smith, and Diane Talley

23. Designing Ability Tests — 527
Gale H. Roid

24. Designing Computerized Adaptive Tests — 543
Tim Davey and Mary J. Pitoniak

25. Designing Tests for Pass–Fail Decisions Using Item Response Theory — 575
Richard M. Luecht

V. TEST PRODUCTION AND ADMINISTRATION

26. Test Production Effects on Validity — 599
Dan Campion and Sherri Miller

27. Test Administration — 625
Rose C. McCallin

28. Considerations for the Administration of Tests to Special Needs Students: Accommodations, Modifications, and More — 653
Martha L. Thurlow, Sandra J. Thompson, and Sheryl S. Lazarus

VI. POSTTEST ACTIVITIES

29. Practices, Issues, and Trends in Student Test Score Reporting 677
Joseph M. Ryan

30. Technical Reporting and Documentation 711
Douglas F. Becker and Mark R. Pomplun

31. Evaluating Tests 725
Chad W. Buckendahl and Barbara S. Plake

32. Roles and Importance of Validity Studies in Test Development 739
Thomas M. Haladyna

VII. EPILOGUE

Epilogue 759
Cynthia Board Schmeiser

Author Index 761
Subject Index 773

Preface

The *Handbook of Test Development* is a systematic and comprehensive source of information about developing tests of knowledge, skills, and ability. The *Handbook* presents the state of the art of developing tests in the twenty-first century. Historically, issues and practices concerning test development have received little scholarly, scientific attention in the academic discipline of educational and psychological measurement; most research and writing has focused on the more statistical issues of testing. Yet the development of tests and all the many issues and practices associated with producing achievement and ability tests occupy a central and critically important role in any testing program.

The field of educational and psychological measurement has changed dramatically in the past decade. Computer-based and computer-adaptive testing, Item Response Theory, generalizability theory, and the unified view of validity are now part of the landscape of many testing programs. Even with such major changes to the theory and practice of educational and psychological measurement and the delivery of tests, the activities associated with high-quality test development remain largely unchanged and mostly undocumented. This *Handbook* seeks to provide information about sound testing practices in a way that will be useful to both test developers and researchers studying issues that affect test development.

The purpose of this *Handbook* is to present a comprehensive, coherent, and scholarly-but-practical discussion of all the issues and sound practices required to construct tests that have sufficient validity evidence to support their intended score interpretations. Well-respected scholars and practitioners of the art and science of developing tests of achievement and ability have contributed chapters to this volume. Each chapter provides practitioners with a useful resource upon which they can rely for well-supported, practical advice on developing tests.

The art and science of test development is usually learned in testing agencies, primarily as "on the job training," with standard practices—based on sound educational measurement theory—handed down from master to apprentice. Graduate educational measurement programs may teach a course or offer a seminar on test development issues, but graduate students often complete doctoral educational measurement programs with little or no insight into or experience with the actual hands-on sound practices associated with developing tests. Psychometric theory presents the foundation for all necessary test development activities, but the nexus between theory and actual practice may not always be readily apparent. The *Handbook* presents a comprehensive guide to test developers for every stage of test development—from the planning stage, through content definition and item or prompt development, to test production, administration, scoring, and reporting.

The *Standards for Educational and Psychological Testing* (AERA, APA, & NCME, 1999) provide a backdrop for all the test development issues discussed in this volume. Chapter authors refer the reader to the relevant *Standards* supporting their discussions, with frequent notation of specific validity evidence that is associated with aspects of test development discussed.

PART I. FOUNDATIONS

Part I of the *Handbook* covers essential aspects of test development that provides a foundation for any testing program. In Chapter 1, Steven Downing introduces the *Handbook of Test Development* by overviewing a detailed model for developing effective tests. Each chapter in this book connects with this chapter in some important way. Robert Linn in Chapter 2 discusses the history of standards in test development and provides a rationale for using the *Standards for Educational and Psychological Testing*, which are imbued throughout this *Handbook*. In Chapter 3, Roger Trent and Edward Roeber discuss the important process of obtaining bids for testing services and contracting for these services. Chapter 4, by Robert Mislevy and Michelle Riconscente, discusses the exiting development known as evidence-centered assessment design. This chapter shows the potential for integrating validity with test development throughout the process of creating a test. James Impara and David Foster, in Chapter 5, present a perspective about security that is becoming increasingly important in high-stakes testing. The last chapter in Part I, by Linda Crocker, deals with the perils and responsibilities of test preparation.

PART II. CONTENT

One primary type of validity evidence comes from knowing the specific content of a test, particularly educational achievement and credentialing tests. Michael Kane in Chapter 7 discusses the evolution of the concept of validity evidence that pertains to test content. Chapter 8 by Norman Webb discusses ways in which educators can more effectively define content, and, thereby, increase content-related validity evidence for their tests. Chapter 9, written by Mark Raymond and Sandra Neustel, provides a complement to Norman Webb's chapter, discussing how essential validity evidence is established for professional credentialing examinations through practice or task analysis. Chapter 10 by Gregory Cizek treats the important topic of standard setting—establishing defensible cut scores for tests.

PART III. ITEM DEVELOPMENT

The heart of any testing program is its item bank. Chapter 11 by David Vale discusses the challenges of item banking and presents an ideal model of how computerized item banking should work. Steven Downing in Chapter 12 discusses the essentials of selected-response item development, and Catherine Welch in Chapter 13 provides a complementary treatment of constructed-response item development. Chapter 14, by Stephen Sireci and April Zenisky, presents ideas about novel item formats that may be useful for newer computerized testing programs.

The next five chapters are complementary and rich in advice about what we need to do to test items before each item becomes operational in a test. In Chapter 15, Rebecca Baranowski discusses the need for professional item and test editing and relates important editorial concerns to validity. In Chapter 16, Michael Zieky presents information about reviewing items for fairness and sensitivity. In Chapter 17, Jamal Abedi advises on the threat to validity posed by unfair reading demands in our test items. In Chapter 18, Ronald Hambleton and Stephen Jirka discuss how item writers and content reviewers might use judgments of expected item statistics to augment traditional methods used to increase the size of item banks. Chapter 19, written by Samuel (Skip) Livingston, shows the importance of item analysis in test development, and he augments this emphasis with newer graphical procedures that promise to make item analysis even more informative for evaluating test items.

PART IV. TEST DESIGN

Principles of test design can be found in statistical treatments, but many pragmatic issues remain that are not found in such sources. This section discusses the importance of test design from many perspectives. Chapter 20, by Cathy Wendler and Michael Walker, provides wisdom on designing large-scale multi-form tests. Michael Young's Chapter 21 explicates the methods for creating vertical scales that span more than a single grade level. Paul Jones, Russell Smith, and Diane Talley, in Chapter 22, provide a unique perspective on test design when the number of persons taking the test is small. Gale Roid in Chapter 23 discusses essential methods required for developing tests of ability. Tim Davey and Mary Pitoniak in Chapter 24 discuss the problems encountered in designing a computer-adaptive test in which each item is selected given the examinee's ability estimate. Chapter 25 by Richard Luecht presents an Item Response Theory design for computer-adaptive testing using multiple test modules, in which each module is adapted to the examinee's estimated ability.

PART V. TEST PRODUCTION AND ADMINISTRATION

Although test production and administration may not seem very important in the spectrum of test development, some of the greatest threats to validity come from inappropriate test production and poor administration. Dan Campion and Sherri Miller in Chapter 26 present concepts, principles, and procedures associated with effective test production. Chapter 27 by Rose McCallin provides a perspective from an experienced test administrator on how to give a test that is seamlessly smooth. Finally, Martha Thurlow, Sandra Thompson, and Sheryl Lazarus provide insight into problems we encounter when giving tests to special needs students in Chapter 28.

PART VI. POSTTEST ACTIVITIES

Although the *Handbook* is not concerned with scoring and analysis of item responses, there are other activities that chronologically follow a test that bear on validity in important ways. Chapter 29 by Joseph Ryan presents new information about reporting test scores and sub-scores. Chapter 30 by Douglas Becker and Mark Pomplun discusses technical reporting and its link to validation. Chapter 31 by Chad Buckendahl and Barbara Plake discuss the important process of evaluating tests, a much recommended but often neglected step in testing. Chapter 32 by Thomas Haladyna argues that research is needed in all testing programs, both for increasing validity evidence but also for solving practical problems that test developers face.

EPILOGUE

Written by Cynthia Board Schmeiser, the epilogue provides indications of where we are in test development as well as what we need to accomplish in the future to make test development activities more sound and meaningful. We hope her comments provide a basis for a new and better *Handbook* in the future.

WHAT DOES THE *HANDBOOK* PROVIDE?

The *Handbook* provides a practical and definitive resource for test developers working in all areas of test development. This *Handbook* can also serve as a text or as supplemental readings for academic courses concerned with test development issues, especially at the graduate level. Finally, the *Handbook* serves as a definitive reference book for researchers who are interested in specific problems associated with test development.

ACKNOWLEDGMENTS

The editors are grateful to Lane Akers of Lawrence Erlbaum Associates, who supported this project from the beginning and assisted the many steps from the birth of this project to its conclusion. We are also grateful to each of the authors who contributed chapters to the *Handbook*, sacrificing time from their busy, productive careers to write these chapters. Their efforts made the *Handbook* possible. We also appreciate all the excellent professional support we received from Ms. Joanne Bowser, our project manager at TechBooks.

We are appreciative of all our instructors and mentors, who encouraged our interest and enthusiasm for the art and science of test development; we especially acknowledge the late Robert L. Ebel of Michigan State University, who highly valued test development and inspired his students to do likewise. And to our spouses, Barbara and Beth, who tolerated us during this extra long year, we continue to be ever thankful.

Finally, the editors and chapter authors wish to thank the National Council on Measurement in Education (NCME) for lifelong professional support. We are happy to provide royalties from this book to support NCME's many important efforts to advance educational measurement as a profession.

—Steven M. Downing
—Thomas M. Haladyna

HANDBOOK
OF
TEST DEVELOPMENT

I
Foundations

1

Twelve Steps for Effective Test Development

Steven M. Downing
University of Illinois at Chicago

Effective test development requires a systematic, detail-oriented approach based on sound theoretical educational measurement principles. This chapter discusses twelve discrete test development procedures or steps that typically must be accomplished in the development of most achievement, ability, or skills tests. Following these twelve steps of effective test development, for both selected-response or constructed-response tests, tends to maximize validity evidence for the intended test score interpretation.

These twelve-steps are presented as a framework, which test developers may find useful in organizing their approach to the many tasks commonly associated with test development—starting with detailed planning in Step 1, carrying through to discussions of content definition and delineation, to creating test stimuli (items or prompts), and administering, scoring, reporting, and documenting all important test development activities. Relevant *Standards* are referenced for each step and validity issues are highlighted throughout.

This chapter provides an overview of the content of the *Handbook of Test Development*, with each of the twelve steps referenced to other chapters.

Effective test development requires a systematic, well-organized approach to ensure sufficient validity evidence to support the proposed inferences from the test scores. A myriad of details and issues, both large and small, comprise the enterprise usually associated with the terms *test development* and *test construction*. All of these details must be well executed to produce a test that estimates examinee achievement or ability fairly and consistently in the content domain purported to be measured by the test and to provide documented evidence in support of the proposed test score inferences.

This chapter discusses a model of systematic test development, organized into twelve discrete tasks or activities. All of the activities and tasks outlined in this chapter are discussed in detail in other chapters of this volume, such that this chapter may be considered an overview or primer for the content of the *Handbook of Test Development*. This chapter is not intended to be a comprehensive discussion of every important issue associated with test development or all of the validity evidence derived from such activities. Rather, this chapter presents a potentially useful model or template for test developers to follow so that each important test development activity receives sufficient attention to maximize the probability of creating an effective measure of the construct of interest.

This particular organization of tasks and activities into twelve discrete steps is somewhat arbitrary; these tasks could be organized differently such that there were fewer or more discrete steps. Each of these steps must be accomplished, at some level of detail, for all types of tests, whether the format is selected response (e.g., multiple choice), constructed response (e.g., short answer essay), or performance (e.g., high-fidelity simulation), and whatever the mode of test administration—traditional paper-and-pencil or computer based. The intensity and technical sophistication of each activity depends on the type of test under development, the test's purpose and its intended inferences, the stakes associated with the test scores, the resources and technical training of the test developers, and so on; but all of the tasks noted in this chapter must be carried out at some level of detail for every test development project.

These twelve steps provide a convenient organizational framework for collecting and reporting all sources of validity evidence for a testing program and also provide a convenient method of organizing a review of the relevant *Standards for Educational and Psychological Testing* (American Educational Research Association [AERA], American Psychological Association [APA], National Council on Measurement in Education [NCME], 1999) pertaining to test development. Each of these steps can be thought of as one major organizer of validity evidence to be documented in a technical report which summarizes all the important activities and results of the test. Each of these steps is also associated with one or more *Standards* (AERA, APA, NCME, 1999) that apply, more or less, given the exact purpose of the test, the consequences of test scores, and the desired interpretation or inferences from the test scores.

Table 1.1 lists the twelve steps of test development and provides a brief summary of tasks, activities, and issues; selected relevant *Standards* (AERA, APA, NCME, 1999) are also noted in Table 1.1 for each step. These steps are listed as a linear model or as a sequential timeline, from a discrete beginning to a final end point; however, in practice, many of these activities may occur simultaneously or the order of some of these steps may be modified. For example, if cut scores or passing scores are required for the test, systematic standard setting activities may occur (or a process may begin) much earlier in the test development process than Step 9 as shown in Table 1.1. Item banking issues are shown as Step 11, but for ongoing testing programs, many item banking issues occur much earlier in the test development sequence. But many of these activities are prerequisite to other activities; for example, content definition must occur before item development and test assembly, so the sequence of steps, although somewhat arbitrary, is meaningful.

Much of the information contained in this chapter is based on years of experience, learning what works and what does not work, in the actual day-to-day practice of test development. The relevant research literature supporting the best practice of test development comes from many diverse areas of psychometrics and educational measurement. The Millman and Greene chapter (1989) and the Schmeiser and Welch chapter (in press) in *Educational Measurement* inspire these 12-steps for effective and efficient test development.

STEP 1: OVERALL PLAN

Every testing program needs some type of overall plan. The first major decision is: What construct is to be measured? What score interpretations are desired? What test format or combination of formats (selected response or constructed response/performance) is most appropriate for the planned assessment? What test administration modality will be used (paper

TABLE 1.1
Twelve Steps for Effective Test Development

Steps	*Example Test Development Tasks*	*Example Related Standards*
1. Overall plan	Systematic guidance for all test development activities: construct; desired test interpretations; test format(s); major sources of validity evidence; clear purpose; desired inferences; psychometric model; timelines; security; quality control	Standard 1.1 Standard 3.2 Standard 3.9
2. Content definition	Sampling plan for domain/universe; various methods related to purpose of assessment; essential source of content-related validity evidence; delineation of construct	Standard 1.6 Standard 3.2 Standard 3.11 Standard 14.8
3. Test specifications	Operational definitions of content; framework for validity evidence related to systematic, defensible sampling of content domain; norm or criterion referenced; desired item characteristics	Standard 1.6 Standard 3.2 Standard 3.3 Standard 3.4 Standard 3.11
4. Item development	Development of effective stimuli; formats; validity evidence related to adherence to evidence-based principles; training of item writers, reviewers; effective item editing; CIV owing to flaws	Standard 3.6 Standard 3.7 Standard 3.17 Standard 7.2 Standard 13.18
5. Test design and assembly	Designing and creating test forms; selecting items for specified test forms; operational sampling by planned blueprint; pretesting considerations	Standard 3.7 Standard 3.8
6. Test production	Publishing activities; printing or CBT packaging; security issues; validity issues concerned with quality control	N/A
7. Test administration	Validity issues concerned with standardization; ADA issues; proctoring; security issues; timing issues	Standard 3.18 Standard 3.19 Standard 3.20 Standard 3.21
8. Scoring test responses	Validity issues: quality control; key validation; item analysis	Standard 3.6 Standard 3.22
9. Passing scores	Establishing defensible passing scores; relative vs. absolute; validity issues concerning cut scores; comparability of standards: maintaining constancy of score scale (equating, linking)	Standard 4.10 Standard 4.11 Standard 4.19 Standard 4.20 Standard 4.21
10. Reporting test results	Validity issues: accuracy, quality control; timely; meaningful; misuse issues; challenges; retakes	Standard 8.13 Standard 11.6 Standard 11.12 Standard 11.15 Standard 13.19 Standard 15.10 Standard 15.11
11. Item banking	Security issues; usefulness, flexibility; principles for effective item banking	Standard 6.4
12. Test technical report	Systematic, thorough, detailed documentation of validity evidence; 12-step organization; recommendations	Standard 3.1 Standard 6.5

Abbreviations: ADA, Americans with Disabilities Act; CBT, computer-based testing; CIV, construct-irrelevent variance.

and pencil or computer based)? One needs to know how exactly and when to begin the program or process, in what sequence tasks must be accomplished, which tasks depend on the successful completion of other tasks, what timeline must be adhered to, who is responsible for carrying out which specific tasks, how to quality control all major aspects of the testing program, plus literally hundreds of other issues, decisions, tasks, and operational details. Step 1, the overall plan, places a systematic framework on all major activities associated with the test development project, makes explicit many of the most important a priori decisions, puts the entire project on a realistic timeline, and emphasizes test security and quality control issues from the outset.

Many of the most fundamental decisions about the testing program must be made prior to beginning formal test development activities. Each of these fundamental decisions, with its clear rationale, ultimately indicate a major source of validity evidence for the test scores resulting from the testing program.

Examples of Step 1–type tasks and decisions include a clear, concise, well-delineated purpose of the planned test. The purpose of testing forms an operational definition of the proposed test and guides nearly all other validity-related decisions related to test development activities. Ultimately, major steps such as content definition, the methods used to define the test content domain, and the construct hypothesized to be measured by the examination are all directly associated with the stated purpose of the test. The choice of psychometric model, whether classical measurement theory or item response theory, may relate to the proposed purpose of the test, as well as the proposed use of the test data and the technical sophistication of the test developers and test users. For example, if the clearly stated purpose of the test is to assess student achievement over a well-defined sequence of instruction or curriculum, the proposed construct, the methods used to select content to test, and the psychometric model to use are each reasonably clear choices for the test developer. Likewise, if the test's purpose is to estimate ability to select students for a national and highly competitive professional educational program, the inferences to be made from test scores are clearly stated, the major constructs of interest are delineated, and the content-defining methods, psychometric model, and other major test development decisions are well guided.

Many other fundamental decisions must be made as part of an overall test development plan, including: Who creates test items for selected-response tests or prompts or stimuli for performance tests? Who reviews newly written test items, prompts or other test stimuli? How is the item or prompt production process managed and on what timeline? Who is responsible for the final selection of test items or prompts? Who produces, publishes, or prints the test? How is test security maintained throughout the test development sequence? What quality controls are used to ensure accuracy of all testing materials? When and how is the test administered, and by whom? Is the test a traditional paper-and-pencil test or a computer-based test? If required, how is the cut score or passing score established, and by what method? Who scores the test and how are the scores reported to examinees? Who maintains an item bank or item pool of secure test items or performance prompts? What are the key dates on the timeline of test development to ensure that all major deadlines are met? Who is responsible for the complete documentation of all the important activities, data results, and evaluation of the test?

In many important ways, Step 1 is the most important step of the twelve tasks of test development. A project well begun is often a project well ended. This critical beginning stage of test development outlines all essential tasks to be accomplished for a successful testing project and clearly highlights all the important sources of validity evidence required for the testing program. Timelines and responsibilities are clearly stated, creating a reasonable and efficient plan to accomplish all necessary tasks, including allowing sufficient time for adequate quality control procedures and a correction cycle for all detected errors. Detailed, clear test program planning is an important first step toward adequately accomplishing the end goal of preparing, administering, scoring, and analyzing a test and presenting reasonable sources of validity evidence to support or refute the intended inferences from test scores. All types of tests, used for whatever purpose, whether using traditional paper-and-pencil selected-response formats or performance tests using constructed-response formats or high-fidelity simulations benefit from the detailed planning activities of Step 1.

The *Standards* (AERA, APA, NCME, 1999) relating to the tasks of Step 1 discuss the importance of clearly defining the purpose of the test, following careful test development procedures, and providing a definitive rationale for the choice of psychometric model for scoring. For example, in discussing validity evidence, the *Standards* (AERA, APA, NCME, 1999, p. 17) suggest that ".... the validity of an intended interpretation of test scores relies on all the available evidence relevant to the technical quality of a testing system. This includes evidence of careful test construction...."

STEP 2: CONTENT DEFINITION

One of the most important questions to be answered in the earliest stages of test development is: What content is to be tested? All ability and achievement tests rely heavily on content-related validity evidence to make fundamental arguments to support (or refute) specific interpretations of test scores (Kane, chap. 7, this volume). No other issue is as critical, in the earliest stages of developing effective tests, as delineating the content domain to be sampled by the examination. If the content domain is ill defined or not carefully delineated, no amount of care taken with other test development activities can compensate for this inadequacy. The validity of inferences for achievement test scores rests primarily and solidly on the adequacy and defensibility of the methods used to define the content domain operationally, delineate clearly the construct to be measured, and successfully implement procedures to systematically and adequately sample the content domain.

The chapter on practice analysis (Raymond & Neustel, chap. 9, this volume) presents a thorough discussion of this empirical method of content definition, especially in the context of credentialing examinations. The *Standards* (AERA, APA, NCME, 1999) clearly endorse the use of empirical job analysis for selection and employment examinations (Standard 14.8), but leave the methodology for content definition more open-ended for other types of examinations. Webb (chap. 8, this volume) addresses the defining of content in achievement tests.

Content defining methods vary in rigor, depending on the purpose of the test, the consequences of decisions made from the resulting test scores, and the amount of defensibility required for any decisions resulting from test scores. For some lower stakes achievement tests, the content-defining methods may be very simple and straightforward, such as instructors making informal (but informed) judgments about the appropriate content to test. For other very high-stakes examination programs, content definition may begin with a multiyear task or job analysis, costing millions of dollars, and requiring the professional services of many testing professionals.

For high-stakes achievement examinations, test content defining methods must be systematic, comprehensive, and defensible. For instance, a professional school may wish to develop an end-of-curriculum comprehensive achievement test covering the content of a two-year curriculum, with a passing score on this test required to continue on to a third year of professional education. In this example, rigorous and defensible methods of content definition and delineation of the content domain are required; all decisions on content, formats, and methods of content selection become essential aspects of validity evidence. In this situation, faculty and administrators may need to develop systematic, thorough methods to define all the content "at risk" for such a high-stakes test, looking to curricular documents, teaching syllabi, instructional materials and content, textbook content, and faculty judgment to behaviorally and operationally define content. The input of professional measurement specialists is desirable for such a high-stakes testing environment. Instructors might be asked to complete empirical methods similar to practice or job analysis to rate and rank "the importance to test" of content statements, after comprehensive lists of all content had first been identified. Their judgments might be further refined by asking representative faculty to rate the "criticality" of content statements or make some judgments about how essential the content statement is to future learning or to the ultimate successful practice of the professional discipline. From such a multistage content-defining process, a complete content domain could result, from which a sampling plan to guide the creation and selection of item content could then be developed.

Credentialing tests in the professions (or occupations) are often required as one of several sources of evidence of competence to be licensed to practice the profession in a jurisdiction. Public safety is typically the greatest concern for licensing tests, such that the persons using the services of the professional have some minimal confidence in the professional's ability to deliver services safely. Clearly, the content-defining and delineation methods used for such high-stakes tests must be much more rigorous and defensible than for many (if not most) other testing situations. Formal practice or task analysis methods (Raymond & Neustel, chap. 9, this volume) are usually required for these high-stakes tests, because the consequences of misclassifications can have serious impact on both society and the individual professional seeking a license to practice.

Certification examinations in the professions share many of the same content-defining requirements as licensening examinations noted above. Traditionally, certification was thought to be voluntary and "over and above" a basic license to practice. More recently, the distinction between licensure and certification has been blurred in many professions. In some professions, like medicine, certification in a medical specialty (such as General Surgery) is essentially required if the individual hopes to practice in the specialty or subspecialty. The content-defining methods required to support (or refute) validity arguments and support the ultimate defensibility for many such certifying examination programs must be extremely rigorous (Raymond & Neustel, chap. 9, this volume).

The defensibility of the content-defining process is associated with the rigor of the methods employed. One essential feature is the unbiased nature of the methods used to place limits around the universe or domain of knowledge or performance. Further, the requirements for defensibility and rigor of content-defining methods is directly proportional to the stakes of the examination and the consequences of decisions made about individuals from the resulting test scores. Rigor, in this context, may be associated with attributes such as dependability of judgments by content experts or subject matter experts (SMEs), qualifications of the SMEs making the content judgments, the inherent adequacy of the judgmental methods employed (lack of bias), the number, independence, and representativeness of the SMEs, and so on. Empirical methods may be used to support the adequacy of the judgmental methods. For example, it may be important to demonstrate the reproducibility of independent SME judgments by computing and evaluating a generalizability coefficient (Brennan, 2001) for raters or some other statistical index of consistency of ratings.

Methods chosen to define test content are critical and depend on the purpose of the test, the consequences of the decisions made on the basis of the test scores, and the validity evidence needed to support test score interpretations. The definition of test content is ultimately a matter of human judgment. Methods and procedures may be developed and used to minimize bias and increase the objectivity of the judgments, but—in the end—professional judgments by content experts shape the content domain and its definition. Such inherent subjectivity can lead to controversy and disagreement, based on politics rather than content.

STEP 3: TEST SPECIFICATIONS: BLUEPRINTING THE TEST

The process of creating test specifications guides detailed test development activities and completes the operational planning for tests in a systematic manner. *Test specifications* and *test blueprint* are sometimes used almost interchangeably. For this chapter, *test specifications* refers to a complete operational definition of test characteristics, in every major detail, and thus includes what some authors call the *test blueprint*. For example, at a minimum, the test specifications must describe (1) the type of testing format to be used (selected response or constructed response/performance); (2) the total number of test items (or performance prompts) to be created or selected for the test, as well as the type or format of test items (e.g., multiple choice, three option, single-best answer); (3) the cognitive classification system to be used (e.g., modified Bloom's taxonomy with three levels); (4) whether or not the test items or performance prompts will contain visual stimuli (e.g., photographs, graphs, charts); (5) the expected item scoring rules (e.g., 1 point for correct, 0 points for incorrect, with no formula scoring); (6) how test scores will be interpreted (e.g., norm or criterion referenced); and (7) the time limit for each item. A *test blueprint* defines and precisely outlines the number (or proportion) of test questions to be allocated to each major and minor content area and how many (what proportion) of these questions will be designed to assess specific cognitive knowledge levels. The higher the stakes or consequences of the test scores, the greater detail should be associated with the test specifications; detailed test specifications provide a major source of validity evidence for the test. But, at minimum, all test specifications must include some range of expected items/prompts to be selected for each major content category and each major cognitive process level (Linn, chap. 2, this volume).

The test specifications form an exact sampling plan for the content domain defined in Step 2. These documents and their rationales form a solid foundation for all systematic test development activities and for the content-related validity evidence needed to support score inferences to the domain of knowledge or performance and the meaningful interpretation of test scores with respect to the construct of interest.

How do the content defining activities of Step 2 get translated into exact test specifications in Step 3? The rigor and sophistication of the blueprinting methods will depend on the consequences of testing. Table 1.2 presents a simple example of a test blueprint for an achievement examination over a curriculum on test development. This simple blueprint operationalizes judgments about the content appropriate for sampling in this achievement test. In this example, the test developer has allocated the item content in proportion to the amount of instructional time devoted to each topic and has further weighted these allocations using some professional judgment about the relative importance of topics. For example, content dealing with "item

TABLE 1.2
Example Test Blueprint—Achievement Examination on Test Development

Content Area	Recall	Application	Problem Solving	Totals
Content define	4	10	6	20
Test specs	3	8	4	15
Item writing	4	10	6	20
Assembly: print administer	2	5	3	10
Test scoring	3	7	5	15
Test standards	4	10	6	20
Totals	20%	50%	30%	100%

writing" was judged to be about twice as important as content dealing with "test assembly, printing, and administration." Such judgments are subjective, but should reflect the relative emphasis in the curriculum as represented by the instructional objectives. This blueprint further suggests that the test developer has some judgmental basis for allocating one half of all test questions to the cognitive level labeled "application," whereas only 20 percent is targeted for "recall" and 30 percent for higher order "problem solving." These cognitive level judgments must reflect the instructional objectives and the instructional methods used for teaching and learning.

For high-stakes, large-scale examinations such as licensing or certifying examinations, the methods used to operationalize the task or practice analysis are much more formal (e.g., Raymond, 2001; Raymond & Neustel, chap. 9, this volume; Spray & Huang, 2000). Webb's chapter (Webb, chap. 8, this volume) addresses many of these issues for other types of achievement tests, especially those used for high-stakes accountability tests in the schools. Typically, the detailed results of an empirical practice analysis are translated to test specifications using some combined empirical and rational/judgmental method. For example, the empirical results of the practice analysis may be summarized for groups of representative content experts, who are tasked with using their expert judgment to decide which content areas receive what specific relative weighting in the test, given their expert experience.

The *Standards* (AERA, APA, NCME, 1999) emphasize documentation of the methods used to establish test specifications and blueprints, their rationale, and the evidence the test developers present to support the argument that the particular test specification fairly represents the content domain of interest. The *Standards* relating to test specifications and test blueprints emphasize the use of unbiased, systematic, well-documented methods to create test sampling plans, such that the resulting examination can have a reasonable chance of fairly representing the universe of content.

STEP 4: ITEM DEVELOPMENT

This step concentrates on a discussion of methods used to systematically develop selected-response items, using the multiple-choice item form as the primary exemplar. Downing (chap. 12, this volume) discusses the selected-response formats in detail in another chapter and Welch (chap. 13, this volume) discusses development of performance prompts.

Creating effective test items may be more art than science, although there is a solid scientific basis for many of the well-established principles of item writing (Haladyna, Downing, & Rodriguez, 2002). The creation and production of effective test questions, designed to measure important content at an appropriate cognitive level, is one of the greater challenges for test developers.

Early in the test development process, the test developer must decide what test item formats to use for the proposed examination. For most large-scale, cognitive achievement testing programs, the choice of an objectively scorable item format is almost automatic. The multiple-choice format (and its variants), with some ninety years of effective use and an extensive research basis, is the item format of choice for most testing programs (Haladyna, 2004). Test developers need not apologize for using multiple-choice formats on achievement tests; there is strong research evidence demonstrating the high positive correlation between constructed-response and selected-response item scores for measuring knowledge and many other cognitive skills (Rodriguez, 2003). (To measure complex constructs, such as writing ability, a constructed response format is typically required.)

The multiple-choice item is the workhorse of the testing enterprise, for very good reasons. The multiple-choice item is an extremely versatile test item form; it can be used to test all levels of the cognitive taxonomy, including very high-level cognitive processes (Downing, 2002a).

The multiple-choice item is an extremely efficient format for examinees, but is often a challenge for the item writer.

The choice of item format is a major source of validity evidence for the test. A clear rationale for item format selection is required. In practice, the choice of item form—selected response versus constructed response—may quite legitimately rest largely on pragmatic reasons and issues of feasibility. For example, for a large-scale, paper-and-pencil examination program, it may not be cost effective or time efficient to use large numbers of constructed response questions. And, given the research basis supporting the use of multiple choice items (e.g., Downing, 2002a, 2004; Haladyna, 2004; Rodriguez, 2003), the test developer need not feel insecure about the choice of a low-fidelity selected-response format, like the multiple choice format, for an achievement test.

The principles of writing effective, objectively scored multiple-choice items are well established and many of these principles have a solid basis in the research literature (Downing, 2002b, 2004; Haladyna, 2004; Haladyna & Downing, 1989a,b; Haladyna et al., 2002). Yet, knowing the principles of effective item writing is no guarantee of an item writer's ability to actually produce effective test questions. Knowing is not necessarily doing. Thus, one of the more important validity issues associated with test development concerns the selection and training of item writers (Abedi, chap. 17, this volume; Downing & Haladyna, 1997). For large-scale examinations, many item writers are often used to produce the large number of questions required for the testing program. The most essential characteristic of an effective item writer is content expertise. Writing ability is also a trait closely associated with the best and most creative item writers. For some national testing programs, many other item writer characteristics such as regional geographic balance, content subspecialization, and racial, ethnic, and gender balance must also be considered in the selection of item writers. All of these item writer characteristics and traits are sources of validity evidence for the testing program and must be well documented in the technical report (Becker & Pomplun, chap. 30, this volume).

Item Writer Training

Effective item writers are trained, not born. Training of item writers is an important validity issue for test development. Without specific training, most novice item writers tend to create poor-quality, flawed, low-cognitive-level test questions that test unimportant or trivial content. Although item writers must be expert in their own disciplines, there is no reason to believe that their subject matter expertise generalizes to effective item writing expertise. Effective item writing is a unique skill and must be learned and practiced. For new item writers, it is often helpful and important to provide specific instruction using an item writer's guide, paired with a hands-on training workshop (Haladyna, 2004). As with all skill learning, feedback from expert item writers and peers is required. The instruction–practice–feedback–reinforcement loop is important for the effective development and maintenance of solid item writing skills (Jozefowicz et al., 2002).

Competent content review and professional editing of test questions is also an important source of validity evidence for high-stakes examinations. All test items should be written against detailed test specifications; these draft or raw items should then be reviewed and edited by a professional test editor, who has specialized editorial skills with respect to testing. Professional editing of test items is an essential validity requirement for high-stakes examinations (see Baranowski, chap. 15, this volume, for a complete discussion). Competent professional editing of test items increases the accuracy and clarity of the questions and often resolves issues or corrects flaws in item content, thus increasing the validity evidence for the test. Professional editors are often responsible for initiating so-called sensitivity reviews for items, with the goal of reducing or eliminating cultural, ethnic, religious, or gender issues or sensitivities, especially in high-stakes tests (e.g., Baranowski, chap. 15, this volume; Abedi, chap. 17, this volume). Professional test editors often find content errors or inconsistencies, which can be clarified by item authors or item content reviewers. Additional content reviews are required, by independent subject matter experts, for high-stakes examinations. Such independent content reviews, after professional editorial review, strengthen the content-related validity evidence for the test.

All test item writers benefit from specialized training. Some of the worst test item examples are found on instructor-developed tests, at all levels of education (e.g., Mehrens & Lehmann, 1991). Poor quality and flawed test items introduce construct-irrelevant variance (CIV) to the assessment, potentially decreasing student passing rates by increasing the mean item difficulty (Downing, 2002b, 2004). Ideally, all item writers with any responsibility for achievement assessment have some special expertise in item writing and test development, gained through effective training and practice. Unfortunately, this is too often not the case and is one of the major failings of educational assessment at all levels of education, from K–12 to graduate professional education.

The creation of effective test items (or performance prompts) is a challenging but essential step in test development. Because the test item is the major building block for all tests, the methods and procedures used to produce effective test items is a major source of validity evidence for all testing programs. This fact is reflected in at least five separate standards with respect to test items and their creation and production.

STEP 5: TEST DESIGN AND ASSEMBLY

Assembling a collection of test items (or performance prompts) into a test or test form is a critical step in test development. Often considered a mundane task, the validity of the final test score interpretation very much relies on the competent and accurate test assembly process. Quality control is the keyword most associated with test assembly. The absence of errors in the test assembly process often goes unnoticed; errors or serious flaws and omissions in the test assembly process can be obviously glaring and have the potential of seriously reducing the validity evidence for examination scores.

The overall design of the test, planned in detail in Step 1, provides a sound rationale related to the purpose of testing and the planned interpretation and use of the test scores. This formal overall test design creates the theoretical basis for Step 5. Several other chapters in this book address test design issues in detail (see Davey & Pitoniak, chap. 24; Luecht, chap. 25; Roid, chap. 23; Jones, Smith, & Talley, chap. 22; Wendler & Walker, chap. 20; Young, chap. 21, this volume).

The specific method and process of assembling test items into final test forms depends on the mode of examination delivery. If a single test form is to be administered in paper-and-pencil mode, the test can be assembled manually, by skilled test developers (perhaps using computer software to assist manual item selection and assembly). If multiple "parallel" test forms are to be assembled simultaneously, human test developers using advanced computer software can assemble the tests. If the test is to be administered as computer-based, more specialized computer software will likely be needed to assemble multiple test forms to ensure proper formatting of the fixed-length test form for the computer-delivery software. If the test is to be administered as a computer-adaptive test, very advanced computer software (automatic test assembly software) will likely be required to adequately manage and resolve multiple test item characteristics simultaneously to create many equivalent test forms (Luecht, chap. 25, this volume).

For most achievement tests, whatever the delivery mode, the most important validity-related issues in test assembly are the correspondence of the content actually tested to the content specifications developed in Step 3 and the high-level quality control of this entire process. The test assembly step operationalizes the exacting sampling plan developed in Steps 2 and 3 and lays the solid foundation for inferential arguments relating sample test scores to population or universe scores in the domain. This is the essence of the content-related validity argument, which, to be taken seriously, must be independently verifiable by independent, noninvested content experts (see Kane, chap. 7, this volume, for a complete discussion).

Other major considerations in test assembly, at least for traditional paper-and-pencil tests, relate to formatting issues (see Campion & Miller, chap. 26, this volume, for a complete discussion). Tests must be formatted to maximize the ease of reading and minimize any additional cognitive burden that is unrelated to the construct being tested (e.g., minimize CIV). Traditional principles such as formatting items such that the entire item, together with any visual or graphical stimuli, appear on the same page (or frame) falls under this rubric of minimizing the potential CIV associated with overly complex item formatting.

Other formatting issues are more psychometric in nature. For example, the placement of pretest (tryout) items within the test form is a formatting issue of interest and concern. Ideally, pretest items are scattered throughout the test form randomly, to minimize any effects of fatigue or lack of motivation (if items are recognized by examinees as pretest only items). (Such random distribution of pretest items is not always practical or feasible.) Both *Standards* cited as relating to Step 5 address pretest or tryout items, suggesting thorough documentation of the item sampling plan and the examinee sampling plan.

Key Balance of Options and Other Issues

Balance of the position or location of the correct answer is an important principle for all selected-response items assembled into discrete test forms. The principle is straightforward: There should be an approximately equal frequency of correct responses allocated to the first position (e.g., A), and the second position (B), and so on. Approximating this goal is sometimes difficult, given other important constraints from the item writing principles. For example, all options containing numbers must be ranked from high to low or low to high, such that the location of the correct answer cannot be rearranged in such an item. The reason for this key balance principle is that both item writers and examinees have a bias toward the middle position, such that item writers tend to place the correct answer in the middle position and examinees tend to select a middle-position answer as a natural testwise inclination (Attali & Bar-Hillel, 2003).

The placement of *anchor* or *common* items used in a common-item equating design is also a formatting issue with validity implications (Kolen & Brennan, 2004). Ideally, the common items used to link test forms in a classical equating design should appear in a similar location in the new test as they did in the prior test to eliminate any potential "order effect" on the common items' difficulty and/or discrimination. (Because of other operational and practical considerations, it is not always possible to place anchor equating items in exactly the same location.)

Throughout the test assembly process, test developers must be keenly aware of test security issues. Although security of tests and test items is a constant concern throughout all steps of test development, the product of the test assembly stage is a nearly final form of a test. If this test form is compromised in any way, the test must be considered insecure. If the stakes are high, the loss of a near final test form is extremely disruptive and costly (see Impara & Foster, chap. 5, this volume).

Quality control procedures are essential for accurate and successful test assembly methods. Unless effective and thorough quality control methods are devised and implemented, errors of test assembly will occur and these errors will reduce the legitimacy of the final test score interpretation, thus reducing the validity evidence for the scores.

Although many of the details of assembling tests into final forms may seem routine and mundane, the product of Step 5 is the test that examinees will encounter. Test assembly errors reduce validity evidence by introducing systematic error—CIV—to the test (Haladyna & Downing, 2004) and may lead to the invalidation of scores for some test items, which potentially reduces the content-related validity evidence for the test.

STEP 6: TEST PRODUCTION

The production, printing, or publication of examinations is another routine step of test development that is often overlooked with respect to its validity aspects. For example, there appear to be no *Standards* that bear directly on this important test development activity. All the prior test development work comes to fruition in Step 6, where the months or years of prior test development work is finally "cast in stone." Campion and Miller (chap. 26, this volume) discuss test production issues and their effect on test validity issues in detail.

All tests, whether large-scale national testing programs or much smaller local testing programs, must ultimately be printed, packaged for computer administration, or published in some form or medium. Test production activities and their validity implications apply equally to performance tests and selected-response tests. Step 5—Test Production—truly operationalizes the examination, making final all test items, their order, and any visual stimuli associated with the test items. This is "the test," as it will be experienced by the examinee, for better or worse. Clearly, what the examinee experiences as the final test form has major implications for how scores on the test can be interpreted, and this is the critical validity aspect associated with test production.

Security issues are prominent for test production. Human error is the most likely source of test security breaches, even in this era of high-tech computer-assisted test production.

During the production process, whether it be physical test booklet printing or packaging activities for computer-based tests, final test items may be available in some form to more individuals that at any prior time during test development. All reasonable security precautions must be taken during test production, during the electronic transmission of secure test items, secure shipping of printed test copy and printed booklets, and secure destruction of excess secure printed materials. Test production security standards and policies must be developed, implemented, and quality controlled for all high-stakes examinations and should reflect the consequences of testing somewhat proportionally. Independent audits of these security procedures should be carried out periodically, by security professionals, especially for all computer-based security systems. All secure test materials must be locked in limited-access files at all times not in direct use by test developers and production staff. For high-stakes tests, staff should have access only to those materials needed for completing their specified tasks and on a time-limited basis; high security control must be maintained and frequently reviewed and updated for all computer systems (Impara & Foster, chap. 5, this volume).

For printed tests, printers usually can provide some type of off-press copy for final review by test development staff. This final preprinting quality control step is important even for tests that are printed directly from camera-ready copy or from a direct electronic file; typographical errors or other major potential item invalidating errors, which were missed at all other proofreading and quality control stages, can often be identified (and corrected) at this late stage.

Other quality control issues are equally important for test production. For example, if a test is being printed by a printing company or service, test development staff (in addition to printer's staff) must take responsibility for many quality assurance procedures. This may mean that test development staff randomly sample some number of final printed booklets to ensure the completeness of test booklets (e.g., no pages missing) and the overall quality (readability) of the final printed copy, including visual material, and so on.

The quality and readability of final test printing or production is important to the validity evidence for the test (Campion & Miller, chap. 26, this volume). If test items or visual stimuli are unclearly printed, test booklet pages are omitted, items are misordered, or options are out of order, such items are potentially invalidated and must be omitted from final scoring. Production and printing errors (or formatting errors for computer-based tests) can seriously reduce the validity evidence for a test and create an aura of distrust and anxiety concerning many other aspects of the test, its construction, and scoring. Great care and effective quality control measures must be exercised during the final production process for all tests, no matter what the modality of delivery. Maintaining complete control over test security, with independently verifiable audit trails, is essential during the production process.

STEP 7: TEST ADMINISTRATION

The administration of tests is the most public and visible aspect of testing. There are major validity issues associated with test administration because much of the standardization of testing conditions relates to the quality of test administration. Whether the test is administered in local school settings by teachers, in large multisite venues by professional proctors, or by trained staff at nationwide computer-based testing centers, many of the basic practices of sound test administration are the same (see McCallin, chap. 27, this volume, for a detailed discussion of test administration issues and Thurlow, Thompson, & Lazarus, chap. 28, this volume, for a discussion of special needs test administration issues, including Americans With Disabilities Act issues.)

Standardization is a common method of experimental control for all tests. Every test (and each question or stimulus within each test) can be considered a mini experiment (van der Linden & Hambleton, 1997). The test administration conditions—standard time limits, proctoring to ensure no irregularities, environmental conditions conducive to test taking, and so on—all seek to control extraneous variables in the "experiment" and make conditions uniform and identical for all examinees. Without adequate control of all relevant variables affecting test performance, it would be difficult to interpret examinee test scores uniformly and meaningfully. This is the essence of the validity issue for test administration considerations.

Security is a major concern for test administration. For most examinations (e.g., large-scale, high-stakes tests), the entire test development process is highly secure, with extremely limited access to test materials. Much effort and expense are devoted to securing examination items and test forms. This "chain of security" is necessarily widened during test production and becomes extremely wide for large-scale test administration. For paper-and-pencil examinations, which are administered in multiple sites, printed test forms and all testing materials must be securely shipped to test sites; securely received and maintained by proctors; distributed to examinees in a secure, controlled, and auditable fashion; collected, accounted for, and reconciled; and securely reshipped back to the test sponsor. Detailed organizational and logistic planning are required for competent, secure test administration.

For paper-and-pencil test administration, proctoring is one of the most critical issues. For large-scale testing programs, testing agencies typically have a cadre of well-trained and well-experienced proctors available to oversee test administration. These professional proctors are key to successful, secure, well-organized and well-administered national examinations. It is generally preferable to designate a single, highly experienced proctor as "chief proctor" for the testing site; this chief proctor assumes full responsibility for all aspects of the secure test, including supervision of other proctors on site (see McCallin, chap. 27, this volume, for detailed discussion of proctoring).

For large-scale computer-based tests, proctoring is generally delegated to the agency providing the computer test administration network. Computer-based testing changes the test security environment. Some security issues associated with paper-and-pencil testing are eliminated, such as printing of test booklets, shipping secure test materials, distributing printed test forms to examinees, and so on. However, other potential test security vulnerabilities are increased, such as the electronic transmission of secure test items and response data, the need to have large numbers of items available on local computer servers, and the possible use of less well-trained and less professional administrative staff in the testing sites.

The *Standards* associated with test administration generally deal with issues of standardization and examinee fairness, such as time limits, clarity of directions to examinees, and standard conditions for testing.

Test administration is an extremely important component of test development. Competent, efficient, and standardized administration of tests provides important validity evidence for test scores. Deficiencies in the detailed planning and logistics required for high-quality test administration can lead to a serious reduction in validity evidence for the examination. The importance of test administration to validity evidence is equally true for a selected-response test as it is for a performance examination; a performance test typically adds many challenges and complex logistics for administration. Security problems during test administration can lead to the invalidation of some or all examinee scores and can require the test developers to retire or eliminate large numbers of very expensive test items. Improper handling of issues pertaining to the Americans with Disabilities Act (ADA) can lead to legal challenges for the test developers. Improper overuse of ADA accommodations can lead to misinterpretations of test scores and other types of validity issues associated with score misinterpretation.

STEP 8: SCORING EXAMINATION RESPONSES

Test scoring is the process of applying a scoring key to examinee responses to the test stimuli. Examinee responses to test item stimuli or performance prompts provide the opportunity to create measurement. The responses are not the measurement; rather an application of some scoring rules, algorithms, or rubrics to the responses result in measurement (Thissen & Wainer, 2001; van der Linden & Hambleton, 1997).

There are many fundamental validity issues associated with test scoring. The most obvious issue relates to accuracy of scoring. If final test scores are to have valid meaning, especially the meaning that was anticipated by the test developers (a measure of the construct of interest, an adequate sample of the domain of knowledge, and so on), a scoring key must be applied with perfect accuracy to the examinee item responses. Scoring errors always reduce validity evidence for the test and can invalidate the results. Validity evidence can be reduced by either a faulty (inaccurate) scoring key or flawed or inaccurate application of the scoring key to responses. Thus, high levels of quality control of the scoring process are essential to validity.

Scoring can be extremely simple or very complex, depending on the type of test item or stimuli. The responses to single-best-answer multiple choice items are easily scored by computer software, whereas responses to complex computer simulation problems can be more challenging to score reliably. Selected-response items are generally more efficiently and objectively scored than constructed-response items and performance prompts; however, constructed-response and performance items can be scored accurately and reliably by competently trained and monitored scorers or computer software.

All scoring issues, for all types of tests and testing formats—from relatively straightforward selected-response formats to extremely complex performance simulations—concern the accurate representation of examinee performance with respect to the measured construct or the domain of knowledge, skills, or ability (e.g., Thissen & Wainer, 2001). Ideally, the scored examination responses correspond closely (nearly one to one) with the examinee's true state with respect to the domain measured by the test or construct of interest. Insofar as the test scores depart from this one-to-one correspondence, random measurement error or systematic construct-irrelevant measurement error (CIV) has been introduced into the measurement.

Much of psychometric theory begins at the "scored response" point of test development. In Step 8, a basic test scoring process, which is appropriate for nearly all achievement tests, is discussed.

Preliminary Scoring and Key Validation

A preliminary scoring and item analysis with a final verification of the scoring key by content experts is an essential quality control procedure for many tests (see Livingston, chap. 19, this volume, for a complete discussion of item analysis issues).

A final "key validation" or key verification step increases the validity evidence for all examinations. This two-step scoring process is essential for tests containing newly written and non-pretested items, because it is possible that such items may contain invalidating flaws that were not detected during the item writing and review process. *Key validation* is the process of preliminary scoring and item analysis of the test data, followed by a careful evaluation of the item-level data to identify potentially flawed or incorrect items prior to final test scoring (Downing & Haladyna, 1997). This key validation process is nearly identical for selected-response tests and performance tests and should be carried out for all types of test modalities, if possible (e.g., Boulet, McKinley, Whelan, & Hambleton, 2003).

After examinee item responses are scanned from paper-and-pencil answer sheets, response strings are provided from computer-based testing administration, or data are computer entered for performance examinations, an initial scoring and item analysis should be completed. Items that perform anomalously should be identified for final review of the scoring key or other potential content problems by subject matter experts. Item difficulty and item discrimination criteria or ranges for key validation item identification should be developed for every testing program (see Haladyna, 2004, p. 228, for example). Typically, items that are very difficult and/or have very low or negative item discrimination indices are identified for further content review. The key validation criteria should be sufficiently sensitive that all potentially problematic questions are identified for final content review. The results of key validation, such as the number and type of questions identified for review, and the disposition of these items (scored "as is," eliminated from final scoring, or key changed) are a source of validity evidence and should be documented in the technical report.

If large numbers of items are identified for key validation procedures, the criteria are either too liberal or there are serious problems with the item writing and review process. If large numbers of items are eliminated from the final scoring, for reasons of poor item quality or incorrectness of content, content-related validity evidence is compromised.

Final Scoring

Final scoring of the examinee responses follows the preliminary scoring and key validation procedures. The final answer key must be carefully proofread and quality controlled for absolute accuracy. Great care must be taken to ensure the complete accuracy of this final scoring key. Subject matter experts who have direct responsibility for the content of the examination must formally approve the final scoring key, especially if testing services are being provided by some outside or contract agency. If multiple forms of the same examination are used, great care must be taken to ensure the use of the correct scoring key for each test form. All pretest or tryout items must be carefully segregated from the final scoring so that pretest questions do not contribute to the final test score in any way (see Livingston, chap. 19, this volume).

A final item analysis should be completed and reviewed carefully. The final item analysis provides another important quality control step to ensure that any changes made at the key validation stage are accurately reflected in the final scoring. A complete final item analysis includes summary test statistics for the test administration. For tests using classical measurement theory, these statistics include the raw score mean and standard deviation, the mean item difficulty (p-value), mean item discrimination (point-biserial or biserial), range of raw scores, the test score reliability (Alpha/Kuder-Richardson 20), plus other appropriate indices of overall test quality such as some index of pass–fail reproducibility (especially for high-stakes examinations). Summary test statistics are critically important validity evidence and must be thoroughly evaluated and documented. Any anomalies identified by final item analysis or final summary test statistical analyses must be thoroughly investigated and resolved prior to reporting test scores.

If test score scaling or equating procedures are to be carried out, these procedures usually follow the final scoring and item analysis (unless pre-equating methods are used).

The standards related to scoring issues discuss ensuring the correspondence of the scoring rules to the stated purpose of testing and clarity of scoring rules to ensure absolute accuracy of final scores.

The most important emphasis in the test scoring step is complete accuracy. Extreme quality control procedures are required to ensure total accuracy of final test scores, especially for very high-stakes examinations. Any scoring errors included in final test scores reduces validity evidence and credibility of the examination and introduces CIV to scores (Haladyna & Downing, 2004)

STEP 9: ESTABLISHING PASSING SCORES

Many, but not all, tests require some type of cut score (passing score) or performance standard. For tests that require cut scores, content standard interpretations, or "grade levels" attributed to certain test scores or score ranges, the methods and procedures used to establish cut scores are a major source of validity evidence and are an integral part of the test development process (see Cizek, chap. 10, this volume, for a complete discussion of standard setting).

For high-stakes tests, the establishment of defensible cut scores is one of the most critical test development issues. For tests of all types, with any consequences for examinees, the legitimacy of the methods used to identify cut scores is a major source of validity evidence.

Step 9 highlights and generally overviews some of the important issues concerning standard setting. Standard setting is a complex issue with a sound basis in the research literature. Also, it must be noted that methods and procedures used to establish passing scores may take place at several different stages of test development, depending on the methods used and the overarching philosophy of standard setting adopted by the test developers and users. The basic decisions on the type of standard-setting method to use should be made early in the test development process, because extensive planning may be required to successfully implement certain types of standard setting procedures. Further, some methods may require multiple exercises or studies, taking place at different times during the test development process and concluding after the test has been administered.

Relative and Absolute Standard-Setting Methods

All methods of establishing passing scores require human judgment and are therefore somewhat arbitrary (e.g., Norcini & Shea, 1997). All examination passing scores answer the question: How much knowledge (skill or ability) is needed to be classified as having passed the examination? Traditionally, standard-setting methods are dichotomized into two major categories: relative or normative methods and absolute methods. But, there are standard-setting methods that blend characteristics of both relative and normative methods, such as the relative–absolute or Hofstee method (Hofstee, 1983).

Relative standard-setting methods—normative methods—use the actual test performance data, usually from some well-defined group of test takers (e.g., first-time takers of the test) to establish a point on the distribution of test scores to designate as the cut score or passing point (Cizek, 2001). The passing score point on the distribution of scores represents a judgment of someone or some group of qualified individuals who are responsible for making such judgments. For example, relative passing scores might be expressed as a score that is exactly one standard deviation below the mean score of all examinees; a T-score of 45, based on all examinees who took the examination for the first time; or a percentile rank of 30. The emphasis of all normative passing scores is on the relative position of the examinee's score in some distribution of scores. All examinees scoring at or above the selected cut point on the distribution pass the test and all those scoring below that point fail. (Note that it is the method used to establish the passing score that makes the chosen score "relative," not the score metric.) Relative passing scores do not address the absolute competency of examinees or make any judgments about what specific knowledge, skill, or ability has been mastered by the examinee.

Absolute passing score methods employ systematic procedures to elicit expert judgments from SMEs, concerning the amount of knowledge (skill or ability) required on a test to be considered a passing examinee. There are many well-established, well-researched methods commonly used to establish defensible and effective absolute passing scores (Cizek, 2001; Cizek, chap. 10, this volume).

All common methods used to establish absolute passing scores on all types of examinations require expert judgments about the expected performance of a borderline examinee. A *borderline examinee* is usually defined as someone who just barely passes or just barely fails the test; the borderline examinee has an exactly equal probability (50–50) of either passing or failing the test. Some commonly used methods are the Angoff method and its modifications (Angoff, 1971; Impara & Plake, 1997; Downing, Lieska, & Raible, 2003), which requires expected passing score judgments about each individual test question; the Ebel method (Ebel, 1972), which requires judges to make expected passing score judgments for sets of items that have been classified into difficulty and relevance categories, and the Hofstee method (Hofstee, 1983), with both absolute and relative characteristics, which asks judges to state their own expected minimum and maximum passing score and failure rate (proportion of examinees failing the test) on the test and then plots those expert judgments onto actual test data.

The absolute methods are not without their critics. For example, Zieky (1997) suggests that the judgments required of content experts, regarding the expected pass score for borderline examinees, represents an impossible cognitive task. Other controversies concern the amount of performance data to provide the content expert judges, although measurement experts tend toward providing more rather than less empirical performance data to standard setting judges (e.g., Zieky, 2001).

Other, more data-centered methods, such as the contrasting groups method and the borderline groups method, are also used for certain types of performance examinations. In the *contrasting groups method*, the actual test performance of a known group of masters, experts, or highly qualified examinees is plotted against the actual test performance of a known group of nonmasters or those who are known to be non-expert or not qualified. The intersection of the two curves describes the passing score, which can be adjusted to minimize false-positive or false-negative error. The *borderline group method* is similar, but requires a direct expert judgment concerning which examinees are "borderline" in their performance; these judgments are then translated into passing scores on the examination (e.g., Wilkinson, Newble, & Frampton, 2001; Kilminster & Roberts, 2003).

The comparability of passing scores across different forms (different test administrations) is a major validity issue (e.g., Norcini & Shea, 1997). If absolute passing scores are used, it is critical that test score equating be used to maintain the constancy of the score scale. If scores are not equated, even slight differences in mean item difficulty across different test administrations make the interpretation of the passing score impossible and may unfairly advantage or disadvantage some examinees (Kolen & Brennan, 2004). Thus, most of the *Standards* (AERA, APA, NCME, 1999) concerning passing scores discuss equating issues. Other standards for absolute passing score determination address issues of ensuring that the task of the standard-setting judges is clear and that the judges can in fact make reasonable and adequate judgments. Fairness of cut score procedures and attention to the consequences or the impact of passing scores are emphasized by the *Standards* (AERA, APA, NCME, 1999).

In summary, different standard-setting methods, whether the traditional relative methods or the more contemporary absolute methods (or other blended methods), produce different cut scores and passing rates. None of these methods is more correct than other methods. The task of content-expert judges, using absolute standard-setting methods, is not to discover some true passing score, but rather to exercise their best professional judgment in answering the question: How much is enough (to pass)? Passing scores reflect policy, values, expert judgment, and politics. The defensibility and the strength of the validity evidence for passing scores relies on the reasonableness of the unbiased process, its rationale and research basis, and the psychometric characteristics of expert judgments.

STEP 10: REPORTING EXAMINATION RESULTS

Score reporting is an important, often complex, step in test development. The contents and format of an examinee score report should be among the many early decisions made for large-scale testing programs. There are multiple validity issues concerning score reporting and several *Standards* (AERA, APA, NCME, 1999) address the adequacy of requirements for score reporting. Ryan (chap. 29, this volume) discusses elements of score reports and the strategies behind different types of score reports.

For large-scale assessments, the score reporting task is complex (e.g., Goodman & Hambleton, 2004) and is often encumbered with nonpsychometric issues. The score reporting issues emphasized by the relevant *Standards* deal with fairness, timeliness, appropriateness of the score, avoidance of score misunderstanding and misuse, and tangentially, issues of test retake (for failing examinees), and test score challenges.

As with so many other prior steps of test development, absolute accuracy is of the highest importance for all reports of scores. Thus, careful and effective quality control measures are critically important. For large-scale, high-stakes examinations, one of the most catastrophic errors is to publicly distribute incorrect score reports, particularly if the pass–fail status of some examinees changes as a result of the scoring errors. Even somewhat trivial errors associated with score reports, such as typographical errors or formatting errors, can call into question the accuracy of the reported score and degrade the credibility of the entire testing program.

For some types of high-stakes examinations, such as licensure and certification examinations, only the pass–fail results of examinations may be reported to examinees. This practice is considered minimally acceptable. However, many high-stakes testing programs report total test scores, the passing score, and some relevant and informative subscale scores. In general, it is usually appropriate to report as much legitimate and useful information as deemed reasonable, without overinterpreting scores.

Examinees have a right to an accurate, timely, meaningful, and useful report of their test performance. Score reports must be written in language that is understandable to recipients and all appropriate cautions and caveats about misuse of test scores must be clearly and unequivocally stated. All anticipated misuses of the test scores should be clearly labeled; those who provide score reports have an obligation to actively discourage misuse of test scores.

The score scale used to report test results varies by the type of test, the purpose of the examination, and the sophistication of the examinees. For score reporting, the choice of raw scores, percent-correct scores, scaled scores, equated scaled scores, or other types of derived scores should be determined solely on the basis of maximizing communication with the examinee. Whatever score scale is used for reporting, the reported metric should be clearly defined and described in language that is easily understood by the examinee and maximizes the probability of avoiding score misinterpretation. If a passing score is applied to the test results, it is appropriate to generally describe the method or procedures used to establish the passing score and to express the passing score on the same scale as the reported score. If weighted composite scores are reported, the method of establishing the passing score for the composite should be clearly described; likewise, if multiple passing "hurdles" are required, the score report must make this clear. If subscale scores are reported to provide feedback to examinees on their relative strengths and limitations, the subscales must be composed of a sufficient number of test items to ensure a reasonable reliability of the score (i.e., at minimum fifteen to twenty items) and some indication of the standard error of measurement of the subscales should be presented. If subscale scores are reported to examinees solely as feedback on performance and are not used to make pass–fail decisions, the score report must clearly state this fact in language that examinees can easily understand.

The reporting of test scores to examinees is an extremely important step for nearly all types of test development projects. A clear rationale for the type of score report and the reported score scale is essential. Accuracy and absolute clarity of the reported score interpretation are important, as is the active discouragement of score misuse or misinterpretation. Documentation of score reporting activities and their rationale is an important aspect of validity; the score report summarizes, in many important ways, the entire test development program, especially for the examinee and any other legitimate users of test scores.

STEP 11: ITEM BANKING

Secure storage of effective test items is an important step for all on-going testing programs. The process of securely storing test items for potential future use is typically referred to as *item banking* (see Vale, chap. 11, this volume, for a complete discussion of item banking issues).

Because effective test questions are so difficult to develop and so many resources must be used to produce useful test items that perform well, it is sensible to store such questions, together with all their relevant performance data, to reuse such questions on some future form of the examination. Item banks can be as simple as a secure file cabinet using paper copies of examination questions, with the appropriate identifying information and test usage data (such as item difficulty, item discrimination). In practice, most item banking is carried out using computer software systems, from fairly simple and inexpensive to very complex and expensive software systems.

All item banking systems, if they are to be effective, must be sufficiently flexible and adaptable to serve the needs of test developers. All item banking systems must have the capability to securely store and retrieve test items (and visual materials associated with test items), using all relevant variables useful for the test developer. The required sophistication of the item banking system depends greatly on the type and purpose of the testing program. But all item banking systems must, at minimum, permit the storage, sorting, and retrieval of several variables, such as a unique item identification number, content classification of the test questions (with several subclassifications of content), a cognitive-level classification of the test item, and historical item usage information such as the test form identification (years, dates) of prior use, the item difficulty and item discrimination indices for each prior use (Item Response Theory parameters, if appropriate), and any indication of other items in the bank that should not be used on the same form as a given item. Performance examination test materials and prompts may require more versatile and sophisticated item banking systems than those used for selected-response item formats.

For complex computer-based tests, sophisticated item banking software is most likely required. Some commercial item banking software systems can also serve as test item presentation software for computer-based tests delivered either via the Internet or on secure networks. Developers of complex computer-based tests, especially certain types of adaptive computer-based tests, require very sophisticated software storage and retrieval systems capable of sorting multiple variables simultaneously to build test forms, each of which is representative of a complex test blueprint.

Security of item banks is paramount, no matter what methods are used to store test items and prompts. There are obvious validity issues associated with the security of items stored for potential reuse, but no standards (AERA, APA, NCME, 1999) appear to bear directly on "item banking." If item banks are compromised, the score inferences from such items can also be compromised and the validity evidence for the examination can be decreased seriously. Given the size of the item bank and the stakes associated with the examinations constructed from such item banks, the costs associated with a complete item bank security breach could be extensive. (Some high-stakes testing programs value test items at well over $1,000 per item; almost all test items would be valued at least $300 per item; see Vale, chap. 11, this volume).

Item banking is an important and useful discrete step in test development. After effective test questions are written, edited, reviewed, pretested, and administered to examinees, the items with the most effective item characteristics and the best content should always be preserved for potential reuse on another version or form of the test. It is far too difficult and costly to create effective test items that are used only once. Secure item banking provides a mechanism for convenient, efficient storage and retrieval of test items and may assist test developers in increasing the validity evidence for examinations by helping to control many relevant variables associated with test items.

STEP 12: TEST TECHNICAL REPORT

Every testing program with meaningful consequences for examinees should be systematically documented and summarized in a technical report describing all important aspects of test development, administration, scoring, reporting, and test analyses and evaluation. The technical report is the culminating test development activity and serves the major, but often ignored, purpose of providing thorough documentation of all the validity evidence for a test, identifies potential threats to validity, and makes recommendations for improvement in the testing program that may strengthen validity evidence.

The *Standards* (AERA, APA, NCME, 1999) address the need for technical reports (chap. 6), emphasizing the documentation aspects of these reports of test development activities (Becker and Pomplun, chap. 30 this volume, address technical reports in detail). Haladyna (2002) presents a validity-based argument for technical reports in relation to the *Standards*.

Test developers are often reluctant to fully document their testing programs. However, the time and effort spent in such documentation activities are rewarded by the ease of retrieval of important validity data and by their support of research efforts on tests (see Haladyna, chap. 32, this volume, for a complete discussion of validity studies). Furthermore, technical reports preserve essential validity evidence for the historical record, including any recommendations for future testing program improvement (Downing & Haladyna, 1997). The overall quality of tests can be improved by focusing careful attention on technical reporting. The examination technical report is also useful in independent evaluations of testing programs, providing a convenient and systematic summary of all important test development activities for review (see Buckendahl & Plake, chap. 31, this volume, for a detailed discussion of the evaluation of testing programs).

One potentially useful model for a technical report is to use the twelve-steps of test development described in this chapter as the major outline headings to organize the report. Depending on the stakes associated with the testing program, each of these twelve-steps requires a significant amount of detailed documentation. Too much documentation is impossible; too little documentation is all too common. The level of detail in the technical report must allow the reader to form clear judgments about the adequacy of each step in test development and about the validity evidence presented for each stage. Some steps may require more documentation than others. For example, for a new high-stakes credentialing examination, it is extremely important to fully document the content definition methods and procedures (and their results), the procedures used to create test specifications, and the methods used to select and train item writers. The methods used to establish the cut score, together with the passing rates associated with implementation of the cut scores, are also important to thoroughly document.

Technical reports must be developed such that all important validity evidence for the testing program is systematically documented in a manner that is easily accessible to all who have a legitimate need to access this information. Reference to the relevant *Standards* (AERA, APA, NCME, 1999) is appropriate in technical documentation, together with the test developer's evaluation of how the test fulfills the recommendations of the *Standards*.

SUMMARY AND CONCLUSION

These twelve-steps for effective test development provide a structured, systematic process for creating effective testing programs of all types. Most of these steps are required for every test. The higher the stakes associated with test scores, the greater the concern for validity (Linn, chap. 2, this volume). Attention to quality control and test security is a pervasive theme running through each of these test development steps. Test development consists of a series of inter-related activities, many of which depend on some prior step or steps of test development. Careful planning and compulsive execution of this detailed plan leads to tests that more validly measure examinee ability or achievement in the well-defined content domain of interest. Adherence to this plan provides validity evidence from multiple sources, as Messick (1989) suggested.

High-quality test development demands great attention to detail. Test validity evidence is increased or decreased, sometimes markedly, as the attention to detail increases or decreases. From the proofreading of item or performance prompt text to the absolute accuracy of test scoring and reporting, effective quality control methods and procedures must be utilized to ensure that the intended inferences from the test scores are achieved and that CIV is minimized. Systematically following these twelve steps for effective test development helps to ensure maximum test validity evidence for the tests we develop.

ACKNOWLEDGMENTS

The author gratefully acknowledges the research assistant contributions of Cherdsak Iramaneerat, MD, MHPE, to this chapter. Also, the critical reviews and suggestions of Thomas M. Haladyna, PhD, and the insight, inspiration, and thoughtful criticism provided by my students in a graduate-level test development course are appreciated.

REFERENCES

American Educational Research Association, American Psychological Association, & National Council on Measurement in Education. (1999). *Standards for Educational and Psychological Testing*. Washington, DC: American Educational Research Association.

Angoff, W. H. (1971). Scales, norms, and equivalent scores. In R. L. Thorndike (Ed.), *Educational measurement* (2nd ed., pp. 508–600). Washington: American Council on Education.

Attali, Y., & Bar-Hillel, M. (2003). Guess where: The position of correct answers in multiple-choice test items as a psychometric variable. *Journal of Educational Measurement, 40*(2), 109–128.

Boulet, J. R., McKinley, D. W., Whelan, G. P., & Hambleton, R. K. (2003). Quality assurance methods for performance-based assessments. *Advances in Health Sciences Education, 8*, 27–47.

Brennan, R. L. (2001). *Generalizability theory*. New York: Springer-Verlag.

Cizek, G. J. (Ed.) (2001). *Setting performance standards: concepts, methods, and perspectives*. Mahwah, NJ: Lawrence Erlbaum Associates.

Downing, S. M. (2002a). Assessment of knowledge with written test forms. In Norman, G. R., Van der Vleuten, C. P. M., Newble, D. I. (Eds.), *International handbook for research in medical education* (pp. 647–672). Dordrecht, The Netherlands: Kluwer Academic Publishers.

Downing, S. M. (2002b). Construct-irrelevant variance and flawed test questions: Do multiple-choice item writing principles make any difference? *Academic Medicine, 77*(10), S103–104.

Downing, S. M. (2004, April). The effects of violating standard item-writing principles: The impact of flawed test items on classroom achievement tests and students. Paper presented at the Annual Meeting of the American Educational Research Association, San Diego, CA.

Downing, S. M., & Haladyna, T. M. (1997). Test item development: Validity evidence from quality assurance procedures. *Applied Measurement in Education, 10*(1), 61–82.

Downing, S. M., Lieska, N. G., & Raible, M. D. (2003). Establishing passing standards for classroom achievement tests in medical education: A comparative study of four methods. *Academic Medicine, 78*, S85–87.

Ebel, R. L. (1972). *Essentials of educational measurement* (2nd ed.). Englewood Cliffs, NJ: Prentice-Hall.

Goodman, D. P., & Hambleton, R. K. (2004). Student test score reports and interpretive guides: Review of current practices and suggestions for future research. *Applied Measurement in Education, 17*(2), 145–220.

Haladyna, T. M. (2002). Supporting documentation: Assuring more valid test score interpretations and uses. In G. Tindal & T. M. Haladyna (Eds.), *Large-scale assessment for all students: Validity, technical adequacy, and implementation* (pp. 89–108). Mahwah, NJ: Lawrence Erlbaum Associates.

Haladyna, T. M. (2004). *Developing and validating multiple-choice test items* (3rd Ed.) Hillsdale, NJ: Lawrence Erlbaum Associates.

Haladyna, T. M., & Downing, S. M. (1989a). A taxonomy of multiple-choice item-writing rules. *Applied Measurement in Education, 1*, 37–50.

Haladyna, T. M., & Downing, S. M. (1989b). The validity of a taxonomy of multiple-choice item-writing rules. *Applied Measurement in Education, 1*, 51–78.

Haladyna, T. M., & Downing, S. M. (2004). Construct-irrelevant variance in high-stakes testing. *Educational Measurement: Issues and Practice, 23*(1), 17–27.

Haladyna, T. M., Downing, S. M., & Rodriguez, M. C. (2002). A review of multiple-choice item-writing guidelines for classroom assessment. *Applied Measurement in Education, 15*(3), 309–334.

Hofstee, W. K. B. (1983). The case for compromise in educational selection and grading. In S. B. Anderson & J. S. Helmick (Eds.), *On educational testing*, (pp. 109–127). San Francisco, CA: Jossey-Bass.

Impara J. C., & Plake B. S. (1997). Standard setting: An alternative approach. *Journal of Educational Measurement, 34*(4), 353–366.

Jozefowicz, R. F., Koeppen, B. M., Case, S., Galbraith, R., Swanson, D., & Glew, H. (2002). The quality of in-house medical school examinations. *Academic Medicine, 77,* 156–161.

Kilminster, S., & Roberts, T. (2003). Standard setting for OSCEs: Trial of borderline approach. *Advances in Health Sciences Education, 8,* 1–9.

Kolen, M. J., & Brennan, R. L. (2004). *Test equating, scaling, and linking: Methods and practices*, (2nd Ed.) New York: Springer-Verlag.

Mehrens, W. A., & Lehmann, I. J. (1991). *Measurement and evaluation in education and psychology.* New York: Harcourt Brace.

Millman, J., & Greene, J. (1989). The specification and development of tests of achievement and ability. In R. L. Linn (Ed.), *Educational measurement* (3rd ed., pp. 335–366). New York: American Council on Education and MacMillan.

Messick, S. (1989). Validity. In R. L. Linn (Ed.), *Educational measurement* (3rd ed., pp. 13–104). New York: American Council on Education and Macmillan.

Norcini, J. J., & Shea, J. A. (1997). The credibility and comparability of standards. *Applied Measurement in Education, 10,* 39–59.

Raymond, M. R. (2001). Job analysis and the specification of content for licensure and certification examinations. *Applied Measurement in Education, 14*(4), 369–415.

Rodriguez, M. C. (2003). Construct equivalence of multiple-choice and constructed-response items: A random effects synthesis of correlations. *Journal of Educational Measurement, 40*(2), 163–184.

Schmeiser, C. B., & Welch, C. (In press). Test development. In R. L. Brennan (Ed.), *Educational measurement* (4th ed.). New York: American Council on Education and Greenwood.

Spray, J., & Huang, C-Y. (2000). Obtaining test blueprint weights from job analysis surveys. *Journal of Educational Measurement, 37*(3), 187–201.

Thissen, D., & Wainer, H. (2001). An overview of *Test Scoring*. In Thissen, D., & Wainer, H. (Eds.), *Test scoring* (pp. 1–19). Mahwah, NJ: Lawrence Erlbaum Associates.

van der Linden, W. J., & Hambleton, R. K. (1997). Item response theory: Brief history, common models, and extensions. In W. J. van der Linden & R. K. Hambleton (Eds.), *Handbook of modern item response theory* (pp. 1–28). New York: Springer-Verlag.

Wilkinson, T., Newble, D., & Frampton, D. (2001). Standard setting in an objective structured clinical examination: Use of global ratings of borderline performance to determine the passing score. *Medical Education, 35*(11), 1043–1049.

Zieky, M. J. (1997). Is the Angoff method really fundamentally flawed? *CLEAR Exam Review, 7*(2), 30–33.

Zieky, M. J. (2001). So much has changed: How the setting of cut scores has evolved since the 1980's. In G. J. Cizek, (Ed.), *Setting performance standards: Concepts, methods, and perspectives* (pp. 19–51). Mahwah, NJ: Lawrence Erlbaum Associates.

2

The Standards for Educational and Psychological Testing: Guidance in Test Development

Robert L. Linn
University of Colorado at Boulder

The 1999 *Standards for Educational and Psychological Testing* are widely recognized as the most authoritative statement of professional consensus regarding the development and evaluation of educational and psychological tests. This chapter highlights the standards most relevant to test development. Standards addressing questions of the purpose(s) of a test, the delineation of the construct or domain to be measured, the development and evaluation of test specifications, item development, scoring, field testing, the analysis and selection of items, and the assembly and evaluation of the test are highlighted and discussed.

The *Standards for Educational and Psychological Testing*, hereafter referred to as the *Standards*, were published in 1999. It is a joint publication of the American Educational Research Association (AERA), the American Psychological Association (APA), and the National Council on Measurement in Education (NCME) and is widely recognized as an authoritative statement of professional consensus regarding standards for testing. The *Standards* enjoy this status, in part, because of the way they have been developed and approved by the sponsoring associations and, in part, because of their relatively lengthy history.

The 1999 *Standards* are the sixth in a series of publications by the three sponsoring associations intended to guide the development, use, and evaluation of tests. The five earlier documents were *Technical Recommendations for Psychological Tests and Diagnostic Techniques* (APA, 1954), *Technical Recommendations for Achievement Tests* prepared by a joint committee of AERA and the National Council on Measurement Used in Education, which later became the NCME, and published by the National Education Association in 1955, *Standards for Educational and Psychological Tests and Manuals* (APA, AERA, & NCME, 1966), *Standards for Educational and Psychological Tests* (APA, AERA, & NCME, 1974), and *Standards for Educational and Psychological Testing* (APA, AERA, & NCME, 1985). Although the titles of the documents changed slightly over the years, the intent has remained constant. Each of the publications represented a professional consensus at the time of the publication regarding desirable test development practices and appropriate uses and evaluations of tests.

The *Standards* recognize that professional judgment is required for the proper interpretation, use, and evaluation of tests. The *Standards* are not intended to be used as a checklist. Rather they are intended to provide a frame of reference that will be useful in the application of professional judgment.

This chapter highlights those aspects of the 1999 *Standards* that are most relevant for test development. Although the process of test development is in many ways iterative in nature, the chapter is organized in the rough sequence in which test development takes place. Hence, we begin with the identification of the purpose(s) of the test and end with a discussion of score reports and interpretive materials.

IDENTIFICATION OF PURPOSE(S) OF THE TEST

The purpose or purposes of a test, as well as the intended uses and inferences to be made from test scores, provide the logical starting point for test development. Purpose(s) are critical to the development of an overall plan for the test that Downing (chap. 1, this volume) identifies as Step 1 of twelve steps for effective test development. They are critical in guiding development and the evaluation of test uses and interpretations. The purpose(s) of a test are important in determining what is, and what is not, appropriate content for the test, in selecting the format of test items and modes of response, and in planning data collection efforts to evaluate the validity of uses and interpretations of test scores, as well as other technical qualities of the test. The types of empirical evidence and logical analysis needed to evaluate the validity of uses and interpretations of the test scores depend on the purpose(s) of the test. This is also true of reliability and questions of fairness of test uses.

Because validity depends on the particular uses and interpretations of test scores, the *Standards* emphasize the need to elaborate the intended uses and interpretations of test scores and to provide evidence relevant to the intended uses and interpretations.

> **Standard 1.1:** A rationale should be presented for each recommended interpretation and use of test scores, together with a comprehensive summary of the evidence and theory bearing on the intended use or interpretation. (AERA, APA, & NCME, 1999, p. 17)

Consider, for example, the development of a test to be used to make high-stakes decisions, such as graduation from high school. If a student must earn a passing score on the test to graduate, then it is clear that multiple forms of the test need to be developed so that students who fail the test have multiple opportunities to retake the test. There is also a greater need to accumulate evidence to justify such a high-stakes use of a test than there would be for a test used for low-stakes formative feedback.

DELINEATION OF THE CONSTRUCT OR DOMAIN TO BE MEASURED

"The first step [in the test development process] is to extend the original statement of purpose(s), and the construct or content domain being considered into a framework for the test that describes the extent of the domain, or the scope of the construct to be measured. The framework, therefore, delineates the aspects (e.g., content, skills, processes, and diagnostic features) of the construct or domain to be measured" (AERA, APA, & NCME, 1999, p. 37). The framework needs to be sufficiently specific so that it is clear whether or not any particular item, content, or skill falls within the scope of the test framework. For example, is an item requiring knowledge of geometry or the comprehension of a scientific passage appropriate for the test? Should a person's test score depend or the speed of their responses? What level of reading difficulty is appropriate for the test?

Standard 1.2 places demands on the test developer to specify both the construct to be measured and the intended uses and interpretations of test scores.

> **Standard 1.2:** The test developer should set forth clearly how test scores are intended to be interpreted and used. The population(s) for which a test is appropriate should be clearly delimited, and the construct that the test is intended to assess should be clearly described. (AERA, APA, & NCME, 1999, p. 17)

A clear description of the construct that the test is intended to assess is needed to evaluate whether the test measures more or less than the specified construct. Reading comprehension, for example, might be considered an ancillary skill for a test intended to measure mathematical problem solving skills. Variation in performance on the test owing to differences in reading comprehension skills is considered *construct-irrelevant variance* (CIV) and undermines the validity of the mathematical problem solving interpretation of the test scores. On the other hand, if the mathematics problem solving construct was intended to cover both algebraic and geometric content, but the test contained only, or a vast preponderance of, algebraic problems then the validity of the intended interpretation of the test is undermined by *construct underrepresentation*.

CIV degrades the validity of the intended interpretation and may raise concerns about fairness for some groups of test takers. Consider, for example, the following standard.

> **Standard 7.7:** In testing applications where the level of linguistic reading ability is not part of the construct of interest, the linguistic or reading demands of the test should be kept to the minimum necessary for valid assessment of the intended construct. (AERA, APA, & NCME, 1999, p. 82)

It is recognized that any written test in English necessarily depends to some extent on the test taker's English language reading ability. The choice of vocabulary and sentence structure can influence the degree of dependence on English language reading ability. Abedi and Lord (2001), for example, have shown ways of reducing the influence of English reading ability on mathematics tests without distorting the construct being measured by the use of simple vocabulary and the direct sentences.

DEVELOPMENT OF TEST SPECIFICATIONS

Once the purpose(s) of the test, the construct to be assessed, and the intended uses and interpretations of test scores have been clarified, the next critical step is the development of test specifications (see, Downing, chap. 1, this volume, Step 3, Test Specifications and Blueprint). According to the *Standards*, "[t]est specifications delineate the format of items, tasks or questions; the response format or conditions of responding; and the type of scoring procedures" (1999, p. 38). These specifications need to be consistent with the construct to be assessed. Test specifications also identify the content domain to be measured and may specify target psychometric characteristics such as distributions of item difficulty and item discrimination.

Content Coverage

The specific delineation of the content to be covered is particularly important for achievement tests or tests of developed ability. The College Board, for example, offers Advanced Placement tests in a variety of subjects corresponding to college courses. One of the subjects is U.S. History. The College Board Web site (http://www.collegeboard.com) lists thirty-three topics such as the civil war, the progressive era, and foreign policy, 1865–1914 that "might appear on any one edition of the exam." It would be inappropriate to include any test items addressing a content topic other than one of the thirty-three that are explicitly listed.

> **Standard 1.6:** When the validation rests in part on the appropriateness of test content, the procedures followed in specifying and generating test content should be described and justified in reference to the construct the test is intended to measure or the domain it is intended to represent. (AERA, APA, & NCME, 1999, p. 18).

In addition to delineating the content coverage for a test, the specifications should also identify the cognitive processes that are essential for adequate measurement of the intended construct.

Cognitive Processes

It is not sufficient for a test intended to measure comprehension of complex concepts or the ability to apply understanding to solve problems, to have adequate content coverage. Measuring simple factual knowledge across the content domain is not a substitute for measuring comprehension of concepts or skill in using content knowledge to solve novel problems. The *Standards* make it clear that evidence is needed to support the interpretations of test scores as reflections of particular cognitive processes.

> **Standard 1.18:** If the rationale for a test use or score interpretation depends on premises about the psychological processes or cognitive operations used by examinees, then theoretical or empirical evidence in support of those premises should be provided. (AERA, APA, & NCME, 1999, p. 19)

The call for evidence that specified cognitive processes are assessed by the test is elaborated in chapter 13 of the *Standards*, which focuses on educational testing and assessment.

> **Standard 13.3:** When a test is used as an indicator of achievement in an instructional domain or with respect to specified curriculum standards, evidence of the extent to which the test samples the range of knowledge and elicits the processes reflected in the target domain should be provided. Both tested and target domains should be described in sufficient detail so their relationship can be evaluated. The analyses should make explicit those aspects of the target domain the test represents as well as those aspects that it fails to represent. (AERA, APA, & NCME, 1999, p. 145)

Because both test content and the cognitive processes are important aspects of test specifications, these two characteristics are often used together to form a two-dimensional (content by process) table of specifications. The 1990–1992 framework for the mathematics assessments for the National Assessment of Educational Progress, for example, identified five broad content areas (numbers and operations; measurement; geometry, data analysis, statistics, and probability; and algebra and functions) by three processes, referred to as mathematical abilities (conceptual understanding, procedural knowledge, and problem solving) (National Assessment Governing Board, 2002, p. 10).

Test specifications vary in characteristics such as granularity, and the degree to which they provide adequate guidance for the development of test items. Thus, it should not simply be assumed that the specifications are adequate. They need to be evaluated.

EVALUATION OF TEST SPECIFICATIONS

How good are the test specifications? Because test specifications provide the blueprint for the development and selection of test items, it is important to evaluate the quality of the specifications. The basis for such an evaluation begins with a consideration of Standard 3.3.

> **Standard 3.3:** The test specifications should be documented, along with their rationale and the process by which they were developed. The test specifications should define the content of the test, the proposed number of items, the item formats, the desired psychometric properties of the items, and the item and section arrangement. They should also specify the amount of time for testing, directions to the test takers, procedures to be used for test administration and scoring, and other relevant information. (AERA, APA, & NCME, p. 43)

Such detailed documentation of test specifications is needed not only to evaluate the specifications, but to provide the basis for the validation of test interpretations, particularly when the validation depends heavily on evidence based on test content.

Validity Evidence Based on Test Content

The *Standards* make it clear that validity is "the most fundamental consideration in developing and evaluating tests" (1999, p. 9). A variety of types of evidence and logical analyses may contribute to the validation of interpretations of scores and intended uses. A critical part of the evidence may be based on test content, and the test specifications provide the natural starting place for content-based validity evidence. According to the *Standards*, content-based evidence "can include logical or empirical analyses of the adequacy with which the test content represents the domain and of the relevance of the content domain to the proposed interpretation of test scores" (AERA, APA, & NCME, 1999, p. 11).

Alignment and Adequacy of Coverage of Content Domain

In educational testing, the content domain for a test is frequently dictated by state-adopted content or curriculum standards. The content of the test is supposed to be aligned with content or curriculum standards. Concerns about alignment of content standards, curriculum materials, instruction, and assessments have received much more attention since the publication of the *Standards* than they did prior to 1999. Hence, alignment is not explicitly addressed in the *Standards*. Several ways of systematically judging alignment have been developed in the last few years (see, for example, Bhola, Impara, & Buckendahl, 2003; Porter, 2002; Rothman, Slattery, Vranek, & Resnick, 2002; Webb, 1999). These techniques are consistent with the intent of the *Standards* to use systematic procedures to collect judgments and empirical evidence for content-based validation, as articulated, for example, in Standard 3.11.

> **Standard 3.11:** Test developers should document the extent to which the content domain of a test represents the defined domain and test specifications. (AERA, APA, & NCME, 1999, p. 45)

ITEM DEVELOPMENT

The nature and quality of test items, tasks, or questions is obviously critical to the development of a test that yields scores that can be validly interpreted and used. As noted by Downing (chap. 1, this volume) item writing is critical to effective test development. There are a variety of types of items that may be used. The choice among item and response formats should be congruent with the purposes and intended uses of the test.

Item Format

A selected-response item format, particularly a multiple-choice format, is the preferred item format for many tests. Multiple-choice items are certainly efficient. A relatively large number of multiple-choice items can be administered in a short time, thereby enhancing reliability, and test taker responses can be scored rapidly and cost effectively by machine. Despite these advantages of multiple-choice and other selected-response item types, they may not be the most suitable item type for some purposes. Constructed-response items involving either short answers or extended responses may provide more valid measurement of some intended constructs. The choice of item format for a test deserves careful consideration. Enhancing the validity of intended uses and inferences should be the primary goal in the selection of item and response formats.

> **Standard 3.6:** The type of items, the response formats, scoring procedures, and test administration procedures should be selected based on the purposes of the test, the domain to be measured, and the intended test takers. To the extent possible, test content should be chosen to ensure that intended inferences from test scores will be equally valid for members of different groups of test takers. The test review process should include empirical analyses and, when appropriate, the use of expert judges to review items and response formats. The qualifications, relevant experiences, and demographic characteristics of expert judges should also be documented. (AERA, APA, & NCME, 1999, p. 44)

Item Review and Editing

Even skilled and experienced item writers sometimes produce flawed items that are ambiguous, have no correct answer, or are unintentionally offensive to some groups of test takers. Hence, it is critical that items be subjected to critical review and editing prior to inclusion in a test. Even with extensive review and editing, however, there is also a need, as discussed next, to conduct tryouts or field tests.

FIELD TESTING

Despite rigorous procedures for development, review, and editing of test items, one cannot be sure how items will work until they have been tried out with a sample of the intended population of test takers. The value of the tryout or field test often depends on the adequacy of the sample.

Sample Selection

> **Standard 3.8:** When item tryouts or field tests are conducted, the procedures used to select the sample(s) of test takers for item tryouts and the resulting characteristics of the sample(s) should be documented. When appropriate, the sample(s) should be as representative of the population(s) for which the test is intended. (AERA, APA, & NCME, 1999, p. 44)

SCORING PROCEDURES

The procedures used to score tests need to be specified and communicated to test takers. With selected-response items the scoring procedure may involve nothing more than counting the number of items answered correctly, but several subscores may also be produced and items may be differentially weighted. With constructed-response items there is a need to specify scoring rubrics, how scorers are trained to score, what procedures are used to monitor the quality of scoring, and how total and any subscores are derived.

Rules for Selected-Response Item Scores

Although number-right scores are the most common for selected response items, *formula scores*, for example, number right minus a fraction of number wrong are sometimes used. Formula scores are intended to reduce guessing, but it is unclear how effective they are for this purpose, and they may put the overly cautious at somewhat of a disadvantage in comparison to other test takers who make better use of partial knowledge. Scores for subdomains of content as well as total scores may be produced, and items may be differentially weighted. For example, some item response models may produce "pattern scores" that take into account estimated item parameters such as discrimination and lower asymptote of the item response curve. Pattern scoring increases accuracy somewhat, but at a cost of making scores harder to explain and defend when two people get the same number of items correct, but receive different scores because of differences in which items they answer correctly. Whatever rules are used, the scoring procedures need to be clearly specified and test takers should be informed about the scoring criteria and such matters as the advisability of omitting responses (see *Standards*, 1999, pp. 85–86).

Rubrics for Judgmentally Scored Items

Although computer scoring of essays and some other constructed-response items has become increasingly common in recent years, constructed-response items are more commonly scored by human judges. This is typically done by creating scoring rubrics and selecting benchmark responses that exemplify each point of the scoring rubric. Test developers should provide descriptions of the scoring rubric together with the benchmark responses that are used to train judges to score the responses to the constructed-response items. The *Standards* address concerns about accuracy, rater training, and rater agreement for judgmentally derived scores.

> **Standard 3:22:** Procedures for scoring and, if relevant, scoring criteria should be presented by the test developer in sufficient detail and clarity to maximize the accuracy of scoring. Instructions for using rating scales or for deriving scores obtained by coding, scaling, or classifying constructed responses should be clear. This is especially important if tests can be scored locally. (AERA, APA, & NCME, 1999, p. 47)

Clear procedures for scoring provide the foundation for obtaining accurate scores, but with judgmentally scored constructed-response items, they must be implemented by human scorers. Hence, the selection, training, qualification, and monitoring of scorers are also critical to achieving to goal of accurate scores.

> **Standard 3.23:** The process for selecting, training, and qualifying scorers should be documented by the test developer. The training materials, such as scoring rubrics and examples of test takers' responses that illustrate the levels on the score scale, and procedures for training scorers should

result in a degree of agreement among scorers that allows the scores to be interpreted as originally intended by the test developer. Scorer reliability and potential drift over time in the raters' scoring standards should be evaluated and reported by the person(s) responsible for conducting the training session. (AERA, APA, & NCME, 1999, pp. 47–48)

TEST ADMINISTRATION INSTRUCTIONS

Uniform administration procedures are critical to standardized testing. The time available for taking the test and conditions for making exceptions (e.g., allowing extra time for persons with particular disabilities) need to be clearly specified. The instructions to test takers need to be clear so that test takers know what they are expected to do. In many cases, it is desirable to provide information about the test content, item formats, scoring rules, and test-taking strategies as well as practice test materials in advance. Consider, for example, Standards 3.20 and 3.21. Standard 3.20 is intended to ensure that test takers understand what is expected when they take the test. Standard 3.21 addresses the basis for allowing variations in administration procedures.

> **Standard 3.20:** The instructions presented to test takers should contain sufficient detail so that test takers can respond to the task in the manner that the test developer intended. When appropriate, sample material, practice or sample questions, criteria for scoring, and a representative item identified with each major area in the test's classification or domain should be provided to the test takers prior to the administration of the test or included in the testing material as part of the standard administration instructions. (AERA, APA, & NCME, 1999, p. 47)

> **Standard 3.21:** If the test developer indicates that the conditions of administration are permitted to vary from one test taker or group to another, permissible variation in conditions of administration should be identified, and a rationale for permitting different conditions should be documented. (AERA, APA, & NCME, 1999, p. 47)

ITEM ANALYSIS

Item analysis can serve several different functions in test development. It can be useful as a means of detecting flawed items. It can be a useful tool in identifying items that contribute the most to test reliability. Analyses of differential item functioning can be useful in identifying items that may put members of particular groups of test takers at a disadvantage.

Item Selection and the Identification of Flawed Items

> **Standard 3.9:** When a test developer evaluates the psychometric properties of items, the classical or Item *Response Theory* (IRT) model used for evaluating the psychometric properties of the items should be documented. The sample used for estimating item properties should be described and should be of adequate size and diversity for the procedure. The process by which items are selected and the data used for item selection, such as item difficulty, item discrimination, and or item information should also be documented. When IRT is used to estimate item parameters in test development, the item response model, estimation procedures, and evidence of model fit should be documented. (AERA, APA, & NCME, 1999, pp. 44–45)

Although item statistics can be useful both in identifying items with the most desirable psychometric properties and the elimination of flawed items, it is important that the item statistics do not distort other fundamental considerations such as the content and cognitive process goals of the test specifications. That is, the criteria for item selection need to include considerations of content, process, and item format in addition to item statistics.

Differential Item Functioning

Questions of fairness to test takers with different backgrounds arise in any test development effort. Reviewing items for language that may be offensive to some groups of test takers or that may cause an item to be more difficult for some groups for reasons irrelevant to the construct that the test is intended to measure are important activities in the test development process. Statistical analyses can also be useful in identifying items that function differently for some groups of test takers. Items that display differential item functioning across groups of test takers may introduce construct-irrelevant variance for some test takers.

> **Standard 7.3:** When credible research reports that differential item functioning exists across age, gender, racial/ethnic, cultural, disability, and/or linguistic groups in the population of test takers in the content domain measured by the test, test developers should conduct appropriate studies when feasible. Such research should seek to detect and eliminate aspects of test design, content, and format that might bias test scores for particular groups. (AERA, APA, & NCME, 1999, p. 81)

SELECTION OF ITEMS FOR THE TEST

The match of items to the content and format of the test specifications is of primary importance for the selection of items for a test. Judgments and evidence that the items assess the cognitive processes and components of the construct that the test is intended to measure are also important. In addition, however, empirical evidence regarding item difficulty, discrimination, and correlations with other variables may also be useful in guiding item selection. If nothing else, the psychometric properties of the items can help to identify flawed items or items that function differently for particular groups of test takers. Overreliance on item statistics has limitations, however, and may be misleading because of capitalization of chance, especially when based on small field-test samples.

> **Standard 3.10:** Test developers should conduct cross-validation studies when items are selected primarily on the basis of empirical relationships rather than on the basis of content or theoretical considerations. The extent to which different studies identify the same item set should be documented. (AERA, APA, & NCME, 1999, p. 45)

TEST ASSEMBLY AND EVALUATION

A number of questions about the overall test can be addressed once items have been selected and assembled into a test. Decisions need to be made about scaling and the types of scores to report. Questions about score comparability or equivalence arise when there are multiple forms of a test and, of course, the reliability and validity of the test can be evaluated.

Scaling

The primary goal in scaling is to create scores that aid interpretation. Scale scores are derived by converting raw or number-right scores to a scale score with certain desired properties that are intended to improve interpretation. *Norm-referenced scale scores,* such as percentile ranks or grade-equivalent scores, attempt to give meaning to scores by comparing a test taker's performance to that of persons in the comparison of norm group. Tests such as the SAT or ACT report test results in terms of a scale established for some reference population of test takers. Subsequent forms of the test are equated and reported in terms of that scale. *Criterion-referenced scales* may consist of just a few performance categories (e.g., advanced, proficient, basic, or below basic). Tests used for licensure or certification may use only two categories (pass or fail). Test developers have the responsibility to clearly describe whatever type of derived scale score they choose to report.

> **Standard 4.1:** Test documents should provide test users with clear explanations of the meaning and intended interpretation of derived scale scores, as well as their limitations. (AERA, APA, & NCME, 1999, p. 54)

When there are multiple forms of a test, test developers need to provide information so that the comparability of scale scores across forms can be evaluated.

> **Standard 4.10:** A clear rationale and supporting evidence should be provided for any claim that scores earned on different forms of a test may be used interchangeably. In some cases, direct evidence of score equivalence may be provided. In other cases, evidence may come from a demonstration that the theoretical assumptions underlying procedures for establishing score comparability have been sufficiently satisfied. The specific rationale and the evidence required will depend in part on the intended use for which equivalence is claimed. (AERA, APA, & NCME, 1999, p. 57)

Evaluation of Reliability

No test is free of measurement error. Scores on different forms of a test or on one part of a test to another will not be perfectly consistent. Estimates of score reliability provide a means of documenting the degree of consistency and, more important, provide a means of evaluating the magnitude of measurement error. Such information is essential to the proper interpretation and use of test scores.

> **Standard 2.1:** For each total score, subscore or combination of scores that is to be interpreted, estimates of relevant reliabilities and standard errors of measurement or test information functions should be reported. (AERA, APA, & NCME, 1999, p. 31)

The type of reliability that needs to be evaluated depends on the intended use and interpretation of the test. Stability over time, for example, is of concern for some uses and interpretations of test scores. For other uses, the main concern may be with consistency of scores from one form of a test to another over a relatively brief period of time. In still other instances, it is sufficient to evaluate the internal consistency of test scores. Although appropriate estimates of reliability provide important information about test scores, the standard error of measurement provides more directly useful information to aide in score interpretation.

> **Standard 2.2:** The standard error of measurement, both overall and conditional (if relevant), should be reported both in raw score or original scale units and in units of each derived score recommended for use in test interpretation. (AERA, APA, & NCME, 1999, p. 31)

Test developers frequently report subscores on a test and encourage the use of difference scores for the identification of strengths and weaknesses or for other purposes. In such instances, the reporting of reliability of the individual subscores is not sufficient because the real concern is with the reliability of the difference scores.

Standard 2.3: When test interpretation emphasizes differences between two observed scores of an individual or two averages of a group, reliability data, including standard errors, should be provided for such differences. (AERA, APA, & NCME, 1999, p. 32)

Validity Evidence

Validity has been discussed fairly extensively above in the context of various aspects of the test development process. Chapter 1 of the *Standards* specifies twenty-four validity standards, only four of which have been specifically discussed. The relevance of the other twenty validity standards varies as a function of the intended uses and interpretations of the test. For example, some standards address the use of subscores or the interpretation of specific items or small subsets of items. Evidence to support recommended uses and interpretations of subscores should be reported according to the *Standards*.

The relevance of other validity standards depends on claims that are made for the test. For example, claims about the effects of coaching may be supported or refuted by results of experiments, whereas claims about the predictive utility of test scores may rely on relationships of test scores to criterion measures. The *Standards* call for evidence to support such claims.

It is recognized in the *Standards* that there may be interpretations of test results for which no validity evidence is available. To the extent possible, test developers are encouraged to acknowledge such limitations.

Standard 1.3: If validity for some common or likely interpretation has not been investigated, or if the interpretation is inconsistent with available evidence, that fact should be made clear and potential users should be cautioned about make unsupported interpretations. (AERA, APA, & NCME, 1999, p. 18)

SCORE REPORTS AND INTERPRETIVE MATERIALS

Test scores cannot be interpreted in isolation. A good deal of information beyond a simple numerical score needs to be provided to make the scores interpretable. A clear description of what the test measures is needed. Properties of the score scale need to be explained and information about the magnitude of measurement error needs to be provided. The preparation of interpretative materials targeted specifically to different audiences that need to understand what the scores mean and how they can be appropriately used is critical.

Standard 5.10: When test score information is released to students, parents, legal representatives, teachers, clients, or the media, those responsible for testing programs should provide appropriate interpretations. The interpretations should describe in simple language what the test covers, what scores mean, the precision of the scores, common misinterpretations of scores, and how the scores will be used. (AERA, APA, & NCME, 1999, p. 65)

Test development is not really complete until the needed interpretive materials have been produced to accompany score reports.

CONCLUSION

The development of a high-quality test that validly serves the intended purpose(s) is not easy. It involves many considerations and there are many pitfalls that need to be avoided. The *Standards* provide helpful guidance for each of the many stages of test development. They also provide an authoritative framework for the evaluation of the degree to which the test development process has achieved the intended goals for a test and the degree to which intended uses and interpretations of test scores are justified. Careful consideration of the *Standards* at each stage of the test development process can contribute to the development of high-quality tests and the valid interpretation and use of test scores.

ACKNOWLEDGMENT

Work on the chapter was partially supported under the Educational Research and Development Center Program PR/ Award #R305B60002, as administered by the Institute of Education Sciences, U.S. Department of Education. The findings and opinions expressed in this paper do not reflect the position or policies of the National Center for Education Research, the Institute of Education Sciences, or the U.S. Department of Education.

REFERENCES

Abedi, J., & Lord, C. (2001). The language factor in mathematics tests. *Applied Measurement in Education, 14*, 219–234.

American Educational Research Association, American Psychological Association, & National Council on Measurement in Education. (1999). *Standards for educational and psychological testing*. Washington, DC: American Educational Research Association.

American Educational Research Association, & National Council on Measurements Used in Education. (1955). *Technical recommendations for achievement tests*. Washington, DC: National Education Association.

American Psychological Association. (1954). *Technical recommendations for psychological tests and diagnostic techniques*. Washington, DC: Author.

American Psychological Association, American Educational Research Association, and the National Council on Measurement in Education. (1966). *Standards for educational and psychological tests and manuals*. Washington, DC: Author.

American Psychological Association, American Educational Research Association, & National Council on Measurement in Education. (1974). *Standards for educational and psychological tests*. Washington, DC: American Psychological Association.

American Psychological Association, American Educational Research Association, & National Council on Measurement in Education. (1985). *Standards for educational and psychological testing*. Washington, DC: American Psychological Association.

Bhola, D. S., Impara, J. C., & Buckendahl, W. (2003). Aligning tests with states' content standards: Methods and issues. *Educational Measurement: Issues and Practice, 22*(3), 21–29.

National Assessment Governing Board. (2002). *Mathematics framework for the 2003 National Assessment of Educational Progress*. Washington, DC: Author.

Porter, A. C. (2002). Measuring the content of instruction: Uses in practice. *Educational Researcher, 31*, 3–14.

Rothman, R, Slattery, J. B., Vranek, J. L., & Resnick, L. B. (2002). *Benchmarking and alignment of standards and testing* (CSE Technical Report 566). Los Angeles: University of California at Los Angeles, National Center for Evaluation, Standards, and Student Testing.

Webb, N. L. (1999). *Alignment of science and mathematics standards and assessments in four states* (Research Monograph No. 18). Madison: University of Wisconsin at Madison, National Institute for Science Education.

3

Contracting for Testing Services

E. Roger Trent
Ohio Department of Education (Retired)

Edward Roeber
Michigan Department of Education

An increasing number of practitioners managing some aspects of large-scale testing programs find themselves responsible for procuring some type of testing services. This chapter describes and illustrates three components of the procurement process: planning; crafting the request for proposals (RFP); and evaluating vendor responses and negotiating the contract. Supporting tools provided include criteria for determining which tasks to complete in house and which to outsource; an outline of requirements to consider for inclusion in the RFP; criteria to consider when evaluating vendor responses; ways to combine evidence across criteria into a single rating; and illustrations of various negotiation strategies. The primary goal is to make the procurement process as defensible and cost effective as possible.

Thousands of state and local agencies, boards, associations, and other entities are currently responsible for developing and implementing testing programs that serve many different purposes. Some of these tests are used for relatively "low-stakes" purposes, such as for career counseling (aptitude measures) or curriculum (achievement tests) decisions. Other tests are developed and used to make decisions that have much higher stakes, for example, determining whether or not a person is admitted to a program, qualified for a job, awarded a credential, or promoted. Most of these test sponsors and developers require outside assistance with one or more aspects of the proposed program. The procurement of such services is vital to the successful development and implementation of the assessment program.

A literature review, web search, and informal survey of several practitioners yielded only a few resources that offer guidance related to the procurement process itself. One report (Accountability Works, Inc., 2002) from a testing summit sponsored by the Education Leaders Council offered model contractor standards and state responsibilities for state testing programs. For example, one of the model contractor standards related to test development addresses the need for a policy ensuring quality of all test instruments developed under the contract. Another contractor standard deals with responsibility for developing a technical manual. In both cases, parallel responsibilities are outlined for the test sponsor.

The Council of Chief State School Officers (CCSSO) has sponsored a State Collaborative on Assessment and Student Standards (SCASS) for Technical Issues in Large-Scale Assessment.

Participants in this SCASS have developed a *Quality Control Checklist for Processing, Scoring, and Reporting* (CCSSO, 2003). This document suggests quality control procedures that test sponsors should consider while monitoring performance of vendors hired to complete various processing, scoring, and reporting functions. The document also identifies the type of expertise or experience that a sponsor's staff members need to ensure the effectiveness of each quality control measure (e.g., content, assessment, psychometric/research, or data management).

Testing program sponsors typically use formal requests for proposals (RFPs) or invitations to bid (ITBs) as tools for procuring the necessary testing services. Any two RFPs or ITBs may differ in several ways, including reasons for the request; type, specificity, and scope of requirements included; timeline for deliverables; and the legal or policy context within which requests are circulated, responses are evaluated, and contracts are executed. Although it is impossible to address all these nuances, the guidance in this chapter is offered from the perspective of an individual or group (referred to as *sponsor*) who seeks assistance through some type of competitive bidding procedure. Some ideas may also be helpful to practitioners who advise those preparing such requests or invitations and to those who respond (referred to as *vendor, contractor,* or *bidder*).

The chapter is divided into three sections. The first focuses on gathering information; defining the total scope of the project; deciding what major tasks to include in the RFP as contractor requirements and what tasks the sponsor will complete; and determining whether any consultants are needed, and if so for what tasks. The second section discusses issues and offers guidance related to estimating expected annual costs of the project, developing the RFP, and identifying which contractors should receive the RFP. The final section deals with issues related to evaluating responses from vendors and negotiating the contract.

PLANNING

A significant proportion of practitioners who develop and use an RFP to procure testing products and services may have had little or no prior experience doing so, and in fact, many may never have reviewed either an RFP or a vendor's response to one. Others who have had some prior experience developing or reviewing an RFP or preparing or examining a contractor's response to one may not have done so recently.

The first priority, therefore, may be to improve one's knowledge and skills regarding the procurement process. Any of the following information-gathering activities may be helpful to someone preparing to write an RFP:

- Review with the sponsor's purchasing/procurement office all policies, regulations, or laws that affect the sponsor's releasing an RFP and executing a contract. Discuss any questions with the sponsor's procurement officer and/or legal counsel.
- Identify a consultant who has prior experience developing an RFP to procure similar products or services. Ask to review a copy of that RFP and if possible any vendor responses to it. *Note*: Such documents are likely subject to public information requests in most publicly funded entities.
- Request copies of recent RFPs and the vendor's responses from colleagues who work for testing service providers. *Note*: Vendors may require a signed confidentiality agreement if the response contains proprietary information.
- After reviewing relevant materials, ask individuals who managed the project for the sponsor or contractor what, if any, changes they would make in the procurement process, the requirements, the timeline, or the evaluation process. Also, inquire about what has and has not worked well in the past.

- If the anticipated development process is complex or any of the anticipated uses is associated with high stakes (e.g., test results to be used in decisions related to licensure, hiring, promotion, graduation, school accreditation, etc.), it may be advisable to obtain the services of a consultant who is knowledgeable about procurement of testing services or to appoint and convene a technical advisory committee (TAC) to offer advice prior to completing the procurement process. *Note*: It may also be advisable to convene the TAC periodically throughout the development and implementation of the program.

Another important part of planning is to define the total scope of the project; that is, to make as many decisions as possible to determine what major tasks must be completed either by the sponsor or by the contractor. Although the following example involves a local education agency, it illustrates a process that any test sponsor can use to define the scope of a test development project.

Example

The school board of a mythical, large city school district establishes a policy that performance on a district-approved end-of-course test will count as a certain percentage of each student's final course grade in all courses required for graduation, and that the policy will become effective for the school year that begins two full years following adoption of the policy. Assume the policy also provides that the district superintendent and curriculum council will approve any test used for this purpose.

Suppose the district superintendent and curriculum council agree the district should construct new end-of-course examinations, rather than purchase tests available commercially, to ensure that the tests are aligned as closely as possible with what students in this district are expected to know and be able to do after completing each required course. Other decisions that may affect the scope of the project include the following:

- Are all students enrolled in a particular course expected to take the test? If so, how will access be ensured for students with disabilities and students who have limited English proficiency (e.g., will Braille and/or enlarged print test forms be available; will English language learners be permitted extra time; etc.)?
- Will each test be administered as a paper-and-pencil measure? Will the test contain constructed-response items? Performance tasks? Will any of the forms be computer administered? When will the first operational test form be administered in the district's high schools? By what date must this form be "camera ready" for printing or ready for computer administration? When will results be available?
- Will students who do not score well on a test be permitted to retake it? If so, when (e.g., after completing a summer class or other intervention program) and where? How often may they retake the test during any given school year? Will they retake the same test or must they take another form (i.e., different test items measuring the same objectives)? How many operational test forms will be needed annually?
- Will any test items be released to teachers, students, parents, and/or community? If so, how many items (or test forms) will be released each year and in what medium (e.g., in the newspaper; or on the district's Web site)?
- How much time will examinees be allowed to complete an operational test form? How many items can most examinees be expected to answer in this amount of time?
- What procedures will be needed to ensure that all tests are valid? That all items are appropriate measures of the course objectives, fair to all examinees required to take the tests, and accurate in terms of content? What procedures will be necessary to ensure that

scoring keys or protocols are accurate and fair? What other types of validity evidence should be collected prior to administering the first operational test form?
- Will the district establish achievement-level standards (e.g., cut scores for each course grade) or offer further guidelines to teachers about incorporating results from this test into the final course grade?
- Is it important to involve any other stakeholders besides educators from the district? If so, what groups? What role(s) should each group have?
- What, if any, additional materials should be developed beside test forms and scoring keys and protocols? For example, will the development effort include informational material for examinees and parents? Test preparation materials? Directions for administering the test? Guidelines for test security? A technical manual? What is the timeline for completing each?
- Who will score the operational tests? What are the reporting requirements? For example, will reporting be limited to individual examinees or include groups? If the latter, what groups or subgroups? What, if any, subscores will be reported for each test? Who will design the score reports and when?
- Who will own each of the products developed during this project? (For more detail, see "Ownership issues" in the next section.)

A third component of planning requires outlining all major tasks and determining which of these will be outsourced (included in the RFP). The following list includes a few of the criteria that could be considered when making these decisions:

- What is the sponsor's "core" business? Does the task align well with this business?
- Does the sponsor's staff have the required expertise and experience to complete a specified task? Does the sponsor have sufficient staff qualified to manage and/or oversee completion of each task?
- Does the sponsor have the technology (e.g., computers, scanners, printers, software, etc.) necessary to complete a specified task?
- Given the context (e.g., policy requirements; timeline; in-house availability of sufficient and appropriate resources; role of consultants, volunteers, the technical advisory committee, and various stakeholder groups; and the estimated level of funding available), is it more cost effective to complete all work in house or to outsource some or all of it?

Recall the illustrative local school board scenario referenced in this section. Which major tasks might be assigned to district staff and which ones might be included in the RFP? Although it is possible to imagine assigning the contractor some role in all major tasks suggested by this example, this sponsor may choose to take the lead role in completing each of the following tasks:

- Define the knowledge and skills that should be measured by each end-of-course test.
- Develop preliminary test and item specifications (including format) for each required test area (perhaps with involvement and advice from a consultant, technical advisory committee, or the contractor).
- Determine what accommodations will be provided to ensure access to all students. (Assumes that students will receive the same accommodations they are provided for classroom tests currently used in the course.)
- Write, review, and revise test items and protocols used in scoring constructed response and/or performance tasks. (Assumes that committees of educators from the district will

complete this task. Perhaps the contractor will be asked to provide assistance with training and to offer technological support as required.)
- Review and approve all operational test forms. (Assumes that the district superintendent or her designee and the curriculum council will do this.)

Conversely, the contractor may be asked to take the lead role in the following tasks:

- Advise the sponsor in developing test and item specifications.
- Provide training for all item writers.
- Provide technological support to track the history of an item as it is reviewed, edited, field tested, and approved or rejected for operational use.
- Collect copyright and permission to use documents.
- Secure an outside, independent review if required.
- Assemble items into field test forms and either print the field test or provide computer support for the field test administration.
- Design and conduct the field test (e.g., design a sampling plan; identify the sample of participating schools, classes, and individuals; print, distribute and collect materials; score the tests; analyze the data; place all items on the same scale; and prepare reports of item statistics for use in final reviews).
- Select items for the required number of operational test forms.
- Deliver camera-ready (or computer-ready) copy of the required number of approved operational test forms and/or the bank of items from which future test forms may be constructed.
- Collect and assemble evidence of test validity (with assistance from the sponsor).
- Develop the technical manual (with input as appropriate from consultants and/or the technical advisory committee, and with approval by the sponsor).

It is important to acknowledge that the scenario used to illustrate decisions, issues, risks, and tasks considered as part of the planning phase does not represent the same level of complexity one might encounter in developing credentialing examinations or examinations used statewide in graduation decisions. However, the process would be the same (i.e., define the complete list of tasks to be accomplished and identify which ones will be completed by the sponsor and which by the contractor).

The illustrative scenario is also modest in scope compared to a project that includes requirements related to the operational aspects of a testing program (e.g., printing, distributing, and collecting materials; administering and scoring tests; developing a score scale; equating results in subsequent years back to the original score scale; setting achievement-level standards; or reporting results). However, the authors' experiences suggest it is reasonable to assume that a process similar to the one illustrated in this section could be used in identifying decisions and determining primary areas of responsibility for each party and that thoughtful planning will likely take weeks or even months, not a few hours or days.

CRAFTING THE RFP

The authors remind readers that this chapter is written from the perspective of the sponsor issuing an RFP or ITB in a competitive bidding environment. Careful planning and a clearly written request/invitation can increase the likelihood the sponsor's expectations of quality are met; make the proposal evaluation process appear easier and fairer; reduce the risks of protests or legal challenges; and help address some known or suspected sources of systematic errors associated with construct-irrelevant variance (CIV) such as those defined by Haladyna and Downing (2004). Although the amount of time needed to prepare an RFP varies with the complexity of the program, the authors recommend allotting at least a month to developing the first draft, followed by several weeks making thoughtful revisions prior to releasing final copy.

In this section on developing the RFP, the following related topics are discussed: judging the adequacy of estimated funding levels; identifying types of requirements and issues that might be addressed in the RFP; and identifying prospective vendors who should be invited to respond.

Determine the Adequacy of Funding

As soon as the scope of the project is known, it is important to begin estimating costs and comparing these estimates to the level of funding currently available or expected for the duration of the project. There are at least two ways to inform this estimate: review the actual cost of the sponsor's most recent test development project, adjusting that estimate both for inflation and for obvious differences in the scope of the two projects; or if the sponsor has no recent experience with test development projects, request the same information from a colleague who is associated with another entity that has such experience.

If the estimated total cost exceeds substantially the estimated level of funding available, the sponsor may choose among several options. For example, the sponsor could seek additional funding; reduce the scope of work by eliminating one or more major tasks; shift one or more major tasks to another fiscal year and seek new funds for that year; assign one or more additional tasks to the sponsor's staff or to unpaid volunteers, assuming they have the required expertise; or specify in the RFP the level of funding available as well as the desired scope of work and ask each prospective contractor to propose what requirements could be met and how for the specified amount of funds. If the difference between estimated costs and available funds is relatively small, the sponsor may elect to proceed with the proposed scope of work and count on competitive bidding to make the project affordable.

Provide a Context for the Proposed Development Effort

If the sponsor has an existing program, give a brief history of that program and describe how the proposed test development project fits into this system. Summarize the policy and legal requirements related to the current program and to the proposed test development effort. Descriptions of the context should make clear the purpose(s) of the test, who will be tested, the timeline for implementation, any requirement to release tests, and a list of allowable accommodations. This section of the RFP should also define beginning and ending dates for the sponsor's "fiscal" or "accounting" year. If applicable, provide links to any laws, regulations, policies, or resolutions that might help respondents better understand the entire program, including the proposed new components.

Make available hard copy or links to electronic copy of previously developed materials, including for example technical manuals; scope and sequence charts, content standards, lists of benchmarks and indicators, or lists of job-related competencies; examples of released tests; examples of test and item specifications; and specific requirements for enlarged print, Braille, and translated test forms.

Outline the Procurement Process

No two sponsors have exactly the same procurement process. To assist respondents, include in the RFP clear descriptions of all procedural requirements. It may be helpful to consult the sponsor's legal counsel, purchasing officer, and procurement specialist for a complete list of such items to include in the RFP. Although the following is not exhaustive, it illustrates the level of detail that should be provided.

Submitting a Response

Is a letter of intent required? If so, when? What is the due date for the proposal? Where must it be sent? Does the due date refer to the date shipped or the date the proposal is received? How many copies of the proposal must be provided? *Note*: Avoid using due dates that immediately follow major holidays. Give vendors at least four weeks to respond to an RFP or ITB, and allow more time if the request is released just prior to a major federal holiday.

Formatting the Response

Can or should vendors describe and offer cost options for different ways to complete one or more of the required tasks? What, if any, format must be followed in the technical and the cost proposal? May the technical and cost sections be combined in one document or must the two be submitted as separate documents? *Note*: To facilitate the evaluation, the sponsor should require a standard format for both the technical and cost sections. The decision regarding separation of the two documents may depend in part on how the cost proposal is weighted in the evaluative process. For more discussion of this process, see the final section of this chapter.

Clarifying RFP Requirements Before an Official Response Is Submitted

What types of questions can individual vendors ask the sponsor? Which sponsor's staff member must be contacted? Which other staff members may answer vendors' questions? How will the sponsor answer such questions (e.g., in writing, with responses shared with all potential vendors)? Will there be a pre-bid meeting (e.g., face-to-face meeting, video conference, or telephone conference)? If so, when (date and time) and where (how to access)? Is participation mandatory? What, if any, restrictions are placed on individuals who may need additional information after the conference? Will answers to such questions be shared with all prospective vendors? *Note*: Pre-bid conferences should be scheduled at least twenty-one days prior to the proposal due date to allow the sponsor time to prepare and distribute to all prospective vendors written summaries of all questions and answers, and to allow contractors time to incorporate any new information into their responses.

Submitting Additional Assurance Forms

Is a respondent required to submit any additional assurance forms? For example, to guarantee the quoted price for a specified time period? Assure that the bidder is a nondiscriminatory employer? Assure that the contractor will involve a specified group of individuals in writing items and/or scoring constructed response or performance tasks? Assure that all products and services will comply with all applicable standards (AERA, APA, & NCME, 1999; International Test Commission, 2001)?

Subcontracting Work

Are there any restrictions on a vendor's ability to subcontract some tasks or functions to other service providers? Will the vendor be required to solicit participation of historically underutilized businesses? Or, businesses from a specific location (e.g., those located in a particular city or state)? What, if any, other provisions may affect such subcontracts? For example, must the contractor identify the subcontractor, describe the work to be performed, and include evidence of corporate capability and staff expertise related to each assigned task? What, if any, other documentation is required?

Performance/Bid Bonds and Penalty/Liquidated Damage Clauses

Must the successful vendor provide evidence that a performance bond will be purchased prior to execution of the contract to protect the sponsor in the event the contractor fails to meet specified performance requirements? Will the sponsor require payment of liquidated damages or other penalties if the vendor fails to deliver products or services in accordance with provisions of the RFP and proposal? If so, what key deliverables should be addressed? What is a reasonable payment level for each failure to perform? Will the number of such clauses, the manner in which they will be used, or the amounts discourage or eliminate potential bidders?

References

What types of references must the vendor provide (e.g., evidence of experience completing tasks similar to those proposed for this project; a list of comparable projects the prospective contractor is currently undertaking in other locations; and evidence of the extent to which the vendor's experienced staff members will be available for key roles as proposed for the new project)? To answer these questions, the sponsor may request references that include name of sponsor, contact information, some indication of the scope and duration of the work, as well as evidence regarding the extent and duration of involvement by the vendor's key staff members who are proposed for lead roles in the new project.

Evaluating Proposals

What steps are used to evaluate responses to this RFP? What criteria or rating scale will be used to judge the technical proposal? The cost proposal? Will ratings be combined in some way to identify the "winner," or must the successful vendor meet minimum requirements on all major factors considered in the evaluation? For example, is the sponsor obligated to award the contract to the lowest bidder whose proposal meets all minimum requirements of the RFP)? Is it possible for the sponsor to reject all proposals submitted (e.g., if no proposal meets all RFP requirements, or if all cost proposals exceed the level of funding available)? If so, what happens? Can the sponsor award contracts to two or more prospective vendors for work described in parts of their proposals? For more detail on the evaluation process, see the last section of this chapter.

Negotiating Requirements and Costs

Will the sponsor consider proposals submitted in response to this RFP to be "best and final offers," or use the results of the initial competition to negotiate "best and final offers" with selected contractors? Will face-to-face meetings be used in the final selection process? If the sponsor considers the first response final, will a vendor be allowed to correct, change, or add any information that the vendor claims represents an unintentional error in the proposal submitted? What, if any, such errors may be corrected before the evaluation process is completed? For more discussion of "negotiation" issues, see the final section of this chapter.

Describe in Detail All Requirements

Ideally, the sponsor should specify clearly all required outcomes (products and services) and let each vendor propose how to accomplish these outcomes. However, sponsors sometimes find it necessary, for a variety of reasons (fiscal, legal, technical, political, etc.), to specify additional procedural requirements. In any case, the RFP should describe requirements in clear, precise language; distinguish clearly between what is mandatory and what is desirable; indicate whether vendors may suggest innovations and improvements in required processes, and if so how and where to describe options and costs; and identify clearly the role and responsibilities of the sponsor's staff in each major task.

Some examples of requirements presented may not apply to all projects. Conversely, the list is not exhaustive. The discussion is intended to identify some requirements that may help eliminate or control some sources of CIV and to illustrate the amount of detail that should be provided regarding any requirement the sponsor decides to include in the RFP. Suggestions regarding requirements have been categorized as follows.

Item Development

Assuming the sponsor has completed some preliminary work developing item specifications, what types of items and tasks will be required? What proportion of items should be selected response, short answer, extended response, or performance tasks? What other item specifications will be needed? Who is responsible for developing these? How many items must be submitted for review? How many must be field tested? How many must "survive" and be available for selection for an operational test form? Can any item that is revised after field testing be counted as a "surviving" item without additional field testing? What are the dates for all deliverables in this category?

Stimulus Materials

Which tests will require stimulus materials (e.g., reading passages, charts, graphs, maps, artwork, etc.)? How many of each type will be needed for each test area? What are the specifications for such materials? For example, must passages used in reading tests be selected from previously published materials; what length of passage should be used; what criteria should be used to judge the grade/age level appropriateness of materials? If any such materials are copyrighted by a third party, who is responsible for securing permission for their use? Must permissions extend to copyrighted materials that are "published" electronically?

Scoring Protocols

Who is responsible for developing scoring protocols for all constructed response and performance tasks? Who will train raters how to use scoring protocols? If composition skills are assessed, who is responsible for coordinating and conducting activities related to identifying range finder responses? Who will score examinee responses? What are the due dates for all deliverables in this category?

Test Forms

Assuming the sponsor has done some preliminary work in developing test specifications, how many operational test forms will be required each year of the contract? Will any test forms be computer administered? If so, which forms? Is the contractor responsible for developing accommodated or alternative test forms? Which tests must be provided in large-print? In Braille? On tape or compact disk? For which test areas must translated forms be provided? For which languages? What types of items and how many of each type will be included in each test form? What other test specifications are required? Who is responsible for developing these? What is the due date for each deliverable?

Ancillary Test Materials

What other materials must be developed? Examples may include answer documents for field test and operational test forms; directions for administering each test form; information booklets and test preparation guides for examinees; application, registration, or enrollment materials (e.g., for certification, licensure, or equivalency diploma programs); surveys used to collect demographic information from examinees, teachers, or institutions; handbooks or guidelines for interpreting and using test results; individual examinee or parent reporting materials; and technical manuals. Who will develop specifications for each such document? What is the due date for each deliverable?

Ownership Issues

Who owns the test items developed for this project? Who owns all test forms and ancillary testing materials developed? Who owns reports of any studies commissioned by the sponsor? What, if any, special provisions are necessary whenever released tests contain materials copyrighted by a third party? Will such ownership issues require revisions in test or item specifications? Who is responsible for resolving each such issue?

Constituting and Convening Committees

What committees must be (or have been) constituted? Examples include technical advisory committee; content and sensitivity review committees; standard-setting committees; program and policy advisory groups; and focus groups to review proposed formats (e.g., for score reports). What tasks are each committee expected to perform? Who is responsible for constituting each committee? For convening each committee? Which committees must the contractor staff? How many contractor staff members are expected (or permitted) to attend? Which stakeholder groups will be represented on each committee? How many of each group? What expenses related to each committee will be the responsibility of the contractor (e.g., meals, lodging, transportation, and stipends for participants; meeting facilities; reimbursement to employers for substitute pay)? Does the sponsor have a policy that establishes maximum rates for any of these expenses, or can the sponsor suggest rates for each vendor to use in figuring costs? Will each committee meet a minimum number of times each year? If so, how many? How many sponsor staff members will attend each meeting?

Field Test Considerations

Is the contractor required to field test a specified number of newly developed test items? What are the anticipated uses of the data collected from this testing (e.g., to inform decisions about the appropriateness of the items for a population of examinees similar to those expected to take the operational tests; to inform content and sensitivity reviews of the items; to pre-equate operational test forms; to inform the standard setting process; or to be used in scaling and/or equating test forms)? When will field testing occur? Is field testing embedded in an operational test administration or is it a stand-alone event? What population should be sampled? What are the other sampling requirements? Is the contractor responsible for notifying participants? If so, are selected individuals and/or institutions required to participate? Is the contractor responsible for selecting and contacting test administration sites? For administering the tests? For scoring the tests? What if any information must be reported? To whom? What are the requirements for storing/retrieving hard copy or images of completed answer documents from the field test (e.g., for later use in scoring operational tests)?

Security Issues

What policies, practices, and procedures related to test security does the sponsor currently have in place? What policies, practices, and procedures related to security will be required for the contractor? For which RFP tasks will prospective vendors be required to propose a security plan? What issues must be addressed in each plan? Will the sponsor need consultative assistance in answering any of these questions or assistance in investigating allegations of security breaches? (See Impara & Foster, chap. 5, this volume.)

Quality Control Issues

What role and responsibilities will the sponsor have for quality control in each major task outlined in the RFP? What sponsor's staff member is assigned responsibility for the quality of each deliverable? What role and responsibilities related to quality control are assigned to the contractor? For which tasks must the prospective vendors propose a plan for quality control? What quality standards must be met in each task? What, if any, penalties or other sanctions may be invoked for failure to meet any of these standards? Will the sponsor employ a third party to verify, check, or replicate results from any process? If so, for which processes (verifying scoring key, rescoring a sample of answer documents, replicating the scaling and/or equating)? What if anything must the contractor provide to the third party?

Operational Program Requirements (If Applicable)

How many test administration dates are anticipated each year? When? How many examinees are expected to take each test form at each test administration date? What is the total number of examinees on each test administration date? How many testing sites are required for each administration? Will prospective examinees be required to apply, register, or enroll to take the test? If so, who is responsible for developing, piloting, and implementing this system? What are the packaging and shipping requirements for all materials distributed to and collected from testing sites? What percentage overage must be printed? Distributed? How many constructed-response and/or performance tasks are included in each test form? Who is responsible for scoring? What are the minimum qualifications for individuals who score constructed responses? How many raters will score each response and how will differences in ratings be resolved? What are the reporting requirements? To whom is each report sent? Is the contractor responsible for tracking the performance of examinees and/or groups over time? If so, who assigns the unique number or other tracking mechanism? What is the timeline for each of these requirements?

Technical Requirements

What, if any, role and responsibility does the contractor have for each of the following: developing field test sampling design; analyzing field test items using specified classical, Item Response Theory (IRT), and/or differential item functioning statistics; placing all field test items on the same scale and using the data to select items for operational test forms; using specified IRT methodology to scale and equate operational test forms; designing a vertical scale; proposing and conducting validity studies; conducting standard-setting meetings; developing a technical manual; and developing and maintaining an item bank? Many sponsors may prefer to require each potential vendor to propose a plan for performing each technical requirement and the rationale for recommending this methodology. Other sponsors, because of legal, historical, political, fiscal, or other factors, may choose to specify a particular methodology for some, if not all, technical tasks. One issue many sponsors encounter is that vendors often use proprietary software in completing technical tasks. The sponsor may wish to require either that all contractors use software that is commercially available (or in the public domain), or provide evidence that results obtained from the proprietary software can be replicated using products available in the public domain or commercially. Before releasing the RFP, the sponsor may wish to discuss with a consultant and/or the TAC the pros and cons of using different methodologies for completing each proposed technical requirement.

Technology Support

Will prospective contractors be required to propose a plan for using technology to track the history of development and use of an item over time? To construct pre-equated operational test forms from an item bank? To administer operational tests online? To score operational tests online? To report results from operational tests online? To store and retrieve images of answer documents? To track examinee results across years? To issue certificates, licenses, diplomas, or other credentials to examinees whose scores meet the minimum performance requirements? To address any other innovative uses? What, if any, other requirements are associated with each proposed use of technology (e.g., requirement to propose plans for maintaining security and quality control; requirement to provide evidence results generated by proprietary software can be replicated using commercially available software)?

Staffing Requirements

What requirements should be included in the RFP regarding staff members assigned as project manager, assistant manager, and lead staff for each task (e.g., require the contractor to identify all such individuals by name; designate the proportion of time each such person will be assigned to this role; and provide written evidence that the assigned individual has previously demonstrated expertise in performing similar tasks for projects of similar size and scope)? What, if any, requirements should be included regarding later substitution for any staff member assigned one of these key roles (e.g., must the substitute have equivalent qualifications; be approved by the sponsor subject to satisfactory performance during a probationary period of a specified number of months)? What other staffing requirements are appropriate? For example, is the project of sufficient size and/or complexity to warrant a requirement that the project manager be assigned full time (100%) for the duration of this project? Is the contractor required to maintain a separate office in a particular location or hire one or more persons to work directly for the sponsor? Are prospective vendors required to provide a staffing plan that shows the number of full-time equivalent employees assigned to each task, the qualifications of such staff members (for their designated roles), and the expected duration of their involvement in the task?

Project Schedule

Although the RFP may provide an overall project schedule, is the contractor responsible for developing and including in its response a comprehensive project schedule? Is the contractor responsible for keeping it up to date? If so, what software should be used to write the schedule; how often should it be updated; who from the contractor or sponsor can change it; and how can it be accessed (e.g., paper only; Web-based read-only format; Web-based changeable format)? How detailed must the initial project schedule be? For example, will it contain only activities completed by the contractor, or will it also cover the work of subcontractors, contractors working on other parts of the same program, and the sponsor? Who should routinely receive updates?

Management Plan and Progress Reporting

What components will be required in each respondent's management plan (e.g., a timeline that includes dates for all required products and services; standards for quality; methods for reporting progress; name of the staff member responsible for delivery of each requirement; and name of the staff member responsible for maintaining and periodically updating the project schedule)? Is a "launch" meeting required at the beginning of the project? If so, who is required to attend? How many other face-to-face meetings will be required each year? Who will document the proceedings of each such meeting? What other types of progress reports are required? How often must such reports be provided? Sponsors will want to err in the direction of requiring progress reports more frequently than might be absolutely necessary rather than to err by requiring too few. For example, weekly reports may seem laborious at times, but at key points in the project schedule, both the sponsor and contractor may agree communication needs to occur at least daily. What components should be required in each type of report? What other documentation requirements should be included (e.g., documentation of all committee meetings, technical processes and procedures, etc.)?

Transition Issues

Any time the sponsor prepares an RFP that includes requirements for continued development of one or more components of an existing program, there is a possibility the current contractor will not be awarded this new contract. It is desirable, therefore, to anticipate and address in the RFP each issue that may be faced in transition. For example, for which tasks should the current vendor be required to collaborate during transition with the new contractor? How is the "transition period" defined? What are the requirements for sharing documentation of all processes and procedures that must be replicated during continued development? Should each prospective vendor be required to demonstrate ability to replicate previous analyses and results? Should all vendors be required to use either commercially or publicly available software, or could a prospective vendor simply demonstrate that results obtained from proprietary software are the same as those obtained using a product that is available to anyone? What, if any, used or unused test materials must be stored by the previous contractor, transported to the new contractor, or destroyed?

Identify Potential Vendors

All other factors being equal, increasing the number of interested vendors can help the sponsor to procure the same products and services for less money, or higher quality products and services for about the same amount. Although including smaller, less well known vendors in the process may increase slightly the possibility a contract may be awarded to a vendor who cannot meet the sponsor's expectations for performance, the likelihood of this happening can be reduced greatly by providing clear requirements, including a requirement that key staff be able to document experience completing similar tasks. Sponsors are encouraged to solicit the interest of as many contractors as possible.

Some sponsors may already have a list of ten or more vendors to whom RFPs are routinely sent. In addition, these same sponsors typically send a copy of an RFP to anyone who requests it. Other sponsors who have never distributed an RFP to procure testing services may first need to develop a list of possible vendor contacts; second, send a letter announcing the intent to distribute an RFP (together with a summary of the primary purposes) to determine vendors' interest in receiving this request; and finally, send a copy of the RFP to all who respond favorably to the letter.

The following strategies may help sponsors to construct a tentative list of potential vendors to whom they might send the letter announcing the pending release of an RFP:

- Place the announcement letter on the sponsor's Web site and invite contacts.
- Contact the Association of Test Publishers (Washington, DC) Web site for links and/or addresses for each current member organization (http://www.testpublishers.org/atpmn.htm).
- Consult a faculty member who teaches test and measurement courses at the nearest university.
- Contact the assessment office of the state education agency or the same office at the Council of Chief State School Officers in Washington, DC.
- Contact an official of Division D or the appropriate special interest group (SIG) of the American Educational Research Association (AERA), the National Council on Measurement in Education (NCME), or Division 5 of the American Psychological Association (APA) in Washington, DC.
- Contact a state, regional, or national consultant with any national testing company.
- Contact any of the authors or editors of this handbook.
- Place an advertisement in *Education Week,* or similar weekly periodicals. If time permits, consider placing a similar advertisement in a quarterly testing periodical (e.g., *Educational Measurement: Issues and Practices*).

Sponsors of small-scale test development projects may need only the assistance of a consultant who has knowledge of test and measurement theory as it is applied in a context similar to that of the sponsor or one who has experience implementing test development tasks similar to those faced by the sponsor. Any of the following sources could likely nominate qualified persons who may be able to help, or at least suggest someone else who may be able to nominate such persons: faculty member who teaches test and measurement courses at the university; officials of NCME, AERA Division D, APA Division 5, or an appropriate SIG; the Association of Test Publishers; or state assessment staff. For each nominee, the sponsor should request some type of documentation of the person's qualifications to fulfill the task requirements. For more discussion of this issue, see "Staffing Qualifications" in the next section.

The ideas presented in this section are intended to help inform and improve the competitive bidding process. The intended final outcome of this process is to select the vendor who submits the most responsive proposal at the fairest price. The evaluation and selection processes discussed in the final section of this chapter should be designed to make this happen.

EVALUATING PROPOSALS AND NEGOTIATING THE CONTRACT

One can conclude from the previous section that it is important to state RFP requirements and evaluation procedures in clear and precise language, so that all bidders have a clear understanding of expectations and of how the new contractor will be selected. Vague or general requirements typically elicit creative responses from vendors, but then each response is unique, making it difficult if not impossible to choose the best among them. Sponsors seeking more creative solutions may wish to consider a two-part solicitation process in which the first step is to request creative design solutions (perhaps rewarding the "winner" with some sort of incentive), and the second phase is to use the most desired creative solution as the basis for the subsequent, more detailed competitive bid.

Clearly specified requirements and evaluation procedures increase the likelihood the sponsor's expectations will be met and reduce the risk that a prospective vendor will file a protest or legal challenge. Three additional factors that can also affect the perceived fairness of the selection process are introduced and described briefly in this section. These include criteria used in evaluating proposals, qualifications and training for raters, and negotiation strategies.

Criteria Used in Evaluating Proposals

Criteria used in the evaluation and selection processes are divided, for purposes of this discussion, into four categories: corporate capability, staff qualifications, responsiveness and/or quality of the technical proposal, and costs. Examples of types of supporting evidence are provided for each of the first three criteria. Illustrations are also provided for how the four criteria might be combined into an overall rating to select the "winning" proposal. These criteria should be outlined in the RFP so that each bidder is aware of the basis for selecting the winning proposal.

Corporate Capability

This term can mean different things to different practitioners. Some vendors are prepared to document their capacity if the sponsor is willing to accept different formats from different vendors. However, a sponsor should expect each vendor to provide, at a minimum, the following evidence of its capacity for delivering the requested products and services in the time allotted.

- **Resources.** Does the vendor have sufficient staff, appropriate and adequate technology, and the necessary financial resources to complete the proposed project within the required timeline?
- **Track record.** Has the vendor previously completed projects of similar size and scope? To document successful completion of similar projects, vendors should be required to provide references listing all previous projects of similar size and scope. References should include the name, address, and telephone number of a contact person for each project. The sponsor should interview at least two or three contacts, especially regarding performance of tasks similar to those proposed in the current RFP.
- **Commitment of top management.** Some sponsors may accept a signature of an authorized official as sufficient evidence of corporate commitment. Other sponsors may prefer a letter containing certain specific assurances of support by top-level management.

Staffing Qualifications

Although adequate staffing may be a component of corporate capability, the qualifications of specific staff members assigned to key positions for this project also affect the ultimate level of success attained. Besides requiring each vendor to provide information about the number of full-time equivalent employees assigned to each task, each vendor might also be asked to submit the following documentation regarding staff qualifications.

- Name of each person assigned to key project positions, and the proportion of that person's time allocated to each assigned task. Key positions include project director, project manager, project assistant, psychometrician, lead content person(s), and others assigned lead responsibility for one or more tasks.
- Resumé for each key staff member identified. Each resumé should include evidence of the individual's qualifications (e.g., training and previous experience) relevant to the proposed role and responsibilities in this project.
- Assurances or other evidence that proposed key staff members will be available to fulfill any major task assigned in the new project.

Technical Proposal

For the purpose of this discussion, *technical proposal* refers to sections of a vendor's response that reflect intent to meet the sponsor's requirements and sections that describe in some detail how each task will be completed (i.e., what processes and procedures are proposed). In evaluating responses, one should distinguish carefully between the quality of writing and the quality of the plan for completing each task of the project. In an effort to ensure that raters address the latter rather than former, the sponsor may ask raters to look for the following types of evidence:

- **Responsiveness to RFP requirements.** As noted, requirements may include mandatory processes and procedures, as well as products and services that are identified as "deliverables." Is each requirement adequately addressed in the response? Has the vendor's staff demonstrated in a previous project their ability to meet each proposed requirement?
- **Adequacy and appropriateness of the proposed processes and procedures.** The technical proposal should also include a description of procedures that will be used to complete each task. These descriptions should not simply repeat language from the RFP, but should indicate precisely how the vendor proposes to complete each specific task. If innovations or improvements are suggested, the vendor should provide a rationale that addresses issues of adequacy and appropriateness for this situation.
- **Adequacy of the vendor's equipment and materials.** Will the equipment that the contractor proposes to use be adequate for the required tasks (e.g., printing, distributing, scanning, scoring, reporting, developing and maintaining an item bank, etc.)? Is there evidence the contractor has previous experience using this equipment to complete similar tasks?

Costs

In most cases, proposed costs are used in some way to help determine which vendor is selected. To facilitate effective use of cost proposals during the evaluation and selection processes, sponsors should specify a standard format for all cost proposals. For example, vendors could be required to indicate costs organized by function or major task to be completed during each fiscal year; or to indicate total cost for each cluster of related tasks completed each fiscal year or during the entire project.

Combining Evidence Into a Single Rating

After determining what criteria raters should use and what types of evidence should be considered for each, sponsors must also decide how to use the supporting evidence related to the evaluative criteria to make a single overall rating of each proposal. The following list, although not exhaustive, illustrates several ways in which evidence from each criterion can be considered during the selection process:

- Assign a specific proportion of total points to each criterion, and provide directions to raters about what evidence to consider and how to award (or deduct) points when evaluating evidence presented in support of each criterion.
- Develop a rating scale or rubric that describes, for each point on the scale, gradations of quality in the supporting evidence related to each of the four criteria. For example, the highest rating on the rubric might contain the following descriptions: "corporate capability and commitment are judged to be excellent"; "all key staff members are highly qualified

to accomplish the assigned tasks, and all are assigned appropriate proportions of time to complete each task"; and "technical proposal is rated superior; is responsive to all RFP requirements; and is considered to offer cost effective solutions."
- Determine which responses meet minimum requirements for corporate capacity, staff qualifications, and quality of the technical proposal; rank by total cost all proposals that meet all minimum requirements specified in the RFP; and award the contract to the highest-rated cost proposal (e.g., the lowest bidder of this group).
- If the criteria are considered to be about equally important, rank proposals on each of the four criteria. Award the contract to the vendor whose proposal received the highest average ranking across all four criteria. *Note*: If there is little variation in ratings across vendors on the first three criteria and several vendors' responses meet all RFP requirements, the cost proposal may well become the dominant factor, even though one or more other factors receive greater weights.

Qualifications and Training for Raters

Some sponsors may have policies governing who can serve on evaluation and selection committees, as well as what processes must be used. If not, sponsors are encouraged to identify as raters at least three qualified persons who are not considered employees of the sponsor, in addition perhaps to others who are. Each rater should understand fully the sponsor's intent regarding each RFP requirement, as well as understand and agree to use as directed the criteria for evaluating proposals. Each rater should also understand each of the tasks described in the RFP. At least one individual should have a thorough understanding of test and measurement theory applied in a setting similar to that described in the RFP. At least one individual (and preferably all) should have experience evaluating responses to RFP's containing similar requirements. As a group, they should have a good understanding of the processes and procedures that may be necessary to complete the tasks. If possible, the sponsor should avoid using raters who might be perceived as having a "conflict of interest" (e.g., an individual who was formerly employed by or who is currently a paid consultant to one or more of the prospective vendors). If information about a possible conflict of interest should arise after ratings are completed, the sponsor is advised, when making the selection decision, to exclude that individual's rating of the proposal in question.

Training opportunities for raters may vary. At the very least, raters should be provided copies of, and asked to study, the following materials: the RFP, all written responses to questions and other documents used to clarify tasks or RFP requirements, criteria used in rating, and any written or oral directions for using the criteria or rating sheets. After raters have had an opportunity to review materials, the sponsor should convene raters by telephone or video conference for a preliminary discussion during which the sponsor reviews all materials, answers questions regarding procedures, and clarifies the sponsor's intent.

Each rater should be asked to assign independently a preliminary rating to each proposal. The sponsor should then reconvene raters (e.g., in a face-to-face meeting, telephone conference call, or video conference) to discuss ratings of each proposal and to allow raters to make their final independent ratings following this discussion. Each individual's final ratings and rationale for each final rating should be part of the documentation collected from this meeting. Although an individual rater's name typically is not included in this documentation, the sponsor may wish to have a coding system through which the sponsor can later identify the person responsible for each set of ratings if this should ever become necessary.

Raters should be encouraged to identify specific issues they had regarding all proposals they read, regardless of their final rating. They should also be asked to identify specific strengths and weaknesses of each proposal, whenever possible relating each strength or weakness to one or more of the criteria used in rating. Descriptions of weaknesses in the proposal or specific issues encountered during the review can be used in debriefing sessions with vendors who are not selected and can point to negotiations that are needed (e.g., in follow-up written questions or face-to-face meetings with one or more finalists) before a "winner" is selected. *Note*: Raters should be advised in advance if documentation from the selection process is subject to release in response to public records requests and in response to protests or legal challenges.

The sponsor should consider in advance how results from raters would be combined and used in the final selection of a contractor. The decision about how to combine results from raters depends in part on the decision about how evidence supporting each of the criteria is combined (see the earlier discussion) and what, if any, negotiation strategies are employed (see the following discussion).

Negotiation Strategies

Some type of negotiation, involving either the cost or technical proposal, or both, may occur before the selection process is concluded. In the earlier section on "Planning," sponsors are encouraged to review with legal counsel or a procurement specialist all policies and regulations that might affect the procurement process. The sponsor should determine during this review whether any negotiation strategy is prohibited and whether one strategy is preferable to others. Following are four examples of situations in which negotiation strategies might be employed.

- **Scenario 1.** No vendor's response meets all RFP requirements, but all are judged acceptable on criteria related to corporate capability and staff qualifications. Beginning with the vendor submitting the lowest bid (and if necessary continuing one at a time), the sponsor could ask whether or not the vendor is willing to meet all requirements of the RFP, including those not addressed satisfactorily in the response, within the timeframe allowed and without increasing the total cost specified in the original cost proposal.
- **Scenario 2.** Six vendors submit responses to an RFP. All responses are evaluated using all criteria except cost. Three vendors whose responses receive the highest overall ratings on the three criteria are invited by the sponsor to discuss possible amendments to their proposals and to submit "best and final offers." In this situation, the contract could be awarded based on the lowest total cost for the revised work plan. In any case, each "best and final offer" and any changes to the bidders' proposals would need to be reevaluated by the original panel that was convened for selection purposes. *Note:* This scenario assumes such negotiations are permitted under existing procurement rules and that the process is described fully in the RFP.
- **Scenario 3.** This scenario is similar to the previous one, except each of the three vendors "called back" is given the total dollar amount available and asked to describe what could be done for this amount (i.e., what products and services could be delivered as well as what processes and procedures would be used to complete each task). The sponsor could then select the highest rated of the three revised proposals. Again, this scenario assumes that each vendor's "best and final offer" and any changes in the proposal will be reevaluated by the original selection panel, and that the process is legitimate and described fully in the RFP.
- **Scenario 4.** The sponsor could cluster related tasks in the RFP and require vendors to provide the proposed cost for each cluster. If raters are required to rate each cluster of tasks in each proposal, it is possible for the sponsor to select multiple vendors. For example, one could select for each cluster the vendor whose technical proposal meets all requirements and whose cost proposal represented the lowest bid for that cluster; one could select the highest-rated technical proposal for that cluster without regard to cost; or one could rank proposals for a particular cluster based on total ratings across all four criteria (including cost).

In an unpublished paper presented at a national conference on large-scale assessment, a representative of one testing contractor estimated that testing companies receive hundreds of RFPs each year and that a small company can spend between $50,000 and $100,000 to prepare a single response (Kahl, 2003). Given this level of investment, not to mention the amount of revenue that is often at stake, it is not surprising that testing service providers may raise questions, submit a formal protest, or even file a legal challenge whenever the selection process appears to be unfair to them. The remainder of this section examines appropriate and inappropriate uses of criteria or negotiation strategies under several different assumptions about the context for the selection process.

First Context Description

The sponsor is an agency, credentialing board, or other organization obligated to award the contract to the lowest bidder whose technical response meets all RFP requirements.

If no vendor meets all requirements, it may be appropriate to provide the lowest bidder a list of requirements not met and ask whether or not the vendor could fulfill all RFP requirements, including those listed, for the same amount of money specified in the original cost proposal. On the other hand, it is likely inappropriate to use the "failure to meet RFP requirements" clause as a way to eliminate some vendors while overlooking similar failures to meet requirements by other vendors.

In this same context, consider a credentialing agency seeking an experienced vendor to develop a new real estate broker's licensing examination. Assume the RFP contained a requirement for the vendor to provide evidence of having previous experience developing similar licensing examinations under similar conditions. If the vendor submitting the lowest bid fails to provide such evidence, it certainly seems appropriate for the sponsor to disqualify the response. Unless this requirement can be waived, it is not an issue that can be resolved by further negotiation.

Second Context Description

The sponsor is not obligated to accept the lowest bidder who meets all RFP requirements, but is committed to getting the best value for the amount of money spent.

In this illustration, a sponsor intending to develop a new testing program may decide to limit RFP requirements primarily to a listing of mandatory products and services. Language could also be provided to encourage vendors to propose alternative processes and procedures, including those considered to be "best practices" and "innovative practices," as well as more traditional methods. Vendors could be asked to provide costs based on using traditional methods, and also to specify how much more (or less) the cost would be to complete a task or function using the proposed alternative method. In this situation, it might be appropriate to identify the highest-rated proposal that did not exceed the sponsor's estimated budget, and select whatever alternative practices were desirable.

Within this same context, it may also be appropriate to disqualify vendors whose proposals are not considered to be responsive to all RFP requirements (assuming all requirements are listed). On the other hand, it may be considered unfair to disqualify one vendor, but not another, for failure to meet all RFP requirements (unless, of course, the sponsor considers some RFP requirements to be more important than others). It might also seem unfair to award the contract to a vendor that proposed no "best" or "innovative" practices if one or more other vendors did propose such alternatives together with compelling evidence such methods have previously produced better outcomes at the same or a lower cost.

Third Context Description

The sponsor has specified an amount of money that is allocated to the project, but is not required to accept the lowest bid that meets all RFP requirements.

In this scenario, it is appropriate for the sponsor to describe the required product(s) and service(s); disclose the amount of funds available; require each vendor to propose how the work will be completed; and require evidence of corporate capability and staff qualifications relevant to the project tasks. It would be appropriate to award the contract to the highest-rated response assuming all requirements are met and the proposed cost is within the amount budgeted. It may also be appropriate to disqualify a vendor who failed to provide evidence that all staff assigned key roles and responsibilities meet staff qualifications requirements of the RFP.

It is not uncommon in one of the scenarios considered in this section for the sponsor to check references provided by the vendor as evidence of corporate capability, only to hear "horror stories" about the shortcomings of the vendor in that earlier project. The key question for the sponsor is, "When should such findings of failure to deliver desired goods or services in a previous project be used to disqualify a vendor?"

In such a situation, the sponsor's first step may be to consult its legal counsel. Legal counselors for some sponsors have indicated their clients could use documentation of past failures to deliver products or services for that sponsor in decisions not to renew the current contract or not to award a new contract to this vendor. On the other hand, complaints about a vendor's unsatisfactory performance elsewhere may not be useful in the current selection process, particularly if the information source is unwilling to serve as a "witness" or the vendor is able to show that past failures to perform may also be explained by contributing factors outside the vendor's control.

It is appropriate, however, for a sponsor to use such historical information to negotiate with the vendor a plan for addressing weaknesses uncovered during such investigations (e.g., weaknesses in quality control processes; inadequate staffing of a particular task; lack of experience for staff assigned to key roles and responsibilities; inappropriate amounts of time allocated for the sponsor to review and approve materials).

SUMMARY

As this chapter points out, it is possible to develop a defensible, cost-effective procurement process that most vendors in a highly competitive environment will consider to be as fair as possible. But, it takes time, careful thought, and planning. Many of the ideas presented in this chapter to accomplish this goal can be summarized in the following statements of advice:

- Define during the planning phase as many aspects of the project as possible.
- Provide clearly written descriptions of RFP requirements, evaluation criteria, and negotiation strategies, as well as clear directions to raters about how each component will be used in the evaluation and selection processes.
- Consider as many context factors as possible (e.g., political, legal, fiscal, and historical) when designing and implementing the evaluation and selection processes.
- At each stage of design and implementation of the procurement system, seek advice from an experienced consultant and/or a carefully constituted panel of technical experts.
- Start early in planning the entire process so there is sufficient time to accomplish well each step of the process.

ACKNOWLEDGMENTS

The authors thank Joseph M. Ryan, Professor, College of Teacher Education and Leadership, Arizona State University West for suggesting this chapter be included in this handbook. The authors acknowledge the helpful suggestions of the editors of this handbook and the following current or former state assessment directors: Reg Allen (MN), Jan Crandell (OH), Jeffrey Nellhaus (MA), Douglas Rindone (CT), and Theresa Siskind (SC). The authors also thank the following persons who offered insightful suggestions after reviewing earlier drafts of this work: Thomas Fisher, former Director of Assessment, Florida Department of Education; Colonel (Retired) Tommy Roberson, United States Army; and Jon Twing, Vice President, Test and Measurement Services, Pearson Educational Measurement.

REFERENCES

Accountability Works, Inc. (2002). *Model contractor standards and state responsibilities for state testing programs.* Washington, DC: Accountability Works, Inc.

American Educational Research Association, American Psychological Association, & National Council on Measurement in Education. (1999). *Standards for educational and psychological testing.* Washington, DC: American Psychological Association.

Council of Chief State School Officers(CCSSO), State Collaborative on Assessment and Student Standards, Technical Issues in Large-Scale Assessment. (2003, January). *Quality control checklist for processing, scoring, and reporting.* Washington, DC: Council of Chief State School Officers.

Haladyna, T. M., & Downing, S. M. (2004). Construct-irrelevant variance in high-stakes testing. *Educational Measurement: Issues and Practice, 23*(1), 17–27.

International Test Commission. (2001). International guidelines for test use. *International Journal of Testing, 1*(2), 93–114.

Kahl, S. (2003, June). The RFP Process Revisited: From Drafting the RFP to Starting the Contract. Paper presented at the annual Large-Scale Assessment Conference of the Council of Chief State School Officers, San Antonio.

4

Evidence-Centered Assessment Design

Robert J. Mislevy
Michelle M. Riconscente
University of Maryland, College Park

Educational assessment is at heart an exercise in evidentiary reasoning. From a handful of things that students say, do, or make, we want to draw inferences about what they know, can do, or have accomplished more broadly. Evidence-centered assessment design (ECD) is a framework that makes explicit the structures of assessment arguments, the elements and processes through which they are instantiated, and the interrelationships among them. This chapter provides an overview of ECD, highlighting the ideas of layers in the process, structures and representations within layers, and terms and concepts that can be used to guide the design of assessments of practically all types. Examples are drawn from the Principled Assessment Design in Inquiry project. An appendix provides annotated references to further ECD readings and examples of applications.

Recent decades have witnessed advances in the cognitive, psychometric, and technological tools, concepts, and theories germane to educational assessment. The challenge is to bring this exciting array of possibilities to bear in designing coherent assessments. This presentation describes a framework that facilitates communication, coherence, and efficiency in assessment design and task creation. It is the evidence-centered approach to assessment design introduced by Mislevy, Steinberg, and Almond (2003)—*evidence-centered design* (ECD). ECD builds on developments in fields such as expert systems (Breese, Goldman, & Wellman, 1994), software design (Gamma, Helm, Johnson, & Vlissides, 1994; Gardner, Rush, Crist, Konitzer, & Teegarden, 1998), and legal argumentation (Tillers & Schum, 1991) to make explicit, and to provide tools for, building assessment arguments that help both in designing new assessments and understanding familiar ones. This section presents the principles underlying ECD. Subsequent sections describe the layers of ECD, and an appendix provides additional resources for the theory and examples of practice that reflect the approach.

Assessment design is often identified with the nuts and bolts of authoring tasks. However, it is more fruitful to view the process as first crafting an assessment argument, then embodying it in the machinery of tasks, rubrics, scores, and the like. This approach highlights an important distinction between testing and assessment as well. Whereas specific tasks and collections of tasks constitute one way of going about gathering information relevant to an assessment, the term *assessment* is broader and refers to processes by which we arrive at inferences or judgments about learner proficiency based on a set of observations (*Standards for Educational and Psychological Testing*, 1999, p. 172). Messick (1994) sounds the keynote:

> A construct-centered approach would begin by asking what complex of knowledge, skills, or other attribute should be assessed, presumably because they are tied to explicit or implicit objectives of instruction or are otherwise valued by society. Next, what behaviors or performances should reveal those constructs, and what tasks or situations should elicit those behaviors? Thus, the nature of the construct guides the selection or construction of relevant tasks as well as the rational development of construct-based scoring criteria and rubrics. (p. 17)

Messick focuses on the construct-centered approach in accordance with his purpose in writing. Salient for our purposes, however, is the chain of reasoning he identifies here. Regardless of the aim of or psychological perspective assumed by a particular assessment (e.g., construct-, domain-, rubric-centered), the same chain of reasoning is central to constructing a valid assessment.

In assessment, we want to make some claim about student knowledge, skills, or abilities[1] (KSAs), and we want our claims to be valid (see Kane, chap. 7, this volume, for a focused discussion of content-related validity evidence). Ideas and terminology from Wigmore's (1937) and Toulmin's (1958) work on argumentation help us to link this goal to the concrete aspects of task development. Both used graphic representations to illustrate the fundamentals of *evidentiary reasoning*, the thinking that links observable but fallible data to a targeted claim by means of a warrant, a rationale or generalization that grounds the inference. In a court case, the target claim might concern whether the defendant stole a particular red car. A witness's testimony that he saw the defendant driving a red car shortly after the time of the theft constitutes evidence to support the claim, because the observation is consistent with the defendant stealing the car and driving it away—but it is not conclusive evidence, because there are alternative explanations, such as that a friend had loaned her a different red car that day. It is always necessary to establish the credentials of evidence—its relevance, credibility, and force (Schum, 1994, p. xiii).

Educational assessment reflects the same fundamental processes of evidentiary reasoning. *Assessment claims* concern a student's capabilities in, for example, designing science experiments, analyzing characters' motives in novels, or using conversational Spanish to buy vegetables at the market. For each claim, we need to present relevant evidence, where criteria for relevance are determined by our warrant—what we know and what we think about proficiency, and what people might say or do in particular situations that provides clues about their proficiency. This chapter discusses how representational forms like Toulmin's and Wigmore's can be used to sketch out assessment arguments and how ECD moves an argument into a design for the machinery of an assessment—tasks, rubrics, statistical models, and the like—in terms of three kinds of models: a student model, evidence models, and task models. As in law, the more complex and interrelated the collection of evidence and warrants becomes, the more helpful it is to have a framework that shows how these elements together contribute to our claim.

Another parallel to legal reasoning arises in complex cases that require a range of expertise in different domains. Depending on the nature of the claim, data, and warrant, it can be necessary to call on expertise in medicine, engineering, or psychology. Communication is a crucial issue here; within each of these fields, a whole world of language and methods

---

[1]Industrial psychologists use the phrase "knowledge, skills, or abilities" (KSAs) to refer to the targets of the inferences they draw. We borrow the term and apply it more broadly with the understanding that for assessments cast from different psychological perspectives and serving varied purposes, the nature of the targets of inference and the kinds of information that will inform them may vary widely in their particulars.

has evolved to face their kinds of problems. However, these languages and methods are not optimized to communicate with other "worlds." We need representations that do not constrain the sophisticated conversations and processes important for each field to do its work, but at the same time help us integrate key intrafield conclusions into the overarching argument. A common language and framework are necessary to orchestrate the contributions of diverse areas of expertise. In a court case, it is the evidentiary argument that weaves together the strands of evidence and their interrelated warrants into a coherent whole (Tillers & Schum, 1991).

In assessment design, expertise from the task design, instruction, psychometrics, substantive domain of interest, and increasingly technology, are all important. Each comes with its own language and methods. The next section describes how the layered framework of ECD affords intrafield investigations while simultaneously providing structures that facilitate communication across various kinds of expertise, each as it contributes in conjunction with the others to instantiate an assessment argument.

Related to the need for a common language is what we refer to as *knowledge representations* (Markman, 1998). To be useful, information must always be represented in some form. Good representations capture the important features of information, in a form that people can reason with, and matched to the purpose the information is to serve. For example, the city map in your car is one representation of the area, and likely to be quite useful to you when lost in an unfamiliar neighborhood. An online mapping application does not need a printed map, but instead uses information presented in digital form, perhaps as a database of street attributes such as global positioning coordinates, name, and speed limit. What is essentially the same information must be represented differently to be useful to different processes or people, for different purposes.

Knowledge representations are important in considerations of complex educational assessment; for various people and stages within the process, different representations of the information are optimal. The ECD framework provides domain-free schemas for organizing these knowledge representations, such as psychometric models and task templates, to support the construction of a solid underlying argument.

In addition to evidentiary reasoning and knowledge representations, the concept of *layers* can profitably be applied to the design and implementation of educational assessment. The driving rationale for thinking in terms of layers is that within complex processes it is often possible to identify subsystems, whose individual components are better handled at the subsystem level (Dym, 1994; Simon, 1969). The components within these subsystems interact in particular ways, using particular knowledge representations, often independent of lower level processes elsewhere in the overall process. The subsystems are related to one another by characteristics such as time scale (as in sequential processes), for which it is possible to construct knowledge representations to support communication across subsystems as required by the overall process. Although certain processes and constraints are in place within each layer, cross-layer communication is limited and tuned to the demands of the overall goal.

Brand's (1994) time-layered perspective on architecture provides an illustration. Drawing on the work of Frank Duffy, Brand considers buildings not as fixed objects but rather as dynamic objects wherein initial construction and subsequent change take place along different timescales, and in varying ways, by people with different roles. These layers, presented in Figure 4.1, serve as an heuristic for making decisions at each step in the life of a building. By employing the layers approach, activities can take place within layers that do not impact the others, yet at certain points need to interface with adjacent layers, as when the installation of a new sink means a change of countertop, cabinet handles, and soap holders to match the new color scheme.

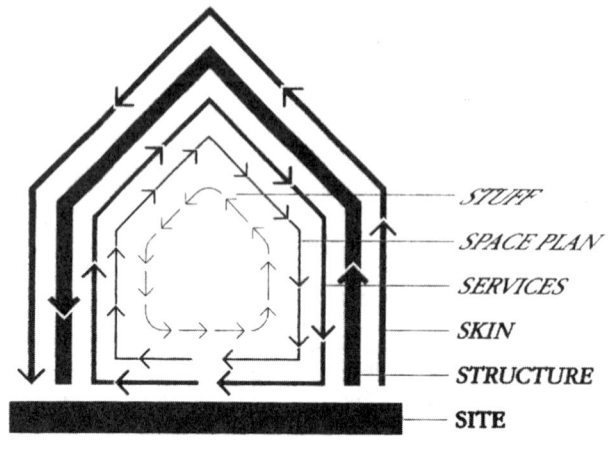

Stuff: Familiar and surface-appointments of an office or living space, such as furniture, artwork, telephones, and appliances.

Space Plan: Layout of living or working space, including partitions, or desks and bookshelves used to delineate different spaces.

Services: Infrastructure elements or systems such as air-conditioning, intercoms, light, power, networks. Often require substantial investment to upgrade (i.e., adding air-conditioning to existing house, or installing an additional telephone line).

Skin: The façade of the building, both aesthetic and functional relevance (e.g., climate will play a role). Changes here are rare and expensive.

Structure: Concrete pillars, steel girders, and wooden frames are all examples, and are fundamental. Changes here are often prohibitively expensive and substantially disruptive to normal activities housed in the building.

Site: Location, and what the structure is built on. Could refer to land, as in sheet rock or clay, or to cultural heritage or way of thinking.

FIG. 4.1. Layers of change in buildings. Diagram by Donald Ryan, from *How Buildings Learn* by Stewart Brand, copyright © 1994 by Stewart Brand. Used by permission of Viking Penguin, a division of Penguin Group (USA) Inc.

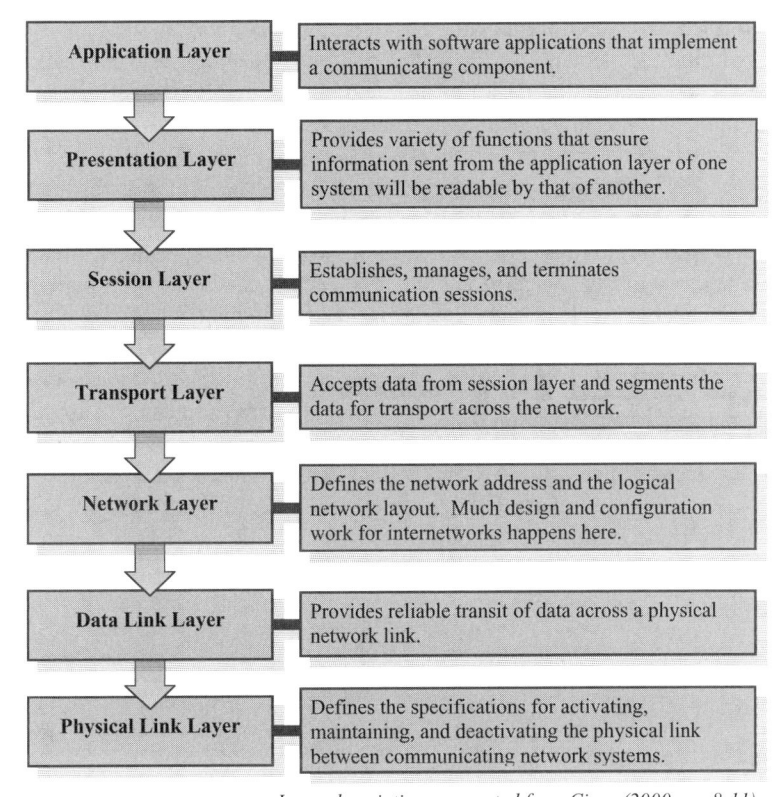

Application Layer	Interacts with software applications that implement a communicating component.
Presentation Layer	Provides variety of functions that ensure information sent from the application layer of one system will be readable by that of another.
Session Layer	Establishes, manages, and terminates communication sessions.
Transport Layer	Accepts data from session layer and segments the data for transport across the network.
Network Layer	Defines the network address and the logical network layout. Much design and configuration work for internetworks happens here.
Data Link Layer	Provides reliable transit of data across a physical network link.
Physical Link Layer	Defines the specifications for activating, maintaining, and deactivating the physical link between communicating network systems.

Layer descriptions excerpted from Cisco (2000, pp. 8-11)

FIG. 4.2. The seven layers of OSI. "The *upper layers* of the OSI model deal with application issues and generally are implemented only in software. The highest layer, the application layer, is closest to the end user. Both users and application layer processes interact with software applications that contain a communications component.... The *lower layers* of the OSI model handle data transport issues. The physical layer and the data link layer are implemented in hardware and software. The lowest layer, the physical layer, is closest to the physical network medium (the network cabling, for example) and is responsible for actually placing information" (Cisco, 2000, 1–4).

Use of layers is also widespread in structuring design and implementation processes in software development. A case in point is Cisco's 7-layer Open System Interconnection (OSI) Reference Model (Figure 4.2), which facilitates the transport of data from a software application on one computer to software on another computer via a network medium.

The Open System Interconnection (OSI) reference model describes how information from a software application in one computer moves through a network medium to a software application in another computer. The OSI reference model is a conceptual model composed of seven layers, each specifying particular network functions.... The OSI model divides the tasks involved with moving information between networked computers into seven smaller, more manageable task groups. A task or group of tasks is then assigned to each of the seven OSI layers. Each layer is reasonably self-contained so that the tasks assigned to each layer can be implemented independently. This enables the solutions offered by one layer to be updated without adversely affecting the other layers. (Cisco, 2000, 3)

ECD invokes the layers metaphor in its approach to assessment. Each layer clarifies relationships within conceptual, structural, or operational levels that need to be coordinated, and are either informed by or hold implications for other levels. Understanding the relationships within layers clarifies decision points and issues involved in making them. Although the layers might suggest a sequence in the design process, good practice is typically characterized by cycles of iteration and refinement both within and across layers.

The depictions of layers and various representations within layers discussed below draw on Mislevy et al. (2003) and on work in the Principled Assessment Design for Inquiry (PADI) project (Mislevy & Baxter, 2005). PADI is a National Science Foundation (NSF)-sponsored project charged with developing a conceptual framework and supporting software to design science inquiry assessments. As representations, however, PADI's design patterns and task templates are applicable across content domains and educational levels.

To illustrate the application of these concepts and structures to assessment design, we take as a running example assessments from a graduate course in the foundations of assessment design, EDMS 738. The assignments in EDMS 738 ask students to analyze aspects of actual assessments of their choice, in terms of the readings and concepts of the course. There are assignments that focus on psychological foundations of the student's example, the measurement model, the task design, and evaluation procedures. A final project requires an integrative analysis of the example incorporating all of these components.

THE ECD LAYERS

This section walks through the ECD layers, noting the kinds of work that take place within and across layers, and offering some examples of knowledge representations in each layer. Veterans of test development are likely to find more familiar terms and concepts in the layers closest to task creation and implementation. Therefore, the discussion focuses on the preceding layers in which the assessment argument is structured—the concept that guides the design choices that guide good task developers but often remains in the background. Figure 4.3 illustrates the relationship among layers, and Table 4.1 summarizes the roles and key entities within the layers that are discussed in this section.

Layer	Key Questions
Domain Analysis	What is important about this domain? What tasks are central to proficiency in this domain? What KRs are central to this domain?
Domain Modeling	How do we represent key aspects of the domain in terms of assessment argument.
Conceptual Assessment Framework	What tools and materials do we need to implement this kind of assessment?
Assessment Implementation	How do we choose and present tasks, and gather and analyze responses?
Assessment Delivery	How do students and tasks actually interact? How do we report examinee performance?

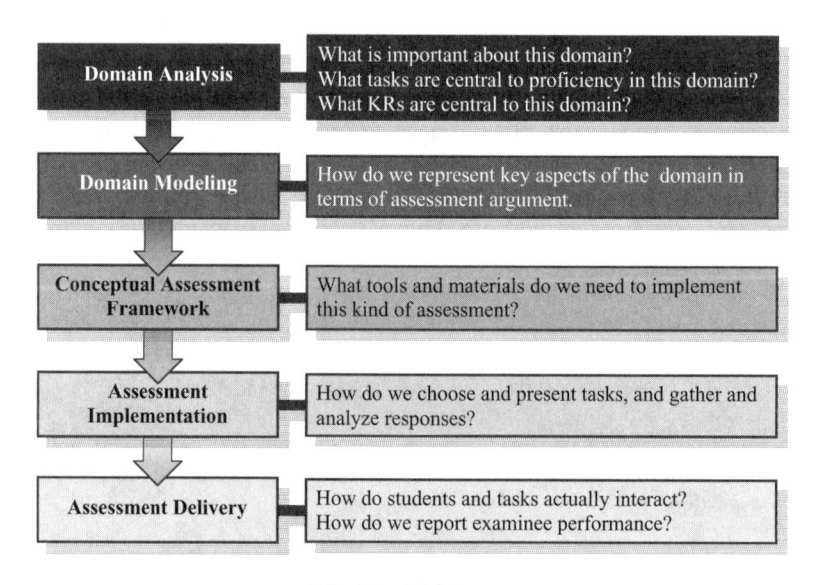

FIG. 4.3. ECD layers.

TABLE 4.1
Summary of ECD Layers

Layer	Role	Key Entities	Examples of Knowledge Representations
Domain analysis	Gather substantive information about the domain on interest that has direct implications for assessment, including how that information is learned and communicated.	Concepts, terminology, tools, and representations forms. Analyses of information use.	All the many and varied representational forms and symbol systems in a domain (e.g., algebraic notation, maps, content standards lists, syllabi).
Domain modeling	Expresses assessment argument in narrative form based on information identified in domain analysis.	KSAs, Potential work products, potential observations.	Toulmin and Wigmore diagrams; PADI design patterns.
Conceptual assessment framework	Expresses assessment argument as blueprints for tasks or items.	Student, evidence, and task models; student-model, observable, and task-model variables; rubrics, measurement models; test assembly specifications; templates.	Algebraic and graphical representations of measurement models; PADI task template object model.
Implementation	Implement assessment, including presenting tasks or items and gathering and analyzing responses.	Task materials (including all materials, tools, affordances), work products, operational data for task-level and test level scoring.	Rendering protocols for tasks; tasks as displayed; IMS/QTI representation of materials and scores; ASCI files of item parameters.
Delivery	Interactions of students and tasks; task- and test-level scoring; reporting.	Tasks as presented; work products as created; scores as evaluated.	Actual renderings of task materials in what forms as used in interactions; numerical and graphical summaries for individual and group-level reports; IMS/QTI compatible files for results.

Domain Analysis

The domain analysis layer is concerned with gathering substantive information about the domain of interest that has implications for assessment. This includes the content, concepts, terminology, tools, and representational forms that people working in the domain use. It may include the situations in which people use declarative, procedural, strategic, and social knowledge, as they interact with the environment and other people. It may include task surveys of how often people encounter various situations and what kinds of knowledge demands are important or frequent. It may include cognitive analyses of how people use their knowledge. Domain analysis echoes aspects of practice analysis for credentials testing as described by Raymond and Neustel (chap. 9, this volume). Through rich descriptions of tasks, practice analysis extracts features of tasks that are important for carrying out the responsibilities of a certain job. These task features in turn inform the kinds of student knowledge, skills, and abilities about which we will want to draw inferences as we proceed in the assessment design process.

Domain analysis also includes, at least implicitly, one or more conceptions of the nature of knowledge in the targeted domain, as Webb (chap. 8, this volume) describes in terms of content domain analysis for achievement testing. How this knowledge is acquired and used, as well as how competence is defined and how it develops is established according to one or more psychological perspectives. Although much may be known about all of these aspects of proficiency in the targeted domain, it has usually not been organized in terms of assessment structures. It is the foundation of assessment arguments, however, and the next layer of assessment design focuses on organizing the information and relationships discovered in domain analysis into assessment argument structures.

The bearing the psychological perspective has on the overall assessment process cannot be emphasized enough; the decisions regarding value and validity about knowledge and learning processes are necessarily determined according to some perspective. Just why is it that level of performance on a given task ought to be useful for the assessment purpose we have in mind? Ideally, the way tasks are constructed, what students are asked to do and which aspects of their work are captured, and how their performances are summarized and reported are all tuned to guide actions or decisions, themselves framed in some perspective of proficiency (Embretson, 1983). The structures of ECD underscore the role of these perspectives, encouraging the test design to make them explicit.

By way of example, imagine the domain of mathematics as seen through the lenses of the behavioral, information processing, or sociocultural perspectives (Greeno, Collins, & Resnick, 1997). In the domain of mathematics, a strict behaviorist perspective concentrates on procedures for solving problems in various classes—possibly quite complex procedures, but ones that could be conceived of, then learned as, assemblages of stimulus–response bonds. An information-processing theorist emphasizes the cognitive processes underlying acquisition of mathematics knowledge, and seeks to identify reasoning patterns that indicate students are on the right track as opposed to caught in common misconceptions (e.g., Siegler's [1981] balance beam tasks). A sociocultural perspective places an emphasis on mathematics as participation in a community of practice and fluency with the forms and protocols of the domain. In each case, the situations that an assessor designs maximize opportunities to observe students acting in ways that give the best evidence about the kinds of inferences that are being targeted, and quite different tasks, evaluation procedures, and reports follow.

Because the content taught, expectations of students, and modes of estimating student progress all rest on the psychological perspective assumed in instruction and assessment, it is important that this be clearly articulated throughout the assessment design process. A mismatch in psychological perspectives at different stages results in substantially less informative assessment. The ECD approach thus suggests that assessment design entails building a coherent argument that is simultaneously consistent with the adopted psychological perspective and the claims one wants to make about examinees. Assessment design can start from a variety of points, such as claims about student proficiency (e.g., "verbal ability") as in the earlier Messick quote, or the kinds of situations in which it is important to see students doing well (e.g., Bachman & Palmer's [1996] "target language use" situations as the starting point for designing language assessment tasks), or the qualities of work at increasing levels of proficiency (e.g., Biggs & Collis's [1982] "structured outcomes of learning" taxonomy). Although the target inferences associated with different starting points vary, all require a coherent chain of observations to arrive at valid claims (Kane, chap. 7, this volume).

With this requirement in mind, we can say a bit more about the work that takes place in domain analysis, and some organizing categories that help a designer to shape the mass of information into forms that lead to assessment arguments; that is, marshalling information, patterns, structures, and relationships in the domain in ways that become important for assessment. We have noted that the psychological perspective(s) the designer assumes for the purpose of the assessment guides this process. More specifically, from the information in domain resources we can generally identify valued work, task features, representational forms, performance outcomes, valued knowledge, knowledge structure and relationships, and knowledge–task relationships. Each of these categories has two critical features. Looking back toward the domain, they are notions that make sense to teachers, domain experts, and researchers in the domain. Looking ahead, they organize information in ways that lead naturally to entities and structures in the next, more technical, design layer, namely domain modeling.

We can identify valued work in a domain by examining real-world situations in which people engage in the behaviors and utilize the knowledge emblematic of a domain. From these situations we can ascertain the kinds of tasks appropriate for assessment, as well as discern which features of the performances themselves may be important to capture in assessment. In EDMS 738, the valued work that forms the basis of the assignments is the explication of actual and particular assessments into the conceptual framework of the ECD models, and explaining these relationships to others. Recurring and salient features of the situations in which this valued work can be observed are referred to as *task features*. Whereas the examinee is in control of the performance itself, the assessment designer plays a decisive role in setting these task features to focus evidence, determine stress on different aspects of knowledge, and preemptively constrain alternative explanations for performance.

In any domain, information takes on a variety of representational forms, depending on the nature of the content and the audience and purpose for which it is used. Learning how to use representational forms to characterize situations, solve problems, transform data, and communicate with others is central to developing proficiency in any domain. In the domain of music, for example, notation has been developed for representing compositions, with some universals and some instrument-specific features; biology uses Punnett squares, and mathematics uses symbol systems and operators. It is necessary to identify the representational forms—such as schematic, graphic, or symbolic systems—that accompany the target domain. Not only is much of the knowledge in the domain built into these representations, but they are what are used to present information and shape expectations for students to work with in assessment tasks (Gitomer & Steinberg, 1999). In EDMS 738, when students study measurement models they must work with algebraic expressions, path diagrams, computer program interfaces, and, importantly, translate information back and forth among these forms. By identifying these representational forms, we make explicit the range of communication tools central to the domain, and set the stage for using them in subsequent layers of the design process.

With *performance outcomes*, we articulate the ways we have of knowing, appropriate to the domain of interest, when someone has arrived at an understanding or appropriate level of knowledge. That is, how do you know good work when you see it? What clues in what students say or do provide insights into the way they are thinking? These characteristics form the criteria that are eventually necessary for crafting rubrics and scoring algorithms. Of course, characteristics of the knowledge, or content, of a domain are also central to assessment design (Webb, chap. 8, this volume). The kinds of knowledge and skill considered important in the domain are referred to as *valued knowledge*. Curriculum materials, textbooks, and concept maps of the domain are all examples of sources of valued knowledge. Of great current interest are content standards for a domain, such as the National Research Council's (1996) *National Science Education Standards*.

In addition, we may be able to specify structures and relationships underlying this valued knowledge in terms of how it tends to develop in individuals or in groups. Artifacts such as curricula and knowledge maps provide insights into this category. Finally, we need to explicate *knowledge–task relationships*, meaning how features of situations and tasks interact with knowledge differences in individuals or groups. With this information, we can then identify features of tasks that prove useful for distinguishing differences in understanding between examinees. If we want to know if a student can choose an effective strategy to solve problems, we must present problems that might be approached in several ways. We must then observe whether the student uses cues in the problem setting to choose a strategy, and recognizes a foundering solution as a signal to change strategies.

The domain analysis layer is furthest from the concrete tasks we ultimately seek to generate in assessment design. But thinking along the lines sketched above underscores the importance of this layer in the overall process, for building validity into assessment outcomes from the start. By making these considerations explicit, we are better able to understand existing tasks and outcomes. More importantly, we are poised to generate new tasks that embody a grounded assessment argument.

Domain Modeling

Work in domain analysis identifies the elements that are needed in an assessment. The *domain modeling layer* consists of systematic structures for organizing the content identified in domain analysis in terms of an assessment argument. Technical details—the nuts and bolts of particular statistical models, rubrics, or task materials—are not the concern yet in this layer. Rather it is the articulation of the argument that connects observations of students' actions in various situations to inferences about what they know or can do. The assessment argument takes a narrative form here: coherent descriptions of proficiencies of interest, ways of getting observations that evidence those proficiencies, and ways of arranging situations in which students can provide evidence of their proficiencies. Whereas content and instructional experts are the foundation of domain analysis, the assessment designer plays a more prominent role in domain modeling. Here the designer collaborates with domain experts to organize information about the domain and about the purpose of the assessment into terms and structures that form assessment arguments.

The concern of ECD at this layer is to fill in an assessment argument schema through which we can view content from any domain. Toulmin's (1958) general structure for arguments, in terms of claims, data, and warrants, provides a starting point; Figure 4.4 shows the basic structure. Adapting these components to assessment design, the claim refers to the target of the assessment, such as level of proficiency in scientific problem solving, or ability to use language appropriately in varying contexts. We provide data, such as quality of responses to questions or behaviors observed in particular situations, to support our claims, and the warrant is the

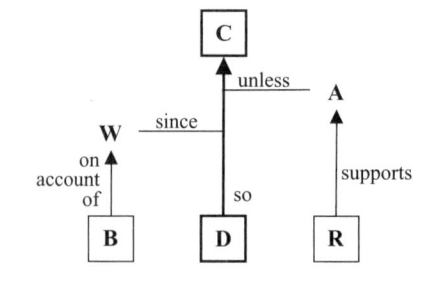

FIG. 4.4. Toulmin's (1958) structure for arguments. Reasoning flows from data (D) to claim (C) by justification of a warrant (W), which in turn is supported by backing (B). The inference may need to be qualified by alternative explanations (A), which may have rebuttal evidence (R) to support them.

4. EVIDENCE-CENTERED DESIGN

```
                    ┌─────────────────────────┐
                    │ C: Sue's configuration of│
                    │    production rules for  │
                    │  operating in the domain │
                    │ (knowledge and skill) is K│
                    └─────────────────────────┘
W₀: Theory about how persons              ▲
with configurations {K₁,...,Kₘ}   since  │
would be likely to respond to items       │
with different salient features.      so  │
                                      and
```

W_0: Theory about how persons with configurations $\{K_1,\ldots,K_m\}$ would be likely to respond to items with different salient features.

C: Sue's probability of answering a Class 1 subtraction problem with borrowing is p_1

  ...

C: Sue's probability of answering a Class n subtraction problem with borrowing is p_n

W: Sampling theory for items with feature set defining Class 1 *since* / *so* / *and*

W: Sampling theory for items with feature set defining Class n *since* / *so* / *and*

D1₁ⱼ: Sue's answer to Item j, Class 1

D2₁ⱼ structure and contents of Item j, Class 1

  ...

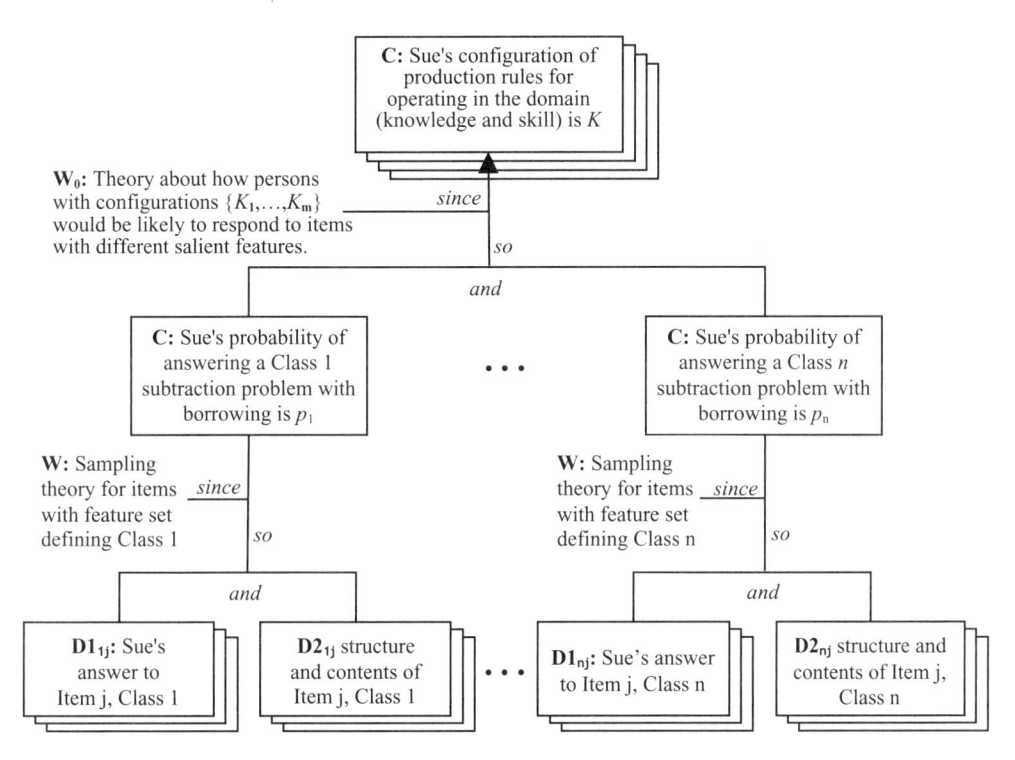

D1ₙⱼ: Sue's answer to Item j, Class n

D2ₙⱼ structure and contents of Item j, Class n

FIG. 4.5. Extended Toulmin diagram in the context of assessment. C, claim; W, warrant; D, data.

logic or reasoning that explains why certain data should be considered appropriate evidence for certain claims. Wigmore (1973) shows how evidentiary arguments in even very complicated legal cases can be expressed with assemblages of these basic structures—recurring structures in the domain or schemas with slots to be filled.

As an illustration, Figure 4.5 adapts Toulmin's and Wigmore's representations to an assessment argument. Here multiple data sources and multiple accompanying warrants are brought to bear on a claim about student mathematical reasoning from an information-processing perspective: Sue has answered a number of subtraction problems that call for a variety of operations involving whole number subtraction, borrowing, borrowing across zeros, and so on. An information-processing perspective characterizes a student in terms of which of these operations they are able to carry out, and posits that they are likely to solve problems for which they have mastered the required operations. This is the warrant, and the backing comes from both classroom experience and cognitive research such as that of VanLehn (1990). Patterns of responses on structurally similar tasks provide clues about the classes of problems Sue does well on and which she has trouble with. These patterns in turn provide evidence for inference about which of the operations Sue has mastered and which she has not.

PADI has adapted structures called design patterns from architecture (Alexander, Ishikawa, & Silverstein, 1977) and software engineering (Gamma et al., 1994; Gardner et al., 1998) to help organize information from domain analysis into the form of potential assessment arguments (PADI, 2003). An assessment design pattern helps domain experts and assessment designers to fill the slots of an assessment argument. Because the structure of the design pattern implicitly contains the structure of an assessment argument, filling in the slots simultaneously renders explicit the relationships among the pieces of information, in terms of the roles they

TABLE 4.2
Design Pattern Attributes and Corresponding Assessment Argument Components

Attribute	Description	Assessment Argument Component
Rationale	Explain why this item is an important aspect of scientific inquiry.	Warrant (underlying)
Focal knowledge, skills, and abilities	The primary knowledge/skill/abilities targeted by this design pattern.	Student model
Additional knowledge, skills, and abilities	Other knowledge/skills/abilities that may be required by this design pattern.	Student model
Potential observations	Some possible things one could see students doing that would give evidence about the KSAs (knowledge/skills/attributes).	Evidence model
Potential work products	Modes, like a written product or a spoken answer, in which students might produce evidence about KSAs (knowledge/skills/attributes).	Task model
Characteristic features	Aspects of assessment situations that are likely to evoke the desired evidence.	Task model
Variable features	Aspects of assessment situations that can be varied in order to shift difficulty or focus.	Task model

play in the argument. We can thus speak of the assessment structure as provided by the design pattern, and the assessment substance as determined by the assessment designer (Mislevy, 2003).

Table 4.2 shows the attributes of a PADI design pattern and their connection to the assessment argument, and Table 4.3 is the design pattern used in our running EDMS 738 example. Design patterns are intentionally broad and nontechnical. Centered around some aspect of KSAs, a design pattern is meant to offer a variety of approaches that can be used to get evidence about that knowledge or skill, organized in such a way as to lead toward the more technical work of designing particular tasks. Here are some additional design patterns PADI has developed for use in assessing science inquiry:

- Formulate a scientific explanation from a body of evidence.
- Analyze data quality.
- Model revision.
- Design under constraints.
- Self-monitoring during inquiry.

To identify each design pattern, there are *title* and *summary* slots that summarize its purpose and basic idea. The *rationale* slot articulates the underlying warrant that justifies the connection between the target inferences and the kinds of tasks and evidence which support them. Focal KSAs come from the valued knowledge identified in domain analysis, and indicate the primary target of the design pattern (and the assessments it will be used to generate); this is the substance of the claim about students that tasks built in accordance with this design pattern address. Focal as well as additional KSAs are cast in terms of the student or examinee; our inference concerns the extent to which the student evidences them. Thus, values of *focal* and *additional KSAs* are phrased as properties of a person (e.g., "ability to...", "knowledge of...", "skill in...",

TABLE 4.3
Model Elaboration Design Pattern

Design Pattern Attribute	Comments
Summary	
This design pattern concerns working with mappings and extensions of given scientific models.	A central element of scientific inquiry is reasoning with models. This design pattern focuses on model elaboration, as a perspective on assessment in inquiry and problem solving.
Rationale	
Scientific models are abstracted schemas involving entities and relationships, meant to be useful across a range of particular circumstances. Correspondences can be established between them and real-world situations and other models. Students use, and gain, conceptual or procedural knowledge working with an existing model.	Students' work is bound by the concept of an existing model (or models) so their work includes an understanding the constraints of the problem. Even though model elaboration does not involve the invention of new objects, processes, or states, it does entail sophisticated thinking and is an analogue of much scientific activity.
Focal knowledge, skills, and abilities	
• Ability to establish correspondence between real-world situation and entities in a given model.	This design pattern focuses on establishing correspondences among models and between models and real-world situations.
• Ability to find links between similar models (ones that share objects, processes, or states).	
• Ability to link models to create a more encompassing model.	
• Ability to have within-model conceptual insights.	
Additional knowledge, skills, and abilities	
• Familiarity with task (materials, protocols, expectations)	According to the designer's purposes, tasks may stress or minimize demand for other KSAs, including content knowledge, familiarity with the task type, and other aspects of model-based reasoning including reasoning within models and revising models.
• Subject area knowledge	
• Ability to reason within the model	
• Ability to conduct model revision	
Potential observations	
• Qualities of mapping the corresponding elements between a real-world situation and a scientific model.	These are examples of aspects of things that students might say, do, or construct in situations that call for model elaboration. They are meant to stimulate thinking about the observable variables the designer might choose to define for assessment tasks addressing model elaboration.
• Appropriateness of catenations of models across levels (e.g., individual-level and species-level models in transmission genetics)	
• Correctness and/or completeness of explanation of modifications, in terms of data/model anomalies	
• Identification of ways that a model does not match a situation (e.g., simplifying assumptions), and characterizations of the implications.	
Potential work products	
• Correspondence mapping between elements or relationships of model and real-world situation	These are examples of things that students might be asked to say, do, or construct, where their actions can provide clues about their proficiencies with model elaboration.
• Correspondence mapping between elements or relationships of overlapping models	
• Elaborated model	
• Written/oral explanation of reasoning behind elaboration	

(Continued)

TABLE 4.3
(Continued)

Design Pattern Attribute	Comments

Characteristic features
  Real-world situation and one or more models appropriate to the situation, for which details of correspondence need to be fleshed out. Addresses correspondence between situation and models, and models with one another.
Variable features
  • Is problem context familiar?
  • Model provided, or to be produced by student(s)?
  • Experimental work or supporting research required?
  • Single model or correspondence among models?
  • How well do the models/data correspond?
	Any task concerning model elaboration generated in accordance with this design pattern indicates a model or class of models the student is to work with, and real-world situations and/or other models to which correspondences are to be established.

or "proficiency as needed to carry out such and such kind of work"). *Additional KSAs* are knowledge, skills, and abilities that might also be required in a task that addresses the focal KSA. The task designer should consider which of these are appropriate to assume, to measure jointly, or to avoid to serve the purpose of the assessment. This is accomplished by design choices about variable features of tasks, as further noted below.

In the case of EDMS 738, the focal KSA is ability to map the particulars of an assessment into the form of a statistical model. Understanding the content area and language of the example assessment is an ancillary but necessary additional KSA. The importance of the additional KSAs becomes clear when we consider what can be inferred from a student's response to a task generated from this design pattern. Because a student's knowledge of the content area and language plays a role in the quality of her or his response, these additional KSAs help us to rule out explanations for poor responses that are based on knowledge or skills that the task demands other than the targeted, focal KSA—sources of construct-irrelevant variance (Messick's, 1989).

Potential work products are kinds of student responses or performances themselves that can hold clues about the focal KSAs. These are things that students say, do, or make; they are thus expressed as nouns. *Potential observations* concern the particular aspects of work products that constitute the evidence. As such, they are adjectives, describing qualities, strengths, or degrees of characteristics of realized work products—the evidence the work products convey about the KSAs (e.g., "number of...," "quality of...," "level of...," "kind of..."). *Potential rubrics* identify the evaluation techniques that could be used or adapted to "score" work products; that is, potential rubrics identify, characterize, and summarize the work products by assigning values to the observations. It is possible that several observations could be derived from the same work product, as in the case of an essay written about a chemical process. If the focal KSA is cast in terms of ability to write a coherent essay, then the potential observations attend to aspects of the work product such as degree to which appropriate grammar is used, not the technical quality of the explanation of the process. In contrast, an assessment in which the focal KSA is knowledge of chemical processes may not note the quality of the writing but focus rather on the accuracy of the processes described. The rubrics for arriving at these observations thus vary in accordance with the features of work that are relevant to the KSAs of interest.

With the *characteristic features* and *variable features* attributes, the assessment designer specifies aspects of the situation in which the work products are elicited. *Characteristic* implies that generally all tasks should bear these features, in some form, to support inference about the focal KSA. *Variable features* pertain to aspects of the task environment that the designer can choose to implement in different ways, perhaps within given constraints. Within the constraints of the characteristic features, choosing different configurations of variable features allows a designer to provide evidence about the focal KSA, while influencing the level of difficulty, the degree of confounding with other knowledge, the quantity of evidence gathered at lesser or greater costs, and so on. One example is the amount of scaffolding a student receives while producing a response. Knowing the degree of scaffolding provided will be important for arriving at appropriate claims about that student's KSAs.

The design pattern structure does not dictate the level of generality or scope an assessment designer may choose to target in filling in the substance. Some PADI design patterns are special cases of more general ones; for example, problem solving is linked to more specific design patterns for solving well-defined problems and solving ill-defined problems. The former can provide better evidence about carrying out problem-solving procedures, but at the cost of missing how students conceptualize problems. The latter is better for getting evidence about conceptualization, but for students who cannot get started or who choose an inappropriate approach, there may be little evidence about how they carry out procedures. The way the designer constructs tasks, therefore, depends on which KSAs are of greatest interest. The design pattern helps by laying out which characteristic features are needed in tasks to learn about those KSAs. Another relationship that can exist among design patterns is for one design pattern to comprise others, such as a general model-based reasoning design pattern linked with using a given model, elaborating a model (the one EDMS 738 uses), and revising models. Design patterns can also be linked with other sources of information such as references, sample tasks, and research. Because PADI focuses on middle-school science inquiry, PADI design patterns are linked with national science standards (National Research Council, 1996).

PADI design patterns also contain a slot for linking the design pattern to templates, the major design structure in the next layer of the system. As the following section describes, *templates* represent the assessment argument in terms of blueprints for the nuts and bolts of operational assessments, reflecting further design decisions that move closer to producing particular tasks.

Conceptual Assessment Framework

The structures in this third layer in the ECD approach to assessment design once again reflect an assessment argument, but they move away from the narrative form of domain modeling and towards the details and the machinery of operational assessments. In the conceptual assessment framework (CAF), we begin to articulate the assessment argument sketched in design patterns in terms of the kinds of elements and processes we need to implement an assessment that embodies that argument. The structures in the CAF are expressed as objects such as variables, task schemas, and scoring mechanisms. The substance takes the form of particular values for these variables, or content and settings.

One way to conceptualize the CAF is as machinery for generating assessment blueprints, by means of a structure that coordinates the substantive, statistical, and operational aspects of an assessment. In the CAF, many design decisions are put into place to give concrete shape to the assessments we generate. These decisions include the kinds of statistical models to be used, the materials that will characterize the student work environment, and the procedures to be used

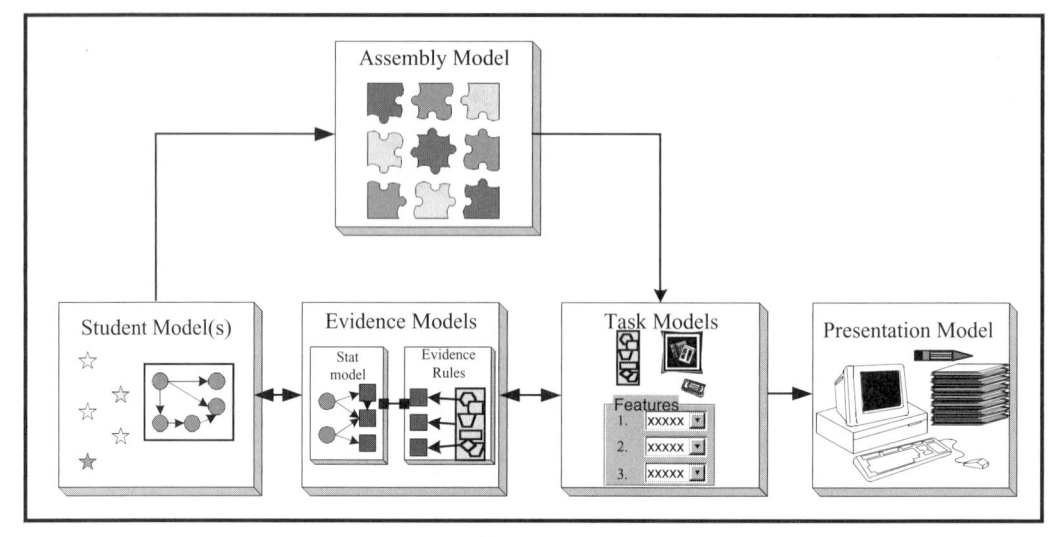

FIG. 4.6. Conceptual assessment framework (CAF).

to score students' work. When we have done the work in the CAF layer, we will have in hand the assessment argument expressed in operational terms, primed to generate a family of tasks and attendant processes that inform the target inference about student proficiency. In addition to assessment expertise, in this layer we may also draw on technical expertise (for details of psychometric models, automated scoring, or presentation of computer-based simulations, for example), as well as on instructional expertise.

The CAF (Figure 4.6) is organized according to three models that correspond to the primary components of the assessment argument. These models work in concert to provide the technical detail required for implementation, such as specifications, operational requirements, statistical models, and details of rubrics. Claims, which in design patterns were expressed in terms of focal and additional KSAs, are operationalized in terms of the variables in the *CAF student model*. There can be one or several variables in a student model, and the student model can take a form as simple as an overall score across items, as complex as a multivariate item response theory or latent class model, or anything in between. What is necessary is that the student model variables link students' performance on tasks to the claim(s) we wish to make about student proficiency. Different values for student model variables indicate different claims about students' proficiencies. A probability distribution over these variables can be used (and is used in formal probabilistic measurement models) to express what one knows about a student at a given point in time.

The *CAF task model* comprises the components necessary to lay out the features of the environment in which the student completes the task. This is where the characteristic and variables features as well as potential work products from design patterns are represented in terms of stimulus materials and values of the variables that describe their salient features. A variety of potential observations and rubrics were identified in design patterns, which linked potential work products to the KSAs. Each may have its own strengths and weaknesses, costs, and learning benefits. Choices among them and specific forms are now chosen to fit the purposes, resources, and context of the particular assessment that is being designed. These more specific forms are expressed in the *CAF evidence model*. Marshalling multiple tasks into an assessment is coordinated by the *assembly model*.

Student Model: What Are We Measuring?

In domain analysis and domain modeling, we described target inference in narratives about content and student abilities, knowledge, and skills. As we have seen, it is not possible to measure these student proficiencies directly; they must instead be inferred from incomplete evidence, in the form of the handful of things that students say, do, or make. The CAF lays out the statistical machinery for making inferences about student proficiencies, which are expressed in terms of probability distributions over a single variable or set of variables.

In the simplest case, where proficiency in some defined domain of tasks is of interest, the student model contains a single student model variable and students are characterized in terms of the proportion of a domain of tasks they are likely to answer correctly. In more complex cases, where more than one proficiency is at issue, a multivariate student model contains a collection of student model variables and a multivariate probability distribution used to express what is known about a student's values.

The CAF contains structures for objects such as the student model, and the schemas for measurement, evaluation, and task elements discussed below. Then, for given assessments, the content or substance of these objects is fleshed out; particular variables are constrained either to a range or fixed value. The relationships among these objects are primed by the way the structures connect to one another.

In the EDMS 738 example, there is a single student model variable. It is a continuous variable in an Item Response Theory (IRT) model, and it is used to accumulate evidence about a student's capability to apply ECD principles to an exemplar, as evidenced by that individual's performance on a series of assignments. A probability distribution (e.g., a maximum likelihood estimate and a standard error, or a Bayes mean estimate and a posterior standard deviation) indicates what is known about a student after evaluating his or her performances. This is the structure of the student model. The meaning of the student model variable is derived from the nature of the student's performances and how they are evaluated; in particular, their reasoning about a real assessment through the lens of ECD. A simplified version of this student model, sufficient and appropriate for, say, classroom testing, is to accumulate a number right or total score and characterize its precision in terms of familiar reliability coefficients and standard errors of measurement.

Evidence Model: How Do We Measure It?

There are two components to the evidence model. The first concerns the qualities of the work products students have produced—quality, accuracy, elegance, strategy used, and so on. The psychological perspective from which the designer views the task informs this component; it determines the criteria for exactly which aspects of work are important and how they should be evaluated. These observable variables, whether quantitative or qualitative, are typically called *item scores*. *Evaluation procedures* define how the values of observable variables are determined from students' work products. Examples of evaluation procedures are answer keys, scoring rubrics with examples, and automated scoring procedures in computer-based simulation tasks. Several features of a single work product may be important for inference, in which case evaluation procedures must produce values of multiple observable variables. In the EDMS 738 example, the student final essay may be scored in terms of use of ECD terminology and application of ECD principles to their chosen assessment.

Although the evaluation component tells us how to characterize the salient features of any particular performance, it remains to synthesize data like these across tasks (perhaps different ones for different students) in terms of evidence for claims about what students know or can do. We need a mechanism to define and quantify the degree to which any given response reveals something about the claim we wish to make. This is the role of the *measurement model*. Each piece of data directly characterizes some aspect of a particular performance, but it also conveys some information about the targeted claim regarding what the student knows or can do. More specifically, a probability-based measurement model characterizes the weight and direction of evidence that observable variables convey about student model variables. Formal psychometric models for this step include IRT models (univariate or multivariate) and latent class models (e.g., for mastery testing). More common is the informal approximation of taking weighted or unweighted scores over items, which suffices when all items contribute relatively independent nuggets of evidence about the same targeted proficiency.

Task Model: Where Do We Measure It?

The *task model* describes the environment in which examinees say, do, or make something to provide the data about what they know or can do as more broadly conceived. Decisions are made from the range of options identified in the domain modeling layer and expressed in design patterns: potential work products and characteristic and variable features of tasks. In the CAF layer, we specify precisely what these work products will be, and narrow down the kinds of features that will be central or optional for grounding the targeted claims about student proficiency, under the particular constraints of the assessment situation at hand.

One decision is the form(s) the work product(s) should take. Will it be a multiple-choice item or an essay, transaction list, or illustration? What materials will be necessary as prompts for the work product? These include directives, manipulatives, and features of the setting such as resources available or scaffolding provided by the teacher. These features of the environment have important implications for assessment. For example, two students may respond to a question, but one may have access to her class notes and textbook, whereas the other may have responded without these resources. Is remembering the details of formulas a focal KSA or not? If it is, then it is appropriate that the setting not provide this information so that the task calls on the students' knowledge in this regard. If not, then providing open-book problems or formula sheets is a better way to focus evidence on using formulas in practical situations. The claims we wish to make about students shape the choices of task features. Sometimes these features are decisions made by students, as in the EDMS 738 example.

Assembly Model: How Much Do We Need to Measure It?

A single piece of evidence is rarely sufficient to sustain a claim about student knowledge. Thus, an operational assessment is likely to include a set of tasks or items. The work of determining the constellation of tasks is taken up by the *assembly model* to represent the breadth and diversity of the domain being assessed. The assembly model thus orchestrates the interrelations among the student models, evidence models, and task models, forming the psychometric backbone of the assessment. The assembly model also specifies the required accuracy for measuring each student model variable. Particular forms an assembly model can take include a familiar test-specifications matrix, an adaptive testing algorithm (e.g., Stocking & Swanson, 1993), or a set of targets for the mix of items in terms of the values of selected task model variables (e.g., the test specifications and blueprints referred to by Webb, chap. 8, this volume).

Sample Knowledge Representations

There are various ways to detail out the general description of the ECD models given, as knowledge representations that support design work in this layer of the system. PADI is one of any number of systems that could be constructed as a vehicle for implementing the principles laid out by ECD. The PADI project has developed structures called *templates* (Riconscente,

4. EVIDENCE-CENTERED DESIGN   79

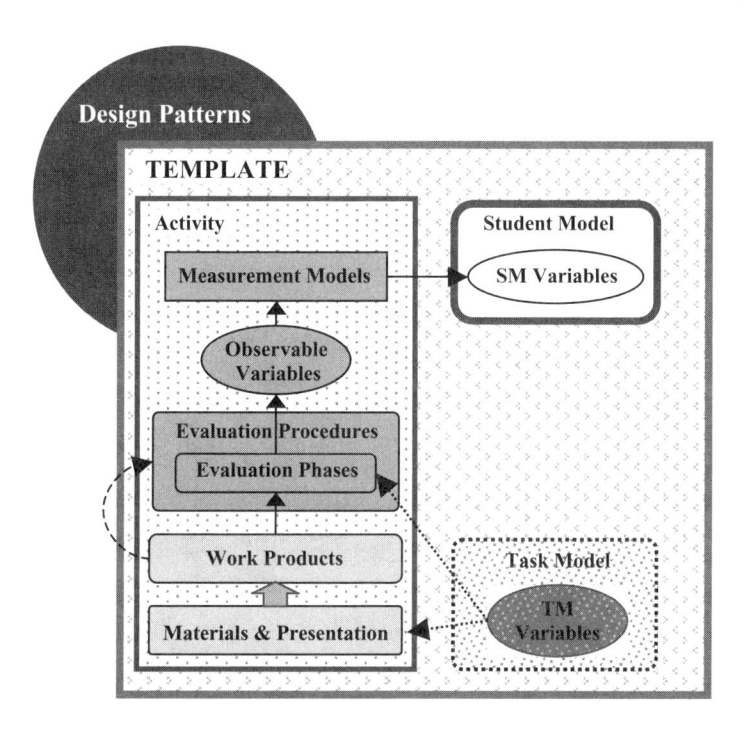

FIG. 4.7. PADI template objects. Patterns map the objects in the PADI design system to the ECD models. Legend: ☐ ECD student model; ☐ ECD evidence model; ☐ ECD task model.

Mislevy, & Hamel, 2005) for doing so. Formally, a PADI template is the central object in the PADI object model, and can be represented formally in unified modeling language (UML; Booch, Rumbaugh, & Jacobson, 1999) or extended markup language (XML) (World-Wide Web Consortium, 1998), or in a more interactive format as web pages in the PADI design system. Within an online design system, the substance of these structures is populated with definitions of student model variables, work products, evaluation procedures, task model variables, and the like, thereby rendering a general blueprint for a family of assessment tasks. Hierarchies of objects and their attributes are defined, in which to detail the objects described in more general form in the student, evidence, and task models described above. Figure 4.7 is a generic representation of the objects in a PADI template. Figure 4.8 summarizes the objects in the EDMS 738 template using the same graphic format. Figures 4.9 through 4.11 show parts of the actual template for EDMS 738 tasks from the perspective of the design system interface. In these figures, screen shots of PADI objects viewed through a web interface are presented. Figure 4.9 shows part of the template object for the EDMS 738 example. In viewing this illustration, it is useful to recall the distinction introduced in the previous section between *structure* and *substance*. The left-most column identifies the attributes of the template object which define its structure; all templates have these attributes. The substance of each attribute is indicated in the right columns. Some of these attributes are narrative descriptions, and others are themselves objects in the PADI object model. Figures 4.10 and 4.11 present objects used as substance for the activities and task model variables attributes in this template.

Assessment Implementation

The next layer in the ECD assessment design scheme is *assessment implementation*, which encompasses creating the assessment pieces that the CAF structures depict: authoring tasks, fitting measurement models, detailing rubrics and providing examples, programming simulations

Design Pattern: Model Elaboration

TEMPLATE: EDMS 738—Basic Structure

Student Model: Understanding of Assessment Foundations
An SM is a collection of one or more SMVs and a probability distribution over them

SMV: Understanding of Assessment Foundations

Activity *Final Version of Essay*

Activity *Outline of Essay* [Since informal, **formative** assessment, no input to SM]

Activity *Presentation to Class*

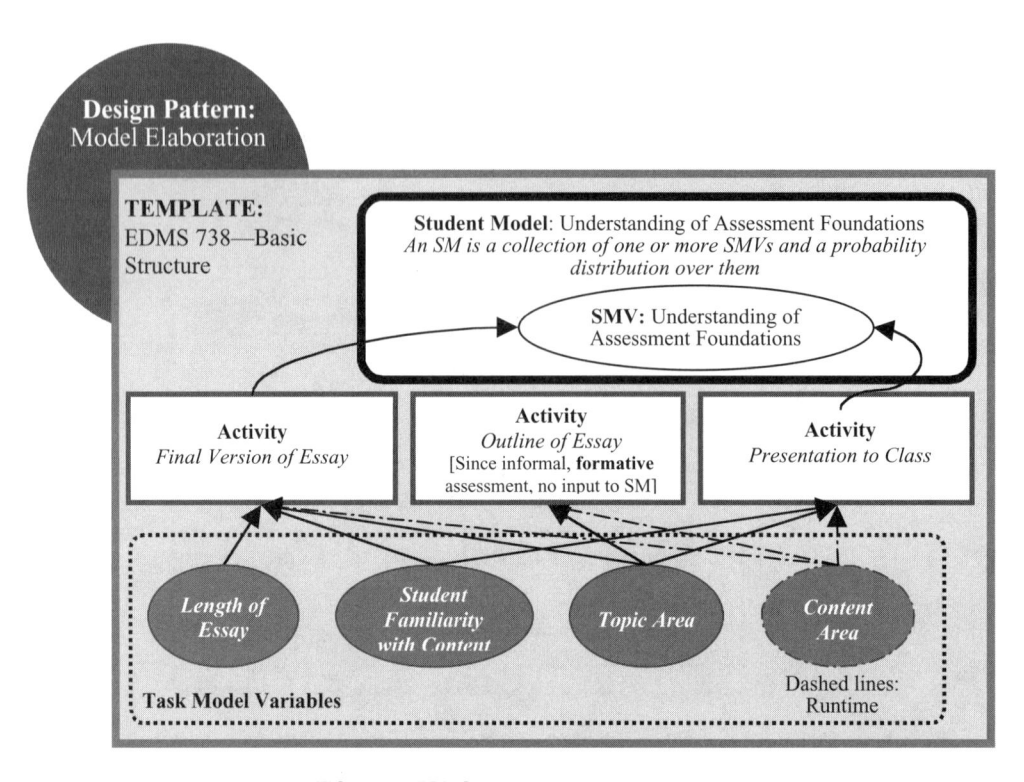

Task Model Variables: *Length of Essay*, *Student Familiarity with Content*, *Topic Area*, *Content Area*

Dashed lines: Runtime

FIG. 4.8. EDMS template collapsed view.

and automated scoring algorithms, and the like. Having invested expertise about the domain, assessment, instruction, and technology in a design process grounded in evidentiary reasoning, the designer is positioned to generate multiple instances of tasks from each template. Although these tasks may vary substantially in their surface features, having been generated from the principled assessment design process, they each embody a shared rationale and assessment argument. Although most of the design decisions are finalized in this layer, some details may remain to be filled in during the subsequent layer, assessment operation. For example, mathematics tasks can be created on the fly, varying only in the values of the numbers used in identical problem structures (Bejar, 2002). In some cases these decisions can be left to the examinee, as in the EDMS 738 example where the students choose their own assessment exemplars to analyze. There, familiarity with the context and domain in an exemplar are required along with ECD principles for good analyses; letting the students choose exemplars with which they are familiar removes demand for this additional knowledge as a source of low performance.

PADI offers support for some of the work in the implementation layer, namely specifying templates fully so they are blueprints for specific tasks. These more specific structures are referred to as *task specifications*, or *task specs*. Although templates are capable of generating families of tasks that may vary in the range of proficiencies assessed (e.g., univariate or complex multivariate) and a host of other features, such as the observable variables or stimulus materials, task specs are final plans for individual tasks. The values of some attributes are selected from among predetermined options. Other attributes will remain unchanged; still others have generic narrative materials tailored to their final forms.

4. EVIDENCE-CENTERED DESIGN   81

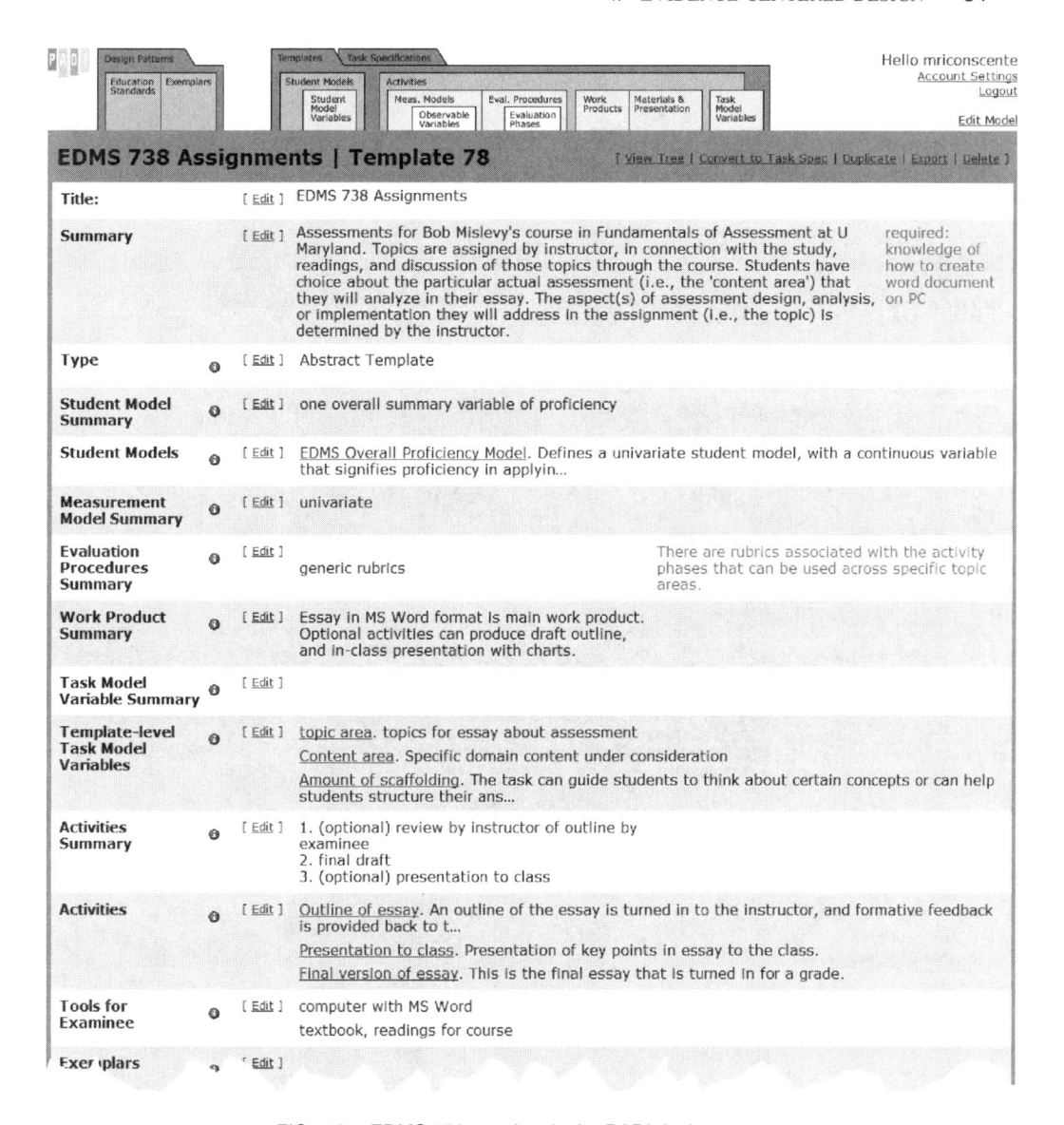

FIG. 4.9. EDMS 738 template in the PADI design system.

Assessment Delivery

The preceding design layers analyze a domain to determine what knowledge and skill is of interest, and how you know it when you see it; how to build an evidentiary argument from this information; how to design the elements of an assessment system that embody this argument; and how to actually build those elements. But the most enviable library of assessment tasks can say nothing about students in and of itself. These libraries provide only potential for learning about what students know and can do, unrealized until students begin to interact with tasks, saying and doing things, which are then captured, evaluated, and synthesized into evidence about the claims at issue. Any assessment requires some processes by which items are actually selected and administered, scores are reported, and feedback is communicated to the appropriate parties.

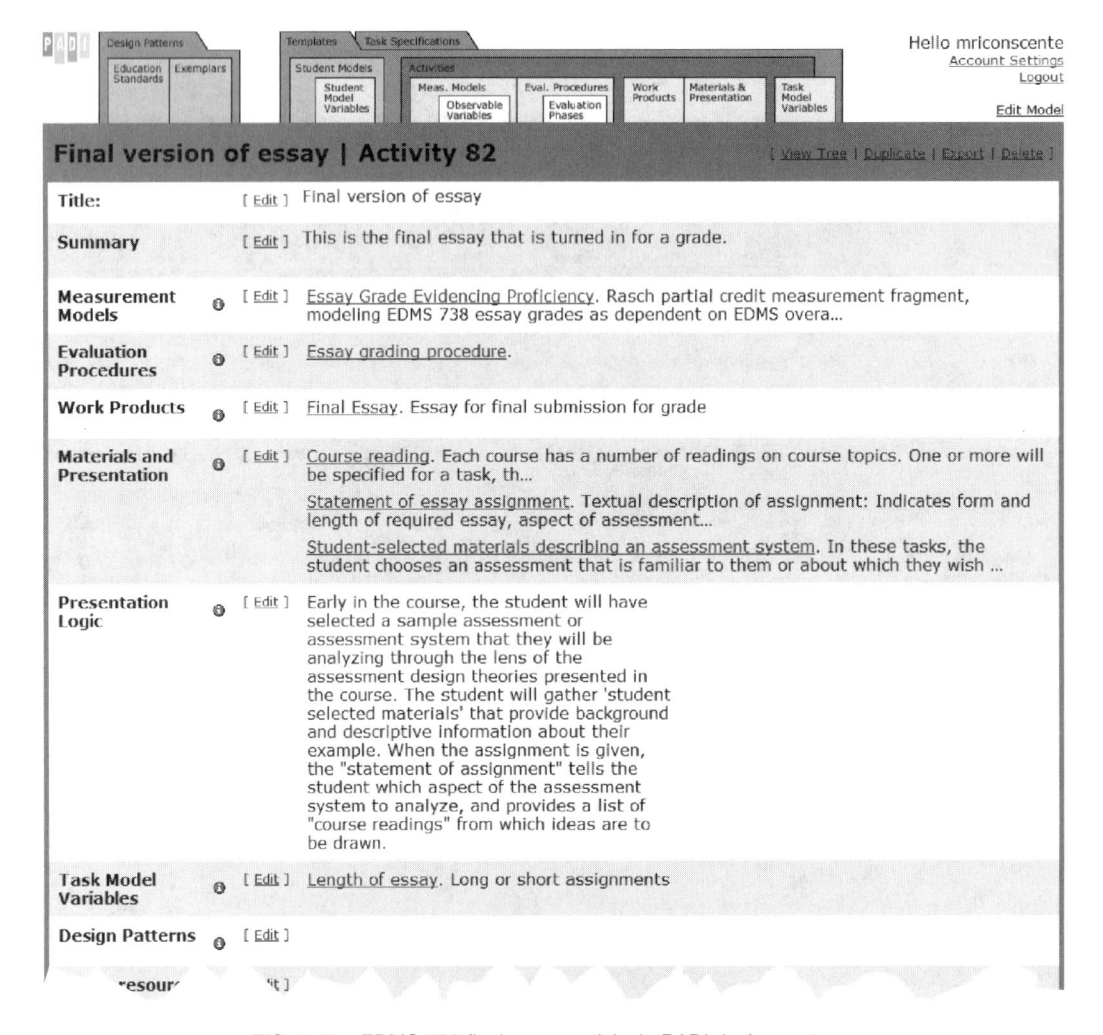

FIG. 4.10. EDMS 738 final essay activity in PADI design system.

Operational processes may differ substantially from one assessment to another, and even within a given assessment system the processes may evolve over time as needs arise. New forms of assessment, such as computer-based simulations, require processes beyond those of familiar multiple-choice and essay assessments. The international standards consortium Instructional Management Systems (IMS) has developed Question and Test Interoperability (QTI) standards to help developers share materials and processes across assessment systems and platforms. The interested reader is referred to the IMS Web site (http://www.imsglobal.org/) for details about QTI standards. Attention here focuses on the conceptual model of the assessment delivery layer that is the basis of the QTI specifications, namely the four-process architecture for assessment delivery shown in Figure 4.12 (Almond, Steinberg, & Mislevy, 2002).

Assessment operation can be represented according to four principal processes. The *activity selection process* selects a task or other activity from the task library. In the case of our EDMS 738 example, the activity selection process—here, the instructor—might select the final essay task. This process then sends instructions about presenting the item to the *presentation process*, which takes care of presenting the item or task to the examinee, in accordance with materials and instructions laid out in the task model. The presentation process also collects responses

4. EVIDENCE-CENTERED DESIGN   83

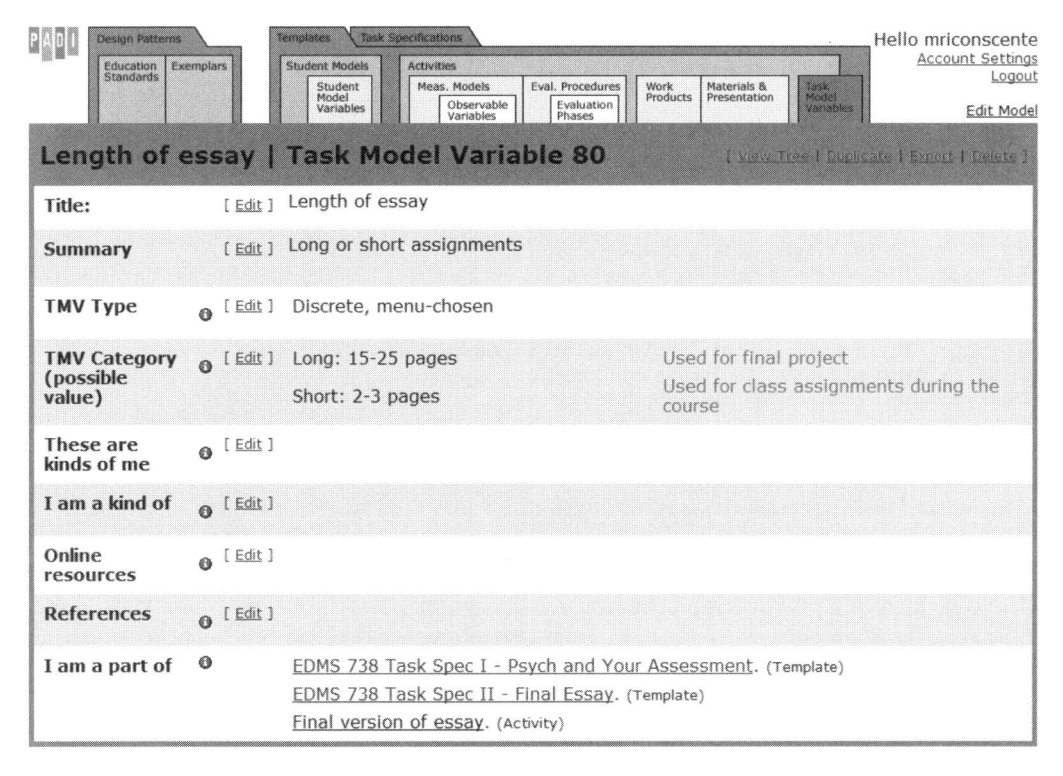

Title:	[Edit]	Length of essay	
Summary	[Edit]	Long or short assignments	
TMV Type	[Edit]	Discrete, menu-chosen	
TMV Category (possible value)	[Edit]	Long: 15-25 pages	Used for final project
		Short: 2-3 pages	Used for class assignments during the course
These are kinds of me	[Edit]		
I am a kind of	[Edit]		
Online resources	[Edit]		
References	[Edit]		
I am a part of		EDMS 738 Task Spec I - Psych and Your Assessment. (Template)	
		EDMS 738 Task Spec II - Final Essay. (Template)	
		Final version of essay. (Activity)	

FIG. 4.11.   EDMS 738 length of essay task model variable in PADI design system.

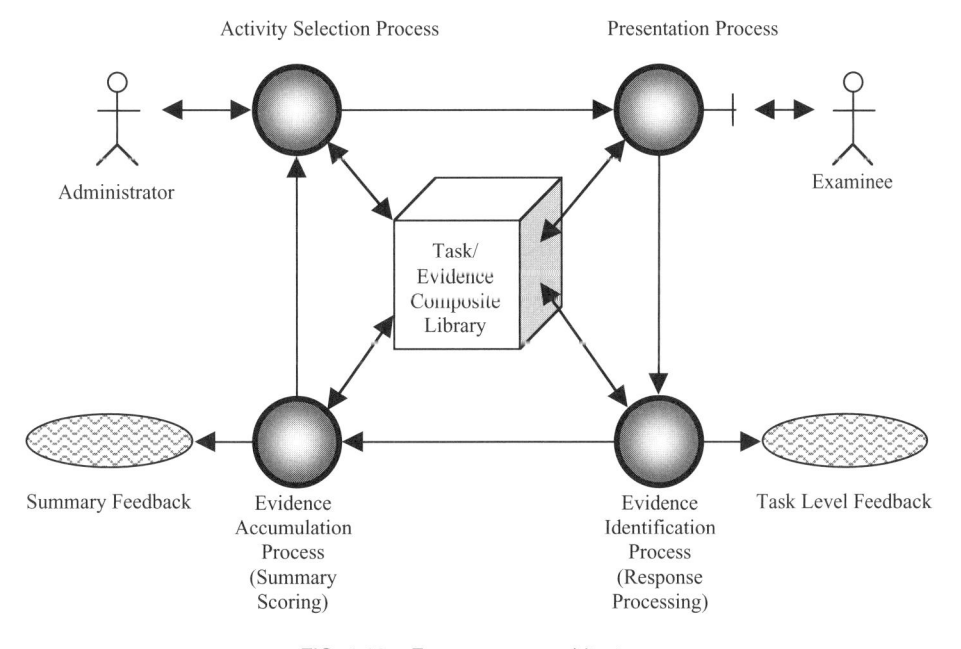

FIG. 4.12.   Four–process architecture.

for scoring and analysis, namely, the work product(s). The work product may be the letter corresponding to a multiple choice option, or it may be a whole series of information including traces of examinee navigation in an online problem-solving environment, final responses, notes, and time spent. The work product in the EDMS 738 example is a student's essay, written in response to the assigned topic in the context of the examinee's exemplar.

Work products are passed to the *evidence identification process,* which performs item-level response processing according to the methods laid out in the evidence model in the CAF. This process identifies the salient outcomes of the task for the assessment purpose, and expresses the outcome in terms of values of observable variables according to the evaluation procedures specified in the evidence model. Possibilities include the quality of writing, accuracy of the content, or degree to which the response reflects critical thinking. One or more outcomes can be abstracted from any given response or set of responses. Depending on the purpose of the assessment, feedback may be communicated at this point to the examinee or a teacher.

Following response processing, the values of observable variables are sent to the *evidence accumulation process,* which is responsible for summary scoring. Here is where we amass the evidence being collected over multiple tasks in accordance with the measurement procedures specified in the CAF via the evidence model. This process updates the probability distributions used to express what is known about the value of an individual's student model variables. Summary feedback based on these results may also be provided immediately or stored for later reporting. Evidence accumulation then informs the activity selection process, which makes a decision about the next task to administer based on criteria that may include current beliefs about examinee proficiency.

Each of these processes relies on information about how items should be presented and scored. What this information is, in abstract terms, and how it is used, was specified in the models of the CAF layer. The particulars for any given item, such as stimulus materials, item parameters, and scoring rules, were specified in the implementation layer. Now, in the operational layer, this information is stored in the *task/evidence composite library,* represented by the cube in the center of Figure 4.12. This library contains information about how each item should be presented, as well as parameters for how examinees will interact with the item. Conditions such as whether examinees can use calculators or spell-checkers are examples of presentation parameters. Additional information in the task/evidence composite library includes how responses are collected and what form they should take, as well as how to extract meaningful features from that work product and translate them into observable variables. Specifications for integrating the evidence into an accumulating student record are also contained in this library. As communication proceeds around this loop, each process communicates directly with the task/evidence composite library, as well as with adjacent processes.

In Figure 4.13 an expanded view shows how data objects are drawn from the library and passed around the cycle. Depending on the application, a wide range of interaction patterns is possible. For example, intelligent tutoring systems, self-assessment, training drills, and multiple-stage investigations use different timeframes for responses and provide different kinds of feedback at different points in the assessment process. Further, this abstract design does not constrain the means by which processes are implemented, their locations, or their sequence and timing (e.g., the interval between evidence identification and evidence accumulation could be measured in weeks or in milliseconds).

Now that this architecture for delivery has been defined, one can see the contribution of the IMS/QTI standards. Even though the content of the messages passed around the processes differs substantially from one assessment system to another, and the nature and interactions of processes vary depending on the assessment system, IMS/QTI focuses on two things that

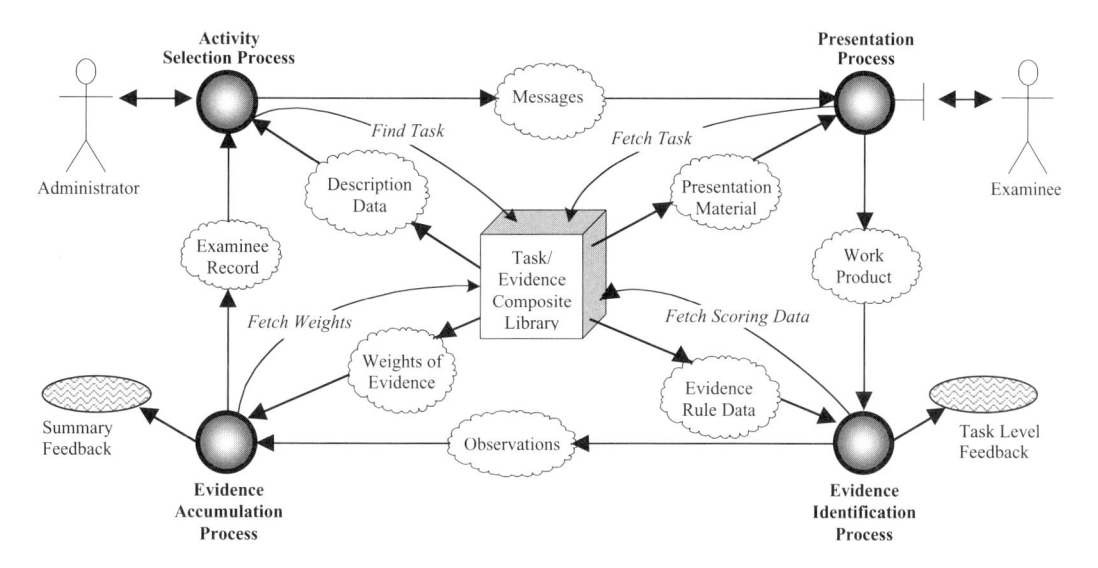

FIG. 4.13. Processes and messages in the delivery cycle.

remain the same: the nature of the processes that are to be carried out, in some fashion, and the kinds of messages (data) that need to be passed from one to another. This is sufficient to define standards for encoding these messages, without restricting their content. Developers of assessment content and assessment processes can create materials and applications that are able to work together with one another, because of a shared conception of the operational layer of assessment.

CONCLUSION

This chapter viewed assessment design as the development of an assessment argument, facilitated by ECD. We showed how the use of layers and attention to various knowledge representations make it feasible for assessment design to coordinate work across wide ranges of expertise and technologies. To illustrate how these principles might be used in real-world assessment development, we drew on experiences and structures emerging from the PADI project. A number of publications provide the interested reader with further ECD-related theoretical considerations as well as practical examples of ECD applications; these resources are identified in the annotated bibliography presented in the appendix.

Today's test developers have at their disposal tools such as the Toulmin structures and design patterns to guide their thinking about assessment design. As we sought to underscore, an essential yet often implicit and invisible property of good assessment design is a coherent evidence-based argument. Simon (1969, p. 5) refers to "imperatives" in the design of "artificial things." *Imperatives* in assessment design translate into the constraints and purposes of the process. The physical nuts and bolts addressed in the CAF—such as time limits, administration settings, and budget—are wont to dominate considerations of constraints in the assessment design process. By engaging in the creation of design patterns, developers are supported to attend to the constraint of making a coherent assessment argument before investing resources at the CAF layer. Currently, tools at the CAF layer are still under development, with some early implementations ongoing at Educational Training Service (ETS) and in PADI. It is our hope that in the near future off-the-shelf (or off-the-web) supports for implementing the particulars of the processes described herein will be available. Even without software supports, however, a test designer at any level, in any content domain, and for any purpose, may benefit from examining test and task development from the perspective discussed in this chapter. The terminology and knowledge representations provide a useful framework for new designers and a useful supplement for experienced ones.

Initial applications of the ideas encompassed in the ECD framework may be labor intensive and time consuming. Nevertheless, the import of the ideas for improving assessment will become clear from (a) the explication of the reasoning behind assessment design decisions and (b) the identification of reusable elements and pieces of infrastructure—conceptual as well as technical—that can be adapted for new projects. The gains may be most apparent in the development of technology-based assessment tasks, such as web-based simulations. The same conceptual framework and design elements may prove equally valuable in making assessment arguments explicit for research projects, performance assessments, informal classroom evaluation, and tasks in large-scale, high-stakes assessments. In this way the ECD framework can serve to speed the diffusion of improved assessment practices.

ACKNOWLEDGMENT

This material is based on work supported by the National Science Foundation under grant REC-0129331 (PADI Implementation Grant). We are grateful for contributions by Larry Hamel and Geneva Haertel and for comments on an earlier version from Thomas M. Haladyna and Steven M. Downing.

REFERENCES

Alexander, C., Ishikawa, S., & Silverstein, M. (1977). *A pattern language: Towns, buildings, construction.* New York: Oxford University Press.

Almond, R. G., Steinberg, L. S., & Mislevy, R. J. (2002). Enhancing the design and delivery of assessment systems: A four-process architecture. *Journal of Technology, Learning, and Assessment, 1*(5). Retrieved August 5, 2005 from http://www.bc.edu/research/intasc/jtla/journal/v1n5.shtml.

Bachman, L. F., & Palmer, A. S. (1996). *Language testing in practice.* Oxford: Oxford University Press.

Baxter, G., & Mislevy, R. J. (2005). *The case for an integrated design framework for assessing science injury (PADI Technical Report 5).* Menlo Park, CA: SRI International.

Bejar, I. I. (2002). Generative testing: From conception to implementation. In S. H. Irvine & P. C. Kyllonen (Eds.), *Item generation for test development* (pp. 199–217). Hillsdale, NJ: Lawrence Erlbaum Associates.

Biggs, J. B., & Collis, K. F. (1982). *Evaluating the quality of learning: The SOLO taxonomy.* New York: Academic Press.

Booch, G., Rumbaugh, J., & Jacobson, I. (1999). *The unified modeling language user guide.* Reading, MA: Addison-Wesley.

Brand, S. (1994). *How buildings learn: What happens after they're built.* New York: Viking-Penguin.

Breese, J. S., Goldman, R. P., & Wellman, M. P. (1994). Introduction to the special section on knowledge-based construction of probabilistic and decision models. *IEEE Transactions on Systems, Man, and Cybernetics, 24,* 1577–1579.

Cisco Systems, (2000). *Internetworking technology basics* (3rd ed.). Indianapolis, IN: Author.

Dym, C. L. (1994). *Engineering design.* New York: Cambridge University Press.

Embretson, S. E. (1983). Construct validity: Construct representation versus nomothetic span. *Psychological Bulletin, 93,* 179–197.

Gamma, E., Helm, R., Johnson, R., & Vlissides, J. (1994). *Design patterns.* Reading, MA: Addison-Wesley.

Gardner, K. M., Rush, A., Crist, M. K., Konitzer, R. & Teegarden, B. (1998). *Cognitive patterns: Problem-solving frameworks for object technology.* New York: Cambridge University Press.

Gitomer, D. H., & Steinberg, L.S. (1999). Representational issues in assessment design. In I. E. Sigel (Ed.), *Development of mental representation* (pp. 351–370). Hillsdale, NJ: Lawrence Erlbaum Associates.

Greeno, J. G., Collins, A. M., & Resnick, L. B. (1997). Cognition and learning. In D. Berliner & R. Calfee (Eds.), *Handbook of educational psychology* (pp. 15–47). New York: Simon & Schuster Macmillan.

Joint Committee on Standards for AERA, APA, and NCME. (1999). *Standards for educational and psychological testing*. Washington, DC: AERA.
Markman, A. B. (1998). *Knowledge representation*. Mahwah, NJ: Lawrence Erlbaum Associates.
Messick, S. (1989). Validity. In R. L. Linn (Ed.), *Educational measurement* (3rd Ed., pp. 13–103). New York: American Council on Education/Macmillan.
Messick, S. (1994). The interplay of evidence and consequences in the validation of performance assessments. *Education Researcher, 32*(2), 13–23.
Mislevy, R. J. (2003). Argument substance and argument structure. *Law, Probability, & Risk, 2,* 237–258.
Mislevy, R. J., Steinberg, L. S., & Almond, R. G. (2003). On the structure of educational assessments. *Measurement: Interdisciplinary Research and Perspectives, 1,* 3–66.
National Research Council. (1996). *National science education standards*. Washington, DC: National Academy Press.
PADI Research Group. (2003). Design patterns for assessing science inquiry. *Technical Report 1*. Menlo Park, CA: SRI, International.
Riconscente, M. M., Mislevy, R. J., Hamel, L., & PADI Research Group. (2005). An introduction to task templates. *Technical Report 3*. Menlo Park, CA: SRI International.
Schum, D. A. (1994). *The evidential foundations of probabilistic reasoning*. New York: Wiley.
Siegler, R. S. (1981). *Developmental sequences within and between concepts*. Monograph of the Society for Research in Child Development, Serial No. 189, 46.
Simon, H. A. (1969). *The sciences of the artificial*. Cambridge, MA: MIT Press.
Stocking, M. L., & Swanson, L. (1993). A method for severely constrained item selection in adaptive testing. *Applied Psychological Measurement, 17,* 277–296.
Tillers, P., & Schum, D. A. (1991). A theory of preliminary fact investigation. *U.C. Davis Law Review, 24,* 907–966.
Toulmin, S. E. (1958). *The uses of argument*. Cambridge: Cambridge University Press.
VanLehn, K. (1990). *Mind bugs: The origins of procedural misconceptions*. Cambridge, MA: MIT Press.
World-Wide Web Consortium. (1998). *Extensible markup language (XML)*. Retrieved August 6, 2005 from http://www.w3c.org/TR/1998/REC-xml-19980210.
Wigmore, J. H. (1937). *The science of judicial proof* (3rd Ed.). Boston: Little, Brown, & Co.

APPENDIX

This chapter provided an overview of ECD—a start, but by no means a sufficient grounding in the subject. This appendix gives suggestions for further reading in publications that were either produced in the ECD research program or address related principles. They are presented below in three groups: publications about the ECD framework itself; applications of these and related ideas; and particular aspects of assessment design and analysis from the perspective of evidentiary reasoning.

The ECD Framework

Almond, R. G., Steinberg, L. S., & Mislevy, R. J. (2002). Enhancing the design and delivery of assessment systems: A four-process architecture. *Journal of Technology, Learning, and Assessment, 1*(5). Retrieved May 1, 2005 from http://www.bc.edu/research/intasc/jtla/journal/v1n5.shtml. Also available as *CSE Technical Report 543*. Los Angeles: The National Center for Research on Evaluation, Standards, Student Testing (CRESST), Center for Studies in Education, UCLA. Retrieved May 1, 2005 from http://www.cse.ucla.edu/CRESST/Reports/TECH543.pdf. [Extended discussion of the four-process delivery system architecture, including explanation of relationships between the design objects of the conceptual assessment framework and the processes and messages in an assessment delivery system.]
Almond, R. G., Steinberg, L. S., & Mislevy, R. J. (2003). A framework for reusing assessment components. In H. Yanai, A. Okada, K. Shigemasu, Y. Kano, & J.J. Meulman (Eds.), *New developments in psychometrics* (pp. 28–288). Tokyo: Springer. [Shorter description of the four-process delivery system, with descriptions of what the four processes do and how they interact in assessments designed to achieve different purposes.]
Mislevy, R. J., Almond, R. G., & Lukas, J. F (2004). A brief introduction to evidence-centered design. *CSE Research Report 632*. Los Angeles: Center for Studies in Education, UCLA. Retrieved June 6, 2005 from http://www.cse.ucla.edu/CRESST/Reports/TR579.pdf. [Brief overview of ECD, focused on the CAF and four-process delivery architecture for assessment delivery systems.]

Mislevy, R. J., Steinberg, L. S., & Almond, R. G. (2002). On the structure of educational assessments. *Measurement: Interdisciplinary Research and Perspectives, 1,* 3–67. Forthcoming as CSE Research Report. [Currently the most comprehensive overview available of evidence centered design, spanning assessment arguments, to design elements, to delivery system architecture, and the connections within and across these levels.]

Applications

Behrens, J. T., Mislevy, R. J., Bauer, M., Williamson, D. M., & Levy, R. (2004). Introduction to Evidence Centered Design and Lessons Learned From Its Application in a Global E-learning Program. *The International Journal of Testing, 4,* 295–301.

Levy, R. & Mislevy, R. J. (2004). Specifying and refining a measurement model for a computer based interactive assessment. *The International Journal of Testing, 4,* 333–369. [Focus on estimation of conditional probability models in the Bayes net psychometric model in Cisco's NetPASS prototype assessment. A fairly technical psychometric paper.]

Mislevy, R. J., Almond, R. G., Dibello, L. V., Jenkins, F., Steinberg, L. S., Yan, D., & Senturk, D. (2002). Modeling conditional probabilities in complex educational assessments. *CSE Technical Report 580.* Los Angeles: The National Center for Research on Evaluation, Standards, Student Testing (CRESST), Center for Studies in Education, UCLA. Retrieved May 1, 2005 from http://www.cse.ucla.edu/CRESST/Reports/TR580.pdf. [Focus on estimation of conditional probability models in the Bayes net psychometric model in the Biomass prototype assessment. A fairly technical psychometric paper.]

Mislevy, R. J., & Gitomer, D. H. (1996). The role of probability-based inference in an intelligent tutoring system. *User-Modeling and User-Adapted Interaction, 5,* 253–282. Also available as *CSE Technical Report 413.* Los Angeles: The National Center for Research on Evaluation, Standards, Student Testing (CRESST), Center for Studies in Education, UCLA. Retrieved May 1, 2005 from http://www.cse.ucla.edu/CRESST/Reports/TECH413.PDF. [Good foundational explanation of the use of Bayesian inference in complex assessments, illustrated with the HYDRIVE intelligent tutoring system for troubleshooting aircraft hydraulics.]

Mislevy, R. J., Steinberg, L. S., & Almond, R. A. (2002). Design and analysis in task-based language assessment. *Language Assessment, 19,* 477–496. Also available as *CSE Technical Report 579.* Los Angeles: The National Center for Research on Evaluation, Standards, Student Testing (CRESST), Center for Studies in Education, UCLA. Retrieved May 1, 2005 from http://www.cse.ucla.edu/CRESST/Reports/TR579.pdf. [ECD perspective on designing task-based language assessments. Includes examples of Bayes nets for tasks that tap multiple aspects or knowledge and skill.]

Mislevy, R. J., Steinberg, L. S., Breyer, F. J., Almond, R. G., & Johnson, L. (1999). A cognitive task analysis, with implications for designing a simulation-based assessment system. *Computers and Human Behavior, 15,* 335–374. Also available as *CSE Technical Report 487.* Los Angeles: The National Center for Research on Evaluation, Standards, Student Testing (CRESST), Center for Studies in Education, UCLA. Retrieved May 1, 2005 from http://www.cse.ucla.edu/CRESST/Reports/TR487.pdf. [Design and conduct of a cognitive task analysis of expertise in dental hygiene, from the perspective of informing the construction of the models in the ECD conceptual assessment framework.]

Mislevy, R. J., Steinberg, L. S., Breyer, F. J., Almond, R. G., & Johnson, L. (2002). Making sense of data from complex assessment. *Applied Measurement in Education, 15,* 363–378. Also available as *CSE Technical Report 538.* Los Angeles: The National Center for Research on Evaluation, Standards, Student Testing (CRESST), Center for Studies in Education, UCLA. Retrieved May 1, 2005 from http://www.cse.ucla.edu/CRESST/Reports/RML%20TR%20538.pdf. [Argument that the way to design and analyze complex assessments, such as computer-based simulations, is from the perspective of the evidentiary argument, not from the perspective of technology. Ideas are illustrated in some detail with the DISC prototype assessment of problem-solving in dental hygiene.]

PADI Research Group. (2002). Design patterns for assessing science inquiry. *PADI Technical Report No. 1.* Menlo Park, CA: SRI International.

Riconscente, M. M., Mislevy, R. J., Hamel, L., & PADI Working Group. (2005). An introduction to PADI task templates. *PADI Technical Report.* Menlo Park, CA: SRI International. [Describes the role of task templates in assessment design and the objects that comprise them as currently implemented in the context of the ECD-based PADI project.]

Songer, N., & Wenk, A. (2003). Measuring the development of complex reasoning in science. Paper presented at the annual meeting of the American Educational Research Association, April 25, 2003, Chicago, IL.

Steinberg, L. S., & Gitomer, D. G. (1996). Intelligent tutoring and assessment built on an understanding of a technical problem-solving task. *Instructional Science, 24,* 223–258. [Concerns the interplay among cognitive analysis, instructional strategy, and assessment design, in the context of the HYDRIVE intelligent tutoring system for troubleshooting aircraft hydraulics.]

Steinberg, L. S., Mislevy, R. J., Almond, R. G., Baird, A. B., Cahallan, C., DiBello, L. V., Senturk, D., Yan, D., Chernick, H., & Kindfield, A. C. H. (2003). *Introduction to the Biomass project: An illustration of evidence-centered assessment design and delivery capability.* Forthcoming CSE Technical Report. Los Angeles, CA: UCLA Center for the Study of Evaluation. [Design rationale for a standards-based, web-delivered assessment of science inquiry, in the areas of transmission genetics and microevolution. Much discussion of working with experts and National Science Education Standards to carry out the ECD design work and then implement a prototype assessment at the level of secondary science.]

Williamson, D. M., Bauer, M., Steinberg, L. S., Mislevy, R. J., & Behrens, J. T. (2004). Design Rationale for a Complex Performance Assessment. *The International Journal of Testing,* 4,303–332. [ECD design rationale for a simulation-based assessment of troubleshooting and design of computer networks. Foundational analysis for the NetPASS online assessment of networking skill, by the Cisco Learning Institute, Educational Testing Service, and the University of Maryland. Includes expert–novice analysis of problem-solving.]

Aspects of Assessment Design and Analysis

Almond, R. G., Herskovits, E., Mislevy, R. J., & Steinberg, L. S. (1999). Transfer of information between system and evidence models. In D. Heckerman & J. Whittaker (Eds.), *Artificial intelligence and statistics* (pp. 181–186). San Francisco: Morgan Kaufmann. Also available as *CSE Technical Report 480.* Los Angeles: The National Center for Research on Evaluation, Standards, Student Testing (CRESST), Center for Studies in Education, UCLA. Retrieved May 1, 2005 from http://www.cse.ucla.edu/CRESST/Reports/TECH480.pdf. [Concerns the technical issue of maintaining student-model and measurement-model fragments of Bayes nets, to be assembled dynamically as is required in adaptive assessments.]

Almond, R. G., & Mislevy, R. J. (1999). Graphical models and computerized adaptive testing. *Applied Psychological Measurement, 23,* 223–237. Also available as *CSE Technical Report 434.* Los Angeles: The National Center for Research on Evaluation, Standards, Student Testing (CRESST), Center for Studies in Education, UCLA. Retrieved May 1, 2005 from http://www.cse.ucla.edu/CRESST/Reports/TECH434.PDF. [Early discussion of the kinds of variables that arise in language assessment, the roles they play in the assessment argument, and where they fit in with Bayes net modeling of performance.]

Collins, A., & Ferguson, W. (1993). Epistemic forms and epistemic games: Structures and strategies to guide inquiry. *Educational Psychologist, 20*(1), 25–42. [Defines epistemic forms as structures that guide inquiry, and epistemic games as the strategies for filling them in.]

DeMark, S. F., & Behrens, J. T. (2004). Using statistical natural language processing for understanding complex responses to free-response tasks . *The International Journal of Testing, 4*(4), 295–301.

Gitomer, D. H., & Steinberg, L.S. (1999). Representational issues in assessment design. In I. E. Sigel (Ed.), *Development of mental representation* (pp. 351–370).Hillsdale, NJ: Lawrence Erlbaum Associates. [Discussion of the key role of representational forms in assessment. Addresses both the use of representational forms to provide information and elicit responses from examinees, and the role of assessments as representations themselves as to what is important in a domain and how it is evaluated.]

Mislevy, R. J. (1994). Evidence and inference in educational assessment. *Psychometrika, 59,* 439–483.Also available as *CSE Technical Report 414.* Los Angeles: The National Center for Research on Evaluation, Standards, Student Testing (CRESST), Center for Studies in Education, UCLA. Retrieved May 1, 2005 from http://www.cse.ucla.edu/CRESST/Reports/TECH414.PDF. [Foundational, not overly technical, discussion of the role that probability-based reasoning plays in assessment and assessment design.]

Mislevy, R. J., Almond, R. G., Yan, D., & Steinberg, L. S. (1999). Bayes nets in educational assessment: Where do the numbers come from? In K. B. Laskey & H. Prade (Eds.), *Proceedings of the Fifteenth Conference on Uncertainty in Artificial Intelligence* (437–446). San Francisco: Morgan Kaufmann. Also available as *CSE Technical Report 518.* Los Angeles: The National Center for Research on Evaluation, Standards, Student Testing (CRESST), Center for Studies in Education, UCLA. Retrived May 1, 2005 from http://www.cse.ucla.edu/CRESST/Reports/TECH518.pdf. [Discussion of Markov Chain Monte Carlo estimation in a binary skills multivariate latent class model for cognitive diagnosis. Illustrated with analysis of data from Kikumi Tatsuoka's studies of mixed number subtraction.]

Mislevy, R. J., Steinberg, L. S., & Almond, R. G. (2002). On the roles of task model variables in assessment design. In S. Irvine & P. Kyllonen (Eds.), *Generating items for cognitive tests: Theory and practice* (pp. 97–128). Hillsdale, NJ: Lawrence Erlbaum Associates. Also available as *CSE Technical Report 500.* Los Angeles: The National Center for Research on Evaluation, Standards, Student Testing (CRESST), Center for Studies in Education, UCLA. Retrieved May 1, 2005 from http://www.cse.ucla.edu/CRESST/Reports/TECH500.pdf.

Mislevy, R. J., Steinberg, L. S., Almond, R. G., Haertel, G., & Penuel, W. (2002). Leverage points for improving educational assessment. In B. Means & G. Haertel (Eds.), *Evaluating the effects of technology in education.* New York: Teachers College Press. Also available as *CSE Technical Report 534.* Los Angeles: The National Center for

Research on Evaluation, Standards, Student Testing (CRESST), Center for Studies in Education, UCLA. Retrieved May 1, 2005 from http://www.cse.ucla.edu/CRESST/Reports/newTR534.pdf. [Looking from the perspective of ECD at ways that assessment can be improved by developments in statistics, technology, and cognitive psychology.]

Mislevy, R. J., Wilson, M. R., Ercikan, K., & Chudowsky, N. (2003). Psychometric principles in student assessment. In T. Kellaghan & D. Stufflebeam (Eds.), *International handbook of educational evaluation* (pp. 489–531). Dordrecht, The Netherlands: Kluwer Academic Press. Forthcoming as a CSE Technical Report. [Exploration of validity, reliability, comparability, and fairness, as viewed from the perspective of evidentiary arguments.]

Williamson, D., Mislevy, R. J., & Almond, R. G. (2000). Model criticism of Bayesian networks with latent variables. In C. Boutilier & M. Goldszmidt (Eds.), *Uncertainty in artificial intelligence 16*, pp. 634–643. San Francisco: Morgan Kaufmann. [An initial investigation into model-fit indices for the use of Bayes nets in educational assessments.]

5

Item and Test Development Strategies to Minimize Test Fraud

James C. Impara
David Foster
Caveon, LLC

This chapter explains why test security is important to both examinees and organizations sponsoring testing in education, admissions, or credentialing settings. Different types of test fraud are described (test pirates who steal items and cheaters who use a variety of nefarious means to get credit when none is deserved). We describe eight strategies for writing items that can help to either make the items harder to memorize, and therefore harder to steal, or to make it harder to copy or collaborate with other examinees to produce inappropriately correct responses to multiple-choice questions. We also discuss methods for producing performance-based items for both computer-based and non–computer-based tests. Finally, we describe four test development strategies that can facilitate higher levels of test security.

This chapter addresses how to develop tests so that test fraud is minimized. Two types of test fraud are of concern. The first is fraud associated with cheating. The second is fraud associated with test piracy, or stealing test items.[1] Clearly, the second type of fraud leads to the first. People steal test items so they can provide them to future test takers who will use the items to gain a higher, but inappropriate, test score. In this chapter, we discuss multiple forms that test fraud may take and how items and tests may be developed to help reduce fraud.

WHY IS TEST FRAUD A CONCERN?

Test fraud is first and foremost a serious threat to the validity of test scores (Haladyna & Downing, 2004). Cheaters' scores do not reflect what the cheaters know and can do; such scores only reflect how a particular set of test questions has been answered or tasks performed through inappropriate means. Cheaters' answers are not a sampling of their behavior that can be generalized to the broader domain that the test is intended to measure. Thus, cheating

---

[1] *Item* is used in its broadest sense. An item may be a multiple-choice item, a writing prompt, a simulated patient station, or a complex set of activities that represent some assessment tasks (e.g., performing a science experiment, trouble shooting a computer network, simulating an accounting problem).

introduces what Messick (1989) characterized as *construct-irrelevant variance* (CIV), which is variance in the test score that is not related to the construct of interest (e.g., the requirement that reading a math word problem may introduce score variance that is not a reflection of math skills). Cheating results in score variance that is not from knowledge of the underlying construct that the test is intended to assess.

In addition to this serious measurement concern are the secondary problems that result from cheating. These problems include the serious impacts to the testing program in terms of loss or damage to its reputation. For example, a credentialing program that has a cheating problem loses credibility with those stakeholders who trust that the tests help to identify qualified individuals. The reputation damage caused by cheating may result in loss of members to professional associations, government licensing agencies may seek alternatives to the testing program (or a new contractor), fewer examinees may seek certification, or examinees may seek certification using alternative methods or programs. Similarly, there are impacts on other organizations that use test scores to help make decisions about examinees such as schools admitting students, organizations hiring certified individuals, and schools advancing unqualified students to the next grade. For example, schools that admit students who are not qualified and who ultimately cannot complete their degree program end up investing money and time in the student only to have him or her leave after a year or two. An employer who hires an unqualified person also invests time and money into bringing that person up to speed, and when the person does not have the knowledge and skills to do the job, there are substantial costs to the organization in time, money, and perhaps customer good will. Often extensive effort is required to remove the student or employee who used fraudulent means to obtain an acceptable passing score, requiring personnel and legal resources best used elsewhere. Another cost of admitting an unqualified student or employing an unqualified person is that such an action takes a student or employee slot that should be given to another qualified applicant.

All of these examples also have fiscal implications to the testing programs. These costs, however, are only a part of the costs that may be incurred if an entire test battery, item pool, or form is exposed. When that happens, scores may be invalidated and a new test battery, item pool, or form must be developed and administered. The testing program, test sponsors, and the examinees suffer direct and indirect costs when scores are invalidated. The cost of test battery, item pool, or test form redevelopment is not trivial. Even testing programs that claim to develop new test forms for each use often use items that overlap with previous tests (for purposes of equating or just to avoid the costs of complete redevelopment). Examinees incur the cost of time lost and energy spent in studying for the retake, in addition to the potential loss of morale. Cheating is an expensive proposition from everyone's perspective.

Preventing fraud also involves other policy and practice issues that increase costs to the testing programs. Such policies and practices include the item and test development strategies discussed in this chapter. Other policies and practices include *item exposure controls* (determining under what conditions an item should be removed from the active item pool due to over exposure with the candidate population), *conducting data forensics* (statistical analyses designed specifically to detect test fraud) to assess the extent of evidence indicative of cheating and where and when it may have taken place, carefully searching the Internet to locate sites that have test items or item pools for sale or discussion forums and chat rooms where items and item pools may be shared, and the establishment of fair retake policies and monitoring of these retakes. Not all of these costs accrue to every testing program (e.g., some large-scale assessment programs in education may not have to set stringent retake policies because the stakes are not too high), but for many testing programs, especially those dealing with credentialing, these concerns loom large in program decision making.

In addition to cost impacts, a secondary effect of invalid examination scores caused by cheating is unfairness to qualified candidates. Cheaters fill job slots and take limited student openings in educational programs, leaving an unidentified percentage of qualified individuals without such opportunities. Test fraud is a problem for testing programs because it results in invalid test scores. Fraud is also destructive to the reputation of the testing program; it may result in consequences of fewer people taking the test, or test users having less confidence in the value and utility of the test. Replacement costs for new items, tests, and item pools may be very high. Examinees may suffer both physical and opportunity costs when they are required to retake an examination when they have done nothing wrong. Test program and test sponsor costs are driven up to ensure protection against test fraud. Qualified individuals lose opportunities they deserve. Thus, any ethical steps that can be undertaken to reduce or even eliminate test fraud are helpful to testing programs, test users, and individual test takers.

This chapter suggests improved methods for developing tests, including writing test items, assembling, and administering tests that may help to reduce test fraud without introducing additional threats to validity associated with CIV. First, we discuss in more detail various types of test fraud, then we elaborate on item types and test development and administration techniques that may help reduce fraud.

TYPES OF TEST FRAUD

As noted, test fraud typically falls into two major classes. The first class is *cheating* (obtaining a score through inappropriate means) and the second class is *piracy* (stealing items, item pools, or tests). In this section, each of these classes of test fraud is elaborated briefly. Some of the ways that people cheat or steal tests or test items cannot be prevented or thwarted by the way the test items are developed or by using various test development or assembly strategies. Some of the methods used to cheat or steal items, item pools, or tests can, however, be made more difficult by using the item and test development and assembly strategies we discuss.

We discuss only two types of cheating, cheating prior to the test and cheating during the test. A third type of cheating is not discussed and that is cheating by others on behalf of the examinee. This third type includes, for example, a teacher changing answers for members of his or her class; hiring a proxy (substitute) to take the test on the examinee's behalf; or having someone electronically hack into the test response file and change the item responses or scores. Item and test development strategies do little to reduce these forms of cheating.

Cheating prior to the test includes such activities as purchasing test items, item pools, or tests from web sites, using a chat room, bulletin board, or discussion forum to solicit and obtain active test items, item pools, or tests; participating in test preparation courses from individuals who are providing or presenting the actual test questions; and collaborating with individuals who take the test during an earlier administration and then provide test items to individuals who take the test at a later time. Some of the item and test development or assembly strategies we discuss help to minimize or at least frustrate these types of efforts to cheat.

Cheating during the test includes such strategies as using various forms of technology (e.g., cell phones, pagers, personal digital assistants (PDAs), pocket personal computers, two-way radios, or other communications devices) to interact with others who may also be taking the test or who are outside the testing environment and find answers; using "cheat" sheets that include information relevant to the test content as an aid to answering questions (e.g., writing answers on rubber bands that are on the examinee's wrist or writing answers or other information on the back of the label on a water bottle); not stopping when the time limit is reached; reviewing sections of the test before receiving directions; using calculators (or information programmed into calculators) that are not permitted by the testing program; and copying other's examinee test responses. There are some excellent item and test development strategies that help to reduce the impact of these and similar cheating strategies.

Stealing test questions (piracy), unlike cheating, is often done with a substantial profit motive in mind for the person(s) doing the pirating. Pirates are either item resellers or are trying to help other examinees to get high scores. Item resellers usually take the test with no intention or interest in attempting to score well. They may attempt only a few test items, but they make no effort at answering correctly. Their only objective is to memorize the specific content and response options for a set of items. If they are working alone, they may take the test on several occasions to steal as many items as they can. If they are working as part of a team, they may take a particular test form only once or twice with the aim of memorizing only a small subset of items (their team mates are stealing the remaining items). These pirates typically resell items to either test preparation organizations or to individuals who put the items on the Internet for resale to future test takers. Those who are taking the test only once, and who are trying to do well, but at the same time are trying to remember as much about the test as they can so they can tell their friends or classmates about the test, also need to be dealt with by using item writing or test development or assembly strategies that may prevent or thwart their efforts. There are some item and test development strategies that can be useful in helping to make the job of a test pirate more difficult, or less fruitful.[2]

ITEM DEVELOPMENT STRATEGIES

We discuss item-writing strategies for multiple-choice, constructed-response, or performance-based items. The strategies associated with multiple-choice items are general; that is, they apply in virtually any context. The strategies for constructed-response and performance-based items follow the discussion of multiple-choice items. The discussion of performance-based items also includes items that rely on computer technology. In a later section, we discuss test assembly strategies.

The item-writing strategies presented herein are not necessarily unique or new. Most of these ways of writing items and assembling tests may have been delineated by others, but not from the perspective of preventing test fraud or making it more difficult to cheat.

In any testing situation item and test development must begin with a proper foundation for item production (see Downing, chap. 1, this volume; Welch, chap. 13, this volume). For an educational test this foundation is the set of standards, learning targets, or objectives that the test is to be written to measure. For employment-related or credentialing tests, this foundation may be derived from a job or practice analysis. Careful selection of the relevant content minimizes the use of items that do not match the construct of interest and helps to ensure the validity of the scores from such items. A content analysis typically provides the objectives necessary to guide correct item development.

Considerable research has been done on the efficacy of different types of multiple-choice items. Much less research has been done that is related to constructed-response or performance-based items or tasks. Our perspective is to look at some of the published research to identify methods of writing test items so that test fraud will be more difficult without introducing construct irrelevant variance. Haladyna and Downing (1989a,b) and Haladyna, Downing, and Rodriguez (2002) have published much of the research on multiple-choice items that we draw on within this section.

---

[2] A typical program marketing strategy is to provide free retakes to test takers. Test takers often take the test the first time without preparation but with the intent to find out as much about the test as possible. They take the test the second time seriously. Test pirates benefit greatly from this and other policies that do not limit the number, timing, and frequency of retakes. Although outside the scope of this chapter, we advise that programs stop the practice of free retakes and that a stringent policy of limited retakes with timing restrictions be instituted.

Multiple-Choice Items—General Strategies

In their taxonomy Haladyna and Downing (1989a) provide forty-three principles associated with the positives and negatives of writing multiple-choice items. They defend these principles (or item writing strategies) in Haladyna and Downing (1989b) by reviewing the literature supporting their application. Some of the principles are supported by the research literature and others were "good ideas" or strategies that make sense on their face, that textbook authors or others thought should be followed. In their limited recent update (Haladyna, Downing, & Rodriguez, 2002) the focus is on a smaller set of thirty-one principles (item-writing strategies) that, although designated for the classroom teacher, have more general applicability.

We follow the taxonomic classifications used by Haladyna et al. (2002) to discuss multiple-choice item-writing strategies that may facilitate improved test security. Of the thirty-one principles suggested by Haladyna, Downing, and Rodriguez (2002) eight are, in our opinion, relevant to test security issues. We do not always agree with the principles or strategies cited by Haladyna and his colleagues. In such cases we explain the conditions under which the principle may be violated and the possible consequences of not following the principle. It is important to note that our agreement or disagreement with the principle is from a security perspective, not necessarily from a psychometric perspective. What makes for good security may not always make for good psychometrics.

We also looked at the original set of forty-three principles proposed by Haladyna and Downing (1989a). The improved test security strategies are shown in Table 5.1 and discussed individually. In some cases the statement of the principles, as shown in Table 5.1, has been modified to generalize them beyond the classroom context.

Each of the eight multiple-choice item-writing strategies is described below. Then each strategy is elaborated in terms of its relationship to improved test security. Our agreement or disagreement with the principle/strategy and the rationale for our position follows the description. It should be noted that although we tend to discuss each strategy separately, the strategies could be combined so that multiple strategies may be used for any particular item or in test assembly.

Strategy 1

> Use novel material to test higher-level concepts. Paraphrase textbook language or language used during instruction to avoid testing for simple recall.

The security issue is that the more directly the item content has come from materials or examples the examinee is familiar with, the easier it is to remember the item content and pass this information about the item (and the answer) to other examinees who are yet to take the test. By using novel materials, content, or testing approaches, the item may be less memorable and less susceptible to cheating or piracy.

Haladyna and his colleagues (Haladyna & Downing, 1989a,b, Haladyna et al. 2002) cited no research to support this strategy. We agree with this strategy and suggest extending it, if possible, to more test situations than using novel material for testing higher level concepts. If higher level concepts are part of the test specifications, then the time it takes to write multiple-choice items that contain novel material is well worth the effort in terms of the accuracy and precision of the item to reveal what the examinee knows or can do. Even if the content requirements are for recall or other factual information, using novel material or novel item formats (see examples later in this chapter) may still be an appropriate way to assess knowledge and skills at lower cognitive levels.

Using textbook or instructional language should be avoided when writing test items because such items do not promote any attempt at meaningful understanding of what is to be learned;

TABLE 5.1
Item-Writing Strategies for Multiple-Choice Items That May Facilitate Test Security

Strategy	Agree With Strategy?	Potential Validity Problem	Type of Cheating Impacted
Content concerns			
1. Use novel material to test higher level concepts. Paraphrase textbook language to avoid testing for simple recall.	Yes	Making item content not reflect the construct of interest	Memorization—piracy of items
2. Avoid overly specific and overly general content.	Yes	Making item content not reflect the construct of interest	Memorization—piracy of items
Style concern			
3. Minimize the amount of reading in each item.	No	Making item content not reflect the construct of interest	Memorization—piracy of items
Writing the item			
4. Avoid window dressing (excess verbiage).	No	Making item content not reflect the construct of interest	Memorization—piracy of items
5. Word the stem positively, avoid negatives such as *not* or *except*. If negatives are used, use the word cautiously and always ensure that the word appears capitalized and boldface.	Yes	Different examinees get different tests	Memorization—piracy of items
Writing the choices			
6. Develop as many effective choices as you can.	Yes	Not typical item-writing style	Memorization—piracy of items; may also deter answer copying
7. Make sure that only one of these choices is the right answer.	No	Not typical item-writing style	Memorization—piracy of items; may also deter answer copying
8. Place choices in logical or numeric order.	No	Not typical item-writing style	Memorization of answer choices; may also deter answer copying

Strategies are adapted from Haladyna, Downing, & Rodriguez (2002).

they just promote memorizing the textbook or notes. There are some obvious exceptions to this suggestion, such as when an exact procedure is the only way to undertake a task; then testing the exact procedures as specified in the learning material is appropriate.

In general, if the test specifications only address factual knowledge and recall, then a review of the test specifications may be in order. Novel content does not always mean that extreme strategies are necessary. For example, in the simple case of trying to determine if an examinee knows what a particular word or phrase means, this can be assessed easily by providing the word or phrase followed by several response choices that might represent a definition. An alternative strategy is to provide the definition and ask which of several words or phrases are correct. A more novel way to assess such information is to use a matching item and have the examinee match several words or phrases to their definition and have the words or phrases all be similar to each other. This kind of item lends itself to the short-answer constructed-response item type. That is, the item can present the definitional text and ask the examinee to provide the word that is defined. Short answer items of this type are not, of course, appropriate for some testing situations where hand scoring of large numbers of examinees may be prohibitively expensive, but such items can be used in computer-based tests that rely on automatic scoring.

Strategy 2

Avoid overly specific and overly general content.

Test security is associated with how easily items can be memorized. When items contain specific terms, technical jargon, or names of people or products, these specifics make the item more easily remembered. Similarly, if the item is so general that it is easy to recall, that also represents a security risk. A blending of being specific enough to make the item meaningful and complex enough to make memorization difficult is the target from a test security perspective.

As with Strategy 1, Haladyna and his colleagues reported no supporting research; however, we believe that this strategy is consistent with good security practices. Clearly, the challenge is to find the appropriate balance between making the item specific enough and complex enough to assess the construct of interest without introducing CIV. This strategy applies not only to the item stem, but also to the response choices.

The stem should use only the specific terms, technical jargon, names, products, situations, and so on, required by the test specifications. However, if the test specifications do not require such specificity, then at times it may be appropriate to add some specifics that do not distract, but add complexity. For example, in a medical context, a vignette may describe certain characteristics of the patient (e.g., a 67-year-old man) that are not pertinent to the problem to be solved. On another test, the patient characteristics may be changed (e.g., a 43-year-old woman) without changing the substance of the vignette. Thus, instead of a problem that is overly simple (e.g., meat $5.59, vegetables $2.35, total $ _____ ?), the item may be expanded to a paragraph with some supplemental details. This strategy should be used consistent with the test specifications and the characteristics of the examinee population. This mathematics example may be just right in its abbreviated form for fifth graders, where there is essentially no security risk, but not for a twelveth grader who is taking an examination needed to graduate from high school.

Thus, some specificity and complexity in the stem (or associated passage and exhibit) may be appropriate to minimize the ease of remembering the items. Corresponding elements of specificity and complexity can be used to make changes in the item form or template to create similar items that can be used on a different form of the test (see Strategy 4 under test assembly related to using item variants or clones on different forms of the test). This complexity must be used judiciously to ensure that it is appropriate and does not introduce CIV. Adding more text, making scenarios and vignettes longer, providing case studies, or using graphics may enhance complexity. Adding options (or using different sets of options for different item variants), for multiple-choice questions can introduce appropriate complexity without introducing CIV. Such a tactic has the additional benefit of making the item more difficult to guess correctly by the uninformed examinee.

When making items more complex it is appropriate that multiple-choice response choices should blend in. In other words, they should have the same level of detail and specificity and be of about the same length. This is an important element of item writing that is one of the principles that Haladyna and Downing's (1989b) report research that justifies keeping options of similar length.

Strategy 3

Minimize the amount of reading in each item.

The test security issue is essentially the same as that stated for Strategy 2. Less complex items are easier to remember. The easier the item is to remember, the more easily someone can steal and resell the item. Clearly, adding a heavy reading load when the construct being assessed is not reading may have a negative impact on the validity of the item. However, in many contexts, the examinee must be able to read and understand what has been read to qualify for taking the test. In such situations, it can be argued that reading is an integral part of the construct, and it is therefore legitimate to write items that have a higher reading load than may be necessary to test a narrow skill or ability. This strategy is related to Strategy 4. Although related, this strategy focuses on the overall length of the item whereas Strategy 4 (avoid "window dressing") relates to the content of the stem, not just how long it is. We should make clear, however, that we are not advocating including verbiage or content that is not at the appropriate level, ambiguous, or overly complex and unrelated to the construct.

We do not agree with this principle. As with the principles discussed, Haladyna and his colleagues do not report any research related to this principle. It is characterized as a value that does not need supporting research. Although in many contexts we would agree with the strategy, especially for low-stakes tests, which have little security risk or tests that are intended to assess content that has no need for reading, for many tests that may lead to a credential, reading and understanding what has been read is an essential element of the profession or occupation being credentialed. In such cases, we have few qualms about a reasonable increase in the reading load to make the item harder to memorize and increase the frustration levels of those who try to memorize it. Clearly, in some contexts, this is a researchable topic. However, until such time as research demonstrates that our position threatens the validity of a test score, we continue to recommend not minimizing an item's verbiage when it seems appropriate.

Strategy 4

Avoid window dressing (excess verbiage).

Once again the principal security issue is the ability to memorize the item. The simpler the item, the more likely an examinee can memorize and recall it. By adding length and complexity, the item is more difficult to remember, and the frustration level of the person trying to remember it is increased. As with Strategy 3, we do not agree that this principle should always be followed.

One way to add length and complexity is to include information that does not contribute to the correct answer, especially if the content of the item is to measure problem solving in a real-world context. As with Strategy 3, however, one must be cautious about the construct being assessed.

Haladyna and Downing (1989b) reported several studies that provide empirical evidence in support of this principle. The findings of the cited research suggest that items having excess verbiage are slightly less valid (correlation with a criterion), slightly more difficult (about 0.03), slightly less reliable (about 0.06), and slightly less discriminating. Moreover, the research suggests that such items take more time to administer and more time to write.

In spite of this research, we believe the psychometric costs are less than the security costs, when adding complexity is appropriate. It is appropriate, we believe, when the purpose of the test is to reflect a real-life application, as might be the case in some mathematics problems and in problems in a credentialing context. In many real-life instances, problems must be solved in context and the context in which the problem appears often requires the examinee to sift out relevant information from nonrelevant information. For example, in a medical context a full patient history may be taken before hypothesizing or diagnosing what may be the patient's problem. The history provides a great deal of information, only some of which may be relevant to the hypotheses or diagnosis. The medical professional must be able to sift through all the information to make tentative hypotheses about what the problem is. Thus, when the item is intended to reflect a real-life application, and such an application may contain more information than is needed to solve the problem, it seems reasonable that judiciously including irrelevant information is appropriate.

Strategy 5

Word the stem positively, avoid negatives such as *not* or *except*. If negatives are used, use the word cautiously and always ensure that the word appears capitalized and boldface.

The security issue once again is related to the ability to memorize items. Because most items are worded positively, using the negative makes the item stand out and easier to recall. Thus, in general we agree with this strategy.

Haladyna and Downing (1989b) and Haladyna et al. (2002) summarized the results of several research studies related to this strategy. In general, the research either supports the rule or is ambiguous. The research suggests that for more complex items, the use of a negative in the stem makes the item more difficult. However, for less complex items, difficulty is either not affected or the negatively stated item is easier. Discrimination and reliability were not affected by the way the stem was expressed, either positively or negatively. Thus, although we agree with the strategy, it is clear that the principle can be violated when appropriate. Such instances are when the objective is that the examinee knows what is not true as well as what is true and when the examinee should know what to avoid. For example, in installing a water pump, it is important to know what amounts of water pressure are excessive for certain different types of pumps. Thus, on a pump installer's licensure examination, some negatively phrased questions may be appropriate. Similarly, on a credentialing examination in the health care field, one may reasonably ask if a particular treatment or medication is contraindicated for a particular patient or condition.

Another instance when the strategy may be violated is when making up alternate forms of the test. Some items may lend themselves to being easily converted from negative to positive. Thus, if on the original form an item was negatively stated (making it more easily memorized), converting that item to a positive may both improve the item and frustrate those who have been sold the negative form of the item.

Finally, if one were testing knowledge of a rule of some sort (e.g., Do not walk on the grass), the negative is part of the rule and would not be emphasized. Although such examples are not common, this illustration is provided to remind the reader that the measurement concern is foremost, not following a rule blindly.

Although we have provided examples of when this strategy may be violated, we do concur with it. If multiple items are written at the same time (creating item variants or clones, see Strategy 4 under test assembly), one such variant may be the negative of the original item and that item may be used on some forms of the test. If this is done, the alternate form may not be parallel because of the psychometric impact of making item stems negatively instead of positively worded.

Strategy 6

Develop as many effective choices as you can.

The security issue once again is to reduce the ability of an examinee to memorize the item stem and its options. The more there is to the item, the more difficult it will be to remember it.

Most test item pirates do not attempt to answer the question correctly. They may not even have the basic knowledge or skill needed to sit for the test. Their job is to memorize items (including the answer options) and replicate them so they can be sold for a profit. The more difficult this task is the less likely they will do it well. We clearly and strongly agree with this strategy. Using paper-based tests where only a single correct choice was available, Haladyna and colleagues found substantial measurement-related research on the effects of increasing the number of incorrect options, or *distractors*. Although it appears that three response choices are sufficient for psychometric soundness, more plausible choices tend to increase reliability, and have a mixed impact on difficulty (in some studies more distractors made the items more difficult and in other studies there was no effect). The number of distractors influenced the discrimination of the item, and this factor seems to be most influential when the distractors are effective distractors. That is, the greater the number of quality distractors (those that drew more unqualified examinees) that were available, the more discriminating the item.

We believe as many as ten answer options (including combinations of correct answers and distractors) would be better than the widely used standard of four or five response options. However, writing large numbers of quality distractors for very many items is at least intimidating, and in some cases may not be possible. Given the difficulty of all items having the same large number of response choices, all alternative forms of the test should be created with similar emphasis on authoring response options. The review process should include a criterion that one form of the test is not clearly different from the others in terms of the number of options (and types of items) included in the other forms.

Although we advocate having as many response options as possible, we also recognize the difficulty, in many contexts, of writing additional, high-quality, plausible distractors. Thus, we emphasize that increasing the number of options not be done unless they are of high quality. Every strategy that increases the amount of material the examinee must read also increases the amount of time it takes to complete the test. Thus, by using various strategies that increase the amount of reading, the number of items that can be incorporated in the test is reduced. Thus, unimportant additional distractors that are not plausible should not be used just to increase the number of response choices.

Strategy 7

Make sure that only one of these choices is the right answer.

We do not agree with this strategy. Having multiple keyed answers helps to confuse those who want to copy answers off the answer sheets of other examinees; it also makes items more difficult to memorize. If an item is memorized, it will be more difficult to determine the keyed answers and more difficult to memorize the answer key.

Haladyna and his colleagues do not cite any research on this strategy, but it is a suggestion often made by textbook authors. Because it is so often followed, examinees are not in the habit of deciding if more than one response choice may be keyed as correct. Clearly if an item has multiple keyed responses, there are some issues that must be considered. First is that the keyed answers must be clearly "correct" answers and not just "best" answers. The following item illustrates our perspective on this strategy:

Q. What two journals are sponsored by the National Council on Measurement in Education (NCME)? (Mark two.)
   1. *Applied Measurement in Education*
   2. *Applied Psychological Measurement*
   3. *Educational and Psychological Measurement*
   4. *Educational Assessment*

5. *Educational Measurement: Issues and Practices**
6. *Educational Measurement Quarterly*
7. *Journal of Educational Measurement**
8. *Journal of International Measurement*
9. *Measurement and Evaluation in Counseling and Development*
10. *Psychological Assessment*
11. *Review of Measurement in Education*

This is a somewhat simplistic item (we would recommend that multiple choice items be used to assess higher level skills), but it illustrates the point that some questions may have more than four or five response choices and that multiple responses may be correct. However, even items with the same number of response options can be made more difficult to memorize by increasing the number of correct options. Consider the following examples:

Q. Which is a mammal?
  1. horse*
  2. snake
  3. bee
  4. shark

Q. Which three are mammals?
  1. horse*
  2. whale*
  3. snake
  4. bear*

A second problem that arises with such items is the issue of scoring. Must an examinee select all correct answers to get any points or is partial credit given for some correct answers? If an examinee selected all the choices, one would not be disposed to give any credit, but in the NCME example above, if the examinee selected both 4 and 7, how would it be scored? First, we suggest that the number of correct answers be prompted in the stem (as we do twice in the example). We further suggest that scoring be all or none. That is, the examinee must respond by entering only the multiple correct keyed responses to obtain credit.

This item type is similar to the multiple true/false item (MTF) that is used in some assessment contexts. There is limited research on MTF items and the research suggests that such items perform well, increasing item difficulty under some circumstances, and also increasing reliability (Haladyna & Downing, 1989b). However, the MTF format tends to be used with items that require less complex cognitive behaviors. Converting the NCME/journal item to an MTF format results in a stem such as the following (the response choices would remain the same).

Q. There are a number of journals that provide insights about measurement theory and practice in education. An organization that promotes enhancing the knowledge and practice of measurement in educational setting is the National Council on Measurement in Education (NCME). NCME sponsors which of the journal(s) named below? (Mark A if NCME is a sponsor. Mark B if NCME is not a sponsor.)[3]

Unlike the previous NCME example, the MTF item is scored such that each response is scored; hence, in the MTF format the item may be worth 11 points (assuming 0-1 scoring)

---

[3] Note that the verbiage has been increased in the stem. If this item were to be used on a credentialing exam for measurement specialists, such an increase may not be unreasonable; however, as a midterm examination in a graduate class, such verbiage should not be included.

instead of only 1 point as would be the case when using standard multiple-choice items with more than one correct answer.

Thus, our position is to combine Strategies 6 and 7 and have as many plausible response choices as are relevant and feasible and to have more than one of the choices be keyed. This can be done with standard form multiple-choice items (using dichotomous scoring), or by using multiple true/false items (where each response option is scored independently). These options potentially lead to greater item difficulty, increased reliability, and enhanced security. These strategies are also likely to require more time for examinees to complete the test.

Strategy 8

Place choices in logical or numeric order.

The security issues are two-fold regarding this strategy. The first is to thwart copying (or having examinees memorize response choice order strings) and the second is to make memorization of items (and answer choices) more difficult and less rewarding. Under certain conditions we do agree with the strategy, but when there is no logical or numerical order, then response choices should be arranged randomly. Moreover, when multiple versions of a test are used in the same testing window (or when computerized testing is being done), the response choices can be randomized within and across test versions. One must use care to keep key balancing in mind when using this strategy (that is, ensure that no response choice is overused across the total test).

Although researchable, Haladyna and his colleagues reported no research on this strategy. They did find research to support key balancing and making the response choices approximately the same length (avoiding making the keyed answer the longest and most detailed). Following the principles of key balancing and homogeneous option length tends to make items more difficult. We suspect that randomizing response choices that have no logical order will have little impact on difficulty or reliability, but it can have an impact on test security, so we recommend randomizing the order of response choices, unless there is a compelling reason (i.e., there is a logical or numerical order) not to do so.

Performance-based Items—General Strategies

Performance-based items have been advocated strongly across a wide array of fields as being more authentic and therefore providing more valid assessments of knowledge and skills. In some content areas such as writing, it is argued that prompts are easy to remember, thus threatening test security (see Powers & Fowles, 1998 for example). It can also be argued that in other contexts the items are not particularly memorable (e.g., in IT certification testing where an examinee must "fix" a network based on a visual and verbal description of the network problem and the problems are sufficiently complex and changeable that remembering the problem is difficult). Thus, there are arguments on both sides of the coin regarding the memorizing of certain types of performance items. If such items are sometimes easy to remember (and thus steal), are there other security concerns that may be compelling enough to justify the use of such items? Yes, however, when considering such issues, one must also examine the overall return on investment for using such items. Return on investment considerations include the cost of replacing items; of developing new scoring keys, rubrics, or algorithms; of training scorers on the new items and rubrics; and of putting new tests in the field when a security breach occurs.

Let us consider for a moment the various security issues. First, memorizing is enhanced for some types of performance items and is less of a concern for other types of performance items. Second, memorizing the answer and repeating it in the test situation is possible, and can be done, if the examinee is sure that the item is the same as the one for which the answer has been memorized. Third, when calculators, especially programmable calculators, are permitted in the testing situation and when examinees bring their own calculators to the test, solutions can be preprogrammed so that the examinee need only insert particular values from the test item to obtain the correct answer. Such an action may mean that the examinee really does not know how to solve the problem because someone other than the examinee may have programmed the calculator. Fourth, copying is made difficult because the answer is often too complex to copy. So, if performance-based items can be written that are difficult to memorize, and if items are "switched out" (new items added and old items rested or retired) frequently, and if computational problems can be made to have different solution strategies across different test forms, then such items can be useful in enhancing test security.

There are other advantages of using performance-based items. If the test specifications are detailed, based on a job or practice analysis that is clear and publicly available, then performance-based items may be disclosed to examinees without concern about copying or sharing. If an examinee has advanced knowledge of the item, the security risk is small because the content is information that has been learned already. In the case of a writing assessment, Powers and Fowles (1998) demonstrated that after releasing a set of operational prompts, examinee performance was no better for the released prompts than for the prompts held in confidence. The current Graduate Management Admissions Council publishes all 280 potential essay topics that are used on the Graduate Management Admissions Test (GMAT), expecting to pull only two for use in any GMAT test administration. The large number of potential writing topics mitigates the security risk. Internet test preparatory organizations even publish high-scoring answers to virtually all of the 280 topics; but that information does little to produce a security risk.

In contrast to the GMAT, testing programs using performance items such as laboratory exercises, simulations of patient–doctor interactions, and essays usually have too few of these items types, thus experiencing a test security risk because of the cost to create and use them. Having relatively few performance tasks allows the examinee population the opportunity to share and memorize the task and practice the skill sufficiently to pass the test. But the examinee's behavior during the test does not generalize to the many other equivalent tasks required at school or in the workplace.

For some performance items, a potential disadvantage is in the increased complexity of scoring. Although automated scoring has made substantial advances, in some contexts hand scoring is still required. This is at substantial cost to the testing program and is not taken lightly. In the sections that follow, we discuss three types of performance-based items and consider the elements of each type that may enhance test security at a reasonable cost. These items are described briefly in the performance-based items shown in Table 5.2.

TABLE 5.2
Item Writing Strategies for Performance-Based and Computerized Items That May Facilitate Test Security

Strategy	Threat to Validity	Type of Cheating Impacted
Performance-based items 1. Short answer or fill in the blank 2. Application of skills 3. Demonstration items	Writing requirement; extraneous elements may influence scoring	Copying, piracy
Computer-based items[a] 1. Drag and drop variants 2. Simple completion item variants 3. Complex problem solving variants	Presentation mode	Memorization, copying

[a] Adapted from Zenisky & Sireci (2002).

Short Answer and Fill-in-the-Blank Items

Short answer or fill-in-the-blank items may require as little as a word or number, or an answer up to a full sentence. For the most part, the writing requirement is minimal, but it still represents a potential source of CIV because the examinee may know the answer, but lack the verbal skills to articulate it in writing. The security issue that such items address is principally that of preventing copying. It is much more difficult to see and read a set of words or numbers than to figure out which bubble is filled in on a multiple-choice answer sheet. Such items can also help to thwart those who claim to have actual test questions.[4] Short answer and fill-in-the-blank questions do not necessarily require a much longer response time than do multiple-choice questions. Moreover, they are often fairly straightforward to write. For these reasons, a test can have a relatively large number of questions and the item bank can be fairly large. The obvious advantage of a large item bank is that new items can be brought online often and item exposure efforts can be effective. Such items may also be relatively easily cloned (making variants that look like and have similar psychometric characteristics to the original item, but have different answers). By having a large item bank and bringing new test forms online often, the security risks associated with test preparation organizations and braindump Web sites are minimized.[5]

Writing short answer items is much like writing multiple-choice items that have closed stems (i.e., present a complete question or problem). Although writing items that have a low cognitive demand is most typical of such items, there is no reason that such items are restricted to that low mental demand. If, however, recall and factual details are important to measure, then the short-answer item is a more secure way to measure than is the multiple-choice item, especially in a paper-and-pencil testing context.[6] The reason for this is that, as noted, we believe it is more difficult to copy the written or numerical answer than it is to copy the answer order from the filled in answer sheet. Of course, the more verbiage that is required in the answer, the more difficult copying will be. If copying does occur, and if more than one word or phrase can be considered correct, then examinees who have exactly the same answers may be suspected of copying (or of using the same test preparation organization or braindump Web site). Use of this strategy can help to discover such security breaches and prevent continued use of the approach or the braindump sites. Such advantages are more difficult to accrue from multiple-choice items.

Fill-in-the-blank items, although seemingly easy to write, require some care to be psychometrically sound. In general, we recommend that the blank be at the end of the item (as is recommended for multiple-choice questions as one of the principles noted by Haladyna & Downing, 1989a). Although the blank may be completed by a number, word, or phrase, our experience suggests that most item writers tend to make such items operate at the recall level. Moreover, they often choose materials that are taken right out of text materials or from lectures. This is not consistent with the recommendations by Haladyna and his colleagues for multiple-choice items and we believe that it is not a good practice for fill-in-the-blank items either, from a security perspective or a psychometric perspective.

---

[4]Some test preparation organizations and "braindump" sites make such claims. A *braindump* is a Web site that provides, for a price, purportedly either live or recently live test items. Both test preparation organizations and braindumps often employ people who take the test with the objective of memorizing test iems. In addition, they may also ask examinees, as they leave the test administration location, about the questions that were on the test.

[5]This, of course, is true no matter what type of item is being used. We mention it here and mention it again in the discussion of test development and assembly.

[6]In the test assembly section we discuss differences in paper-and-pencil testing strategies and computer-based testing strategies.

Application of Skills and Performance Items

Items testing the application of knowledge and skills are those in which a vignette or other scenario that reflects a reality-based situation is presented. These items may be presented in a paper-and-pencil or computer-based context. Typically, these items represent complex tasks that require specific skills to solve. Such items may be mathematical (e.g., in an engineering context where a stress problem must be solved), verbal (e.g., in a medical context where a patient presents with a problem and the various appropriate next steps must be described), or visual (e.g., in a networking problem where a plan/schematic is presented and the examinee must diagnose and troubleshoot a solution).

Performance items require actual or simulated performance in the context that such performance might occur; for example, a simulated patient examination in the medical arena. Other examples include such things as writing a check in a mathematics or daily living class, installing a pump, soldering a circuit, or almost any other instance in which actual physical or cognitive performance is demonstrated.

The test security issues related to such performance items are, as with short answer items, difficulty of copying (not really relevant for many performance items that are administered individually), and the complexity of the items can make performance items hard to remember in sufficient detail to make them useful for test preparation organizations or braindump web sites. Moreover, many performance items can be changed in minor ways to make new items without changing the psychometric characteristics (difficulty, discrimination, and/or guessability). Because of the complexity of the responses, if test preparation organizations have breached the security of the test, then individuals who have participated in such courses may have answers that are so similar to each other that discovery of the breach may be facilitated. Although this does not protect the test's security retroactively, it can be useful to know when to change test forms and it may lead to action against such organizations for violation of copyright.

Of course, performance item types often take substantial time to administer and score; thus, relatively few can be administered in a short testing period. These items are often very difficult to construct, develop a manageable scoring rubric, and very expensive to score. Clearly, when some of these difficulties can be overcome, the utility of these item types is very high from both a psychometric and a security perspective.

Computer-Based Items—General Strategies

The item types already discussed—multiple-choice, short answer, fill-in-the-blank, application of skills, and performance—can all be presented in either a paper- or computer-based context. There are, however, some modes of item presentation that are unique to or facilitated by computer delivery. Zenisky and Sireci (2002) presented twenty-one different innovative item-writing applications that can be classified into three broad categories (see Table 5.2). These categories are drag and drop, simple completion, and complex problem solving. See Sireci and Zenisky (chap. 14 this volume) for a more complete discussion of these item formats and their rationale.

Drag-and-drop items require the use of a mouse. The examinee "selects" something on the screen, clicks on that selection and, while holding down the mouse key, drags that item to another location on the screen and releases the mouse key. There are a wide array of variations on the drag-and-drop item, some of which are discussed below. The simple completion item has multiple forms, some of which are familiar (as described previously) and some of which are innovative. We will have little to add about the more familiar forms of the completion items other than to echo Zenisky and Sireci's "collecting such answers via computer can be effective for data management purposes..." (p. 346). Some of the more innovative item types are discussed below. The complex constructed response item types are illustrated by such licensure examinations as those used for architects and certified public accountants. These complex item types tend to be both complex for the examinee in terms of a response and complex in structure and therefore are more difficult for potential cheaters or pirates to remember.

Drag-and-Drop Variants

These item types range from simple to complex. They can be in the form of matching-type items to more complex graphical completions. The security issue related to these and virtually all of the computer-based item types is the ability to remember the item and subsequently reveal it to future examinees either for free or for a price. The more difficult it is to recall the item, the more difficult it will be to steal it.

Drag-and-drop items can readily employ some of the strategies already discussed. For example, a simple drag and drop item task is to provide a list with some missing elements. The missing elements are displayed outside the list and the examinee is instructed to select each item and place it in its proper location in the list. For example a list of events could be displayed (see example below) along with the events that are "missing" and need to be placed in the proper order.

Place the conflicts listed below in their proper position in the timeline shown.[7] Korean Conflict, Spanish-American War, War of 1812, Desert Storm

Timeline: French and Indian War; American Revolution; _?_ ; Mexican-American War; Civil War; _?_ ; World War I; World War II; _?_; Viet Nam Conflict; _?_ ; War in Iraq

In addition to sequencing and other sorts of matching items, mathematical problems (like those that would require a graphing calculator) can be presented, as can other types of problems that employ graphics. More complex items can also be used.

A variation on the drag-and-drop item is the highlighting of text or graphics. For example, an examinee could be presented with a reading passage and asked to highlight the words or sentence that best represents the main idea. These item types can be extended to require the examinee to make multiple selections. Such items have advantages similar to those noted with the multiple-choice items requiring multiple responses.

Simple Completion

This item type is much like the performance-based items discussed. In addition, there is at least one innovative strategy that Zenisky and Sireci (2002) discuss. Although described by Zenisky and Sireci as a novel item type, it is a variation on items used to assess creativity. This item presents a scenario or problem and asks the examinee to provide as many solutions as possible. It can also ask for causes of the problem, hypotheses about why the problem exists, and multiple mathematical solutions to complex problems. As in the discussion of performance-based items, if two or more examinees come up with virtually identical response choices in the same order, it may serve as a flag to alert the test sponsor to the possibility of collusion either through an exam preparation organization or a chat room, discussion forum, or bulletin board where examinees have posted the item. Thus, a careful analysis of examinee

---

[7]Items such as this can also be presented in a multiple-choice format that can be used in either a computer-based or a paper-and-pencil administration.

responses may facilitate discovery of a security breach and permit taking appropriate actions to shut down the offending web site and schedule required changes in the test.

Complex Problem Solving

These item types are used for presenting authentic types of problems in very close to real-life contexts that permit using tools that are exactly the same as or very similar to those used in everyday settings. Such items are used on the Architectural Registration Exam (ARE) and in the Certified Public Accountant (CPA) examination. The ARE requires examinees to design structures that meet certain requirements and specifications or to solve specific design problems. The nature of the solution necessitates that more than one answer can be correct. Thus, the evaluation of the variety of potential responses is a major challenge. The enhanced security of such an item lies in the complexity of the presentation of the item and complexity of the responses. The CPA examination presents various simulations of accounting problems that have unique correct answers. The high security of these complex problem solving items is because there are numerous simulations that look similar (they are clones of each other) and there are multiple responses required by the examinee on each simulation (some are numerical responses as on a spread sheet, some are verbal responses, some are information search and retrieval, and some are drag-and-drop responses). Thus, these item types can combine the various ways to make items realistic yet complex without introducing CIV (assuming the examinee has taken advantage of using the practice examinations to learn the various manipulations that are required). In addition to the strategies noted to make items both complex and realistic, other means to achieve this end include the use of graphics, calculators, and reference tools (dictionaries, special occupational tools). All of these elements have the benefit of making the problems more realistic and less easily memorized or recorded.

Test Assembly Strategies to Minimize Test Fraud

There are several test development strategies that we believe will facilitate maintaining and improving test security (Table 5.3). Note that one of these strategies has been touched on in the discussion on multiple-choice items (randomly ordered response choices). One of the

TABLE 5.3
Test Assembly Strategies That May Facilitate Test Security

Strategy	Threat to Validity	Type of Cheating Impacted
1. Randomly order response choices (see strategy 8 related to multiple choice items)	Not typical item writing style	Answer copying, memorization of response string
2. Use multiple versions or forms (e.g., randomly order items)	Item order effect, if any	Test piracy, answer copying, memorization of response string
3. Use computer-based tests (e.g., LOTF or adaptive models)	Mode of delivery	Answer copying, memorization of response string
4. Use item variants/clones on alternate forms of tests	Not all items may have equal psychometric characteristics	Answer copying, memorization of response string

Abbreviation: LOTF, linear-on-the-fly.

other strategies is not really just a test development strategy (using item variants/clones), but is a combination of item writing and test assembly strategies. The other two strategies, using multiple versions or forms, and using computer-based testing, are test assembly and administration strategies. We report briefly on some of the research that supports (or suggests limits for) our suggested strategies.

Randomly-Ordered Response Choices

Randomizing the order of response choices increases security of tests by hindering easy and consistent copying. It also helps to thwart those who have obtained copies of the items (or answer key) in advance of testing and who have memorized the answer key. Thus, this strategy is a useful one in situations noted under Strategy 8 related to multiple-choice items.

A problem with using this strategy for paper-and-pencil testing is that each variation of response choices requires a unique answer key. Because of the complexity of printing and scoring the multiple variations, this strategy can be cumbersome with paper-and-pencil tests. Perhaps the new one-by-one printing technologies will join with test design specialists and create individualized exams where item response options are randomized. However, this problem may be substantially reduced in a computer-based testing environment where the item presentation algorithm can be adapted to present the response choices in various sequences and be scored correctly each time. Because copying is of less concern with many applications of computer-based tests, one advantage of this strategy is to thwart using the advanced memorization of items and answer keys. Another advantage is to make less effective the text messaging capability of cell phones, pagers, pocket personal computers, and PDAs to get answers from outside the testing context without entering all response choices, which is likely to take excessive time. Randomizing response choices, when used in combination with the following strategy makes it very difficult to cheat by memorizing an answer key or by using various technological tools to try to get answers from someone else who is outside the testing context (or another examinee).

When the response choices have some logical order (e.g., a numerical sequence), the use of this strategy is not recommended. The security advantages do not outweigh the psychometric advantages of providing response choices in an expected logical order. However, when there is no particular logical order this strategy can be used. Thus, in many tests some items may have the response choices varied across forms, whereas the response choices for other items are the same across forms.[8]

Use Multiple Versions or Forms

In this section, we discuss two basic strategies that may be considered independently or in combination. The first strategy is that of different versions of the test and the second strategy is using different forms of the test. Either strategy would be appropriate within a testing window. A *version* has the same test items, but with items in a different order. A *form* has some percentage of completely different items and is equated to some "base" form. These two strategies have much in common from a security perspective, but the research focuses on the use of different versions, rather than different forms. In the discussion of these strategies note that they focus on testing situations that assume fixed testing windows and that may permit opportunities for examinees to cheat by copying, as is the case in many paper-and-pencil testing situations and

---

[8]*Forms* is used here in the most general sense. In paper-and-pencil testing, it literally means different forms. In computer-based testing, it means for the same items that are administered to different examinees either in the context of a linear test or an adaptive test.

in some web-based testing situations. We discuss some computer-based testing strategies in the next section (adaptive testing and linear-on-the-fly (LOTF)[9] test assembly).

As is the case with randomly ordering the response choices, the test items may also be randomly ordered such that there may be a number of different variations of item orders in the test that are used at the same test centers for examinees taking the test at essentially the same time. In the case of multiple forms there may be some overlap of test items between or among forms, but some percentage of the items (typically 60% to 75%) are unique to each form. The same security issues are addressed with these strategies as were addressed by randomly ordering response choices. That is, copying answers will not result in a positive score, and trying to anticipate a similar order of questions for a colleague will be frustrating. Trying to use technology to obtain answers from within or outside the testing context or memorizing an answer key or even test items (unless they are performance-type items) will not result in an enhanced score for examinees who try to beat the system in either of these ways. Similarly, when testing across time zones, the different versions or forms also make communication of what is on the test more difficult. One substantive difference however, is that, when using multiple forms, if there is a security breach the cost may be much higher than if using only multiple versions. This is especially true in a paper-and-pencil testing context where the loss of a single box of tests that represent multiple test forms may result in a substantial exposure of items in the entire active item pool.

Multiple Versions. Like the random ordering of response choices, this strategy is researchable and there have been several studies that have looked at this topic. Leary and Dorans (1985) did a review of the research in this area, as did Brennan (1992). A summary of their findings suggests that under some conditions the ordering of items has an impact on the difficulty of the items, which may also have an impact on the extent that changing the item order may introduce CIV, thus impacting the validity of the scores for some examinees.

The principal results reported by Leary and Dorans (1985) were that when items were ordered from easy to hard, then reordered, that the difficulty changed on some of the items (easy items became more difficult and hard items became less difficult). This result may be most highly influenced when there is a speed factor associated with the test. Leary and Dorans noted that even a modest speed factor had an influence on both the difficulty and discrimination values associated with items when item order was changed. Brennan (1992) found additional evidence supporting Leary and Dorans's contention that some item types were more influenced by item-order effects than others. In particular, items associated with a reading passage when scrambled within the set associated with the passage may have different difficulty levels resulting from different orders. Brennan discourages item reordering under almost all conditions, but suggests strategies for equating when item ordering changes the psychometric characteristics of the test.

There have also been studies that examined the order effect when items are presented in blocks consistent with instruction or in random order. Although the results have been mixed, with most studies showing no effect, there is some indication that there may be an interaction between test anxiety and item order. Neely, Springston, and McCann (1994), for example, found that if the items are presented on a final examination in the same order as the instruction (i.e., if addition was taught first, the addition items were first on the test) that item ordering matters more for the more anxious examinees. Because many high-stakes tests are very anxiety producing, this potential impact is important when there is a well-defined order of presentation of materials. It may also have implications for keeping items that assess similar content together, even when such content is not associated with a reading passage or vignette.

---

[9] Linear, LOTF, and computer-adaptive tests are defined in a later section of this chapter.

To examine the possibility of an order effect when using multiple versions of a test that has items in different (e.g., random) order some experimentation may be done if items are pretested in an operational context. That is, when items have been pretested by placing them in an operational administration of the test as unscored items, we advise randomly ordering the items in the pretest context. Thus, when pretesting a new passage (or vignette) with multiple items, one should randomly order the new items/passages across different forms and place the passage in various positions in the test (beginning, middle, end). This means that only programs large enough to have from three to six different operational forms during a testing window can take advantage of this strategy.

We believe that randomly ordering items or using multiple forms is an excellent way to enhance security; however, we recommend that it be done judiciously for several reasons. First, for paper-and-pencil testing, it increases the cost of testing because of the need for printing multiple versions and for scoring with multiple keys. Clearly, a study of the return on investment will be helpful to determine if the costs associated with using multiple versions or forms is less than the cost of security breaches. We believe these physical costs are relatively low for most testing programs and will be less than the cost of a security breach. Second, for computer-based tests the costs associated with using more complex scoring algorithms than are used for direct linear tests may be higher.[10]

Multiple Forms. We were unable to find explicit research on the impact of using different forms of a test other than the research on equating and equating error, which is not considered in this chapter. There are many variations of this option. For paper-and-pencil testing, the options include having as few as two forms that are used in a spiraled order with examinees who are in adjacent seats, to as many as six to ten different forms for use within a test center and in test centers across different time zones. Of course, examinees who take a computer-based test that is adaptive or that is assembled as a LOTF test, are also taking different forms. We were unable to find any literature on LOTF or adaptive testing that tried to assess the item order effect (other than a brief discussion by Brennan, 1992). Moreover, it is clear that the more able examinees who take an adaptive test (and thus, are exposed to increasingly difficult items) often attempt fewer items and they believe the test to be more difficult than the typical test they take (tests that are not adaptive). These two types of test (adaptive and LOTF) are discussed in the next section.

A testing program could attempt to combine both of these strategies by having multiple versions across different forms, but this seems to us to be excessive. It is not suggested to modify the placement of items to be used in equating across forms, so the number of items that could be randomly ordered is limited and the complexity of keeping track of such variations is likely to be more costly than the associated benefits.

The costs associated with using multiple test forms outside of a computer-based testing context are developing and using multiple keys (and for security purposes, scoring all tests with all keys to try to detect cheating) and equating across forms. Thus, the use of multiple forms is more costly than the use of different versions of the same test, which may not require equating.

Validity Concerns for Both Multiple Versions and Multiple Forms. The cost of the potential for reduced validity is an important issue. If changing item order across versions produces versions with different psychometric characteristics, then some examinees may be

---

[10] At this point we are not considering either LOTF, adaptive, or multistage tests. These tests may also have order effects, but such effects are not readily assessable. Brennan (1992) has considered this impact and suggests the need for more research.

disadvantaged by virtue of the version of the test they took. Similarly, if different forms of the test are used, an equating strategy must be used and such strategies have equating error, which may disadvantage some examinees. Equating is also much more problematic if the test includes performance-type items. These are clearly validity issues and should to the extent possible be avoided.

In summary, randomly ordering items within passages or across the range of items in a test results in different versions of the test. The research literature suggests that such variation will, in some cases, have an impact on the difficulty and discrimination of the items. However, the security benefits of this strategy can also be high to the overall testing program. To assess the impact of item order, we advise proceeding cautiously and pretesting the impact of item order whenever possible. If there is no item order effect, then items should, to the extent that it is affordable, be administered in different order on different versions of the test within any testing window. Regarding the use of different forms of the test, this can be an effective strategy for reducing cheating, but the cost of repairing a major security breach could be higher than the cost of using different versions. Moreover, the need for equating also adds to the costs of testing (and there may be validity issues if there are performance items) and may delay score reporting. We strongly recommend using multiple versions of a test and recommend multiple forms under certain conditions (when there are multiple time zones and when the item pool is large).

Use Computer-Based Tests

There are several basic forms of computer-based tests: linear, LOTF, and adaptive. A *linear computer-based test* is one that is like a paper-based test, but is administered using a computer. It is fixed length and items are in the same order for all examinees. A *LOFT computer-based test* is a test that is fixed length, but the items are drawn randomly from the item pool so that each examinee takes a different set of items (the item selection strategy or algorithm may be set to be a stratified random sample to insure content coverage). A computer adaptive test (CAT) is one that adjusts the difficulty of the items so that the examinee's score best reflects the examinee's ability. Davey and Pitoniak (chap. 24 this volume) discuss this format, and Luecht (chap. 8 this volume) discusses the use of this format for decision-based testing. Items are selected from the pool so that if an examinee misses an item, the next item presented is easier than the previous one, or if the examinee answers correctly the next item administered is harder. Adaptive tests may or may not be fixed length. CATs are a recommended design for two major security reasons: overall reduced item exposure and reduced risk of exposure to item pirates.

To achieve a score with similar accuracy to a nonadaptive test, a CAT needs to present fewer questions. Some programs (e.g., Novell's certification program; http.//www.novell.com/training/) experienced as much as two-thirds reduction in the number of items needed. The National Council of State Boards of Nursing licensure examination (NCLEX) reduced their lengthy test covering two days to just seventy-five test items administered in a half day. Logically, this means that fewer items in the original pool are exposed on a regular schedule, extending the life of the pool and individual items. Even without the dedicated efforts of item and test pirates, general item exposure is a security risk because test takers often share general information about items they have seen with others, or they use the information they gained from taking the test the first time if they need to take the test again.

As has happened often in the past, an unscrupulous test preparation organization may use the tactic of sending unknowledgeable test takers to the test to memorize items. Because of the CAT's design, these individuals will likely only see the items on the lower end of the difficulty scale, protecting the items in the moderate and difficult ranges of proficiency. This design feature of CATs makes the theft of questions very difficult and unprofitable. Anecdotal information from some test program personnel suggests that to protect the item pool from exposure, it must be large and have an item selection algorithm that selects from the total pool, not just items that are the most discriminating or the most informative. If these conditions are not in place, then there is greater risk of theft of the entire item pool.

CATs also increase exposure risks because the items that exist in the item pool are not presented an equal number of times. A few items may be presented an abnormally large number of times and may be considered overexposed. The majority are presented at rates that would be less than in the equivalent traditional linear exam. And a few items are shown rarely (some items in CAT pools may never be presented). Obviously, care must be taken to reduce the exposure of those highly discriminating items that are overexposed. Usually an item exposure constraint can be added to the CAT algorithm to reduce the levels for those items at risk or randomization from a set of several highly informative items at a designated ability level.

If the CAT can be established as a valid measurement of the construct of interest and if the rate of exposure of the more "popular" items can be reduced (usually accomplished by adding more items to the pool and more items that discriminate well), the CAT offers substantial security benefits over linear forms–based testing.

LOTF test are fixed length, and created by selecting items at random from an item pool (hence, *on-the-fly*). The item selection algorithm is often constrained to select items so that the final test represents the test specification and items are selected using a stratified random sample of items rather than a simple random sample. Tests are constructed to be equivalent with each other in difficulty and content. Essentially, the LOTF (and the CATs for that matter) can be viewed as tests with an unlimited number of equivalent forms and versions. As such they have the same advantages for security as multiple versions and multiple forms, in that they protect against copying. Davey and Nering present a fairly gloomy prospect for computerized testing and managing item pools in their chapter in *Computer-Based Testing: Building the Foundation for Future Assessments* (Davey & Nering, 2002):

> The fight for pool security is ultimately a losing battle, with a temporary holding action or stalemate being the best that can be hoped for. In some way, on some day, examinees will inevitably learn enough about a pool to render it useless. Whether they learn from each other or from a coaching school is unimportant. A pool is just as useless either way. (p. 187)

They go on to say:

> ...the adaptive testing process may itself hold the key to its salvation. A CAT is smarter than a conventional test, but it can be made a lot smarter still. It must be taught to recognize the unusual response patterns produced by examinees who have been exposed to some of a pool. It must be taught to treat these examinees fairly but differently from examinees who are responding in more predictable ways. The psychometrics underlying adaptive testing can and must be substantially improved. It is a human trait to believe today's problems will be solved by tomorrow's technology. It is just possible that adaptive testing may turn out to be one of the few cases where this faith is warranted. (p. 189)

Use Item Variants/Clones on Alternate Forms of Tests

Although this is an item construction strategy, it is included here as a test assembly strategy because the use of item variants across forms of a test is what enhances the security-related elements. The security issue is one of preventing memorization of items and of the answer key. By using item variants examinees who purchase items or item components (or get them free from forums and chat rooms) can be led into thinking that the item they are seeing is a different one, even though the essential components of the items are the same. There are a number of examples of this that come quickly to mind, especially in quantitative areas where the numbers can change or the item context can change and the number stay the same. Such variants are relatively easy to construct. Item variants can also be constructed in many other fields that are not quantitative.

An example may help to clarify how such variations can be developed. Suppose you have a question that starts with the sentence, "Several teams of wildlife officers receive training on a new strategy for increasing the survival rates of stocked trout in high mountain lakes." If examinees saw this question on a forum or purchased it from a web site, the phrases "wildlife officers" and/or "increasing the survival rate of stocked trout" or even "high mountain lakes" may cue them to recall the specifics of (and the answer to) the item. These surface characteristics provide important clues to help recall the question. If the question is rewritten and the following substitutions were made "neonatal care nurses" for "wildlife officers" and "decreasing the incidence of sudden infant death syndrome in hospitals" for "increasing the survival rate of stocked trout in high mountain lakes," the number of helpful clues from the original question would be very few, thwarting the cheater's efforts to use hints that aid in producing the right answer. As is noted in a recent article about this technique,

> Some subtleties should be considered. First, we need to recognize that this contextual-reminding process is not necessarily a conscious phenomenon. If we, as question designers, are relying on our intuitions about how to deliver questions, we may unintentionally create exams that don't measure what we think they're measuring. As always, it's good to have a research-based understanding of these veiled learning processes. Second, the danger of having repeated questions trigger contextual hints recedes with time. If the final exam questions were delivered two months after the quiz questions, for example, then they would be much less likely to provide contextual hints. Finally, these contextual hints will produce their most damage when learners have to produce their own answer responses. They'll have less of an effect on multiple-choice questions. On the other hand, we ought to recognize that multiple-choice answer choices provide their own sense of context (QuestionMark, 2004, 2).

Thus, the use of item variants can be applied across a wide array of content areas and types of tests. The use of such variants helps to make equivalent tests even when the items do not, on the surface, appear to be similar. This represents a significant step in increasing the security of the test and also helps to offset the high cost of generating new test questions. It may also help to reduce costs of pretesting items if a history exists of how the item variants (sometimes called *clones*) behave psychometrically.

SUMMARY

This chapter explains why test security is important to both examinees and organizations that sponsor testing in education, admissions, or credentialing settings. Different types of test fraud are described (test pirates who steal items and cheaters who use nefarious means to get credit when none is deserved). We described eight strategies for writing items that can help to either make the items harder to memorize, and therefore harder to steal, or to make it harder to copy or collaborate with other examinees to produce undeserved correct responses to multiple-choice questions. We also discuss methods for producing performance-based items for both computer-based and non–computer-based delivery. Finally, we describe four test development strategies that can facilitate higher levels of test security. We note that sometimes there is a conflict between good psychometrics and good security.

This chapter emphasizes that the way we create items and tests has a bearing on the security of the tests. If test developers are not thoughtful about how items are written and how tests are constructed, they could be inadvertently making the test easier to steal. Test developers spend a lot of money to make sure the content is accurate and cut scores are set properly, only to give the test and items away with poor item and test design. With a few changes in strategy, test developers can help protect the tests and ensure a fair testing environment for the examinees.

ACKNOWLEDGMENT

The authors express profound appreciation to the external reviewers, Barbara S. Plake, Thomas M. Haladyna, and Steven M. Downing for their excellent suggestions to improve this chapter.

REFERENCES

Brennan, R. L. (1992). The context of context effects. *Applied Measurement in Education, 5,* 225–264.

Davey, T., & Nering, M. (2002). Controlling item exposure and maintaining item security. In C. Mills, M. Potenza, J. Fremer, & W. Ward (Eds.), *Computer-basted testing building the foundation for future assessments* (pp. 165–191). Mahwah, NJ : Lawrence Erlbaum Associates.

Haladyna, T. M., & Downing, S. M. (1989a). A taxonomy of multiple-choice item-writing rules. *Applied Measurement in Education, 2,* 37–50.

Haladyna, T. M., & Downing, S. M. (1989b). The validity of a taxonomy of multiple-choice item-writing rules. *Applied Measurement in Education, 2,* 51–78.

Haladyna, T. M., & Downing, S. M. (2004). Construct-irrelevant variance in high-stakes testing. *Educational Measurement: Issues and Practices, 23*(1), 17–27.

Haladyna, T. M., Downing, S. M., & Rodriguez, M. C. (2002). A review of multiple-choice item-writing guidelines for classroom assessment. *Applied Measurement in Education, 15,* 309–334.

Leary, L. F., & Dorans, N. J. (1985). Implications for altering the context in which test items appear: A historical perspective on an immediate concern. *Review of Educational Research, 55,* 387–413.

Messick, S. (1989). Validity. In R. L. Linn (Ed.), *Educational measurement* (3rd ed., pp. 13–104). New York: American Council on Education and Macmillan.

Neely, D. L., Springston, F. J., & McCann, S. J. H. (1994). Does item order affect performance on multiple-choice exams? *Teaching of Psychology, 47,* 513–522.

Powers, D. E., & Fowles, M. E. (1998). Effects of preexamination disclosure of essay topics. *Applied Measurement in Education, 11*(2), 139–157.

QuestionMark. (2004). Should quiz questions be used again. Retrieved August 13, 2004 from http://www.questionmark.com/newsletter/newsus1022.htm.

Zenisky, A. L., & Sireci, S. G. (2002). Technical innovations in large scale assessment. *Applied Measurement in Education, 15,* 337–362.

6

Preparing Examinees for Test Taking: Guidelines for Test Developers and Test Users

Linda Crocker
University of Florida

Preparing examinees for college admissions tests or K–12 assessment testing is an area of growing concern for educators and measurement experts. Research and practice on this topic span more than 50 years. The *Standards for Educational and Psychological Testing* address responsibilities of test developers and test users in this area in ten separate standards. From the test developer's perspective, these standards deal with coachability of test item formats, test instructions, and test preparation materials. For test users, relevant standards deal with maintaining test security, respecting intellectual property of test content, and preparing examinees for upcoming tests. Illustrative practices that operationalize these standards are described. Finally, five criteria are identified for evaluating the appropriateness of strategies for preparing examinees for tests, and a research agenda is proposed based on these criteria.

No activity in educational assessment raises more instructional, ethical, and validity issues than preparation for large-scale, high-stakes tests. Historically, college admissions examinations and professional licensure examinations have been targets of the most concerted test preparation efforts. The primary responsibility of preparing for such tests generally rests with individual examinees who often purchase special "test prep" materials or enroll in private coaching schools. Now, however, K–12 students are subject to high-stakes testing situations where graduation or promotion to the next grade may depend on their performance on state assessment tests in reading, writing, or mathematics. Furthermore, in this age of accountability, teachers and school administrators now shoulder major responsibility for preparing students for various academic assessment programs with ensuing rewards or sanctions for these educators based on their students' performance. In this environment demand for test preparation materials and programs flourishes as debate about appropriate examinee test preparation practices intensifies (Jones, Jones, & Hargrove, 2003; Smith, Smith, & Delisi, 2001; Wilson, 2002). Most debate focuses on three fundamental measurement issues:

1. Validity of inferences drawn from test scores when coaching and test preparation contribute to test performance (Allalouf & Ben-Shakhar, 1998; Haladyna & Downing, 2004; Messick, 1989; Powers, 1985a,b; Shepard, 1990);

2. Fairness to examinees who have differential access to test preparation opportunities (Bond, 1989; Crocker, 2003; Linn, 1990; Rogers & Bateson, 1991); and
3. Consequences of test use when instructional time and resources are dedicated to examinee test preparation (Cizek, 1998; Koretz, McCaffrey, & Hamilton, 2001; Popham, 2003; Smith & Rottenberg, 1991; Stecher, 2002).

To address these issues, measurement experts and educators need to be well-acquainted with the history and research base on preparing examinees for high-stakes tests. In this chapter, we introduce some basic terms and concepts from literature on test-taking preparation. Then in the areas of admissions testing and K–12 assessment programs, we briefly review the history of preparing examinees for such tests. Standards of practice relating to examinee test preparation are highlighted, and illustrative practices consistent with those standards are identified. Finally, directions for needed research are suggested.

BASIC TERMINOLOGY

Professional literature on preparing examinees for tests contains a variety of terms that do not always have standard meaning. *Examinee test preparation*, as defined here, refers to activities, beyond normal classroom instruction or study, specifically undertaken to (a) review content likely to be covered on a test and (b) practice skills necessary to demonstrate that knowledge in the format of the test (or tests) anticipated.

Coaching refers to activities specifically undertaken to prepare examinees for a particular test with the intent of helping the students to improve their scores. Coaching may include instruction in both content and test-wiseness strategies (American Educational Research Association, [AERA], American Psychological Association [APA], & National Council on Measurement in Education [NCME], 1999), but is commonly considered as a supplement to initial instruction in the content tested. A common example of coaching has been when high school English students are assigned to study published lists of vocabulary words that are frequently used on the Scholastic Aptitude Test (SAT; a content strategy). Coaching may also involve administration of practice tests to give students experience with time management, use of answer sheets, and decisions regarding item omission (a test-wiseness strategy). Finally, an example of coaching for performance assessments occurs when a teacher requires students to practice writing essays in a particular structure to prepare for an upcoming writing assessment (a combination of content and test-wiseness practice).

Test wiseness traditionally refers to the ability of examinees to use test-taking strategies to enhance their scores without an actual increase in knowledge of the content or ability domain covered by the test. Test-wiseness strategies include time management, developing familiarity and adeptness with multiple item formats, and effective employment of metacognitive strategies in responding to assessment exercises (Sarnacki, 1979). Some test-wiseness strategies may be strictly related to test-taking situations; for example, eliminating clearly incorrect options and then making an informed guess among the remaining responses on multiple choice items (Millman, Bishop, & Ebel, 1965). Other strategies, however, represent effective work habits or problem-solving techniques that generalize to other academic or work situations. For example, underlining the main idea of a paragraph or checking to see that numbers have been correctly copied from the problem when setting up a solution are sound study and work habits that benefit the examinee beyond the testing situation.

Test study guides are materials and activities designed to help students perform well on a particular test. These may include instructional material geared to test content, lists of topics to review, sample test items, practice tests, and lists of test-taking tips.

Curricular alignment refers to adapting a planned instructional curriculum to ensure that topics from the tested domain of knowledge are included systematically in the normal course of instruction. This practice goes beyond short-term test preparation, review for an upcoming test, or practice in test taking because it includes selection of topics, materials, and learning activities that constitute the initial instruction.

SOURCES OF INFORMATION ON DESIRED PROFESSIONAL PRACTICES

Charting an appropriate course of action by test developers and test users with regard to test preparation is a significant challenge. The following documents offer guidance to measurement professionals on a broad range of issues, including those that affect test preparation:

1. *Standards for Educational and Psychological Testing* (AERA, APA, & NCME, 1999);
2. *Code of Fair Testing Practices* (Joint Committee on Testing Practices, 2004);
3. *Code of Professional Responsibilities* (NCME, 1995); and
4. Professional literature (e.g., Mehrens & Kaminski, 1989; Mehrens, Popham, & Ryan, 1998; Popham, 1991; Schmeiser, 1998).

Collectively, these sources address responsibilities of both test developers and test users with respect to appropriate practices in preparing examinees for high-stakes tests. In subsequent sections of this chapter, we address two different types of high-stakes testing situations: college admissions testing and K–12 assessment programs.

TEST PREPARATION IN COLLEGE ADMISSIONS TESTING

Background

According to Linn (1990), "If the topic of bias ranks first among controversial issues related to admissions testing, coaching, at least in recent years, probably ranks second" (p. 313). Linn noted that most college bound students are required to take tests offered by the American College Testing Program (the ACT) or the College Board's SAT. He also noted that applicants for graduate school or for law, medical, or business schools confronted similar examinations; namely, the Graduate Record Examination (GRE), Law School Admissions Test (LSAT), the Medical College Admissions Test (MCAT), and the Graduate Management Admission Test (GMAT).

At least four concerns over admissions testing are documented in measurement literature. A primary concern has been the effectiveness of coaching and test preparation for admissions tests. Research on the magnitude of score increases attained by examinees who retake examinations after some form of preparation has yielded considerable variation in estimates of effects (see Powers & Rock, 1999). In part, this is caused by a lack of uniformity in the types of preparation, the duration of the preparation, the subject areas, and the methodology of the studies. A summary of findings reported by Linn (1990) and Bond (1989) suggests that somewhat greater gains have been reported for studies that (a) have treatments that are longer in duration; (b) involve instruction in content in addition to test-wiseness skills; and (c) focus on mathematics rather than verbal reasoning. Studies with more rigorous experimental designs, using control groups and random assignment, tended to yield lower effect sizes.

Validity is the second concern. If test preparation can increase examinee's scores, then the question is whether the increases achieved by coaching result in improvements in future examinee academic performance. If not, then variation in test scores owing to coaching effects is construct-irrelevant variance (CIV; see Haladyna & Downing, 2004) and detracts from the quality of admissions decisions. CIV has been defined by Messick (1989) as systematic error variance in test scores resulting in over- or underprediction of an examinee's standing on the construct of interest owing to differences among the examinees on some other variable (unrelated to the construct of interest). This critical issue remains largely unresolved in part because of limited research on the topic (Linn, 1990) and because findings from the few studies conducted have been mixed. For example, Powers (1985b) reported a negative effect of coaching on validity evidence for the GRE analytic reasoning subtest; however, Allalouf and Ben-Shakar (1998) found neither a reduction in validity nor in a prediction bias against uncoached examinees, despite a gain of nearly 0.25 standard deviations in the scores of coached examinees.

A third concern is fairness (Zwick, 2002). Critics of college admissions testing have suggested that unequal access to costly test preparation programs and materials may contribute to the performance gap between majority and minority subgroups, who generally come from less affluent backgrounds (Linn, 1990).

Finally, a long-standing concern has been the method by which those who offer test preparation services obtain information about test contents. Lemann (1999) summarized the origins of the two major coaching schools. The founding father of examinee test preparation as a commercial enterprise was Stanley Kaplan who began to tutor public high school students in Brooklyn for the SAT during the 1940s. Kaplan created his study guides using information gleaned from written descriptions of the test and by interviewing students who had just taken the test to learn about item content and format. Later John Katzman, who founded the Princeton Review, followed a similar strategy. Lemann (1999) quoted Katzman, "We'd send people in to take tests.... I'd take ten, fifteen kids and say: I'll buy you Chinese food if you tell me as many questions as you can remember" (p. 229). Developers of the early SAT had designed their item formats to test verbal and quantitative reasoning in novel problems and thus viewed coaching based on information obtained through memorization of "live" items as a threat to score comparability and valid test score interpretation. Today, the SAT is considered primarily an achievement test, and the test description and item formats are well publicized. In addition, coaching and test preparatory services have become more circumspect in their approaches to tracking test content and format. Thus, the present relationship between testing companies and coaching schools might be described as one of vigilant coexistence. As we shall see in subsequent sections, current professional standards reflect an awareness of these controversial aspects of test preparation.

Relevant Standards and Illustrative Practices for Test Developers

Although most test developers agree that the best form of test preparation for college admissions tests is completing a rigorous high school curriculum (Schmeiser, 2001), they typically encourage examinees to develop sound test-taking skills as well. In addition, they have become more proactive in attempts to "level the playing field" with respect to access to test preparation for all examinees. Most test developers pursue a multifaceted strategy to offer all examinees equitable opportunities for test preparation and practice: (a) Topical content areas tested are publicized so that examinees (and their teachers) can review these areas as needed; (b) Sample test forms are released and often packages of multiple released forms with problem solution strategies can be purchased directly from test publishers; and (c) New item formats are tested empirically to assess their vulnerability to coaching prior to use (e.g., Powers, 1986; Powers & Swinton, 1984). The *Standards for Educational and Psychological Testing* (AERA, APA, & NCME, 1999) and the *Code of Fair Testing Practices* (Joint Committee on Testing Practices, 2004) delineate responsibilities of test developers to communicate with test takers and test users regarding

TABLE 6.1
Standards for Test Developers Regarding Test Preparation of Examinees

Standard 1.9	If a test is claimed to be essentially unaffected by practice and coaching, then the sensitivity of test performance to change with these forms of instruction should be documented (AERA, APA, & NCME, 1999, p. 19).
Standard 3.20	The instructions presented to test takers should contain sufficient detail so that test takers can respond to the task in the manner that the test developer intended. When appropriate, sample material, practice or sample questions, criteria for scoring, and a representative item identified with each major area in the test's classification or domain should be provided to the test takers prior to the administration of the test or included in the testing material as part of the standard administration instruction (AERA, APA, & NCME, 1999, p. 47).
Standard 5.5	Instructions to test takers should clearly indicate how to make responses. Instructions should also be given in the use of any equipment likely to be unfamiliar to test takers. Opportunity to practice responding should be given when equipment is involved, unless use of the equipment is being assessed (AERA, APA, & NCME, 1999, p. 63).
Standard 8.1	Any information about test content and purposes that is available to any test taker should be available to all test takers.... Comment: ... More detailed information, such as practice materials, is sometimes offered for a fee. Such offering should be made to all test takers (AERA, APA, & NCME, 1999, p. 85).
Code of Fair Testing Practices in Education. D.1	Inform test takers in advance of the test administration about the coverage of the test, the types of question format, the directions, and appropriate test-taking strategies. Make such information available to all test takers (Joint Commission for Test Taking, 2004, p. 6).

test content, format, and administration procedures and to assure equitable access to resources describing the test. These standards include communication about examinee test preparation (Table 6.1).

The following list offers a sample of sound practices that test developers may use during the test development and administration stages that demonstrate the spirit of the standards listed in Table 6.1. This list is intended to be neither restrictive nor exhaustive; nor is the full list of practices applicable to any single testing program.

- All items are reviewed for their susceptibility to coachability according to common item-writing principles, for example, avoid making the correct answer longer, and so on (see Downing, chap. 12, this volume.)
- Novel item formats are reviewed and then tested empirically for susceptibility to short-term coaching or experience with the format.
- Material sent to examinees prior to testing indicates recommended test preparation strategies and indicates the value of coaching for this test (as shown from research).
- Prior to testing, examinees have access to sample items with solutions and explanations of the problem-solving process.
- All testing sessions begin with complete instructions on how to respond to each item format used in that session and examinees have the opportunity to practice with one or more sample items of each type before testing commences.
- Instructions address time limits, guessing, penalties for guessing that are applied, and other scoring rules (e.g., partial credit).
- When tools such as computers or calculators are used during the test administration, examinees have use of these tools during the item practice session. When possible, examinees have the opportunity to practice with these tools in advance of the testing session.

- Upon registration for the examination, examinees receive practice materials that include one or more complete copies of released forms of the test with scoring key.
- When the test includes performance exercises, examinees receive advance practice exercises with scoring rubrics and sample responses that illustrate different levels of proficiency according to that rubric.

In addition to these practices, test developers are increasingly exploring the use of technology to enhance test preparation; a few examples are practice tests on CD-ROMS that simulate computer-based testing situations, web sites that are continually refreshed with new practice items and solution strategies, and diagnostic score reporting for individuals or groups from a particular school site.

PREPARING EXAMINEES IN K–12 ASSESSMENT PROGRAMS

Background

For much of the 20th century, concerns about examinee test preparation were rare in the context of large-scale achievement testing for public schools. Most research on test wiseness in children and youth focused on helping classroom teachers write items for their own tests that contained no inadvertent clues to the correct answer (e.g., Carter, 1986). The focus of test-taking preparation shifted, however, because of three major events in the assessment scene:

1. The 1965 Elementary and Secondary Education Act provided federal funding for state and local school districts to enhance education of children from low-income families. Its evaluation requirements for objective measurement of educational achievement resulted in widespread use of nationally normed, commercially published achievement tests (see Linn, 2000; Stecher, 2002).
2. The statewide assessment movement using minimum competency testing for high school graduation and school accountability began in the 1970s. This assessment movement relied on criterion-referenced tests, based on explicitly stated instructional objectives and preset performance levels for mastery that were linked to the score scale on the test so that no child's score depended on its relationship to others' scores (see Hambleton, 1994; Popham, 1992).
3. The No Child Left Behind (NCLB) Act of 2001 requires statewide testing of nearly all students in mathematics and reading in grades three through eight and once in high school by 2005–2006 using statewide, standards-based assessment tests with testing in science at selected grade levels by 2007. *Standards-based assessments* are linked to state content standards in each tested subject and have performance standards for proficiency set by the state. A key feature of NCLB is *Annual Yearly Progress* (AYP), which establishes targets for the percentage of students scoring at above the proficient level over time (see Linn, Baker, & Betebenner, 2002). NCLB also allows states to use sanctions or rewards for districts and schools to promote accountability and ensure annual yearly progress (No Child Left Behind Act of 2001, 2002).

These events have spurred intense interest in how to prepare students for high-stakes tests. At least four major themes emerge in measurement literature on preparation of school children for high stakes testing since that first Title I legislation.

The first issue to arise was whether test preparation efforts would be effective in raising test scores. Two major reviews and meta-analyses in the 1980s concluded that test preparation typically raised student scores on average by approximately one quarter of a standard deviation. The greatest benefits accrued to longer programs incorporating frequent opportunities to practice and stressing broad cognitive skills (Bangert-Drowns, Kulik, & Kulik, 1983; Scruggs, White, & Bonnur, 1986).

A second issue has been the nature of appropriate test preparation practices and the extent to which teachers may go beyond acceptable boundaries. For example, when Cannell (1987) questioned how all fifty states could report "above average" performance of their students on nationally normed, standardized achievement tests, some measurement experts suggested that overzealous test preparation by teachers was a contributing factor (Linn, Graue, & Sanders, 1990; Shepard, 1990). Such concerns prompted Mehrens and Kaminski (1989) to propose a continuum for appropriate test preparation practices. The most appropriate practices enhance student knowledge of subject matter as well as improving their test performance (e.g., using estimation skills in mathematics to check on the accuracy of a solution); the most inappropriate raise student scores on a particular test with no increase in generalizable knowledge (e.g., practice on a parallel test form or advance practice on items from the test actually used). In one well-known study, Nolen, Haladyna, and Haas (1992) revealed that approximately 10% of a large sample of teachers reported giving students practice on the current test form, and 25% taught vocabulary words that were used in the test.

The third issue is the potentially negative impact on learning caused by teaching to the test and drilling on test-taking skills (e.g., Madaus, 1998; Popham, 2003; Smith & Rottenberg, 1991). *Teaching to the test* refers to instruction that narrows the focus of instruction to only that content covered by the test and preparing students to demonstrate their knowledge only in the format used by that particular test. A concomitant fear is that untested, yet important, parts of the curriculum are neglected as teachers use class time for practice tests and test-taking skills. Studies by Herman and Golan (1993) and Smith and Rottenberg (1991) support this concern. Some evidence further suggests that the problem is greater in schools serving poor and minority students (Herman & Golan, 1993; Lomax et al., 1995). Cizek (2002) and others have noted that the body of evidence for these claims is limited, but Stecher (2002) noted the difficulty of distinguishing excessive test preparation from content instruction. This concern seems unlikely to subside unless clearer definitions and guidelines emerge.

RESPONSIBILITIES OF TEST USERS IN SCHOOL SETTINGS

In K–12 testing programs, test developers have little direct communication with the examinees. However, the responsibility for handling test materials and communicating with examinees in ways that preserve the validity of score interpretations passes to the teachers and administrators who are the primary test users. Standards focused on these test user responsibilities, with respect to preparing examinees for tests, fall into two categories: (a) security of test content and (b) preparing students.

Respect of Intellectual Property and Test Security

Public credibility of high-stakes accountability systems is jeopardized when teachers or students are accused of gaining unauthorized access to test items and using that access to boost scores. Individual or group scores may be nullified and sanctions may be imposed on those found guilty of legal or academic misconduct. Table 6.2 displays excerpts from the *Standards for Educational and Psychological Testing* that specifically address tests user obligations to avoid this problem by respecting intellectual property of test material and secure handling of these materials.

TABLE 6.2
Standards for Test Users Regarding Intellectual Property and Test Security

Standard 11.8	Test users have the responsibility to respect test copyrights (p. 115).
Standard 11.7	Test users have the responsibility to protect the security of tests to the extent that developers enjoin users to do so (p. 115).
Standard 11.9	Test users should remind test takers and others who have access to test materials that the legal rights of test publishers, including copyrights, and the legal obligations of other participants in the testing process may prohibit the disclosure of test items without specific authorization (p. 115).

From the AERA, APA, & NCME, 1999.

At the school or district level, testing directors or building administrators play an important role in helping teachers and students meet these standards. A list of illustrative practices that can protect test content intellectual property and promote test security includes the following activities:

- When teachers are permitted to review test materials, they should have clear, consistent definitions of acceptable and unacceptable practices. Guidelines should specifically address issues such as retaining copies of tests, making photocopies of test materials, or making notes regarding test content or format.
- Have systematic procedures for storing test materials securely, retaining counts of test booklets and answer sheets, and clear policies for who may handle these materials.
- Provide guidelines for unacceptable, acceptable, and recommended test handling and preparation practices, with examples of each.
- Arrange testing schedules to minimize the opportunity for examinees to pass on information regarding test item content to those who have yet to take the test. This is particularly critical for essay or performance exercises.
- Offer professional development experiences on (a) effective test preparation practices, (b) how to integrate test preparation into meaningful classroom instruction activities, (c) the distinction between desirable curricular alignment and "teaching to the test," and (d) establishing a positive climate for assessment and use of test score information for advancing children's learning.
- Monitor the type and frequency of test preparation activity at the classroom level from perspectives of teachers, students, and parents.
- Examine school academic honor codes to assess whether and how test preparation and test-taking behavior are addressed. Consider modifications if needed.

Preparing Examinees for Upcoming Tests

In K–12 assessment, teachers are in the "front line" of examinee test preparation and have greatest accountability for the performance of their students on high-stakes assessment. As noted, there is concern among researchers and practitioners that some teachers may engage in test preparation practices that are inappropriate and counterproductive to the purpose for which the assessment scores will be used (Schmeiser, 1998). The *Standards for Educational and Psychological Testing* have three broad standards that address this (see Table 6.3.) At the classroom level, teachers can engage in a number of legitimate test preparation practices that enhance student learning as well as their test-taking skills while conforming to the standards in Table 6.3. Crocker (2005) has identified various sources on teaching test-taking skills and compiled a list of recommendations for classroom teachers from those sources. Most suggestions

TABLE 6.3
Standards for Test Users Regarding Test Preparation

Standard 13.11	In educational settings, test users should ensure that any test preparation activities and materials provided to students will not adversely affect the validity of test score inferences (p. 148).
Standard 15.7	...It is the responsibility of those who mandate the use of tests to identify and monitor their impact and to minimize potential negative consequences.... Comment: ...An example of negative consequences is the use of strategies to raise scores artificially (p. 168).
Standard 15.9	The integrity of test results should be maintained by eliminating practices designed to raise test scores without improving performance on the construct or domain measured by test (p. 168).

From the AERA, APA, & NCME (1999).

provided below originated from that list. The suggestions are grouped by type of test—generic to all types of tests, objective-item format, and essay/performance assessment exercise.

The following suggestions apply generically to all types of test formats:

- Express a positive attitude in talking with students and parents about testing to encourage motivation and reduce possible test anxiety.
- Over time, lengthen in-class seat assignments, tests, or quizzes, until students are accustomed to maintaining sustained silent concentration for the length of the standardized test period and have practice in budgeting time.
- Give instructions for classroom assignments in ways that require students to model how they should behave in the testing milieu; for example, listening to and reading instructions for standardized tests, including working sample exercises, and asking questions before they start if they do not understand the directions.
- Make sure that students can read and comprehend "terms of art" that they may encounter on tests at their grade levels in each subject. For example, in mathematics, students should read and understand terms such as *digit, numeral, direction, decimal, estimate, solve,* and *multiply*.
- Administer practice tests as provided by the district; review correct responses and explain why incorrect answers are incorrect; model good problem-solving strategies when demonstrating how to approach test items. Note that use of such tests should be limited, perhaps as needed for formative evaluation, not to the extent that they supplant instruction.

When preparing students for tests with objective item formats, these recommendations may be useful:

- Use a variety of item formats on teacher-made assessments or homework assignments, including but not restricted to those used on major assessment tests.
- Vary the difficulty level of items within tests or assignments so that students learn to persist if they encounter some items that they cannot answer.
- Teach students to use systematic strategies for choosing one best answer for multiple-choice items; encourage discussion in which students explain to each other why one answer is more correct than others.
- Have students practice in reviewing their work and deciding when response change is indicated.
- Occasionally use separate answer sheets that require bubbling or circling the correct response on teacher-made tests or homework assignments.

For essay or performance assessments, the following suggestions may be helpful in preparing examinees (adapted from Mehrens et al., 1998):

- Keep in mind the broader domain to which inference will be drawn from the score on a particular performance exercise.
- When teaching students how to respond to performance exercises using sample exercises, focus student attention on the content of the domain being tested, rather than the context of the exercise. For example, if students are being tested on interpreting data using a table in a magazine article, focus on the mathematical skills and concepts they must apply more than the topic of the article.
- Identify evaluative criteria in advance of instructional planning and communicate these to students.
- Give students practice using performance exercises of various types.
- Explain how score rubrics are used to score performance exercises and have students learn to evaluate their own responses using such rubrics.
- Point out how the knowledge being applied a particular task can be transferred to other tasks or situations.

Three points about these test preparation strategies are noteworthy. First, these techniques should not impinge heavily on class instructional time. They can be integrated into almost any instructional content unit where the teacher wants to assess student learning. Second, practicing these skills should enhance study habits and future learning. Third, these activities should not enable students who know nothing about the content domain to achieve high scores but should allow students to demonstrate what they know (or do not know) about the material without interfering "noise" (CIV) in the scores resulting from lack of familiarity with the assessment format.

BEYOND THE CURRENT STANDARDS: POSSIBLE RESEARCH DIRECTIONS

Professional standards for test development and test preparation steadily evolve as the educational and political context of assessment changes. New practices and methods of test preparation emerge that may not always be covered in any given edition of standards that are revised periodically. Nevertheless, over time, five general criteria seem to be embodied in various standards. These criteria suggest possible directions for fruitful research that would have substantial application in practice. These basic principles are as follows:

1. *Validity:* Test preparation in test-taking skills should improve validity of test score interpretations by allowing only examinees who have knowledge or partial knowledge of content being tested to benefit from the preparation (AERA, APA, & NCME, 1999). For example, strategies that teach examinees how to receive partial credit by attempting to answer essay items even when not completely sure, how to manage time, how to avoid careless errors, or how to minimize distraction because of test anxiety should contribute to the accuracy of inferences based on test scores. In essence, sound test preparation strategies should reduce effects of random measurement error or CIV.
2. *Academic ethics:* Test preparation activities should be consistent with the ethical canons of the education profession, dealing with cheating, misrepresentation, and respect for intellectual property or work of others (Popham, 1991). For example, making copies of

a secure test form or memorizing items for the purpose of instructing students in how to respond to these or similar items is a clear violation of this criterion.
3. *Fairness:* Fairness requires that similar scores have equivalent meaning for all individuals and that all individuals have equal access to preparation opportunities. When a particular test preparation strategy is effective, it should be available to all examinees, not limited to those who can afford special services to acquire it. It also suggests that the possibility of differential impact of test preparation strategies for various subgroups should be investigated prior to across-the-board implementation.
4. *Educational value:* Content-focused test preparation that leads to improvement in examinee scores should simultaneously increase examinee mastery of the content domain tested (AERA, APA, & NCME, 1999; Popham, 1991, Reeves, 2001; Wilson, 2002). For example, review of word-decoding skills, teaching examinees to work with number operations in both vertical and horizontal presentations, or finding the main idea in a paragraph of text in preparation for an upcoming test have educational value that generalizes beyond the testing situation, as opposed to teaching a few isolated facts or word meanings that are known to be covered on a particular test.
5. *Transferability:* Test preparation focused on test-taking skills should provide examinees with skills that have applicability to a broad range of testing situations (Crocker, 2003; Mehrens et al., 1998; Popham, 1992). Examples of transferable skills are time management, identifying and eliminating obviously incorrect options, or labeling graphs properly, because these skills are applicable to a wide gamut of tests and offer the student some long-term benefits beyond the immediate testing situation.

Measurement practitioners who confront new situations in test preparation may find that one or more of these criteria provide a useful litmus test for proposed activity. In addition, however, these criteria can suggest new research directions or extensions in the investigation of examinee test preparation. Illustrations of the types of questions that could be formulated using these five criteria, respectively, are as follows:

1. What are the longitudinal effects of preparation for college admissions tests on subsequent academic performance (either on overall grade point average [GPA] or performance in specific courses)? Is the relationship between test score and academic performance moderated by type and amount of test preparation?
2. Can professional development on appropriate strategies for improving examinee test performance affect reported incidence rates of inappropriate practices, based on teacher self-reports and classroom observations?
3. Does the type and amount of examinee test preparation affect differential subgroup performance of examinees? Can it alter the relationship between test performance and other criteria of academic achievement (e.g., GPA)? How do patterns of test preparation differ in schools with different student body characteristics?
4. Can various content-focused test preparation strategies be placed on a continuum of "long-range academic value" and can immediate and longitudinal effects be determined for corresponding categories of this continuum?
5. Can the transfer effects of various strategies for test preparation be evaluated over different tests at the same grade level and for similar tests taken at different grade levels to assess horizontal and vertical transferability?

These questions are not intended as a definitive list. Rather, they are intended to stimulate thought about a more in-depth research agenda on preparing examinees for high-stakes tests. To date, most research in this area has examined only the impact of any particular practice on increasing examinee scores without considering more important or long-range outcomes and consequences. As a greater proportion of limited instruction time and fiscal resources are devoted to examinee test preparation, the answers to such questions seem long overdue.

SUMMARY

Preparing examinees for high-stakes tests is a growing enterprise in education both for college admissions testing and for K–12 assessment programs. Commensurate with this increase in test preparation activity, the *Standards for Educational and Psychological Testing* and other professional literature have begun to address the responsibilities of test developers and test users in this arena. For test developers in college admissions, standards have addressed test developer responsibilities to develop clear instructions, provide practice opportunities, and support claims regarding how scores are (or are not) affected by coaching with empirical research. Major issues in preparation for college admissions tests are (a) the extent to which such preparation may introduce CIV into test scores, thereby reducing the predictive usefulness of the test scores and (b) equality of access to test preparation opportunities for all examinees. In K–12 assessment programs, tests users have obligations regarding intellectual property of test material and secure handling of these materials. In addition, they have the responsibility for preparing students for upcoming assessment tests in ways that are educationally appropriate to preserve and enhance the validity of the inferences and decisions that may be based on student test scores.

Five general criteria can be used to assess the appropriateness of proposed activity for preparing examinees for high-stakes tests. These criteria are validity, academic ethics, fairness, educational value, and transferability. An agenda for research using these criteria was recommended to expand our knowledge of the outcomes and consequences of examinee test preparation.

REFERENCES

Allalouf, A., & Ben-Shakhar, G. (1998). The effect of coaching on the predictive validity of scholastic aptitude test. *Journal of Educational Measurement, 35,* 31–47.

American Educational Research Association (AERA), American Psychological Association (APA), & National Council on Measurement in Educatiion (NCME). (1999). *Standards for educational and psychological testing.* Washington DC: Author.

Bangert-Drowns, R. L., Kulik, J. A., & Kulik, C. C. (1983). Effects of coaching programs on achievement test performance. *Review of Educational Research, 53,* 571–586.

Bond, L. (1989). The effects of special preparation on measures of scholastic ability. In R. L. Linn (Ed.), *Educational measurement* (3rd ed., pp. 429–444). New York: American Council on Education/Macmillan.

Cannell, J. J. (1987). *How public educators cheat on standardized achievement tests.* Albuquerque, NM: Friends for Education.

Carter, K. (1986). Test-wiseness for teachers and students. *Educational Measurement: Issues & Practice, 5*(4), 20–23.

Cizek, G. J. (2002). More unintended consequences of high-stakes testing. *Educational Measurement: Issues & Practice, 20*(4), 19–27.

Crocker, L. (2005). Teaching for the test: how and why test preparation is appropriate. In R. P. Phelps (Ed.). *Defanding standardized testing*, Mahwah, NJ: Lawrence Erlbaum Associates.

Crocker, L. (2003). Teaching for the test: Validity, fairness, and moral action. *Educational Measurement: Issues & Practice, 22*(3), 5–11.

Haladyna, T. M., & Downing. S. M. (2004). Construct irrelevant variance in high stakes testing. *Educational Measurement: Issues & Practice, 23*(1), 17–27.

Hambleton, R. K. (1994). The rise and fall of criterion-referenced measurement? *Educational Measurement: Issues & Practice, 13*(4), 21–26.

Herman, J. L., & Golan, S. (1993). The effects of standardized testing on teaching and schools. *Educational Measurement: Issues & Practice, 12*(4), 20–25, 41–42.

Joint Committee on Testing Practices. (2004). *Code of fair testing practices*. Washington, DC: American Psychological Association.

Jones, M. G., Jones, B. D., & Hargrvove, T. Y. (2003). *The unintended consequences of high-stakes testing*. Lanham, MD: Rowman & Littlefield.

Koretz, D., McCaffrey, D., & Hamilton, L. (2001). *Toward a framework for validating gains under high-stakes conditions*. (CSE tech. Rep. No. 409). Los Angeles: Center for the Study of Evaluation, University of California.

Lemann, N. (1999). *The big test*. New York: Farrar, Strauss, & Giroux.

Linn, R. L. (1990). Admissions testing: Recommended uses, validity, differential prediction, and coaching. *Applied Measurement in Education, 3,* 297–318.

Linn, R. L. (2000). Assessments and accountability. *Educational Researcher, 29*(2), 4–16.

Linn, R. L., Baker, E. L., & Betebenner, D. W. (2002). Accountability systems: Implications of requirements of the No Child Left Behind Act of 2001. *Educational Researcher, 31*(6), 3–16.

Linn, R. L., Graue, M. E., & Sanders, N. M. (1990). Comparing state and district test results to national norms: The validity of the claims that "everyone is above average." *Educational Measurement: Issues and Practice, 9*(3), 5–14.

Lomax, R. G., West, M. M., Herman, M. C., & Madaus, G. (1995). The impact of mandated standardized testing on minority students. *Journal of Negro Education, 64,* 171–184.

Madaus, G. (1998). The distortion of teaching and testing: High-stakes testing and instruction. *Peabody Journal of Education, 65,* 29–46.

Mehrens, W. A., & Kaminski, J. (1989). Methods for improving standardized test scores: Fruitful, fruitless, or fraudulent? *Educational Measurement: Issues and Practice, 8*(1), 14–22.

Mehrens, W. A., Popham, W. J., & Ryan, J. M. (1998). How to prepare students for performance assessments. *Educational Measurement: Issues & Practice, 17*(1), 18–22.

Messick, S. (1989). Validity. In R. L. Linn (Ed.), *Educational measurement* (3rd Ed. pp. 13–103). American Council on Education. New York: Macmillan.

Millman, J., Bishop, C. H., & Ebel, R. L. (1965). An analysis of test wiseness. *Educational and Psychological Measurement, 25,* 707–726.

National Council on Measurement in Education. (1995). *Code of professional responsibilities in educational measurement*. Washington, DC: Author.

No Child Left Behind Act of 2001, P. L. No. 107–110, 115 Stat. 1425. (2002).

Nolen, S. B., Haladyna, T. M., & Haas, N. S. (1992). Uses and abuses of achievement test scores. *Educational Measurement: Issues & Practice, 11*(2), 9–15.

Popham, W. J. (1991). Appropriateness of teachers' test-preparation practices. *Educational Measurement: Issues and Practice, 10,* 12–15.

Popham, W. J. (1992). A tale of two test-specification strategies. *Educational Measurement: Issues & Practice, 11*(2), 16–17, 22.

Popham, W. J. (2003). Seeking redemption for our psychometric sins. *Educational Measurement: Issues and Practice, 22*(1), 45–48.

Powers, D. E. (1985a). Effects of test preparation on the validity of a graduate admissions test. *Applied Psychological Measurement, 9*(2), 179–190.

Powers, D. E. (1985b). Effects of coaching on GRE aptitude test scores. *Journal of Educational Measurement, 22*(2), 121–136.

Powers, D. E. (1986). Relations of test item characteristics to test preparation/test practice effects: A quantitative summary. *Psychological Bulletin, 100*(1), 67–77.

Powers, D. E., & Rock, D. A. (1999). Effects of coaching on SAT I: Reasoning test scores. *Journal of Educational Measurement, 36,* 93–118.

Powers, D. E., & Swinton, S. S. (1984). Effects of self-study for coachable test item types. *Journal of Educational Psychology, 76,* 266–278.

Reeves, D. B. (2001). Standards make a difference: The influence of standards on classroom assessment. *NASSP Bulletin, 85,* 5–12.

Rogers, W. T., & Bateson, D. J. (1991). The influence of test-wiseness on performance of high school seniors on school leaving examinations. *Applied Measurement in Education, 4,* 159–183.

Sarnacki, R. E. (1979). An examination of test wiseness in the cognitive domain. *Review of Educational Research, 49,* 252–279.

Schmeiser, C. B. (1998). Professional responsibility: Does the end always justify the means? *Educational Measurement: Issues & Practice, 17*(4), 5–8.

Schmeiser, C. B. (2001). Promoting a healthy environment for college admissions testing. *NASSP Bulletin, 85,* 27–36.

Scruggs, T. E., White, K. P., & Bonnur, K. (1986). Teaching test-taking skills to elementary grade students: A metanalysis, *The Elementary School Journal, 87,* 69–82.

Shepard, L. A. (1990). Inflated test score gains: Is the problem old norms or teaching the test? *Educational Measurement: Issues & Practice, 9*(3), 15–22.

Smith, M. L., & Rottenberg, C. (1991). Unintended consequences of external testing in elementary schools. *Educational Measurement: Issues & Practice, 12*(4), 20–25, 41.

Smith, J. K., Smith, L. F., & DeLisi, R. (2001). *Natural classroom assessment.* Thousand Oaks, CA: Corwin.

Stecher, B. M. (2002). Consequences of large-scale, high-stakes testing on school and classroom practice. In L. S. Hamilton, B. M. Stecher, & S. P. Klein (Eds.), *Making sense of test-based accountability in education* (pp. 79–100). Santa Monica: Rand.

Wilson, L. W. (2002). *Better instruction through assessment.* Larchmont, NY: Eye on Education.

Zwick, R. (2002). Fair game? *The use of standardized admission tests in higher education.* New York: Routledge Falmer.

II
Content

7

Content-Related Validity Evidence in Test Development

Michael Kane
National Conference of Bar Examiners

Content-related validity evidence is closely tied to test development. The proposed interpretation and use of test scores guides the development of the test and the inferences leading from test scores to conclusions and decisions. This process typically involves the specification of a target domain of observations that either defines the attribute of interest or an indicator to be used in estimating the attribute of interest. In either case, it is necessary to draw samples from the target domain or a subset of the target domain for inclusion in the test. The nature of the sampling procedures (e.g., a representative sample from the target domain) can provide justification for inferences from sample means to the expected value over the target domain. Empirical analyses of variability over tasks, raters, and conditions of observation can provide support for the generalizability of scores, and efforts to control systematic error can help to rule out alternative interpretations. As a result, much of the evidence needed to support the interpretations of test scores as measures of observable attributes may be generated during test development as the content domain for the test is specified, data collection procedures are defined, and samples of tasks and conditions of observations are drawn.

According to the most recent edition of the *Standards for Educational and Psychological Testing* (AERA, APA, NCME, 1999), "Validity refers to the degree to which evidence and theory support the interpretations of test scores entailed by proposed uses of test scores" (1999, p. 9). To validate a proposed interpretation or use of test scores is to evaluate the claims being based on the test scores. The specific mix of evidence needed for validation depends on the inferences being drawn and the assumptions being made.

Some basic inferences and assumptions in test score interpretations are most readily evaluated by examining the procedures used to generate the scores. For example, inferences from an observed score based on a sample of observations of some activity to conclusions about typical performance on that activity generally rely on assumptions about the representativeness of the sample, and these claims are based on the procedures used to draw the sample. Inferences about latent attributes (e.g., constructs) and proposed uses of test scores also rely on judgments about the relevance of the observed performances to the proposed interpretations and uses. The ruling out of alternative interpretations of test scores (e.g., in terms of bias) generally relies on a careful review of the assessment tasks and data collection procedures. Much of this procedural and judgmental evidence is produced during test development, and has generally been referred to as *content-related validity evidence*.

Content-related validity evidence has been criticized from a number of points of view, most of which are discussed later in this chapter. In particular, the judgments that constitute a major part of content-related evidence tend to have a confirmationist bias, especially when they are generated by the persons who developed the test. However, it is also clear that analyses of the structure and content of the test provide critical evidence in the evaluation of some inferences and assumptions in test score interpretations. The analyses in this chapter suggest that all validation strategies rely on content-related evidence in evaluating claims about relevance, representativeness, and the impact of systematic errors. In most cases, the content-related evidence does not in itself fully justify the proposed interpretation, but it is an essential part of the overall analysis of validity.

The next section of this chapter provides a brief review of the evolution of content-related evidence over the last century, and of the major criticisms of content-related validity evidence. The following section outlines an argument-based model for validity, and the section after that focuses on observable attributes, which are defined in terms of domains of possible observations. The subsequent analyses of direct and standardized measures of observable attributes indicate that the validation of measures of observable attributes tends to be heavily dependent on content-related evidence.

THE EVOLVING ROLE OF CONTENT-RELATED VALIDITY EVIDENCE

For most of its history, testing involved the assessment of knowledge and skills that were considered important to the community. In the earliest high-stakes assessment, Adam and Eve faced a fairly simple performance task—choosing the fruit that could be eaten and leaving that which should not be eaten. This was probably an important skill for early humans. The Greeks valued excellence in many activities (sports, literature, etc.) and sponsored competitions designed to identify the best practitioners in each area; the Greeks seem to have had a passion for high-stakes, norm-referenced assessment. The Chinese civil service examinations focused on calligraphy, poetry, and other forms of elegant expression. More recent civil service examinations as well as various kinds of licensure and certification examinations have tended to have a more pragmatic and mundane orientation, with an emphasis on knowledge and skills relevant to the activity under consideration. In education, most testing has focused on the content taught in a specific course or program.

The common thread that runs through all of these examples is an interest in an individual level of proficiency in some valued area of activity. The areas of activity and the reasons for valuing these areas of activity vary, but in all cases, the immediate focus is on the activity. Any hypotheses about explanatory mechanisms or latent attributes that might account for performance seem to have been implicit.

A defining characteristic of the modern testing movement beginning in the 1880s was a focus on inferences about latent attributes or traits (e.g., mental ability). Mental ability was to be estimated from performance on certain tasks but was not defined in terms of the tasks. It was recognized that the estimates contained error, and accuracy was evaluated mainly in terms of the consistency among the different measures of the trait. The tasks included in these tests were designed to reflect the developers' conceptions of the nature of mental ability. Some researchers (e.g., Galton) focused on simple discrimination tasks and reaction times, and others (e.g., Binet) emphasized more complex problem-solving tasks, but the general intent was to infer level of mental ability from level of performance on the tasks (Shepard, 1993). The argument for interpreting scores in terms of mental ability rather than some other variable (e.g., quality of prior education) depended on the researchers' views about the nature of mental ability as a latent attribute, or trait, of the person, as reflected in performance on the tasks.

Evaluations of these early measures of mental ability depended on the perceived relevance of test tasks to mental ability and on the consistency among different measures that were considered equally relevant. Evaluations of relevance were based on the judgments of qualified "experts" (e.g., content specialists, teachers). These judgments about relevance can be considered early prototypes of content-related validity evidence. They followed the age-old interest in evaluating significant performances but introduced a trait, mental ability, that was assumed to account for the performances. In measuring mental ability, the performance was of interest mainly as an indicator of an otherwise unobservable trait, but adequate sampling of the relevant task performances was an essential characteristic of the assessment.

The new trait-based interpretations did not displace the older content-based interpretations. Rather, the two models complemented each other. In this context, content-related validity evidence operated in two ways. Some test scores were interpreted as measures of expected performance in some area of activity, and the central question of validity focused on how well the test represented the area of activity. Other test scores were used to estimate some nontest performance (e.g., some latent ability), and in these cases, content-related validity evidence played a more limited role in evaluating some aspects of the testing procedure.

The Criterion Model

The earliest explicit model for validity, the criterion model, was introduced before 1920 (Scott, 1917) and was based on correlations of the test scores with scores on some criterion measure (Angoff, 1988; Cureton, 1951; Moss, 1992; Shepard, 1993). The criterion model is very appealing in many contexts, because it seems to be completely objective. Once the criterion scores and test scores are collected, the correlation between the test scores and the criterion scores can simply be computed. Of course, the choice of the criterion and of a sample of persons for the validity study involve judgments, but these decisions are in the background. In many high-stakes contexts, the formal objectivity of the criterion model has great appeal (Porter, 2003).

The Achilles' heel of the criterion model is the need for a clearly valid criterion for the attribute of interest. In many contexts, acceptable criterion measures are not available, and if a criterion is identified, how can it be validated? The criterion measure could be compared to another criterion, but how would that criterion be validated? If criterion-related evidence is adopted as the basic model of validation, the result is either infinite regress or circularity (Ebel, 1961). At some point, some criterion measures have to be validated without appealing to a new criterion.

Content Model

The traditional way to avoid circularity and infinite regress is to justify some criteria in terms of the procedures used to generate them. Reasonable conclusions about level of skill in an activity can be derived from observations of performance of the activity (Cronbach, 1971; Cureton, 1951; Ebel, 1961; Kane, 1982). If an adequate sample of performances in some area of activity has been evaluated in an appropriate way, and random and systematic errors seem to be under control, it is reasonable to accept the scores as valid measures of level of proficiency in the area of activity (Kane, Crooks, & Cohen, 1999). Such interpretations can be questioned on various grounds, but they do not require external criteria for their validation.

The traditional content-based model uses expert judgment to justify inferences from observed samples of performance to conclusions about levels of proficiency in a domain of performances from which the samples were drawn. In practice, the interpretation is often extended to claims about a trait, which is assumed account for observed regularities in performance. As discussed in some detail later in this chapter, even if the first of these inferences is quite solid, the second may not be justified.

The content model tends to work especially well for tests of specific skills, where it is relatively easy to define a performance domain and draw representative samples from the domain. For more broadly defined areas of achievement, it is more difficult to make a case for the validity of any test as a direct measure of proficiency, but it is still possible. For example, Newmann (1992) proposed using performance on a sample of discourse tasks in social studies to draw inferences about skill in social studies discourse, and Crooks and Flockton (1996; Flockton & Crooks, 2002a,b) have developed measures of various kinds of proficiency for use in New Zealand's national assessment program.

The Construct Model

Cronbach and Meehl (1955) developed the construct validation model in terms of constructs that are implicitly defined by their roles in a theory. The constructs are linked to observable attributes that serve as indicators of the constructs, but the constructs are not defined by these indicators.

The construct model was initially proposed as an alternative to the content and criterion models (Cronbach & Meehl, 1955), but was subsequently extended to a general model of validity subsuming all kinds of validity evidence, including content-related evidence and criterion-related evidence. Content-related evidence plays a critical role in the construct model, as it does in the criterion model, where it is used to justify the criterion measures. The justification for linking certain kinds of observations to certain constructs in the theory is typically based on judgments about the appropriateness of these choices.

Criticisms of the Content Model

Content-related evidence supports inferences from a sample of observation to a domain of observations. The definition of the domain of interest may be based on practice analyses (Raymond & Neustel, chap. 9, this volume), on studies of curricula and textbooks, or on conceptual analyses by panels of experts (Webb, chap. 8, this volume). Typically, expert panels develop test specifications based on the domain definition and produce test tasks that reflect the test specifications. Judgments about the relevance of the domain, the adequacy of the test specifications given the domain, and the representativeness of the tasks are typically made during test development.

The traditional content model is liable to a number of criticisms. First, content-related validity evidence is necessarily based on judgment, and therefore, it appears to lack the kind of objectivity available in criterion-related evidence and construct-related evidence. In particular, content-based studies do not generally pose empirical challenges to proposed interpretations. A criterion or construct study can easily yield results that contradict expectations (e.g., a nonsignificant or negative correlation where a strong positive correlation is expected); analyses of content-related validity evidence do not provide such empirical challenges and do not yield crisp yes/no answers. However, because criterion-related studies require the development or acceptance of a criterion and because construct studies require the development of indicators for the constructs, criterion and construct evidence also depend on judgment.

Second, it seems that content-related evidence has more of a confirmationist bias than other kinds of validity evidence, because it relies on judgments that are usually rendered by the test developers. This concern can be partially addressed by having some of these judgments made by content experts who are not associated with the test development effort.

In fact, some of the judgments could be obtained from critics, thus giving due consideration to advocates of alternative interpretations. Nevertheless, most content-based studies are part of test development and therefore tend to confirm the proposed interpretations.

Third, Messick (1989) raised the fundamental objection that, because content-related validity evidence does not involve test scores or the records of performance on which the scores are based, it cannot justify conclusions about the interpretation of test scores. According to this view, content-related evidence, which focuses on test content and procedures, supports claims about the test, but not claims about the interpretation or use of the scores. Messick (1989) described content-related validity evidence as providing support for "the domain relevance and representativeness of the test instrument" (p. 17), but saw it as playing a limited role in validation because it does not provide direct evidence for "inferences to be made from test scores" (p. 17). Messick's criticism can be mitigated by expanding the focus of the validation effort beyond content per se, to include any other aspects of performance (e.g., the context and conditions of observation and the rules used to generate scores) that are relevant to the interpretation of observed performances. This gets us beyond limited notions of content, but it does not include analysis of scores (beyond that involved in initial pilot testing of the instrument and preliminary generalizability studies).

Although content-related evidence does not apply directly to test scores, it can support interpretations of scores in terms of expected performance over some performance domain. If the domain is specified clearly, and a representative sample of performances is drawn from the domain, it is legitimate to draw conclusions from the observed performances to expected performance over the domain.

A fourth concern about content-related evidence is the tendency for it to be used to justify interpretations that go beyond those for which the evidence is relevant. Rozeboom (1966) complained that content-related validity evidence was often used to justify an interpretation in terms of a, "a *theoretical* variable hypothesized to unify the composite's domain" (p. 205). Cronbach (1971) and Linn (1979) expressed similar concerns, and Messick (1989) maintained that the inferences involved in content validity are likely to "invoke, even if only tacitly psychological processes or behaviors rather than mere surface content" (p. 36). These authors are all expressing a concern that content-related evidence is used to justify conclusions that go beyond those that can be justified by this kind of evidence.

This last criticism does not suggest that there is anything intrinsically wrong with content-related evidence; the concern being raised is that the conclusions based on content-related evidence may go beyond those that are justified by this evidence. Content-related evidence can justify an interpretation of test scores in terms of the expected value over a domain of possible performances, but it cannot justify a construct interpretation. The analyses in this chapter suggest that content-related evidence, broadly conceived, can provide justification for content-based score interpretations, and it can provide essential support for more ambitious interpretations (e.g., in terms of latent attributes) but cannot fully evaluate these more ambitious interpretations.

VALIDITY AS ARGUMENT

Validation requires the evaluation of the proposed interpretations and uses of test scores based on all available evidence (Cronbach, 1988; House, 1980; Messick 1989) and therefore requires a clear statement of what is being proposed. The proposed interpretation and uses can be made explicit by specifying an interpretive argument that lays out the inferences and assumptions leading from the test scores to the conclusions and decisions based on the test scores (Crooks, Kane & Cohen, 1996; Kane, 1992; Shepard, 1993).

To say that a score interpretation or use is *valid* is to say that the interpretive argument is coherent (in the sense that reasoning leading from the score to the conclusions hangs together) and that its inferences and assumptions are plausible. The validity argument provides an overall evaluation of the proposed interpretation and uses of test scores, and of any plausible alternative interpretations or uses of the scores (Cronbach, 1988). A serious validation effort involves a critical evaluation of all inferences and assumptions in the interpretive argument. As Cronbach has suggested, "a proposition deserves some degree of trust only when it has survived serious attempts to falsify it" (Cronbach, 1980, p. 103).

The interpretive argument provides a framework for validation by determining the issues that need to be addressed in the validity argument. If the interpretive argument includes a statistical generalization from a sample of performances to the expected value over a universe of possible performances, the validity argument needs to examine the justification for this generalization. If the interpretation does not claim that scores are generalizable over some facet (e.g., the occasion on which observations are made), empirical evidence for generalizability over that facet may be interesting but is not particularly relevant to the validity argument. If the interpretation suggests that level of performance should change in response to some events (e.g., intensive instruction or practice), consistency in scores before and after such events constitutes evidence against the proposed interpretation. In general, evidence for a particular assumption supports a claim for validity if and only if the interpretive argument includes that assumption.

DEVELOPING AND EVALUATING INTERPRETIVE ARGUMENTS

The interpretive argument specifies the proposed interpretation and use of test scores. It is applied every time a test score is interpreted and used. A validity argument that yields a positive evaluation of the interpretive argument (i.e., that suggests that its structure is coherent and that its inferences and assumptions are plausible in some population and under some range of conditions) provides support for the proposed interpretation and use of test scores in that population and under those conditions; it establishes a presumption in favor of the proposed interpretation.

An explicitly stated interpretive argument serves three critical functions. First, it provides a framework for test development by indicating the assumptions that need to hold, and, therefore, indicates issues (e.g., adequacy of sampling) that need to be addressed in test development. Second, it provides a framework for the development of the validity argument by indicating the inferences and assumptions that need to be evaluated. Third, it provides a basis for evaluating the validity argument by indicating the questions that an adequate validity argument would address. A clearly stated interpretive argument thereby provides some protection against a confirmationist bias in validation research (Kane, 1992; Shepard, 1993). An interpretive argument that has survived serious criticism can be accepted as being plausible, just as a scientific theory that has survived serious attempts to refute it is presumptively adopted (Popper, 1962).

The interpretive argument is evaluated by checking its completeness and coherence and by evaluating the evidence for and against its inferences and assumptions, especially its most questionable assumptions. One (a) decides on the conclusions and decisions to be based on test scores, (b) specifies the inferences and assumptions leading from the test scores to these conclusions and decisions, (c) identifies potential competing interpretations, and (d) evaluates all of the evidence for and against the proposed interpretive argument. Just as a scientific theory provides guidance in interpreting observable phenomena, the interpretive argument provides a framework for interpreting test scores and the performances on which they are based. Like scientific theories, interpretive arguments are evaluated in terms of their clarity, coherence, and plausibility in light of the available evidence.

The validation of an interpretive argument can be separated into two stages. In the *development stage,* the measurement procedure and the interpretive argument are developed. In the *appraisal stage,* the interpretive argument is critically evaluated. Most of the data and analyses generated during the development stage are produced by the test developers, and therefore, this stage tends to have a legitimate confirmationist bias. The test developers are trying to make the assessment program as good as it can be, and if they discover a weakness in the testing program or in the proposed interpretation, their natural and appropriate response is to fix it. However, at some point, a more arms-length and critical stance is needed to provide a convincing evaluation of the proposed interpretation and uses, and this occurs in the appraisal stage. Note that, in Kane (2004), the development and appraisal stages were labeled the "formative" and "summative" stages.

Developing the Test and Interpretive Argument

The development of the test and a plausible and coherent interpretive argument to represent the proposed interpretation and use of the scores is a creative effort. In most cases, more than one interpretive argument could be used to meet a general goal (e.g., to assess level of proficiency in an activity like writing). The test developer has to decide on a general approach to achieving the goal at hand and then has to develop a measurement procedure and an interpretive argument that seem to achieve the goal. Preferably, the test and the interpretive argument are developed together and designed to be consistent with each other and with the intended interpretation and use of the scores.

For example, an assessment of writing proficiency could go in any one of several directions. The student could be required to write several essays on different topics, and ratings of these performances could be generalized to a conclusion about writing proficiency, with the interpretation focusing mainly on a generalization from a sample of performance to the expected value over the range of writing activities that are of interest. Alternately, the assessment might consist of a series highly standardized exercises involving the editing of existing passages or objective questions on grammar, sentence structure, and so on. For each of these approaches, efforts to identify and control possible sources of extraneous variance (e.g., content of writing tasks, time limits) can help to rule out certain alternative interpretations.

Each of these approaches to the assessment of writing requires a different interpretive argument. The direct approach, involving a representative sample of writing performances, has a very simple interpretive argument involving two main inferences—the scoring of the performances and the generalization of the resulting score to the domain of interest. Assessment strategies that rely on editing tasks or objective questions provide less direct assessments of writing proficiency, and therefore require more elaborate interpretive arguments to get from the observed performances to conclusions about writing proficiency. Note that the more direct approach is not necessarily better than the less direct approaches, particularly if some inferences or assumptions (e.g., representative sampling, adequate generalizability) are more questionable for the direct approach (Kane et al., 1999).

A basic iterative strategy for developing a test and an interpretive argument can be described in terms of five steps. First, the proposed interpretation and use are specified in terms of a preliminary interpretive argument, and test specifications are developed to fit this interpretive argument (see Raymond & Neustel, chap. 9, this volume; Webb, chap. 8, this volume). If a reasonable interpretive argument and a feasible test design cannot be developed for the proposed interpretation, it may be necessary to adjust the interpretation or to cancel the project. It is not sensible to move forward until a plan that is likely to work reasonably well is in place.

Second, a preliminary version of the test is developed to fit the test specifications and interpretive argument. If the preliminary interpretive argument includes inferences about mastery of certain skills, it makes sense to design the test tasks so that they require these skills (Embretson, 1984). If inferences are to be drawn about a particular performance domain, the test tasks are presumably sampled from this domain.

Third, the overall plausibility of the interpretive argument is evaluated by examining whether its inferences and assumptions provide a clear and coherent basis for drawing the proposed interpretation and use of test scores.

Fourth, to the extent possible during the development stage, the plausibility of the inferences and assumptions in the interpretive argument are evaluated. Those inferences and assumptions for which data can be obtained during the development stage are also checked empirically. For example, generalizability over tasks is likely to be questionable for many assessments and deserves attention during test development.

Fifth, any conflicts between the test, the interpretive argument, and the proposed interpretation and use of test scores are fixed if possible by making suitable adjustments. If substantial changes are made, the new test and the new interpretive argument need to be evaluated. The third, fourth, and fifth steps are repeated until the interpretive argument is considered coherent and palusible.

This iterative approach to test development is much like the process of theory development and refinement in science, with the interpretive argument playing the role of the theory. Preliminary versions of the test and the interpretation are developed and analyzed. Any weaknesses identified in the interpretive argument or the measurement procedure are corrected if possible, just as a scientific theory is adjusted in response to new data.

The development stage has a strong confirmationist tendency. The goal is to develop a measurement procedure and an interpretive argument that are consistent with each other and with the proposed interpretation and use of the test scores. If this developmental effort is successful, the steps taken to link the observed scores to the proposed interpretation provide a plausible interpretive argument for the scores, and in so doing, they generate a preliminary validity argument for the proposed interpretation and use of scores.

Evaluating the Proposed Interpretive Argument

After the testing program and its interpretive argument are fully developed, it is appropriate to subject them to a more critical evaluation. During this appraisal stage, the proposed interpretive argument is subjected to empirical challenges. Some of its inferences and assumptions may be plausible a priori and some may be adequately supported by evidence generated during the developmental stage. Inferences and assumptions that are less well established deserve further examination. In general, studies of the weakest assumptions in the interpretive argument are likely to be most informative, but it is also prudent to check any inferences and assumptions that are easy to check.

Choices about how to distribute resources across studies involve a number of tradeoffs. Cronbach (1989) proposed four criteria for identifying the empirical studies to be pursued by the test evaluator:

1. **Prior uncertainty:** Is the issue genuinely in doubt?
2. **Information yield:** How much uncertainty will remain at the end of a feasible study?
3. **Cost:** How expensive is the investigation in time and dollars?
4. **Leverage:** How critical is the information for achieving consensus in the relevant audience (Cronbach, 1989, p. 165).

These criteria could apply to both the developmental and appraisal stages, but they are especially useful in choosing among empirical studies that might be conducted during the appraisal stage. Such studies tend to be time consuming and expensive, and therefore the tradeoffs are of utmost concern.

At the appraisal stage, the interpretive argument generated during the development stage can be considered a conjecture, which is subjected to empirical evaluation and possible refutation. To the extent that the interpretive argument can withstand serious challenges, confidence in the claims being made increases. If it cannot withstand these challenges, then either the measurement procedure or the proposed interpretation and use have to be modified.

Criteria for Evaluating Interpretive Arguments

The interpretive argument provides a general framework for interpreting test scores. Therefore, it should be clearly stated; it should be complete and coherent; its inferences and assumptions should be plausible; and any competing interpretations should be less plausible than the proposed interpretation.

Clarity of the Proposed Interpretation

The interpretive argument should be stated clearly and completely. The inferences and assumptions used to get from test scores to the proposed conclusions and decisions should be stated explicitly.

Coherence of the Proposed Interpretation

The interpretive argument is expected to be coherent in the sense that the conclusions follow from the test scores and the supporting assumptions. Interpretive arguments are informal or presumptive arguments. They are not expected to provide a logical or mathematical proof of any conclusions, but rather, to establish a strong presumption in favor of the proposed interpretation and uses of the test scores (Kane, 2004).

Plausibility of the Assumptions

The assumptions included in the interpretive argument should be plausible. Some assumptions may be established well enough that they can be taken for granted. Other assumptions must be supported by various kinds of evidence (e.g., expert opinion on scoping criteria, generaliability studies).

Evaluating Alternative Interpretations

Any plausible alternative interpretations of test scores, including potential sources of construct-irrelevant variance (CIV), should be identified and eliminated if possible. One of the most effective ways to challenge an interpretive argument is to propose an alternative argument that is more plausible.

ROLE OF CONTENT-RELATED EVIDENCE IN VALIDATION

Content-related evidence is most relevant to inferences from samples of observation to conclusions about attributes that are defined in terms of the domains of observations from which these samples are drawn. An *observable attribute* is the expected score over a domain of possible observations. The attribute is observable in the sense that it is defined in terms of how well a person performs some kind of task or how the person responds to some kind of stimulus situation and is not defined in terms of any underlying trait or construct. It may be linked to latent variables in various ways, but it is not defined in terms of these latent variables. Cronbach and Meehl (1955) referred to such attributes as "inductive summaries."

Observable attributes can serve two functions. They can be used to describe some characteristic of a person or they can be used as indicators of some latent variable. *Descriptive attributes* are designed to describe a person's expected performance or behavior over some range of tasks or stimuli and some range of conditions of observation. Descriptive attributes are of interest to the extent that the area of activity being described is considered important. *Indicators* are designed to estimate some latent attribute (e.g., mental ability) and are of interest mainly as estimates of these variables. Indicators are observable attributes, but are used mainly to estimate variables that are not observable.

Target Domains

The value of an observable attribute for a person, the *target score*, is the person's expected score over a target domain of possible observations. The *target domain* is defined in terms of a range of tasks or stimuli, of conditions of observation, and of rules for scoring responses. All that is required for an observable attribute to be well defined is the clear specification of the target domain.

A descriptive attribute is designed to provide a measure of some disposition or proficiency that is of interest in itself. The target domains for descriptive attributes tend to be broadly defined, and they tend to depend on prior conceptions of the attribute. For example, the state might want to determine whether applicants for a driver's license can drive safely. This application suggests a target domain that is defined in terms of proficiency in driving a car under a variety of conditions. The boundary of the domain is defined by the range of conditions under which driving occurs and involves various driving tasks, times of day and year, roads, weather conditions, traffic conditions, and so on.

The fact that some observations in the target domain might be difficult to include in a test does not make them any less important in our conception of the attribute and does not indicate that they be excluded from the target domain. The target domain specifies what is meant by the observable attribute. It does not necessarily indicate how to assess the attribute. As noted, assessments of writing proficiency may involve samples from the target domain of writing performances (a direct assessment of writing) or may be based on measures of specific skills that are used in writing (a relatively indirect measure of writing), but in either case, writing proficiency is defined in terms of a large and varied domain of writing performances.

At the other end of the spectrum, indicators are of interest mainly as estimates of some other variable, and therefore they can often be specified in terms of relatively narrow and homogeneous target domains. For example, Butterfield, Nielsen, Tangen, and Richardson (1985) defined a domain of series-completion tasks in some detail with the understanding that scores on the tests derived from this domain were to be used as measures of inductive reasoning.

The target domains for descriptive attributes are often proposed to provide a clearer and more definite meaning for existing concepts, like literacy, achievement in some academic subject, proficiency in some activity, or a disposition to behave in some way (e.g., aggressiveness or motivation to achieve). They are broadly defined and have implications that go beyond the specification of a domain of observations.

The indicators are created to serve a specific purpose, and do not necessarily have any implicit assumptions attached to their labels. Operational definitions provide extreme examples of this lack of excess meaning. The goal in creating operational definitions was to eliminate implicit assumptions (Bridgeman, 1927) from science. For operationally defined variables that are used as indicators, the observations included in the target domain do not have to be of any special interest in themselves; rather, the score is of interest mainly as an estimate of some latent attribute.

These two uses of observable attributes, as indicators and as descriptive attributes, are not mutually exclusive. An attribute can be of interest in itself (level of achievement in an algebra course), and can serve as one indicator of some other attribute (readiness for a particular science course).

Implications of Attribute Labels and Verbal Descriptions

The fact that an observable attribute is described in a particular way or is intended to serve some purpose and is labeled to reflect this purpose adds certain implications or connotations to the interpretation of the observable attribute. Assuming that the observable attribute is defined in terms of its target domain, any implications in its label, verbal description, and proposed use can be considered *excess meaning*.

The label and verbal description of an observable attribute often claims (usually implicitly) that the attribute has a broad target domain, is related to other variables in certain ways, or is suitable for an intended purpose (Shepard, 1993). Suppose, for example, that a test asks students to make choices about word usage, grammar, and punctuation within prose passages. To label the test as a measure of word usage, grammar, and punctuation provides a reasonable description of the performances covered by the test. To label the test as a measure of proficiency in writing implies a target domain that is broader than that represented in the test. To label the test as a measure of editing skills falls somewhere between these two extremes. The excess meaning in labels and verbal descriptions is part of the interpretation to be evaluated by a validity argument.

The lure of operational definitions (Bridgeman, 1927) was that they were supposed to eliminate any implications that would go beyond the operations used to generate scores. Such excess meaning was seen as rash speculation. In practice, indicators can be operationally defined (although their effectiveness in estimating the variable of interest cannot be established in this way), but descriptive attributes typically carry a number of (often implicit) assumptions and inferences in their wake.

Measurement Procedures and Universes of Generalization

Observable attributes are observable in the sense that they are defined in terms of the expected value over a target domain of possible observations. However, in most cases, it is not possible to draw random or representative samples from the target domain, and, therefore, the expected value over the target domain has to be estimated in some less direct way (Kane, 2002; Loevinger, 1957).

Even if the test tasks are drawn from the target domain, they are typically drawn from a subset of the target domain that is standardized and thereby restricted in many ways (Kane, 1982; Messick, 1994). Some restrictions are imposed for practical reasons (e.g., time limits), some for safety reasons, and some to facilitate objective scoring. In the typical case where the measurement procedure does not involve random or representative samples from the target domain, it is useful to distinguish between the target domain about which conclusions are to be drawn and the domain from which observations are actually sampled.

For example, a reasonable conception of adult literacy would tend to include a wide range of possible performances (responding orally or in writing, taking some action) based on a variety of texts (fiction, instructional manuals, magazines, memos, signs, etc.), in a wide range of contexts (at home, in school, at work, or on the street), and the target domain would include the full range of possible observations of literate behavior. However, a typical assessment of literacy involves objective questions about short passages and is administered under standardized conditions with strict time limits. The assessment includes a sample of literate behavior, but the sample is drawn from a restricted subset of the target domain for literacy.

The domain from which the observations are actually drawn is referred to as the *universe of generalization* for the measurement procedure, and a person's expected score over this universe of generalization is referred to as the person's *universe score* (Brennan, 2001; Cronbach, Gleser, Nanda, & Rajaratnam, 1972; Shavelson & Webb, 1991).

For descriptive attributes, the universe of generalization is typically a standardized subset of the target domain (Fitzpatrick & Morrison, 1971; Kane, 1982, 2004). For indicators, the universe of generalization is the target domain, because there is generally no broader domain to which scores will be generalized. Indicators are defined by their universes of observations.

Inferences From Universe Scores to Target Scores

In cases where the observations made by the measurement procedure are drawn from a standardized subset of the target domain, a simple generalization from observed scores to target scores is not justified by statistical sampling theory, because the required sampling assumptions are clearly violated (Kane, 2002). Statistical generalization from the observed score to the mean over the universe of generalization may be reasonable, but generalization to the target domain is not plausible. A second inference, which is referred to as an *extrapolation* is required to extend the interpretation from the universe score to the target score. *Extrapolation* involves an inference from one variable to a conceptually related variable, but it is not a simple generalization from a sample to a domain. The observed score is generalized to the universe score and is then extrapolated to the target score.

The differences between the universe of generalization and the target domain are most pronounced for objective tests, but standardization is also required for performance testing (Messick, 1994). Students taking a performance assessment in science are likely to be presented with highly standardized tasks. The tasks are to be completed within some fixed time limit, using standard setups, and with no help from anyone else. This kind of stylized performance is part of the target domain for science proficiency, but a sample of such activities is not representative of the target domain defining proficiency in science.

For standardized measures of descriptive attributes, the interpretation involves two domains. One of these, the universe of generalization, defines the measurement procedure. The other, the target domain, defines the observable attribute of interest. Given an interpretation in terms of the expected score over the target domain, the goal is to define the measurement procedure (i.e., the universe of generalization) so that it supports inferences from observed scores to the target score.

DIRECT MEASURES OF OBSERVABLE ATTRIBUTES

In developing measurement procedures and interpretive arguments, it is often useful to start at the end, with the proposed interpretation and use of the scores, and to work backward to the kind of observations that would support the proposed interpretation and use. The interpretive argument can then be stated in the forward direction.

An observable attribute is defined in terms of the expected score over the target domain, and therefore, the observed score for a random or representative sample of observations from the target domain provides a direct measure of the observable attribute. If the test scores are to be given a very expansive interpretation like language proficiency, the target domain should presumably include speaking, listening, and writing as well as reading, and should involve a variety of tasks in a variety of situations. Writing proficiency is a narrower attribute, but it is still quite broad. The definition of the target domain for an indicator tends to rely on expert judgment and on the nature of the variable to be estimated by the indicator. Specifying the target domain is easier for indicators than it is for descriptive attributes.

The label and verbal description assigned to the attribute can add assumptions and inferences to the interpretation. This kind of implicit extension of the interpretation can occur for any attribute, but tends to be most important for broadly defined descriptive attributes. Descriptive attributes tend to carry connotations that go beyond the target domain, especially when they are assigned labels, like "literacy," that have a long history of usage in the language. These implications should be addressed initially during test development as the measurement procedures and attribute labels are developed.

One way to estimate a target score is to draw a random or representative sample from the target domain, and to use performance on this sample (the observed score) to estimate the expected level of performance in the target domain (the target score). The sample should be large enough to be reasonably free of random errors. This approach is generally not feasible for broadly defined descriptive attributes, but is possible for narrowly defined indicators.

Before generalizing the observed score to the target score, it is necessary to determine the person's observed score by evaluating their test performances against appropriate criteria. The scoring criteria are typically developed by experts and their evaluation is based on expert judgment.

Running this argument in the forward direction, there are three major inferences in direct measures of observable attributes, *scoring*, *generalization*, and *implication*:

I1: **Scoring:** The observed performance is evaluated, yielding an observed score.
I2: **Generalization:** The observed score is generalized to an estimated target score.
I3: **Implication:** The estimated target score is translated into a verbal. description.

Scoring involves an inference from a set of observations to an observed score. Generalization extends the interpretation from the observed score for a particular sample of observations to an estimate of the expected score over the target domain; the score remains the same, but its interpretation is broadened from the sample to the domain. The label and verbal descriptions of the attribute can add various implications to the interpretation of the scores. For the interpretation to be considered valid, all of these inferences have to be acceptable.

VALIDATION OF DIRECT MEASURES OF OBSERVABLE ATTRIBUTES

The evidence needed to validate a direct measure of an observable attribute depends on the details of the proposed interpretation and use, and on the context of use, but basically, the validation effort needs to evaluate the three main inferences in the interpretive argument.

Scoring

The scoring inference uses a scoring key or rubric to assign scores to observed performances, and the plausibility of the scoring inference depends on the appropriateness of the scoring rule and the care with which it is applied. The criteria used to evaluate observed performances are generally based on expert judgment (Clauser, 2000). For essays and performance tasks, content experts develop a scoring rubric reflecting the qualities considered most important in evaluating performance. For high-stakes, objective tests, a committee of content experts writes the questions and develops the answer key.

Support for the scoring inference tends to be based on expert judgments indicating that the scoring criteria are reasonable and applied appropriately, and on evidence indicating that nothing went wrong in scoring. Evaluations of the scoring rule tend to focus on the qualifications of the experts who develop the rule, the methods used to select them, and the procedures they use to develop the assessment tasks and the scoring rule for each task. Additional evidence can be developed through subsequent reviews of the tasks and scoring rules by outside experts and by representatives of various groups of stakeholders.

Evidence indicating how carefully and consistently the scoring rules are applied can be generated by documenting the procedures used in scoring. In cases where scoring involves judgment, the consistency of scoring can be evaluated by examining generalizability over raters (*interrater reliability*). Various quality control procedures (e.g., careful calibration of scorers) can be employed to enhance confidence that the scoring criteria are being applied correctly and consistently.

Confidence in the scoring inference can be challenged on various grounds. A critic might argue that the scoring key includes inappropriate criteria or omits some important, relevant criteria. The selection or training of scorers may be challenged. Quality control procedures (e.g., periodic checks on the scorers' consistency and accuracy in applying the scoring rubrics) may be inadequate. Challenges to the scoring inference may also be based on specific problems (e.g., a rater was found to be negligent or biased).

The expert judgment and procedural evidence used to justify the scoring inference cannot establish the plausibility of the interpretive argument, but any lapse in procedure can refute the interpretive argument. If the procedures have not been followed correctly (e.g., the wrong scoring key was used, or the sample of scores used to generate norms is inappropriate) or if the procedures themselves are clearly inadequate (e.g., no training for raters who are asked to make complex decisions), the interpretive argument is effectively undermined. If the scoring rule and its implementation are carefully reviewed and no problems are identified, confidence in the scoring inference increases.

Generalization

The generalization inference is based on statistical sampling theory. It assumes that the observations are a random or representative sample from the target domain and that the sample is large enough to control sampling error. If both of these assumptions are met, sampling theory supports generalization of the observed score to the target score. These requirements are easier to meet for indicators that are operationally defined in terms of homogeneous domains than they are for direct assessments of broadly defined descriptive attributes.

For broadly defined descriptive attributes, claims that the observed performances constitute a random sample from the target domain are typically implausible (Loevinger, 1957). Claims for representative sampling tend to be more plausible (Kane, 2002). Such claims can be considered reasonable if it can be shown that the measurement procedure is unlikely to substantially undersample any major parts of the target domain (i.e., construct underrepresentation) or to include observations that are not in the domain (CIV).

For direct measures of observable attributes, the measurement procedure is designed to yield representative samples from the target domain (e.g., by following specific test plans). The goal is to sample all parts of the domain in more or less the right proportions. In some cases, empirical evidence can be helpful in defining the domain and the test plan (e.g., practice analyses, job analyses, and curricula and textbook surveys) given the proposed interpretation and use. It is not possible to ensure representative sampling. However, if a serious effort has been made to draw a representative sample from the target domain, and there is no indication that this effort has failed, it is reasonable to assume that the sample is representative enough. The evidence for representativeness is largely negative in the sense that it involves ruling out possible sources of bias (Eisner, 1991; Kane, 2002).

Although evidence supporting sampling assumptions is always open to question (e.g., if a new source of potentially significant bias is identified), evidence indicating that sampling is not representative can decisively refute inferences from observed scores to the target scores. If the observations did not occur under conditions consistent with the definition of the target domain (e.g., because of poor environment, faulty equipment, or inappropriate help from other persons), they do not constitute a sample from the target domain. If the observations were drawn from a small part of the target domain (e.g., short reading passages on a test of literacy), they are not representative of the target domain, and therefore do not support a simple generalization to the target domain. In such cases, a more complex interpretive argument, involving extrapolation as well as generalization, is called for.

The sampling of any facet in the target domain (e.g., tasks, occasions, and conditions of observation) introduces some sampling error. The measurement procedure needs to draw a large enough sample of observations to control these sampling errors (Brennan, 2001; Cronbach et al., 1972; Feldt & Brennan, 1989). Claims that observed scores can be generalized to target scores rely on the assumption that the variability caused by to sampling errors is small.

Implication

The third inference, implication, is an extension of the interpretation beyond the expected value over the target domain. The label or description attached to the target variable often involves implicit claims about the attribute. As noted, these claims tend to be more significant for descriptive attributes than they are for observable attributes used as indicators.

The proposed interpretation and use of an observable attribute suggests the kinds of observation that should be included in the target domain, as well as the kinds of observations that should be excluded. The validation of a measure of an observable attribute includes an evaluation of the appropriateness of the domain definition given the attribute label and description, or conversely, the appropriateness of the label and description given the domain. It is, of course, possible to stipulate, via an operational definition, that a particular domain of observations defines the attribute of interest, but to do so in some arbitrary way while employing a label (e.g., "literacy") that is already in use is to invite misinterpretation and misuse.

If the observable attribute serves mainly as an indicator for the estimation of some latent attribute, the additional inferences leading from the indicator to the latent attribute are, presumably, explicitly included in the interpretive argument for that attribute. In such cases, the need to evaluate implications of attribute labels and descriptions apply mainly to the variable being estimated by the indicator.

The implications of the label and description are especially important for labels drawn from "folk psychology," which tend to carry many connotations and values with them, and for labels that suggest particular uses of test scores (Shepard, 1993). For example, labeling a test a measure of "reading readiness" extends the interpretation beyond the domain of task performances included in the test by implicitly claiming that the skills measured on the test are prerequisites for learning to read.

Direct Assessments of Indicators and Descriptive Attributes

Direct assessments of observable attributes are easier to implement for indicators than they are for general descriptive attributes. The operationally defined indicators can be precisely defined and systematically sampled. For a homogeneous domain, like series-completion tasks (Butterfield et al.,1985), the selection of representative samples is relatively easy (Kane, 2002). If the performances are carefully scored and a large sample of observations is included, validating the interpretation of observed scores as measures of performance on this kind of task is relatively straightforward.

Direct assessments of broadly defined descriptive attributes are difficult to implement, because it is difficult to draw a representative sample from the domain. Returning to the example of language proficiency, a representative sample of observations includes a range of stimulus materials (e.g., spoken or written requests, books, movies, signs), responses (e.g., written or spoken response to questions, actions taken in response to requests), and contexts (e.g., in a classroom, restaurant, theater, bus). Collecting an adequate sample from this kind of broadly defined domain is generally not feasible. As a result, most measures of descriptive attributes tend to be highly standardized, and a different kind of interpretive argument is needed for such standardized measures.

STANDARDIZED MEASURES OF OBSERVABLE ATTRIBUTES

As noted, it is generally difficult if not impossible to draw representative sample of observations from broadly defined target domains, and, as a result, descriptive attributes are usually estimated by sampling a subset of the target domain. Some of the conditions of observation may be standardized to enhance consistency and thus eliminate some sources of systematic error. Some restrictions may be imposed for practical reasons. In any case, because the observations are drawn from a subset (often a small subset) of the target domain, the observed performances cannot be considered a random or representative sample from the target domain.

For a standardized measurement procedure, it is not appropriate to generalize from the observed score to the target score (Kane, 1982). In cases where the universe of generalization is a standardized subset of the target domain, evidence for generalization from an observed score to a universe score does not, in itself, justify the further inference to the target score. It is certainly not obvious that scores on a test consisting of short passages followed by multiple-choice questions can be generalized to the much broader target domain associated with literacy, even if generalization over replications of the measurement procedure has been empirically verified.

Interpretive Arguments for Standardized Measures of Observable Attributes

Starting from the proposed interpretation and working backward, the first step is to define the target domain. Assuming that it is not feasible to draw representative samples from the target domain, a universe of generalization that is more amenable to representative sampling has to be developed for the measurement procedure. The goal in designing the measurement procedure for standardized measures of observable attributes is to specify a universe of generalization that can be sampled in a way that controls random sampling errors and systematic errors and yet includes enough of the target domain to support an extrapolation from the universe score to the target score. The universe score is essentially an indicator for the target variable. Generalization from the observed score to the universe score tends to be quite plausible for standardized measures, because the universe of generalization can be fairly narrow and well defined and therefore amenable to representative sampling.

The scoring inference is also likely to be more plausible for highly standardized measures, because it is easier to develop clear scoring rules for standardized performances. The ultimate in standardization, multiple-choice questions, can be scored quickly and unambiguously.

Although the adoption of a standardized measurement procedure tends to make the scoring and generalization inferences more plausible, it introduces a need for extrapolation from the universe score to the target score. As a measurement procedure becomes more highly standardized, confidence in the adequacy of scoring and generalization is likely to increase, but confidence in extrapolation to the target domain tends to become more questionable (Kane et al., 1999).

Assuming that the universe of generalization for the measurement procedure is a subset of the target domain, the interpretive argument employs four inferences:

I1: **Scoring:** from observed performance to the observed score.
I2: **Generalization:** from observed score to universe score.
I3: **Extrapolation:** from universe score to target score.
I4: **Implication:** from target score to verbal description.

As noted, the scoring and generalization inferences tend to be more plausible for standardized measures of observable attributes than for direct measures of these attributes. The implication inference is similar to the corresponding inference for direct assessments of observable attributes. The extrapolation inference adds a new wrinkle, and merits further attention.

EXTRAPOLATIONS FROM UNIVERSE SCORES TO TARGET SCORES

Extrapolation from the universe score to the target score extends the interpretation from expected performance over the universe of generalization (i.e., over the assessment tasks) to expected performance over the full target domain. The score does not change, but its interpretation is extended from a claim about the universe of generalization to a claim about the target domain.

Support for the extrapolation inference tends to be of two kinds, analytic and empirical. Analytic evidence relies on judgments about the relationship between the universe of generalization and the target domain and therefore falls under the heading of content-related evidence (Cronbach, 1971). Much of this evidence tends to be generated during the development stage, as the interpretive argument and the test are created.

The empirical evaluation of extrapolation inferences examines relationships between scores on the test and criterion scores based on representative samples from the target domain or with measures of performance in different parts of the target domain. These empirical studies of the extrapolation inference fall under the headings of criterion-related or convergent evidence (Cronbach, 1971).

Analytic Evaluation of Extrapolation Inference

Confidence in the extrapolation inference is likely to depend in part on how similar the universe of generalization is to the target domain. If the universe of generalization covers a large part of the target domain, the inference from the universe score to the target score is likely to seem quite safe. If the universe of generalization constitutes a highly restricted subset of the target domain, the extrapolation inference is likely to seem more questionable.

Alternately, the relationship between the skills needed to complete the test tasks and those needed for other tasks in the target domain can be analyzed. If the skills needed for good performance in the universe of generalization seem to be more or less the same as, or are a critical subset of, those needed in the full target domain, extrapolation from the universe score to the target score could be quite reasonable, even if the universe of generalization does not cover most of the target domain. Basically, claims for extrapolation are similar to claims for transfer in educational programs and rest on the same kinds of assumptions.

The argument for extrapolation may be based on fairly loose notions of similarity or on a more detailed analysis of the specific processes used by persons in responding to various tasks (Snow & Lohman, 1989). One way to examine the skills needed for specific tasks is to collect "think-aloud" protocols from examinees as they respond to these tasks. This data could be collected in one-on-one sessions with researchers recording the candidate's self-description of how they approach each task (Cronbach, 1971; Ohlsson, 1990). If the processes used in responding to the test tasks are similar to those needed for most tasks in the target domain, confidence in the extrapolation is enhanced. To the extent that the test performances are found to be substantially different from those in the target domain, the extrapolation is suspect.

An explicit evaluation of the processes involved in the performances in the universe of generalization and those in the rest of the target domain can provide strong support for extrapolation, but this kind of detailed analysis is not always necessary. It is sufficient to argue that anyone who performs well on the assessment should also perform well in the target domain, and anyone who performs poorly on the assessment should also perform poorly in the target domain.

In practice, the analytic component of the argument for extrapolation is often a negative argument. If a serious effort is made to identify performance differences that are likely to interfere with extrapolation to a substantial degree, and no such differences are found, the extrapolation is likely to be accepted.

Differences between the universe of generalization and the target domain tend to contribute systematic error to estimates of the target score based on the observed score. For example, to the extent that the test involves task or response formats that are different from those in the target domain, irrelevant method variance may be introduced (Messick, 1989, 1994). Inferences from highly standardized test tasks to a target domain that includes a wide range of nontest performances are riskier than inferences from a broader sample of observations (e.g., multiple formats, simulations) to the target domain.

Empirical Evaluation of Extrapolation Inference

Inferences from universe scores to target scores can be evaluated empirically by comparing observed scores to criterion scores based on representative samples of performance from the target domain. Criterion-related validity evidence seeks to establish such a direct link between test scores and a demonstrably valid criterion (Cronbach, 1971; Messick, 1989). In the past, this approach has been widely recommended and sometimes implemented for objective tests interpreted as measures of observable attributes. In an operational testing program, it is generally not possible to observe a large and representative sample of performances from the target domain, but it may be possible to do so in special validity studies.

In cases where it is not feasible to develop a clearly valid measure of the target score for use as a criterion measure, it may be possible to develop measures based on several different subsets of the target domain. High correlations among measures based on different parts of the target domain indicate that the different parts of the target domain are closely related, and therefore that extrapolation from test scores to target scores is reasonable.

Generally, the most effective evaluations of extrapolation inferences combine analytic evidence and empirical evidence. Extrapolation could be supported in several ways during the development stage, in particular, by making the universe of generalization as similar as possible to the target domain. During the appraisal stage, various kinds of empirical evidence that might challenge the extrapolation inference could be examined, using criterion-related evidence or convergent evidence.

CONTENT-RELATED VALIDITY EVIDENCE

An observable attribute is defined by a target domain of possible observations and its value is given by the target score, the expected value over the target domain. The target score can be estimated by drawing samples of observations from the target domain or from a standardized subset of the target domain. The statistical inferences in the interpretive arguments for observable attributes are fairly simple. For direct estimates of the target variable, the only statistical inference is a generalization from the observed score to the target score. For standardized measures of observable attributes, the interpretive argument includes a generalization from the observed score to the universe score and an extrapolation from the universe score to the target score.

In evaluating the plausibility of the interpretive argument for observable attributes, it is the substantive assumptions surrounding the statistical inferences that tend to be most problematic. The target domain has to be compatible with the interpretation implied by the attribute label and any verbal description. Empirical data can often be helpful in defining target domains, but ultimately the process is largely judgmental (see Raymond & Neustel, chap. 9, this volume; Webb, chap. 8, this volume). Target domains do not exist in nature; they are constructions, as are universes of generalization. For high-stakes testing programs, both the target domain and the universe of generalization are developed by panels of experts who rely on many different kinds of information in making their decisions. The justification for the scoring rules and for the procedures used to implement the scoring rules is also judgmental.

The analytic evidence supporting extrapolations from the universe score to the target score can also be based on expert judgment, which may be informed by various kinds of evidence, including studies of the processes involved in different performances and studies of the impact of various factors on scores (e.g., impact of length and content of passages on measures of literacy). If extrapolation is supported by empirical studies of the relationship between observed scores and a criterion measure of the target variable, questions about the representativeness of sampling and the accuracy of scoring have to be addressed for the criterion measure as well as the test. The interpretive argument for an observable attribute draws inferences from observed performances to conclusions about expected performance over the target domain, and most of the evidence supporting this interpretive argument has generally been included under the heading of content-related validity evidence.

Guion (1977) rejected the notion of "content validity" as an alternative kind of validity, but recognized the pervasive importance of judgment in validation. He listed five conditions that he considered necessary, "for the acceptance of a measure on the basis of its content" (Guion, 1977, p. 5).

1. The content domain must be rooted in behavior with a generally accepted meaning (Guion, 1977, p. 6).
2. The content domain must be defined unambiguously (Guion, 1977, p. 6).
3. The content domain must be relevant to the purposes of measurement (Guion, 1977, p. 6).
4. Qualified judges must agree that the domain has been adequately sampled (Guion, 1977, p. 7).
5. The response content must be reliably observed and evaluated (Guion, 1977, p. 7).

The approach taken here is in close agreement with Guion's (1977) views. His first two conditions suggest the need for a well-defined target domain. His first and third conditions require that this domain be relevant to the proposed interpretation and use of the test scores. His fourth condition calls for representative sampling, and his fifth condition requires that performances be scored accurately and that the observed scores be generalizable.

The analysis of the role of content-related evidence in supporting interpretive arguments for observable attributes suggests two conclusions. First, the argument-based analyses of measures of observable attributes do not postulate any special kind of validity or special kind of evidence in validating these interpretations. Evaluation, generalization, extrapolation, and implication play important roles in many interpretive arguments, and the evidence required to support these inferences is required whenever they are included in an interpretive argument (Kane, 2004).

Second, explicitly stating the proposed interpretation and uses of scores tends to make the limited nature of an observable attribute as the expected value over the target domain relatively clear. The evidence needed to validate measures of observable attributes is not as extensive as that expected for some more ambitious interpretations (e.g., trait or construct interpretations), because the claims being made for the observable attributes are quite limited.

CONCLUDING REMARKS

Validity is a property of the interpretation and uses of test scores. It is not a property of tests or of test scores. To say that an interpretation or use is valid is to say that it is justified by appropriate evidence. This view of validity suggests that it is critically important to state the proposed interpretation and uses of test scores clearly. To the extent that the claims based on test scores are ambiguous, it is not possible to evaluate them decisively. The proposed interpretation or use can be explicitly stated as an interpretive argument, a network of inferences and assumptions leading from test scores to conclusions and actions. Validation requires an evaluation of the coherence of the interpretive argument and of the plausibility of its inferences and assumptions.

Validation can be thought of as occurring in two stages. In the development stage, the measurement procedure and the interpretive argument are developed in tandem. This stage tends to be confirmationist, because its goal is to develop a workable measurement procedure and a plausible interpretive argument. Any flaws uncovered at this stage are corrected to the extent possible so that the resulting interpretive argument is as plausible as possible. The validity evidence generated during the development stage tends to be based on expert judgment, documentation of the procedures used for test development, and empirical evidence for the generalizability over various conditions of observation. If all goes well, the development stage yields a measurement procedure, an interpretive argument, and a preliminary validity argument for the proposed interpretive argument.

The appraisal stage evaluates the proposed interpretation and uses against plausible alternative interpretations and uses. Although validation begins with efforts to develop the measurement procedure and the interpretive argument, it cannot be considered satisfactory until the proposed interpretive argument has been subjected to critical evaluation. As noted, a proposed interpretation deserves our trust "only when it has survived serious attempts to falsify it" (Cronbach, 1980, p. 103). The appraisal stage involves the development and evaluation of challenges to the proposed interpretation and use.

The interpretive argument is analogous to a scientific theory. During the development stage, the infant theory is nurtured and refined. During the appraisal stage, the mature theory is subjected to a trial by fire.

Content-related validity evidence, broadly conceived, plays a major role in validating interpretations in terms of observable attributes. For direct measures of target scores based on representative samples from the target domain, validity depends on the appropriateness and clarity of the target domain, the representativeness of the sample of observations, the appropriateness of the scoring rule and procedures, and the dependability of generalizations from observed scores to target scores. Evaluations of the first three of these assumptions rely mainly on procedural evidence and on expert judgment. The generalizability of observed scores tends to be evaluated empirically during test development. For standardized measures of descriptive attributes, where the test observations are drawn from a universe of generalization that is a subset of the target domain, the validity of the interpretation also depends on the plausibility of the proposed extrapolation from the universe score to the target score. Evaluations of the extrapolation inference typically rely on both judgment and empirical evidence.

Content-related validity evidence also plays an essential role in validating indicators of latent attributes (e.g., theoretical constructs). The validity of interpretations in terms of a latent attribute is determined by examining whether the observed scores function in the ways that they would be expected to function if they were accurate estimates of the latent attribute. However, it is also necessary to evaluate the performance of the indicator as an observable attribute. Content-related evidence generated during the development of the indicator can provide support for the reasonableness of the target domain specified for the indicator, the appropriateness of the scoring rules and procedures, the adequacy of the sampling of the target domain, and the generalizability of the resulting scores. This evidence is not, in itself, sufficient to establish the validity of an interpretation in terms of a latent attribute, but it is an essential part of the validity argument for such interpretations.

Performance on a test can be interpreted as a sample from the target domain for a descriptive attribute or as a sign of some underlying construct or trait (Goodenough, 1949; Loevinger, 1957; Messick, 1989). Content-related validity evidence can support a test score interpretation in terms of the target domain for an observable attribute, but it does not justify further inferences to latent attributes that may be postulated to account for performance in the target domain (Cronbach, 1971; Cronbach & Meehl, 1955; Linn, 1979; Messick, 1989; Rozeboom, 1966).

ACKNOWLEDGMENT

I would like to thank Steven M. Downing, Thomas M. Haladyna, and Mark R. Raymond for their comments and suggestions on a draft of this chapter.

REFERENCES

American Educational Research Association, American Psychological Association, & National Council on Measurement in Education (1999). *Standards for educational and psychological testing.* Washington, DC: American Psychological Association.

Angoff, W. H. (1988). Validity: An evolving concept. In H. Wainer & H. Braun (Eds.), *Test validity* (pp. 9–13). Hillsdale, NJ: Lawrence Erlbaum Associates.

Brennan, R. (2001). *Generalizability theory.* New York: Springer-Verlag.

Bridgeman, P. (1927). *The logic of modern physics.* New York: Macmillan.

Butterfield, E., Nielsen, D., Tangen, K., & Richardson, M. (1985) Theoretically based psychometric measures of inductive reasoning. In S. E. Embretson (Ed.), *Test design: Developments in psychology and psychometrics* (77–148). New York: Academic Press.

Clauser, B. (2000). Recurrent issues and recent advances in scoring performance assessments. *Applied Psychological Measurement, 24,* 310–324.

Cronbach, L. J. (1971). Test validation. In R. L. Thorndike (Ed.), *Educational measurement* (2nd ed., pp. 443–507). Washington, DC: American Council on Education.

Cronbach, L. J. (1980). Validity on parole: How can we go straight? New directions for testing and measurement: Measuring achievement over a decade. *Proceedings of the 1979 ETS Invitational Conference* (pp. 99–108). San Francisco: Jossey-Bass.

Cronbach, L. J. (1988). Five perspectives on validity argument. In H. Wainer & H. Braun (Eds.), *Test validity* (pp. 3–17). Hillsdale, NJ: Lawrence Erlbaum Associates.

Cronbach, L. J. (1989). Construct validation after thirty years. In R. E. Linn (Ed.), *Intelligence: Measurement, theory, and public policy* (pp. 147–171). Urbana: University of Illinois Press.

Cronbach, L. J., Gleser, G. C., Nanda, H., & Rajaratnam, N. (1972). *The dependability of behavioral measurements: Theory of generalizability for scores and profiles*. New York: Wiley.

Cronbach, L. J., & Meehl, P. E. (1955). Construct validity in psychological tests. *Psychological Bulletin, 52*, 281–302.

Crooks, T., & Flockton, L. (1996). *Science assessment results 1995*. Dunedin, New Zealand: Educational Assessment Research Unit, University of Otago.

Crooks, T., Kane, M., & Cohen, A. (1996). Threats to the valid use of assessments. *Assessment in Education, 3*, 265–285.

Cureton, E. E. (1951). Validity. In E. F. Lingquist (Ed.), *Educational measurement*. Washington, DC: American Council on Education.

Ebel, R. (1961). Must all tests be valid? *American Psychologist, 16*, 640–647.

Eisner, E. (1991). *The enlightened eye: qualitative inquiry and the enhancement of educational practice*. New York: Macmillan.

Embretson, S. (1984). A general multicomponent latent trait model for measuring learning and change. *Psychometrika, 49*, 175–186.

Feldt, L. S., & Brennan, R. L. (1989). Reliability. In R. L. Linn (Ed.), *Educational measurement* (3rd ed., pp. 105–146). New York: American Council on Education & Macmillan.

Fitzpatrick, R., & Morrison, E. J. (1971). Performance and product evaluation. In R. L. Thorndike (Ed.), *Educational measurement* (2nd ed., pp. 237–270). Washington, DC: American Council on Education.

Flockton, L., & Crooks, T. (2002a). *Social studies assessment results 2001*. Dunedin, New Zealand: Educational Assessment Research Unit, University of Otago.

Flockton, L., & Crooks, T. (2002b). *Information skills: Assessment results 2001*. Dunedin, New Zealand: Educational Assessment Research Unit, University of Otago.

Goodenough, F. (1949). *Mental testing*, New York: Rinehart,

Guion, R. (1977). Content validity: The source of my discontent. *Applied Psychological Measurement, 1*, 1–10.

House, E. R. (1980). *Evaluating with validity*. Beverly Hills, CA: Sage.

Kane, M. T. (1982). A sampling model for validity. *Applied Psychological Measurement, 6*, 125–160.

Kane, M. (1992). An argument-based approach to validation. *Psychological Bulletin, 112*, 527–535.

Kane, M. (2002). Inferences about G-study variance components in the absence of Random Sampling. *Journal of Educational Measurement, 39*(2), 165–181.

Kane, M. (2004). Certification testing as an illustration of argument-based validation. *Measurement: Interdisciplinary Research and Perspectives, 2*, 135–170.

Kane, M. T., Crooks T. J., & Cohen, A. S. (1999). Validating measures of performance. *Educational Measurement: Issues and Practice, 18*, 2, 5–17.

Linn, R. L. (1979). Issues of validity in measurement for competency-based programs. In M. Bunda & J. Sanders (Eds.), *Practices & problems in competency-based measurement* (pp. 108–123). Washington, DC: National Council on Measurement in Education.

Loevinger, J. (1957). Objective tests as instruments of psychological theory. *Psychological Reports, Monograph Supplement, 3*, 635–694.

Messick, S. (1989). Validity. In R. L. Linn (Ed.), *Educational measurement* (3rd ed., pp. 13–103). New York: American Council on Education & Macmillan.

Messick, S. (1994). The interplay of evidence and consequences in the validation of performance assessments. *Educational Researcher, 23*, 13–23.

Moss, P. (1992). Shifting conceptions of validity in educational measurement: Implications for performance assessment. *Review of Educational Research, 62*, 229–258.

Newmann, F. M. (1992). The assessment of discourse in social studies. In H. Berlak, F. Newmann, E. Adams, D. Archbald, T. Burgess, J. Raven, & T. Romberg (Eds.), *Toward a new science of educational testing and assessment* (pp. 53–69). Albany: State University of New York Press.

Ohlsson, S. (1990). Trace analysis and spatial reasoning: An example of intensive cognitive diagnosis and its implications for testing. In N. Frederiksen, R. Glaser, A. Lesgold, & M. G. Shafto (Eds.), *Diagnostic monitoring of skill and knowledge acquisition* (pp. 251–296). Hillsdale, NJ: Lawrence Erlbaum Associates.

Popper, K. R. (1962). *Conjecture and refutation: The growth of scientific knowledge*. New York: Basic Books.

Porter, T. (2003). Measurement, objectivity, and trust. *Measurement: Interdisciplinary Research and Perspectives, 1*, 241–255.

Rozeboom, W (1966). *Foundations of the theory of prediction*. Homewood, IL: Dorsey Press.

Scott, W. (1917). A fourth method of checking results in vocational selection. *Journal of Applied Psychology, 1,* 61–66.

Shavelson R. J., & Webb, N. M. (1991). *Generalizability theory: A primer.* Newbury Park, CA: Sage.

Shepard, L. A. (1993). Evaluating test validity. In L. Darling-Hammond (Ed.), *Review of research in education* (Vol. 19, pp. 405–450). Washington, DC: American Educational Research Association.

Snow, R. E., & Lohman, D. E. (1989). Implications of cognitive psychology for educational measurement. In R. L. Linn (Ed.), *Educational measurement* (3rd ed., pp. 263–332). New York: American Council on Education & Macmillan.

8

Identifying Content for Student Achievement Tests

Norman L. Webb
University of Wisconsin

Content specification is a conceptual framework that delineates the targeted content domain for a student achievement test. This framework is an important part of the more encompassing test specifications that include item format, distribution of items among reporting categories, scoring rubrics, psychometric properties, and other test characteristics. Clear content specifications are necessary because of the number of limitations imposed on any student achievement test, such as the amount of testing time available and the costs of developing good test items. It is critical that test developers who are interpreting expectations for student learning be aware of learning theories, the beginning point for writing clear content specifications. Four alignment criteria can help frame the content for a test. These criteria provide guidelines for (1) the content topics to be included on a test, (2) the complexity of the test items, (3) the range of content to be covered, and (4) the degree of emphasis to be given to specific content expectations. In addition, other factors that should be considered include equity, fairness, content integrity, level of precision, and the nature of the assessment. The chapter concludes with a description and examples of information that could be included in test specifications in addition to content specifications.

Identifying the content of a test designed to measure students' content knowledge and skills is as much an art as it is a science. The science of content specification draws on conceptual frameworks, mathematical models, and replicable procedures. The art of content specification is based on expert judgments, writing effective test items, and balancing the many tradeoffs that have to be made. This chapter describes in some detail guidelines that can be used for blending the science and the art of test design. Although the intent of explicating some basic guidelines and important issues for content specifications is to make the process more objective, the many refined subtleties that remain ensure that a test designer's creativity still is crucial. The chapter begins by explaining the importance of articulating clear content specifications rooted in the uniqueness of the content area and of understanding the psychology of learning. This explanation is followed by a discussion of specifying learning expectations or targets. The discussion is greatly influenced by the academic standards movement that has shaped national policies. Critical to standards-based assessment is the importance of alignment between the standards at issue and assessment. The third section of this chapter describes four criteria for framing test content that were derived from those used for judging the alignment of a test with a set of curriculum standards. The fourth section discusses other factors to be considered in specifying the content for a test. The fifth section explains how carefully crafted content specifications for a test contribute and fit into the more general test specifications. The chapter concludes with an overall summary.

Designating precise content for a test is an important component of the test specifications. The Joint Committee on Standards for Educational and Psychological Testing (1999) defines test specifications as

> ... a detailed description for a test, often called a test blueprint, that specifies the number or proportion of items that assess each content and process/skill area; the format of items, responses, and scoring rubrics and procedures; and the desired psychometric properties of the items and test such as the distribution of item difficulty and discrimination indices. (p. 183)

As one part of test specification, content specification is a conceptual framework for a student achievement test that delineates students' knowledge, constructs, concepts, skills, reasoning, and, in some cases, disposition that are intended to be measured by the test. The need for clear content specification and the assurance that the inferences made from the test scores about student achievement are appropriate for the stated purposes of the test (see Kane, chap. 7, this volume) are both critical to test validity. Because of the close link between these factors in establishing the validity, content specification is integral to the content validation process. *Test framework* and a test's *conceptual framework* are other terms that have been used for describing content specifications (Joint Committee on Standards For Educational and Psychological Testing, 1999). For the purposes of this chapter, *content specifications* is used to embody all of these representations of content definition for test design.

In measuring student achievement, curriculum documents and other input on expectations for student learning generally are the underpinnings for test content specifications. Curriculum standards as one of the basics in test design are very prevalent in the current political climate. The national No Child Left Behind Act requires that all states develop challenging academic content and student achievement standards as well as tests aligned to these standards in the core academic areas of reading/language arts, mathematics, and science (U.S. Department of Education, 2003). At the state level, academic content standards typically are written by committees and approved by the legislature. These standards communicate to educators, students, and the public what content is valued and what students are expected to know and do within a content area at specific points during their formal education.

Content standards can be very specific, describing in detail learning objectives by grade level, or they can be more general, providing statements of expectations by grade ranges. Curriculum frameworks are based on the content of academic standards. As such, curriculum frameworks explicate what students are to know and do in a content area at specific points in their educational career by clearly delineating scope and sequence in content knowledge, skills, and dispositions. In developing test content specifications for student achievement, it is possible to primarily use the content standards. However, if content standards are written very generally, it may be necessary to use more detailed curriculum frameworks to define more precisely what content should be tested.

Tests are prepared and used for specific purposes. Test specifications, content specifications, and validity all are strongly influenced by the purpose of the test and how the results from the tests are used. Four general purposes of tests include (1) monitoring students' progress (e.g., diagnosis of student learning needs); (2) making instructional decisions (based on student attainment of standards, student mastery of content, and grade-to-grade promotion); (3) evaluating students' achievement and goals (e.g., high school diploma and college admissions);

and (4) evaluating programs (e.g., comparison of two or more curricula) (National Council of Teachers of Mathematics, 1995). The two most important purposes for tests for the discussion of test specifications in this chapter are making instructional decisions and evaluating students' achievement.

With this brief background in some of the differences in terminology, we are now ready to embark on a more detailed discussion of content specifications. This discussion begins with clarification of the importance of attending to content specifications and ensuring that these specifications are clear and concise. Because content areas differ, some effort is made to point out the differences and how these differences can influence content specifications. Also, student achievement in specific content areas is closely linked to theories of learning. The intent of this chapter is not to go into great detail on learning theories. However, learning theory is closely connected to delineating what content students are to know, what they are to be able to do, how they are to demonstrate their knowledge, and what interpretations can be made (National Research Council, 2001b). Thus, the next section begins with a brief discussion of learning theory and its importance to content specifications.

THE IMPORTANCE OF CLEAR CONTENT SPECIFICATIONS

Appropriate identification of content is critical for testing at any level, from informal tests in the classroom to high-stakes mandated school district and state tests. Any test is limited in the number of tasks that can be included and, consequently, the amount of content that can be assessed. The very nature of a test as an evaluative device or procedure is to collect a sample of students' behavior and knowledge in a content area (American Educational Research Association [AERA], American Psychological Association [APA], & National Council on Measurement in Education [NCME], (1999). This limitation forces a test to measure only a sample of students' content knowledge. What content to include on a test and what content to exclude are important decisions that impact significantly the inferences that can be made from students' responses.

Information produced from a test is one of many sources of information used for the purpose of assessing students' learning. In education, assessment is a comprehensive and systematic accounting of an individual's or group's functioning within a specified content domain (Webb, 1992a,b; Wood, 1987). Educators use tests as a means of gathering information about what students know and can do in order to make decisions. These decisions can be about educational policies, programs designed for use with students, the quality of these programs, or the evaluation of individual students. Content specifications for tests are not only important for the immediate instructional decisions that can be made from test results, but also for more comprehensive assessment applications. The degree to which the decisions derived from a test are valid and appropriate depends both on what content knowledge is being assessed and what content is included on the test.

The extent to which valid inferences (see Kane, in chap. 7, this volume; Cronbach, 1971) can be made from a test is closely linked to confidence that the appropriate content is included on the test and that the tasks that are included adequately sample the body of content knowledge from which inferences are made about students. Thus, appropriate content identification for a test depends on the inferences to be made, the purpose of the test, the structure of the content area being assessed, and the desired precision of the test.

Content areas—such as mathematics, language arts, science, social studies, and music—differ in how topics within the content area are structured and relate to each other (National Research Council, 2001a); how students accumulate or build their knowledge; how instruction is provided; and how students' knowledge in the content area develops over time. The differences in the underlying structure of content and curricular areas have important implications for how content should be identified for assessments.

In mathematics, students build on their growing understanding of numbers, from whole numbers to integers to rational numbers and on to the real numbers. In geometry, students' understanding of geometric figures develops from recognizing topological similarities to more refined specifications of attributes and distinctions, such as the difference between a square and a rectangle, lines of symmetry in figures, similar and congruent figures, and on to multiple dimensions and manifolds. School mathematics is structured hierarchically; the aim of mathematics education is to have students develop a growing sophistication in knowing and applying this structure. It needs to be noted that even though a field such as mathematics has a hierarchical structure, this does not imply that instruction has to be organized in a strictly hierarchical manner. Developing a test to measure students' knowledge of a hierarchically structured content area requires attending to prerequisite knowledge as well as to more advanced knowledge that builds on the underlying concepts and skills. Test developers need to attend to how students build this structure of content and what the indicators of more advanced understanding are.

Language arts is less hierarchical as a content area than mathematics. Over the grades, students progress in their use of language by applying many of the same skills and procedures, gradually increasing in the sophistication of language use. Once students acquire the underlying principles and skills for reading, they depend less on explanations from others and may refine their skills from reading more. In mathematics, the majority of students require detailed explanations of unfamiliar topics for most of their educational career. Complexity in language arts increases through broadening vocabulary, using more complex sentence structures, and applying more complex analyses and inferences. In specifying content for tests in language arts, test developers are required to think about what is less complex and what is more complex based on word usage, sentence structure, passage length, and the number of inferences required. They also need to consider students' background and experiential knowledge, which may strongly interfere with measuring students' competency in language arts.

In the sciences, on the other hand, distinct content areas become specialized fields of study, such as chemistry, biology, physics, astronomy, and the variety of subfields under each of these. As students develop understanding in each of these areas, they learn specific concepts and scientific principles that may or may not relate to concepts and principles in other areas. The scientific method or way of thinking is used throughout all areas of science, as are specific processes such as observing, reflecting, justifying, and generalizing. Early phases of learning in science begin with students experiencing different scientific phenomena in their environment. Students' understanding of science grows as a result of their involvement in performing increasingly complex experiments, and in making inquiries and observations. As they progress, they encounter scientific laws and principles of greater complexity. This knowledge builds on prerequisite content, but increased understanding enables students to branch out into the separate science areas as they advance through the curriculum. Developing tests of scientific knowledge requires that test designers attend to an increasing understanding of scientific inquiry while identifying the specific concepts and principles that comprise the different fields of science.

The content area of social studies consists of distinct disciplines, including history, economics, psychology, and geography, to name a few of the most basic. Although certain common processes apply across these disciplines, they are generally learned as distinct areas. There is less *spiraling*—or attention to hierarchy—in social studies curricula than in the other content areas. Specific content and topics are taught at specific grades and are generally not taught at other times in the curriculum. For example, the history of the state is taught in third or fourth grade. World history is taught as one course in high school. Across the disciplines that comprise social studies, a common expectation is that students acquire knowledge of civic responsibility and what is required to be a member of a democratic society. Inquiry in social sciences draws on applying skills from other content areas, including language arts, mathematics, and science. In developing tests in social studies, it is important to know what students have had the opportunity to learn in specific social studies fields, as well as skills that can be applied from other content areas. It is also important for test developers to be aware of the level of abstract thinking and the types of inferences students should be able to make in the different social studies disciplines. It is unreasonable to expect students to necessarily have the same competence in higher-order reasoning in one area of social studies (such as history) as in other areas of social studies (such as geography or economics).

As can been seen in these brief descriptions, content areas differ in how they are structured and in what students are expected to know and do within each of them. Because of these differences, it is important to take content structure into consideration when specifying the content for a test, particularly when identifying the range of content to be assessed and what content a test should cover.

Another consideration in specifying content for assessments is the desired generalizability of the test results. Some tests are developed solely to measure what students know about a very narrow range of content knowledge, such as the addition of whole numbers up to ten or the spelling of a given set of words. Other tests are designed to measure students' mastery or attainment of the content knowledge specified by curriculum standards or required for graduation from high school. The span of content knowledge targeted by a test can vary greatly, ranging from very specific content to more general content. The procedures used for specifying content for a test may also vary significantly, depending on whether the test is to measure a narrow or very specific area of content, or whether the test is to measure students' knowledge of a broad and varied area of study. Whereas the procedures for identifying content for a narrow and specific test are readily defined by the content to be measured, the procedures for selecting content on a test designed to measure knowledge in a large content domain require sampling procedures and decision rules so that the appropriate inferences can be made (see Young, chap. 21, this volume).

How Students Learn

Understanding how students learn and how students will portray that learning is another critical factor in specifying content for a test (National Research Council, 2001b). There are different psychological learning theories and perspectives that influence expectations for student learning and for tests. Test developers with a *differential* perspective in the early 20th century produced tests to differentiate those at different levels of intelligence or with specific mental abilities.

A *behaviorist* perspective emphasizes more specific skills, concepts, and principles. Students acquire these through stimulus–response associations and become more proficient as a result of combining simpler components of skills and acquiring more complex skills. Memorization is an important means of learning from a behavioral perspective, with students engaging in repetitively working with samples of a skill, concept, or principles, and then practicing these skills.

In contrast, a *cognitive* approach emphasizes the relationships among skills, concepts, and principles and how all of the pieces fit together. From this perspective, students develop structures of knowledge by building on prior knowledge and understandings. Important to a cognitive perspective is having students develop an understanding of the relationships among skills, concepts, and principles. Students develop the meaning of these learning outcomes through experiencing and working with different representations of skills, concepts, and principles. These skills and concepts are not ends in themselves, but components in the construction of more meaningful structures. Learning is about how these ideas relate to each other and to students' current understandings. Viewing student learning from a cognitive approach, test developers consider different models of how students develop conceptual understanding and how specific learning experiences help them to see the similarities and differences among concepts, skills, reasoning, and problem solving. These developers consider content areas to be assessed by addressing different modes of representation, including verbal descriptions, pictorial depictions, and concrete modeling.

A *situative* or *sociocultural* perspective, which stresses the social aspects of knowing a content area, posits that people develop their knowledge of a content area through activity, interactions with others, and in context (National Research Council, 2001b; Wertsch, 1998). Important in this approach is having individual students work with other students in meaningful activities as a means of advancing their understanding of the skills, concepts, and principles of the content area. Working with other students on activities derived from students' real-life contexts contributes to the learning of all of the students.

These four perspectives on learning represent only a few of the different perspectives that exist. In most cases, it must be noted that learning and instruction in practice can be interpreted by some combination of two or more psychological learning theories. The theories have much in common and complement each other in fully describing how students learn. Test developers need to be aware of the learning theories both to interpret expectations for student learning and for selecting tasks and activities that produce evidence about what students know and are able to do. In defining the content for tests designed to differentiate among individuals—the differential perspective—the underlying construct or trait (e.g., intelligence) to be measured needs to be described very carefully. Such definitions are necessary to select test items that can distinguish individuals with the focused trait from those who do not have the trait or with lesser degrees of the trait. Experimentation is an important step to identifying items from a differential perspective. Tests based primarily on a behaviorist perspective describe content more as isolated facts and concepts. Such tests require students basically to reproduce or recall the correct response. Tests based primarily on a cognitive approach toward learning describe the relationship among facts and concepts, where students show their underlying thinking about these facts and concepts. A social constructivist, or sociocultural, approach includes expressing the content students are to perform and know in a social context. Here the focus is on contextual knowledge and identifying evidence of how students are able to apply their knowledge to a realistic situation.

Summary

In summary, it is critical to establish accurate and comprehensive content specifications for a test to ensure that accurate inferences can be made from the test results. A clearly articulated theory of learning in the content area should underlie the selection of content and activities for any test. Making valid inferences from test results begins with accurate content specifications informed by relevant learning theory. In addition, any test has a number of limitations imposed on it by the amount of content knowledge from a given content area that can be sampled by the test. Accurate content specifications are essential, therefore, to ensure that the content sampled by a test is representative and that results from the test can be generalized to the full range of the knowledge being assessed. However, how content for a test should be specified varies in part on the basis of the specific content area and desired levels of learning, the purpose of the test, the extent to which the results can be generalized, and the understanding of how students learn, as well as the epistemological structure of knowledge in the content area.

SPECIFICATIONS OF LEARNING EXPECTATIONS

Content specification for a test generally begins with some statement of what students are expected to know and to do in the content area. Curriculum or content standards are currently a common form of stating learning expectations, expressing what learning is of value, and defining what constitutes quality. These statements generally explicate what students are to know and to do for one grade level (e.g., grade four), or for a grade range (e.g., kindergarten through grade four). Set standards, in most cases, are structured by presenting embedded levels of learning expectations with the most general statement of the standard, and where the lower levels of expectations list more detailed statements of what students are to know and do to fully meet the standards. One set of standards could consist of six or seven standards students are to achieve in a grade level. Each of these general expectations of learning can be further described, or delineated, by subcategories or goals. Content under each of these can then be further described by learning objectives. Some states—for example, West Virginia—uses topics as standards and then more explicitly describes the content as objectives under the standards (Table 8.1).

Not all frameworks for identifying the content that students are expected to know provide great detail in specifying that content. Some frameworks only list the topics, as found in the table of contents for a textbook. If the content students are expected to know is not explicitly stated by a framework, then greater demands are placed on the test developer to generate content specifications to describe the content that should be assessed. Thus, content specifications for a test have to compensate for lack of clarity in the curriculum content framework used to define the learning expectations. In more comprehensive standards, the set of goals under a standard fully covers or spans the range of knowledge under that standard; and the set of objectives under

TABLE 8.1
Two of West Virginia's Grade Six Science Standards

SC.S.1 History/Nature
- SC.6.1.1 Explain that scientists formulate and test their explanations of nature using observation and experiments.
- SC.6.1.2 Recognize that scientific knowledge is subject to modification as new scientific information challenges current theories.
- SC.6.1.3 Examine the careers and contributions of men and women of diverse cultures to the development of science.
- SC.6.1.4 Articulate the historical significance of scientific discoveries as influenced by technological demands, competition, controversy, world events, personalities and societal issues.

SC.S.2 Inquiry
- SC.6.2.1 Cooperate and collaborate to ask questions, find answers, solve problems, and conduct investigations to further an appreciation of scientific discovery.
- SC.6.2.2 Formulate conclusions through close observations, logical reasoning, objectivity, perseverance, and integrity in data collection.
- SC.6.2.3 Apply skepticism, careful methods, logical reasoning, and creativity in investigating the observable universe.
- SC.6.2.4 Use a variety of materials and scientific instruments to conduct explorations, investigations, and experiments of the natural world (e.g., barometer, anemometer, microscope, computer).
- SC.6.2.5 Demonstrate safe techniques for handling, manipulating, and caring for science materials, equipment, natural specimens, and living organisms.
- SC.6.2.6 Utilize experimentation to demonstrate scientific processes and thinking skills (e.g., formulating questions, predicting, forming hypotheses, quantifying, and identifying dependent and independent variables).

a goal covers or spans the range of knowledge under that goal. In less rigorously structured standards, given goals and objectives are only examples of more explicit content under a standard. It is important for the test developer to know just how the standards are structured to ensure that the content specifications incorporate the full content domain.

Grain size is frequently used to describe the degree of specificity of content. The smaller the grain size, the more specific the description of the content is. In the West Virginia science standards, each standard is stated using a very large grain size, whereas the objectives are stated in a smaller and more explicit grain size. In specifying content for a test, it is not always preferable to have explicit grain size or detailed statements of content. More explicit content statements represented in multiple levels of statements can increase the demands on a test to cover all of the desired content. This is particularly true if the test is expected to produce results that can provide inferences about students' knowledge and understandings, or to report results at this lower grain size. A more moderate level of content specifications with an illustrative sample of items permits the use of a greater variety of assessment approaches. A moderate level of specificity also increases the likelihood that classroom teachers as well as test designers of large-scale high-stakes tests can use the content specifications to guide their assessments (Popham, 1992).

Some tests are designed to sort students on the basis of their knowledge of a content area rather than to indicate whether students have met certain levels of learning expectations, or whether students have made adequate progress in learning content. For example, tests designed for competitions, to select students who have achieved a certain level of knowledge, or to compare students to a norm, do not require as detailed a description of content as a basis for developing the tests. In cases where test scores are interpreted in terms of relative standards (Klein & Hamilton, 1999), test characteristics such as item-discrimination factors are more important than content coverage. As such, a general statement of content is adequate because the inclusion of test items is determined more by statistical parameters, such as item difficulty level, and by how the item discriminates between students who have exceptional content knowledge and those who have average or below average knowledge. Parallel forms of such tests are based more on statistical qualities of the test than on the degree to which the test measures the full range of students' content knowledge (Wendler & Walker, chap. 20, this volume).

Computer-based assessments that are designed to identify a student's ability level may be driven more by content coverage than by an attempt to identify the precise level of tasks a student can successfully perform as opposed to those the student cannot perform. On the other hand, Item Response Theory (IRT) is a method more frequently used to determine the difficulty level of items on a test and attends less to the specific content. Davey and Pitoniak (chap. 24, this volume), as well as Luecht (chap. 25, this volume), discuss ways to design computer-based tests for a variety of purposes.

Diagnostic tests also vary in how content is specified—compared to tests designed to cover a range of content, or to sort students by achievement. Diagnostic tests are designed to identify the learning problems students are having or whether a student meets a certain level of educational attainment. In these cases, the content to be specified on the test depends heavily on what is to be measured or diagnosed. For example, a fourth grade teacher may want to know whether her students can apply the addition algorithm if one of the numbers includes a zero as one of the digits. In this case, the teacher selects a very narrow range of tasks with two- or three-digit numbers, including a zero, as one of the digits. Test items are selected on the basis of common errors that students make, or to distinguish what students know from what they do not know. Such assessments are used most frequently in the classroom to give teachers timely information on students and their learning (Webb, 1993), (NRC, 2001c).

ALIGNMENT: FOUR CRITERIA FOR FRAMING THE CONTENT OF A TEST

When specifying the content for any student achievement test, multiple factors can be taken into consideration. As shown, content specification depends on a number of features of the test, such as the purpose of the test and the desired generalizability of the test results. A specific model of learning should be paramount in any test design. In general, the content to be included in a test needs to be clearly identified by defining decision rules for the development and selection of test items. Such decision rules can then be used to define the domain, or universe, of all possible items measuring students' content knowledge related to the learning expectations and to identify a procedure for selecting tasks so that the desired inferences can be made.

Since the early 1990s, standards-based education has become the dominant approach to structuring state and local education systems in the United States. Central to a standards-based education system are (1) curriculum or content standards that express what students are to know and do and (2) alignment among all system components. Components are held to be aligned when they serve in conjunction with one another to guide the education system toward students learning what they are expected to know as stated in the content standards (Webb, 1997, 2002). Test developers who design student achievement tests for the classroom, school, district, or state need to attend to the alignment of the tests with the content standards and other system components, including instruction, policy, and curriculum. Specific *criteria,* or means for judging the degree of alignment between test and content standards, are helpful in guiding the development of content specifications for a test. Below, four alignment criteria—categorical concurrence, depth-of-knowledge consistency, range-of-knowledge correspondence, and balance of representation—are described, followed by a discussion of how these criteria can inform test content specifications.

Categorical Concurrence

An important aspect of alignment between standards and tests is whether both address the same content categories or topics. The criterion of categorical concurrence between standards and assessment is met if the same or consistent categories of content appear in both documents. A very simplistic approach to identifying the content for a test is to specify the major content topics to be included on the test and the distribution of items by topic. For example, a language arts teacher assessing students' knowledge of reading and writing may choose these two general topics, both identified on state standards, as the major focus for instruction during the school year and the two major topics to be assessed. Such broad statements of content topics provide only very general directions for selecting assessment tasks. But these topics do provide some parameters for the development of assessments and serve as a beginning point for content identification. For example, the *2005 Mathematics Assessment Framework* of the National Assessment of Educational Progress (NAEP; National Assessment Governing Board, 2004) lists the following content topics or strands for designing the tests:

1. Number sense, properties, and operations
2. Measurement
3. Geometry and spatial sense
4. Data analysis, statistics, and probability
5. Algebra and functions

TABLE 8.2
Percentage of Items, by Grade Level, Allocated to Each Content Strand

Content Area (2005)	Grade 4 (%)	Grade 8 (%)	Grade 12 (%)
Number sense, properties, and operations	40	20	10
Measurement	20	15	30
Geometry and spatial sense	15	20	30
Data analysis, statistics, and probability	10	15	25
Algebra and functions	15	30	35

NAEP's *2005 Framework* goes further and specifies the percentage of items at each grade level that should be allocated to each of these content strands (Table 8.2).

The most general criteria used in the design of tests should also have some bearing on how the results from the test are to be reported and interpreted. If the purpose of the test is to report on student learning after a year of instruction, then very general topics, such as reading and writing, may be appropriate for reporting on students' competency. However, if the test is to report on student learning from a four-week unit of instruction, or to provide diagnostic information on students' understanding, then the test needs to be designed to produce evidence of student learning on more detailed topics, such as reading comprehension, word meaning and usage, and literature elements. The reporting categories are very important to the specification of test content.

Specifying the main topics for inclusion on the test and thinking about how results from the test are to be reported can be very useful in guiding other important decisions for assessment development. One major decision to be made in the construction of any assessment involves the number of tasks to be included on the test. Some constraints are imposed on most assessments, such as the amount of time students are allocated to take the test. Because instructional time is precious and limited, an inordinate amount of time cannot be spent on *measuring* students' knowledge. Again, depending on the purpose for the test, the allocated time may be one 45-minute class period, or 15 minutes at the beginning of a class period. High-stakes tests, semester tests, or end-of-year tests may be designed to give students two or three hours to complete the test. Time limitations on a test, along with the task format and difficulty, govern the total number of items that can be included. The limited number of items on any test then places some constraints on the number of content topics that can be reliably used to make inferences regarding students' learning on those content topics. Including too many topics on a test administered with a time constraint lowers the reliability of results that can be reported on any one of the topics.

The exact number of tasks needed to make reliable inferences regarding students' understanding of a topic can be computed using statistical models. In general, the greater the number of items, the more reliable the inferences. However, most tests designed to measure knowledge students gained from curriculum and to judge their content-area knowledge require a tradeoff between the number of topics included on the test and the reliability of inferences that can be made about student learning on any one of these topics. There is some question about the minimum number of assessment tasks that may be required to reliably report on student learning within a content topic. One assessment task is clearly insufficient. Many factors have to be considered in determining what a reasonable number is, including the reliability of the subscale, the mean score, and cutoff score for determining mastery.

Using a procedure developed by Subkoviak (1988) and assuming that the cutoff score is the mean and that the reliability of one task is 0.10, it was estimated that six tasks would produce an agreement coefficient of at least 0.63. This indicates that about 63% of the group would be consistently classified as masters or nonmasters if two equivalent test administrations were employed. The agreement coefficient would increase if the cutoff score is increased to one standard deviation from the mean to 0.77 and, with a cutoff score of 1.50 standard deviations from the mean, to 0.88. The estimate of the minimum number of tasks needed to reliably make and report inferences regarding students' understanding, the total number of topics, and the time available for the test can be used as a basis for estimating the total number of tasks for a test.

Of course, if a content topic is both broad and complex, a greater number of assessment tasks are needed to ensure that adequate inferences can be made. One process that can be used to determine the total number of items and content topics for a test is to first determine the total amount of time students need to take the test, say 40 minutes, and the average amount of time students need to complete each item. If the test items consist of multiple-choice items measuring specific skills and concepts, then the average amount of time required for a single item may be as low as 1 minute. If the tasks on the test are constructed-response items, as used on performance assessments, then a task may require students to spend a longer time, such as 5 minutes, or more, on each task. Field testing of items is generally required to determine the average amount of time students require to complete a test item. If students have 40 minutes to complete a test and if the students average about one minute an item, then the test can consist of about 40 assessment items. If the reliability for determining a student's mastery of content of 0.63 is sufficient, then six tasks per topic is reasonable. This means that student knowledge of six topics can each be reasonably measured on the test. It is very difficult to make reliable inferences on a large number of topics on a test administered within a typical class period of 60 minutes or less.

Summary of Categorical Concurrence Criterion

In summary, an acceptable level on the categorical concurrent criterion is achieved if major topics on a test match the major topics in the content standards and there is a sufficient number of items on the test to report out by those topics. The identification of the general topics on a test can be used to make some basic decisions regarding the test and what content should be included on it. The number of topics, total time for the test, and average time for each item can be used to make some content judgments about what is reasonable to include on the test. It may be found that there are too many general topics to include to make reliable inferences. If this is the case, then some of the topics need to be combined to reduce the number. Of course, most test development requires an iterative process that involves trying different versions of the test and analyzing what is feasible. It is vital that educators not make inferences about students' knowledge of content using an insufficient number of items.

Depth-of-Knowledge Consistency

Tests for measuring student learning of a content area should be based on solid understanding of a specific conception of learning within the content area. Belief in the nature of learning will strongly influence selection of content for a test (National Research Council, 2001b, p. 43). Content topics identify areas for study, but not what students are to know or do within the area, or how students are to think about the content areas. A description of content complexity or cognitive demand is necessary to indicate what students are to do with the content. A number of frameworks have been identified that can be used to analyze the content complexity or cognitive demand of assessment tasks (Bloom, 1956; Gagne, 1965; Marzano et al., 1997; National Assessment Governing Board, 2004; National Research Council, 2001a). Frameworks do not have to be hierarchical, but can be categorical. For example, in science education, Solano-Flores and Shavelson (1997) identified six types of science knowledge for defining a shell for developing performance assessments (planning investigations, designing investigations, conducting a hands-on investigation, analyzing data, interpreting data, and applying science knowledge). These frameworks outline levels or categories of complexity or sophistication based on what students are expected to know and do and the cognitive or content area functioning students are likely to apply when doing a task. However, be aware that different frameworks may attach different meanings to the same word or idea.

One framework that has been used to analyze the alignment of standards and assessment provides an example of levels of content complexity. Four levels are used to identify content complexity. The lowest level describes recall or recognition of information, facts, and skills. Here, a *skill* is a behavior or sequence of behaviors generally learned through practice and performed easily. The next level describes the application of skills and concepts, procedural understanding, and conceptual understanding. A *concept* is a class of stimuli, such as objects, events, or persons, that have common characteristics (DeCecco, 1968). *Conceptual understanding* generally refers to the integration and application of concepts and other ideas of a content area. *Procedural understanding* denotes knowledge about skills and sequence of steps, when and how these should be used appropriately, and their efficient and accurate applications. The third level requires more sophisticated reasoning and analysis. Assessment tasks and objectives at this level require students to solve problems; draw conclusions given the data, arguments, situations, and other information presented; and construct mental models translating among different representations, justifying from evidence, or summarizing a body of text. The fourth level involves extended thinking that requires the integration of knowledge from multiple sources and the ability to represent knowledge in a variety of ways. *Extended thinking* usually requires work over a period of time, including gathering information, analyzing findings, preparing reports, and presenting findings.

Depth-of-Knowledge Levels for Mathematics

A more precise description of the four depth-of-knowledge levels (Webb, 1997, 2002) for mathematics are provided in Table 8.3. The four depth-of-knowledge levels for mathematics specify the degree of complexity of mathematical content. The lowest level of knowledge complexity is rote or routine use of mathematical procedures, concepts, and ideas. The levels increase in complexity to solving multifaceted problems or doing projects that require students to apply multiple mathematical ideas and skills, generally over an extended period of time. Levels of knowledge complexity vary by age. In judging the depth-of-knowledge level of a test item or a curriculum standard, the mathematical complexity is adjudged on the basis of performance of an average student at the targeted grade level.

The distribution of tasks by complexity on a test depends on a variety of factors. If a state test is designed to determine whether students have achieved at the level identified in state standards, and if state law requires it, the depth-of-knowledge level of each of the test items should be the same as the depth-of-knowledge level of the standard or objective the test item is designed to measure. That is, if the depth-of-knowledge level of the work required to satisfy a content standard is for students to think and reason with content, Level 3 as defined, then all of the items used to measure students' attainment of that standard should also be at Level 3. An exact agreement between the depth-of-knowledge level of the standard and the test items is particularly appropriate if the test is designed only to make a dichotomous decision regarding whether students have or have not attained the required standard. Rarely is this the case.

TABLE 8.3
Definition of Depth-of-Knowledge Levels for Mathematics

Level 1 (Recall)	Includes the recall of information such as a fact, definition, term, or a simple procedure, as well as performing a simple algorithm or applying a formula. That is, in mathematics a one step, well-defined, and straight algorithmic procedure should be included at this lowest level. In science, a simple experimental procedure including one or two steps should be coded as Level 1. Other key words that signify a Level 1 include *identify, recall, recognize, use,* and *measure*. Verbs such as *describe* and *explain* could be classified at different levels, depending on what is to be described and explained.
Level 2 (Skill/Concept)	Includes the engagement of some mental processing beyond a habitual response. A Level 2 assessment task requires students to make some decisions as to how to approach the problem or activity, whereas Level 1 requires students to demonstrate a rote response, perform a well-known algorithm, follow a set procedure (like a recipe), or perform a clearly defined series of steps. Keywords that generally distinguish a Level 2 task include *classify, organize, estimate, make observations, collect and display data,* and *compare data*. These actions imply more than one step. For example, to compare data requires first identifying characteristics of the objects or phenomenon and then grouping or ordering the objects. Some action verbs, such as *explain, describe,* or *interpret* could be classified at different levels depending on the object of the action. For example, interpreting information from a simple graph, requiring reading information from the graph, also is at Level 2. Interpreting information from a complex graph that requires some decisions on what features of the graph need to be considered and how information from the graph can be aggregated is a Level 3. Level 2 activities are not limited to just number skills, but can involve visualization skills and probability skills. Other Level 2 activities include noticing and describing nontrivial patterns; explaining the purpose and use of experimental procedures; carrying out experimental procedures; making observations and collecting data; classifying, organizing, and comparing data; and organizing and displaying data in tables, graphs, and charts.
Level 3 (Strategic Thinking)	Requires reasoning, planning, using evidence, and a higher level of thinking than the previous two levels. In most instances, requiring students to explain their thinking is a Level 3. Activities that require students to make conjectures are also at this level. The cognitive demands at Level 3 are complex and abstract. The complexity does not result from the fact that there are multiple answers, a possibility for both Levels 1 and 2, but because the task requires more demanding reasoning. An activity, however, that has more than one possible answer and requires students to justify the response they give would most likely be a Level 3. Other Level 3 activities include drawing conclusions from observations; citing evidence and developing a logical argument for concepts; explaining phenomena in terms of concepts; and using concepts to solve problems.
Level 4 (Extended Thinking)	Requires complex reasoning, planning, developing, and thinking most likely over an extended period of time. The extended time period is not a distinguishing factor if the required work is only repetitive and does not require applying significant conceptual understanding and higher order thinking. For example, if a student has to take the water temperature from a river each day for a month and then construct a graph, this would be classified as a Level 2. However, if the student is to conduct a river study that requires taking into consideration a number of variables, this would be at Level 4. At Level 4, the cognitive demands of the task should be high and the work should be very complex. Students should be required to make several connections—relate ideas within the content area or *among* content areas—and select one approach among many alternatives on how the situation should be solved, in order to be at this highest level. Level 4 activities include developing and proving conjectures; designing and conducting experiments; making connections between a finding and related concepts and phenomena; combining and synthesizing ideas into new concepts; and critiquing experimental designs.

Most standards-based assessments are designed to identify the level that students have attained vis a vis a standard, or standards, using categories such as *below basic*, *basic*, *proficient*, and *advanced*. There is always some variation in achievement levels within any group of students. Because of this, a test designed to more accurately identify the achievement of individual students needs to provide some range in the complexity of the items. Without definition of such a range, the information about students produced by the test is of limited value.

There is no set rule for deciding exactly what the range of complexity of items on a test should be. The greater the number of items at a given complexity level that are comparable to a student's ability level in that content area, the more accurately a test can gauge what a student knows and can do. However, most tests are designed to provide information about groups of students, students who may vary greatly in their content area competence. Tests that are designed to produce measures of the range in student achievement in a large population need sets of items that vary in their complexity.

One way of deciding on the range of items by complexity, or depth-of-knowledge level, is to think about the approximate number of test items a student would have to answer correctly to be judged proficient. Whatever this number, it is reasonable to expect that if a student is to be judged proficient, at a minimum the student would have answered correctly at least one item at the depth-of-knowledge level that is the same as or above the depth-of-knowledge represented by the standard. For example, consider a content standard in science with a depth-of-knowledge level that requires students to have some understanding of skills and concepts (Level 2). Also, assume that of the ten items on the test designed to measure students' proficiency on this standard, it is judged that a student needs to answer six items correctly to be judged proficient. Then at least five of the ten test items should have a complexity level of 2 or higher to ensure that a student has to answer correctly at least one item with a complexity level that is the same or higher than that on the standard. Thus, the set of ten items related to this standard could have five Level 1 items and five Level 2 items. Ensuring that students who are judged proficient on a standard have answered correctly at least one test item at a comparable depth-of-knowledge level as a standard is a very weak criterion. Most tests are likely to have a greater number of items with the same or higher depth-of-knowledge levels than those of the standard.

A test that consists of items at a lower than appropriate level of complexity may be given if the test is only a test of the skills used to determine whether students have competencies in recall of information and the use of skills and concepts. However, if one purpose of the test is to judge whether a student has some breadth of knowledge related to the standard, then it is appropriate to include one or two test items with a higher degree of complexity. In this case, the set of ten items may include five Level 1 items, three Level 2 items, and two Level 3 items. Or, there could be three Level 1 items, four Level 2 items, and three Level 3 items. Both of these distributions of items by complexity has a sufficient number of items (five) so that if a student was judged proficient by answering at least six items correctly, then the student would have to answer at least one item correctly that has a level of complexity that is the same as or higher than that indicated by the content standard. The second set of items—three Level 1, four Level 2, and three Level 3—requires a student to answer correctly a greater number of items at a comparable complexity (Level 2) of the content standard. This set of items is preferable on a standards-based assessment designed to give some indication of the breadth of student knowledge related to the content standard. Of course, some standards are very narrow in that the domain of items that can be used to assess students' knowledge related to the standard mainly contains items with the same level of complexity. Other content standards can have a very broad domain of possible items by level of complexity. For most tests, the items measuring students' content knowledge as represented by a standard should have a distribution in complexity that is representative of the domain of possible items.

The complexity of a test item is related to the difficulty of the item, but this should not be mistakenly assumed to mean that it is the same as the difficulty of an item. The difficulty of an item depends on many factors, including the complexity of the content. A test item can be more difficult because of students' opportunity to learn the content needed to respond to the test task correctly. An item that requires additional actions by a student, even if those actions are repetitive, can be more difficult. For example, a grade four computation task to add two three-digit numbers such as that shown below requires that grade four students recall an algorithm and facts. However, the item can be difficult for students because of the number of computations that are required. The item could be even more difficult if it required regrouping:

$$\begin{array}{r} 342 \\ +154 \\ \hline \end{array}$$

According to the depth-of-knowledge level definitions given, both of the computation tasks, with and without regrouping, would be considered to have a depth-of-knowledge level of 1—recall and recognition. Making the distinction between *complexity* and *difficulty* is important in specifying the content for a test. The range of complexity of the items on a test should correspond to the range of complexity of the content as expressed by curriculum standards, or other descriptions of the content domain being tested. This range can be specified, as indicated, based on what students should be expected to know and do to demonstrate their proficiency in the content domain. Such a decision is primarily determined by an analysis of the content, or an analysis of students' thinking as they complete the item. Item difficulty, on the other hand, is more a statistical attribute that is determined by the results of students taking the test. Clearly, item difficulty is to be considered in specifying content for a test, particularly if it is associated with students' opportunity to learn the content tested. However, considering content complexity and how representative this complexity is of the content knowledge to be assessed is more important in developing a test to measure students' proficiency within the specified content domain than in sorting students in a group by content knowledge.

Summary of the Depth-of-Knowledge Consistency Criterion

Four depth-of-knowledge levels are used to describe levels of complexity of content standards, other expectations for learning, and for test items. The four levels, with only some variation by content area, are recall and reproduction, concepts and skills, strategic thinking, and extended thinking. A rationale is given for determining the distribution of items by depth-of-knowledge levels for a standard, or some other reportable category. At a minimum, 50% of the items should have the same or higher depth-of-knowledge level as the corresponding standard. This is based on the assumption that a student who answers at least half of the items measuring content related to this standard is considered to demonstrate the minimum acceptable level. Of course, this minimal level of 50% of the items with a depth-of-knowledge level at or above the level of the standard can vary with the rigor of the performance students are required to demonstrate to indicate the proficiency of the standard and the distribution of items by depth-of-knowledge in the domain of items measuring the standard. Caution is warranted to avoid equating depth-of-knowledge or content complexity with item difficulty. Although related, these two characteristics of test items are different. Content complexity is judged by a content analysis or cognitive laboratory. Item difficulty is determined experimentally by pilot testing and can be related to opportunity to learn and number of actions required. Depth-of-knowledge, or some representation of cognitive demand, is an essential consideration in specifying the content for a test to ensure that the performance required to answer the test items is comparable to the performance of the content knowledge being assessed.

Range-of-Knowledge Correspondence

A third criterion to consider in specifying content on a test is the range or breadth of knowledge as measured by the test compared to the range of content in the domain being assessed. The two prior criteria—categorical concurrence and depth-of-knowledge levels—address the number of assessment tasks to include and the complexity of these tasks. The range-of-knowledge criterion is used to ensure that the comparable span of knowledge expected of students by a standard is the same as, or corresponds to, the span of knowledge that students need to correctly respond to the tasks on the test. Theoretically, range is not an issue if a representative sample of items could be drawn from a sample, as discussed by Kane (chap. 7, this volume) and Messick (1989). However, it is often difficult to describe the universe of items in sufficient detail to select items that are representative without some other decision rule. Attending to range-of-knowledge correspondence in the context of content standards provides such a decision rule. The criterion for correspondence between span of knowledge for a standard and a test considers the number of objectives within the standard, or other logical partitions of a content domain. The test should include tasks that measure students' knowledge and ability to some degree on having a sufficient number of the content partitions or objectives under a standard in a standard-based assessment. This also applies to tests based on some other content framework beside standards alone.

What is considered sufficient coverage of content has to be decided in relation to the other criteria, in particular through a consideration of the number of assessment tasks measuring content that can be included on a test. A test designed to measure students' knowledge related to three or four standards can measure a greater range of knowledge under each standard than a test that is required to produce information on students' knowledge of ten or twelve standards. It is reasonable to expect that 50% of the objectives for a standard have at least one related assessment item for at least some alignment to exist between a test and the standard. This level is based on the assumption that students' knowledge should be tested on content from over half of the domain of knowledge for a standard. This assumes that each objective for a standard is given equal weight. Depending on the balance in the distribution of items and the need to have a low number of items related to any one objective, the requirement that assessment tasks need to be related to more than 50% of the objectives for a standard increases the likelihood that students have to demonstrate knowledge on more than one objective per standard to achieve a minimal passing score.

As with the other criteria, practical considerations may put a strain on achieving the acceptable level of 50% of the objectives under a standard. A more rigorous acceptable level of objectives with at least one item can be required if it is judged necessary to have information on students' knowledge related to a higher percentage of the objectives. This occurs when a standard is subdivided into a smaller number of objectives, three or four, all considered critical for students to demonstrate their knowledge. Any restriction on the number of items included on the test places an upper limit on the number of objectives, or other partitions of content, that can be assessed. Thus, the range-of-knowledge correspondence is more difficult to attain if the content expectations are partitioned among a greater number of standards and with a large number of objectives under each.

Balance of Representation

The range-of-knowledge correspondence criterion only considers the number of objectives within a standard with one or more corresponding items. The range criterion does not take into consideration how the test items are distributed among or within these objectives. In addition to comparable depth (complexity) and breadth of knowledge, the test may have a similar emphasis on different objectives or partitions of content, as in a content standard or content domain. The balance-of-representation criterion for specifying assessment items is used to indicate the degree to which one objective is given more emphasis on the test than another. Not all objectives under a standard or subdivision of content are of equal importance. The more important or more encompassing objectives should be given greater emphasis by including a greater number of assessment items that measure knowledge related to these objectives. In practice, this is not always the case. Some item banks only include a specific type of item measuring knowledge related to one standard or one content domain. As a consequence, a test developed by selecting items from such an item bank may only include a disproportionately large number of items of one kind that measure one objective under a standard. For example, the test may include an inordinate number of assessment items related to the main idea on a reading assessment, while placing less emphasis on using meaning clues, making comparisons between characters and events, and paraphrasing. The imbalance could be caused by an insufficient number of assessment items on students' knowledge of using meaning clues and making comparisons.

Summary for Criteria for Framing Content Specifications

In summary, four criteria for specifying content are described. These criteria of categorical concurrence, depth-of-knowledge consistency, range-of-knowledge correspondence, and balance of representation apply to any form of assessment. They apply to any of the different ways in which expectations for student learning can be expressed either by content topics, standards or framework, statistical properties, or by which student learning problems are being diagnosed. These criteria provide some practical guidelines for creating a blueprint for assessment and establishing the needed parameters. For example, for a test to measure students' knowledge of five standards, each standard should have eight to ten items, with over half of the items for each standard at or above the depth-of-knowledge level of the objectives under the standard, with items measuring content knowledge related to at least half of the objectives, and with the items evenly distributed among the objectives to achieve balance.

OTHER CONTENT ATTRIBUTES TO CONSIDER IN CONTENT SPECIFICATIONS

In addition to the discussed criteria for the distribution of items, there are other content attributes that can influence the content specifications for a test of student learning. These attributes of content range from very theoretical considerations, such as the structure of knowledge, to more practical considerations, such as the precision with which student learning is to be assessed. The importance of any one of these factors varies according to the purpose of the test. A teacher designing a test to diagnose students' learning problems associated with a specific content topic considers some of these factors in greater detail than others compared to a colleague designing a high-stakes assessment to measure students' attainment of curriculum standards. However, given underlying content specifications in general, it is necessary to develop a test that can produce evidence upon which desired inferences can be made about student learning that are based on some theory of learning in the content area.

Structure of Knowledge

As noted, specification of content for a test needs to be developed on the basis of a theory of learning for the content area. Such a theory of learning needs to clarify how students' knowledge of the content area develops, how their knowledge deepens through forming relationships among the concepts and skills in the content area, and the pathways students can use to become competent in the content area. For tests to be theoretically based and aligned with more complex expectations, test developers must attend not only to the facts, concepts, skills, and reasoning process in the content area, but they must also consider how all of these relate to each other and form a system of knowledge.

Content specifications for tests attend to the structure of knowledge by clearly identifying the most important connections among the main ideas in the content area at the level being assessed. The connections and relationships among content ideas that students are to know can be overtly identified in curriculum standards, or inferred from a deep understanding of the content area and how students learn. For example, standards in mathematics and science have expressed expectations that students "see mathematics as an integrated whole" (National Council of Teachers of Mathematics, 1989, p. 84), or "science as inquiry" (National Research Council, 1996, p. 105). An underlying rationale for assessment, as stated in the content specifications, that measures skills, concepts, and processes in isolation from each other falls short if students are to understand content areas such as mathematics as an integrated whole or science as inquiry.

Not only should the specification of content consider the structure of knowledge or the relation of the important content ideas at the grade level of the test, but these specifications should also take into consideration prior and future learning. Test items at a given grade level should be consistent with how students' knowledge in that content area develops and with the articulation of the content area over the grades. Students' knowledge in content areas grows and matures over time with increased experiences and cognitive development. Tests, particularly those that are a part of a testing system to measure students' knowledge at a number of grade levels, should advance a common view of how students develop in their knowledge of content. The tests across grades should include items measuring students' understanding and applications of content that can be used to infer students' development in content knowledge over time. As noted in the No Child Left Behind nonregulatory guidelines (U.S. Department of Education, 2003), the sophistication of the content assessed should increase as students' growth in knowledge and learning becomes more sophisticated. In the language of the criteria for framing content, it is reasonable to expect that the proportion of items with a higher depth-of-knowledge level will increase with grade level.

As students' increased understanding of concepts and processes matures over time, they are able to perform at higher levels of analysis and to work with a greater tolerance of criticism and uncertainty. In mathematics, for example, students' increased understanding of number, operations, and generalizations across the grades leads toward more abstract and algebraic thinking. Tests, then, at different grade levels need to be based on sound developmental principles and research on how students learn within the content area.

Equity, Inclusiveness, and Fairness

A classroom teacher who develops a test for a class of 20 to 30 students generally has a good understanding of her students, their backgrounds, and their learning needs. She can gather information on her students' learning by assuring that the test tasks are written or constructed to avoid words and contexts her students may not understand or be familiar with. If students do have difficulty understanding a test item, she can ask probing questions and provide some assistance to reduce any misunderstandings that may arise from other reasons besides the content understanding being assessed. In this way, the teacher can make real-time adjustments to be sure that the test is fair and equitable for all of her students.

Real-time adjustments are not possible on large-scale assessments, such as those developed to be administered to all students in a district or state. In the development of large-scale tests, special attention needs to be given to ensuring that the test items are fair and equitable to all students who take the test. In constructing the content specifications for a test, special note needs to be made if any content topic or context other than a variation in the content knowledge being assessed may result in an unfair advantage or disadvantage to students in some subpopulation. Other authors in this volume discuss this issue of equity and fairness in more detail. Abedi (chap. 17, this volume) addresses problems related to English language learners. Zieky (chap. 16, this volume) discusses the review of items to make tests fairer. Thurlow, Thompson, and Lazarus (chap. 28, this volume) discuss test administration issues related to students with disabilities and language limitations.

Content specifications for large-scale assessments, in particular, need to have some description of the population of students being assessed. Such a description should include identification of the differences in the population attributed to different life experiences, physical conditions, gender, and ethnic, cultural, and social backgrounds. Then the content specifications need to have some directions for developing or selecting test items in appropriate and inappropriate contexts for items and the type of test items most likely to yield information needed for ensuring that valid inferences can be made about each student or groups of students given the test. There are psychometric methods, such as differential item analyses, that can be used to identify statistically biased tasks for groups of students (see Livingston, chap. 19, this volume). It is important to use these. However, these statistical methods do not eliminate the need to provide some control over the content on a test in relationship to equity and fairness. The most common method for analyzing the equity and fairness of a test is to employ a panel of experts, given a clear description of the students to be tested, to perform a content analysis of the test.

Content Integrity

Any assessment is limited in the number of items that can be included on the instrument and in the amount of content knowledge that can be measured. Thoughtful choices are needed in specifying the content for a test to be sure that items that measure the most important content knowledge are included on the test and not only items that measure content knowledge that is the easiest to assess. Messick (1989) has described this phenomenon as *construct underrepresentation*. Content specifications for any test should lead toward content integrity by assigning priorities to specific content topics in the domain being assessed. Concepts, skills, and reasoning should form the basis for developing test items because these skills are important for students to acquire per se, and they are essential prerequisites for future learning. The inclusion of obscure facts, minor details, content ideas of marginal importance, outdated information, and creative but marginally useful transfers of knowledge on tests may successfully spread students across a continuum. However, the inclusion of such peripheral content uses valuable testing time that could be more productively used to provide evidence of students' deep understanding of more central content. In specifying content for a test and to ensure content integrity, the most important content to be assessed needs to be clearly identified, as do the ways in which choices are made for including items on the test.

Level of Precision

Any form of content knowledge, including topics, skills, concepts, processes, and reasoning in all content areas, exists as a continuum—from the most detailed bits of information and refined ideas to broad and overarching principles. The degree of precision included in different sets of curriculum standards can vary greatly in the generality with which content is specified, from a precisely defined fact (students know the addition fact family of 2, 3, and 5) to a more general range of knowledge (students are able to compute with whole numbers less than 20). In developing tests, even those that are to be aligned with very detailed expectations, content specifications need to state clearly what the level of detail, or grain size, of the test items is and the distribution of test items by detail. It is very likely that if too many of the test items in an instrument are of a fine grain size, then other areas are not assessed. Of course, the grain size of test items varies based on the purpose of the test. A classroom quiz or diagnostic test, for very good reasons, could consist entirely of items of small grain size, whereas annual district tests are more likely to include test items that measure multiple ideas in one item, or require student understanding of underlying principles. Finally, the level of precision of the test items is related to other factors, including content integrity.

The Nature of Assessment

There are a number of ways in which tests can be administered. A major proportion of large-scale tests are paper-and-pencil instruments. An increasing number of tests are computer based and administered to students electronically. In this environment, the test items that a student faces could vary on the basis of prior levels of performance, each choice selected to better estimate the ability level of the student within the content domain. In a computer-based test environment, each student could be administered different test items, or take the test items in different order (see Davey & Pitoniak, chap. 24, this volume; Luecht, chap. 25, this volume).

Another form of assessment embeds test items in instruction so that students produce information on what they are learning as they proceed with instructional activities. These different forms of assessment have implications for specifying content. In paper-and-pencil tests, where all of the students have the same opportunity to do all of the items, the content specifications need to attend to all of the above factors to ensure that the set of test items are chosen on the basis of an underlying theory of learning and to adequately cover what students are expected to have learned. The content specifications for a branching computer-based test must address all of these factors, but also needs to be more specific about how different items relate to each other and whether different subsets or pathways through the available items produce a coherent assessment. If the purpose of the computer-based test is to sort students according to their ability, then the statistical difficulty levels and statistical modeling are more important than the precise content substance. If a computer-based test is to produce some indication of students' competence within a content area, then the relationship of the items and how they fit a coherent structure becomes more important. For instruction-embedded tests, the content specifications need to frame items that have both instructional and measurement value. This may require specifying that the test items have multiple entry points, while producing information on one concept or on the ability to problem solve. The different types of tests are too numerous to describe here. With regard to content specifications, the main point is that along with the purpose of the test, the nature of the test needs to be considered in developing the specifications for content.

Summary of Content Specifications

A number of considerations have been presented to guide the formulation of content specifications for a test. The principle underlying content specifications is to define a knowledge domain precisely and clearly enough for a test designer to select items or tasks that can gather information from students that then can be used to make valid inferences about the students' knowledge in this domain. Here a test designer could be a classroom teacher, a member of a state assessment staff, or some others who have the responsibility for developing a test for a given purpose. The first step in specifying content is development of some statement or document expressing what students are expected to know and do. These expectations could be stated as content standards, a curriculum scope and sequence, or a course syllabus.

Next, criteria need to be specified for judging the degree to which the test being developed corresponds to or is aligned with the stated expectations for student learning. The four criteria for framing test content, along with decision rules for judging an acceptable level for each, are presented. Categorical concurrence is achieved if the same content topics are addressed by the test as those that are included in the learning expectations. Depth-of-knowledge consistency is obtained if the complexity as expressed in the content expectations or standards is the same as that required of students by the test items. The criterion of range-of-knowledge correspondence is met if a test covers an adequate breadth of content as expressed in the learning expectations. A fourth criterion, balance of representation, is met if the degree of emphasis of content and complexity is the same on the test as that expressed in the learning expectations. The four criteria given are not the only possible criteria that could be use for specifying content for a test. They are offered as an example of one possible set of criteria and of important considerations in content specification—topic, complexity, breadth, and emphasis. Depending on the purpose of the test, other criteria may be selected. The key point is that a set of criteria be operationalized to ensure that the content on a test has a high degree of correspondence with the student learning expectations being measured.

Finally, other content attributes need to be considered to fully specify the content for a test. Any statement of content expectations has an implied structure of knowledge. This structure of knowledge is related to the implied underlying theory of learning and how content topics and ideas are linked within the content area. The structure of knowledge as implied by the learning expectations should be the same as that represented on the test. Content specifications also need to be created with a clear understanding of the population of students being assessed to ensure the test is fair, inclusive, and equitable. In addition, content knowledge measured by a test should have content integrity by including items that measure the most important knowledge and not obscure facts. Along with the other attributes, the degree of precision at which content knowledge is assessed needs to be at a level that is appropriate for the purpose of the test, as well as the specifications of content. Finally, the content specifications vary by the nature of the test and the technical requirements imposed by how the test is constructed and administered, either as a paper-and-pencil test, a performance test, a computer-based test, or another test form.

TEST SPECIFICATIONS

The main purpose of this chapter is to describe in some detail what needs to be considered in developing content specifications for a test. A well-delineated content specification for a test helps to ensure, but not fully guarantee, that valid inferences can be made from test results. Beside specification of the content, for example, the test domain or universe to be assessed, a number of other attributes of the test needs to be defined. These attributes are identified in the test specifications in addition to specifying the content of the test. As noted, test specifications provide a detailed description of the number or proportion of items that assess each content and process or skill area; the format of items, responses, and scoring rubrics and procedures; and the desired psychometric properties of the items and test such as the distribution of item difficulty and discrimination indices, as suggested in the *Standards for Educational and Psychological Testing* (AERA, APA, & NCME, 1999).

Test specifications are used to communicate to different audiences the structure and content of a test. One important purpose of such specifications is for an agency, such as a department of education, to communicate to a testing contractor what the parameters are for the tests to be developed. Sometimes the most detailed test specifications are restricted in use to prevent teachers from teaching to the test and specifications, rather than keeping their focus on the curriculum standards. Many states and districts make test specifications public to teachers, principals, parents, and students as an additional means of communicating to these audiences what it is important for students to know and do. Some states have question-and-answer sections written to parents that describe what content is used for designing its state tests and indicating that the acadamic content standards are the starting point.

Well-constructed test specifications are critical for ensuring that the tests are developed to measure the intended content and for developing multiple forms needed for retesting or testing in other years. Detailed test specifications increase the likelihood that the different forms of the tests measure different subtopics in the same proportion and with similar task formats.

Because test specifications can have different purposes and audiences, what is included in the specifications and the detail that is used varies. However, there are common features to most test specifications. One common feature is some statement or reference to the content expectations or curriculum with a description of what students are to know and do. They list the reportable areas. Generally, a total score is reported that expresses a measure of a student's attainment of content standards or achievement in a content area. But, other scores may also be reported, such as scores for each content standard, a cluster of standards, or for different categories of knowledge (problem solving, skills, and concept). For norm-referenced tests, scores may be reported by percentile and normal curve equivalents. Based on the reportable areas, the test specifications generally indicate the proportion of assessment tasks or weight that should be given to each reportable category or major content area. More detailed specifications indicate the task format (selected response and constructed response) and the number for each under each reportable category. Reading level, the number of choices for selected response tasks, the type of distractors, and the time students have to take the test are other forms of information that can be included in specifications.

Item Format

A number of different formats for test items are available for any developer of a test. The format of items on a test is integrally related to the content of an assessment, how much content knowledge can be measured by a test, and the overall cost of a test. The general types of item formats are discussed by Downing (chap. 12, this volume) and Welch (chap. 13, this volume). Test specifications need to delineate not only what item content knowledge should be measured, but what item format should be used and how the different formats should be distributed among the items. Multiple-choice items are commonly used on many tests, particularly on large-scale assessments (Haladyna, 2004). Well-designed multiple-choice items, with thoughtful distractors, can be very effective in producing information on students' conceptual knowledge, procedural knowledge, and reasoning. However, constructed-response items are more appropriate for measuring students' capabilities to perform, such as writing an essay (Bennett & Ward, 1993). Kane (chap. 7, this volume), Messick (1989), and Mislevy and Riconscentes (chap. 4, this volume) consider this construct-centered measurement, where the object of the test item is some complex learned ability, such as we see in writing.

In defining the specifications for a test, the different item formats should be listed, along with the proportion of the different formats that should be represented on the test. This decision needs to be based on the content knowledge the test is designed to measure. If the expectation for students is to "write a grammatically correct sentence," then a valid test would have students write a sentence that has no grammatical errors. Multiple-choice items could assess whether students can identify a grammatical mistake in a sentence, or a sentence that does not have any grammatical errors. However, neither of these types of evidence of student knowledge would fully indicate whether students can write a grammatically correct sentence.

In deciding on what the appropriate item formats are, the test developer needs to consider first what inferences are to be made based on the test results about students' knowledge. Practical consideration needs to be given to the time students have to complete the test, the resources available for scoring student work, and the psychometric qualities of the test. There are tradeoffs that need to be considered in the increased reliability obtained from a large number of multiple-choice items on a test and the increased validity of test items that more closely produce evidence on the expectations for students. Also, constructed-response items, like other formats of activities, can vary in quality. For tests measuring students' achievement in reading and language arts, test specifications should describe in some detail the characteristics of the reading passages to be used. These characteristics should include the length of the passages, their general content, reading levels, and other specific characteristics (e.g., type of author, setting, etc.). The Oregon test specifications for reading and literature knowledge and skills are provided as one example (Table 8.4) (Oregon Department of Education, 2001).

Scoring Rubrics and Procedures

In specifying the attributes for a test, including the formats for the items, it is important to consider the scoring rubrics for constructed-response items that will be used and samples of student work to illustrate how the scoring rubrics will be used. In some cases, scoring rubrics do not give full credit for the deep intellectual work required by a standard or objective. Rather, the rubric gives full credit for any response that reproduces information given in the prompt. In cases where the full application of scoring of a constructed-response item is underserved, then multiple-choice tasks may produce more reliable and valid evidence of student learning.

Other Information in Test Specifications

Test specifications can vary considerably in the amount of information included. Some limits can be given for the item difficulties and the reliability for the tests. Including sample items can often be helpful, with a caution. Sometimes the sample items can be interpreted too narrowly and the test is developed with too limited a format of items. The test specifications should be clear about the conditions under which the test should be administered, including the use of materials such as calculators, list of formulas, use of dictionaries, and permissible accommodations for students with special needs.

If a test is to be aligned to curriculum standards, then all of the standards should be measured by the test. In some cases, such as having students prepare and give a speech or conduct a scientific experiment, it may not be possible to fully assess all standards with an on-demand test. The test specifications should be clear as to which standards are included and which standards are not included. If students are not to be assessed on specific standards, but yet students are to be held accountable for these standards, then test specifications should make some note of how students will be assessed. If it is the responsibility of teachers to assess students' attainment of some standards, then the test specifications should make this clear to fully address all of the standards.

TABLE 8.4
2001–2002 State of Oregon Test Specifications for Reading and Literature Knowledge and Skills

Overview: Reading/Literature

Knowledge and Skills Test Specifications

Knowledge and Skills test questions each have a single correct answer. A computer scans the "fill-in-the-bubble" answer sheets. The scanned results are scored against the answer key to produce a raw score. The raw score is converted to a scale score called a Rasch UnIT or RIT score. Students receive a scale score based on the number of questions answered correctly compared to the total number of questions on the form—taking into account the difficulty of the questions. Students are not penalized for guessing.

On the reading and literature knowledge and skills tests there are three levels of tests at benchmarks 1, 2, 3, and CIM (Certificate of Initial Mastery). The three levels overlap, sharing a common measurement range and some test items. They each deal with the same content and concepts, but individual test items are selected for each level to match student achievement more closely.

Level tests produce more accurate scores for all students, including many students with disabilities. With level tests, as many as 70 percent of students receiving special education will be able to participate in state tests under standard conditions.

On the Knowledge and Skills Reading and Literature Tests
- A variety of types of reading selections will be included in the test. Selections will reflect that reading serves three basic purposes:
  - Reading for literary experience (literary selections—fiction, drama, poetry);
  - Reading to gain information (informative selections—articles, biographies, autobiographies); and
  - Reading to perform a task (practical selections—instructions, reference materials).
- Each selection will be free of age, gender, geographic, ethnic, socioeconomic, physical disability, or religious stereotypes. In fact, many selections have been chosen specifically to show diverse peoples, cultures, and time periods.
- No materials that include religious themes, violence, or controversial subject matter will be used.
- Each benchmark level will have some selections by Oregon and/or Northwest authors.
- Selections will vary in length from a few paragraphs to a few pages, and will be appropriate in length, reading level, experience, and interest for the benchmark level tested. Notwithstanding the preceding, some selections and items will be shared between benchmark levels, so that students are appropriately challenged if they are reading well above or below their grade of enrollment.
- Excerpted selections will contain enough substance to "stand alone" and to support the test items which are based on them. In most cases, this will mean that selections have a beginning, middle, and end.
- Each selection will be preceded by a title and an introduction that provides the source of the selection and is designed to stimulate interest in reading the selection.
- Whenever possible, reading selections, visual aids, and their corresponding test items and answer choices will appear on the same page or facing pages of the test. Because many selections require multiple pages of text, however, it is usually not possible to accomplish this.
- Illustrations that are integral to the passage (i.e., they show incidents from the story) are included in many, but not all, third and fifth grade reading selections. In other benchmarks, smaller illustrations that relate to the content of the passages—but are not integral to them—appear in the margins of some, but not all, selections.
- Type size will be appropriate for the benchmark level.
- Selections will be similar in format to excerpts from content textbooks, literature or practical reading tasks.

The Test Items
- Each reading selection will be followed by at least 3 and no more than 10 knowledge and skills test items.
- Each test item will measure only one State Reporting Category:

	Percent of Questions	
Score Reporting Category	*Benchmark 1*	*Benchmarks 2, 3 $ CIM*
Word meaning	18%	16%
Literal comprehension	18%	16%
Inferential comprehension	18%	16%
Evaluative comprehension	18%	16%
Locating information	10%	11%
Literary form	7%	9%
Literary elements and devices	11%	16%

(Continued)

TABLE 8.4
(Continued)

Overview: Reading/Literature

- Each test item will be followed by a set of four answer choices. "None of the above" will not be used as an answer choice.
- Test items, including answer choices, may contain extraneous information.
- Test items will be stated in the clearest manner possible.
- Words which qualify the choice in test items (least, most, first, best, except, probably) will be printed in small capitals when it is likely that students may otherwise overlook the qualifier.
- When testing word meaning, words will be underlined in the reading selection and in the quote of the sentence or portion of the sentence when it appears in the test question. If the tested word is repeated in the test question, it will be italicized.
- Students will be told in the test directions to choose the best answer from among the choices.

SUMMARY

This chapter described in some detail guidelines that can be used for blending the science and the art of test design. Specific criteria were described for making decisions about content to include on a test, given a clear understanding of the purpose of the test and target content domain of the test. The categorical concurrence criterion attends to the content topics on the test. The depth-of-knowledge consistency criterion addresses the complexity on the test compared to the complexity in the target content domain. The range-of-knowledge correspondence criterion is considered to determine if the test has an adequate breadth of content as expressed in the learning expectations or target content domain. The balance-of-representation criterion is met if the degree of emphasis of content and complexity is the same on the test as that expressed in the learning expectations. With acceptable levels for each, these four criteria provide specific guidance for developing tests that align with learning expectations or a target content domain.

The more encompassing test specifications are used to delineate additional information that can be used to develop tests including item format, scoring procedures, reporting categories, accommodations, distribution of items by reporting categories, and statistical parameters. But even with very detailed content and test specifications, the art of developing or selecting good items assumes a critical role. Developing good items requires a thorough knowledge of the content along with considerable creativity. Field testing and revising items is essential to the process, but having those who can think of creative ways of asking questions, developing interesting contexts for questions, and engaging items is very much an art. Item development is discussed in great detail in other parts of this volume. What is essential to assure that valid inferences can be made from the collection of items on a test is for items to be developed based on clear content specifications.

REFERENCES

American Educational Research Association (AERA), American Psychological Association (APA), & National Council on Measurement in Education (NCME). (1999). *Standards for educational and psychological testing.* Washington, DC: AERA.

Bennett, R. E., & Ward, W. C. (Eds.). (1993). *Construction versus choice in cognitive measurement: Issues in constructed response, performance testing, and portfolio assessment.* Hillsdale, NJ: Lawrence Erlbaum Associates.

Bloom, B. S. (Ed.). (1956). *Taxonomy of educational objectives, Handbook I: Cognitive domain.* Preading, MA: Addison Wesley.

Cronbach, L. J. (1971). Test validation. In R. L. Thorndike (Ed.), *Educational measurement* (2nd ed., pp. 443–507). Washington, DC: American Council on Education.

De Cecco, J. P. (1968). *The psychology of learning and instruction: Educational psychology.* Englewood Cliffs, NJ: Prentice-Hall.

Gagne, R. M. (1965). *Conditions of learning.* New York: Holt, Rinehart & Winston.

Haladyna, T. M. (2004). *Developing and validating multiple-choice test items* (3rd ed.). Mahwah, NJ: Lawrence Erlbaum Associates.

Joint Committee on Standards for Educational and Psychological Testing. (1999). *The standards for educational and psychological testing.* Washington, DC: Author: American Educational Research Association, American Psychological Association, and National Council on Measurement in Education.

Klein, S. P., & Hamilton, L. (1999). *Large-scale testing. Current practices and new directions.* Santa Monica, CA: RAND. Retrieved August 13, 2005 from http://www.rand.org/publications/IP/IP182/.

Marzano, R. J., Pickering, D. J., Arrendondo, D. E., Blackburn, G. J., Brandt, R. S., Moffett, C. A. (1997). *Dimensions of learning teacher's manual* (2nd ed). Alexandria, VA: Association for Supervision & Curriculum Development.

Messick, S. (1989). Validity. In R. L. Linn (Ed.), *Educational measurement* (3rd ed., pp. 13–103). New York: American Council on Education MacMillan.

National Assessment Governing Board. (2004). *Mathematics framework for the 2005 National Assessment of Educational Progress.* Washington, DC: U.S. Department of Education. Retrieved August 13, 2005 from http://www.nagb.org/pubs/m_framework_05/.

National Council of Teachers of Mathematics. (1989). *Curriculum and evaluation standards for school mathematics.* Reston, VA: Author.

National Council of Teachers of Mathematics. (1995). *Assessment standards for school mathematics.* Reston, VA: Author.

National Research Council. (1996). National science education standards. National Committee on Science Education Standards and Assessment. Washington, DC: National Academy Press.

National Research Council. (2001a). In J. Kilpatrick, J. Swafford, & B. Findell (Eds.). Adding it up: Helping children learn mathematics. Mathematics Learning Study Committee, Center for Education. Division of Behavioral and Social Sciences and Education. Washington, DC: National Academy Press.

National Research Council (2001b). In J. Pellegrino, N. Chudowsky, & R. Glaser (Eds), *Knowing what students know: The science and design of educational assessment.* Committee on the Foundations of Assessment. Board on Testing and Assessment, Center for Education. Division of Behavioral and Social Sciences and Education. Washington, DC: National Academy Press.

National Research Council. (2001c). In J. Myron Atkin, P. Black, and J. Coffey (Eds.), *Classroom assessment and the National Science Education Standards.* Committee on Classroom Assessment and the National Science Education Standards. Center for Education. Division of Behavioral and Social Sciences and Education. Washington, DC: National Academy Press.

Oregon Department of Education. (2001). General test specifications. Salem, Oregon: Author. Retrieved August 13, 2005, from http://www.ode.state.or.us/teachlearn/testing/dev/testspecs/overviewreadkstestspecs.pdf.

Popham, (1992). A tale of two test-specification strategies. *Educational Measurement: Issues and Practices, 11*(2) 16–17, 22.

Solano-Flores, G., & Shavelson, R. J. (1997). Development of performance assessments in science: Conceptual, practical, and logistical issues. *Educational Measurement: Issues and Practices, 16*(3) 16–25.

Subkoviak, M. J. (1988). A practitioner's guide to computation and interpretation of reliability indices for mastery tests. *Journal of Educational Measurement, 25*(1), 47–55.

U.S. Department of Education. (2003). *The school improvement knowledge base.* Standards and assessments, Non-regulatory guidance. Washington, DC: Author.

Webb, N. L. (1992a). Assessment of students' knowledge of mathematics: Steps toward a theory. In D. A. Grouws (Ed.), *Handbook of research on mathematics teaching and learning* (pp. 661–683). New York: Macmillan.

Webb, N. L. (1992b). Visualizing a theory of assessment of students' knowledge of mathematics. In M. Niss (Ed.), *Investigations into assessment in mathematics education* (pp. 253–263). Dordrecht, The Netherlands: Kluwer Academic Publishers.

Webb, N. L. (1993). Assessment for the mathematics classroom. In N. L. Webb & A. F. Coxford (Eds.), *National Council of Teachers of Mathematics 1993 yearbook* (pp. 1–6). Reston, VA: National Council of Teachers of Mathematics.

Webb, N. L. (1997). *Criteria of alignment of frameworks, standards, and student assessments for mathematics and science education* (Research Monograph No. 6). Council of Chief State School Officials and National Institute for Science Education. Madison: University of Wisconsin.

Webb, N. L. (2002). *Alignment study in language arts, mathematics, science, and social studies of state standards and assessments for four states.* Washington, DC: Council of Chief State School Officers.

Wertsch, J. V. (1998). *Mind as action.* New York: Oxford University Press.

Wood, R. (1987). *Measurement and assessment in education and psychology.* London: The Falmer Press.

9

Determining the Content of Credentialing Examinations

Mark R. Raymond
Sandra Neustel
American Registry of Radiologic Technologists

The purpose of a credentialing examination is to assure the public that individuals who work in an occupation or profession have met certain standards. To be consistent with this purpose, credentialing examinations must be job related, and this requirement is typically met by developing test specifications based on an empirical job or practice analysis. The first two sections of this chapter describe methods of practice analysis, emphasizing the task inventory questionnaire. We present editorial guidelines for writing task statements and discuss the development of scales for rating tasks and other job requirements. The remaining sections of the chapter describe various approaches to translating the results of practice analysis questionnaires into test specifications. We present models for combining data from different rating scales (e.g., task frequency, task criticality) to obtain weights for test specifications. We also discuss frameworks for organizing test specifications and offer a few observations on the utility of these different frameworks. The chapter concludes with an illustration of four methods for establishing weights for test specifications for a credentialing examination.

The goal of licensure and certification is to assure the public that individuals who work in a profession have met certain standards and are qualified to engage in practice (American Educational Research Association [AERA], American Psychological Association [APA], and National Council on Measurement in Education [NCME], 1999). To meet this goal, it is important that requirements for certification and licensure be based on the requirements for safe and effective practice (AERA, APA, & NCME, 1999; Kane, 1982; Shimberg, 1981; Smith & Hambleton, 1990). This is typically accomplished by conducting an empirical job or practice analysis to identify the job responsibilities of those employed in the profession. Once the job responsibilities have been determined, it is possible to postulate the knowledge, skills, and abilities (KSAs) required to effectively carry out those responsibilities. These KSAs then serve as the basis for test plans or test specifications. Practice analysis and the development of test specifications are two related, but distinct, activities (Harvey, 1991; Harvey & Wilson, 2000; Raymond, 2001).[1]

---

[1] Notes on terminology: Like the *Standards* (AERA, APA, & NCME, 1999) we use *credentialing* to refer generically to licensure and certification. Although *licensure* and *certification* have different functions (Shimberg, 1981), the ideas

This chapter describes procedures for conducting a practice analysis and translating those results into test specifications. In the first half of the chapter, we provide guidelines for developing practice analysis questionnaires. Although emphasis is given to the task inventory method of job analysis, other methods are also discussed. The second half of the chapter addresses procedures for developing test specifications from the results of a practice analysis. We first describe conceptual frameworks for organizing test specifications, and then describe various statistical and judgmental methods for obtaining weights for test specifications using data from an actual practice analysis of radiography quality control managers.

As with many research projects, conducting a practice analysis for a credentialing program is a complex undertaking. It requires general skills related to project management, survey construction, data analysis, and report writing, as well as specific knowledge of job analysis techniques. To limit the length of the chapter, we focus on those topics that (1) are most important to a successful outcome; (2) readers are least likely to be familiar with; or (3) have been the source of debate. The chapter does not cover topics to which most readers have been exposed. For example, although we do not discuss sampling and routine data analysis, we do give thorough treatment of statistical models for deriving weights for test specifications.

METHODS OF JOB ANALYSIS

Literally dozens of methods of job analysis have been described in the literature over the years. Some of the more popular approaches to job analysis in the general field of industrial/organizational psychology include the Job Element Inventory (Harvey, Friedman, Hakel, & Cornelius, 1988), the Position Analysis Questionnaire (McCormick, Jeanneret, & Mecham, 1972), and the Ability Requirements Scales (Fleishman & Quaintance, 1984). These methods are off-the-shelf instruments applicable to a wide variety of jobs; they generally are not suitable for credentialing examinations because they focus on human abilities or personality traits, and are intended for personnel selection, job design, or other human resource activities. However, they are worthy of study because most have been carefully developed and thoroughly researched.

A variety of practice analysis methods have been used within the context of professional credentialing. These methods are not the types of off-the-shelf instruments just described, but represent general methodological approaches to practice analysis. Two methods that have seen wider use in the context of professional credentialing are the professional practice model (LaDuca, 1980, 1994) and the critical incident technique (Flanagan, 1954; Jacobs, Fivars, Edwards, & Fitzpatrick, 1978; Levine, McGuire, Miller, & Larson, 1968). However, the most common method of practice analysis is the task inventory and its variations (Newman, Slaughter, & Taranath, 1999). Given the popularity of the task inventory and the suitability of its framework for studying many occupations, this chapter focuses primarily on that method of practice analysis.

A *task inventory* is a list of tasks or activities thought to be performed by those who work in a particular profession. The task inventory is formatted into a questionnaire and mailed to a large sample of individuals who are asked to rate each task on certain scales. The scales might ask, for example, how often each task is performed, how difficult it is, or how important it is for successful practice. A task inventory provides an efficient way of obtaining information

---

presented here apply to both. We also use *occupation* and *profession* interchangeably, although the two have different meanings. Finally, *practice analysis* is used here to refer to the types of job analyses conducted within the context of professional credentialing programs. Distinctions between job analysis and practice analysis are discussed elsewhere (Knapp & Knapp, 1995; Raymond, 2001).

about a wide variety of work-related activities across numerous locations. This is especially important, because credentialing examinations are intended to gauge an individual's readiness for a wide range of activities in a variety of settings (Kane, 1982). Another benefit is that a typical task inventory questionnaire generates a large amount of data that can be analyzed in many ways. Further discussion of the merits and limitations of the task inventory and other methods of practice analysis can be found in Kane, Kingsbury, Colton, and Estes (1986) and Raymond (2001).

Task Inventory Questionnaires

The central piece of most practice analysis questionnaires is a task inventory. The following describes procedures for writing task statements and discusses the types of rating scales commonly used on task inventory questionnaires. However, practice analysis questionnaires often consist of other sections as well. For example, it can be important to obtain information about the contextual factors that influence job performance such as the practice setting, types of clients seen, types of equipment used, and so on. Some questionnaires also seek to elicit judgments regarding the importance of various KSAs thought to be required for practice. We address these topics in the section Other Questionnaire Content.

Procedures for Writing Task Statements

Editorial Guidelines. Gael (1983) defines a *task* as a unit of work performed by an individual that has a definite beginning and end and results in a product or service (pp. 9, 50). Although this definition emphasizes physical activities, many tasks also involve cognitive activities, and therefore may not necessarily be observable (Equal Employment Opportunity Commission, 1978; Harvey, 1991). Cognitive activities should still be included as part of a task inventory as appropriate. Figure 9.1 depicts a portion of a typical task inventory questionnaire. The task statements in Figure 9.1 were taken from a questionnaire for radiography quality management (RQM). Note that most task statements follow the grammatical form of subject, verb, and object, with the subject usually an implied first person. Task statements may also contain qualifiers that indicate how the task is done, the tools required to complete it, its purpose, and where or under what circumstances it is performed. Such qualifiers should be included only if necessary to clarify the task statement. For example, task 2 in Figure 9.1 contains the qualifier *using fluoroscopy*, which is an essential component of the task.

Task statements must be written clearly and precisely if they are to provide useful information. In general, task statements should have only one action and one object; contain action verbs; use precise words; describe practice activities, not prescribe how the activities should be done; and be written at a consistent level of specificity. The following discussion elaborates on each of these guidelines; they are guidelines, not hard and fast rules. Gael (1983) presents a similar list of recommendations.

In general, it is desirable for a task statement to contain just one action and one object. However, this guideline can be violated on occasion. Consider the second statement in Figure 9.1. It contains three objects (aprons, gloves, and other shielding devices). All three objects have similar physical construction, and are used to protect people from scattered radiation. More important, it is common to evaluate them together as a single activity using the same technique. The same is true for task 4.c, which also contains two objects. It can also be acceptable for statements to contain two or more verbs. If two activities are almost always performed together, either because they occur in close sequence or are otherwise interdependent, then it makes sense to include two verbs in the statement. However, in general any activity statements

		High							
IMPORTANCE		Moderate							
		Low							
		Daily							
FREQUENCY		Weekly							
		Monthly							
		Yearly							
Not Responsible for This Task:									
			NR	Y	M	W	D	L	M	H

1. Instruct personnel about regulatory requirements (e.g., OSHA, NRC, FDA)... o | o | o | o | o | o | o | o

2. Evaluate lead aprons, gloves and other shielding devices for cracks or holes using fluoroscopy............ o | o | o | o | o | o | o | o

3. Determine optimal temperature for film processor....... o | o | o | o | o | o | o | o

4. Perform the following quality control tests on radiographic equipment:

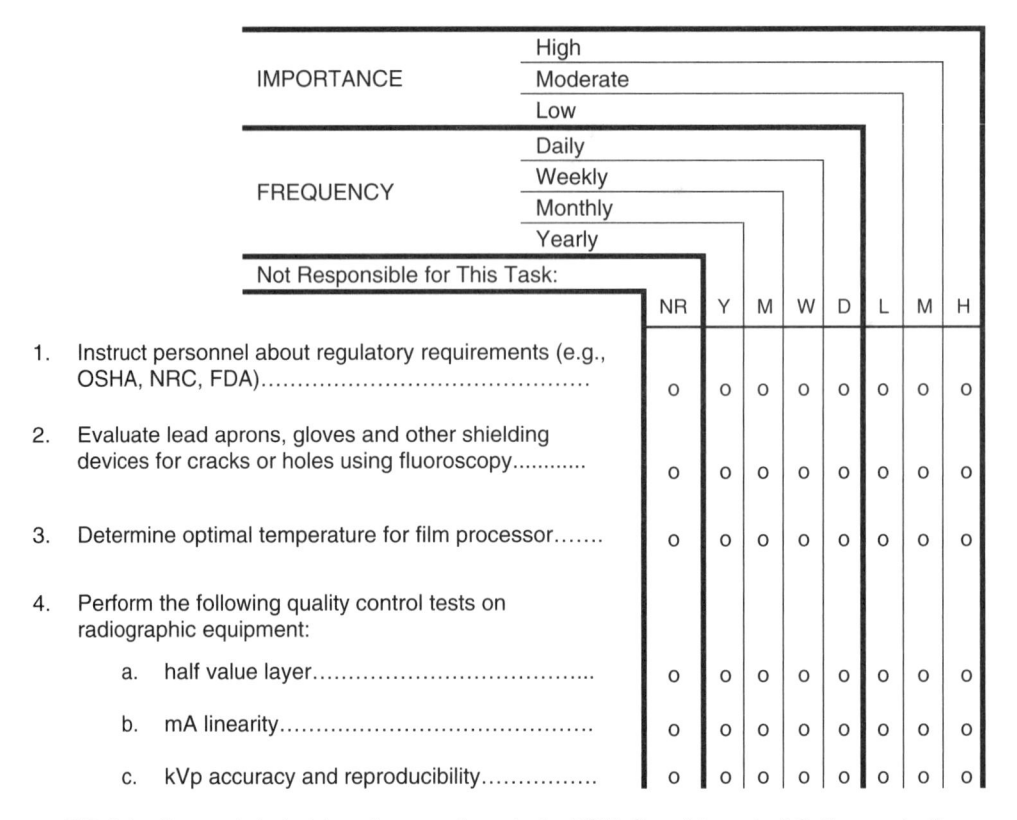

    a. half value layer... o | o | o | o | o | o | o | o

    b. mA linearity... o | o | o | o | o | o | o | o

    c. kVp accuracy and reproducibility................. o | o | o | o | o | o | o | o

FIG. 9.1. Segment of a task inventory questionnaire for RQM. Complete scale definitions and rating instructions would appear on a previous page.

that contain the words *and* or *or* should be scrutinized. Also, slashes should be avoided because it is difficult to determine whether they mean *and* or *or*.

It is important for task statements to use action verbs. This applies to both physical and cognitive activities. Given that cognitive activities involve attending to and processing information, the task statement might also describe the type of information being acted upon. The task statement might also indicate the product, information, or service resulting from the cognitive task. "Apply knowledge of basic statistics when analyzing quality control (QC) results" is not useful because it is so broad and the verb *apply* does not denote a specific action. It might be replaced by something like "Calculate mean and standard deviations when evaluating QC results" or even "Read and evaluate reports containing basic statistics (e.g., means, standard deviations, proportions)."

Precise word choice is essential for self-administered questionnaires. Note that the first task statement in Figure 9.1 contains the phrase, *Instruct personnel*. Does this mean to hold a seminar or simply to stop by someone's office and tell them about a new regulation? Maybe this statement requires clarification, maybe not; either way, survey developers need to pay attention to such issues. Cognitive tasks require special attention. Terms such as *analyze* and *instruct* have different meanings for different people. It may be necessary to pilot test terms such as these to ensure that respondents have similar interpretations. Desimone and LaFloche (2004) recommend the use of cognitive interviews—similar to the think-aloud protocol used in problem-solving studies—to evaluate the wording of survey questions.

A problem that frequently arises when developing practice analysis questionnaires is the tendency to write task statements that prescribe correct practice. It is tempting to write task statements like, "Obtain medical history from patient using appropriate interview technique," or "Perform physical assessment in a manner that maintains patient dignity." Statements such as these can result in positive or negative response bias, rendering the data uninterpretable. In general, individuals are predisposed to respond positively to statements that contain socially desirable content (Morgeson & Campion, 1997). The wording of these particular statements almost begs a positive response, even from those who may not perform the activities. Furthermore, what can be concluded about respondents who assign low ratings to such statements? Is it because they infrequently obtain medical histories, or because they did not understand which interview techniques were regarded as appropriate? A related issue pertains to the use of qualifiers such as, *as needed* or *when required*, which tend to elicit positive responses even if the task is seldom performed. The purpose of practice analysis is to describe practice, not prescribe it. Using a task inventory questionnaire as a vehicle for communicating effective or appropriate practice, even though well intentioned, produces ambiguous data.

The last guideline in the list has to do with writing task statements at a consistent and useful level of specificity. Achieving consistency, although tedious when there are a couple of hundred task statements, is straightforward. For example, the task, "Perform QC tests on radiographic equipment," would not be included on the task inventory in Figure 9.1 because it is far more general than, and overlaps with, other statements. Deciding on the appropriate level of specificity can be a challenge. The task, "Obtain patient's vital signs," has appeared on task inventories for many health professions. Although this activity seems straightforward, it involves many psychomotor and cognitive activities related to both acquiring and evaluating four physiologic measurements (pulse, respiration, blood pressure, and temperature). Is it necessary to break this general task into several component tasks? There is no definitive answer, but if the personnel who perform one of the component tasks also perform the others, then numerous statements probably are not necessary. Task statements should be written at the level of specificity required to accomplish some discernible goal that is important to the profession being studied and consistent with the purpose of the practice analysis. A task inventory that consists of 25 statements is likely to provide very general information of limited utility, whereas a questionnaire consisting of 400 statements may be overly specific. Level of specificity is a recurring theme in practice analysis, and is an important source of variation among different job analysis methods (McCormick, 1976; Raymond, 2001). It may be that traditional task inventories are too detailed and discrete to provide a coherent view of professional practice (e.g., LaDuca, 1994), making it difficult to see the forest through the trees. In a later section we describe other types of questionnaire content that help get at other aspects of practice.

Generating Task Statements

Identifying tasks to include on a questionnaire requires involvement from subject matter experts (SMEs). Their work is often coordinated by a behavioral researcher serving in the role of project director. The project director might initiate questionnaire development by mailing job-related materials to SMEs for review and input. SMEs can be given previous job analysis reports, job descriptions, performance evaluation forms, curricula, lists of training objectives, and any other documentation that sheds light on the nature of the profession being studied. Existing records such as billing statements, patient charts, and insurance records are also excellent sources of practice-related information. A note of caution: by relying too much on existing materials or on experts who may be removed from everyday practice, there is some risk of including tasks that are not relevant to most practitioners. However, it is safer to be overly inclusive (rather than exclusive); the survey results will identify irrelevant tasks.

Some projects require a preliminary survey to identify tasks to include on the final questionnaire. This might be the case for emerging professions that have not been studied extensively or those that experience rapid change. A preliminary project might involve site visits to observe and interview those who perform the job, or collecting critical incidents from a small sample of practitioners. In the early 1990s, staff at ACT, Inc. conducted a practice analysis of secretaries and administrative assistants. Although the project team had access to previous practice analysis reports and job descriptions, most information was outdated and did not reflect the changing responsibilities of secretaries resulting from recent advances in office technology. To identify emerging secretarial tasks and technologies, 150 secretaries were asked to complete work diaries summarizing their work activities for one half day. To ensure a representative sample of tasks, respondents were directed to record activities for certain times of the day (morning or afternoon) or on certain days of the week. Tasks obtained from completed work diaries were then edited and included as part of the final task inventory questionnaire.

Once SMEs generate a preliminary list of tasks, the project director can collate, revise, and eliminate redundant tasks. Even after an initial culling of task statements, it is not uncommon for early drafts of a task inventory to consist of 300 or more statements. It is natural for these drafts to include redundant tasks, or to have tasks written at different levels of specificity. To manage overlap and identify omissions it is helpful have a framework for classifying and sorting tasks. At this early stage, it is not essential to have a formal taxonomy for task classification, unless a useful framework happens to be available. One convenient way to organize tasks is sequentially, according to when they get performed in the course of a day, week, or some other time frame. An example of a sequential scheme is the nursing process, under which tasks would be classified as assessment, diagnosis, planning, intervention, evaluation. Alternatively, tasks can be classified conceptually, with similar activities placed in the same category regardless of when they are performed in the sequence of events. Tables of contents or subject matter indices from major textbooks in a profession might suggest a conceptual framework. For example, the major categories of a task inventory for nurses might consist of neurologic conditions, trauma, cardiovascular, obstetrics, and so on. Tasks can even be categorized according to two or more frameworks (e.g., one sequential and the other conceptual). This is quite easy, assuming the task list is entered into a spreadsheet or word processing table. The use of multiple classification schemes allows the project team to view the task list sorted in various ways, making it easier to discern and resolve different levels of specificity among task statements. One of the classification schemes may even provide a useful framework for the final questionnaire or test specifications.

Rating Scales

A casual review of task inventory questionnaires that have been used over the years quickly reveals that there has been no shortage of creativity in the development of rating scales. Scales vary in the attributes measured (e.g., task difficulty, task frequency), the number of scale points, and the types of anchors used (verbal versus numeric; relative versus absolute). Although some questionnaires include just one or two scales, others may have four or more scales for rating each task. Here we offer suggestions regarding the types of scales to include and factors to consider when constructing these scales.

Types of Rating Scales. Listed below are several scales likely to be useful for professional credentialing. For examples of other scales, see Gael (1983), Harvey (1991), Knapp and Knapp (1995), and Raymond (2001).

- **Task responsibility**. Almost any job analysis needs to determine whether the respondent is personally responsible for performing each task. Although a simple dichotomous scale (yes, no) can be used, it is often convenient to incorporate task responsibility into other scales. In Figure 9.1, for example, the lowest point of the frequency scale is *not responsible for this task*.

- **Need at entry**. This type of scale is intended to determine the extent to which each task is required of entry-level practitioners. There are many variations of this scale. Some address simple task responsibility (yes, no); others get at attributes like level of competence required or when mastery is expected (e.g., competence not required at entry; task should be learned within first six months). An apparent advantage of the need-at-entry scale is that it can be completed by anyone familiar with the job—it merely asks the respondent to make a judgment. However, another way to obtain information about entry-level practice is to develop a standard questionnaire using any of the other scales described here, and then being sure to include entry-level practitioners in the sample. In other words, the most direct method for determining if a task is required for entry-level practice is to ask entry-level practitioners if they perform it.
- **Level of responsibility**. A scale that measures level of responsibility can be useful for determining the depth of knowledge at which certain skills should be assessed, with higher levels of responsibility implying the need for deeper understanding. These scales might consist of response categories such as 1—assist with, 2—perform under direct supervision, and 3—independently perform. Respondents are instructed to check just one response. This type of scale assumes that response categories can be ordered from lowest to highest degree of responsibility.
- **Type of responsibility**. Type of responsibility scales generally allow for multiple responses. Consider a task inventory questionnaire that lists several QC procedures. The response categories might include four options such as recognize when to perform the QC test, perform the QC test, interpret results of the QC test, and take corrective action based on QC results. When respondents can legitimately check more than one category, the end result is a set of nominal scales with dichotomous values. Interpreting these scales can be challenging. For example, 50 tasks rated on a type of responsibility scale that consists of five response categories results in 250 dichotomous variables.
- **Where or when learned**. It is sometimes useful to determine if certain skills are acquired during training or after one has worked in the field for some period of time (Rosenfeld and Leung, 1999). Such scales are not particularly useful for deriving test content, but can be very useful for establishing curriculum standards, for differentiating entry-level from advanced practice, or for identifying continuing education needs.
- **Time spent**. A common method for determining the amount of time individuals spend performing work activities is to ask them to rate the time spent on each activity compared to all others (Knapp & Knapp, 1995). Table 9.1A presents a typical scale for relative time spent. Although time spent scales are popular, it must be a challenge for respondents to provide accurate ratings given that they are required to first determine how much time they spend performing an individual task and then compare it to the time spent for all other tasks. Time spent scales can be useful if respondents are required to judge a limited set of more general activities (e.g., administration, teaching, research). The type of scale presented in Table 9.1B seems to function effectively so long as the categories are mutually exclusive and not too numerous. If many tasks are to be rated, a frequency scale probably provides more accurate information, and such information can be useful for making decisions about test content.
- **Task frequency**. Task frequency is one of the most common scales used in job analysis questionnaires (Newman et al., 1999). The utility of this scale derives from the notion that a credentialing exam should give greater emphasis to activities performed more often. Table 9.2 presents two types of frequency scales. The first is a relative frequency scale; the second measures absolute frequency.

TABLE 9.1
Sample Rating Scale: Time Spent

Marginally Acceptable	*Improved*
A. *Relative Time Spent on Each Task*	B. *Relative Time Spent in Categories of Activities*
For each task on the following pages, indicate how often you spend performing that task compared to all other tasks. Use the 5-point scale below to guide your ratings.	Indicate the percent of time you spend producing medical images for each of the modalities listed below. Your percentages should sum to 100%.
1 = much less time than on other tasks 2 = less time than on other tasks 3 = about the same amount as on other tasks 4 = more time than on other tasks 5 = much more time than on other tasks	general radiography ___ % mammography ___ % CT ___ % MR ___ % nuclear medicine (including PET) ___ % general ultrasound ___ % Total 100 %

TABLE 9.2
Sample Rating Scale: Task Frequency

Marginally Acceptable	*Improved*
A. *Relative Frequency*	B. *Absolute Frequency*
Use the scale below to indicate how often you personally perform each activity. If you are not responsible for an activity, simply check NR and proceed to the next one. Check only one box for each activity.	Use the scale below to indicate how often you personally perform each activity. If you are not responsible for an activity, simply check NR and proceed to the next one. Check only one box for each activity.
0 = never perform 1 = seldom perform 2 = occasionally perform 3 = perform fairly often 4 = perform very often	N = never perform Y = about once per year or less M = about once per month W = about once per week D = about once per day SD = several times per day

- **Task complexity or difficulty**. Scales such as these might be helpful in identifying skills that should be included on a credentialing examination because they are particularly difficult to perform or master. Although these scales are common in business and industry, they do not yet enjoy widespread use in credentialing. See Fleishman and Quaintance (1984) for examples of task complexity scales.
- **Criticality**. Criticality scales get at the importance of a task by asking how essential it is to successful job performance. Criticality scales are usually phrased in the negative, by asking what the consequences would be if an activity is performed poorly or not at all. The rationale for these scales is that credentialing examinations should address those skills most crucial to public protection, even if those activities are rarely performed (Kane,

TABLE 9.3
Sample Rating Scale: Overall Importance

Marginally Acceptable	*Improved*
A. *Overall Importance*	B. *Critically*
Use the scale below to rate how important competent performance of each activity is to the safety and protection of the public.	Use the scale below to rate the criticality of each task to the well-being of clients, staff, or your employer. In other words, if the task is performed incorrectly (or not at all), what would be the risk of an adverse consequence such as injury or litigation?
0 = of no importance	0 = no risk of adverse consequences
1 = of little importance	1 = slight risk of adverse consequences
2 = moderately important	2 = moderate risk of adverse consequences
3 = extremely important	3 = very high risk of adverse consequences

1982). Respondents should be given a clear definition of the scale, and anchors must be consistent with that definition. *Criticality* is usually defined in terms of either the risk or likelihood of a negative consequence or as the severity of the negative consequence, although some scales may confound risk and severity. For professions that involve interactions with patients, the negative consequences are often defined in terms of harmful outcomes such as distress, complications, or impairment of function. For other professions, negative consequences can be stated in terms of flawed products, financial harm to the organization, risk of litigation, and other undesirable outcomes. Table 9.3B presents a criticality scale that gets at the risk of negative consequences.

- **Overall importance**. Scales that measure overall task importance are very similar to the criticality scales presented, but are broader and focus on successful outcomes. Scale points are usually relative in nature, as illustrated in Figure 9.1 and Table 9.3A. Importance appears to be used more often than any other scale in the context of professional credentialing (Newman et al., 1999). Its use is consistent with the *Standards*, which note that the content of credentialing exams should be defined and justified in terms of the importance of that content for effective practice (AERA, APA, & NCME, 1999, p. 161). The limitation with these scales is that overall importance is multidimensional, and tends to elicit subjective judgments (Harvey, 1991; Raymond, 2001; Sanchez & Levine, 1989). One task might be judged as important because it is performed on a daily basis, whereas another task is viewed as important because it is difficult to perform, and yet another task may elicit high ratings because mistakes are very costly. In a policy-capturing study designed to understand respondents' reasoning process when rating overall task importance, Sanchez and Levine (1989) found that judgments of importance were most influenced by task criticality and difficulty of learning, but there was considerable variability from person to person.

Rating Scale Design and Use. When designing rating scales, it is first important to consider how the practice analysis results will be used. If the goal of the study is to determine which activities are most critical, then the scales can be constructed that measure one or more aspects of task importance or task criticality. If the study needs to get at task frequency in addition to criticality, then a second scale may be needed. Some studies may have multiple purposes, for example, to develop both curricula and test specifications. In such instances multiple scales, or even multiple questionnaires, may be required.

It is also necessary to consider the possible sources of information (i.e., the respondents) before deciding which rating scales to use. Some scales—such as relative time spent, criticality, complexity, or overall importance—have high cognitive processing demands if taken seriously by respondents. Cognitively complex judgments are necessary for some practice analysis studies, but collecting these judgments may impact sampling, scale design, and data collection strategies. Although typical practitioners are the best source of information for ratings of task frequency or task difficulty, judgments about task criticality or overall importance might better be left to seasoned SMEs (Kane, 1997; Raymond, 2002a). A questionnaire is not always the most effective method for collecting job-related data. It may be more productive to gather complex judgments in the context of a live meeting where SME panels have the benefit of discussing and refining their definitions of rating scales such as criticality or importance.

Once the purpose of the study and sources of information have been determined, the study should be designed in a way that requires individuals to respond to the least number of scales possible. Most job analysis questionnaires are long to begin with; those with multiple scales are tedious to complete and may suppress response rates. In instances for which it has been decided that the questionnaire will include only a single scale, overall importance appears to be the scale of choice (Newman et al., 1999), although our objections to this scale were just noted. If the questionnaire does not contain too many tasks, then two scales can be used. In such instances, the *Standards* (AERA, APA, & NCME, 1999, p. 160) suggest that frequency and criticality should be used, as does prior research (Kane, Kingsbury, Colton, & Estes, 1989). For example, the frequency and criticality scales in Table 9.2B and Table 9.3B could be combined to create a meaningful index of overall importance. Studies have generally found that composites of task importance created from two or more scales are more reliable than the holistic judgments of overall importance (Hughes & Prien, 1989; Sanchez & Levine, 1989). Although this finding is consistent with psychometric theory, it was not replicated in a follow-up study (Sanchez & Fraser, 1992). The reliability of the derived importance index is influenced by the covariances among scales, which was not controlled in these studies. Both research and common sense suggest that the simultaneous use of importance and criticality scales is not cost effective and should be avoided; those two scales are highly correlated and provide redundant information (Sanchez & Levine, 1989).

In addition, some attention should be given to the psychometric features of the rating scales. We limit our discussion to four notable scaling issues. The first pertains to the verbal descriptors or values used to label the rating scales. The scale points need to be clearly defined, and should be meaningful for the profession being studied. A study of accountants, for example, might include *yearly* and *quarterly*, as some accounting activities occur at those intervals. Numeric and verbal labels also need to be consistent with the intended meaning of the scale. Numeric codes should be used only when a number is appropriate. Anchor labels such as *0, 1, 2, 3* are probably acceptable for scales like importance, criticality, or level of responsibility (e.g., Table 9.2A, Table 9.3A or Table 9.3B). However, numeric labels should be avoided for response categories that do not have an implied ordering from low to high. Even when numeric codes are technically suitable, they may not be the most effective way to label a scale. For example, the absolute frequency scale in Table 9.2B is better defined by verbal anchors that serve as useful mnemonic (e.g., *W* for *weekly*).

A second scaling issue has to do with the use of relative versus absolute rating scales. In general, scales with absolute anchors are preferable to relative scales. Relative scales, such as that depicted in Table 9.1A, interfere with meaningful comparisons across jobs and people (Harvey, 1991), and are prone to response bias and halo error (Harvey & Wilson,

2000; Raymond, 2001, 2002b). However, we must often rely on relative scales because many characteristics of interest just do not lend themselves to absolute scales.

A third issue has to do with the level of measurement of the rating scales used in practice analysis (e.g., nominal, ordinal, interval, ratio). Most rating scales produce data with ordinal properties. Although one can be confident that *extremely important* should receive a higher value than *moderately important*, it is not possible to ascertain the magnitude of the difference between those two scale points, or if that difference is the same as the difference between *moderately important* and *somewhat important*. It is nonetheless customary in practice analysis to assign values like 0 through 3 to such scales, and then proceed with routine statistical analyses such as computing the mean rating for each task. However, if the scale has drastically unequal intervals, means and standard deviations will not adequately summarize the data. It is also important to acknowledge that the assumptions required by inferential statistics like t-tests and analyses of variance (ANOVAs) may not be met by ordinal data. Some consideration should be given to using methods intended for categorical data analysis (e.g., proportions, chi-square tests, logistic models). The practice of treating ordinal scales as if they have interval or ratio properties is probably acceptable in most instances, but should be carefully evaluated in others. The values assigned to an ordinal scale can have a notable impact when converting ratings to weights for test specifications (Spray & Huang, 2000, Table 1).

The final scaling issue is the practice of treating absolute rating scales as ordinal scales. Consider the frequency scale presented in Table 9.2B. It is common to transform frequency ratings such as this to a simple ordinal scale where 1 = yearly 2, = monthly, 3 = weekly, and so on. However, it could be argued that the responses actually approximate a ratio scale corresponding to the number of times per week an activity is performed. If a task is never performed, it is assigned a value of zero, whereas a task performed daily might be given a value of 5 on a times-per-week scale. Similarly, a task performed weekly would be given a value of 1. The challenge occurs when deciding what quantity to assign to *several times per day* or *yearly*. In such instances, SMEs may be able to help settle on a useful approximation. It is apparent that times-per-week scale is rather coarse; however, it is preferable to the distortion introduced by using a simple ordinal scale that runs from 0 to 5 or some similar range of values.

Other Questionnaire Content

Practice Context. The task inventory has been criticized as not being a particularly useful tool for understanding the requirements of professional practice analysis. The final product—a list of discrete tasks—provides an incomplete and fragmented description of practice, and may overlook the cognitive complexity of many professions (LaDuca, 1994). To address this limitation, LaDuca (1980, 1994) advocates a method of practice analysis referred to as the *professional practice model*. This model characterizes practice by the types of problems that professionals are called on to solve and the contexts in which those problems occur. The professional practice model is based on principles of facet design. A simplified model of practice for a healthcare worker might consist of two dimensions: care setting and type of medical problem. The care setting facet could be composed of categories such as trauma center, long-term care facility, and physician's office, whereas the medical problems might be organized according to organ systems (e.g., endocrine, skeletal, etc.). The cells produced by crossing the facets give rise to numerous practice-related situations.

Perhaps the trouble with typical practice analysis questionnaires is not so much that they represent a flawed approach to understanding professions, but rather that they may not be asking the types of questions that encourage a coherent description of practice. One way to add depth to practice analysis questionnaires is to ask more about the respondents' practice environment, the types of clients they see, the problems they solve, and the tools they use in their daily work to solve those problems (e.g., instrumentation, technology, models, and theories). Such an approach to practice analysis, although not common, is nothing new. D'Costa (1986) used a multidimensional competency model to delineate the role of dietitians. More recently, Kane (1997) described the use of model-based practice analysis. In both of these instances, principles of facet design were used to conceptualize and organize job responsibilities.

Recent studies of nurse anesthesia practice illustrate a facet-based approach to practice analysis questionnaires (McShane & Fagerlund, 2004). That questionnaire included over 300 survey items, or practice descriptors, organized under six dimensions: (1) practice setting; (2) patient characteristics such as age and gender; (3) patient medical condition; (4) type of procedure being performed; (5) anesthesia agents and technique; and (6) anesthesia equipment and instrumentation required. For example, the section pertaining to patient medical conditions included descriptors such as *myocardial infarction, hypertension, acute renal failure*, and so on. The section on anesthesia technique listed various types of inhalants, intravenous agents, and local anesthetics. Questionnaire respondents rated each descriptor in terms of frequency of encounter and level of skill required, and ratings were translated into weights for test specifications (i.e., the same six dimensions were used to organize the test specifications). It is interesting to note that the questionnaire did not include any traditional task statements.

KSA Requirements. Traditional task inventories focus on tasks that are actually performed in the practice setting. In contrast, most credentialing examinations assess cognitive knowledge and skills. This means that test specifications often consist not of tasks, but of topics and KSAs—information likely to be absent from a typical task inventory. One way to expedite the process of developing test specifications is to include KSAs as part of the practice analysis questionnaires. For example, a list of KSAs for a questionnaire for psychologists included topics such as theories of learning, personality inventories, counseling and guidance techniques, group dynamics, and reliability concepts (Rosenfeld, Shimberg, & Thornton, 1983). Once a complete list of KSAs is generated, it can be formatted into a questionnaire with rating scales. Many of the scales for rating tasks also apply to KSAs. Scales that get at KSA importance or relevance appear to be the most popular choice, although other scales might be used as well (e.g., where learned, frequency of use).

Including KSAs on practice analysis questionnaires appears to be straightforward; however, it is deceptive in its simplicity. KSAs are both complex and abstract, which makes them difficult to define in a mail-out questionnaire. What is meant by the KSA *reliability concepts*? Does it refer to classical test theory or IRT? one parameter model or three? single-faceted generalizability designs or multi-faceted? Respondents may wonder about such things. Furthermore, KSA ratings are prone to positive response bias (Landy, 1988; Morgeson & Campion, 1997; Morgeson, Delaney-Klinger, Mayfield, Ferrara, & Campion, 2004; Raymond, 2001).

These limitations have implications for questionnaire design. First, to ensure that each KSA has a similar meaning for all respondents, it may be necessary to provide definitions or clarifying examples for each KSA. Second, special consideration should be given to the types of scales used. Because credentialing examinations are intended to assess KSAs at the level required for competent practice (Kane, 1982), scales that get at level of knowledge may be more suitable than importance scales for eliciting KSA judgments. For example, Bloom's (1956) taxonomy was used as the framework for KSA rating scales for a job analysis of psychologists (Rosenfeld et al., 1983). Third, the use of scales with concrete behavioral anchors, rather than general abilities and traits, can be a useful strategy for managing bias in ratings (Fleishman & Quaintance, 1984). We recently developed a set of level-of-knowledge scales for the radiologic sciences. Each scale was designed around behavioral anchors specific to each KSA to be rated. One of the scales appears in Figure 9.2; there were 33 such scales in all. Although the ratings produced by these types of scales are helpful for various test development activities, the time and effort required to develop them is significant. Fourth, obtaining accurate KSA judgments

Radiologic Science Knowledge Requirements Scales:
Shoulder Positioning

The rating scale below lists *sample* behaviors corresponding to different levels of knowledge and skill related to positioning for radiographs of the **shoulder**. Please select two points on the scale that identify your expectations for the entry-level technologists you hire.

- The first point on the scale should correspond to the level of skill you expect of the *typical* entry-level radiographer that you hire. Use the letter **T** to indicate this rating.

- The second point on the scale should indicate the *minimal* level of skill you are willing to accept of a *marginally qualified* entry-level radiographer. In other words identify the *lowest* level of skill that you consider acceptable for a new hire. Use the letter **M** for this rating.

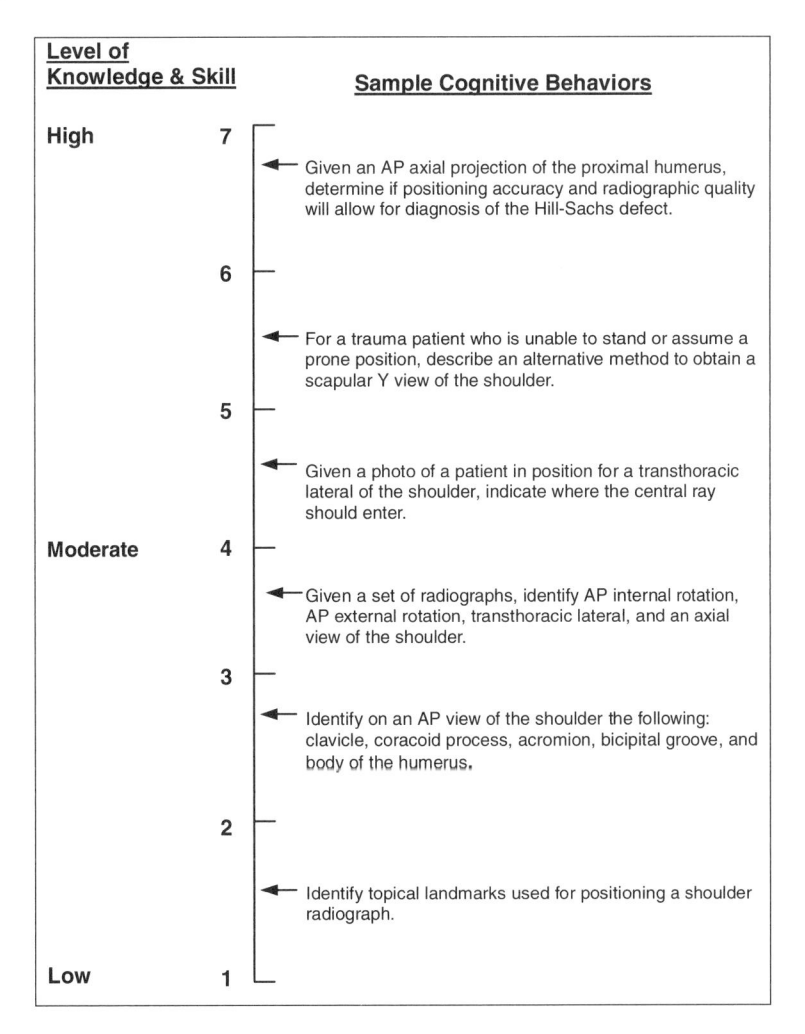

Level of Knowledge & Skill		Sample Cognitive Behaviors
High	7	← Given an AP axial projection of the proximal humerus, determine if positioning accuracy and radiographic quality will allow for diagnosis of the Hill-Sachs defect.
	6	
		← For a trauma patient who is unable to stand or assume a prone position, describe an alternative method to obtain a scapular Y view of the shoulder.
	5	
		← Given a photo of a patient in position for a transthoracic lateral of the shoulder, indicate where the central ray should enter.
Moderate	4	
		← Given a set of radiographs, identify AP internal rotation, AP external rotation, transthoracic lateral, and an axial view of the shoulder.
	3	
		← Identify on an AP view of the shoulder the following: clavicle, coracoid process, acromion, bicipital groove, and body of the humerus.
	2	
		← Identify topical landmarks used for positioning a shoulder radiograph.
Low	1	

FIG. 9.2. A behaviorally anchored rating scale for judging the level of knowledge required for the topic of shoulder positioning. A similar scale was developed for each of 33 topics.

may require special efforts related to data collection. Although entry-level practitioners can be relied on to indicate how often they apply a KSA in their work, they may not be the best group to judge the importance of KSAs or the depth of knowledge required in practice. This is another instance where a meeting of SMEs might be a more effective data collection strategy

(Kane, 1997; Raymond, 2001). Procedures for eliciting SME judgments are covered in a later section when we describe methods for developing test specifications.

Demographics. Most job analysis questionnaires include one or more pages devoted to characteristics related to the respondent's background and work environment. The demographics section of a survey might include questions on practice setting (size and type of facility); demographic characteristics (population density, regional socioeconomics); age; gender; ethnic background; employment status; educational preparation (e.g., type of degree, coursework); years of experience; hours worked; access to support services; availability of equipment and technology; types of support personnel or colleagues in work setting; general practice activities or specialties (e.g., research, teaching, or client services); and characteristics of patients, clients, or other users of service. These types of questions are essential for describing the sample of respondents and comparing them to the population to investigate the possibility of sampling bias. In addition, demographic questions can be used as the basis for comparing subgroups of respondents. It may prove interesting to compare the practice activities of those who work in different settings or who see different types of clients. It can also be useful to investigate how practice changes as a function of experience, as a way to understand how entry-level practice compares to advanced practice. Such analyses can inform interpretation of the data in important ways.

Questionnaire Administration and Data Analysis

Whether a questionnaire is to be mailed out or administered over the Internet, it is necessary to attend to many details related to questionnaire layout, sample selection, data entry procedures, and so on. One of the more important activities is to conduct a pilot study to make certain that questions and response categories are interpreted as intended (Bourque & Fielder, 2003; Desimone & LaFloche, 2004). These activities, although very critical, are beyond the scope of this chapter. Readers interested in a general perspective on questionnaire design and administration can consult Dillman (2000) or Fink (2003). Raymond (2005) discusses these topics within the context practice analysis, and presents numerous guidelines for both mail-out and Internet questionnaires.

Many questionnaires consist of more than 100 tasks rated on multiple scales; thus, it is not uncommon for the resulting data files to consist of 500 to 1,000 variables. Before data are subjected to analysis, they must be screened for coding errors, missing data, response bias, and response validity (Colton, Kane, Kingsbury, & Estes, 1991). Then a wide variety of routine data analysis methods may be used to summarize the activities that define the profession. In addition, multivariate procedures may be helpful for data reduction, developing concise models of practice, or distinguishing among subspecialties (D'Costa, 1986; Kane et al., 1986; Raymond & Williams, 2004; Rosenfeld et al., 1983). With few exceptions, there is nothing unique about practice analysis data that requires discussion of these quantitative methods beyond what can be found in statistics textbooks. One of those exceptions pertains to the practice of combining ratings from multiple scales to create an index of overall importance. This issue, which is especially germane to practice analysis, is addressed below.

DATA ANALYSIS: COMBINING RATINGS FROM MULTIPLE SCALES

Although practice analyses are typically conducted for the purpose of developing test specifications, the results can also be used for other endeavors such as curriculum development, establishing educational requirements, and determining eligibility criteria. Developing test specifications involves making decisions about the topics to cover on an examination and the emphasis to allocate to each topic. The challenge is to sift through the mountains of practice analysis data—ratings from several hundred respondents on two or three rating scales for a couple of hundred tasks—in a manner that facilitates making well-informed and consistent decisions about test content.

One approach to data interpretation is to develop decision rules for each of the scales deemed relevant for a study. A study that includes a criticality scale and a need-at-entry scale might be guided by this two-stage rule: (1) any task for which at least 60% of the sample indicates that it is needed at entry into the profession will be included in the test plan; and (2) the amount of emphasis to be received on the test plan will be directly proportional to that task's rating on the criticality scale. A second approach to data management is to combine the multiple scales into a single index using a formula or some other mathematical model. The second approach seems to be more common and makes more complete use of the rating data. We discuss four statistical models for combining ratings scales: the additive model, multiplicative model, hierarchical ranking scheme, and the Rasch model. Although the statistical model is the most important factor to consider when combining scales, there are other issues to resolve, such as the scales to include in the model, the weight given to each scale, the statistical properties of the scales, and the manner in which data are aggregated.

Statistical Models

Various models for combining practice analysis ratings have been proposed over the years. The additive, or linear, model appears to be the most popular approach to combining ratings, owing perhaps to its simplicity (Raymond, 1996; Sanchez & Fraser, 1992). Each task's overall importance is determined by summing across all rating scales included in the model. This model is fully compensatory: a low rating on one scale can be offset by a high rating on another scale. The effects of compensation are most notable when either frequency or criticality, but not both, have a value of zero. For example, if a task has a criticality of 0 and a frequency of 5, its importance index is still 5. This outcome illustrates one potential limitation of the additive model. In addition, Kane et al. (1989) noted that there is no clear interpretation of a scale formed by adding frequency and importance. Despite these limitations, there is literature supporting the use of simple linear models over more complex ones when using statistical models in decision making (Dawes & Corrigan, 1974; Sanchez & Fraser, 1992).

Kane et al. (1989) offer a compelling rationale supporting the use of multiplicative models for combining ratings. It is based on the premise that criticality can be regarded as the importance of an activity per occurrence of a task. It then follows that the overall importance of a task can be obtained by summing criticality over all occurrences of that task. Further, if task frequency can be assumed to correspond to all occurrences of a task, then overall importance can be estimated by multiplying task criticality by frequency. The multiplicative model offers an elegant interpretation not afforded by other models. That is, importance is based on a task's criticality each time it is performed. Given two tasks with equal criticality, if task A is performed twice as often as task B, then it should receive twice the weight. Although it is compensatory, it is does not compensate if one or more of the scales contain a zero.

Ranking methods use a conversion table to transform ratings from multiple scales into a single index. The most well-developed ranking method is the hierarchical ranking scheme proposed by Spray and Huang (2000). Their method combines multiple ratings into a single scale by recoding ordered pairs of responses into a single rank or score. The scales are nested such that the most highly valued scale takes precedence. Assuming criticality is to receive more emphasis than frequency, then values for frequency are nested within criticality, as illustrated in

TABLE 9.4
Hierarchical Recoding of Criticality
(C) and Frequency (F) scales

(C, F)	Rank
(2, 4)	15
(2, 3)	14
(2, 2)	13
(2, 1)	12
(2, 0)	11
(1, 4)	10
(1, 3)	9
...	...
(0, 0)	1

Table 9.4. This recoding is based on a criticality scale with three values (2, 1, 0) and frequency scale with five values (4, 3, 2, 1, 0). From these two scales, a total of 15 ranks are possible. Once frequency and criticality ratings have been converted to ranks for each respondent, it is possible to summarize the data using a variety of methods and statistical indices. Spray and Huang (2000) suggest that the Rasch rating scale model (RRSM) (Andrich, 1978) be used. This model requires only rank order data, which is what most practice analysis scales produce, and requires no assumptions about the specific values assigned to the ratings. The hierarchical ranking method, because of its reliance on an explicit conversion table, is very straightforward and is likely to appeal to lay audiences and SMEs. Like the additive model, the hierarchical ranking method is fully compensatory. In fact, this method can be represented as an additive model.

The RRSM has also been used as a method for combining scales, specifically the multi-faceted RRSM (see Joseph & Taranath, 1999). The influence of each scale on overall importance is determined by the statistical properties of the rating data. Therefore, a notable limitation is that the user does not have explicit control in determining the contribution of each scale in the formation of the importance scale. The contributions to be made by criticality and frequency should be a matter of SME judgment, not the empirical properties of the data (Kane et al., 1989). Furthermore, most ratings probably are not locally independent (Spray & Huang, 2000), and the multiple scales to be combined may not represent a unidimensional construct (Raymond, 2001), both of which are assumptions of the RRSM. Although the RRSM has many useful applications, combining ratings from different types of rating scales is not one of them.

Other Factors Affecting Choice of Method

Once the mathematical model has been determined, there remain a few other substantive and methodological issues to address before combining ratings. Given that task ratings are available from multiple scales, someone needs to decide which scales to include in the model as well as the relative contribution (weight) assigned to each scale. It is beneficial to obtain input from both SMEs and researchers at this point, because there may be both substantive and empirical reasons to give certain scales more or less weight in the determination of overall importance. It might be suggested that task frequency be included in the model and given substantial weight.

In addition, some research suggests that difficulty of learning should be part of the equation that comprises overall importance. Alternatively, criticality might be given most of the weight, particularly for licensure examinations. The purpose of licensure is to protect the public by identifying those who lack critical knowledge or skills necessary for safe and effective practice (Kane, 1982), which implies that criticality be given greater emphasis (Kane et al., 1989; Rakel, 1979). It is obvious that the choices are many, and rationales such as these should be used to guide the manner in which scales are selected and weighted.

The statistical properties of rating data also influence the manner in which the scales are combined. There are two issues. First, it is not beneficial to combine scales that provide similar information. If two scales have similar profiles over tasks (i.e., similar means and high correlation), then the scales are redundant, and there is little need to use both (Sanchez & Fraser, 1992). Second, for the additive and multiplicative models, the variances and covariances of the scales affect the emphasis a scale has on the calculated importance index. The effective contribution of a scale (its true contribution) to a single importance index does not necessarily equal its nominal contribution (the contribution we assign). In a model with two scales, a scale's effective contribution equals its nominal contribution only if the variances for the two scales are equal. This is generally true of any composite created by combining scores on other variables. For example, test items with greater variance contribute more to total test score than items with less variance. To maintain control of the relative contributions of each scale, it is necessary to equalize their variances prior to combining them. Transformations for equalizing variances are described later.

Another factor to consider when implementing a method for combining scales is the sequence for aggregating the rating data. Determining the overall importance of a task requires that data be aggregated in two directions: over rating scales and over respondents. The obvious approach is to first combine the rating scales (e.g., frequency, criticality) at the level of the individual. This produces an importance index for each respondent on each task. A task's overall importance is then determined by calculating the mean importance over all respondents. Alternatively, data can first be aggregated over respondents, by computing the mean frequency and the mean criticality for each task. The resulting vectors for mean frequency and criticality are then combined to determine overall importance for each task. A key advantage of aggregating data before combining scales is that it allows one to combine ratings from different groups of respondents. For example, frequency ratings could be obtained from a large sample of entry-level practitioners, while criticality ratings are obtained from a panel of SMEs during a meeting. The four models presented earlier have different requirements related to order of aggregation. Both the hierarchical ranking scheme and RRSM expect that ratings be combined at the level of the individual respondent. The additive model and the multiplicative model can be applied to either individual ratings or to vectors of mean ratings.

Application of Models

The following text illustrates additive and multiplicative models for combining ratings from practice analysis rating scales. The models are applied to frequency and criticality ratings for ten tasks taken from the same RQM questionnaire depicted in Figure 9.1. All ten tasks fall within the general domain of image processing. A sample task is "determine optimal temperature for the film processor." For all examples, calculations are performed as if the ten tasks were the entire questionnaire. We first present two versions of the additive model, followed by two versions of the multiplicative model. Both models are applied to ratings that have been aggregated over respondents.

Additive Model

The additive, or linear model is the simplest and most common method (Sanchez & Levine, 1989) for combining scales. The model may be stated as:

$$I_i = C_i + F_i \tag{9.1}$$

where: I_i = importance index for task i,
C_i = mean criticality rating for task i, and
F_i = mean frequency rating for task i.

Equation 9.1 gives criticality and frequency equal contribution to the importance index. It is also common to weight the terms in the model to reflect SME consensus regarding the contribution each term should make to the overall importance of each task. If, for example, SMEs judged criticality to be three times more important than frequency, the resulting linear combination would be:

$$I_i = 3C_i + F_i \tag{9.2}$$

The importance scale resulting from either of these models is not immediately useful for determining the amount of weight each task receives on the test specifications. The proportional weight of an individual task, W_i, can be obtained by dividing its importance rating by the sum of all importance ratings. The general formula is:

$$W_i = \frac{I_i}{\sum_i I_i}, \tag{9.3}$$

which results in weights that sum to 1.0. It is convenient to multiply W_i by 100 to put the weights on a percent scale.

As noted, the variances of criticality and frequency ratings influence their relative contributions to importance. To give criticality and frequency the emphasis specified by Equation 9.1 or Equation 9.2, it is necessary to transform one of the scales to equalize their variances. A linear transformation that preserves the location of each scale (i.e., lowest rating of zero) can be obtained by multiplying each value by the ratio of the standard deviations, or

$$C_i^* = \frac{s_f}{s_c} \times C_i \tag{9.4}$$

where: C^* = the transformed criticality ratings,
s_f = the standard deviation of the vector of mean frequency ratings over all tasks,
s_c = the standard deviation of the vector of mean criticality ratings over all tasks, and
C_i = the mean criticality rating of task i.

Equations 9.1, 9.2, and 9.3 were used to compute importance indices and weights for the ten tasks after equalizing the variances. The left and central portions of Table 9.5 present the results. The table contains the original frequency and criticality ratings, the transformed criticality rating (C^*), as well as the importance weights for each task. The bottom rows of the table present summary statistics as an interpretive aid. Before attending to the weights, note that the original criticality ratings had considerably less variability than the frequency ratings. We have observed this in many sets of practice analysis data. The results of transforming criticality

TABLE 9.5
Importance Indices and Weights for Two Versions of the Additive Model and Two Versions of the Multiplicative Model

| | Mean Ratings | | | Additive Model | | | | Multiplicative Model | |
| | | | | Weights (W_i) | | | | Weights (W_i) | |
Task	Frequency	Criticality	C^*	$C^* + F$	$3C^* + F$	$C^{3.34}$	$C^{7.89}$	$C^{3.34}F$	$C^{7.89}F$
1	3.75	1.21	5.66	.129	.109	1.89	4.50	.178	.088
2	0.71	1.27	5.94	.091	.098	2.22	6.59	.040	.024
3	0.63	1.25	5.85	.089	.096	2.11	5.82	.033	.019
4	2.06	1.49	6.97	.124	.121	3.79	23.26	.196	.250
5	0.80	1.36	6.36	.098	.105	2.79	11.32	.056	.047
6	1.56	1.43	6.69	.113	.114	3.30	16.82	.129	.137
7	0.54	0.67	3.14	.050	.052	0.26	0.04	.004	.000
8	3.00	1.51	7.07	.138	.128	3.96	25.84	.298	.405
9	0.34	1.08	5.05	.074	.082	1.29	1.84	.011	.003
10	1.22	1.19	5.57	.093	.095	1.79	3.95	.055	.025
Mean	1.46	1.25	5.83	.100	.100	2.34	10.00	.100	.100
SD	1.15	0.25	1.15	.027	.022	1.15	9.05	.097	.132

are seen in the column labeled C^*. A scaling factor of 4.68, obtained from Equation 9.4, was required to equalize the variances. The effectiveness of the transformation in equalizing the variances can be verified in the bottom row of the table, where it is evident that the standard deviation (SD) of C^* is equal to that of the original frequency ratings.

Of most interest are the two columns of importance weights under the additive model (see Equation 9.3). Most tasks were minimally affected by giving three times more weight to criticality. The differential weighting had the most effect on task 1, which dropped from 0.129 to 0.109. Under the equal weight model; the high frequency rating for task 1 (3.75) had notable influence on overall importance. However, weighting criticality by a factor of 3 diluted the influence of task frequency, and increased the influence of the criticality rating (1.21), which was lower than average. All other differences between the two sets of weights were 0.01 or less. The correlation between the two columns of weights is 0.96. One noteworthy finding is that both additive models seemed to produce limited variability in weights. If weights were arbitrarily assigned, we would pick a value of 0.10 for each task (i.e., the mean). It is apparent that actual weights deviate very little from this mean, ranging from about .050 to .138.

Multiplicative Model

The multiplicative model proposed by Kane et al. (1989) can be expressed as:

$$I_i = C_i F_i \tag{9.5}$$

This version of the model indicates that criticality and frequency have equal influence on overall importance, which implies that the two scales have equal variances. As indicated in Table 9.5, they do not. To account for differences in the variability of the two scales, Kane et al. (1989) proposed modifying Equation 9.5 to incorporate the necessary transformation:

$$I_i = C_i^a F_i \tag{9.6}$$

In other words, criticality and frequency can be given equal emphasis in determining overall importance by raising mean criticality to the power a. The transformation could be applied to either criticality or frequency; however, given that frequency scales are generally more readily interpretable as they stand (particularly if it is an absolute scale), then it may be desirable to leave frequency in its original form. The formula for the exponent a is:

$$a = \sqrt{\frac{\text{var}(\ln F_i)}{\text{var}(\ln C_i)}} \qquad (9.7)$$

where: $\text{var}(\ln F_i)$ = the variance of the natural logarithm of the mean frequency ratings, and
$\text{var}(\ln C_i)$ = the variance of the natural logarithm of the mean criticality ratings.

To calculate the exponent, it is necessary to first take the natural log of the mean frequency and mean criticality of each task, and then find the variance of the transformed values. We performed the necessary transformation on the ten frequency and criticality ratings and found that $\text{var}(\ln F) = 0.613$ and $\text{var}(\ln C) = 0.055$. Inserting these values into Equation 9.7, gives $a = 3.34$. Finding the exponent is more complex if there are more than two rating scales in the model, or if one of the scales is to receive greater emphasis. Computational details for these extensions of the multiplicative model can be found in Kane et al. (1989). We completed the calculations necessary to give criticality three times the emphasis of frequency, which resulted in $a = 7.89$.

The multiplicative model as presented in Equation 9.6 was applied to frequency and criticality ratings for the same ten tasks. The right portion of Table 9.5 presents the weights for a model that gives criticality and frequency equal emphasis and another that gives criticality three times the emphasis. These two models result in notably different weights for tasks 1 and 8, as well as for task 4. The weight for task 1 dropped from 0.178 to 0.088 for the 3C model. Recall that task 1 was affected in a similar way for the additive model. Meanwhile, the weight for task 8 increased from .298 to .405 as a consequence of criticality receiving more weight, whereas task 4 increased from 0.196 to 0.250. Both of these tasks were at the high end of the original criticality scale, and increasing their emphasis by raising them to a power of 7.89 exaggerates their already high values. In spite of these differences, the two sets of multiplicative weights still had a correlation of 0.94.

Before leaving this example, it is useful to look at the summary statistics in the bottom rows of Table 9.5. First note that the standard deviations for the original criticality ratings and the transformed ratings ($C^{3.34}$ and $C^{7.89}$) are dramatically different, giving an indication of the magnitude to which the original criticality ratings had to be adjusted to have their intended effect. Second, there is far more variability in weights for the $C^{7.89}$ model. This runs counter to the outcome for the additive model, where giving criticality more emphasis resulted in a slight decrease in variability of weights.

Summary of Models

The four methods for combining weights were created by manipulating two independent factors: the statistical model (additive versus multiplicative) and the emphasis given to each scale (equal emphasis versus increasing criticality by a factor of three). Although the data in Table 9.5 are based on only ten tasks, the results are generally consistent with what might be observed for complete sets of practice analysis data. In general, the statistical form of the model has a notable impact on weights, whereas varying the emphasis given to each scale matters little. The most noteworthy feature of the multiplicative model is that it stretches the distribution of importance weights, thereby allowing them to exhibit more variability. Another way to think about the relationships among models is through the use of scatterplots. For example, if pairs of weights produced by two additive models are plotted, the weights generally fall close to a straight line, with occasional outliers (like task 1). Plotting two multiplicative models gives a similar result. The plot is not strictly linear, and it still has its occasional outlier. Meanwhile, a plot of additive and multiplicative weights exhibits a strong, but fairly uniform, curvilinear relationship.

Although the additive model is most common in practice, we tend to favor the multiplicative model, particularly when used in conjunction with scales that have quasi-ratio properties (e.g., absolute frequency or criticality that have a meaningful zero). The added complexity of the multiplicative model is offset by the interpretive advantages noted by Kane et al. (1989). In addition, the restricted variability in weights for the additive model may be cause for concern. Although the methods should not be evaluated on this basis alone, it does seem reasonable to question a method that produces very similar weights for most tasks.

THE NATURE AND USE OF TEST SPECIFICATIONS

Practice analysis is a straightforward process resulting in a fairly objective documentation of job responsibilities. In contrast, developing test specifications is subjective in nature and requires that assumptions be made about the KSAs required for effective practice. In other words, practice analysis is a descriptive activity, whereas establishing KSA requirements is an inferential activity. To help ensure that test specifications are linked to the requirements of practice, it is important that they be developed using systematic procedures. This section provides an overview of conceptual frameworks for organizing test specifications. It is followed by a discussion of strategies for evaluating the effectiveness and utility of test specifications. The last section presents a detailed illustration of different methods for converting the results of practice analysis into test specifications. Some methods rely exclusively on SME judgments of topic importance, whereas other methods derive test specifications from the results of the practice analysis questionnaire.

Types of Test Specifications

Test specifications describe the important features of an examination and are an essential piece of the test development process (AERA, APA, & NCME, 1999, p. 43). At a minimum, test specifications list the topics or behaviors to be covered by an examination and indicate the emphasis given to different categories of topics or behaviors. Many test specifications document additional features of the examination such as the format of the test items (e.g., multiple choice, matching, or essay), the difficulty of different sections, the cognitive complexity of the test items, and features of the test stimuli or intended responses (Millman & Greene, 1989; Osterlind, 1998). Test specifications can be written at various levels of specificity, with more detail generally being preferred (Popham, 1984). All test specifications are ultimately built on a foundation of process, content, or both. *Process-based test specifications* emphasize the cognitive behaviors and practice activities required in the work setting. In contrast, *content-based test specifications* specify the knowledge required for practice. It is often convenient to integrate both tasks and KSAs into a single set of test specifications, with the content-by-process matrix being the most common way to accomplish this (Millman & Greene, 1989; Osterlind, 1998).

Process-Based Test Specifications

One way to help ensure that credentialing examinations are job related is to use test specifications that are directly tied to the tasks performed in the practice setting. Process-based test specifications are common in fields as diverse as nursing (Millman & Green, 1989, Figure 8.2), architecture, and medicine. For example, the licensure test for architects is organized around the major tasks associated with design and construction (National Council of Architectural Registration Boards, 2002). Included are activities such as "develop project schedule," "analyze soils and foundation," and "identify and calculate loads." The critical incidents study of orthopedic surgery resulted in a classic example of a process-based test plan (Levine et al., 1968; Miller, 1968). The final test plan consisted of the nine major performance domains such as gathering clinical data, performing diagnostic procedures, implementing a treatment plan, and so on. These nine domains were divided into subcategories (e.g., obtain information by physical assessment), which in turn listed several practice requirements (e.g., perform orthopedic evaluation). The final report from that project also identified critical incidents under each practice requirement, with each incident serving as the foundation for test items.

Readers whose background is specific to educational achievement testing likely have a different understanding of process-based test specifications. In educational assessment, process usually refers to some framework for describing cognitive behaviors, such as Bloom's (1956) taxonomy or some other model of cognitive processing (e.g., Fleishman & Quaintance, 1984; Millman & Greene, 1989; Osterlind, 1998). This is because much of the educational performance domain is cognitive in nature. It is common for educational test specifications to contain words such as *recall*, *apply*, or *analyze*. However, in professional credentialing, process generally refers to practice-related behaviors such as *assess* or *diagnose*. This reflects an interest in developing examinations that simulate what occurs in the practice setting.

Whether the assessment context is educational testing or professional credentialing, a key feature of process-based test specifications is that they generally consist of either verbs (e.g., *analyze*, *diagnose*) or nominal forms of verbs (e.g., *analysis*, *diagnosis*). Therefore, one advantage of process-based test specifications stems from their obvious link to the real-world setting. In addition, they encourage the development of test items that assess an examinee's ability to apply concepts and principles to practical problems (D'Costa, 1986). Another advantage is that it is relatively straightforward to translate the results of a practice analysis into the test plan because the test plan often consists of the very same descriptors that appeared on the practice analysis questionnaire. As we later illustrate, process-based test specifications are developed by organizing tasks into categories and assigning weights to those categories.

Content-Based Test Specifications

It is common to arrange test specifications for credentialing examinations much in the way that academic disciplines are organized: as an outline of the topics that examinees are expected to master. Consider the test plan for the *Fundamentals of Engineering Exam*, the first of a series of licensing examinations taken by engineers (National Conference of Examiners for Engineering and Surveying, 1999a). This 180-item examination addresses the basic sciences that apply to a variety of engineering specialties. The twelve major sections of the test plan consist of topics such as chemistry, dynamics, electric circuits, fluid mechanics, and mathematics. The test plan also indicates the percentage of questions allocated to each section. Then, each section is broken down into its constituent topics. For example, the section on chemistry is made up of fourteen specific topics including acids and bases, equilibrium, kinetics, and so on. It is interesting that the words and phrases that typically make up content-based test specifications are often nouns.

Some content-based test specifications are organized around the types of problems encountered in practice. The second set of examinations taken by engineers is called the *Principles and Practice of Engineering*. The examination in civil engineering, for example, covers topics such as transportation systems, waste systems, and water resources (National Conference of Examiners for Engineering and Surveying, 1999b). Then, within each of these systems, different classes of engineering problems are specified (e.g., traffic interchanges, parking). Problem-based test specifications are also common in the health professions (LaDuca, Downing, & Henzel, 1995). For example, the test plan in emergency medicine is organized primarily around organ systems (cardiovascular, gastrointestinal, etc.), with specific medical problems nested within each system (e.g., acute gastritis).

The underlying strength of content-based test specifications is that they describe the content of an examination in a way that most users can understand. They are often organized around well-established, logically structured frameworks that resemble the way content is organized for instructional purposes. This probably benefits educators and examinees in their preparation efforts, and probably helps item writers to locate the references they require.

Integrating Content With Process

The two-dimensional content-by-process matrix is probably the most common way for incorporating both tasks and topics into a single test plan. For most content-by-process matrices, the *content dimension* identifies the topics to be covered by the test items, whereas the *process dimension* describes the examinee behaviors presumably required to correctly answer those test items (Millman & Greene, 1989; Osterlind, 1998). The cells of the matrix typically indicate the number of test items allocated to each content–process combination, but they could also convey other information. Table 9.6 illustrates a portion of a content-by-process matrix that might be used for credentialing examination in a health profession. The content dimension runs down the left side of the table and consists of patient problems nested within organ systems. The process dimension is represented by the columns and identifies classes of practice-related behaviors. This is a very useful way to describe the context of a credentialing test. While one dimension specifies the practice-related problem to be addressed, the other dimension provides information about the context of the problem.

There are many variations of the test plan in Table 9.6. For example, cognitive behaviors such as recall, interpret, or analyze could be used instead of, or in addition to, the practice-related behaviors. Some credentialing agencies have even found that three dimensions are required to adequately describe test content (American Board of Physical Medicine and Rehabilitation, 1998, D'Costa, 1986; LaDuca, Taylor, & Hill, 1984). It is useful to note that content and process can be combined using frameworks other than a matrix. Tasks can be nested within topics, or vice versa (Millman & Greene, 1989, Figure 8.2; Prekeges, Sawyer, & Wells, 1999). It is sometimes desirable to mix frameworks. For example, one part of a test plan might consist of a topic outline that covers academic disciplines such as basic sciences, and a second part of the test plan that addresses professional practice might use a content-by-process matrix. The framework chosen for organizing a test plan is an important decision that can affect many activities related to test development and scoring. We have probably given the impression that most test specifications are either content or process, or some highly structured combination of the two. In reality, content and process are often combined a less coherent fashion, resulting in test specifications with redundant or overlapping categories. Although less-structured test specifications are useful, limitations such as overlap or lack of specificity can interfere with activities such as item classification, equating, or reporting section scores.

TABLE 9.6
Sample Content-by-Process Matrix for a Health Profession

Organ System / Patient Condition	Obtain Clinical Data		Evaluate Diagnostic Studies		Prescribe Treatment		Total
	Patient Interview	Physical Assessment	Lab Studies	Medical Images	Medical Management	Surgical Intervention	
CV disorders Angina Myocardial infarction And so on	3	5	3	4	6	4	25
GI disorders Acute gastritis Appendicitis And so on	1	2	3	2	5	2	15
Neurologic disorders Encephalitis Meningitis And so on	3	6	2	5	3	1	20
Additional conditions	XX	XX	XX	XX	XX	XX	XX
Total	10	20	20	20	90	40	200

Values in the cells specify the emphasis (e.g., number of questions) given to each section. A variation of this matrix replaces practice-based columns with cognitive processes such as comprehension, application, synthesis and so on. *Abbreviations:* CV, cardiovascular; GI, gastrointestinal.
Table from Raymond, M. R. (2002a). A practical guide to practice analysis for credentialing examinations. *Educational Measurement: Issues & Practice, 21*(3), 25–37. Reprinted with the permission of Blackwell Publishing.

The Utility of Test Specifications

A test plan can be viewed as a system for describing and classifying the behaviors to be elicited by the assessment tasks presented to the examinee (Messick, 1989, pp. 37–38). As such, they are really behavioral taxonomies (Fleishman & Quaintance, 1984; Schaefer, Raymond, & White, 1992). Bloom's (1956) taxonomy, the Ability Requirements Scales (Fleishman & Quaintance, 1984), and the test plan for orthopedic surgery described are fine examples of behavioral taxonomies based on carefully explicated theories of performance. Even test specifications that correspond to traditional academic disciplines (e.g., chemistry, fluid mechanics, trigonometry) can be regarded as taxonomies.

Fleishman & Quaintance (1984) proposed several criteria for evaluating behavioral taxonomies, and these criteria apply equally well to test specifications. First, the taxonomy should lead to reliable classification. One way to evaluate reliability is to determine the extent to which two or more individuals classify test items or assessment tasks into the same content domain. Another strategy is to have SMEs sort topics from lower levels of ordination of a test plan into their parent categories. Second, test specifications should lead to mutually exclusive classification of topics. Although this is certainly a desirable property for any classification system, it is difficult to satisfy with behavioral taxonomies (Fleishman & Quaintance, 1984, p. 83). Third, the underlying features that distinguish categories should be obvious to knowledgeable reviewers. In other words, the test plan and the logic underlying its structure should make sense. SMEs should be able to explain why two topics appear near or distant from each other in a test plan, or why one topic is subordinate to another. Fourth, behavioral taxonomies should achieve their intended objectives. This criterion is obviously broader and more difficult to evaluate than the previous three. We consider three broad uses of test specifications—test development, scoring and scaling, and informing the public—and discuss methods for evaluating the extent to which test specifications meet these objectives.

Examination Development

Test specifications are an essential part of the examination development process (AERA, APA, & NCME, 1999, Standards, 3.2, 3.3). They provide direction to item writers and are used by SMEs to review and judge the appropriateness of test items for operational use. SMEs rely on test specifications for classifying test items, and test assembly personnel depend on thorough test specifications to construct examination forms that are parallel in terms of content, difficulty, and other characteristics. Test specifications are especially important for automated test assembly, computer-adaptive testing, and other instances for which test forms are assembled and administered without first being reviewed by humans (Wightman, 1998). It is apparent that to serve these functions the categories on a test plan must have sufficient detail, minimal redundancy, and be conducive to reliable item classification. It is easy to design empirical studies to investigate item classification accuracy. Evaluative information also surfaces through anecdotal reports from testing specialists and SMEs who work with the test plan on a routine basis. Well-designed studies have made use of both empirical and judgmental criteria when evaluating computerized item selection procedures. Predictably, even the most elaborate item selection algorithms produce uneven test forms when the framework for classifying test content is not sufficiently detailed (e.g., Stocking, Swanson, & Pearlman, 1993).

Scoring and Scaling

Test specifications are also used for statistical activities such as scoring, equating, item calibration, scaling, and even standard setting, all of which influence score interpretations. Sound test specifications are one of the requirements for accurate equating (Cook & Petersen, 1987; Kolen & Brennan, 1995). To effectively implement the common item equating design, for example, the test items common to the forms to be equated (i.e., the equating link) should mirror the entire examination in terms of content and statistical properties. Vague or ambiguous test specifications, or those that do not adequately model the content domain of interest, can lead to inaccurate equating results because the common items may not be representative of the complete test (Klein & Jarjoura, 1985). Test specifications also provide the basis for section scores, which are usually interpreted as representing relatively unidimensional constructs. The manner in which total scores are partitioned may in turn guide other analyses, such item bank calibration, standard setting, and the organization of various statistical reports. For example, it is common to compare groups of examinees (based on gender, type of training, state of residence, etc.) on various sections of a test. If sections of the test represent more-or-less random collections of items rather than homogeneous behavioral constructs, the comparisons will be inaccurate, misleading, or both.

In short, sections of a test generally correspond to constructs that represent behavioral processes (Messick, 1989). Claims that tests measure behavioral processes such as clinical reasoning or analysis should be supported by evidence that the assessment tasks actually elicit those behaviors from examinees (AERA, APA, & NCME, 1999, p. 12). Credentialing organizations often lack the resources required for the types of thorough experimentation and investigation required to support such claims. There are, however, a variety of practical approaches for evaluating the extent to which test specifications and test items represent the intended constructs. SMEs can be asked to judge the relevance and representativeness of test items when reviewing new items or assembling forms. Hambleton (1984) describes systematic methods for obtaining SME judgments and computing statistical indices of item–domain congruence and content representation. Messick (1989) describes successful applications of factor analysis and multidimensional scaling to judgments of item relevance. Even the linkage matrix presented in Table 9.9 could be subjected to multivariate procedures to investigate the perceived structure of the content domain.

In addition to methods that rely on SME judgment, it is also informative to evaluate examinee responses to test items to determine if patterns of responses are consistent with expectations based on the test specifications. Haladyna and Kramer (2004) present several strategies for investigating the validity of interpretations of subscores from credentialing examinations, including correlational studies, factor analysis, and various other methods for evaluating score profiles. However, factor analysis of item responses is seldom as informative as one would hope. It is also useful to compare competing classification systems. Item responses can be scored according to two or more test specifications, and the section scores subjected to various logical and empirical analyses in search of the classification framework that makes the most sense, produces subscores that correlate least with others, and results in subscores with the highest measures of internal consistency. Although more research is needed, studies of process-oriented test specifications suggest that their subscores do not hold up to empirical scrutiny. Subscores tend to vary and covary not because of skills such as application, analysis, diagnosis, or interpersonal skills (Cizek, Webb, & Kalohn, 1995; Seddon, 1978), but because of examinees' level of knowledge of trigonometry, physics, or the renal system. In other words, test performance seems to be context or domain specific in academic disciplines (Perkins & Salomon, 1989), and case or problem specific in the professions (Colliver, Markwell, Vu, & Barrows, 1990; Elstein, Shulman, & Sprafka, 1978).

Public Information

Test specifications and abbreviated versions of them also make their way into the hands of students, educators, policy makers, and other consumers. Educators use test specifications to help determine what to cover in their courses, while examinees use test specifications to study for examinations. Test-coaching schools and authors of review books hopefully rely on test specifications when developing their preparation materials.[2] Educators and examinees use section scores derived from test specifications to identify strengths or weaknesses in specific content areas. However, the feedback is of limited use if the section scores are based on poorly formulated content domains or domains that use labels that really do not provide the student or educator with remedial guidance. We suspect that a student who receives a low score in "problem solving" on a credentialing examination will have very little idea about what he or she should study when preparing for his or her next attempt. Evaluating the utility of score reports is an important, but often neglected, activity (Goodman & Hambleton, 2004; Haladyna & Kramer, 2004). In addition to completing the types of analyses described in the preceeding paragraph, users of score reports can be surveyed regarding utility of the information they receive. Test specifications also inform policy decisions and serve other public interests. It is crucial that licensing agencies have access to detailed test specifications prior to using test results to make pass/fail decisions (AERA, APA, & NCME, 1999, p. 83). Finally, well-developed test specifications can help credentialing agencies to address legal challenges. Not only is it important for test specifications to be based on an empirical practice analysis, but the

---

[2] Admittedly, a questionable use. However, providing the public with detailed test specifications can help to ensure that all examinees have equal access to the same information, and may perhaps discourage them from obtaining the information in less honorable ways.

link between the specifications and practice responsibilities should be evident and supported by documentation.

In sum, those test specifications with the greatest utility share three characteristics. First, they provide a comprehensive description of the practice-related behaviors to be covered by the examination, with those behaviors being derived from a practice analysis. Second, the sections of the test plan represent a meaningful taxonomy of the constructs sampled by the test. Third, the test plan has the specificity required to fulfill its uses by various audiences. Given that test specifications are used for different purposes, a single document may not be adequate. Whereas test developers require a very detailed version, an abbreviated version may meet the needs of the public and consumers.

Types of Test Specifications Revisited

Table 9.7 summarizes the features of each of the three major frameworks for organizing test specifications. The advantages of process-based test specifications stem from their obvious link to practice. They encourage test developers and the public to think not just in terms of academic subject matter, but how those textbook concepts and principles apply to practical problems. On the surface, process-based test specifications provide convincing support for content-related interpretations of scores on credentialing examinations. On more thorough inspection, they have limited utility when applied to multiple choice questions and other types of written assessments. The tasks presented by most written examinations—as useful as they are for assessing knowledge and cognitive skills—really do not elicit the behaviors that occur in the practice setting, such as interviewing a patient or performing a surgical procedure. Process-based test specifications may capture the essence of actual practice, and may tell us something about the behavioral domain about which we wish to make inferences, but they do not effectively describe the actual content of test items that make up an examination. They often provide inadequate specificity to item writers, test assemblers, and examinees in terms of actual test content, and may not accurately describe the constructs measured by multiple-choice questions. However, for performance-based examinations that directly sample practice behaviors, test specifications organized around process are a natural choice.

The contribution of content-based test specifications is that their language more closely mirrors the actual content of most credentialing examinations; that is, multiple-choice test items and other types of written tasks. Such examinations generally do not assess actual practice behaviors,[3] but instead sample the KSAs required to effectively perform those practice behaviors. The major weakness of content-based test specifications is that their relationship to practice may not be immediately apparent. Likewise, item writers may find it challenging to write test questions that apply to practice, and may instead write items that assess recall of isolated concepts and principles. Another limitation is that the process for translating the results of an empirical practice analysis into content-based test specifications is very tedious.

Choosing between content-based and process-based specifications is a matter of matching the framework with examination format: content-based test specifications are effective for written examinations, whereas process-based test specifications are likely to have greater utility for performance assessments. But it may not be necessary to make a choice. It is evident that the content-by-process matrix capitalizes on the strengths of both types of frameworks, and can be adapted to meet the needs of most types of assessments. A content-by-process matrix can be useful for organizing entire test specifications or even just parts of the test plan that apply most directly to practice.

---

[3] Exceptions include those professions that depend extensively on written language.

TABLE 9.7
Summary of Frameworks for Organizing Test Specifications

	Content	*Process*[a]	*Content and Process*
Primary characteristics	List of topics, academic subjects, or classes of problems. Consist of nouns (e.g., biology, economics, traffic systems, neurologic disorders). Emphasize cognitive knowledge and skills.	List of practice activities, performance domains, or cognitive processes. Consist of verbs or nominal form of verbs (e.g., analyze, diagnosis). Emphasize behaviors or processes required in practice settings.	Topics and practice activities are integrated into a single framework. Nouns and verbs often crossed to create a matrix, but nesting also possible. Emphasize application of knowledge to practice activities.
Benefits	Similar to curriculum outlines, textbook chapters, and indexing systems. Direct specification of test item content; helpful for item writing. Section scores correspond to recognized domains.	Similar to job descriptions and other documents that summarize practice. Direct link to practice; high face validity. Useful for developing materials for performance assessments (tasks, rating forms, etc).	Suggest how cognitive knowledge is applied to practice activities. Useful for developing various assessment tasks. Allows for thorough item classification. Section scores possible for content and process.
Limitations	Identifying the topics to include is tedious and subjective. Items classified only on content dimension. Relationship of topics to actual practice is not always obvious.	The content of actual test items is not directly specified and must be inferred. Categories often overlap. Section scores may represent unproven cognitive processes; highly correlated section scores owing to case specificity.	Extensive detail and complex formatting can be difficult for users. Section scores possible for both dimensions, but score dependence is a problem.
Overall utility	Effective for written assessments (e.g., multiple choice, matching, essay).	Effective for performance assessments (e.g., work samples, simulations, orals).	Can be applied to most types of assessments.

[a] In educational assessment, *process* often refers to the types of activities listed in Bloom's taxonomy and other models of cognitive processing. In professional credentialing, *process* can also refer to the behaviors required in the practice setting.

Table from Raymond, M. R. (2002a). A practical guide to practice analysis for credentialing examinations. *Educational Measurement: Issues & Practice, 21*(3), 25–37. Reprinted with permission of Blackwell Publishing.

FROM PRACTICE ANALYSIS TO TEST SPECIFICATIONS: FOUR EXAMPLES

Procedures for converting the results of a job analysis into test specifications range from simple to complex. The specific steps depend on numerous factors, including the framework for the test specifications, their specificity, the type of information produced by the practice analysis, and the source of information for determining weights (SME panels versus large samples of practitioners). In this section, we illustrate the development of test specifications using four approaches. We first use a multiplicative model to demonstrate procedures for obtaining weights for a process-based test plan. Next, we address the development of content-based test specifications. Content-based test specifications require that a topic outline already exist. To this end we describe how to work with SMEs to identify the KSAs to be included on a test plan. We then present three systematic methods for establishing weights for those content-based test specifications. All examples utilize data from the RQM practice analysis described below.

Background of RQM Project

The RQM practice analysis is typical of many projects in terms of sample size, questionnaire length, and types of rating scales. The questionnaire consists of 144 task statements addressing two classes of job responsibilities. About two thirds of the tasks pertain to specific QC tests for different types of imaging equipment, and the remaining one third pertain to the types of continuous quality improvement (QI) and managerial activities common to many industries. Given that RQM was a relatively new specialty within radiology, the questionnaire was intentionally broad. Two rating scales were included, similar to those depicted in Figure 9.1. The frequency scale consists of four response categories (yearly, monthly, weekly, daily); the criticality scales had three response categories (little or no harm, moderate harm, serious harm). The rating scale also provided an oval for individuals to indicate if they were not responsible for a task.

Another section of the questionnaire consisted of 29 topics, referred to as *KSA statements*. The SMEs who developed the questionnaire believed most KSAs to be relevant to quality management; however, three were thought not to be relevant and were included as control items (foils) to help determine the presence of response bias. A four-point rating scale was used for recording KSA judgments (not at all important, of slight importance, moderately important, absolutely essential). The KSA section of the survey is discussed later the chapter.

The questionnaire was mailed to 1,500 individuals in April 1995. Six hundred forty-seven questionnaires were returned for a response rate of 43%. All results reported here are based on 286 individuals who reported spending a significant portion of their time performing activities directly related to RQM.

Weights for Process-Based Test Specifications

Once frequency and criticality ratings have been combined to form an overall importance weight, developing process-based test specifications from a task inventory is a very straightforward process. All that remains are two sets of related activities: organizing tasks into an outline or taxonomy, and computing weights for each section of the outline based on the importance of each task. Steps for creating process-based test specifications are summarized below, although the order may differ from what is presented here.

1. **Finalize the task list**. It is typical for the final test plan to consist of a subset of the tasks appearing on the questionnaire. Tasks might be dropped for various reasons (e.g., frequency or criticality ratings did not exceed some cutoff). For the RQM project, tasks were dropped if fewer than 40% of the sample indicated they were responsible for performing it, although a few exceptions were made based on SME consensus. A total of 85 tasks appeared on the final task inventory and were considered legitimate content for the test plan.
2. **Classify tasks into performance domains**. SME judgment or multivariate procedures can be used to classify tasks into domains (Raymond, 2001). For the RQM project,

cluster analysis of task frequency ratings was used to suggest initial groupings, with final categories based on SME consensus. The 85 tasks were sorted into 11 categories, which were further classified under 4 major domains.

3. **Calculate** an importance index, I, and importance weight, W, for each task. We use the multiplicative model.
4. **Sum the weights**. Weights can be summed within each subcategory and major domain. The weights indicate the degree of emphasis, or proportion of test items, allocated to each category of the test plan. The weights should total 1.00 when summed over all 85 tasks. It is convenient to convert them to percentages by multiplying by 100.

Table 9.8 presents importance indices and weights for the first two levels of the test plan. The two categories with the largest weights are C.3 and D.2. The weight for category C.3 can be explained primarily by the large number of tasks within the category. Although category D.2 has only five tasks, all five were among the top seven tasks in criticality ratings. Adhering to regulations is apparently central to the job of radiography quality management. Note that Table 9.8 illustrates the test plan only for the major domains and categories. In practice, it is desirable to include all 85 tasks as part of the final test plan.

We recommend that statistical weights be evaluated by SMEs and adjusted based on their judgments (Kane et al., 1989; Raymond, 1996). For example, most experts would agree that categories D.1 and D.2 should receive less weight. Although both categories are critical, the knowledge associated with these activities is not extensive when compared to the knowledge requirements for the other categories. Similarly, the weight for category C.3 may be overly influenced by the relatively large number of fairly specific tasks in that category. One systematic method for obtaining judgments from SMEs is through the use of a hierarchically structured

TABLE 9.8
Task-Oriented Test Plan and Weights for RQM

Task Domain	Tasks (n)	ΣI	ΣW
A. QI activities			.20
1. QI problem solving methods	11	4.6	.02
2. Collection and analysis of QI data	15	29.0	.13
3. Ongoing QI administration	6	10.5	.05
B. QC of radiographic equipment			.13
1. Development of QC protocols	7	9.2	.04
2. Performance of QC tests	11	19.0	.09
C. QC of ancillary equipment			.35
1. Shielding devices	5	32.4	.15
2. Film and screens	4	5.9	.03
3. Image processing equipment	10	38.0	.17
D. QC administration			.32
1. Records management	7	26.5	.12
2. Assurance of regulatory compliance	5	36.4	.17
3. Staff development	4	6.8	.03
Sum	85	218.4	1.00

Abbreviations: QC, quality control; QI, quality improvement.

Test Weights for Radiography Quality Management

Instructions: The purpose of this survey is to obtain your judgments regarding the percentage of questions to allocate to each section, category, and subcategories of the test plan. Before completing the survey, it is important to review the complete test plan (enclosed) to have full appreciation of the specific topics included within each subcategory.

For the 3 <u>major sections</u> listed below, please indicate the percentage of test questions you believe should be allocated to each section. Your percentage should add to 100%.

    A. Radiographic Quality Control   _____

    B. Quality Improvement   _____

    C. Regulations and Program Standards   _____

                                           Total =   100%

For the 3 <u>categories</u> within *Radiographic Quality Control,* indicate the percentage of test questions that you believe should be assigned to each category. The percentages should add to 100%

    A. Radiographic Quality Control

        1. Physical Principles   _____

        2. Collection and Analysis of QC Test Data   _____

        3. Test Instrumentation   _____

                                           Total =   100%

For the 4 <u>subcategories</u> within *Physical Principles,* indicate the percentage of test questions that you believe should be assigned to each category. The percentages should add to 100%.

    1. Physical Principles

        a) radiation production   _____

        b) x-ray beam characteristics   _____

        c) screen-film characteristics   _____

        d) film processing   _____

                                            Total =   100%

(questionnaire continues)

FIG. 9.3. First page of a questionnaire for obtaining holistic judgments for topic weights from SMEs.

questionnaire that asks SMEs to assign percentages to various domains and categories of the test plan (e.g., analogous to the questionnaire depicted in Figure 9.3).

Weights for Content-Based Test Specifications

We now turn to content-based test specifications. Because KSAs typically are not directly observable, there is ample opportunity for content-based test specifications to be influenced by the biases of those who develop them (Levine, Ash, & Bennett, 1980; Morgeson & Campion, 1997; Morgeson et al., 2004). The use of systematic procedures involving multiple groups of stakeholders can help to ensure that content-based test specifications are practice related, fair, and replicable. The development of content-based test specifications requires two sets of activities. First, SMEs need to identify and organize the KSAs required for practice. The procedures described below represent one of many possible systematic approaches; something like it has worked for us and colleagues in the past. Next, it is necessary to assign weights to sections of the test plan. We illustrate three very different procedures for assigning weights.

Identifying KSA Requirements

Cataloging the KSAs required for professional practice typically involves obtaining opinions from panels of SMEs. This usually requires that SMEs work independently and as a panel, and may require two or three meetings. The process described below assumes that one person is designated to coordinate the work of SMEs. We refer to that person as the *project director,* although it could be a committee chair, consultant, or other project staff.

1. **Acquire relevant documentation**. The project director locates reference materials such as task inventories, job descriptions, textbooks, review articles, results of other practice analyses, curricula, and course objectives. Many of these materials may have been used when developing the task inventory questionnaire.
2. **Obtain input from SMEs**. The project director can prepare a preliminary list of ten or fifteen topics covered in major textbooks, along with a task inventory. This list is then mailed to SMEs, who are assigned specific sections to work on. SMEs are asked to list the KSAs required to perform each task. The product might be a short outline for each of their major topics.
3. **SMEs develop first draft of outline**. SMEs should meet to review materials and prepare a working first draft. The first part of the meeting should focus on identifying major categories. Then, major sections can be assigned to individual SMEs for detailed development. If necessary, SMEs can continue their work at home and mail materials to the project director.
4. **Develop second draft**. SMEs should review and revise the outline at home or during a meeting. A number substantive and formatting and editorial issues may need to be addressed during the course of the meeting (e.g., level of specificity, redundancies, topics assigned to multiple sections). To ensure a single, coherent editorial style, it is best if a single individual serves as editor.
5. **Review topics for job relevance**. SMEs should verify that all topics appearing on the outline are practice related. This is best accomplished by reviewing the outline vis-à-vis the task inventory. One method for accomplishing this—the linkage exercise—is described later.
6. **Assign content weights**. After a complete and near-final draft has been developed, it is necessary to assign weights to indicate the number of test items allocated to each section of the test plan. Three methods for establishing weights are described below.
7. **Stakeholder review and finalization of draft**. It is always a good idea to mail the final draft to the professional community for review and comment. To help focus the review and increase the likelihood of response, it is helpful to ask specific questions related to content, organization, and topic weights. Comments can be incorporated into a final version as appropriate.

Although this general approach works well in practice, one limitation of relying exclusively on SME panels is that the test plan may reflect little more than conventional wisdom, and may include KSAs that really are not required for public protection, but appear because of tradition. A class of research methods known as knowledge elicitation represents a more rigorous approach to identifying KSA requirements. *Knowledge elicitation* is the process of explicating the domain-specific knowledge underlying the performance of specific tasks and the solutions to specific real-world problems (Cooke, 1999, p. 479). It has its roots in the fields of cognitive psychology and human engineering, and has been used in the design of expert systems, intelligent tutoring systems, and human–computer interfaces. Given these uses, it is not surprising that knowledge elicitation is a very detailed method for identifying KSAs requirements. Knowledge elicitation studies are not widely used in credentialing. However, the method can be helpful in instances for which there is uncertainty about certain aspects of practice (e.g., new technology, or a KSA topic that is being challenged). Methods for eliciting knowledge fall into four general categories: direct observation, interview, process tracing, and conceptual methods (Cooke, 1999). Most procedures require the researcher to observe or interact with experts, either concurrent with task performance or retrospectively, immediately following task performance. The think-aloud protocol, a variant of process tracing, is one of the more popular methods of knowledge elicitation. It has been used to study problem solving in medicine and other professions (vanSomeren, Barnard, & Sandberg, 1994).

Establishing Content Weights

Methods for weighting test specifications range from the informal and subjective to the detailed and mechanical. For example, weights are sometimes established by asking an SME panel to discuss the different sections of a test plan and eventually reach consensus about the number of test questions for each section. Although there is nothing inherently wrong with this approach, it runs the risk of being overly influenced by one or two individuals. We advocate a more systematic approach to obtaining SME judgments, and describe three approaches below. The first method is based on holistic judgments from panels of SMEs. The second method utilizes ratings of KSA importance obtained from a national sample of practitioners as the basis for weights. The final method statistically combines two types of data to obtain weights: (a) ratings from the task inventory questionnaire and (b) SME judgments regarding the strength of relationships between tasks from the questionnaire and KSAs appearing on the test plan.

Holistic Judgments From SME Panels. Judgmental weights require that a group of experts provide direct, holistic judgments regarding the number or percentage of test items per section. The more systematic approaches resemble the manner in which standard-setting judgments are obtained. Experts are first oriented to the exercise and are then asked to express their individual judgments. They receive feedback, provide additional judgments, and then reach consensus. Any judgmental method should encourage experts to consider the information available from practice analyses and related studies. Experts might also benefit from discussing ideas such as the complexity of the topics on the test plan, the difficulty of learning those topics, and so on. A distinguishing feature of the judgmental methods is that, although SMEs are asked to consider various types of practice-related information, they are not specifically told how to use that information in the assignment of weights (Hughes & Prien, 1989).

There are two basic approaches to eliciting judgmental weights from experts: top down or bottom up. In the *top-down approach*, a questionnaire is designed that leads SMEs through the categories of the test plan. SMEs first assign percentages to each of the major sections such that the percentages sum to 100%. Next, they assign percentages to categories at the second level of ordination. Again, it is convenient if the weights within each second level category sum to 100%. This process continues until weights have been assigned to the desired level of specificity. Figure 9.3 presents an excerpt from a questionnaire for obtaining weights for test specifications. Note how SMEs first assign percentages so each of the major sections, and later to each of the categories. Although this questionnaire could be completed as a group activity, we prefer that individuals complete it on their own and then discuss findings. The questionnaire depicted in Figure 9.3 contained three levels and required a total of 46 ratings. Such questionnaires can typically be completed in one half hour or less. A notable advantage, especially when compared to methods that use importance scales, is that the weights are constrained to sum to 100%. This controls the tendency to rate everything as very important (Landy, 1988).

After data are collected from SMEs, ratings can be summarized by tabulating the averages, highs and lows for each section and category. SMEs are given feedback and encouraged to discuss their ratings. SMEs can then either be asked to reach consensus on a final set of weights, or they can complete the weighting exercise again, and use those results to arrive at a final set of weights. At some point it is necessary to express category weights as values that correspond to a percentage of the total test rather than a percentage of the section. This is done by multiplying percentages for subordinate categories by the percentages for their corresponding parent category. If, for example, the percentage for section A is 55% and the percentage for category A.1 is 25%, the final weight for A.1 is .55 × .25 = .14, or 14% of the entire test.

One limitation of the top-down questionnaire is that the simplicity of assigning percentages may not provide SMEs with a realistic sense of the actual number of questions that will ultimately be assigned to each task or content domain. A related problem is that more specific topics at lower levels of ordination are not rated until later in the process. Therefore, topics at lower levels may end up with erroneous weights because they depend on the percentages assigned to their parent categories. Reviewing the results in terms of actual number of test questions provides an important reality check.

With the *bottom-up approach,* weights are assigned in reverse order by leading SMEs through the test plan one section at a time, starting with specific topics at lower levels of ordination (e.g., level 4). Weights for the major categories and sections (e.g., levels 1 and 2) are determined by summing over weights assigned to the lower levels. The bottom-up approach seems to work more effectively by asking SMEs to indicate actual numbers of test items rather than percentages. The bottom-up method is a bit tedious and can be expected to require more time and SME interaction than the top-down approach. The two methods complement one another, and it is often feasible to use both approaches. The limitation of both methods is that, although SMEs might be asked to consider results of a practice analysis when making their judgments, they are not instructed how to use that information.

KSA Ratings. Recall that one section of the RQM questionnaire consisted of 29 KSA statements (topics) rated on a 0 to 3 importance scale. The KSAs were taken from an early draft of the test plan. The list included topics such as philosophy and concepts of QI (Deming, CQI versus QC, etc.), physics of image production, and graphing techniques (bar charts, trend charts, control charts, etc.). Although most of these KSAs appeared on the final test plan at the second level of ordination, the KSA list was not a perfect representation of the test plan. Converting KSA importance ratings to weights is very similar to the process for converting task importance indices into task weights.

1. **Screen data and evaluate the rating scale**. Ratings should be screened for response bias and other threats to validity. For the RQM project, the survey included three KSAs (potential foils) that were expected to receive ratings at or near zero. The means for these three KSAs were 0.85, 1.23, and 1.25. Although the committee could formulate a rationale to explain mean ratings of 1.23 and 1.25, the KSA with a mean of 0.85, which

was "advanced statistics," was determined to have zero value on the importance scale. Therefore, all original ratings were adjusted by subtracting 0.85.[4]

2. **Revise the KSA list**. KSAs might be excluded if the ratings did not exceed a certain threshold or if the final test plan no longer includes that KSA. For RQM, five KSAs were dropped from the original list of 29, leaving 24.
3. **Calculate the average importance** (I_i). We obtained means for each KSA based on the scale adjusted for response bias. The means for the 24 KSAs ranged from 0.40 to 1.82 on the 0 to 3 scale, with an overall mean of 1.13. Recall that the scale was adjusted by subtracting 0.85 from all ratings.
4. **Obtain proportional weights**. The mean importance index for each KSA was transformed into a proportional weight, W_i, where $W_i = I_i/27.08$.
5. **Classify KSAs according to test plan**. This step was straightforward. The 24 KSAs were classified into the 14 level 2 content categories comprising the test plan. (*Note*: Given the general nature of the KSAs, it was not possible to assign them to level 3 categories.)
6. **Sum the weights within sections**. The weights indicate the degree of emphasis, or proportion of test items, to allocate to each category of the test plan, and will total 1.00 when summed over all 24 KSAs. The proportional weights can be converted to percentages for convenience. The final weights based on KSA ratings appear in Table 9.12 and are discussed later.

Task-by-Topic Linkages. The KSA ratings previously described are holistic in that they do not correspond to specific tasks. The purpose of a linkage exercise is to delineate the relationships between KSAs that appear on the test plan and the tasks that comprise the task inventory questionnaire. The linkage exercise serves at least three functions. One is to identify KSAs that are not practice related so that they can be deleted from the test plan. Another is to ensure that the list of KSAs is sufficiently comprehensive (e.g., that at least one KSA is specified for each relevant task). An additional use, as described below, is to combine linkage information with task ratings to produce weights for test specifications. The use of linkage data in this manner is based on the rationale that the weight for a content category should be a function of the number of tasks linked to that category and the importance of the tasks associated with that category (Raymond, 1996).

Various forms of the linkage activity have been described in published reports (Fleishman & Quaintance, 1984; Hughes & Prien, 1989; Landy, 1988; Slaughter & Newman, 1999; Spray & Chai, 2000; Wang, Schnipke, & Witt, 2005). Figure 9.4 presents a conceptual diagram of the process. SMEs are asked to make a judgment about the relationship between each KSA and task. The judgments may be dichotomous (yes, no) or may consist of ratings on a scale that corresponds to the strength or intensity of the relationship. A significant problem with the linkage activity is that it becomes unmanageable if there are many tasks and KSAs. The RQM task inventory consisted of 85 tasks, and the test plan consisted of about 120 separate topics, which is relatively short as far as test specifications go. The linkage exercise would require over 10,000 judgments. To make the linkage activity more manageable, tasks and KSAs can be classified into broader categories (Landy, 1988). This seems to work well so long as the two lists are not condensed to only a few categories. Another strategy is to double the number of SMEs who participate and then have each SME complete only half the matrix. The nature of the rating task depends, in part, on whether the judgments are dichotomous or polytomous.

---

[4]It is important to note that this linear transformation has a nontrivial impact on the final weights—it actually increased the variability of the weights. Ordinal scales can be affected by linear transformations weights when such scales are later subjected multiplication and division. See Spray and Huang (2000) for additional discussion.

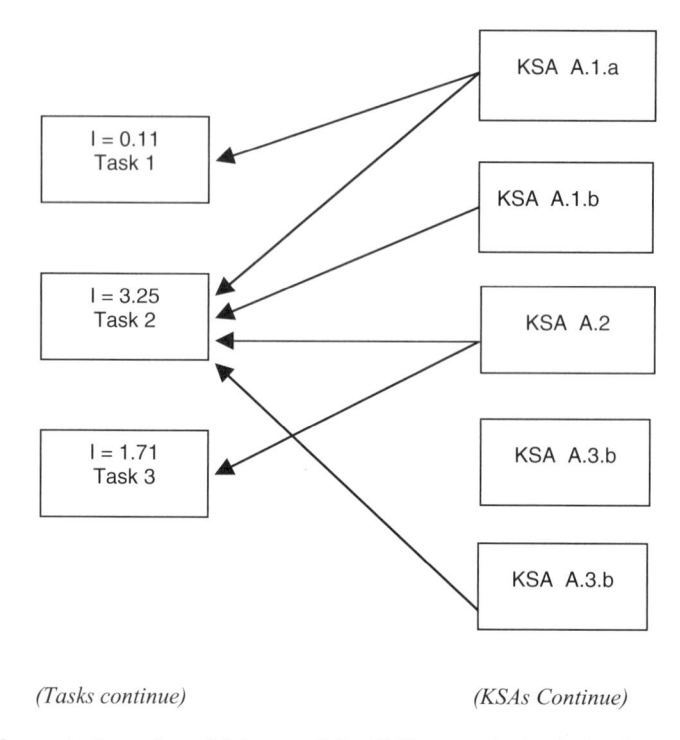

```
                                          ┌─────────────┐
                                          │  KSA A.1.a  │
                                          └─────────────┘
    ┌──────────┐
    │ I = 0.11 │
    │  Task 1  │                          ┌─────────────┐
    └──────────┘                          │  KSA A.1.b  │
                                          └─────────────┘

    ┌──────────┐
    │ I = 3.25 │
    │  Task 2  │                          ┌─────────────┐
    └──────────┘                          │   KSA A.2   │
                                          └─────────────┘

    ┌──────────┐
    │ I = 1.71 │                          ┌─────────────┐
    │  Task 3  │                          │  KSA A.3.b  │
    └──────────┘                          └─────────────┘


                                          ┌─────────────┐
                                          │  KSA A.3.b  │
                                          └─────────────┘
```

(Tasks continue)   *(KSAs Continue)*

FIG. 9.4. Conceptual overview of linkage activity. SMEs are asked to judge the extent to which each KSAs is required to successfully perform each task. Importance values appear above the task number.

If the exercise is structured to obtain polytomous ratings, SMEs can be asked to consider questions such as: How important is knowledge of topic X for performing task Y? To what extent is performance of task Y influenced by knowledge of topic X? If a student has not mastered topic X, how likely are they to demonstrate inadequate performance on task Y? Does extensive knowledge of topic X enhance performance of task Y? What depth of knowledge is required of topic X in order to be proficient at task Y?

The following describes the process used to elicit linkage judgments for the RQM project, and explains methods for calculating topic weights from linkage judgments and task weights. The discussion assumes that an importance index for each task has been calculated and that a topic outline has already been developed.

1. **Plan the exercise**. We structured the rating task so that SMEs would not become fatigued. For the present study, we classified 85 tasks into 14 task domains based on cluster analysis and SME consensus. The activity was further limited to 34 KSAs by including just those from the first three levels of the outline (e.g., A.1.a). Therefore, the linkage activity required 476 judgments.
2. **Develop rating scales**. For the present study, we used a 0 to 3 point scale that asked SMEs to indicate the depth of knowledge required of a particular topic to successfully perform the tasks within each of the 14 task domains. As part of their orientation, SMEs discussed questions similar to those listed above.
3. **Obtain linkage judgments**. The linkage exercise was presented to SMEs as a matrix consisting of 14 columns of task domains and 34 rows of KSAs. SMEs were asked to start with a task domain and assign linkage ratings for each of 34 KSAs before proceeding to the next task domain. For example, assume an SME is reviewing the task

9. CONTENT OF CREDENTIALING EXAMINATIONS

TABLE 9.9
Mean Linkage Ratings (0 to 3 scale) Provided by SMEs to a Segment of the Task-by-Topic Linkage Matrix

	QI Charting Tools (3.04)	QI Admin (10.50)	Radiographic QC (19.04)	Film Processing (38.00)	Others
A. Radiography QC					
1. Physical principles					
a) Radiation production	0	0.7	2.5	0.2	...
b) X-ray beam characteristics	0	0.8	2.8	0.3	...
c) Screen–film characteristics	0	0.9	1.6	1.5	...
d) Film processing	0	1.0	1.5	3.0	...

Note: Table extends for 28 content (e.g., A.1.a) categories and 14 task domains. Rows correspond to content categories (through level 3), and columns correspond to 14 task domains. The value in parentheses under the column label is the sum of the importance values over the tasks in that domain.

Abbreviations: QC, quality control; QI, quality improvement.

domain *Film Processing* (fourth column in Table 9.9). When the SME encounters the row corresponding to radiation production (topic A.1.a), he or she might reason that only a little knowledge of x-ray production is required to perform tasks related to film processing, which might lead the SME to assign a rating of 1 to that cell. To be sure, this type of rating activity could be structured differently. It may be helpful to present each task-by-KSA combination one at a time in an effort to encourage independence among ratings. Spray and Chai (2000) discussed the use of a computer program to present and record linkage judgments.

4. **Summarize linkage judgments**. The mean rating for each cell was obtained, although other summary values could have been used (e.g., median, trimmed mean). For dichotomous judgments, the proportion of SMEs indicating the presence of a link might be the summary value. Table 9.9 shows the mean ratings for a portion of the matrix.

5. **Calculate products for each cell and row sum**. We multiplied the summary value (e.g., mean linkage rating) by the importance index for that task. Because we were working with task domains consisting of many individual tasks, we multiplied the mean linkage rating by the sum of the importance indices for that task domain. Each row was summed, with the sum being interpreted as an index of the overall importance of each KSA. Table 9.10 presents sample results for these operations.

6. **Convert row sums to percentages**. Each row sum was converted to a proportion by dividing the sums by the total taken over all rows. For the present example, each row sum in Table 9.10 was divided by 8440.70, which is the sum over all 28 KSA categories. For convenience, proportions were multiplied by 100. The results appear in Table 9.11.

Although these weights could be accepted as final, we advocate that they be subject to review and revision by an SME panel and other stakeholders. One reason is that the linkage method is sensitive to, and may be adversely affected by, factors such as tasks written at varying levels of specificity, overlapping KSAs, and response bias in linkage judgments (Raymond, 1996). A holistic evaluation of the weights may identify results that do not make sense. A second reason is that there are many ways to structure the linkage activity and numerous methods for

TABLE 9.10
Product of the Mean Linkage Rating and the Column Importance Index (from Table 9.9) for a Segment of the Linkage Matrix

	QI Charting Tools	QI Admin	Radiographic QC	Film Processing		Sum
A. Radiography QC						
1. Physical principles						
a) Radiation production	0.0	7.4	47.6	7.6	...	233.59
b) X-ray beam characteristics	0.0	8.4	53.3	11.4	...	240.47
c) Screen-film characteristics	0.0	9.5	30.5	57.0	...	295.92
d) Film processing	0.0	10.5	28.6	114.0	...	372.10

Sum over all 14 task domains and 28 content categories = 8440.70

Abbreviations: QC, quality control; QI, quality improvement.

TABLE 9.11
Topic Weights for a Segment of the Test Plan Value[a]

	Level 3 Weight (%)	Level 2 Weight (%)
A. Radiography QC		
1. Physical principles		13.5
a) Radiation production	2.8	
b) X-ray beam characteristics	2.8	
c) Screen–film characteristics	3.5	
d) Film processing	4.4	

Table extends for 28 Level 3 content categories.

[a] Obtained from values in Table 9.10 (each row sum divided by the overall sum of 8440.70).
Abbreviations: QC, quality control.

tabulating the data (Spray & Chai, 2000; Wang et al., 2005). Each variation gives different results, with no particular method being viewed as correct.

Summary of Weighting Methods

We presented four methods for obtaining weights for test specifications. The first method can be used for process-based test specifications; the remaining methods are intended for content-based test specifications. Obtaining weights for process-based specifications is straightforward. It requires combining ratings from two or more scales to create an index of overall importance and then summing the weights within the categories of the test plan. Perhaps the most challenging activity is determining the framework for categorizing tasks. The results of using the multiplicative model to derive weights for test specifications were presented in Table 9.8. As noted, process-based specifications are optimal for performance assessment. For example, the

TABLE 9.12
Weights (in percentages) for RQM Test Plan Obtained from Three Content-Based Methods[a]

	Weighting Method		
	KSA Ratings	Top-Down Survey	Linkage Activity
A. Radiographic QC	52	55	56
1. Physical principles	19	14	14
2. Collection and analysis of QC test data	28	27	19
3. Test instrumentation	5	14	24
B. QI	33	30	17
1. Concepts and principles of QI	15	12	7
2. Collection and analysis of QI data	18	18	10
C. Regulations and program standards	15	15	27
1. NCRP recommendations	—	7	10
2. ACR standards for mammography	—	8	17

[a]*Note:* Although weights for just the first two levels are presented here, they were also obtained for level three.

Abbreviations: ACR, American College of Radiology; NCRP, National Council on Radiation Protection and Measurements; QC, quality control; QI, quality improvement.

specifications in Table 9.8 would be an excellent resource for guiding the development of an instrument to rate clinical performance. However, that same test plan would have limited utility for written assessments.

The three methods for obtaining content-based weights differed in terms of the source of the judgments, the type of judgments obtained, and the specificity of those judgments. The top-down KSA questionnaire required that SMEs provide holistic ratings on each section and subcategory of the test specifications (Figure 9.3). Given that ratings within sections and subcategories are constrained to sum to 100%, this method may help to control positive response bias and ceiling effects. The second method for obtaining weights for content-based specifications relied on KSA ratings from the sample of practitioners who completed the RQM practice analysis questionnaire. The third method was organized around an exercise that required SMEs to link topics from the test specifications to specific job responsibilities. Weights were based on a combination of task ratings from the practitioners who completed the RQM questionnaire and the linkage judgments from a panel of SMEs.

Table 9.12 compares the results of the three weighting methods for content-based test specifications. We restrict the table to just the first two levels of the test plan because one of the methods (KSA ratings from RQM questionnaire) did not include three levels of ordination. As indicated in the first two columns of Table 9.12, the two methods based on direct judgments of KSAs give similar results for this example, particularly for the three major sections. Meanwhile, the linkage activity provided notably different results for sections B and C. We believe the smaller weight for category B and larger weight for category C are due, in part, to methodological artifacts.

Which method is to be preferred? Obtaining KSA ratings from practice analysis questionnaires is a convenient way to collect data from many practitioners. However, the results must be interpreted in light of the numerous limitations of that method of data collection (e.g., bias, ambiguous KSAs). Therefore, weights based on KSA ratings might be regarded as secondary to other sources. The holistic ratings obtained from the top-down survey are easy to implement and seem to produce meaningful results. Their effectiveness depends on the procedures being carried out in a systematic manner, as well as the inclusion of SMEs who represent multiple stakeholder groups. In addition, it is important to build a final check into the procedures to assure that each KSA included in the test specifications is truly required for safe and effective practice. It is all too easy to include topics that seem relevant to the profession, but may be difficult to justify in terms of competent task performance. That brings us to the linkage method. It is clearly the most detailed, systematic, and costly of the procedures for establishing weights. Its primary advantage is that it requires SMEs to carefully consider each KSA in light of specific tasks known to be required for the job. In other words, it provides the reality check missing from the other methods. However, given the potential limitations noted in other studies (Raymond, 1996) and summarized above, this method warrants some degree of skepticism. The real benefit of the linkage exercise may be in the process, not the product. As such, it may be a useful procedure to use in addition to, or even before, the top-down and bottom-up holistic methods. Although all of the methods described here are informative and helpful, no single method is deserving of our unquestioning trust. The use of multiple methods and multiple groups of stakeholders still seems to be the prudent approach to developing test specifications.

ACKNOWLEDGMENTS

We are grateful to the ARRT for supporting work on this chapter. We would also like to thank the editors, as well as Michael Kane, Michael Rosenfeld, and Judy Spray for their many helpful comments. The responsibility for any oversights or overstatements remains with us.

REFERENCES

American Board of Physical Medicine and Rehabilitation. (1998, December). The SCI medicine exam outline: A closer look. In *Diplomate news*. Rochester, MN: Author.

American Educational Research Association (AERA), American Psychological Association (APA), & National Council on Measurement in Education (NCME). (1999). *Standards for educational and psychological testing*. Washington DC: American Educational Research Association.

Andrich, D. (1978). A rating formulation of ordered response categories. *Psychometrika, 43*, 561–573.

Bloom, B. S. (Ed.). (1956). *Taxonomy of educational objectives, handbook 1: The cognitive domain*. New York: McKay.

Bourque, L. B., & Fielder, E. P. (2003). *How to conduct self-administered and mail-out questionnaires* (2nd ed.). Newbury Park, CA: Sage.

Cizek, G. J., Webb, L. C., & Kalohn, J. C. (1995). The use of cognitive taxonomies in licensure and certification test development: Reasonable or customary? *Evaluation and the Health Professions, 18*, 77–91.

Colliver, J. A., Markwell, S. J. Vu, N. V., & Barrows, H. S. (1990). Case specificity of standardized patient examinations. *Evaluation and the Health Professions, 13*, 252–261.

Colton, D. A., Kane, M. T., Kingsbury, C., & Estes, C. A. (1991). A strategy for examining the validity of job analysis data. *Journal of Educational Measurement, 28*, 283–294.

Cook, L. L. & Petersen, N. S. (1987). Problems related to the use of conventional and item response theory methods of equating in less than optimal circumstances. *Applied Psychological Measurement, 11*, 225–244.

Cooke, N. J. (1999). Knowledge elicitation. In F. T. Durso, R. S. Nickerson, R. W. Schvaneveldt, S. F. Dumais, & M. T. H. Chi (Eds.), *Handbook of applied cognition* (pp. 479–509). New York: John Wiley & Sons.

D'Costa, A. (1986). The validity of credentialing examinations. *Evaluation and the Health Professions, 9*, 137–169.

Dawes, R. M. & Corrigan, B. (1974). Linear models in decision making. *Psychological Bulletin, 81*, 95–106.

Desimone, L. A., & LeFloch, K. C. (2004). Are we asking the right questions? Using cognitive interviews to improve surveys in education research. *Educational Evaluation and Policy Analysis, 26*, 1–22.

Dillman, D. A. (2000). *Mail and Internet surveys: The tailored design method.* New York: John Wiley & Sons.

Elstein, A. S., Shulman, L. S., & Sprafka, S. A. (1978). *Medical problem solving: an analysis of clinical reasoning.* Cambridge, MA: Harvard University Press.

Equal Employment Opportunity Commission, Civil Service Commission, Department of Labor, & Department of Justice. (1978). Adoption by four agencies of uniform guidelines of employee selection procedures. *Federal Register, 43*(166), 38290–38315.

Fink, A. (2003). *How to sample in questionnaires* (2nd ed.). Newbury Park, CA: Sage.

Flanagan, J. C. (1954). The critical incident technique. *Psychological Bulletin, 51,* 327–358.

Fleishman, E. A., & Quaintance, M. K. (1984). *Taxonomies of human performance: The description of human tasks.* New York: Academic Press.

Friedman, L. (1990). Degree of redundancy between time, importance and frequency task ratings. *Journal of Applied Psychology, 75,* 748–752.

Gael, S. (1983). *Job analysis: A guide to assessing work activities.* San Francisco: Jossey-Bass.

Goodman, D. P., & Hambleton, R. K. (2004). Student test score reports and interpretive guides: a review of current practices and suggestions for future research. *Applied Measurement in Education, 17,* 145–220.

Haladyna, T. M., & Kramer, G. A. (2004). The validity of subscores for a credentialing test. *Evaluation and the Health Professions, 27,* 349–368.

Hambleton, R. K. (1984). Validating the test scores. In R. A. Berk (Ed.), *A guide to criterion-referenced test construction.* Baltimore, MD: The Johns Hopkins University Press.

Harvey, R. J. (1991). Job analysis. In M. Dunnette & L. Hough (Eds.), *Handbook of industrial and organizational psychology* (Vol. 2, 2nd ed., pp. 71–163). Palo Alto, CA: Consulting Psychologists Press.

Harvey, R. J., Friedman, L., Hakel, M. D., & Cornelius, E. T. (1988). Dimensionality of the Job Element Inventory (JEI), a simplified worker-oriented job analysis questionnaire. *Journal of Applied Psychology, 73,* 639–646.

Harvey, R. J., & Wilson, M. A. (2000). Yes Virginia, there really is an objective reality in job analysis. *Organizational Behavior and Human Performance, 21,* 829–854.

Hughes, G. L., & Prien, E. P. (1989). Evaluation of task and job skill linkage judgments used to develop test specifications. *Personnel Psychology, 42,* 283–292.

Jacobs, A. M., Fivars, G., Edwards, D. S., & Fitzpatrick, R. (1978). *Critical requirements for safe/effective nursing practice.* Washington, DC: American Nurses' Association.

Joseph, M. J., & Taranath, S. N. (1999, April). *Obtaining task measures from job analysis data.* Paper presented at the annual meeting of the National Council on Measurement in Education, Montreal, Canada.

Kane, M. T. (1982). The validity of licensure examinations. *American Psychologist, 37,* 911–918.

Kane, M. T. (1997). Model-based practice analysis and test specifications. *Applied Measurement in Education, 10,* 5–18.

Kane, M. T., Kingsbury, C., Colton, D., & Estes, C. (1986). *A study of nursing practice and role delineation and job analysis of entry-level performance of registered nurses.* Chicago: National Council of State Boards of Nursing.

Kane, M. T., Kingsbury, C., Colton, D., & Estes, C. (1989). Combining data on criticality and frequency in developing plans for licensure and certification examinations. *Journal of Educational Measurement, 26,* 17–27.

Klein, L. W., & Jarjoura, D. (1985). The importance of content representation for common-item equating with nonrandom groups. *Journal of Educational Measurement, 22,* 197–206.

Knapp, J., & Knapp, L. (1995). Practice analysis: Building the foundation for validity. In J. C. Impara (Ed.), *Licensure testing: Purposes, procedures, and practices* (pp. 93–116). Lincoln, NE: Buros Institute of Mental Measurements.

Kolen, M. J., & Brennan, R. L. (1995). *Test equating. Methods and practices.* New York: Springer-Verlag.

LaDuca, A. (1980). The structure of competence in the health professions. *Evaluation and the Health Professions, 3,* 253–288.

LaDuca, A. (1994). Validation of professional licensure examinations: Professions theory, test design, and construct validity. *Evaluation and the Health Professions, 17,* 178–197.

LaDuca, A., Downing, S., & Henzel, T. (1995). Test development: Systematic item writing and test construction. In J. C. Impara (Ed.), *Licensure testing: Purposes, procedures, and practices* (pp. 117–148). Lincoln, NE: Buros Institute of Mental Measurements.

LaDuca, A., Taylor, D. D., & Hill, I. K. (1984). The design of a new physician licensure examination. *Evaluation and the Health Professions, 7,* 115–140.

Landy, F. J. (1988). Selection procedure development and usage. In S. Gael (Ed.) *The job analysis handbook for business, industry, and government* (Vols. I and II, pp. 271–287). New York: John Wiley & Sons.

Levine, E. L., Ash, R. A., & Bennett, N. (1980). Exploratory comparative study of four job analysis methods. *Journal of Applied Psychology, 65,* 524–535.

Levine, H. G., McGuire, C., Miller, G. E., & Larson, C. (1968). *The orthopaedic training study: Final report.* Chicago: University of Illinois, Center for the Study of Medical Education.

McCormick, E. J. (1976). Job and task analysis. In M. D. Dunnette (Ed.), *Handbook of industrial and organizational psychology* (pp. 651–696). Chicago: Rand McNally.

McCormick, E. J., Jeanneret, P. R., & Mecham, R. C. (1972). A study of job characteristics and job dimensions as based on the Position Analysis Questionnaire. *Journal of Applied Psychology, 56,* 347–368.

McShane, F., & Fagerlund, K. A. (2004). A report on the council on certification of nurse anesthetists 2001 professional practice analysis. *Journal of the American Association of Nurse Anesthetists, 72,* 31–52.

Messick, S. (1989). Validity. In R. L. Linn (Ed.), *Educational measurement* (3rd ed., pp. 13–103). New York: American Council on Education MacMillan.

Miller, G. E. (1968). The orthopaedic training study. *Journal of the American Medical Association, 206,* 601–606.

Millman, J., & Greene, J. (1989). The specification and development of tests of achievement and ability. In R. L. Linn (Ed.) *Educational measurement* (3rd ed. pp. 335–366). New York: American Council on Education & MacMillan.

Morgeson, F. P., & Campion, M. A. (1997). Social and cognitive sources of potential inaccuracy in job analysis. *Journal of Applied Psychology, 82,* 627–655.

Morgeson, F. P., Delaney-Klinger, K. D, Mayfield, M. S., Ferrara, P., & Campion, M. A. (2004). Self-presentation processes in job analysis: A field experiment investigating inflation in abilities, tasks and competencies. *Journal of Applied Psychology, 89,* 674–686.

National Conference of Examiners for Engineering and Surveying. (1999a). *Fundamentals of engineering (FE) examinations: Morning session specifications.* Clemson, SC: Author.

National Conference of Examiners for Engineering and Surveying. (1999b). *PE examination formats: Principles and practice of engineering examinations.* Clemson, SC: Author.

National Council of Architectural Registration Boards. (2002). *ARE guidelines.* Washington, DC: Author.

Newman, L. S., Slaughter, R. C., & Taranath, S. N. (1999, April). *The selection and use of rating scales in task surveys: A review of current job analysis practice.* Paper presented at the annual meeting of the National Council on Measurement in Education, Montreal, Canada.

Osterlind, S. J. (1998). *Constructing test items: Multiple choice, constructed response, performance, and other formats.* Boston, MA: Klewer Academic Publishers.

Perkins, D. N., & Salomon, G. (1989). Are cognitive skills context-bound? *Educational Researcher, 18*(1), 16–25.

Popham, W. J. (1984). Specifying the domain of content or behaviors. In R. A. Berk (Ed.), *A guide to criterion-referenced test construction,* Baltimore, MD: The Johns Hopkins University Press.

Prekeges, J. L., Sawyer, N. S., & Wells, P. C. (1999). Components of preparedness for nuclear medicine technologists. *Journal of Nuclear Medicine Technology, 27,* 237–245.

Rakel, R. (1979). Defining competence in specialty practice: The need for relevance. In *Definitions of competence in specialties of medicine, conference proceedings.* Chicago: American Board of Medical Specialties.

Raymond, M. R. (1996). Establishing weights for test plans for licensure and certification examinations. *Applied Measurement in Education, 9,* 237–256.

Raymond, M. R. (2001). Job analysis and the specification of content for licensure and certification examinations. *Applied Measurement in Education, 14,* 369–415.

Raymond, M. R. (2002a). A practical guide to practice analysis for credentialing examinations. *Educational Measurement: Issues & Practice, 21*(3), 25–37.

Raymond, M. R. (2002b, April). *The influence of rating scale format on rater errors in practice analysis surveys.* Paper presented at the annual meeting of the American Educational Research Association, New Orleans, LA.

Raymond, M. R. (2005). An NCME instructional module on Developing and administering practice analysis questionnaires . *Educational Measurement: Issues and Practice, 24*(2), 29–42.

Raymond, M. R. & Williams, C. O. (2004) Empirically mapping the subspecialties of cardiovascular-interventional technology. *Journal of Allied Health, 33,* 95–103.

Rosenfeld, M., Shimberg, B., & Thornton, R. F. (1983). *Job analysis of licensed psychologists in the United States and Canada.* Princeton, NJ: Educational Testing Service.

Sanchez, J. I., & Fraser, S. L. (1992). On the choice of scales for task analysis. *Journal of Applied Psychology, 77,* 545–553.

Sanchez, J. I. & Levine, E. L. (1989). Determining important tasks within jobs: A policy-capturing approach. *Journal of Applied Psychology, 74,* 336–342.

Schaefer, L., Raymond, M. R., & White A. S. (1992). A comparison of two methods for structuring performance domains. *Applied Measurement in Education, 5,* 321–335.

Seddon, G. M. (1978). The properties of Bloom's taxonomy of educational objectives for the cognitive domain. *Review of Educational Research, 48,* 302–323.

Shimberg, B. (1981). Testing for licensure and certification. *American Psychologist, 36,* 1138–1146.

Slaughter, R. C., & Newman, L. S. (1999, April). *Developing test specifications from job analysis data.* Paper presented at the annual meeting of the National Council on Measurement in Education, Montreal, Canada.

Smith, I. L., & Hambleton, R. K. (1990). Content validity studies of licensing examinations. *Educational Measurement: Issues and Practice, 9*(4), 7–10.

Spray, J. A. & Chai, S (2000). *PDD job analysis seminar* (training manual). Iowa City, IA: ACT, Inc.

Spray, J. A. & Huang, C. (2000). Obtaining test blueprint weights from job analysis surveys. *Journal of Educational Measurement, 37,* 187–201.

Stocking, M. L., Swanson, L., & Pearlman, M. (1993). Application of item selection method to real data. *Applied Psychological Measurement, 17,* 167–176.

vanSomeren, M. W., Barnard, Y. F., & Sandberg, J. A. C. (1994) *The think aloud method: A practical guide to modeling cognitive processes.* London: Academic Press.

Wang, N. Schnike, D., & Witt, E. A. (2005). Use of knowledge, skill and ability statements in developing licensure and certification examinations. *Educational Measurement: Issues and Practice, 24*(1), 15–22.

Wightman, L. (1998). Practical issues in computerized test assembly. *Applied Psychological Measurement, 22,* 292–302.

10

Standard Setting

Gregory J. Cizek
University of North Carolina–Chapel Hill

This chapter describes one of the most visible and critical elements in the test development process: the setting of performance standards (i.e., cut scores). The first portion of the chapter presents background on the concept and theory of standard setting. The second section presents a brief description of the contexts in which standard setting occurs. The third section provides and overview of common, foundational elements that are part of nearly all standard setting procedures. The fourth, and most extensive, section comprises detailed treatment of several commonly-used standard setting procedures.

Standard setting refers to the process of establishing cut scores on examinations. In some arenas—licensure and certification testing programs, for example—only a single cut score may be required. In these cases, standard setting helps to create categories such as pass/fail, allow/deny a license, or award/withhold a credential.

In other contexts, a standard-setting procedure may be used to create more than two categories. For example, in elementary and secondary education, the categories of performance labeled *Basic, Proficient,* and *Advanced* are commonly used to connote differing degrees of attainment vis à vis a set of content standards or objectives.

Standard setting is arguably one of the most important tasks in the test development, administration, and reporting process. Although often mistakenly incorporated very late in the process, standard setting is best considered early enough to align with the identified purpose of the test, the selected test item or task formats, and when there is ample opportunity to identify relevant sources of evidence bearing on the validity of the categorical assignments and to gather and analyze that evidence.

An abundance of information sources are available to those seeking information on standard setting.[1] Much of this information, however, is found in scholarly or technical journals and books, and tends to present the topic in a more academic fashion. By contrast, this chapter is intended to provide concrete, practical information to those who oversee or conduct standard

---
[1]This chapter draws on several of those sources, including Cizek (1993, 1996a, 1996b, 2001c) and Cizek, Bunch, and Koons (2004).

setting. Although necessary theoretical foundations are included at relevant junctures, the focus is clearly on the mechanics of standard setting.

The chapter is organized into five parts. The first section presents additional information on the concept and theory of standard setting. The second section provides a more extensive introduction to the contexts of standard setting. The third section discusses common, foundational elements that are part of nearly all standard setting procedures. The fourth (and most extensive) section comprises detailed treatment of several commonly used standard-setting procedures. The chapter ends with a brief conclusions section.

WHAT IS STANDARD SETTING?

At the risk of sounding fatuous, *standard setting* can be defined as the process by which a standard or cut score is established. The simplicity of that definition, however, belies the complex nature of standard setting. For example, it is common—although inaccurate—to say that a panel that meets for the purpose of engaging in standard setting *sets* a standard(s). In fact, such panels derive their legitimacy from the entities that authorize them—namely, professional associations, academies, boards of education, state agencies, and so on. It is these entities that solely possess the responsibility for setting standards. Thus, it is more accurate to refer to the process of standard setting as one of "standard recommending" in that the panels engaging in a process only provide reasoned guidance to those actually responsible for the act of setting standards, or of approving, rejecting, adjusting, or implementing any cut scores.[2]

One definition of standard setting has been suggested by Cizek (1993). According to this definition, *standard setting* "is the proper following of a prescribed, rational system of rules or procedures resulting in the assignment of a number to differentiate between two or more states or degrees of performance" (p. 100). The definition highlights the procedural aspect of standard setting and draws on the legal framework of due process and traditional definitions of measurement.[3]

Kane has provided another definition of standard setting that highlights the conceptual nature of the endeavor. According to Kane, "It is useful to draw a distinction between the *passing score*, defined as a point on the score scale, and the *performance standard*, defined as the minimally adequate level of performance for some purpose.... The performance standard is the conceptual version of the desired level of competence, and the passing score is the operational version" (1994, p. 426, emphasis in original).

Two observations are warranted related to Kane's (1994) notions about standard setting. First, despite Kane's preference, *performance standard* is routinely used as a synonym for *cut score, achievement level,* or *passing score*. Throughout this chapter, those terms are used interchangeably. Second, the concept of *content standards* has recently been introduced. Content standards are not *standards* in the sense that the term is used elsewhere in this chapter. Rather,

---

[2]It seems somewhat cumbersome and out of touch with current usage of the phrase *standard setting* to insist that the replacement *standard recommending* be used. Therefore, in the balance of this chapter, the more common usage is employed.

[3]It should be noted that this definition addresses only one aspect of the legal theory known as due process. According to the legal theory, important decisions about a person's life, liberty, or property must involve due process—that is, a systematic, open process, stated in advance, and applied uniformly. The theory further divides the concept of due process into procedural due process and substantive due process. Whereas procedural due process provides guidance regarding what elements of a procedure are necessary, substantive due process characterizes the result of the procedure. The notion of substantive due process demands that the procedure lead to a decision that is fundamentally fair. Whereas Cizek's (1993) definition clearly sets forth a procedural conception of standard setting, it fails to address the result of standard setting. This aspect of fundamental fairness is similar to what has been called the "consequential basis of test use" (Messick, 1989, p. 84).

content standards describes the set of outcomes, objectives, or specific instructional goals that form the domain from which a test is constructed.

Finally, any explication of what standard setting is must also acknowledge what it is not; namely, that the work of standard setting is not a search for a knowable boundary that exists *a priori* between categories, with the task of standard-setting participants[4] being simply to discover it. Such a view may have prevailed in the minds of early standard-setting theorists. However, modern standard-setting theory recognizes that standard-setting procedures simply enable participants to bring to bear their judgments in such a way as to translate the policy positions of authorizing entities into locations on a score scale. It is these translations that define the categories.

These translations are seldom, if ever, purely statistical, psychometric, impartial, apolitical, or ideologically neutral activities. How could they be? In education contexts, social, political, and economic forces cannot help but impinge on the standard-setting process when participants decide what level of performance on a mathematics test should be required to earn a high school diploma. In licensure contexts, standard-setting participants cannot help but consider the relative cost to public health and safety posed by awarding a license to an examinee who may not truly have the requisite knowledge or skill, and of denying a license—perhaps even a livelihood—to an examinee who is truly competent.

Standard setting is rightly seen as a statistical and procedural necessity, that is unavoidably conducted in contexts that challenge any claims to the pure objectivity of the process. As noted in the *Standards for Educational and Psychological Testing,* standard setting "embod[ies] value judgments as well as technical and empirical considerations" (American Educational Research Association [AERA], American Psychological Association [APA], & National Council on Measurement in Education [NCME], 1999, p. 54). And, as Cizek (2001b) has observed: "Standard setting is perhaps the branch of psychometrics that blends more artistic, political, and cultural ingredients into the mix of its products than any other" (p. 5).

STANDARD SETTING: AN ENDURING NEED

Before embarking on any standard setting enterprise, it is worthwhile to ask the fundamental question: "What is the purpose of setting these standards?" The question may be answered reflexively in cases such as when a legislative or regulatory action has been taken that mandates an examination program and corresponding cut scores. A deeper analysis suggests, however, that there is a need for standard setting—even in the absence of guiding legislation or regulations—simply because decisions must be made. As stated elsewhere:

> There is simply no way to escape making decisions.... These decisions, by definition, create categories. If, for example, some students graduate from high school and others do not, a categorical decision has been made, even if a graduation test was not used. (The decisions were, presumably, made on *some* basis.) High school music teachers make decisions such as who should be first chair for the clarinets. College faculties make decisions to tenure (or not) their colleagues. We embrace decision making regarding who should be licensed to practice medicine. All of these kinds of decisions are unavoidable; each should be based on sound information; and the information should be combined in some deliberate, considered, defensible manner. (Cizek, 2001a, p. 21)

To say that standard setting is a necessary part of decision making sidesteps the objection that decisions could still be made without formal tests, without standard setting, and so on.

---

[4]Some sources refer to participants in standard-setting procedures *as judges*. Throughout this chapter, *participants* is used and can be considered as synonymous with *judges*.

Indeed, the *Standards for Educational and Psychological Testing* state that "a decision or characterization that will have a major impact on a student should not be made on the basis of a single test score" (AERA, APA, & NCME, 1999, p. 146).

To some extent, it is a truism that no decision is ever really made based solely on a single test score. For example, a single measure such as the SAT for college admissions is used with other criteria (e.g., high school graduation, grade point average [GPA], and so on). Candidates for a credential in a medical specialty must also provide evidence of appropriate training. Exceptional performance on a high school graduation test is of no avail if the student has not accumulated the requisite credit hours, GPA, and met other requirements. Although clearly not the sole criterion, it is certain that information yielded by tests plays an important part in decisions as diverse as placement in a remedial or gifted program, selection or promotion of employees, scholarship awards, licensure to practice in a profession, and certification or recertification in a specialized field.

The test component in categorical decision making such as pass/fail or license/deny license decision adds an independent, objective, and rigorous piece of evidence to the process. This is likely because the information provided by tests is of knowable quality—and often of higher quality than other sources of information. Tests can—and should—be subjected to accepted standards of analysis that reveal the worth of the information they yield. According to the *Standards for Educational and Psychological Testing*, "the proper use of tests can result in wiser decisions about individuals and programs than would be the case without their use and also can provide a route to broader and more equitable access to education and employment" (AERA, APA, & NCME, 1999, p. 1). In the end, cut scores are the mechanism that results in category formation on tests. Thus, the importance of deriving defensible cut scores and their relevance to sound decision making seem obvious.

STANDARD-SETTING STANDARDS

In addition to fundamental clarity about the purpose for setting standards, a critical step in planning for a standard setting activity is to become familiar with professionally recommended quality control steps that should be built into the process. A number of sources provide a compilation of guidelines related the conduct of standard setting. Two such sources are Cizek (1996b) and Hambleton (1998).

Another authoritative source of guidance related to standard setting is the *Standards for Educational and Psychological Testing* (AERA, APA, & NCME, 1999). This document represents the joint effort of the three sponsoring professional associations,[5] whose missions include the advancement of sound testing practice. The latest edition is the sixth version of test standards documents that originated with the *Technical Recommendations for Psychological and Diagnostic Techniques* published by the APA in 1954.

As Linn (chap. 2, this volume) describes, the *Standards* provide guidance on a wide range of test-related activities. However, they give specific attention to the process of standard setting. According to the *Standards*:

> A critical step in the development and use of some tests is to establish one or more cut points dividing the score range to partition the distribution of scores into categories.... [C]ut scores embody the rules according to which tests are used or interpreted. Thus, in some situations, the validity of test interpretations may hinge on the cut scores. (AERA, APA, & NCME, 1999, p. 53).

---

[5]For this reason, the *Standards for Educational and Psychological Testing* are frequently referred to as the *Joint Standards*.

TABLE 10.1
AERA, APA, & NCME *Standards* Related to Setting Cut Scores

Standard Number	Standard
1.7	When a validation rests in part on the opinions or decisions of expert judges, observers or raters, procedures for selecting such experts and for eliciting judgments or ratings should be fully described. The qualifications and experience of the judges should be presented. The description of procedures should include any training and instructions provided, should indicate whether participants reached their decisions independently, and should report the level of agreement reached. If participants interacted with one another or exchanged information, the procedures through which they may have influenced one another should be set forth.
2.14	Where cut scores are specified for selection or classification, the standard errors of measurement should be reported in the vicinity of each cut score.
2.15	When a test or combination of measures is used to make categorical decisions, estimates should be provided of the percentage of examinees who would be classified in the same way on two applications of the procedure, using the same or alternate forms of the instrument.
4.19	When proposed interpretations involve one or more cut scores, the rationale and procedures used for establishing cut scores should be clearly documented.
4.20	When feasible, cut scores defining categories with distinct substantive interpretations should be established on the basis of sound empirical data concerning the relation of test performance to relevant criteria.
4.21	When cut scores defining pass/fail or proficiency categories are based on direct judgments about the adequacy of item or test performances or performance levels, the judgmental process should be designed so that judges can bring their knowledge and experience to bear in a reasonable way.
6.5	When relevant for test interpretation, test documents ordinarily should include item level information, cut scores, [and so on].
14.17	The level of performance required for passing a credentialing test should depend on the knowledge and skills necessary for acceptable performance in the occupation or profession and should not be adjusted to regulate the number or proportion of persons passing the test.

Adapted from AERA, APA, & NCME (1999).

In the special context of licensure and certification testing, the *Standards* note that "the validity of the inferences drawn from the test depends on whether the standard for passing makes a valid distinction between adequate and inadequate performance" (p. 157).

A number of specific statements regarding standard setting can be found in the *Standards*. Table 10.1 provides an abbreviated summary of these statements (also called "Standards"). Two caveats are in order related to Table 10.1. First, although Table 10.1 lists each standard related to setting cut scores, it is abbreviated in the sense that, in the full document, each individual standard is followed by more detailed, elaborative commentary designed to assist the user in applying the Standard appropriately. Second, the listing shown in Table 10.1 should not be relied on as the entirety of essential information. Any entity responsible for planning, conducting, or implementing standard setting should be familiar with the full *Standards* document and the standards beyond those for establishing cut scores.

COMMON CONSIDERATIONS IN STANDARD SETTING

In a subsequent section of this chapter, several methods for setting cut scores are presented. First, however, this section describes six common considerations that are not unique to the specific method chosen. Rather, these issues include those that must be addressed regardless of the standard-setting approach selected.

Identifying the Purpose of Standard Setting

It is first important to consider the need for standard setting and when, in the test development process, standard-setting activities should occur. As mentioned, an initial question to be answered relates to the purpose of establishing standards in the first place. Kane (1994) has summarized the primacy of purpose:

> Before embarking on any standard setting method, however, it is important to consider the fundamental issue of whether it is necessary or useful to employ a passing score.... Assuming that it is necessary or useful to employ a passing score, it is important to be clear about what we want to achieve in making pass/fail decisions, so that our goals can guide our choices at various stages in the standards-setting process. (p. 427)

A common practice in all standard setting is to begin the actual standard-setting meeting with an orientation for participants to the purpose of the task at hand. This orientation is a pivotal point in the process and provides the frame participants are expected to apply in the conduct of their work.

Linn (1994) has suggested that standard setting can focus on one of four purposes: (1) exhortation, (2) exemplification, (3) accountability, or (4) certification of achievement. Depending on the purpose, the orientation to participants can differ substantially. For example, standard setting might involve exhortation. If the purpose were to "ratchet up expectations to world-class levels" for elementary school students studying mathematics, the orientation provided to standard-setting participants might focus on describing the low level of current knowledge and skill, the evolving needs of the work force, and so on. Certification of achievement is the purpose ordinarily served by credentialing examinations. Standard setting with an orientation of exemplification focuses more on providing concrete examples to educators of the competencies embedded in the content standards.

By contrast, for licensure and certification examinations, protecting the public from incompetent or unsafe practice is often of primary concern. As such, the oreintation to the standard-setting process might focus on the relative costs of incorrect credentialling decisions. For example, the entitiy responsible (e.g., the licensure board, state agency) might establish a policy position that the consequence of licensing an unsafe practitioner (referred to generally as a *false-positive decision*) is a more serious error than failing to license a truly competent person (referred to as a *false-negative decision*). The entity may rely on such a stated policy regarding public protection and comparative seriousness of a false-positive credentialling decision to, for example, reject a standard-setting panel's recommended cut score in favor on a higher performance standard. Of course, adjusting a cut score so as to reduce the probability of one type of decision error necessarily increases the probability of the other.

Scheduling the Standard-Setting Activity

A second difficult issue that must be confronted is whether to conduct a standard-setting activity before or after the administration of a "live" test form; that is, a test form for which performance has real consequences for examinees.

Downing (chap. 1, this volume, Table 1.1) has provided a generic list of 12 key steps in the test development process. Although Downing places the standard-setting activity as the ninth step in the process, following test administration and scoring, it is desirable and probably more common for cut scores to be established before actually administering an examination. According to Downing's sequence, this would locate standard setting at some stage between steps 5 and 7.

The ideal time for standard setting is not a settled question, however, and there are benefits to locating it earlier or later in the test development process. The placement of standard-setting activities early in the test development process reflects an implicit issue of fundamental fairness. Namely, it seems somewhat inappropriate to require examinees to submit to an examination requirement without being able to communicate to them in advance about the level of performance required to pass. On the other hand, establishing cut scores after an operational test has been administered is likely to yield more dependable results. Because many standard-setting procedures involve the provision of impact data to those who participate in the process, actual performance data from an operational test administration is necessary. Impact data based on results from a field test are notorious for their instability, and unknown degree of bias because the data are collected during a "no-stakes" test administration for which motivation levels of examinees are not likely equivalent to those of examinees who will take the test under standard conditions.

Standard-Setting Referents

A third cross-cutting aspect of standard setting is the creation and use of *performance level labels* (PLLs) and *performance level descriptions* (PLDs) or the creation and use of a referent examinee or group. Regardless of the standard-setting method selected, participants must either rely on a verbal description of a specified level of performance and make their judgments with respect to that level, or they must rely on a conceptualization of a hypothetical examinee (or group of examinees) and express their judgments as to how such an examinee would be expected to perform on a collection of items or tasks.

PLLs refer to the (usually) single-word terms used to identify performance categories: for example, *Basic*, *Proficient*, or *Advanced*. Although PLLs have little theoretical underpinning, they clearly carry rhetorical value as related to the purpose of the standard setting. Such labels have the potential to convey a great deal in a succinct manner vis à vis the meaning of classifications that result from the application of cut scores. It is obvious from a measurement perspective that PLLs should be carefully chosen to relate to the purpose of the assessment, to the construct assessed, and to the intended, supportable inferences arising from the classifications.

PLDs are an elaboration of PLLs. PLDs usually consist of several sentences or paragraphs that provide a fuller, more complete illustration of what performance within a particular category comprises. PLDs vary in their level of specificity, but have in common the verbal elaboration of the knowledge, skills, or attributes of test takers at a performance level. PLDs may be developed in advance by a separate committee for use by standard-setting panels, or may be created in the course of a standard-setting procedure by participants in the process. Sample PLDs, in this case those used for the National Assessment of Educational Progress (NAEP) Grade 4 reading assessment, are shown in Figure 10.1.

Other standard-setting methods require participants to think of a real or hypothetical group or individual test takers who possess specific characteristics. For example, the Angoff (1971) method requires the conceptualization of a "minimally competent" examinee. The need for such conceptualizations may have origins in the Nedelsky (1954) method, which requires participants to consider multiple-choice item options that a hypothetical "F/D student" would recognize as incorrect. According to Nedelsky, the *F/D student* is on the borderline between passing and failing a course; hence, the notion of a point differentiating between a failing grade of "F" and a passing grade of "D." When using the Borderline Group method (Livingston & Zieky, 1982), participants must identify specific examinees that they judge to be on the border between clearly failing or incompetent, and clearly able or competent.

In summary, all standard-setting methods require reference to one hypothetical conceptualization or another, whether it be in the form of an hypothetical examinee, a distilled description

Performance Level Label	Performance Level Description
Advanced	Fourth-grade students performing at the Advanced level should be able to generalize about topics in the reading selection and demonstrate an awareness of how authors compose and use literary devices. When reading text appropriate to fourth grade, they should be able to judge texts critically and, in general, give thorough answers that indicate careful thought. For example, when reading **literatry** text, Advanced-level students should be able to make generalizations about the point of the story and extend its meaning by integrating personal experiences and other readings with ideas suggested by the text. They should be able to identify literary devices such as figurative language. When reading **informational** text, Advanced-level fourth graders should be able to explain the author's intent by using supporting material from the text. They should be able to make critical judgments of the form and content of the text and explain their judgments clearly.
Proficient	Fourth-grade students performing at the Proficient level should be able to demonstrate an overall understanding of the text, providing inferential as well as literal information. When reading text appropriate to fourth grade, they should be able to extend the ideas in the text by making inferences, drawing conclusions, and making connections to their own experiences. The connections between the text and what the student infers should be clear. For example, when reading **literary** text, Proficient-level fourth graders should be able to summarize the story, draw conclusions about the characters or plot, and recognize relationships such as cause and effect. When reading **informational** text, Proficient-level students should be able to summarize the information and identify the author's intent or purpose. They should be able to draw reasonable conclusions from the text, recognize relationships such as cause and effect or similarities and differences, and identify the meaning of the selection's key concepts.
Basic	Fourth-grade students performing at the Basic level should demonstrate an understanding of the overall meaning of what they read. When reading text appropriate for fourth graders, they should be able to make relatively obvious connections between the text and their own experiences, and extend the ideas in the text by making simple inferences. For example, when reading **literary** text, they should be able to tell what the story is generally about—providing details to support their understanding—and be able to connect aspects of the stories to their own experiences. When reading **informational** text, Basic-level fourth graders should be able to tell what the selection is generally about or identify the purpose for reading it, provide details to support their understanding, and connect ideas from the text to their background knowledge and experiences.

FIG. 10.1. Sample NAEP Grade 4 Performance Level Descriptions.

of acceptable performance, or an abstract borderline between two categories of performance. Thus, standard-setting participants are usually selected based on their possesion of both content area expertise and familiarity with the target group of examinees to whom the test will be administered.

Selecting and Training Standard-Setting Participants

A fourth pervasive issue in standard setting involves the need to identify and train qualified participants to engage in the judgmental task. It has long been known that the participants in the standard-setting process are critical to the success of the endeavor and are a source of variability of standard setting results. The *Standards for Educational and Psychological Testing*

(AERA, APA, & NCME, 1999) provide guidance on representation, selection, and training of participants. For example, the *Standards* indicate that "a sufficiently large and representative group of judges should be involved to provide reasonable assurance that results would not vary greatly if the process were repeated" (p. 54). The *Standards* also recommend that "the qualifications of any judges involved in standard setting and the process by which they are selected" (p. 54) should be fully described and included as part of the documentation for the standard setting process. The *Standards* also address training, indicating that:

> Care must be taken to assure that judges understand what they are to do. The process must be such that well-qualified judges can apply their knowledge and experience to reach meaningful and relevant judgments that accurately reflect their understandings and intentions. (p. 54)

There is a tension present in the selection of standard-setting participants. Although it is often recommended that participants have special expertise in the area for which standards will be set, in practice this can mean that standard-setting panels consist of participants whose perspectives are not representative of all practitioners in a field, all teachers at a grade level, and so on. Such a bias might be desirable if the purpose of standard setting is exhortation, though less so if the purpose of standard setting is to certify competence of students for awarding a high school diploma. For some standard-setting contexts, such as in licensure and certification, the pool of potential participants may be very small and limited to those subject matter experts (SMEs) with advanced preparation and experience in the field.

In other contexts, such as elementary and secondary school math achievement testing, the pool of potential participants may be quite large and include nearly any citizen with a stake in deciding what level of subject matter mastery is important for, say, high school graduation. In contexts such as this, it may be that relying only on those with advanced training and experience in mathematics (e.g., high school honors calculus teachers) would be a serious mistake. Only somewhat tongue in cheek, a psychometric colleague of mine has opined that the optimal participant for a standard-setting panel to decide on cut scores for a graduation test in mathematics would be a typical high school English teacher.[6]

Much has been written on how to identify a pool of potential participants, how to select participants from that pool, and how to conduct efficient and effective training of participants. Considerable detail on this topic is provided by Raymond and Reid (2001), and readers are referred to that source for further information on the topic.

Providing Feedback to Participants

A fifth common element in most standard setting procedures involves the additional information that will be provided to participants to help them accomplish the task of generating meaningful, realistic, and useful judgments. Once standard-setting participants have been selected and trained and the procedure has begun, feedback is routinely provided to participants that provides them with normative information (i.e., comparisons with other participants), reality information (data on the actual performance of examinees), or impact information (the effect of their judgments on the examinee group).

Many standard-setting approaches are composed of "rounds" or iterations of judgments. At each round, participants may be provided various kinds of information, including a summary of their own judgments; a summary of their internal consistency; an indication of how their

---

[6]I first heard this observation offered by Professor William Mehrens, while discussing standard setting for a high school graduation test.

judgments compare to the judgments of other participants; an indication of variability in participants' ratings; and the likely impact of the individual or group judgment on the examinee population (e.g., the overall passing or failure rates, the percentages of examinees likely to be classified in each of the performance levels, the differential impact on examinees from various demographic categories, etc.).

There are many ways of providing such feedback. And the kind, amount, timing, and format of feedback depends on the standard-setting method used and the purpose of the activity. A complete treatment of the topic of providing feedback to participants is beyond the scope of this chapter. As with the issue of training of participants, the topic of feedback is covered in detail elsewhere, and readers are referred to the work of Reckase (2001) for in-depth treatment of this topic.

Evaluating the Standard-Setting Process

The sixth common element in all standard setting is evaluation. It is important that any standard-setting process gather evidence bearing on the manner in which any particular approach was implemented and the extent to which participants in the process were able to understand, apply, and have confidence in the eventual performance standards. An equivalent degree of attention should be devoted to planning the standard-setting evaluation, a priori, as is devoted to identifying the method, selecting and training participants, and carrying out the procedure itself.

Evaluation of standard setting is a multifaceted endeavor. A complete listing of possible evaluation elements is provided in Table 10.2. Evaluation of standard setting can be thought of as beginning with a critical appraisal of the degree of alignment between the standard-setting method selected and the purpose and design of the test, the goals of the standard-setting agency, and the characteristics of the standard setters. This match should be evaluated by an independent body (such as a technical advisory committee) acting on behalf of the entity that authorizes the standard setting and is responsible ultimately for the choice of cut scores.

Evaluation continues with a close examination of the application of the standard-setting procedure: To what extent did it adhere faithfully to the published principles of the procedure? Did it deviate in unexpected, undocumented ways? If there are deviations, are they reasonable adaptations, specified and approved in advance, and consistent with the overall goals of the activity?

The preceding questions reflect an "external" focus of the evaluation. Other evaluation activities can be thought of as more "internal" to the process. For example, a measure of the degree to which standard-setting participants seem to achieve consensus or converge toward a common standard from one round of judgments to the next can indicate that the selected method is working as intended. Trained facilitators can assess the extent to which deliberations or discussions are freely engaged in by all participants or are driven by one or more influential participants.

In-progress evaluations of the process of standard setting also serve as an important internal check on the validity and success of the process. Minimally, two evaluations should be conducted during the course of a standard-setting meeting, and both usually consist of mainly forced-choice survey questions with a few open-ended items. The first evaluation occurs after initial orientation of participants to the process, training in the method, and (when appropriate) administration to participants of an actual test form. This first evaluation serves as a check on the extent to which participants have been adequately trained, understand key conceptualizations and the task before them, and have confidence that they will be able to apply the selected method. The second evaluation is conducted at the conclusion of the standard-setting meeting and mainly serves the purpose of gathering information on participants' level of confidence in and agreement with the final to-be-recommended standard. A sample survey, which includes

TABLE 10.2
Standard-Setting Evaluation Elements

Evaluation Element	Description
Procedural	
Explicitness	The degree to which the standard-setting purposes and processes were clearly and explicitly articulated a priori
Practicability	The ease of implementation of the procedures and data analysis; the degree to which procedures are credible and interpretable to relevant audiences.
Implementation	The degree to which the following procedures were reasonable, and systematically and rigorously conducted: selection and training of participants, definition of the performance standard, and data collection
Feedback	The extent to which participants have confidence in the process and in resulting cutscore(s)
Documentation	The extent to which features of the study are reviewed and documented for evaluation and communication purposes
Internal	
Consistency within method	The precision of the estimate of the cutscore(s)
Intra-participant consistency	The degree to which a participant is able to provide ratings consistent with the empirical item difficulties, and the degree to which ratings change across rounds
Inter-participant consistency	The consistency of item ratings and cut scores across participants
Decision Consistency	The extent to which repeated application of the identified cutscores(s) would yield consistent classifications of examinees
Other measures	The consistency of cut scores across item types, content areas, and cognitive processes
External	
Comparisons to other standard-setting methods	The agreement of cut scores across replications using other standard-setting methods
Comparisons to other sources of information	The relationship between decisions made using the test to other relevant criteria (e.g., grades, performance on tests measuring similar constructs, etc.)
Reasonableness of cut scores	The extent to which cut score recommendations are feasible or realistic (including pass/fail rates and differential impact on relevant subgroups)

Adapted from Pitoniak (2003).

both kinds of questions and which users should modify to their particular context, is shown in Figure 10.2.

Much of the preceding information on evaluation has focused on process-related aspects of standard-setting. Of course, the product or result (i.e., the actual cut scores) of standard-setting is arguably even more important. Two commonly employed evaluation criteria related to results include reasonableness and replicability.

The reasonableness aspect can perhaps first be assessed in the first "product" of standard setting, which in most instances are PLLs and PLDs or written description of referent examinees or groups. The utility and comprehensibility of these descriptions are essential. For a given field, subject, or grade level, they should accurately reflect the content standards or credentialing objectives. They should be reasonably consistent with statements developed by others with similar goals.

Reasonableness can be assessed by the degree to which cut scores derived from the standard-setting process classify examinees into groups in a manner consistent with other information about the examinees. For example, suppose it could be assumed that a state's eighth-grade

Directions: Please check to indicate your level of agreement with each of the following statements and add any additional comments you have on the process at the bottom of this page. Thank you.

Item	Statement	Strongly Disagree	Disagree	Agree	Strongly Agree
1	The orientation provided me with a clear understanding of the purpose of the meeting.				
2	The workshop leaders clearly explained the task.				
3	The training and practice exercises helped me understand how to perform the task.				
4	Taking the test helped me to understand the assessment.				
5	The performance level descriptions (referent examinee descriptions) were clear and useful.				
6	The large and small group discussions aided my understanding of the process.				
7	There was adequate time provided for discussions.				
8	There was an equal opportunity for everyone in my group to contribute his/her ideas and opinions.				
9	I was able to follow the instructions and complete the rating sheets accurately.				
10	The discussions after the first round of ratings were helpful to me.				
11	The discussions after the second round of ratings were helpful to me.				
12	The information showing the distribution of examinee scores was helpful to me.				
13	I am confident about the defensibility and appropriateness of the final recommended cut scores.				
14	The facilities and food service helped create a productive and efficient working environment.				

15 Comments: _____

FIG. 10.2. Sample evaluation form for standard-setting participants. (Adapted from Cizek, Bunch, & Koons, 2005.)

reading test and the NAEP were based on common content standards (or similar content standards that had roughly equal instructional emphasis). In such as case, a standard-setting procedure for the state test resulting in 72% of the state's eighth graders being classified as *Proficient*, while NAEP results for the same grade showed that only 39% were Proficient, would cause concern that one or the other set of performance standards was inappropriate.

Local information can also provide criteria by which to judge reasonableness. Do students who typically do well in class and on assignments mostly meet the top standard set for the test, and students who struggle fall into the lower categories? In licensure and certification contexts,

TABLE 10.3
Generic Steps in Setting Performance Standards

Step	Description
1	Select a large and representative group of participants.
2	Choose a standard-setting method; prepare training materials and standard-setting meeting agenda.
3	Prepare descriptions of the performance categories (i.e., PLDs) or referent candidate or group.
4	Train participants to use the standard-setting method.
5	Compile item ratings or other judgments from participants and produce descriptive or summary information or other feedback for participants.
6	Facilitate discussion among participants of initial descriptive or summary information.
7	Provide an opportunity for participants to generate revised ratings/judgments; compile information; repeat Steps 5 and 6.
8	Provide for a final opportunity for participants to review information, arrive at final recommended performance standard(s)/cutscore(s).
9	Conduct an evaluation of the standard-setting process, including gathering participants' confidence in the process and resulting performance standard(s).
10	Assemble documentation of the standard setting process and other evidence, as appropriate, bearing on the validity of resulting performance standards.

Adapted from Hambleton (1998).
Abbreviation: PLD, performance level description.

past experience with the proportions of candidates who have been deemed competent, and the experiences of those who oversee pre-service internships, residencies, or have other interactions with candidates for the credential can be brought to bear to assess reasonableness.

Replicability is another aspect in the evaluation of standard setting. For example, in some contexts where substantial resources are available, it is possible to conduct independent applications of a standard-setting process to assess the degree to which replications of the procedure yield similar results. Evaluation might also involve comparisons between results obtained using one method and an independent application of one or more different methods. Interpretation of the results of these comparisons, however, is far from clear. For example, Jaeger (1989) noted that different methods yield different results, and there is no way to determine that one method or the other produced the wrong results. Zieky (2001) noted that there is still no consensus as to which standard-setting method is most defensible in a given situation. Again, differences in results from two different procedures would not be an indication that one was right and the other wrong; even if two methods did produce the same or similar cut scores, we could only be sure of precision, not accuracy.

Other Cross-Cutting Concerns

In addition to the six issues set apart for special consideration in the preceding sections, a number of other issues are common to most standard setting activities. Hambleton (1998) has provided a list of general steps to consider in the standard setting process; an adaptation of his list is provided in Table 10.3.

An examination of Table 10.3 reveals that the preceding sections have focused most on Steps 1 through 5 of the general process. In a subsequent section of this chapter additional attention is given to Step 9 (evaluating the standard-setting process). Throughout this chapter, Step 10 (documenting the standard-setting process) is referred to as an essential element that forms the basis for communicating about the meaning of the standards, and for providing validity evidence to support the use of the standards. In the next section of this chapter, however, the focus is on providing "how-to" information related to several, specific methods.

STANDARD-SETTING METHODS

According to the *Standards for Educational and Psychological Testing*, "There can be no single method for determining cut scores for all tests or for all purposes, nor can there be any single set of procedures for establishing their defensibility" (AERA, APA, & NCME, 1999, p. 53). Put another way, the particular approach to standard setting selected may not be as critical to the success of the endeavor as the fidelity and care with which it is conducted.

There exists an extensive and growing list of methodological options for setting standards. Several classification schemes have been suggested for categorizing the options. For example, Jaeger (1989) has categorized the alternatives as either grounded in judgements about test content or test items (*test centered*) or in judgments about test takers themselves (*examinee centered*). Clearly, however, any standard-setting procedure necessarily requires both kinds of judgments and information about both test content and test takers. It would not be possible for a standard setting participant to make a judgment about the difficulty of an item or task without relying on his or her knowledge or expectations of the abilities of examinees in the target population. Conversely, it would not be possible for a participant to express judgments about examinees without explicit consideration of the items or tasks the examinee is administered. Thus, although both so-called test-centered and examinee-centered methods are described in the following portions of this chapter, it is important to realize that such labeling serves more as a convenient way of grouping methods than as conceptual or essential distinctions between methods.

Although both test-centered and examinee-centered methods are detailed in the following sections, space considerations dictate that only a subset of the potential options is described. However, page limitations are only a comparatively minor rationale for any omissions, and other considerations played a larger role in making the difficult decisions about which methods to include and which to exclude. First, some methods (although often encountered in professional literature) do not appear to be actually used in practice. The choice of methods described in the following sections represents an attempt to err on the side of frequency of use. Second, some methods appear to be more prevalent for licensure and certification applications; others are more often encountered in K–12 education settings. In deciding which methods to cover in this section, attention was given to representing options for both of these contexts. Finally, some of the selected methods are included because they represent new approaches carrying potential advantages over more established methods; for example, they may be more holistic (they require standard-setting participants to make holistic judgments about items or examinee test performance); they may be intended to reduce the cognitive burden on participants; or they may be applied to a wide variety of item and task formats. As the consequences and costs of standard setting have escalated, researchers have developed new methods that are more intuitively appealing to participants and stakeholders, and that can be implemented efficiently. The ultimate goal of all the standard-setting methods described in the following sections is to aid participants in bringing their judgments to bear in ways that are reproducible, informed by relevant sources of evidence, and fundamentally fair to those affected by the process.

Before turning to specific description of individual methods, three important caveats are in order. First, the choice of method should always be made with the purpose and format of the examination in mind. Some methods are more appropriate for, say, multiple-choice format tests; others are more appropriate for performance tasks. The scoring model used for the test should also align with the purpose and format of the examination. *Scoring model* refers to the way in which test responses are combined to arrive at a total score or classification decision. For example, suppose a test of ophthalmic knowledge consisted of three subtests, each covering a specific portion of the anatomy of the eye (e.g., lens, retina, cornea). An examinee's score on the examination (and, hence, the pass/fail decision) could be based on the examinee's total raw score computed across each of the three sections. In effect, this would mean that comparatively strong performance in one of the subareas could compensate for weak or inadequate knowledge on one of the other areas. Such an approach is called a *compensatory model*. An alternative is to require a minimum score in each of the subareas to be obtain in addition to a minimum total score. Such a scoring model, called a *conjunctive model*, effectively precludes comparatively strong performance in one area from compensating for comparative weakness in another. Clearly the choice of the scoring models is a policy decision that must be made by the entity responsible for the testing program. However, the choice of scoring model is also inextricably related to the purpose of the test and to the relative costs of incorrect decisions (see the preceeding discussion of false-positive and false-negative decisions).

Second, only the most basic information needed to conduct a particular standard-setting method is presented. Once a method has been identified, potential users should seek additional information on the method via the original source for the method cited in each section, or in a more elaborate treatment of standard setting generally (e.g., Cizek, 2001c). Users may also require assistance with other "nuts-and-bolts" activities, including designing and preparing training materials, setting up data collection mechanisms to gather participants judgments, creating software or routines for analyzing those judgments, developing sources of and procedures for providing feedback to participants, designing process evaluations, and so on.

Third, the descriptions of each method focus mainly on the procedures used to actually obtain one or more cut scores. As should be evident from the preceding sections, much more is required of a defensible standard-setting process, including identification and training of appropriately qualified participants, effective facilitation, monitoring, feedback to participants, and well-conceived strategies for gathering support for whatever validity claims are made. We now turn to description of 10 methods for obtaining cut scores on tests.

The Angoff Method

What may be the most widely used (and certainly most thoroughly researched and documented) standard-setting method is attributed to William Angoff (1971) and bears his name. Since its introduction, a number of variations of the original Angoff method have also come into wide use. Thus, it is perhaps best to think of the method as a family of related approaches.

The basic Angoff method requires participants to review the individual items that comprise a test and to provide estimates, for each item, of the proportion of a subpopulation of examinees who would answer the items correctly. In Angoff's words:

> A systematic procedure for deciding on the minimum raw scores for passing and honors might be developed as follows: keeping the hypothetical "minimally acceptable person" in mind, one could go through the test item by item and decide whether such a person could answer correctly each item under consideration. If a score of one is given for each item answered correctly by the hypothetical person and a score of zero is given for each item answered incorrectly by that person, the sum of the item scores will equal the raw score earned by the "minimally acceptable person." (1971, pp. 514–515)

In practice, a variation to the procedure suggest by Angoff in a footnote has become the typical application of the method. According to Angoff:

> A slight variation of this procedure is to ask each judge to state the probability that the "minimally acceptable person" would answer each item correctly. In effect, judges would think of a number of minimally acceptable persons, instead of only one such person, and would estimate the proportion of minimally acceptable persons who would answer each item correctly. The sum of these probabilities would then represent the minimally acceptable score. (1971, p. 515).

In this description, Angoff was obviously not referring to the acceptability of an examinee as a person, but to the qualifications of the examinee vis à vis the purpose of the test. Subsequent to Angoff's introduction of this method, *minimally competent examinee* has been substituted when the Angoff procedure is used. It should be clear, however, that this idea—that is, the minimally competent or borderline examinee—is a key referent for this standard-setting method. It is common for much of the beginning time afforded to the actual standard-setting meeting to be devoted to helping participants refine and acquire this essential conceptualization.

Although the conceptualization of the minimally competent examinee is somewhat unique to the Angoff method, the other aspects of implementing the method are common to most other standard-setting approaches. Namely, qualified participants are selected and are oriented to the task; they are grounded in the content standards or essential knowledge, skills, and abilities upon which the test was built; they are (usually) required to take the test themselves; and they generate performance estimates for a group of examinees in an iterative process over two or more rounds or ratings.

The purpose of the iterative rating process is to permit participants to discuss their opinions, view normative data, get feedback on their ratings, and reduce group variability in the estimates (i.e., to promote movement toward a consensus standard of performance). Normative data are often presented in the form of actual item difficulty indices (e.g., p-values) based on total group performance if operational test data are available. In theory and if practicable, however, it is preferable that the p-values be based on a subset of examinees whose performance locates them in a borderline region. Because the exact location of the border is unknown until the process is completed, it is possible to use participants' first round ratings to identify a preliminary cut score. With this cut score in hand, those conducting the standard-setting meeting can recalculate p-values for feedback to participants based only on the performance of examinees scoring within, say ± 1 standard error of measurement of the preliminary cut.

Table 10.4 illustrates a scaled-down, hypothetical example of the data that might be collected as part of a basic Angoff standard-setting procedure, along with some key summary statistics. The table shows two rounds of ratings of 13 multiple-choice items by 10 participants. As is often the case when using the Angoff approach, participants were instructed to imagine a group of 100 minimally competent examinees, and to estimate the number out of that 100 who would answer a given item correctly. To make the task easier, participants were given a form on which to record their estimates, and they were asked to provide their estimates in multiples of 10 only (although this is not a requirement of the Angoff method).

The data for a single participant consists of two lines of data; the first line represents the participant's item ratings of each item in the first round of ratings; the second line is the participant's Round 2 ratings. The means for each participant and for each item are also presented by round. These values reveal that, for example, in Round 2, Rater 1 produced the most stringent ratings ($M = 88.5$) and Rater 2 the most lenient ($M = 66.9$). Across all raters in Round 2, Item 13 was judged to be the easiest ($M = 79.0$) and Item 10 the most difficult ($M = 63.0$).

TABLE 10.4
Hypothetical Data for Angoff Standard-Setting Method

Rater ID Number	*Item Number*													
	1	*2*	*3*	*4*	*5*	*6*	*7*	*8*	*9*	*10*	*11*	*12*	*13*	*Means*
1	90	90	100	100	100	90	90	90	90	60	90	100	90	90.8
	80	90	90	100	90	90	100	90	80	70	90	90	90	88.5
2	60	80	50	60	70	90	70	60	30	40	40	50	70	59.2
	70	80	60	70	80	90	80	70	40	50	60	60	60	66.9
3	90	70	80	80	100	60	80	80	80	60	50	90	80	76.9
	90	80	90	70	80	60	70	80	80	60	60	90	70	75.4
4	70	60	70	80	90	80	80	70	70	60	50	90	90	73.9
	70	70	60	70	80	80	70	70	70	70	70	80	80	72.3
5	90	60	90	40	80	60	80	70	60	60	90	70	80	71.5
	80	70	90	60	80	60	70	70	70	70	80	70	70	72.3
6	60	60	80	60	70	70	80	80	60	50	70	80	90	70.0
	70	60	70	70	70	70	70	80	60	50	70	80	90	70.0
7	90	50	80	60	60	70	70	70	70	60	80	80	70	70.0
	80	60	80	70	60	70	60	80	80	50	80	70	80	70.8
8	80	50	70	80	40	90	70	70	60	60	70	70	80	68.5
	70	50	80	70	50	90	70	80	70	70	70	80	80	71.5
9	80	70	60	70	60	80	50	60	60	30	50	60	90	63.1
	90	70	70	70	60	80	60	70	70	60	60	70	80	70.0
10	80	90	90	40	100	80	100	70	80	90	100	70	80	82.3
	80	70	90	60	100	80	90	80	70	80	80	80	90	80.8
Means	79.0	68.0	77.0	67.0	77.0	77.0	77.0	72.0	66.0	57.0	69.0	76.0	82.0	72.6
	78.0	70.0	78.0	71.0	75.0	77.0	74.0	77.0	69.0	63.0	72.0	77.0	79.0	73.8

Derivation of a recommended passing score using the Angoff method is accomplished by averaging either the rater or item means. Usually the calculations are based on the final round of ratings. Using the Round 2 ratings shown in Table 10.4, the recommended passing score would be 73.8% correct, or approximately 9.6 of the 13 items on the test.[7] The decision about how to handle non-integer results is a policy decision. For example, if the context were one in which protecting the public was a primary concern, an examinee's raw score of 9 would not be at or above the level that SMEs had indicated was the minimum level of performance required. Thus, the recommended cut score of 9.6 might be rounded to 10. In other situations, where a false negative decision was deemed to be a greater potential harm, a decision rule might be adopted to truncate the obtained value, round to the nearest integer value, or some other rule.

One advantage of the Angoff method is that it can be used in a variety of applications beyond traditional multiple-choice and other select-response formats, including constructed-response items and performance tasks. In these modifications to the original method, participants estimate expected scores for minimally proficient examinees on whatever score scale is used. For

---

[7]The decision about how to handle non-integer results is a policy decision. For example, if the context were one in which protecting the public was a primary concern, an examinee's raw score of 9 would not be at or above the level that SMEs had indicated was the minimum level of performance required. Thus, the recommended cut score of 9.6 might be rounded to 10. In other situations, where a false-negative decision was deemed to be a greater potential harm, a decision rule might be adopted to truncate the obtained value, round to the nearest integer value, or some other rule.

example, Impara and Plake (1997) described what they call the *Yes/No method*; Hambleton and Plake (1995) have described the use of an *Extended Angoff procedure*.

Angoff Variations

There are numerous ways in which the Angoff method has been modified. Two variations of the method described above are presented in the following subsections. The first method, called the *Yes/No method*, involves a simplification of the rating task so that participants are not required to estimate probabilities. The second method is an adaptation of the Angoff method used in dichotomous-scoring contexts (e.g., multiple-choice formats) to situations that involve polytomous scoring (e.g., constructed-response items, performances).

The Yes/No Method

The Yes/No method is highly similar to the original Angoff (1971) approach. Although the footnoted version has come to be known as the widely used Angoff method, Angoff's original idea was that standard setters simply judge whether a hypothetical minimally competent examinee would answer an item correctly or not. Thus, the question addressed by standard-setting participants can be answered "Yes" or "No" for each item. In the Yes/No method described by Impara and Plake (1997; see also Downing, Lieska, & Raible, 2003), participants are directed to

> Read each item [in the test] and make a judgment about whether the borderline student you have in mind will be able to answer each question correctly. If you think so, then under Rating 1 on the sheet you have in front of you, write in a Y. If you think the student will not be able to answer correctly, then write in an N. (pp. 364–365)

There are two variations of the Yes/No method. One variation requires participants to form the traditional conceptualization of a hypothetical borderline examinee; the other requires participants to reference their judgments with respect to an actual examinee on the borderline between classifications (e.g., between *Basic* and *Proficient* or between Fail and Pass).

Implementation of the Yes/No method comprises the same features as most common standard-setting approaches. After training and discussion of the characteristics of the minimally competent candidate, participants rate a set of operational items (usually an intact test form) to complete a first round of judgments. Following this, participants are provided with feedback on their Round 1 ratings, then begin a second round of yes/no judgments on each item. If not provided previously, at the end of Round 2, participants receive additional feedback, which ordinarily includes impact data (i.e., the percentages of examinees predicted to pass/fail based on their judgments). Regardless of how many rounds of ratings occur, calculation of the final recommended passing score is based on data obtained in the final round.

One of the appealing features of the Yes/No method is its simplicity. In typical implementations of modified Angoff procedures, participants must maintain a concept of a group of hypothetical examinees and must estimate the proportion of that group that will answer an item correctly. Clearly, this is an important—although perhaps difficult—task. The Yes/No method simplifies the judgment task by reducing the probability estimation required to a dichotomous outcome. Impara and Plake (1998) found that the Yes/No method ameliorated some of the difficulty of the probability estimation task. They reported that

> We believe that the yes/no method shows substantial promise. Not only do panelists find this method clearer and easier to use than the more traditional Angoff probability estimation procedures, its results show less sensitivity to performance data and lower within-panelist variability. Further, panelists report that the conceptualization of a typical borderline examinee is easier for them

than the task of imagining a group of hypothetical target candidates. Therefore, the performance standard derived from the yes/no method may be more valid than that derived from the traditional Angoff method. (p. 336)

To date, the Yes/No method has only been applied in contexts where the outcome is dichotomous (i.e., with multiple-choice or other dichotomously scored formats) and has not yet been subjected to extensive scrutiny. In one study, it was compared to other standard-setting methods (e.g. Angoff and Hofstee) and found to perform reasonably well in a classroom testing situation (Downing, Lieska, & Raible, 2003). One potential weakness of the method lies in the potential for either positive or negative bias in item ratings, depending on the clustering of item difficulty values in the test. The potential for bias arises because the method is based on an implicit judgment of whether the probability of correct response at the cut score is greater than .5. To illustrate, suppose that a test were composed of identical items that all had a probability of correct response at the cut score of .7. An accurate rater would assign ratings of 1 to each item, and the resulting performance standard would be a perfect score—clearly not the intent of the intent of the rater, nor a realistic expectation based on the difficulty of the test.

The Extended Angoff Method

Another variation of Angoff's approach has been created to address tests that include a mix of constructed- and selected-response items. Hambleton and Plake (1995) describe what they have labeled an *Extended Angoff procedure*. Participants in this method, in addition to providing conventional probability estimates of borderline examinee performance for each selected-response item, participants also estimate the number of scale points that they believe borderline examinees will obtain on each constructed-response task in the assessment. Cut scores for the extended Angoff approach are calculated in the same way as with traditional Angoff methods although, as Hambleton (1998) notes, more complex weighting schemes can also be used for combining components in a mixed-format assessment.

Table 10.5 presents hypothetical data for the ratings of 20 items by 6 participants in two rounds of ratings using the Yes/No and Extended Angoff methods. The upper and lower entries in each cell of the table represent participants' first and second round ratings, respectively. The table has been prepared to illustrate three scenarios: (1) calculation of cut scores that would result from use of the Yes/No method alone for a set of dichotomously scored selected-response items (the first 12 items listed in the table); (2) calculation of cut scores based on the extended-Angoff method alone for a set of constructed-response items scored on a 1 to 4 scale (the last eight items in the table); and (3) cut scores based on a combination of Yes/No and extended-Angoff (for the full 20-item set).

The means for each rater and item are also presented for each round. Using the Round 2 ratings shown in Table 10.5, the recommended Yes/No passing score for the 12-item selected response test is approximately 58% of the total raw score points (.58 × 12 items = 6.96), or approximately 7 out of 12 points possible. The recommended passing score on the eight-item constructed-response test is 22 out of a total of 32 possible score points (2.69 × 8 items = 21.52). A recommended passing score for the full 20-item test comprising a mix of selected- and constructed-response items is approximately 28 of the 44 total possible raw score points [(.58 × 12) + (2.69 × 8) = 28.48].

The Nedelsky Method

Although not as commonly implemented as the Angoff method, a method proposed by Nedelsky (1954) for setting cut scores on multiple-choice tests remains in use today. The longevity of the method is perhaps because it is intuitive and easily performed by participants,

TABLE 10.5
Hypothetical Data and Examples of Yes/No and Extended-Angoff Standard-Setting Methods

Item	\multicolumn{6}{c}{Rater ID Number}	Means
	1	2	3	4	5	6	
1	1	0	0	1	0	1	0.50
	1	1	0	0	0	1	0.50
2	0	0	0	0	0	0	0.00
	0	0	0	1	0	0	0.17
3	1	1	0	1	1	1	0.83
	1	1	0	1	1	1	0.83
4	1	1	1	1	1	1	1.00
	1	1	1	1	1	1	1.00
5	0	0	0	0	0	0	0.00
	0	0	0	0	0	0	0.00
6	0	0	0	0	0	0	0.00
	0	0	0	0	0	0	0.00
7	1	1	1	1	1	1	1.00
	1	1	1	1	1	1	1.00
8	1	1	1	1	1	1	1.00
	1	1	1	1	1	1	1.00
9	1	1	1	1	1	1	1.00
	1	1	1	1	1	1	1.00
10	1	1	1	0	1	1	0.83
	1	1	1	0	1	1	0.83
11	0	0	0	0	0	0	0.00
	0	0	0	0	0	0	0.00
12	0	0	1	0	0	0	0.17
	1	0	1	1	1	0	0.67
Means	.58	.50	.50	.50	.50	.58	.53
	.67	.58	.50	.58	.58	.58	.58
13	2	3	2	2	3	1	2.17
	3	3	3	3	3	2	2.83
14	1	2	1	2	2	1	1.50
	2	2	2	2	3	2	2.17
15	2	2	2	2	2	2	2.00
	3	3	3	3	3	2	2.83
16	3	3	2	2	3	2	2.50
	3	3	3	3	3	3	3.00
17	1	1	2	1	2	1	1.33
	2	2	2	2	2	1	1.83
18	2	3	3	2	3	2	2.50
	3	3	3	3	3	2	2.83
19	3	2	2	2	3	2	2.33
	3	3	3	3	3	3	3.00
20	2	3	3	2	3	2	2.50
	3	3	3	3	3	3	3.00
Means	2.00	2.38	2.13	1.88	2.63	1.63	2.10
	2.75	2.75	2.75	2.75	2.88	2.25	2.69

it is comparatively time efficient, and the kind of item format it can be applied to—multiple choice—remains a format of choice for many testing programs. Nedelsky's method tends to be used more so in credentialing contexts than in education contexts.

It was in an education context, however, that the Nedelsky method was proposed. It was, in its day, perhaps the first widely disseminated criterion-referenced method for setting cut scores. At the time of its introduction, standards were often established, grades were assigned, and so on, using norm-referenced methods; that is, methods by which passing or failing are determined not so much by an individual's actual achievement, but by achievements of others in a group and the relative standing of the individual within that group. In most situations today, norm-referenced procedures are judged as fundamentally unfair, and suffer serious validity concerns.

Nedelsky's (1954) method was one of the first to shift the focus from relative performance to what he termed "absolute" levels of performance. To use the Nedelsky method, participants assign values to multiple-choice test items based on the likelihood of certain examinees being able to rule out incorrect options. The examinees used as a reference group are hypothetical examinees on the borderline between inadequate mastery and acceptable mastery of some area. Nedelsky's term for this borderline examinee was the "F-D student" where F and D refer to clearly failing and just passing grades in a course. The F-D student lies right on the cusp of these two categories. According to Nedelsky, on an individual item,

> Responses which the lowest D-student should be able to reject as incorrect, and which therefore should be attractive to [failing students] are called F-responses... Students who possess just enough knowledge to reject F-responses and must choose among the remaining responses at random are called F-D students. (1954, p. 5)

The first portion of a standard-setting meeting in which the Nedelsky method is used consists of participants' discussion and clarification of the borderline examinee. Participants then review each item in a test form and, for each item, identify the options that they believe a hypothetical minimally competent examinee would rule out as incorrect. The reciprocal of the remaining number of options becomes each item's "Nedelsky value". That value is interpreted as the probability that the borderline examinee will answer the item correctly. For example, on a five-option item for which borderline examinees would be expected to rule out two of the options as incorrect, the Nedelsky rating would be 1/(3 remaining options) = .33. The sum of these values can be directly translated into the passing score.[8]

To illustrate the method, consider the hypothetical data presented in Table 10.6. The table shows the ratings of 15 items by 6 participants. In the example, participants were not required to reach consensus about the Nedelsky values for each item; rather, the mean of their judgments is used as the final rating for each item. The sum of the 15 ratings, 6.89, yields a recommended passing score of approximately 7 out of 15 items correct. This is the number of items that the borderline examinee would be expected to answer correctly.

In addition to illustrating the method, Table 10.6 illustrates some of the limitations of the Nedelsky method that have been noted in the literature. As mentioned, the method can only be used with multiple-choice format items. Additionally, the method only permits raters to assign a very limited number of probabilities (.20, .25, .33, .50, and 1.00 for a five-option item) and there are not equal intervals between those possibilities. Because raters tend not to assign probabilities of 1.00, this may tend to create a downward bias (i.e., result in lower passing scores compared to other methods) when the Nedelsky method is used.

---

[8]Nedelsky's original work proposed a further adjustment of the simple sum of the ratings which, in essence, would take into account the relative costs of incorrect pass/fail decisions.

TABLE 10.6
Hypothetical Data for Nedelsky Standard Setting Method

| | \multicolumn{6}{c|}{Rater ID Number} | |
Item	1	2	3	4	5	6	Item Means
	\multicolumn{6}{c	}{Nedelsky Values}	
1	.33	.50	.50	.33	.33	.33	.39
2	.50	1.00	.50	.25	1.00	1.00	.71
3	.25	.33	.25	.25	.25	.33	.28
4	1.00	1.00	.50	1.00	.50	1.00	.83
5	.33	.33	.33	.33	.25	.33	.32
6	.25	.33	.25	.25	.25	.33	.28
7	.25	.20	.25	.33	.20	.20	.24
8	1.00	.33	1.00	.50	1.00	.50	.72
9	.20	.33	.25	.20	.33	.25	.26
10	.50	1.00	1.00	.50	.50	1.00	.75
11	.50	.50	.50	1.00	.50	.50	.58
12	.50	.33	.33	.50	.33	.33	.39
13	.20	.20	.20	.20	.20	.20	.20
14	.25	.20	.33	.25	.33	.25	.27
15	1.00	.50	.50	.50	1.00	.50	.67
							Sum = 6.89

The Bookmark Method

The Bookmark method, described by Mitzel, Lewis, Patz, and Green (2001), has rapidly become widely used in K–12 education assessment contexts. Among the advantages of the Bookmark method are the comparative ease with which it can be explained to and applied by standard-setting participants, the fact that it can be applied to tests composed of both constructed- and selected-response items, and the fact that it can be used to set multiple cut scores on a single test.

The Bookmark method derives its name from the activity that participants are asked to engage in; namely, they identify cut scores by placing markers in a specially prepared booklet consisting of the items and tasks that appear in a test form. However, the items and tasks do no appear as an intact form, but are reordered, appearing one per page, according to their individual difficulty levels, from easiest to hardest.

This specially prepared set of items has come to be referred to as an *ordered item booklet* (OIB). The ordering of multiple-choice or other selected-response items in an OIB is straightforward, particularly if an item response theory model was used to obtain item difficulty parameter estimates (i.e., b-values), in which case items appear in the OIB in increasing b-value order.[9] When a test contains both constructed- and selected-response items, they are interspersed in the OIB, with the selected-response items appearing once (in increasing difficulty order) and each constructed-response item appearing once for each of its score points; each location in the OIB depends on the difficulty of obtaining each particular score point. The stimulus or prompt for each selected-response item, the scoring rubric, and sample responses illustrating each score point are also provided to participants.

---

[9]It is also possible to create OIBs based on other item difficulty indices (e.g., classical p-values, but this is much less common).

As is common in other standard-setting methods, the Bookmark procedure begins with selection of qualified participants, an orientation to the purpose of the test, familiarization with relevant content standards and performance level descriptions, and so on. Training in the method informs participants that the will progress through the OIB, in which each succeeding item is harder than the one before, and their task is to place one (or more, depending on the number of cut scores required) marker at the point in their booklets at which they believe a specified level of probability is passed. Specifically, as they review each item (or constructed-response score point) in the OIB, participants ask themselves: "Is it likely that an examinee on the borderline between passing and failing (or between performance categories X and Y) will answer this item correctly or earn this score point?" Mitzel, Lewis, Patz, and Green (2001) recommend that the probability judgment be referenced to a 67 percent likelihood, which they refer for as the *response probability* (RP). According to Mitzel et al. (2001), an RP of .67 can be interpreted in the following way: "For a given cut score, a student with a test score at that point will have a .67 probability of answering an item also at that cut score correctly" (p. 260). Thus, participants are instructed to place a marker on the first page in their OIB at which, in their opinion, the RP drops below. 67.

Although some applications of the Bookmark procedure have translated the bookmark positions directly into cut scores based on the number of raw score points prior to the bookmark (see Buckendahl, Smith, Impara, & Plake, 2002), this modification has received little research attention and comparatively much less frequent use. The more common method of deriving Bookmark cut score(s), described by Mitzel et al. (2001) is to obtain, for each participant, the scale value (usually an Item Response Theory [IRT] ability estimate) corresponding to a .67 probability of answering the bookmarked item correctly. The ability estimates implied by each participants' bookmark locations for a performance level are averaged, and the raw score corresponding to that average is used as the cut score. If cut scores for more than one performance level are required, the ability estimates implied by the bookmarks for each level are averaged and translated into raw cut scores in the same way.[10]

In the simplest case, applying a one-parameter logistic item response model for a test composed of select-response items, the probability of a correct response ($Px_j = 1$) for an SR item, i, is a function of an examinee's ability (θ), and the difficulty of the item (b_i). The model for this probability is:

$$P(x_i = 1|\theta) = \exp(\theta - b_i)/[1 + \exp(\theta - b_i)] \qquad (10.1)$$

where exp represents the natural logarithm e (2.71828...) raised to the power of the parenthetical expression that follows.

For select-response items, the basic standard-setting question is whether or not an examinee just barely categorized into a given performance level has a .67 chance of answering a given selected-response item correctly. Thus, starting with a probability, $P(x_i = 1|\theta)$, of .67 and solving Equation 10.1 for the ability (θ) needed to answer an item correctly, results in:

$$\theta = b_i + .708 \qquad (10.2)$$

---

[10]The basic Bookmark procedure, as described here, can be easily applied to tests composed of multiple-choice or other selected-response formats using the b-values, response probabilities, and associated ability (i.e., theta) estimates corresponding to bookmark placements. The situation becomes is more complicated when a test includes polytomously scored items, though the logic of deriving any cut score(s) is exactly the same. Because of space considerations, the mechanics for calculating a cut score in the more complicated case are not presented here. The interested reader can locate the relevant formulas and information in Cizek, Bunch, and Koons (2004).

where the values of b_i are taken from the parameter estimates of the item bookmarked by each participant and the resulting values of θ are then averaged to obtain the average recommended cut score(s). Equation 10.2 is interpreted to mean that the ability level required for an examinee to have a .67 probability of answering a given selected-response item correctly is .708 logits greater than the difficulty of the item.

The preceeding discussion is limited, however, to identification of one or more cut scores on the ability (i.e., θ) metric for OIBs composed of selected-response items. When constructed-response items are included in the OIB, derivation of the cut scores is conceptually the same, although the actual calculations become somewhat more complex as the location in the OIB of each constructed-response item is not based on an overall difficulty of the item, but on the probabilities of obtaining each of however many possible score points are associated with the item. Although somewhat beyond the scope of this chapter, readers interested in the relevant formulas appropriate for such a situation are referred to Cizek, Bunch, and Koons (2004).

The Contrasting Groups and Borderline Group Methods

Each of the preceding standard-setting methods described has required participants to consider each item or task in a test, or the collection of items and tasks, and to estimate the probable performance on those items and tasks by an examinee at or above a given level of performance. In contrast to that general approach to standard setting, other methods focus participants' judgments not on the items or tasks, but on examinees themselves. The latter methods have been termed "examinee centered" (Jaeger, 1989). Some researchers believe that examinee-centered methods represent a task that participants are more accustomed to; that is, the task of judging whether a specific student or examinee possesses adequate knowledge, skill, or ability with respect to a set of content standards (Livingston & Zieky, 1989).

Two examinee-centered methods are described in this chapter: the Borderline Group method and the Contrasting Groups method. Both methods require participants to make direct judgments about the status of real (i.e., not hypothetical) test takers. Essentially, each method derives a passing score for the test by combining the judgments about examinees with information about their actual performance on an examination. The methods differ in how the specific judgments that participants are required to make and in how those judgments are analyzed to derive cut scores.

The Contrasting Groups Method

The Contrasting Groups method has been described by Berk, who referred to it as "an extension of the familiar known-groups validation procedure" (1976, p. 4) that could be used to obtain a cut score differentiating between instructed and uninstructed students. To implement the method, two groups of examinees—those who were known to have received effective instruction covering the content to be tested and those who had not been so instructed—were administered a test over the content of instruction. Distributions of the total test scores for the two groups could be plotted and examined to find a point on the score scale that maximized the differentiation between those examinees who had received effective instruction ("true masters") and those who had not ("true nonmasters").

In its most common adaptation, the Contrasting Groups method requires examinees to take a test before any cut score(s) are yet known. Participants are empaneled who have personal knowledge of individual examinees' level of knowledge or skill level with respect to the characteristic being assessed. The participants—unaware of examinees' actual test scores—make judgments about each examinee as to their mastery/nonmastery status. As Berk suggested,

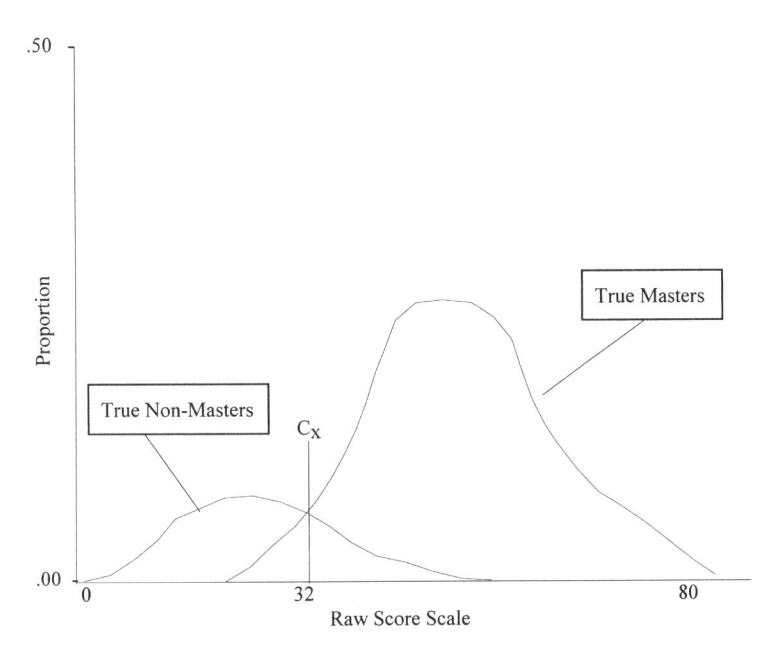

FIG. 10.3. Hypothetical distributions illustrating the Contrasting Groups method.

participants judgments are used to form two distributions based on the total test scores for the two groups. The distributions are then plotted and analyzed (Figure 10.3).

Depending on the sample sizes of the group judged to be masters and the group judged to be nonmasters, the plotted distributions may be rather "toothy" and not conforming to easy analysis. At least theoretically, the jaggedness of the distributions can be attributed to sampling error, so a common recommendation is that a smoothing procedure be implemented prior to locating a cut score (Livingston & Zieky, 1982). Using the smoothed distributions (such as those illustrated in Figure 10.3), a common strategy for deriving a cut score is to select the point of intersection of the two distributions. This point is indicated as C_x in Figure 10.3.

It is important to note at least two cautions with respect to the Contrasting Groups method. First, the strategy for identifying a cut score illustrated in Figure 10.3 implicitly assumes that the consequences of misclassifications are equally serious. In this case, a false-negative misclassification occurs when an examinee judged to truly have mastery of the content (a "true master") obtains a test score that falls below C_x. A false-positive misclassification occurs when an examinee judged to have an unacceptable level mastery of the content (a "true nonmaster") obtains a test score above C_x. The cut score identified illustrated in Figure 10.3, because it was set at the point of intersection of the two distributions, treats the two misclassifications as being of equal relative cost. In all cases, however, an explicit policy should be established in advance with respect to the relative costs of each type of classification error, and the actual location of C_x should be derived with respect to that policy decision.

Second, the Contrasting Groups method relies on the accuracy and reliability of participants' judgments about the examinees—essentially treating those judgments as a perfect criterion. Of course, this cannot be the case; human judgments that classify examinees as "true masters" or "true nonmasters" are susceptible to the same kinds of error as other classifications schemes (e.g., such as the test itself). Thus, when using the Contrasting Groups method, it is perhaps even more important than with other methods to devote time to selection and training of participants to assist them in making these critical judgments.

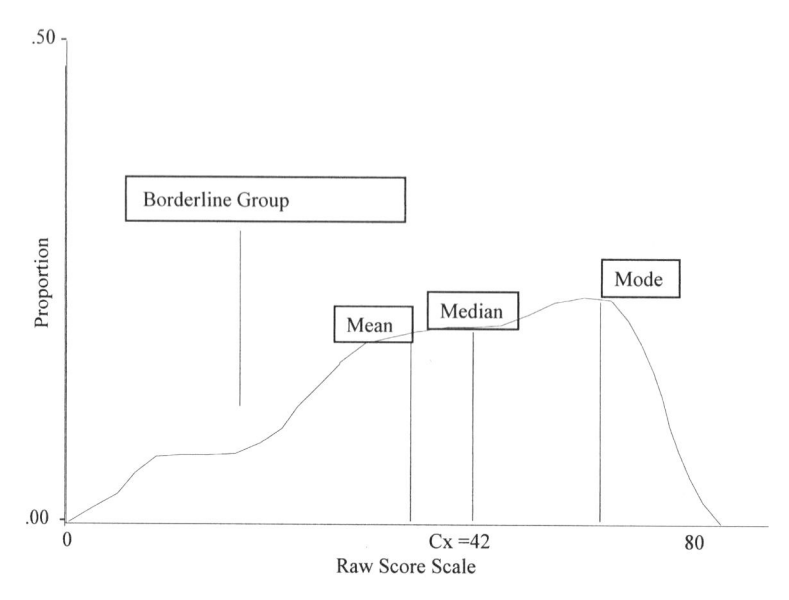

FIG. 10.4. Hypothetical distributions illustrating the Borderline Group method.

The Borderline Group Method

An even more straightforward judgment about examinees is made by participants using the Borderline Group method (Zieky & Livingston, 1977). Like the Contrasting Groups method, participants are selected who are familiar with the content tested and who have specific knowledge of the knowledge, skills, and abilities of individual examinees who are subject to the examination. To implement this method, participants first engage in an extended discussion to develop a description of an examinee on the borderline between mastery and nonmastery. With this conceptualization in mind, and again without knowledge of examinees' test performance, participants using the Borderline Group method to identify specific examinees whom they believe to lie at the borderline separating acceptable and unacceptable competence. (Alternatively, participants may be asked to sort examinees into three categories, one whom they believe to be clearly competent, one they believe to be clearly inadequately prepared, and one they believe to be on the cusp between competent and not competent.) A distribution of the borderline examinees' performances is formed and the median of the distribution is often used as the recommended standard. Figure 10.4 illustrates a cut score obtained using the Borderline Group method. In this case, the median (42) is identified as the cut score.

As with the Contrasting Groups method, the Borderline Group method has as one advantage its intuitive nature. On the other hand, a major limitation of the method lies in the fact that the size of the group judged to be on the borderline may be quite small, making estimates of the cut score unstable. Conversely, Jaeger (1989) has worried that participants who do not have sufficient knowledge about individual examinees may be susceptible to errors of central tendency and might assign a disproportionately large number of examinees to the borderline group. Although perhaps yielding a more stable estimate of C_x, such a tendency has the potential to bias the estimate in unknown ways.

The Body of Work Method

Within the last 20 years, many testing programs—particularly those focused on measuring achievement in K–12 school subject areas—have evolved to involve a diversity of item formats (i.e., other than uniformly multiple choice). These include short-response items, essays, performances, show your work, written reflections, grid-in responses, and others. At least in principle, this evolution has offered the potential for more faithful measurement of complex constructs; including a mix of item formats can help to avoid the validity threat known as construct underrepresentation.

Of the standard-setting methods with the greatest history of use, most were developed in the context of exclusively multiple-choice testing. And, although many of those methods can be adapted to tests that include a mix of item and task formats, some could only be applied to multiple-choice formats. A new genre of methods, called "holistic," has developed specifically to allow participants to make judgments about complex samples of evidence and to make judgments about samples of evidence that are heterogeneous in terms of item or task format. The so-called holistic methods require participants to focus their judgments on a collection of examinee work greater than a single item or task at a time. Although a number of methods can be classified as holistic, the differences between holistic methods can be appreciable. The following description applies to the holistic method known as the Body of Work method, proposed by Kingston, Kahl, Sweeney, and Bay (2001).

The basic approach to the Body of Work method is similar in conceptualization to the Contrasting Groups technique. However, rather than assigning examinees to categories such as "master" or "nonmaster," the Body of Work method requires participants to assign samples of examinees work (i.e., test performances) to the categories.

To implement the Body of Work method, participants are first familiarized with the purpose of the test, the characteristics of examinees, and the definitions of any relevant categories, in much the same way as training would occur for other methods. Participants are then presented with a large number of real, complete examinee work samples or test performances. Typically, these work samples are scored prior to standard setting; they are selected to span the range of obtainable total scores; and they cover the likely ways those total scores could be obtained by combinations of scores on the various components or formats of the total test.[11] Participants, again without knowledge of the actual scores assigned to the work samples, then rate each work sample holistically and classify it into one of the required categories (e.g., *Pass/Fail* or *Basic*, *Proficient*, *Advanced*).

To illustrate computation of cut scores using the Body of Work method, we consider a hypothetical test consisting of two extended constructed-response items scored using a 0 to 6 rubric, five short constructed-response items scored on a 0 to 3 scale, and 24 multiple-choice items scored 0 if incorrect, 1 if correct. Thus, the total possible raw score on this test is 51 points, and samples of real student work are selected to span raw scores ranging from approximately 7 to 50.[12] Further, let us assume that two cut scores are needed to distinguish between *Low*, *Medium*, and *High* levels of performance.

Using the Body of Work method, each participant categorizes each work sample into the three requisite categories. Figure 10.5 shows the hypothetical distributions of work samples grouped according to how they were classified by participants at the end of an initial round of ratings. In the current example, the process yields two preliminary cut scores—one to separate *Low* from *Medium* performance, and one to separate *Medium* from *High*.

---

[11] The number of work samples ultimately selected depends on the number of score points possible on the total test.

[12] Under an assumption of random guessing, chance performance on the 24 multiple-choice items is a total score of approximately 6. It is unlikely an efficient use of participants' time to require judgments for work samples composed of total scores not likely to be observed. Additionally, even if it was decided that judging samples across the entire raw score range was desirable, because raw scores less than 7 are unlikely, it would be difficult to identify such samples for inclusion.

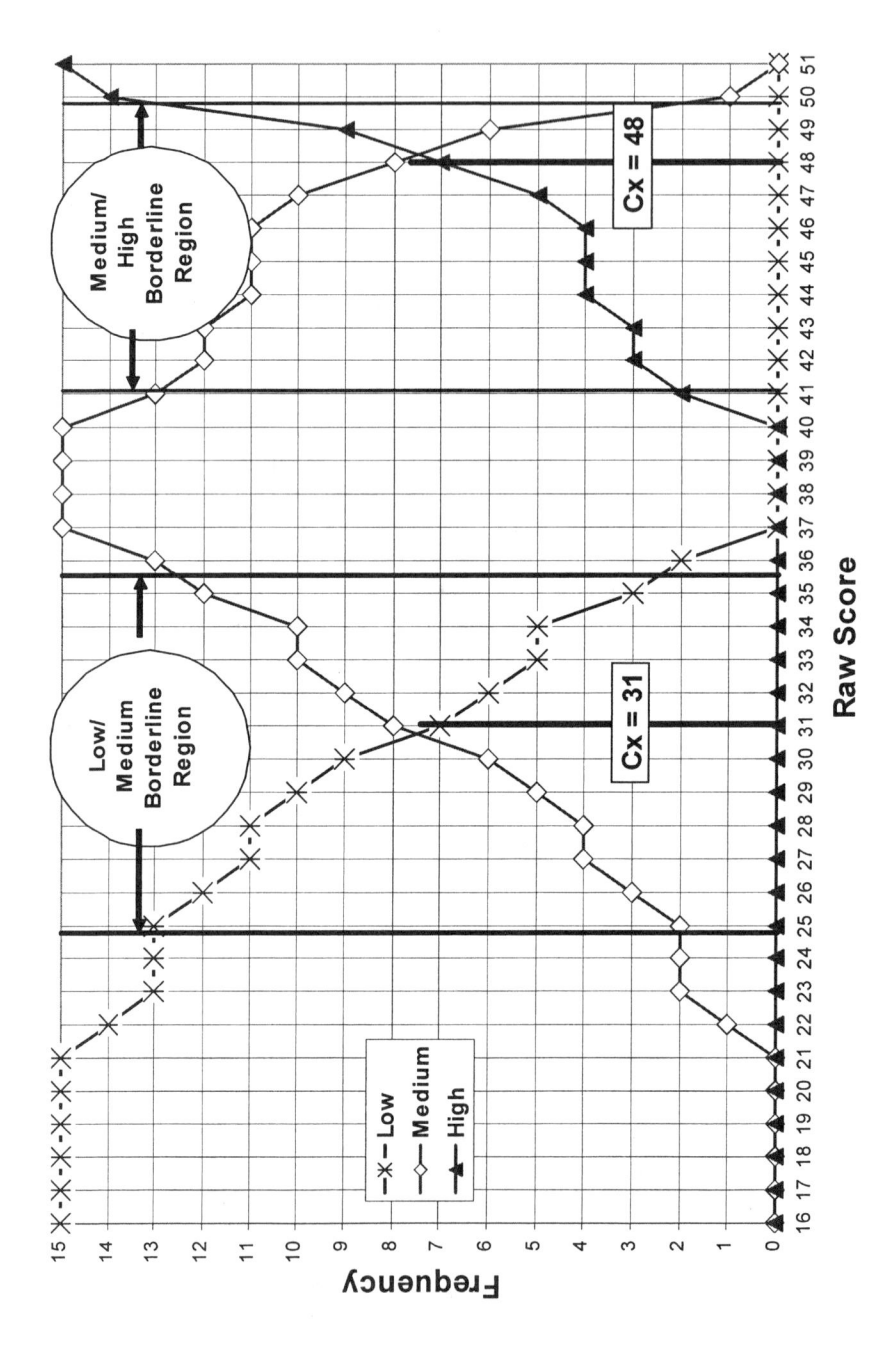

FIG. 10.5. Hypothetical distributions of Body of Work classifications.

As might be imagined, data analysis at the end of the first round of ratings provides a narrower range of possibilities for each of the three cut scores. For this reason, the first round of ratings using the Body of Work method is sometimes referred to as *range finding*. In the example shown in Figure 10.5, all participants identified work samples with a total score below 21 as belonging to the *Low* category. However, in the region bounded by total raw scores of 25 and 36, there was some disagreement among participants regarding whether those work samples should be classified as *Low* or *Medium*. Similarly, a range of uncertainty exists between total raw scores of 41 and 50 regarding the boundaries for the *Medium* and *High* performance categories. These areas are labeled "Low/Medium Borderline Region" and "Medium/High Borderline Region," respectively, in Figure 10.5.

As a result of the range-finding round, work samples with total raw scores outside of the borderline regions are eliminated from further consideration, and additional work samples are added to illustrate performances within the borderline regions and a second round of classifications ensues. Because the work samples classified by participants in Round 2 are more narrowly focused on the likely areas of the eventual cut scores, this round of ratings is sometimes referred to as *pinpointing*.

As with other standard-setting methods, following the rounds of ratings, it is common for participants using the Body of Work method to receive feedback regarding how other participants classified work samples, discuss their classifications, receive feedback on the likely impact of preliminary cut scores, and have opportunities to modify their judgments across the rounds of classifications.

There are at least two possibilities for obtaining final recommended cut scores using holistic methods such as the Body of Work method. A holistic method called *Analytic Judgment*, proposed by Plake and Hambleton (2001), involves classification of work into fairly fine-grained categories. For example, if performance standards at the *Basic*, *Proficient*, and *Advanced* levels are required, participants sort work samples into categories that included low-*Basic*, mid-*Basic*, high-*Basic*, low-*Proficient*, mid-*Proficient*, high-*Proficient*, and so on. This process results in some papers being assigned to the borderline categories (i.e., high-*Basic*/low-*Proficient*, and high-*Proficient*/low-*Advanced*). Deriving a cut score using the Analytic Judgment method requires only that the mean total scores of work samples classified into these adjacent borderline categories be averaged. Alternatively, the midpoint between the mean of the two adjacent borderline categories could by used.

The developers of the Body of Work method (Kingston et al., 2001) suggest the use of logistic regression to derive cut scores. Use of a logistic regression procedure results, roughly, in the approximate cut score locations shown in Figure 10.5. The two vertical lines in the figure with the associated labels $C_x = 31$ and $C_x = 48$ indicate the tentative cut scores separating the Low/Medium and Medium/High performance levels.

Methods for Adjusting Cut Scores

Ultimately, standard-setting participants do not themselves set standards. Rather, they follow procedures designed to result in a defensible recommendation to an agency, board, or other entity with the authority to accept, reject, or modify the recommendation. Assuming that the psychometric procedures for standard setting using some defensible method were carried out with fidelity, any adjustments of standards are necessarily based more on policy considerations than technical bases. For example, an entity may wish to adjust a panel's recommended cut score(s) based on their concerns about and percieved relative costs about the previously described reality that false-positive and false-negative decisions will occur. The measurement literature contains comparatively far fewer details for adjusting standards than for setting them in the first place.

One strategy for adjustment that has substantial logical and empirical foundation is based on the standard error of measurement (SEM) of observed test scores. This statistic takes into account variability in examinee performance attributable to random errors of measurement. However, the amount and direction of an adjustment based on the SEM are not determined for all situations. The amount and direction of any adjustment should be based on consideration of the relative costs of errors (see below), expert knowledge of the characteristics of examinees, previous pass/fail rates, and other factors involving human judgment.

It is not automatically known in what direction to apply an adjustment based on the SEM, or what multiple (or fraction) of an SEM should be used. These decisions relate to the judgments, by the responsible board, as to the relative seriousness of making false-negative decisions (i.e., denying a credential, diploma, license, and so on to a truly deserving examinee) or false-positive decisions (i.e., awarding a credential to a truly inadequately prepared examinee). Explicit consideration of the relative costs of each type of error, along with the purpose of the examination, should be translated into an explicit policy that helps to guide standard-setting decisions and any adjustments.

Two other methods have been proposed in the psychometric literature for striking a compromise between the kinds of standards that might be established using one of the methods described in this chapter (which are sometimes referred to as "absolute methods"), and more norm-referenced approaches. Both of the two compromise methods essentially ask participants to explicitly state the pass and fail rates that they believe to be reflective of the "true" proportions in the sample of examinees and tolerable from political, economic, or other perspectives. The following sections describe these compromise methods.

The Beuk Method

Beuk realized that all standard setting "is only partly a psychometric problem" (1984, p. 147). He suggested that standard-setting procedures take into account the level of content mastery judged to be essential, as well as comparative information about examinees.

To implement Beuk's (1984) method, each participant is asked to answer two straightforward questions: (1) What should be the minimum level of knowledge required to pass an examination? and (2) What passing rate should be expected? Participants express their answers to these questions as a raw score percent correct for the total test and as a percentage of the examinee population. When the examination is administered, these expectations can be compared with the actual performance of the examinees. To the extent that the expectations differ from the observed results, a compromise between the two can be struck using the answers provided by the participants to the two questions.

Figure 10.6 shows a hypothetical application of the Beuk method. Suppose, for example, that participants, on average, judged that the minimum percent correct should be 70% and they judged, on average, that 90% of examinees should pass. In Figure 10.6, these points are labeled $\bar{x}$ and $\bar{y}$, respectively. Then, the intersection of points $\bar{x}$ and $\bar{y}$ is determined; it is labeled "A" in the figure. Further suppose that, based on data actually obtained following the test administration, that the relationship between passing score used and percentage of examinees that would pass was represented by the monotonically decreasing function shown with the solid, curved line. The line indicates (as is necessarily true) that the percentage of examinees passing the test decreases as the percent correct required to pass increases.

The next step in applying the Beuk method is to calculate the standard deviations of participants' answers to the two questions related to expected percent correct and passing rates. The ratio of these two standard deviations (S_x/S_y) is used to construct a line with a slope equal to that ratio and which, passing through point A, is projected onto the distributional curve. The point at which the line intersects the curve is labeled B in the figure. The adjusted values of $\bar{x}$

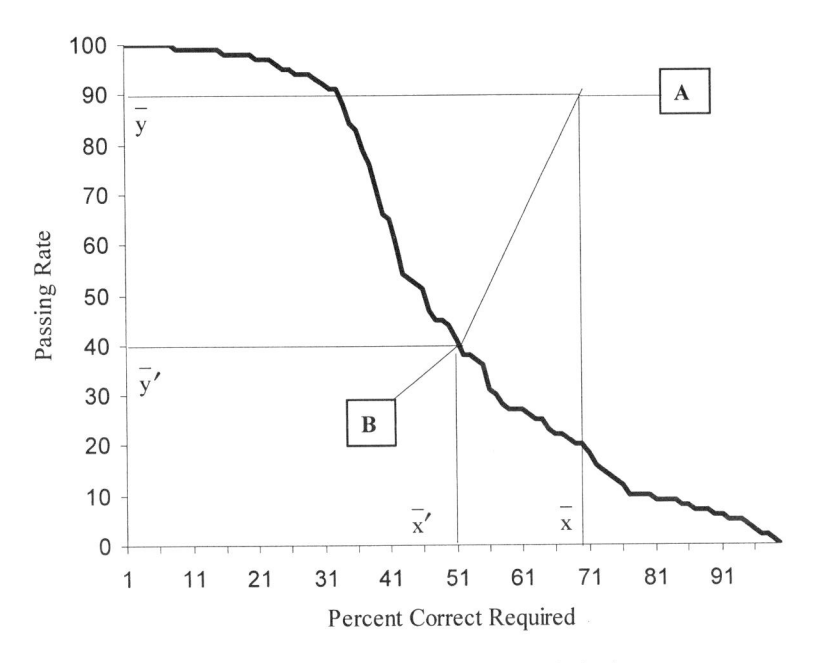

FIG. 10.6. Illustration of Beuk cut score derivation.

and $\bar{y}$ associated with B are then obtained by projecting point B on the two axes to determine the adjusted or "compromise" percent correct (i.e., the cut score) and the associated passing rate, labeled $\bar{x}'$ and $\bar{y}'$, respectively, in the figure. In the illustration shown, the projection yields an recommended percent correct (i.e., cut score) of 51% correct and the corresponding passing rate of 40%. The raw cut score is obtained by multiplying the adjusted percent correct ($\bar{x}'$) by the total number of possible points on the examination.

The Hofstee Method

Hofstee's (1983) compromise method is another approach to striking a balance between absolute and norm-referenced data. Hofstee proposed a model that applies "to the situation in which a cutoff score on an achievement test is set for the first time.... [and when] no agreed-upon prior or collateral information is available on the difficulty of the test, the quality of the course, or the amount of preparation by the students" (p. 117). The Hofstee approach is implemented by asking each standard-setting participant to respond to four questions:

1. What is the lowest cutoff score that would be acceptable, even if every student attained that score on the first testing?;
2. What is the lowest acceptable cutoff score, even if no student attained that score on the first testing?;
3. What is the maximum tolerable failure rate?; and
4. What is the minimum acceptable failure rate?

The mean values of the responses to these questions, across participants are referred to, respectively, as k_{min}, k_{max}, f_{max}, and f_{min}. Figure 10.7 illustrates a hypothetical application of the Hofstee method in which the participants' mean judgments about k_{min}, k_{max}, f_{max}, and f_{min} are approximately 15, 90, 80, and 35, respectively.

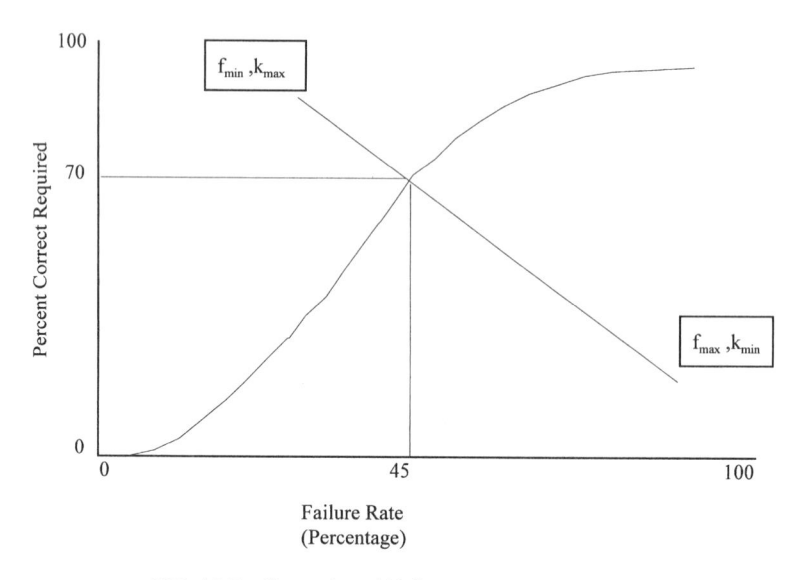

FIG. 10.7. Illustration of Hofstee cut score derivation.

To derive the cut score, the points (f_{min}, k_{max}) and (f_{max}, k_{min}), which in this case correspond to the points (35, 90) and (80, 15) are used to plot a line which, like the Beuk (1984) method, is projected onto the distribution of observed test scores. Figure 10.7 identifies the locations of (f_{min}, k_{max}) and (f_{max}, k_{min}) and illustrates the projection of the resulting line onto a curve showing the functional relationship between percentages of failing examinees (on the abscissa) and the percentage of correct responses on a test (on the ordinate). The percent correct required to pass is found by following the horizontal line to the ordinate; the failure rate that corresponds to that cut score is found by following the vertical line to the abscissa. In the hyothetical illustration shown in Figure 10.7, the percent correct required and corresponding failure rates would be 70 and 45, respectively.

CONCLUSION

Setting performance standards has been called "the most controversial problem in educational assessment today" (Hambleton, 1998, p. 103). It is clearly one of the most critical—and visible—steps in the test development process. When a legal challenge arises for a testing program, it almost always arises because it is alleged that incorrect or unfair decisions were made as a result of applying a cut score. Thus, agencies responsible for testing programs must recognize that, as long as important decisions must be made, and as long as test performance plays a part in those decisions, it is likely that controversy will remain. At least to some degree, however, the defensibility of those decisions can be maximized by crafting well-conceived methods for setting performance standards, implementing those methods faithfully, and gathering sound evidence regarding the validity of the process and the result.

REFERENCES

American Educational Research Association (AERA), American Psychological Association (APA), & National Council on Measurement in Education (NCME). (1999). *Standards for educational and psychological testing.* Washington, DC: American Psychological Association.

American Psychological Association. (1954). *Technical recommendations for psychological and diagnostic technequies.* Washington, DC: Author.

Angoff, W. H. (1971). Scales, norms, and equivalent scores. In R. L. Thorndike (Ed.), *Educational measurement* (pp. 508–600). Washington, DC: American Council on Education.

Berk, R. A. (1976). Determination of optional [sic] cutting scores in criterion-referenced measurement. *Journal of Experimental Education, 45*, 4–9.

Buckendahl, C. W., Smith, R. W., Impara, J. C., & Plake, B. S. (2002). A comparison of Angoff and Bookmark standard setting methods. *Journal of Educational Measurement, 39*, 253–264.

Beuk, C. H. (1984). A method for reaching a compromise between absolute and relative standards in examinations. *Journal of Educational Measurement, 21*, 147–152.

Cizek, G. J. (1993). Reconsidering standards and criteria. *Journal of Educational Measurement, 30*(2), 93–106.

Cizek, G. J. (1996a). Setting passing scores. *Educational Measurement: Issues and Practice, 15*(2), 20–31.

Cizek, G. J. (1996b). Standard setting guidelines. *Educational Measurement: Issues and Practice, 15*(1), 13–21, 12.

Cizek, G. J. (2001a). More unintended consequences of high-stakes testing. *Educational Measurement: Issues and Practice, 20*(4), 19–27.

Cizek, G. J. (2001b). Conjectures on the rise and call of standard setting: An introduction to context and practice. In G. J. Cizek (Ed.), *Setting performance standards: Concepts, methods, and perspectives* (pp. 3–17). Mahwah, NJ: Lawrence Erlbaum Associates.

Cizek, G. J. (Ed.). (2001c). *Setting performance standards: Concepts, methods, and perspectives*. Mahwah, NJ: Lawrence Erlbaum Associates.

Cizek, G. J., Bunch, M., & Koons, H. (2004). Setting performance standards: Contemporary methods. *Educational Measurement: Issues and Practice, 23*(4), 31–50.

Downing, S. M., Lieska, N. G., & Raible, M. D. (2003). Establishing passign standards for classroom achievement tests in medical education: A comparative study of four methods. *Academic Medicine, 78*(10), S85–S87.

Hambleton, R. M. (1998). Setting performance standards on achievement tests: Meeting the requirements of Title I. In L. N. Hansche (Ed.), *Handbook for the development of performance standards* (pp. 87–114). Washington, DC: Council of Chief State School Officers.

Hambleton, R. M., & Plake, B. S. (1995). Using an extended Angoff procedure to set standards on complex performance assessments. *Applied Measurement in Education, 8*, 41–56.

Hofstee, W. K. B. (1983). The case for compromise in educational selection and grading. In S. B. Anderson & J. S. Helmick (Eds.), *On educational testing* (pp. 109–127). San Francisco: Jossey-Bass.

Impara, J. C., & Plake, B. S. (1997). Standard-setting: An alternative approach. *Journal of Educational Measurement, 34*, 353–366.

Impara, J. C., & Plake, B. S. (1998). Teachers' ability to estimate item difficulty: A test of the assumptions in the Angoff standard setting method. *Journal of Educational Measurement, 35*, 69–81.

Jaeger, R. M. (1989). Certification of student competence. In R. L. Linn (Ed.), *Educational measurement* (3rd ed., pp. 485–514). New York: Macmillan.

Kane, M. (1994). Validating the performance standards associated with passing scores. *Review of Educational Research, 64*(3), 425–461.

Kingston, N. M., Kahl, S. R., Sweeney, K., & Bay, L. (2001). Setting performance standards using the body of work method. In G. J. Cizek (Ed.), *Setting performance standards: Concepts, methods, and perspectives* (pp. 219–248). Mahwah, NJ: Lawrence Erlbaum Associates.

Linn, R. L. (1994, October). *The likely impact of performance standards as a function of uses: From rhetoric to sanctions.* Paper presented at the Joint Conference on Standard Setting for Large-Scale Assessments, Washington, DC.

Livingston, S. A., & Zieky, M. J. (1982). *Passing scores*. Princeton, NJ: Educational Testing Service.

Livingston, S. A., & Zieky, M. J. (1989). A comparative study of standard-setting methods. *Applied Measurement in Education, 2*, 121–141.

Messick, S. (1989). Validity. In R. L. Linn (Ed.), *Educational measurement* (3rd ed., pp. 13–104). New York: Macmillan.

Mitzel, H. C., Lewis, D. M., Patz, R. J., & Green, D. R. (2001). The bookmark procedure: Psychological perspectives. In G. J. Cizek (Ed.), *Setting performance standards: Concepts, methods, and perspectives* (pp. 249–281). Mahwah, NJ: Lawrence Erlbaum Associates.

Nedelsky, L. (1954). Absolute grading standards for objective tests. *Educational and Psychological Measurement, 14*, 3–19.

Pitoniak, M. J. (2003). *Standard setting methods for complex licensure examinations.* Unpublished doctoral dissertation, University of Massachusetts, Amherst.

Plake, B. S., & Hambleton, R. K. (2001). The analytic judgment method for setting standards on complex performance assessments. In G. J. Cizek (Ed.), *Setting performance standards: Concepts, methods, and perspectives* (pp. 283–312). Mahwah, NJ: Lawrence Erlbaum Associates.

Raymond, M. R., & Reid, J. B. (2001). Who made thee a judge? Selecting and training participants for standard setting. In G. J. Cizek (Ed.), *Setting performance standards: Concepts, methods, and perspectives* (pp. 119–157). Mahwah, NJ: Lawrence Erlbaum Associates.

Reckase, M. D. (2001). Innovative methods for helping standard-setting participants to perform their task. The role of feedback regarding consistency, accuracy, and impact. In G. J. Cizek (Ed.), *Setting performance standards: Concepts, methods, and perspectives* (pp. 159–174). Mahwah, NJ: Lawrence Erlbaum Associates.

Zieky, M. J. (2001). So much has changed: How the setting of cut scores has evolved since the 1980s. In G. J. Cizek (Ed.), *Setting performance standards: Concepts, methods, and perspectives* (pp. 19–52). Mahwah, NJ: Lawrence Erlbaum Associates.

Zieky, M. J., & Livingston, S. A. (1977). *Manual for setting standards on the Basic Skills Assessment Tests*. Princeton, NJ: Educational Testing Service.

III

Item Development

11

Computerized Item Banking

C. David Vale

Computerized item banking has emerged as an essential activity in the development of commercial and other large-scale tests. Thus, the item banker has become an indispensable tool of the test developer. Although a significant proportion of the test items in use today reside in electronic item banks, such item banks do not generally follow a standard of structure or representation. Standards are emerging, however. This chapter explores the conceptual underpinnings of item banks and item bankers. These include the concept of objects, formulations of items as objects, a social order of items, and standards of representation. Additionally, models of bank organization, methods of securing an item bank, and structural concepts applicable to tests are considered. The chapter discusses these in light of the leading item-banking standard and provides some examples of elements often found in item banks and desired in item bankers.

The idea of computerized item banking is at least 30 years old (e.g., Choppin, 1976). It has been almost that long since I first programmed a computerized item banker. Thirty years ago, computerized item banking concepts were simple. The source material consisted of either a collection of old tests or those same tests cut apart, item by item, pasted on cards, and somehow organized in one or more shoeboxes. The vast majority of the items were of the textual multiple-choice variety. Virtually any form of computerization was an improvement, usually resulting in reduced clerical time for producing future tests. Of course, the computer systems were simple as well. My first item banker was housed on a mainframe, accessed through a CRT at 30 characters per second, and budgeted for two megabytes of disk storage. Baker (1986), by comparison, noted that the storage problem had become a thing of the past with as much as 30 megabytes then available on a microcomputer. As further comparison, today's commodity home computers routinely offer at least 60 gigabytes—about 2,000 times what Baker referenced.

Item banking was not an overnight success, however. In fact, the whole idea of computer use in testing was still suspect 20 years ago (e.g., Hiscox, 1985). First, the value of a computerized system that just printed tests appealed primarily to small-scale, technically oriented users who did not type very well. The technical support for a production system staffed by clerical workers could be daunting. Second, the value of item banking seemed interrelated with Item

Response Theory (IRT) (Hambleton & Swaminathan, 1985). Van der Linden, for example, suggested that "The practice of item banking and the theory of item response models are interdependent" (1986, p. 331). The implementation of two technologies required a level of technical sophistication beyond the comfort level of many test developers of the era.

But then, about 20 years ago, computerized testing began to catch on. The armed services (Sands, Waters, & McBride, 1997) and the National Association of Securities Dealers were among the first to field significant operational programs, followed by insurance and real estate testing. Commercial software systems became available, not just for item banking but for the complete process of computerized test administration (cf. Baker, 1989). Then the Federal Aviation Administration and The American College changed the nature of computerized testing by endorsing multiple delivery vendors for their licensure and certification examinations. Finally, a massive interest by most of the hardware and software vendors in the information technology industry offered the experience of computerized testing to millions. And adaptive testing (van der Linden & Glas, 2000), used in several of these programs, changed the inherent structure of tests from fixed forms to custom collections of test items drawn, for each examinee at test time, from a larger item bank.

Where an electronic item bank represented a potential labor-saving device for a paper-and-pencil test, it became an essential precursor of a computer-administered one. To those who must manage significant banks of test items, an item banker has taken on a status similar to the word processor, the spreadsheet, and the telephone: It has become a tool for doing an essential job. But unlike the telephone system, item banking tools have not achieved a uniformity of function or a standard of interface necessary to readily support the transfer of item banks from one venue to another. This, of course, is changing.

Several articles have enumerated and discussed the benefits of item banking as well as provided basic guidelines for developing banks and selecting bankers (e.g., Bergstrom & Gershon, 1995; Rudner, 1998; Umar, 1999; Ward & Murray-Ward, 1994). In this chapter, I take a different slant on the topic and focus on some core concepts of item banking, commonalties among different applications, and efforts toward standardization of efforts. With many organizations sharing development and delivery resources, standardization of item bank representation is inevitable. Thus, part of this chapter is devoted to discussion of the evolving standards for item banks and item bankers. Although test developers have been accustomed to standards (e.g., for validity and mastery), the new standards have taken on a level of complexity totally unfamiliar to many in the test-development community.

This chapter starts at the most basic (i.e., elemental, not elementary) and works up. Most basic is the *test item*, a concept that becomes less well defined as more forms of testing become possible. Organization of the items into banks is next, followed by the characteristics and requirements of the item bankers that support them. This is followed by a discussion of the products of item banking, including tests and structured pools for newer forms of computerized tests. Finally, practical issues important to individuals managing item resources are discussed, including the portability of resources and the provision for their security. The appendix to this chapter includes a list of some of the currently available item-banking programs. This chapter does not review the software nor does it offer any recommendations for the purchase of such software. Neither does it offer explicit guidance on how to create such a system. However, it does present conceptual underpinnings necessary to understand the issues in organizing an item bank and selecting and/or designing item-banking software to manage it.

This chapter makes heavy reference to the evolving standards developed by the IMS Global Learning Consortium (IMS, 2002a, 2002b, 2002c, 2004a). IMS is a nonprofit organization with members from a variety of sectors of the electronic learning community, including hardware and software developers, educators, publishers, and government. Its mission is to support the adoption and use of learning technology by providing a forum for collaboration on issues of interoperability (IMS, 2004b). Discussion here remains at a more conceptual level than does the IMS specification, however. This is in part because the specification is evolving and some of the details will change. It is also because the specification is much longer, more complex, and more detailed than is appropriate for a chapter such as this one. Finally, the IMS specification represents a standard of information exchange and, although it may drive the conceptual organization of an item bank, it is not a standard for item bank organization or a requirement for internal representation. I do endeavor, insofar as is possible, to remain consistent with the spirit and terminology of the IMS specification in the discussions that follow.

ITEMS

Definition

Definition and organization are central to any discussion of item banking and we face a challenge of definition with the concept of the *item,* considered by many to be the most basic element in an item bank. The difficulty with basic elements is that they tend, with the passage of time and the extension of knowledge, to no longer be basic. Consider the atom, the basic chemical element, composed of more basic particles such as protons, themselves composed of more basic particles like quarks, and so on. The item similarly is composed of subelements, but can function as an elemental concept around which concepts both larger and smaller are discussed.

Note that *item* is a term of art. Lay people think of tests as consisting of questions and our use of *item* often requires explanation. Of course the term exists because tests are not always collections of questions, but may also consist of problems to solve and assertions to evaluate. *Item*, like *element* or *component*, encompasses a variety of things.

Items have been variously described and classified (see Downing, chap. 12, and Welch, chap. 13, this volume for discussions of selected-response and constructed-response items). Although the descriptions and classifications in most of the testing literature have psychological or substantive significance, the definition of an item for purposes of item banking has a more concrete purpose of facilitating its representation in the bank. Thus, the definition offered here is not intended as a replacement for those definitions, but a working definition useful for the construction of item banks.

An *item,* most basically, must include a stimulus. That stimulus can be a simple question. Or it can be a question followed by several alternative answers. It may be part of a larger structure, consisting of other stimuli, such as a passage of text or some other form of reference material. And it may occur in concert with other items, either optionally or as a requirement.

The IMS Global Learning Consortium (2002a, 2002b, 2002c, 2004a, 2004b) has invested a considerable amount of effort to describe what an item is and how items may be organized into banks and tests (*assessments*, in IMS terminology). Its goal is to provide a representation in which items and tests can be readily exchanged among users working with a wide variety of computer types and instructional management software. In the IMS conceptual structure, the *item* is defined as "the fundamental block that contains one or more questions and responses" (IMS, 2002b, p. 10). It is given the status of the "smallest exchangeable object" within the Question and Test Interoperability Specification (IMS, 2004a). The IMS specification represents the most thorough attempt to date to provide a standard by which different vendors of item banks and item bankers may exchange information. Note that, in the interest of a readable presentation, I take some liberties with the details of the specification, deviating from the specification where it is in the interest of clarity. Readers desiring a faithful interpretation of the specification are directed to the public specification itself.

The IMS specification represents items and assessments as object models. Object modeling grows out of the discipline of Object-Oriented Programming (OOP) (Booch, 1994). OOP has been a religion in computer science circles for well over a decade. Defining and understanding OOP is an art, the subject of countless philosophical and practical books, seminars, and conventions. The goal of OOP is to provide a set of tools for managing the overwhelming complexity that characterizes much modern-day software development by organizing programs into an interrelated set of entities called *objects*. Although item banks almost never take on the degree of complexity found in a significant programming effort, some of the OOP concepts and methods are useful in thinking about item banking. Furthermore, much of the language finds its way into discussions of communication among item bankers. Thus, a brief lay description is in order.

Classically, an object model was thought to have four major elements or characteristics: abstraction, encapsulation, modularity, and hierarchy (Booch, 1994). *Abstraction* is essentially definition, the denotation of essential properties that describe an object, distinguish it, and give it meaning relative to the system developer. *Encapsulation* separates external functionality from internal implementation. An object is a black box to the user of its functionality because the details of how the functionality is achieved are hidden or encapsulated. *Modularity* refers to the decomposition of a system into separate chunks or modules. Objects are modular by their nature, but modularity generally refers to larger chunks of program code. Modularity was once essential for all computer programs of any size because of the time it took to compile or translate the source program into executable code. As computers have become faster, this is now an issue for only really large systems. Finally, *hierarchy* refers to a cascading of objects or abstractions, such that child abstractions can inherit characteristics of their parents.

Objects have *properties* that characterize their unique features. They offer *methods*, that is, procedures for doing things subject to the values of certain properties. And they respond to *events*, a class of external stimuli that they recognize. In a more concrete example, a brick is an object that can be considered to have properties of height, speed, and support. The method, drop, changes support from true to false and formulaically increases the speed property and reduces the height property until the event, hit ground, occurs. That event reasserts support and reduces height and speed to zero.

Software objects are a combination of data and procedural instructions. Like their physical counterparts, they can serve as building blocks for larger structures. An *object class* is like a blueprint or prototype. With an object class defined, instantiations of objects can be created in the image of the object class. By changing the properties of the instantiations, a variety of different objects can be created.

Major motivations behind OOP are the ideas of reusability and portability. *Reusability* refers to the prospect of reusing major segments of program code by changing a few parameters. *Portability* is the idea that, by changing a few minor characteristics, major software systems could be used on a variety of platforms. The idea of reusability is somewhat akin to creating a jig to build window frames. Portability is like being able to use the window frames built in the jig for houses all over the country.

The trick to making OOP work is in the development of the base object classes, the structuring of a hierarchy of object classes, and in getting everyone working on the process to use the base classes as building blocks for the necessary functionality. In the case of an item bank, the first challenge is in creating base classes to represent the extreme variation in item types that the creativity of test developers supports. The second challenge is in getting those producing item-banking software to develop it using the base classes.

The general body of work in computer science most closely related to the application of OOP to item banking is the field of document modeling (cf., Bradley, 2004, chap. 2). Initially of interest to developers of word processors and related utilities, the efforts have focused on the development of common document base classes and the specification of program interfaces to process them, with the majority of the effort being conducted by the W3C working group on the document object model (DOM) (W3C, 2004). The emerging standard language in which documents are specified is the extensible markup language (XML) (Young, 2002), and the IMS specifications are in terms of XML.

The IMS specification is an attempt to provide a base class of objects for describing items and assessments. It is a work in progress and, as such, is likely to be found somewhat unstable and incomplete. It does, however, provide the most focused and comprehensive attempt to provide an object class for building items and assessments. The presentation here should be considered an attempt to describe the model in consistent lay terms. To accomplish that, I have taken some liberties with the details of the evolving standard, attempting in some cases to extrapolate features it will ultimately need.

A few definitions provided by IMS (2004a, Section 3) serve to both clarify the concept of an item and illustrate the complexity inherent in the definition. An *item* is the smallest exchangeable object. A *basic item* contains a single interaction. An *interaction* is the method by which the candidate selects or creates a response. An *attempt* is the process by which the candidate interacts with an item. A *candidate session* is the time during which a candidate interacts with a single item as part of an attempt. An *item session* is the accumulation of all attempts a candidate makes to an item. A *composite item* contains more than one interaction. An *adaptive item* adapts its appearance, its scoring, or both in response to the candidate's attempt(s). Note that an item (in the 2004 specification) does not contain a response, per se, but rather defines response processing by which response variables are judged or scored and converted to outcome variables.

Items, broadly described, consist of two classes of element: material and interactions. *Material* is anything that is presented to the examinee (others might call it the stimulus). I would deviate slightly from the IMS definition to suggest that an item consists of a stimulus and, optionally, an interaction. An optional interaction allows support material and instructions to be represented using the structures available for items. Note that the concept of an adaptive item allows not only simple formats such as answer until correct, but conceptually embodies the elements necessary to represent a simulation.

An item may consist of any combination of material and interaction that the medium of presentation supports. In the case of a paper-and-pencil test, the material is limited to what can be displayed on a printed page and the interaction is usually limited to what marks the examinee can make with the pencil. (Note that the answer-until-correct format, an adaptive item format, existed in paper-and-pencil form, usually implemented through scratch-offs or latent ink.) A computerized test may contain anything supported by the computer hardware, including graphics, video, sound, and multiple or continuous interactions comparable to those found in computer games.

Although some items exist independently, others establish relationships with other items in the bank. These relationships, characteristic of the items themselves, rather than the bank in which they appear, can be thought of as a *social order* among items. Three relationships, along with their variations, are important in the social order of an item bank: friends, enemies, and dependents. *Friends* are items that must appear together in a test. *Antagonists* must not appear near each other. *Dependent* items cannot appear without their *supporters*. *Close friends* cannot appear without all of their other close friends. *Snobs* must appear in a designated order. *Enemies* must not appear in the same test. These relationships are summarized in Table 11.1.

To illustrate, reading comprehension items are dependent friends; the passage is their supporter. The items must appear together, following their supporter. If the order of item

TABLE 11.1
Social Order Among Items

Relationship	Meaning	Examples
Friends	Items that must appear together because of substantive similarity or reliance on common support material.	Reading comprehension items, story problems that exploit a common theme.
Close friends	Items that must appear as a complete block; if one is included, all (or a minimum number) must be.	Reading comprehension items may, by policy, require at least three items per passage.
Snobs	Close friends that must appear in a defined order.	Grammar or punctuation items that constitute single lines in a larger paragraph; if presented out of order, the paragraph would be incomprehensible.
Dependents	Items that can appear only with support.	Reading comprehension items, that require a passage.
Supporters	Items without interactions that provide support to other items.	Instructions; reading passages.
Antagonists	Items that cue each other and must be separated in presentation.	"Which is a primary color?" and "All the following are primary colors except."
Enemies	Items that cannot appear in the same test.	Clones or questions with minor variations that ask essentially the same thing.

presentation is important, the items are dependent snobs. Items that represent lines of text in a larger paragraph (in a grammar test, for example) are close snobbish friends; all must appear together and in the right order. Two items that may cue each other are antagonists. Two items that ask exactly the same question using trivially different words are enemies. Obviously, the banker must occasionally intervene to avoid problems in test construction if friends have friends who are enemies. (This may occur, for example, when items associated with a reading passage cue each other or are clones.) Social order is not explicitly supported in the IMS specification.

Item properties or ancillary information support the administration and scoring process and may consist of scoring keys, characteristic parameters, and other information that directs the delivery or scoring of an item (e.g., substantive content assignment). Table 11.2 lists some of the most common item properties. This table falls far short of providing a complete specification of properties, as the IMS specification attempts.

Items may also be represented as *item templates*, within the IMS specification, an item with structure but lacking certain elements of content. Item templates (elsewhere referred to as *shells* [e.g., Haladyna & Shindoll, 1989]) are converted to actual items by filling in the *template variables*. An example of an item template is an arithmetic story problem in which the actual numbers (e.g., the numbers and/or types of fruit Dick ate) are supplied at the time of test production or administration.

An abundance of item types are possible. Haladyna (2004) enumerated a variety of multiple-choice item types and Parshall, Davey, and Pashley (2000) discussed some of the "innovative" types, including several with multimedia stimuli, high-fidelity simulation, and haptic (three-dimensional touch) responses. Sireci and Zenisky (chap. 14, this volume) also present innovative formats that are in a computer-administered environment. The IMS specification does not explicitly classify items according to type of item, but rather by type of response processing

TABLE 11.2
Partial Listing of Item Properties

Property	Meaning	Example
Ancestry	Items that may have provided a base for revision that resulted in this item. Different from social order in that ancestry is informational and social order is actionable.	RC0000234 required counting apples; this item requires identical operations but is based on oranges.
Classification	The (usually hierarchical) sequence of classification codes that places an item in a unique category.	Nutrition/food groups/fats/saturated fats
Identifier	A unique identifier for an item.	RC0001234
IRT Parameters	Numbers characterizing an item within the framework of an IRT model (e.g., a, b, c)	1.739
Item-total or item-scale correlation	The statistical correlation between the item score and total score or a scale score. Most often this is a biserial or point-biserial correlation. Sample specific, this statistic often has an associated test date or identifier.	0.34 in TDK1102 0.31 in TDK1103
Proportion correct	The proportion of candidates who answered the item correctly. This statistic is also sample specific.	0.89 in TDK1102 0.78 in TDK1103
Response rationales	Explanations for each response in an objective item, documenting how the alternative was obtained and justifying it as a correct or incorrect choice.	A. Incorrect; failure to carry. B. Correct; computation verified.
Response type	A code or description indicating the type of response.	LID-1: Multiple choice
Reviewers	Documentation of who reviewed the item and his or her comments. Should include a date of review. May reference a reviewer biographical database.	D.Vale (6/21/04): Both B and C are correct.
Revision history	Documentation of the changes made to the item.	6/30/04: Alternative C changed to "12".
Scoring key	In an objective item format, an indication of the response that is considered to be correct.	B
Scoring rubric	For a subjectively scored, constructed-response item, the features characteristic of right and wrong answers.	1. Notes that the Rasch model does not accommodate guessing. 2. Recognizes that God intended items to have three parameters.
Social order	Lists of all items of this item's social order, one list for each type of relationship.	Friends: RC0001235, RC0001236 Enemies: RC0001237
Source reference	Reference to one or more authoritative documents that may support the scoring key or rubric, should it be challenged. May also support incorrectness of distractors.	Haladyna (2004, p. 228)
Usage history	A listing of the forms and dates in which the item was used.	TDK1102; 11/04/02. TDK1103; 11/01/03.
Writer	The name or other identifier of the individual who authored the item, along with the date of authorship. This often refers to a more extensive biography of the individual including affiliations, qualifications, and contact information.	J. Smith Professor of Education Oxblood University 11/22/03

TABLE 11.3
IMS Response Types

Response Type	Meaning	Example
Logical identifier (LID)	Responses are made by selecting or positioning a clearly defined visual element.	Selecting a check box or positioning a slider. (Multiple-choice items use this response type.)
X–Y coordinates (XY)	Responses are made by identifying an area on the displayed item that may not be explicitly demarcated as a response option.	Mouse clicking image hotspots.
String (STR)	A string of text is supplied by the candidate.	Short-answer and essay item responses.
Numerical (NUM)	The examinee enters a number as a response.	A free-response arithmetic item.
Logical groups (GRP)	The examinee responds in a way that associates elements with each other.	A matching item.

required. The specification anticipates that all simple item types can be classified according to five general response-processing types (Table 11.3).

Version 1.2 of the specification (IMS, 2002b) allowed composite responses to be built from multiple basic types. The draft of Version 2.0 (IMS, 2004a) appears to have dropped that concept in favor of the composite item, one that contains multiple interactions between the examinee and the item stimulus.

Basic items do not contain methods or events, except in the trivial sense of displaying a stimulus, storing a response, and ending. Adaptive items, depending on their implementation, may encapsulate methods for responding to response events and changing the stimulus as a result.

An item banker does not need to and invariably does not support all types of items. An item banker is considered compliant with the IMS specification if it is capable of exporting all the item features it supports within the constraints of the specification and is capable of recognizing all of these features in the specification. A compliant banker is not required to recognize features it does not support.

Organization

An *item bank* is an organized collection of items. Organization, or classification, is important for at least two reasons. First, organization allows one to find, count, and inventory items of various types and functions. Second, organization into groups allows one to discuss and allocate higher level representations of items.

Booch (1994) describes three historical approaches to the problem of classification: classical categorization, conceptual clustering, and prototype theory. *Classical categorization,* a method attributed to Plato, groups entities according to their similarities as determined from their properties. For example, has leaves, has claws, and has teeth. A major challenge in the classical method is the selection of properties, which should have a degree of granularity appropriate to the task at hand and should be rather orthogonal, that is, they should not be redundant as a result of being too similar either functionally or statistically. Classical categorization generally results in a hierarchical organization of entities.

Conceptual clustering is a variation of the classical approach. It differs not so much in concept, but rather in the certainty with which entities may be classified according to properties.

Whereas the classical and conceptual approaches require all members of a classification to possess all common properties, *prototype theory* allows classification based on similarity of a collection of properties, rather than possession of all. Prototype theory classifies entities based on overall family resemblance, classifying each with the category it most closely resembles. For example, a classification based on prototype theory would most likely consider an emu to be a bird, even though it does not possess the ability to fly, a feature common to most other birds; classical and conceptual classifications might not.

The items in an item bank should be organized in a manner that is logical to those who need to find the items. Although the Dewey Decimal System and the Library of Congress Classification are suitable for organizing libraries, their use in video rental stores is rare. All classification systems have several things in common. First, they are conceptual structures based in human judgment; different humans may produce different judgments. Second, a specific classification system is designed for a specific task; the properties or prototypes, as well as their granularity, are determined by their function. Third, all classification systems change over time, because of changes in judges, judgments, or the state of knowledge about the entities involved.

The properties of items may be categorical or continuous. Content areas, cognitive levels, and response types tend to be categorical, for example. Quantitative parameters, such as the IRT a, b, and c parameters, tend to be continuous. Continuous properties can be readily made categorical, but categorical properties can be made continuous only if they have an implicit order. Classification can only be done using categorical properties.

Properties may be *crossed* or *nested,* terms that have the same meaning here as in experimental design. *Crossed properties* are defined in the same way across all conditions. *Nested properties* are defined differently across items according to their other properties. Substantive content properties are usually nested. This results in a hierarchy of properties, often reflected in a content outline. Most other properties are crossed.

Licensure and certification banks are generally organized hierarchically by topic, usually in approximate correspondence to content outlines distributed to prospective examinees. Aptitude banks may be organized according to cognitive traits and levels, which may be fully crossed across several dimensions. Educational banks may be organized by content, grade level, cognitive level, and other pedagogical characteristics. See Raymond and Neustel (chap. 9, this volume) for a discussion of methods of structuring credentialing test plans and Webb (chap. 8, this volume) for discussion of structuring student achievement.

Most item classifications I have encountered could be considered a combination of conceptual and prototype philosophies of classification. The top levels tend to be concepts such as verbal, quantitative, history, and so on. However, items tend to blend categories at some level in the organizational hierarchy. Story problems, for example, cross verbal and quantitative categories at a top level. Such items may be classified according to family resemblance, that is, prototypes. Or if a sufficient number of items confound the classification scheme, the classification system may require change.

A key feature of all organizing characteristics is that the items they define must fall unambiguously in one category of each characteristic; that is, the categories of a characteristic used for classification must be mutually exclusive. Although the concepts or prototypes may be fuzzy, a decision must be made and the item must be placed in one category and not in the others. That is, if the categories of a characteristic are animal, vegetable, and mineral, each item must be assigned to one and only one kingdom. Or, getting more realistic, if the categories are executive, management, and supervisory, an item dealing with supervision of managers by an executive must be placed in one category, not all three. Although I have seen such multiple assignment done, it plays havoc when constructing a test that is supposed to contain 10% of its items from each of the three categories. (The solution proposed to this conflict was to conditionally assign the item, at test construction time, to whatever area had an item shortage, an approach of dubious validity.)

Revisiting our concrete example, consider colored bricks being sorted prior to filling specific customer orders. Red bricks go in bin 1, blue bricks in bin 2, and white bricks in bin 3. If a multicolored brick is encountered with sides variously red, white, and blue, it cannot be split three ways and probably should not be tossed at random into one of the three bins. One good solution for dealing with these bricks is to add a fourth bin for multicolored bricks. Another satisfactory solution is to reject the multicolored bricks as defective and not put them into any bin. The solution of randomly assigning the bricks or placing them in the emptiest bin may ultimately result in the construction of an otherwise white brick wall with red and blue spots on it.

Note that the requirement for unambiguous categories is a requirement only if the property is used for classification. There are two good solutions to the classification of the executive–management–supervision item. If it is important that items be classified according to those properties, then either a prototype approach can be taken (in which each item is assigned to the prototype it most closely matches) or executive, management, and supervision can be made three binary properties, rather than categories of a single ternary one. (This approach results in eight categories, rather than three.) If the goal is not classification but rather to assemble tests consisting of executive, management, and supervisory knowledge, items can be awarded increments of executive, management, and supervisory contribution, depending on the relative importance of each bit of knowledge in their solution. This approach results in making the properties continuous, and thus precludes classification based on them.

The content outlines that drive test specifications are routinely revised. To minimize impact on the bank, it is often desirable to disconnect the item bank organization from the content outline, to some degree. The item bank organization should support the specification outline, insofar as it goes. However, it is often desirable to extend the organization of the bank to a greater degree of detail than specified in the outline. If the substance of the items is described to the greatest degree possible, the classification nodes can be collected into buckets assigned to the outline points and, when the outline changes, the nodes can be reassigned to new buckets without requiring a reclassification based on detailed review of the item content.

I am familiar with one testing program that found a hierarchical organization of its item banks too limiting and preferred to organize its items into buckets or modules and to only assign the buckets to hierarchical outlines at the time of test construction. This is an acceptable form of organization to the extent that the test developers using the item bank can remember the names and/or contents of all of the modules. However, as the bank grows large enough that the test developers cannot do this, I can see the buckets being placed on "pallets" and the pallets being grouped into "truckloads," which is, of course, another hierarchical metaphor. I can also see using old tests, in which the modules were previously assigned to nodes of a related outline, as a guide for the assignment of modules to the new test. Of course this substitutes organization by proxy for true item bank organization. Hierarchy provides mnemonic support to those of us with limited memory capacity. It should provide support rather than constraint.

Item characteristics and categories should be afforded meaningful names. Preferences differ in whether the names should be short or long. But they should have intuitive meaning: Red, white, and blue rather than 1, 2, and 3. I have encountered item banks in which items were named according to the numbers associated with their terminal node in the outline. This required complete renaming of the items each time the outline changed. It also made re-use in multiple tests with different outlines extremely cumbersome. (Not to mention the mental challenge of remembering that 6.4.3.1 referred to Parol Evidence.)

The purpose of including the statistics in the item banker is to support decisions, automated assembly, and downstream processing. When data storage was expensive and processing was slow, item bankers sometimes contained intermediate computations so that statistics could be updated rather than recomputed. With modern computing capabilities, this is unnecessary and probably unduly cumbersome. An item bank should be considered a repository of statistical information for ultimate consumption, not an intermediary in the computation of statistics.

ITEM BANKERS

What to Bank

The use of the computer to administer tests has led to an explosion of item types. Where paper-and-pencil tests were limited to a few objective formats (notably multiple-choice, true–false, and matching) and a few constructed-response formats (e.g., short-answer, essay, fill-in-the-blank), the computer has opened the door to active multimedia formats and interactive simulations. And although the IMS specification appears general enough to support most of the imaginable item types, even a banker capable of supporting the full specification cannot support all item types. One of the first tasks in implementing an item bank is thus determining which types of items the bank must include and the banker must support.

Two factors worth considering are the number of items to be managed and the complexity of those items. An item banker is useful for organizing and managing relatively large numbers of items. If the tests encompass 10,000 multiple-choice items and five stand-alone computer simulations, for example, an item banking system that only manages the multiple-choice items is of significant value. However, if the tests encompass thirty distinct item types, each with 300 items, the determination of how many types a banker must support is less clear.

An item banker has two functions: to author and to organize the items in the bank. *Authoring* refers to the initial entry and ongoing editing and maintenance of the item. In the case of simple objective items, the authoring function amounts to a word processor, usually with stylistic controls to ensure that the item conforms to the established format standards. In the case of a graphic item, the authoring function must allow for the importation and editing of drawings and pictures. The complexity of the required functionality grows rapidly as items include multimedia stimuli and the continuous examinee interaction that characterizes some simulations. The authoring function of an item banker must support entry and editing of all items included in the bank. Furthermore, it must support them with facility comparable to state-of-the-art standalone editors. It is reasonable for an item banker to rely on external functionality for authoring, if that functionality is integrated in a reasonably seamless manner. For example, it would be unusual (and probably unwelcome) for an item banker to include a complete multimedia editing studio. However, it would not be unusual to expect an item banker to link to a popular commercial video editor, storing and retrieving the video material from the item bank. If the banker cannot support a certain functionality, the item types requiring that functionality should probably be excluded from the bank. This does not suggest that the items should not exist (clearly they do), but rather that they should be supported external to the item bank.

Deciding which item types an item banker should accommodate is a design decision, one for which there is no single correct answer. In making that decision for an item type, however, several things should be considered.

- Is an adequate external editor available for this item type? That is, can the item be authored outside the banking system? Can the banker seamlessly link to the external editor?
- How many items of this type will be excluded from the bank if their authoring is not supported?
- Are items of this type required in concert with other types of items? If all groups that include this item type are excluded the test, how many other items must be managed outside of the bank?

Authoring items in an item banker will never be as simple as typing items on paper. A certain amount of computer capability among the user group is expected. Thus, *seamless* does not necessarily mean as simple as pushing a button. But neither should a user have to write a transfer program to get items from the banker to a supported auxiliary editor.

Item Organization

Items in the bank are organized according to intuitive structures and schemata devised by test developers. Whatever the internal structure of the data, the external view must match the minds of the test developers. And those minds change from time to time, occasionally on whim, but more often based on changes in knowledge, regulation, or pedagogy that drives the organization of the bank.

An item bank can be thought of as a database. But, as databases go, item banks are small and accessed infrequently. Mapping the conceptual structure of an item bank into a fully normalized relational structure that can be managed using state-of-the-art database software is not a requirement of a viable item banker. An item bank can also be thought of as a structured document. Most modern mechanisms for item and test exchange are based on a document model embodied in a structured markup language, the structure of which is inherently hierarchical.

Whatever structure is used, it should be designed to allow for frequent recoding. Where a payroll or personnel database must be designed for speed of access, an item bank must be designed for flexibility and change. Recoding includes both renaming and restructuring. Characteristics are renamed as a result of whim, regulation, or other impetus. *Renaming* is a simple process of name substitution. Structures are also recoded, however, which may take the form of new categories, new characteristics, or the splitting and assignment of old categories to new characteristics. Support should be provided for the automatic reclassification of old characteristics and branch segments to new ones. Acceptable methods include a textual correspondence list and cutting and pasting of graphical representations of organizational structures. Obviously, an audit trail is necessary to allow the user to determine where an old item in a new classification came from.

Note also that the organizational structure should be kept apart from the item identification. Items are assembled into tests by reference identifier. If that reference identifier is based on the item's node in the classification structure and the classification is changed, reassembly of the test then requires reconstruction of the prior classification scheme. It is a better plan to use the organizational scheme to find items and assign them to tests, but to then use a unique reference number, say an item serial number, for unambiguously identifying the item.

Also be aware that retrieval by traversing an organizational structure is only one method of retrieval. Classic database design considered search to be a retrieval method of last resort. However, search is the predominant method by which the current generation of computer users find things on the World Wide Web. Thus, search should be a prominent capability among the "organizational" tools provided by an item banker. One should be able to search on formal keywords as well as all words in the text of an item. Where the organizational structure of an item bank is extremely useful in providing higher order classifications for discussing and weighting items, the predominant mode of locating items is probably through search.

Item Representation

Item stimuli, for the most part, are visual or auditory. An item's stimulus representation consists of a logical instantiation of its visual and auditory counterpart. At a basic level, this consists of a string of computer bits that is translated by a computer program into the desired display or sound. But such a string of bits is generally deficient in terms of portability and accessibility.

That is, different output devices require different strings of bits to produce comparable end results. Fortunately, there are standard exchange protocols available, although they differ in their portability and accessibility.

Rich text format (RTF) is a standard developed and supported by Microsoft and used to transfer word processor documents from one program to another. It supports most of the content and formatting information used in a typical word processing document, including graphics. It is a text-based encoding scheme that, unlike a Microsoft Word document file, can usually be read (without formatting) by a standard text editor. Its drawbacks as a representation for item bank data are that (1) it is primarily a display language, ill suited for representing other data characteristics of items; (2) although it is possible to read the text using a text editor, it is very difficult to decipher or modify the formatting using one; and (3) it is a standard controlled by a private company and historically revised with each new version of Microsoft Word.

HyperText markup language (HTML) is the display language used for most Web pages on the Internet. It supports formatting and hyperlinks, is the standard display language on all Internet browsers, and can readily be read and modified using a standard text editor (although this is clearly not the easiest way to do it). As a representation standard for an item bank, its biggest drawbacks are that it offers limited formatting capabilities and was designed for video display, offering only limited support for print.

Extensible markup language (XML) is a data representation language, explicitly designed to specify data structures and represent data according to those structures. It can be viewed and modified using a standard text editor (although, again, this is the hard way to do it) and it can represent data of almost any imaginable structure. Although it is not a display language, it can be structured for automatic translation to HTML for display. It is evolving as the base standard for all exchange of information on the Internet. The IMS Question and Test Interoperability standard, discussed above, is expressed in XML.

Extended hypertext markup language (XHTML) is the latest version of HTML and is expressed in XML. It is the current Web standard for all new Web pages (Tanenbaum, 2003). The most significant advantages of XHTML over HTML are extensibility and portability. *Extensibility* refers to the inclusion of formal methods for extending the language to meet emerging needs. *Portability* essentially refers to the standard being "standard," that is a well-defined specification that can be interpreted by all XHTML-compliant devices. Extensibility and portability have historically been antagonistic, the need for extensibility resulting in versions that are not universally interpretable. XHTML purports to have solved that problem.

Standard generalized markup language (SGML) is the parent of all modern markup languages. It is variously described as a meta-language (i.e., a language for describing languages) and a markup language too complicated for general use on the Internet. HTML and XML are more practical languages, but both are described by SGML. SGML is probably too complex to use as a representational language for an item bank.

Unicode (The Unicode Consortium, 2004) is a set of standards for character representation and is the modern successor to earlier character standards such as ASCII and EBCDIC. Unicode standards represent characters in blocks of 8 bits (UTF-8), 16 bits (UTF-16), or 32 bits (UTF-32). It provides a standard in which the characters of all the world's languages can be represented. The level of Unicode support is determined to some extent by the processor reading the data file, but HTML processors uniformly support at least UTF-8 and XML processors support at least UTF-16 (Young, 2002).

It is not essential that an item banker use any of the standards for internal representation. It is also possible to use one standard internally and another externally. However, for ease of development and interoperability in a growing network of uses, XML appears to be the standard of choice for representing an item bank. All of these standards, except for RTF, are formally described in the web site of the World Wide Web Consortium (www.w3c.org).

Item Authoring

Item authoring is one of the essential functions that an item banker must perform. In developing an item banker, providing an acceptable authoring capability is something of a challenge. Virtually every item component that must be edited (e.g., text, graphic, photograph, video segment, audio clip) has a counterpart outside of the item banker. Generally the market is larger for the counterpart function and a highly capable editor is commercially available and known to users of the item banker. The capability of the counterpart editor sets the standard for how the item banker must perform. In general, item bankers follow rather than lead the state of the art in all forms of editing capability.

Acceptability issues of an editor can be grouped into three categories: functionality, navigation, and speed. *Functionality* refers to what the editor can accomplish. A text editor lacks the functionality to change the colors in a photograph. A photo editor most likely has this functionality. *Navigation* refers to how the functionality is achieved by the user. The key issue in navigation is how much skill and input is required on the part of the user to achieve a function. Changing colors in a photograph could, for example, be achieved using an editor that allowed the user to modify the RGB (red, green, and blue color) values for each pixel. The navigation of an editor that chose colors from a color wheel or palette and dropped them with a mouse click to all contiguous pixels of a common color is considered vastly superior. *Speed* refers to the computer processing time required to achieve a function. Users have some tolerance for processing delays when dealing with databases, but much less tolerance when using word processors. An item banker is a hybrid of a database manager and a word processor. Although some modest delay in the selection of items for retrieval or the retrieval of an item from disk may be acceptable, there should be no perceptible delay in actions taken to edit an item. Tolerable database delays are measured in seconds; tolerable editing delays are measured in milliseconds.

Design of the authoring user interface is far beyond the scope of this chapter, other than to note a few essential design concepts. Broadly speaking, the item author needs two views of the materials he or she edits. The first is the candidate's view, often characterized as the WYSIWYG (what you see is what you get) view. This is an essential view. No modern editor can expect to be viable without the capability to display the item in the candidate view. An item author should not be expected to refer to a second program to see how the item will be rendered for the candidate. Generally, this view is appropriate for most editing of the item.

Usually, an editor should also supply one or more technical views of the item and its components. A *technical view* is one that provides special tools and a look behind the scenes to fine-tune the item. A word processor view that shows spaces, paragraph marks, paragraph styles, and a ruler is a technical view. In editing audio clips, it is nearly impossible to seamlessly merge separate clips by listening to them. But this can often be done cleanly, with little effort, when waveform diagrams can be viewed and edited graphically. Because the capabilities of an item banker follow the state of the art, the necessary capabilities should be discerned from the best stand-alone editors available for the component types.

State-of-the-art editing capability may seem a lot to expect from an item banker, a tool with a relatively small market (from the perspective of software marketing). However, the state of the art of software development has changed dramatically over the past thirty years, as well. Microsoft's active document technology, for example (e.g., OLE, ActiveX, COM, .Net), provides a mechanism through which the best independent tools can be linked together into one seamless application. Unfortunately, this approach is sometimes cumbersome and expensive; cumbersome because the independent applications generate a notable delay when they are launched and expensive because each separate application requires a separate license. Regarding expense, the collection of programs necessary to support an item banker capable of managing and authoring a collection of multimedia items could easily cost in excess of $1,000 per copy.

Interoperability

Serious item banks do not exist in isolation. A test owner who contracts test development with others can change vendors; vendors typically do not use the same item banker. A testing company that develops its own tests may be acquired. In either case, the management of an item bank is likely to be accomplished with a different item banker. *Interoperability,* the ability to use an old bank with a new banker, is highly desirable.

The internal structure of items used to be very idiosyncratic. This is probably less so in modern item bankers, because developers tend to make use of tools for displaying and editing common data formats. Regardless, the internal representation of items and tests is of little interest to anyone other than those who design, develop, and maintain the programs that facilitate item banking. Modern interoperability requires that item bankers have at least the capability to import and export items in formats that allow the relatively easy transfer of item banks.

Thirty years ago, when the major special feature was underlined text, a simple text file with a few special formatting characters was adequate. With modern complexity and expectations, XML has emerged as the fundamental language of exchange. However, XML is a language for representing data, and its tags and structures must be interpreted. The IMS specification is based on XML and is intended to provide a common set of tags and structures with common interpretations to facilitate the transfer of item banks.

The IMS specification, like many software standards, is complex and remains a work in progress. Commercial item bankers advertising IMS compliance are available, however. This suggests that developers of new item bankers would be wise to design IMS compliance into their products. Test owners contracting bank management to outsiders should consider requiring an IMS-compliant version of their item banks as a deliverable final product in any item management contract. Testing contractors should be advised to use IMS-compliant item bankers. And independent test developers should expect their tests (and companies) to be more valuable (e.g., in an acquisition) if they were all available in an IMS-compliant format. It seems that significant pressure for IMS compliance will develop.

Item Bank Security

A recent analysis of insurance policy schedules suggested that licensure and certification test items are valued at, on average, approximately $300 each. Certain types of test items, especially those relying on extensive statistical data (e.g., IRT parameters) or involving complex processes such as simulations, may cost $1,000 or more each to develop. Even the lower value suggests that a bank containing a few thousand items, not an atypical number, may be worth in excess of a million dollars. And unlike other computerized data, whose ongoing value can be ensured by an adequate system of backups, items retain value only to the extent their confidentiality can be assured.

There are three threats to the security of an item bank: theft, disappearance, and exposure. *Theft* refers to someone deliberately stealing test items, presumably for some nefarious purpose such as sale or self-preparation. *Disappearance* refers to the mysterious disappearance of items, tests, or item banks. Disappearance may result from theft, carelessness, or act of God (e.g., the plane carrying the tests crashes). *Exposure* is the inevitable disclosure of items to candidates for the purpose of testing, some of which will be memorized and stolen. Impara and Foster (chap. 5, this volume) discuss methods of test construction that can minimize the effects of exposure and the effectiveness of item theft. However, the prevention of item theft and disappearance is within the purview of item bank management. The primary methods of prevention are access control and encryption of material.

Access Control

Access control can be achieved through physical and/or logical means. *Physical means* include separation of secure areas via locked doors and security guards. *Logical means* include software systems restricting access to those with appropriate hardware and software keys (i.e., passwords). Modern item banks are routinely shared across a wide range of geography. Physical security is essential around the physical representations of the test data (e.g., the network servers) and desirable around areas of display (e.g., the test-development department). Logical security is essential for all access that may not be physically controlled or controlled to the level desired for a program (e.g., access to a client program by specific personnel within the test-development department).

M-Tech (2003) suggests three approaches to logical access security: *secrets,* such as a password or a personal identification number (PIN); *tokens,* such as a card or other electronic key; and *biometrics,* such as a voiceprint, fingerprint, or retinal scan. According to M-Tech, biometrics are the most secure and secrets the least. Nevertheless, because of the cost of biometrics and their incompatibility with most legacy systems, secrets are likely to remain the logical access-control method of choice for some time.

There is an art to the design of a password system that is well beyond the scope of this chapter. The challenge in such a design is in achieving a system that preserves the secret, that is, a system that makes the password hard to guess without making it hard to remember. Long passwords that are changed frequently and incorporate most of the characters available on the keyboard are hard to guess. They are also hard to remember, leading users to leave them on notes beneath their keyboards.

Readers interested in the art of password management are directed to M-Tech (2003) and the old, but still standard FIPS Standard 112 (FIPS, 1985). To superficially summarize the FIPS standard:

- Characters in passwords should be drawn from an alphabet consisting of not less than ten characters (e.g., 0 to 9).
- The length and composition of the password should provide a minimum of 10,000 possible passwords.
- Passwords should have a maximum lifetime of one year and be deactivated immediately if compromise is suspected.
- Users who create their own passwords should be instructed to create them at random, or at least refrain from including elements of their identities in them.
- Only individuals entrusted with the protection of the information the passwords secure should know passwords.
- Access to shared data should not require a common password from different users sharing the data.
- Password distribution methods must ensure that only the intended recipient sees the password.
- The password user should be able to enter the password in secret and should be given a limited number of tries to get it right.

Note that these standards are from another era and generally provide a somewhat less restrictive scheme than expected today.

The essential point for this discussion is that all item bankers should require passwords for access. Ideally, they should support rings of access such that developers can have access to items and tests in specific programs, supervisors can have access to the programs of all their subordinates, and managers can have access to the programs of an entire department. Individuals should be able to access all data within their authority by a single password, but no two users should share a password.

Encryption

In addition to controlling access to the item bank with a password, the bank files themselves must be secured. A passworded banker with plaintext item files is like a locked gate without a fence. The item database must be encrypted using one of the modern encryption standards. Computers are routinely stolen and networked databases are routinely accessible by a number of people. It is a common practice for the systems department to restrict network access to an item bank, limiting access to those few test developers working on a program. It is also common practice for most of the systems department to be able to access that same restricted bank. Although systems personnel are probably as honest as any, they have no need to access the substance of an item bank. Encrypting the bank such that only privileged test developers can decrypt it can preclude such access.

Amateur item bank developers, not well versed in encryption technology, occasionally attempt to custom design an encryption technology (say a character-substitution algorithm or an exclusive-or mask). A home-brew encryption scheme is never acceptable in a serious item banker. A body of research exists on encryption and a principal tenet of knowledgeable cryptographers is that a useful encryption algorithm must be public, open to challenge, and not successfully defeated. It is the encryption key (the password) that must be kept secret, not the method of encryption.

There are two general categories of encryption algorithms: symmetric-key and public-key algorithms (Tanenbaum, 2003, chap. 8). *Symmetric-key algorithms* use a common secret key for encryption and decryption of information. They are generally fast in execution and are the method of choice for encryption of databases. *Public-key algorithms* have separate keys for encryption and decryption. This allows the sender to encrypt a message using the recipient's public encryption key, but only the recipient is able to decrypt the message using his or her secret decryption key. Public-key algorithms are much slower in execution and are primarily used to distribute secret symmetric keys.

Only two or three symmetric-key algorithms are considered acceptable. The Data Encryption Standard, using a 56-bit key, was the method of choice for several years, but it has now been broken using a brute-force attack and modern processor speeds. Thus, it is no longer considered acceptable for serious encryption. A triple-encryption variation that effectively lengthens the key to 112 bits (three encryptions but only two keys) is considered acceptable, but the new standard is the Advanced Encryption Standard based on the Rijndael algorithm (Tanenbaum, 2003). An item bank should be protected using one of these three algorithms, preferably one of the latter two.

The encryption key applied to the item bank is, in a sense, a password. However, a password should be personal and memorable, two features incompatible with an encryption key. Several test developers may work on an item bank. The areas of the item bank that they are authorized to access may differ, although some parts may overlap. If the encryption key was the same as the password, all would need to use the same password, or they could not decrypt the portions of the bank to which they share access. All using the same password undoes the value of partitioned access. The personal password must control access to personal privileges in the bank, but thereafter a separate key must control encryption and decryption of the data.

TEST CREATION

The goal of all item banking is the creation of tests (assessments, in the IMS model). These may be conventional tests administered in paper or computer format or they may be customized linear tests or adaptive tests created from a specification while the test is being given. Although items have representational needs similar to materials in disciplines other than testing (and thus have a number of methods and standards on which to build), tests are unique.

All item bankers, of which I am aware, offer tools for the creation of tests. Tests have a conceptual structure, an internal representation, and an external representation. The conceptual structure may be an object model. IMS (2002c) has begun to develop a specification for test blueprints and presents its object models with examples in XML. At the time of this writing, the models available do not extend beyond fixed and random selection of items and examples of even those specifications are too bulky to include here. Readers interested in that theoretical object structure of assessments are referred to IMS (2002c). However, to provide a flavor of test specification, simplified concepts and simplified versions of specifications used with an operational testing system I designed a few years ago are illustrated. Note that the specifications are for illustration only and may exclude key elements required for actual implementation.

Structures, Conventional and Unconventional

The structure of a conventional test is logically quite simple. Conventional tests are linear. Thus, most of the content of a conventional test can be represented by a list. A list of item numbers pretty well specifies a conventional test, although additional functions assist in formatting the test. If all text and graphic material is represented as an item, the only additions necessary in the conventional specification are functions to repeat items periodically (for headers and footers), insert variables into items (e.g., page numbers and client-specific references), and direct breaks (page breaks for paper tests and restroom breaks for computerized tests). Unconventional tests comprise everything other than the conventional format and, necessarily, are almost always administered on a computer. The specification of an adaptive test, for example, does not need to be substantially more complicated than that of a conventional test. Changing the scoring method to an IRT-based score and denoting that a subset of the total item list should be selected according to a specified adaptive algorithm are the only essential changes. As noted, the IMS specification of test structures is in the early phases of development. Past practical attempts to specify tests for computer-based testing (CBT) implementations pale by comparison to that effort. Nevertheless, I describe some of the structural concepts that have proven useful in the description of CBTs in the past.

Test Block

The test defines the environment within which the items are administered and the test block statement sets the attributes of that environment. Among the environmental attributes set in the test block statement are:

- **Skip:** Can the candidate skip items?
- **Mark:** Can the candidate mark items for review?
- **Backup:** Can the candidate back up to previous items?
- **Break:** When and how long does the candidate get a break?
- **Pilot:** When and how many pilot or pretest items to administer?

Section Block

The section block statement groups items for special consideration. A section may identify the order in which items should appear, the priority with which they should be selected, or the minimum and maximum number of them to be selected.

- **Strategy statement:** The strategy statement specifies the method by which items should be selected (e.g., by information, by listed order, or randomly).
- **Score statement:** The score statement(s) specifies how candidate responses should be scored.
- **Conditional statements:** Conditional statements (e.g., If, ElseIf) control the selection of items or the branching among sections. (Branching, long abandoned by much of computer science, continues in test strategy design.)
- **Display statements:** Modern computer-based testing environments allow some control over the display presented to the candidate and the interaction capabilities (e.g., buttons) afforded.
- **Report statements:** Many test specifications include detailed instructions regarding how to format and report results, both to the candidate and to the test owner.

Although a specification for adaptive tests was scheduled for Version 2.0 of the IMS specification, it has not yet appeared in the draft form. Such specification are difficult to achieve in any meaningful way because computer-based test designs are continuously evolving and have little analogy with any other, better developed discipline.

Formats, Paper and Electronic

Computer-administered tests always have to be published in electronic form, and for the time being in the peculiar format specified by the test delivery provider. Fortunately, these formats are usually built on one of the standard material representation formats and the item banker can at least assist in producing them.

Figure 11.1 is an example of a specification of a conventional test for computer administration. It is a slight abstraction of an actual computer-based test specification. The specifications of a conventional test for paper production and computer administration are typically somewhat different. This is because the specification for computer-based testing usually must specify not only what items to give and their order (as in paper form), but must also specify the administration process, minimally specifying a time limit, a scoring method, and how to report the results. Note that the essential core of the specification is the list of items. Were this a specification for a paper test, the environmental details would relate to formatting rather than time limits. Figure 11.2 illustrates the additions necessary to make the test adaptive. Although the core is still the item list, more detail regarding selection must be given.

The output from the banker for a computer-based test usually amounts to the test specification and an export of the item content, in an appropriate format. For paper tests, the final output from the item banker may be a printed master. Or it may be another electronic format. The Adobe Portable Document Format (PDF) offers a universal format in which users, regardless of computer platform, can reproduce virtually identical copies of a document. The PDF format can be sent directly to the laser printer or to the printing vendor, with virtual assurance that the document produced will match the document sent. The format offers the added advantage of being lockable by the creator so it cannot be modified, being encrypted with a password, and being assured of authenticity with a digital signature. Furthermore, the PDF format is an open standard, so item bankers can be designed to create them directly.

Test LIN0001	Name the test
Set TimeLimit 7200	Set a 2-hour time limit
Strategy Linear	Administer the items in the order listed
Section 1	Divide into sections; no real function here
Item SMFF2384	List items in Section 1
Item SMFF2758	
Item SMFF3311	
.	
.	
.	
EndSection	End of Section 1
Section 2	Start Section 2
Item SDXX2110	
Item SDXX3827	
Item SDXX2118	
.	
.	
.	
EndSection	End of Section 2
EndTest	End of the test specification

FIG. 11.1. Specification of a conventional test.

History and Lockdown

An item bank is an evolving entity; the tests created from an item bank are frozen in time. This presents a challenge in preserving history. A few examples may clarify the problem. Say a test is created from a bank in January and given immediately. A bank review is conducted in February and some of the items are changed and the changes are entered into the bank. Item statistics for the January examination are computed in March and entered into the bank. When a new test is created in April, the revised items are used. However, the statistics available are for the old items. If management policy is to create a new item each time an item is modified, then the modified items are without statistics. If the statistics are IRT parameters, required for incorporation of the item into a test, this presents a problem.

  Consider a slightly different scenario. Items are approved for incorporation into a test in January but the test is not created until March. Meanwhile, in February, an item review results

Test CAT0001	Name the test
Set TLim 7200	Set a 2-hour time limit
Set Done ((ATime >=TLim) OR (NAdm = 60))	Quit at time or item-count limit
Score ModalBayesian MBScore	Bayesian MAP scoring
Strategy MaxInfo MBScore	Max Info selection based on Bayesian score
Section 1 1 30	Select 30 items from Section 1 first
Item SMFF2384	List items in Section 1
Item SMFF2758	
Item SMFF3311	
.	
.	
.	
EndSection	End of Section 1
Section 2 2 30	Select 30 items from Section 2 next
Item SDXX2110	
Item SDXX3827	
Item SDXX2118	
.	
.	
.	
EndSection	End of Section 2
EndTest	End of the test specification

FIG. 11.2. Specification of an adaptive test.

in revisions to some of the items. If the revised items are not given new identities, the test created is different from the test approved. On the other hand, if they are given new identities, the test does not benefit from improvements that resulted from the review.

There are numerous approaches to solving the problem. Rather than enumerating them all, let me suggest a conceptual model that can be adopted in whole or in part. First, consider three levels of item revision: correction, improvement, and cloning. A *correction* changes some minor aspect of the item (say a misspelled word) that a liberal test developer might say should not affect the item's substantive or statistical performance. An *improvement* is a more substantive change that may, for example, clarify the exposition of the question and, it is hoped, improve the psychometric character of the item. One could reasonably expect, however, that the substantive content the item was intended to assess had not changed. Finally, the *clone* is an item that borrows significant portions of the item, but may not even assess the same content.

A capable item banker is able to track the history of an item and identify degrees of change. With this information, tests could be assembled from specifications using the most recent improvements. (An assembled test here refers to a paper test at the time of printing or a computer-based test item pool at the time of fielding.) However, if item statistics were critical (e.g., IRT parameters), perhaps only corrections should be allowed. Once a test had been given, only the original item should be allowed in further reproductions. Clones should never be substituted in test assembly, but perhaps should be marked as enemies to limit their joint use in future forms.

CONCLUSION

An item bank is a significant piece of intellectual property with considerable monetary value. The elements that make it valuable are the content of the items, the organization of those items into meaningful categories that can be externally related, and the documentation that supports the validity of the included tests and items for real-world inferences. An item banker is a program entrusted with managing that valuable property.

Item banks and item bankers are no longer the toys of intellectuals and hackers, but rather form the core of several significant modern businesses. As business properties, prone to changing management and ownership, the idiosyncratic nature of item bank representation is waning. Modern item banks, and the item bankers that support them, will increasingly achieve a level of interoperability that makes transfer of electronic banks as simple as handing off the legendary shoebox. Computerized item banking is no longer the future of test construction, it is the status quo.

ACKNOWLEDGMENTS

This chapter was written, in part, during the time I was employed by Capstar Learning, LLC. However, the information contained herein is solely my responsibility and may or may not reflect the views and perspectives of Capstar or its successors.

I would like to thank Susan Davis-Ali and Linda Waters for their reviews and insightful comments on an earlier version of this chapter. Their suggestions, as well as those of the *Handbook* editors, have served to make this chapter more lucid and comprehensive.

REFERENCES

Baker, F. B. (1986). Item banking in computer-based instructional systems. *Applied Psychological Measurement, 10*(4), 405–414.

Baker, F. B. (1989). Computer technology in test construction and processing. In R. L. Linn (Ed.), *Educational Measurement*. New York: MacMillan.

Bergstrom, B. A., & Gershon, R. C. (1995). Item Banking. In J. C. Impara (Ed.), *Licensure testing: Purposes, procedures, and practices*. Lincoln, NE: Buros.

Booch, G. (1994). *Object-oriented analysis and design with applications* (2nd ed.). New York: Addison-Wesley.

Bradley, N. (2004). *The XML schema companion*. New York: Addison-Wesley.

Choppin, B. H. (1976). Item banking development. In D. N. M. DeGruiter, & van der L. J. T. Kamp, (Eds.), *Advances in psychometrics and educational measurement*. London: Wiley.

FIPS. (1985). *Federal information processing standard publication 112: Password usage.* Springfield, VA: National Technical Information service. Retrieved July 30, 2005 from http://www.itl.nist.gov/fipspubs/fip112.htm.

Haladyna, T. M. (2004). *Developing and validating multiple choice test items* (3rd ed). Mahwah, NJ: Lawrence Erlbaum Associates.

Haladyna, T. M., & Shindoll, R. R. (1989). Item shells: A method for writing effective multiple-choice items. *Evaluation and the Health Professions, 12,* 97–104.

Hambleton, R. K., & Swaminathan, H. (1985). *Item response theory: Principles and applications.* Boston: Kluwer-Nijhoff.

Hiscox, M. D. (1985). Computer-based testing systems: Much ado about nothing. *Educational Measurement: Issues and Practice, 4,* 27–28.

IMS Global Learning Consortium, Inc. (IMS). (2002a). *IMS question & test interoperability: An overview (Final specification version 1.2).* Burlington, MA: Author. Retrieved July 30, 2005 from http://www.imsglobal.org/question/qtiv1p2/imsqti_oviewv1p2.html.

IMS Global Learning Consortium, Inc. (IMS). (2002b). *IMS question & test interoperability: ASI information model specification (Final specification version 1.2).* Burlington, MA: Author. Retrieved July 30, 2005 from http://www.imsglobal.org/question/qtiv1p2/imsqti_asi_infov1p2.html.

IMS Global Learning Consortium, Inc. (IMS). (2002c). *IMS question & test interoperability: ASI selection and ordering (Final specification version 1.2).* Burlington, MA: Author. Retrieved July 30, 2005 from http://www.imsglobal.org/question/qtiv1p2/imsqti_asi_saov1p2.html.

IMS Global Learning Consortium, Inc. (IMS). (2004a). *IMS question and test interoperability: Information model (Version 2.0 public draft).* Burlington, MA: Author. Retrieved July 30, 2005 from http://www.imsglobal.org/question/qti_item_v2p0pd/infomodel.html.

IMS Global Learning Consortium, Inc. (IMS). (2004b). *IMS Global Learning Consortium home page.* Retrieved July 30, 2005 from http://www.imsproject.org/.

M-Tech. (2003). *Password management best practices.* Calgary, Alberta: M-Tech Information Technology, Inc. Retrieved July 30, 2005 from http://www.psynch.com/docs/best_practices.pdf.

Parshall, C. G., Davey, T., & Pashley, P. J. (2000). Innovative item types for computerized testing. In W. J. van der Linden & C. A. W. Glas (Eds.), *Computerized adaptive testing, theory and practice* (pp. 129–148). Dordrect, The Netherlands: Kluwer.

Rudner, L. (1998). Item banking [Electronic version]. *Practical Assessment, Research, & Evaluation, 6*(4). Retrieved July 30, 2005 from http://www.ericdigests.org/1999-2/item.htm.

Sands, W. A., Waters, B. K., & McBride, J. R. (Eds.). (1997). *Computerized adaptive testing: From inquiry to operation.* Washington, DC: American Psychological Association.

Tanenbaum, A. S. (2003). *Computer networks.* Upper Saddle River, NJ: Prentice Hall.

Umar, J. (1999). Item banking. In G. N. Masters & J. P. Keeves (Eds.), *Advances in Measurement in Educational Research and Assessment.* New York: Pergamon.

The Unicode Consortium. (2004). *The Unicode standard: A technical introduction.* Retrieved July 30, 2005 from http://www.unicode.org/standard/principles.html.

van der Linden, W. J. (1986). The changing conception of measurement in education and psychology. *Applied Psychological Measurement, 10*(4), 325–332.

van der Linden, W. J., & Glas, C. A. W. (Eds.). (2000). *Computerized adaptive testing, theory and practice.* Dordrect, The Netherlands: Kluwer.

Ward, A. W., & Murray-Ward, M. (1994). Guidelines for the development of item banks. *Educational Measurement: Issues and Practice, 13*(1), 34–39.

W3C. (2004). *Document object model (DOM).* Retrieved July 30, 2005 from http://www.w3.org/DOM/Overview.html.

Young, M. J. (2002). *XML step by step.* (2nd ed). Redmond, WA: Microsoft.

APPENDIX

Table 11.4 provides a sample of item banking software currently available for sale. The products included represent the results of a modestly comprehensive search of the World Wide Web in late 2004. They are provided as a starting point for readers wishing to explore item-banking software further. Inclusion in this list in no way represents endorsement of these products and the exclusion of products from the list implies a limitation in the search rather than a deficiency in the product.

TABLE 11.4
A Sample of Current Item Banking Software

Product Name	Description	Source	Price
CQuest db	An item banker for printed and computer-administered tests including item editing, storage, formatting, and rudimentary statistical analysis. Part of a more comprehensive package for managing a small testing program.	http://www.assess.com/	$300–$2,850
Exam Manager	An item banker for printed and computerized tests, including editing, storage, test assembly, and test administration.	http://www.assess.com/	$350–$1,500
Examiner	An item banker for printed and computerized tests, including editing, storage, test assembly, and test administration. Includes statistical test analyses.	http://www.assess.com/	$875–$1,295
FastTest	An item banker intended primarily for printed tests with capabilities for item editing, item storage, test assembly, test printing, and IRT support.	http://www.assess.com/	$399–$599
FastTest Professional	An extended version of FastTest, adding capabilities for statistical analysis, computerized test administration, and adaptive testing.	http://www.assess.com/	$999–$3,995
MicroCAT	An item banker embedded in a complete system for creating, administering, and analyzing computerized and printed tests. Somewhat aged, at this time, and running only in MS-DOS.	http://www.assess.com/	$700–$4,900
Perception	An item banker designed primarily to create computerized tests. Items may include multiple-choice, essay, drag-and-drop, and several other formats. Tests may be conventional, random, or adaptive.	http://www.pearsonncs.com/perception/index.htm	
Perception	An item banker intended primarily for computer-administered tests. Part of a comprehensive testing system.	http://www.questionmark.com/	
Random Test Generator Pro	An item banker intended primarily for computerized tests. Includes graphic and sound capability.	http://www.hirtlesoftware.com/	$100
SkillCheck Professional Plus Testmaker	An item banker for creating multiple-choice tests to be administered on a computer. Includes test administration capability.	http://www.hrpress-software.com/testmake.html	$299
Test Creator	An item banker and supporting system for creating printed or computerized multiple-choice tests.	http://www.centronsoftware.com/tcpage.html	$37–$130
Test Generator	An item banker supporting ten item formats and printed and computerized test administration. Includes feedback and reporting capabilities.	http://www.testshop.com/	$79–$699

(Continued)

TABLE 11.4
(Continued)

Product Name	Description	Source	Price
Testmaker	An item banker and test construction tool intended primarily to allow customization of a set of pre-packaged personnel selection tests.	http://www.totaltesting.com/	
TestPro 7	An item banker for the creation of printed and computer-administered tests. Internet licensing is available.	http://www.atrixware.com/	$109–$1,395
Unitest System	An item banker intended primarily for computer-administered tests. Includes capabilities for keyword scoring of constructed-response items.	http://www.sight2k.com/	$34–$798
WinAsks Professional	An item banker and test administration system intended primarily for surveys and questionnaires.	http://www.assess.com/	$99

12

Selected-Response Item Formats in Test Development

Steven M. Downing
University of Illinois at Chicago

This chapter discusses the use of selected-response item formats in developing tests of achievement and ability. The chapter reviews some important research evidence to support the use of selected-response item forms as a major building block for written and computer-based tests. Validity evidence for the selected-response item format is emphasized. Strengths and limitations of the selected-response formats are overviewed and specific formats, such as multiple-choice, extended matching, and special uses of selected-response formats in testlets or context-dependent item sets are discussed.

The selected-response item format is the best choice for test developers interested in efficient, effective measurement of cognitive achievement or ability. This statement is supported by approximately 90 years of research and development activities for the selected-response format (Downing, 2002a). Although selected-response formats are certainly not without their critics, most of this criticism follows from examples of poorly written items and is not attributable to the selected-response item form per se (Downing, 2002c).

Selected response is accurately descriptive of item forms such as the multiple-choice item and all its many variants. In the selected-response format, examinees are required to choose an answer to a question or a statement from a listing of several possible answers. The selected-response item format may be considered a simulation of reality, albeit a very low-fidelity simulation.

This chapter focuses on developing test items to measure cognitive achievement or ability objectively and efficiently, in a manner that maximizes validity evidence for tests (Messick, 1989) and conforms to the *Standards for Educational and Psychological Testing* (AERA, APA, NCME, 1999). Item formats such as the multiple-choice item, multiple-choice variants such as extended matching formats, and special uses of selected-response–type items in sets, typically called *context-dependent item sets* (Haladyna, 1992a, 1992b) or *testlets*, are all common item forms useful to test developers.

TEST ITEMS TO MEASURE COGNITIVE ACHIEVEMENT

Selected-response items are the most appropriate item format for measuring cognitive achievement or ability, especially higher order cognitive achievement or cognitive abilities, such as problem solving, synthesis, and evaluation (Haladyna, 2004). Selected-response items are extremely useful and appropriate for tests intended to make inferences to a large domain of knowledge, ability, or cognitive skills. Kane (chap. 7, this volume) describes the content basis for domains, and the importance of sampling from the appropriate domain as a sound source of validity evidence. For example, if inferences are to be made to the domain of knowledge about the anatomy of the head and neck, a test composed of selected-response items written at the appropriate cognitive levels, using relevant diagrams and photographs, may be appropriate. However, the selected-response format is not useful or appropriate to develop tests of very complex abilities that require the application and integration of high-level complex skills, abilities, and other noncognitive abilities (such as written communication). For example, if inferences are to be made about specialized psychomotor skills, which require complex cognitive and psychomotor abilities applied in integrative ways to novel problem sets, a higher fidelity performance test is needed. (See Welch, chap. 8,13 this volume, for a discussion of prompt development for performance examinations.)

Constructed-response items, such as short or long essays, can be used to test knowledge, achievement, and abilities. However, compared to selected-response items, these items are much less efficient, typically produce less reliable scores, and may inadequately sample the content of the target domain, thus reducing content-related validity evidence for the test. Constructed-response items should be used to test only those content skill areas that cannot be measured by selected-response items.

The theoretical orientation of this chapter is straightforward and behavioral, considering human cognition to be a continuum of knowledge, skills, and abilities (KSAs). *Knowledge* consists of the foundational basics, such as concepts, facts, principles and their manipulation and application to novel situations, including problem solving (e.g., Bloom, Engelhart, Furst, Hill, & Krathwohl, 1956). Knowledge is specific and can be delineated and specified readily. *Abilities* are more general, leaving aside any discussion of innateness, genetics, or environmental issues such as nature–nurture. Abilities tend to require the integration of more basic knowledge into a complex "whole." Human communication, especially written communication, is a good example of a complex ability, requiring the integration of many specific bits of knowledge and some specific psychomotor skills. *Skills* refer to physical, psychomotor activities. Cognitive knowledge is a foundation for many skills, but the essence of a skill has to do with performance. True psychomotor skills must be measured by a performance test. Cognitive abilities, such as "problem solving," can be measured in either the knowledge domain or the psychomotor skills domain (leaving aside any discussion of whether or not "problem solving" can be measured purely and absolutely, outside of some problem-space context).

SELECTED-RESPONSE ITEM FORMAT

This section discusses some of the important general characteristics of the selected-response item format and considers the multiple-choice form as the prototypic selected-response item. Selected-response formats can be classified in many different ways: by their stimulus material (item stems), by the number of options presented, by the manner in which their text is presented on the page (i.e., the matching or multiple-choice form), and so on. However selected-response items are classified, the prototypic or generic parent for most of the objectively scored selected-response formats is the multiple-choice item. For example, consider the multiple-choice item, with a variable number of choices or options (two to twenty or more choices). Depending on exactly how this item is presented on the test page, it could be considered a multiple-choice item or an extended matching item. Because the multiple-choice item can be presented in so many different forms and because of its flexibility and versatility in a wide range of testing applications, the multiple-choice item can be used to test all levels of the cognitive domain, from simple recall to very high-level problem solving, synthesis, or evaluation.

STRENGTHS OF SELECTED-RESPONSE FORMATS

Why are selected-response formats recommended for most large-scale achievement test? Beside their well-known efficiency for automated scoring, the validity evidence for this format is strong. For example, a recent meta-analysis by Rodriguez (2003) demonstrated conclusively that "stem equivalent" constructed-response and selected-response items correlate nearly perfectly, after correction for unreliability. Thus, when designed to measure the same construct (a domain of knowledge and skill), the selected- and constructed-response formats produce nearly equivalent scores.

Selected-response formats have many validity advantages in the measurement of cognitive achievement and ability. They encourage content validity evidence by allowing a thorough and representative sampling of the cognitive domain; this is especially important for large domains of knowledge that should be sampled at multiple cognitive levels. Such representativeness of the content sampling process strengthens the validity evidence for inferences to the domain and reduces one major threat to validity—construct underrepresentation (Haladyna & Downing, 2004; Messick, 1989). Selected-response item responses are also efficiently machine or computer scored, typically demonstrating nearly perfect agreement among content experts concerning the correctness of the keyed answer, which achieves objectivity in scoring and eliminates subjectivity as a threat to validity, producing strong and desirable educational measurement characteristics. Objectivity is an essential characteristic of all effective measurement and adds to validity evidence, defensibility, and efficiency in the test development process. This characteristic of objectivity is obtained at much lower cost per unit of testing time for selected-response items as compared to constructed-response items.

Because of its extensive research base, well-written selected-response items can be easily defended against challenges and threats to validity (Downing & Haladyna, 2004). These items are efficient for both test developers and examinees, and if securely maintained in item banks, test items are reusable, which adds significantly to their efficiency and their strong measurement properties. Scores from selected-response formats are readily statistically equated, maintaining the constancy of the measurement scale across multiple test forms and reducing construct-irrelevant variance (CIV) from changes in mean item difficulty across test forms (Haladyna & Downing, 2004). Subjectively scored constructed-response or performance test formats can be statistically equated, but educational measurement professionals may have less experience using these newer equating methods than they have using the more common selected-response equating procedures (Kolen & Brennan, 2004).

On the other hand, constructed responses are necessarily subjectively scored. Subjectivity is introduced into scores by human raters, who may suffer from a whole host of biasing predispositions or traits, such as leniency or severity error, halo or logical error, or the tendency to rate all examinees as "average" or in the middle of the scale (central tendency error). All such rater errors introduce CIV to the constructed-response ratings, thus reducing the validity evidence for the CR scores (e.g., Haladyna & Downing, 2004). Careful training, calibration, and monitoring of human constructed-response raters can reduce, but probably not totally eliminate, the CIV error caused by subjectivity. Computer constructed-response scoring systems are currently being developed, tested, and used in production with great potential by large testing agencies such as Educational Testing Service (ETS) (Burstein, 2003).

Because of the strong measurement properties of well-constructed selected-response items, validity evidence for tests composed of these item formats is more readily assembled and evaluated than for constructed-response items. For example, it is much more straightforward to assess the content-related validity evidence for a 100-item multiple-choice test sampling some discrete cognitive knowledge domain than it is to evaluate the validity evidence for an essay test over the same domain of content. The inferences to the domain of interest are likely to be more readily made (i.e., stronger validity evidence) for the multiple-choice test compared to the constructed-response test on the same content. Kane (chap. 7, this volume) discusses problems in identifying target domains and the chain of inference required to make the essential connections between item responses and an underlying latent trait or construct. With the selected-response format, such a validity claim is usually easier to make as compared to constructed-response formats.

Selected-response item formats are defensible if they are carefully created by content experts, reviewed, edited, administered and scored. If selected-response items are maintained securely, items can be reused on future test forms. Pretesting or new item tryout is also more easily carried out for selected-response items than for constructed-response items; it is may be more difficult for examinees to memorize many selected-response items than a few constructed-response items.

LIMITATIONS OF SELECTED-RESPONSE FORMATS

Selected-response item formats are useful only for the assessment of cognitive knowledge; these formats are useless for the measurement of psychomotor skills, such as the production of original writing. For complex production tasks like writing, only a constructed-response format will suffice. Yet, many of the foundations or precursors to complex production tasks (like writing) can be effectively and efficiently measured by selected-response items. For instance, knowledge about standard sentence structure, grammar, and spelling can be efficiently tested by the selected-response formats. The fidelity of this approach may not be as high as a more direct method, such as scoring based on a student's actual writing sample, but the efficiency is considerably better with the selected-response format, and correlation with the higher fidelity performance test can be very high.

One of the greatest limitations of the selected-response formats derives from the creation of flawed selected-response items. Although this is generally not an issue for large-scale tests produced by professional testing agencies, poorly written or flawed items are a major source of CIV for many smaller scale tests that must be developed with fewer resources. The principles of effective item writing are well delineated (e.g., Haladyna, Downing, & Rodriguez, 2002); these principles, based on a consensus of the educational measurement textbook authors and empirical research studies, can be considered the "evidence-based" principles of effective item writing. Developers of large-scale assessments generally adhere to these essential principles. The negative effect of violations of these evidence-based principles has been demonstrated (Downing, 2002b; Downing, 2005). For example, it has been shown that flawed multiple-choice items are up to 15 percentage points more difficult than standard items (items that conform to the standard principles) testing the same content, with median passing rates about 3.5 percentage points lower for flawed items as compared to standard items (Downing, 2005). These research results reinforce the necessity for test developers to carefully monitor the creation of new item material, to ensure competent content editing and content review of new items (see Baranowski, chap. 15, this volume).

What are some other limitations of selected-response formats? Possible cluing of the keyed correct answer is frequently noted as a potential negative. But, cluing of correct answers implies flawed items or use of implausible incorrect answer options. Certainly, it is possible to present selected-response items that contain clues to the correct answer, but well crafted and well-edited selected-response items do not exemplify such item flaws, if the standard principles of effective item writing are followed. Critics sometimes cite the artificiality of presenting examinees the task of selecting a correct or best answer from a predefined listing of possible answers. Typically, selected-response items are somewhat easier than same-content constructed-response items (e.g., Heim & Watts, 1967), but the subjectivity bias of the readers also influences the scores and the scale. The differential difficulty of selected- and constructed-response items is a scaling issue and can be compensated for during any standard-setting process, if cut scores are applied to the test scores. The meta-analysis work on stem-equivalent (content equal) constructed- and selected-response items, showing the near unity of disattenuated correlations between the two formats, lays to rest any legitimate controversy on this issue (Rodriguez, 2003).

Trivial content of selected-response items is sometimes cited as an inherent flaw of the item type. Although it is certainly true that the educational world is awash in trivial item content (e.g., Downing, 2002c), the selected-response format can be utilized to test all levels of the cognitive taxonomy, including very high levels such as problem solving, judgment, and synthesis. Selected-response formats can be used to effectively and efficiently test many higher order abilities and skills, once thought to be the exclusive domain of the constructed-response item format (Haladyna, 1997). However, selected-response items cannot be used to test production skills, such as writing or human traits, or abilities, such as creativity. Trivial item content is not a necessary property of the item form, but rather a weakness introduced by the item writer. Novice item writers, without any specialized training or educational intervention, tend to write flawed selected-response items testing trivial content, at lower cognitive levels such as recall or recognition of facts. The adage, "Absent intervention, teachers teach the way they were taught and test the way they were tested" is very true. Special expertise in the content discipline is a necessary but not sufficient condition for expertise in selected-response item writing.

Random guessing is sometimes alleged to be a major weakness of selected-response items. Guessing is possible on any of the selected-response formats, but is often overestimated as a serious problem in well-constructed tests composed of sufficient numbers of test items. Random guessing is less common than feared; however, examinees may use partial knowledge to eliminate incorrect answers (Ebel & Frisbie, 1991). In high-stakes examinations, for which examinees are typically well prepared and item difficulty is targeted appropriately, examinees rarely need to randomly guess. If random guessing were a serious problem in selected-response tests, score reliability estimates would be attenuated by the introduction of random measurement error. This is typically not the case in well-developed tests (Downing, 2003). Further, the statistical probability of achieving a good score on even a very short test through random guessing alone is extremely low (e.g., the random probability of obtaining 70% correct on a thirty-item, three-option test is 0.0000356.)

NUMBER OF OPTIONS

The total number of options in a test item determines the statistical probability of randomly guessing the one correct answer. With three options, the probability of randomly guessing the correct answer is 0.33. However, the probability of getting two of these three-option test items right by random guessing alone is 0.11, three correct is 0.04, four correct is 0.01 and five correct is 0.004. This leads to the logical and intuitive conclusion that more options are better than fewer options. This would be correct if every incorrect option had an equal probability of being chosen and had a monotonic negative response curve (Livingston, chap. 19, this volume), but this is rarely true. A study by Haladyna and Downing (1993) shows that three options are typically sufficient, because even in very well-developed tests it is rare that more than three options are statistically functional. Functionality of incorrect options is defined empirically as an option that is selected by at least some small percentage of examinees (e.g., 5%) and also demonstrates a monotonically decreasing option response curve or trace line (Wainer, 1989). Few test items, even very well written and edited items, in large-scale, high-stakes tests have more than three functional options. The tradition of using four or five options for multiple-choice items is strong, despite the research evidence suggesting that it is nearly impossible to create selected-response test items with more than about three functional options.

A recent meta-analysis of 80-years of published empirical studies on the appropriate number of options to use for multiple-choice items concludes: "... MC items should consist of three options, one correct option and two plausible distractors. Using more options does little to improve item and test score statistics and typically results in implausible distractors" (Rodriguez, 2005, p. 11).

Thus, if test items are reasonably well constructed and tests have a sufficient number of total items which are appropriately targeted in difficulty to the examinees' ability, test developers can confidently use three-option multiple-choice items for most tests of achievement or ability.

DIFFICULTY OF DEVELOPMENT

The difficulty and cost of developing effective selected-response items is sometimes cited as a limitation of the format. Typically, it is easier and less costly to write constructed-response questions than selected-response items, but these economies tend to evaporate when scoring issues and difficulties are considered. Selected-response item writer training is an essential component of the validity evidence required for achievement tests (Downing, chap. 1, this volume; Downing & Haladyna, 1997). Such training adds to the cost of producing effective selected-response items. Further, writing effective selected-response items is a nontrivial skill, requiring a great deal of costly professional time and effort from content experts. But, if effective selected-response items are created, reviewed, edited, and pretested and their security is maintained, items can be reused—effectively amortizing the cost per item over many uses. (Per item costs are variable, but it is not unreasonable for a very high-stakes testing program to value its items at more than $1,000 per item.)

SELECTED-RESPONSE FORMATS

This section overviews the common or traditional selected-response formats: multiple-choice forms, including their special use in context-dependent item sets (testlets) and their variants such as the extended-matching format. The discussion is limited to these high-usage, high-utility formats, because the vast majority of test development applications (both traditional paper-and-pencil tests and computer-based tests) are well served by these primary item forms.

Some more innovative selected-response formats, potentially useful for computer-based tests, are discussed by Sireci and Zenisky (chap. 14, this volume). Other selected-response formats, such as the multiple true–false format, are excluded from discussion here, because their use has a mixed research basis (Frisbie, 1992; Frisbie & Becker, 1991; Haladyna et al., 2002). All complex multiple-choice formats are excluded from discussion because they lack the research support to recommend their use (Haladyna et al., 2002). All true–false formats, including alternate-choice formats (e.g., Downing, 1992) are excluded because of their limited utility in large-scale testing, although they can be used effectively in some testing applications. Novel formats, such as the key features format (Bordage, Carretier, Bertrand, & Page, 1995; Bordage & Page, 1987), are excluded from this discussion because the format has been used only in medical education settings and may be difficult to adapt to large-scale tests in non-medical disciplines.

The Multiple-Choice Format

Multiple-choice items are the workhorse of the testing enterprise throughout much of the world, at least the Western world. This familiar item format is the most common selected-response item form because of its great versatility; its efficiency in testing all levels of knowledge, achievement, and ability; its usefulness in both paper-and-pencil and computer-based testing applications; and its relative ease for item writers to produce and test developers to use, secure, store, and reuse in the test development process.

The multiple-choice item format was introduced out of the necessity of efficiency during World War I, for the U.S. Army Alpha test of "general intelligence." The army had a need to sort and classify large numbers of trainees into ability classifications, matching recruits to tasks for which they had some aptitude or ability. Constructed-response items would be very inefficient and time and resource intensive for screening large numbers of recruits quickly, efficiently, and validly. The multiple-choice item form was ideal for this first major large-scale testing project, overseen by the great early testing psychologists such as Yerkes, Terman, and Otis (Ebel, 1972).

The multiple-choice item format (and objective testing in general) has always had its critics, from the time the format was "coming of age" in the 1960s (e.g., Hoffmann, 1962) to the present (e.g., FairTest: The National Center for Fair & Open Testing, 2004). And, critics have much legitimate ammunition; the world is awash in poorly written multiple-choice items (Downing, 2002c), which assess only the most basic factual information and do so with poorly crafted items that frequently violate even the most obvious standard principles of sound item development.

However, large-scale testing programs typically produce high-quality, effective multiple-choice items for their tests. What are the qualities of a good multiple-choice item? The answer to this question has been studied thoroughly in the last two decades (e.g., Haladyna & Downing, 1989a, 1989b; Haladyna et al., 2002). A major text (Haladyna, 2004) is devoted entirely to a detailed, academic review of multiple-choice items and all their many variants. And, many excellent item-writer training guides, based on these "evidence-based" principles of effective item writing, are readily available (e.g., Case & Swanson, 1998).

Table 12.1 lists thirty-one consensus principles of effective multiple choice item writing and is quoted from the Haladyna et al. (2002) review paper. All but one of these principles is endorsed by some or all of the twenty-seven educational measurement textbooks reviewed in this study and about half of these principles have some empirical research basis (Haladyna & Downing, 1989a, 1989b).

Item writing is both art and science. There are scientifically sound principles of item writing, but the creation of effective multiple-choice items requires the skillful application of these principles to the content to be tested. That is the art. Content expertise is an absolute essential for effective item writers, but expertise in the subject matter is no guarantee of excellence in item writing, unless the content expert is first trained in the art of producing effective test items. The training of expert item writers is an essential component of validity evidence and the training materials used to guide item writers should be well documented (see Downing, chap. 1, this volume).

TABLE 12.1
A Revised Taxonomy of Multiple-Choice Item Writing Guidelines

Content

1. Every item should reflect specific content and a single specific mental behavior, as called for in the test specifications.
2. Base each item on important content; avoid trivial content.
3. Use novel material to test higher level learning. Do not use exact textbook language in test items to avoid testing only recall of familiar words and phrases.
4. Keep the content of each item independent
5. Avoid overly specific and overly general content.
6. Avoid opinion-based items.
7. Avoid trick items.
8. Keep vocabulary simple and appropriate for the examinees tested.

Formatting concerns

9. Use the question, completion, and best answer versions of conventional multiple-choice items, the alternate choice, true–false, multiple true–false, matching, and the context-dependent item and item set formats, but avoid the complex multiple-choice format.
10. Format the item vertically, not horizontally.

Style concerns

11. Edit and proof items.
12. Use correct grammar, punctuation, capitalization, and spelling.
13. Minimize the amount of reading in each item.
14. Ensure that the directions in the stem are very clear.
15. Include the central idea in the stem, not the options.
16. Avoid window dressing (excessive verbiage).
17. Word the stem positively; avoid negatives such as not or except. If negative words are used, use the word cautiously and always ensure that the word appears capitalized and in bold type.

The options

18. Develop as many effective choices as you can, but research suggests three are adequate.
19. Make sure that only one of these choices is the correct answer.
20. Vary the location of the correct answer according to the number of choices. Balance the answer key, insofar as possible, so that the correct answer appears an equal number of times in each answer position.
21. Place the choices in logical or numerical order.
22. Keep choices independent; choices should not be overlapping in meaning.
23. Keep choices homogeneous in content and grammatical structure.
24. Keep the length of choices about equal.
25. *None of the above* should be used carefully.
26. Avoid *All of the above*.
27. Phrase choices positively; avoid negatives such as not.
28. Avoid giving clues to the right answer, such as
    a. Specific determiners including *always, never, completely,* and *absolutely.*
    b. Clang associations, choices identical to or resembling words in the stem.
    c. Grammatical inconsistencies that cue the test taker to the correct choice.
    d. Conspicuously correct choice.
    e. Pairs or triplets of options that clue the test taker to the correct choice.
    f. Blatantly absurd, ridiculous options.
29. Make all distractors plausible.
30. Use typical errors of students to create distractors.
31. Use humor if it is compatible with the teacher and the learning environment.

Quoted from and adapted from Haladyna, Downing, & Rodriquez (2002, p. 312).

Anatomy of a Multiple-Choice Item

A multiple-choice item consists of a stem, lead-in, or stimulus, containing all the information required to answer a question, including the "lead line," which poses a specific question (see Baranowski, chap. 15, this volume). Ideally, the stem ends with a direct question (or a strongly implied question). Every item should have a very clear "testing point" or objective that can be stated in a simple phrase, sentence, or proposition. The stem (question) should be phrased in positive form, avoiding negation unless the negative term is essential to the testing point (e.g., the contraindication for a medication). The options or all the possible answers follow the stem and are identified by alphanumeric letters or numbers, only one of which is best or correct (in the recommended form). The general directions for multiple-choice items usually require selecting the best answer from those presented, although some tests require selecting the single correct answer from those given. The "best answer" format is most common, because it is most defensible. See Figure 12.1 for example multiple-choice items.

Most of the information should be contained in the item stem or lead-in, such that the options contain fewer words, relative to the stem. Stem length can vary from very short one-sentence questions ("Who was the first president of the National Council on Measurement in Education?) to a very long scenario or vignette composed of several paragraphs of information. The stem must contain sufficient information to answer the question posed, but should not contain superfluous "window dressing," because reading burden can introduce CIV into the measurement (see Abedi, chap. 17, this volume.)

---

1. Dr. Aziz, a United States citizen and Professor of Internal Medicine at the University of Chicago, is detained by United States law enforcement agents for questioning concerning her association with certain faculty members from the College of Medicine at the University of Baghdad in Iraq. Dr. Aziz is not permitted to speak with her attorney and is being held in an undisclosed location. She is not charged with any crime and no warrant for her arrest has been issued, but she is being held as a "material witness" for an indefinite period of time. Which document forbids this action of the government against Dr. Aziz?

  A. The First Amendment
  B. The Fourth Amendment
  C. The Fourteenth Amendment

2. "Where it is an absolute question of the welfare of our country, we must admit of no considerations of justice or injustice, or mercy or cruelty, or praise or ignominy, but putting all else aside must adopt whatever course will save its existence and preserve its liberty."
  This quote is most likely from which of the following?

  A. John Aschcroft
  B. Desiderius Erasmus
  C. King Henry VIII
  D. Niccolo Machiavelli
  E. Karl Rove

3. A Surgery clerkship coordinator initiates a new observational system for the clinical performance assessment of third-year medical students. The new system requires faculty and residents to rate clerkship students on their overall clinical performance, using a global rating scale, on three separate occasions over the course of a 12-week clerkship. The Associate Dean for Undergraduate Education has demanded evidence that this new system is "valid." Which type of reproducibility is most important to estimate?

  A. Rater stability over time
  B. Intra-rater agreement over occasions
  C. Inter-rater agreement across students
  D. Internal consistency of ratings

FIG. 12.1 Multiple-choice item examples.

The set of answer options should be homogenous in content, all relating to the same general class, and should be of about equal length, to avoid cueing testwise examinees. Options should be worded positively. Every option should be a plausible correct answer for the uninformed examinee. One universal recommendation is that the examinee should be able to answer the test question with all of the options covered. This principle ensures that the stem of the item poses a clear and direct question, which focuses the examinee on the exact problem to be solved. (If the item is unfocused, the examinee first must determine what question is being posed before even beginning the process of problem solving. This additional cognitive burden may add CIV to the measurement and tends to artificially increase the difficulty of the question.)

The research evidence suggests that three plausible options are sufficient (one best answer and two incorrect answers), especially for high-ability examinees (Haladyna & Downing, 1993; Lord, 1977; Rodriguez, 2005). A common recommendation is to use as many options as reasonable for the item. Plausibility of options leads to functionality (as defined), but ultimately both characteristics are empirically determined by administration of the item to a sample of examinees (Haladyna, 2004). (Also see Livingston, chap. 19, this volume).

Technology of Test Item Generation

The difficulty of creating effective selected-response items has encouraged the development of techniques to increase the efficiency of item production. Roid and Haladyna (1982) discussed many methods to maximize the production of large numbers of effective selected-response items. Methods such as the use of item shells (Haladyna & Shindoll, 1989) and item modeling techniques (e.g., LaDuca, 1994; LaDuca, Downing, & Henzel, 1995; LaDuca, Staples, Templeton, & Holzman, 1986) are commonly used in large-scale testing programs to effectively and efficiently maximize the number of test items available for multiple test forms (see Haladyna [2004] for a complete description of item shells and item-modeling techniques).

The item shells method gives item writers a template of common and useful item stem questions or suggests the particular type of information to include in stem questions for a variety of cognitive levels. Item modeling, expressed in a number of different techniques, presents a prototypic test item that can be systematically modified in various ways to produce items that are "parallel" (or almost identical) in content but are superficially different in appearance.

Methods for effectively and efficiently producing large numbers of high-quality test items are needed for many large-scale testing programs, especially computer-based testing programs that are available to examinees "on demand" or nearly constantly. Computer-adaptive testing programs are the most item needy, requiring the constant production of large numbers of high-quality selected-response items that meet exacting content specifications and have specific psychometric characteristics. Almost all large-scale tests require multiple test forms, which increases the need for a constant inflow of newly written test items. As the complexity of the testing program increases, the need for newly created items grows. So, for example, a computer-adaptive test, offered to large numbers of examinees as an "on demand" test, requires large numbers of new items constantly. Test developers have become very creative in meeting these new item needs, by expanding on techniques such as the use of item shells and item modeling, to create new item social order classifications, such as item "clones," "friends," "dependents," "enemies," and "archenemies"—all from a need to create large numbers of effective test items with highly specified content and particular measurement characteristics (see Vale, chap. 11, this volume). Large testing agencies, such as ETS, continue to research methods to "automatically" create high-quality test items through computer generation (e.g., Deane & Sheehan, 2003), but these methods are still in their infancy and are not likely to replace creative human item writers with particular content expertise anytime soon.

Item Sets

Special sets or groupings of test items have been used in tests for many years. Recently, there has been an increased interest in special applications of selected-response items, as "context-dependent item sets" (Haladyna, 1992a) or "testlets" (Wainer & Kiely, 1987). The concept is straightforward: Common stimulus material, such as a paragraph or two containing a scenario, vignette, or situation, provides a common stem or lead-in for multiple selected-response items. For example, in a medical certification examination, the common stimulus material could be a clinical situation, describing a patient's relevant history or presenting problem in sufficient detail for examinees to respond to several independent selected-response questions, all related to the common stem, asking for diagnosis, management decisions, laboratory tests, likely complications, and so on.

The obvious benefit of item sets is efficiency. It is usually somewhat easier to write a series of related items around a common theme or stimulus than the same number of unrelated or stand-alone items. And it is possible to probe a content area very thoroughly using the testlet technique. Further, it is possible to write a large number of items relating to a common stimulus and then mix and match items from a particular item set on various forms of the test. Sophisticated item-banking software (Vale, chap. 11, this volume) makes the creation and flexible use of item sets possible.

With all item sets, care must be exercised to ensure that all the items in the set are as independent of one another as possible. That is, no item may cue or give away the answer to any other item in the set and the items cannot be so tightly linked that getting one item incorrect causes the examinee to get another item (or all the rest of the items) incorrect. Statistical independence of items is a fundamental assumption for all measurement theory models. Item sets typically violate this assumption of local independence, such that the item scores within the testlet correlate more highly with one another than with items outside of the testlet. Such a lack of local independence can lead to an overestimation of test score reliability (Wainer & Thissen, 1996). Thus, Thissen and Wainer (2001) show that a testlet score (the sum of item scores within a testlet) is the proper unit of reliability analysis for testlets.

Another important caveat in using context-dependent item sets is to take care not to oversample particular content areas, skewing the test content specifications by sampling only one small facet of some particular content area tested by the item set. For example, because all item sets use a common stimulus for a number of unique test items, all items in the set sample the same general content area, which is likely to represent one small piece of the entire test content specifications. Many such context-dependent item sets can set up the possibility of an extremely narrow sampling of the content domain, thus reducing the validity evidence for the test and compromising inferences to the larger domain of interest.

Testlets or context-dependent item sets are useful for test developers, especially if item banking software allows the test developers to mix and match various items from a large set to a common stimulus on various forms of a test. Overall, the benefits of using item sets very likely outweigh the potential limitations of such use, if test developers remain vigilant about oversampling and take care to limit dependence or linking of items to one another within the set.

Extended Matching Items

Extended matching items can be considered a variant of the multiple-choice item, a variant of the traditional matching item, a special type of context-dependent item set, or a unique item form. However one classifies this item format, it is a useful and versatile format, first popularized by Case and Swanson (1993, 1998) at the National Board of Medical Examiners.

> **Theme: Diagnosis of Complications of Liposuction**
>
> A. Vasovagal reaction
> B. Anaphylaxis
> C. Lidocaine toxicity
> D. Allergic contact dermatitis
> E. Stroke
>
> **Which is the most likely diagnosis for each patient who is undergoing or has recently undergone pure tumescent liposuction?**
>
> 1. Immediately post operatively, a 47-year-old woman says that she "feels sick." Her blood pressure is 126/70 and her pulse is difficult to detect; her skin is pale, cool and diaphoretic.
> 2. Six hours post operatively, a 26-year-old man is agitated and has tingling around his mouth. His speech is rapid.
> 3. During surgery, a 32-year-old woman says she "feels sick." She has generalized pruritus, her blood pressure begins to decrease and her pulse rate is rapid. Her skin is red and warm.

FIG. 12.2 Extended matching item example. This extended matching item example has been trimmed to fit a typical 5-response answer sheet. Exemplar extended matching items have 10 to 20 or more "options," with much longer items—sometimes comprising two or three sentences.

The extended matching item is similar to the traditional matching item in that it consists of a set of homogeneous options to which a set of item stems is matched. There is typically a lead-in type sentence that sets up the exact task or question for the examinee. Each extended matching item has a common theme, which unifies both the options and the items or questions. See Figure 12.2 for an example of an extended matching item.

A major strength of the extended matching item form is that it typically forces the item author to write a question testing some higher order knowledge, such as problem solving, evaluation, or application. Whereas the traditional matching format usually tests lower level cognitive processes such as recognition or recall of facts, the extended matching format forces the item writer to formulate content in such a way that higher order cognitive processes are assessed. Also, item writers who are well trained and experienced with this item form typically find it relatively easy to produce effective extended matching items as compared to multiple-choice items. As with testlet item sets, clever use of sophisticated item banking software allows the test developers to mix and match extended matching items to the same set of options on different forms of a test. There is no reason to believe that more time is required for examinees to complete extended matching items as compared to multiple-choice items; thus, differential weighting of extended matching item scores should not be required when combining extended matching scores with traditional multiple-choice item scores.

The limitations of extended matching item sets are similar to those noted for other item sets, such as testlets or context-dependent item sets. Because, by definition, the extended matching item set has a common theme and all options must be sampled from a homogeneous class, it is possible to oversample a tiny portion of the content specifications at the expense of other appropriate content. Thus, a judicious use of extended matching items across a test form is generally recommended (as a mix of item types within a test form). It is generally not recommended to attempt to sample an entire content domain using only extended matching items.

If extended matching items are used on paper-and-pencil tests and answered on traditional optically scanned answer sheets, test developers must take care to ensure that the available answer sheets accommodate the total number of options presented. For example, if a test is composed of a mixture of three-, four-, and five-option multiple-choice items, plus three extended-matching sets of twelve, fifteen, and twenty options, the test developer must be sure that the answer sheet accommodates twelve-, fifteen- and twenty-option answers. Usually, this requires custom-printed answer sheets and special scoring and item analysis software (or the appropriate work arounds). Because custom answer sheets are more expensive than standard answer sheets, the extended matching item may be more expensive to use than the typical multiple-choice item. If extended matching items are used on computer-based tests, the user interface must accommodate this item form and may require some special attention to ensure the availability of options and items on the same screen.

The basic principles of writing effective extended matching items are similar to traditional matching items. There should always be more options than items, such that there is not a one-to-one correspondence of items to options. The general directions for extended matching items, like traditional matching, typically read: "Options may be selected once, more than once, or not at all." The major organizing principle of the extended matching item set is that there must always be some common or homogeneous theme to the item set as expressed in the options. The items are usually one- to two-sentence scenarios describing the essence of the problem or task to be solved; all of the options must be sampled from the same general class such as "types of reproducibility."

SUMMARY AND CONCLUSION

The selected-response item format is extremely useful for developers of achievement and ability tests. The multiple-choice item, a primary exemplar of the selected-response item type, is widely used throughout the world, largely because of its versatility and utility in assessing KSAs, including the highest levels of problem solving, synthesis, and evaluation. The principles for creating effective multiple-choice items are well documented and research based. The multiple-choice item type is frequently derided as fostering the assessment of trivial and low-level knowledge, but the research evidence suggests that the fault lay not with the multiple-choice item per se, but with item writers who fail to follow the principles of effective item design (Downing, 2005; Jozefowicz et al., 2002).

Variants of the multiple-choice item, such as the extended matching item, offer additional selected-response formats for the creative test developer. One strength of the extended matching item is that it encourages assessment of higher level knowledge and, if used properly, almost guarantees such higher order measurement.

The use of context-dependent item sets or testlets can increase efficiency for test developers, because multiple selected-response items can be created for common introductory stimuli. Judicious use of testlet items, with different items of the set used in various test forms, can effectively increase the number of useful selected-response items available for test form construction.

Techniques such as using item shells or using item modeling methods can assist test developers in creating the large number of effective test items needed to construct ongoing multiple test forms. The ever-increasing transition of large-scale tests from infrequently offered, fixed-date, paper-and-pencil administrations to "on demand" (nearly continuous) computer administrations requires test developers to find methods to greatly expand useable item pools to meet the demands for new test items and limit the exposure of previously used test items.

The technology of selected-response item writing has evolved little over the long history of the format's use, despite the best efforts of researchers such as Roid and Haladyna (1982) and Bormuth (1970). Out of necessity, test developers are now finding creative ways, such as using item-cloning techniques, to increase the useable number of test items in the most efficient and cost-effective way possible. The trend toward ever-increasing computer-based testing applications is likely to accelerate the need for the development of item-writing technologies. Perhaps the innovative computer-based item generation techniques being developed by agencies such as ETS (e.g., Deane & Sheehan, 2003) will ultimately provide the solution to the problem of creating large numbers of unique high quality selected-response test items.

ACKNOWLEDGMENTS

The author gratefully acknowledges the critical review and helpful suggestions of Thomas M. Haladyna, PhD, and the insight, inspiration, and thoughtful criticism provided by my students in a graduate-level test development course.

REFERENCES

American Educational Research Association (AERA), American Psychological Association (APA), & National Council on Measurement in Education (NCME). (1999). *Standards for educational and psychological testing.* Washington DC: American Educational Research Association.
Bloom, B. S., Engelhart, M. D., Furst, E. J., Hill, W. H., & Krathwohl, D. R. (1956). *Taxonomy of educational objectives.* New York: Longmans Green.
Bordage, G., Carretier, H., Bertrand, R., & Page, G. (1995). Comparing times and performances of French- and English-speaking candidates taking a national examination of clinical decision-making skills. *Academic Medicine, 70*(5), 359–365.
Bordage, G., & Page, G. (1987). An alternative approach to PMPs: The key features concept. In I. Hart & R. Harden (Eds.), *Further developments in assessing clinical competence* (pp. 57–75). Montreal, Canada: Heal.
Bormuth, J. R. (1970). *On a theory of achievement test items.* Chicago: University of Chicago Press.
Burstein, J. (2003). The *e-rater* scoring engine: Automated essay scoring with natural language processing. In M. D. Shermis & J. Burstein (Eds.), *Automated essay scoring: A cross-disciplinary perspective.* Hillsdale, NJ: Lawrence Erlbaum Associates.
Case, S., & Swanson, D. (1998). *Constructing written test questions for the basic and clinical sciences.* Philadelphia: National Board of Medical Examiners.
Case, S. M., & Swanson, D. B. (1993). Extended matching items: A practical alternative to free response questions. *Teaching and Learning in Medicine, 5*(2), 107–115.
Deane, P., & Sheehan, K. (2003). *Automatic item generation via frame semantics: Natural language generation of math word problems.* Princeton, NJ: Educational Testing Service.
Downing, S. M. (1992). True-False, alternate-choice and multiple-choice items: A research perspective. *Educational Measurement: Issues and Practice, 11,* 27–30.
Downing, S. M. (2002a). Assessment of knowledge with written test forms. In G. R. Norman, C. P. M., Van der Vleuten, & D. I. Newble, (Eds.) *International handbook of research in medical education* (pp. 647–672). Dordrecht, The Netherlands: Kluwer Academic Publishers.
Downing, S. M. (2002b). Construct-irrelevant variance and flawed test questions: Do multiple-choice item-writing principles make any difference? *Academic Medicine, 77*(10), S103–104.
Downing, S. M. (2002c). Threats to the validity of locally developed multiple-choice tests in medical education: Construct-irrelevant variance and construct underrepresentation. *Advances in Health Sciences Education, 7,* 235–241.
Downing, S. M. (2003). Guessing on selected-response examinations. *Medical Education, 37,* 670–671.
Downing, S. M. (2005). The effects of violating standard item writing principles on tests and students: The consequences of using flawed test items on achievement examinations in medical education. *Advances in Health Sciences Education, 10,* 133–143.
Downing, S. M., & Haladyna, T. M. (1997). Test item development: Validity evidence from quality assurance procedures. *Applied Measurement in Education, 10,* 61–82.
Downing, S. M., & Haladyna, T. M. (2004). Validity threats: Overcoming interference with proposed interpretations of assessment data. *Medical Education, 38,* 327–333.
Ebel, R. L. (1972). *Essentials of educational measurement.* Englewood Cliffs, NJ: Prentice Hall.
Ebel, R. L., & Frisbie, D. A. (1991). *Essentials of educational measurement.* Englewood Cliffs, NJ: Prentice Hall.
FairTest: The National Center for Fair & Open Testing. (2004). The dangerous consequences of high-stakes standardized testing. Retrieved November 22, 2004, from http://fairtest.org/facts/Dangerous%20Consequences.html.
Frisbie, D. A. (1992). The multiple true-false item format: A status review. *Educational Measurement: Issues and Practice, 5*(4), 21–26.

Frisbie, D. A., & Becker, D. F. (1991). An analysis of textbook advice about true-false tests. *Applied Measurement in Education, 4*, 67–83.

Haladyna, T. M. (1992a). Context-dependent item sets. *Educational Measurement: Issues and Practice, 11*, 21–25.

Haladyna, T. M. (1992b). The effectiveness of several multiple-choice formats. *Applied Measurement in Education, 5*, 73–88.

Haladyna, T. M. (1997). *Writing test items to measure higher level thinking*. Needham Heights, MA: Allyn & Bacon.

Haladyna, T. M. (2004). *Developing and validating multiple-choice test items*. Mahwah, NJ: Lawrence Erlbaum Associates.

Haladyna, T. M., & Downing, S. M. (1989a). A taxonomy of multiple-choice item-writing rules. *Applied Measurement in Education, 1*, 37–50.

Haladyna, T. M., & Downing, S. M. (1989b). The validity of a taxonomy of multiple-choice item-writing rules. *Applied Measurement in Education, 1*, 51–78.

Haladyna, T. M., & Downing, S. M. (1993). How many options is enough for a multiple-choice test item. *Educational and Psychological Measurement, 53*, 999–1010.

Haladyna, T. M., & Downing, S. M. (2004). Construct-irrelevant variance: A threat in high-stakes testing. *Educational Measurement: Issues and Practice, 23*(1), 17–27.

Haladyna, T. M., Downing, S. M., & Rodriguez, M. C. (2002). A review of multiple-choice item-writing guidelines for classroom assessment. *Applied Measurement in Education, 15*(3), 309–334.

Haladyna, T. M., & Shindoll, R. R. (1989). Item shells: A method for writing effective multiple-choice test items. *Evaluation and the Health Professions, 12*, 97–104.

Heim, A. W., & Watts, K. P. (1967). An experiment on multiple-choice versus open-ended answering in a vocabulary test. *British Journal of Educational Psychology, 37*, 339–346.

Hoffmann, B. (1962). *The tyranny of testing*. New York: Crowell-Collier-Macmillan.

Jozefowicz, R. F., Koeppen, B. M., Case, S., Galbraith, R., Swanson, D., & Glew, H. (2002). The quality of in-house medical school examinations. *Academic Medicine, 77*, 156–61.

Kolen, M. J., & Brennan, R. L. (2004). *Test equating, scaling, and linking: Methods and practices*. New York: Springer-Verlag.

LaDuca, A. (1994). Validation of a professional licensure examination: Professions theory, test design, and construct validity. *Evaluation and the Health Professions, 17*(2), 178–197.

LaDuca, A., Downing, S. M., & Henzel, T. R. (1995). Test development: Systematic item writing and test construction. In J. C. Impara & J. C. Fortune (Eds.), *Licensure examinations: Purposes, procedures, and practices* (pp. 117–148). Lincoln, NE: Buros Institute of Mental Measurements.

LaDuca, A., Staples, W. I., Templeton, B., & Holzman, G. B. (1986). Item modelling procedure for constructing content–equivalent multiple-choice questions. *Medical Education, 20*, 53–56.

Lord, F. M. (1977). Optimal number of choices per item—A comparison of four approaches. *Journal of Educational Measurement, 14*, 33–38.

Messick, S. (1989). Validity. In R. L. Linn (Ed.), *Educational measurement* (3rd ed., pp. 13–104). New York: American Council on Education & MacMillan.

Rodriguez, M. C. (2003) Construct equivalence of multiple-choice and constructed-response items: A random effects synthesis of correlations. *Journal of Educational Measurement, 40*(2), 163–184.

Rodriguez, M. C. (2005). Three options are optimal for multiple-choice items: A meta-analysis of 80 years of research. *Educational Measurement: Issues and Practice, 24*(2), 3–13.

Roid, G. H., & Haladyna, T. M. (1982). *Toward a technology of test-item writing*. New York: Academic Press.

Thissen, D., & Wainer, H. (Eds.). (2001). *Test scoring*. Mahwah, NJ: Lawrence Erlbaum Associates.

Wainer, H. (1989). The future of item analysis. *Journal of Educational Measurement, 26*, 191–208.

Wainer, H., & Kiely, G. (1987). Item clusters and computerized adaptive testing: A case for testlets. *Journal of Educational Measurement, 24*, 185–202.

Wainer, H., & Thissen, D. (1996). How is reliability related to the quality of test scores? What is the effect of local dependence on reliability? *Educational Measurement: Issues and Practice, 15*(1), 22–29.

13

Item and Prompt Development in Performance Testing

Catherine Welch
ACT, Inc.

Assessment programs are moving toward the integration of performance assessment items with the traditional multiple-choice items to provide a better coverage of the standards being assessed. This chapter describes the process of performance assessment development including the content, technical, and logistical decisions that must be considered prior to the development of any assessment items. The chapter discusses the processes to be followed in the development of performance assessment items including the selection and training of prompt writers, topic selection, and technical considerations. The chapter also provides a discussion of the development of the scoring rubrics, the prompt-review process, and the ultimate field testing of the items. The chapter concludes with a discussion of issues surrounding the test assembly process when performance assessment items are being included.

The primary purpose of this chapter is to describe the item and prompt development process and to identify various considerations that test developers should take into account as they design and develop performance assessments. This chapter is intended for the test developer. It is intended to assist the test developer to focus on various considerations of the development process, particularly those that are relevant to the inclusion of performance assessments. This chapter begins with the characteristics of various item types, includes a discussion of the item and prompt and scoring rubric development processes, and presents information about the test assembly process when performance assessment items are to be included.

The test development process involves many varied, yet related, considerations (see Downing, chap. 1, this volume). Key among these are considerations of purpose, content, item format, and the uses of the assessment. The test developer must begin the development process by specifying the purpose of the test and the content or construct to be measured. Once the purpose of the assessment is specified, the test developer must define the specifications for the test. The test specifications should identify the content domain for the test, the proposed number of items to be developed, the desired psychometric characteristics of the test, the logistical restrictions for the test and the appropriate item format (American Educational Research Association [AERA], American Psychological Association [APA], & National Council of Measurement in Education [NCME], 1999, Standard 3.3). Test developers and users may typically choose between performance assessment item types and multiple-choice item types when developing a test to measure a body of knowledge or a set of skills (see Downing, chap. 12, this volume, for a discussion of selected-response items). The choice of item format to be developed is typically driven by the content and cognitive demand desired in the test specifications as well as the depth and breadth of the knowledge to be assessed. Logistical restrictions (i.e., turnaround time, resources for scoring, available testing time) must also be considered in the item format decision. Lindquist (1951) argued that the item type should match the criterion of interest. He indicated that the test developer should make the item format as similar to the criterion format as possible, recognizing the constraints of efficiency, comparability, and economy. The same argument is still true today.

Messick (1996) stated that the assessment should be worthwhile and meaningful to the students. Performance assessment tasks can accomplish this by communicating clearly what is expected of the examinees and how the responses are ultimately evaluated.

The test developer should evaluate each item format to identify those that might be preferable for reasons of content and cognitive demand coverage, economy, precision, response time, development and scoring costs, delivery constraints, and feasibility. More than one item format might be appropriate and needed if the content and cognitive demand in the test specifications are broad and diversified. The matching of item format to the test domain can conflict with other constraints such as scoring ease, reliability targets, and development time, but above all the test developer needs to promote the item formats that are most consistent with and most likely to provide the best measures of content and skill test specifications. All aspects of the knowledge content and skill domains need to be considered in selecting the item format.

Finally, the test developer must consider how the item format, including stimulus materials, are affected by the delivery platform. If the test is to be delivered on computer, the developer needs to consider how the screen resolution, navigational interface, and screen layout work with the various item formats. Some formats that work well on paper may be more difficult for students to take on computer. For example, a history assessment could present a description of a battle and accompany the description with maps and charts displaying the results of the battle. The stimulus materials could then be followed by a series of items. When displayed in a test booklet, the entire item set can be printed on adjoining pages, but on computer the student needs to scroll through the passage while juggling the charts and maps. The difficulty or ease of navigating that students have when taking tests on computer must be considered when item formats are selected. Sireci and Zenisky (chap. 14, this volume) discuss the strengths and weaknesses of computer-based item formats and their potential to improve performance testing.

This chapter assumes that the test developer has selected performance assessment items for inclusion in their assessment. The purpose of this chapter is to present the considerations and issues related to the development of effective performance assessment items and prompts and the assembly of these performance assessment items into tests.

TYPES OF ITEMS AND PROMPTS

There are many names identified in the literature with regard to performance assessment items or prompts. There is often confusion about the terminology used and there appears to be no industry standard with regard to the definition of performance assessments. To help address this omission in the field, numerous authors have attempted to provide their own definitions of performance assessment items. A few of these are presented here as background information for the test developer.

1. Haladyna (2004) divided item formats into the two general categories of multiple choice and constructed response. The constructed-response formats are offered in two varieties: high-inference format (requiring expert judgement about the trait being observed) and low-inference format (involving observation of the behavior of interest). The low-inference format includes short-answer items, essay items, and checklists of observations.
2. Martinez (1999) provided a summary of the characteristics of multiple-choice, discrete constructed-response, and extended performance categories. Discrete constructed-response formats require a short response. Extended performance requires more complex performance, such as written essays or science experiments.
3. Millman and Greene (1989) divided item types into objective type items, performance assessments, and simulation exercises. Within each of these broad categories are subcategories that include item types such as true/false, matching, or supply item types (i.e., completion, short answer, and essay).
4. Cronbach (1984) used *constructed response* to refer to a broad class of test item formats in which a response must be generated by the examinee rather than being selected from a list of options.
5. Bennett, Ward, Rock, and LaHart (1990; see also Bennett, 1993) proposed a scheme for categorizing various constructed-response and performance formats. Formats were ordered along a continuum of possible range of responses (selection/identification, reordering/rearrangement, substitution/correction, completion, construction, and presentation) from lowest to highest.
6. Osterlind (1998) provided a list of performance assessment item formats that includes the very basic (short answer, fill in the blank) to the very complex (portfolios, research papers, oral reports).
7. The *Standards for Educational and Psychological Testing* (AERA, APA, & NCME, 1999) defined short-answer items to require a response that is no more than a few words. Extended-response formats required a more extensive response of several sentences or paragraphs. Performance assessments go beyond the extended response and try to simulate the context in which the actual knowledge is being applied.

Regardless of the definition adopted by the test developer, there are certain characteristics common to the performance assessment format. For the purposes of this chapter, it is assumed that a performance assessment item or prompt must include the following characteristics:

- The opportunity for the examinee to generate or create a response.
- The opportunity to go beyond the requirements of a multiple-choice test (i.e., examinees may be given the chance to revise work, seek consultation, work with a cooperative group).
- The resulting response is evaluated by comparing the response to developed criteria.
- The evaluation criteria has a range of values.

For the sake of simplicity, this chapter uses *items* and *prompts* interchangeably. Both *item* and *prompt* refer to the task that is being requested of the examinee. It may include a set of stimulus materials or may simply be the statement of the task.

CONSIDERATIONS FOR THE PROMPT AND ITEM DEVELOPMENT PROCESS

Considering that items are the backbone of the assessment industry, there is relatively little research on item writing. This concern was raised over 40 years ago by Ebel (1951) and to a large extent has remained true until only recently. Prior to 1990, item writing was viewed not as a science but simply a collection of guidelines (Bormuth, 1970; Cronbach, 1971; Nitko, 1985). The second and third editions of *Educational Measurement* (Thorndike, 1971; Linn, 1989) contributed to this body of research but did not address the actual item writing process in depth.

Since 1990 the research on item writing has increased substantially (Haladyna, 1997; Linn & Gronlund, 1995; Popham, 1997). Although the majority of research is focused on multiple-choice item development, many of the principles and recommended processes hold true for the development of performance assessment items. Haladyna and Downing (1989) took the current knowledge about writing multiple-choice items and created a taxonomy of item-writing rules. Haladyna, Downing, and Rodriguez (2002) updated their taxonomy and reduced the taxonomy to 31 guidelines for effective item writing. However, Haladyna (2004) indicated that the research on item writing is still asystematic and limited only to several rules. Encouraging research continues to be done, showing that there is some interest in advancing the science of item writing (p. 212). Regardless of the type of development, the prompt development process is very much an iterative process, but it can be defined and completed in a standardized manner (Schmeiser & Welch, in press).

Osterlind (1998) stated that item writers are routinely left to their own devices because there is no developed theory to guide item writing, nor is there a comprehensive resource identifying the distinctive features and limitations of test items, the function of test items in measurement, or even basic editorial principles and stylistic guidelines (p. 5). Haladyna (1994) stated the concern that item writing has not received the same attention that statistical theories of test scores have received.

Research on the development and scoring of performance assessment item types has greatly evolved since 1990 because of a greater application of performance assessments in large-scale testing programs. In 2004, more than 95% of the state testing programs (Council of Chief State School Officers, 2003), the two college admissions assessments (ACT and SAT), and the three graduate school admissions (MCAT, LSAT, and GMAT) tests support the use of performance assessments. This body of research indicates that performance assessments can be developed in a systematic manner and can produce dependable results (Stiggins, 1995).

Sound test development makes the assumption that the item development process is well defined and defensible. Sound item development is critical for providing the quality and consistency necessary for both valid and reliable assessments. Item development occurs incrementally in a series of steps that are often reiterated. There is not one sequence for these steps that is best in all cases. Each situation should be analyzed, and the consequences of various alternative plans considered. This section discusses various considerations of the item and prompt development process including the identification of the writers, development of both prompts and scoring rubrics, item review and refinement, field testing, and forms assembly.

Qualifications of Prompt Writers

The determination of the source of the prompt content depends on test purpose and the inferences that need to be made based on that content. The most appropriate source is typically the expert who is knowledgeable about both the specifics of the content as well as the appropriate difficulty level for the intended audience. The identification of the content expert to assist in this process can depend on political, fiscal, or logistical considerations. However, the ultimate goal is to identify content experts who can serve as writers and produce testing materials that are directly tied to the test specifications and appropriately targeted in difficulty.

In a large-scale assessment program there is a need for identifying, selecting, and contacting prompt writers to maintain, expand, and renew the pool of potential item writers on a regular basis. In addition, there is the need for maintaining a pool of talented and experienced item writers who can offer consistency across development cycles for a testing program. A key consideration in the generation of performance assessment items is to ensure that no individual author contributes too greatly to the pool of the performance assessment items that are being developed. Unlike multiple-choice testing where there is often a large pool of items and item writers, the pool of performance assessment items tends to be much smaller. However, it is critical that the pool of item and prompt writers remain as diversified and large as possible.

The ongoing process of prompt-writer identification and selection may be accomplished according to a specified set of procedures designed to select writers who meet the particular qualifications and requirements of the testing program. For example, a particular state may want teachers from their state to write the items for their assessment program. Or, another state, concerned about the security or compromise of the items, may restrict teachers from their state from participating in their item production. A high-stakes admissions testing program may recruit prompt writers who have experience testing the appropriate coursework. However, the same testing program may eliminate from prompt writing any individuals who have had experience providing preparation courses for the test of interest.

As with multiple-choice item development, the process for identifying those individuals who are qualified to develop performance assessment items should reflect a need for specified professional credentials, the geographic representation of the examinees, the representation of the racial/ethnic backgrounds of the examinee population, and the representation of the gender backgrounds of the examinee population. Contributions from each of these are essential to help the assessment accurately measure the knowledge and skills judged to be necessary. Standard 3.6 indicates that these qualifications, relevant experiences, and demographic characteristics of the prompts writers must be documented.

These criteria for the identification of prompt writers are intended to reflect the general and institutional characteristics of the entire pool of writers; however, criteria reflecting the writer's individual characteristics may also be considered. Such criteria include knowledge of, and training in, the particular subject matter; accomplishments within the particular area of expertise; current teaching responsibilities; and background and experience in writing items. The racial/ethnic background and gender of the writers may also be considered to ensure proportional representation of both genders and all ethnic groups as exhibited by the examinee population.

A systematic search for individuals to contribute diversity to its prompt-writer pool results in diversity in test materials. Given the limited number of performance assessment items that are developed relative to multiple-choice testing, the issues of diversity and fairness are an even greater concern for test developers.

Prompt writers are typically drawn from relevant educational levels. Knowledge of the curriculum and of examinee ability levels is mainly derived from actual teaching experience. Knowledge of examinee capabilities should help prompt writers to target appropriate levels of difficulty for test materials and be able to anticipate the types of responses the examinees of interest produce.

Training of Prompt Writers

The prompt-writing process is continuous and varies substantially according to the test program and the availability of resources to support this aspect of item development. However, once test specifications are developed and approved, the move to prompt-writing training is the next logical step in the development process. There are a variety of approaches for prompt writing that range from an "item drive" conducted via the web among volunteers untrained as prompt writers to a long-term effort by trained prompt writers under contract for pay. Whatever the approach, it must be compatible with the purpose and use(s) of the test, good test development practice, resources, and timelines. Each approach offers its own advantages and, depending on the level of security required for the program, the level of exposure that is acceptable for the program, and the logistical concerns such as development timelines, a single approach is generally accepted for a given testing program.

Web-based approaches offer the advantage of providing training to a large number of prompt writers according to their own schedule without incurring the travel costs associated with bringing writers together for a workshop. This approach can be very efficient in involving a large number of prompt writers and tends to be very effective when the content specifications are well defined. Most web-based approaches allow prompt writers to interact with the trainers and to raise questions about the process. After training is completed, the prompt writers create, review, and comment on items via the Internet. Writers are given access to create and edit new prompts, using predefined templates to control such variables as formatting, numbering, and structure.

Mail-out approaches require prompt writers to work through written training materials to internalize the test specifications and draft test materials. This approach offers a secure approach to recruiting materials from selected individuals. Prompt writers typically submit materials to the test developers for review and comment. Prompt writers are often asked to revise their materials and resubmit the materials based on comments from the test developers. Workshops offer the opportunity for prompt writers to come together as a group to receive in-person training and to generate items. Workshops offer the opportunity for immediate feedback to prompt writers concerning the quality of their materials. Prompts can be immediately revised and re-reviewed. Large numbers of prompts can be generated in a short period of time. Workshops tend to be the preferred approach for testing programs where the prompt writing is viewed as a professional development opportunity.

Regardless of how the prompt writing is completed, the training process is an absolutely critical step. The training materials must be of high quality and consistently applied. If the training process is of poor quality or poorly applied, the quality of the items suffers. If the quality of items suffers, the survival rates for the items from the field test are reduced, leading to increased expenses and possibly lower quality assessments. This section describes the considerations of the prompt-writing training process. Critical to the success of this prompt development process is an opportunity for feedback to review and revise items throughout the training and development process.

After the prompt writers have agreed to develop materials, the prompt-development process begins with training prompt writers in the construction of technically sound sample items. Because prompt writing is not an easy skill, there should be a well-defined process to train all writers contributing to a particular testing program. This process can be customized according to the needs of the testing program (i.e., credentials of prompt writers, development timelines, resources) but should be uniformly presented to all prompt writers who are contributing to a pool of performance assessment items. The prompt writers for the performance assessment items may be a different group of individuals than those used for the multiple-choice item development. If the performance assessment items are designed to measure different skills

TABLE 13.1
Proposed Prompt-Writing Workshop Agenda

Discuss the purpose and audience of the assessment.
Present test specifications and test development process.
Provide general guidelines for prompt writing (timelines, sources, copyrights).
Present the structure of the prompts (the template, the item shell).
Present examples of successful prompts.
Provide examples of prompts that were not successful (too broad, inaccessible, vague, misinterpreted).
Articulate successful prompts and nonsuccessful prompts.
Writers generate topics for consideration.
Review and approve or revise topics.
Writers generate prompts from the approved topics.

---

than the multiple-choice items, the necessary credentials for the prompt writers may also be different. The test specifications, including a description of the system for classifying items by content area and cognitive demand, should form the basis for the training materials. In addition, sharing examples of technically sound performance assessments is a critical component of the training process. The training should include a discussion of the positive features of these exemplar performance assessments. Each prompt writer must be provided with training materials relevant to the particular test for which the author will develop prompts. The training materials should also address general item writing issues such as fairness-related issues (fair portrayal, accessibility and comparability of prompts, fairness in language, cultural sensitivity) and content-related issues (audience, difficulty, effectiveness of prompts, assumptions for background knowledge). Table 13.1 proposes an outline for an item-writing workshop that may extend from a self-directed, abbreviated session to a more extensive multiple-day session. The duration of the workshop is a direct function of the level of sophistication and complexity of the items that the prompt writers are expected to generate and the experience of the prompt writers.

DEVELOPMENT OF PERFORMANCE ASSESSMENT ITEMS

The development of successful performance assessment items relies on the definition of at least three different types of specifications. These include content specifications, technical specifications, and logistical specifications. Prior to any development activities, all specifications should be developed with the assistance of experts from the field of interest. The experts should agree on the specific purpose of the test, the content domain, and the acceptable topics that can be included in the test. Detailed content specifications are critical because performance assessment tasks tend to be more unique than multiple-choice items. The content specifications must include timing requirements (which may vary for each prompt), administration directions and conditions, and specific materials needed to complete the task or prompt (Haertel & Linn, 1996). The content coverage, the number of items included on each test, and the amount of testing time should reflect the emphasis of the body of knowledge or the curriculum that is being assessed.

The use of various types of performance assessments raises questions concerning fairness. Some believe that the use of performance assessments provides a more fair approach to assessing ability than traditional multiple-choice methods (Hambleton & Murphy, 1992). However, the very nature of a performance assessment introduces the possibility of extraneous error from sources unfamiliar to multiple-choice tests such as those that may arise owing to readers, topic selection, and the approach to scoring (Linn, Baker, & Dunbar, 1991; Sackett, 1987). These sources of error need to be taken into account during the prompt development process. Brossell (1986) categorizes sources of error as major situational variables that include topic, writer, and procedural variables. It is these types of error that make questions of fairness as important for performance assessment as for multiple-choice tests (Linn et al., 1991). So, in addition to the typical procedures followed for good multiple-choice item development, test developers of performance assessments should consider topic and writer issues as well as the sensitivity of materials. The close monitoring of these areas in the test development and scoring processes is critical to minimizing extraneous sources of error.

A general approach to the development of prompts should be guided by the following principles:

1. There must be thorough and open participation by all relevant populations in the prompt development process;
2. The prompt development process must be carefully designed, technically sound, rigorously implemented, and appropriately validated;
3. The prompt development process must be comprehensible to all interested parties and easily implemented by the participants; and
4. The stakeholders must approve of the process and be kept fully informed of all major prompt development activities.

The development of technically sound performance assessment items is an iterative process that relies on the delineation of clear and concise test specifications and the adequate training. Test developers should strive to develop prompts that follow good item-writing guidelines, but also address issues specific to the development of performance assessments. Table 13.2. highlights some of the issues that are particularly important to the initial prompt development.

TOPIC SELECTION

Topic selection is an issue that is more problematic for developers of performance assessments than it is for multiple-choice assessments. Bennett (1993) indicated that success depends, in part, on context-bound skills, as well as on knowledge of the context itself (p. 9). Because of the interaction between the prompt and the examinee, the selection, specific wording, and context of the topic becomes extremely important and has implications for the overall fairness of the assessment (Bond, Moss, & Carr, 1996).

Given the limited number of prompts that are typically contained on a performance assessment, new prompts need to constructed to be as parallel as possible (Haertel & Linn, 1996). When multiple forms of an assessment are operational, performance assessment topics need to be "interchangeable" for examinees (i.e., no examinee should be advantaged or disadvantaged from the inclusion of a particular prompt on an assessment). For example, some high-stakes writing assessment programs require examinees to respond to a pair of prompts. Given that the testing program offers the assessment on multiple test dates throughout the year, it is imperative that the pair of prompts administered during the first administration is as comparable as possible to the pair of prompts given during a later administration.

Other research that supports the criticality of topic selection includes Breland, Camp, Jones, Morris, & Rock (1987) and Quellmalz, Capell, and Chou (1982) who found that examinees who write well on one topic may not do as well on another topic. Consistent with this finding,

TABLE 13.2
General Guidelines for Prompt Writers

Issue	Prompt Development Guideline
Accessibility	• Prompts should be accessible to all examinees, regardless of gender, culture, or ethnic background. • Differences in prompt performance should be directly tied to the differences in the skills being assessed and not to any other factors such as group expectations or background knowledge.
Fairness	• No mention of any group or its members should appear derogatory or detrimental to that group. • All references to individuals within prompts should be accurate, fair, and free from stereotyping. • All social and cultural issues should be addressed within the general knowledge of the examinees
Audience	• The prompts should accurately and fairly reflect the audience in terms of gender, ethnic, and cultural background, socioeconomic status, geographic location, educational background, work experience, and religious beliefs.
Difficulty	• Prompts should be sufficiently complex to support the examinee's development of original writing. • Provide examinees the opportunity to go beyond the simple restatement of the prompt. • Responding to a prompt should not be confounded by the difficulty of the language or concepts used in the prompt.
Background knowledge	• Prompts should be free of "weighting" toward examinees with certain backgrounds or experiences. • Prompts should be fair and accessible to examinees with a variety of backgrounds.

Brown, Hilgers, and Marsella (1991) reported that differences in writing performance are attributable to differences in topic types.

Unlike multiple-choice tests, where a large number of items are combined to create a test, and tests can be equated to help eliminate any differences across forms, performance assessments must rely on the detail contained in the content specifications and the field test data to support topic selection decisions. Results from generalizability studies help to determine whether topics are interchangeable. If possible, field test administrations should be designed to assist in the collection of data to inform test developers about the interactions between examinees and specific topics.

The precise effects of the wording of the topics, the subject matter of the topics, and the influences of the modes of discourse are not known (Brossell, 1986). However, it is safe to assume that although a prompt is identical for all examinees, each examinee's understanding of it is somewhat different, and "the idea that such an assessment is a fair measure of each respondent's performance is thus open to challenge" (Brossell, 1986, p. 175). Changing a single word or direction to the examinee can have a substantial impact on student performance. To guard against such changes, all prompts that are changed after the field test administration should be field tested again prior to their operational use to establish the most accurate performance statistics for that particular item.

Performance assessments lend themselves to situations where examinees are offered a degree of choice in the selection of a prompt. The issue of choice poses a specific threat to comparability and the ramifications must be weighed against the advantage of offering the choice. Wainer, Wang, and Thissen (1994) examined the question of how well scores on test forms that are constructed by examinee topic selection can be compared. They concluded that an item performs differently when examinees are able to select the topic.

TECHNICAL CONSIDERATIONS

In addition to the development and content considerations that must guide the test developer, the developer should also be aware of the technical considerations that accompany the development and use of performance assessments, particularly within the large-scale testing environment. All assessments must continue to satisfy the *Standards for Educational and Psychological Testing* (AERA, APA, & NCME, 1999), regardless of the item format to be used. However, the test developer of performance assessments should also consider the needs for reliability, comparability, and generalizability associated with the performance assessment development issues. One of the primary questions that the test developer must address is how far can the performance assessments be generalized beyond the specific tasks and readers? How indicative is performance on a particular item of the broader domain that is being measured? Performance assessments are often less generalizable than scores on multiple-choice tests (Brennan, 2001) because of their uniqueness and limited numbers. The nature of performance assessments makes it more difficult to control psychometric and measurement characteristics across multiple forms and therefore generalizability becomes questionable. As stated, quality field test data are critical and essential to building assessments that produce the generalizability necessary to support the decisions of interest. Table 13.3 identifies some very general technical considerations and strategies that may help to shape the development process and subsequent inferences.

DEVELOPMENT OF SCORING RUBRICS

The test developer needs to provide a clear description of the scoring criteria to ensure that the intended purpose of the test is consistent with the appropriateness of the scoring (*Standard for Educational and Psychological Testing,* AERA, APA, & NCME, 1999, Standard 3.14). This standard dictates that the development of performance assessments requires the development of prompts as well as the development of the procedures and criteria to be used during the scoring process. Consistent with the sentiment of Standard 3.14, Gitomer (1993) indicates that the more important issue is coming to an agreement on what the scoring criteria should be and how inferences should be made. Again, this is support for the need for clean, well-articulated content specifications.

Performance assessments are often criticized because they cannot be scored objectively like multiple-choice tests. However, with well-articulated scoring rubrics and well-defined and monitored scoring processes, acceptable levels of reliability of the scoring process can be obtained for all types of inferences. To help guarantee the reliable scoring of performance assessment items, the scoring rubrics are generally developed simultaneously with the items. The prompt writer is the primary source for identifying the types of responses to be elicited from a particular item and to identifying the necessary components of the response for evaluation.

Writers of performance assessment items must adhere to the same rules of item writing used in the development of multiple-choice test items. In addition to the item, the development of successful scoring rubrics is critical to the success of the item. A reliable scoring rubric must

- be consistent with the decisions/inferences to be made with the results;
- define the characteristics of the response to be evaluated along a continuum;
- convey performance criteria in an understandable way;

TABLE 13.3
Considerations and Strategies for Maximizing Technical Characteristics

Technical Consideration	Possible Strategy
Reliability	• Increase testing time and therefore increase the number of items per examinee. • Design field test administrations to allow for generalizability studies to predict the reliability for different length tests.
Comparability	• Maximize the size of the performance assessment prompt pool (to the extent possible) to allow for adequate selection in the test assembly process. • Standardize administration conditions to the extent possible. • Increase the number of items to achieve the best possible domain representation. • Structure the development process to include a small-scale pilot administration prior to the field test. • Structure the development process to include a robust field test administration to provide information on the generalizability of the items.
Validity	• Identify the performance criteria at the same time that the performance assessment items are being written. • Align the performance criteria with the curriculum standards being assessed. • Complete an independent evaluation of the alignment. • Maintain alignment for all new development.
Scoring accuracy	• Design the scoring rubrics to be aligned with the performance criteria that are being assessed. • Design scoring rubrics to be prompt specific and customized for each prompt that is developed. • Finalize the scoring rubrics after the field test papers have been evaluated. • Maximize the number of readers per response on the field test papers to help ensure accuracy of the scoring. • Implement a scoring audit process to verify the accuracy of the results.
Generalizability	• Examine the interprompt correlations based on a preliminary pilot administration to determine the extent of content coverage. • Examine the prompt-by-examinee variance component based on field test results. • Refine content specifications to minimize the prompt-by-examinee variance. • When scores are being reported at the group level rather than the individual level, institute matrix sampling procedures to increase the dependability of the generalization (Brennan, 2001).

• use items that elicit a range of performance; and
• be aligned with the content standards that are being assessed.

There are many different types of scoring rubrics that can be used with performance assessment items. The different rubrics serve different purposes and the determination of the type of rubric should also be a part of the development of the test specifications. Two common types are analytic and holistic scoring. The *analytic rubric* provides information on a number of dimensions and may be most useful for diagnostic testing and the identification of student strengths and weaknesses. The *holistic rubric* provides a single score on overall performance and may be most appropriate when the skills being assessed are highly correlated. However, test developers should know that there are many variations and combinations of rubrics that exist. As with the content of the items themselves, the rubrics must align themselves with the stated purpose of the assessment.

Holistic scoring involves the evaluation of a response for the total effect of the response. The overall quality of the response is valued more than the discrete elements of the response; the primary advantage of holistic scoring is the simultaneous consideration of all components of the response. White (1985) stated that holistic scoring has made the direct testing of writing both practical and reliable, and contends that it effectively embodies a concept of writing that is responsible. Holistic scoring is also an efficient approach to large-scale scoring where readers are trained to read a paper every three to four minutes. A commonly cited disadvantage of this approach is that holistic scoring does not necessarily attain the interpretability that is seen with analytic scoring (Huot, 1990; Veal & Hudson, 1983). Figure 13.1 provides an illustration of a holistic scoring rubric. As noted in the language of the rubric, all characteristics of writing are treated simultaneously and the reader assigns a single score to the response.

Analytic scoring has been considered a more interpretable scoring approach because it assesses the examinee's specific strengths and weaknesses and identifies the particular components of writing that an examinee needs to develop. Erwin (1991) reported that holistic scores provide valuable information for an overall categorization of writing ability, but analytic scores provide more diagnostic information. Other cited advantages of analytic scoring are immediate and well-defined understanding of scores and additional ease in deciding the appropriate level of a response. Disadvantages of analytic scoring often cited are its tendencies to reduce and oversimplify the components of writing, and to emphasize the flaws rather than the strengths of writing (Fowles, 1978). White (1985) cited other limitations of analytic scoring: the lack of agreement about what separable traits exist and its tendency to complicate the assignment of scores for readers, increasing time and therefore costs. These implications for increased costs were confirmed by Spandel and Stiggins (1980). Figure 13.2 provides an illustration of an analytic scoring rubric. Using this rubric as a guide, scores are assigned individually for each characteristic of writing that is being assessed (focus, complexity, development, organization, and language). Each characteristic is evaluated by comparing it to the definitions for each of the six-point scales.

At this point in the development process, the scoring rubric is a description of the types of responses that are expected. This version of the scoring rubric serves as a placeholder in the development process until the field test responses are available. With the assistance of the field test responses, the test developer is able to more fully define and refine the scoring rubric.

ITEM AND PROMPT REVIEWS

Once new prompts and scoring rubrics have been developed, they should be subjected to a multistage, multipurpose review for match to specifications, content accuracy, universal design, editorial style, fairness, and psychometric concerns. The various stages of these reviews are described below. It is critical that the prompt reviewers be experts in the area of review for which they are being recruited. Reviewers should also be selected based on their ability to represent the examinees. Reviewers, as with prompt writers, should receive standardized training on the attributes of the prompts and scoring rubrics that they are being recruited to evaluate. After the prompts and scoring guides have been evaluated by these reviewers, any testing material that falls short of meeting all of the review criteria is either revised or discarded. All procedures used to review the prompts and scoring guides should be documented throughout the process. This documentation becomes a critical element of the information provided to help a potential user evaluate the appropriateness and defensibility of a testing program for a given purpose (AERA, APA, & NCME, 1999, Standards 3.7 and 6.1).

Match-to-Specifications Review

Each prompt should be classified according to the content specifications and the cognitive demand required to respond to it. This is typically completed during the development process. After new prompts and scoring guides are generated, content specialists should review the

Papers at each level exhibit *all* or *most* of the characteristics described at each score point.

Score = 6 Essays within this score range demonstrate effective skill in responding to the task.
The essay shows a clear understanding of the task. The essay takes a position on the issue and may offer a critical context for discussion. The essay addresses complexity by examining different perspectives on the issue, or by evaluating the implications and/or complications of the issue, or by fully responding to counter-arguments to the writer's position. Development of ideas is ample, specific, and logical. Most ideas are fully elaborated. A clear focus on the specific issue in the prompt is maintained. The organization of the essay is clear: the organization may be somewhat predictable or it may grow from the writer's purpose. Ideas are logically sequenced. Most transitions reflect the writer's logic and they are usually integrated into the essay. The introduction and conclusion are effective, clear, and well developed. The essay shows a good command of language. Sentences are varied and word choice is varied and precise. There are few, if any, errors to distract the reader.

Score = 5 Essays within this score range demonstrate competent skill in responding to the task.
The essay shows a clear understanding of the task. The essay takes a position on the issue and may offer a broad context for discussion. The essay shows recognition of complexity by partially evaluating the implications and/or complications of the issue, or by responding to counter-arguments to the writer's position. Development of ideas is specific and logical. Most ideas are elaborated, with clear movement between general statements and specific reasons, examples, and details. Focus on the specific issue in the prompt is maintained. The organization of the essay is clear, although it may be predictable. Ideas are logically sequenced, although simple and obvious transitions may be used. The introduction and conclusion are clear and generally well developed. Language is competent. Sentences are somewhat varied and word choice is sometimes varied and precise. There may be a few errors, but they are rarely distracting.

Score = 4 Essays within this score range demonstrate adequate skill in responding to the task.
The essay shows an understanding of the task. The essay takes a position on the issue and may offer some context for discussion. The essay may show some recognition of complexity by providing some response to counter-arguments to the writer's position. Development of ideas is adequate, with some movement between general statements and specific reasons, examples, and details. Focus on the specific issue in the prompt is maintained throughout most of the essay. The organization of the essay is apparent but predictable. Some evidence of logical sequencing of ideas is apparent, although most transitions are simple and obvious. The introduction and conclusion are clear and somewhat developed. Language is adequate, with some sentence variety and appropriate word choice. There may be some distracting errors, but they do not impede understanding.

Score = 3 Essays within this score range demonstrate some developing skill in responding to the task.
The essay shows some understanding of the task. The essay takes a position on the issue but does not offer a context for discussion. The essay may acknowledge a counter-argument to the writer's position, but its development is brief or unclear. Development of ideas is limited and may be repetitious, with little, if any, movement between general statements and specific reasons, examples, and details. Focus on a general topic is maintained, but focus on the specific issue in the prompt may not be maintained. The organization of the essay is simple. Ideas are logically grouped within parts of the essay, but there is little or no evidence of logical sequencing of ideas. Transitions, if used, are simple and obvious. An introduction and conclusion are clearly discernible but underdeveloped. Language shows a basic control. Sentences show a little variety and word choice is appropriate. Errors may be distracting and may occasionally impede understanding.

Score = 2 Essays within this score range demonstrate inconsistent or weak skill in responding to the task.
The essay shows a weak understanding of the task. The essay may not take a position on the issue, or the essay may take a position but fail to convey reasons to support that position, or the essay may take a position but fail to maintain a stance. There is little or no recognition of a counter-argument to the writer's position. The essay is thinly developed. If examples are given, they are general and may not be clearly relevant. The essay may include extensive repetition of the writer's ideas or of ideas in the prompt. Focus on a general topic is maintained, but focus on the specific issue in the prompt may not be maintained. There is some indication of an organizational structure, and some logical grouping of ideas within parts of the essay is apparent. Transitions, if used, are simple and obvious, and they may be inappropriate or misleading. An introduction and conclusion are discernible but minimal. Sentence structure and word choice are usually simple. Errors may be frequently distracting and may sometimes impede understanding.

Score = 1 Essays within this score range show little or no skill in responding to the task.
The essay shows little or no understanding of the task. If the essay takes a position, it fails to convey reasons to support that position. The essay is minimally developed. The essay may include excessive repetition of the writer's ideas or of ideas in the prompt. Focus on a general topic is usually maintained, but focus on the specific issue in the prompt may not be maintained. There is little or no evidence of an organizational structure or of the logical grouping of ideas. Transitions are rarely used. If present, an introduction and conclusion are minimal. Sentence structure and word choice are simple. Errors may be frequently distracting and may significantly impede understanding.

© 2004 by ACT, Inc. All rights reserved.

FIG 13.1. Six-point holistic rubric for ACT assessment writing test.

| | Focus
Sustain a position by focusing on the topic throughout the essay. | Complexity
Show the ability to make and articulate judgments by taking a position on the issue and by demonstrating the ability to grasp the complexity of issues by considering implications or complications. | Development
Develop a position by presenting support or evidence using specific details and by using logical reasoning to distinguish between assertions and evidence and to make inferences based on support or evidence. | Organization
Organize and present ideas in a logical way by logically grouping and sequencing ideas and by using transitional devices to identify logical connections and tie ideas together. | Language
Communicate clearly by using language effectively and by observing the conventions of standard written English. |
|---|---|---|---|---|---|
| 6 | The essay shows a clear understanding of the purpose of the essay by articulating a position and by clearly explaining the issue. The essay may offer a broad context for discussion. Clear and consistent focus on the specific prompt issue is maintained. | The essay addresses complexity by critically examining alternate points of view, posing and responding to counter-arguments, or evaluating the implications or complications of its position. | Development of ideas is ample, specific, and logical. Most ideas are fully elaborated, with strong movement between the general and specific. | The organization of the essay is clear; it may be predictable or may grow from the writer's purpose. The introduction and conclusion are effective, clear, and well developed. Ideas are logically sequenced and transitions are usually integrated into the essay. | The essay shows a good command of language. Sentences are varied and word choice is varied and precise. There are few, if any, language errors to distract the reader. |
| 5 | The essay shows a clear understanding of the purpose of the essay by articulating a position and by explaining the issue. The essay may offer a context for discussion. Focus on the specific prompt issue is maintained. | The essay shows recognition of complexity by considering alternate points of view or by partially evaluating implications and/or complications of its position. | Development of ideas is specific and logical. Most ideas are elaborated, with movement between the general and specific. | Organization is clear although it may be somewhat formulaic. The introduction and conclusion are clear and generally well developed. Progression of ideas is logical although obvious transitions may be used. | Language is competent. Sentence structure is somewhat varied and word choice is sometimes precise. There may be a few errors, but they rarely distract the reader. |
| 4 | The essay shows an understanding of the purpose of the essay by articulating a position and by partially explaining the issue. The essay may offer some context for discussion. Focus on the specific prompt issue is maintained throughout most of the essay. | The essay is unlikely to show clear recognition of complexity, but acknowledges alternate points of view or complications without weakening its position on the issue. | Development of ideas is adequate and shows some movement between the general and the specific. | Organization is apparent. The introduction and conclusion are somewhat developed. Some evidence of logical sequencing is apparent. Transitions show an attempt to connect ideas in a logical way. | Language is adequate, with some sentence variety and appropriate word choice. There may be some distracting errors, but they do not impede understanding. |

3	The essay shows some understanding of the purpose of the essay. The essay takes a position on the issue but does not explain the issue or set a context for the discussion. Focus on the general topic is maintained but focus on the specific issue may not be maintained.	If present, consideration of complexity is confusing or unclear. Any acknowledgement of alternate points of view or complications weakens the essay's position or makes the discussion less clear.	Some development of the writer's assertions is present, but development is limited or repetitious, and examples may be general. There is little, if any, movement between the general and the specific.	There is a simple organizational structure, but ideas are not always logically sequenced. The introduction and conclusion are clearly discernible but are underdeveloped. Transitions, if used, are predictable.	Sentences show a little variety and word choice is clear. Errors may or may not be frequently distracting and may sometimes impede understanding.
2	The essay shows a weak understanding of the purpose of the essay. The essay does not take a position on the issue, takes a position but does not convey reasons to support that position, or at first appears to take a position but does not maintain a stance. Focus on the general topic is maintained but focus on the specific issue may not be maintained.	The essay recognizes alternate points of view or complications only superficially, perhaps only mentioning these in passing.	The essay is thinly developed. If examples are given, they are general and may not be clearly relevant. The essay may include excessive repetition of the writer's ideas or ideas in the prompt. Assertions may be contradictory.	There may be some indication of organizational structure, but there is little or no logical grouping of ideas. Transitions, if used, are simple and may be inappropriate or misleading.	Sentence structure and word choice are simple. Errors may or may not be frequently distracting and may or may not significantly impede understanding.
1	The essay shows little or no understanding of the purpose of the essay. The essay does not identify the issue or does little more than repeat the language in the prompt. Focus on the general topic is maintained but focus on the specific issue may not be maintained.	There is no recognition of complexity or alternate points of view.	Ideas related to the topic are minimally developed.	There is little or no evidence of an organizational structure; transitional devices are rarely used.	Sentence structure and word choice are simple. Errors are frequently distracting and/or significantly impede understanding.

© 2004 by ACT, Inc. All rights reserved.

FIG. 13.2. Analytical rubric for ACT assessment writing test.

assigned content and cognitive demand. The purpose of the review is to verify the accuracy of the classifications. This review process often takes a participatory approach where many interested persons (teachers, test developers, practitioners, etc.) are involved in classifying the prompts that have been developed. Depending on the level of reporting that is required by a testing program, the match-to-specifications review can be very critical to interpreting total scores, subscores, and domain scores associated with an assessment.

Content Review

Each new prompt and scoring guide should be reviewed first for content and grammatical accuracy and for sound measurement characteristics according to the established standards of the measurement profession (Osterlind, 1998). The content reviewer systematically checks each prompt to ensure that it fulfills the general requirements of the test specifications. In addition, the content reviewer reviews each prompt, scoring guide, and set of stimulus materials to ensure that all are clear, unambiguous, and grammatically consistent. Any problems in the technical quality of the stimulus materials (e.g., passage, tables, graphs) or prompts are detected and recorded at this early stage and immediately revised.

For all types of assessments, the editing of artwork and the production of graphics are important tasks in the preparation of test materials. Editorial staff contributes to the accuracy of all processing of artwork with numerous checks concerned with identification, accuracy, and accessibility of the artwork. Different quality control steps should be established according to the mode of delivery whether it is paper-and-pencil or computer-based delivery.

Content reviewers are asked to review the prompts according to a set of criteria. Developers may use guidelines that provide explicit instructions on how to review prompts emphasizing the characteristics most important to the intended inferences. The guide instructs reviewers to scrutinize prompts for (1) alignment with the content domain; (2) match to the specified classifications; (3) content accuracy; (4) accessibility of the prompt language; (5) clarity of the prompt language; and (6) adherence to the specified item format. The content reviewers must be familiar with the population being tested.

After the content reviewers have evaluated the prompts, they may be re-edited to meet all of the criteria. If editors require additional technical assistance to properly evaluate a prompt in light of the comments received from the technical reviewers, they may resubmit the revised prompt to additional reviewers. All prompts judged by the reviewers to be accurate in terms of content should be prepared for another editorial review.

Universal Design Review

Assessments based on universal design principles (Center for Universal Design, 1997) help to ensure that optimal, standardized conditions are available for all students. Good test design is inclusive and should be "designed and developed from the beginning to allow participation of the widest possible range of students, and to result in valid inferences about performance for all students who participate in the assessment" (Thompson, Johnstone, & Thurlow, 2002, p. 5). According to Thompson et al. (2002, p. 3), the seven critical elements of universal design for assessments, regardless of whether the items are multiple-choice or performance assessments are:

- **Inclusive assessment population:** All test takers, including people with disabilities and English language learners, should be considered at test design and included in field tests.

- **Precisely defined concepts:** The construct must be clear so that construct-irrelevant material can be eliminated.
- **Accessible, nonbiased items:** Item types that are not accessible by people with disabilities are not selected for use in the test, unless required for valid measurement.
- **Amenable to accommodations:** Items that cannot be put into Braille or be scripted are eliminated from the test, unless required for valid measurement.
- **Simple, clear, and intuitive instructions and procedures:** The directions for taking the test should be clear to all examinees.
- **Maximum readability and comprehensibility:** Text is clearly written with vocabulary, sentence length, and required reasoning skills appropriate for grade level.
- **Maximum legibility:** Text and visual materials should be large enough for easy visibility, spaced to increase ease of comprehension, and have a minimum of distractions.

Individuals familiar with the principles of universal design should be used as part of this review process.

Thurlow, Thompson, and Lazarus (chap. 28, this volume) stated that the essential idea behind universally designed assessments is that assessments are designed to measure the relevant construct. The principles of universal design are consistent with the principles for the selection of item types. The test developer must select the item format that provides the most valid measure of the knowledge and skills to be assessed.

Soundness Reviews

Soundness reviewers should be given explicit instructions on how to review the prompts and scoring rubrics. The training materials should explain how to scrutinize the testing materials for technical correctness, effectiveness of the prompts, effectiveness of the scoring rubric, clarity of expression, and adherence to the specified item format.

Sensitivity Reviews

All development should be committed to fairness both in principle and in the interest of accuracy in all tests. Fairness should be a concern in all steps of the test development process from the defining of the construct to be measured, to the specifications of the development process, to the development and review of the items, and to the final assembly of the test forms. Test developers should endorse the *Code of Fair Testing Practices in Education* (1988), a statement of the obligations to test takers of those who develop, administer, and use educational tests and data. The *Code* sets forth criteria for fairness in four areas: developing and selecting appropriate tests, interpreting test scores, striving for fairness, and informing test takers. According to the *Code*, test developers should develop tests that are as fair as possible for all test takers. Individuals with relevant experience in fairness issues should be recruited from various subgroups of the examinee population to serve as reviewers. Members of the fairness review team should evaluate each prompt and scoring rubric for characteristics that might give any examinee group an advantage or disadvantage.

The training materials for the sensitivity reviews should ensure that test developers avoid potentially insensitive content or language and enact procedures that help to ensure that differences in performance are related primarily to the skills under assessment rather than to irrelevant factors.

Ensuring fairness is an essential goal of all assessment programs and unfairness must be prevented whenever possible. The work of ensuring test fairness starts with design of the test and test specifications. It then continues through every stage of the test development process, including prompt writing and review, field testing, item selection and forms construction, and forms review. The multistage item development and review process is a highly interactive and complex system; each of the stages included in the process focuses on a somewhat different aspect or characteristic of the items. This process helps to ensure that prompts and scoring guides developed are reviewed and evaluated from diverse viewpoints.

All prompts should be reviewed prior to the field test and again after the field test. The sensitivity review that occurs before field testing involves examination of the test materials by external sensitivity reviewers who give feedback to the editorial staff concerning potential overt sensitivity problems or sensitivity issues. Sensitivity reviewers may be recruited through a variety of sources and should be representative of the testing population. The ideal reviewer is an expert in the content of the test, measurement, and written communication, and brings to the review process a relevant perspective. Sensitivity review is particularly critical with performance assessment items in that both the prompts and the scoring rubrics should be evaluated for issues related to accessibility and fairness. Sensitivity reviewers should be provided with guidance as to what they should look for when reviewing prompts. Topics that disproportionately advantage or disadvantage examinees owing to gender or racial/ethnic background should be eliminated. In addition, all sensitive topics including religious, sexual, or highly emotional or personal topics should be eliminated from testing programs. It is commonly understood that test material that is inflammatory, insulting, slanted, pejorative, or otherwise unfair can seriously impair examinees' efforts to perform to the best of their knowledge and abilities and should be avoided.

The post–field test item review should include the review of statistics generated from the field test administration to help ensure that all test material is fair and free of sensitivity. If sample sizes allow, prompt-level performance should be examined for all demographic variables of interest (i.e., gender, racial/ethnic, language). If there are large differences in performance between groups, the prompts and scoring rubrics should be reexamined with this information as a guide.

In addition to the post–field test statistics, developers may also examine differential item functioning (DIF) statistics on performance assessment results if the sample sizes are large enough to permit this comparison. The measurement literature has identified numerous statistical approaches for determining the degree of DIF between two or more groups on multiple-choice tests (Dorans & Holland, 1992; Dorans & Schmitt, 1993). To the extent that these procedures are sensitive to actual DIF, they can be useful in determining the appropriateness of an examination for a given subgroup of examinees. DIF may occur if the content of an item is less appropriate for one group of examinees than for the other. DIF refers to the differential impact of an item on the performance of one subgroup when compared to that of another subgroup. Using this definition, it is possible to use statistical procedures to identify multiple-choice items that appear to be biased against a particular subgroup of examinees. However, work to extend these procedures to performance assessment tests has been limited, in part because of the limitations of selecting a matching criterion that is measuring the same underlying trait as the item of interest in a reliable manner. Traub and MacRury (1990) concluded that multiple-choice and performance assessments are measuring different knowledge and abilities, thereby questioning the use of a matching variable based on multiple-choice performance. A second limitation is the relatively large, equal sample sizes that are necessary to perform some of these procedures (Welch & Hoover, 1993). Overall, given the relatively small number of performance assessment items typically found on assessments, the questionable nature of using a multiple-choice matching variable, and the need for large sample sizes, DIF analyses on performance assessment items can be a difficult task.

Item Refinement

The item evaluations of the sensitivity, content, and technical reviewers must be collated, and a comprehensive evaluation of each prompt and scoring rubric must be made by the test developers. If revisions are determined to be necessary, they should be made and the material should be resubmitted, if needed, to an appropriate reviewer for final approval.

Materials that are judged to be acceptable, having successfully passed all the stages of review process, are prepared for field testing. Testing development staff should ensure that all suggestions made by reviewers have been addressed and are well documented. As with all stages of development, documentation of the item refinement process is critical. Chapter 6 of the *Standards* (AERA, APA, & NCME, 1999) emphasizes the need for documentation, indicating that the ultimate purpose of documentation is to provide potential users with the information they need to evaluate a testing program.

Summary of Item Review

There are many essential stages of the item development and review process. Although each stage takes time in the developmental schedule, each contributes unique perspectives and insights into the development process and should not be ignored. Prompts and scoring rubrics that satisfactorily pass all review stages should be considered eligible for field testing. All evaluations and comments made during each of these stages should be carefully documented and retained for use in the test assembly process.

All prompts should be written by individuals judged to be qualified according to specified criteria. The writers should represent, as closely as possible, the various requirements considered to be representative of the target examinee population. Extensive prompt-writer training materials help to produce prompts and rubrics that are technically sound, while preserving the security and confidentiality of the test materials themselves. The training of writers is further enhanced by direct communication with psychometric and testing specialists who can offer specific suggestions and recommendations for further technical improvement of the materials. An intensive review by experts helps ensure that the items comply with the *Standards for Educational and Psychological Testing* (AERA, APA, & NCME, 1999). Such reviews serve to detect and correct deficiencies in the technical qualities of the items before content experts review the items. In addition, possible problems with race, gender, or other sensitivities can be detected at this early stage and corrected. Content evaluations assess the accuracy, clarity, relevance, and significance of the test materials. Review of prompts and scoring rubrics by reviewers sensitive to cultural and gender issues helps to detect and eliminate any apparent unfairness in the language, population references and characterizations, and content or format of the test materials. This evaluation should be given careful and deliberate attention.

FIELD TESTING OF PERFORMANCE ASSESSMENT ITEMS

As with multiple-choice tests, field testing is an essential and critical step in the development of performance assessments. However, unlike multiple-choice tests, the field test responses of a performance assessment provide the necessary information to construct the training sets and refine the scoring rubrics that are essential to the evaluation of future operational assessments. The training sets and scoring rubrics serve as the "key" for the performance assessment items. Just as an item analysis program helps to identify the multiple-choice items that are not functioning as hoped, the field test responses help to identify the performance assessment items that are not functioning satisfactorily.

The best possible predictor of operational performance on a prompt is the field test performance of similar prompts on a representative sample of examinees. The most technically attractive approach to field testing is the ability to administer the field test prompts in a spiraled administration design where every nth examinee receives the same field test prompts. This type of design allows for the creation of randomly equivalent groups. The randomly equivalent groups design allows the test developer the ability to compare performance across prompts to more competently evaluate the performance of the item and not the examinee population. However, unlike multiple-choice assessments, performance assessments often introduce the possibility of peer decisions, peer reviews, small group work, or teacher-directed assessments. In these cases, spiraling is not a viable option as directions are most often specific to the prompt that is being administered. If spiraling is not an option, field test sample sizes need to be increased. Classrooms or individual settings become the unit for collecting the data. In this case, balancing the distribution of the field test prompts across classrooms with respect to the ability levels of the examinees and the demographic characteristics of the examinees help to make the results more usable.

Field testing tends to be a very expensive and time-consuming component of the performance assessment development process. Examinees must be recruited, time to administer assessment must be allocated, and scoring must be completed. Incorporating a pilot administration into the test development procedures prior to the field test helps the test developer to collect information on the item format and scoring rubric before assuming the expense of a full-scale field test. A pilot test can use prototype performance assessment items administered to a small sample of examinees to gather valuable information concerning the success of the item format, the time requirements and administration requirements. Pilot test samples can be as small as 15 to 20 examinees per prompt and still provide very valuable information to test developers. In testing programs where new item formats or new time requirements are being introduced, pilot administrations should be considered prior to the finalization of the test specifications.

Whenever possible, test developers should construct the field test forms to approximate operational forms in terms of item formats, time requirements, and administration requirements. Because of the restrictions of the field test administration design, this may not always be an option. However, if field test forms can be constructed to mirror the operational test, issues of time and overlap between item types can be analyzed prior to the construction of the operational test.

Test developers should consider the effects of context and position of the performance assessment items when constructing field test forms. For example, if the operational assessment includes performance assessment items mixed with multiple-choice items, the test developer should attempt to replicate the same order in the field test design.

The field test sample needs to be adequate in size to provide stable estimates of performance on various items. Most critical to the field test is identifying a sample that provides a typical range of expected skill levels. Given that most of the papers used to train for an operational administration of the test are pulled from the field test administration, it is critical that both the high and low levels of performance are represented. The field test administration samples should be selected to be as representative of the operational sample as possible.

If possible, test developers should field test an adequate number of prompts to minimize editing and changes between the field test and the operational test. Any change in prompts between these two stages of development can drastically impact the responses generated from the operational testing. If a testing program needs to be able to predict operational test performance from the field test performance, then editing should not be allowed between these two stages.

Test developers must also consider the implications for security and exposure of performance assessment items during the pilot and field test administrations. Unlike multiple-choice tests where examinees are exposed to a large number of items, examinees may be able to remember the performance assessment items following the pilot test or field test administrations. Test developers must evaluate and compare the risks associated with item exposure to the value of the information collected during these special administrations.

There are a variety of approaches for field testing items. Two common approaches are embedded field test administrations and special stand-alone studies. The embedded field test could be carried out during the operational administration either embedded within or appended to the operational test. This type of field test tends to produce the most useful information. Examinees tend to be motivated to complete the field test because they are often unaware of which items are field tested and which are operational. Given that the field test is either embedded or appended to an operational administration, the test developer can be sure that the ability level and demographic characteristics of the examinee population are appropriate. Test forms built using items field tested as part of an operational assessment are more stable and predictable in their performance than those built using field test items from special studies.

Stand-alone field testing models tend to be more expensive and time consuming than embedded field test administrations. Examinees must be recruited and compensated for their efforts. Test developers are always concerned about the appropriateness of the sample being recruited. The quality of the resulting item statistics is typically less stable than those obtained through a field test process included in the operational assessments. However, because of changing testing programs (i.e., change in content or format specifications), security and exposure concerns, or concerns about the amount of time that students spend testing, stand-alone field tests may be the only viable option.

Following the field test, evaluation of items should be conducted with the assistance of the field test data. Typical information for performance assessment items elicited from the field test includes the descriptive statistics, such as the frequency distributions of responses, and the minimum and maximum responses, and the mean and standard deviation for the response. In addition to the item-level information, test developers should examine the accuracy statistics associated with the scoring process. For example, if multiple readers have been used in scoring, the correlation between readers, the percent of time readers agree with one another in the scoring process, and the percent of time readers disagree with one another in the scoring process need to be examined. If the performance assessment items have been used in conjunction with multiple-choice items, the correlations between item formats are also of interest to the test developer.

Performance assessment items and scoring rubrics should be reviewed again after field test administration, as part of the process of selecting those that will appear in the operational assessment. Any item and scoring rubric that statistical evaluation reveals to be technically flawed should be eliminated or reworked for another field test administration. Those items that pass all criteria and perform well at the field test stage should be put into the available pool for future forms construction.

TEST ASSEMBLY

As stated, the design and development of any performance assessment must consider content, technical, and logistical factors simultaneously. It is the recommendation of this author that the content specifications be the first priority of the test developers in the test assembly process. Beyond the content specifications, an iterative development process should be used where the test developers and psychometricians work collaboratively with content specialists to assemble a test that has good content-related validity evidence (see Kane, chap. 7, this volume).

The rigor of the training and scoring process is a critical point in the development of valid and reliable performance assessment items and the ultimate selection for forms. Standardized procedures should guide the training and scoring to ensure that the reported scores are accurate and reflect the intended specifications. For each performance assessment item, test developers should construct an extensive scoring guide. Based on the need to deliver consistent and accurate performance assessment scores in a timely manner, procedures must be developed that address the scoring procedures and the assembly of training materials following each assessment administration.

After the field test administration for performance assessment items and prior to final test assembly, test developers typically engage in a range-finding process where the responses from the field test are read and evaluated according to the scoring rubric. This process helps to define the characteristics along the scoring rubric scale from the very lowest levels of performance to the highest levels of performance. This process typically involves not only the test developers, but representatives of the scoring vendor as well as content experts. The outcome of the range-finding process is the identification of papers along the scoring rubric continuum used to train and monitor readers to evaluate the performance assessment responses. These papers typically include the identification of anchor papers (exemplar responses at each score point), training papers, qualifying papers, and monitoring papers. Each set of papers serves a unique purpose in the scoring process. For example, the training papers are typically scored by the range-finding experts and are used to help explain the various characteristics of a response to potential readers. Qualifying papers are used to help ensure readers are prepared to operationally score the performance assessment responses. Monitoring papers are those used by the test developers to help ensure readers are consistently applying the scoring rubric across time and across papers.

Decisions about distributions of responses, difficulty, and discrimination and intercorrelations should be made as a collaborative effort between the test developer's technical and content staff, after the field test results have been scored and analyzed. Precise recommendations for distributions, intercorrelations, and levels of difficulty are not always appropriate for delineating in the technical specifications document; however, appropriate ranges should be provided as guides for the test developers.

The ultimate use of the results of an assessment should determine the technical specifications that are necessary. The higher the stakes, the higher standards we have for the technical specifications (Linn, 2000). Low-stakes decisions, such as group decisions, should also be consistent with the technical specifications on assessments designed to serve in a low-stakes capacity. Test developers also need to consider the generalizability of the results. Regardless of the stakes associated with the test, test developers want a level of confidence that the test results are generalizable beyond the specific task.

Test developers may consider the following strategies for addressing technical specifications issues.

- Critical to the technical specifications is the absolute adherence to the content specifications. Test developers should consider content specifications as their primary responsibility.
- Assuming adherence to the content specifications, field test an adequate sample of prompts to allow for the identification and selection of the best possible prompts.
- Given the design of the field test, select prompts within the pool of field-tested prompts that demonstrate a reasonable level of inter-item correlation. Selected prompts should not be so unique that the generalizability of the results is limited.

- Encourage appropriate analyses and data explorations following the field test administration.
- Test developers should use observable statistics such as means, variances, and frequency distributions to help select operational prompts. Information on the distribution, difficulty, and other variables relevant to judging the quality of each performance assessment item should be considered. This information is critical to the selection of items that are equivalent in difficulty. The results of the field test should help test developers to revise or eliminate performance assessment items that do not elicit the appropriate distributions.
- Agreement statistics should be examined in addition to interrater correlations to ensure variability across the scoring rubric and consistency of assigned scores. Test developers should consider the impact of the interaction between score-point distributions and interrater agreement. High agreement statistics between readers may indicate the use of a limited number of score points.
- If decisions are to be made based on the rank order of examinees, identify prompts that elicit a range of responses. The standard deviation of the items should be large enough to help ensure a spread of responses.
- Consider the balance between variety and the generalizability of the prompts. The prompts should not be so unique from one another that they limit the ability to generalize beyond the particular prompt.
- Consider the impact of the interaction between score-point distributions and interrater agreement. High agreement statistics between readers may indicate the use of few score points. Agreement statistics should be examined in addition to interrater correlations to ensure variability across the scoring rubric and consistency of assigned scores.
- If rank ordering is of interest, seek prompts that broadly discriminate over the entire scoring rubric. Prompts should elicit responses at all possible score points. Some percent of the respondents should be found in each of the extreme values. Based on the field test results, revise or eliminate prompts that do not elicit responses at all score points, assuming adherence to the content specifications.

A final form of a test may include both performance assessment items and multiple-choice items. After the selection of the performance assessment items, test developers should determine the appropriate method for combining the multiple-choice and performance assessment scores into a single reported score. Test developers should model the various combinations of scores to produce the most reliable score while still retaining the most appropriate content coverage.

SUMMARY

The development of any test is a complex process. The test developer is responsible for taking a definition of what a test is intended to measure and working that definition into test specifications. The test developer must be confident that the necessary inferences can be supported by the specifications. The specifications must address the content coverage, technical quality, and logistical parameters of the test. In performance tests, the determination of the test specifications is complicated by logistical concerns such as scoring resources, turnaround time, and required testing time. This is why it is even more critical for the test developer to articulate the content, technical, and logistical specifications prior to the development of the items. Threats to validity and technical soundness of a performance assessment are more prevalent than similar threats to a multiple-choice assessment. The test developer must be fully aware of these threats and must address them throughout the process.

This chapter raised a number of issues for the test developer's consideration when designing a performance assessment. The *Standards for Educational and Psychological Testing* (AERA, APA, & NCME, 1999, chap. 3) identifies twenty-seven standards that test developers should consider as they develop, assemble, and implement their testing programs. Each of these standards addresses an important concept regardless of the type of item that is being developed or the inference to be made. It is critical that the test developer remember that regardless of the development process used, performance assessments are evaluated by the same standards as all other types of tests.

ACKNOWLEDGMENT

I wish to acknowledge the helpful assistance of Tim Miller, Marnita Beal, and Tim Hazen for their valuable contributions and review of this chapter.

REFERENCES

American Educational Research Association (AERA), American Psychological Association (APA), & National Council on Measurement in Education (NCME). (1999). *Standards for educational and psychological testing*. Washington, DC: American Psychological Association.

Bennett, R. E. (1993). On the meaning of constructed response. In R. E. Bennett & W. C. Ward (Eds.), *Construction versus choice in cognitive measurement: Issues in constructed response, performance testing, and portfolio assessment* (pp. 1–27). Hillsdale, NJ: Lawrence Erlbaum Associates.

Bennett, R. E., Ward, W. C., Rock, D. A., & Lahart, C. (1990). Toward a framework for constructed response items. Princeton, NJ: Educational Testing Service.

Bond, L., Moss, P., & Carr, P. (1996). Fairness in large-scale performance assessments. In G. Phillips (Ed.), *Technical issues in large-scale performance assessment* (pp. 117–140). Washington, DC: National Center for Educational Statistics.

Bormuth, J. R. (1970). *On the theory of achievement test items*. Chicago: University of Chicago Press.

Breland, H. M., Camp, R., Jones, R. J., Morris, M. M., & Rock, D. A., (1987). *Assessing writing skill*. New York: The College Board.

Brennan, R. L. (2001). *Generalizability theory*. New York: Springer-Verlag.

Brossell, G. (1986). Current research and unanswered questions in writing assessment. In K. K. Greenberg, H. S. Weiner, & R. A. Donovan (Eds.), *Writing assessment: Issues and strategies* (pp. 168–182). New York: Longman.

Brown, J. D., Hilgers, T., & Marsella, J. (1991) Essay prompts and topics: Minimizing the effect of differences. *Written Communication, 8,* 532–555.

Center for Universal Design. (1997). *What is universal design?* Raleigh: Center for Universal Design, North Carolina State University.

Code of Fair Testing Practices in Education. (1988). Washington, DC: Joint Committee on Testing Practices.

Council of Chief State School Officers. (2003). *State student assessment programs annual survey: Amended summary report*. Washington, DC: Council of Chief State School Officers.

Cronbach, L. J. (1984). *Essential of psychological testing* (4th ed.). New York: Harper & Row.

Cronbach, L. J. (1971). Test validation. In R. L. Thorndike (Ed.), *Educational measurement* (2nd ed.). Washington, DC: American Council on Education.

Dorans, N. J., & Holland, P. (1992). DIF detection and description: Mantel-Haenszel and standardization. In P. W. Holland, & H. Wainer (Eds.), *Differential item functioning: Theory and practice* (pp. 35–66). Hillsdale, NJ: Lawrence Erlbaum Associates.

Dorans, N. J., & Schmitt, A. P. (1993). Constructed response and differential item functioning: A pragmatic approach. In R. E. Bennett & W. C. Ward (Eds.), *Construction versus choice in cognitive measurement: Issues in constructed response, performance testing, and portfolio assessment* (pp. 135–165). Hillsdale, NJ: Lawrence Erlbaum Associates.

Ebel, R. (1951). Writing the test item. In E. F. Lindquist (Ed.), *Educational measurement* (pp. 185–249). Washington, DC: American Council on Education.

Erwin, T. D. (1991). *Assessing student learning and development*. San Francisco: Jossey Bass.

Fowles, M. (1978). *Manual for scoring the writing sample*. Princeton, NJ: Educational Testing Service.

Gitomer, D. H. (1993). Performance assessment and educational measurement. In R. E. Bennett & W. C. Ward (Eds.), *Construction versus choice in cognitive measurement: Issues in constructed response, performance testing, and portfolio assessment* (pp. 241–263). Hillsdale, NJ: Lawrence Erlbaum Associates.

Haertel, E. H., & Linn, R. L. (1996). Comparability. In G. Phillips (Ed.), *Technical issues in large-scale performance assessment* (pp. 59–78). Washington, DC: National Center for Educational Statistics.

Haladyna, T. M. (1994). *Developing and validating multiple-choice items.* Hillsdale, NJ: Lawrence Erlbaum Associates.

Haladyna, T. M. (1997). *Writing test items to evaluate higher order thinking.* Boston: Allyn & Bacon.

Haladyna, T. M. (2004). *Developing and validating multiple-choice test items* (3rd ed.). Mahwah, NJ: Lawrence Erlbaum Associates.

Haladyna, T. M., & Downing, S. M. (1989). A taxonomy of multiple-choice item-writing rules. *Applied Measurement in Education, 2,* 37–50.

Haladyna, T. M., Downing, S. M., & Rodriguez, M. C. (2002). A review of multiple-choice item-writing guidelines for classroom assessment. *Applied Measurement in Education, 15*(3), 309–334.

Hambleton, R. K., & Murphy, E. (1992). A psychometric perspective on authentic measurement. *Applied Measurement in Education, 5*(1), 1–16.

Huot, B. (1990). Reliability, validity, and holistic scoring: What we know and what we need to know. *College Composition and Communication, 41*(2), 201–213.

Kane, M. T. (1992) An argument-based approach to validity. *Psychological Bulletin, 112,* 527–535.

Lindquist, E. F., (Ed.), (1951). *Educational measurement.* Washington, DC: American Council on Education.

Linn, R. L. (2000). Assessments and accountability. *Educational Researcher, 23*(9), 4–14.

Linn, R. L. (Ed.). (1989). *Educational measurement* (3rd ed.). New York: American Council on Education & MacMillan.

Linn, R. L., Baker, E. L., & Dunbar, S. B. (1991). Complex, performance-based assessment: expectations and validation criteria. *Educational Researcher, 20*(8), 15–21.

Linn, R. L., & Gronlund, N. E. (1995). *Measurement and assessment in teaching.* Upper Saddle River, NJ: Merrill.

Martinez, M. E. (1999). Cognition and the question of test item format. *Educational Psychologist, 34,* 207–218.

Messick, S. (1989). Validity. In R. L. Linn (Ed.), *Educational measurement* (3rd ed., pp. 13–104). New York: American Council on Education & MacMillan.

Messick, S. (1996). Validity of Performance Assessments. In G. Phillips (ed.), Technical issues in large-scale performance assessment (pp 1–99). Washington, DC: National Center for Educational Statistics.

Millman, J., & Greene, J. (1989). The specification and development of tests of achievement and ability. In R. L. Linn (Ed.), *Educational measurement* (3rd ed., pp. 335–355). New York: American Council on Education & MacMillan.

Nitko, A. J. (1985). A technology for test item writing. *Journal of Educational Measurement, 21,* 201–204.

Osterlind, S. J. (1998). *Constructing test items: Multiple-choice, constructed-response, performance, and other formats (Evaluation in education and human services, 47).* Boston: Kluwer Academic Publishers.

Popham, W. J. (1997). What's wrong—and what's right—with rubrics. *Educational Leadership, 55*(2), 72–75.

Sackett, P. R. (1987). Assessment centers and content validity: Some neglected issues. *Personnel Psychology, 40,* 13–25.

Schmeiser, C. B., & Welch, C. (In press). Test development. In R. L. Brennan (Ed.), *Educational measurement* (4th ed.). New York: American Council on Education & Greenwood.

Spandel, V., & Stiggins, R. J. (1980). *Direct measure of writing skill: Issues and applications.* Portland, OR: Northwest Regional Educational Development Laboratory.

Stiggins, R. J. (1995). Assessment literacy for the 21st century. *Phi Delta Kappan,* November 1995.

Thompson, S. J., Johnstone, C. J. & Thurlow, M. L. (2002). *Universal design applied to large scale assessments* (Synthesis Report 44). Minneapolis: University of Minnesota, National Center on Educational Outcomes. Retrieved October 13, 2004 from http://education.umn.edu/NCEO/OnlinePubs/Synthesis44.html.

Thorndike, R. L. (Ed.). *Educational Measurement* (2nd ed). Washington, DC: American Council on Education.

Traub, R. E., & MacRury, K. (1990). Multiple-choice vs. free-response in the testing of scholastic achievement. In K. Ingenkamp & R. S. Jager (Eds.), *Tests and trends: Eighth yearbook of educational measurement* (pp. 128–159). Weinheim and Basel, Germany: Beltz Verlag.

Veal, L., & Hudson, S. (1983). Direct and indirect measure for large scale evaluation of writing. *Research in the Teaching of English, 17,* 285–296.

Wainer, H., Wang, X., & Thissen, D. (1994). How well can we compare scores on test forms that are constructed by examinees' choice? *Journal of Educational Measurement, 31*(3), 183–199.

Welch, C., & Hoover, H. D. (1993). Procedures for extending item bias detection techniques to polytomously scored items. *Applied Measurement in Education, 6,* 1–19.

White, E. M. (1985). *Teaching and assessing writing.* San Francisco, CA: Jossey-Bass.

14

Innovative Item Formats in Computer-Based Testing: In Pursuit of Improved Construct Representation

Stephen G. Sireci
April L. Zenisky
University of Massachusetts, Amherst

When test developers construct a test to be administered in a computer-based environment, the measurement possibilities before them are far different than what can be done with a traditional paper test. At a computer, an examinee can complete familiar tasks such as multiple-choice and free-response questions, and in the course of the same examination, be asked to engage in creative activities to demonstrate skills and abilities in highly dynamic and contextualized scenarios. Much of the promise associated with innovative item formats and their components (including high-resolution graphics, video, and audio) lies in the potential for improved construct representation. In this chapter, specific innovations in computerized item formats are reviewed, with a focus on the implications of such technologies on test score validity. Examples from testing programs currently using technologically innovative items are presented and discussed, as is the limited research in this area. Promising directions for future research are also discussed.

Computer-based testing is revolutionizing how tests are assembled and delivered. One of the most exciting and promising aspects is the inclusion of new item formats, often called *innovative item formats*. These new formats are promising because they may help to address a long-standing criticism of standardized tests—namely, that the testing process is too artificial and does not measure knowledge, skills, and abilities (KSAs) in a realistic way. Furthermore, innovative item formats available in computer-based testing have the potential to measure important attributes that are not measurable using traditional item formats. In this chapter, we review the potential advantages and disadvantages of innovative item formats within the framework of test score validity. We begin with a discussion of the limitations of traditional item formats. Next, we describe innovative computer-based item formats currently in use or proposed for use. We also review the research on the advantages and limitations of these new formats. Finally, we conclude that, if implemented properly, the newer item formats made possible by computerized testing can greatly enhance the validity of interpretations made on the basis of test scores.

TRADITIONAL VERSUS INNOVATIVE ITEM FORMATS

Standardized tests are often criticized because the tasks presented to examinees do not look like the tasks people are presented with in everyday life. This artificial impression stems from the ubiquitous multiple-choice item format. More "authentic" items, such as essays and other constructed-response item formats that require examinees to produce a response, increase the realism of testing tasks. By striving to give examinees opportunities to generate solutions and explore out-of-the-box ideas, non–multiple-choice formats can in some cases bring some of the "real world" back into the artificiality of a test administration. With the drive toward more authentic item formats, the onus is placed on the examinee to use skills and abilities in more applied ways. This approach to developing and using test items is guided by a need to more fully represent skills associated with the construct measured by the test to facilitate more valid test score interpretations (see Kane, chap. 7, this volume).

This increased realism, however, may come at great expense. Constructed-response items are often accompanied by increased scoring costs, increased testing time, and decreased test score reliability. These limitations explain the popularity of multiple-choice items, which are efficient with respect to testing time because examinees can answer many items in a relatively short time period. This feature allows for measurement of more content per given unit of testing time. They are straightforward and economical to score, and they promote test score reliability, relative to other item formats (Wainer & Thissen, 1993).

To summarize our discussion of traditional item formats, multiple-choice items are inexpensive to score, can efficiently test a great deal of content, and promote test score reliability. At the same time, however, this format can be limiting. First, although it is possible to write multiple-choice items to evoke more complex cognitions (Braswell & Kupin, 1993; Martinez, 1999), the task is not easy to accomplish. Second, they are limited with respect to the nature of the performances they can measure (e.g., multiple-choice items cannot measure the ability to write an essay or conduct an experiment). Constructed-response items, on the other hand, allow for measurement of more complex knowledge and skills, but they take up a great deal of testing time (e.g., 45 minutes to write an essay), which limits the degree to which the different areas of a content domain can be measured. In addition, the subjectivity introduced in scoring examinees' responses leads to reductions in test score reliability. Add increased scoring costs to the list of the disadvantages of constructed-response items and it can be seen how the choice of item format is a difficult one when both costs and accuracy in measurement must be considered.

Like multiple-choice and traditional constructed-response item formats, computer-based innovative item formats have their advantages and disadvantages. However, their advantages are exciting because they offer a compromise between the strengths and limitations of the more traditional item formats. Although we discuss validity issues with these newer item formats in greater detail later, the advantages and disadvantages are best framed within the context of two related validity concepts—construct representation and construct-irrelevant variance (CIV). *Construct representation* is the ability of a test to fully represent all the knowledge, skills, and abilities inherent in the construct measured. *Construct-irrelevant variance* refers to the other attributes unintentionally measured by a test that affect test scores (e.g., English proficiency affecting math test performance; see Haladyna & Downing, 2004, for further examples). As Messick (1988) put it, "tests are imperfect measures of constructs because they either leave out something that should be included... or else include something that should be left out, or both" (p. 34). Leaving something out results in construct underrepresentation and including something that should be left out results in measuring something irrelevant to the construct. The ability to increase construct representation is perhaps the greatest potential of innovative item formats in computer-based testing. However, the ability to interact with the computer (computer literacy) may be a source of CIV. Some empirical research on this point has been done: for example, one study by Taylor, Jamieson, Eignor, and Kirsch (1998) found no statistical or practical differences in test scores on a computer-based test with respect to varying levels of computer familiarity, and the use of well-developed and explicit tutorials is critical to the successful introduction and use of computers in large-scale testing contexts.

In the next section we describe and illustrate specific computer-based testing innovative item formats. As will become evident, many of these formats can measure knowledge and skills not measurable by multiple-choice items in a way that is efficient with respect to testing time and can be scored objectively (and inexpensively) by the computer. We return to issues of computer literacy in a subsequent section.

AVAILABLE ITEM FORMATS

The range of possibilities of various item formats is a significant part of the appeal of computer-based testing. Rather than being constrained by what can be represented in two dimensions on static paper forms, computerized tests can seamlessly integrate high-resolution graphics, realistic audio, and a library's worth of resource literature into the simplest or most complex task. Indeed, the tasks themselves can reflect everything from what items look like in the familiar paper-and-pencil forms to activities that simulate real-life situations and allow for testing unique problem-solving skills. In addition, even familiar item types can be "formatted" in a number of ways, which can add significant benefits compared to the traditional presentation on a paper-based test. (A simple example of this is allowing examinees to manipulate the onscreen text size to meet their visual needs.) In this section, we provide an overview of many of these tasks and review the format components that test developers can draw on in the course of creating innovative computerized assessments.

Item Formats Defined

The classic way of thinking about test item formats divides all item types into two groups—items that require examinees to select a response (selected-response items) and items that require examinees to generate a response (constructed-response items). In this approach, the nature of the response dictates the characterization of an item. Must the examinee select from what is presented, or construct a unique answer given the parameters of the question? As straightforward as this question sounds, with the advent of certain new formats that involve skills such as ordering information or classifying objects according to some defined dimension, the line between how much is selected and to what extent examinees are generating their own responses becomes blurred. An alternate approach to item format categorization described by Bennett, Ward, Rock, and LaHart (1990) stipulates seven categories of item formats: multiple-choice, selection/identification, reordering/rearrangement, substitution/correction, completion, construction, and presentation. This list reflects a continuum of item formats that generally vary from most to least constrained in terms of responses. In addition, it more clearly characterizes the nature of tasks associated with the different item formats within each level of response constraint.

What is an item format, though? Simply put, the *format* of a test item encompasses all aspects of the specific task an examinee is to complete. The first part of any test item is referred to as the *stimulus* or the *item stem*. The stem is where a question is asked of examinees, or a task to be completed is laid out. When the item stem is taken together with the directions for completing the item, it should be explicit to each examinee what must be done to answer the item. The second part of test items, clearly, is the *response*, where examinees answer as directed. For a multiple-choice item, the examinee must choose a single answer among presented alternatives given an item stem; the essay format directs an examinee to write a text-based response of some length in response to a presented question or statement serving as an item stem.

In addition to the format of the response, the nature of the response is also important. Parshall, Davey, and Pashley (2000) highlighted the need to consider both the input devices to be used and the response action the examinee must take to complete a test item. At the level of identifying the value added by integrating computerized tasks, some of which may be highly novel for test takers, there are several angles by which the validity of using such technologies can be evaluated. This involves consideration of what examinees should know and be able to do relative to the construct of interest, what kind of information is needed from examinees to make those determinations about the knowledge and skills acquired, how that information can best be represented by examinees, and how that information is represented electronically by examinees.

The input devices most commonly found in current computer-based testing applications are the mouse and the keyboard. However, Parshall et al. (2000) note that other possibilities, such as touch screens, light pens, joysticks, trackballs, and speech recognition software, hold promise for some specialized testing contexts. In terms of response actions, the computer mouse allows the examinee to direct an onscreen cursor to click on onscreen items such as pictures, text, or radio buttons; trigger pull-down menus; draw onscreen images; and drag and drop objects as needed. With the keyboard, some of what an examinee can be asked to do is type text-based responses, enter numerical answers, or navigate a screen using arrow keys. It is clear that with some consideration of these input devices and the universe of associated response actions, computerized testing has the potential to gather and store measurement information well beyond the capabilities of traditional standardized test methods.

Innovative Formats

There are many specific types of item formats presently found in different large-scale testing contexts. These types include formats modeled on those used in paper-and-pencil testing, those that are creatively presented in the context of real-life situations to help enhance the fidelity of the measurement with the construct being assessed, and those that are entirely unique and only logistically feasible through technology. As we proceed in our discussion of item formats, we highlight some of these kinds of format variations that are options for test developers.

In this section, we provide an overview of selected formats that are either novel to testing, can be administered to examinees in novel ways through computer-based testing, or both. We describe fourteen item formats used in computer-based testing, beginning with the multiple-choice item. We illustrate the item formats we believe are most likely to improve construct representation while balancing the need for automatically scoreable formats. Illustrations of other item types can be found in Zenisky and Sireci (2002).

Multiple Choice

To answer multiple-choice questions on many traditional standardized tests, examinees generally read an item in a test booklet and then "bubble in" the letter of the chosen answer on a separate piece of paper. Clearly, computerized testing eliminates the need for examinees to solve a test question and then transfer that answer from the test booklet to a separate answer sheet; an examinee can use the computer mouse to select an answer onscreen directly in the physical location of the test item. A further feature of computer-based multiple-choice formats concerns how an examinee selects an answer among presented alternatives. For example, this

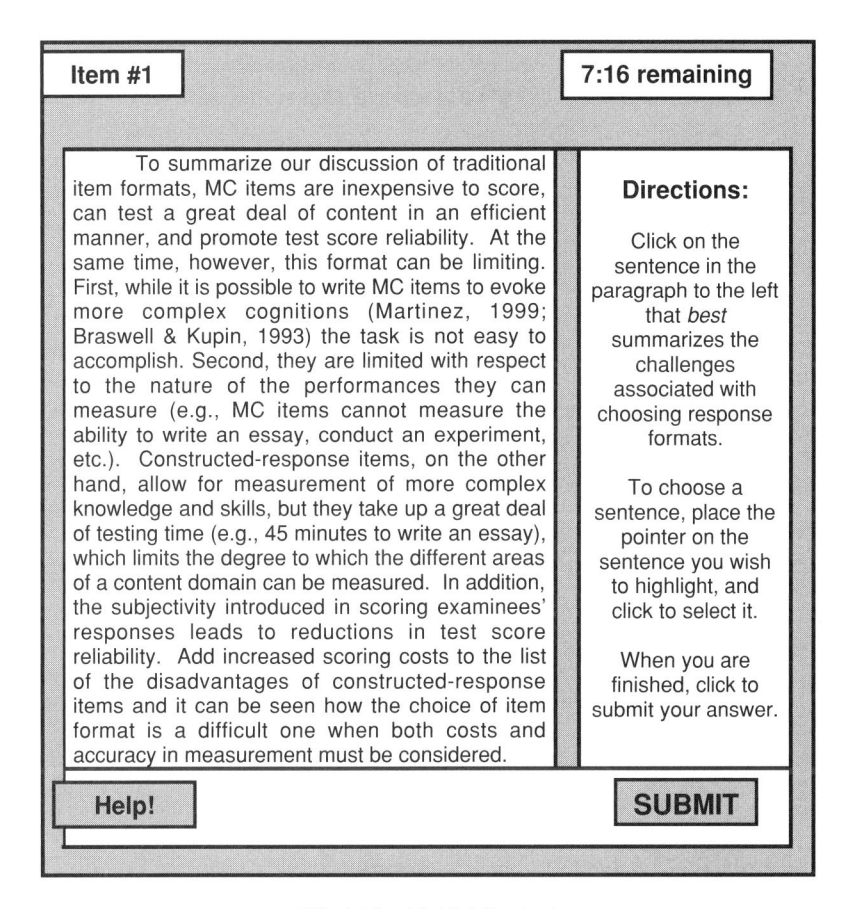

```
┌─────────────────────────────────────────────────────────┐
│  Item #1                                 7:16 remaining │
│                                                         │
│  ┌──────────────────────────────────┬─────────────────┐ │
│  │     To summarize our discussion  │                 │ │
│  │ of traditional item formats, MC  │   Directions:   │ │
│  │ items are inexpensive to score,  │                 │ │
│  │ can test a great deal of content │   Click on the  │ │
│  │ in an efficient manner, and      │   sentence in the│ │
│  │ promote test score reliability.  │  paragraph to the│ │
│  │ At the same time, however, this  │   left that best │ │
│  │ format can be limiting. First,   │   summarizes the │ │
│  │ while it is possible to write MC │    challenges    │ │
│  │ items to evoke more complex      │   associated with│ │
│  │ cognitions (Martinez, 1999;      │  choosing response│ │
│  │ Braswell & Kupin, 1993) the task │     formats.     │ │
│  │ is not easy to accomplish.       │                  │ │
│  │ Second, they are limited with    │    To choose a   │ │
│  │ respect to the nature of the     │  sentence, place │ │
│  │ performances they can measure    │   the pointer on │ │
│  │ (e.g., MC items cannot measure   │   the sentence   │ │
│  │ the ability to write an essay,   │  you wish to     │ │
│  │ conduct an experiment, etc.).    │ highlight, and   │ │
│  │ Constructed-response items, on   │ click to select  │ │
│  │ the other hand, allow for        │       it.        │ │
│  │ measurement of more complex      │                  │ │
│  │ knowledge and skills, but they   │  When you are    │ │
│  │ take up a great deal of testing  │ finished, click  │ │
│  │ time (e.g., 45 minutes to write  │ to submit your   │ │
│  │ an essay), which limits the      │    answer.       │ │
│  │ degree to which the different    │                  │ │
│  │ areas of a content domain can be │                  │ │
│  │ measured. In addition, the       │                  │ │
│  │ subjectivity introduced in       │                  │ │
│  │ scoring examinees' responses     │                  │ │
│  │ leads to reductions in test      │                  │ │
│  │ score reliability. Add increased │                  │ │
│  │ scoring costs to the list of the │                  │ │
│  │ disadvantages of constructed-    │                  │ │
│  │ response items and it can be     │                  │ │
│  │ seen how the choice of item      │                  │ │
│  │ format is a difficult one when   │                  │ │
│  │ both costs and accuracy in       │                  │ │
│  │ measurement must be considered.  │                  │ │
│  └──────────────────────────────────┴─────────────────┘ │
│   [Help!]                              [SUBMIT]         │
└─────────────────────────────────────────────────────────┘
```

FIG. 14.1. Highlighting text.

could involve clicking on a letter of an answer, on an unlettered radio button next to the answer, on the answer itself (which could be text or a picture), or scrolling to an answer on a drop-down menu.

Extended Multiple Choice

This format is similar to multiple-choice but, as typically implemented, the number of presented answer choices is large enough to render the probability of guessing correctly extremely low. The *highlighting text* format (Carey, 2001; Walker & Crandall, 1999) shown in Figure 14.1 is a variation on extended multiple-choice in which the examinee is supposed to select a sentence from a passage that best matches what the stem requires (i.e., the main idea of the paragraph, the meaning of a specialized term, etc.). The analyzing situations item format gives examinees the opportunity to critically evaluate a situation and make a judgment using the presented options (Ackerman, Evans, Park, Tamassia, & Turner, 1999).

Multiple Selection

In this format, examinees are directed to select more than one answer from the answer choices given the context or question presented in the item stem. It might be that examinees must explicitly identify all the correct answers, or the question might be framed such that there

334   SIRECI AND ZENISKY

```
Directions:
Marco has $7.00 to spend on his lunch.
Click on one drink, one sandwich, and one side dish that Marco could
have for lunch so that the price of the three items adds up to $7.00 or
less.
You may only click on one item in each column.
Click on Submit when you are finished.
```

DRINKS		SANDWICHES		SIDE DISHES	
$1.25	Milk	$3.75	Veggie	$1.50	Chips
$.95	Tea	$4.50	Turkey	$1.00	Cookies
$1.50	Soda	$4.75	Roast Beef	$1.75	Rice
$1.25	Juice	$5.00	Pastrami	$1.50	Green Salad
$.95	Coffee	$4.75	Ham	$1.50	Fruit Salad

SUBMIT

FIG. 14.2. Multiple selection.

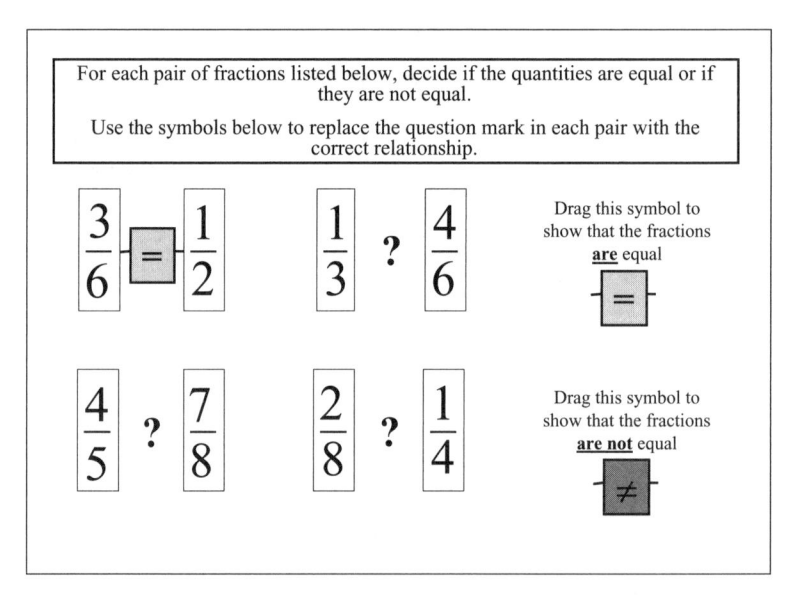

For each pair of fractions listed below, decide if the quantities are equal or if they are not equal.
Use the symbols below to replace the question mark in each pair with the correct relationship.

$\frac{3}{6} = \frac{1}{2}$ $\frac{1}{3} \: ? \: \frac{4}{6}$

Drag this symbol to show that the fractions **are** equal

$=$

$\frac{4}{5} \: ? \: \frac{7}{8}$ $\frac{2}{8} \: ? \: \frac{1}{4}$

Drag this symbol to show that the fractions **are not** equal

$\neq$

FIG. 14.3. Specifying relationships item format.

are multiple correct (and incorrect) answers and the examinee should select one set of answers to meet the parameters of the question (Figure 14.2).

Specifying Relationships

In specifying relationships-type items, the task is to identify the relationship between presented sets of onscreen items (Fitzgerald, 2001) (Figure 14.3). The relations specified might be mathematical or otherwise.

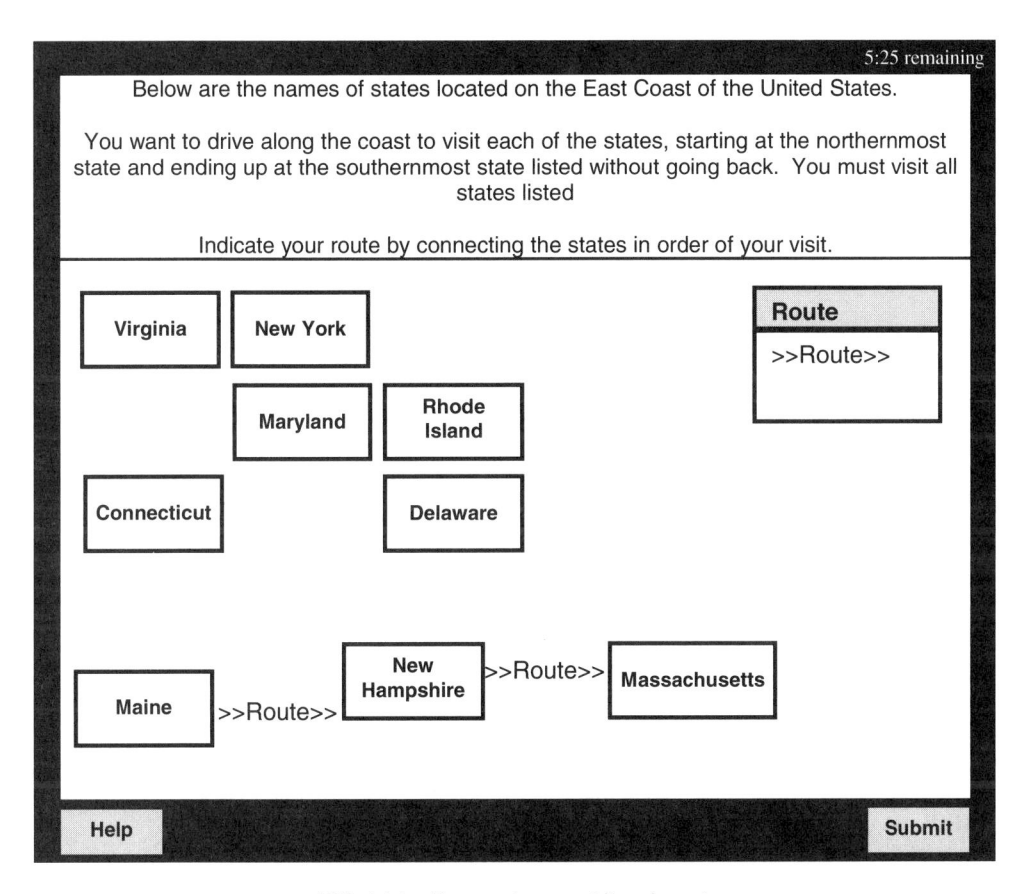

FIG. 14.4. Drag-and-connect item format.

Drag-and-connect

The drag-and-connect format (Fitzgerald, 2001) is analogous to specifying relationships, but rather than establishing a linkage between pairs of item the task is broadened to connect multiple items (Figure 14.4).

Ordering Information

The ordering information format (Figure 14.5) reflects an effort to evaluate the extent to which an examinee can reorder or rearrange things in a specified order (Fitzgerald, 2001; Walker & Crandall, 1999). Conceptual examples of ordering information tasks include ordering sentences, constructing anagrams, arranging mathematical expressions to form a proof, arranging pictures in sequence, or putting together a puzzle. This general format of ordering information is one that is significantly aided by the use of technology for administration, because items are ordered not by placing numbers next to objects to signify an order but rather by using the mouse to drag-and-drop onscreen items to form a more coherent whole.

Select and Classify

In the select-and-classify item format, examinees are required to categorize onscreen items. The task is, to drag the item, using the mouse, to the appropriate onscreen repository (Microsoft Corporation, 1998) (Figure 14.6). Bennett and Sebrechts' (1997) "sorting information" format

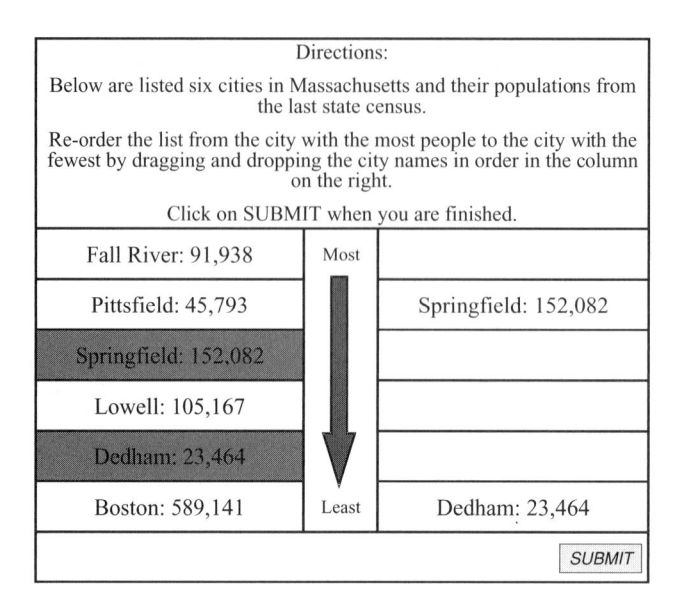

FIG. 14.5. Ordering information item format.

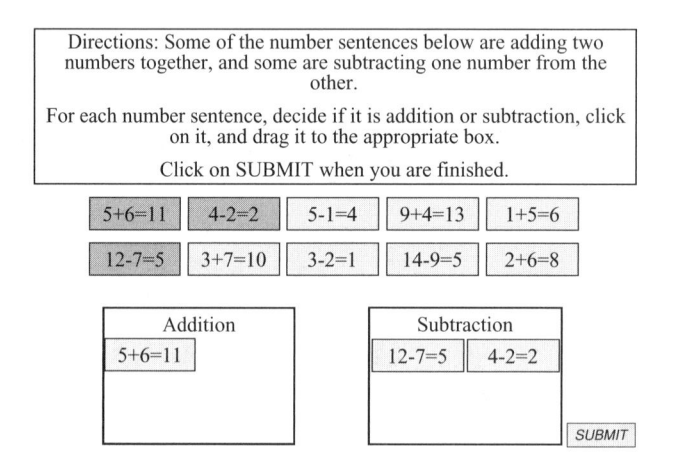

FIG. 14.6. Select-and-classify item format.

falls into this category. The create-a-tree item format is a visual variation on select-and-classify (Figure 14.7). The task here is for examinees to consider each element in a list, and after dragging and dropping to classify each element, each item appears linked to its classification label as a branch from a tree (Fitzgerald, 2001; Walker & Crandall, 1999).

Inserting Text

This format has the examinee drag and drop a presented sentence into a logical place within an onscreen passage (Taylor, Kirsch, Eignor, & Jamieson, 1999). A sentence is presented to the examinee separate from a passage, and the directions instruct the examinee to place the sentence into the passage where appropriate (e.g., where a sentence gives an example of an idea raised in the previous statement).

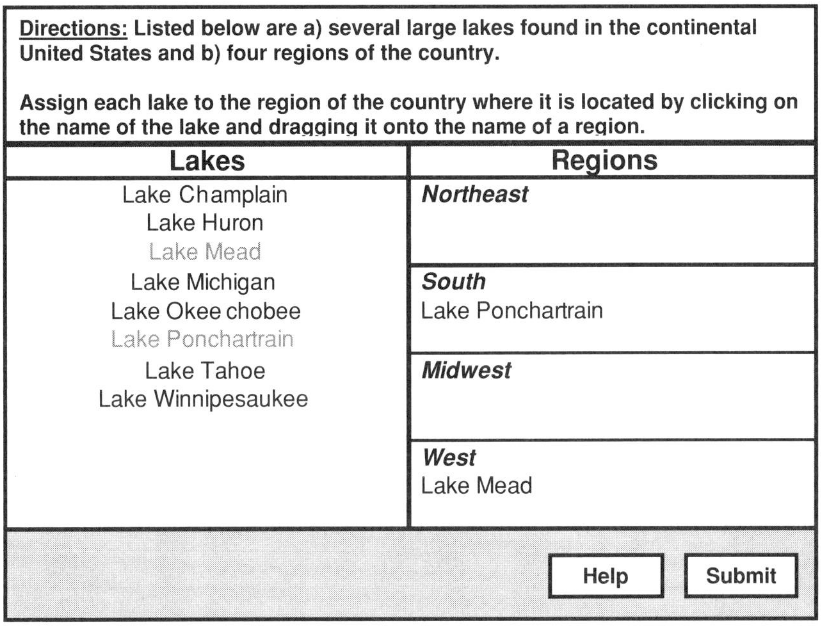

Lakes	Regions
Lake Champlain Lake Huron Lake Mead Lake Michigan Lake Okeechobee Lake Ponchartrain Lake Tahoe Lake Winnipesaukee	**Northeast** **South** Lake Ponchartrain **Midwest** **West** Lake Mead

Directions: Listed below are a) several large lakes found in the continental United States and b) four regions of the country.

Assign each lake to the region of the country where it is located by clicking on the name of the lake and dragging it onto the name of a region.

FIG. 14.7. Create-a-tree.

Corrections and Substitutions

Items formatted as corrections and substitutions direct examinees to replace what is presented to them with a self-generated alternative. For example, if an examinee is given an incorrectly spelled word, the task is to type in a correct spelling for that word. Other conceptual examples include fixing grammatical errors or other editing tasks and solving bugs in computer programs.

Completion

The number of possible contexts for simple completion items is significant. When an incomplete stimulus is presented, examinees must self-generate the answer rather than fix what is already there. Examples include free-response mathematics (Braswell & Kupin, 1993), sentence completion, grid-in, numerical equations, and short answer-type questions. *Multiple numerical response* is a variation on completion, where an examinee might have to complete multiple free response items en route to solving a problem.

Graphical Modeling

Formalized by Bennett, Morley, and Quardt (2000), graphical modeling items offer examinees the chance to model data by completing a graph. This might include shading a portion of a geometric shape, drawing a line graph to represent trends in data, or extending a bar graph (Figure 14.8).

Formulating Hypotheses

This item format presents a context or situation for which examinees must generate as many plausible reasons or hypotheses about the situation as possible (Bennett & Rock, 1995). A similar variation on this is the generating examples format researched by Bennett et al.

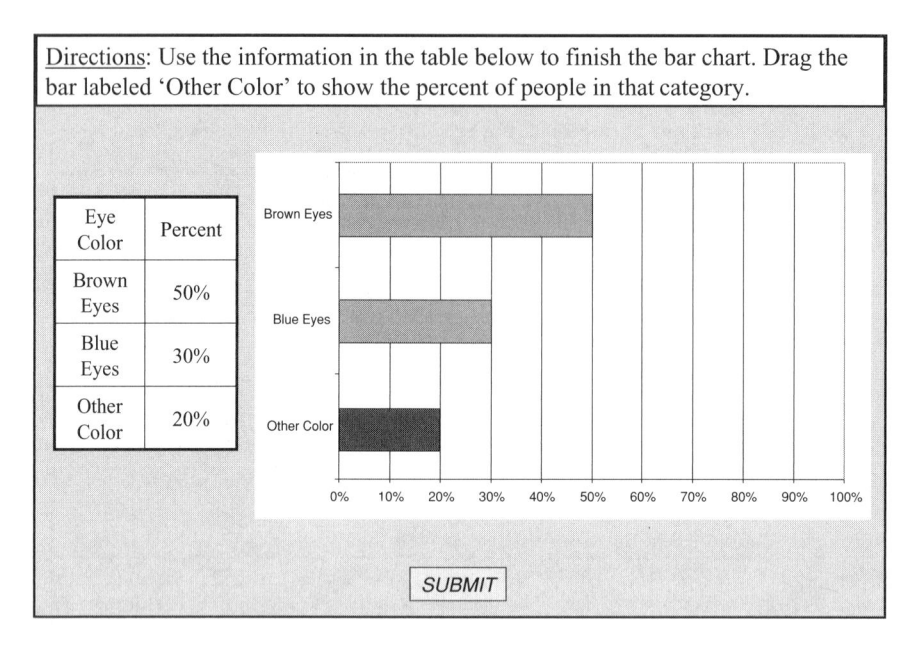

FIG. 14.8. Graphical modeling.

(1999), where instead of hypotheses the task is to come up with examples of a given condition or proposition.

Computer-Based Essay

The computer-based essay can be implemented much the way it is used in paper-based tests, where examinees generate a written response of some length to answer a writing prompt. However, some features of writing on the computer that might be included are editing features such as cut, copy, and paste, as well as a spellcheck and/or a thesaurus.

Problem-Solving Vignette

This format is actually not necessarily a unique item format (in terms of a simple stimulus followed by response) but rather is of particular note in computer-based testing given the flexibility of administering a test by computer. An example of this is the standardized patient vignette used by the National Board of Medical Examiners (Clauser, Margolis, Clyman, & Ross, 1997), in which examinees work through a medical case from initial diagnosis to case management as the clock ticks down in real time. The consequences of medical decisions made by the examinee can be negative as well as positive. The National Council of Architectural Registration Boards also has a test based in part on vignette performance as well, where candidates for architectural licensure use onscreen tools to design a building from the ground up given building codes and client specifications (Bejar, 1991). Another example of problem-solving vignettes is the newly revised Uniform CPA Exam that presents realistic accounting scenarios to candidates, and requires them to access onscreen resources to solve a problem (Devore, 2002). A demonstration of this Uniform CPA exam can be found online at http://www.cpa-exam.org/lrc/exam_tutorial.html.

Innovations in Item Format Components

As much as the many possibilities for test item formats discussed above have made computer-based testing a very different and exciting experience as compared to traditional paper testing, using the computer for test administration also allows for multimedia features to be incorporated in a much more appropriate, efficient, and individualized way. Rather than playing a video or audio component aloud in a large room full of people, each individual test taker can listen to an audio or video clip at his or her own computer terminal at his or her own pace. Still pictures and other graphics can also be reproduced in color and in more detail than they might otherwise appear on paper. The ability to increase the size of such graphics and the font size for text allows for the integration of some principles of universal test design (Thompson, Thurlow, & Malouf, 2004; Thompson, Thurlow, & Moore, 2003). For example, with such capabilities, special "large-print" versions of test forms may not be needed for many students with some types of visual disabilities.

In addition, the use of calculators is simplified in computer-based testing. Rather than having to specify and check what kinds of calculators examinees bring into test centers (simple, scientific, or graphing), test developers can include the option for examinees to use a calculator for some questions by simply clicking on a button to access an onscreen calculator. Calculator use can be allowed on some items and not others. A spellcheck feature can be similarly implemented or not implemented on a per-item basis as desired.

Another component that is increasingly finding application in credentialing testing is the use of authoritative literature. The architectural licensing examination allows examinees to access pages upon pages of building codes at the click of an onscreen button, and the Uniform CPA Examination similarly provides access to tax code and other such relevant materials. A unique set of such materials cannot usually be provided to each examinee in a paper-based test.

RESEARCH ON THE VALIDITY OF INNOVATIVE ITEM FORMATS

As mentioned, the greatest promise of innovative item formats in computer-based testing is improved construct representation. That is, these item formats may allow for measurement of KSAs that are not measurable using traditional item formats. In the preceding section, we described some situations in which this is already occurring. For example, on the Uniform CPA Examination candidates are required to use electronic resources to research the answer to a presented problem. However, as also mentioned, a potential problem is the possibility that when examinees interact with a computer, computer proficiency may introduce CIV. If test scores are influenced by how well an examinee can navigate the computerized testing system, accurate measurement of the intended proficiencies is hindered.

In this section, we review research on the degree to which computer-based item formats have affected the validity of interpretations made on the basis of test scores. However, the unfortunate state of affairs is that not much research has been done in this area. As Huff and Sireci (2001) pointed out, the vast majority of research on innovative item formats in computer-based testing has focused on developing these formats, rather than on their validation. Two important questions should drive the validity research on innovative item formats in computer-based testing: What is the value added of these item formats in terms of construct representation? and Do these item formats decrease validity by introducing CIV? These are important validity issues because, if not implemented properly, the added complexity of a computer-based test could confuse candidates rather than allow them to demonstrate their capabilities.

Research conducted on the validity of innovative item formats in computer-based testing has focused primarily on two issues: (a) the comparability of a newly introduced computer-based test to its paper-based predecessor and (b) the degree to which innovative item formats possess desirable measurement properties such as discrimination and information.

Research on Test Comparability

When computer-based tests were first introduced, the validity research focused on evaluating the comparability of paper-and-pencil and computerized versions of a test (e.g., Greaud & Green, 1986; Green, 1988; McBride & Martin, 1983; Sympson, Weiss, & Ree, 1983, 1984). Many of the first computer-based tests, such as the Armed Services Vocational Aptitude Battery (ASVAB), were designed to replace paper-and-pencil versions of a test. An important validity question for these new tests was the extent to which they measured the same construct as the paper versions and the degree to which they increased measurement efficiency.

Most of these comparability studies reported positive results. For example, McBride and Martin (1983) investigated the benefits of the computer-based version of the ASVAB. They randomly assigned Marine Corps recruits to computer- or paper-based versions of the verbal ability subtest. Each group took two parallel forms of each test, as well as a criterion measure of verbal ability. Their analyses focused on reliability comparisons as a function of the number of items administered and on concurrent validity with the criterion test. With respect to parallel forms reliability, they found that the computer-based version was more than twice as efficient as the paper test when fewer than twenty items were administered, but that this efficiency declined as the number of items administered increased (e.g., at thirty items, the reliability associated with the computer-based test was only slightly higher than that associated with the paper test). They also found that the computer-based version of the test exhibited slightly higher correlations (validity coefficients) with the criterion test. Although this study involved the same item formats on both tests (multiple choice), the results indicate that, if implemented carefully, computer-based tests can meet or exceed the psychometric qualities of traditional testing programs. Obviously, however, validation of a computerized version of a paper-and-pencil examination must be done on a case-by-case basis.

The issue of the comparability of scores from paper- and computer-based testing is directly addressed multiple times in the *Standards for Educational and Psychological Testing* (American Educational Research Association [AERA], American Psychological Association [APA], & National Council on Measurement in Education [NCME], 1999). The *Standards* highlight the need to for test developers to be clear about what levels of comparability across forms can be expected and the extent to which differences may affect test score interpretations. For example, Standard 6.11 states

> If a test is designed so that more than one method can be used for administration or for recording responses... the manual should clearly document the extent to which scores arising from these methods are interchangeable. If the results are not interchangeable, this fact should be reported, and guidance should be given for the interpretation of scores obtained under the various conditions... (p. 70)

Ultimately, in transitioning from one administration mode to another, test developers must be aware of the extent to which comparability is reasonably ensured, and regard the compilation of such evidence as a critical aspect of validity. In many cases, however, a new computerized version of a test is not designed to exist in parallel fashion to a paper-based examination, or to substitute for it. Rather, it is expected to replace the traditional examination and introduce improvements such as better measurement of the construct. In such cases, comparability is not to be expected, and so the evaluation changes from a focus on comparability to a focus on the value added by the new administration format.

Research Evaluating Innovative Item Formats

Jodoin (2003) conducted a comprehensive evaluation of two relatively new innovative item types in computer-based testing. Using data from an information technology certification examination, he compared the relative item information (i.e., measurement precision within an item response theory context) of multiple-choice and innovative items. The innovative items in this study were drag-and-connect and create-a-tree items (illustrated in Figures 14.4 and 14.7). The multiple-choice items included both traditional items and multiple response items. He found that the innovative item types provided much more information compared to multiple-choice items; however, it took examinees three to four times longer to complete an innovative item. When the amount of time it took to answer an item was taken into account, Jodoin found that multiple-choice items provided more than twice the amount of information per unit of testing time. He concluded "... given a fixed amount of testing time, a test composed of only multiple-choice items would provide more than twice as much information compared to a test with only innovative items" (p. 9). He also explored different hybrid options because many test developers use both item formats on a test to improve construct representation without sacrificing testing time or measurement precision. In most of these cases, selected response items represent a much larger proportion of the test, in terms of both testing time and weight associated with the total test score (Wainer & Thissen, 1993).

Bennett and Sebrechts (1997) investigated a computer-based innovative item format proposed for the Graduate Record Exam (GRE) that assessed examinees' "representational skill." Essentially, the task presented to examinees was to match a target item to one of four prototype items. The target and prototype items were presented simultaneously on the same screen. This item format was based on research in cognitive psychology regarding novice–expert differences in quantitative problem solving. Their comprehensive evaluation focused on (a) criterion-related validity evidence (the relationship between scores on the representational skills items and several criterion measures), (b) the reliability of the representational skills test scores, and (c) examinees' perceptions of this new item format.

Bennett and Sebrechts' (1997) results generally supported the validity of this item format. Although the reliability estimates for the subscores were lower than those associated with multiple-choice GRE items, examinees scoring well on the representational skills items tended to have higher GRE scores and college grades ($r > .50$). In addition, more than half of the examinees preferred the sorting items to the multiple-choice items on the relevant section of the GRE, and the vast majority thought this item format was a "fairer measure of their ability to undertake graduate study" (p. 74). The results of this study are particularly encouraging because this item format represented measurement of a new cognitive skill called *representational ability*. The study also illustrates how cognitive theory and traditional validity evidence can be used to build a validity argument for a new item format. As Bennett and Sebrechts stated, a "cognitive psychological underpinning helps bolster the argument for construct validity. (Most large-scale testing programs lack an explicit theoretical rationale, which weakens the validity argument)" (pp. 65–66).

In a similar study, Bennett et al. (1999) evaluated the validity of the generating examples item format. Once again, a central focus of the analysis was construct representation. In this format, all the information to find a unique solution for an item is not presented and so "examinees must use a 'generate-and-test' approach" (p. 234). The generating examples items led to scores of sufficiently high reliability (projected alpha was 0.90 for a forty-item test). The disattenuated correlation of the generating examples scores with the scores from the GRE sections were around 0.70, which suggests these items were measuring related, but distinct, skills. Thus, these results are consistent with an argument of increased construct representation. This study was also impressive in that it investigated the differential impact of this item format across men and women. The results indicated similar sex differences to other GRE item types. One negative result of this study was that about 75% of the examinees preferred traditional multiple-choice items to the generating examples item format.

Evaluating Effects of Computer Proficiency

When the Test of English as a Foreign Language (TOEFL) was computerized, the degree to which computer proficiency may affect test scores was an issue of serious concern. To evaluate the potential presence of CIV caused by differential computer proficiency among TOEFL examinees, a comprehensive study of the effects of computer familiarity on TOEFL performance was conducted. Taylor et al. (1999) used a measure of examinee's initial English proficiency (based on a paper-and-pencil TOEFL administration) as a covariate to adjust for preexisting differences when comparing computer-familiar and computer-novice examinees with respect to their scores on the computerized version of the TOEFL. They found that although group differences on the test favored the computer-familiar group, the effect sizes associated with these differences were negligible. They concluded that CIV from computer proficiency would not be a problem for the computerized TOEFL.

PRACTICAL ISSUES

In the preceding sections, we introduced various innovative item formats in computer-based testing, discussed their advantages and limitations, and summarized some of the research on innovations. In this section, we discuss the practical issues that must be considered when developing or implementing a computer-based test.

Implementing a large-scale computerized test is a tremendous undertaking, and it is made more so by the use of innovative item formats. These complexities arise in two ways: first, in the course of test development activities, and second, in test administration.

Test Development

One significant challenge to widespread implementation of novel formats is the lack of research and guidance for test developers and item writers. Whereas much has been written about the properties of and item-writing guidelines for multiple-choice items (see Haladyna, 2004; Haladyna & Downing, 1989), essays, and other more traditional formats, comparatively little information is available with respect to innovative item formats. In testing contexts where novel formats have been used with varying degrees of success, the item-writing guidelines produced are largely context specific and often proprietary. More research is needed to identify the kinds of measurement information gathered by these items and the extent to which such novel item formats contribute to the overall testing goals. Research is needed, for example, to demonstrate these new item formats (a) measure KSAs that were not previously measurable using selected-response item formats, (b) are understandable to all examinees, (c) are not susceptible to sources of CIV such as computer literacy, and (d) do not increase performance gaps across subgroups for reasons such as differential coaching. Innovative item formats that involve sets of items also require research on the best ways to score the items, particularly if a response to one item affects how a student answers a subsequent item (i.e., research on handling local item dependence).

Training and Tutorials

The use of innovative item formats and computerized format components (such as onscreen calculators and spellchecks, among others) has made the importance of developing pretesting preparation materials as well as tutorials a critical concern for test developers. To ensure that examinees are familiar with the specific nature of the tasks being used in a given testing context as well as the use of all "clickable" options presented, test developers must work to create CDs and other electronic resource material that can be distributed to examinees well in advance of the date of test administration, or to develop informative downloadable pages that can be accessed via the Internet. In addition, tutorial time must be budgeted into the actual test setting to allow the examinee an opportunity to become familiar with the computer, the testing environment, and the response actions required to complete the test.

Implementation and Delivery

The delivery of computerized tests at any level of complexity is a challenging undertaking. In the first place, computerized tests can be sent out via the Internet (with accompanying security difficulties) or be given in secure test centers (with escalating costs for examinees). Although the Internet is an attractive option for some test developers and testing contexts, many testing applications using the kinds of technological innovation detailed in this chapter must be aware of things like the speeds at which individuals connect to the Internet and the feasibility of faithfully transmitting test takers' answers to the server and recording them without error. Standardization of browsers and plugins is a fundamental step. In addition, there remain a number of basic equity concerns relating to infrastructure for computerized testing, such as improving access to testing centers and quality hardware. This is particularly the case in international testing contexts, but is also a significant issue domestically for large-scale testing programs.

Scoring

When considering how to score innovative item formats in computer-based testing, the possibilities are exciting. In many cases, computerized examinations are desired primarily so that examinee responses can be gathered and stored electronically, and scored instantaneously. These advantages apply to both the simple and more complex item formats. Recent advances in automated scoring mechanisms extend well beyond simple "key matches" to intelligent systems that can process text and/or judge test takers using a multitude of rule-based algorithms (Dodd & Fitzpatrick, 2002). For example, computerized scoring systems have been shown to score essays and other constructed responses reliably and validly (Khaliq & Sireci, 2004).

Test Security and Task Memorability

One issue that has curbed wide use of performance tasks in even a noncomputerized testing mode is the potential threat to test security posed by having examinees work on single, potentially highly memorable test items for extended lengths of time. In computerized testing, although the actual time spent on an innovative item might vary depending on the nature of the task, the experience of working through such an item, coupled with the novelty of the format, might combine to make items in a new format more memorable than more traditional items. Advances in item cloning techniques (Habbick, 1999; Hambleton, 2002) are one method by which test developers can try to minimize the impact of task memorability, but the creation of item variants is challenging, as is ensuring the similarity of clones with respect to their statistical properties.

As described in detail by Impara and Foster (chap. 5, this volume), concentrated efforts to "beat the test" also pose significant threats to the validity of computer-based testing. If examinees memorize items and post them in chat rooms and on web sites, validity is certainly compromised. In addition, the use of impersonators may become more prevalent in Internet-based testing, because on-site proctors may be infeasible.

Cost

Creating and administering innovative items to examinees in large-scale testing is typically an expensive endeavor. The need to create templates and models that may not exist make the process of developing items using novel formats a significant challenge, and the sheer numbers of those items needed to support a secure testing program means test developers must significantly invest in item writing. Likewise, choosing and validating scoring systems that can handle complex responses that may be represented many ways within a database is another investment. The computer-based administration modes of choice (stand-alone applications versus Internet) each have associated development costs, and, depending on the complexity of other features of the test (i.e., adaptive), may pose additional difficulties with respect to programming in item selection rules given content constraints as well as item difficulty values.

THE FUTURE OF INNOVATIVE ITEM FORMATS

In this chapter, we illustrated specific innovative item formats in computer-based testing and discussed their advantages and limitations. We also discussed the factors that should be considered in implementing such items in a computer-based test. Innovative item formats hold much promise, and in many cases, such as the Uniform CPA Examination (http://www.cpa-exam.org/), the Architecture Registration Examination (http://www.ncarb.org/are/overview.html), and the United States Medical Licensing Exam (http://www.usmle.org/step3/default.htm), they are already producing benefits. The web addresses provided for each of these credentialing programs include links that provide examples of the format innovations that are being used in high-stakes contexts. In each of these cases, the innovative item formats were implemented to increase construct representation and great strides were made to familiarize examinees with these formats to minimize the possibility of construct-irrelevant variance being introduced. Modern test developers are aware that computerizing an examination may introduce problems. For example, the *Standards for Educational and Psychological Testing* (AERA, APA, & NCME, 1999) explicitly urge developers of computer-based tests to be aware of the validity issues associated with computerized testing. For example, Standard 13.18 states

> Documentation of design, models, scoring algorithms, and methods for scoring and classifying should be provided for tests administered and scored using multimedia or computers. Construct-irrelevant variance pertinent to computer-based testing and the use of other media in testing, such as the test taker's familiarity with technology and the test format, should be addressed in their design and use. (p. 149)

Clearly, computer and multimedia testing need to be held to the same requirements of technical quality that all tests must meet.

There is, of course, an important counterexample that supports the exploration and expansion of computerized testing in some contexts. Increasingly, many skills used in real life are done in a computer environment. Without movement toward greater use of computer-based testing, the potential exists for CIV to creep into a paper-based testing environment because of unfamiliarity with paper test methods. For example, if a student who has become quite accustomed to using a keyboard and word processor to write is asked to compose an essay by hand, it is possible that he or she may be placed at a disadvantage owing to this "unfamiliar" testing condition.

The successful implementation of innovative item formats by many testing organizations indicates these problems are considered at the test design and use stages. For example, most of the examination programs that implemented a computer-based test began a long series of research before making the examination operational.

Although we are excited about the possibilities of innovative item types in computer-based testing and of the current progress in this field, we remain disappointed that there is not more research supporting the validity of these new formats. In particular, there is very little research on the social considerations of innovative item formats. This is unfortunate because computer familiarity is likely to be associated with socioeconomic status and other demographic variables. Rabinowitz and Brandt (2001) point out that opportunity to learn applies to taking a computerized test, too. As they describe:

> The first access factor is the need to assess using a mode of instruction the student commonly experiences.... If the first time students [encounter specific content is] during the actual test administration, the results would not be valid. Just as curriculum and instruction must incorporate the content standards to properly prepare students for tests, so, too, must students be familiar with the actual technology used for assessment... (p. 7)

More research is also needed on examinees' impressions of innovative item formats. Some important work has been done in this area (e.g., Bennett & Sebrechts, 1997; Bennett et al., 1999), but much more is needed. Further analysis of the cognitive demand employed by examinees when responding to innovative items will help to evaluate the degree to which they enhance construct representation.

In closing, it is safe to say that computer-based testing will increasingly become the testing medium of choice in the future. In many respects, the future is now; most large-scale testing programs are either computerized or moving toward implementation. The use of innovative item formats that take advantage of computerized technology to measure KSAs, and that make the measurement process more reflective of the real-world tasks they are designed to represent, is an important part of this technological transformation. Our hope is that innovative item formats prove to be more valid for measuring intended constructs. The possibilities technology offers for improving construct representation leaves us optimistic that innovations in item formats continue, and they lead to improvements in the accuracy of the decisions we make on the basis of test scores. However, these "improvements" are subject to empirical verification, and can only win the hearts of the measurement profession if they truly accomplish the objectives of increased construct representation and improved measurement efficiency.

ACKNOWLEDGMENT

Center for Educational Assessment Research Report No. 555. Amherst, MA: Center for Educational Assessment, University of Massachusetts. The authors thank Michael G. Jodoin for his comments on an earlier draft of this chapter.

REFERENCES

Ackerman, T. A., Evans, J., Park, K., Tamassia, C., & Turner, R. (1999). Computer assessment using visual stimuli: A test of dermatological skin disorders. In F. Drasgow and J. Olson-Buchanan (Eds.), *Innovations in computerized assessment* (pp. 137–150). Mahwah, NJ: Lawrence Erlbaum Associates.

American Educational Research Association (AERA), American Psychological Association (APA), & National Council on Measurement in Education (NCME). (1999). *Standards for educational and psychological testing*. Washington, DC: American Educational Research Association.

Bejar, I. (1991). A methodology for scoring open-ended architectural design problems. *Journal of Applied Psychology, 76*(4), 522–532.

Bennett, R. E., Morley, M., & Quardt, D. (2000). Three response types for broadening the conception of mathematical problem solving in computerized tests. *Applied Psychological Measurement, 24*(4), 294–309.

Bennett, R. E., Morley, M., Quardt, D., Rock, D. A., Singley, M. K., Katz, I. R., & Nhouyvanisvong, A. (1999). Psychometric and cognitive functioning of an under-determined computer-based response type for quantitative reasoning. *Journal of Educational Measurement, 36,* 233–252.

Bennett, R. E., & Rock, D. A. (1995). Generalizability, validity, and examinee perceptions of a computer-delivered formulating-hypotheses test. *Journal of Educational Measurement, 32,* 19–36.

Bennett, R. E., & Sebrechts, M. M. (1997). A computer-based task for measuring the representational component of quantitative proficiency. *Journal of Educational Measurement, 34,* 64–77.

Bennett, R. E., Ward, W. C., Rock, D. A., & LaHart, C. (1990). *Toward a framework for constructed-response items* (RR-90-7). Princeton, NJ: Educational Testing Service.

Braswell, J., & Kupin, J. (1993). Item formats for assessment in mathematics. In R. E. Bennett & W. C. Ward (Eds.), *Construction versus choice in cognitive measurement* (pp. 167–182). Hillsdale, NJ: Lawrence Erlbaum Associates.

Carey, P. (2001, April). *Overview of current computer-based TOEFL*. Paper presented at the annual meeting of the National Council on Measurement in Education, Seattle, WA.

Clauser, B. E., Margolis, M. J., Clyman, S. G. & Ross, L. P. (1997). Development of automated scoring algorithms for complex performance assessments: A comparison of two approaches. *Journal of Educational Measurement, 34,* 141–161.

Devore, R. (2002, April). *Considerations in the development of accounting simulations*. Paper presented at the annual meeting of the National Council on Measurement in Education, New Orleans, LA.

Dodd, B. G., & Fitzpatrick, S. J. (2002). Alternatives for scoring CBTs. In Mills, C. N., Potenza, M. T., Fremer, J. J., & Ward, W. C. (Eds.), *Computer-based testing: Building the foundation for future assessments* (pp. 215–236). Mahwah, NJ: Lawrence Erlbaum Associates.

Fitzgerald, C. (2001, April). *Rewards and challenges of implementing an innovative CBT certification exam program*. Paper presented at the annual meeting of the National Council on Measurement in Education, Seattle, WA.

Greaud, V., & Green, B. F. (1986). Equivalence of conventional and computer presentation of speed tests. *Applied Psychological Measurement, 10,* 23–34.

Green, B. F. (1988). Construct validity of computer-based tests. In H. Wainer & H. Braun (Eds.), *Test validity* (pp. 77–86). Hillsdale, NJ: Lawrence Erlbaum Associates.

Habbick, T. (1999, April). *Item variants in computer-based tests*. Paper presented at the annual meeting of the American Educational Research Association, Montreal, Canada.

Haladyna, T. M. (2004). *Developing and validating multiple-choice test items* (3rd ed.). Mahwah, NJ: Lawrence Erlbaum Associates.

Haladyna, T. M., & Downing, S. M. (1989). A taxonomy of multiple-choice item-writing rules. *Applied Measurement in Education, 2*(1), 37–50.

Haladyna, T. M., & Downing, S. M. (2004). Construct-irrelevant variance in high-stakes testing. *Educational Measurement: Issues and Practice, 23*(1), 17–27.

Hambleton, R. K. (2002). New CBT technical issues: Developing items, pretesting, test security, and item exposure. In C. N. Mills, M. T. Potenza, J. J. Fremer, & W. C. Ward (Eds.), *Computer-based testing: Building the foundation for future assessments* (pp. 193–203). Mahwah, NJ: Lawrence Erlbaum Associates.

Huff, K. L., & Sireci, S. G. (2001). Validity issues in computer-based testing. *Educational Measurement: Issues and Practice, 20*(3), 16–25.

Jodoin, M. G. (2003). Measurement efficiency of innovative item formats in computer-based testing. *Journal of Educational Measurement, 40,* 1–15.

Khaliq, S. N., & Sireci, S. G. (2004, April). *Evaluating essay scoring programs: Beyond percent agreement and Pearson correlations*. Paper presented at the annual meeting of the National Council on Measurement in Education, San Diego, CA.

Martinez, M. E. (1999). Cognition and the question of test item format. *Educational Psychologist, 34,* 207–218.

McBride, J. R., & Martin, J. T. (1983). Reliability and validity of adaptive ability tests in a military setting. In D. J. Weiss (Ed.), *New horizons in testing: Latent trait test theory and computerized adaptive testing* (pp. 223–236). New York: Academic Press.

Messick, S. (1988). The once and future issues of validity: Assessing the meaning and consequences of measurement. In H. Wainer & H. I. Braun (Eds.), *Test validity* (pp. 33–45). Hillsdale, New Jersey: Lawrence Erlbaum Associates.

Microsoft Corporation. (1998, September). *Procedures and guidelines for writing Microsoft Certification Exams.* Redmond, WA: Author.

Parshall, C. G., Davey, T., & Pashley, P. (2000). Innovative item types for computerized testing. In W. J. van der Linden and C. Glas (Eds.), *Computer-adaptive testing: Theory and practice* (pp. 129–148). Boston: Kluwer Academic Publishers.

Rabinowitz, S., & Brandt, S. (2001). Computer-based assessment: Can it deliver on its promise? *WestEd Knowledge Brief.* Downloaded January 30, 2005 from http://www.wested.org/cs/we/view/rs/568.

Sympson, J. B., Weiss, D. J., & Ree, M. J. (1983). *A validity comparison of adaptive testing in a military technical training environment* (AFHLR-TR-81-40). Brooks AFB, TX: Manpower and Personnel Division, Air Force Human Resources Laboratory.

Sympson, J. B., Weiss, D. J., & Ree, M. J. (1984). *Predictive validity of computerized adaptive testing in a military training environment.* A paper present at the annual convention of the American Educational Research Association, New Orleans, LA.

(AFHLR-TR-81-40). Brooks AFB, TX: Manpower and Personnel Division, Air Force Human Resources Laboratory.

Taylor, C., Jamieson, J., Eignor, D., & Kirsch, I. (1998, March). *The relationship between computer familiarity and performance on computer-based TOEFL test tasks* (TOEFL Research Reports 61). Princeton, NJ: Educational Testing Service. Retrieved January 17, 2005 from http://www.ets.org/ell/research/toeflresearch.html.

Taylor, C., Kirsch, I., Eignor, D., & Jamieson, J. (1999). Examining the relationship between computer familiarity and performance on computer-based language tasks. *Language Learning, 49,* 219–274.

Thompson, S., Thurlow, M., & Malouf, D. B. (2004). Creating better tests for everyone through universally designed assessments. *Journal of Applied Testing Technology.* Retrieved November 1, 2004 from http://www.testpublishers.org/atp_journal.htm.

Thompson, S., Thurlow, M., & Moore, M. (2003). Using computer-based tests with students with disabilities. *NCEO Policy Directions.* Minneapolis: University of Minnesota, National Center on Educational Outcomes.

Wainer, H., & Thissen, D. (1993). Combining multiple choice and constructed response test scores: Toward a Marxist theory of test construction. *Applied Measurement in Education, 6,* 103–118.

Walker, G., & Crandall, J. (1999, February). *Value added by computer-based TOEFL test* [TOEFL briefing]. Princeton, NJ: Educational Testing Service.

Zenisky, A. L., & Sireci, S. G. (2002). Technological innovations in large-scale assessment. *Applied Measurement in Education, 15,* 337–362.

15

Item Editing and Editorial Review

Rebecca A. Baranowski
American Board of Internal Medicine

If item writing is considered an art, then item editing is a craft, which can improve the overall validity of a test. A skilled editor should be much more than a proofreader and grammarian, however. The item writer and editor should work together throughout the test-development process, beginning with item-writer training. If writers learn and follow basic guidelines and principles, test items tend to be of higher quality. Editors should provide feedback as items are developed, allowing ample time for revisions. Then, as the test-development process nears completion, the editor should direct a multicomponent review to evaluate item content, format and structure, grammar, and fairness or bias. Field testing of items also is strongly recommended. Item revision after field testing remains a problematic aspect of test development. "Bad" items may be fixable, but "good" items may not necessarily become better.

Item writing frequently is referred to as an art (Cantor, 1987), the principles of which may be passed down from teacher to student (Downing & Haladyna, 1997). Item editing is an essential but often-neglected aspect of item development. Significant attention generally is focused on test content, administration, and scoring, all of which have clearly recognized links to test validity. Skilled editing improves the appearance, readability, and fairness of test items. Moreover, poor editing poses a threat to a test's validity. Items that are inaccurate, confusing to examinees, or otherwise flawed should not be included in scoring. They also generate bad feelings among examinees. Downing and Haladyna discuss important qualitative evidence for item editing and its implications for validity. They encourage a team approach: the item writer and professional editor working together to achieve high-quality questions. All too often, editing is seen as a final hurdle over which items and item writers must jump. This places the editor in an adversarial position, and the test items potentially suffer.

The relationship between item writer and editor should begin early in the test-development process. (See Downing, chap. 1, this volume, for a compete discussion of the process.) The editor should play a prominent role in the training of item writers. Thorough training makes the task of writing items less onerous and makes the editor's job easier as well. Activities such as developing style guidelines, preparing written instructions for item writers, conducting item-writing workshops, and providing feedback to writers introduce the editor as a partner, rather than a disciplinarian or enforcer of arcane rules. The editor should remain involved throughout the test-development process, providing advice and guidance as items are written, reviewed, and revised.

ITEM-WRITING PRINCIPLES

The item editor ideally should have an extensive knowledge of item-writing principles. A standard format and styles guidelines should be established by the test developer, and these then should be followed (Marrelli, 1995). This is particularly important when test items are generated by more than one person. Testing agencies typically have an in-house style manual that is distributed to item writers. A variety of general resources also are available to provide basic grammatical information and inform decisions regarding use of abbreviations, numerals, specialized terminology, and so on. Some frequently used texts include the *American Medical Association Manual of Style* (1998), *The Chicago Manual of Style* (University of Chicago Press Staff, 2003), *Strunk and White's Elements of Style* (Strunk, White, 2000), the American Mathematical Society's *Mathematics into Type* (Swanson, 1999), and the *Publication Manual of the American Psychological Association* (2001).

What constitutes a high-quality test item? Do we know one when we see one, or can we only identify one based on its performance statistics? The ideal item assesses appropriate content accurately, concisely, and consistently. Successful item writers are skilled communicators who are knowledgeable of subject matter and of their examinee population (Cantor, 1987). A well-constructed and well-written multiple-choice item can assess simple cognitive processes (i.e., recall knowledge), as well as higher order thinking: *synthesis* (the ability to recall specific knowledge, interpret information, and reach a conclusion) and *judgment* (the ability to recall specific knowledge, interpret information, reach a conclusion, and take an action). The multiple-choice item has high reliability per hour of testing time (Schuwirth & van der Vleuten, 2003). This chapter focuses on single-best-answer multiple-choice items, although much of the information is applicable to other item formats (see Haladyna, Downing, & Rodriguez, 2002), including performance assessments.

The multiple-choice item has two or three components: the *stem* (problem/case presentation), the *lead line* (question task), and the *response options* (correct answer/key and foils/distractors). Items assessing recall knowledge do not have a stem. Rather, they simply pose a question directly. For example:

> Which of the following is the most important responsibility of the item editor?

Item writers may attempt to justify the importance of or otherwise disguise a recall question by adding a stem. For example:

> The editor plays an important role in the test-development process. The editor and item writer should work together to develop a high-quality test. Which of the following is the most important responsibility of the item editor?

This introduction does not enhance the item or transform it into an assessment of higher order thinking. The additional sentences waste valuable examinee time and may decrease test performance. Frary (1995) suggests that this may be an unconscious attempt to continue teaching while testing, so item writers should be reminded of the important distinction between these tasks.

Items assessing synthesis and judgment do require a stem that presents a problem or scenario. Avoid "window dressing"—the stem should be clear, concise, and free of superfluous details, but it must include all information necessary for a competent examinee to select the correct answer. Writing complex stems, such as for medical tests, can be particularly challenging in this regard because of the natural tendency to use a real patient as the basis for a test item. It is important to remember that clinical stems are "convenient fictions not reflections of real-world ambiguity" (R. F. LeBlond, personal communication, September 19, 2003). A better tactic is to abstract the important principle from a patient case, then write an item that tests that principle directly. Avoid "red herrings" intended to confuse or trick the examinee.

Interpretation of audio/visual material may form the basis for a multiple-choice item. However, the material should convey the intended point clearly and should not deal with trivia. The item should be designed so that the examinee must utilize the material to answer the question correctly. Examinees may tend to overinterpret such material, so it should be reproduced carefully, with as little distortion as possible.

The lead line poses a precise task for the examinee, who should know what is being asked before reading the options (Marrelli, 1995). In other words, after reading the stem and lead line, an examinee should be able to state the correct answer, even before seeing the options. Thus, "Which of the following statements is correct?" is a particularly flawed lead line. "Which of the following statements is correct regarding X?" is little better because it also fails to focus the examinee's thinking adequately. A complete sentence is favored as the lead line, rather than a phrase intended to be completed by the correct option. Examples of well-written lead lines include the following:

Which of the following best explains this situation? — Assesses synthesis
Which of the following is the most likely diagnosis? — Assesses synthesis
Which of the following is the best management plan? — Assesses judgement
Which of the following actions should you take next? — Assesses judgement

Negative language should be avoided in the lead line. For example:

Which of the following statements is FALSE regarding X?
Which of the following outcomes is LEAST likely to occur?
All of the following actions are indicated EXCEPT...

Invariably, when such an item is reviewed by a group of content experts, at least one person misinterprets it. With the added pressure during a test administration, anxious examinees may be even more prone to misreading and selecting the wrong response. As Cantor (1987) reminds the testing community, "A good test item measures examinees' ability to recall a central theme, not their ability to take tests."

The response options are the final component of a test item. In addition to the correct answer, several incorrect but plausible distractors must be written. The options should be homogeneous—parallel in construction and of roughly the same length and complexity. Textbook, verbatim phrasing, and stereotyped phraseology should be avoided (Haladyna, 2004; Kehoe, 1995b). These serve to clue even less-proficient examinees. Another common flaw in item writing is to make the correct answer more detailed than the distractors. For example:

Which of the following activities is the most important responsibility of the item editor?
(A) Scheduling dates for test administration
(B) Ensuring that test items conform to recognized principles of test construction, are grammatically sound, and assess content accurately and concisely
(C) Arranging payment for item writers
(D) Developing rationales for test items

Option (B), the correct answer, is more complex than the other options. This level of detail serves as a strong clue for the testwise examinee. This items also is flawed because "most important" is a highly subjective concept—an item writer may select option (C) as the correct answer!

The appropriate number of options has been the subject of considerable debate. Four or five options—the correct answer plus three or four distractors—traditionally have been recommended. Kehoe (1995b) suggests that the struggle to find a fifth option often outweighs any benefit that option might have on item performance. Fewer functional distractors (i.e., those selected by some examinees) are preferable to more options that remain unselected. But, how few are too few? A cursory review of many tests often shows that only three of the four or five options attract more than 3% to 5% of examinees (S. M. Downing, personal communication, July 28, 2004). Three-option items have strong advocates (Delgado, 1998; Downing & Haladyna, 1997; Haladyna, 2004; Haladyna & Downing, 1993; Trevisan, Sax, & Michael, 1994), although they are most appropriate for high-ability examinees. Aamodt and McShane (1992) found that three-option items are slightly easier than four-option items and require significantly less time to complete. One three-option item is useful in a variety of settings:

Which of the following outcomes in feature Y is most likely to occur with event X?
(A) Increase
(B) Decrease
(C) No change

The number of options may vary from item to item within a test; no psychometric advantage has been documented when all items have the same number of options (Frary, 1995). Options should be ordered logically: in alphabetical or numeric order, by time sequence, or other subject grouping. Distractors should reflect common misconceptions or outdated information. They may be partially correct, but the correct answer must be the best response to the question. Distractors should not focus on trivia or be nonsensical. As with lead lines, options should be phrased positively. If it is absolutely necessary to use a word such as NOT or EXCEPT, it should be highlighted (e.g., capitalized) to minimize the possibility of being misread by examinees. Negative options following a negative lead line are especially problematic. Although such items may appear to perform adequately, it is likely that the better examinees, who tend to score higher on the overall test, are more capable of sorting out the complexities of a double negative (Frary, 1995). Imprecise probability terms such as *often, frequently, rarely,* and *occasionally* are interpreted differently by individuals and should be used cautiously (Case, 1988; Kong, Octo Barnett, Mosteller, & Youtz, 1986). More precise terms, but not overly so, are preferable. For example:

At least 75% — more specific than *frequently* but less of a clue than 77%
The majority of cases — more specific than *often* but less of a clue than 54%
Less than 5% — more specific than *rarely* but less of a clue than 2%

Ranges also may be used, but be sure that the values do not overlap and are separated by sufficient magnitude. Absolute terms such as *all, always, never,* and *only* should not be used. A testwise examinee knows that such absolutes are rare, so options containing these words are easily recognized as incorrect.

Avoid *All of the above* as an option. Its use can enable examinees who have only partial knowledge to answer the item correctly. *None of the above* also should be discouraged because it too it rewards examinees with knowledge deficiencies or misinformation (Gross, 1994). It is impossible to know what the examinee is thinking when he or she selects this option—it might be exactly what the item writer was thinking, or it could be a completely different response. The best response should be listed among the options to prevent examinees from receiving undeserved credit. If an item writer argues that the best response would be too obvious among the distractors, then perhaps better distractors are needed or the entire item should be reworked. (See Livingston, chap. 19, this volume, for a discussion of statistical methods to evaluate test items, including distractors.)

REVIEWING TEST ITEMS

Even the most carefully written test items, including those crafted by experienced item writers, should be reviewed extensively prior to their administration. Asking a colleague to review items can be helpful to the writer and ultimately the items. Kehoe (1995b) acknowledges the feeling of relief that comes over writers after their item-writing assignment is completed, but cautions against regarding the items as finalized. Rather, item writers should be encouraged to "review, reflect, and rewrite" (R. F. LeBlond, personal communication, September 19, 2003).

Haladyna et al. (2002) presented an extensive taxonomy of "Guidelines/Rules/Suggestions/Advice" that covers all aspects of item writing. This comprehensive list is an excellent resource for both experienced and novice item writers. One point, "Allow time for editing and other types of item revisions," is particularly relevant to the current discussion. Proofreading is essential as a final check of items, but editing and revising should occur throughout the test-development process, not just before the test is published or administered. Late changes may be made hastily and could do more harm than good. Experienced writers often put aside newly written items for a brief period of time. Then, when they re-read the items, flaws can become more apparent. This, of course, assumes that item writing begins well in advance of the deadline or examination date.

Haladyna (2004) describes several specific steps that should occur during the item-review process. A review of content is an appropriate initial step. Specifically, the reviewer(s) should confirm that each item assesses appropriate and important information. A detailed content outline for the test and specific item-writing assignments help to steer the test-development process in the right direction. If item content is deemed unacceptable, the item—no matter how well written—should not be used. Such drastic action can be difficult for both the item writer and the test developer, given that a considerable amount of time and effort likely has been invested.

A review for adherence to accepted item-writing principles also should occur. Items that violate one or more of the principles should be examined closely and revised as needed or discarded. Schrock and Mueller (1982) studied test items that violated several item writing principles, including complete versus incomplete lead lines and presence versus absence of extraneous material in the stem. They found no significant difference between items with a complete sentence as the lead line and those with an incomplete sentence. However, inclusion of extraneous material resulted in lower mean scores and longer completion times. Inclusion of such material likely places too much importance on reading comprehension (Kehoe, 1995b). Downing (2002) found that flawed items were approximately seven percentage points more difficult than nonflawed items measuring the same content. Further, lower achieving students had greater difficulty with these flawed items than did their higher achieving peers. A number of other studies (e.g., Board & Whitney, 1972; Crehan & Haladyna, 1991; Rachor & Gray, 1996; Schmeiser & Whitney, 1975; Sireci, Wiley, & Keller, 1998; Violato, 1991; Weiten, 1984) also have explored the effects of rule violation. Most of these authors report no or very weak overall effects of rule violations.

An editorial review is another essential aspect of the overall item-review process. The *Standards for Educational and Psychological Testing* (American Educational Research Association [AERA], American Psychological Association [APA], & National Council on Measurement in Education [NCME], 1999) do not specifically address item editing—an oversight that fails to recognize sloppy writing as a nuisance variable that can threaten test reliability and validity. Computer spelling checkers can identify some spelling and grammatical problems, but errors in technical language are missed. A correctly spelled word that is used in the wrong context is also not identified; for example, a *correctly spilled word* or a *correctly spelled work* are both acceptable to a computer. The professional editor should address mechanics (e.g., spelling, use of abbreviations), grammar, clarity, and style (e.g., active voice, positive statements in lead lines and options). Computation of the reading level of test items also may be appropriate. In a test of general knowledge administered to nearly 1,000 undergraduate students, Green (1983) reported that language difficulty had an insignificant effect on item difficulty. Nevertheless, Marrelli (1995) recommends a reading level that is at least two grade levels below that of the examinee population. Unnecessary linguistic complexity is particularly important if the population includes examinees who are less proficient in English (see Abedi, chap. 17, this volume).

The answer key also must be checked carefully. Item editing often necessitates reordering of options, and the key must be updated to reflect such changes. Content experts should ensure that the keyed answer is absolutely correct. Many testing agencies require item writers to submit references to document the correct answer. This can be helpful in resolving concerns about the accuracy of the items. If reviewers ultimately disagree, however, the item should not be used. Some testing experts suggest that the correct answer be positioned on as random a basis as possible (Kehoe, 1995b). Others argue that placement of correct answers does not significantly affect validity (Bresnock, Graves, & White, 1989).

Another facet of item review is a sensitivity analysis to ensure fairness and eliminate bias. *Bias* occurs when some characteristic of an item results in differential performance for individuals of the same ability but of different genders or from different ethnic or cultural groups. Classic examples of potentially biased items are ones that refer to machinery- or sports-related information, which may be less familiar to female than to male examinees. Tests should include an appropriate balance of multicultural material and an appropriate gender representation (Educational Testing Service, 2003). Further, items should not contain "offensive, demeaning, or emotionally charged" material (Hambleton & Rogers, 1995). Stereotyping should be avoided. Such material may result in differential item functioning, which jeopardizes the validity of the test. (See Zieky, chap. 16, this volume, for a complete discussion of fairness reviews.)

The final element of item review is that provided by the examinees themselves. It is nearly impossible to estimate how an item will perform until it actually is used in a test. In a classroom setting, students should have the opportunity to review and discuss a test after it has been administered and scored. Ambiguous wording, alternative correct answers, or other item flaws may surface during these discussions. Large-scale and high-stakes examinations generally conduct a field test or pretest of new items. Field testing also may help to uncover flawed items. A convenient rule of thumb is to write at least twice as many items as ultimately needed, so that all flawed items can be discarded (Marrelli, 1995). It also may be useful to generate more items in areas that have been difficult to test in the past.

"IMPROVING" TEST ITEMS

After items have been field tested or after an examination has been administered, test developers face the difficult issue of what to do about flawed items. They can be discarded, of course, but this represents a substantial loss of time and effort. Thus, attempts generally are made to improve items. Further, the *Standards* (AERA, APA, & NCME, 1999) recommend periodic review of tests to ensure that items remain valid. This may be particularly important for tests in fields such as medicine, where scientific knowledge advances rapidly.

Testing experts often recommend eliminating or replacing options that are not selected by examinees because the unselected options do not contribute to the item's ability to discriminate among examinees (Kehoe, 1995a). A further justification for eliminating nonfunctioning options is to reduce overall reading time for examinees (Reshetar, Mills, Norcini, & Guille, 1998). Changes involving options suggest the need for another field test.

Overall, though, little is known about the impact of rewriting items, and it is difficult to determine which types of changes require repeat field testing (Brown, Frank, Pownall, & Anderson, 2003). O'Neill (1986) reported no significant difference in item performance when "stylistic manipulations" (i.e., abbreviations, symbols, generic versus proprietary drug names) were made. Dawson-Saunders et al. (1992) found that changes in English usage and medical terminology resulted in small but sometimes significant effects on item performance. It, therefore, seems unwise and inappropriate to assume that "minor" changes do not alter performance. Examinees are best served when all changes are field tested again, but this may not be practical or feasible in all situations. Brown and colleagues (2003) recommend taking adequate time for reviewing and revising prior to field testing. Similarly, Reshetar and colleagues (1998) suggest that time is better spent in generating new items rather than rewriting flawed ones. Further research is needed to clarify the effects of item revision; at this time, "if it ain't broke, don't fix it" clearly is the safest approach to rewriting test items.

SUMMARY

Many elements come together to create a high-quality, valid test. Among these are well-trained item writers and well-edited items. Adequate time must be allowed for both of these activities, in addition to the time allotted for item writing. Editing is much more than proofreading and is best accomplished by a professional editor who is knowledgeable of item-writing principles. Writers and editors should work together throughout the test-development process, then should undertake a comprehensive review of the items as the test nears completion. Items should be field tested whenever feasible. Finally, revising items is best done prior to field testing; when revisions are made after field testing, item performance may be affected adversely.

ACKNOWLEDGMENTS

The author gratefully acknowledges the critical reviews and suggestions of Steven M. Downing, PhD, Linda E. Mills, and Thomas M. Haladyna.

REFERENCES

Aamodt, M. G., & McShane, T. D. (1992). A meta-analytic investigation of the effect of various test item characteristics on test scores and test completion times. *Public Personnel Management, 21*(2), 151–160.

American Educational Research Association (AERA), American Psychological Association(APA), & National Council on Measurement in Education (NCME). (1999). *Standards for educational and psychological testing.* Washington, DC: American Educational Research Association.

American Medical Association. (1998). *Manual of style.* (9th ed.). Chicago: Williams & Wilkins.

American Psychological Association. (2001). *Publication manual of the american psychological association.* (5th ed.). Washington, DC: American Psychological Association.

Board, C., & Whitney, D. R. (1972). The effect of selected por item-writing practices on multiple choice and validity. *Journal of Educational Measurement, 9*(3), 225–233.

Bresnock, A. E., Graves, P. E., & White, N. (1989). Multiple-choice testing: Question and response position. *Journal of Economic Education, 20*(3), 239–245.

Brown, L. M., Frank, L. A., Pownall, M. T., & Anderson, S. (2003). Do revisions to medical test questions change examinees' chances of answering the question correctly? Unpublished manuscript, American Board of Internal Medicine, Philadelphia, PA.

Cantor, J. A. (1987). Developing multiple-choice test items. *Training and Development Journal, 41*(5), 85–88.

Case, S. M. (1988). How often is "often"? The use of imprecise terms in exam items. Paper presented at the Annual Meeting of the Eastern Education Research Association; Miami Beach, FL.

Crehan, K., & Haladyna, T. M. (1991). The validity of two item-writing rules. *Journal of Experimental Education, 59*(2), 183–192.

Dawson-Saunders, B., Reshetar, R. A., Shea, J. A., Fierman, C. D., Kangilaski, R., & Poniatowski, P. A. (1992). Alterations to item text and effects on item difficulty and discrimination. Paper presented at the Annual Meeting of the National Council on Measurement in Education; San Francisco, CA.

Delgado, A. R. (1998). Further evidence favoring three-option items in multiple-choice tests. *European Journal of Psychological Assessment, 14*(3), 197–201.

Downing, S. M. (2002). Construct-irrelevant variance and flawed test questions: Do multiple-choice item writing principles make any difference? *Academic Medicine, 77*(1), S103–104.

Downing, S. M., & Haladyna, T. M. (1997). Test item development: Validity evidence from quality assurance procedures. *Applied Measurement in Education, 10*(1), 61–82.

Educational Testing Service (2003). Fairness Review Guidelines. Retrieved August 17, 2004, from http://www.ets.org.

Frary, R. B. (1995). More multiple-choice item writing do's and don'ts. *ERIC Digests 398238*. Retrieved March 16, 2004, from http://www.ericfacility.net/ericdigests/ed398238.html.

Green, K. E. (1983). Multiple-choice item difficulty: The effects of language and distracter set similarity. Paper presented at the Annual Meeting of the American Education Research Association; Montreal, Quebec.

Gross, L. J. (1994). Logical versus empirical guidelines for writing test items: The case of "none of the above." *Evaluation and the Health Professions, 17*(1), 123–126.

Haladyna, T. M. (2004). *Developing and validating multiple-choice test items* (3rd ed.). Hillsdale, NJ: Lawrence Erlbaum Associates.

Haladyna, T. M., & Downing, S. M. (1993). How many options is enough for a multiple-choice test item? *Educational and Psychological Measurement, 53*, 999–1010.

Haladyna, T. M., Downing, S. M., & Rodriguez, M. C. (2002). A review of multiple-choice item-writing guidelines for classroom assessment. *Applied Measurement in Education, 15*(3), 309–334.

Hambleton, R., & Rodgers, J. (1995). Item bias review. *ERIC Digests 398241*. Retrieved March 16, 2004, from http://www.ericfacility.net/ericdigests/ed398241.html.

Kehoe, J. (1995a). Basic item analysis for multiple-choice tests. *ERIC Digests 398237*. Retrieved from March 16, 2004, from http://www.ericfacility.net/ericdigests/ed398237.html.

Kehoe, J. (1995b). Writing multiple-choice tests items. *ERIC Digests 398236*. Retrieved March 16, 2004, from http://www.ericfacility.net/ericdigests/ed398236.html.

Kong, A, Octo Barnett, G., Mosteller, F., & Youtz, C. (1986). How medical professional evaluate expressions of probability. *New England Journal of Medicine, 315*(12), 740–744.

Marelli, A. E. (1995). Writing multiple-choice test items. *Performance and Instruction, 34*(8), 24–29.

O'Neill, K. A. (1986). The effect of stylistic changes on item performance. Paper presented at the Annual Meeting of the American Educational Research Association, San Francisco, CA.

Rachor, R. E., & Gray, G. T. (1996). Must all stems be green? A study of two guidelines for writing multiple choice stems. Paper presented at the Annual Meeting of the American Educational Research Association, New York, NY.

Reshetar, R., Mills, L., Norcini, J., & Guille, R. (1998). Is it worth the time to attempt fixing an item? Paper presented at the Ottawa Conference in Medical Education, Philadelphia, PA.

Schmeiser, C. B., & Whitney, D. R. (1975). Effect of two selected item-writing practices on test difficulty, discrimination, and reliability. *Journal of Experimental Education, 43*(3), 30–34.

Schrock, T. J., & Mueller, D. J. (1982). Effects of violating three multiple-choice item construction principles. *Journal of Educational Research, 75*(5), 314–318.

Schuwirth, L. W., & van der Vleuten, C. P. M. (2003). Written assessment. *British Medical Journal, 326*(7390), 643–645.

Sireci, S. G., Wiley, A., & Keller, L. A. (1998). An empirical evaluation of selected multiple-choice item writing guidelines. Paper presented at the Annual Meeting of the Northeastern Education Research Association, Ellenville, NY.

Strunk, W., Jr, White, E. B., & Angell, R. (2000). *The elements of style.* (4th ed.). Needham Heights, MA: Allyn & Bacon.

Swanson, E., O'Sean, A., & Schleyer, A. (1999). *Mathematics into type* (Updated ed.). Providence, RI: American Mathematical Society.

Trevisan, M. S., Sax, G., & Michael, W. B. (1994). Estimating the optimum number of options per item using an incremental option paradigm. *Educational & Psychological Measurement, 54*(1), 86–91.

University of Chicago Press Staff. (2003). *The Chicago manual of style* (15th ed.). Chicago: The University of Chicago Press.

Violata, C. (1991). Item difficulty and discrimination as a function of stem completeness. *Psychological Reports, 69*(3, Pt 1), 739–743.

Weiten, W. (1984). Violation of selected item constructin principles in education measurement. *Journal of Experimental Education, 52*(3), 174–178.

16

Fairness Review in Assessment

Michael Zieky
Educational Testing Service

Until the 1960s little attention was paid to fairness in assessment. From the 1960s onward, however, fairness has become a major concern in the design, development, and use of assessments. A major tool in making fair tests is a fairness review to find construct-irrelevant sources of difficulty that may interfere with validity for various groups of test takers. This chapter discusses six fairness review guidelines: (1) Treat people with respect; (2) Minimize the effects of construct-irrelevant knowledge or skills; (3) Avoid material that is unnecessarily controversial, inflammatory, offensive, or upsetting; (4) Use appropriate terminology to refer to people; (5) Avoid stereotypes; and (6) Represent diversity in depictions of people. In addition to completing fairness reviews, test developers should treat all test takers equally, provide accommodations for people with disabilities, obtain diverse input, use an empirical indicator of item fairness, obtain validation information, and help score recipients use the test results appropriately.

This chapter describes what a fairness review is, why it is done, and how to do it. This chapter is intended for test developers. The focus is on the actions that test developers should take to help ensure the fairness of the tests that they make, rather than on theoretical discussions or descriptions of research studies. Some references are included for readers interested in more detailed information. This chapter is not intended to be a general treatise on good test development practices; however, because fairness and validity are so closely intertwined, the procedures required to make a fair test overlap considerably with the procedures required to make a good test.

The chapter begins with a brief review of the rapid growth of interest in test fairness since the 1960s. The chapter then discusses some of the more common meanings of fairness in assessment because it is impossible to have a rational discussion of test fairness unless there is some agreement about what is meant by a fair test. Unfortunately, there is still a great deal of disagreement about the meaning of fairness in the context of assessment. Many arguments about whether or not a test is fair have no resolution because the participants are using different definitions of fairness. The chapter describes in detail a definition of fairness based on validity because it is the most meaningful and useful definition for test developers.

Following a description of the rationale supporting fairness reviews, the bulk of the chapter focuses on important guidelines for performing fairness reviews and on procedures for maintaining the integrity of the fairness review process.

Fairness review alone, however, is insufficient to ensure that tests are fair. Fairness should be an important factor in decisions made about assessments from the planning stages through the uses made of the scores. Therefore, the chapter briefly discusses the actions that should be taken, in addition to fairness review, to help ensure the fairness of assessments.

BRIEF HISTORY

Burst of Interest

Measurement professionals paid little attention to fairness during the first half of the 20th century (Green, 1982). In the 1960s, however, fairness suddenly became a widespread concern among psychometricians and test developers. Cole (1993, p. 25) credited the civil rights era for the rush of interest in fairness, "because test and item bias concerns in their modern form grew out of this era, were responses to it, were influenced by it, and took their role as a standard part of the testing enterprise because of it." As Berk (1982, p.1) noted, "In the late 1960s and early 1970s psychometricians hastened to provide definitions of bias in terms of objective criteria, to develop rigorous and precise methods for studying bias, and to consider empirical investigations of test bias."

During that era, test publishers instituted fairness reviews, and many also began to use some empirical measures to help identify items that might be unfair. (See Angoff, 1993, for a discussion of the development of indicators of item bias. See Ramsey, 1993, for a discussion of the development of fairness review.)

Acceptance

During the 1980s and 1990s, fairness review became a widespread, expected aspect of professional test development. States that commissioned tests commonly established their own fairness review committees. Empirical measures to help identify items that might be unfair became widely used. The 1999 edition of the *Standards for Educational and Psychological Testing* (American Educational Research Association [AERA], American Psychological Association [APA], & National Council on Measurement in Education [NCME], p. 73) summarized the work on fairness in assessment at the end of the 20th century with considerable understatement by writing, "the amount of explicit attention to fairness in the design of well-made tests compares favorably to that of many alternative selection or evaluation methods." In fact, the amount of attention paid to the fairness of professionally made tests far exceeded and still exceeds the attention paid to the fairness of grades, interviews, letters of recommendation, and the like. For example, reviews of the fairness of every grade, empirical measures of the fairness of interview results whenever sample sizes permit, and ongoing studies of the reliability of letters of recommendation for various groups of applicants are unheard of, but all of those efforts to ensure fairness are commonly applied to professionally made items and tests.

Current Status

At the beginning of the 21st century, even though fairness remains a concern among test developers, the intense interest that psychometricians had shown in the topic appears to have abated somewhat (Cole & Zieky, 2001). Public interest in fairness, however, has been piqued by the No Child Left Behind (NCLB) legislation of 2001 and the concomitant increase in the use of tests for highly visible and controversial purposes. NCLB keeps group differences in test scores in public view because the law requires reporting of scores separately for different demographic groups such as Black students and White students. (See www.ed.gov/nclb [n.d.] for detailed information about NCLB.)

After more than a third of a century of intense work on fairness issues, how much progress has been made? As noted, by the end of the 20th century useful actions to help ensure fairness had become common among professional test developers. As I discuss in the next section, however, people still do not agree on what fairness is. In fact, some of the definitions in the literature are mutually contradictory so that a test that is fair by one definition is unfair according to other definitions. There is still no statistic that can prove whether or not a test item or a test is fair. Furthermore, attempts at maintaining fairness through fairness review have been attacked as censorship.

MEANINGS OF FAIRNESS

Lack of a Universal Definition

There is no definition of fairness in assessment that all people accept. The *Standards for Educational and Psychological Testing* (AERA, APA, & NCME, 1999, p. 80) states that fairness "is subject to different definitions and interpretations in different social and political circumstances." To add to the confusion, there is a large difference between the way many members of the measurement profession define fairness and the way many members of the general public define fairness (Cole & Zieky, 2001).

Score Differences

Many members of the general public define test fairness as equality of average scores across groups. According to that definition, if women score lower than men on average, then the tests are biased against women. If Black test takers score lower than White test takers on average, then the tests are biased against Black test takers, and so on.

The definition of fairness as equality of scores across groups is clear, popular, and wrong. It is wrong because it overlooks the possibility that there may be valid (real and relevant) differences between the groups in what the test is appropriately measuring. To demonstrate that differences alone are not proof of bias, consider yardsticks. Even though men and women have different average heights, yardsticks are not necessarily biased.

Psychometricians have for many years clearly and consistently rejected the definition of fairness based on equality of scores. Thorndike (1971, p. 64) stated, "The presence (or absence) of differences in mean score between groups ... tells us nothing directly about fairness." Shepard (1987, p. 178) was very clear in stating, "mean differences are not evidence of bias...." Cole and Zieky (2001, p. 375) summarized the issue by writing, "If the members of the measurement community currently agree on any aspect of fairness, it is that score differences alone are not proof of bias."

Mean score differences may indicate a problem with fairness, but the differences are only an indication that further review is needed, rather than proof of bias. If mean score differences are not a correct definition of fairness in assessment, what definition should be used?

Prediction and Selection

In the late 1960s and through the 1970s, psychometricians tried to define fairness in empirical terms. I describe four of the many proposed definitions to illustrate the different ways that fairness in assessment has been conceptualized.

In one of the earliest and most widely recognized attempts, Cleary (1968) defined fairness for tests used as predictors as a lack of systematic underprediction[1] or overprediction[2] for any group. Darlington (1971), however, proposed a model of fairness that purposefully overpredicted the criterion scores of selected groups to achieve what the users of the model considered fair representation for those groups.

Several other empirical definitions of fairness were based on the effects of using tests to select people. Two examples illustrate such definitions. Cole (1973) defined selection tests as fair if applicants in different groups who are able to succeed have the same chance of being selected. Linn (1973) defined selection tests as fair if the proportion of those accepted who succeed is the same across groups. Although the two definitions both seem appropriate (and seem to be quite similar to non-statisticians), no test is likely to satisfy both definitions simultaneously.

The empirical definitions of fairness have had little impact on actual test development practice because they are often mutually contradictory, because they depend on criteria that may be biased and unreliable, and because they depend on data that can be difficult to obtain. (See Petersen & Novick, 1976, and Shepard, 1982, for more information about empirical models of test fairness.)

The empirical definitions of fairness did not directly affect test construction because they are based on the outcomes of the use of completed tests. It is ironic that the empirical definitions of fairness produced by trained psychometricians and published in refereed journals have had very little practical effect on test construction, whereas, as discussed in the next section, the unsophisticated, subjective idea that fairness depends on how an item looks has had a major impact on test content in the United States.

Item Appearance

Many people believe that an item is unfair if it looks unfair. They believe that items are unfair if the items look as though they could cause a group of test takers to become alienated, angry, distracted, disturbed, fearful, offended, or otherwise upset. The definition of fairness based on the appearance of items is less than satisfactory because it is clearly subjective. Furthermore, there is seldom a match between reviewers' perceptions of item fairness and the actual performances of people in different groups on the item (Bond, 1993; Elliott, 1987).

In spite of its lack of objectivity and its lack of empirical justification, the definition of fairness based on the way items look has strongly influenced tests developed over the last 30 years or so because it led to the process of fairness review. Given the definition of fairness based on the way an item looks, the rationale for fairness review is clear and compelling. If it is possible to identify potentially unfair items by the way they appear, then test developers have a professional and moral obligation to find and replace or revise such items before the tests are administered.

---

[1] *Underprediction* is predicting a criterion score that is, on average, lower than the score actually achieved.
[2] *Overprediction* is predicting a criterion score that is, on average, higher than the score actually achieved.

Validity

The definition of fairness in assessment that is most meaningful and useful for test developers is based on validity. Shepard (1987, p. 179) made the point as clearly and as succinctly as possible, "Bias is defined as invalidity."

Anything that is construct irrelevant—not part of what the test is supposed to measure—is not valid. Therefore, "fairness requires that construct-irrelevant personal characteristics of test takers have no appreciable effect on test results or their interpretation" (ETS, 2002, p. 17). In short, anything that lowers the validity of a test for a group of test takers reduces the fairness of the test. Because fairness is linked to validity and validity is linked to the purpose of a test, an item may be fair for one purpose and unfair for a different purpose. Consider the following items:

1. How much is $1.8 \times 1,000$?
2. How many meters in 1.8 kilometers?

If the purpose of the item is to measure the ability to multiply with a decimal number, then item 1 is likely to be considered fair. Even though item 2 requires exactly the same mathematical operation, it is unfair for that purpose because it requires construct-irrelevant knowledge of the metric system and because such knowledge is not equally distributed across groups. Item 2 is fair, however, if the purpose of the item is to measure the ability to make conversions within the metric system. Note that the fairness of the item depends on its validity for a particular purpose rather than merely on its appearance.

The linking of fairness with validity has provided a meaningful theoretical and practical basis for fairness review. Rather than identifying test content that looks unfair to them, fairness reviewers have the much more defensible task of trying to identify test content that may cause invalid differences between groups. For example, even if it looks fair, an unnecessary graphic display in an item may make the item invalidly (and unfairly) more difficult for test takers with vision problems. Even if it looks fair, language in an item that is more difficult than necessary to meet the purpose of the item may make the item invalidly (and unfairly) more difficult for test takers who are deaf or who are English language learners. Even if it looks fair, construct-irrelevant knowledge that is required to answer an item correctly may make the item invalidly (and unfairly) more difficult for groups of people who tend to lack the construct-irrelevant knowledge.

The construct-irrelevant factors may be emotional as well as cognitive. As noted in the *ETS Fairness Review Guidelines* (2003)

> Offensive content may make it difficult for test takers to concentrate on the meaning of a reading passage or the answer to a test item, thus serving as a source of construct-irrelevant difficulty. Test takers may be distracted if they believe that a test advocates positions counter to their beliefs. Test takers may respond emotionally rather than logically to needlessly controversial material. (p. 7)

FAIRNESS REVIEW

Purpose of Fairness Review

The purpose of fairness review is to identify any construct-irrelevant factors in tests that might plausibly prevent the members of a group of test takers from responding to the tests in ways that allow appropriate inferences about the test takers' knowledge, skills, abilities, or other attributes. The driving force behind fairness review is validity, not political correctness.

Major test publishers in the United States have instituted some form of fairness review in an attempt to avoid content judged to be unfair and in an attempt to include content that reflects the diversity of the test-taking population. In fact, the process of fairness review has become so pervasive and encompassing that a backlash has formed. Ravitch (2003, p. 3) described fairness review as "an elaborate well-established protocol of beneficent censorship, quietly endorsed and broadly implemented by textbook publishers, testing agencies, professional associations, states, and the federal government."

The linkage of fairness and validity, however, weakens the claim that fairness review is censorship because when fairness review is done correctly anything required for valid measurement is allowed. As stated clearly in the *ETS Fairness Review Guidelines*, "material required for valid measurement is acceptable even if it includes topics, ideas, attitudes, images, or other content that the guidelines would otherwise prohibit" (2003, p. 8). The elimination of potentially construct-irrelevant factors in items is good test development practice, not inappropriate censorship.

There is a useful distinction between skills tests and content tests with respect to fairness review. Skills tests measure general skills such as reading comprehension, logical reasoning, or quantitative ability. Content tests measure specific subject matter such as biology, psychology, or history. Because general skills can be measured in many different contexts, there is very rarely a need to include material out of compliance with the guidelines. Content tests, on the other hand, must include whatever is required for valid measurement. A test for licensing physicians, for example, might contain material about abortion that would be inappropriate in a test of reading comprehension.

Groups

In the United States, test publishers have tended to focus their fairness reviews on groups of people defined on the basis of gender, race, ethnicity, national or regional origin, disability, religion, age, and economic status. There has been an emphasis on ensuring fairness for groups that have been historically disadvantaged: African Americans, Asian Americans, Hispanic Americans, Native Americans, and women.

FAIRNESS REVIEW GUIDELINES

Need for Guidelines

Fairness review should be done with respect to written guidelines. The guidelines serve several purposes. They make the reviews less subjective and help to ensure that all aspects of fairness are considered. In addition, written guidelines lessen the inevitable disputes between item writers and fairness reviewers. Saying that an item is unfair because it violates Guideline 2 in specified ways is much more defensible than saying an item is unfair because a reviewer happens to think it is unfair. More importantly, if the guidelines are shared with item writers and test development committees, the guidelines help to keep unsuitable material from being generated in the first place.

There are many sets of fairness review guidelines in use. The *Publication Manual of the American Psychological Association* (APA, 2001, pp. 370–374) cites 17 documents in its list of suggested readings concerning "nondiscriminatory language." Ravitch (2003, pp. 201–202) reviewed more than 20 different sets of guidelines from testing agencies, publishers, and government agencies. The various guidelines tend to be quite similar to one another. Often the same wording is found in different documents. As Ravitch (2003, p. 57) observed following her reviews of many sets of guidelines, "all test and textbook bias guidelines start to look alike."

Given the similarity of the various guidelines, I use the *ETS Fairness Review Guidelines* (2003) as the primary source in the following discussion of guidelines because the *ETS Guidelines* have been used operationally by hundreds of test developers as the basis for a formal, documented fairness review process since 1980, they have been applied to a large variety of widely used and highly prominent tests, and they have been expanded and refined over the years based on experience with their use. (The *ETS Fairness Review Guidelines* are available at www.ets.org.)

- **Guideline 1:** Treat people with respect.
- **Guideline 2:** Minimize the effects of construct-irrelevant knowledge or skills.
- **Guideline 3:** Avoid material that is unnecessarily controversial, inflammatory, offensive, or upsetting.
- **Guideline 4:** Use appropriate terminology to refer to people.
- **Guideline 5:** Avoid stereotypes.
- **Guideline 6:** Represent diversity in depictions of people.

Application of the Guidelines Outside of the United States

The discussions of the guidelines and the examples given below apply to fairness reviews of tests designed for use primarily in the United States. The discussions and examples reflect the concerns for fairness in a very diverse, democratic country. The six guidelines treated as general principles are likely to be appropriate in all countries, however. For example, it is difficult to conceive of a country that would deliberately include unnecessarily offensive or upsetting material in its tests, but what is considered offensive or upsetting is likely to vary from country to country. What is considered offensive in Saudi Arabia may be perfectly acceptable in Sweden. Therefore, for use outside of the United States, the six guidelines need to be augmented with locally appropriate interpretations and examples. The additions should be made by people who are very familiar with the culture(s) of the country in which the test will be used. (For more information about fairness review for tests constructed primarily for use in countries other than the United States, see *ETS International Principles for Fairness Review of Assessments*, 2004, available at www.ets.org.)

Treat People With Respect

The first guideline is very general and is intended to ensure that test takers are not distracted from their tasks on tests by content that they find insulting. Do not confront test takers with any words or images that are contemptuous, degrading, exclusionary, mocking, or the like concerning them, their families, or people they value, unless such content is required for valid measurement. Because test takers in the United States are so heterogeneous, the best practice is to treat all groups with respect unless doing so would interfere with valid measurement. (A history test, for example, may include source documents from the struggle for women's suffrage that would currently be considered derogatory toward women, if necessary to measure the intended construct.)

Avoid overrepresenting members of any group in contemptible, foolish, or criminal activities. For example, do not consistently show women as compulsive shoppers and men as educated consumers. Do not trivialize the real problems of a group by making fun of them. For example, do not use the debilitating effects of old age as a source of humor. Do not treat a group's strongly held beliefs as nonsensical. If it is necessary to point out that certain beliefs may be questionable, use an objective rather than a mocking tone.

Do not treat any group of people as innately superior to others. Avoid ethnocentrism, the attitude that one's own group is superior to other groups. For example, the phrase *culturally deprived* carries the ethnocentric implication that departures from the majority culture necessarily result in deprivation.

Do not treat the dominant majority's point of view as though it were held by all people, either overtly or by unstated assumptions. For example, the statement "All social workers should learn Spanish" is based on the inappropriate, unstated assumption that there are no social workers who are native speakers of Spanish. (There is also the problematic implication that an inordinate number of Spanish speakers are in need of help from social workers.)

Sometimes the problems in showing respect can be subtle. Consider the sentence, "The Navajo prefer to be called the Dineh." The sentence is inappropriate because it implies that the real name of the group is Navajo, but that the members of the group prefer a different name. Consider the sentence, "The Dineh are often referred to as the Navajo." The second sentence shows respect because it accepts the name preferred by the group as correct. (For more information about the first guideline, see ETS, 2003, pp. 10–11.)

Minimize the Effects of Construct-Irrelevant Knowledge or Skills

The point of the second guideline is to avoid requiring any knowledge, skill, or ability to answer an item unless it is relevant to the construct that is being measured. (See Haladyna & Downing, 2004, for a discussion of sources of construct-irrelevant variance.)

Avoiding construct-irrelevant material is an important aspect of good test development practice and contributes to validity for all test takers. If the construct-irrelevant knowledge or skill is not equally available to all groups of test takers, however, the items that require the construct-irrelevant material contribute to invalid group differences. In short, the items are unfair.

Among common sources of potentially construct-irrelevant sources of difficulty are the unnecessary uses of visual stimuli. Unless the intent of the item is to measure skill in reading maps, charts, or graphs, do not include such materials in an item. (It is, of course, acceptable to include maps, charts, or graphs, if skill in reading such materials is part of the intended construct.)

Similarly, avoid unnecessarily difficult words, figures of speech, idioms, or syntactic structures. Use the most common vocabulary, the most straightforward language, and the most uncomplicated syntax consistent with valid measurement. For tests that measure occupational knowledge and skills, the linguistic demands of the test should not exceed the linguistic demands of the occupation. (Difficult language is, of course, acceptable if it is the purpose of the test to measure the ability to comprehend such language. See Abedi, chap. 17, this volume, for more information on avoiding unnecessarily difficult language.)

Tests of general verbal skills should not measure specialized vocabulary better known by members of some groups than by members of other groups. It is difficult, however, to differentiate between words that are part of the construct of general vocabulary and words that are too specialized to be included in that construct.

For example, male test takers are currently more likely to be familiar with specialized words related to tools and machinery than are female test takers. Most test developers would probably agree that *nail* is acceptable as general vocabulary and that *brad* is too specialized; that *drill* is acceptable and that *chuck* is too specialized. Test developers might well disagree about *bit*, however. Even though the borderlines between general vocabulary and specialized vocabulary are fuzzy, strive to avoid specialized vocabulary unless knowledge of such words is part of the construct to be measured.

In addition to tools and machinery, the types of vocabulary likely to cause construct-irrelevant difficulty include elitisms such as *penthouse*, uncommon financial vocabulary such as *arbitrage*, uncommon farm-related words such as *thresher*, specialized legal words such as *tort*, specialized words related to weapons such as *rapier*, specialized political words such as *alderman*, and regionalisms such as *grinder* or *hoagie*, in place of *sandwich*.

Technical terms such as *lumen* or *vacuole* are not acceptable if the construct is general vocabulary. Furthermore, avoid requiring knowledge of specialized vehicles such as *ketch*, or of parts of vehicles such as *cam* to answer an item correctly in a general skills test. Do not require specialized knowledge of words associated with sports unless such knowledge is part of the intended construct.

In a country as diverse as the United States, assuming knowledge of a common religion is a likely source of construct-irrelevant difficulty. Do not require knowledge of a religion to answer an item correctly unless the knowledge is part of the intended construct. A complication is that much art, music, and literature include religious themes. In such cases, items may include the aspects of religion taught in art, music, or literature courses, but not the aspects of religion taught only in religion courses. In any case, materials about religion should be as objective as possible. Do not favor or disparage any religion in tests made for use in the United States.

If tests are to be administered outside of the United States or to people who are new to the United States, do not assume that all test takers are familiar with unique aspects of United States culture. Unnecessarily requiring knowledge of United States geography, institutions, branded products, and the like may be a source of construct-irrelevant differences between groups.

Illustrations designed to aid understanding may actually confuse test takers from countries other than the United States and cause construct-irrelevant difficulty if the illustrations contradict cultural expectations. For example, in illustrations of college classrooms, students with little experience in the United States may become confused about the roles depicted if the professors are dressed as informally as the students.

It is important to keep in mind that the lists of topics to be avoided apply only when the topics are not required for valid measurement. Tests made for many military occupational specialties validly include specialized words related to weapons; tests made for mechanics validly include specialized words related to tools and machinery; tests made for physical education teachers validly include many specialized terms related to sports; tests made for accountants validly include specialized financial terminology; and so forth. (For more information about the second guideline, see ETS, 2003, pp. 11–14.)

Avoid Material That Is Unnecessarily Controversial, Inflammatory, Offensive, or Upsetting

The third guideline is what many people still think of as the sole purpose of fairness review. Early work on fairness review focused on items that were offensive or upsetting because such items looked unfair. The current rationale is that such material might serve as a source of construct-irrelevant difficulty by distracting test takers at a time when they should be devoting their full attention to demonstrating what they know and can do.

What people consider too controversial, inflammatory, offensive, or upsetting for use in assessments differs in different groups and in different localities. Some states, for example, believe that the theory of evolution is too sensitive to include on tests for school children, whereas other states accept it (Ravitch, 2003). There are some topics, however, that are so commonly considered problematic in the United States that they should be included on tests only if required for valid measurement. For example, avoid the unnecessary inclusion of topics as controversial, offensive, or upsetting as abortion, genocide, rape, and torture.

In addition, there are aspects of some topics that should be avoided unless required for valid measurement, even though other aspects of those topics might be acceptable. For example, avoid the shocking or horrible effects of accidents, illnesses, or disasters even though it is acceptable to include other aspects of those topics such as the prevention of accidents. Similarly, avoid the gruesome details of death, suicide, or violence unless they are required to measure the intended construct.

Do not use test content as a platform to support one side of a controversial issue unless required to do so for valid measurement. Test takers who hold opposing views may be unfairly disadvantaged.

If tests are to be used in several countries, it is important to consider regional differences in what might be considered offensive or controversial. For example, many images considered appropriate in the United States, such as adolescent girls playing sports in shorts and T shirts, may be offensive in some other countries. Certain topics considered normal in the United States, such as women working outside of the home, may be highly controversial in some other countries.

Culture-specific taboos should be honored to the extent possible in tests if validity can be maintained. For example, some groups do not eat pork and other groups do not eat beef. Therefore, if the stimulus material for a set of comprehension items is a recipe, use a recipe for a vegetarian dish rather than for a pork or beef dish.

Some states have specified numerous topics to avoid in their skills tests. The states appoint people to fairness review committees who are sensitive to the concerns of various constituencies within the state. The results of the committees' deliberations are sometimes surprising to people who are less familiar with the concerns of the state's citizens. For example, state fairness review committees have excluded topics such as birthday celebrations, social dancing, fossils and geologic ages, Halloween, junk food, snakes, spiders, and supernatural beings (Ravitch, 2003). Test developers who are working on tests commissioned by a state should determine which topics the state chooses to exclude. (For more information about the third guideline, see ETS, 2003, pp. 14–17.)

Use Appropriate Terminology

The fourth guideline is included because people, including test takers, are very sensitive about the labels used to describe them. If labels are necessary, try to use the terms that group members prefer.

Because group members may prefer different labels and because the preferred labels may change over time, it is safest to avoid labeling people. For example, *African American* and *Black* are currently both acceptable even though some members of the group prefer one or the other of the terms. *Negro* and *Colored*, however, are acceptable only in historical contexts or in the names of organizations. In any case, avoid derogatory labels even if some group members use the terms. If labels are used, it is generally preferable to use group names as adjectives rather than nouns. For example, "Black students in college" is preferable to "Blacks in college."

In general, refer to people objectively. Avoid both derogatory terms and euphemisms. For people with disabilities, put the emphasis on the person rather than on the disability. For example *people who are blind* is preferable to *the blind*. Use objective terms rather than emotionally loaded labels. For example, *person with AIDS* is preferable to *victim of AIDS*. Avoid overly euphemistic, condescending language such as *special* or *challenged*.

Use specific group labels rather than more general ones whenever the specific terms are more informative. For example, when group identification is relevant, *Japanese American* or

Chinese American is preferable to *Asian American*; *Cuban American* or *Mexican American* is preferable to *Hispanic American*; and so forth.

Parallelism is a very important concept in the treatment of labels for men and women in test materials used in the United States. Address men and women in the same way. For example, if men are addressed by last name and title, women should be addressed by last name and title as well. If women are addressed by first name only, men should also be addressed by first name only. Refer to women as *wives* or *mothers* only in contexts in which men would be called *husbands* or *fathers*. Do not describe the members of one group in terms of their accomplishments and members of the other group in terms of their appearances. Do not refer to adult women as *girls*, and do not refer to adult men as *boys*.

Terms for occupations and roles should include both genders. *Scientist*, for example, includes both men and women. It is not appropriate to refer to a *woman scientist*. Replace terms such as *fireman* and *mailman* with inclusive terms such as *fire fighter* and *mail carrier*. Use of generic *man* to refer to human beings has become unacceptable. Replace terms such as *man made* with gender free words such as *synthetic*.

When valid measurement requires people to be identified by sexual orientation, use *bisexual, gay, lesbian,* or *transgendered* as appropriate. Use *homosexual* only in a scientific or historical context. Avoid *queer* in the context of sexual orientation. (For more information about the fourth guideline, see ETS, 2003, pp. 17–22.)

Avoid Stereotypes

Stereotypes assign characteristics to people solely on the basis of group membership and overlook individual differences within a group and similarities across groups. Stereotypes are so pervasive that they are at times difficult to recognize. A reference to a *man-sized job*, for example, invokes stereotypes about male and female capabilities. Avoid stereotyping groups as superior or inferior to other groups with respect to attributes such as honesty, generosity, wisdom, industriousness, squeamishness, and the like.

Do not use stereotypes to make the wrong answers in multiple-choice items attractive. Test takers who select the wrong answer do so because they believe it to be correct, which serves to reinforce the stereotype.

It is important to distinguish between a portrayal that shows members of a group in a traditional role and a portrayal of a stereotype. For example, showing a woman engaged in a traditional role such as child care or cooking is not necessarily stereotypical. If the only depictions of women are in traditional roles, however, then the test is inappropriately reinforcing a stereotype. (For more information about the fifth guideline, see ETS, 2003, pp. 22–23.)

Represent Diversity

The sixth guideline is meant to allow test takers to see themselves reflected in the test. Test takers who are not members of the dominant group should not be made to feel excluded or alienated from the test. For example, in skills tests made for use in the United States, try to have roughly half the items that mention people represent women. To the extent possible, try to balance the status of the men and women mentioned in the test. The mention of a famous man (e.g., Einstein) is not appropriately balanced by the use of a generic female name (e.g., Jane).

For content tests, the gender balance is generally determined by the content. For example, a licensing test for nurses should more or less reflect the gender distribution of members of the occupation and include fewer men than women.

Some proportion of the items that mention people should portray members of racial and ethnic groups in the test-taking population that have historically been underrepresented. Ideally, for example, if Black people are 12% of the test-taking population, roughly 12% of the items that mention people in a skills test should depict Black people. Realistically, however, it is probably not possible to proportionately represent all groups in the test-taking population in every test. For example, in a test with only a single reading passage that mentions people, it is possible that only one group could be represented in each form. Try to represent the test-taking population across test forms as well as possible within the constraints imposed by the test specifications. (For more information about the sixth guideline, see ETS, 2003, pp. 23–24.)

PROCEDURES FOR FAIRNESS REVIEW

Need for Procedures

Merely having fairness review guidelines is insufficient. The guidelines must be applied as consistently and objectively as possible. There must be an agreed-upon way of resolving the disputes that inevitably occur when the guidelines are applied. Therefore, it is important to have a set of written procedures to shape the application of the fairness review guidelines.

Given the wide variety of tests and the wide variety of ways in which those tests are constructed, there is no single set of procedures that is appropriate for all fairness reviews. There are, however, certain broad principles that should guide the development of the procedures.

Principles

The following principles for conducting fairness review are based on the procedures that evolved over more than 20 years at ETS. The procedures are fully described in the *ETS Fairness Review Guidelines* (2003, pp. 25–27).

Train item writers and fairness reviewers to follow the written fairness review guidelines that have been adopted. Training item writers as well as reviewers increases the likelihood that acceptable items will be written. Training in the application of the guidelines should focus on marginal items that lead to disagreements rather than on obviously flawed items.

The fairness reviewer should have no incentive to provide favorable reviews. For example, a person responsible for completing a test that is behind schedule is not an appropriate reviewer. To help ensure that the fairness reviewer is as objective as possible, do not allow the person who requests a fairness review to select the particular person who will do the review.

Give the fairness reviewer the test specifications and a description of the construct to be measured. The reviewer should see the version of the items that the test takers will see, including any related stimulus materials. (It is often useful to obtain a fairness review of stimulus materials before time and money are spent writing items based on potentially inappropriate materials. Therefore, include a provision in the fairness review procedures for reviewing stimulus materials without items. The items that are eventually written still need a fairness review.)

Document the results of the reviews. The reviews should be done with respect to the fairness review guidelines. An item should not be challenged merely because a reviewer does not like it. An item should be challenged only if it is out of compliance with one or more of the written guidelines, and the reviewer should cite the guideline(s) involved. If possible, the reviewer should indicate what needs to be done to bring the item into compliance.

A fairness challenge may not be ignored. If an item has been challenged, either the item must be replaced or revised, or the challenge must be disputed. (A new item used to replace a challenged item must receive a fairness review.) If the challenge is disputed, then previously agreed-upon resolution procedures should be followed.

Because equally intelligent, good-willed, and well-trained people are likely to disagree about the fairness of certain items, a procedure to resolve disputes is required. The procedure depends on the structure of the testing organization and on the role desired by the client who commissioned the test. Some states, for example, want their own fairness review committees to make the final decisions about which items meet the state's criteria for fairness. One reasonable resolution procedure involves three stages:

1. Begin with discussions between the reviewer and the person in charge of the item, usually the test assembler or the item writer. In most cases, the disagreements can be resolved at this stage.
2. If the discussions fail to resolve the problem, ask an experienced fairness reviewer with no stake in the outcome to help the disputants reach a resolution.
3. If agreement is not reached even after third-party mediation, submit the dispute to the individual or group, such as a state's fairness review committee, with the authority to make a final decision about fairness review issues.

Document the fairness disputes that go beyond the first stage. If any consistent issues emerge, use the information to identify ambiguities in the fairness review guidelines or weaknesses in the fairness review training. Finally, document any procedures that have been adopted and make the written procedures available to all who will be involved in writing items and in reviewing items for fairness.

OTHER FAIRNESS ACTIONS

Rationale

No matter how well it is done, fairness review by itself is insufficient to ensure the fairness of a test. Fairness requires attention from the initial planning stages of testing through the uses made of the scores. According to the *ETS Standards for Quality and Fairness* (2002, p. 18), it is necessary to "address fairness in the design, development, administration, and use" of a test.

Equal Treatment

Fairness requires that all groups of test takers be treated equally to the extent possible. (An exception is the special treatment required for some test takers with disabilities, which is actually intended to "level the playing field" and result in greater equality.) Give useful information about the test equally to all test takers.

Establish equivalent test registration procedures for all groups of test takers. Make sure that administration sites are accessible to all groups of test takers, including test takers with disabilities. Do not give the people who are scoring items access to information about any test taker's gender, ethnicity, race, and so forth. If scoring involves direct observation of test takers or videotapes of test takers' performances, then train scorers specifically to reduce any biases that may affect the scores that they give.

Test Design

Willingham and Cole (1997) showed that the constructs measured can have a large effect on group differences. If it is possible to design equally valid and practical tests to meet the same purpose, and those tests have different effects on group differences in performance, then set the test specifications with some regard given to reducing group differences. For example, spatial reasoning tends to show large male–female differences (Willingham & Cole, 1997). Therefore, if it is possible to meet the purpose of a test equally as well with and without the measurement of spatial reasoning ability, fairness suggests that spatial reasoning be excluded. (Note that this does not require the exclusion of spatial reasoning if it is needed to meet the purpose of a test.)

An important contributor to fairness at the initial stage of test development is the concept of universal design, a sensible concept that began in architecture and is being applied to assessment. The primary idea is that both structures and tests should be designed from the beginning to be as appropriate as possible for all users. (See Thurlow, Thompson, & Lazarus, chap. 28, this volume, and Thompson, Johnstone, and Thurlow, 2002, for a good introduction to the principles of universal design for assessments.)

During the test design process, consider the suitability of item types for all groups of test takers, including test takers with disabilities and English language learners. How difficult would it be for a blind person to navigate the item type in Braille, or with voicing software? Is the language more difficult than it needs to be to measure the intended construct?

UD is not only for people with disabilities. For example, making sure that a math problem does not contain unnecessarily complicated language results in a fairer item for test takers who are deaf, and it results in a better measure of the intended construct for all other test takers as well.

Diverse Input

Involve people with diverse points of view in the test development process to help ensure that the resulting test is appropriate for all of the intended test takers. Because most test development organizations are not large enough to include all relevant points of view, it has become common practice to use committees of external subject matter experts to help with test design, item writing, and item review. Ethnic diversity, racial diversity, and gender diversity are important on such committees, but it is also important to represent people from different geographic areas, from different types of educational institutions, and from different schools of thought within a discipline. If time and budget constraints allow, it may be helpful to establish a separate group devoted solely to fairness concerns. Many states, for example, have separate fairness review committees in addition to their subject matter committees.

Provision of Accommodations

Fairness requires providing accommodations as necessary for people with disabilities. The goal is to measure the intended construct rather than the irrelevant effects of a test taker's disability. For example, a test taker who is blind may request a Braille version of the test. The topic of when and how to provide accommodations is complicated, has become highly politicized, and is subject to a great deal of litigation. (See Koretz & Barton, 2003/2004, for a discussion of the issues involved in testing people with disabilities.)

Some of the actions that test developers should take to ensure the fairness of accommodations are clear. Establish rules for identifying who is qualified for an accommodation. Generally, those who qualify for accommodations in school or at work should qualify for similar accommodations in testing. Consult a lawyer when establishing criteria for accommodations because the laws governing who is eligible are wide ranging, complicated, and not intuitively clear to lay people.

It is generally straightforward to provide an accommodation for a disability that is not related to the construct being measured. For example, providing a large-type version of a foreign language test for a person with limited vision obviously helps to remove the irrelevant effect of the person's disability while not interfering with measurement of the construct in any way. Fairness requires the provision of accommodations when test takers can document the existence of a disability unrelated to the construct being tested that might interfere with valid inferences about the test takers.

The issue becomes much more complicated when the accommodation does interfere with measurement of the intended construct. Consider, for example, the request of a test taker who is dyslexic to have a test of reading comprehension read aloud as an accommodation. If the intended construct is the ability to comprehend and reason with language regardless of the input mode, then fairness requires that the accommodation be made. In that case, the written text happens to be part of the test, but it is not a necessary part of the construct. If, however, the intended construct includes the ability to decode written text, then the requested accommodation of reading aloud to the test taker may be considered inappropriate because it would significantly alter the construct being measured.

The best advice that can be offered within the scope of this chapter is to be sure that the construct to be measured has been clearly defined, to involve a lawyer in writing the policies to be followed to ensure that the policies are congruent with the various applicable laws, and to scrupulously follow the written policies. (See *Standards for Educational and Psychological Testing,* AERA, APA, & NCME, 1999, chap. 10, for information on testing people with disabilities.)

Differential Item Functioning

Use some empirical measure of the performance of people in different groups to help evaluate the fairness of items. Raw differences in percent correct are not an appropriate measure simply because there may be real and relevant differences in knowledge of the measured construct. Good items reflect real and relevant differences between groups just as they reflect real and relevant differences between individuals. Therefore, test developers have widely adopted measures of differential item functioning (DIF).

The concept of DIF is straightforward and sensible. If people know the same amount about the construct being tested, then they should perform similarly on an item measuring that construct regardless of irrelevant group membership. For example, if men and women know the same amount about the construct measured by a mathematics test, then they should perform the same way on an item that measures that construct, regardless of their differences in gender. The matching is most often done on the basis of test scores. Differences in item performance by matched people in different groups result in differential item functioning. DIF is a sign that the item may be measuring something other than the intended construct and may be unfair. DIF, however, is not proof of bias. A fair item may show DIF merely because the matching variable has not matched test takers well on the knowledge, skill, or ability measured by the item. (See Livingston, chap. 19, this volume; Holland & Thayer, 1988; Dorans, 1989; and Dorans & Holland, 1993, for more information about DIF.)

The procedures in use at ETS will serve as an example of how test developers can use DIF statistics to help ensure fairness. When sample sizes permit, data for DIF comparisons are gathered for African American, Asian American, Hispanic American, Native American, White, and male and female test takers. Items are placed in one of three categories based on the magnitude and significance of the DIF statistics. Items in the first category have statistically insignificant or small values of DIF. Items in the second category have moderate levels of DIF, and items in the third category have larger than moderate values of DIF.

If DIF data are available before tests are assembled, items in the first category are selected first. If items in the second category are needed to meet test specifications, they may be used, but preference is given to the items with less DIF. Items in the third category are to be avoided unless they are judged to be fair and are required for valid measurement.

If DIF data are not available before tests are assembled, DIF is calculated after the administration of the test, but before scores are reported. Any items that fall in the third category must be reviewed to determine if they are fair. If items are judged to be unfair, they are removed from the set of items on which scores are based. The judgments should be made by people with no vested interest in retaining the items. (See Zieky, 1993, for more information about the use of DIF statistics in test development.)

Validation

Because invalid differences are unfair, making sure that evidence exists to support the inferences made on the basis of the test scores is probably the most important fairness activity. A clear definition of the intended construct is a crucial starting point because it is impossible to determine if a source of score variance is construct relevant or not without a well-defined construct. Because fairness depends on the elimination of construct-irrelevant material, it is necessary to know exactly what has been included in the intended construct and what has been purposefully excluded.

For all types of tests, build a chain of reasoning using documented evidence to support the fairness of the intended uses of the test scores. The chain of evidence should begin with test design. What evidence is there that fairness issues were considered at the test design stage? Were the people who set the specifications reasonably diverse? What kind of training and experience did they have? Did they have information about whether or not learning opportunities might vary by group, or about previous research on how various groups react to different aspects of the construct? If task analyses or curriculum surveys were used to provide information to test developers, did the samples of participants include people from various groups?

Include in the chain of evidence answers to questions such as the following: What were the qualifications of the item writers? Were they trained to consider fairness issues? Were items reviewed specifically for fairness? Were written fairness review guidelines followed? What happened to items that were challenged for fairness concerns? Were any procedures followed to ensure that the linguistic demands of the test do not exceed the linguistic demands of the construct?

After administration, answer questions such as the following: Was any empirical measure of group performance included in the analyses of the items? If so, what happened to items that were flagged for inordinate differences? Which groups were included in the analyses of group performance? If the tests were used for prediction, do the regression lines differ significantly for different groups? Does predictive validity differ for people in different groups for reasons other than statistical artifacts? (For example, all other things being equal, a group with less score variance is likely to show lower predictive validity than a group with more score variance. This does not necessarily mean the test is unfair to the group with less score variance.)

Are the consequences of measurement different for people in different groups? For example, do failure rates differ greatly? If so, is there evidence that the differences are caused by construct-relevant factors? (Note that differences in failure rates are not proof of unfairness. A test is unfair if the differences in failure rates are caused by construct-irrelevant sources of variance.)

The call for validation evidence related to fairness is insatiable because it is always theoretically possible to gather more evidence and to gather evidence on more groups. In practical terms, given real world limitations on schedules and budgets, test developers have to decide which groups to study, and what information to obtain for each particular test. (See Messick, 1989; Haladyna, chap. 32, this volume; and Kane, chap. 7, this volume, for more detail on the kinds of validity evidence to obtain.)

Test Use

Even a fair test can be used unfairly. For example, interpreting the scores on a test as a measure of innate ability when people in different groups did not have an equal opportunity to learn the material being tested is unfair. Interpreting the same scores as a measure of current level of knowledge, however, may be perfectly fair. Make sure that score recipients receive information about appropriate uses of the test scores and warn score recipients of likely misuses of the scores.

CONCLUSION

In 1999, the *Standards for Educational and Psychological Testing* (AERA, APA, & NCME, p. 80) stated that, "it is unlikely that consensus in society at large or within the measurement community is imminent on all matters of fairness in the use of tests." It is still unlikely.

There is consensus, however, that test developers must strive to ensure fairness throughout the test creation process. Fairness should be a concern as constructs are selected, as test specifications are set, as items are written and reviewed, as tests are assembled and reviewed, as tests are administered and scored, and as scores are interpreted.

Test developers will never be able to prove that that their tests are fair, but following the actions described in this chapter will help them to make their tests as fair as possible for all of the people who take them.

ACKNOWLEDGMENT

I wish to acknowledge the helpful reviews of Brent Bridgeman, Sydell Carlton, Dan Eignor, Samuel Livingston, William Monaghan, and the editors of this volume.

REFERENCES

American Educational Research Association (AERA), American Psychological Association (APA), & National Council on Measurement in Education (NCME). (1999). *Standards for educational and psychological testing.* Washington, DC: American Psychological Association.

American Psychological Association (APA). (2001). *Publication manual of the American Psychological Association.* Washington, DC: Author.

Angoff, W. H. (1993). Perspectives on differential item functioning methodology. In P. Holland, & H. Wainer (Eds.), *Differential item functioning.* Hillsdale, NJ: Lawrence Erlbaum Associates.

Berk, R. A. (1982). Introduction. In R. A. Berk (Ed.), *Handbook of methods for detecting test bias.* Baltimore, MD: The Johns Hopkins University Press.

Bond, L. (1993). Comments on the O'Neill & McPeek paper. In P. Holland, & H. Wainer (Eds.), *Differential item functioning.* Hillsdale, NJ: Lawrence Erlbaum Associates.

Cleary, T. A. (1968). Test bias: Prediction of grades of Negro and White students in integrated colleges. *Journal of Educational Measurement, 5,* 115–124.

Cole, N. S. (1973). Bias in selection. *Journal of Educational Measurement, 10,* 237–255.

Cole, N. S. (1993). History and development of DIF. In P. Holland, & H. Wainer (Eds.), *Differential item functioning.* Hillsdale, NJ: Lawrence Erlbaum Associates.

Cole, N. S., & Zieky, M. J. (2001). The new faces of fairness. *Journal of Educational Measurement, 38,* 4.

Darlington, R. B. (1971). Another look at "culture fairness." *Journal of Educational Measurement, 8,* 71–82.

Dorans, N. (1989). Two new approaches to assessing differential item functioning: standardization and the Mantel-Haenszel method. *Applied Measurement in Education, 2,* (3), 217–233.

Dorans, N., & Holland, P. (1993). DIF detection and description: Mantel-Haenszel and standardization. In P. Holland & H. Wainer (Eds.), *Differential item functioning.* Hillsdale, NJ: Lawrence Erlbaum Associates.

Elliott, R. (1987). *Litigating intelligence.* Dover, MA: Auburn House.
Educational Testing Service (ETS). (2002). *ETS standards for quality and fairness.* Princeton, NJ: Author.
Educational Testing Service (ETS). (2003). *ETS fairness review guidelines.* Princeton, NJ: Author.
Educational Testing Service (ETS). (2004). *ETS international principles for fairness review of assessments.* Princeton, NJ: Author.
Green, D. R. (1982). Methods used by test publishers to "debias" standardized tests. In R. A. Berk (Ed.), *Handbook of methods for detecting test bias.* Baltimore, MD: The Johns Hopkins University Press.
Haladyna, T., & Downing, S. (2004). Construct irrelevant variance in high stakes testing. *Educational Measurement: Issues and Practice, 23* (1), 17–27.
Holland, P., & Thayer, D. (1988). Differential item performance and the Mantel-Haenszel procedure. In H. Wainer & H. Braun (Eds.), *Test validity.* Hillsdale, NJ: Lawrence Erlbaum Associates.
Koretz, D., & Barton, K. (2003/2004). Assessing students with disabilities: Issues and evidence. *Educational Assessment, 9* (1&2), 29–60.
Linn, R. L. (1973). Fair test use in selection. *Review of Educational Research, 43,* 139–161.
Messick, S. (1989). Validity. In R. L. Linn (Ed.), *Educational measurement.* Washington, DC: American Council on Education.
No Child Left Behind (NCLB). (n.d.). Retrieved September 2, 2004, from, http://www.ed.gov/nclb.
Petersen, N. S., & Novick, M. R. (1976). An evaluation of some models for culture fair selection. *Journal of Educational Measurement, 13,* 3–29.
Ramsey, P. (1993). Sensitivity review: The ETS experience as a case study. In P. Holland, & H. Wainer (Eds.), *Differential item functioning.* Hillsdale, NJ: Lawrence Erlbaum Associates.
Ravitch, D. (2003). *The language police: How pressure groups restrict what students learn.* New York: Knopf.
Shepard, L. A. (1982). Definitions of bias. In R. A. Berk (Ed.), *Handbook of methods for detecting test bias.* Baltimore, MD: The Johns Hopkins University Press.
Shepard, L. A. (1987). The case for bias in tests of achievement and scholastic aptitude. In S. Modgil & C. Modgil (Eds.), *Arthur Jensen: Consensus and controversy.* London: Falmer Press.
Thompson, S. J., Johnstone, C. J., & Thurlow, M. L. (2002). *Universal design applied to large scale assessments.* Minneapolis: University of Minnesota, National Center on Educational Outcomes.
Thorndike, R. L. (1971). Concepts of culture fairness. *Journal of Educational Measurement, 8,* 63–70.
Willingham, W. W., & Cole, N. S. (1997). *Gender and fair assessment.* Mahwah, NJ: Lawrence Erlbaum Associates.
Zieky, M. J. (1993). Practical questions in the use of DIF statistics in test development. In P. Holland & H. Wainer (Eds.), *Differential item functioning.* Hillsdale, NJ: Lawrence Erlbaum Associates.

17

Language Issues in Item Development

Jamal Abedi
University of California, Davis

Unnecessary linguistic complexity of content-based test items may be a source of construct-irrelevant variance and may threaten the validity of assessment. This threat is more serious when it affects the performance of subgroups differently. Research literature suggests that English language learners (ELLs) may not possess language capabilities sufficient to demonstrate their content knowledge in areas such as math and science when assessed in English. Thus, the level of impact of language factors on assessment of ELL students is greater in test items with higher level of language demand.

To provide fair and valid assessment for all students, and particularly for ELL students, the impact of language unrelated to content-based assessments must be controlled. This chapter explains the concept of linguistic complexity as it applies to test items, helps test item writers to identify sources of linguistic complexity that are judged to be unnecessary or irrelevant to the content and construct being assessed, and assists writers in modifying test items to control for such sources of variations.

THEORETICAL FRAMEWORK

Assessment outcomes may be confounded with nuisance variables that are unrelated to the construct being measured. These variables, sometimes referred to as *extraneous variables* or *contaminants*, come from many different sources. The variability of assessment outcomes owing to these variables is often referred to as *construct-irrelevant variance* (CIV). Construct-irrelevant sources of variance threaten the validity of assessment, particularly when they impact the performance of subgroups differently. Among the most influential sources of CIV is the impact of unnecessary linguistic complexity of test items on student assessment outcome.

Research has shown that language factors affect the assessment outcome of all students, particularly those who are not highly proficient in the language. English language learners (ELLs) generally perform lower than non-ELLs on reading, language arts, math, science, and social sciences—an indication that English language proficiency may affect assessment. Assessment tools that are less influenced by the unnecessary linguistic complexity of test items may provide a more valid picture of what students know and can do. Research shows that the assessment outcomes of ELL students, particularly those at the lower end of English proficiency spectrum, suffer from lower reliability and validity. That is, language factors may be a source of measurement error in the assessment of ELL students and may affect the reliability of the test. Language factors as a source of CIV (Messick, 1994) may also affect the test's construct validity.

The *Standards for Educational and Psychological Testing* (American Educational Research Association [AERA], American Psychological Association [APA], & National Council on Measurement in Education [NCME], 1999) reminds us that

> Test use with individuals who have not sufficiently acquired the language of the test may introduce construct irrelevant components to the testing process. In such instances, test results may not reflect accurately the qualities and competencies intended to be measured. [Therefore] special attention to issues related to language and culture may be needed when developing, administering, scoring, and interpreting test scores and making decisions based on test scores. (p. 91)

This chapter explains the concept of linguistic complexity of test items, provides information on the linguistic features that affect test performance, and explains the process of linguistic modification of test items. Samples of linguistically complex items that have been used in past national assessments are presented along with their linguistically modified versions. These examples of original and linguistically modified test items help item writers to identify linguistically complex items and avoid such complexity when developing new items.

Nuisance Variables

Nuisance variables as sources of threat to reliability and validity of tests are sometimes referred to as *extraneous variables* (Linn & Gronlund, 1995), *contaminants,* or *construct irrelevant* (Haladyna & Downing, 2004; Messick, 1984). Zieky (chap. 16, this volume) indicates that a fairness review to identify construct-irrelevant sources is a major effort in constructing fair tests. "During the development of an assessment, an attempt is made to rule out extraneous factors that might distort the meaning of the scores, and follow-up studies are conducted to verify the success of these attempts" (Linn & Gronlund, 1995, p. 71).

There are many different nuisance variables that may affect the reliability and validity of assessment outcomes. Problems that affect readability of assessment instruments, issues surrounding test instructions, and inconsistencies in test administrations and scoring are examples of nuisance variables. The effects of these variables on assessment outcomes may be more serious when they differentially impact subgroups of test takers. This differential impact is of particular concern in cognitive assessments.

For example, if a test is administered in a noisy condition and the level of noise during the test administration affects everyone equally, then the noise may not have a serious impact on the relative standing of students under a norm-referenced testing condition. However, under a criterion-referenced testing condition, the noise may affect students' content mastery level outcome. The effects of this nuisance variable on the assessment outcome are more serious when it has differential level of impact on subgroups of test takers. For example, if some students are more sensitive to noise than others, and if those students happen to be mostly from a particular subgroup, then differential impact of a nuisance variable occurs. This may be true for some bilingual students. Partial bilinguals who are proficient in their native language, but not in the second language, are likely to perform more poorly if the assessment is in their weaker language. This occurs because of less efficient language processing (Dornic, 1979), especially under adverse environmental conditions such as a noisy room (Figueroa, 1989).

Because nuisance variables are systematic sources of variation on the assessment, one may control for these sources if the magnitude of their effects is known and if this magnitude is the same for all test takers in different subgroups. However, the major issue in dealing with the impact of nuisance variables on the assessment outcome is the possibility that these variables have different level of impacts on different subgroups of test takers. Controlling for differential impact of these variables can be extremely complex.

Although nuisance variable may be sources of systematic error, measurement error in classical test theory is considered random. A short discussion follows on the random error in classical test theory and the assumptions associated with the randomness of such errors.

Error of Measurement in Classical Test Theory

In classical test theory, reliability is defined as the ratio of the true-score variance (σ^2_T) to the observed-score variance (σ^2_X) (Allen & Yen, 1979). This observed score variance (σ^2_X) is a sum of two components, the true-score variance (σ^2_T) and the error variance (σ^2_E).

$$\sigma^2_X = \sigma^2_T + \sigma^2_E \qquad (17.1)$$

In a perfectly reliable test, the error variance (σ^2_E) is zero; therefore, the true-score variance (σ^2_T) is equal to the observed-score variance. However, in measurement involving human subjects, there is always an error component, whether large or small, which is referred to in the classical test theory as the *measurement error* (see Allen & Yen, 1979; Crocker & Algina, 1986; Linn & Gronlund, 1995; Salvia & Ysseldyke, 1998). Understanding the nature of measurement error is important in any type of assessment, whether in the traditional multiple-choice approach or in performance-based assessments (Linn, 1995; see also AERA, APA, & NCME, 1999). Many different sources (e.g., occasion, tasks, test administration conditions and scoring of open-ended items) may contribute to measurement error in assessment. In the classical approach to estimating reliability of assessment, the level of contribution from different sources to measurement error may be indeterminable. Through the application of generalizability theory, one would be able to determine the extent of the variance each individual source contributes (such as occasion, tasks, items, scorers) to the overall measurement error (see Brennan, 2001; Cronbach, Gleser, Nanda, & Rajaratnam, 1972; Shavelson & Webb, 1991).

A major assumption in classical test theory is that the "Error-of measurement is an unsystematic, or random, deviation of an examinee's observed score from a theoretically expected observed scores." (Allen & Yen, 1979, p. 59). That is, there is no correlation between the true scores and the error scores. This assumption of the error of measurement being random is the foundation of classical test theory. As stated earlier, based on this assumption the reliability of a test ($\rho_{XX'}$) is defined as (Allen & Yen, 1979, p. 73)

$$\rho_{XX'} = \sigma^2_T / \sigma^2_X \qquad (17.2)$$

Also, as indicated, a major issue with nuisance variables is that they add a systematic source of score variance to the observed score. Because these sources of nuisance variables are systematic, they are correlated with the observed and error scores. Although some authors do not consider this systematic source of variation as *measurement error* in classical test theory (Allen & Yen, 1979), this source undoubtedly impacts the reliability and validity of assessments. Thus, the definition of observed score variance in the classical test theory should be modified if there is substantial impact of nuisance variables (CIV) on the assessment outcome:

$$\sigma^2_X = \sigma^2_T + \sigma^2_E + \sigma^2_S + \sigma_{ES} \qquad (17.3)$$

The new component (σ^2_S) is the source of variance from systematic effects of nuisance variables (see also Haladyna & Downing, 2004, p. 18). Because this component is correlated with the observed and error scores, another component to represent this correlation is added. This component which is shown as σ_{ES} is the covariance between the nuisance variable and the error score.

Haladyna and Downing (2004) elaborated on the impact of CIV on the validity of high-stakes testing. They provided a taxonomy of different sources associated with CIV, and cited twenty-one possible sources. These sources were grouped into four major categories: (1) sources owing to uniformity and types of test preparation; (2) test development, administration, and scoring; (3) sources owing to individual student participation; and (4) sources owing to cheating (Table 1, p. 20).

A major source of nuisance variables or CIV that falls under Haladyna and Downing's first category described is the unnecessary linguistic complexity of test items. This source may have serious consequences on assessment validity not only because it affects the assessment outcome considerably but because its effect is different across student subgroups. Assessment results for ELLs and students with learning disabilities may be negatively impacted by this source of CIV.

Research Linking Language Factors With Content Assessment Outcomes

Research suggests that language factors affect performance outcomes, especially for ELLs. Students' content knowledge in areas such as mathematics, science, or history may not be truly demonstrated if students cannot understand the vocabulary and linguistic structures used in the test. Language barriers can threaten the validity and reliability of content-based assessments (Abedi, 2002, 2004; Abedi, Leon, & Mirocha, 2003; Abedi & Lord, 2001). Minor changes in the wording of content-related test items can raise student performance (Abedi & Lord, 2001; Abedi, Lord, Hofstetter, & Baker, 2000; Abedi, Lord, & Plummer, 1997; Cummins, Kintsch, Reusser, & Weimer, 1988; De Corte, Verschaffel, & DeWin, 1985; Durán, 1999; Hudson, 1983; Riley, Greeno, & Heller, 1983). For example, rewording a verbal problem can make semantic relations more explicit, without affecting the underlying semantic and content structure; thus, the reader is more likely to construct a proper problem representation and solve the problem correctly.

Modifying language features such as sentence length can also make a difference in a reader's ability to comprehend content. When test items from the National Assessment of Educational Progress (NAEP) were grouped into long and short items, Abedi et al. (1997) found that ELL students performed significantly lower on the longer test items regardless of the items' level of content difficulty. Results also suggested that English Language Learners (ELLs) had higher proportions of omitted/not-reached items and experienced more difficulty with the items that were judged to be linguistically complex.

In analyzing existing test data from four different locations in the nation, Abedi et al. (2003) compared the performance of ELL and non-ELL students in several different content areas. Among these content areas, reading has the highest level of language demand because language is central to the construct being measured. However, in the science and math tests, understanding of the science and math content—not the language—is the focus of assessment. ELL students in grade 10 of one of the data sites had a mean reading score of 24.0 (SD = 16.4) as compared with a mean reading score of 38.0 (SD = 16.0) for non-ELL students, a difference of 14 score points. The difference between ELL and non-ELL mean normal curve equivalent scores for science was 9.7, substantially less than the 14 score points difference in reading. For math, the difference between ELL and non-ELL was 2.8.

The substantial disparity between reading and the other two content areas of science and math can probably be accounted for by the difference in language demand between the subjects. Among these content areas, reading has the highest level of language demand because language is central to the construct being measured. This is different from science and math tests in which the science and math content, not the language, is the focus of assessment. As these data show, the performance gap between ELL and non-ELL students diminishes as the level of language demand of test items decreases. For eleventh-grade students, the ELL/non-ELL performance difference was 15.9 for reading, 11.2 for science, and close to 0 for math computation. These results were consistent with the results of analyses from the other data sites.

Although subsections of standardized achievement tests attempt to measure students' knowledge of specific content areas, analyses of mathematics and science subsections of the Test of Achievement and Proficiency by Imbens-Bailey and Castellon-Wellington (1999) show that two thirds of the items included general vocabulary considered uncommon or used in an atypical manner. One third of the items included syntactic structures that were evaluated as complex or unusual in their construction. To accurately assess knowledge within content areas, students must comprehend what the items are asking and understand the response choices.

By reducing the impact of language barriers on content-based assessments, the validity and reliability of assessments can be improved, resulting in fairer assessments for all students, including ELLs (see Abedi & Lord, 2001; Abedi, Lord, Hofstetter, & Baker, 2000; Hansen & Mislevy, 2004; Kiplinger, Haug, & Abedi, 2000; Maihoff, 2002). When math test items were modified to reduce the level of linguistic complexity, over 80% of middle-school students who were interviewed preferred the linguistically modified over the original English version of the test items (see Abedi et al., 1997).

Recent studies using items from NAEP compared student scores on actual NAEP items with the parallel modified items in which the content task and content terminology were retained but the language was simplified. One study (Abedi & Lord, 2001) of 1,031 eighth-grade students in southern California found small but significant improvements in the scores of students in low- and average-level math classes using the linguistically modified test items. Among the linguistic features that appeared to contribute to the differences were low-frequency vocabulary and passive voice verb constructions (see a description of the linguistic features below; for a discussion of the nature of and rationale for the modifications see Abedi et al. [1997]).

Providing equitable access to special needs student population in large scale assessment is a major step toward a fair assessment for all. Well-designed assessments are better measures for all students, including students with disabilities and ELLs (Thurlow, Thompson, & Lazarus, chap. 28, this volume). Linguistic modification as a form of accommodation makes the assessment accessible to larger populations of students. In a study (Abedi, Lord, & Hofstetter, 1998) of 1,394 grade 8 students in schools with high enrollments of Spanish speakers showed that modification of language of the items contributed to improved performance on 49% of the items; the students generally scored higher on shorter problem statements. A third study (Abedi, Lord, Hofstetter, & Baker, 2000) tested 946 grade 8 students with different accommodations including modified linguistic structures, provision of extra time, and provision of a glossary. Among the different options, only the linguistic modification accommodation narrowed the performance-gap between ELL and non-ELL students significantly (Abedi et al., 1998; Abedi, Lord, Hofstetter, & Baker, 2000).

Another study consisting of 422 students in eighth grade science classes (Abedi, Lord, Kim-Boscardin, & Miyoshi, 2000) compared performance on NAEP science items in three test formats: one booklet in original format (no accommodation); one booklet with English glosses and Spanish translations in the margins; and one booklet with a customized English dictionary at the end of the test booklet. The customized dictionary included only the noncontent words that appeared in the test items. With the language needs addressed, ELL students scored the highest on the customized dictionary accommodation (their mean score for the customized dictionary was 10.18 on a 20-item test as compared with means of 8.36 and 8.51 for the other two accommodations).

In a study on the impact of accommodation on grade 8 students in math, Abedi, Lord, Hofstetter, and Baker (2000) applied four different types of accommodations: linguistically modified English version of the test, standard NAEP items with glossary only, extra time only, and glossary plus extra time. Students were also tested using standard NAEP items with no accommodation. The non-ELL students in this study, who happened to be among the low-performing student population, also benefited from the linguistic modification of test items, suggesting that clarifying the language of instruction and assessment may be helpful not only to ELL students but to low-performing non-ELL students as well (Durán, Escobar, & Wakin, 1997).

To accurately assess knowledge within content areas, students must comprehend what the items are asking and understand the response choices. Research to date suggests that a productive teaching and assessment approach for helping students, particularly ELL students, must be examined for unnecessary linguistic complexities. What can we say with confidence at this time?

1. The performance gap between ELL students and other students on content area tests can be narrowed by modifying the language of the test items to reduce the use of low-frequency vocabulary and language structures that are incidental to the content knowledge being assessed. This strategy has been shown to be effective in reducing the performance gap between high- and low-performing students as well.
2. All students should have content area assessments that use clear language and provide sufficient time for them to demonstrate their knowledge.
3. The development of future instructional materials and large-scale content area assessments should consider ELL students from the outset rather than as an afterthought. The use of clear language, free of unnecessary complexity, can and should be a part of good instructional planning and assessment practice.
4. The specific language demands of academic materials and assessment tools should be identified and provided to teachers so that they can ensure that students have the language resources to demonstrate their content area knowledge and skills.

Research Findings on Language as a Source of Measurement Error

The internal consistency approach is frequently used for estimating the reliability of an instrument. The main limitation of the internal consistency approach, however, is the assumption of unidimensionality. For example, the literature has indicated that Cronbach's alpha, which is a measure of internal consistency, is extremely sensitive to the multidimensionality of test items; it assumes all items measure the same construct (see, for example, Abedi, 1996; Cortina, 1993). The unnecessary linguistic complexity of test items may introduce a new dimension that may not be highly correlated with the content being assessed. It may also create a restriction of range problem by lowering achievement outcomes for ELL students that itself may lower internal consistency of test performance. To demonstrate this point, item-level Stanford 9 data were analyzed at different grade levels.

Internal consistency (Cronbach's alpha) coefficients for the Stanford 9 data were compared across ELL categories (ELL versus non-ELL). For grade 2 students the difference between reliability coefficients for ELL and non-ELL was .058 in reading, .013 in math, and .062 in language as compared with the ELL/non-ELL reliability difference of .109 for reading, .096 for math, and .120 for language in grade 9. The difference between the overall reliability coefficient of ELL and non-ELL for grade 9 was .167, which was substantially higher than the respective difference of .043 in grade 2. Thus, the reliability gap between ELL and non-ELL students increases with increase in the grade level. This may be from the use of more complex language structures in higher grades. The results of these analyses suggest that students' language background factors may have a profound effect on their assessment outcomes.

Research Findings on Language as a Source of Construct-Irrelevant Variance

As illustrated, complex language in the content-based assessment for non-native speakers of English may reduce the validity of inferences drawn about students' content-based knowledge. That is, the linguistic factors in content-based assessments (such as math and science) may be considered a source of CIV as discussed; it is not conceptually related to the content being assessed (Messick, 1994; Sandoval & Durán, 1998).

> With respect to the distortion of task performance, some aspects of the task may require skills or other attributes having nothing to do with the focal constructs in question, so that limitations in performing construct-irrelevant skills might prevent some students from demonstrating the focal competencies. (Messick, 1994, p. 14)

To examine the possible differences in the validity of standardized achievement tests between ELL and non-ELL students, a multiple group confirmatory factor analysis model was used in a study by Abedi et al. (2003). The results of analyses indicated that the correlations of item parcels with the latent factors were consistently lower for ELL students than they were for non-ELL students. This finding was true for all parcels regardless of which grade or which sample of the population was tested. For example, for grade 9 ELL students, the correlation for the four reading parcels ranged from a low of .719 to a high of .779 across the two samples. In comparison, for non-ELL students, the correlation for the four reading parcels ranged from a low of .832 to a high of .858 across the two samples. The item parcel correlations were also larger for non-ELL students than for ELL students in math and science. Again these results were consistent across the different samples. (See Abedi et al., 2003, for a detailed description of the study; see also Kane, chap. 7, this volume, for a discussion of content-related validity).

The correlations between the latent factors were also larger for non-ELL students than they were for ELL students. This gap in latent factor correlations between non-ELL and ELL students was especially large in test items where there was more language demand. For example, for grade 9, the correlation between latent factors for math and reading for non-ELL students was .782 compared to just .645 for ELL students. When comparing the latent factor correlations between reading and science from the same population, the correlation was still larger for non-ELL students (.837) than for ELL students (.806), but the gap between the correlations was smaller. This was likely because of language demand differences. Multiple group structural models were run to test whether the differences between the non-ELL and ELL students mentioned were significant. There were significant differences for all constraints tested at the .05 nominal level.

The results of simple structure confirmatory factor analyses also showed differences in factor loadings and factor correlations between the ELL and non-ELL groups. The hypotheses of invariance of factor loadings and factor correlations between the ELL and non-ELL groups were tested. Specifically, we tested the following null hypotheses:

H_{01}: Correlations between parcel scores and a reading latent variable are the same for the ELL and non-ELL groups.
H_{02}: Correlations between parcel scores and a science latent variable are the same for the ELL and non-ELL groups.
H_{03}: Correlations between parcel scores and a math latent variable are the same for the ELL and non-ELL groups.
H_{04}: Correlations between content-based latent variables are the same for the ELL and non-ELL groups.

The results of multiple group factor analysis for reading and math tests for students in grade 10 indicated significant differences between the ELL and non-ELL groups at or below .05 nominal level. There were several significant differences between ELL and non-ELL students on the correlations between parcel scores and latent variables. For example, on the math subscale, differences in factor loadings between ELLs and non-ELLs groups on parcels 2 and 3 were significant. These results indicate that:

1. Findings from the two cross-validation samples are very similar and provide evidence on the consistency of the results.
2. Structural models show a better fit for non-ELL than for ELL students.
3. Correlations between parcel scores and the content-based latent variables are generally lower for ELL students.
4. Correlations between the content-based latent variables are lower for ELL students.
5. These results suggest that language factors may be a source of CIV in the assessment of ELL students.

The research evidence presented clearly shows the impact of linguistic factors on assessments particularly for ELL students. Thus, a valid assessment for ELL students must be free of unnecessary linguistic complexity. In the next section, we discuss approaches for dealing with the linguistic complexity of test items.

LINGUISTIC MODIFICATION OF TEST ITEMS: PRACTICAL IMPLICATIONS

Linguistically modified assessments may facilitate students' negotiation of language barriers. Linguistic modification of test items involves simplifying or modifying the language of a text while keeping the content the same. This may be accomplished, for example, by shortening sentences, removing unnecessary expository material, using more familiar or more frequently used words, using grammar thought to be more easily understood—including using present tense, and using concrete rather than abstract situations. This is elaborated below.

In the first part of this chapter, we presented a theoretical framework for the concept of linguistic complexity of test items. The second part of this chapter is devoted to the practical aspects of this concept. In this part, we (1) present a brief description of some of the linguistic features that are shown to impact students' performance on content-based assessments; (2) discuss procedures for modifying test items to reduce linguistic complexity of items; (3)

describe a rubric for assessing the level of linguistic complexity of existing items; and (4) provide instructions for test developers on how to write test items that are free from unnecessary linguistic complexity. The first two sections are based partly on language difficulty analyses and modification strategies by Carol Lord described in Abedi et al. (1997); see also Lord (2004).

LINGUISTIC FEATURES THAT MAY AFFECT COMPREHENSION

A summary of linguistic features that may affect comprehension follows. These features slow down the reader, make misinterpretation more likely, and add to the reader's cognitive load, thus interfering with concurrent tasks. Before discussing each of these individual linguistic features, it must be noted that this list is by no means exhaustive of the linguistic features that could affect students' performance. Researchers, linguists, and measurement experts may add other pertinent features. However, the purpose of this chapter is not to provide a comprehensive linguistic analysis of content-based test items. Rather, it is to introduce the concept of linguistic complexity and to discuss methodology to control for such threats to the reliability and validity of assessment tools for all students, particularly for those with greater language needs.

It must also be noted that there are naturally circumstances where the grammar in an item is too challenging to modify. In such cases, we can only remind ourselves to not create items in such a manner for the future, and try our best to modify other parts of the item. The more we can linguistically modify items to make them easier to be understood the greater the chances of adequately gauging an ELL's content knowledge. Later we provide examples of linguistic modification that specifically address these language concerns.

Word Frequency and Familiarity

Word frequency was an element in early formulas for readability (Dale & Chall, 1948; Klare, 1974). Words that are high on a general frequency list for English are likely to be familiar to most readers because they are encountered often. Readers who encounter a familiar word are likely to interpret it quickly and correctly, spending less cognitive energy analyzing its phonological component (Adams, 1990; Chall, Jacobs, & Baldwin, 1990; Gathercole and Baddeley, 1993). On a test with math items of equivalent mathematical difficulty, eighth-grade students scored higher on the versions of items with vocabulary that was more frequent and familiar; the difference in score was particularly notable for students in low-level math classes (Abedi et al., 1997).

Word Length

As frequency of occurrence decreases, words tend to be longer. Accordingly, word length can serve as an index of word familiarity (Kucera & Francis, 1967; Zipf, 1949). Additionally, longer words are more likely to be morphologically complex. In one study, language minority students performed better on math test items with shorter word lengths than items with longer word lengths (Abedi et al., 1997).

Sentence Length

Sentence length serves as an index for syntactic complexity and can be used to predict comprehension difficulty; linguistic definitions of complexity based on the assumption that word depth correlates with sentence length (Bormuth, 1966; MacGinitie & Tretiak, 1971; Wang, 1970).

Voice of Verb Phrase

People find passive voice constructions more difficult to process than active constructions (Forster & Olbrei, 1973), and more difficult to remember (Savin & Perchonock, 1965; Slobin, 1968). Furthermore, passive constructions can pose a particular challenge for non-native speakers of English (Celce-Murcia & Larsen-Freeman, 1983). Passive voice constructions tend to be used less frequently in conversation than in formal writing such as scientific writing (Celce-Murcia & Larsen-Freeman, 1983). In one study, eighth-grade students (native and non-native English speakers) were given equivalent math items with and without passive voice constructions; students in average math classes scored higher in the versions without passive constructions (Abedi et al., 1997).

Length of Nominals

Noun phrases with several modifiers have been identified as potential sources of difficulty in test items (Spanos, Rhodes, Dale, & Crandall, 1988). Long nominal compounds typically contain more semantic elements and are inherently syntactically ambiguous; accordingly, a reader's comprehension of a text may be impaired or delayed by problems in interpreting them (Halliday & Martin, 1993; Just & Carpenter, 1980; King & Just, 1991; MacDonald, 1993). Romance languages such as Spanish, French, Italian, and Portuguese make less use of compounding than English does, and when they do employ such a device, the rules are different. Consequently, students whose first language is a Romance language may have difficulty interpreting compound nominals in English (Celce-Murcia & Larsen-Freeman, 1983).

Complex Question Phrases

Longer question phrases occur with lower frequency than short question phrases, and low-frequency expressions are in general harder to read and understand (Adams, 1990).

Comparative Structures

Comparative constructions have been identified as potential sources of difficulty for non-native speakers (Jones, 1982; Spanos, Rhodes, Dale, & Crandall, 1988) and for speakers of non-mainstream dialects (Orr, 1987; see also Baugh, 1988).

Prepositional Phrases

Students may find interpretation of prepositions difficult (Orr, 1987; Spanos et al., 1988). Languages such as English and Spanish may differ in the ways that motion concepts are encoded using verbs and prepositions (Slobin, 1968).

Sentence and Discourse Structure

Two sentences may have the same number of words, but one may be more difficult than the other because of the syntactic structure or discourse relationships among sentences (Finegan, 1978; Freeman, 1978; Larsen, Parker, & Trenholme, 1978).

Subordinate Clauses

Subordinate clauses may contribute more to complexity than coordinate clauses (Botel & Granowsky, 1974; Hunt, 1965, 1977; Lord, 2002; Wang, 1970).

Conditional Clauses

Conditional clauses and initial adverbial clauses have been identified as contributing to difficulty (Spanos et al., 1988; Shuard & Rothery, 1984). The semantics of the various types of conditional clauses in English are subtle and hard to understand even for native speakers (Celce-Murcia & Larsen-Freeman, 1983). Non-native speakers may omit function words (such as *if*) and may employ separate clauses without function words. Separate sentences, rather than subordinate *if* clauses, may be easier for some students to understand (Spanos et al., 1988). In fact, some languages do not allow sentences with the conditional clause in sentence-final position (Haiman, 1985). Consequently, this positioning may cause difficulty for some non-native speakers.

Relative Clauses

Because relative clauses are less frequent in spoken English than in written English, some students may have had limited exposure to them. In fact, Pauley and Syder (1983) argue that the relative clauses in literature differ from those in spoken vernacular language (Schachter, 1983).

Concrete versus Abstract or Impersonal Presentations

Studies show better performance when problem statements are presented in concrete rather than abstract terms (Cummins et al., 1988). Information presented in narrative structures tends to be understood and remembered better than information presented in expository text (Lemke, 1986).

Negation

Mestre (1988) observed that a considerable number of research studies indicate that sentences containing negations (e.g., no, not, none, never) are harder to comprehend than affirmative sentences. One of the reasons for its complexity may be because there is a lack of parallelism in the use of negation between English and other languages. In Spanish, for example, double negative constructions retain a negative meaning instead of reverting to an affirmative meaning, as would be the case in grammatically correct English. Mestre found that Spanish-speaking students processed negations from left to right, which works for natural discourse but does not always work for mathematics texts.

Procedures for Linguistic Modification of Test Items

The process of identifying the potentially problematic linguistic features in test items must be based on the knowledge of content/linguistic experts and the actual characteristics of test items. The process can also be informed by research literature (see, for example, Abedi et al., 1997) and knowledge of the type of linguistic features likely to cause problems for learners of English as a second language. Finally, the linguistic features that were introduced can guide the process of linguistic modification. This list of linguistic features can be modified as new linguistic features emerge.

To illustrate the process of identifying the potentially problematic linguistic features in assessment, a summary of linguistic modification implemented in a study is presented (Abedi et al., 1997). In this study, 69 NAEP math items for eighth-grade students were examined for linguistic complexity. The research literature, expert knowledge, and the actual characteristics of the NAEP items led to the identification of the features.

Each of the 69 items was read and the mathematical operations attempted. Items in which the language was considered potentially difficult for students to understand were flagged and analyzed; linguistic features likely to contribute to the difficulty were identified and categorized. Simplified forms of linguistically complex items were drafted to make these items easier for students to understand. From this set of features, only the most salient and frequent language problems were selected for investigation in the field study.

Changes were made to the language of the original NAEP items in the following seven categories: familiarity/frequency of nonmath vocabulary, voice of the verb phrase, length of nominals (noun phrases), conditional clauses, relative clauses, question phrases, and abstract or impersonal presentations. Changes in each of these areas are described and illustrated below.

Familiarity/Frequency of Nonmath Vocabulary

Potentially unfamiliar, low-frequency lexical items were replaced with more familiar, higher frequency lexical items.

Original: A certain reference file contains approximately six billion facts.
Revision: Mack's company sold six billion hamburgers.
Original: census
Revision: video game

In the student's world, for example, the concepts of "company" and "hamburger" are probably more familiar, and are probably encountered more frequently, than "certain reference file" and "facts." If a student does not understand all the words in a test item, she or he may not understand what the item is asking and may be unable to solve it. If an item contains unfamiliar vocabulary, it may take the student longer to read and understand the item, and the student may be at a disadvantage compared to other students on a timed test. The accuracy and speed of written word recognition depend on the reader's familiarity with the word in print (Adams, 1990). A task places greater demands on a student if her or his attention is divided between employing math problem-solving strategies and coping with difficult vocabulary and unfamiliar content (Gathercole & Baddeley, 1993).

In revising the items, estimates of familiarity/frequency of vocabulary were made based on established word frequency sources as well as research staff judgments of the students' familiarity with the words and concepts. For example, *The American Heritage Word Frequency Book* (Carroll, Davies, & Richman, 1971), based on 5 million words from textbooks and library materials for grades 3 through 9, and the *Frequency Analysis of English Usage: Lexicon and Grammar* (Francis & Kucera, 1982), based on the 1 million-word Brown University Corpus, listed *company* as occurring more frequently than *reference* or *file*, a result that was consistent with our intuitions.

Voice of Verb Phrase

Verbs in the passive voice were replaced with verbs in the active voice.

Original: A sample of 25 was selected.
Revision: He selected a sample of 25.
Original: The weight of 3 objects were compared
Revision: Sandra compared the weights of 3 rabbits

Passive constructions occur less frequently than active constructions in English (Biber, 1988; Celce-Murcia & Larsen-Freeman, 1983). Children learning English as a second language have more difficulty understanding passive verb forms than active verb forms (Bever, 1970, deVilliers, & deVilliers, 1973).

Length of Nominals

The number of prenominal modifiers in a noun phrase was reduced, as in the example below:

Original: ...last year's class vice president...
Revision: ..., vice president...
Original: ...the pattern of puppy's weight gain...
Revision: ...the pattern above

In processing novel nominal compounds, people use lexical information as well as knowledge of the world and the context to rule out implausible readings. Faced with the task of interpreting a long nominal, a student with a limited English vocabulary is at a disadvantage.

Postmodifiers can be similarly ambiguous; for example, in a noun phrase followed by two prepositional phrase modifiers, such as "the man in the car from Mexico," the man may be from Mexico, or the car may be from Mexico. Adding more modifiers multiplies the possibilities for ambiguity.

Conditional Clauses

Some conditional *if* clauses were replaced with separate sentences. In some instances, the order of the *if* clause and the main clause was reversed.

Original: If x represents the number of newspapers that Lee delivers each day...
Revision: Lee delivers x newspapers each day.
Original: If two batteries in the sample were found to be dead.
Revision: He found three broken pencils in the sample.

In this item, in addition to removing the conditional clause, unfamiliar vocabulary (dead batteries) was replaced with familiar vocabulary (broken pencils). Separate sentences, rather than subordinate *if* clauses, may be easier for some students to understand (Spanos et al., 1988). Some languages do not allow sentences with the conditional clause in last position (Haiman, 1985). Consequently, sentences with the conditional clause last may cause difficulty for some non-native speakers.

Relative Clauses

Some relative clauses were removed or recast.

Original: A report that contains 64 sheets of paper...
Revised: He needs 64 sheets of paper for each report.

In this example, the original version contains information in a relative clause, whereas the revised item contains the same information in a separate, simple sentence. Although the number of sentences in the revised item is increased, the number of clauses per sentence is reduced. Students process shorter sentences with lower information density levels more easily.

ELLs may find that English employs unfamiliar devices such as relative pronouns instead of particles or affixes. In English, relative clauses follow the noun, but relative clauses precede the noun in other languages such as Chinese and Japanese. Relative clauses in English may be difficult for a non-native speaker to interpret if her or his first language employs patterns that are different from those of English.

Complex Question Phrases

Some question structures were changed from complex question phrases to simple question words.

Original: At which of the following times...?
Revision: When...?
Original: Which is the best approximation of the number...?
Revision: Approximately how many...?

In the first example, the complex question phrase in the original version was replaced with a single question word in the revision. The single-word structure is simpler syntactically, and the placement of the question word at the beginning of the sentence gives it greater salience. The longer question phrases occur with lower frequency, and low-frequency expressions are generally harder to read and understand (Adams, 1990).

Concrete Versus Abstract or Impersonal Presentations

In some instances, an abstract presentation mode was made more concrete.

Original: The weights of three objects were compared using a pan balance. Two comparisons were made...
Revision: Sandra compared the weights of three objects using a pan balance. She made two comparisons...

In this example, the problem statement was made more story-like by the introduction of "Sandra." Abstract or nonsituated items may employ the passive voice, but not all passive constructions are abstract or nonsituated; abstract or impersonal presentations may also employ modals or generic nominals, for example. A problem expressed in concrete terms may be easier for students to understand than an abstract problem statement (see, for instance, Lemke, 1986).

A Rubric for Assessing the Level of Linguistic Complexity of the Existing Test Items

The first step in modifying test items for linguistic complexity is to identify which of the linguistic features mentioned are present in the item and how serious are their effects. For identifying these features in our studies, we developed a rating system for evaluating the level of linguistic complexity of test items. The rating system consists of two different rating scales: (1) an analytical scale, and (2) a holistic scale. Each test item may be rated on both scales. We elaborate on each of these rating approaches below.

Analytical Rating

Individual test items are examined for existence of each of the 14 linguistic complexity features explained earlier in this chapter. The ratings are based on a 5-point Likert scale, with 1 indicating no complexity present with respect for that particular feature and 5 suggesting a high level of linguistic complexity with that feature. Therefore, each test items receives 14 ratings, one for each linguistic feature. For example, with respect to linguistic feature number 1 "Word frequency/familiarity," if the words used in the item are "very familiar' and "frequently" being used, then the item receives a rating of 1, or "no complexity." However, if the word is unfamiliar, or being used less frequently, then depend on the level of unfamiliarity and low frequency, it receives a rating between 2 and 5. The highest rating of 5 in this example refers to a word that is extremely unfamiliar and used the least. Judgments on the familiarity/frequency of the word can be made based on sources such as *The American Heritage Word Frequency Book* (Carroll et al., 1971) and the *Frequency Analysis of English Usage: Lexicon and Grammar* (Francis & Kucera, 1982).

For analytical rating, a rater or a group of raters is trained. They then rate a set of items in a practice session. It is desirable that each item be rated on each of the 14 features by more than one rater. However, if this is not possible or not logistically feasible, then at least a small set of items should be rated by more than one rater. The interrater reliability coefficients should be computed and based on the results of interrater reliability analyses, decisions should be made on how many ratings each test item may need. If, for example, the interrater reliability indices are low, then more than one rating of each item is needed. The commonly used approaches for estimating interrater reliability are percent of exact and within points agreement, PM correlation, intraclass correlation, kappa coefficient, alpha coefficient, and Williams' index of agreement (for complete description of interrater reliability coefficients and their limitations; see Abedi, 1996).

If a small set of test items, say 10, are rated by two raters and a kappa coefficient of 0.80 (or above) is obtained, then one can proceed with only one rater scoring each item. However, if the interrater coefficients (e.g., kappa, alpha, or intraclass correlation) are lower than 0.70, then more training should be conducted and more ratings of the items should be obtained. Figure 17.1 shows the analytical linguistic modification rubric.

Linguistic Feature	Degree of Complexity				
	Not Complex 1	2	3	4	Most Complex 5
1. Word frequency/ familiarity	–	–	–	–	–
2. Word length	–	–	–	–	–
3. Sentence length	–	–	–	–	–
4. Passive voice constructs	–	–	–	–	–
5. Long noun phrases	–	–	–	–	–
6. Long question phrases	–	–	–	–	–
7. Comparative structures	–	–	–	–	–
8. Prepositional phrases	–	–	–	–	–
9. Sentence and discourse structure	–	–	–	–	–
10. Subordinate clauses	–	–	–	–	–
11. Conditional clauses	–	–	–	–	–
12. Relative clauses	–	–	–	–	–
13. Concrete vs. abstract or impersonal presentations	–	–	–	–	–
14. Negation	–	–	–	–	–

FIG. 17.1. Rubric for rating the level of linguistic complexity.

LEVEL	QUALITY
1	**EXEMPLARY ITEM** *Sample Features:* • Familiar or frequently used words; word length generally shorter • Short sentences and limited prepositional phrases • Concrete item and a narrative structure • No complex conditional or adverbial clauses • No passive voice or abstract or impersonal presentations
2	**ADEQUATE ITEM** *Sample Features:* • Familiar or frequently used words; short to moderate word length • Moderate sentence length with a few prepositional phrases • Concrete item • No subordinate, conditional, or adverbial clauses • No passive voice or abstract or impersonal presentations
3	**WEAK ITEM** *Sample Features:* • Relatively unfamiliar or seldom used words • Long sentence(s) • Abstract concept(s) • Complex sentence/conditional tense/adverbial clause • A few passive voice or abstract or impersonal presentations
4	**ATTENTION ITEM** *Sample Features:* • Unfamiliar or seldom used words • Long or complex sentence • Abstract item • Difficult subordinate, conditional, or adverbial clause • Passive voice/ abstract or impersonal presentations
5	**PROBLEMATIC ITEM** *Sample Features:* • Highly unfamiliar or seldom used words • Very Long or complex sentence • Abstract item • Very difficult subordinate, conditional, or adverbial clause • Many passive voice and abstract or impersonal presentations

FIG. 17.2. Holistic Item Rating Rubric.

Holistic Rating

In addition to the ratings for each of the 14 linguistic features, an overall rating of linguistic complexity of each test item is recommended. Similar to the ratings that are assigned based on the analytical procedure, this rating is on a 5-point Likert scale, 1 representing items with no or minimal level of linguistic complexity and 5 shows an item with an extremely complex linguistic structure. Figure 17.2 shows the Holistic Rating Rubric. As Figure 17.2 shows, a test item free of unnecessary linguistic complexity (with a rating of 1) does not suffer from any of the 14 linguistic complexity threats. For example, the item uses familiar or frequently used words, the words as well as sentences in these items are generally shorter, there are no complex conditional and/or adverbial clauses, and there are no passive voices or abstract presentations. On the contrary, an item with a severe level of linguistic complexity contains all or many sources of threats.

Ratings on the linguistic modification (both analytical and holistic) provide diagnostic information on the linguistic barriers present in test items. This information may help item writers or test developers to identify problem items. These items can then be corrected for such problems. Because linguistic modification ratings are on a Likert scale, median ratings can be computed and can be used for decisions on how the items should be modified.

Once again, it must be noted that the 14 linguistic features we present in this section are defined based on the limited number of test items we used in our past studies and also based on limited number of research reports that we reviewed. Linguists, measurement experts, and classroom teachers may provide insight into a more comprehensive list of linguistic features might affect students' performance.

Instructions for the Incorporation of Linguistic Modification When Developing New Test Items

Item writers should be trained to be sensitive to the linguistic complexity of items. In training sessions, a key topic area that should be discussed is the impact of language factors on assessment outcomes (see Downing, chap. 1, this volume, for a comprehensive discussion of item-writer training issues as a validity aspect). The results of research showing the impact of linguistic complexity may be summarized. Several examples of released test items from national and state large-scale assessments may be used to demonstrate the existence of linguistic features that could make items difficult to comprehend. Examples of the linguistically complex items and their revised versions that were presented above can be used for demonstrating the linguistic modification concept. In training sessions, test items that are linguistically complex can be modified by participants individually and then shared and discussed with the group.

Thus, training sessions should present a description of the concept of linguistic complexity and provide opportunity for item developers to participate in a hands-on modification. This way, participants can then apply what they learned to develop new test items (see, Baranowski, chap. 15, this volume, for a comprehensive discussion of item editing).

SUMMARY AND DISCUSSION

Unnecessary linguistic complexity of test items is a source of systematic CIV and threatens the reliability and validity of assessment for many students, especially for ELLs. To provide a valid and fair assessment for all students, it is imperative to bring this issue to the attention of test item writers and developers. To be effective in presenting this issue to the measurement and assessment community, the foundation for this claim must be justified by research findings. This chapter introduces the concept of linguistic complexity of test items, provides some research support for this concept, and offers practical suggestions to address reliability and validity issues as related to the impact of language on assessment.

Past research findings coupled with findings from our own studies have informed us of the serious impact that unnecessary linguistic complexity of test items may have on content-based assessments. We differentiate between language that is an essential part of the question content and language that makes the question incomprehensible to many students, particularly to ELLs. We understand and value the richness of language in an assessment system; however, we also believe that students with limited English proficiency and other students with similar language needs should not be penalized for their lack of English proficiency in areas where the target of assessment is not language. Although we understand the views of some language modification critics in not "dumbing down" assessment questions by simplifying the language, we also recognize the distinction between necessary and unnecessary linguistic complexity.

We believe that content assessment specialists should make these distinctions when creating test items.

In developing the linguistic complexity rating rubrics that are introduced in this chapter, we utilized past research findings to provide practical suggestions in addressing language issues in assessments. Because past research has consistently found the linguistic modification approach to control for sources of assessment validity threats, we hope this chapter helps test item writers develop more valid assessments for every student as required by the *No Child Left Behind Act* (2002) and similar policies.

REVIEW EXERCISES

Below is a set of three math items that were released from a national assessment test items. For this exercise, you should try to do the following:

1. Modify the items to remove unnecessary linguistic complexity of the items. In this linguistic modification, you need to make sure that the language related to math content is retained. To ensure retaining of content-related language, you need to consult with math and linguistic content experts.
2. Use the analytical and holistic rubrics to rate the level of linguistic complexity of each item.
3. You may consider a small-scale study in which you randomly assign the original and revised test items to a group of about 100 eighth-grade students (four classes) and then compare their performance.

To help you with this process, we have provided our linguistically modified version of items. However, we strongly suggest that you prepare your own modified version of the items first and then review our suggested modifications.

ORIGINAL ITEMS

1. Raymond must buy enough paper to print 28 copies of report that contains 64 sheets of paper. Paper is only available in packages of 500 sheets. How many whole packages of paper will he need to buy to do the printing?

Answer: _____

2. Harriet, Jim, Roberto, Maria, and Willie are in the same eighth-grade class. One of them is this year's class president. Based on the following information, who is the class president?

   1. The class president was last year's vice president and lives on Vince Street.
   2. Willie is this year's class vice president.
   3. Jim and Maria live on Cypress Street.
   4. Roberto was not last year's vice president.

   A. Jim
   B. Harriet
   C. Roberto
   D. Maria
   E. Willie

3. The census showed that three hundred fifty-six thousand, ninety-seven people lived in Middletown. Written as a number, that is:

   A. 350,697
   B. 356,097
   C. 356,907
   D. 356,970

4. Steve was asked to pick two marbles from a bag of yellow marbles and blue marbles. One possible result was one yellow marble first and one blue marble second. He wrote this result in the table below. List all of the other possible results that Steve could get.

y stands for one yellow

b stands for one blue marble

First Marble	Second Marble
y	b

LINGUISTICALLY REVISED ITEMS

1. Raymond has to buy paper to print 28 copies of a report. He needs 64 sheets of paper for each report. There are 500 sheets of paper in each package. How many whole packages of paper must Raymond buy?

   Answer: _____

2. Harriet, Jim, Roberto, Maria, and Willie ran for president of their eighth-grade class. One of them won. Who is president?

   1. The president now was vice president last year and lives on Vince Street.
   2. Willie is vice president now.
   3. Jim and Maria live on Cypress Street.
   4. Roberto was not vice president last year.

   A. Jim
   B. Harriet
   C. Roberto
   D. Maria
   E. Willie

3. Janet played a video game. Her score was three hundred fifty-six thousand, ninety-seven. Written as number, that is:

   A. 350,697
   B. 356,097
   C. 356,907
   D. 356,970

4. Steve had a bag with yellow and blue marbles in it. He took out two marbles. The first marble was yellow, and the second marble was blue. He wrote this result in the table below. List all of the other possible results that Steve could get.

y   stands for one yellow

b   stands for one blue marble

First Marble	Second Marble
y	b

ACKNOWLEDGMENT

The author acknowledges valuable contribution of colleagues in preparation of this work. Professor Richard Duran contributed to this chapter with his thorough review and very helpful comments and suggestions. Professor Carol Lord also reviewed this chapter and provided excellent comments and suggestions. The author is also grateful to Professor Steve Downing and Professor Thomas Haladyna for their valuable feedback and suggestions. Gary Ockey also provided very helpful comments and suggestions. For this, I am thankful to him. Jenny Kao contributed substantially with comments and assistance in structuring and revising the paper.

REFERENCES

Abedi, J. (1996). The interrater/test reliability system (ITRS). *Multivariate Behavioral Research, 31*(4), 409–417.

Abedi, J. (2002). Standardized achievement tests and English language learners: Psychometrics issues. *Educational Assessment, 8*(3), 231–257.

Abedi, J. (2004). The No Child Left Behind Act and English language learners: Assessment and accountability issues. *Educational Researcher, 33*(1), 4–14.

Abedi, J., Leon, S., & Mirocha, J. (2003). *Impact of student language background on content-based performance: Analyses of extant data* (CSE Tech. Rep. No. 603). Los Angeles: University of California, National Center for Research on Evaluation, Standards, and Student Testing.

Abedi, J., & Lord, C. (2001). The language factor in mathematics tests. *Applied Measurement in Education, 14*(3), 219–234.

Abedi, J., Lord, C., & Hofstetter, C. (1998). *Impact of selected background variables on students' NAEP math performance* (CSE Tech. Rep. No. 478). Los Angeles: University of California, National Center for Research on Evaluation, Standards, and Student Testing.

Abedi, J., Lord, C., Hofstetter, C., & Baker, E. (2000). Impact of accommodation strategies on English language learners' test performance. *Educational Measurement: Issues and Practice, 19*(3), 16–26.

Abedi, J., Lord, C., Kim-Boscardin, C., & Miyoshi, J. (2000). *The effects of accommodations on the assessment of LEP students in NAEP* (CSE Tech. Rep. No. 537). Los Angeles: University of California, National Center for Research on Evaluation, Standards, and Student Testing.

Abedi, J., Lord, C., & Plummer, J. (1997). *Language background as a variable in NAEP mathematics performance* (CSE Tech. Rep. No. 429). Los Angeles: University of California, National Center for Research on Evaluation, Standards, and Student Testing.

Adams, M. J. (1990). *Beginning to read: Thinking and learning about print*. Cambridge, MA: MIT Press.

Allen, M. J., & Yen, W. M. (1979). *Introduction to measurement theory*. Monterey, CA: Brooks/Cole.

American Educational Research Association (AERA), American Psychological Association (APA), & National Council on Measurement in Education (NCME). (1999). *Standards for educational and psychological testing*. Washington, DC: American Educational Research Association.

Baugh, J. (1988, August). Review of the article *Twice as less: Black English and the performance of black students in mathematics and science*. *Harvard Educational Review, 58*(3), 395–404.

Bever, T. (1970). The cognitive basis for linguistic structure. In J. R. Hayes (Ed.), *Cognition and the development of language* (pp. 279–353). New York: John Wiley.

Biber, D. (1988). *Variation across speech and writing*. New York: Cambridge University Press.

Bormuth, J. R. (1966). Readability: A new approach. *Reading Research Quarterly, 1*(3), 79–132.

Botel, M., & Granowsky, A. (1974). A formula for measuring syntactic complexity: A directional effort. *Elementary English, 1,* 513–516.

Brennan, R. L. (2001). *Generalizability theory*. New York: Springer.

Carroll, J. B., Davies, P., & Richman, B. (1971). *The American Heritage word frequency book*. Boston: Houghton Mifflin.

Celce-Murcia, M., & Larsen-Freeman, D. (1983). *The grammar book: An ESL/EFL teacher's book*. Rowley, MA: Newbury House.

Chall, J. S., Jacobs, V. S., & Baldwin, L. E. (1990). *The reading crisis: Why poor children fall behind*. Cambridge, MA: Harvard University Press.

Cortina, J. M. (1993). What is coefficient alpha? An examination of theory and applications. *Journal of Applied Psychology, 78*(1), 98–104.

Crocker, L., & Algina, J. (1986). Introduction to classical and modern test theory. New York: Holt, Rinehart.

Cronbach, L. J., Gleser, G. C., Nanda, H., & Rajaratnam, N. (1972). *The dependability of behavioral measurements: Theory of generalizability for scores and profiles*. New York: John Wiley.

Cummins, D. D., Kintsch, W., Reusser, K., & Weimer, R. (1988). The role of understanding in solving word problems. *Cognitive Psychology, 20,* 405–438.

Dale, E., & Chall, J. S. (1948). A formula for predicting readability. *Educational Research Bulletin, 27,* 11–20, *28,* 37–54.

De Corte, E., Verschaffel, L., & DeWin, L. (1985). Influence of rewording verbal problems on children's problem representations and solutions. *Journal of Educational Psychology, 77*(4), 460–470.

deVilliers, J., & deVilliers, P. (1973). Development of the use of word order in comprehension. *Journal of Psychological Research, 2,* 331–341.

Dornic, S. (1979). Information processing in bilinguals. *Psychological Research, 40,* 329–348.

Durán, R. P. (1999). Directions in assessment of linguistic minorities. In S. Messick (Ed.), *Assessment in higher education: Issues in access, quality, student development, and public policy*. Hillsdale, NJ: Lawrence Erlbaum Associates.

Durán, R., Escobar, F., & Wakin, M. (1997). Improving classroom instruction for Latino elementary school students: Aiming for college. In M. Yepes, (Ed.). *Proceedings from the 1996 Educational Testing Service Invitational Conference on Latino Education Issues*. Princeton, NJ: Educational Testing Service.

Figueroa, R. A. (1989). Psychological testing of Linguistic-Minority Students: Knowledge gaps and regulations. *Exceptional children, 56*(62), 145–152.

Finegan, E. (1978, December). *The significance of syntactic arrangement for readability*. Paper presented to the Linguistic Society of America, Boston, MA.

Forster, K. I., & Olbrei, I. (1973). Semantic heuristics and syntactic trial. *Cognition, 2*(3), 319–347.

Francis, W. N., & Kucera, H. (1982). *Frequency analysis of English usage: Lexicon and grammar*. Boston: Houghton Mifflin.

Freeman, G. G. (1978, June). *Interdisciplinary evaluation of children's primary language skills*. Paper presented at the World Congress on Future Special Education, First, Stirling, Scotland. (ERIC Document Reproduction Service No. ED157341)

Gathercole, S. E., & Baddeley, A. D. (1993). *Working memory and language*. Hillsdale, NJ: Lawrence Erlbaum Associates.

Haiman, J. (1985). *Natural syntax: Iconicity and erosion*. New York: Cambridge University Press.

Haladyna, T. M., & Downing, S. M. (2004). Construct-irrelevant variance in high-stakes testing. *Educational Measurement: Issues and Practice, 23*(1), 17–27.

Hansen, E. G. & Mislevy, R. (2004, April). *Towards a unified validity framework for ensuring access to assessments by individuals with disabilities and English language learners*. Paper presented at the annual meeting of the National Council on Measurement in Education, San Diego, CA.

Hudson, T. (1983). Correspondences and numerical differences between disjoint sets. *Child Development, 54,* 84–90.

Hunt, K. W. (1965). *Grammatical structures written at three grade levels* (Research Rep. No. 3). Urbana, IL: National Council of Teachers of English.

Hunt, K. W. (1977). Early blooming and late blooming syntactic structures. In C. R. Cooper & L. Odell (Eds.), *Evaluating writing: Describing, measuring, judging*. Urbana, IL: National Council of Teachers of English.

Imbens-Bailey, A., & Castellon-Wellington, M. (1999, September). *Linguistic demands of test items used to assess ELL students*. Paper presented at the annual conference of the National Center for Research on Evaluation, Standards, and Student Testing, Los Angeles, CA.

Jones, P. L. (1982). Learning mathematics in a second language: A problem with more and less. *Educational Studies in Mathematics, 13,* 269–287.

Kiplinger, V. L., Haug, C. A., & Abedi, J. (2000, April). *Measuring math—not reading—on a math assessment: A language accommodations study of English language learners and other special populations*. Presented at the annual meeting of the American Educational Research Association, New Orleans, LA.

Klare, G. R. (1974). Assessing readability. *Reading Research Quarterly, 10,* 62–102.

Kucera, H., & Francis, W. N. (1967). *Computational analysis of present-day English*. Providence, RI: Brown University Press.

Larsen, S. C., Parker, R. M., & Trenholme, B. (1978). The effects of syntactic complexity upon arithmetic performance. *Educational Studies in Mathematics, 21,* 83–90.

Lemke, J. L. (1986). *Using language in classrooms.* Victoria, Australia: Deakin University Press.

Linn, R. L. (1995). *Assessment-based reform: Challenges to educational measurement.* Princeton, NJ: Educational Testing Service.

Linn, R. L., & Gronlund, N. E. (1995). *Measuring and assessment in teaching* (7th ed.). Englewood Cliffs, NJ: Prentice-Hall.

Lord, C. (2002). Are subordinate clauses more difficult? In J. Bybee & M. Noonan (Eds.), *Subordination in discourse.* Amsterdam: John Benjamins.

Lord, C. (2004). *Language structure and difficulty: Hypotheses for empirical investigation.* Unpublished manuscript.

MacGinitie, W. H., & Tretiak, R. (1971). Sentence depth measures as predictors of reading difficulty. *Reading Research Quarterly, 6,* 364–377.

Maihoff, N. A. (2002, June). *Using Delaware data in making decisions regarding the education of LEP students.* Paper presented at the Council of Chief State School Officers 32nd Annual National Conference on Large-Scale Assessment, Palm Desert, CA.

Messick, S. (1984). Assessment in Context: Appraising student performance in relation to instructional quality. *Educational Reseacher, 13*(3), 3–8.

Messick, S. (1994). The interplay of evidence and consequences in the validation of performance assessments. *Educational Researcher, 23*(2), 13–23.

Mestre, J. P. (1988). The role of language comprehension in mathematics and problem solving. In R. R. Cocking & J. P. Mestre (Eds.), *Linguistic and cultural influences on learning mathematics* (pp. 200–220). Hillsdale, NJ: Lawrence Erlbaum Associates.

No Child Left Behind Act of 2001. Public Law No. 107-110, 115 Stat. 1425 (2002).

Orr, E. W. (1987). *Twice as less: Black English and the performance of black students in mathematics and science.* New York: W. W. Norton.

Pauley, A., & Syder, F. H. (1983). Natural selection in syntax: Notes on adaptive variation and change in vernacular and literary grammar. *Journal of Pragmatics, 7,* 551–579.

Riley, M. S., Greeno, J. G., & Heller, J. I. (1983). Development of children's problem-solving ability in arithmetic. In H. P. Ginsburg (Ed.), *The development of mathematical thinking* (pp. 153–196). New York: Academic Press.

Salvia, J., & Ysseldyke, J. (1998). *Assessment.* Boston: Houghton Mifflin.

Sandoval, J., & Durán, R. P. (1998). The influence of language: Interpreting tests given to non-native English speakers. In J. Sandoval (Ed.). *Test interpretation and diversity.* Washington, DC: American Psychological Association.

Savin, H. B., & Perchonock, E. (1965). Grammatical structure and the immediate recall of English sentences. *Journal of Verbal Learning and Verbal Behavior, 4,* 348–353.

Schachter, P. (1983). *On syntactic categories.* Bloomington: Indiana University Linguistics Club.

Shavelson, R. J., & Webb, N. M. (1991). *MMSS generalizability theory: A primer* (Vol. 1). Newbury Park, CA: Sage.

Shuard, H., & Rothery, A. (Eds.). (1984). *Children reading mathematics.* London: J. Murray.

Slobin, D. I. (1968). Recall of full and truncated passive sentences in connected discourse. *Journal of Verbal Learning and Verbal Behavior, 7,* 876–881.

Spanos, G., Rhodes, N. C., Dale, T. C., & Crandall, J. (1988). Linguistic features of mathematical problem solving: Insights and applications. In R. R. Cocking & J. P. Mestre (Eds.), *Linguistic and cultural influences on learning mathematics* (pp. 221–240). Hillsdale, NJ: Lawrence Erlbaum Associates.

Wang, M. D. (1970). The role of syntactic complexity as a determiner of comprehensibility. *Journal of Verbal Learning and Verbal Behavior, 9,* 398–404.

Zipf, G. K. (1949). *Human behavior and the principle of least effort.* Cambridge, MA: Addison-Wesley.

18

Anchor-Based Methods for Judgmentally Estimating Item Statistics

Ronald K. Hambleton
Stephen J. Jirka
University of Massachusetts at Amherst

Flexibly scheduled computer-based tests require test developers to expand their item banks or overexposure of test items lowers the validity of their tests. An increase in the number of test items adds a cost to the testing program, as does the expanded amount of necessary pretesting of new test items. It has been suggested that perhaps item writers, item reviewers, or test specialists might judgmentally estimate item statistics, and these estimates could be combined with some empirical data (but not as much data as would be required without the judgmental evidence) to obtain item statistics of acceptable precision and accuracy. In this chapter, we review some of the pertinent literature on the topic of judgmentally estimating item statistics, and describe one recent study to collect judgmentally estimated item statistics. Although the available research literature suggests mixed results in estimating item statistics judgmentally, our review suggests that some of that literature may be flawed, and more recent research, including research from the fields of standard setting and score reporting, suggests that there may be several promising directions for future development of methods. Among the best suggestions for improving the quality of judgments of item statistics include (1) using judges who are familiar with the item content, (2) providing judges with extensive training and practice, (3) including feedback to judges during the judgmental process, and (4) asking judges to provide their ratings on meaningful (i.e., anchor-based) scales. We can expect substantially more research and use of judgmental methods for estimating item statistics in the future. Some suggestions for additional research are included at the end of the chapter.

One important lesson learned from the controversy several years ago between the Educational Testing Service (ETS) and Stanley H. Kaplan Educational Centers Ltd. about the computer-based version of the Graduate Record Examination (GRE) was that larger item banks than had been initially assumed necessary are needed to support flexibly scheduled computer-based tests. Large item banks are needed to keep conditional item exposure levels low to protect the validity of test scores (Davey & Nering, 2002). Of course, one consequence is the increased cost to produce the extra test items, and another is the increased cost to field test substantially more test items.

Testing agencies are faced with a dilemma: Large and heterogeneous samples of candidates for field testing new or revised test items are highly desirable because precision and accuracy are needed in the item statistics, but large candidate samples are associated with higher costs, and a potential loss of item security (the concern is that the more candidates who see items during a field test, the less likely they are to remain secure). One possible solution to the dilemma might be to use item writers, item reviewers, or other test specialists to estimate item statistics. Such a solution could lower the costs associated with obtaining item statistics and ensure item security, at least until items become a part of an item bank and are available for use in a computer-based test. Of course, this possible solution has merit only if it can be shown that item writers, reviewers, or test specialists are capable of accurately estimating item statistics.

The use of judgmentally determined item statistics is not uncommon in test construction in the credentialing field. When, for example, field testing new items is not possible because of concerns about item security or because of the limited availability of suitable candidates, judgmentally determined item statistics are sometimes used to help in the construction of test forms parallel to previous forms. Item writers or item reviewers code items as, for example, "easy," "medium," or "hard," or sometimes they directly estimate classical item difficulty values (or p values). But, rarely are investigations in these test agencies carried out to determine the closeness of the judgmental estimates to the empirical estimates, and often there is little or no sophistication in the training of persons to make the estimates. In fact, the tendency is for persons to consistently underestimate the difficulty of new test items, and little is done to correct their judgments. For example, it is easy enough to provide a bit of training to item writers about the factors that influence item statistics and show them some examples of their judgments and actual item statistics. One bit of good news is that group estimates of item difficulties, and these are common in practice, are often substantially better estimates than individual estimates, although the positive bias in the estimates often remains.

Following a test administration, proper item calibration of new or revised test items can take place, and with the availability of some common items from a previous administration, new tests can be equated to previous test forms. But test score equating is better accomplished if the score adjustments from one form to another are small, and this means, therefore, that judgmental item statistics need to be fairly accurate and, at a minimum, unbiased.

The use of item writers, item reviewers, or test specialists to estimate item statistics has not been a guarantee of success in the past; the balance of the research evidence suggests that they are not especially good at estimating item difficulties or other item statistics unless certain procedures are followed (Hambleton, Sireci, Swaminathan, Xing, & Rizavi, 2003). These procedures are described in detail later in the chapter.

This chapter has two purposes. First, we provide a review of some of the research literature for using judges to estimate item statistics. Judges, from this point forward in the chapter, may be item writers, item reviewers, or other test specialists who are being used by a testing agency to estimate item statistics. Second, we describe the findings from one of our own studies (Hambleton et al., 2003) with anchor-based methods, for improving judges' estimates of item difficulty. *Anchor-based methods* include scales that provide ratings made meaningful by, for example, several clearly described score points along the rating scale. The anchors serve much the same purpose as 32° and 68° Fahrenheit on the temperature scale: We judge temperatures in relation to the ones we know. For example, if judges are being asked to estimate item difficulties (p-values), one way to anchor the scale is to describe the types of items and provide samples of items that have p-values at 0.25, 0.50, and 0.75 on the 0 to 1.00 proportion-correct scale.

Support for an anchor-based approach to item statistics estimation comes from recent research in standard setting and score reporting: The standard-setting process is improved with clear descriptions of the performance levels (Cizek, 2001) and the meaning of score scales can be enhanced with items "mapped" to the reporting scale (Hambleton, 2002). Performance-level descriptions are used to describe, say, "basic," "proficient," and "advanced" levels, and then judges attempt to determine scores on the test that match these descriptions. Clear performance-level descriptions are one of the most important elements of a defensible standard-setting process. Item mapping was introduced in the 1990s with the National Assessment of Educational Progress (NAEP) to help define selected score points (150, 200, 250, etc.) and the performance standards on the NAEP scale (Loomis & Bourque, 2001) and make score reporting to the public more meaningful. A point on the score scale could be made more meaningful by describing the sorts of items candidates could answer correctly or not correctly with some stated probabilities.

How might the judgmentally determined item statistics be used in practice? In some instances, they might be used simply to build new tests that are more parallel to the tests they are being linked to than might be possible were these statistics not available. There are a surprisingly large number of test agencies currently trying to build parallel tests with only the most superficial judgmental estimates of item statistics. They can almost certainly do much better. At other times, the goal might be to prepare randomly equivalent blocks of items for field testing. Some judgmentally determined item statistics are helpful in producing more or less equivalent blocks of items. Also, for many test agencies, the goal is to use judgmentally determined item statistics to set prior distributions to assist in the IRT item parameter estimation process. A good prior on an unknown item parameter such as item difficulty makes it possible to estimate the item parameter with a specified degree of precision and accuracy with a smaller candidate sample size than would be possible were the prior not available. Swaminathan, Hambleton, Sireci, Xing, and Rizavi (2003) were able to show that field test samples of candidates could be cut in half if judgmental data about the item statistics were reasonably valid when used as priors in Bayesian IRT item parameter estimation. Bayesian estimation of item statistics can be quite effective with well chosen priors for the unknown item parameters (see, for example, Mislevy, 1986, 1988; Swaminathan & Gifford, 1982, 1985, 1986).

ESTIMATING ITEM DIFFICULTY BY JUDGMENTAL METHODS: A REVIEW OF THE LITERATURE

Implementing a testing program involves many steps. One of these steps involves the field testing of many test items with (preferably) large numbers of candidates. This process can be both expensive and time consuming. Test agencies prefer to use fewer candidates; item security is tighter as well. This brings up the question, "Is it possible to gather the same type of information from a judgmental process as from an empirical process?" This question, and many related ones, have presented significant challenges for psychometricians for decades. Sheehan and Mislevy (1994) have shown that it can be done via "a tree-based analysis," but this complex cognitive analysis of test items appears to be very labor intensive. It may eventually prove to be feasible on a large scale, but the method is not considered further in this chapter because it does not involve content experts making direct judgments of item statistics.

Research has been ongoing for over 70 years and has resulted in significant findings about how judges can estimate item statistics through judgmental methods and the factors that contribute to the difficulty of items. We review studies herein that fall roughly into five categories: (1) studies on judging item difficulty, (2) studies on other item characteristics, (3) studies on item-writing rules, (4) research on other attributes affecting item characteristics, and (5) a mixture of judgment and factor studies.

Studies on Judging Item Difficulty

One of the first studies in this area was done by Farmer (1928). He asked judges to estimate the difficulty of candidates completing tasks. He found there was some agreement between the group of judges' estimates and how candidates actually performed on the tasks. This was the first study we could find on the topic, and it has given researchers ever since some hope about judges estimating the difficulty of test items. It was the first study in a long line that have showed that a group estimate is nearly always better than individual judges' estimates.

Beginning in the 1950s, a series of studies were carried out by Lorge and his colleagues. First, they had two groups of judges (four in each) estimate the difficulties of a set of mathematics test items (Lorge & Kruglov, 1952). These judges were advanced graduate students in a test construction course, so they did not have specific content knowledge. They were asked to estimate the absolute difficulty (percent getting the item correct) and the relative difficulty (ranking of the items). One group was told about the difficulty of 30 of the items (a first study aimed at providing anchors for subsequent ratings), whereas the other group received no information about the empirical statistics of any of the items. The results indicated that both groups estimated relative difficulty equally well, but the group with information on the 30 items did a bit better in judging absolute levels of item difficulty. Also, the group with additional information made more consistent ratings (i.e., agreement in the judges' ratings of item difficulty was higher), so the researchers reported that fewer judges with such additional information would do about as well as more judges without such information. This finding itself supports the use of additional anchoring information for estimating item statistics. Our own suspicion is that 30 items may have been too many for the group to use as anchors for their judgments. We are also unclear about the directions given to the group who had the extra information, or the time they had to study the 30 items and provide their ratings. But the study provided some promising results.

One major limitation of the study, namely the limited familiarity of judges with teaching mathematics and the specific content, led Lorge and Kruglov (1953) to carry out an extension of their first study by using experienced high school mathematics teachers. The researchers found that these judges made more errors when they were given no information than when they were given information on a few items to anchor their estimates. Specifically, there was a reduction in the tendency of judges to underestimate item difficulties. This remains a problem today in many practical initiatives to estimate item difficulties—judges tend to underestimate the difficulty of test items. But this study did not take into account any possible inequity in the ability to judge the items by the two different groups. This led them to conduct a final study.

The final study in this series by Lorge and Diamond (1954) considered the competency of judges as it relates to the estimation of item difficulty. Competency was defined by correlations between (1) estimated and empirical rank-ordering of items by their difficulty, and (2) estimated difficulties and actual item difficulties. The researchers concluded that the anchor information helped the poor judges the most and the more experienced judges the least. The researchers felt that the additional information made up for the lack of experience of some of the judges. Again, the inclusion of anchor items into the judgmental process had a positive effect on the validity of the judgmental estimates of item difficulty.

Thorndike (1982) made the excellent suggestion that if anchor items were included in the rating process, unknown to the judges, then after the ratings process, they could be used to statistically adjust the judges' ratings to the new items to make them comparable to item statistics based on empirical data. For example, if judges were to consistently underestimate item difficulties (by, say, 10%), this would be known from their ratings of the anchor items, and so all of their estimates of item difficulty for new items could be statistically adjusted upward by 10%. (Of course, even better statistical adjustments such as linear equating are available, with both empirical and judgmental item statistics estimates available for a small set of the test items.) He offered two suggestions consistent with our own methods introduced later in the chapter: (1) select better judges, and (2) train the judges. He also suggested that research be done on how best to choose anchor items (e.g., perhaps the best anchors may be items that judges have been successful in estimating difficulty), and on the placement of the anchor items—hidden away in the set of items being judged so that statistical adjustments can be made after the ratings have been completed, or highlighted for the judges to use as references in making their ratings. It is the latter suggestion that we have pursued in our research, but the other suggestion requires research as well. It seems like a promising idea. In fact, there is really no reason why both ideas could not be included in a study when judges are estimating item statistics.

Studies on Other Item Characteristics

After a gap of almost 15 years in the research literature, other studies began to appear in the measurement literature examining other item statistics in addition to item difficulty. Ryan (1968) conducted a study using teacher's judgments of items to obtain judgments of difficulty, discrimination, and content relevance. A group of high school mathematics teachers were asked to judge multiple-choice items from two achievement tests. The teachers were asked to make judgments in reference to their mathematics classes. One class was a conventional mathematics class program and the other was experimental. Detailed definitions of the characteristics of the items that were to be judged and the procedures themselves were sent to the teachers in advance of the rating process.

Item relevance to the instructional content was determined to be a major factor in determining overall item quality, but not item difficulty or discrimination. A number of the teachers were able to provide statistically reliable estimates of item difficulties. However, the accuracy of the ratings varied and was not consistent over all judgment conditions. Teachers did best when the test items were similar to those they might use on their own tests. There was a positive correlation between judgmental and empirical difficulty when the test content was perceived to be familiar to their students. A limitation to this study was the way discrimination was determined by the teachers. Methodological shortcomings including an awkwardly worded question to the teachers may have contributed to the less than satisfactory findings. At the same time, with only one exception, no one in any studies we have read has been successful at getting judges to estimate item discrimination indices well. This seems surprising because it seems, for example, that test items with distractors consisting of common mistakes and misconceptions are more discriminating than test items with irrelevant or obviously incorrect answer choices even to poorly performing candidates. Judges could be trained to watch for the quality of distractors and use the information in their estimates of item discrimination.

Studies on Item-Writing Rules

Some studies have taken the perspective that violations of the rules of writing multiple choice items may provide clues to item statistics. Board and Whitney (1972) examined how violations of four principles of writing multiple-choice items might influence item statistics. Three of the four violations had no effect on the difficulty of the items. The following conclusions were offered: Adding extraneous material in the item stems made items easier for poor candidates but more difficult for better candidates, so there was little overall influence on item difficulty because the two factors more or less canceled each other. Incomplete stems made the items more difficult. Having an answer that was longer than the distractors did not make the items less difficult. Finally, grammatical consistency between stem and the correct response did not have a major influence on item difficulty. A flaw in this study was that the candidates knew which test was the experimental one and which was the actual one, so motivation may have been a factor in the findings. It certainly seems unlikely that the findings are generalizable to studies with well-coached test candidates. Spotting grammatical clues and overly long correct answers are two of the standard rules that coaching schools teach (correct grammar usage is more likely to be associated with correct answers, and incorrect grammar usage is more likely to be associated with incorrect responses; the longest answer choice is most likely to be associated with a correct answer), and item statistics are surely affected. Clearly, more research along these same general lines is worthwhile, to check the validity of the findings. We suspect that the findings would not be replicated on credentialing examinations and other high-stakes tests. Some evidence to support our position is offered later in this review.

Dudycha and Carpenter (1973) also conducted a study that looked at some of the rules for writing multiple-choice items and their effect on item difficulty and discrimination. The factors they investigated were positive or negative item stem orientation, open versus closed structure, and the presence or absence of inclusive alternatives. The authors found that all three affected item difficulty and that some influenced the level of item discrimination. These results seem much more in line with reasonable expectations.

These two studies provide some information about the specific attributes that can contribute to item difficulty and discrimination and these attributes could be taught to judges during their training to estimate item statistics. Fortunately, even more and better designed studies followed in the late 1970s and 1980s.

Quereshi and Fisher (1977) undertook a study that attempted to consolidate the findings of previous studies such as those carried out by Lorge and his colleagues. The researchers incorporated written feedback by the judges on how they based their judgments to gain better insight into the process. This study used items from a general abilities test. There were five judges and 186 psychology student participants. The judges were advanced graduate students in psychology who rated 44 test items. These students were considered experienced experts in the content.

The results seem to confirm earlier research and add new information. There was a significant correlation between judgmental estimates and empirical estimates for ranking of items and difficulty of items. However, there were large variations in the ratings of judges, with some making much better judgments than others. The guidelines given to the judges were a major determining factor in the quality of the ratings. Not surprisingly, pooling of judges' ratings resulted in better ratings than using the ratings of any of the individual judges.

A study by Willoughby (1980) assessed the validity of estimates of item characteristics. A total of 30 items that included the lowest and highest 15 items based on item discrimination indices from an achievement test were used. Both professors and students provided ratings. Two of the major findings were that (1) all judges showed consistency of ratings between moderate and high, and (2) these ratings were not significantly correlated to the empirical values. Perhaps the major limitation of the study was that the judges were not content experts. Accordingly, the researcher suggested that in a next study real content experts should be used, and that these experts should study the logic and syntax of items.

Another researcher in the area, Bejar (1983), wanted to determine the degree to which subject matter experts could predict item difficulty and discrimination for writing assessments and he came out with mixed results. The *Test of Standard Written English* was used, and the experts were test development staff from ETS. Bejar concluded that he could not use ratings as a substitute for pretesting of writing items because of the low correlation between the empirical and judgmental data. More raters would be needed to get better results, and he was concerned that this would lead to higher costs. He speculated that more training might help the raters to better estimate the item difficulty and discrimination indices, so lack of training may have been the key factor in the less than encouraging results.

Bejar did note that he expected that predicting performance on writing test items would be especially difficult because of the relatively large number of factors that can impact on the item statistics compared to factors affecting the difficulty of, say, mathematics test items. This is an important finding and suggests that research findings may be, in the main, specific to particular content areas and item types. Generalizability of findings may be quite limited.

Research on Other Attributes Affecting Item Characteristics

Additional studies have looked at the specific factors that may influence item statistics. Green conducted two studies that explored the validity of judgmental estimates, as well as other factors that influenced item difficulty besides content knowledge. In her first study, Green (1983) looked at estimates of validity and reliability of judgmental estimates of five characteristics of multiple-choice items. Judges rated 10 items selected from a 40-item astronomy test by using the method of paired comparisons. After judging one criterion, judges repeated their ratings with another. The five factors were item difficulty, language complexity, content importance or relevance, response set convergence, and process complexity.

Green found that item complexity judgment was the most consistent and might be used in place of item difficulty. Item complexity correlated with both empirical and judgmental difficulty. So Green showed that judges are capable of estimating relative difficulties, and can also make judgments about other factors. Item relevance was also found to be a predictor of item difficulty. Item phrasing was not found to be a predictor of difficulty, so cognitive processes could be the major contributor, not language difficulty. One shortcoming of this study may have been the small number of items that judges compared, and the sparseness of the available data (each judge provided only 45 of the 780 possible comparisons).

Green wanted to explore other factors that may influence item difficulty besides content knowledge. Green (1984) described an experimental study. Language difficulty and answer choice set convergence were experimentally manipulated to see how they affected item difficulty. Difficulty of language was manipulated by increasing stem length, syntactic complexity, and using less familiar words in the item stems. Answer choice convergence entailed varying the similarity of the answer choices from very similar to less similar. Answer choice convergence was found to have a significant effect, whereas language difficulty did not. There may be a small effect of language difficulty on the individual items, but it was not significant. The findings from this study regarding the importance of answer choice convergence will come as no surprise to item writers.

One of the most useful pieces of research that we located was work carried out by Chalifour and Powers (1989). They attempted to identify content characteristics that were related to item difficulty and discrimination using 1,400 items from the analytic reasoning section of the GRE. Participants in the study were item reviewers, subject matter experts, and clerical staff.

Interestingly and importantly, several of the content characteristics were good predictors of item difficulty, and to a lesser extent, item discrimination. Content characteristics that were predictors included features such as the usefulness of drawings in obtaining a correct answer, number of words in the stimulus material for the item, the number of rules or conditions in the test item, and so on. Content characteristics and the one expert in the study predicted item difficulty with about the same accuracy (the correlations were about 0.70) and the content characteristics predicted item discrimination with somewhat lower accuracy (the correlation was about 0.40). These results were about the best that we saw in our review of the literature, and provide hope for predicting item discrimination levels in addition to item difficulty levels. The interesting feature of the content characteristics that were good predictors of item difficulty is that they can be coded and provided by trained clerical staff.

It was noted by the researchers that if you can identify the factors that influence item statistics, then you can begin to write test items that might meet statistical specifications as well as content specifications. We see this as one of the immensely important benefits of this general line of research to predict item statistics. With greater understanding of the factors that influence item statistics, then it ought to be possible to construct items in the future to meet statistical specifications. In this way, item writers could be focused on the development of test items that are needed to meet statistical criteria such as the production of test items that function optimally near a cut-off score on a proficiency scale.

Mixture of Judgment and Factor Studies

Impara and Plake (1998) investigated the main assumption of the Angoff standard-setting method, and that is that judges are capable of accurately estimating the difficulties of test items. In the Angoff method, judges are not actually asked to estimate the difficulty of items in the population for whom the item is intended but instead they are asked to estimate the difficulties of items for borderline basic, proficient, and advanced candidates, but the same processes are needed to provide the estimates. With certification examinations, the task is estimating item difficulties for borderline candidates. Impara and Plake determined that judges (in their study, 26 sixth-grade classroom teachers) were not very good at estimating either the performance of a total group of students or the performance of borderline students. They were quite pessimistic actually of teachers' abilities to estimate item difficulties. At the same time, their findings highlight again the importance of defining "experts," and ensuring effective training and feedback. In their study, no one was eliminated on the grounds of not being an expert in judging item difficulty, training of teachers was minimal, and there was no feedback or discussions allowing the teachers to reconsider their ratings.

We located several studies in the literature that used regression models to study factors that may contribute to the statistical characteristics of items. One study by Rupp, Garcia, and Jamieson (2001) combined multiple regression, classification, and regression tree analysis techniques to study the factors that contributed to the difficulty of second language reading and listening comprehension items. Over 200 items administered by computer were completed by 87 non-native English speakers. The data were analyzed twofold. First, multiple regression was used to model the data with 12 text and item interaction predictor variables. Next, the data were used to build models with classification and regression tree analysis techniques (introduced by Sheehan & Mislevy [1994]). Rupp and his colleagues were able to identify, among other things, characteristics of items falling in different ranges of difficulty.

A study by Roccas and Moshinsky (2003) also examined the factors that affect the difficulty of items, specifically, verbal analogy items. They looked at knowledge and process attributes, and examined the factors that were determined to contribute to the difficulty of the analogies. Results from studies like this one can be used to train judges to make better estimates of difficulty of analogy-type items.

Several research studies dealing with the prediction of item difficulty were conducted by Freedle and Kostin (1993, 1996), two of which dealt with attempting to predict the difficulty of items in the *Test of English as a Foreign Language* (TOEFL). The authors used a mixture of judgment and factor studies. The first looked at reading comprehension items and investigated main idea, inference, and supporting statement items. Based on a literature review, the authors made a list of variables that can be considered to predict item difficulty and placed them into 12 categories, with some overlap among the categories for some items. For categories that required subjective judgment, two raters were used. Data from a sample of examinees were used to calculate item difficulty indices and z-scores for these examinees, who were then divided into five ability groups. Several statistical analyses were applied to the sample of items. In short, the results showed that, in general, almost all categories had some influence on item difficulty, with the variance of the low ability group explained more than that of the high ability group. The second study examined the prediction of item difficulty for listening comprehension passages. While the authors noted some differences in the factors for predicting difficulty for listening versus reading comprehension passages, they also noted that many of the same variables that successfully accounted for reading item difficulty also accounted for listening item difficulty.

Nearly all of the previous research has used items that were already written in post hoc analyses to estimate item difficulty. Enright, Morley, and Sheehan (2002) wanted to study the impact of systematic item feature variation on item statistics and how this information could be used as collateral information to supplement candidate performance information and reduce pretest sample sizes. Rate and probability word problems from the GRE were used. Item difficulty, discrimination, and guessing were all affected for the rate problems, whereas only difficulty was affected for the probability problems.

Some of the major findings were that all of the item features affected the difficulty for rate problems, but some aspects of context facilitated or impeded the performance of lower performing candidates, but not among the higher performing candidates. For probability problems, increasing the complexity of the counting task had the greatest impact on difficulty. Some aspects of context did affect difficulty but others did not.

Some Final Thoughts

Our literature review left us with strong views about the research that has been carried out on the topic of judgmentally estimating item statistics. First, our view is that a number of the studies we reviewed had fairly substantial methodological limitations or seemed doomed to failure before they were initiated. It is hard to imagine, for example, why anyone would expect judges lacking content knowledge to be proficient at estimating item statistics. It is not even interesting to know that they cannot do it, because we doubt that a test agency would proceed with such judges anyway. Second, all too often in the studies we reviewed, training appeared to be modest or missing with little focus on any general or specific factors that might influence item difficulty or discrimination. Third, none of the studies we reviewed provided feedback to judges with the expectation that they would reconsider and reestimate the item statistics. Such feedback, for example, is routinely done with many standard-setting methods. Finally, in a number of the studies, researchers suggested that more accurate results might be expected with content experts and some good training.

In the next section of this chapter, we briefly describe one of our studies to have judges estimate item statistics. Our research was based on some suggestions made by Thorndike (1982), our own ideas about how the estimation process might be improved, and some of the findings from the literature review:

1. With training, judges do a more accurate job of estimating item statistics. (They develop more complex models of the concept of "item difficulty" and can apply these models when training is provided.)
2. Component models of item difficulty (e.g., estimating item readability, suitability of distractors, consistency of items with the item writing rules) are not typically as good predictors of item difficulty as more global ratings (i.e., estimate the level of difficulty of this item).
3. In many studies, raters are asked to use unfamiliar scales (delta scale, latent ability, 1 to 10, etc.) in judging item difficulty. These scales are often problematic for judges. They have no frame of reference, for example, for a delta of (say) 11.3. Anchor-based rating scales appear to be more useful to them.
4. Predictors of item difficulty (factors that influence item difficulty) vary as a function of the item type (e.g., what works with verbal analogies may not work with reading comprehension or analytical reasoning). Effective training may need to consist of two

aspects: generic training (e.g., item readability is important, or the number of steps required to complete a problem is important) and specific training for particular item types (e.g., with reading comprehension items, asking candidates to identify purpose is harder if it is implied rather than stated in the passage).

5. Securing judge agreement about item difficulty (obtained through discussion and feedback) provides more accurate estimates of item statistics than averaging totally independent judges' ratings and using the averages as the estimates.
6. Some types of items are easier to judge than others (e.g., quantitative items are easier to judge item difficulty than verbal items). Basically, item complexity impacts on the accuracy with which item statistics can be estimated.
7. Administration details can be influential in estimating item difficulty (e.g., Is the test slightly or moderately speeded? Are candidates permitted the use of calculators?). Also, judges may underestimate the difficulty of items when items appear toward the end of a slightly or moderately speeded test.
8. Judges need to be trained to look at (1) structural characteristics (e.g., item format, number of answer choices, number of operations needed to solve the problem), (2) surface features (e.g., sentence lengths, use of uncommon words), and (3) the psychological component (e.g., which cognitive skills are needed to answer the question?) of test items. The common shortcoming of judges is to focus their judgments of item statistics on only one of the dimensions.
9. The candidate population is important (e.g., the age, gender, and ethnic group of candidates; levels of test anxiety and motivation to perform well are also important). Judges either need to know the candidate population well, or time must be spent in training to ensure that they have detailed information about the candidate population.
10. Item placement in a test is important (especially if a test is speeded). Item statistics may vary as a function of their placement in a test.
11. There is considerable evidence to suggest that item difficulty levels can be predicted, but predicting item discrimination has been much more difficult to do with any accuracy. (Our own thought here is that the average level of item discrimination in an item bank could serve as a good estimate perhaps modified a bit by the well-known negative relationship between item discrimination and item difficulty—basically, hard items tend to be more discriminating.).
12. Average ratings of item difficulty statistics across judges (raters) are much more highly correlated with actual item difficulties than individual judges ratings. (The conclusion that follows is: Use multiple judges in judging item statistics.)

All of these results are found in the available literature, and appear to be important for researchers to consider in the design of new studies to estimate item statistics.

ONE MORE RESEARCH INITIATIVE

Hambleton et al., (2003) reviewed the relevant research on judgmentally estimating item statistics, and felt there were promising signs in the research literature for improving the estimation of item statistics. Several good suggestions came from the literature and they were identified in the last section. Most influential in their thinking were several lessons learned from effective standard setting (Cizek, 2001) and score reporting (Hambleton, 2002). First, judges need to know the test content, receive effective training to understand their tasks, and receive feedback during the rating process so that they can modify their ratings, if necessary, and second, they need to understand the rating scale they are using. On the first point, this means that judges ought to be familiar with the item content, and training needs to be focused on the general and specific factors that influence item difficulty. Effective training requires practice in rating items and receiving some feedback about how well they are doing. Too often we found in the research literature that judges did not know the content of the items they were judging, were not well trained to complete their ratings, and received no feedback on the quality of their ratings. In practice, this is easily done by having judges rate items for which item statistics are known. Also, just as in standard-setting studies, judges might be expected to discuss their ratings with colleagues, and be given the opportunity to revise their estimates based on group feedback. On the second point, it is important that judges understand the scale being used to item judgments. This can be accomplished, for example, by (1) asking for judgments on the percent-correct scale, and (2) providing examples of test items with difficulty values at different points on the percent-correct scale. Explaining percent scores to judges is easy—it is bounded by 0% and 100%, and judgments are the expected percentage of candidates who will answer the test item correctly (including some percentage who will guess the correct answer). It is also important to describe as clearly as possible the reference group, for example, all 10th-grade students in Massachusetts, or candidates about to sit for a credentialing examination. The literature review showed that judges always provided more accurate ratings when familiar with the test candidates. The populations can be described by their demographics, motivation to do well, and so on. Providing examples of items and the percent-correct for these items helps to anchor the scale for judges. For example, when they see three or four items with p-values around .25 they presumably get a better idea of the kinds of items that candidates find very hard.

In the past, it appears that researchers have asked judges to estimate statistics on the reporting scale that they were needed on (e.g., deltas, latent ability). Our view is that a scale should be used that is meaningful to judges, and then later, the estimates can be transferred by psychometricians to the desired scale. For example, it is easy to transfer p-values to the delta scale or p-values to the latent ability scale. Any assumptions that must be made to make the transformations seem preferable to asking judges to work with confusing or mysterious rating scales. The goal should be to make the task as easy and as meaningful as possible for the judges.

Hambleton and his colleagues carried out three studies for the Law School Admissions Council (LSAC) (summarized in Hambleton et al., 2003). The design and results from only the first study are described, focusing on the results and how well the various aspects of the methods actually worked.

Design

A big element of the study concerned training on the factors that we believed influenced item difficulty. Basically, factors affecting item difficulty were organized around three major categories: the item itself (e.g., novelty of item format, reading difficulty, cognitive complexity, number of near correct answer choices, item placement in the test), administration (administration mode, test speededness, etc.), and test candidates (e.g., age, gender, ethnic group, candidate test sophistication). Our literature review enabled us to train judges on the factors that have generally contributed to item difficulty. Judges were made aware of the 10 specific factors listed, and others in estimating item difficulty levels:

1. Negations: they nearly always make test items harder than they are without the negations.
2. Referential: the greater the number, the more difficult the test item.
3. Vocabulary: the more multisyllabic words and hard words used, the more difficult the test item is.

4. Sentence and paragraph lengths affect item difficulty; in general, the more sentences and the longer the paragraphs, the more difficult the associated test item is for candidates.
5. Abstraction of text: the more abstract the text, the harder the test item is.
6. Location of relevant text: apparently, when the relevant material is in the middle of a passage, the item is harder for candidates.
7. The levels and numbers of cognitive skills needed to answer a test item affect item difficulty. Problem complexity is an important factor in determining item difficulty.
8. The novelty of the item type to candidates makes test items more difficult.
9. Item placement in the test: items appearing late in a test are more difficult than when they appear early or in the middle of a test. This may be caused by an examinee's tendency to ignore time limits, or simply that examinees are not capable of answering the test items at the pace required to finish the test within the available time limit.
10. Closeness of the best distractors to the correct answer. This is especially important; an item with a near correct distractor is more difficult than a test item with a correct answer and three or four answer choices that can easily be distinguished from the correct answer.

Judges

The six judges who participated in the training and item rating process were test specialists for the LSAC. Though they were generally familiar with the three subtests on the Law School Admissions Test (LSAT), all were specialists with respect to only one of the three subtests. Some of the specialists indicated later that they would have preferred to rate only items from the subtest they normally addressed in their work. This finding, again, reinforces the important matter of judges knowing the item content.

Anchor-Based Methods

Anchor Based and Item Mapping

Before gathering the judgments of item difficulty, a 2-hour interactive training session was held to describe item attributes related to item difficulty. The purpose of this training session was to inform the judges of item characteristics that previous research demonstrated were related to item difficulty.

Two procedures were used to collect the judgments of item difficulty. The first method, called the *anchor-based method*, featured a discussion of the attributes of items at three points along the item difficulty (p-value) scale: 0.25, 0.50, and 0.75. After discussing the attributes of "difficult," "moderate," and "easy" items around these three scale points, a booklet of 27 reading comprehension items was distributed to the judges. The empirical item difficulties (i.e., actual item p-values) for 6 of these 27 items were revealed to the judges. These six items were chosen to be representative of items characterizing each of the three anchor points of the item difficulty scale.

The first task for the judges was to place each of the remaining items into one of the four categories delineated on the item difficulty scale (<0.25, ≥ 0.25 but <0.50, ≥ 0.50 but <0.75, or ≥ 0.75). The appendix contains the training materials for the reading comprehension items. (The training materials, except for information on the specific factors that make logical reasoning items difficult, were the same.) Next the judges were asked to provide an exact estimate of the difficulty for each item, ranging from .00 (no one would get the item correct) to 1.00 (everyone would get the item correct). After the judges had completed these ratings, the individual ratings were shared with the group, item by item, and the judges were asked to explain their item difficulty ratings. The judges were then given an opportunity to revise their initial difficulty estimates based on the group discussions. Basically, the study was carried out in a way similar to the setting of performance standards.

The second rating method, called *item mapping*, but which is really just another form of scale anchoring, presented the judges with an entire booklet of 27 logical reasoning items. The empirical item difficulty (p-value) for each item was included in the booklet. The judges were told to use these actual item difficulties as a reference for estimating the difficulties of other logical reasoning items. The item difficulties associated with these items essentially spanned the item difficulty scale, and so more "anchor points" were provided than in the anchor-based method. The judges were then presented with a booklet of 21 logical reasoning items and were asked to provide difficulty estimates for each item. The judges first provided their ratings individually, then met as a group to discuss their individual ratings. They were encouraged to revise their initial ratings based upon the group discussions as they felt necessary.

Brief descriptions of the two related methods and how they were implemented follow. Very specific details are provided in the appendix.

Anchor-Based Method Steps

1. Review the three anchor point descriptions (chosen to be 0.25, 0.50, and 0.75 on the item difficulty scale for this field test) in terms of content, cognitive skills, item format, and a sample item or two (in total, item difficulty estimates for six items were given during the training), and so on.
2. Read each set of items (associated with a common stimulus such as a passage or problem statement) and then sort each item into one of the four categories: category 1, 0.00 to 0.24; category 2, 0.25 to 0.49; category 3, 0.50 to 0.74; and category 4, 0.75 to 1.00. Record your ratings on the Round 1 Rating Form. Estimate item difficulty and place this estimate in the column provided on the Rating Form. (Round 1)
3. Receive feedback on judges' placement of items and item difficulty estimates, and discuss this information, and ultimately revise the category placement and item difficulty estimates. (Round 2)

Item Mapping Method Steps

1. Review the 27 test items mapped onto the item difficulty scale for this field test. Try to determine what makes some items more difficult or easier than others.
2. Read each item or set of items (associated with a common stimulus such as a passage or problem statement) and then decide whether individual test items are harder or easier than those with known item difficulty levels. Estimate item difficulty for these new items and place this item difficulty estimate in the column provided on the Rating Form. (Round 1)
3. Receive feedback on judges' item difficulty estimates, and discuss this information, and ultimately revise your item difficulty estimates if you feel revisions are in order. (Round 2)

Results

Reading Comprehension

Table 18.1 presents some descriptive statistics summarizing the results of the item difficulty ratings for the reading comprehension items. As described, these item difficulty ratings were gathered using the anchor-based method. The statistics presented in Table 18.1 include the

TABLE 18.1
Descriptive Statistics for Reading Comprehension Items (Anchor-Based Method)

Item	"True p"	Mean p Round 1	Median p Round 1	Mean p Round 2	Median p Round 2	"True p" − Round 2 Mean
1	.51	.58	.58	.57	.55	−.06
2	.69	.57	.57	.56	.57	.13
3	.64	.66	.73	.69	.73	−.05
4	.43	.64	.69	.59	.58	−.16
5	.60	.72	.73	.78	.78	−.18
6	.54	.41	.38	.43	.40	.11
7	.37	.37	.36	.36	.36	.01
8	.48	.57	.57	.60	.57	−.12
10	.39	.47	.48	.48	.46	−.09
12	.44	.57	.54	.52	.52	−.08
13	.60	.62	.60	.62	.60	.02
14	.49	.61	.63	.62	.63	−.13
15	.61	.41	.43	.41	.43	.20
16	.39	.49	.50	.48	.45	−.09
19	.59	.67	.63	.65	.63	−.06
20	.64	.71	.70	.71	.70	−.07
21	.62	.73	.75	.73	.75	−.11
22	.68	.66	.68	.66	.68	.02
25	.60	.49	.47	.49	.47	.11
26	.36	.52	.50	.47	.45	−.11
27	.55	.71	.75	.71	.75	−.16
Mean	.53	.58	.58	.58	.57	−.04

mean and median estimates of item difficulty (calculated over judges) for the first round (initial ratings) and second round (revised ratings), and the difference between the empirical item difficulty and the mean revised item difficulty estimate for each item.

The results in Table 18.1 illustrate that the judges rated two thirds of the items to be easier than the actual item difficulty estimates showed. The data also show that although the average judges' ratings did not change very much from round 1 to round 2 (time for discussion had been more limited than we had hoped or planned for), there was a consistent improvement in average difficulty estimates from round 1 to round 2. The group discussions appeared to improved the estimates. The group discussions also brought the judges closer to consensus. The interrater reliability index for the round 1 ratings was 0.71 for round 1 and 0.87 for round 2. It was also apparent that judges' means typically moved in the direction of the "true" item p-values, the p-values based on actual examinee data (this was the case for seven of eight items where shifts in access of 0.02 were noted).

In terms of the precision of the estimated difficulties, 9 of the 21 items had mean (round 2) estimates within 0.10 of the actual item difficulties. The largest discrepancy was for item number 15, which was one of the few (7) items estimated to be harder than its empirical difficulty. The correlation between the empirical item difficulties and the mean and median estimated difficulties improved from round 1 to round 2. The correlation between "true" and mean estimated difficulty was 0.50 for round 1 and 0.55 for round 2. The correlation between the "true" and median estimated difficulty was 0.47 for round 1 and 0.59 for round 2. These correlations, and the data presented in Table 18.1, indicate that the judges were somewhat successful in estimating the item difficulties. The higher correlation observed for the median

TABLE 18.2
Descriptive Statistics for Logical Reasoning Items (Item Mapping Method)

Item	"True p"	Mean p Round 1	Median p Round 1	Mean p Round 2	Median p Round 2	"True p" − Round 2 Mean
1	.42	.58	.55	.56	.55	−.14
2	.72	.68	.70	.68	.69	.04
3	.56	.78	.78	.78	.78	−.22
4	.48	.62	.66	.60	.64	−.12
5	.47	.63	.65	.61	.62	−.14
6	.45	.58	.59	.51	.51	−.06
7	.61	.66	.73	.59	.65	.02
8	.51	.53	.55	.49	.50	.02
9	.48	.40	.39	.36	.35	.12
10	.20	.54	.47	.45	.45	−.25
11	.24	.40	.37	.35	.35	−.11
12	.28	.42	.43	.41	.43	−.13
13	.54	.61	.62	.60	.59	−.06
14	.81	.75	.75	.78	.80	.03
15	.83	.81	.83	.83	.83	.00
16	.82	.70	.69	.68	.69	.14
17	.72	.70	.72	.71	.74	.01
18	.83	.72	.74	.74	.74	.09
19	.81	.79	.78	.80	.81	.01
20	.77	.65	.64	.63	.64	.14
21	.50	.57	.58	.57	.58	−.07
Mean	.57	.62	.63	.61	.62	−.03

difficulty estimates from round 2 suggest that some judges provided better estimates than others.

Not presented are the summary statistics for each of the six judges. The results confirmed the improvement in difficulty estimation from round 1 to round 2, and illustrated the relative success in item difficulty estimation for the judges.

Logical Reasoning

Table 18.2 summarizes the results of the item difficulty ratings for the logical reasoning items. As described, these item ratings were gathered using the item mapping procedure. The predominance of estimating items to be easier than their empirical difficulties did not occur. About half of the items (10) were judged to be easier than their empirical difficulties; the other half (11) were judged to be harder than their empirical difficulties. This was an encouraging finding, and may suggest that the training and sample items were helpful in removing the common finding of negatively biased estimates.

As with the reading comprehension ratings, the estimates improved from round 1 to round 2. The round 2 mean difficulty estimates for 11 items were within 0.10 of their empirical difficulties; however, two items (numbers 3 and 10) were judged to be greater than 0.20 easier than their empirical difficulties. And again, it was noted that when there were shifts in the judges' mean estimates (.02 or more), the shifts were consistently toward the actual item p-values (10 of 12 cases).

The correlations between the empirical item difficulties and the average estimated item difficulties were much higher for the logical reasoning items than for the reading comprehension items. The correlation between the mean estimated difficulties and empirical difficulties was 0.81 for round 1 and 0.84 for round 2 (compared to 0.55 for the reading comprehension items). The correlation between the median estimated difficulties and the empirical difficulties were 0.83 for round 1 and 0.84 for round 2. These correlations are higher than any we saw in our literature review.

The interrater reliabilities were also higher for the logical reasoning ratings for both round 1 and round 2. The interrater reliability was 0.84 for the round 1 ratings, and 0.95 for the round 2 ratings. Once again, the group discussions brought the judges closer to consensus.

The results for the individual judges' logical reasoning difficulty estimates are not presented here. The data reflected the higher correlation between the true and estimated difficulties across all judges and revealed the relative successes of the judges in terms of their difficulty estimates.

For the logical reasoning items, the empirical difficulty estimates and the deviations between mean difficulty estimates and true difficulties were highly correlated, but this correlation was reduced from round 1 (0.82) to round 2 (0.72). This finding indicated that the judges' estimates of the easier logical reasoning items were relatively poorer than their estimates of the harder items.

From a comparison of the data in Tables 18.1 and 18.2, it is evident that more precise difficulty estimates were provided for the logical reasoning items. However, because different procedures were used for the reading comprehension (anchor-based procedure) and the logical reasoning items (item mapping procedure), these results do not tell us if the improved results are due to item type (reading comprehension versus logical reasoning) or estimation procedure (anchor based versus item mapping).

Evaluation

In all three of our studies for the LSAC, we compiled evaluations and suggestions from the judges for improving the process. In this first study there was consensus about the adequacy of the training and discussions of the factors that influenced item difficulty. The biggest criticism—and it is one we have encountered in all of our efforts—has to do with the shortage of time to complete the work. It appears that if judges are serious and intend to use the anchor methods, they need more time than might be estimated to make all of the necessary comparisons. We have misjudged the needed time in all four of our studies—three with the LSAC and one with a credentialing agency in the fall of 2004.

The judges also provided information regarding the item characteristics they used to make their difficulty judgments. Some factors listed were length and ambiguity of the item stems and item choices, the plausibility of the distractors, the overall difficulty level of the passage associated with an item, and the presence of negations in the items. It was also clear from their ratings that specific factors tied to item type were important. The judges also drew on their differential experience with reading comprehension and logical reasoning items in making their difficulty ratings.

The judges were consistent in praising group review of the initial item ratings. However, there was also consensus that the time devoted to the group discussions was too short. Still, the judges indicated moderate-to-strong confidence in the procedures.

Conclusions

Many things were learned from the first field test. First, we were encouraged by the results. Despite the hurried and less-than-ideal training and the speed with which judges were expected to provide their ratings, the evidence seemed clear that judges were able to provide item difficulty estimates that might be useful in a Bayesian IRT item parameter estimation process. We were also encouraged by the role of discussion. For the reading comprehension subtest, seven of the eight items showing shifts (of 0.02 or greater) were in the direction of the actual item difficulty estimates (see Table 18.1). For the logical reasoning subtest, 10 of 12 items showing shifts (of 0.02 or greater) were in the direction of the actual item difficulties (see Table 18.2). Clearly, the discussions and feedback had an effect.

We also felt that there was no clear separation between the two methods. In the course of introducing the anchor-based method, statistics for a small sample of items were given. This amounted to a modest attempt at item mapping. This was especially important because the anchors we attempted to develop were not very sophisticated for the judges who were experts on one of more of the three major components of the test.

In sum, the main suggestions for future studies to improve the item judgmental process included extending the time for training, discussing the role of cognitive complexity on item difficulty during training, emphasizing the role of item distractors in item difficulty, and retaining and emphasizing group discussion. Nearly all of the judges felt that with good and extended training, and with discussions and feedback during the process, they would be capable of judging item difficulties fairly accurately. The results suggest that their perceptions on this point are accurate. These changes were incorporated into two additional field tests that, generally, provided more insights in the training and implementation of procedures for estimating item statistics.

CONCLUSIONS

This chapter reviewed the literature on the topic of judgmentally estimating item statistics and described the findings from one study that has advanced two related, promising anchor-based methods. Our own view is that some of the early research literature on the topic is very mixed, with a number of the studies showing methodological weaknesses. Perhaps the most notable problems with some of the early efforts have been associated with the use of judges without content expertise, failure to provide adequate training and feedback, and using scales for reporting that may not be clear to the judges. But there have also been some studies that have shown promising results, including our own.

It would be incorrect to leave the impression that the research by Hambleton and his colleagues produced a set of validated methods for estimating item difficulty. The total of four field tests (three with the LSAT subtests) reveals that there is still much to learn about the process of training judges to estimate item statistics. At the same time, some of the results are very encouraging: Judges indicated that they thought they could be trained to complete the item difficulty estimation process with accuracy and they demonstrated this, at least to some degree. Judges also demonstrated that they benefited from discussions with other judges. Some recentering of ratings was clearly taking place, and judges gained new insights about the factors that make items easy or hard. Almost always, item statistics estimates, after discussion, were more accurate than estimates before discussion. Judges indicated too that they found the discussions of item judgments useful. Perhaps the major failing in the Hambleton et al. studies, including the fourth one, has been the underestimation of time needed by judges to carry out the necessary tasks correctly.

We were able to demonstrate that judges are capable of producing anchor descriptions that more closely met their needs than those produced by the researchers. Perhaps this point should have been obvious to us but we missed it. The use of a sequential process involving the review of many items and the continued refinement of the descriptions seemed to work.

Another important point learned was that judges brought to the task their own experiences and ideas about how to judge item difficulties. In future studies, these experiences might

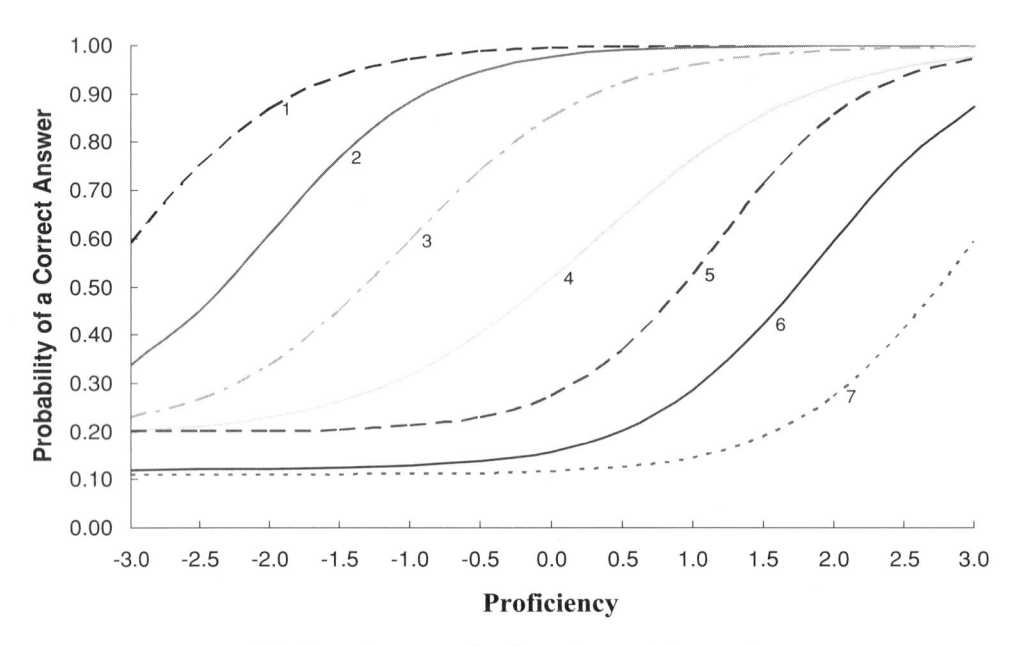

FIG. 18.1. Item exemplars (item characteristic curves).

be incorporated directly into the process of judging items (rather than collected during the evaluation period or in a haphazard way during the course of the meeting). Research findings are perhaps a good starting point for identifying factors to consider in judging item difficulty, but what we learned from our research so far is that with each item type there are very specific factors that influence item difficulty, that a unique set of factors would almost certainly be needed to guide judges through the estimation process. General factors gleaned from previous research are helpful, but much more needs to be done with specific item types.

We began our own research with the idea that we had two methods to study: one based on anchor descriptions and the other based on item mappings to help define the p-value scale. Producing usable anchor descriptions was helpful in our work, but judges benefited from the item mapping information as well. Even when we applied the anchor-based descriptions, we found it useful to provide sample items to further articulate the p-value scale. At this time, our conclusion is that both defining anchor points (such as 0.25, 0.50, and 0.75) along the p-value scale and providing exemplar test items either at the anchors or other points along the scale will be valuable information for judges. Item characteristic curves (ICCs) (Hambleton, Swaminathan, & Rogers, 1991) like those shown in Figure 18.1 could be valuable in helping to clarify the descriptions at anchor points and selecting test items. These ICCs might be used to define what candidates can and cannot do at selected points on the proficiency continuum.

We conclude this chapter with a strong feeling that our general line of research will produce promising results. Clearly, however, more research is needed. More needs to be learned about what factors contribute to item difficulty so that judges can be better trained. More work especially should be committed to the prediction of item discriminating power. This line of research will not only be important for the training of judges, but will be invaluable in training item writers to produce items not only to meet content requirements but to meet statistical specifications as well. The days are long gone when item writers can be pragmatic about the statistics associated with their items. They are going to be asked to write items to a particular level of difficulty (perhaps a passing score), and so research as sketched out here will address two important problems in testing.

We reiterate that our main interest is using judgmental data about item statistics in a Bayesian IRT item parameter estimation procedure where the information provided by the test specialists serves as a prior distribution. The combination of the prior beliefs about the item statistics with item response data from a reduced sample of candidates may function about as well as item statistics based upon considerably larger candidate samples. This point is demonstrated in the paper by Swaminathan, et al., (2003).

APPENDIX: TRAINING MATERIALS

ESTIMATING THE DIFFICULTY OF LSAT READING COMPREHENSION ITEMS

Workshop Handout (Day 1)

Goals of the 1-Day Meeting

There are two goals for this one-day workshop with LSAT test specialists:

1. You will receive training on the estimation of test item difficulties. (Morning)
2. You will estimate item difficulties on one section of the LSAT. (Afternoon)

Item Difficulty

For our purposes, *item difficulty* is defined as the proportion of candidates in the national sample of candidates taking the LSAT who answer the item correctly. For example, an item difficulty of 0.65 means that 65% of the candidates answered the item correctly. Easy test items have high numbers (say, 0.70 and 0.80) and hard test items have low numbers (say, 0.25 and 0.35). Over the course of this workshop, the expectation is that test specialists like yourself will be trained in the accurate estimation of item difficulty and then you will apply your estimation skills to some new test items.

Factors That May Influence the Difficulty of Test Items

In helping test specialists make estimates of item difficulty, two sets of factors have been identified: (1) those factors that are general and are often cited in the measurement literature for use in estimating the difficulties of lots of different types of items (e.g., the reading difficulty of the test item), and (2) specific factors concerning reading comprehension test items.

General Factors. There are several general factors in the measurement literature that can help in the prediction or estimation of the difficulty of test items. Probably the ones most relevant to reading comprehension test items are the following:

1. **Negations:** The greater the number, the more difficult the test item. For example, "Except-type" test items are generally harder than "Which statement is true...".
2. **Vocabulary:** The more multisyllabic words used, the more difficult the test item.
3. **Length:** Sentence and paragraph length affect test item difficulty (because length often introduces more points of complexity, rules, etc.).
4. **Abstraction:** Abstract (or nonintuitive) texts/concepts affect test item difficulty.

5. **Skill level:** In general, the level and number of cognitive skills needed to solve a problem affects the test item difficulty.
6. **Distractors:** The degree of correctness of the distractors affects item difficulty. When distractors and the correct answer are close in meaning, the test item is more difficult. On the other hand, even the most difficult concept for candidates is made easier if the distractors for the test item measuring the concept have little or no relationship to the correct answer and become easy to identify as incorrect answers.

Specific Factors for Reading Comprehension Test Items. In reviewing the measurement literature (e.g., Freedle & Kostin, 1993), a number of factors were suggested that can assist in the prediction of the difficulty of reading comprehension test items:

1. Look for surface features such as number of words in the stimulus, item stem, answer choices, and number of hard words.
2. Watch for connective propositions such as *and, but, however, since, because*. These rhetorical devices tend to influence item difficulty.
3. Negations influence item difficulty.
4. The use of referential expressions influences item difficulty.
5. Main ideas expressed early in a passage (first paragraph) tend to be easier than when they appear in the middle of passages.
6. Vocabulary level, sentence length, passage length, number of paragraphs, paragraph length, and abstraction of text have all been found to influence item difficulty.
7. Inference test items, too, are harder when the relevant material appears in middle paragraphs of the passage.
8. Overlap of words in the passage and the correct answer reduces item difficulty.

Steps in the Item Difficulty Estimation Process

The plan to be followed today consists of nine steps:

1. **General orientation:** very brief (10 minutes maximum) description of the purpose of the study and *p*-values.
2. **Practice test:** test specialists will work through about 20 items; 45 minutes.
3. **General rules** for estimating item difficulty: these are specific to the section of the test; 15 minutes.
4. **Practice** in estimating item difficulty: 5 to 7 items, first ratings, discussion, second ratings, discussion of factors affecting difficulty; 30 minutes.
5. **Continued practice** in estimating item difficulty: repeat Step 4 with the next 5 to 7 items in the Practice Test; 30 minutes.
6. **Development** of anchors or descriptions: based on the first 10 to 14 items; 30 minutes.
7. **Continued practice** in estimating item difficulty: repeat Step 4 with the next 5 to 7 items in the Practice Test, focusing special attention on the anchors and sample items—we want test specialists to be using the Anchors and the item statistics for the first 10 to 14 items; 30 minutes.
8. **Final revisions** to the anchors and review of sample item statistics; 30 minutes.
9. **Implementation** of the estimation of item difficulty process: review the items, provide initial ratings, discuss the ratings, provide second ratings; 120 minutes.

We think the nine steps should ensure that test specialists understand the procedure for judging item difficulty, have confidence in applying the procedure (because of the practice and feedback received), and have sufficient time to complete the procedure in an unhurried way.

REFERENCES

Bejar, I. I. (1983). Subject matter experts' assessment of item statistics. *Applied Psychological Measurement, 7,* 303–310.

Board, C., & Whitney, D. R. (1972). The effect of selected poor item writing practices on test difficulty, reliability, and validity. *Journal of Educational Measurement, 9,* 225–233.

Chalifour, C. L., & Powers, D. E. (1989). The relationship of content characteristics of GRE analytical reasoning items to their difficulties and discriminations. *Journal of Educational Measurement, 26*(2), 120–132.

Cizek, G. (Ed.). (2001). *Setting performance standards: Concepts, methods, and perspectives.* Mahwah, NJ: Lawrence Erlbaum Associates.

Davey, T., & Nering, M. (2002). Controlling item exposure and maintaining item security. In C. N. Mills, M. T. Potenza, J. J. Fremer, & W. C. Ward (Eds.), *Computer-based testing: Building the foundation for future assessments* (pp. 165–191). Mahwah, NJ: Lawrence Erlbaum Associates.

Dudycha, A. L., & Carpenter, J. (1973). Effects of item format on item discrimination and difficulty. *Journal of Applied Psychology, 58,* 116–121.

Enright, M. K., Morley, M., & Sheehan, K. M. (2002). Items by design: The impact of systematic feature variation on item statistical characteristics. *Applied Psychological Measurement, 15,* 49–74.

Farmer, E. (1928). Concerning subjective judgment of difficulty. *British Journal of Psychology, 18,* 438–442.

Freedle, R., & Kostin, I. (1993). *The prediction of TOEFL reading comprehension item difficulty for expository prose passages for three item types: main idea, inference, and supporting ideas items* (Research Report 93-13). Princeton, NJ: Educational Testing Service.

Freedle, R., & Kostin, I. (1996). *The prediction of TOEFL listening comprehension item difficulty for minitalk passages: Implications for construct validity* (Research Report 96–29). Princeton, NJ: Educational Testing Service.

Green, K. (1983, April). *Multiple-choice item difficulty: the effects of language and distracter set similarity.* Paper presented at the meeting of the AERA, Montreal.

Green, K. (1984). Effects of item characteristics on multiple-choice item difficulty. *Educational and Psychological Measurement, 44*(3), 551–561.

Hambleton, R. K. (2002). How can we make NAEP and state test score reporting scales and reports more understandable? In R. W. Lissitz & W. D. Schafer (Eds.), *Assessment in educational reform* (pp. 192–205). Boston: Allyn & Bacon.

Hambleton, R. K., Sireci, S. G., Swaminathan, H., Xing, D., & Rizavi, S. (2003). *Anchor-based methods for judgmentally estimating item difficulty parameters* (Law School Admission Council Computerized Testing Report 98-05). Newtown, PA: Law School Admissions Council.

Hambleton, R. K., Swaminathan, H., & Rogers, H. J. (1991). *Fundamentals of item response theory.* Newbury Park, CA: Sage.

Impara, J. C., & Plake, B. S. (1998). Teachers' ability to estimate item difficulty: A test of the assumptions in the Angoff standard setting method. *Journal of Educational Measurement, 35*(1), 69–81.

Loomis, S., & Bourque, M. L. (2001). From tradition to innovation: Standard-setting on the National Assessment of Educational Progress. In G. Cizek (Ed.), *Setting performance standards: Concepts, methods, and perspectives* (pp. 175–218). Mahwah, NJ: Lawrence Erlbaum Associates.

Lorge, L., & Diamond, L. (1954). The value of information to good and poor judges of item difficulty. *Educational and Psychological Measurement, 14,* 29–33.

Lorge, L., & Kruglov, L. (1952). A suggested technique for the improvement of difficulty prediction of test items. *Educational and Psychological Measurement, 12,* 554–561.

Lorge, L., & Kruglov, L. (1953). The improvement of estimates of test difficulty. *Educational and Psychological Measurement, 13,* 34–36.

Mislevy, R. J. (1986). Bayes modal estimation in item response models. *Psychometrika, 49,* 359–381.

Mislevy, R. J. (1988). Exploiting auxiliary information about items in the estimation of Rasch item difficulty parameters. *Applied Psychological Measurement, 12*(3), 281–296.

Quereshi, M. Y., & Fisher, T. L. (1977). Logical versus empirical estimates of item difficulty. *Educational and Psychological Measurement, 37,* 91–100.

Roccas, S., & Moshinsky, A. (2003). Factors affecting difficulty of verbal analogies. *Applied Measurement in Education, 16*(2), 99–113.

Rupp, A. A., Garcia, P., & Jamieson, J. (2001). Combining multiple regression and CART to understand item difficulty in second language reading and listening comprehension test items. *International Journal of Testing, 1,* 185–216.

Ryan, J. J. (1968). Teacher judgment of test item properties. *Journal of Educational Measurement, 5,* 301–306.

Sheehan, K. M., & Mislevy, R. J. (1994). *A tree-based analysis of items from an assessment of basic mathematics skills* (ETS Research Report 94-14). Princeton, NJ: Educational Testing Service.

Swaminathan, H., & Gifford, J. (1982). Bayesian estimation in the Rasch model. *Journal of Educational Statistics, 7,* 175–191.

Swaminathan, H., & Gifford, J. (1985). Bayesian estimation in the two-parameter logistic model. *Psychometrika, 50,* 349–364.

Swaminathan, H., & Gifford, J. (1986). Bayesian estimation in the three-parameter logistic model. *Psychometrika, 51,* 589–601.

Swaminathan, H., Hambleton, R. K., Sireci, S. G., Xing, D., & Rizavi, S. M. (2003). Small sample estimation in dichotomous item response models: effects of priors based on judgmental information on the accuracy of item parameter estimates. *Applied Psychological Measurement, 27,* 27–51.

Thorndike, R. L. (1982). Item and score conversion by pooled judgment. In P. W. Holland, & D. B. Rubin (Eds.), *Test equating* (pp. 309–317). New York: Academic Press.

Willoughby, T. L. (1980). Reliability and validity of a priori estimates of item characteristics for an examination of health science information. *Educational and Psychological Measurement, 40,* 1141–1146.

19

Item Analysis

Samuel A. Livingston
Educational Testing Service

Item analysis consists of statistical analyses of the data produced when test takers respond to test items—analyses conducted for the purpose of providing information about the items, rather than the test takers. Item analysis results can be presented graphically or numerically. The graphic presentation consists of response curves showing the test taker's estimated probability of a particular response (e.g., a correct answer) as a function of the test taker's score on a measure of the general type of skills or knowledge measured by the item. The numerical presentation includes statistics that measure the difficulty of the item and the extent to which it discriminates between strong and weak test takers. *Differential item functioning* describes the extent to which the item is particularly difficult (or easy) for a specified demographic group of test takers, after controlling for between-group differences in the knowledge or skills tested.

This chapter explains what item analysis is and what information it provides, why test makers do it, when they do it, and how they do it. This chapter explains what item response curves are and what information they provide, with examples to show how the response curves differ for different items. It describes two different approaches to estimating the response curves—weighted moving average and item response theory (IRT). It presents some of the statistics used to describe the performance of test items, and it discusses the strengths and limitations of each one. And it explains the concept of differential item functioning (DIF) and briefly describes the procedures used to measure it.

WHAT IS ITEM ANALYSIS?

Item analysis is a term that seems to have been defined more often implicitly than explicitly. In this chapter, the term refers to a group of statistical analyses having these two characteristics:

1. The data consist of (a) the actual responses of individual people to individual test items or (b) the scores of individual people on individual test items; and
2. The primary purpose of the analyses is to gain information about the items, rather than about the people.

The items can be questions, exercises, or problems on a test, questionnaire, or performance assessment. They can require the test taker to select a response from a list of options presented or to generate a response. What makes them "items" is the way they are used to provide information about the people responding to them. The items are not used individually, but are combined (in some way) to produce a total score.

This chapter refers to the collection of items as a *test*, to the people responding to the items as *test takers*, and to the characteristics that the items are intended to indicate as *knowledge* or *skills*. However, many of the same principles and techniques that apply to tests of knowledge and skills apply also to questionnaires, observation checklists, and other types of measures.

WHAT DOES ITEM ANALYSIS TELL US ABOUT THE ITEMS?

Item analysis provides three kinds of important information about the items: difficulty, discrimination and DIF. *Difficulty* is exactly what the term implies, how hard the item is. For most tests, the test developers need to know which test items (if any) are so hard that almost none of the test takers can answer them correctly and which items (if any) are so easy that nearly all the test takers can answer them correctly. Knowing the difficulty of the items helps the test makers to avoid making a test so hard or so easy that it fails to provide much information about individual test takers. Also, an item that proves to be much harder or much easier than anticipated may be flawed in some way. An unexpectedly hard item may be ambiguous, or it may have a wrong answer option—a *distractor*—that is too nearly correct. An unexpectedly easy item may contain some kind of information that makes the correct answer apparent even to test takers who do not have the knowledge the item is intended to test.

Discrimination is the tendency of the item to be answered correctly by test takers who are generally strong in the skills or type of knowledge the item is intended to measure and to be answered incorrectly by test takers who are not. To evaluate the discriminating power of the item, it is necessary to have a measure of the test takers' proficiency in those skills or that type of knowledge. This measure is the *item analysis criterion* or simply the *criterion*. Usually, it is the test taker's score on the full test or on a portion of the test. An item that does not discriminate between test takers who are strong on the criterion and those who are weak on the criterion is likely to be a bad item. It may be ambiguous or misleading. It may have wrong answer options that are too nearly correct. It may test an obsolete skill or point of knowledge. On the other hand, it may be a perfectly good item that measures a specific skill or point of knowledge that happens to be known by many test takers who are not especially strong in the other skills or knowledge the test measures.

What are the advantages of using the full test as the item analysis criterion, and what are the advantages of using only a portion of the test? There are two main advantages of using the full test: (1) The total score is a more reliable measure of the test taker's proficiency, because it is based on more observations. (2) The total score is less affected by the inclusion of the item. If the item is included in the criterion, the test taker's score on the criterion depends partly on the test taker's score on the item. The smaller the number of items in the criterion, the greater is this dependency. For example, if the criterion is a 10-item subtest that includes the item, the item accounts for one tenth of the test taker's score on the criterion. If the criterion is the total score on a 50-item test, the item accounts for only one fiftieth of the test taker's score on the criterion. However, in one common situation it is advantageous to use a subscore as the item analysis criterion. This situation occurs when the full test measures two or more different skills or types of knowledge and test takers who are strong at one of them are not especially likely to be strong at the others. For example, a science test may test knowledge of biology, chemistry, and physics, and test takers who are particularly strong in biology may not be particularly strong in physics.

DIF stands for *Differential item functioning*. DIF is the tendency of an item to function differently in different groups of test takers, groups defined by something other than their proficiency in the subject of the test. An item shows DIF against a group of test takers if it is particularly difficult for members of that group—more difficult than expected from the general performance of that group and the general difficulty of that item. The most common reason for DIF analysis is to identify and remove from the test any items that are particularly difficult for test takers who are members of specified demographic groups: women, African Americans, Asian Americans, Hispanic or Latino Americans, and Native Americans. However, DIF analysis can also be used to identify items that are particularly difficult (or items that are particularly easy) for students who have attended a particular type of school or studied a particular type of curriculum. DIF is a secondary form of item analysis that is sometimes conducted after the primary item analysis, which focuses on the difficulty of the items and their discrimination between generally strong and generally weak test takers.

HOW ARE ITEM ANALYSIS RESULTS USED?

The information provided by item analysis helps test developers select the items to be included in each form (edition) of the test, and to identify items that need to be revised before they are included in any form of the test. Item analysis also serves as a quality-control step—a last chance to catch errors in the scoring key or items that should be excluded from the scoring of the test. (Statistics alone cannot determine which items on a test are good and which are bad, but statistics can be used to identify items that are worth a particularly close look.) Item analysis helps test developers decide which items from a current form of a test to use in a future form of the test. It helps the test developers identify items that might be substantially improved by revisions. And it helps the test developers learn what types of items tend to work well and what types tend not to work well in a particular type of test.

The ways in which the item analysis results are used depend on when the results are available. In large-scale testing programs, there are three points in the measurement process at which item analysis is often done.

After Pretesting

In many large-scale testing programs, items are pretested by administering these items to a group of test takers like those who will take the test, before the items are included in an actual form of the test. Item analysis based on pretesting allows the test developers to identify and correct any flawed items before they are included in an operational version of the test.

In some testing programs, items are pretested by administering them at a regular test administration along with the operational test. Testing programs that pretest items often administer several versions of the test at the same time, with the different versions having the same operational items but different pretest items. In some cases, the items being pretested are placed in a separately timed section of the test. In other cases, the pretest items are embedded—interspersed with the operational items on the test. Putting the pretest items in a separately timed section eliminates the possibility of having them interfere with the test takers' performance on the operational items. However, it may lead the test takers to suspect that the separately timed items do not count in the final score, and the test takers may not make a genuine effort in answering them. Embedding the pretest items in the operational test solves this problem, but it may result in test takers spending too much of their limited time on the pretest items and running short of time for the operational items.

After Administration, but Before Scoring

Item analysis done at this stage of the process helps the test developers identify errors in the scoring key or serious defects in the items—errors or defects serious enough to exclude the item from scoring. The information provided by the item analysis enables test developers to focus their attention on a relatively small subset of items, helping them to make any necessary corrections in the scoring key before the test takers' scores are computed. Item analysis at this stage is especially important for tests in which the items have not been pretested, but it is a useful quality-control step on any test.

After Scores Have Been Reported

Item analysis done at this stage of the process helps test developers select items for reuse in future forms of the test. If the scores on a future form of the test will be linked to scores on the current form through common items, item analysis is especially useful in selecting a set of common items that represents the full range of difficulty of the items on the test.

HOW ARE ITEM ANALYSIS RESULTS PRESENTED?

Item analysis results can be presented graphically or numerically. Each method has its advantages. A graphic presentation enables the test developer to take in a lot of information about the item very quickly. The test developer can see how likely test takers are to answer the item correctly and how this tendency varies with their scores on the criterion. If the item is a multiple-choice item, the graph can also show how likely the test takers are to choose each wrong answer option and how those tendencies vary with their scores on the criterion. If the item is scored to allow partial credit, the graph can show how likely test takers are to attain each possible score on the item and how those tendencies vary with their scores on the criterion.

A numerical presentation is useful for creating programmable decision rules to provide the test developer with a computer-produced list of items for special attention—something that is especially useful when the number of items to be reviewed is large. Numerical item statistics also enable the test developers to establish statistical specifications for difficulty by dividing the range of the difficulty statistic into intervals and requiring each form of the test to have a specified number of items in each interval.

WHAT DOES A GRAPHIC PRESENTATION OF ITEM ANALYSIS RESULTS LOOK LIKE?

A graph for presenting item analysis results consists of one or more *response curves*. A response curve shows a test taker's probability of a particular response to the item as a function of the test taker's score on the criterion. The horizontal axis represents the score scale for the criterion; the height of the curve indicates the probability of a correct response. Many item analysis graphs contain only one response curve—the response curve for answering the item correctly. The response curve for the correct answer indicates both the difficulty and the discrimination of the

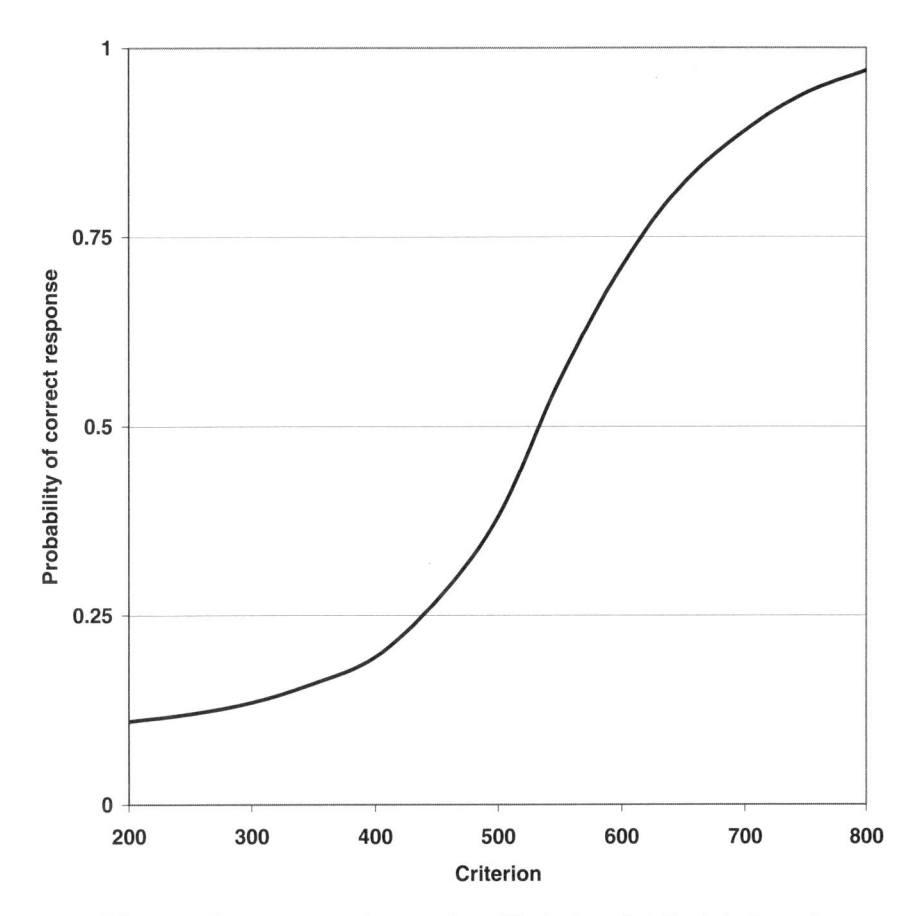

FIG. 19.1. Response curve for a medium-difficulty item that discriminates well.

item. The higher the response curve (in any given range of the criterion), the easier the item (for test takers whose performance on the criterion places them in that range). The lower the response curve, the more difficult the item. The more steeply the height of the curve increases from left (weaker test takers) to right (stronger test takers), the greater the discriminating power of the item.[1]

Figures 19.1 to 19.4 show some examples. Each of these figures shows the response curve for the correct answer to a five-option multiple-choice item. The item illustrated in Figure 19.1 is a medium-difficulty item that discriminates effectively throughout most of the range of scores on the criterion. Test takers with low scores on the criterion have a very low probability of answering the item correctly; test takers with high score on the criterion have a high probability of answering correctly. The curve rises steeply between criterion score 400 and criterion score 700, indicating that the item discriminates well among test takers with criterion scores in this range.

Figure 19.2 shows the response curve for an easy item. It discriminates well among the weaker test takers, but it is too easy to discriminate among the rest. Almost no test takers with criterion scores above 500 miss this item.

---

[1] The author first encountered this graphic approach in 1981; Charles Pine, a physics professor at Rutgers University at Newark, was using it to analyze items on the New Jersey College Basic Skills Placement Test.

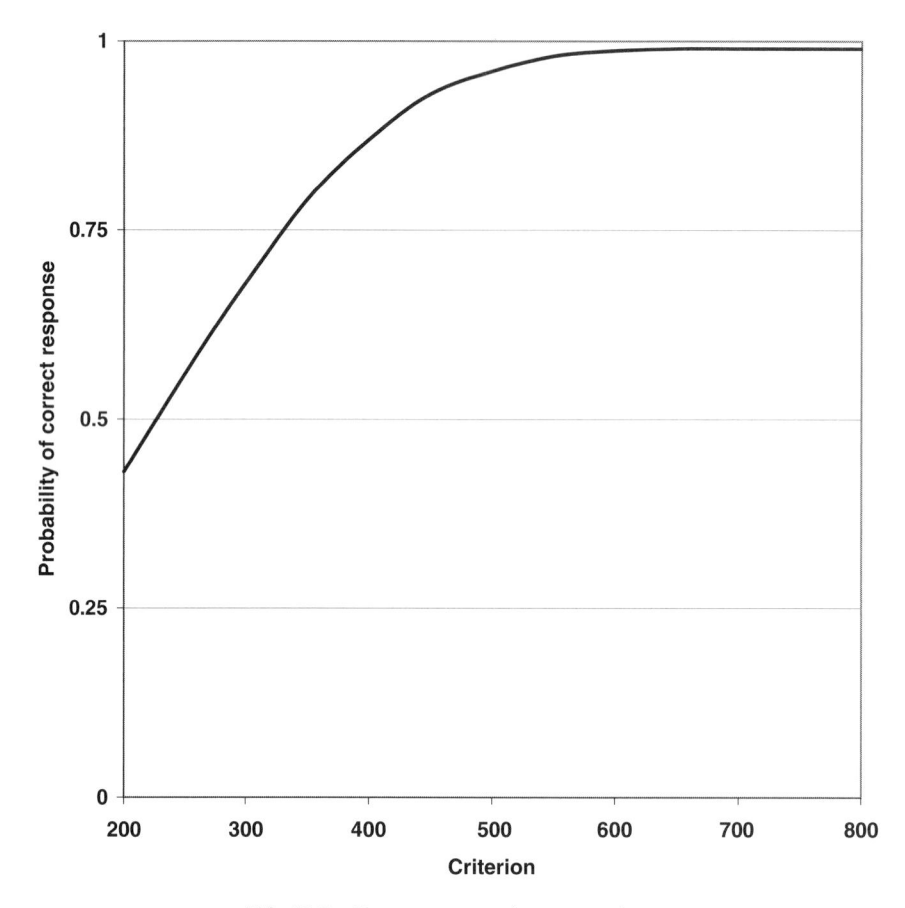

FIG. 19.2. Response curve for an easy item.

Figure 19.3 shows the response curve for a difficult item. It discriminates well among the stronger test takers, and it separates them from the rest of the test takers. But it is so difficult that the test takers with criterion scores of 500 or lower have only about a 20% probability of choosing the correct answer. As a group, those test takers could have done about as well on this item if they had answered it without bothering to read it! This item is too hard to discriminate the test takers in the middle of the criterion score range from those at the bottom.

Figure 19.4 shows the response curve for an item that is too difficult to be of any use in this test. Even the strongest test takers have less than a 40% probability of answering it correctly. Test takers with criterion scores in the upper middle portion of the criterion score range are the least likely to answer this item correctly! For an item like this one, it would be especially useful for the test developers to see the response curves for the distractors as well as for the correct answer.

Figure 19.5 shows all the response curves for this item in a single graph. Distractor C appears to be the most popular choice, especially among the stronger test takers, but there is no single distractor that most of the test takers are choosing.

Figure 19.6 shows the response curves for a *partial-credit item*, an item on which the test taker's response is not scored simply right or wrong. On this item, the test taker can receive a score of 0, 1, 2, 3, or 4. There is a separate response curve for each score except 0, the lowest possible score. The height of the curve indicates the probability that the test taker's response to the item receives at least that score. In Figure 19.6, the response curve for a score of at least

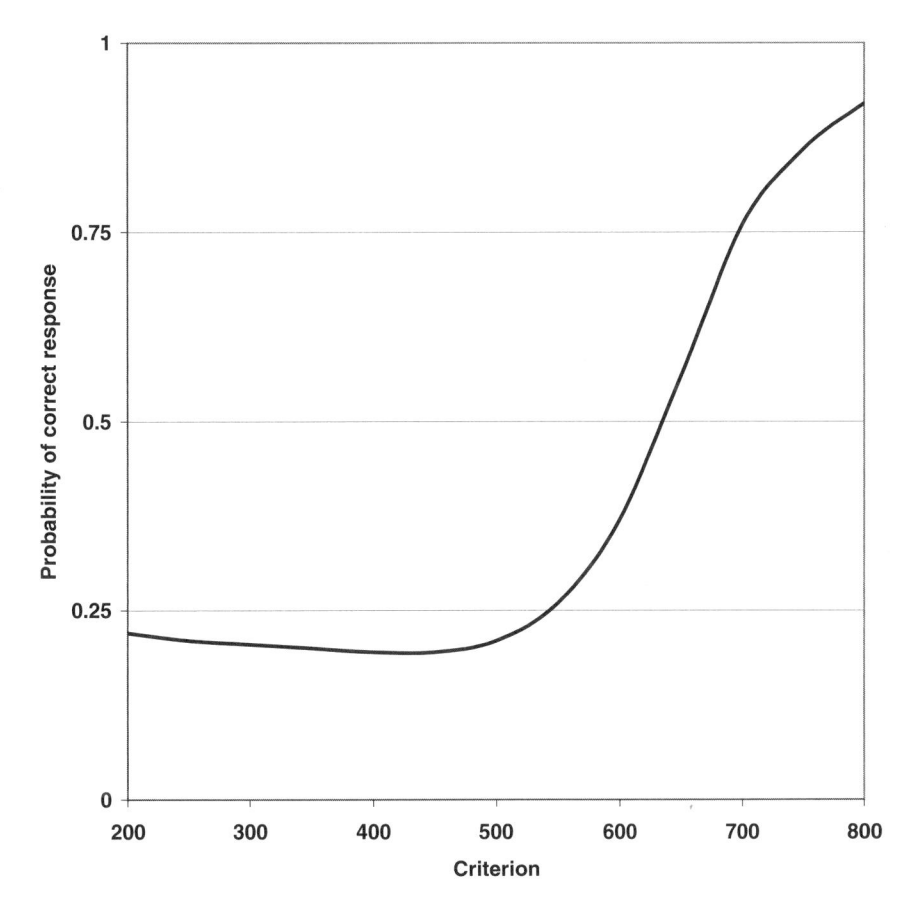

FIG. 19.3. Response curve for a difficult item that discriminates well.

1 looks like a response curve for an easy item. The response curve for a score of at least 2 looks like a response curve for a medium-difficulty item. The response curve for a score of at least 3 looks like a response curve for a difficult item. And the response curve for a score of 4 (the highest possible score) looks like a response curve for a very difficult item.

HOW ARE ITEM RESPONSE CURVES ESTIMATED?

There are at least two ways to estimate item response curves. These two methods, when applied to the same data, often produce similar results—item response curves that look essentially the same—but sometimes they do not. The response curves in Figures 19.1 to 19.6 were estimated by a method that statisticians call *weighted moving-average smoothing*.[2] This method does not make strong assumptions about the way test takers respond to test items. It assumes only that (1) a small change in the test taker's criterion score does not lead to an abrupt change in the probability of the response, and (2) information from test takers with a particular criterion score is relevant for estimating the response probability for test takers with nearby criterion scores.

---

[2]The particular type of weighted moving-average smoothing used to produce Figures 19.1 to 19.6 is called *Gaussian kernel smoothing*. It was pioneered by Ramsay (1995).

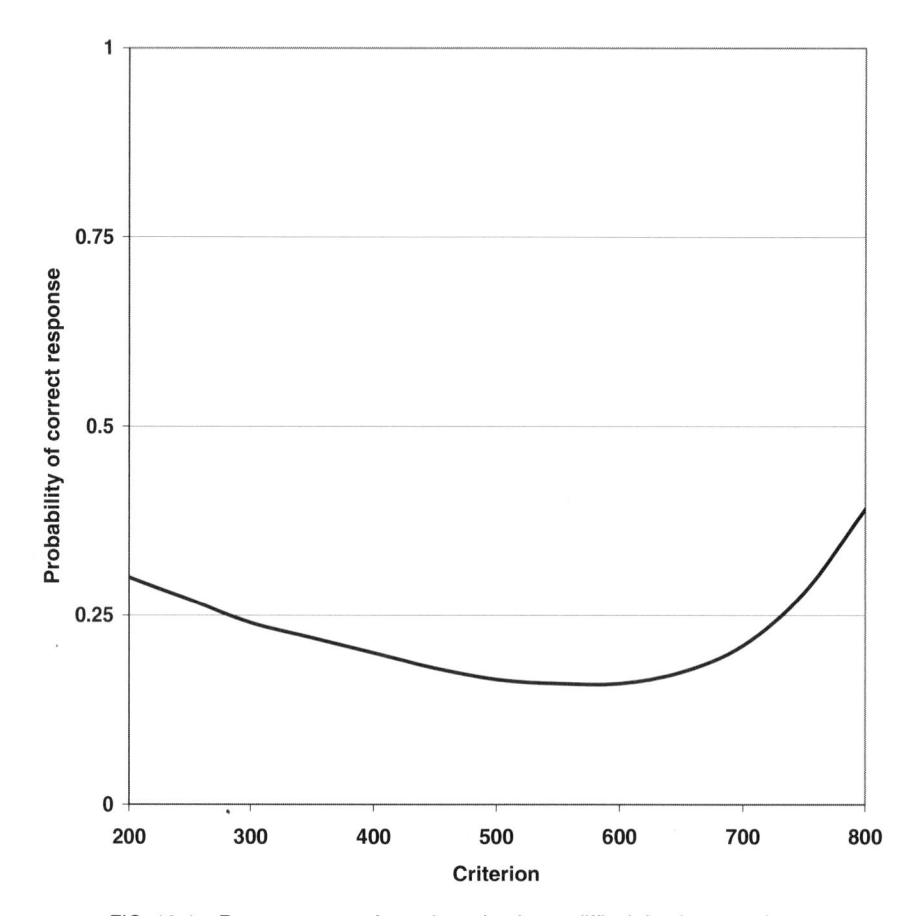

FIG. 19.4. Response curve for an item that is too difficult for the test takers.

There is another commonly used statistical approach to estimating response curves: Item Response Theory (IRT).[3] IRT makes some strong assumptions about the way test takers respond to test items. The commonly used versions of IRT assume that a test taker's probability of answering an item correctly depends on only two kinds of things: (1) the test taker's general ability in the subject of the test, and (2) a small number of characteristics of the item—one, two, or three, depending on the version of IRT. Each version of IRT assumes that there is a general formula for the response curve, a formula that applies to all the items. One consequence of this assumption is that the estimated response curves for all the items have the same general shape.[4]

Figures 19.7 to 19.9 are examples of the graphs of the response curves produced by an IRT analysis. Each graph shows the response curve for the correct answer only. The most important difference between these graphs and those in Figures 19.1 to 19.4 is the criterion. In Figures 19.1 to 19.4, the criterion is a score that can actually be observed for every test taker in the analysis. In Figures 19.7 to 19.9, the criterion is an unobservable variable called *Ability*, which is a short way of saying, "the characteristic that enables test takers to answer items on this test correctly."[5] The IRT analysis results in a mathematical formula for each item, giving

---

[3]Response curves estimated by IRT are sometimes called *item characteristic curves* or *trace lines*.
[4]See Lei, Dunbar, and Kolen (2004) for a comparison of these two approaches to item analysis.
[5]The test taker's ability is commonly represented in formulas by the Greek letter θ (theta).

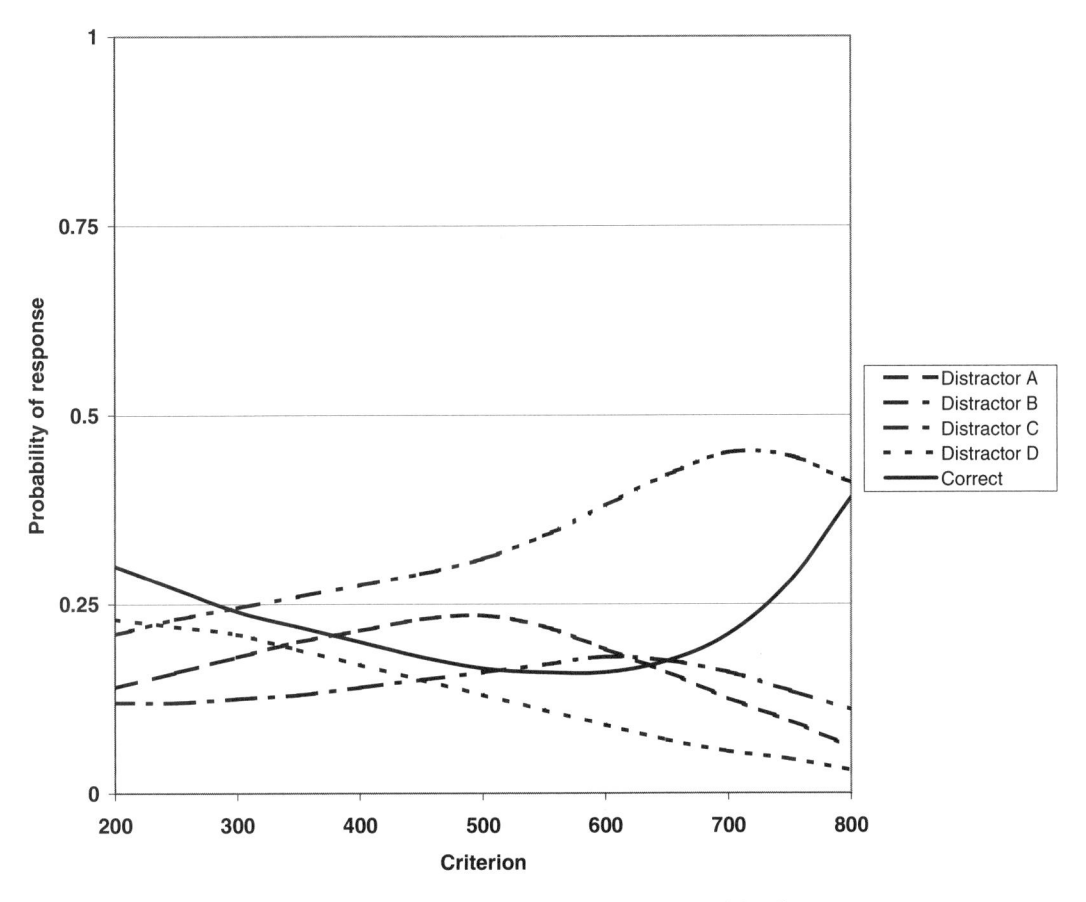

FIG. 19.5. Response curves for the correct answer and the distractors.

the estimated probability of a correct answer by a test taker at any given level of ability. The IRT analysis also estimates an ability value for each test taker whose responses are included in the analysis.

The most commonly used versions of IRT assume that the ability variable has a normal distribution, with a mean of 0 and standard deviation of 1, in the population of test takers. Figures 19.7 to 19.9 reflect this assumption. Negative numbers on the ability scale represent below-average ability, positive numbers represent above-average ability, and about two thirds of the test takers have estimated ability values between −1 and +1. Figure 19.7 shows the estimated response curve for an item that discriminates strongly in the low-average-ability to high-ability range (from −1 to +2). Figure 19.8 shows the estimated response curve for a much easier item. This item discriminates strongly in the low-ability to average-ability range (from −2 to 0). Figure 19.9 shows the estimated response curve for an item that discriminates throughout the entire ability range but does not discriminate strongly in any part of the ability range.

The version of IRT used to produce the graphs in Figures 19.7 to 19.9 assumes that the items can differ in three ways: (1) difficulty, (2) discriminating power, and (3) the tendency for a test taker with absolutely no knowledge of the subject to answer the item correctly. This version of IRT is commonly referred to as the *three-parameter model*. The three parameters are numbers that determine the shape and position of the response curve. They

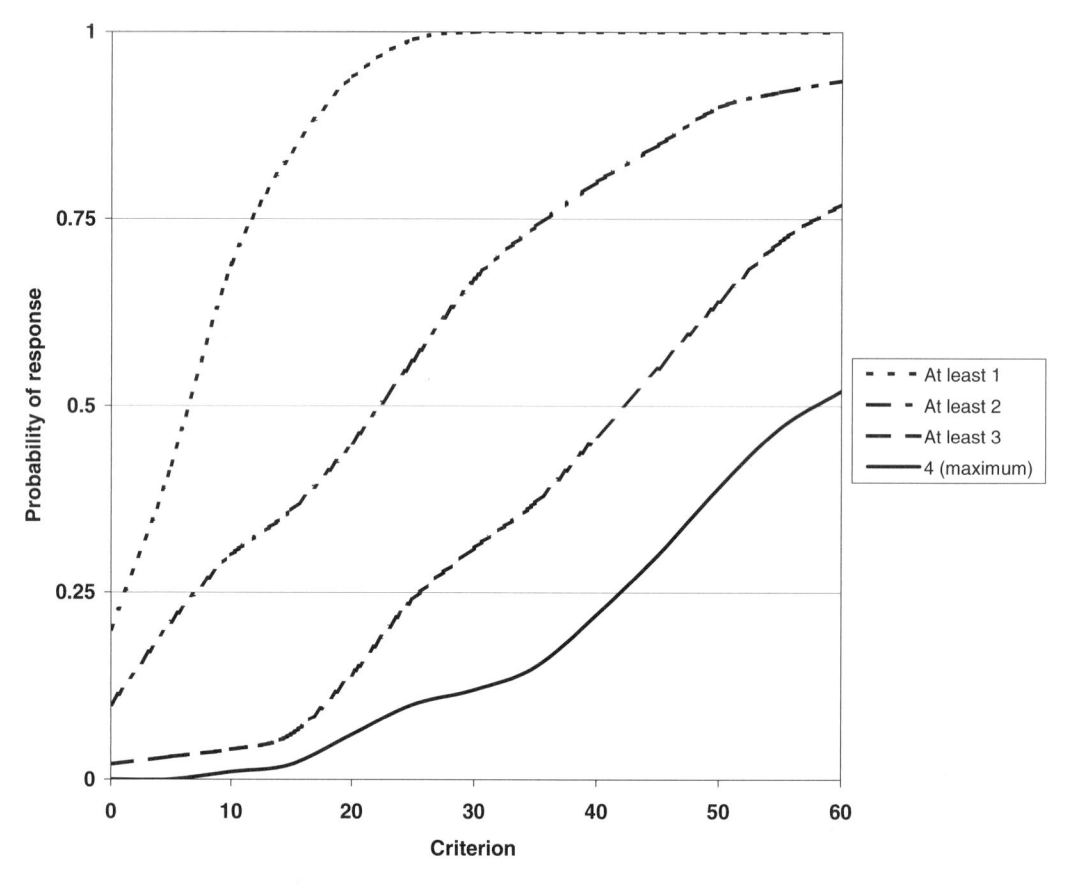

FIG. 19.6. Response curves for a partial-credit item.

are sometimes referred to as the *difficulty parameter*, the *discrimination parameter*, or the *guessing parameter*. The three-parameter model requires data from a fairly large number of test takers, because of the number of parameters to be estimated (three parameters for each item).

There is another frequently used version of IRT, one that does not require as large a number of test takers as the three-parameter model. It is called the *one-parameter model* (or *Rasch model*), and it assumes that the items differ only in difficulty. This version of IRT makes all the assumptions of the three-parameter model, plus two more: (1) that all the items have the same discriminating power and (2) that a test taker with absolutely no knowledge of the subject has absolutely no chance of answering any of the items correctly, not even by a lucky guess. Figures 19.10 to 19.12 show the response curves estimated by this version of IRT for the same items as in Figures 19.7 to 19.9. Notice that the curves produced for these three items by the one-parameter model are all equally steep, whereas the curves produced by the three-parameter model (Figures 19.7 to 19.9) are not.

There are other versions of IRT in addition to the two mentioned above. One of them is the two-parameter model, which assumes that the items can differ in their discriminating power but that a test taker with no knowledge has no chance of answering any items correctly. There are also versions of IRT that apply to partial-credit items, to estimate a response curve for each possible score on the item.

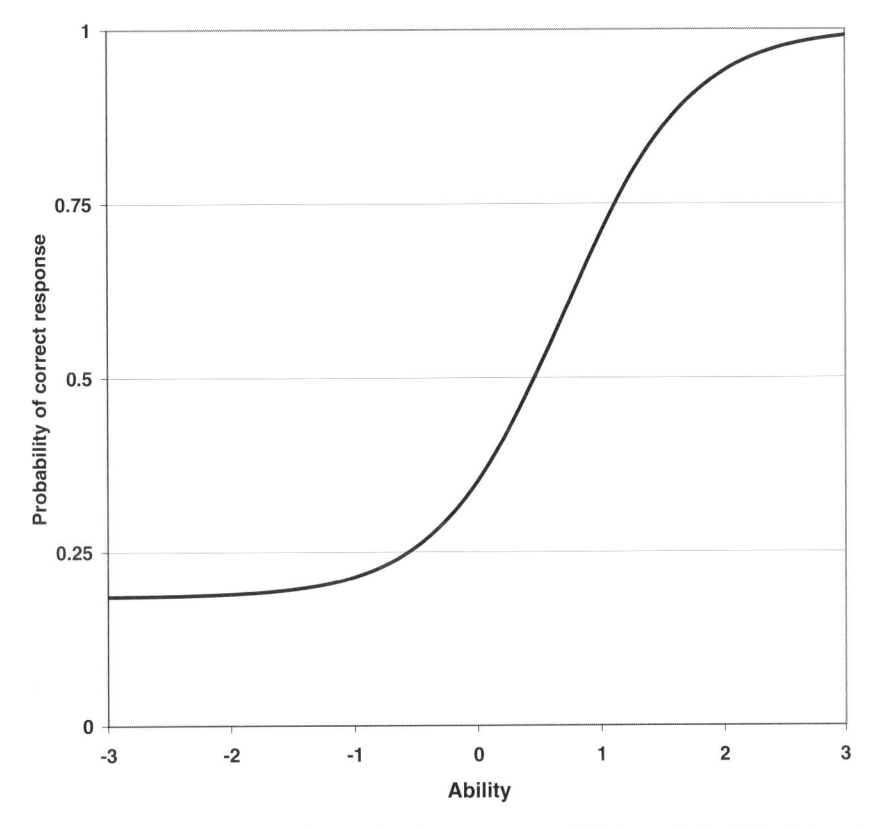

FIG. 19.7. Response curve estimated by three-parameter IRT for a fairly difficult item that discriminates well.

WHAT STATISTICS DOES AN ITEM ANALYSIS INCLUDE?

Difficulty

Probably the simplest and most obvious measure of the difficulty of an item for a group of test takers is their average score on the item. If the only possible scores on the item are 1 (for a correct answer) or 0 (for an incorrect answer or a missing response), this statistic is equal to the percentage of the group who answer the item correctly. In this case, it is often called the p-value. Of course, the average item score is meaningful only if you know something about the group of test takers that it refers to. Average item scores can be very misleading if they are computed from the responses of an unusually strong or unusually weak group of test takers.

If the items are partial-credit items, it is often useful to report the percentage of test takers earning each possible score on the item. It may also be useful to report cumulative percentages, accumulating from the top down. For example, if the item has possible scores of 0, 1, 2, and 3, what percent of the test takers earned scores of 3? What percent earned scores of at least 2? What percent earned scores of at least 1?

In an IRT analysis, the difficulty of an item is usually indicated by the value of its "difficulty parameter."[6] In a one-parameter IRT analysis, this statistic says it all. However, in a three-parameter IRT analysis, two items can have the same difficulty parameter and yet differ

---

[6]In an IRT analysis of partial-credit items, there is a different difficulty parameter for each possible score on the item.

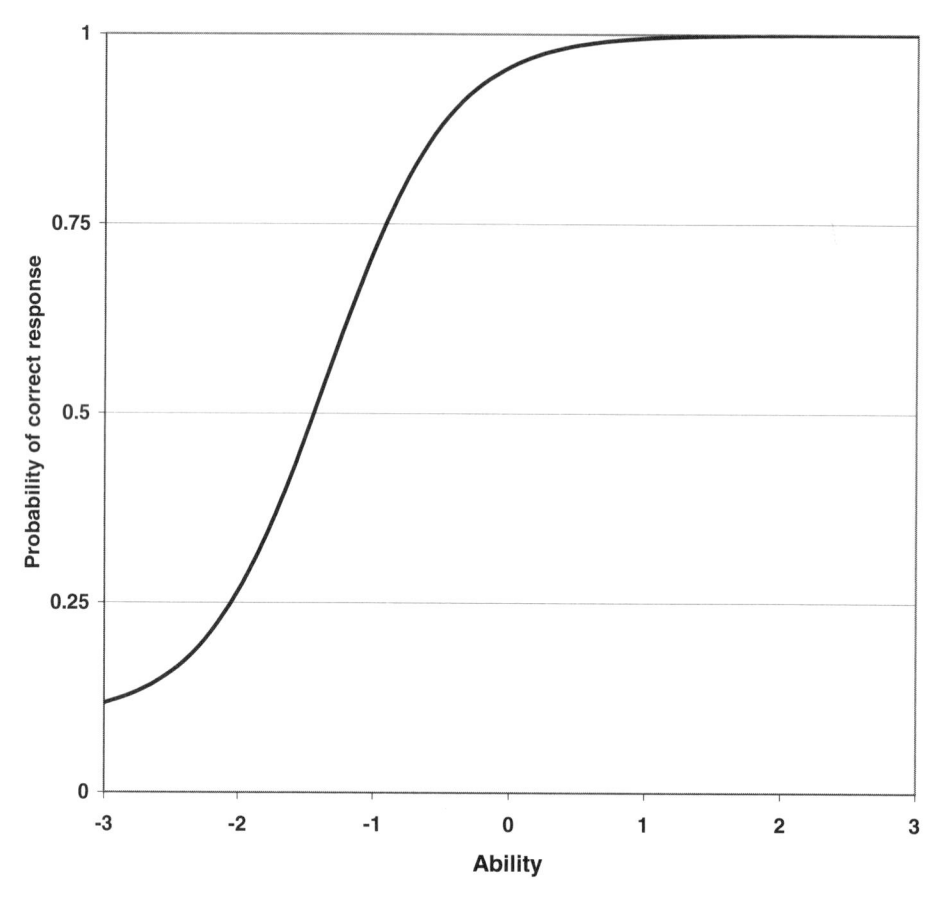

FIG. 19.8. Response curve estimated by three-parameter IRT for an easy item that discriminates well.

considerably in the proportion of correct responses expected in a large group of test takers like those the test is intended for. It is also possible for two items to have noticeably different difficulty parameters and yet have response curves that are very similar in the range of ability that includes most of the test takers.[7]

Discriminating Power

The usual statistic for describing the discriminating power of an item is the correlation between scores on the item and scores on the criterion. However, in the case where the only possible item scores are 1 and 0, there are two kinds of correlations that are used, and they do not produce the same results. One is simply the correlation between the 0/1 scores on the item and the scores on the criterion. The other type of correlation, called a *biserial correlation*, treats the 0/1 scores on the item as an indicator of an underlying proficiency, which the test takers can have to varying degrees.[8] Because this underlying proficiency is not observable, its correlation with test takers' scores on the criterion cannot be computed. However, with certain

---

[7] A possible solution to this problem is to compute a different kind of IRT difficulty statistic: the ability value that corresponds to a specified probability of answering the item correctly.

[8] This underlying variable resembles the Ability variable in IRT, but the calculation of a biserial correlation does not imply all of the assumptions of IRT.

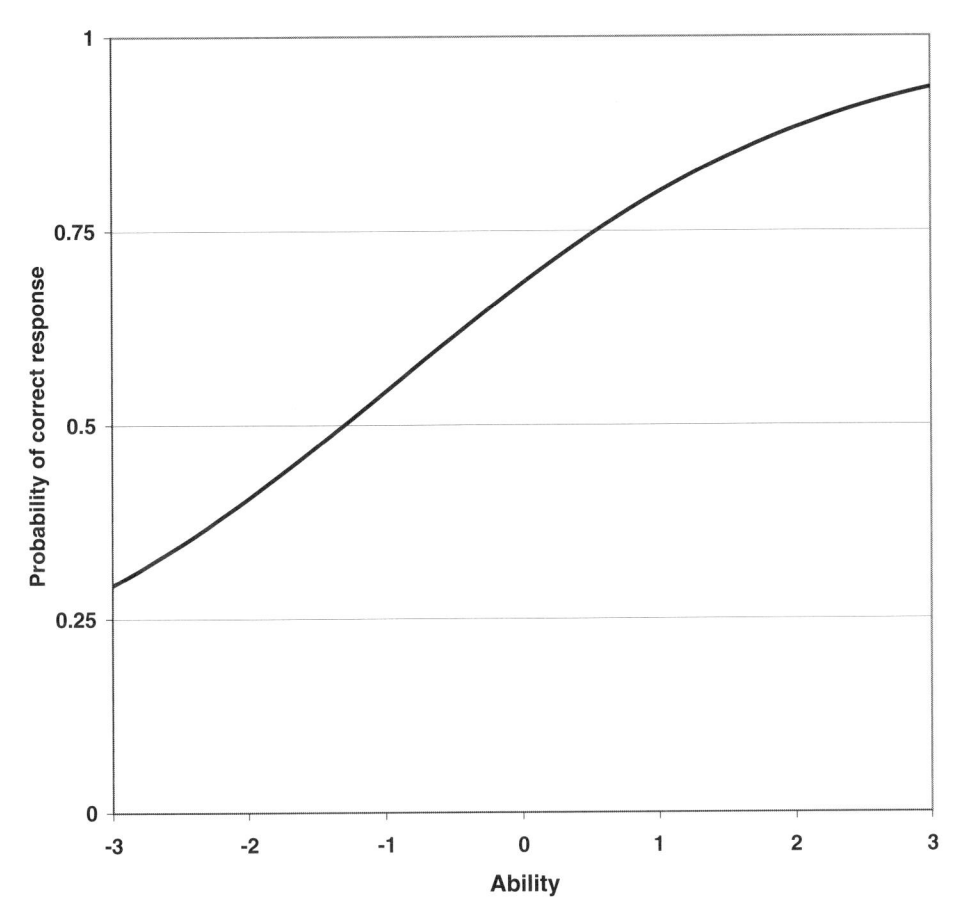

FIG. 19.9. Response curve estimated by three-parameter IRT for an item that does not discriminate well.

assumptions, the correlation can be estimated. Many statisticians prefer to use the biserial correlation, rather than the observed correlation between scores on the item and the criterion, because the observed correlation is unduly influenced by the difficulty of the item.

At this point, the terminology becomes confusing, because the actual correlation between the 0/1 item scores and the scores on the criterion is sometimes called the *point-biserial correlation*. To summarize the distinction,

- The biserial correlation is an estimate of the correlation between test takers' scores on the criterion and an unobservable variable underlying their performance on the item;
- The point-biserial correlation is the observed correlation between test takers' scores on the criterion and their actual scores on the item (0 or 1).

In general, the biserial correlation is larger than the point-biserial correlation. To understand why, think about an item that discriminates perfectly: every test taker at or above a particular score on the criterion gets the item right, and every test taker below that score on the criterion misses the item. In this case, the biserial correlation is a perfect 1.00, but the point-biserial correlation is not. For the point-biserial correlation to be a perfect 1.00, all the test takers who got the item right must have exactly the same score on the criterion, and all the test takers who missed the item must have exactly the same score (a lower score) on the criterion.

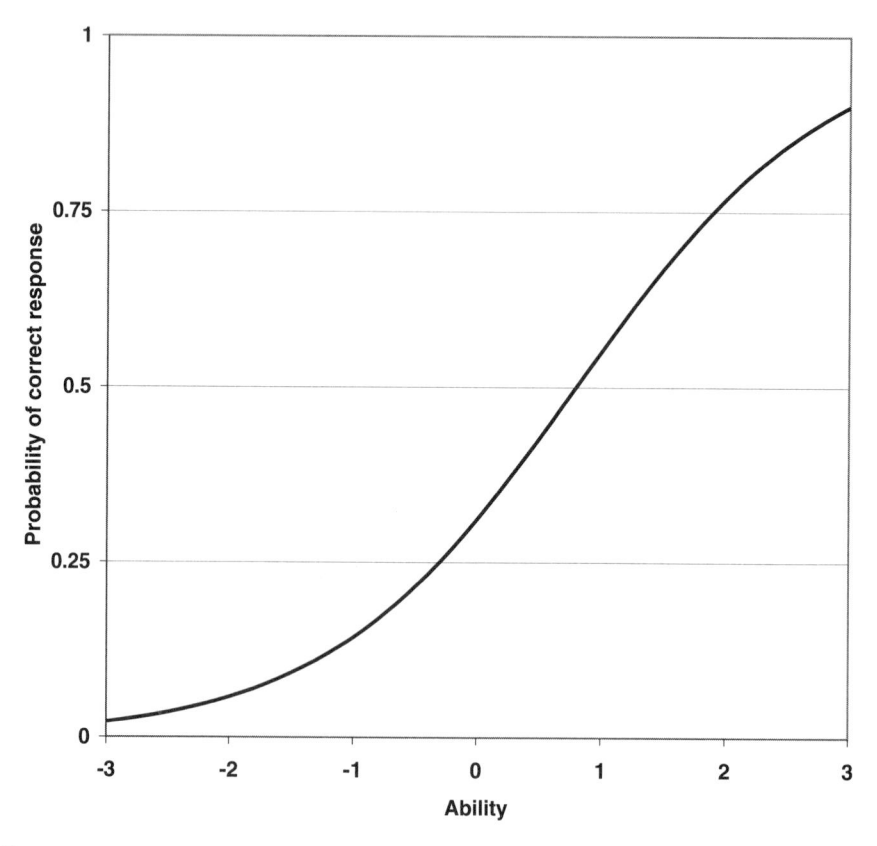

FIG. 19.10. Response curve estimated by one-parameter IRT for a fairly difficult item that discriminates well.

As a practical matter, either the biserial correlation or the point-biserial correlation can serve the purpose of identifying the items that are not measuring the same qualities as the criterion. The important thing to remember is that these two correlation procedures are not the same, and the numbers they produce are not comparable.

In a two- or three-parameter IRT analysis, the discriminating power of the item is indicated by the discrimination parameter. The larger the value of the discrimination parameter, the steeper the slope of the curve—and the more sharply the item discriminates, in the part of the ability range where it discriminates best.[9] In a one-parameter IRT analysis (a Rasch analysis), there is no statistic to indicate the discriminating power of an item, because all the items are assumed to have the same discriminating power.

Discrimination at a Cut Point

Some tests are built for the purpose of classifying test takers into two groups—a high-scoring group and a low-scoring group. Sometimes it is possible, in constructing these tests, to pretest the items on a group of test takers who can each be identified as belonging in the high group

---

[9]The discrimination parameter indicates the slope of the response curve for the item at the point where curve inflects—where it stops rising faster and begins to rise more slowly. The difficulty parameter indicates the value on the ability scale that corresponds to this inflection point on the curve. Thus, the discrimination parameter indicates the slope of the curve in the region of the difficulty parameter.

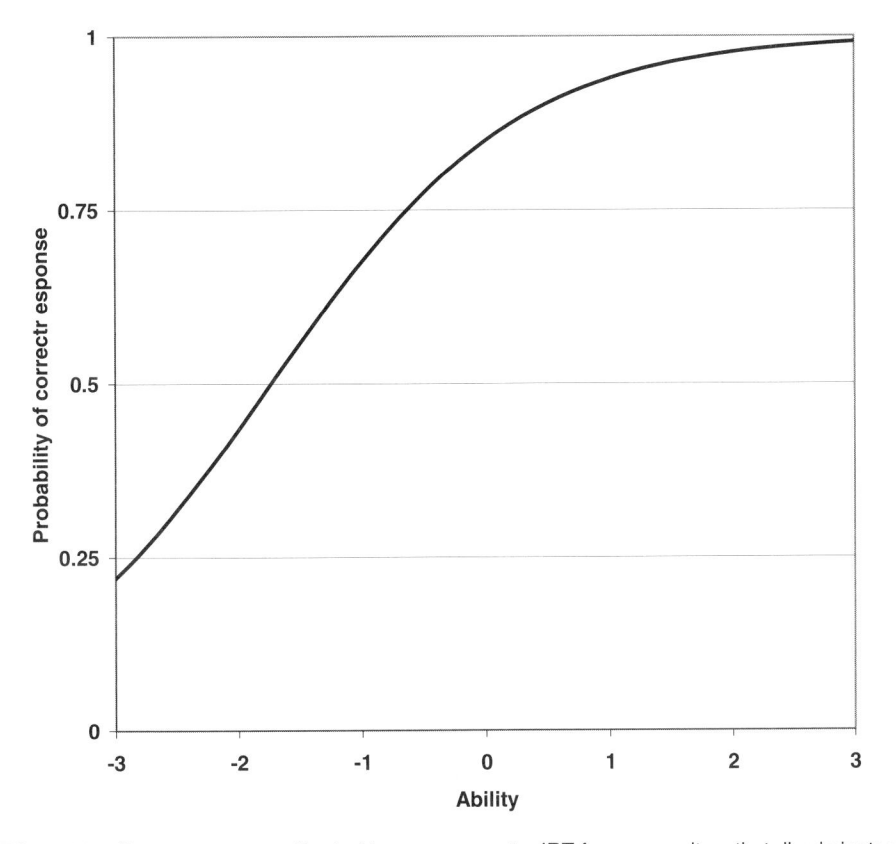

FIG. 19.11. Response curve estimated by one-parameter IRT for an easy item that discriminates well.

or the low group. For example, if new items are embedded in the test for pretesting, the high group and the low group can be formed on the basis of the operational scores. In this case, it is useful to report statistics that indicate the extent to which the information provided by an individual item is consistent with the classification of the test takers. How likely are the members of the high-scoring group to answer the item correctly? How likely are the members of the low-scoring group to miss the item? There are a number of statistics that test makers use to answer these questions. They look at the percentage of test takers in each group who answer the item correctly and at the difference between these two percentages. They also look at the correlation between the scores on the item (0 or 1) and the classifications (a score of 0 for the low group and 1 for the high group).

Comparing the Test Takers Who Choose Different Options

In the item analysis for a multiple-choice test, some test developers like to see the mean score on the criterion (e.g., the total test score) for the group of test takers who chose each option. There are some problems with this approach. The group of test takers who chose the correct answer is likely to include some who knew the correct answer, some who reasoned incorrectly but arrived at the correct answer, and some who chose it by guessing at random, and there is no way to know how many of each. Similarly, the group of test takers who chose a wrong answer is likely to include some who thought the answer was correct and some who were just guessing. A much better way to compare the distractors with each other and with the correct

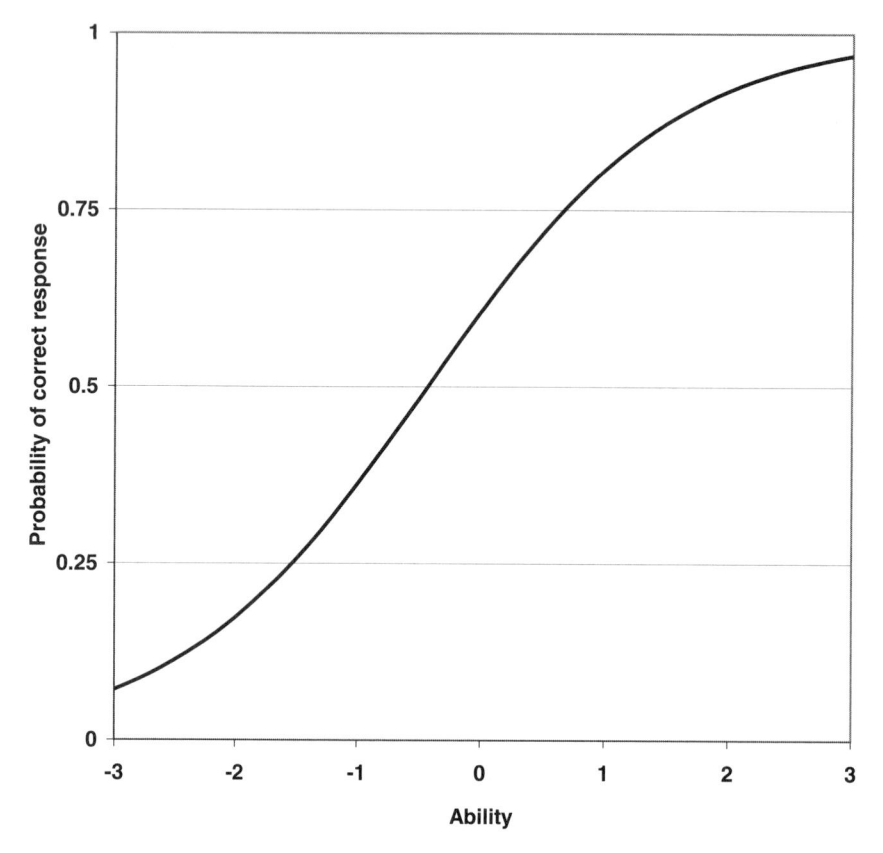

FIG. 19.12. Response curve estimated by one-parameter IRT for an item that does not discriminate well.

answer is to compute a response curve for each option (see Figure 19.5). However, if response curves for the distractors are not available, the mean scores on the criterion for the test takers choosing each response to the item can be informative.

IS IT ACCEPTABLE TO COMPARE ITEM STATISTICS COMPUTED ON DIFFERENT GROUPS OF TEST TAKERS?

Test developers sometimes want to compare item analysis results for items that were administered to different groups of test takers. But are such comparisons meaningful? If the groups of test takers are very similar in the types of knowledge and skills measured by the test, the comparisons should be meaningful. Sometimes it is possible to implement a data collection plan that results in the different sets of items being taken by similar groups of test takers. Even in the absence of such a systematic plan, there may be strong evidence that the groups are highly similar. For example, the groups may have performed equally well on a test that measures the same kinds of knowledge and skills as the items being analyzed.

But what if this kind of evidence is available, and the data indicate that the groups of test takers who took different forms of the test are not equally strong? Is there any way to make the item statistics comparable? Yes, if the criterion variable has the same meaning for all the groups of test takers—for example, if it is an equated total score. The estimation procedure requires an assumption—that if the comparison is based on *only the test takers having a particular score on the criterion*, then the probability of answering the item correctly is the same in the groups of test takers taking different forms of the test.

Notice that the response curves in Figures 19.1 to 19.4 indicate the probability of a correct response to the item for test takers with each possible score on the criterion. If you know the distribution of the criterion scores in a group of test takers, you can use the response curves to estimate difficulty and discrimination statistics for the item in a group of test takers, even if the response curves were estimated in a stronger group or a weaker group.

Estimating the difficulty of the item for a group of test takers—the percentage of the group who would answer the item correctly—is fairly simple. The estimated percent correct on the item is simply a weighted average of the percent correct at all the score levels of the criterion. The weight for each score level is the proportion of the group having that score on the criterion.

It is not so easy to estimate the correlation of the item with the criterion when you do not actually have the test takers' scores on both the item and the criterion. There is a procedure for estimating the biserial correlation in this case, but it cannot be expressed in a single simple formula or described in one or two sentences (Lewis, Thayer, & Livingston, 2003).

WHAT FACTORS COMPLICATE AN ITEM ANALYSIS?

One factor that can make the results of an item analysis difficult to interpret is *speededness*—the effect of time pressure on the test takers' performance. Typically, speededness is reflected in the test takers' responses to items near the end of the test (or near the end of each separately timed section of the test). The items near the end of the test are more likely to be left unanswered than they would be if they had been placed earlier in the test. They are also more likely to be answered incorrectly, because many test takers will answer them without taking the time necessary to consider them carefully. However, the items near the end of the test are typically harder than the items placed earlier in the test, because the test makers want to make sure that slower test takers have the opportunity to answer the items they are most likely to be able to answer correctly. Therefore, in reviewing the results of an item analysis, it is difficult to separate the effects of speededness from the effects of the difficulty of the items. Another complicating factor is that measures of speededness and difficulty differ from one group of test takers to another. Generally, a test is more speeded in a less able group of test takers.

Some item analyses make a distinction between items omitted and items not reached, in classifying the items that a test taker did not answer. An item is considered *not reached* if the test taker did not respond to that item or any item placed later in the test. The item is considered *omitted* if the test taker did not respond to that item but did respond to at least one item placed later in the test. This distinction can be misleading, for at least two reasons. First, a test-wise test-taker who is running out of time will answer all the remaining items as quickly as possible and then go back and consider carefully as many items as time permits, changing the answers if necessary. If an incorrect answer receives the same score as an omitted item (i.e., 0), this strategy can only increase the test taker's score. But even if each incorrect answer decreases the test taker's score slightly (by subtracting a fraction of a point), this strategy will usually result in enough correct answers to yield a net gain. Second, some test-wise test takers do not answer the items in numerical order. Instead, they read through the test quickly, answering the items they can answer quickly. They then make a second pass through the test, answering the items that take more time—but still leaving for last those items that will take them much longer than the others.

For these reasons, it is wrong to assume that, by limiting the analysis to the test takers who reached the item, you can remove the effects of speededness. The analysis will still include some test takers (you cannot know how many) who left the item unanswered or answered it incorrectly but would have answered it correctly if given enough time to think. At the same time, the analysis will exclude the slowest test takers, and many of them will be the ones least likely to know the answers to the items at the end of the test.

Given these problems, can you trust the item analysis information for an item at or near the end of a speeded test? Yes, but only if you recognize the limitations of the information—that it applies only to that item placed in the same position (or very nearly the same position), in that same test or an equally speeded test, taken by a group of test takers similar to the group in the item analysis. You cannot generalize the results to a less speeded test, in which the test takers' responses to the item would be less hurried. In general, it is best to set time limits that give all the test takers time to answer all the items. Otherwise, the scores will be partly the result of guessing, and the test will be partly a measure of the test takers' ability to work quickly.[10]

Another factor that complicates the interpretation of an item analysis is content stratification. On a test of knowledge, the test takers who are strongest in one kind of knowledge may not be strongest in the other kinds. On a science test, the test takers who know the most about biology may not know the most about physics, chemistry, or geology; On a biology test, the test takers who know the most about cell biology may not know the most about population biology, and so on. As a result, the relationship between performance on an item and performance on the full test tends to be weaker than it would be if all the items on the test tested the same kind of knowledge. This effect is especially noticeable when there is a content category that represents a relatively small portion of the test and the test takers who are strongest in that category are not especially strong in the other content categories. For example, in tests of musical knowledge, it often happens that the test takers who know the most about jazz are not stronger than the other test takers in their knowledge about other types of music.

If the test is long enough, it may be worthwhile to separate the items in the test into two or more content categories and perform a separate analysis for each content category. The relationship between each item and the criterion tends to be stronger in this analysis than in an analysis that combines all the content categories. However, to do a separate analysis for a content category, you need enough items in the category to produce a criterion score that separates the test takers who are strong in that content category from those who are not. (Twenty items would probably be enough; 10 items probably would not.)

In general, it is not a good idea to use an item analysis criterion based on a small number of items. A score based on a small number of items is not very reliable. Also, the smaller the number of items, the more the test taker's total score is affected by each item. Removing the item from the total score solves this problem but creates another problem; it results in an analysis in which each item is analyzed against a somewhat different criterion!

Another factor that can complicate an item analysis, especially when the data come from pretesting the items, is the presence of bad items in the criterion—items that would not be included in an operational version of the test. These items might be unclear, ambiguous, or simply wrong. The criterion for an item analysis should be the best available measure of the knowledge or skills that the test is intended to measure. A test or (especially) a collection of items being pretested can contain some bad items that went unnoticed until the test developers looked at the item analysis information. In that case, it may be worthwhile to remove these items from the criterion and rerun the item analysis, so that the results will be a better indicator of the quality of the remaining items.

---

[10]There is a version of IRT that is designed to estimate the effects of time limits and the position of the item in the test, separately from those of the difficulty and discrimination of the item (Yamamoto, 1995; Yamamoto & Everson, 1995).

WHAT IS DIF?

On most tests, the items that are easy for one group of test takers—easy in comparison to the other items—tend to be the same items that are easy for other groups of test takers. The items that are hard for one group (in comparison to the other items) tend to be hard for other groups. For example, the items that are hardest for boys tend to be hardest for girls. The items that are easiest for students in urban schools tend to be the easiest for students in suburban or rural schools. Any exception to this general tendency is referred to as *differential item functioning* or "DIF". DIF occurs when a test item is particularly difficult (or particularly easy) for a group of test takers—easier (or harder) than would be implied by its difficulty for test takers who are not members of that group.

DIF does not mean simply that an item is harder for one group of test takers than for another group. If test takers in one group tend to know more about the subject than test takers in another group, they tend to perform better on all the test items. DIF occurs when an item is substantially harder for one group than for another group after these overall differences in knowledge of the subject are taken into account.

An item that has DIF against a particular group may be unfair to test takers who are members of that group, or it may not. Whether or not the item is unfair depends on whether the specific skill or point of knowledge it measures is an important part of the content being tested.

One way to look at DIF is to estimate two sets of response curves for each item—a separate response curve for each of the two test-taker groups to be compared (e.g., boys and girls). If the two response curves for the correct answer are different (by enough to matter), the item has DIF for those two groups of test takers. For a statistic that measures the amount of DIF, take the difference between the two response curves at each criterion score level, multiply by the proportion of the test takers at that criterion score level, and sum over the criterion score levels. (For an alternative approach, see the appendix to this chapter.)

In many DIF analyses, test developers are particularly concerned about the difficulty of the item for one of the two groups. That group is called the *focal group*. In the computation of the DIF statistic, the proportion of test takers with scores at each criterion score level is computed in the focal group. The resulting DIF statistic compares the focal group's performance on the item with the performance of a reference group that is matched to the focal group on the criterion. For that reason, the criterion in a DIF analysis is often referred to as a *matching criterion*.

SUMMARY

Item analysis includes several different kinds of statistical analyses of the data produced when test takers respond to test items. What these analyses have in common is that (1) they require as input the scores or the responses of individual test takers to individual items and (2) their purpose is to provide information about the items, rather than the test takers. Item analysis results can be presented graphically or numerically. The graphic presentation takes the form of response curves, which show the test taker's estimated probability of a particular response (e.g., a correct answer) as a function of the test taker's score on a criterion—a measure of the general type of skills or knowledge that includes the specific skill or point of knowledge measured by the item. The numerical presentation includes statistics that measure the difficulty of the item and the extent to which it discriminates between test takers who are generally strong and those who are generally weak in the knowledge or skills tested. DIF describes the extent to which the item is particularly difficult (or easy) for a specified demographic group of test takers, after controlling for between-group differences in the knowledge or skills tested.

ACKNOWLEDGMENT

Any opinions expressed in this chapter are those of the author and do not necessarily reflect the position of Educational Testing Service or any of its clients. I thank Neil J. Dorans for his many contributions to both the form and the substance of this chapter and Michael J. Zieky for his helpful suggestions in response to an earlier draft.

APPENDIX

ALTERNATIVE APPROACHES TO ESTIMATING ITEM RESPONSE CURVES

Procedures for estimating response curves can be classified in two ways:

- Procedures that require an observed criterion measure and procedures that use an implied unobservable criterion.
- Descriptive procedures and formula-based procedures.

Formula-based procedures assume a particular mathematical form for the relationship between performance on the item and performance on the criterion. This assumption requires the response curves for all the items to have a particular shape. The response curves for different items can differ only in certain specific ways.

The smoothing procedure used to produce Figures 19.1 to 19.4 uses an observed criterion measure. It is not formula based; it allows the response curves for different items to differ in any way that the data indicate. IRT procedures use an implied, unobservable criterion and are formula based; they allow the response curves for different items to differ only in certain specified ways. An example of a formula-based procedure that uses an observed criterion measure is the use of logistic regression for DIF analysis (Swaminathan & Rogers, 1990). An example of a descriptive procedure for DIF analysis that uses an implied unobservable criterion is SIBTEST (Shealy & Stout, 1993).

ALTERNATIVE APPROACHES TO DIF MEASUREMENT

DIF statistics based on the estimation of two response curves for each item can be computed with any method of estimating the response curves, including IRT, as long as the distribution of the criterion scores in each group of test takers can be computed or estimated. (For the details of an IRT approach to DIF, see Thissen, Steinberg, & Wainer ([1993]).

In addition to DIF statistics based on estimating two response curves for each item, there is a statistic called the *Mantel-Haenszel* statistic that is sometimes used to measure DIF. The computation of this statistic is based on the estimation of a 2 × 2 table at each score level of the matching criterion. The format of the table looks like this:

	Number answering item correctly	Number answering item incorrectly
Group 1	*a*	*b*
Group 2	*c*	*d*

In this diagram, *a* represents the number of test takers in Group 1 who had scores at this particular level of the matching criterion and who answered this item correctly, and similarly for b, c, and d. If you choose a test taker at random from the test takers in Group 1 who had this score on the matching criterion, the odds of choosing one who answered the item correctly are a/b. If you choose a test taker at random from those in Group 2 who had this score on the matching criterion, the odds are c/d. The odds ratio is the ratio of these two quantities: $(a/b)/(c/d)$. If the item has absolutely no DIF for Groups 1 and 2 at this score level of the matching criterion, the odds ratio is exactly 1. If the item has DIF in favor of Group 1 (or against Group 2), the odds ratio tends to be greater than 1. Combining the data over all levels of the matching criterion yields an overall odds ratio for the item. This overall odds ratio can be used to estimate the difference, in the proportion answering the item correctly, between the focal group and a group of test takers selected from the reference group to match the focal group on the matching criterion. (For more detail on this procedure, see Dorans & Holland, 1993.)

REFERENCES

Dorans, N. J., & Holland, P. W. (1993). DIF detection and description: Mantel-Haenszel and standardization. In P. W. Holland & H. Wainer (Eds.), *Differential item functioning*. Hillsdale, NJ: Lawrence Erlbaum Associates.

Lei, P., Dunbar, S. B., & Kolen, M. J. (2004). A comparison of parametric and nonparametric approaches to item analysis for multiple-choice tests. *Educational and Psychological Measurement, 64*, 565–587.

Lewis, C., Thayer, D., & Livingston, S. A. (2003). *A regression-based polyserial correlation coefficient.* Unpublished manuscript.

Ramsay, J. O. (1995). *TestGraf: A program for the graphical analysis of multiple choice test and questionnaire data* (Technical Report). Montreal, Quebec, Canada: McGill University.

Shealey, R. T., & Stout, W. F. (1993). An item response theory model for test bias and differential test functioning. In P. W. Holland & H. Wainer (Eds.). *Differential item functioning*. Hillsdale, NJ: Lawrence Erlbaum Associates.

Swaminathan, H., & Rogers, H. J. (1990). Detecting differential item functioning using logistic regression procedures. *Journal of Educational Measurement, 27*, 361–370.

Thissen, D., Steinberg, L., & Wainer, H. (1993). Detection of differential item functioning using the parameters of item response models. In P. W. Holland & H. Wainer (Eds.), *Differential item functioning*. Hillsdale, NJ: Lawrence Erlbaum Associates.

Yamamoto, K. (1995). *Estimating the effects of test length and test time on parameter estimation under the HYBRID model.* (Research Report RR-95-02). Princeton, NJ: Educational Testing Service.

Yamamoto, K., & Everson, H. T. (1995). *Modeling the mixture of IRT and pattern responses by a modified hybrid model.* (Research Report RR-95-16). Princeton, NJ: Educational Testing Service.

IV
Test Design

20

Practical Issues in Designing and Maintaining Multiple Test Forms for Large-Scale Programs

Cathy LW Wendler
Michael E. Walker
Educational Testing Service

This chapter focuses on key psychometric and development issues related to creating and maintaining large-scale testing programs that require multiple versions of the same test. Large-scale testing programs give versions of the same test at different administrations but scores from each of the administrations must be comparable. Three broad areas of interest to test developers and statisticians are covered, namely, preliminary, operational, and maintenance requirements. Preliminary concepts that drive the ultimate design of the test are discussed, including use considerations (e.g., test purpose, target population, and criteria for score use), content considerations (e.g., content-related validity evidence, item format, and content specifications), and psychometric considerations (e.g., statistical specifications, scoring methods, choosing a reporting scale, and test length). Issues dealing with routine operational requirements for maintaining a viable testing program are also explored. Test delivery platform and security issues are discussed briefly. Greater attention is given to item and test development considerations, particularly considerations related to creating an optimal test inventory and determining the appropriate number of test items to write. Three basic methods for item tryouts are detailed and the pros and cons of each method described. Finally, requirements for maintaining a large-scale program are presented. Processes for building equivalent forms are described, test equating methods considered, and methods for maintaining the meaning of the scale discussed.

Each summer, Educational Testing Service (ETS) hosts a summer intern program consisting of graduate students seeking degrees in research and measurement fields. This opportunity provides them with a chance to learn about the "real world" of testing. A frequent question from this group is "How do you go about figuring out the work for a testing program?" This question reflects precisely what this chapter is about: the psychometric-related planning, issues, and concerns that surround creating and maintaining testing programs that require multiple versions of the same test.

Although a number of sources over the years have offered guidelines to the practitioner for item writing (e.g., Haladyna & Downing, 1989; Haladyna, Downing, & Rodriguez, 2002; Krypsin & Feldhusen, 1974; Roid & Haladyna, 1982; Roid & Wendler, 1983), few guides exist that detail the technical requirements for creating and maintaining multiple test forms needed to support large-scale testing programs. For purposes of this chapter, *large-scale tests* are defined as those that are administered to groups of examinees over multiple administrations. The administrations take place multiple times within a specified period of time (usually by month or year) and across multiple years. Although the administration schedules may differ, all require that the meaning of the test scores remain steady so that appropriate comparisons can be made and trends measured. The scores received from these multiple administrations must be comparable regardless of the test form given, the date of the administration, or the group of examinees who take the test on a specific administration. They are not individually administered tests, as one would find with some psychological or educational tests. Examples of such tests include college admissions tests given multiple times in a school year, high school exit examinations given once a year but over multiple years, and K–12 tests given at multiple grade levels. The tests described in this chapter are linear (nonadaptive), with parallel forms of the test given across the different administrations. The specific method of delivery (e.g., computer, paper-pencil, Internet), although a consideration in test design, is not important for the concepts discussed here.

PRELIMINARY CONSIDERATIONS

A number of key considerations that drive the ultimate design of the testing program and the multiple forms that support it must be established first. We have grouped these preliminary considerations into three major categories: (1) Use considerations, (2) content-related validity evidence considerations (see also Kane, chap. 7, this volume), and (3) psychometric considerations.

Use Considerations

Purpose of the Test

The first and cornerstone consideration is the use that will be made of the test scores. The purpose of the test must be clearly identified. It is important to identify not just the primary use of the test scores, but secondary uses as well. For example, a college admission test's primary purpose may be to predict how well a student is likely to do at a specific college. But individual departments at the college may wish to use the test scores for decisions regarding course placement and scholarship programs may use the results for award decisions. No single test can be designed to support a wide variety of purposes; therefore, it is important to clearly define the purpose of the assessment and build it to support that purpose. Tests that purport to have multiple uses must be validated for each of those uses (American Educational Research Association [AERA], American Psychological Association [APA], and National Council on Measurement in Education [NCME], 1999).

A determination of whether the scores from the test are considered high or low stakes is also important. High-stakes decisions affect future opportunities for a particular examinee. For example, the ability to receive a high school diploma, to obtain a license in a particular occupation, to attend a specific college, or to be promoted to the next grade in school are high-stakes decisions that are often based on a test score, in addition to other criteria. It is imperative that when decisions like these are being made, multiple forms of the test be as parallel as possible, scores across administrations be as equivalent as possible, and measurement error be as small as possible so that all examinees are given an equal opportunity to perform. Tests that result in low-stakes decisions may allow the test developer to relax some of the psychometric and content considerations that are required of multiple forms. However, this is not to imply that such tests are, by default, of lower quality or less valid. The need for stricter content and statistical guidelines and the effort put toward validity evidence increases as the stakes regarding test use increase (Linn, 2000). The higher the stakes, the greater this effort should be.

Target Population

The identification of the target population is also an important preliminary decision. The *target population* is the group for whom the test is designed. The *testing population* is the group who actually takes the test. Ideally, the testing population and target population are identical. For many tests, there is a high degree of overlap between the target and testing populations. For example, a 4th-grade end-of-year test given at all elementary schools in a state has a high percentage of the target population actually take the test because it is fairly easy to make sure that third or fifth graders are not administered the test. However, for most tests, there is some general mismatch with those for whom the test is designed and those who show up on test day.

For some tests, there are major differences in the target and testing populations. A test designed to measure proficiency in a world language taught at a high school level may be taken by examinees who are native speakers of that language. The native speakers may represent the greatest percentage of the testing population, whereas fewer students who are part of the target population may take the test. If the target group is used for equating purposes, ensuring equivalent scores across administrations and reducing measurement error becomes more difficult as the proportion of the target population in the testing population drops.

Criteria for Score Use

Finally, the criteria for test score use must be acknowledged. Providing only aggregate scores to schools or districts requires different decisions than if individual student scores are to be provided as well. Individual results that are used to advance or place students into the next grade level require different information be provided than if those results are only given back to the teacher to help in understanding a student's strengths and weaknesses in a particular subject. A note of caution here: It is a frequent occurrence that tests designed for one purpose are applied to a multitude of uses. It is impossible to stop the ranking of schools or real estate based on The College Board's SAT® (College Board, 2005) scores, number of students taking tests from the Advanced Placement® Program (College Board, 2005) or percent of students passing a high school exit examination. The creator of the test must be very clear about the limitations of the assessment and must detail the particular criteria under which the test scores may be used (AERA, APA, & NCME, 1999). This brings us to the next group of preliminary considerations—content-related validity evidence concerns.

Content Considerations

Test Content and Validity

To develop multiple versions of a test that can be equitably given to examinees at different administrations, it is important that each version sample content from the same content domain. This ensures that each form of the test accurately measures what it should and thus establishes the test's validity. Validity is an essential concept and allows judgment as to the usability and meaningfulness of test scores. As stated by Messick (1993, p. 13), "Validity is a unitary concept... [it] refers to the degree to which empirical evidence and theoretical rationales support the adequacy and appropriateness of interpretations and actions based on test scores."

Our focus here is on content-related validity considerations, which focus on understanding the content domain that is measured by a particular test and the ability to design and sustain multiple test forms.

It is important that the content domain of a test be clearly defined to maximize content-related validity evidence. The determination of the appropriate content for an assessment depends on the target population. For example, the content of a test of general mathematics ability should greatly differ for a 4th-grade target population versus a 10th-grade population. Within the 10th-grade target population there are finer distinctions: Should the content include concepts drawn from algebra, geometry, or trigonometry if not all 10th-grade students have been exposed to such classes? (Also see Kane [chap. 7, this volume] for a discussion on validity evidence related to the content of tests.) Focusing and documenting the range of content to be covered must also take into account the potential use of the test scores. A test designed to assess student knowledge across a variety of concepts in a subject area needs to include a wider breadth of topics than one designed to place students into a particular class that requires in-depth knowledge of specific concepts.

Choosing Item Formats

Once the content domain is established, the practitioner needs to determine the item formats that most appropriately measure the content. The most common type of item format is the standard multiple-choice item. This type of item has both benefits and limitations. Not all content is sufficiently covered by a multiple-choice item, and thus the established content domain may not be sufficiently assessed if the choice is made to use only this type of item. Nevertheless, scoring for this type of item is fairly straightforward, and it continues to be an efficient method for testing large numbers of examinees within a prescribed time period. In addition, tools for calculating classical and simple item statistics (e.g., difficulty indices, discrimination, item bias indicators) with these types of test items are readily accessible to practitioners (see Livingston, chap. 19, this volume).

Although many test developers intuitively lean toward more "innovative" item formats, considerations of scoring feasibility, the ability to sustain such item types, and the mechanisms for producing particular item formats must be considered. For example, although constructed-response items may seem at first glance easy to write, each item requires a scoring guide be established at the same time to ensure that all examinee responses are equitably scored. In addition, plans must be made to ensure that all answers are examined in terms of their probability of being correct. A simple example: A constructed-response type item commonly used in mathematics testing is an item that has a stem but no answer choices. Examinees write down their answer, sometimes indicating the answer by completing a special grid or coding in a special section on an answer sheet. This type of item is ideal for testing in a way that standard multiple-choice items cannot (e.g., ranges, questions that have multiple answers, etc.) and may seem straightforward to score. However, decisions regarding the form of the answer must be considered—fractions or decimals, rounding or trailing digits, number of digits allowed, right or left justification, and so on. And even once these issues are resolved, there needs to be a plan to consider unexpected correct answers that might be given. At ETS, for those tests using this item type, content specialists review the answers provided by examinees for each constructed-response question after a test administration to ensure that no unexpectedly correct answer is given that is not picked up by the scoring key.

The task becomes even more complex for constructed-response questions that require longer, essay-type responses. The task of scoring such questions becomes time consuming and expensive. But the biggest challenge is to keep the scoring criteria from shifting within a scoring

TABLE 20.1
Example of Content Specifications Blueprint for a General Mathematics Test

Testing Time: 60 Minutes	Number of Items	Percent of Test
Multiple choice (5-choice)	20 items	40%
Multiple choice (4-choice)	20 items	40%
Constructed response	10 items	20%
Total	50 items	

Number and operations
    Properties of integers
    Elementary number theory
    Rational numbers
    Arithmetic word problems
    Sequences and series
    Sets
    Counting problems
	18–19 items	30–32%

Algebra and functions
    Operations on algebraic expressions
    Algebraic representations, translation
    Linear equations and inequalities
    Systems of linear equations and inequalities
    Quadratics
    Basic concepts of algebraic functions
	17–19 items	28–32%

Geometry and measurement
    Points and lines in the plane
    Angles in the plane
    Triangles (interior and exterior angles, area, perimeter)
    Special triangles (30–60–90, isosceles, equilateral, etc.)
    Circles (area, circumference)
    polygons
    Solid geometry (volume, surface area)
	16–18 items	27–30%

session and across scoring sessions. This is especially important if test questions are reused in subsequent administrations. Downing (chap. 12, this volume) and Welch (chap. 13, this volume) provide extensive advice on item development for selected-response and constructed-response formats.

Once the content domain and item types are decided upon, the practitioner can formalize the test specifications. These test specifications act as a blueprint for the test and serve an important function in ensuring all subsequent versions of the test are built from the same blueprint. This way all examinees, regardless of when they take the test or which version of the test they take, are provided with appropriate content coverage so that appropriate and fair interpretations of their level of knowledge can be made. These test specifications specify the level of content, the type of item formats, and the percentage of each content-item type on each test form in enough detail that a content specialist can generate items from it as well as assemble a finished product. In essence, the central focus of test specifications is to make sure that the test appropriately represents the content domain (Messick, 1993). Table 20.1 provides an example of a simple content specifications blueprint.

A formal framework for test design used at ETS is *evidence-centered design* (ECD) (Mislevy, Almond, & Lukas, 2003; Mislevy & Riconscentes, chap. 4, this volume). ECD approaches the construction of assessments in terms of evidentiary arguments, and the validity argument for the test becomes part of its formal development. It allows the test developer to (1) consider the skills the are to be measured, (2) identify the evidence that indicates that the skills are present, and (3) construct test items that reflect this evidence. The full ECD framework has several phases (Mislevy, Steinberg, & Almond, 2002). This framework ensures that all versions of the test follow the same test specifications.

Psychometric Considerations

Statistical Specifications

In addition to identifying appropriate content and created test specifications from which to develop the test, statistical specifications for the assessment must be established. These specifications set the technical requirements for the test and help to ensure parallelism across multiple versions of the test. The average test difficulty and distribution of difficulty (i.e., spread of item difficulty and shape of the item distribution) must be established so that it is appropriate for the purpose of the test. For example, the general rule for a test that rank-orders examinees on a specific scale, such as a subject-based test used for college admissions, is that the level of difficulty is appropriate if the target population can correctly answer 50 to 60% of the test items.

The distribution of item difficulty must also be established. The difficulty of a test question is a function of the percent of examinees who responded correctly to it (p-value). However, p-values are influenced by the group of examinees who responded to the question. For example, a test item given to more able group of examinees shows that items are somewhat easier than if the same test item is given to a less able group. Generally, p-values are converted to a standard scale that avoids negative values and decimals (Anastasi, 1976). At ETS, p-values are converted onto a standard scale called the *delta index*, which is based on the percent of examinees correctly answering the item, where 1 minus the p-values are converted to z scores and transformed to a scale with a mean of 13 and a standard deviation of 4. Deltas are inversely related to p-values: The more difficult the item, the higher the value of the delta and the lower the p-value.

The ideal distribution of the p-values (or deltas) must also be considered. If the test has mostly easy test items, the majority of the examinees answer them correctly and the test is not able to distinguish among examinees with different levels of ability. The same is true for a test with only difficult items; only a few examinees can answer them correctly. As a result, the test only distinguishes between the examinees at the top of the score scale; all others fall into one group. A test having only test items that are of medium difficulty is of limited use for examinees beyond the middle range of ability, because there are no difficult items to allow further distinction among examinees at the top end of the scale. Having some easier and some more difficult test items allows for finer distinctions among examinees at the tails of the reporting scale. In general, it is best to create an item difficulty distribution that has a moderate spread of difficulty around a mean p-value of .50.

The shape of the distribution of item difficulty is also important because it allows the greatest precision on the reporting scale to be at the place where decisions are made. For example, if a cut score is being used as in the case of a licensing test, the greatest precision needs to be at the point on the reporting scale where a "pass" or "no pass" decision is made. In this case, the distribution is likely more skewed, in that there are more items at a higher level of difficulty. (See Luecht, [chap. 25, this volume] for a lengthier discussion on information for cut scores.) If the purpose of the test is to measure where examinees' abilities fall across the entire scale range, the distribution of item difficulty resembles a normal distribution.

For a test containing more than one item type, the spread of item difficulty must take into account characteristics of the item format or content being measured. Items covering a particular content might, by their nature, be more difficult than items covering other content. And particular item formats may in general be more difficult than others. Thus it is important to consider both question content and format when determining the appropriate distribution of item difficulty.

Item discrimination, expressed as a correlation between the item and the total test score, must also be considered (see Livingston [chap. 19, this volume] for a detailed discussion of item discrimination indices). Item discrimination is vital to a test in that it allows examinees with different ability levels to be distinguished from each other. Correlations range from +1.00 to −1.00. For item discrimination, the more positive the correlation, the more the test item distinguishes examinees with high scores from those with low scores. Correlations close to zero indicate that high and low scorers have the same chance of answering the test item correctly; negative correlations indicate that low scorers are more likely to answer the question correctly than high scorers. It is best to avoid using test questions with low or negative biserials!

The correlation provides an indication of the extent that performance on a specific item relates to the total test score (i.e., the homogeneity of the test items). If the correlation is close to +1.00, it indicates that the information provided by that item is redundant with the information provided by other test items. Items with moderate correlations (+0.30 to +0.80) allow distinction among ability levels of examinees while still providing unique information. Items should relate to the total test score the same way for all examinees at the same score level; that is, individual items are expected to perform similarly for examinees with the same score.

Once the statistical specifications for the test are finalized, the practitioner can draw up the specifications into a blueprint similar to that used for content specifications. Table 20.2 provides an example of test specifications showing statistical specifications for a general mathematics test. (Note that this table provides an example for a testing program that can support precise statistical specifications. Many testing programs cannot support this level of precision for a number of reasons.)

Scoring Method

Another psychometric consideration is the scoring method used. The simplest method for scoring a test, and the one most familiar to most people, is the total number of correct items, which is also known as *rights scoring*. Under rights scoring, an examinee receives no penalty for incorrect responses. Thus, the best way to maximize the test score is to answer every item, even if the examinee must guess on some items. Instructions for such tests usually inform the examinee that there is no penalty for a wrong response and that the optimal strategy is to answer all items. Such instructions are referred to as *rights scoring directions*.

A deterrent to the use of rights scoring is the guessing component. If an examinee guesses the answers to items about which the examinee knows nothing, then these guesses add noise to the measurement of knowledge or ability. Arguments against rights scoring and the accompanying directions on philosophical grounds exist as well: "Many educators argue that to encourage guessing on the part of examinees is poor educational practice, since it fosters undesirable habits" (Thorndike, 1971, p. 59).

As a correction for random guessing, some tests use a method called *formula scoring* (Thurstone, 1919). In formula scoring, a fraction of the number of wrong responses is subtracted from the number of correct responses:

$$y = R - \frac{W}{k-1}, \tag{20.1}$$

TABLE 20.2
Example of Statistical Specifications Blueprint for
General Mathematics Test

Multiple-Choice (5- and 4-Choice)

Equated Delta	Number of Items
≥ 19	
18	1
17	2
16	2
15	4
14	6
13	6
12	6
11	6
10	5
9	4
8	3
7	2
6	2
≤ 5.9	1
N	50
Mean delta	12.2
Standard deviation	3.0

Constructed Response

Equated Delta	Number of Items
	10
18–20	1
16–17	2
14–15	2
12–13	2
10–11	2
8–9	1
6–7	
≤ 5.9	
N	10
Mean delta	13.6–14.2
Standard deviation	3.0

where R is the number of correct responses (the rights score), W is the number of wrong responses, and k is the number of response options per item.[1] Under this scoring system, an examinee who randomly guesses on a group of items can expect to receive a score of zero for those items. In this case, test instructions encourage examinees to answer items to which they

---

[1] Other mathematically equivalent formula scores are possible: for example, $y' = R + O/k$, where O is the number of omitted items.

know the answer, to omit items about which they have no knowledge, and to guess only on an item for which they can eliminate one or two possible answers. Such instructions are referred to as *formula scoring directions*.

There are disagreements about which scoring method is preferable. Both scoring methods distinguish between right and wrong responses. Formula scoring as outlined here may be viewed as having potential psychometric advantages over rights scoring because it extracts more information from item responses than rights scoring. In addition, formula scoring separates items answered incorrectly, to which examinees believe they know the answer but do not, from omitted items, to which presumably examinees know they do not know the answer.

One of the major arguments against formula scoring is the intractability of the random guessing model. The random guessing model posits that examinees either know an answer (in which case they respond correctly) or they do not (in which case they guess randomly). However, the model fails to acknowledge nonrandom guessing based on partial information. Lord (1975) showed that under rights scoring directions both the formula score and the rights score are unbiased estimators of examinee knowledge. However, he felt the formula score to be preferable because it had smaller sampling error than the rights score. Furthermore, if there are any omitted items, the formula score is more reliable than the rights score.

The hypothesis that under formula scoring directions examinees omit only those items on which they would perform at chance levels under rights scoring directions has been called the *invariance hypothesis*. A competing hypothesis, that examinees omit some items under formula scoring directions about which they have partial knowledge, such that the examinees would perform better under rights scoring directions, has been termed the *differential effects hypothesis*. Angoff and Schrader (1984) examined these competing hypotheses and determined that when the tests were formula scored for groups receiving both directions, the average performance was equivalent.

A possible limitation of formula scoring involves individual differences in risk preferences. Risk-averse individuals tend to choose a guaranteed outcome over a gamble with an equal or larger expected payoff (Kahneman & Tversky, 1979). On a formula-scored test, a risk-averse examinee prefers to omit an item, guaranteeing a zero gain, rather than guess and risk a small loss (or a 1-point gain).

The formula scores described are but two of many possible formula scores (see McDonald, 1999). Several widely used formula test scores follow from the class of models developed within the framework of Item Response Theory (IRT; see Hambleton, Swaminathan, & Rogers [1991] for an extensive treatment). These models posit a mathematical relationship between the probability of an observable examinee response to an item and the examinee's unobservable ability. The relationship may be different for each item on the test. The nature of these relationships, as well as the particular pattern of item responses, determines the relative importance of each item in determining a person's IRT score. IRT subsumes numerous models, which can conveniently be classified as linear or nonlinear, unidimensional or multidimensional, and dichotomous or polytomous (McDonald, 1982).

Proponents of IRT scoring point to several advantages of the models over conventional scoring methods. First, test item statistics (e.g., difficulty level and item discrimination) are independent of the particular sample of examinees upon which the statistics are computed. However, it is possible to adjust item statistics to a reference population so that they remain fairly stable across different samples from the population even with conventional scoring methods. Second, although IRT item parameters are theoretically invariant, the parameter estimates are not necessarily so (Cook & Petersen, 1987; Fan, 1998).

A second advantage often mentioned for IRT models is that, once model assumptions are met and once an item bank has been calibrated (i.e., the item parameters have been estimated), the estimated ability of an examinee is independent of the particular set of items upon which the estimate is based. Herein lies the true power of IRT models. Whereas conventional scores on different versions of a test must be adjusted (via test equating) before they yield comparable estimates of ability, any number of test forms built from a calibrated item pool yield equivalent ability estimates. (The precision of those estimates, however, depends on the items appearing on the test forms.)

A third advantage of IRT models is that an IRT score uses more information in the test items and therefore provides more information about the examinee than other test scores. A score derived from rights scoring, for example, only uses information from those items an examinee answered correctly. Formula scoring further distinguishes between items that the examinee attempts but gets incorrect and items the examinee chooses to omit. An IRT score (such as a pattern score) uses not just the number of correct responses, but also information about the particular items that were answered correctly, to estimate an examinee's ability.

Given the tradeoffs involved in various scoring strategies, which is the best one to choose? Rights scores are simplest to explain but may provide the least information in many situations. Formula scores provide more information about the examinee but require more explanation about how to take the test and what the resulting scores mean. IRT scores potentially offer more information about the examinee than either rights scores or formula scores, but their complexity makes them nearly impossible to explain to test score users. Prior to the launch of a new testing program, it is highly desirable to examine several scoring methods and to compare the results directly as part of a pilot study or field test. The method chosen is the simplest scoring method that is viable in a given testing situation, yields an acceptable level of information, and can be maintained by the testing program.

Determining the Score Scale to Report

For every test, scores must be presented on a reporting scale in particular units. This score reporting scale is the foundational infrastructure of a testing program (Dorans, 2002). The reporting scale becomes the test's face to the public (Walker & Liu, 2004). Because of this, it is important to align the scales with the intended use of the scores. (Also see Ryan [chap. 29, this volume] for a detailed discussion on score scales, subscores, and score reports.)

There are many kinds of score scales. Most are numeric, although some may incorporate verbal labels. Some are norm referenced, in the sense that the scores on the scale indicate relative standing in a particular population. Other scales are criterion referenced: Each score on the scale represents a particular level of mastery of a specified domain of knowledge or skills.

The *raw score scale* is the simplest; it usually involves rights scores but can also consist of formula scores. The raw score scale has limited generalizability, because it is limited to the particular test form on which it is based. Raw scores cannot be compared across different forms of the same test because the test forms differ in difficulty. Related to the raw score scale is the *percent mastery scale*, which represents the percentage of tested material the examinee has mastered, and is easily computed by dividing the number of correct responses on a test by the number of items. Although percent correct scores on various tests appear to be on the same scale, they are not comparable.

Often a score reporting scale is established with the first edition of a test by linearly or nonlinearly transforming the raw scores. One popular scale is the *linear transformation*, or *standard score*, scale, which is usually established by administering a test form to a specific population, and then setting the mean and standard deviation of the resulting score distribution to specified values. Such a scale incorporates normative meaning in the sense that an examinee's score indicates relative standing in the reference population

The linear transformation preserves the shape of the raw score distribution. Sometimes, however, it is desirable to have a score scale with a specific shape in the reference population.

Such a scale is independent of the particular characteristics of the test items used to establish the scale. A *normalized scale*, for example, converts the original raw score distribution into a scaled score distribution with the familiar bell shape and a particular mean and standard deviation.

The *percentile rank scale* represents another fairly familiar scale for reporting scores; this scale gives the percentage of people in the reference population scoring below the score (or at and below the score) received by a given examinee. This scale is often used as an auxiliary rather than a primary score scale. Although the scale is self-interpreting, the intervals between the percentiles are not equal and therefore the scale is not amenable to arithmetic operations.

The score scales listed are norm referenced in the sense that they are established on a specific population of examinees. Criterion-referenced scales, such as a *proficiency scale,* relate the test score to the content of the test (Petersen, Kolen, & Hoover, 1989). One method of achieving this is via use of subjective techniques such as standard setting (Livingston & Zieky, 1982). Another method is to tie test score to performance on the criterion of interest.

The type of score scale adopted for a particular test should facilitate meaningful score interpretation across the score range. Too many score points on the scale, for example, may suggest more precision than actually exists in the test; too few points may lead to loss of valuable information (Petersen et al., 1989). Supporting materials for the test should provide clear explanations of score meaning, as well as the method used to establish the scale (AERA, APA, & NCME, 1999). The score scale also should be chosen so as to avoid confusion with other score scales that are widely used in the same population (ETS, 1987).

Test Length

Test length is an additional psychometric issue that must be considered. When constructing a new test, it is necessary to be concerned with at least three interrelated issues. The first is content-related validity evidence considerations (see the section on Content Considerations). The second issue is speededness. Usually we want to test examinees' knowledge or ability rather than how fast they work. In that case, we want a test that is essentially unspeeded. At the same time, most tests used in large-scale assessment must fit into a time window that is small enough to reduce issues of fatigue, inconvenience, and administrative constraints. Finally, reliability or test score precision is an issue. The test should accurately measure what examinees know. If examinees were to take the test on another occasion, or if they were to take another version of the test, their scores should be about the same each time.

There are a few possibilities for reducing speededness. If the allotted time remains the same then it may be necessary to use a less "authentic" item type (e.g., multiple choice versus essay for measuring writing skills), possibly lowering validity. Alternatively, the test must be shortened, thereby lowering test score precision. If neither precision nor validity can be decreased, then it may be necessary to increase the allotted time.

Given a fixed test length, it is possible to construct a test that maximizes precision through judicious use of test items. In a classical framework, selection of items exhibiting higher correlations with the total test score tends to raise reliability estimates, as compared with items having lower correlations with the total. IRT models lend themselves particularly well to optimal item selection strategies (see Davey and Pitoniak, chap. 24, this volume; Luecht, chap. 25, this volume).

Every test, whether IRT scoring is used or not, has a *test information function* that represents the precision with which the test can measure at each test score level (i.e., at each level of person ability). If the test score is plotted on the horizontal axis, the height of the curve at each score point represents the amount of information the test provides about people scoring at that level on the test. Points at which the curve is relatively high represent scores for which it is more certain that the observed score represents the person's true ability. That is, these scores have relatively lower measurement error. The shape of the test information curve should reflect the purpose for which the test is designed. A test used to make a pass/fail decision (e.g., a certification or licensure examination) should have an information curve that is highest in the area of the decision point (see Leucht, chap. 25, this volume). A test of general ability has a test information curve that is relatively uniform across the range of ability.

Similarly, every item has an *item information function*, which represents how well the item can discriminate among examinees of similar abilities, at different levels of ability. The point where the item information function is highest represents the ability level at which the item is most useful for distinguishing among different examinees. The test information function is simply the sum of the item information functions of the items on the test. The test information curve is highest at the point where the discrimination ability of the test items is most concentrated. Lord (1980) suggests a four-step procedure for test construction, based on the item information curves:

1. Decide on the shape desired for the test information function, which Lord terms the *target information curve*.
2. Select items with item information curves that fill in the spaces under the target information curve.
3. Continue to add item information curves, monitoring the resulting subtest information function for the already selected items.
4. Continue to add (and possibly subtract) items until the target information curve is satisfactorily approximated.

Lord's procedure makes use of the relationship between item and test information functions. Following this procedure ensures that the items chosen for the test form are sufficient for accomplishing the task for which the test is designed. Even if IRT scoring is ultimately not used, a test constructed in the manner outlined above should exhibit greater score precision (and higher reliability) than a test constructed by randomly selecting items from an item pool.

OPERATIONAL CONSIDERATIONS

Preliminary issues that must be considered for a large-scale assessment containing multiple versions of a test were discussed previously. These considerations allow test developers to ensure adequate test design as a first step. However, the ability to develop a test is not the only consideration that must be taken into account. Other issues dealing with routine operational needs for maintaining the test as a viable program must be considered as well. A number of key operational considerations exist: (1) The delivery platform for the test, (2) item and test development requirements, (3) methods available for item tryouts, and (4) test security issues.

Choice of Delivery Platform

There are currently a number of delivery platforms available. The traditional paper-and-pencil platform has been around for many decades and offers an efficient way to test large numbers of examinees in a single setting. Computer-based delivery is becoming more common and provides great opportunity for the delivery of innovative item formats as well as tailoring a test to an individual examinee. See Sireci and Zenisky (chap. 14, this volume) for examples of innovative item formats. Other methods, such as Internet-based delivery, are emerging and offer much in the way of testing large numbers of examinees globally as well as providing the opportunity for innovative assessment.

The pros and cons of each of these platforms are not discussed in this chapter. However, it is important to note that the ultimate choice of delivery platform impacts the ability to design and sustain multiple test forms in large-scale assessments as well as support the required test administration schedule.

Test and Item Development Considerations

Item and test development considerations are the elements most critical to the effective maintenance of a testing program. Determining the number of test items that must be created depends on the number of test forms that are needed. The number of test forms needed is driven by the number of times the test is given, whether examinees test more than once, the costs of multiple administrations, and a plethora of test security issues. The ability to successfully launch a new testing program requires meeting the requirements detailed in this chapter; the ability to sustain that program has the additional requirement of continuously developing sufficient numbers of items resulting in an item pool or item bank that allows the creation of many versions of the same test using the same test blueprint. Vale (chap. 11, this volume) discusses the considerable requirements of an item banking system.

The Test Inventory

The *test administration schedule* has the most impact on determining the number of test forms, or test inventory that is required. Testing programs that test multiple times in a given time period, especially those that result in high-stakes decisions, must determine the optimal number of new test forms that must be created as well as determining whether the reuse of test forms is acceptable. New test forms have an obvious advantage: Items are unique[2] so that examinees who test later are not advantaged by having an opportunity to learn about the items from examinees who were tested at earlier administrations. Although it might seem desirable to develop new versions of each test for all administrations, use of new test forms have a number of disadvantages as well. As new versions of each test are developed, new items are required to populate them and the cost of item development and tryout can be prohibitive, especially for some types of items. So too, ensuring that all versions of the test remain true to the test specifications becomes more complex as the number of individual versions of the test increases. Often one of the new tests cannot exactly match the requirements of the test specifications and a decision must be made as to whether or not the version is close enough to cover adequately the content domain or statistical specifications of the test. Finally, an unrepresentative or small examinee volume at some administrations can make it technically challenging to equate adequately the new form so that the meaning of the test scores remains steady across all administrations. Jones, Smith, and Talley (chap. 22, this volume) discuss the problems and recommend procedures for producing equivalent forms when the number of examinees is very small.

Reusing a test form (referred to here as a *reprint*) often helps to avoid the disadvantages described. With a reprint test, the same items are given to examinees, and raw-to-scaled score conversions determined at the time the version of the test was first administered are used to score the test. For example, college admission tests serve large numbers of students and are offered

---

[2]Some items, used for equating purposes, are not necessarily unique from one form to the next.

a number of times throughout the year. Some administrations, such as Sunday administrations or makeup administrations, generally do not have sufficient numbers of examinees to allow for adequately equating a new test form. In these cases, the use of a reprint test is ideal because it ensures the accuracy of the score for a small number of examinees.

An additional consideration for testing programs is determining how long a particular version of a test can be used. If appropriate scheduling and security considerations are accounted for, test forms may be used multiple times. However, although the test specifications may not change, it is still important to evaluate the test and items periodically. Changes in the outside world, in teaching practices, or in the content itself may alter the usability of particular items. At ETS, items and tests are generally reviewed at least every 5 years to ensure that they have not become outdated. Items determined to be outdated are removed and replaced with more appropriate items. This revised, or *refurbished,* test is readministered to examinees at an administration that allows it to be equated again prior to being placed back into the test inventory.

Developing Adequate Numbers of Test Items

Once the number of new test forms required for the test inventory is established, the number of test items needed to support the development of new test forms can be determined. Downing (chap. 12, this volume) and Welch (chap. 13, this volume) deal with issues relevant to item development, and other authors provide insight as to the many important activities, such as having sufficient numbers of trained item writers, required to maintain an adequate item bank (Abedi, chap. 17, this volume; Baranowski, chap. 15, this volume; Zieky, chap. 16, this volume).

Developing an adequate supply of test items should not be perceived as simply writing a set of test items. Although the most pressing need for new items comes from the number of new test forms required in the test inventory, other requirements also impact the number of new items available for development needs.

Items may become unavailable for a number of reasons. Subsequent reviews for item content, editorial style, and fairness result in the loss of some test items. Item tryouts (see below) may result in unacceptable item discrimination values or difficulty levels. Some item types may be more likely than others to show unacceptable statistical properties and this must be taken into account when planning item development. For example, very difficult or very easy items are more likely to have low item discrimination values than medium difficult items. Therefore, item-writing targets and item tryouts may need to include proportionally more difficult items than easy or medium ones.

To maintain the meaning of the scores from one administration to the next, equating is required (see Test Equating Methods). All equating designs require the use of additional test items identified as anchor items. When taken together, the anchor items must reflect the content and difficulty level of the test itself. Although there is no hard-and-fast number, the general rule is that the anchor test consist of no fewer than 20 items or 25% of the total test, whichever is larger (Dorans, Kubiak, & Melican, 1998; Kolen & Brennan, 2004). Thus, item development must also take into account the need for anchor items.

Other potential uses of items must be taken into account as well. For example, items provided as part of test preparation materials are not available for test assembly. Items are invariably lost as part of legislated test disclosure or retirement of intact test forms. Although such uses are secondary in driving item development, they must be considered as part of the total number of needed items. Otherwise, it is possible for the item bank to become too lean, and this presents a challenge to the assembly of subsequent versions of a test that successfully meet test content specifications.

Methods for Item Tryouts

Whenever possible, some type of item tryout should be done prior to the item being made available for use in test assembly. Item tryouts are often referred to as *pretesting* or *field testing*. The goal of an item tryout is to ensure that items function as expected. Information about item difficulty and item discrimination can be determined if the tryout sample is large enough and adequately represents the test-taking population. Most importantly, item tryout information can indicate unnoticed flaws in an item (e.g., a negative relationship with other items or a very high omission rate). Even without a particularly large sample, item tryouts may provide information about whether there is a single best answer in a multiple-choice item, likely responses to an open-ended item, and so on. In addition to evaluating the statistical properties of items, the statistical information obtained during item tryouts is also used to ensure the construction of multiple equivalent forms (see Maintenance Considerations). There are three basic models for item tryouts: (1) An embedded section within a test, (2) embedded items within a section of a test, and (3) external to the test itself. Performance on items that are part of an item tryout typically do not count toward an examinee's score.

The use of an *embedded section* within a test is thought to be the ideal method to use for item tryouts. The greatest advantage to this method is that the same examinees who take the test also take the new items, ensuring adequate sample sizes and representativeness of the test-taking population. In addition, the use of a separate section allows a relatively large number of items to be evaluated at the same time. However, if examinees are able to discern which section is being used for item tryouts (and thus not count toward their score), they are likely to be less motivated to perform as well as they would on other test sections that do count toward their score. Therefore, it is important that item tryout sections mimic the design of other test sections to provide usable information. This requirement limits the number and type of items included in the section and may limit the placement of the section within the test itself. Trying out innovative, new item types within an embedded section is often not possible because examinees might recognize it as the "unscored" section. Because the tryout section must mimic other test sections, the ability to include more items of a particular type or content, or items noticeably different in difficulty level, is limited.

The use of *embedded items* within a test section also has the advantage of ensuring adequate sample sizes and representativeness with the test-taking population. This method is preferable when the test design does not allow for a separate embedded section within the test. However, including items within a test section either increases the length of the total section or decreases the number of items used to generate examinees' scores. Adding to the testing time might be administratively unacceptable. If, however, tryout items are simply added to the test section, the amount of time examinees are given per item is decreased, and this might be detrimental to performance. Replacing operational items with tryout items allows the timing of the section to remain steady but may call into question adequate content coverage. In any case, including tryout items within the test section may result in examinees unknowingly spending too much time on individual items that do not count toward their score. As with the embedded section method, embedded items within a test section does not allow for the tryout of innovative or new item types.

Often items are evaluated *outside of the test administration* completely. The use of a field trial is warranted when it is not possible to create a separate section within a test or to embed items within a test section. There are a number of challenges that must be faced when employing this method of item tryout. Most importantly, it may be difficult to motivate examinees to perform the same way they would during the actual test administration unless they perceive some type of reward for performing well. It also may be difficult to find a sample that accurately reflects the test-taking population along important demographic, experience, and ability levels. So too, obtaining an adequate sample size so that full item analysis statistics can be generated is often financially prohibitive. Although this method is ideal for a one-time data collection effort, such as establishing an initial item bank, it tends to be less successful and more expensive for maintaining large-scale testing programs that require multiple test forms.

Test Security Issues

Test security issues influence the ideal number of test forms required by a testing program. New technology and global testing have dramatically changed the focus of test security considerations over the years. (See Impara and Foster [chap. 5, this volume] for a discussion of the many issues surrounding test security.) The key to test security as it relates to maintaining large-scale testing programs is to understand the test-taking behavior of examinees. For example, the use of a reprint test has a serious drawback if there is opportunity for large numbers of examinees to retake the test and they are administered the same test twice. The successful use of test reprints requires understanding when examinees are likely to retake a test so that reprints of tests can be scheduled at administrations where few examinees are likely to see the same test again. If a number of examinees repeat a test, a routine score change analysis can be implemented. This type of analysis evaluates, at an individual examinee level, changes in performance from one test administration to the next and determines the probability of the magnitude of change. Score changes that exceed a particular probability threshold may be questioned and investigated further.

MAINTENANCE CONSIDERATIONS

Most large-scale testing programs develop and administer multiple test forms across multiple administrations. The major goal of any such testing programs should be to ensure the valid interpretation or use of the test scores for all examinees. This means guaranteeing that the score an examinee receives on the test reflects only the examinee's ability and not extraneous, construct-irrelevant factors such as the test form, the time of year, or who else completed the test administration.

Building Equivalent Forms

The process of increasing evidence supporting validity begins with a strong test design and continues by building multiple forms of the test that match the test design. In large-scale testing programs, all forms of the test should be built to be as similar as possible, so that it would be a matter of indifference to the examinee which test form were administered (cf. Lord, 1980; see below). Nearly equivalent forms are best achieved by building all forms using strict content and statistical specifications, both of which have been discussed previously. However, because examinees may respond to specific item content in different ways, it is unlikely that examinees are totally indifferent to different forms of the test. For example, a reading passage on astronomy may be preferred by examinees whose hobby is astronomy, even if another science reading passage is statistically equivalent.

In principle, the process of building equivalent forms is fairly straightforward, if the content and statistical specifications are well defined and there is an adequate bank of items. A trade off must be acknowledged at this point, however. Obviously, the simplest way to achieve equivalent forms is to make the forms identical. Security issues demand, however, that test forms be as different as possible to avoid memorization of the items. Thus, test forms with identical items, or even with items that are clones of each other (identical except for certain words or numbers) become less ideal. Instead, different versions of a test must include items that measure the same concepts in different ways. Test specifications must be flexible enough to allow for such differences among test forms.

The item and test review processes are critical to the production of equivalent forms. Items must be reviewed on two levels: the judged content of the item and the observed responses to the item. The determination of whether or not an item falls within a content specification relies on the opinions of expert judges. These judges provide opinions on the specific topics covered by each item, the correctness of the keyed response, the clarity and appropriateness of the language, the plausibility of the various distractor responses, and possibly the difficulty of the item.

Judges also evaluate the items in the context of the entire test form to determine the extent to which the form meets the content specifications. The test developer takes care not to place items covering overly similar content, or items including identical distractors, in the same form; the judges determine if this attempt has been met. The judges review the consistency of the placement of item types across forms, as well as the comparability of forms in terms of reading load and physical item layout. Millman and Greene (1989) offer a general discussion of content evaluation in the context of the entire test development process.

Item tryouts offer several distinct advantages for the test construction process. The resulting item statistics indicate the difficulty of the items for the examinees (as often as not, what examinees find difficult is not the same as what experts predicted would be difficult). Statistics can indicate how strongly each item is related to the construct being measured. Item statistics generated from pretest data are used to construct test forms that meet the statistical specifications. In addition to meeting basic specifications such as average difficulty and the range of difficulty of the items, test forms are usually constructed to conform to certain other constraints. For example, the items in a section might proceed from easiest to hardest. The actual number of items of a particular difficulty might also be specified.

Careful review of content and statistical characteristics of individual items and of test forms helps to produce test forms that are very close to each other in content coverage and difficulty. However, even such careful procedures cannot guarantee that the test forms are truly equivalent. Fortunately, test equating can be used to statistically adjust for small variations in test difficulty.

Test Equating Methods

The purpose of test equating is to ensure that the reported scores on two forms of a test are comparable. In other words, it should not matter which version of a test an examinee takes—the score the person receives should be an accurate reflection of that examinee's ability assuming that the different versions of the test are assembled from the same set of test specifications. The test equating process removes score differences owing to small variations in test form difficulty. In this way, only examinee ability is reflected in the test score.

According to Lord (1980) four conditions must be met for successful equating to take place:

a. **Equal constructs**: Both tests must measure the same characteristic.
b. **Symmetry**: The function equating scores on Form Y to Form X should be the inverse of the function equating Form X to Form Y.
c. **Equity**: Once tests have been equated, it should not matter to a test taker which form is given. This condition subsumes another condition often listed in the literature (e.g., see Dorans & Holland, 2000), namely that the tests be of equal reliability.
d. **Population invariance**: The equating function linking form Y to form X should be the same, no matter which population the equating data come from.

In its strictest form, the equity requirement formed the basis for Lord's (1980) Theorem: "Under realistic regularity conditions, scores x and y on two tests cannot be equated unless either (1) both scores are perfectly reliable or (2) the two tests are strictly parallel [in which case $x(y) \equiv y$] (p. 108)." In other words, equating is either impossible or unnecessary. Fortunately, most practitioners do not consider the situation so hopeless. In any event, the satisfaction of these four conditions should be checked to whatever extent possible.

When discussing equating, it is important to bear in mind that the methods are generally designed to adjust for small differences in test difficulty and sometimes across populations exhibiting small differences in ability. To use a carpentry analogy, test equating is more like sandpaper than a saw. Equating methods are not designed to correct for gross differences in test difficulty. In this respect, test equating really begins with test construction (see Mislevy, 1992). This concept is represented in condition (a) above and to some extent in condition (c). As for the other conditions, (b) is usually met trivially because the equating methods impose symmetry. Condition (d) has received a large amount of attention in recent years, beginning with indices developed by Dorans and Holland (2000) to evaluate the departure from invariance, and including a special issue of the *Journal of Educational Measurement* (Dorans, 2004). The increasingly widespread availability of diagnostic indices should help to ensure successful equating.

There is not just one equating method, but rather a variety of methods that attempt in various ways to solve very practical problems. Fortunately, work by Braun and Holland (1982), and more recently by von Davier, Holland, and Thayer (2004), have provided a unified theoretical framework for most of the observed-score equating models. This section sketches out some practical considerations for establishing equating designs and evaluating the success of equating.

In practice, equating cannot adjust scores correctly for every individual examinee (hence Lord's bleak 1980 pronouncement). One examinee may find Form X easier, while another finds Form Y easier. No adjustment can correct for both people. Equating can adjust scores correctly for a group of examinees. However, it cannot adjust for every possible group. For example, one group may include more examinees who find Form X easier, while another group may include more examinees who find Form Y easier. No adjustment can correct for both groups. Fortunately, if an equating adjustment is correct for one group, it is likely to be approximately correct for other groups. It is important to consider the group for which the equating should be as correct as possible—the target population. This is the population from which the equating samples should be drawn.

All equating designs try to separate the effects of examinee ability from the effects of test difficulty, so that test difficulty may be adjusted. Single-group and equivalent-groups designs control for ability directly by holding it constant across test forms. In single-group designs, each examinee receives both the old and the new forms of the test. The order may be counterbalanced so that carryover effects may be assessed. In equivalent-groups designs, the two forms are randomly distributed to examinees so that ability level is randomly equivalent across the two test forms. When the testing situation permits, either of these two designs is preferable to other designs.

In some cases, it is impossible to administer both tests to the same sample. In such cases, the groups cannot be considered equivalent in ability. For non-equivalent groups, the ability level of the two groups must be adjusted statistically using a set of common items, or an anchor test. This anchor test is used to determine the difference in ability between the two groups. Thus, it is important that this anchor test be a miniature version of the total test, both in content and in difficulty.

The number of items to include in the anchor tests depends on a number of factors, both content related and statistical. One important factor is the correlation between the anchor test and the total test. If the anchor test is external to the old form and to the form to be equated (i.e., the anchor test indeed constitutes a totally separate test), as opposed to being embedded within the two test forms, then more items are needed to ensure the same level of correlation with the total tests. If the anchor test is embedded within the total test forms, then fewer items may suffice. Results by Dorans (2000) suggest that a correlation of 0.87 be considered a minimum target for the correlation between the anchor and total tests. Other work by Dorans et al. (1998) suggests that the number of items in the anchor test be no fewer than 20 items or 25% of the total test, whichever is larger (Kolen & Brennan [2004], offer similar suggestions).

Placement of the anchor items is also an issue. If the anchor test is external to the total test, then the items should be kept in the same order. If the items are embedded within the total test, then care should be taken to place the items in similar locations in both the old form and the form to be equated to avoid possible context effects. For a speeded test, items that are affected by speed should be avoided as common items. For an unspeeded test, except for a long test in which fatigue may be an issue, exact placement of items may be less of an issue. It may be wise to avoid using the first item on a test form as an anchor item, to give examinees a chance to become acclimated to the test. These steps do not guarantee that the anchor items will behave in the same way across both testing groups. Item statistics can be examined to check for items that may be behaving differently for the two testing groups (Harris, 1993).

As mentioned, non-equivalent groups equating methods are designed to adjust for small differences in group ability. Cook and Petersen (1987), for example, found that when the two testing groups differed greatly in ability, even anchor tests containing almost 60% of the items on the tests could not adjust correctly for group difficulty. For this reason, it is essential that the old form and new form groups be as similar in ability as possible. In large-scale testing programs with multiple administrations per year, it may be the case that certain administrations routinely attract examinees of higher ability, and other administrations attract examinees of lower average ability. If this is the case, it may be wise to equate a new form to an old form that was given at the same time of year (e.g., equate a Spring form to a Spring form used the previous year, equate a Fall form to a Fall form) (Cook & Petersen, 1987).

Equating test forms in separate administrations as suggested may have undesirable side effects. Because equating methods contain some error, a certain amount of scale drift may take place over time (Dorans, 1985). To the extent that the populations represented by the different administrations differ, and to the extent that population invariance cannot hold exactly, the possibility exists for certain strains of equated tests to develop, each with a slightly different reporting scale. The development of such strains can be avoided by incorporating safeguards into the equating plan. One such safeguard involves using a test as an old form in an administration different from the one in which it was originally equated. For example, if a test is originally equated in the Fall, it is readministered in the Spring and used as an old form for a test to be equated in the Spring. Another method of avoiding the development of strains is to periodically equate a new form to two or more old forms, which themselves were equated in different administrations.

All of these methods require careful consideration as to how new versions of a test and any reprints are scheduled to be given. The method chosen directly impacts the development of new tests because sufficient numbers of new and old versions of the test must be in the test inventory to sustain the method.

Rescaling to Maintain Scale Meaning

As discussed, test score reporting scales often derive meaning by being linked to some reference group or to some specific criterion. Over time, as new versions of a test become farther and farther removed from the original reference group or criterion, a reporting scale can begin to drift and lose meaning. The SAT Reasoning test (SAT) provides a dramatic example of this phenomenon (see Dorans, 2002). In 1941, the means for both the Verbal and Math tests were set at 500 on the 200 to 800-point reporting scale, for that year's population of approximately 10,000 examinees. Over time, most score users continued to believe that the mean Verbal and Math scores were 500 in the testing population. However, as the test-taking population became less selective, the score means gradually decreased; by 1990 the means for the more than 1 million college-bound seniors who took the test were 424 for Verbal and 476 for Math. Clearly, the meaning of the scale had changed dramatically.

There are several reasons that score scales lose their meaning over time. An example of shifting test-taking populations was just described. In addition, the test content specifications may change (e.g., to remain aligned with shifting school curricula). Even if the test specifications do not change, test content may drift, perhaps imperceptibly as new forms are equated to old, but possibly quite dramatically over a long period of time. Even when no population or content shifts take place, the imperfect nature of test score equating can introduce scale drift.

The nature of large-scale testing programs requires that the meaning of scores across many versions of the test from multiple administrations remain invariant. Scores on scales that have drifted from the original scale invite misinterpretation. This difficulty led Angoff (1984) to argue in favor of score scales free of normative references, claiming that scales can be quite useful without any inherent meaning. He used by way of example the fact that the original definitions of units of physical measurement such as feet and inches have been lost over time; nevertheless, the measures continue to be useful.

For cases in which a non-normative scale is neither desired nor possible, it is essential that the scale remain properly aligned to avoid confusion and misinterpretation. For this reason, Dorans (2002) urges that the score scale be viewed as a testing infrastructure in need of periodic adjustment. Any effort to rescale a test on a regular basis may meet with a certain amount of resistance, however; the realignment of a misaligned score scale necessarily disrupts score continuity and year-to-year trend data. In that sense, scaling contravenes the very goals that equating works to preserve. For that reason, it may be advisable to rescale a test often enough so that the disruption is not perceptible, but not so often that cross-year comparisons become impossible.

Several methods for test score rescaling exist. Which one is appropriate depends on the nature of the test. Licensure examinations, for example, may repeat the initial study in which the cut-score was set. For criterion-referenced tests, scaling studies can likewise be repeated on a regular basis. For normative tests, the scaling procedure can be carried out on a more recent norming population.

In the case of a test battery, using similar methods for scaling and norming all the tests in the battery can facilitate comparison of examinee performance on different tests. Typically, the entire test battery is administered to the entire norm group. If the scaled score distributions for the individual tests in the battery are all set to be identical in the norm group, then the scores on different tests can be compared without reference to norm tables (Petersen et al., 1989).

Sometimes not all tests can be administered to the norm sample simultaneously. For example, a test may be added to a battery after scales for the other tests have been set. Such a situation offers a special challenge. A similar problem arises when not all examinees take all tests in a battery (such as with the SAT Subject tests). In these cases, the scales for the tests must be set indirectly.

One method of indirect scaling was attributed to Tucker by Gulliksen (1987, pp. 299–304). The method makes use of linear regression techniques (with the new test as the criterion and the already normed tests as covariates) to estimate the performance of the norm sample on the new test. The score scale for the new test can then be adjusted so that its estimated mean and standard deviation in the norm sample match some desired values.

TABLE 20.3
Questions for the Test Developer

Preliminary Questions	Operational Questions	Maintenance Questions
What **use** will be made of the test? • What is the test's purpose? • Is it high or low stakes?	What **delivery platform** will be used?	What procedures will be used to build **equivalent forms**? • Item-level reviews? • Test-level reviews?
What is the **target population** for the test? • Who is the test designed for? • Who is likely to take the test?	What is the optimal **test inventory**? • How many new test forms must be developed? • What is the test administration schedule? • Will reprints be used?	What **test equating** methods will be used? • How many anchor items are needed? • What is the placement of the anchor items? • How is test form scheduling affected?
How will the **test scores** be used? • What is the primary use of the scores? • What are secondary uses?	What is the optimal **item bank**? • How many new test forms are required? • What is the requirement for anchor items? • What item tryout method will be used? • What is the expected item loss from reviews and tryouts? • What other uses of items will be required?	Is the possibility of **scale drift** important? • How will scale drift be monitored? • How frequently is rescaling acceptable? • What rescaling method will be used?
What are the **content specifications** for the test? • What is the content domain? • What are the question formats?		
What are the **statistical specifications** for the test? • What is the average test difficulty? • What is the distribution of item difficulty? • What is acceptable item discrimination?		
What **scoring method** will be used? • Will a pilot study be used to examine various scoring methods?		
What **score scale** will be used to report scores? • What type of scale is most appropriate? • What are the optimal number scale points?		
What is the appropriate **test length**? • How does the length impact validity? • How does the length impact test score precision (reliability)? • How does the length impact test speededness?		

In some cases, such as when a test is added to an existing battery that all examinees take in total, it is possible to observe directly the extent to which the scaling was successful by examining all test score distributions in some population similar to the reference population (e.g., by using the data from all examinees in a subsequent testing year). In other cases, such as when each test is taken by a different subset of examinees, it is difficult to know if the scaling was successful. Perhaps the best that can be done is to repeat the scaling procedure using several scaling samples and assess the degree of similarity among all of the results.

PRACTICAL GUIDELINES

The issues explored in this chapter focus on the psychometric-related planning and maintenance concerns surrounding large-scale testing programs that require the use of multiple test forms across multiple administrations. Attention to test design and technical procedures at the initial stage helps to ensure that the testing program is kept technically sound over many years. Such requirements are used actively at ETS and many other test publishing companies in support of large-scale testing programs. Table 20.3 offers a set of guidelines as a checklist to assist the practitioner in considering important decision points as part of start up or maintenance of a large scale testing program.

ACKNOWLEDGMENT

The authors are grateful for the thoughtful reviews and insights provided by Rosemary Reshetar and Michael Zieky. We also thank Tom Haladyna and Steve Downing for their feedback on the draft chapter and Eric Wendler for his review and editorial comments. Errors of fact or interpretation are those of the authors.

REFERENCES

American Educational Research Association (AERA), American Psychological Association (APA), & National Council on Measurement in Education (NCME) (1999). *Standards for educational and psychological testing*. Washington, DC: AERA.

Anastasi, A. (1976). *Psychological testing* (4th ed.). New York: MacMillan.

Angoff, W. H. (1984). Scale, norms, and equivalent scores. Princeton NJ: Educational Testing Service.

Angoff, W. H., & Schrader, W. B. (1984). A study of hypotheses basic to the use of rights and formula scores. *Journal of Educational Measurement, 21*(1), 1–17.

Braun, H. I., & Holland, P. W. (1982). Observed-score test equating: A mathematical analysis of some ETS equating procedures. In Holland, P. W., & Rubin, D. B. (Eds.). *Test equating* (pp. 9–49. New York: Academic Press.

College Board. (2005). *Advanced Placement Program*. New York: College Entrance Examination Board.

College Board. (2005). *SAT Resoning Test*. New York: College Entrance Examination Board.

Cook, L. L., & Petersen, N. S. (1987). Problems related to the use of conventional and item response theory equating methods in less than optimal circumstances. *Applied Psychological Measurement, 11*(3), 225–244.

Dorans, N. J. (1985). *Achievement test rescaling: Help or hindrance?* (Educational Testing Service Statistical Report SR-85-92). Princeton, NJ: Educational Testing Service.

Dorans, N. J. (2000). *Distinctions among classes of linkages* (College Board Research Note RN-11). New York: The College Board.

Dorans, N. J. (2002). Recentering and realigning the SAT score distributions: How and why. *Journal of Educational Measurement, 39*(1), 59–84.

Dorans, N. J. (Ed.) (2004). Special Issue: Assessing the population sensitivity of equating functions. *Journal of educational measurement, 41*(1), 1–68.

Dorans, N. J., & Holland, P. J. (2000). Population invariance and the equatability of tests: Basic theory and the linear case. *Journal of Educational Measurement, 37*(4), 281–306.

Dorans, N. J., Kubiak, A., & Melican, G. J. (1998). *Guidelines for selection of embedded common items for score equating.* (Educational Testing Service Statistical Report SR-98-02). Princeton, NJ: Educational Testing Service.

Educational Testing Service (ETS). (1987). *ETS standards for quality and fairness.* Princeton, NJ: ETS.

Fan, X. (1998). Item response theory and classical test theory: An empirical comparison of their item/person statistics. *Educational and Psychological Measurement, 58*(3), 357–381.

Gulliksen, H. (1987). *Theory of mental tests.* Hillsdale, NJ: Lawrence Erlbaum Associates.

Haladyna, T. M., & Downing, S. M. (1989). Validity of a taxonomy of multiple-choice item-writing rules. *Applied Measurement in Education, 2*(1), 51–78.

Haladyna, T. M., Downing, S. M., & Rodriguez, M. C. (2002). A review of multiple-choice item-writing guidelines for classroom assessment. *Applied Measurement in Education, 15*(3), 309–334.

Hambleton, R. K., Swaminathan, H., & Rogers, H. J. (1991). *Fundamentals of item response theory.* Newbury Park, CA: Sage.

Harris, D. J. (1993). *Practical issues in equating.* Paper presented at the annual meeting of the American Educational Research Association, Atlanta, GA.

Kahneman, D., & Tversky, A. (1979). Prospect theory: An analysis of decision under risk. *Econometrica, 47,* 263–291.

Kolen, M. J., & Brennan, R. L. (2004). *Test equating, scaling, and linking: Methods and practices,* 2nd edition. New York: Springer.

Kryspin, W. J., & Feldhusen, J. F. (1974). *Developing classroom tests. A guide for writing and evaluating test items.* Minneapolis, MN: Burgess.

Linn, R.L. (2000). Assessment and accountability. *Educational Researcher, 29*(2), 4–16.

Livingston, S. A., & Zieky, M. J. (1982). *Passing scores: A manual for setting standards of performance on educational and occupational tests.* Princeton, NJ: ETS.

Lord, F. M. (1975). Formula scoring and number-right scoring. *Journal of Educational Measurement, 12*(1), 7–11.

Lord, F. M. (1980). *Applications of item response theory to practical testing problems.* Hillsdale, NJ: Lawrence Erlbaum Associates.

McDonald, R. P. (1982). Linear versus non-linear models in item response theory. *Applied Psychological Measurement, 6,* 379–396.

McDonald, R. P. (1999). *Test theory: A unified treatment.* Mahwah, NJ: Larence Erlbaum Associates.

Messick, S. (1993). Validity. In R. L. Linn (Ed.), *Educational measurement* (3rd ed. pp. 13–103). Phoenix: The Oryz Press.

Millman, J., & Greene, J. (1989). The specification and development of tests of achievement and ability. In Linn, R. L. (Ed.). *Educational measurement* (3rd ed., pp. 335–366). New York: MacMillan.

Mislevy, R. J. (1992). *Linking educational assessments: Concepts, issues, methods, and prospects.* Princeton, NJ: ETS Policy Information Center.

Mislevy, R. J., Almond, R. G., & Lukas, J. F. (2003). *A brief introduction to evidence-centered design.* (Educational Testing Service Research Report RR-03-16). Princeton, NJ: ETS.

Mislevy, R. J., Steinberg, L. S., & Almond, R. G. (2002). On the roles of task model variables in assessment design. In S. Irvine, & P. Kyllonen (Eds). *Generating items for cognitive tests: Theory and practice* (pp. 97–128). Hillsdale, NJ: Lawrence Erlbaum Associates.

Petersen, N. S., Kolen, M. J., & Hoover, H. D. (1989). Scaling, norming, and equating. In Linn, R. L. (Ed.). *Educational measurement* (3rd ed.), pp. 221–262 New York: MacMillan.

Roid, G. H., & Haladyna, T. (1982). *A technology for test-item writing.* New York: Academic Press.

Roid, G. H., & Wendler, C. LW. (1983). *Item bias detection and item writing technology.* Paper presented at the annual meeting of the American Educational Research Association, Montreal, Canada.

Thorndike, R. L. (1971). The problem of guessing. In Thorndike, R. L. (Ed.), *Educational measurement* (2nd ed., pp. 59–61). Washington, D.C.: American Council on Education.

Thurstone, L. L. (1919). A method for scoring tests. *Psychological Bulletin, 16,* 235–240.

von Davier, A. A., Holland, P. W., & Thayer, D. T. (2004). *The kernel method of test equating.* New York: Springer.

Walker, M. E., & Liu, J. (2004). *Scaling issues associated with the new SAT: Writing Test.* Paper presented at the annual meeting of the National Council on Measurement in Education, San Diego, CA.

21

Vertical Scales

Michael J. Young
Harcourt Assessment, Inc.

A *vertical scale* is an extended score scale that spans a series of grades and allows the estimation of student growth along a continuum. As states and school districts report on the adequate yearly progress of student performance as required by the *No Child Left Behind Act of 2001* (NCLB), there is increasing emphasis on documenting student progress within selected subject areas. Using a vertical scale can meet this need for a common interpretive framework for test results across grades and yield important information that informs individual and classroom instruction.

Although there is no consensus on what constitutes best professional practice for developing and validating vertical scales, this chapter provides a series of questions that can be used as a framework for the issues that need to be addressed while creating vertical scales. Among some of the matters addressed in this overview are the definition of *growth* that should be employed in establishing a vertical scale; the kinds of test content appropriate for the vertical scale; designs for collecting data for creating the vertical scale; methodologies for linking together tests at different levels; and techniques for evaluating the resulting vertical scale. The chapter concludes with some practical advice on creating vertical scales for state and school district testing programs.

As states and school districts report on the adequate yearly progress of student performance as required by the *No Child Left Behind Act of 2001* (NCLB), there is increasing emphasis on documenting student progress within selected subject areas. Using a vertical scale can meet this need for a common interpretive framework for test results across grades and yield important information that informs individual and classroom instruction.

A *vertical scale* (also referred to as a *developmental scale*) is an extended score scale that spans a series of grades (typically from Kindergarten through grade 12) and allows the estimation of student growth along a continuum (Nitko, 2004). These scales are distinct from *horizontal* or *within-grade scales* that are derived by equating different forms of the same test that are assumed to be assessing the same content at the same level of difficulty. Although vertical scales may be created using the same kinds of statistical methods as in horizontal equating, the process involved is more accurately described as *calibration;* the test forms involved are designed for different grades with different content and difficulty levels (Kolen & Brennan, 2004).

Typically, vertical scales have had their provenance with test publishers, who establish a separate vertical scale for each subtest or content area for their achievement test batteries, such as the *Stanford Achievement Test Series* (Harcourt Educational Measurement, 2003), the *Metropolitan Achievement Tests* (Harcourt Educational Measurement 2002), the *Iowa Tests of Basic Skills* (Petersen, Kolen, & Hoover, 1989), and *TerraNova* (CTB/McGraw-Hill, 1996).

Vertical scales can be used in a variety of ways (cf. Angoff, 1984; Petersen et al., 1989; Schulz, Perlman, Rice Jr, & Wright, 1992). Through the use of a vertical scale, student progress can be monitored as new skills are developed or new knowledge is acquired within a content area, and scores earned by students on different assessment instruments administered at different times can be directly compared. In addition, growth patterns for individual students or groups of students may be measured in terms of changes in performance and variability from grade to grade.

A vertical scale also allows for a comparison of the test difficulties across grade levels. This feature is especially useful because it allows "out-of-level" testing, that is, the administration of a test that most closely matches a student's ability level regardless of grade level.

Beside examining the difficulty of tests, a vertical scale can also be used to benchmark assessment items consistent with content standards or curriculum frameworks at different levels. Such an approach was used with the "scale anchors" of the National Assessment of Educational Progress (NAEP), which were used to describe what a student knew and was able to do at specified NAEP scale scores (Beaton & Allen, 1992).

Finally, when cut scores for passing criteria are developed for a criterion or standards-referenced assessment system, a vertical scale can be used to check on the consistency of achievement expectations across grade levels.

Unfortunately, there is no consensus in the measurement community on what constitutes best professional practice for developing and validating vertical scales. The *Standards for Educational and Psychological Testing* (American Educational Research Association [AERA], American Psychological Association [APA], & National Council on Measurement in Education [NCME], 1999) mention vertical scaling only in passing, and the only relevant standards deal with scales in general rather than vertical scales in particular. Specifically, Standard 4.1 states that test users should be provided with "clear explanations of the meaning and intended interpretation of derived score scales, as well as their limitations" (AERA, APA, & NCME, 1999, p. 54); Standard 4.2 affirms that the "construction of scales used for reporting scores should be described clearly in test documents" (AERA, APA, & NCME, 1999, p. 54). Finally, Standard 4.3 warns that if "specific misinterpretations of a score scale are likely, test users should be explicitly forewarned" (AERA, APA, & NCME, 1999, p. 54). Although these standards address the need to document carefully the construction, interpretation, and misinterpretation of all scales, they provide no guidance to practioners wishing to develop their own vertical scales.

The most up-to-date summaries of the literature (Harris, Hendrickson, Tong, Shin, & Shyu, 2004; Kolen & Brennan, 2004) provide an almost bewildering array of questions that need to be addressed with respect to creating a vertical scale. Among the most important of these questions are the following:

- What definition of *growth* should be employed?
- What test content is most appropriate for developing a vertical scale?
- What design should be used to collect the data needed for creating the vertical scale?
- What methodology should be used to link tests at different levels to form the vertical scale?
- How should one evaluate the resulting vertical scale?

These questions are used as a framework for providing practioners an overview to the information they need to create vertical scales for their own testing programs. The next section examines alternative definitions of growth along a vertical scale and the development and selection of test content that is most suitable for creating vertically scaled tests. Data collection designs are then examined; methods for creating vertical scales are reviewed; and evaluating the resulting vertical scale is discussed. Finally, developing vertical scales in practice is discussed.

DEFINING GROWTH AND TEST CONTENT FOR VERTICAL SCALES

As stated, above, one of the primary uses of a vertical scale is to measure student progress in a content area across time. Ideally, the construct being measured on a vertical scale should be identical at any point along it. Consider the results on two tests that indicate the levels of achievement for a content area at two grades: To place the scores from these tests on the same vertical scale and interpret differences as growth, we must assume that the knowledge and the skills being measured at those grade levels are similar enough to be placed on the same developmental continuum (Vukmirovic, 2004). Creating a vertical scale and justifying the inferences to be drawn from it depend on several factors:

- The subject matter to be covered by the vertical scale: Certain content areas lend themselves more readily to the creation of vertical scales than others. For example, reading and mathematics are taught and learned continuously across the grades. A vertical scale might be more reasonable for these subjects than for a subject such as science, where the content can change dramatically from grade to grade (e.g., from life to physical science; Lissitz & Huynh, 2003).
- The relationship of the subject matter of the test to the educational curriculum: As Kolen and Brennan (2004) point out, students show different amounts of growth depending on how closely tied the subject matter of the test is to the educational curriculum. When the test is closely tied to the curriculum, students show more growth on new subject matter introduced near the end of the year it is emphasized than on subject matter introduced in previous years.
- How widely separated the test levels are from which the scores are taken: Interpreting score differences as gains is more justified for test levels at adjacent grades than for test levels that are widely separated. It was this issue among others that led to the scrutiny of the across-grade scaling at grades 4, 8, and 12 for NAEP (Haertel, 1991; Hunyh & Schneider, 2004).
- The definition of growth used. Kolen and Brennan (2004) provide two conceptual definitions of growth along a vertical scale: The *domain definition* defines growth over the all of content assessed by the levels of a vertically scaled series of tests. The domain includes the content taught at a specific grade level together with the content that is taught at other grade levels. Under this definition, grade-to-grade growth is defined over the entire range of content within the domain. In contrast, the *grade-to-grade definition* defines growth over the content at a specific grade level. *Grade-to-grade growth* is the change from one grade level to the next over the content taught at a certain grade level. The operationalization of these definitions of growth requires the use of different data collection designs and leads to different vertical scales when the subject matter areas tested are closely tied to the educational curriculum.

Each of these factors should be considered prior to developing a vertical scale. In light of NCLB, state testing programs considering vertical scales probably need to focus their attention on developing scales that span grades 3 through 8 inclusively, rather than at a few, separated grades. State testing programs should carefully examine their content standards at each grade level and articulate the relationship of those standards to the standards of the preceding and succeeding grades. Many state testing programs have found that the easiest way to do this is to create a cross-walk between the standards at a pair of adjacent grade levels.

A *cross-walk* is a chart with the listing the standards of one grade down the left-most column of the page with the standards of the next higher grade across the top row. The cells of the chart are used to indicate where a standard is present at the lower grade but not the higher grade, is present at the higher grade but not the lower grade, or is present at both grades. Such a technique can also be used to examine the test specifications or blueprints that are developed to test students with respect to a set of content standards.

Test developers are used to creating test specifications that are essentially one dimensional—that is, showing a distribution of the numbers of items across content to be tested—or two-dimensional—that is, showing both the distribution of content as well as the cognitive demand to be tested (see Nitko, 2004, pp. 107–110 for examples of one- and two-dimensional test specifications and blueprints, and Webb, chap. 8, this volume, on the importance of clear content specifications). Developing vertical scales requires test developers to think three dimensionally, with the third dimension being the change in emphasis in the knowledge and skills being tested from one grade to the next. Creating test specification cross-walks (also called *content* or *assessment scatter plots* [Lissitz & Huynh, 2003]) is an important way of checking on changes to a construct as it is being assessed across the grades, and can serve as an important source of validity evidence for the use and interpretation of the vertical scale (see Kane, chap. 7, this volume; Messick, 1989).

DATA COLLECTION DESIGNS

After examining the content from an item pool for its suitability for constructing a vertical scale, the next step in the process is to choose a design to collect the data needed to construct the vertical scale. In general, a data collection design uses one of three approaches:

1. A common set of items is present on the test forms taken by different groups of examinees;
2. A common group of examinees take different test forms; or
3. Equivalent groups of examinees take different test forms.

Common Item Designs

In the *common item design,* test forms are administered across the grade levels that target the content appropriate to that level. Common items are embedded into these test forms from the levels immediately above and below each target level to allow the scale to be constructed. This data collection design is shown in Figure 21.1 for the construction of a hypothetical vertical scale for grades 3 through 8. The rows of the figure represent the grades of the examinees taking the test, and the level of the test taken is shown in the columns. The boxes in the figure represent the groups of examinees taking the content targeted to their grade with linkages to the content at the adjacent grades. Thus 5th-grade examinees take a test that is targeted for 5th-grade content, while also answering items that are from the 4th and 6th grades. When the common items are administered as a separate test rather than embedded in the on-level test, this design is often called an *anchor test design*.

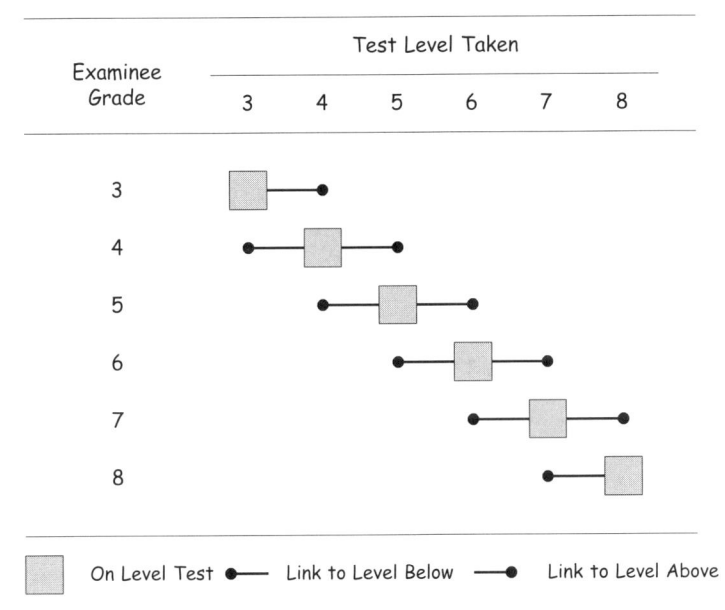

FIG. 21.1. Common item design.

FIG. 21.2. Scaling test design.

In the *scaling test design,* a special test form is created that takes representative content across a span of grades and places all the items on a single form. This scaling test is administered to examinees along with the test level that is appropriate to their grade, and provides the common item link across levels. The difference between the scaling test design and the common item design is that the examinees are all administered the same set of common items. Figure 21.2 depicts this design. In this figure, examinees at each grade take a test targeted to their grade level (i.e., the boxes along the diagonal in the figure) while taking the same scaling test (i.e., the boxes at the far right).

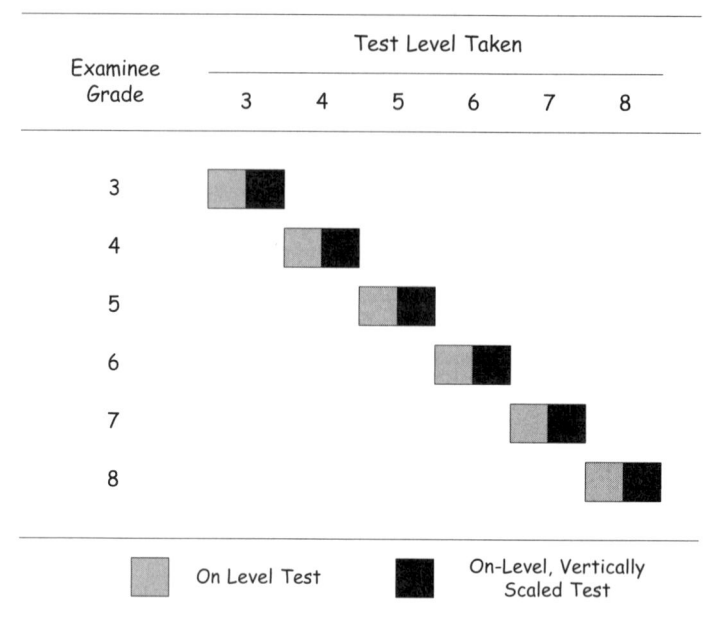

FIG. 21.3. Quasi-common item design.

When an external anchor is taken from a series of tests that are already vertically scaled, this anchor can be used to equate test forms to the preexisting scale using the *quasi-common item design*. This design has its origin in Angoff's discussion (1984) of the common item design. Angoff noted that an external anchor test, denoted U, may be used to equate two test forms, X and Y, and that Form U may be a quasi-common test. That is to say, it may actually be two different forms of a test, one administered to (one group) and the other to (another group). The only restriction is that the two forms be expressed on the same scale, so that appropriate comparisons and adjustments may be made for differences between the two groups in the process of equating the tests (Angoff, 1984, p. 112).

As shown in Figure 21.3, examinees take the appropriate on-grade level of the test that is to be vertically scaled (the light boxes) along with the on-grade level of a test on a preexisting vertical scale (the dark boxes). Horizontal linkages at each level are used to place the new tests onto the same vertical scale as the pre-existing test.

Common Person Design

In the *counterbalanced single group design,* each grade is administered both the "on-level" form of a test and the test level immediately below it. In many cases, the order in which the tests are administered may have an effect on the examinees. Counterbalancing can be used to ensure that the scores on both test forms are equally affected by such factors as learning, fatigue, and practice (Petersen et al., 1989). Counterbalancing can be achieved by spiraling, that is, by alternating the order of test forms before distributing them to examinees. In this way, half of the examinees take the on-level form of the test followed by the lower test level, and the other half of the examinees take the lower test level followed by the on-level test. As shown in Figure 21.4, each group of examinees (except for the lowest test level) takes both the on-grade test level as well as the test level below. Numbers indicating the order of testing explicitly show the counter-balancing in this design.

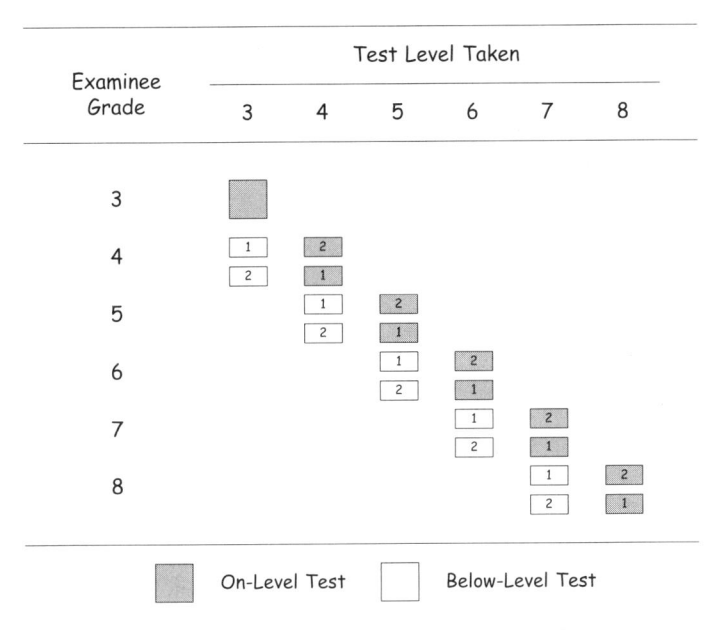

FIG. 21.4. Counterbalanced single group design.

Equivalent Groups Design

The *equivalent groups design* represents another approach to gathering data for constructing a vertical scale. In this design, examinees from each level are randomly administered tests either from the level appropriate to their grade or the level below. The random administration is achieved by spiraling the tests before giving them to the examinees. This design is shown in Figure 21.5, where except for the lowest grade, half of each grade of examinees is administered one of two levels of the test.

Choosing a Data Collection Design

The choice of data collection design to create a vertical scale is affected by several concerns, both theoretical and practical, including:

- The impact of definition of growth on data collection method. As Kolen and Brennan (2004) point out, the domain definition of *growth* is defined over the entire range of test content for a given subject area. Only the scaling test design explicitly adopts this definition of growth, because students at every level take a test whose content spans the grades. The grade-to-grade definition of growth can be operationalized by the common-item, single-group counterbalanced, and equivalent-groups designs. Note that adopting the quasi-common item design implicitly adopts the definition of growth used to develop the test with the preexisting vertical scale.
- The difficulty of test items. Administering a scaling test requires that items be administered that some examinees find too difficult and others find too easy. This may prove to be frustrating for examinees and be questioned by teachers, principals, and parents. A state trying to create a vertical scale might want to choose a design where the items administered more nearly target the ability level of the examinees.

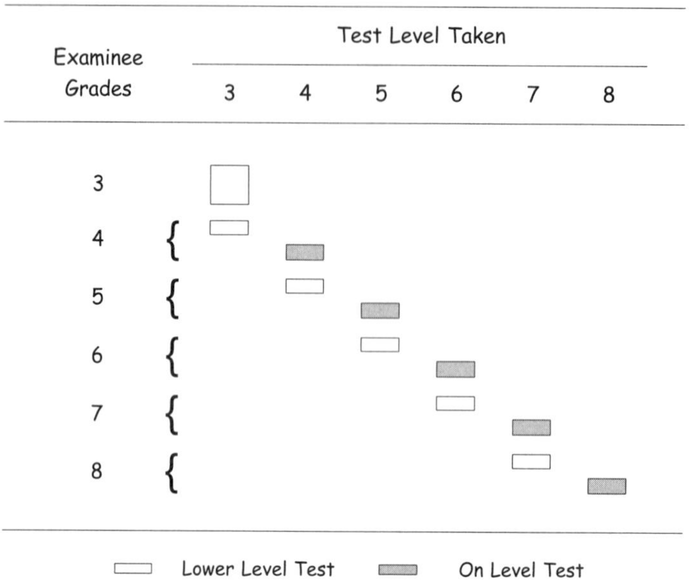

FIG. 21.5. Equivalent groups design.

- The amount of student testing time required by the data collection design. The single-group counterbalanced, quasi-common item and scaling test designs require the most amount of testing time; each examinee must take two complete tests. The equivalent-groups design takes up the least amount of testing time; each examinee is administered a single form at random. The testing time using the common-item design falls somewhere in between.
- The need for additional item development. The scaling test design requires a special test that spans the content across the grade levels. Test developers need to consider carefully their test specifications across the grade levels to create the test specifications for the scaling test. The items for the scaling test need to reflect changes in content emphasis for different areas of the content domain across the domain. The item development for this test is added to the development of the test items for each test level of the vertical scale.

The use of the common-item design may also require additional item development, especially if the common items are administered as a separate, external anchor test. Kolen and Brennan's (2004) rule of thumb for the number of common items needed for horizontal equating can be adapted for vertical equating. They state that "a common item set should be at least 20% of the length of a total test containing 40 or more items, unless the test is very long, in which case 30 items might suffice" (p. 271). However, in the case of vertical scaling it might be wise to increase the number of common items, since differences in content and difficulty levels across grades might have an impact on the precision of the linkage (McBride & Wise, 2000).

Although the single-group counterbalanced design requires that each student take two test levels, no additional item development is necessary because the design uses existing forms. The quasi-common item design requires that a test on a preexisting vertical scale be administered along with each test that needs to be vertically scaled. Using the abbreviated or survey form of a publisher's vertically scaled achievement test battery can serve quite nicely for this role.

METHODOLOGIES FOR LINKING TEST FORMS

Virtually every approach that can used to equate test forms can be used to link test forms to create a vertical scale. Typically, a given test level is designated as a base level and the other test levels are sequentially linked to it. For example, the base level might be chosen to be the lowest test level to be administered, with the other levels linked up the scale. Test publishers often choose one of the middle test levels as a base, and build the links downward to the lowest level and upward to the highest level. Linear and equipercentile equating for different data collection designs are discussed in several sources including Angoff (1984), Tong and Harris (2004), and Kolen and Brennan (2004). This section describes two classical approaches to scaling, namely the methods attributed to Hieronymous and Thurstone, and then focuses on factors that need to be taken into account when creating vertical scales using Item Response Theory (IRT). These include the IRT scaling model used, the estimation strategy employed, and how estimates of person ability are obtained.

Hieronymous Scaling

As described by Petersen et al. (1989), *Hieronymous scaling,* also called *grade-equivalent scaling,* is the procedure used to develop the score scale for the *Iowa Tests of Basic Skills*. This procedure consists of the following steps.

A scaling test is designed by taking test items from each test level for a span of grades (e.g., grades 3 through 8). The items are chosen to be representative of the content being assessed, and the entire test is designed to be short enough to be administered in a single sitting. The scaling test is then administered to representative samples of students from the span of grades. The tests are scored and the distribution of raw scores is obtained for each grade level.

Next, true score distributions are obtained from the observed raw score distributions by assuming that the true score distributions have the same means and shapes as the observed score distributions, but with smaller variances. Specifically, the variance of the true score distribution at a given grade is assumed to be equal to the scaling test reliability at that grade multiplied by the variance of the observed raw score distribution.

For all grades, the scaling test score medians of the true score distributions are calculated. These medians are used together with the true score distributions to construct a table that lists the percentile ranks of grade medians across grades. The column headings indicate the grade and time of year for which the median was calculated, and the columns themselves show for a fixed median, the percentages of students falling below that median at each grade. Thus, a table heading of 4.5 indicates the grade equivalent for the median calculated during the 5th month of the fourth grade, and the column entries show the percentile ranks for the median at grades 3 through 8. The rows of the table are the within-grade percentile ranks on the grade-equivalent scale for each of the medians.

The final step is to establish raw score to grade-equivalent score tables. This is done by first administering to representative samples of students the appropriate full-length, on-level versions of their tests. Next, percentile ranks are calculated for each level of the test. For a given grade, a raw score is assigned the grade equivalent with the same percentile rank as that of the grade equivalent from the scaling test.

Thurstone's Absolute Scaling Method

A different approach to creating a vertical scale can be found in *Thurstone's absolute scaling method,* which requires that data be collected for two groups of examinees on a common set of items in addition to the items of the forms to be scaled. This technique hypothesizes that the raw scores on tests are monotonically related to trait values, and normalizes the raw scores to create an equal interval scale (Allen & Yen, 1979).

Once this is done, the raw score distributions on the set of common items for the two examinee groups are obtained separately. The percentiles are computed for each of the raw scores and transformed to the deviates z, of the standard normal distribution. Next, the z-scores for each of the groups are then plotted against each other, and the resulting scatterplot is examined to see if they are linearly related. If the correlation between the z-scores is high, and the scatterplot shows reasonable linearity, then the scaling continues.

Finally, the means and standard deviations of the z-scores for the groups are calculated and used to create the linear function that transforms the z-scores from one group into z-scores with same mean and standard deviation in the other group. An additional transformation can be applied to obtain the final reporting scale.

Item Response Theory Approaches

It is beyond the scope of this introduction to vertical scaling to delve into the intricacies of IRT. Rather, the following focuses on a few of the issues that can affect the creation of vertical scales when using item response theory methods. General introductions to IRT can be found in Hambleton and Swaminathan (1985), Hambleton, Swaminathan, and Rogers (1991), and Embretson and Reise (2000). A discussion of IRT methods in the context of equating can be found in Kolen and Brennan (2004).

Item Response Theory Scaling Models

Among the IRT scaling models that can be used to create vertical scales when the tests involved consist of dichotomously scored multiple-choice items are the *Rasch model* (Rasch, 1960) (also known as the *one-parameter logistic model*) and the *two-* and *three-parameter logistic models* (Hambleton & Swaminathan, 1985). Models for polytomously scored constructed response items include the *partial-credit model* (Masters, 1982), the *generalized partial-credit model* (Muraki, 1992), and the *graded response model* (Samejima, 1969). A discussion of these models can be found in Embretson and Reise (2000). More recent IRT models for creating vertical scales have considered modeling growth across the test levels as a part of the model specification (Patz & Hanson, 2002; Yao, Patz, Chia, Lewis, & Hoskens, 2003) or using multidimensional, multigroup models (Yao et al., 2003).

The literature to date is inconsistent with respect how well different IRT models perform when creating vertical scales. For example, Schulz et al. (1992), Shen (1993), and Lee (2003) have successfully used the Rasch model to create vertical scales, whereas Slinde and Linn (1978) and Loyd and Hoover (1980) have recommended against using the model. More research needs to be done to address this issue.

Estimation Strategies

There are three principal IRT estimation strategies that can be used to create vertical scales, namely, separate estimation, fixed estimation, and concurrent estimation (Patz & Hanson, 2002). These strategies are also referred to as separate, fixed, or concurrent calibration procedures. Assuming a common item data collection design, in *separate estimation,* the data from each level of the test are used to independently estimate the item parameters for that level, and results in item parameter estimates for each level being on a separate scale. After a base level is chosen, the sets of item parameters at the base level and an adjacent level are used to create the transformation that translates the scale of the adjacent level to that of the base scale. This process continues with pairs of adjacent levels until all the levels are on the same scale as the base level. The mean/mean, mean/sigma, or an item characteristic curve method such as the Stocking-Lord procedure can be used to effect the scale transformation between test levels (Kolen & Brennan, 2004).

Fixed estimation begins with the estimation of the item parameters of the base level. Next, the item parameter estimates for the items at an adjacent level that are common to the base level are fixed at the values obtained for the base level. The calibration of the remaining items of the adjacent level together with the fixed parameters, places the parameter estimates of all of the items on the scale of the base form. For each pair of adjacent levels, the process of fixing the common items of an adjacent level to the values of the common items from previously calibrated level is repeated until all of the levels are on the same scale.

Unlike the separate and fixed estimation procedures that require independent runs of the calibration software for each level, *concurrent estimation* estimates the parameters of all of the items across levels in a single run by placing all of the examinee responses across the test levels into one data matrix, where items not taken by an examinee are treated as missing. When calibrated, all of the item parameters are simultaneously estimated and are on the same scale.

It is important to note that when marginal maximum likelihood estimation is used, the estimation software required for concurrent calibration must be able to provide estimates for multiple groups (DeMars, 2002). Single group estimation assumes that all examinees are sampled from the same population. When single group estimation is applied to a sample comprised of groups from different populations, this can result in biased item parameter estimates. Multiple group estimation is required in the case of vertical scaling, because different populations of examinees take the test levels.

A hybrid of the separate and concurrent estimation procedures is the *pair-wise method* (Karkee, Lewis, Hoskens, Yao, & Haug, 2003). In this procedure, concurrent estimation is applied independently to pairs of adjacent grades. One grade pair is identified as the base scale and then the separately calibrated grade pairs are linked to it using common items as under the separate estimation procedure.

Kim and Cohen (1998) studied the relative performance of concurrent versus separate estimations and recommended the use of separate estimations over concurrent estimation when the number of common items is small. However, in a later simulation study examining the graded response model, Kim and Cohen (2002) found that concurrent estimation provided consistent, although only slightly better, parameter recovery than did separate estimation. Hanson and Bèguin (2002) in their simulation studies found that concurrent estimation resulted in lower error than separate estimation. However, they did not recommend abandoning separate estimation in favor of concurrent estimation. Karkee et al. (2003) compared separate, concurrent, and pair-wise methods of estimation using data obtained from an operational state assessment program, linked via a common-item design. They found that separate estimation produced "consistently better results than did the concurrent or pair-wise concurrent estimation methods in terms of convergence of items, model fit, and differential item functioning analyses (Karkee et al., 2003, p. 28).

Given the diversity of these results, there is no clear consensus regarding which IRT estimation strategy performs the best. Kolen and Brennan (2004) argue that separate estimation may be the safest of the alternatives. With separate estimation, violations of the IRT unidimensionality assumption may have less impact on the parameters estimates because the parameters are estimated for only one grade level at time.

Person Ability Estimation

When IRT methods are used, a decision must be made as to how person ability will be estimated. When the entire response string for an examinee is used to estimate his or her ability (a procedure called *pattern scoring*), then two common options for producing ability estimates are *maximum likelihood* (ML) *estimation* and *expected a posteriori* (EAP) *estimation*.

Each option has its advantages and disadvantages. Whereas ML estimates are unbiased, ML estimates do not exist for zero or perfect raw scores on dichotomously scored tests. EAP estimates, although biased, do provide estimates for these raw scores. EAP estimates are derived via Bayesian procedures and are regressed or shrunk to the mean. Because of this, EAP estimates are typically less variable than ML estimates.

Choosing a Linking Methodology

There is no clear choice available as to which linking methodology produces the best results in the context of vertical scaling; there is no necessary reason to prefer one method such as Thurstone scaling over another such as an IRT-based method. What is clearly needed are additional simulation studies wherein a vertical scale is simulated with know properties, and different linking methodologies are used to "recover" this structure. The results from a series of such studies could be invaluable in aiding the practitioner in selecting a linking methodology to use.

Barring such studies, the choice of linking methodology is often made on pragmatic grounds. Most state testing programs use IRT models to equate and scale their assessments. In addition, they have used these models to create extensive banks of calibrated items. For these reasons, the most practical choice may be for state testing programs to continue to use the IRT methodology they currently have in place to vertically scale their tests.

As stated, if the IRT approach is adopted, it is recommended that the separate estimation procedure be followed. This procedure may be somewhat safer than concurrent estimation in that there may less impact on parameter estimates when the assumptions of IRT unidimensionality are violated.

EVALUATING VERTICAL SCALES

Kolen and Brennan (2004) describe three properties of score scales that have been used to evaluate the results of vertical scaling. These properties are average grade-to-grade growth, grade-to-grade variability, and the separation of grade distributions.

Grade-to-grade growth usually focuses on the differences of either the means or medians of the scale score distributions at adjacent grades. In a similar fashion, *grade-to-grade variability* centers on examining the differences in standard deviations or other measures of variability such as interquartile ranges (IQRs) between adjacent grades. Both properties can be inspected visually through the use of growth curve plots.

The third property of score scales is the separation of grade distributions. An index proposed by Yen (1986) is the effect size for grade-to-grade differences. This is given as difference of the means of adjacent grades divided through by the pooled within-grade standard deviation:

$$\textit{effect size} = \frac{\overline{x}_{upper} - \overline{x}_{lower}}{\sqrt{(n_{upper}s^2_{upper} + n_{lower}s^2_{lower})/(n_{upper} + n_{lower})}}, \qquad (21.1)$$

where $\overline{x}_{upper}$, s^2_{upper}, and n_{upper} are the mean, variance, and sample size of the upper grade's distribution, and $\overline{x}_{lower}$, s^2_{lower}, and n_{lower} are the mean, variance, and sample size of the lower grade's distribution. The effect size shows mean grade-to-grade differences in standard deviation units.

Total Mathematics

Total Reading

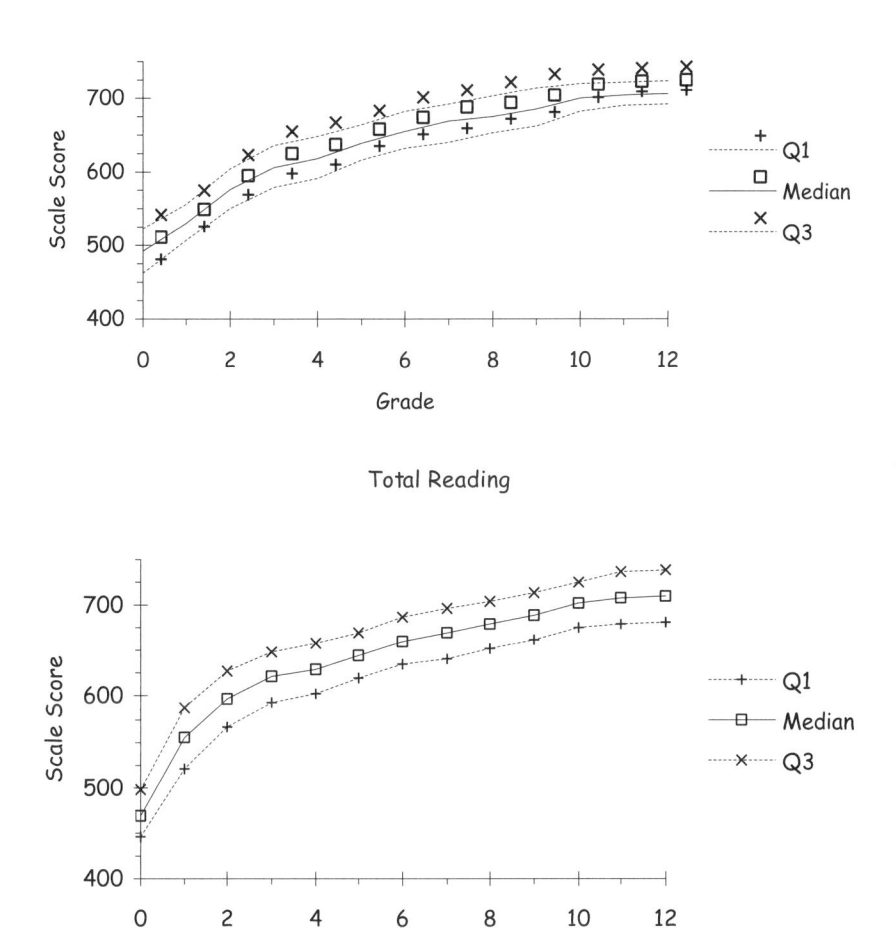

FIG. 21.6. Stanford 10 scaled scores for Total Mathematics and Total Reading at key percentile ranks by grade—Spring norms. (*Source data:* Harcourt Educational Measurement, 2003.)

As an example of how these properties can be used to evaluate the results of a vertical scaling, consider the growth curve plots shown in Figure 21.6. The data for these plots are taken from the Total Mathematics and Total Reading scales of the *Stanford Achievement Test Series* (Harcourt Educational Measurement, 2003). In these plots, the median scale scores are shown at each grade level from Kindergarten (denoted Grade 0) through grade 12. The curves are steepest at the lower grades where the differences between the medians at adjacent grades are greatest. The curves progressively flatten out at the higher grades where the differences between medians are smallest. The plots also indicate that between Kindergarten and Grade 1, the average grade-to-grade growth for Total Reading is greater than that for Total Mathematics. By having the quartiles plotted along with the medians, one can inspect the grade-to-grade variability as well, since the difference between the 1st and 3rd quartiles is the interquartile range. For these data, the variability is with a few exceptions, generally constant across the grades. Unlike Total Reading, the variability of the Total Mathematics scores lessens at the highest grades.

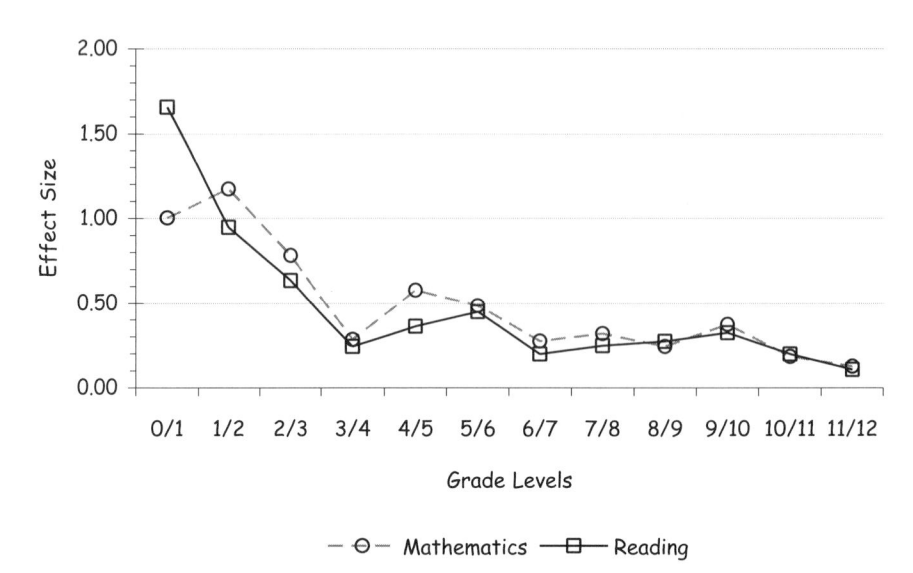

FIG. 21.7. Effect sizes versus grade levels for Stanford 10 Mathematics and Total Reading scores—Spring norms. (*Source data:* Harcourt Educational Measurement, 2003.)

The index in Equation 21.1 was used to calculate effect sizes for the Total Mathematics and Total Reading scales. The results were plotted against grade level and are shown in Figure 21.7. In general, the effect sizes for the two content areas decrease as the grade level increases. In the comparison of the lower grades, the effect sizes show that the grade-to-grade growth are over 1 standard deviation unit in size, and decrease at the higher grades to around 0.10 standard deviation units. The grade distributions for the Total Mathematics scale tend to show as much or more separation than the grade distributions for Total Reading. The exception is in the comparison of the Kindergarten (Grade 0) distribution to the Grade 1 distribution: The greater grade-to-grade growth for Total Reading over Total Mathematics noted above shows up in the effect size for this comparison.

DEVELOPING VERTICAL SCALES IN PRACTICE: ADVICE FOR STATE AND SCHOOL DISTRICT TESTING PROGRAMS

Test publishers have been developing vertical scales for many years; state and larger school district achievement testing programs have only begun to do so recently. Table 21.1 shows the data collection designs and methodologies for linking test forms that were used to create the vertical scales for several publishers' tests and state programs: It is clear that there is no agreed upon method.

The comments that follow are addressed to state testing programs. They may well have fewer resources and more limitations than test publishers. As described, the choice of a data collection design, a linking strategy, and so forth is likely decided by balancing several constraints. Some final practical points to consider follow.

State Your Assumptions

It is important that practioners developing vertical scales make as explicit as possible their assumptions regarding growth along the scale, their choice of data collection design, how they

TABLE 21.1
Data Collection Designs and Scaling Models Used by Several Test Publishers and State Assessment Programs

Assessment	Source	Data Collection Design	Scaling Model
Iowa Test of Basic Skills	Petersen et al. (1989); Kolen & Brennan (2004)	Scaling test	Hieronymous scaling
Metropolitan Achievement Tests	Harcourt Educational Measurement (2003)	Single group, counterbalanced	Rasch model
Stanford Achievement Test Series	Harcourt Educational Measurement (2003)	Single group, counterbalanced	Rasch model
Delaware Student Testing Program (DSTP)	Lau (personal communication, 2004)	Quasi-common item (linked to *Stanford Achievement Test Series*)	Rasch model
Mississippi Curriculum Test (MCT)	Tomkowicz & Schaeffer (2002)	Quasi-common item (linked to *TerraNova*)	Three-parameter logistic IRT model
TerraNova	CTB/McGraw-Hill (1996)	Single group, counterbalanced	Three-parameter logistic IRT model
Florida Comprehensive Assessment Test (FCAT)	Hoffman et al. (2003)	Common item	Three-parameter logistic IRT model

link the tests at different levels, and how they evaluate the resulting vertical scale. Harris et al. (2004) provided a useful checklist of the assumptions that practioners should make clear before creating a vertical scale. They recommended that practitioners should specify:

- How the pattern of growth may vary across grades and subject areas;
- Whether variability in examinee achievement should increase or decrease over time;
- Whether high achieving students should logically show more growth than low achieving students;
- How *adequate yearly progress* and *proficient progress* are defined;
- What common content should be covered in adjacent grades; and
- Whether test content should be developed to meet a preexisting growth model or a growth model is based on empirical information taken from tests built to a particular curriculum.

The Choice of Data Collection Design

Most of the points regarding the issues involved in choosing among data collection designs have been made above. Ultimately, the choice of a data collection design comes down to a balancing act among the definition of *growth* to be used, a match of test item difficulty to examinee level of ability, the amount of testing time one is willing to give up, and the need for additional item development that can be supported by the test developer.

The Choice of Linking Methodology

As stated, most state testing programs use IRT models to equate and scale their assessments. On practical grounds, states would do well to continue using their current IRT models when creating vertical scales for their tests. If this approach is accepted, then separate estimation procedures may be somewhat safer to use than concurrent estimation procedures.

Tying the Vertical Scale to Performance Standards

In most state testing programs, test content is directly tied to state standards and student achievement on tests is used to indicate progress towards meeting those standards. When conducting standard settings, state testing programs should consider the placement of cutscores along the vertical scale along with other evidence such as student impact data, before arriving at a final set of proficiency level cutscores. Doing this allows a check on the consistency of achievement expectations across the grade levels. For example, one might reasonably expect that the proficiency level cut score at each grade level should be greater than or equal to the proficiency level cut scores of the grades below it. If this does not occur—if there are "reversals" of the cutscores—then a careful analysis needs to be made why the standard setting judges chose the cutscores that they did.

Vertical scaling is an intricate measurement process. Growth definitions, scale assumptions, data collection designs, and linking methods combine to produce vertical scale in ways that are not always clear. However, what is clear is the need to carefully document the construction of any vertical scale. With respect to the need for documentation, Standard 6.5 of the *Standards* states in part that "... When relevant for test interpretation, test documents should ordinarily include ... a description of the procedures used to equate multiple forms (AERA, APA, & NCME, 1999, p. 69). The valid use and interpretation of vertical scales requires nothing less.

REFERENCES

Allen, M. J., & Yen, W. M. (1979). *Introduction to measurement theory*. Monterey, CA: Brooks/Cole.
American Educational Research Association (AERA), American Psychological Association (APA), & National Council on Measurement in Education (NCME). (1999). *Standards for educational and psychological testing*. Washington, DC: AERA.
Angoff, W. H. (1984). *Scales, norms, and equivalent scores*. Princeton, NJ: Educational Testing Service.
Beaton, A. E., & Allen, N. L. (1992). Interpreting scales through scale anchoring. *Journal of Educational Statistics, 17,* 191–204.
CTB/McGraw-Hill. (1996). *TerraNova prepublication technical bulletin*. Monterey, CA: Author.
DeMars, C. (2002). Incomplete data and item parameter estimates under JMLE and MML estimation. *Applied Measurement in Education, 15,* 15–31.
Embretson, S. E., & Reise, S. P. (2000). *Item response theory for psychologists*. Hillsdale, NJ: Lawrence Erlbaum Associates.
Haertel, E. (1991). *Report on TRP analyses of issues concerning within-age versus cross-age scales for the National Assessment of Educational Progress* [ERIC Clearinghouse Document Reproduction Service No ED404367]. Washington, DC: National Center for Education Statistics.
Hambleton, R. K., & Swaminathan, H. (1985). *Item response theory: Principles and applications*. Boston: Kluwer Nijhoff.
Hambleton, R. K., Swaminathan, H., & Rogers, H. J. (1991). *Fundamentals of item response theory*. Newbury Park, CA: Sage.
Hanson, B. A., & Bèguin, A. A. (2002). Obtaining a common scale for item response theory parameters using separate versus concurrent estimation in the common-item equating design. *Applied Psychological Measurement, 26,* 3–24.
Harcourt Educational Measurement. (2002). *Metropolitan Achievement Tests: Technical manual* (8th ed.). San Antonio, TX: Author.
Harcourt Educational Measurement. (2003). *Stanford Achievement Test series: Spring technical data report* (10th ed.). San Antonio, TX: Author.
Harris, D. J., Hendrickson, A. B., Tong, Y., Shin, S.-H., & Shyu, C.-Y. (2004, April). *Vertical scales and the measurement of growth*. Paper presented at the annual meeting of the National Council on Measurement in Education, San Diego, CA.

Hoffman, R. G., Wise, L. L., Thacker, A. A., & Ford, L. A. (2003, January). *Florida Comprehensive Assessment Tests: Technical report on vertical scaling for reading and mathematics.* A HumRRO report under subcontract to Harcourt Assessment, San Antonio, TX.

Hunyh, H., & Schneider, C. (2004, April). *Vertically moderated standards as an alternative to vertical scaling: Assumptions, practices, and an odyssey through NAEP.* Paper presented at the annual meeting of the National Council on Measurement in Education, San Diego, CA.

Karkee, T., Lewis, D. M., Hoskens, M., Yao, L., & Haug, C. (2003, April). *Separate versus concurrent calibration methods in vertical scaling.* Paper presented at the annual meeting of the National Council on Measurement in Education, Chicago, IL.

Kim, S., & Cohen, A. S. (1998). A comparison of linking and concurrent calibration under item response theory. *Applied Psychological Measurement, 22,* 131–143.

Kim, S., & Cohen, A. S. (2002). A comparison of linking and concurrent calibration under the graded response model. *Applied Psychological Measurement, 26,* 25–41.

Kolen, M. J., & Brennan, R. L. (2004). *Test equating, scaling, and linking: Methods and practices* (2nd ed.). New York: Springer-Verlag.

Lee, O. K. (2003). Rasch simultaneous vertical equating for measuring growth. *Journal of Applied Measurement, 4,* 10–23.

Lissitz, R. W. & Huynh, H. (2003). Vertical equating for state assessments: Issues and solutions in determination of adequate yearly progress and school accountability [on-line]. *Practical Assessment, Research, and Evaluation, 8*(10). Retrieved March 12, 2004 from http://PAREonline.net/getvn.asp?v=8&n=10.

Loyd, B. H., & Hoover, H. D. (1980). Vertical equating using the Rasch model. *Journal of Educational Measurement, 17,* 179–193.

Masters, G. N. (1982). A Rasch model for partial credit scoring. *Psychometrika, 47,* 149–174.

Messick, S. J. (1989). Validity. In R. L. Linn (Ed.), *Educational measurement* (3rd ed., pp. 13–103). Englewood Cliffs, NJ: Prentice Hall.

McBride, J., & Wise, L. (2000, May). *Developing a vertical scale for the Florida Comprehensive Assessment Test (FCAT).* A HumRRO report under subcontract to Harcourt Assessment, San Antonio, TX.

Muraki, E. (1992). A generalized partial credit model: Application of an EM algorithm. *Applied Psychological Measurement, 16,* 159–176.

Nitko, A. J. (2004). *The educational assessment of students* (4th ed.). Englewood Cliffs, NJ: Prentice Hall.

Patz, R. J., & Hanson, B. A. (2002, April). *Psychometric issues in vertical scaling.* Paper presented at the annual meeting of the National Council on Measurement in Education, New Orleans, LA.

Petersen, N. S., Kolen, M. J., & Hoover, H. D. (1989). Scaling, norms, and equating. In R. L. Linn (Ed.), *Educational measurement* (3rd ed.). Englewood Cliffs, NJ: Prentice Hall.

Rasch, G. (1960). *Probabilistic models for some intelligence and attainment tests.* Copenhagen: Danish Institute for Educational Research.

Samejima, F. (1969). *Estimation of latent ability using a response pattern of graded scores.* (Psychometrika Monograph, 17) Richmond, VA: Psychometrics Society.

Schulz, E. M., Perlman, C., Rice Jr, W. K. & Wright, B. D. (1992). Vertically equating reading tests: An example from the Chicago Public Schools. In Wilson, M. (Ed.). *Objective measurement: Theory into practice* (Vol. 1). Norwood, NJ: Ablex.

Shen, L. (1993, April). *Constructing a measure for longitudinal medical achievement studies by the Rasch model one-step equating.* Paper presented at the annual meeting of the American Educational Research Association, Atlanta, GA.

Slinde, J. A., & Linn, R. L. (1978). An exploration of the adequacy of the Rasch model for the problem of vertical scaling. *Journal of Educational Measurement, 15,* 23–35.

Tomkowicz, J., & Schaeffer, G. A. (2002, April). *Vertical scaling for custom criterion-referenced tests.* Paper presented at the annual meeting of the National Council on Measurement in Education, San Diego, CA.

Tong, Y., & Harris, D. J. (2004, April). *The impact of linking methods and choice of scales on vertical scales.* Paper presented at the annual meeting of the National Council on Measurement in Education, San Diego, CA.

Vukmirovic, Z. (2004). *Vertical scaling: The issues in construction and interpretation.* (Unpublished manuscript). San Antonio, TX: Harcourt Assessment.

Yao, L., Patz, R. J., Chia, M., Lewis, D. M., & Hoskens, M. (2003, April). *Hierarchical and multidimensional models for vertical scaling.* Paper presented at the annual meeting of the National Council on Measurement in Education, Chicago, IL.

Yen, W. M. (1986). The choice of scale for educational measurement: An IRT perspective. *Journal of Educational Measurement, 23,* 299–325.

22

Developing Test Forms for Small-Scale Achievement Testing Systems

Paul Jones
Russell W. Smith
Thomson Prometric

Diane Talley
University of North Carolina

This chapter discusses the problem of modeling items and tests and then assembling items into one or more forms of an achievement test when relatively few test takers are available. The focus is on test forms that are assembled nonadaptively to have specific content and statistical characteristics and strategies for coping with small data sets and small item pools. The discussion begins with the collection of pretest data to perform preliminary item analysis. We then consider the available small-n measurement models and the data requirements for various development applications. We discuss the concept of test form assembly and illustrate an algorithm for assembling one or more test forms from a small item pool. Finally, we consider the issues of equating new forms to a concurrently or previously administered reference form. The chapter is meant to be a practical guide for the measurement professional charged with sponsoring or developing small-scale achievement testing systems.

This chapter discusses the problem of modeling items and tests and then assembling items into one or more forms of an achievement test when relatively few test takers are available. *Achievement tests* are tests developed for purposes such as certification or licensure judgments, measurement of knowledge acquisition from a course of study, or decisions about whether a person has adequate prerequisite knowledge to be admitted to an educational opportunity, advance in a career development track, or be considered for a particular job. *Small-scale* is arbitrarily defined as pretest data obtained from 0 to 200 representative test takers. It is assumed that relatively few test takers are available to participate in the development process, either because the testing program is new or because the target population is inherently small. A *testing system* includes the procedures used to develop the test forms, the infrastructure used to deliver the test forms and record test-taker behavior, and the decision-making policies and procedures that are implemented to evaluate and use the test results. The testing system creates, administers, maintains, and ultimately revises or retires test forms.

The emphasis of this chapter is on developing one or more test forms. We confine our discussion to test forms that are assembled nonadaptively to have specific content and statistical characteristics. Although we touch on other aspects of development in passing, particularly as they impact the validity of the small-scale testing system, we focus on the characteristics of the set of items assembled and administered to an individual examinee and how the test form may be imbued with these characteristics. This chapter discusses how the validity argument may be enhanced in support of the testing system by how test forms are developed. It is meant to be a practical guide for the measurement professional charged with sponsoring or developing small-scale achievement testing systems.

We organize our discussion around the following test development scenario: An achievement test has been defined for a specific credentialing purpose. A practice analysis has been undertaken to define the construct domain of interest (Messick, 1989) and test specifications have been generated based on this analysis. Test items have been written, linked to the test specifications, and reviewed. We now wish to pretest the items and use the resulting pretest data to perform preliminary item analysis, select items for inclusion in the examination, and use those data to assemble one or more forms to support credentialing. In addition, we consider how we might equate the new forms to a concurrently or previously administered reference form.

THE TWIN GOALS OF TEST DEVELOPMENT: VALIDITY AND REALITY

We begin by considering the twin goals of an achievement testing system. The first goal is that we use the test to make valid judgments. The second goal is that the test used to make those judgments actually is developed on time and within budget using available resources. In many cases only the test developer, drawing on all his or her powers of communication and evangelistic zeal, can convince the test sponsor that the first goal is as important as the second. We consider these two goals in turn.

Supporting Validity

Practitioners often regard validity as the extent to which a test "measures what it is supposed to measure." The *Standards for Educational and Psychological Testing* (American Educational Research Association [AERA], American Psychological Association [APA], & National Council on Measurement in Education [NCME], 1999) define validity more precisely as "the degree to which evidence and theory support the interpretations of test scores entailed by proposed uses of tests" (p. 9). All achievement-testing systems seek to make more or less the following score interpretation:

> An increasing score on the achievement test indicates increasing competency in the "construct domain of reference" (see Messick, 1989).

Achievement tests used for selection seek to make the following additional score interpretation:

> A test score at or above the cut point justifies classification in a higher level category. A test score below the cut point justifies classification in the lower level category.

Support for these inferences depends on evidence:

> Ultimately, the validity of an intended interpretation of test scores relies on all the available evidence relevant to the technical quality of a testing system. This includes evidence of careful test construction; adequate score reliability; appropriate test administration and scoring; accurate

score scaling, equating, and standard setting; and careful attention to fairness for all examinees, as described in subsequent chapters of the *Standards*. (AERA, APA, & NCME, 1999, p. 17)

The *Standards* go on to describe validity in terms of evidence for specific propositions that must be supported in order to sustain the proposed interpretation(s) of scores. Jones (2004a) identified 31 such validity propositions for certification testing systems. The authors feel that these propositions pertain to all classification testing systems and most pertain to any achievement testing system, including the small-scale systems we are discussing here. Table 22.1 summarizes these propositions along with relevant quotes from Messick (1989) and the *Standards*.

Developing a Real Test in Real Time

It is usually not possible to address all of these propositions at once or to give them equal weight in the actual development process. As the *Standards* point out, "Evaluating the acceptability of a test or test application does not rest on the literal satisfaction of every standard in this document, and acceptability cannot be determined by using a checklist. Specific circumstances affect the importance of individual standards, and individual standards should not be considered in isolation" (p. 4). Likewise with the list of validity propositions in Table 22.1. This is especially the case in small-scale systems where both data and resources are usually limited. Because of this fact, the test sponsor and test developer must sit down together to negotiate how to address these validity propositions and still create a real test. This requires assessing potential risks and available resources, in some cases prioritizing certain validity propositions over others, deferring the completion of some parts of the validity argument, and wisely limiting the scope of the testing system so that certain unattainable arguments are not attempted. This can be an especially agonizing process for the developer who must usually take the lead in assessing risks and recommending compromises in the face of realities posed by the sponsoring agency. However, as the *Standards* make clear, the test sponsor bears responsibility for validity jointly with the developer. This validity negotiation between the sponsor and developer must not degenerate into a long series of capitulations by the developer for the sake of expediency. The integrity and professional judgment of both parties are clearly on the line, as well as the legal defensibility of the test, and in the end the developer may have to decide that developing the test under tight data and resource constraints is too risky.

Now a word about test design and development. This chapter emphasizes the validity propositions highlighted in Table 22.1 as they pertain to small-scale systems. Because this chapter focuses on dealing with the constraint of limited data, we emphasize the psychometrics of items and tests. However, as shown in Table 22.1, high-validity testing systems require support for a number of propositions that relate to the test design, domain analysis, and item development effort. The test sponsor may have limited funds as well as few data. If so, prioritizing the front end of test development and providing strong test definition, domain analysis, design, and item development is likely to pay more dividends than doing a mediocre job of both test development and analysis. The test sponsor should pay the price to have legitimate, representative subject matter experts participate in practice analysis (Propositions 2 and 3), test design (Propositions 1, 4, and 5) and coached, supervised item development (Proposition 6). Above all, competent, representative subject matter experts (SMEs) must review each item prior to final acceptance. A strong item review process verifying linkage between items and content specifications, appropriate reading demands, clarity, relevance, correctness of keys and incorrectness of distractors, lack of irrelevant cues, and lack of biasing or offensive content absolutely cannot be skirted (Propositions 7, 6, 9, and 10). In-person, group reviews with a

TABLE 22.1
Validity Propositions for Achievement Testing Systems

Proposition	Explanation
1. Intended interpretation and use of test scores is clear.	The test developer clearly describes the intended interpretation and use of test scores, the populations for which the test is appropriate, and the construct domain of reference (see AERA, APA, & NCME, 1999, Standard 1.2).
2. SMEs are qualified and their views are representative.	The qualifications and experience of subject matter experts participating in test development, the training and instructions they receive, and the ways in which they interact to make decisions all lend support to the decisions made and provide evidence of the representativeness of the views expressed (Messick, 1989).
3. The construct domain of reference is based on practice analysis (Raymond & Neustel, chap. 9, this volume) or content analysis (Webb, chap. 8, this volume).	The construct domain of reference is completely described through a job or practice analysis procedure, "including boundaries, logical subdivisions and psychological subdivisions" (Messick, 1989, p. 39; AERA, APA, & NCME, 1999, Standard 14.8).
4. Knowledge and skills covered are important and relevant.	The knowledge and skills to be covered by the test are important for credential-worthy performance in the focal occupation and are consistent with the purposes of the test (see AERA, APA, & NCME, 1999, Standard 14.14).
5. The test specifications are based on defined rules.	The defined frequency or weight of items in each content category "duplicates or reproduces the essential characteristics of the universe [of generalization], in their proper proportion and balance" (Lennon, 1956, p. 301) as determined by defined rules such as job criticality, importance or frequency (Messick, 1989, p. 39; AERA, APA, & NCME, 1999, Standard14.10).
6. The test items are appropriate.	The type of items, response formats, scoring procedures, and test administration procedures are selected based on the purposes of the test, are germane to the construct domain of reference, and are equally appropriate for all intended test takers, including those of different gender, ethnic, cultural, or geographical groups (AERA, APA, & NCME, 1999, Standard 3.6; Messick, 1989, p. 39). "To the extent possible stimulus and response specifications for test items" are "based on what is known about nontest stimulus and response properties in the behavioral or trait domain under scrutiny" (Messick, 1989, p. 38).
7. The test items are linked to the test specifications via judgment by SMEs.	Empirical evidence and/or high-consensus expert judgment are used to classify items according to categories of the test specifications (AERA, APA, & NCME, 1999, p. 44; Messick, 1989, p. 38).
8. Item reading and response demands are reasonable (Abedi, chap. 17, this volume).	"The linguistic or reading demands of the test are kept to the minimum necesary for the valid assessment of the intended construct" (AERA, APA, & NCME, 1999, Standard 7.7, 9.8). All test takers can reasonably be assumed to have the skills necessary to choose or construct item responses, or are provided the necessary training to do so (AERA, APA, & NCME, 1999, Standard 5.5).
9. Items are apparently well formed (Downing, chap. 12, this volume; Welch, chap. 13, this volume).	Ambiguity, irrelevancy, and unintended cues to the correct answer are controlled (Messick, 1989).
10. Offensive content is eliminated (Zieky, chap. 16, this volume).	Language, symbols, words, phrases, and content that are generally regarded as offensive by members of racial, ethnic, gender, or other groups are eliminated from the item content (AERA, APA, & NCME, 1999, Standard 7.4).

TABLE 22.1
(Continued)

Proposition	Explanation
11. Pretest takers are drawn from the population of live test takers or a population that is similar enough to the live population to allow the developer to preview the performance of test items and forms.	When appropriate, research test taker sample(s) are representative of the population(s) for which the test is intended (AERA, APA, & NCME, 1999, Standard 3.8).
12. Items are selected based on response consistencies within each dimension of the construct. The nature and dimensionality of the interitem structure reflect the nature and dimensionality of the construct domain of reference.	Apparently well-formed items are selected based on response consistencies between items within each dimension of the construct, and the content of the included items provides a good account of the original construct domain of reference. The degree of homogeneity in the test is commensurate with the characteristic degree of homogeneity associated with the construct. The nature and dimensionality of the interitem structure reflects the nature and dimensionality of the construct domain (Messick, 1989, pp. 43–44).
13. Test content represents the construct domain of reference and the test specifications.	The content of the test represents the defined domain and test specifications (AERA, APA, & NCME, 1999, Standard 3.11). Content categories for which satisfactory performing items cannot be created after multiple attempts are revised or eliminated from the specifications (Messick, 1989, p. 43).
14. The reported test scores capture the dimensionality of the test.	Every effort is made to capture the dimensionality of the test at the level of test scoring and interpretation (Messick, 1989, pp. 43–44).
15. The test scores correlate with other variables in expected ways.	The constructs represented in the test rationally account for the external pattern of test correlations (Messick, 1989).
16. Reported scores and subscores are reliable (Ryan, chap. 29, this volume)	Each total score, subscore, or combination of scores that is interpreted has adequate reliability (AERA, APA & NCME, 1999, Standard 2.1).
17. Cut scores are defensible. (Cizek, chap. 10, this volume)	The rationale and procedures used for establishing cut scores are clearly documented and are based on empirical relationships between test performance and relevant criteria, when feasible. Expert judgments about the adequacy of item or test performance are made only after judges "have formed clear conceptions of adequacy or quality"(AERA, APA, & NCME, 1999, p. 60, Standards, 4.19–4.21).
18. Cut score judgments are reliable (Cizek, chap. 10, this volume).	The amount of variation in cut scores that might be expected if the standard setting procedure were replicated is tolerable (AERA, APA, & NCME, 1999, pp. 60).
19. The standard error of measurement near the cut score is adequate and the reliability of pass–fail decisions is adequate.	Conditional standard errors of measurement in the vicinity of the cut score are adequate (AERA, APA, & NCME, 1999, Standards 2.14). Reliability of test-based credentialing decisions is adequate (AERA, APA, & NCME, 1999, Standards 2.15,14.15).
20. Candidates have sufficient time to complete the test.	
21. Different forms of the test can be used interchangeably.	Different forms of the test can be used interchangeably (AERA, APA, & NCME, 1999, Standard 4.10).
22. Sources of item bias are detected and eliminated (Zieky, chap. 16, this volume).	"When credible research reports that differential item functioning exists across age, gender, racial/ethnic, cultural, disability, and/or linguistic groups... test developers" conduct "appropriate studies when feasible. Such studies... seek to detect and eliminate aspects of test design, content, and format that might bias scores for particular groups" (AERA, APA, & NCME, 1999, Standard 7.3).

(Continued)

TABLE 22.1
(Continued)

Proposition	Explanation
23. Test translations are adequate, scores of translated tests are reliable, and interpretations of translated test scores are valid.	When a test is translated, "methods used in establishing the adequacy of the translation" are described. "Empirical and logical evidence" is provided for the translated test's score reliability and the validity of score inferences "in the linguistic groups to be tested" (AERA, APA, & NCME, 1999, Standard 9.7).
24. Instructions are adequate (Campion & Miller, chap. 26, this volume).	The instructions presented to test takers contain sufficient detail so that test takers can respond to a task in the manner that the test developer intended (AERA, APA, & NCME, 1999, Standard 3.20).
25. Test takers receive equitable treatment (Abedi, chap. 16, chap. 28, this volume: Thurlow, Thompson, & Lazarus, chap. 16, this volume: Zieky, this volume).	"Test takers receive comparable and equitable treatment during all phases of the testing or assessment process" (AERA, APA, & NCME, 1999, Standard 7.12).
26. The test environment furnishes reasonable comfort and minimal distractions.	The test environment furnishes "reasonable comfort and minimal distractions" (AERA, APA, & NCME, 1999, Standard 5.4).
27. Score reports are timely and understandable (Ryan, chap. 29, this volume).	A "timely," "understandable" report of test results is provided "to the test taker and others entitled to receive this information" (AERA, APA, & NCME, 1999, Standard 11.6).
28. Misinterpretations of test scores and unintended negative consequences of test use are avoided.	Steps are taken to "avoid foreseeable misinterpretations of test scores" and "unintended negative consequences" of test use (AERA, APA, & NCME, 1999, Standard 11.15).
29. Test security is maintained. (Impara & Foster, chap. 5, his volume).	"Reasonable efforts" are made to eliminate "opportunities for test takers to obtain scores by fraudulent means" (AERA, APA, & NCME, 1999, Standard 5.6). The security of test materials is protected at all times (AERA, APA, & NCME, 1999, Standard 5.7).
30. Any material errors are corrected quickly.	If a "material error is found in test scores or other important information released by a testing organization . . . a corrected score report is distributed as soon as practicable to all known recipients who might otherwise use the erroneous scores as a basis for decision making" (AERA, APA, & NCME, 1999, Standard 5.14).
31. Revisions to the test, the conceptual framework, and the construct are made in response to new evidence.	"As validation proceeds, and as new evidence about the meaning of a test's scores becomes available," appropriate revisions are made in "the test, in the conceptual framework that shapes it, and even in the construct underlying the test" (AERA, APA, & NCME, 1999, p. 9).

trained facilitator are best, although Webcasting solutions are possible. In the opinion of the authors, test sponsors and their programs have suffered the most when they have short-changed this item review and revision step.

In the next section, we discuss the problem of collecting pretest data so that it can be leveraged to preview and evaluate the performance of test items and forms (Proposition 11). We then discuss four measurement models that might be applied to items and test forms, the limitations imposed by small datasets and strategies for selecting items and assembling forms under these limitations (Propositions 6, 9, 12, 16, and 19). Next, we describe different approaches to assembling forms and highlights an assembly algorithm that is especially useful for small item pools (Propositions 16, 19, 20, and 21). Finally, we address the problem of equating multiple forms of small-volume tests (Proposition 21).

GATHERING PRETEST DATA FOR SMALL-SCALE TESTS

Here we discuss the problem of collecting data to evaluate item and test performance and to provide impact data for standard setting. These same data may also be used to equate test forms and issues surrounding that purpose are discussed in the section on equating multiple forms.

Pretest data collection may be the most difficult phase of test development. Parshall (2002) provides a good review of the issues, particularly related to pretesting in a computerized environment. The size and representativeness of the field test sample heavily impact the validity of the inferences made about test item quality, item parameters, test form characteristics, and form equivalence (Proposition 11). What makes data collection so difficult is that the test developer must place himself or herself in the position to make sound statistical inferences while working within the constraints imposed by the testing system; namely, that there are fewer than 200 test takers available to participate in field testing—perhaps far fewer. This imposes some serious restrictions on the data collection strategies we will want to consider.

The first restriction on data gathering is that we know in detail what kind of pretest takers we are looking for. Standard 3.8 AERA, APA, NCME (1999) makes this clear:

> When item tryouts or field tests are conducted, the procedures used to select the sample(s) of test takers for item tryouts and the resulting characteristics of the sample(s) should be documented. When appropriate, the sample(s) should be as representative as possible of the population(s) for which the test is intended. (p. 44)

This means that the sample should be drawn from the population for which the test was constructed if at all possible. A clearly defined testing audience is critical to ensure a representative sample and a well-defined test. If the test is meant for credentialing, as in this scenario, we should know what the purpose of the test is, what job roles our candidates will have and what job tasks these entail, the training or educational prerequisites required by the test sponsor, and the characteristics of test takers that are clearly qualified, borderline qualified, and informed but not qualified. Because the pretest activity is advertised among people who are likely credentialing candidates, either immediately or in the near future, information on these candidate dimensions can be collected so that pretest candidates can be qualified in advance. In some cases, test sponsors know specific potential candidates and can recruit them for participation. No measurement model is expected to work with data taken from test takers outside the target population; thus, in the case of a small pretest sample, where each additional observation has a proportionally large impact on test and item statistics, it is important that all the observations be legitimate. If at all possible, the pretest sample should be as geographically dispersed as the target population. Particular intact classrooms of pretest takers can be quite nonrepresentative of the population as a whole and should be avoided if possible (Farish, 1984).

Millman and Greene (1989) suggested a preliminary tryout of items with a small sample, prior to the field test, when possible. This may be conducted with five or six members of the target population or with SMEs who are familiar with that population. The developer can observe these people taking the test in a secured environment and then interview them about the test, its instructions, and individual test items. Such a tryout can greatly improve the quality of the test and ensure that the field test is not bogged down by avoidable technical glitches, unclear instructions, formatting problems, and even content errors.

In cases where the potential initial candidate population is well known to the test sponsors, it is sometimes possible to recruit a stratified sample of pretest takers that is distributed similarly to the projected target population (e.g., 60% borderline candidates with approximately 15% above borderline and 15% below borderline). This strategy can help to ensure that the sample is diverse enough to provide a basis for evaluating the discrimination properties of the items and provides a better sample for Rasch or one-parameter IRT calibration.

In an operational field test all items are administered, but only items meeting certain criteria are then incorporated into the final form(s) of the test and used for scoring. This is a good approach for small-scale programs because it does not require separate sets of test takers for item tryout versus operational testing. The operational field test strategy may be difficult to implement with large item pools. Typically, more items are developed than needed for the final examination because all items will not be of the desired quality. If the required number of items exceeds that which test takers can realistically answer within a specified amount of time, multiple field test forms need to be developed (see the section on equating multiple forms in small-scale systems). The requirement of multiple tryout forms exacerbates the problem of low pretest data availability; a larger number of observations per item is needed to achieve comparable item statistics across pretest samples than would be the case if data were obtained from a single sample.

Larger item pools are usually a response to continuous examination administration and the need to control exposure. From a measurement standpoint, it would be well if small-scale systems could deliver their examinations within controlled administration windows, thus easing the pressure to pretest many items.

Another field test option is to imbed new items within existing live tests (Millman & Greene, 1989). In this case, the new items—perhaps 20% of the test—do not contribute to the final score. Test takers are made aware of the presence of unscored items being delivered for research purposes but do not know which are scored and which are not. This option is appropriate for systems administering live tests in an ongoing fashion, or for windowed testing systems where instantaneous scoring of qualified items is needed and interruptions in administration cannot be tolerated. However, neither of these scenarios is congenial to small-scale development. With low system throughputs, (e.g., 20 or fewer live test takers per month or per administration), it would be impractical to build up one or more entire new test forms solely from embedded items. In many quickly evolving technical domains, the pace of field testing would never keep up with new item development.

Finally, items can be tried out in a field test completely separate from the operational test (Millman & Greene, 1989). This is the least desirable option for small-scale testing systems because it requires a set of representative test takers for the field testing who will not receive a score for taking the examination. This not only puts obvious strain on scarce data resources but also calls into question the "representativeness" of the tryout sample. Recruiting tryout test takers is also a considerable administrative burden and may entail additional expenditures for honoraria, prizes, advertising, and so on to attract tryout candidates.

It is better to conduct an operational field test where the additional cost and time of administering a separate test are avoided and there is little question of how representative the test takers are of the intended audience. Ideally, new items can be administered in a single pretest form to test takers from the target population who can be scored and graded following item analysis, selection, and final forms assembly. This may be repeated with every test administration, in the case of programs with discrete administration windows, or prior to publication of the final live forms, which are then continuously administered.

If a larger item pool is needed (e.g., more than 180 items) consideration should be given to a two-part field test administration with one part administered before a midday break and the second after the midday break. Order of administration of parts could be counterbalanced and order of item selection within parts could be randomized within randomly selected content sections. The ability of the test taker to review items could be restricted to items within a given part. The challenge, of course, is to attract persons who are willing to participate in a 6-hour tryout test, when a final form might run only 1 to 2 hours. However, it may be worth the effort; you may need data from four to six times as many test takers in a two-form pretest as you would if you were only administering one pretest form (Table 22.2).

TABLE 22.2
Pretest Sample Sizes Indicated for Various Test Development Applications

Application	Indicated N Per Item
Estimate pass-fail decision consistency using single-administration methods on a test of about 50 dichotomously-scored items with a standard error of about .02 to .03 (Subkoviak, 1978).	≥30
Rank-order a set of items given to a single pretest sample by difficulty using classical theory (Nevo, 1980).	≥32
Assemble a single form of the exam from the best available items using classical test theory when one third of the available items will be used (Thayn, 2001).	≥50 to 80
Assemble multiple final forms from a single pretest form for pass–fail decision purposes when two thirds of the available items will be used (using classical theory or Rasch modeling; Smith & Jones, 2002).	
Perform linear equating on multiple forms delivered to a single group when the cut score is near the mean (assumes a normal distribution and a standard error of equating of .1 SD unit [exact $N = 60$]; Kolen & Brennan, 2004).	
Estimate the alpha reliability of newly assembled forms (see Kromrey & Bacon, 1992).	
Choose items that are significant positive discriminators under classical test theory (see Kromrey & Bacon, 1992).	
Calibrate items using a Rasch or modified one-parameter IRT model for the purpose of test taker ability estimation using IRT methods with a test of at least 50 items (see Barnes & Wise, 1991: Linacre, 1994; Wright & Tennant, 1996).	
Use a restricted two-parameter model (with a narrow prior distribution on the a parameter) to estimate abilities of subsequent test takers using IRT methods and a test of 80 items (Parshall et al. 1997).	≥100
Justify using the Rasch model to estimate test taker ability as opposed to an unrestricted two-parameter IRT model (Lord, 1983).	100–200
Obtain relatively stable p-value estimates under classical test theory (see Millman & Green, 1989; Sireci, 1991).	≥100–250
Obtain relatively stable b-value estimates under the two-parameter model (Sireci, 1991).	
Obtain stable Rasch item measures (see Farish, 1984; Forster, 1978; Whitely, 1980; Wright & Stone, 1979)	
Use measurement decision theory to classify test takers versus a cut score with at least 85% accuracy (Rudner, 2003).	≥100–200
Rank-order items based on their classical discriminating power and choose items at or above a certain discrimination threshold (see Nevo, 1980)	≥128–256
Perform linear equating on multiple equivalent forms administered to randomly equivalent sets of candidates, with the pass–fail point located near the mean score (assumes normal distributions and a standard error of equating =.1 SD units; for two groups the total required $N = 400$; see Kolen & Brennan, 2004).	≥200
Obtain relatively stable classical item statistics (Crocker & Algina, 1986; Kromrey and Bacon, 1992) (but, perhaps as high as $N = 3,000$, depending on the population; see Conrad, 1948; Henrysson, 1971; Swineford, 1974).	≥200–300
Have a stable correlation matrix on which to perform a factor analysis (see Loo, 1983).	≥200
Confirm or reject unidimensionality of an dichotomously scored test of 20–40 items with the computer program NOHARM (De Champlain & Gessaroli, 1998; Fraser & McDonald, 1988).	≥250
Obtain stable calibrations for the two-parameter model using Bilog (see Harwell & Janowski, 1991; Hulin, Lissak, & Drasgow, 1982).	≥250–500
Choose items with a particular distribution of item difficulties (see Nevo, 1980).	≥256–1024

(Continued)

TABLE 22.2
Pretest Sample Sizes Indicated for Various Test Development Applications

Application	Indicated N Per Item
Choose items with a particular distribution of item difficulties and that also meet or exceed a threshold point-biserial discrimination value (see Nevo, 1980).	
Perform linear equating of multiple final forms that have been delivered to a single group of candidates when the cut score is two standard deviations away from the mean (assumes a normal distribution and a standard error of equating =.1 SD unit; Kolen & Brennan, 2004).	≥264
Estimate pass–fail decision consistency using single-administration methods on a test of about 50 dichotomously-scored items with a standard error of about .01 (Subkoviak, 1978).	≥300
Perform equipercentile equating of multiple equivalent forms administered to randomly equivalent sets of candidates, with the pass–fail point located near the mean score (assumes a normal distribution and a standard error of equating =.1 SD unit; for two groups the total required $N = 628$; see Kolen & Brennan, 2004).	≥314
Perform a DIF analysis on pretest items, with at least 100 test takers in the smaller of the two groups being compared (Zieky, 1993).	≥500
Assess the dimensionality of a polytomously scored test (De Champlain et al., 1998).	
Perform linear equating of multiple equivalent forms administered to randomly equivalent sets of candidates, with the pass–fail point located two standard deviations away from the mean score (assumes a normal distribution and a standard error of equating =.1 SD unit; for two groups the total required $N = 1,200$; see Kolen & Brennan, 2004).	≥600
Identify half or more of the items in a sample exhibiting item parameter drift over time (Donoghue & Isham, 1998)	
Obtain stable calibrations for the 3-parameter model (Hulin et al., 1982; Lord, 1968; Mislevy & Stocking, 1989; Millman and Greene, 1989. Thissen and Wainer, 1982).	≥1000
Perform equipercentile equating of multiple equivalent forms administered to randomly equivalent sets of candidates, with the pass–fail point located two standard deviations away from the mean score (assumes a normal distribution and a standard error of equating =.1 SD unit; for two groups the total required $N = 3,056$; see Kolen & Brennan, 2004).	≥1528

MODELING ITEMS AND TESTS IN SMALL-SCALE SYSTEMS

Once data have been collected on prospective test items, the test developer must apply one or more measurement models to those data as a basis for selecting items for inclusion in the final form(s). Measurement models provide a means for deciding whether test items are apparently well formed after they have been rigorously and systematically reviewed by subject matter experts, editors, test developers, and perhaps others (Proposition 9). Measurement models define how individual item responses combine to create a test score and the kind of response consistency among items that is expected in each construct dimension (Proposition 12). They thus provide a rationale for selecting some items over others (because some assemblies result in greater response consistency among selected items), thereby leading us to maximize important score or decision reliabilities (Propositions 16 and 19). Standard 3.9 specifies the responsibilities of the test developer:

> When a test developer evaluates the psychometric properties of items, the classical or item response theory (IRT) model used for evaluating the psychometric properties of items should be documented.

The sample used for estimating item properties should be described and should be of adequate size and diversity for the procedure. The process by which items are selected and the data used for item selection, such as item difficulty, item discrimination, and/or item information, should also be documented. When IRT is used to estimate item parameters in test development, the item response model, estimation procedures, and evidence of model fit should be documented. (AERA, APA, & NCME, 1999, pp. 44–45)

In this section we first summarize the literature on data requirements for various measurement models and applications. Based on this analysis, we briefly describe four measurement models that might be available to the small-scale test developer. Finally, we summarize practical strategies that the small-scale test developer might use to deal with data sets of various sizes.

Data Requirements for Various Test Development Applications

Table 22.2 shows a summary compiled by Jones (2004b) of minimum sample sizes that have been indicated in the measurement literature for various test development applications. In most cases the "Indicated N per item" is based on the conclusion of the study authors given specific assumed conditions; in other cases, Jones drew conclusions based on findings reported in the study. Of course, the generality of findings such as these is open to continual investigation and refinement. Readers are encouraged to review these and other sources along with the characteristics of their own testing system to draw their own conclusions regarding data requirements.

Given these indications regarding needed sample sizes for various test development applications, we now consider the model selection and development strategy options that may be available to small-scale achievement testing systems.

Measurement Models for Small-Scale Test Development

Based on Table 2 there appear to be four measurement model options available to small-scale test developers: (1) the classical test theory model which seems useable in some situations with single pretest data samples as low as $N = 50$ test takers and more generally with multiple samples of $N \geq 150$ to 200 test takers each; (2) the Rasch model, whose applicability seems to parallel that of the classical test theory model; (3) the modified one-parameter and restricted two parameter IRT models, the first of which has applicability similar to the Rasch model, the second of which may be useful for scoring subsequent test takers based on a calibration sample of $N \geq 100$; and (4) the decision theory model which may be usefully applied to classification tests based on a calibration sample of $N \geq 100$.

One of the main goals of item and test modeling is to allow the test developer to estimate test score reliability or information. Standard 2.1 states

> For each total score, subscore, or combination of scores that is to be interpreted, estimates of relevant reliabilities and standard errors of measurement or test information functions should be reported. (AERA, APA, & NCME, 1999, p. 21)

The method of estimating score reliability is to be clearly described and estimated in terms of statistics (Standard 2.4). In our credentialing scenario, the conditional standard error of measurement, particularly near the cut score, and pass/fail decision reliability are also to be estimated (Standard 2.2, 14.15). We next briefly review each of the candidate measurement models.

The Classical Test Theory Model

Under the Spearman single-factor interpretation of the classical model (McDonald, 1999), the goal of test form assembly using classical test theory is to select appropriate, apparently well-formed items that meet the content specifications of the test while maximizing the value of coefficient ω, which is

$$\omega = \frac{\left(\sum_{j=1}^{m} \lambda_j\right)^2}{\sigma_Y^2} \tag{22.1}$$

where λ_j is the loading of item j on the common factor measured by all the items and σ_Y^2 is the total test variance. The numerator Equation 22.1 is the true score variance of test Y, so omega is the ratio of true score to total test variance.

Coefficient omega is also (a) the correlation between the total test score Y and the common factor, (b) the correlation between the scores on two tests Y and Y' that have the same sum of loadings on the same common factor and have the same sum of unique variances, and (c) the squared correlation between the test scores Y and the mean scores on the infinite set of items from a homogeneous domain of which the m items used in the test are a subset (McDonald, 1999). Thus, ω it is not only an indicator of reliability, but also of the response consistency within a given content dimension that is validity evidence (Proposition 12).

The problem with using the single-factor model for small-scale development is that usually there are not sufficient data to verify essential unidimensionality and estimate the factor loadings (see below). However, if we are willing to assume unidimensionality and the simplifying assumption that each item loads equally on the common factor, we can use coefficient α as an approximation of coefficient ω

$$\hat{\omega} = \left(\frac{m}{m-1}\right)\left(1 - \left(\frac{\sum_{j=1}^{m} s_j^2}{s_Y^2}\right)\right) \tag{22.2}$$

where m is the number of items and s_j^2 is the variance of item j (McDonald, 1999, p. 208). To maximize coefficient α we choose items with high item reliability indices (Crocker & Algina, 1986)

$$\sigma_{x_j Z} = \sigma_{x_j} \rho_{x_j Y} \tag{22.3}$$

where σ_{x_j} is the item standard deviation and $\rho_{x_j Y}$ is the Pearson correlation between the raw item scores and the raw total test scores (the point-biserial correlation for dichotomous items), which is the most commonly used measure of item discrimination. The sum of Equation 22.3 over all the selected items is an estimate of the total test standard deviation.

Of course, increasing coefficient alpha has the effect of reducing the average standard error of measurement (SEM; Proposition 16). The average SEM for a raw score, σ_{E_Y}, is given by

$$\sigma_{E_Y} = \sqrt{\sigma_Y^2 (1 - \hat{\alpha})} \tag{22.4}$$

and the conditional standard error or measurement (CSEM) for a given (dichotomous) raw score, $\hat{\sigma}_{E.Y_p}$, can be estimated by

$$\hat{\sigma}_{E.Y_p} = \sqrt{\frac{(m - Y_p)(Y_p)(1 - \alpha)}{(n - 1)(1 - KR_{21})}} \quad (22.5)$$

where KR_{21} is a simplification of alpha assuming dichotomous items all of equal difficulty,

$$KR_{21} = \left(\frac{m}{m - 1}\right)\left(1 - \frac{\mu_Y(m - \mu_Y)}{n\sigma_Y^2}\right) \quad (22.6)$$

(Keats, 1957; Lord & Novick, 1968; see Feldt, Steffen, & Gupta [1985] for descriptions of other CSEM methods).

The remaining challenges for small-scale test developers, then, are obtaining stable values of item and option difficulty and discrimination against which to judge item appropriateness and well-formedness and obtaining stable values of coefficient alpha.

The Rasch Model

The Rasch model (Rasch, 1960; Wright & Masters, 1982; Wright & Stone, 1979) expresses the probability of person n obtaining a score of x (or reaching x out of k possible steps on an item) as

$$\pi_{nix} = \frac{\exp \sum_{j=0}^{x} (\beta_n - \delta_{ix})}{\sum_{k=0}^{m_i} \exp \sum_{j=0}^{k} (\beta_n - \delta_{ij})} \quad (22.7)$$

where π_{nix} is the probability of person n scoring x on item i, x is the count of steps completed, β_n is the ability of person n, δ_{ij} is the difficulty of completing step j of item i, k and m_i are the number of steps possible for item i, and the denominator of Equation 22.7 is the sum of all possible numerators (Wright and Masters, 1982). The Rasch model requires that all items conform, within tolerance, to the relationship expressed in Equation 22.7. Rasch proponents claim that the Rasch model embodies characteristics that are essential for all good measurement, and thus prefer to use the Rasch model to other alternatives no matter the size of the data set. Not only is the Rasch model always preferred by Rasch proponents, but also items that conform to the Rasch model. Consequently, Rasch proponents discard items that might be judged acceptable under classical test theory because they do not conform to the expectations of the Rasch model (see Hambleton, Wright, Crocker, Masters, & van der Linden, 1992). This philosophical stance may thus have practical consequences for small item pools.

The goal of form assembly under the Rasch model is to select content-appropriate items that fit the Rasch model so that the standard error of measurement is minimized over the score range of interest. Rasch person standard error is described by

$$SEM_{(b_r)} = \left[\sum_{i=1}^{L}\left[\sum_{k=1}^{m} k^2 P_{rik} - \left(\sum_{k=1}^{m} k P_{rik}\right)^2\right]\right]^{-1/2}. \quad (22.8)$$

where P_{rik} is the probability of person with raw score r (corresponding to achievement level b) achieving a score of k on item i (Wright & Masters, 1982). (*Note*: this formula pertains to the dichotomous Rasch model and the Rasch rating scale model; see Wright & Masters [1982] for the standard error for other Rasch models). To do this, the developer selects items that maximize test information for achievement level b, the quantity inside the brackets of equation 22.8. The challenge for small-scale Rasch development is to obtain stable enough measures of person ability and item difficulty to assemble forms and score test takers.

The Modified One-Parameter and restricted Two-Parameter Item Response Theory models

The dichotomous, unidimensional three-parameter Item Response Theory (IRT) model (Hambleton, 1989, Hambleton, Swaminathan, & Rogers, 1992; Lord 1980; McDonald, 1999; Thissen & Orlando, 2001) expresses the probability of person n answering item i correctly as

$$P_i(\theta_j) = c_i + \frac{(1-c_i)}{1+e^{-Da_i(\theta_j-b_i)}} \qquad (22.9)$$

where $P_i(\theta_j)$ is the probability of person j with true ability or achievement θ_j answering item i correctly, a_i is the discrimination parameter of item i, b_i is the difficulty or location parameter, c_i is the probability of a correct response by a very-low-ability test taker, and $D = 1.7$ if the results are scaled in the normal metric or $D = 1.0$ if the results are scaled in the logistic metric. Equation 22.9 is said to describe the item characteristic curve or (ICC) of item i. The sum of ICCs across θ_j produces a test characteristic curve (TCC),

$$P(\theta_j) = \sum_{i=1}^{L}\left[c_i + \frac{(1-c_i)}{1+e^{-Da_i(\theta_j-b_i)}}\right], \qquad (22.10)$$

which associates every level of θ_j with an expected *raw score* or *true score* on the test.

The sensitivity of an item to changes in person ability is quantified as item information

$$I_i(\theta_j) = \frac{D^2 a_i^2 (1-c_i)}{\left(c_i + e^{Da_i(\theta_j-b_i)}\right)\left(1+e^{-Da_i(\theta_j-b_i)}\right)} \qquad (22.11)$$

The sensitivity of the total test to differences in latent ability is described by the test information function (TIF). The TIF is the sum of the individual item information functions

$$I(\theta_j) = \sum_i \frac{D^2 a_i^2 (1-c_i)}{\left(c_i + e^{Da_i(\theta_j-b_i)}\right)\left(1+e^{-Da_i(\theta_j-b_i)}\right)^2} \qquad (22.12)$$

The SEM of θ_j is the reciprocal of the square root of test information

$$SEM(\theta_j) = \frac{1}{\sqrt{I(\theta_j)}}. \qquad (22.13)$$

The philosophical stance of IRT practitioners is directly opposite to that of Rasch proponents. Whereas Rasch users hold items up against the standard of the Rasch model, IRT practitioners seek to use the item response models that best fit the data. The goal of form assembly under IRT is to select well-formed items that conform to the test specifications of the test and fit the chosen IRT model while maximizing test information and minimizing SEM along the important range of person abilities, or matching a preestablished TIF target as closely as possible. The challenge of using IRT for small-scale test development is that of confirming essential unidimensionality and obtaining stable item and person parameter estimates. As we saw in Table 22.2, research has suggested that multiparameter item response models may not be appropriate for cases where $N \leq 200$ observations. However, a one-parameter item response model that forces $a_i = 1$ and $c_i = 0$ has been shown to be useful in small N situations (Barnes & Wise, 1991; De Gruijter, 1986; Wainer & Wright, 1980). IRT proponents have criticized the one-parameter model because it assumes that all item discriminations are the same, which is demonstrably not true except in rare cases, and that the probability of correctly answering selected response items with low levels of achievement is 0, which is also often not true. Although research has shown that the one-parameter model is robust to moderate variations in item discrimination (Dinero & Haertel, 1977; Hambleton & Cook, 1983; Hambleton & Traub, 1973) it is not as robust to violations of the assumption of non-zero lower asymptotes. In item parameter recovery studies, the one-parameter model appears to do an adequate job of tracing the empirical item response function at theta values of between −1 and +1, but tends to underestimate the ability of low-ability test takers and overestimate the difficulty of easy items (Barnes & Wise, 1991; Divgi, 1986; Hambleton & Cook, 1983; van de Vijver, 1986). A modified version of the one-parameter model may be more appropriate in certain situations. In the modified one-parameter model the lower asymptote, c_i, is fixed at a non-zero value to account for correct responding with very low levels of knowledge (Barnes & Wise, 1991; De Gruijter, 1986; Divgi, 1986; Wainer & Wright, 1980).

Parshall, Kromrey, Chason, and Yi (1997) in a parameter recovery study using a six-dimensional multi-dimensional item response theory (MIRT) model to generate item response data found that an 80-item test modeled with a restricted unidimensional two-parameter IRT model (with a tight prior distribution placed on the a parameter) based on a calibration sample of $N = 100$ examinees provide suitably accurate measures of test-taker ability on a subsequent cross-validation samples of test takers. We include the restricted two-parameter model here as a possibility for small-n test development, particularly if the goal is to provide IRT ability estimates on subsequent test takers (as opposed to the calibration sample test takers) using long tests.

The Measurement Decision Theory Model

Rudner (2003) proposed a simplified model for test development in cases where the goal of testing is to make classification decisions about individuals. His approach, which he terms *measurement decision theory,* aims to make a "best guess" as to the test taker's mastery state or latent classification based on the person's item responses, prior item information and prior information about population classification proportions. Rudner's research to date has shown the applicability of the model to sample sizes of $N = 100$ to 200 and possibly lower, depending on the desired classification accuracy.

The model assumes that the test developer has in hand k mastery states that have values m_k, a set of L items conforming to a set of content specifications, and an response vector $z = [z_1, z_2, \ldots z_L]$ from each of a calibration sample of test takers. A pass–fail or other decision point is established on the raw score scale. The probability of a randomly selected test taker falling in each of the k mastery states is calculated, $P(m_k)$. Finally, the probability of a score z_i given the kth mastery state, $P(z_i|m_k)$, is calculated for each item i.

Subsequent test takers are then classified into one of k mastery states using the prior probabilities calculated on the calibration sample and their response vectors. Assuming that the item responses are independent, the probability of a response vector z given a classification of m_k is given by

$$P(\mathbf{z}|m_k) = \prod_{i=1}^{N} P(\mathbf{z}_i|m_k). \tag{22.14}$$

Then, the probability of a test taker's classification m_k is calculated using Bayes' theorem

$$P(m_k|\mathbf{z}) = cP(\mathbf{z}|m_k)P(m_k). \quad (22.15)$$

where c is a normalizing constant. The test developer calculates k separate values of Equation 22.15 for each test taker, one for each classification. Rudner (2003) suggested several methods for determining the test taker's classification, the simplest of which is to assign the test taker to the classification with the maximum a posteriori probability by Equation 22.15.

Using Measurement Models With Small Data Sets

We now look at how these models may be used in the context of small data sets. First, we consider the problem of dimensionality. We then discuss modeling strategies under three different conditions: (a) when there are no pretest data, (b) when we have a pretest sample up to $N = 100$, and (c) when we have a pretest sample of $N = 100$ to 200. We then acknowledge certain test development applications that cannot be done with pretest $N \leq 200$. Finally, we comment on grading extended responses with human scorers and consider methods of estimating pass–fail reliability. Options for equating with $N \leq 200$ are discussed in the next section.

Dealing With Dimensionality

The Spearman single-factor, Rasch, and IRT models described all assume that the test is essentially unidimensional. The risk of assuming essential unidimensionality when it does not exist is a problem that must be grappled with at the form development stage by the small-scale developer. Loo (1983) recommended a sample size of $N \geq 200$ to obtain a stable correlation matrix for factor analysis. De Champlain and Gessaroli (1998) examined the utility of three dimensionality assessment procedures in small test (20 versus 40 items) and small-volume ($N = 250$ versus 500 versus 1,000) situations. They compared the ability of TESTFACT (Wilson, Wood, & Gibbons, 1991), LISREL8 (Jöreskog & Sörbom, 1993), and NOHARM (Fraser & McDonald, 1988) to correctly reject the unidimensionality assumption when it did not hold, and the type I error rates for those procedures when unidimensionality did hold for dichotomous tests. Rejection rates for two-dimensional data sets were high for all sample sizes, but only NOHARM did not suffer inflated type I error rates as the tests got shorter and the data sets got smaller. How well NOHARM would have worked with $N \leq 200$ test takers is not known. In a similar investigation of methods for assessing dimensionality of tests with polytomously scored responses, DeChamplain, Gessaroli, Tang, and De Champlain (1998) found that neither LISREL8 nor Poly-DIMTEST (Li & Stout, 1994, 1995) worked well for samples of less that $N = 500$ test takers.

To mitigate this risk of uncertain dimensionality, it appears that the small-scale developer must depend on careful test and item design and then carefully consider the logic of the test specifications. For example, if the test content covers multiple courses from multiple disciplines, then it is likely that different dimensions of ability will control success on the test items from these different sections. In this case, it makes more sense to treat each section as a separate test, analyzing and selecting items one section at a time. On the other hand, if the section represents the content from a single 3-day course, the chances of having essential unidimensionality across the item pool are increased; in many cases, the different segments of content are conceptually interdependent (e.g., Smith, 2002).

Modeling Strategies When There Are No Item Response Data

In situations where no pretest data can be collected on item and test performance before scores have to be reported, we must rely on rigorous item review procedures to ensure that the test items are appropriate (Proposition 6), are linked to the test specifications (Proposition 7), impose no inappropriate reading and response demands (Proposition 8), are apparently well formed (Proposition 9), are free of offensive content (Proposition 10), are representative of the construct domain of reference (Proposition 13), are unbiased (Proposition 22), and have adequate instructions (Propositions 24). As mentioned, a preliminary tryout test by a handful of test takers can be very helpful in this regard. By adding a thorough review process to a good practice or domain analysis and test specification process, we hope to increase our chances of producing appropriate, well-formed items (Propositions 6 and 9) that exhibit response consistency within logical content dimensions (Proposition 12), even though we do not have empirical evidence for these properties at item selection time. Long consulting experience has shown that improved care for the test design, item development, and item review processes does, in fact, result in a higher proportion of empirically sound items.

As for test forms created with no data, statements cannot be made about the equivalence of these forms to concurrent or previous forms along any appreciable segment of the score scale. Thus, it is recommended that only one form of such tests be delivered at a time. Each form thus produced must essentially stand alone because it cannot be equated to other forms. In addition, because even carefully reviewed item pools can lose 20 to 30% of their items because of poor or negative discrimination, inappropriate distracter function, or inappropriate difficulty, it is wise in these situations to develop oversized test forms if possible; that is, forms that are 50 to 100% larger than the anticipated need based on generalizability or Spearman-Brown reliability analysis. Such a strategy may help to mitigate the degrading effects of poor items on reliability and allows later opportunity to reduce the test size by eliminating inefficient or even malignant items. The single form may even be divided into two alternate forms after sufficient data have been collected to support equating. The model used in those cases depends on the amount and type of data available and the purposes of measurement.

Under circumstances of few or no data, it might be preferable to avoid noncompensatory scoring strategies, as, for example, when a certification candidate is required to meet or exceed a cut score for each section of an examination. Such a strategy holds the candidate hostage to the least reliable of the separately graded sections and is not prudent when that level of reliability cannot be assessed. Hambleton and Slater (1997) show how noncompensatory scoring and standard-setting strategies can actually cause the reliability and validity of pass–fail decisions to decrease as the number of separately scored sections is increased.

Occasionally, it may be the case that a larger-than-average number of SME judges are available to the test developer when pretest takers are not. In such cases, it may be useful to have the judges independently sort items into ordinal difficulty categories and then examine the median rating and midrange of ratings for each item. It might be argued that items with wide midrange values are difficult to place on the scale and that such items are not part of the same construct as the others (Wright & Masters, 1982). Of course, the generalizability of such ratings from a small sample of judges may be open to question.

Although equating along any appreciable span of the score scale is not possible without item response data, it may be feasible to equate at the cut score using SME judgment data. Smith and Carlson (1995) used Angoff (1984) ratings from 19 trained judges engaged in a two-pass procedure to assemble three nonoverlapping 50-item forms from a pool of 228 items. Each of these experimental examinations was built to match the cut score of a target operational examination and was also built to have a similar distribution of Angoff ratings as the target exam (the target examination ratings being provided by the same group of judges). The experimental forms were compared with three randomly selected operational forms that had been previously constructed using classical statistics to be equivalent with the target examination. The three experimental forms and the three randomly selected operational forms were equated with the target form using IRT based equating on $N = 2,000$ candidates. Both sets of examinations were found to have judgmental cut scores that underestimated the raw equated cut scores by a little over 1.5 raw score points. The average variation between judgmental and equated cut scores was less for the experimental forms than for the operational forms. Smith and Carlson (1995) concluded that

> the use of judgmental ratings as 'statistical' specifications proved to be as successful as classical statistics in the construction of parallel forms given content sampling constraints. However, comparisons between judgmental and equated cut scores showed the judgmental cut scores to differ from cut scores obtained through equating the test forms to a degree that would be acceptable only if the sample sizes for equating are extremely small. (p. 9)

Thorndike (1982) suggested a method for filling in missing item difficulty and discrimination estimates for new items by either interpolation or regression. This approach requires previously administered items with known difficulty and discrimination parameters from the same achievement domain as the new items and item difficulty ratings by "several" judges. Thorndike based his method on work by Lorge and Kruglov (1952, 1953), who found that although judges are poor estimators of absolute item difficulty, their appraisals of difficulty correlate reasonably well with empirical difficulty estimates and with one another; that is, they are better judges of relative item difficulty.

To begin, previously administered anchor items with known difficulties and discriminations are selected from across the ability scale. New, untested items from the same achievement domain are added. The combined set of old and new items are presented to judges who independently rate the difficulty of each item. The average difficulty rating of each item, $\bar{g}_i$, is calculated. The old and new items are arranged in descending order of $\bar{g}_i$. The empirical difficulty parameters for the old items, b_i (based on Rasch or IRT calibration) are compared with $\bar{g}_i$ for rank-order consistency. If the rank-order correlation between b_i and $\bar{g}_i$ is high, estimated b_i values for the new items, b_i^* are calculated either by linear interpolation or by regressing b_i on $\bar{g}_i$. The new b_i^* values could be used "as is" in the assembly of new forms, or they could be used to estimate classical item difficulties (p-values).

To estimate p-values for the new items, an estimation spreadsheet with two input variable cells and one output cell per item is prepared. The input cells are the estimated discrimination parameter for the new item, a_i, and the estimated difficulty parameter for the new item, b_i. The output cell is the expected proportion correct for the new item, P_i. The estimated a_i value is either the average or fixed a_i value of the anchor items, or a value estimated from the known biserial correlation, r_{bis_i}, between the anchor item scores and an achievement measure (e.g., a previous achievement test score from the same domain) using the following relationship

$$a_i^* = \frac{r_{bis_i}}{\sqrt{1 - r_{bis_r}^2}}. \tag{22.16}$$

The spreadsheet is prepared to take the input values a_i and b_i, insert them into Equation 22.9 and calculate the expected proportion of correct answers, $P_i(\theta_j)$, at k equally spaced levels of θ. These proportions are multiplied by the expected proportion of test takers at each value of theta, g_j, and summed across θ levels to obtain the total estimated proportion correct, P_i, for the combination of a_i and b_i,

$$P_i = \sum_{j=1}^{k} P_i(\theta_j) g_j. \qquad (22.17)$$

Once estimated P_i and r_{bis_i} values are obtained for each new item, the expected mean raw score, standard deviation, and α values are calculated for the test form. First, we calculate the estimated point-biserial values, ρ_{xY}, for the new items by the relationship

$$r_{bis} = \rho_{xY} \frac{\sqrt{P_i(1-P_i)}}{\mu} \qquad (22.18)$$

where μ is the ordinate of the unit normal curve at the z value that divides the distribution into the proportions P_i and $1 - P_i$. Then, test variance can be estimated as the square of the sum of the products of the individual item standard deviations by their point-biserial values, with individual dichotomous item standard deviations $\sigma_{x_i} = \sqrt{P_i Q_i}$. Equation 22.2 can then be used to estimate coefficient α. The estimated mean raw test score is the sum of P_i.

The Thorndike method may be useful in test revision situations where no pretesting of items is possible, but where both expert judges and previously administered anchor items are available. The method could be used to guide selection of appropriate items for a test form, although it might not be appropriate for assembling parallel test forms.

Modeling Strategies for Sample Sizes up to $N = 100$ Observations per Item

Rasch proponents recommend beginning a small-scale item analysis with a visual examination of the matrix of item-by-person scores (Wright & Masters, 1982; Wright & Stone, 1979). The developer orders this item-by-person matrix (items across the top, persons down the side) by decreasing person score going from top to bottom and decreasing item score going from left to right. The developer expects to see approximately two triangular half matrices, the upper left one filled with larger numbers, the lower right one filled with smaller numbers. Any departures from the expected pattern are examined and noted. Persons exhibiting unusual response patterns (unexpected correct or incorrect answers) may have been cheating, distracted, or employing some inappropriate response strategy not reflective of their true ability. Likewise, items exhibiting unexpected responses might need to be flagged as susceptible to guessing, or may be malformed or compromised in some way. Such persons and items are said to be *misfitting*, meaning they do not conform to the model's expectations, and both may be dropped from further analysis if it is determined that they are injecting noise into the process of building a good achievement measure, much like automobile components that exceed design tolerances might be rejected from an assembly line. Rasch analysis programs such as WINSTEPS (Linacre, 1992–2004) apply special statistical tests to item and person fit. Of course, although items may be permanently dropped, test takers cannot be disregarded. Once the measurement has been constructed using items and persons that fit model expectations, poorly fitting persons are usually given a score. However, unlike the situation in classical test theory, the developer is aware that the scores of these persons may not signify the same achievement that was modeled during item analysis.

With sample sizes in this range, we may come close to obtaining stable item difficulty measures, particularly as we near the top end. However, at $N \geq 32$ we may have the stability we need to rank-order items by their classical difficulties, which may be enough to allow selection of the most appropriately test items for a single final form, or to support a modified bookmark standard-setting procedure. Although classical item discriminations are apparently much harder to estimate than difficulties (Nevo, 1980), Farish (1984), in a real-data study, found that with random sampling of pretest candidates, the average point-biserial discrimination values converged on population values with $N = 40$. It was when clustered sampling was used, such as when whole classrooms were administered test items, that the point-biserial estimates became much more unstable. In any case, $N = 100$ should be useful for discerning items that are significant positive discriminators (Kromrey & Bacon, 1992). In a small item pool with limited choices, this may be all the information that the test developer needs.

In the end, if the item pool is small, sample sizes as low as $N = 50$ may provide enough information to select desirable test items for inclusion in test forms. Thayn (2001), in a real-data simulation, found that he could assemble test forms based on random samples of $N = 50$ candidates that yielded 0.86 of the information available in the maximally informative form. With random samples of $N = 200$, the resulting forms were .96 as informative as the maximally informative test form.

Fewer than 100 pretest observations from a single sample similar to a randomly selected sample are probably sufficient to assemble two forms that are reasonably comparable at the cut score using any of the models discussed, except the multiparameter IRT models, if the cut score is not too far from the middle of the score distribution. Smith and Jones (2002), in a real-data simulation, found that 64-item forms assembled from the first $N = 40, 60, 100,$ and 200 pretest candidates all yielded pass–fail decisions that agreed $p_o = 0.90$ to 0.93 with decisions made by a canonical form on a cross-validation sample of $N = 445$ candidates. Forms assembled using Rasch methodology performed comparably with forms assembled using classical theory. Pass–fail agreement between forms in the validation sample ranged from 0.85 to 0.93 and fluctuated up and down as pretest sample size on which the assembly was based increased from $N = 40$ to $N = 200$. Smith and Jones did not investigate to what extent increasing test length might have improved these results.

Rudner (2003), in a real-data simulation, found that forms built based on $N = 100$ candidates using measurement decision theory agreed with a canonical form $p_o = .86$ on a cross-validation sample of $N = 1,000$ candidates. Agreement rose to $p_o = .901$ when forms were built based on $N = 200$ candidates.

Estimates of coefficient α, which may be used to evaluate score reliability, SEM, and CSEM, and drive the selection of items under the classical model, may be usefully stable at $N \geq 50$ to 80 (Kromrey & Bacon, 1992).

These sample sizes may be appropriate for scaling items under the dichotomous Rasch and modified one-parameter IRT models for the purpose of doing response pattern scoring of test takers, especially if the test is long (over 50 items). Linacre (1994) suggested that $N = 50$ pretest takers is an adequate calibration sample.

Modeling Strategies for $N = 100$ to 200 Observations per Item

The closer we come to the top end of our data range in this chapter, closer we come to stability in classical item statistics and Rasch item parameters (Crocker & Algina, 1986; Farish, 1984; Kromrey & Bacon, 1992; Wright & Stone, 1979). Per-item samples near the top of this range may be a reasonable basis for combining data from two or more randomly equivalent groups of pretest takers. This is important because it allows the test developer to think of splitting a single pretest form into two pretest forms, thus shortening the test and, in some situations, perhaps attracting greater pretest participation.

With sample sizes in this range we may be able to identify items that meet or surpass quality thresholds in terms of classical discrimination (Nevo, 1980). This facilitates making reliable item selection decisions within a larger item pool, although it may not be until more data are collected that we can target a particular distribution of item difficulties and at the same time select items with discriminations above a particular threshold (Nevo, 1980).

Finally, we note the research results of Parshall et al. (1997), who obtained accurate ability estimation performance on a cross-validation sample of simulated test takers after calibrating an 80-item test on a sample of 100 simulees using a restricted two-parameter IRT model. The restrictions were represented by a tight prior distribution placed on the a parameter. Their results are interesting because the response generation model used was a six-dimensional MIRT model, producing more realistic response data than in studies where the unidimensional three-parameter model is taken as "truth," and because modeling of item responses was better on the cross-validation sample than on the original calibration sample. Their conclusion was that restricted models fit the calibration data less exactly than the unrestricted models, but are useful in the ability estimation of subsequent test takers because they are less prone to distortion from the overfitting of idiosyncrasies in the calibration data set.

Future research into the use of priors in IRT item parameter estimation may prove relevant to small-scale test developers. For example, Swaminathan, Hambleton, Sireci, Xing, and Rizavi (2003) showed that Bayesian prior distributions for item difficulty parameters could be derived from SME predictions as to the proportion of examinees who would answer an item correctly. These priors, along with sample-free priors on item discrimination and guessing parameters, were applied to Rasch, two-, and three-parameter IRT models and used with BILOG to calibrate items on samples of $N = 100, 150, 200, 300, 400,$ and 500 test takers. The use of judgmental priors led to a slight improvement in Rasch item parameter estimation and two-parameter b-value estimation, at the smallest sample sizes, but the improvement in a-value accuracy at a sample size of $N = 100$ was more substantial; a 50% improvement in accuracy over the no-prior condition. The improvements in the performance of the three-parameter model were even more dramatic: at $N = 100$ a 50% improvement in b-value accuracy was obtained over the no-prior condition, a 100% improvement in a-value accuracy was obtained over the no-prior condition, and a 500% improvement in c-value accuracy was obtained. Swaminathan et al. (2003) suggest that "considerable improvement" might result from being able to obtain judgmental predictions of item discrimination and lower asymptote parameters as well as the difficulty parameter. Research continues in this area.

Applications Requiring More Data Than $N = 200$ Observations per Item

IRT applications involving use of the unrestricted two-parameter model are usually thought to require $N \geq 250$ to 500 test takers per form. Unrestricted three-parameter IRT applications may require $N \geq 1,000$ test takers for stable parameter estimates. Again, however, we note the results of Parshall et al. (1997) who obtained reasonable ability estimation performance for a cross-validation sample of simulated examinees using various restricted and unrestricted IRT models and a calibration sample of $N = 250$. Item parameter drift and differential item functioning studies probably require more data than we are considering here (Donoghue & Isham, 1998; Zieky, 1993).

Human Scoring of Extended Responses

Many small-scale achievement tests require extended responses, including essays, multistep solutions where intermediate work must be shown, observed performances, manipulations of equipment, creation of products, and other authentic performances. Although some large-scale systems have successfully implemented machine scoring of extended responses, for small-scale programs the scoring responsibility most likely falls to a small committee of human scorers. Human scoring requires not only requires a *scoring rubric* (a set of explicit rules for assigning scores to performances), it requires that the appropriate implementation of that rubric be modeled for the scorers using benchmark exemplars and so-called range-finder exemplars (instances of the highest and lowest quality work that qualify for each score). APA Standard 3.23 specifies the responsibility of the test developer in training human scorers:

> The process for selecting, training, and qualifying scorers should be documented by the test developer. The training materials, such as the scoring rubrics and examples of test takers' responses that illustrate the levels on the score scale, and the procedures for training scorers should result in a degree of agreement among scorers that allows for the scores to be interpreted as originally intended by the test developer. Scorer reliability and potential drift over time in raters' scoring standards should be evaluated and reported by the persons responsible for conducting the training session. (AERA, APA, & NCME, 1999, p. 48)

Training of human scorers is best done in a workshop setting where supervisors can explain the rubric to the scorers and explain why benchmark and range-finder exemplars merit particular scores. The trainees can score additional benchmark cases independently, then reunite to report the scores they gave, explain their rationale, and receive corrective feedback. When scorers are able to score benchmark exemplars to within a certain degree of accuracy, they can score actual performances independently. Normally, two trained scorers score each performance independently. In cases where the scorers do not agree to within a preestablished level of tolerance, say 1 score point, the performance is scored independently by a third trained person, usually a supervisor. Scores can be monitored electronically as they are given and consistency among scorers can be tracked in real time. Should inconsistent behavior emerge from one or more scorers, retraining can take place. For multiday scoring sessions, each day can begin with scoring of benchmark cases to make sure that scorer consistency is maintained from day to day.

Small-scale testing systems require fewer trained human scorers than larger systems, which reduces training costs and makes consistent performance easier to achieve. The complication is that there may be fewer benchmark and range-finder instances available for training purposes than is desirable. To compensate, small-scale test developers need to create scoring rubrics that are as explicit as possible. For example, instead of holistic rating scales that could require many exemplars for training, small-scale developers might consider using analytical scoring rubrics where each feature of each performance is examined and evaluated according to precise, case-specific criteria.

Pass–Fail Reliability

Once test forms are assembled and a cut score is established, pass–fail decision consistency is estimated. The seemingly most straightforward way to measure pass–fail consistency is to administer parallel forms of a test to the same test takers and observe the proportion of test takers classified the same way on both tests, p_o (Hambleton & Novick, 1973), or the proportion of pass–fail agreement beyond chance agreement using coefficient κ (Cohen, 1960; Swaminathan, Hambleton, & Algina, 1974),

$$\hat{\kappa} = \frac{\hat{p}_o - \hat{p}_c}{1 - \hat{p}_c} \qquad (22.19)$$

where $\hat{p}_c$ is the proportion of pass–fail agreement expected by chance.

Of course, it is not often possible for any testing system to administer two forms of the same examination to all test takers, or even to a research sample, much less a small-scale system. Fortunately there are methods available for estimating $\hat{p}_o$ and $\hat{\kappa}$ based on data from a single test administration. Methods proposed by Huynh (1976), Subkoviak (1976), and Marshall and Haertel (1976) are useful for equally weighted, dichotomously scored items. Methods by Breyer and Lewis (1994) and Livingston and Lewis (1995) can be used with tests scored by any method.

Subkoviak (1978) provided some information on the sensitivity of these statistics to small sample sizes. He compared the mean estimated $\hat{p}_o$ values from the Swaminathan et al. (1974), Huynh (1976), Subkoviak (1976), and Marshall–Haertel (1976) methods to pass–fail parameters calculated over a population of 1,586 students. Each student in the population took parallel forms of 10, 30, and 50 items and the observed pass–fail consistencies across these forms served as the population parameters for each study condition. Subkoviak drew 50 samples of either $N = 30$ or $N = 300$ test takers with replacement from the population and applied the four methods to each sample. This procedure was repeated at cut points of 50%, 60%, 70%, and 80% for tests of 10, 30, and 50 items.

For tests of 50 items Subkoviak (1978) found that the Swaminathan et al. (1974) method was unbiased. The Huynh (1976) and Subkoviak (1976) methods showed slight bias with different patterns. The Huynh (1976) method underestimated $\hat{p}_o$ by 1 or 2 points at the two low cut scores in the $N = 30$ condition and overestimated $\hat{p}_o$ at the 90% cut score by 1 point in the $N = 300$ condition. The Subkoviak (1976) method showed a 1- to 2- point bias upward for all cut scores in the $N = 30$ condition, and a 1 or 2 point bias upward for the two high cut scores in the $N = 300$ condition. The Marshall–Haertel (1976) method showed virtually no bias.

In terms of standard error—that is, average deviation from the population parameter—the two-administration procedure by (Swaminathan et al., 1974) performed more poorly than the single-administration methods. For samples of $N = 30$, the standard error ranged from 0.05 to 0.08. For samples of $N = 300$, the standard error ranged from 0.01 to 0.02. By contrast, the Huynh (1976) method had a standard error of 0.02 for all cut scores in the $N = 30$ condition and 0.01 for all cut scores in the $N = 300$ condition. The other methods had standard errors of .02 to .03 in the $N = 30$ condition and .01 in the $N = 300$ condition. The results were only slightly worse for tests of 30 items. Ten-item tests showed standard errors of 0.03 to 0.08 across all methods in the N= 30 condition and .01 to .06 in the $N = 300$ condition.

These results suggest that for tests of around 50 items even $N = 30$ test takers may yield reasonable estimates of pass–fail reliability using single-administration procedures. By contrast, the test–retest method seems much less appropriate for small samples, even if it is feasible.

ASSEMBLING PARALLEL TEST FORMS IN SMALL-SCALE SYSTEMS

Once an appropriate measurement model has been selected and the items have been psychometrically evaluated, items are selected for the final form(s). If a single, stand-alone form is created then items are selected based on the criteria of the model used. Because selecting a good, content-balanced set of items from a pool to populate a single form is the least demanding development application, it is the one recommended for small-n test development. If multiple concurrent forms are needed, an attempt is made to make those forms parallel.

APA Standard 4.10 states, "a clear rationale and supporting evidence should be provided for any claim that scores earned on different forms of a test may be used interchangeably." The commentary on that standard goes on to say "Score equivalence is easiest to establish when different forms are constructed following identical procedures, then equated statistically" (AERA, APA, & NCME, 1999, p. 57).

In this section, we define *parallelism* and *assembly algorithm* and then describe an assembly algorithm useful for constructing several forms simultaneously, using identical procedures, particularly in small-*n* situations. In the following section, we discuss equating. First, we consider the need to assemble forms that meet the specifications for the test.

Assembling Forms That Meet Test Specifications

Millman and Greene (1989) provide a good overview of the sorts of test specifications that might be developed. These include the legitimate sources of test content, the desired test dimensionality, the specificity or broadness of the domain of reference, the distribution of items across content categories, the item formats used, the target test length, the desired psychometric characteristics of the items, the item evaluation and selection criteria, the way items are arranged, the scoring methodology, and the desired psychometric properties of the test. This chapter has focused on quantitative properties; however, it is the qualitative properties of the test form that the test sponsor, and test takers, and the test consumers care most about—and with good reason. Imagine a new building that meets or exceeds measurable building code requirements in every way, but departs from the intended purpose, function, or even the blueprint envisioned by the property owner. Quantitative excellence is always subservient to the test's purpose, function, and blueprint.

Consequently, we take the opportunity here to highlight the importance of Proposition 13: "Test content represents the construct domain of reference and the test specifications." If test content specifications are ignored in assembling the test form, then even with a very unidimensional set of items, there is risk that individual test takers will be done an injustice or will do the system an injustice. If the practice analysis mandates that Content Category A should have five items to Content Category B's one item, and if the actual item distribution on the test is reversed (five items in Content Category B, one item in Content Category A) then the individual who is competent in B but incompetent in A is unjustly and inaccurately scaled as being more competent than he or she would be if the test conformed to the blueprint. Likewise, the person weak in category B is unjustly penalized. Of course, for the content specification to have real meaning, it must be based on a set of rules (Proposition 5) that "duplicates or reproduces the essential characteristics of the universe in their proper proportion and balance" (Lennon, 1956, p. 301).

Assembling Parallel Forms

Parallel forms measure the same construct and have scores that can be interpreted the same way, so achieving parallel forms pertains to Proposition 21. If sufficient parallelism cannot be achieved in the assembly, equating of forms may be needed, as discussed in the next section.

A *form assembly algorithm* is a routine for assigning test items to forms. The algorithm may be implemented by hand or computer. Its task is to build forms with certain predefined statistical and qualitative properties, and, when multiple forms are constructed at once, to ensure that the forms are as parallel as possible under some specific notion of parallelism.

Feldt and Brennan (1989) describe different degrees of parallelism under classical test theory. Strictly parallel forms in classical test theory are defined as forms having equivalent true scores, equivalent error variances, and equivalent internal reliability. *τ-Equivalent forms* assume equivalent true scores, but do not assume equal error variances. The resulting score distributions have the same means and score reliability but potentially different variances. *Essentially τ-Equivalent* forms are assumed to be equivalent with the exception that true scores are allowed to differ by an additive constant. Observed score distribution means and variances may differ, but the internal reliabilities remain the same. *Congeneric forms* allow the true scores to vary by an additive and a multiplicative constant, as if the forms were of different lengths. Observed score means, variances, and reliabilities may differ, but there is a perfect linear relationship between the scores.

It is desirable for an assembly algorithm using classical test theory to be able to construct concurrent forms with a high degree of parallelism while conforming to multiple content targets and other constraints (such as total test time), while balancing these features between forms. Adema and van der Linden (1989) and Sanders and Verschoor (1998) provide examples of assembly algorithms using classic test theory that can perform these tasks. Are parallel forms a reasonable goal for small-n forms assembly?

As we can see in Table 22.2, achieving comparable mean test scores is probably within the reach of many small-scale development situations (Millman & Greene 1989; Nevo, 1980; Sireci, 1991), as are relatively stable values of coefficient α (Kromrey & Bacon, 1992), particularly if a single pretest data sample is used. As mentioned, total test variance is the square of the sum of individual item point-biserial correlations multiplied by their item standard deviations. There is evidence that point-biserial discriminations stabilize more slowly than item difficulties (Nevo, 1980), and hence we can expect it to be more difficult to equalize test score variances than score means as test forms are assembled in a small-n environment. We are likely do a better job creating parallel forms near the mean of the score distribution than toward the tails. This may be enough when assembling parallel forms for decision making with a moderate cut score and a small item pool (Smith & Jones, 2002).

In latent trait theory, forms are considered strictly parallel if each item on one form has a one-to-one correspondence with an item on another form that has equivalent parameters. McDonald (1999, p. 350) refers to such forms as *item parallel*. In practice, achieving such strict parallelism is next to impossible. Lesser degrees of parallelism have been defined under latent trait theory, as with classical test theory. *Weakly parallel forms* measure the same construct and have identical TIFs (Equation 22.12), but do not require a one-to-one correspondence between items or even the same number of items (Samejima, 1977). *TCC-parallel forms* measure the same construct and have identical TCCs (Equation 22.10), but may have different TIFs (McDonald, 1999). It is desirable for concurrent achievement test forms to have matching TIFs and TCCs, with test information maximized at important regions of the achievement scale, while still matching targets for content and other important features and balancing these across forms. For examples of latent trait assembly algorithms see Ackerman (1989) and Adema (1989).

Again we may ask, are TCC and TIF parallel forms possible in small-n situations? TIFs and TCCs depend on the stability of item parameters, and, under the Rasch model, there is evidence of relative stability at the top end of the small-n data range (Farish, 1984; Forster, 1978; Whitely, 1980; Wright & Stone, 1979). The Smith and Jones (2002) study found evidence that TCC/TIF parallel forms of a certification test with a moderate cut score could be built as effectively using Rasch as using classical test theory in a small-n situation with a modest item pool.

Available Assembly Algorithms

Most assembly algorithms, independent of the measurement model, involve either the use of linear programming or heuristics designed to "dramatically reduce computational demand" of linear programming models (Luecht & Hirsch, 1992, p. 41). For examples of assembly algorithms using linear programming see Adema and van der Linden (1989), Adema, Boekkooi-Timminga, and van der Linden, (1991), Baker, Cohen, and Barmish (1988), and Thuenissen (1985). Examples of algorithms that have employed heuristics include Luecht (1998), Swanson and Stocking (1993), and Stocking, Swanson, and Pearlman (1993).

An Assembly Algorithm for Small-Scale Tests

One of the problems with simply trying to match a target test information function with a limited item pool is that by the time the algorithm has assigned items to best match the target TIF, the forms themselves are not equivalent. We now illustrate an heuristic-based assembly algorithm, a so-called greedy algorithm (Leucht, 1998) developed by Smith (2005) that may be used with the Rasch, modified one-parameter, or constrained two-parameter model. This algorithm is particularly suited to small-scale tests in that it is flexible enough to deal with limited item pools and balances the twin goals of matching a target TIF and maintaining equivalence between the forms.

The advantage of the proposed algorithm is that it attempts to match a target test information function while balancing the form TIFs (creating weakly parallel forms) and controlling any number of other content constraints. This is done through the use of a weighted dynamic target test information function (WDT-TIF). Such an algorithm is especially applicable to small item pools, such as may be the case in many small-volume testing systems, because it attempts to match a target TIF for each form while trying to achieve parallelism between forms. The usefulness of this algorithm depends directly on the robustness of the calibration as discussed in the previous section.

The essence of the current algorithm is to select the weakest form, defined as the form with the weakest weighted test information, and select from all the possible items (those that meet all the other constraints) either the item that provides the most weighted information or the item that minimizes the distance between the form TIF and the weighted dynamic target TIF.

To accomplish this, the user must first choose a number of quadrature points ($k = 1, \ldots, K$) along the ability continuum (θ) and apply weights to each of them ($w = 1, \ldots, W$). In theory, the range of K is infinite, but in practice is kept relatively small, less than 40. The process of assigning weights along the ability continuum is analogous to defining a target TIF. By way of example, one may choose to weight the points in a pattern centered around the cut score, use the number of quadrature points and weights provided by calibration software such as BILOG-MG (Zimowski, Muraki, Mislevy, & Bock, 1996) and MULTILOG (Thissen, Chen, & Bock, 2004), or any other user defined shape such as a rectangular distribution.

The weights are multiplied by the information provided by each item ($j = 1, \ldots, J$) at each quadrature point to calculate weighted item information such that

$$I_j^*(\theta_k) = w_k^* I_j(\theta_k). \tag{22.20}$$

where $I_j^*(\theta_k)$ is the weighted information for item j at the kth quadrature point, w_k is the weight applied to the kth quadrature point for all items, and $I_j(\theta_k)$ is the item information for item j at the kth quadrature point. The total weighted item information, denoted W_j^*, is the sum of the weighted item information across K quadrature points, where

$$W_j^* = \sum_{k=1}^{K} I_j^*(\theta_k) \tag{22.21}$$

The weighted test information function for test form $l(l = 1, \ldots, L)$ at each quadrature point k, denoted, F_{lkm}^* is calculated by summing the weighted item information functions for the m items on that form. This is represented in the formula

$$F_{lkm}^* = \sum_{j=1}^{m} I_j^*(\theta_k) \tag{22.23}$$

The total weighted information for form l, T_{lm}^* is the sum of weighted item information values across the m items assigned to the form.

$$T_{lm}^* = \sum_{j=1}^{m} W_j^* \qquad (22.24)$$

The weighted dynamic target test information function, D_{kn}, is determined by selecting the maximum form information function at each quadrature point, k, from among the L forms, after n total items have been assigned. That is

$$D_{kn} = Max[F_{lkm}^*] \; l = 1, 2, \ldots L \text{ and } k = 1, 2, \ldots K \qquad (22.25)$$

The weighted item information functions only need to be calculated once, prior to implementing the algorithm. The other calculations need to be updated each time an item is assigned to a form. The algorithm is described here through two iterations.

1. Assume each of the L forms has m items already assigned and that $n - 1$ total items have been assigned. To make the nth item assignment:
   a. Select the form to receive the nth item assignment.
      i. If $m = 0$, select one of the forms at random.
      ii. If $m > 0$, select the form with the smallest total weighted test information $[T_{lm}^*]$.
   b. Select the nth item and assign it to the selected form.
      i. Of all the items that do not violate any qualitative constraints for the form, select the item with the highest total weighted item information $[W_j^*]$ and assign it to the selected form
   c. Update the weighted dynamic target TIF, from D_{kn-1} to D_{kn}.
2. To make the $n + 1$th item assignment:
   a. Select the form to receive the n + 1th item assignment
      i. If only one form has m items, that form is selected.
      ii. If more than one form has m items, the form with the smallest weighted test information $[T_{lm}^*]$ is selected from among those forms.
   b. Select the $n + 1$th item and assign it as the $m + 1$ item on the selected form.
      i. Of all the items that do not violate any constraints for that form, select the item, j, that minimizes the absolute difference between that form's resulting weighted TIF and the weighted dynamic target TIF, d_{jm+1}. This is done by computing

$$d_{jm+1} = \sum_{k=1}^{K} |D_{kn} - [F_{lkm}^* + I_d^*(\theta_k)]| \qquad (22.26)$$

for each viable item (those that do not violate any constraints) and selecting the item (j) that results in the smallest value.
   c. Update the dynamic target TIF from D_{kn} to D_{kn+1}.

Equation 22.26 can easily be replaced by a formula that uses the root of the mean squared error (RMSE) instead of the sum of the absolute differences. In practice, the problem of finding the item that minimizes Equation 22.26 value is transformed into finding the maximum by subtracting the result of Equation 22.26 by the maximum result from Equation 22.26 for all items such that

$$e_{jm+1} = Max\left(Max(d_{jm+1}) - d_{jm+1}\right) j = j - m \text{ to } j. \qquad (22.27)$$

There are many ways to implement constraints on other variables ($v = 1, \ldots, V$). One simple approach to this is to dichotomize (0 or 1; viable or not viable) each variable you want to control for. This is done for each item on each form. For example, if there are to be no more than five items on a form from the first objective and a form already has five items placed on it from that objective, then make all items from the first objective non-viable (0) for that form. The product of all the dichotomous variables and the result of Equation 22.27 can then be sorted for use in an algorithm. If an item is not viable due to any single constraint and there is a viable question, non-viable questions will never be selected. If other constraints are to be prioritized, Equation 22.27 can also be transformed into a ratio using the minimum and maximum values.

Summary

When possible, it is recommended that a single form be used for small-scale testing systems. When it is necessary to assemble multiple forms using classic test theory statistics or a latent trait theory, greedy algorithms work fairly well, particularly if the target TIF or reliability can be driven by the properties of the limited item pool as well as prior goals. Finally, the use of one algorithm or one theory does not preclude the use of another. The authors often use a combination of classic test theory and latent trait theory and a mixture of assembly algorithms to assemble and evaluate forms for small-scale testing programs.

EQUATING MULTIPLE FORMS IN SMALL-SCALE SYSTEMS

In the previous section, we discussed forms assembly algorithms that could be applied to constructing a single form or multiple forms. Parallel forms may have score distributions that are so similar they cannot be statistically distinguished. Such *pre-equated* forms do not require further equating adjustments before scores and decisions are reported. Pre-equating may or may not be possible in a given instance, depending on the size and characteristics of the source item pool and the score range over which scores must be equated. It may be that concurrently assembled forms need additional statistical adjustment before they may be used interchangeably (Proposition 21). Or, it may be that successive forms of a test need to be statistically transformed to the scale of an original reference form for the purpose of maintaining the same pass–fail standard over time.

Equating Defined

Equating is a statistical method that allows scores on one form of a test to be converted to scores on another so-called reference form when the forms differ only in difficulty. The purpose of equating is to ensure that test scores from different forms of the same test can be treated the same, regardless of which form is taken. How forms are equated and whether they can truly be used interchangeably impacts the validity of the test scores. Equated forms may be administered concurrently with the reference form; consecutively, after the reference form has been administered; or both.

APA Standard 4.11 describes the responsibility of the test developer who performs statistical equating:

> When claims of form-to-form score equivalence are based on equating procedures, detailed technical information should be provided on the method by which equating functions or other linkages were established and on the accuracy of equating. (AERA, APA, & NCME, 1999, p. 57)

In this section we consider equating in more detail. Our purpose is not to provide instructions on how to equate forms, but to provide a general discussion of equating considerations for small-scale testing. For a comprehensive discussion of equating methods see Kolen and Brennan (2004).

On Having a Single Form of the Test

When it seems that a testing system requires multiple forms of a test, consideration should be given to the impact of multiple forms on validity. We have made the point several times that it is much easier for a small-scale testing system to field a single form of a test than two or more equivalent forms. We have noted that a single form does not require item or test parameters be known with the same degree of precision as in the case of multiple forms. When constructing a single form, we usually do not need to forecast item difficulties and discriminations with great precision; we are only concerned about choosing good items that are reasonably efficient and free of fatal errors. We need a good idea of the SEM and reliability, but only to the extent that we know that the error is tolerable and the reliability adequate (Kane, 1996). We may or may not feel the need to forecast mean scores and pass rates, but for small-scale programs this is usually a luxury rather than a necessity. Being content with a single test form simplifies the process of test development and eliminates the possibility of additional error introduced by the equating process.

Equating Concurrent Forms

That being said, testing systems that allow failing candidates to retake the test usually require concurrent equated forms. The decision to create concurrent forms for a very small testing program is difficult because of the expense involved and the risk of not doing it well. However, as the test sponsor and developer assess the validity propositions in Table 22.2, they may legitimately conclude that security concerns (Proposition 29) warrant equating, even when the conditions for equating are not ideal (see Kolen & Brennan [2004] for a summary). Even if the testing system administers 25 tests per year, if candidates are permitted to retake tests within a few days or months, a second form may be necessary to ensure that the test items are "equally appropriate for all test takers" (including those who have tested before; see Proposition 6) and that the knowledge and skills actually being tested are "important and relevant" (see Proposition 4).

Linking Consecutive Forms Over Time

Equating multiple generations of forms across time is known as *linking*. Linking forms is useful when a different form of a test is administered during each test administration or window. A typical large-scale example of this is the Scholostic Aptitude Test (SAT) (Kolen & Brennan, 2004). Because a different form of the SAT is used for each test administration in an effort to ensure test security, forms must be linked using equating methods so that scores have the same interpretation, regardless of when the test is taken. With very small numbers of test takers it may not be necessary to use a different equated form or set of forms at each test administration, particularly if test administration windows are narrow and widely spaced. For rapidly evolving technical domains it is often the case that changes in examination specifications obviate the need to link forms backward in time. Revised test specifications necessitate new test content, which results in new candidate expectations, and, consequently, new pass–fail standards. Under these conditions, a new standard-setting procedure may be required for each new test edition rather than an equating.

If the test developer and test sponsor determine that multiple forms are necessary, there are several things that should be considered before undertaking an equating project: (a) whether or not to use identity equating (b) how to collect the data needed to equate forms if equating is needed, and (c) selecting an appropriate equating method. Small-scale testing situations present a unique set of problems and limit the options available to address them.

To Equate or Not to Equate

Once it is determined that multiple forms are needed, the next step is to determine what equating method to use. However, in some cases, especially with small sample sizes, it may be preferable not to try to implement a statistical transformation of raw scores from one scale to another, but to simply assume that a given number correct score has the same meaning on both forms. This is known as *identity equating*. To understand the issues regarding whether to equate or not it is important to first discuss the standard error of equating.

The standard error of equating is important because it provides an estimate of equating error owing to sampling error. *Standard error of equating* is "the standard deviation of equated scores over hypothetical replications of an equating procedure in samples from a population or populations of examinees" (Kolen & Brennan, 2004, p. 232). If an infinite number of random samples were taken from a population and an equated score of Y_p^* was generated from a raw score of X_p for each sample, the standard error is the standard deviation of the equated scores Y_p^*. The standard error of equating is thus conditional on raw score X_p of the form to be equated. The larger the sample size, the smaller the standard error of equating.

There are two primary methods for estimating standard error of equating: the bootstrap method and the delta method. *Bootstrap methods* involve repeatedly and randomly sampling scores from the population, equating those scores to the reference form using an appropriate method, then calculating a standard deviation of the equated scores at each score point across all samples. As many as 1,000 or more samples may need to be generated to accurately calculate standard errors (Kolen & Brennan, 2004). Kolen and Brennan (2004) describe variations on this method for improving the accuracy of standard errors for equipercentile equating. Additionally, they provide multiple procedures and formulas for implementing the so-called delta method of equating error estimation. The *delta method* uses complex formulas that embody specific assumptions about the population distributions involved and the equating method being used.

There are two basic approaches to determining whether or not test forms need to be equated. The first is to estimate the bias that would be injected by not equating in the available sample then estimating the standard error of equating that would be obtained from an appropriate equating method. If the estimated standard error of equating is greater than the bias that would result from identity equating, then statistical equating is inappropriate. If the standard error of equating is less than the bias injected by identity equating, then equating is appropriate (Kolen & Brennan, 2004; Tsai, 1997).

A second approach is to statistically evaluate the observed raw score distributions resulting from multiple forms to determine if they can be assumed to be equivalent. If the distributions cannot be assumed to be the same, then statistical equating is performed.

Hanson (1996a) developed a set of procedures for testing the equivalence of score distributions. The rationale for these procedures is this: If the difference between two observed distributions is not greater than would be expected by sampling error, then statistical equating only introduces additional error. The Hanson procedures predict the log expected count of each possible test score on each of two or more alternate test forms using three different log-linear models (see Hanson [1996a] for details). Full and reduced versions of each model are fit to the score distributions and that fit is described using a likelihood-ratio χ^2 statistic. The "full" version of each model contains independent variables to model each test score distribution separately. The "reduced" model assumes that the distributions are the same. The full and reduced versions of each model are compared using χ^2 difference tests, where significance indicates the superiority of the full model and the need to reject the null hypothesis of equivalent distributions. Hanson (1996b) developed a small DOS-based program that calculates each of the three tests with the user providing only the score distributions. The Hanson tests are potentially useful adjuncts to the parallel forms assembly process described in the previous section.

Data Collection for Equating

We assume that small-scale test developers do not have the luxury of an equating study separate from the pretest data gathering as described. In this discussion of data collection, we assume that the context is pretest data gathering prior to final item selection, forms assembly, and scoring.

There are a number of equating data collection designs available, including the random groups, single group with counterbalancing, common-item random groups, and common-item nonequivalent groups designs. Kolen and Brennan (2004) and Petersen, Kolen, and Hoover (1989) provide comprehensive descriptions of all these designs. Which of these approaches make sense for small-scale testing systems? In light of our earlier discussion on pretest data collection, it is not surprising that we recommend the single group, single group with counterbalancing, and random groups with common items designs for concurrent equated forms, and, for equating over time, the common-item nonequivalent groups design. Random groups designs are best used with larger sample sizes (see Table 22.2 for a comparison of single-versus-multiple random group requirements) and are not considered in this discussion.

Single Group and Counterbalanced Random-Groups Designs

In a single group design, all forms are administered to all test takers. This design may be the most sound if, as discussed, there is a small item pool and all forms can be delivered in one sitting. Computerized test delivery is a great advantage in this situation. Most test drivers allow topical sections of items to be randomly selected and items selected in a random exhaustive manner within sections, with a new section selected after the previous one is complete, thus nullifying the effects of practice and fatigue on individual items while maintaining topical context. The benefits of the single group design are its efficient use of test takers, ease of administration, and lack of assumptions. There is no need to assume equivalence between groups taking different forms or to prepare blocks of representative anchor items to adjust for group differences. This design is a natural fit for systems that have a single intact cohort of examinees, such as a classroom or a workgroup. It is also useful if there is access to the entire geographic population of test takers and nonbiased participation can be solicited from the entire group in a pretest exercise. This is possible if, for example, the test is being uniformly administered through a worldwide network of proctored computerized testing centers.

The single group design can also be used to administer multiple intact tryout forms consecutively. This can be done if the test developer is concerned about holding within-form item position constant for all test takers and may be the most economical choice for equating small-n paper-and-pencil forms. One of the weaknesses of this design for multiple intact forms is that the scores on the form taken last may be affected by test fatigue or practice. To compensate for the effects of fatigue and practice, two or more counterbalanced delivery blocks can be constructed and members of the group can be randomly assigned to blocks. In this case, the examinees are randomly divided into two groups and the groups are randomly assigned to blocks. For example, Random Block 1 takes Form X, and then Form Y; Block 2 takes Form

Y, then Form X. Test takers can also be assigned to blocks using the spiraling method rather than random assignment.

Common-Item Random Groups and Common-Item Nonequivalent Groups Designs

As mentioned, a single-group design is preferred in small-n situations, particularly if the item pool is not large and can be administered to all candidates, because a single-group design is not subject to the additional sampling error caused by group differences in ability or item difficulty (Kolen & Brennan, 2004; Petersen et al., 1989). In cases where multiple intact forms cannot be avoided, common item designs can help to compensate for differences between samples of test takers and differences in form difficulty. The degree of compensation will depend on the quality of the anchor test of common items.

Regarding anchor test equating methods, APA Standard 4.13 states

> In equating studies that employ an anchor test design, the characteristics of the anchor test and its similarity to the forms being equated should be presented, including both content specifications and empirically-determined relationships among test scores. If anchor items are used, as in some IRT-based and classical equating studies, the representativeness and psychometric characteristics of anchor items should be presented. (AERA, APA, NCME, 1999, p. 58)

In the case where different forms of the examination are administered in different testing windows, representative items from the original test form are selected as common or anchor items to appear on the next test form to allow for equating of scores (linking). When concurrent forms are to be constructed using classical test theory, the use of common items can ameliorate some of the effects of sampling error with small sample sizes by accounting for some of the random differences between groups of test takers. When alternate forms are constructed using Rasch or IRT methods, common items can be used to calibrate items on the same scale.

The characteristics of the common items and their location on the test can have a decisive influence on the quality of the equating. The literature has urged that common items be proportionally representative of the overall test content, perform in the same manner as other items on the test, and appear in the same location on all forms of the test to ensure that the common items perform similarly on all forms (Cook & Petersen, 1987; Kolen & Brennan, 2004; Parshall, Dubose, & Kromrey, 1995). The number of common items is also important. In their analysis of linear equating with small samples, Parshall et al. (1995) demonstrated that a larger number of common items produced better equating results. In this study, the best equating results (lowest amount of equating error) occurred when at least 50% of total test items were common items. Kolen and Brennan suggest that common items should constitute at least 20% of the total test items. In cases where the item pool is very large, there should be at least 30 common items. With many small-scale programs, there are more items available than test takers. In that case, we recommend large item overlap between intact forms to improve equating precision, assuming that the increased item exposure is a reasonable risk in a situation where the threat to test security is not as great as the threat of non-equivalent forms.

Additional Considerations for Collecting Equating Data

Some additional considerations when selecting a data collection design are the location of the cut score (if there is one), the target test length, and method of test administration.

It is easier to equate scores near the mean of the score distribution than at the tails; that is, all else being equal, it takes fewer test scores to equate to a given level of precision near the mean of the score distribution using any method than it does to use that same method to equate scores far away from the mean. Table 22.2 shows us that an acceptably precise single-group linear equating of multiple forms near the mean may take 50 to 80 test takers, whereas a single group equating at two standard deviations away from the mean to the same level of precision may take over 264 test takers. To perform an acceptable linear equating near the mean score with randomly equivalent groups may take 200 to 300 test takers per form, whereas the same precision of equating two standard deviations from the mean may require over 600 test takers per form. The demands of equipercentile equating are more severe, but follow a similar pattern. Again, these are not hard-and-fast rules, but the clear test design message for small-n test developers is that if the testing system demands multiple equivalent forms, try to build the test so that the region of interest (e.g., the cut score) is near the mean of the score distribution).

Test length affects the required number of field test forms and test takers. If you have a smaller item pool (such as can be delivered in 2 or 3 hours), the single-groups design may be applied. With a larger item pool, it may be necessary to administer different forms to different groups, in which case you have to be concerned with the equivalency of the groups. As mentioned, it may be more economical to administer one longer tryout form rather than multiple forms given that the data requirements for the single-group design are much less severe.

The method of test delivery, whether a test is administered by paper and pencil or electronically, can affect the available sample. For example, custom administration by paper and pencil to groups of test takers places limits on the geographical reach of a field test. The population may be scattered throughout the United States, but because custom paper-and-pencil administrations are costly to conduct, secure, and attend it may become necessary to limit the field test to only a few locales. Electronic administration across a wide network of preexisting testing centers may allow access to a larger number of examinees and a more representative sample.

Selecting an Equating Method

Earlier in this section, we discussed how to determine when to use identity equating. If identity equating is not appropriate then another method must be selected.

The primary consideration in selecting an equating method in a small-sample situation is the size of the available sample and the robustness of the method to small sample sizes. Typically, one tries to compensate for meager data by making strong assumptions. Two equating methods that make the strongest assumptions are mean and linear equating (Kolen & Brennan, 2004; Livingston, 1993). Both methods assume a linear relationship between the score distributions of the two forms. With mean equating, the distributions are assumed to have the same spread and shape and differ only in their mean value. Scores are equated by finding the difference between the mean score for the reference form and the mean score for the form that is being equated, then subtracting this difference from every score from the form that is being equated. This is a simple procedure to implement, but one based on assumptions so rigid they are likely to be wrong as one moves away from the center of the score distributions. Kolen and Brennan (2004) suggested that mean equating might be useful when only one or a few scores need to be equated, such as the scores surrounding a cut point, particularly if that cut point is located near the center of the distribution.

Linear equating assumes that the shapes of the score distributions for Forms X and Y are the same, and that only the mean and standard deviations differ. If the shapes of the asymptotic score distributions for the two forms are too different then linear equating may not afford an adequate solution. Methods for calculating linearly equated scores for the different designs can be found in Crocker and Algina (1986) and Kolen and Brennan (2004).

Linear equating may be feasible for small-n testing systems for scores near the middle of the score distribution and a single group design is used (Kolen & Brennan, 2004). Linear equating with randomly equivalent or non-equivalent groups is more problematic at small-n, even for scores near the middle of the distribution.

The equipercentile method equates scores that correspond to the same percentile ranking and is appropriate for nonlinear score distributions, but is not typically recommended for small sample sizes. With small sample sizes, the larger sampling error tends to result in irregular distributions. One approach to dealing with these irregular distributions is to use a smoothing method. Presmoothing estimates the distribution of raw scores for the population prior to equating while postsmoothing estimates the distribution of the equated scores. Livingston (1993) showed that using log-linear smoothing with three moments could reduce by half the number of test takers necessary to achieve a given degree of equating accuracy using equipercentile equating. The study suggests that using equipercentile equating with smoothing may be feasible when sample sizes are small.

IRT true score equating equates expected true scores on one form to expected true scores on another using the TCCs of the two forms. A true raw score X_p is linked to a corresponding value of θ_p using the test characteristic curve for Form X. That same value of theta is linked to a true raw score of Y_p^* using the test characteristic curve for Form Y. Because fairly robust Rasch item measures may be estimated based on $N = 200$ test takers per form (see Table 22.2), true score equating might be reasonable for small-scale testing systems, using a Rasch model or modified one-parameter model (if guessing is involved and lower ability scores need to be equated). Again, the solution is likely to be better if the scores of interest are not far from the mean and the test forms are long (see Kolen & Brennan, 2004). True score equating is really the basis of weakly parallel forms construction using the algorithms in the previous section.

Finally, if Rasch or IRT ability estimation methods are used to score the test then equating between forms is not necessary because of the principle of person parameter invariance. However, items calibrated with different samples of pretest takers must be linked to the same scale either by calibrating the item sets concurrently or by calibrating separately and then transforming the calibrations from one item set onto the scale of the first item set (see Kim & Cohen, 1998; Vale 1986).

SUMMARY AND RECOMMENDATIONS

We recommend that the small-scale test developer define the test-taking population in detail prior to designing the test and certainly prior to pretesting. Steps should be taken to ensure that each pretest taker is a member of the population of interest and that the sample is representative along important dimensions such as ethnicity, gender, geography, competence level, and so on. For national or global testing systems, a widely distributed network of proctored computerized testing centers is very helpful in this regard.

It can be very useful to conduct a preliminary tryout test with a few test takers who either know or represent the target population. The tryout can be observed by the test developer, who can then interview the test takers and gain valuable insights into test content, presentation, function, and instructions. If very few pretest takers are available, or if members of the target population cannot see the test prior to the live administration and only expert reviewers are available for pretesting, this may be the best use of those resources.

When pretest data resources are scare, the test sponsor must invest financial resources into careful test design and thorough item and test review by SMEs. Experience has shown that rigorous design and development results in a greater proportion of well-formed items with useful psychometric properties.

When a pretest can be conducted, it should be given as a single operational test form if at all possible, with test takers being scored and judged following subsequent item analysis and selection and assembly of the final form(s). The pretest form should be as long as practically possible to offset the influence of any ill-formed items and to shore up reliability in the face of greater statistical uncertainty. The oversized form may be divisible into two or more forms at a later time or pared down in size after supporting data are gathered. If multiple pretest forms are necessary, a large amount of item overlap can help to relieve the effects of sampling error and may be worth the risk of greater item exposure, particularly if tests are administered in discrete time windows.

It may be wise to avoid noncompensatory scoring and grading models, if possible, in the face of greater uncertainty about item quality and test reliability. Noncompensatory models require minimum performance on each section of an examination and subject the test taker to the reliability of the least reliable of the sections. It may be safer to apply all items to a single score and a single decision.

If possible, the test should be administered in narrow, discrete windows of time so as to concentrate the available data for item analysis and form building and minimize exposure of the small item pool. Scoring and grading should be delayed until after item analysis, selection, and final form assembly. New test items should be regularly developed and included in these administrations.

Several measurement models are possible and options increase as the pretest sample size increases. Selection of a model depends on the purpose of the test, the number of data sources, the philosophy of the developer, and professional judgment. If items have been administered to one pretest sample, classical test theory, Rasch modeling, or decision theory may be useful approaches. If pretest items come from multiple forms and are being mixed and matched to create new forms, a Rasch or constrained IRT model is necessary. It may be reasonable to use a constrained two-parameter model if the object of pretesting is to model items to score subsequent test takers, as opposed to scoring the calibration sample.

Small-scale development is not congenial to developing multiple test forms where parallelism along the entire score scale is important. If the test is being used for measurement rather than classification, we recommend that only one form at a time be used and that no claims of equivalence between successive forms be made. If the test is being used for decision making, as in a credentialing examination, parallelism of multiple forms and equating near the cut score may be possible if the cut score is not too far from the mean. The need for equating forms should be carefully evaluated before proceeding. If two score distributions cannot be statistically distinguished, or if the standard error of equating is greater than the bias resulting from identity equating, identity equating is indicated. Means equating, linear equating, or Rasch-based IRT equating may be useful if identify equating cannot be supported.

REFERENCES

Ackerman. T. (1989, March). *An alternative methodology for creating parallel test forms using IRT information function.* Paper presented at the 1989 National Council on Measurement in Education annual meeting, San Francisco.

Adema, J. J. (1989). Methods and models for the construction of weakly parallel tests. *Applied Psychological Measurement, 16,* 53–63

Adema, J. J., Boekkooi-Timminga, E., & van der Linden, W. J. (1991). Achievement test construction using 0-1 linear programming. *European Journal of Operational Research, 55,* 103–111.

Adema, J. J., & van der Linden, W. J. (1989). Algorithms for computerized test construction using classical item parameters. *Journal of Educational Statistics, 14,* 279–289.

American Educational Research Associations (AERA), American Psychological Association (APA), & National Council on Measurement in Education (NCME). (1999). *Standards for educational and psychological testing.* Washington, DC: American Psychological Association.

Angoff, W. H. (1984). *Scales, norms, and equivalent scores.* Princeton, NJ: Educational Testing Service.

Baker, F. B., Cohen, A. S., & Barmish, B. R. (1988). Item characteristics of tests constructed by linear programming. *Applied Psychological Measurement, 12,* 189–199.

Barnes, L. L. B., & Wise, S. L. (1991). The utility of a modified one-parameter IRT model with small samples. *Applied Measurement in Education, 4,* 143–157.

Breyer, F. J., & Lewis, C. (1994). *Pass-fail reliability for tests with cut scores: A simplified method.* Research Report ETS-RR-94-39. Princeton, NJ: Educational Testing Service.

Cohen, J. A. (1960). A coefficient of agreement for nominal scales. *Educational and Psychological Measurement, 20,* 37–46.

Conrad, S. H. (1948). Characteristics and uses of item-analysis data. *Psychological Monographs, 62,* 1–48.

Cook, L. L., & Petersen, N. S. (1987). Problems related to the use of conventional and item response theory equating methods in less than optimal circumstances. *Applied Psychological Measurement, 11,* 225–244.

Crocker, L., & Algina, J. (1986). *Introduction to classical and modern test theory.* New York: Harcourt Brace Jovanovich.

De Champlain, A., & Gessaroli, M. E. (1998). Assessing the dimensionality of item response matrices with small sample sizes and short test lengths. *Applied Measurement in Education, 11,* 231–253.

De Champlain, A., Gessaroli, M. E., Tang, K. L., & De Champlain, J. E. (1998, April). *Assessing the dimensionality of polytomous item responses with small sample sizes and short test lengths: A comparison of procedures.* Paper presented at the annual meeting of the National Council on Measurement in Education, San Diego.

De Gruijter, D. N. M. (1986). Small N does not always justify the Rasch model. *Applied Psychological Measurement, 10,* 187–194.

Dinero, T. E., & Haertel, E. (1977). Applicability of the Rasch model with varying item discriminations. *Applied Psychological Measurement, 1,* 581–592.

Divgi, D. R. (1986). Does the Rasch model really work for multiple choice items? Not if you look closely. *Journal of Educational Measurement, 23,* 283–298.

Donoghue, J. R., & Isham, S. P. (1998). A comparison of procedures to detect item parameter drift. *Applied Psychological Measurement, 22,* 33–51.

Farish, S. J. (1984). *Investigating item stability: An empirical investigation into the variability of item statistics under conditions of varying sample design and sample size.* Occasional Paper No. 18. Hawthorn, Australia: Australian Council for Educational Research.

Feldt, L. S., & Brennan, R. L. (1989). Reliability. In R. L. Linn (Ed.), *Educational measurement,* (3rd ed., pp. 105–146). New York: MacMillan.

Feldt, L. S., Steffen, M., & Gupta, N. C. (1985). A comparison of five methods for estimating the standard error of measurement at specific score levels. *Applied Psychological Measurement, 9,* 351–361.

Forster, F. (1978, March). *Research on the Rasch measurement model.* Paper presented at the annual meeting of the American Educational Research Association, Toronto, Ontario, Canada.

Fraser, C., & McDonald, R. P. (1988). NOHARM: Least squares factor analysis. *Multivariate Behavioral Research, 23,* 267–269.

Hambleton, R. K. (1989). Principles and selected applications of item response theory. In R. L. Linn (Ed.), *Educational measurement,* (3rd ed., pp. 147–200). New York: MacMillan.

Hambleton, R. K., & Cook, L. L. (1983). The robustness of item response models and effects of test length and sample size on the precision of ability estimates, In D. Weiss (Ed.), *New horizons in testing* (pp. 31–49). New York: Academic Press.

Hambleton, R. K., & Novick, M. R. (1973). Toward an integration of theory and method for criterion-referenced tests. *Journal of Educational Measurement, 10,* 159–170.

Hambleton, R. K., & Slater, S. C. (1997). Reliability of credentialing examinations and the impact of scoring models and standard-setting policies. *Applied Measurement in Education, 10,* 19–38.

Hambleton, R. K., Swaminathan, H., & Rogers, H. J. (1992). *Fundamentals of item response theory.* Thousand Oaks, CA: Sage.

Hambleton, R. K., & Traub, R. E. (1973). Information curves and efficiency of three logistic test models. *British Journal of Mathematical and Statistical Psychology, 24,* 195–211.

Hambleton, R. K., Wright, B. D., Crocker, L., Masters, G., & van der Linden, W. J. [speakers], (1992, April). *IRT in the 1990s: Which models work best.* Invited debate presented at the annual meeting of the American Educational Research Association, Chicago.

Hanson, B. A. (1996a). Testing for differences in test score distributions using loglinear models. *Applied Measurement in Education, 9,* 305–321.

Hanson, B. A. (1996b). *Dist Diff Test: A program for testing for differences in score distributions* [Computer Program].

Harwell, M. R., & Janowski, J. E. (1991). An empirical study of the effects of small datasets and varying prior variances on item parameter estimation in BILOG. *Applied Psychological Measurement, 15,* 279–291.

Henrysson, S. (1971). Gathering, analyzing, and using data on test items. In R. L. Thorndike (Ed.), *Educational measurement* (2nd ed., pp. 130–159). Washington, DC: Council on Education.

Hulin, C. L., Lissak, R. I., & Drasgow, F. (1982). Recovery of two- and three-parameter logistic item characteristic curves: A Monte Carlo study. *Applied Psychological Measurement, 6,* 249–260.

Huynh, H. (1976). On the reliability of domain-referenced testing. *Journal of Educational Measurement, 13,* 253–264.

Jones, P. E. (2004a). *Validity propositions that must be supported in a certification exam.* Baltimore, MD: Thomson Prometric.

Jones, P. E. (Ed.) (2004b). *Thomson Prometric test development services and philosophy.* Baltimore, MD: Thomson Prometric.

Jöreskog, K. G., & Sörbom, D. (1993). *LISREL8 user's reference guide.* Chicago: Scientific Software.

Kane, M. (1996). The precision of measurements. *Applied Measurement in Education, 9,* 355–379.

Keats, J. A. (1957). Estimation of error variances of test scores. *Psychometrika, 22,* 29–41.

Kim, S., & Cohen, A. S. (1998). A comparison of linking and concurrent calibration under item response theory. *Applied Psychological Measurement, 22,* 131–143.

Kolen, M. J., & Brennan, R. L. (2004). *Test equating methods and practices.* New York: Springer-Verlag.

Kromrey, J. D., & Bacon, T. P. (1992, April). *Item analysis of achievement tests based on small numbers of examinees.* Paper presented at the annual meeting of the American Educational Research Association, San Francisco.

Lennon, R. T. (1956). Assumptions underlying the use of content validity. *Educational and Psychologic Measurement, 16,* 299–304.

Li, H. H., & Stout, W. (1994, April). *Assessment of dimensionality for partial credit polytomous items: A modification of DIMTEST.* Paper presented at the annual meeting of the National Council on Measurement in Education, New Orleans, LA.

Li, H. H., & Stout, W. (1995, April). *A version of DIMTEST to assess latent tra unidimensionality for mixed polytomous and dichotomous item response data.* Paper presented at the annual meeting of the National Council on Measurement in Education, San Francisco.

Linacre, J. M. (1992–2004). *WINSTEPS: Rasch-model computer program.* Chicago Winsteps.com.

Linacre, J. M. (1994). Sample size and item calibration stability. *Rasch Measurement Transactions, 7,* 328.

Livingston, S. A. (1993). Small-sample equating with log-linear smoothing. *Journal of Educational Measurement, 30,* 23–39.

Livingston, S. A., & Lewis, C. (1995). Estimating the consistency and accuracy of classifications based on test scores. *Journal of Educational Measurement, 32,* 179–197.

Livingston, S. A., & Zieky, M. J. (1982). *Passing scores: A manual for setting standards of performance on educational and occupational tests.* Princeton, NJ: Educational Testing Service.

Loo, R. (1983). Caveat on sample sizes in factor analysis. *Perceptual and Motor Skills, 56,* 371–374.

Lord, F. M. (1968). An analysis of the verbal scholastic aptitude test using Birnbaum's three-parameter logistic model. *Educational and Psychological Measurement, 28,* 989–1020.

Lord, F. M. (1980). *Applications of item response theory to practical testing problems.* Hillsdale, NJ: Lawrence Erlbaum Associates.

Lord, F. M. (1983). Small N justifies the Rasch model. In D. J. Weiss (Ed.), *New horizons in testing* (pp. 51–62). New York: Academic Press.

Lord, F. M., & Novick, M. R. (1968). *Statistical theories of mental test scores.* Reading, MA: Addison-Wesley.

Lorge, I., & Kruglov, L. (1952). A suggested technique for improvement of difficulty prediction of test items. *Educational and Psychological Measurement, 12,* 554–561.

Lorge, I., & Kruglov, L. (1953). The improvement of estimates of test difficulty. *Educational and Psychological Measurement, 13,* 34–46.

Luecht, R. M. (1998). Computer-assisted test assembly using optimization heuristics. *Applied Psychological Measurement, 22,* 224–236.

Luecht, R. M., & Hirsch, T. (1992). Item selection using an average growth approximation of target information functions. *Applied Psychological Measurement, 16,* 41–51.

Marshall, J. L., & Haertel, E. H. (1976). The mean split-half coefficient of agreement: A single administration index of reliability for mastery tests. Unpublished manuscript, University of Wisconsin.

McDonald, R. P. (1999). *Test theory: A unified treatment.* Mahwah, NJ: Lawrence Erlbaum Associates.

Messick, S. (1989). Validity. In R. L. Linn (Ed.), *Educational measurement,* (3rd ed., pp. 13–103). New York: MacMillan.

Millman, J., & Greene, J. (1989). The specification and development of tests of achievement and ability. In R. L. Linn (Ed.), *Educational measurement,* (3rd ed., pp. 335–366). New York: MacMillan.

Mislevy, R. J., & Stocking, M. L. (1989). A consumer's guide to LOGIST and BILOG. *Applied Psychological Measurement, 13,* 57–75.

Nevo, B. (1980). Item analysis with small samples. *Applied Psychological Measurement, 4,* 323–329.

Parshall, C. G. (2002). Item development and pretesting in a CBT environment. In Mills, C. N., Potenza, M. T., Fremer, J. J., & Ward, W. C. (Eds.), *Computer-based testing: Building the foundation of future assessments* (pp. 119–141). Mahwah, NJ: Lawrence Erlbaum Associates.

Parshall, C. G., Dubose, P., & Kromrey, J. D. (1995). Equating error and statistical bias in small sample linear equating. *Journal of Educational Measurement, 3,* 37–54.

Parshall, C. G., Kromrey, J. D., Chason, W. M., & Yi, Q. (1997, June). Evaluation of parameter estimation under modified IRT models and small samples. Paper presented at the annual meeting of the Psychometric Society, Gatlinburg, TN.

Petersen, N. S., Kolen, M. J., & Hoover, H. D. (1989). Scaling, norming and equating. In Linn, R. (Ed.), *Educational measurement.* (3rd ed. pp. 221–262). New York: MacMillan.

Rasch, G. (1960). *Probabilistic models for some intelligence and attainment tests.* Copenhagen: Danish Institute for Educational Research.

Rudner, L. (2003April). *The classification accuracy of measurement decision theory.* Paper presented at the annual meeting of the National Council on Measurement in Education, Chicago.

Samejima, F. (1977). Weakly parallel tests in latent trait theory with some criticisms of classical test theory. *Psychometrika, 42,* 193–198.

Sanders, P. F., & Verschoor, A. J. (1998). Parallel test construction using classical item parameters. *Applied Psychological Measurement, 22,* 212–223.

Sireci, S. G. (1991, October). *"Sample-independent" item parameters? An investigation of the stability of IRT item parameters estimated from small data sets.* Paper presented at the annual meeting of the Northeastern Educational Research Association, Ellenville, NY.

Smith, R. L., & Carlson, A. B. (1995). *Using judgmental estimates of item difficulty to assemble test forms with equivalent cut scores.* [Educational Testing Service Research Memorandum]. Princeton, NJ: Educational Testing Service.

Smith, R. W. (2002, April). *A multitrait-multimethod validity investigation of responses from borderline survey questions.* Paper presented at the annual meeting of the National Council on Measurement in Education, New Orleans, LA.

Smith, R. W. (2005, April). *Automated test assembly using a weighted dynamic target test information function.* Paper presented at the Annual Meeting of the National Council on Measurement in Education: Montreal, Quebec, Canada.

Smith, R. W., & Jones, P. E. (2002, April). *The robustness of forms assembly using small n: A comparison of classical methods versus Rasch.* Paper presented at the annual meeting of the National Council on Measurement in Education, New Orleans, LA.

Stocking, M. L, Swanson, L., & Pearlman, M. (1993). Application of an automated item selection method to real data. *Applied Psychological Measurement, 17,* 167–176.

Subkoviak, M. J. (1976). Estimating reliability from a single administration of a mastery test. *Journal of Educational Measurement, 13,* 265–276.

Subkoviak, M. J. (1978) Empirical investigation of procedures for estimating reliability for mastery tests. *Journal of Educational Measurement, 15,* 111–116.

Swanson, L., & Stocking, M. L. (1993). A model and heuristic for solving very large item selection problems. *Applied Psychological Measurement, 17,* 151–166.

Swaminathan, H., Hambleton, R. K., & Algina. (1974). Reliability of criterion-referenced tests: A decision-theoretic formulation. *Journal of Educational Measurement, 11,* 263–267.

Swaminathan, H., Hambleton, R. K., Sireci, S. G., Xing, D., & Rizavi, S. M. (2003). Small sample estimation in dichotomous item response models: Effect of priors based on judgmental information on the accuracy of item parameter estimates. *Applied Psychological Measurement, 27,* 27–51.

Swineford, F. (1974). *The test consultant manual.* Princeton, NJ: Educational Testing Service.

Thayn, K. S. (2001). *The effects of small sample sizes in item selection.* Unpublished masters thesis, Brigham Young University.

Theunissen, T. J. J. M. (1985). Binary programming and test design. *Psychometrika, 50,* 411–420.

Thissen, D., Chen, W., & Bock, D (2004). MULTILOG: Multiple, categorical item analysis and test scoring using item response theory (version 7) [Computer software and manual]. Chicago, Scientific Software.

Thissen, D., & Orlando, M. (2001). Item response theory for items scored in two categories. In D. Thissen & H. Wainer (Eds.), *Test scoring* (pp. 73–140). Mahwah, NJ: Lawrence Erlbaum Associates.

Thissen, D., & Wainer, H. (1982). Some standard errors in item response theory. *Psychometrika, 47,* 397–412.

Thorndike, R. L. (1982). *Applied psychometrics.* Boston: Houghton Mifflin.

Tsai, T. (March, 1997). *Estimating minimum sample sizes in random groups equating.* Paper presented atthe Annual Meeting of the National Council onMeasurement in Education, Chicago.

Vale, C. D. (1986). Linking item parameters onto a common scale. *Applied Psychological Measurement, 10,* 333–344.

van de Vijver, F. J. R. (1986). The robustness of Rasch estimates. *Applied Psychological Measurement, 10,* 45–57.

Wainer, H., & Wright, B. D. (1980). Robust estimation of ability in the Rasch model. *Psychometrika, 45,* 373–391.

Whitely, S. E. (1980). Latent trait models in the study of intelligence. *Intelligence, 4,* 97–132.

Wilson, D., Wood, R., & Gibbons, R. (1991). *TESTFACT: Test scoring, item statistics, and item factor analysis* [computer program]. Morresville, IN: Scientific Software International.

Wright, B. D., & Masters, G. N. (1982). *Rating scale analysis*. Chicago, : Institute for Objective Measurement.
Wright, B. D., & Stone, M. H. (1979). *Best test design*. Chicago, : Institute for Objective Measurement.
Wright, B. D., & Tennant, A. (1996). Sample size again. *Rasch Measurement Transactions,* 9:4, 968.
Zieky, M. (1993). Practical questions in the use of DIF statistics in test development. In P. W. Holland & H. Wainer (Eds.), *Differential item functioning* (pp. 337–347). Hillsdale, NJ: Lawrence Erlbaum Associates.
Zimowski, M. F., Muraki, E., Mislevy, R. J., & Bock, R. D. (1996). *BILOG-MG 3: Multiple-group IRT analysis and test maintenance for binary items* [computer program]. Chicago, IL: Scientific Software International.

23

Designing Ability Tests

Gale H. Roid
George Fox University

Historically, educational and psychological tests have been constructed to measure a wide range of abilities, particularly in the cognitive, physical (motor skills), and language areas. Four major steps in designing ability tests are discussed: planning, research, psychometrics, and pragmatics. Emphasis is placed on the development of individually administered and nationally standardized test batteries, based on the author's 25 years of experience in test development. The design of ability tests can be complex and involve multiple research steps conducted over a period of several years. Because these steps are rarely covered in measurement textbooks, this chapter describes important practical and technical aspects of each design phase. Also, the chapter emphasizes an important method of creating test scales using item response theory to provide test scores that are sensitive to developmental growth and change across time within the individual examinee. With focus on the steps indicated in this chapter, test developers can draw on the accumulated history of ability tests, as well as the promise of the "new rules of measurement" emerging from the refinement of item response theory methods.

Abilities are enduring characteristics of individuals, sometimes called *ability traits,* because they show considerable stability in the individual across time. Abilities can be seen in many domains of individual differences, including intellectual, cognitive, physical, athletic, communicative (e.g., language), visual, auditory, musical, mechanical, job-related, and daily-living domains. Historically, educational and psychological tests have been constructed to measure a wide range of abilities, particularly in the cognitive, physical (motor skills), and language areas (Carroll, 1993). In his classic textbook on psychological tests, Cronbach (1970) noted that ability tests are usually seen by examinees as tests on which they should "do their best." Examinees often feel that ability tests measure something more innate and less dependent on schooling in contrast with achievement tests or other types of measures. This perception seems to be common in society despite the fact that research shows mixed results on the exact degree of genetic or "innate" basis of abilities. Also, examinees usually know that there are "correct" answers and an implied standard of performance within the resulting score; thus, they may be more concerned about their responses as compared to personality, interest, and attitude scales.

Some of the most widely used ability tests are intelligence batteries such as the *Stanford-Binet Intelligence Scale* (5th ed.) (SB5; Roid, 2003) and Wechsler scales (WAIS-III; WISC-IV; Harcourt Assessment, 1997, 2003); career aptitude tests such as the *Differential Aptitude Test* (DAT; Bennett, Seashore, & Wesman, 1990) and the *Armed Services Vocational Aptitude Battery* (Larson, 1994); and motor-skills assessments such as the *Bruininks-Oseretsky Test of Motor Proficiency* (Bruininks, 2000) and the *Toddler and Infant Motor Evaluation* (Miller & Roid, 1994). Another category of widely used ability tests focuses on the development of cognitive, language, and motor abilities of infants and children (e.g., the *Bayley Scales of Infant Development* [2nd ed.], [Bayley, 1993] or the *Merrill-Palmer Revised Scales of Development*, [Roid & Sampers, 2004]).

Note that the examples of tests listed are classified as individually administered, commercially developed, and nationally standardized test batteries, mostly norm referenced, as compared to group-administered, locally developed, or criterion-referenced tests. This chapter emphasizes the design of such tests because of my 25 years of experience working as a developer or author of this type of ability test. My goal has been to compile and describe some of the most important practical and technical steps in designing publishable ability tests. I hope that the lessons I have learned from the development of published tests assists local developers, researchers, and students of testing, as well as readers who are professional test developers.

DEFINITIONS OF TERMS

In his comprehensive study of human abilities, Carroll (1993) defined *ability* in the following way:

> ...ability refers to the possible variations over individuals in the liminal levels (thresholds) of task difficulty... at which, on any given occasion in which all conditions appear favorable, individuals perform successfully on a defined class of tasks. (p. 8)

Carroll referred to *tasks* as activities in which people engage so as "to achieve a specifiable class of objectives, final results, or terminal states of affairs (p. 8)." Tasks may be self-imposed or imposed by other people or the environment, and tasks with similar attributes may form a class of tasks. If a test evaluates performance on a task, it is usually in terms of the task performance exceeding some threshold of quality such as in the measurement of task mastery or minimum competency; hence, Carroll's emphasis on task difficulty and thresholds of individual variation. The interaction of person ability and task difficulty is a fundamental notion in modern item response theory or IRT (Embretson & Reise, 2000; Lord, 1980; Rasch, 1980). Item Response Theory (IRT) is a contemporary alternative to classical test theory and has several advantages as compared to traditional psychometric methods (Embretson, 1996; Embretson & Hershberger, 1999). Advantages of IRT include sophisticated item analysis methods, prior calibration of item difficulty, and collecting a bank of precalibrated items useful for test design and computerized testing. IRT is discussed at greater length in the other sections of this chapter including the section on Designing Measures of Growth and Change under the topic of Psychometrics and also in the chapter on Designing Tests for Pass–Fail Decisions using IRT in Part IV of this book.

Some other terminology used in ability tests include examinees, examiners, items, scales, raw scores, scaled scores, standard scores, profiles, and factor indexes. *Examinees* is a general category of all people that could be examined, including any infant, child, adolescent, or adult, or anyone from a clinical or special population that is tested. The *examiner* (the professional assessor) presents the items and materials to the examinee, observes and scores the test performance, and has a critical role in the validity and authenticity of the testing session. Characteristics of both the examinees and the examiners are extremely important to specify as part of test design. *Items* are the questions or tasks administered to examinees. Sets of items form *scales* when responses are scored and summed into total raw scores.

Usually, ability test batteries have several subscales and composite scores so that several dimensions of ability are measured instead of a single total score. A typical scoring method is to count 1 point for correct answers, and form raw scores by calculating the total number of correct responses. *Scaled scores* are normalized standard scores, usually with a mean of 10 and standard deviation (SD) of 3, useful for forming a *profile* (graph of examinees' scores). Scaled scores are normalized (with distributions of scores converted to a normal curve) because many abilities are normally distributed in the population. *Normalized scores* allow comparisons among and between the scores and can reveal strengths and weaknesses in the examinee's abilities. Standard scores may be *conventional* (corrected for mean and SD in the population, such as those with mean 50 and SD 10) or *normalized* (fitted to the normal curve with specified mean and standard deviation, e.g., the intelligence quotient metric of mean 100 and SD of 15). *Factor indexes* have become more popular in recent years and are often unit-weighted sums of subscales that cluster together, as demonstrated by factor analysis (Harcourt Assessment, 2003). For additional information on factor analysis, see the section on Psychometrics, Factor Analysis.

OVERVIEW

The design of ability tests can be complex and involve multiple research steps conducted over a period of several years. Because the steps in ability test design are rarely covered in measurement textbooks, the most comprehensive source of information on a specific ability test is the published technical manual for the instrument, available separately from the test publisher (e.g., Harcourt Assessment, 1997, 2003; Roid, 2003). If the reader is developing an ability test in a field not mentioned in this chapter, the technical manual of an existing test in that field should be consulted. Publishers control the distribution of these manual to professionals, so that students may have to seek the assistance of a practicing professional or faculty member to obtain copies. The technical manual for a major test describes the planning and design steps, details of the theory, validation (including reliability of the test), and will have a chapter on the development of the instrument.

Although the steps in ability test design are varied across different domains (cognition, language, motor skills, etc.), there are some essential steps that can be grouped into four main areas: planning, research, psychometrics, and pragmatics. Each of these four areas will be discussed in turn, and major issues within each area will be listed and described.

STEP 1: PLANNING

Test development should be planned as a research project with multiple phases and substudies, and a commitment to data-based decision making. Items and tasks that seem reasonable to test developers may not capture the attention of examinees or result in a smooth test administration for examiners. For these reasons, research studies with various examinees and examiners, including computerized data analysis of results of trial testing sessions, are crucial to the design and development of an acceptable ability test. In some cases, as much as a year of planning is required before the test design can be finalized, and even then, adjustments may have to be made during subsequent steps in test development. Some key steps in planning include the definition of the purpose (or uses) of the test, specification of the users and applications expected, scheduling, and determination of the degree of specificity versus generality that should be designed into the test and its scoring system (see the Downing, chap. 1, this volume).

Definition of Purpose(s)

Most professionals use tests to make decisions about examinees. The purpose of the test may be to diagnose a condition, document strengths and weaknesses, select people for treatments or jobs, or place people in various groups or interventions. One of the classic books in psychometrics is the study of psychological tests and personnel decisions by Cronbach and Gleser (1965), which describes the characteristics and statistical methods for various testing decisions. Also, Cronbach and Gleser made a distinction between tests that have a broad versus narrow *bandwidth* (degree of generality). They showed that a test with a narrow bandwidth (e.g., a single, specific scale) may have high reliability, but less "fidelity" for evaluating a range of decisions as compared to a more broad-based battery of scales, because of the advantages gained by the intercorrelations among scales within a multiscore battery. For these reasons, the test designer should specify all of the possible decisions and purposes of the test and broaden the focus of the test (e.g., providing multiple subscores) to increase its usefulness.

Many test design projects are revisions of existing tests that already have established purposes and uses. Even when the uses are widely known (e.g., for an intelligence battery), surveys of users and experts should be conducted to assess the subtleties of these uses and their relative frequency among assessors. In some cases, two or more uses of a test may be so different that test design becomes complex, as in the case of a widely used cognitive battery for young children and adults, including the elderly (Roid, 2003). These multiple purposes may require a complex design, with different tasks and items used at various "levels," a wide range of task difficulty, and specific planning to include pilot studies with diverse examinee groups. Additionally, a new emphasis on including "teaching items" within ability batteries has emerged, where initial items in each section of the test are introduced to examinees using a teaching mode (as compared to a testing mode) with the correct answer being revealed in some cases (Roid & Miller, 1997). This method allows diverse examinees to learn the task requirements, resulting in a "level playing field" for examinees from culturally diverse backgrounds (Roid, 2003). In these cases, the test design is altered to include introductory items that are easy, straightforward, and effective as demonstrations.

Specifying the purposes of a test also has implications for planning of the validation studies. Decision-consistency reliability indexes, such as those used for criterion-referenced tests (Berk, 1984) may be required to assess the reliability of dichotomous decisions (e.g., presence or absence of mental retardation) across testing occasions. Extensive clinical studies of various special groups may have to be planned, including access to examiners and examinees in clinical or special education settings. Decisions about the type of scaling for the test scores is also important. Normative scores have some limitations, for example, for tracking growth across time, especially for low-functioning individuals or those with disabilities because they may not "catch up" with their age peers and remain at low percentile levels. In contrast, some type of criterion-referenced or IRT scale may be helpful for documenting change and growth (see the section on Psychometrics, Designing Measures of Growth and Change; also see Roid, 2003).

Specification of Users and Applications

Once the purposes of the test have been set, users of the test can be specified, including examinees, examiners, administrators who order or obtain the tests, coordinators at local sites who administer and score tests, and professionals who may review or conduct research on the instrument. Planning for the design of the test should include some type of survey of these users leading to a definition of their current needs, preferences for types of scores, styles of score reporting, materials, and ancillary products (e.g., training materials, computer software). Interviews can be obtained by phone, in focus groups, or in small groups of professionals organized at various professional meetings. Printed questionnaires can be mailed to lists of potential users. As simple as these steps may seem, they may have profound implications for the type of items, scores, format, materials, and general "look and feel" of the test. To ignore the wishes of the users is clearly unwise because the huge effort expended on a multiyear development project could be wasted and result in a test that is not used! In technical terms, the validation, and particularly the consequential validity of the test (Messick, 1980, 1989, 1995), may be compromised if it is difficult for users to administer, score, and apply to local needs.

Design in Relationship to Age or Functional Level

One of the first steps in planning an ability tests is to review the research on the developmental progression of the ability as it emerges from infancy to adulthood. If a test is used in the infant and toddler or preschool range in particular, the types of items, materials, formats, scoring, and examiner directions may be qualitatively different for different age levels. If the test is used for individuals with developmental delays, retardation, or any condition that results in performance levels that differ from the expected performance at each chronological age, test design should be sensitive to the possibility of out of level testing. In *out of level testing,* the reliability of the test can be enhanced by adapting the test items to the functional ability of the examinee, rather than to the age level or grade level of the individual (van der Linden & Glas, 2001; Wainer, 2000). This condition applies to gifted individuals as well as those with delays or disabilities (Ruf, 2003).

Conventional psychometrics and classical test theory may be less helpful than IRT models for adapting tests to the examinee's functional level (Embretson & Hershberger, 1999). In such a case, planning should include the provision of software such as WINSTEPS by Linacre and Wright (2000), BILOG and BILOG-MG by Zimowski, Muraki, Mislevy, and Bock (2003), or, for multicategory items, the MULTILOG program by Thissen, Chen, and Bock (2002).[1] With these software packages, test items can be calibrated in difficulty (and other attributes) so that performance levels can be predicted in advance and various difficulty levels designed into the test structure. Also, a thorough item collection can be assembled, field tested, and precalibrated before the final test forms are actually assembled.

Schedules and Time Frames

Experience in test development shows that each step, and particularly those requiring data collection and analysis, take longer than expected. Planning must include the setting of a time frame for each step in development, but also specify the contingencies by planning major review-and-revision points between each of the development steps. Examples of contingencies include the discovery of weak sections of a test, lack of clear dimensionality (unclear factor structure), or tryout editions of a test that are too lengthy or difficult to administer. Ample time should be given at the end of the project for a comprehensive manual (and all the data analysis required) to be completed, as required by the American Educational Research Association

---

[1]Many more programs of for IRT analysis are available including RASCAL, CONQUEST, PARSCALE, and various European versions. Updates of these programs are frequently published. The reader should consult Web sites that advertise IRT and this software, including Scientific Software International (ssicentral.com), Assessment System Corporation (assess.com), or organizations promoting the Rasch methods (rasch.org, MESA Press).

(AERA), American Psychological Association (APA), and National Council on Measurement in Education (NCME) technical standards (1999). Writing and producing a proper test manual could involve as much as 6 months to a year for a complex cognitive battery, for example (see Buckendahl & Plake, chap. 31, this volume).

Degree of Diagnostic Sensitivity

The design of a test may vary greatly depending on the degree to which test scales are designed for maximum diagnostic information versus global normative comparison of examinees. When detailed diagnostic information is needed, many subabilities and components of performance must be measured and test scores provided for them. In tests designed for more global comparisons (e.g., general cognitive status measures, screening tests, and brief or "short form" assessments), the number of subscales or profile scores may be minimized in favor of global composite scores. Creating an effective diagnostic tool requires a solid grounding of the instrument in a research-based theory or expert clinical method, and, thus, should include provision for consultation with experts in those theories or methods. One of the new approaches to diagnostic sensitivity is to examine the "quality of performance" (Roid & Sampers, 2004) as compared to emphasis on the correctness or mastery of task performance. For example, when a small child stacks a set of blocks, the quality of his or her grasp and finger dexterity may vary greatly, even among children who stack the same number of blocks. Mild developmental delays and subtle disability conditions may be diagnosed when the quality of the examinee's response is measured, not just its correctness or age appropriateness (Miller & Roid, 1994).

STEP 2: RESEARCH

Tests become more useful when they are based on a theoretical and research foundation and documentation of that foundation is provided (see Haladyna, chap. 32, in this volume). A theory of abilities in a specific domain can guide the design of the types of items and scores in a test. The theory and a body of published research on the theory can assist test users in the interpretation of the test and the pattern of resulting scores for an individual examinee. Experts familiar with a theory can serve as consultants. Future uses of the test in research can contribute to progress in the science of human abilities. For these reasons, research and the review of ability theories is an essential part of test planning.

Theory or Rationale

A foundational concept in the validation of a test is the idea that test scores measure theoretical constructs (Cronbach & Meehl, 1955; Messick, 1980, 1989, 1995) not simply a test-specific skill or factor. For example, a test of short-term verbal memory might involve the recall of a brief story presented in English. Such a test should be designed to measure the construct of short-term verbal memory of textual (or aurally perceived) language, not the specific ability to recall a specific story or set of stories. The challenge to test design is that constructs are not directly observable, but, instead, are inferred from a pattern of relationships among various measures and indicators. In test validation, measures of the same and different constructs should be correlated to verify that the test being developed does measure the targeted construct (Campbell & Fiske, 1959). Thus, in research on an intelligence battery, correlations among other intelligence tests and achievement tests should be examined. The newly developed intelligence test should correlate highly with other intelligence scales but moderately with achievement tests (Roid, 2003).

Designing a test to measure the dimensions of a specific theory of abilities assists the developer in collecting evidence of construct validity. So, for example, plans should be made in advance to be sure that a given test can be validated by correlating it with another (independently developed) measure of the same construct whether it is in the same test battery or in a test given concurrently. This is easier when the published literature includes several examples of measures of the same construct (e.g., the many short-term memory measures described by Lezak [1995]). The modern emphasis on *cross-battery assessment* in which an examinee is given tests of the same cognitive factor (construct) taken from multiple published tests is based on the same rationale (Flanagan & Ortiz, 2001). A good example of the benefits of theory-based test design is richness of assessment possible for school psychologists when they use any one of the several tests now based on the Cattell–Horn–Carroll model of cognitive abilities (McGrew & Woodcock, 2001). Subtests from several cognitive batteries can be administered to the same child and compared, including subtests from the Kaufman Assessment Battery for Children (2nd ed.) (Kaufman & Kaufman, 2004), the SB5 (Roid, 2003), or the Woodcock-Johnson Tests of Cognitive Abilities (3rd ed.) (Woodcock, McGrew, & Mather, 2001). If all three test batteries show a similar pattern of strengths and weaknesses in the child's cognitive abilities, interpretation of results would be given a strong, construct-valid basis.

Research-Based Item Writing

There is a technology of item writing that provides a research-based approach to creating items aligned with specific theories and designs (see Part III, Item Development, this volume; Haladyna, 2004; Roid & Haladyna, 1982). Schemata called *item forms* can be specified to guide item writers (or computer software) to create collections of items to measure a domain of skills. Existing items from similar ability tests or experimental measures of the targeted constructs can be "cloned" in form and function by specifying their essential form and then replacing key words, quantities, examples, situations, and so on. In my experience, it is wise to have extensive human review of any automated item collection because odd patterns of wording can result. Also, high-quality item writers can be found and contracted to write items that have creative content not found in other tests. Most publishers produce a list of topics for item writers to avoid, such as *nuclear war, death, injury to animals,* and so on (see Zieky, chap. 16, this volume). Again, in this author's experience, it is wise to hire a number of item writers on a per-item contract, as a way to identify those who show particular skill in producing effective items.

Expert Consultation

Another planning step that increases the usefulness and diagnostic power of a test is the use of experts to guide the early design of items and scales. Experts in the research literature can be combined with experts who frequently test individuals and are sensitive to tests that "work" in a clinical or applied setting. Taking an initial year for planning, literature review, and consultation at the beginning of a test design project can pay huge dividends in the usefulness of the final product. When a published test is being revised into a new edition, another type of expert is the professional who has given the test to many examinees over a long period of time. These experienced examiners can provide many practical tips and reveal any subtle flaws in the design of a previous edition. Many publishers, for example, keep files of all inquiries and correspondence in which a test is critiqued or errors documented (either real or supposed errors) to use in the design of future editions of an instrument.

Pilot Studies

Because test design is a data-based process, ideally, it is wise to conduct pilot studies to examine various test design options in the early stages of development project. Some pilot studies may involve new data collected on draft sections of the new test, or analyses of existing data sets of previous versions of the test (or tests similar to the new test). Many characteristics of test design, such as number of items in each subscale or level, can be examined through data simulation where designs are varied and compared on existing data. The best development projects study many more types of items and scales than ever reach the final published edition. Initially, pilot studies may require the drafting of three or four times as many items as are needed for the final version of a test. Long tryout editions are essential when a test is designed for a wide age range or comprehensive diagnostic system. (See Roid [2003] for a description of the multiple steps taken during the seven years of development invested in the Fifth Edition of the Stanford-Binet).

STEP 3: PSYCHOMETRICS

Ability tests have some special characteristics that require emphasis on several important psychometric methods in their design. One of the principle methods of analysis applied to ability tests is factor analysis (Gorsuch, 1983). Factor analysis and related methods such as cluster analysis and structural equation modeling (confirmatory factor analysis) are methods of determining the demonstrable dimensions among the items or subtests of an ability battery (Grimm & Yarnold, 2000). Determining dimensions is a key step when an ability test is designed to measure a specific theory or research model of abilities. If a multiscore test battery claims to be based on a theory with multiple dimensions, clearly, the data must show that the score dimensions actually approximate the theory. Early in the development of the test design, previous research findings, pilot study data, or some combination of information must suggest strongly that the test design will result in the theoretical dimensions being measured by the final version of the test. If this is not the case, the final version of the test will be open to severe criticism by psychometric reviewers.

In addition to factor analysis, other psychometric issues to resolve during test design include the choosing of a measurement (scaling) model, item analysis strategies including differential item functioning studies, plans for validation methods that will shape the test design, and fairness (e.g., fairness of interpretation across ethnic groups) of the measure. Different types of validity evidence should be collected including evidence bearing on dimensionality, item quality, scaling, and comparability, among others (see Haladyna, chap. 32, this volume). Some of these issues are briefly discussed along with suggested statistical methods that are otherwise difficult to locate in the psychometric literature. The reader should also consult the *Standards for Educational and Psychological Testing* (AERA, APA, & NCME, 1999).

Choosing a Scaling Model or Models

The nature of the ability being measured may dictate the type of scaling models considered for use. For example, when speed of performance is a critical element of an ability, timed items must be used and, yet, the distributions of response latencies (e.g., in seconds) can be non-normal and unusual indeed. Dichotomizing such distributions into slow and fast times (or "correct" versus "incorrect" speed) produces a crude scaling, so distributions of time scores need to be preserved or divided into quartiles or multipoint (integer) scales. When these timed items are mixed with conventional correct/incorrect items, a scaling model that allows for both dichotomous and polychotomous items must be found. Fortunately, many of the current IRT programs such as WINSTEPS (Linacre & Wright, 2000) and MULTILOG (Thissen et al., 2002) allow for such mixtures.

Another practical approach to ability test design is to use a mixture of different psychometric methods for certain development phases or certain sections of the test. Because a majority of test users are unfamiliar with the interpretation and use of IRT scales, using of conventional classical test-theory methods is wise for certain steps in developing the test. This author recommends presenting both classical and IRT reliability evidence, for example, because so many school districts and institutions have written standards for test selection that rely on classical reliability indexes (e.g., internal consistency indexes or test–retest correlations). If certain subscores in a test battery can be treated separately (e.g., as a supplemental diagnostic section), and they require a complex scaling model (with multipoint items, timed items, or error counts), separate methods could be employed for that section of the test as long as this practice is clearly documented in the technical manual.

Designing Measures of Growth and Change

An important new emphasis in ability test design is to create test scales that are sensitive to developmental growth and change across time within the individual examinee. Growth in ability includes the expected maturation of cognitive ability as a child develops into an adult. Growth may also be caused by educational and training experiences that enhance the individual's ability. Change in ability includes the loss of function (and its possible recovery) after accidental head injury, stroke, or other neurologic conditions. Individuals who have been in bicycle, motorcycle, or other vehicle accidents, for example, may sustain a traumatic head injury and require treatment and repeated testing to assess their loss of cognitive ability and subsequent recovery. Such conditions require IRT scaling for optimum sensitivity of the test scores to growth and change, as discussed. Also, examiners need to be alerted to the benefits of repeated testing and archiving of scores across time. Obviously, growth and change should be measured by studying the results of multiple testing sessions.

Growth is the incremental improvement in ability (e.g., cognitive functioning) across age or time span, however small the improvement may be. Growth is most obvious with repeated, individual (longitudinal) testing. Increments of growth are analogous to the changes in performance noted across age groups, from birth to adulthood, as measured by "growth curves" of test scores. *Change* is any increment of improvement, decline, or recovery in the level of ability functioning. Change may be caused by typical development, injury or illness, or response to treatment or intervention. Based on the Rasch model of item response theory (Rasch, 1980), *change-sensitive scores* were developed for the SB5 and are described in detail by Roid (2003). In developmental testing of infants and young children, change-sensitive assessment can best be implemented by using a "quality of performance" approach to item construction (Roid & Sampers, 2004). For example, a fine motor test of ability includes an item in which a young child builds a tower by stacking blocks to match a model created by the examiner. A change-sensitive assessment includes a checklist of the quality of behavior, such as the method of grasping and the alignment of blocks in the tower. Children with borderline or mild developmental delays may build the tower but show unusual methods of grasping or aligning the blocks. Change-sensitive assessment with IRT scaling improves the identification of these developmental delays and their subsequent improvement from treatment intervention. Such an assessment also identifies children who meet "milestones" (correct responses at a given age level, such as walking by 12 months of age), but still identify children with mild deficits in the quality of their performance.

Collins and Sayer (2001), Lohman (1993), and Thompson et al. (1994) have called for refined methods of measuring growth, change, and recovery of function that go beyond traditional age-normed scores. Researchers in special education desire to have a stronger link between assessment and early intervention (Bagnato, Neisworth, & Munson, 1989). Goldstein and Levin (1984) highlight the need for tests that provide fine-grained analysis of deficits in traumatic brain injury. Parents of children with disabilities and the professionals who care for them often express concern that the majority of cognitive ability measures currently available do not adequately document the quality and magnitude of potential gains by these children during the course of treatment. Most age-standardized test scores are unable to document these gains because (a) children with mild-to-moderate disabilities are functioning in the lowest standard-score categories (three standard deviations below the mean) where measurement is imprecise; or (b) age-standardized, normative scores continue to categorize the child in the lowest score ranges at each successive year of age; hence no "progress" is evident.

Change-sensitive scales and growth scores can be developed by applying IRT analyses to form an IRT scale within each domain of ability being measured (Roid, 2003). In the design of scales sensitive to growth and change in the infant or child, preliminary analyses should be conducted on pilot data using some of the commonly available IRT software (e.g., Linacre & Wright, 2000; Zimowski et al., 2003). With extensive data analysis, selection of items that fit the IRT model, and computer calibration of the difficulty of each item within each domain of ability, estimates of the ability level (the θ in IRT terms) for each examinee can be derived. These ability estimates can be converted from the z-score form used in the software into common scales used in testing (e.g., scales centered at 100, 200, or even 500 as recommended by Woodcock & Dahl [1971] and widely used today). These ability estimates allow for growth scale estimation across different sets of items at different levels of difficulty (as long as issues of vertical equating and model-data-fit are solved). Such scales are believed to have excellent scaling properties (Embretson, 1996; Woodcock et al., 2001) in comparison to age-normed scores, percentiles, or other scores derived from normative comparisons. Also, as each child increases in age, and is exposed to increasingly more difficult items, IRT scaling "corrects" for differences in sets of items by allowing transformation of raw scores onto the latent-trait dimension represented by the ability scale. Where items fit the model, estimates of ability based on different sets of items are consistent and allow for growth comparisons across time and across sets of items (Embretson & Reice, 2000; Hambleton & Swaminathan, 1985; van der Linden & Hambleton, 1997).

The Rasch model (one-parameter logistic model) fits ability-test data well, produces stable estimates of item difficulty, and provides straightforward hand scoring of tests (Linacre & Wright, 2000). In contrast, more complex models usually depend on computer scoring of patterns of item responses. The Rasch model has advantages because of its simple transformation from raw score total to IRT ability estimate (and, thus, from raw score to growth or change scale). Even with advances in portable computers, many examiners are very mobile and must be able to score tests "on the go," in hospitals or schools, and this often requires rapid hand scoring. Complex IRT models require computer estimation of the ability score because multiple item parameters (difficulty, discrimination, guessing, etc.) are taken into account. With complex IRT models, item responses are weighted and the pattern of right and wrong responses is taken into account. This complexity clearly requires computer scoring. Interestingly, the resulting computer-generated score is likely to be highly correlated with scores generated from a simpler model (such as the Rasch one-parameter model) where both complex and simple models are applied to the same test for research purposes. At this point in history, with computer software not universally available for all mobile situations, the simpler IRT models have the practical advantage.

Another advantage of growth scores is that an increasing number of published tests have now included change-sensitive scales employing the same metric—the *W*-scale originally developed by Woodcock and Dahl (1971). This Rasch-based IRT scale is centered at 500 to represent the performance of a typical fifth-grade student (10 years, 0 months), with an expansion factor of 9.1024, which allows for meaningful differences of approximately 10 points up and down the scale. This scale is used in several recently published ability tests including the *Leiter International Performance Scale—Revised* (Roid & Miller, 1997), all editions of the Woodcock-Johnson batteries (e.g., McGrew & Woodcock, 2001; Woodcock & Johnson, 1989), the SB5 (Roid, 2003), and the *Merrill-Palmer Revised Scales of Development* (Roid & Sampers, 2004). Madsen, Pomplun, Carson, and Roid (2004) recently reported an amazing consistency of the age-equivalent IRT scores from these four test batteries (e.g., values of 425 at age 2 years, 0 months, approximately 470 at age 5, as well as the expected 500 at age 10 years). Consistency in change-sensitive scores across published test batteries allows for the longitudinal tracking of examinees across time and instrumentation.

Item Analysis Approaches

One of the best methods of item analysis is to employ a comprehensive chart of item data at important stages in test design and development. The chart can include some computerized collection of item statistics, such as conventional or IRT item difficulties and model-fit statistics (Embretson & Reise, 2000; van der Linden & Hambleton, 1997), but presentation on a large, handwritten chart, or printed notebook of findings is helpful when a test design team meets in person to select items for preliminary or final editions of a test. When the test is designed for a wide age range, the chart of item statistics must be divided by age groupings so that trends across age can be determined. The chart should include statistics on differential item functioning (Holland & Wainer, 1993) across gender and ethnic groups so that fairness of assessment can be evaluated along with psychometric characteristics. Also, including comments from expert reviewers who judge the ethnic or religious bias or fairness of items is an important addition to the evaluation. Such reviews allow for screening of inappropriate illustrations, names, and depictions of ethnic individuals, topics, and content of items (e.g., note the methods used in the development of the SB5; Roid, 2003).

Including preliminary reliability statistics on groupings of items that may form subscales or total scores is an important goal in the early stages of test research. Comments from examiners in the field who have given preliminary versions of the test items should be included, perhaps in a separate collection of questionnaire responses. It is always wise to collect written feedback from any experienced examiners who administered items during the development of the test. Examiners should be asked to rate items in terms of their ease of administration and scoring and their perceptions of how the items were received by examinees. These examiners are also sensitive to subtleties in the wording of directions and formats for item scoring.

Design Strategies for Test Validation

Test design should always include test validation studies during the early stages of the test development project (AERA, APA, & NCME, 1999). This may include analyses such as preliminary calculation of internal consistency, IRT reliability across sets of items, or use of clinical validity groups to show discriminant validity at the item level. One simple index of construct validity for most ability tests is the sensitivity of items to the developmental trend across age levels. So, good approaches include χ^2 analyses of the relationship between age groupings and item responses, one-way analysis of variance of score means across age groups, or graphs of item and score means across ages or developmental levels.

To ensure reliability of an ability test, the sections of the test used to tabulate total scores (e.g., subscales, subtests, scales, or testlets as described by Wainer & Lewis [1990]) need to be of sufficient length to produce reliabilities above 0.70 (for components or testlets used as parts of summative scores), or ideally above 0.80 for subtests and above 0.90 for total scores. Adaptive tests can be designed with sections having different levels of difficulty and a preliminary estimate of ability given by an initial "routing test" (Roid, 2003). Use of a routing test may allow for more efficient measurement with higher reliability because of the advantages of adaptive the test to the ability level of the examinee (van der Linden & Glas, 2001).

STEP 4: PRAGMATICS

If you want a test to be widely used, design the test to be as practical and easy to administer and score as possible. The test cannot be so lengthy that the busy professional avoids using it on a regular basis. Most school psychologists, for example, have heavy caseloads and many students to evaluate in a given week. Most testing sessions are less than 1 hour, ideally, and even shorter for young children. Assessment professionals often travel between locations to reach examinees who may be hospitalized, at home, or elsewhere, so the test must be as portable and lightweight as possible. Any survey of assessment professionals quickly reveals these realities. For these reasons, test designers must be pragmatic and design an ability test within the time, weight, and portability constraints of the average assessment professional if there is any hope of widespread implementation of the test.

Specify the Audiences

Test design should take into account the audiences for the test, including the types of examinees and examiners, their settings and practical constraints, as well as the nature of professionals that review and select tests for these settings. The test development project must be designed to produce the quantitative evidence of test validation required by these professionals as well as producing a practical test for the examiners. The great challenge in developing publishable tests is to find creative solutions to the dilemmas that arise in the balancing of technical quality with practicality. Fortunately, the test designer has many examples of published tests to study and discover how these dilemmas have been resolved. A review of published test manuals shows that these documents are intended for several types of professionals among test users. Introductory sections are often written for readers who need a quick overview of the test, followed by test-administration details written for the practitioner involved in giving the tests. The technical sections of test manuals are often included toward the end of the manual or in separate technical supplements because they are often addressed to reviewers. Reviewers might include measurement researchers, experts writing professional test reviews (e.g., Buros Institute, 2003), selection committees, and textbooks authors.

One of the best ways to specify the audience(s) for your ability test is to conduct the surveys of users, as mentioned in the section on Planning, Specification of Users, and Applications. Mailing lists of professionals who might be targeted for survey questionnaires include a wide range of individuals representing examiners, trainers, professors, researchers, administrators, and other professionals. A purposeful tabulation of your respondents should reveal the audiences for your test, and can be used to sort responses by category to analyze varying opinions about ability tests in your content area.

Examinee Friendliness

Saying that tests can be challenging but fun for examinees is nearly an oxymoron. However, the test designer must find ways to engage the examinee and increase his or her motivation to "do their best." For young children, brightly colored materials, toys, and manipulatives (puzzles, blocks) have often been used to increase the child friendliness of ability tests (Roid, 2003). At the same time, an ability test may be used for low-functioning older individuals who perform in the child range of ability, causing the dilemma that manipulatives cannot be too babyish. Much of examinee friendliness is achieved by proper rapport building by the professional examiner, and directions for building rapport prior to testing should always be discussed in detail in the test manual. Basically, examinee friendliness is created by modernizing materials, keeping the flow of testing quick and easy, and finding age- or functional-level appropriate tasks for the examinee. Thus, adaptive tests have huge advantages in matching the functional characteristics of examinees to the proper difficulty level of items. Adaptive strategies should definitely be considered for any individually administered test, and are often implemented simply by having various age-appropriate starting and ending points in a conventional point-scale test. More sophisticated methods of adaptation include two-stage testing with a screening or routing test given first (Roid, 2003).

Another aspect of examinee friendliness is test design that anticipates the need for accommodations for disabilities. Some examinees may request changes in test administration procedures based on their legal right to accommodations, whether by extending time or changing the allowable methods of responding. At a minimum, the test manual for any ability test should provide options for accommodating examinees with severe physical or communication difficulties (see Braden & Elliott, 2003; Elliott, Braden, & White, 2001). There is a distinction between a proper test accommodation and test modifications (Thurlow, Elliott, & Ysseldyke, 1998). With *accommodations*, the basic construct validity of the ability test is retained because the focus on targeted skills (e.g., fluid reasoning, working memory, finger dexterity) remains intact. Test *modifications* are those procedures that alter the task requirements of an ability test (e.g., using easier items; making tasks into measures of attention rather than reasoning; providing clues to correct responses) (see Thurlow, Thompson, & Lazanis, chap. 28, this volume).

According to professional guidelines given in Braden and Elliott (2003), the AERA, APA and NCME (1999) standards, and other sources, the following general methods of test accommodation should be anticipated in test design:

1. **Presentation format:** For example, using sign language or other communication methods for deafness or hard-of-hearing conditions; using Braille versions of verbal items; Allowing magnification for visual impairments; or allowing repetition of items that are not repeated in standard administration.
2. **Response format:** For example, allowing examinees to gesture or point rather than use expressive language; allowing technological response devices or handwriting of verbal responses; or, for orthopedic disabilities, assisting with hand movements and responses.
3. **Using Sections of the Test:** Examples of accommodations include using only nonverbal items or subtests for examinees with English-as-a-second-language, or selecting certain tasks for individuals with severe autism, or concentrating on the more verbal sections for examinees with restricted visual capabilities.
4. **Timing:** Examples include modifying time limits, durations, lengths of testing sessions, or intervals for items and subtests.

Examiner Friendliness

Several methods of test design can enhance the possibility that examiners will find the resulting test easy to use, and, hence "friendly" to them. First, the materials of the test (stimulus pictures, manipulatives such as toys, blocks, etc., printed test booklets, and forms) must be designed with an eye to "human factors"—reading level, simplicity of design, and ease of use. For example, many published tests use similar formats for the record form (the document on which item responses, scores, and notes of test administration are written) so that examiners do not have to learn (or relearn) new formats and notations for each new test. Many ability tests have employed an "easel" type of stimulus book in which the pictures or questions for the examinee are printed on one side of an upright booklet (with built-in cardboard easel) and examiner directions on the other side. This easel format has been warmly received because it give examiners structure and clear directions (right in front of their eyes instead of in a test manual) for testing. The challenge remains to design pages, directions, scoring guides, and illustrations that examiners find easy to use.

CONCLUSIONS

Ability tests pose some difficult challenges for the test developer. Fortunately, the long history of test development, going back to the early developments of Binet and Simon (1916), Terman (1916) and the subsequent 90 years of ability test publishing provides the test designer with many models and methods. This chapter has taken a particular viewpoint, from experience in the development of more than 40 published tests, and has emphasized the individually administered, nationally standardized ability tests as models. The published technical manuals for these instruments (listed in the references) remain the most comprehensive resource for the developer, even though they are sometimes overlooked when students attempt to learn the process of test development. In this author's view, published test manuals represent a sophisticated collection of highly empirical studies of test development and validation, with each manual equivalent to multiple published articles on test characteristics.

Sadly, test manuals are sometimes seen as "advertising" by some test reviewers, and their contents and empirical studies are passed over in favor of research articles in refereed journals. Perhaps this is fair, given the potential for bias among test developers and publishers, but based on 25 years of experience, developers of published tests are typically highly competent researchers who also publish articles, and the contents of their test manuals could be published if they were divided into smaller segments. However, ethical concerns keep these authors from publishing the same studies in both the test manuals and in published articles, an admirable action, which also works to their disadvantage. My hope is that readers of this chapter find the published test manual of ability tests as a valuable, professional source of ideas for test design, rather than as commercial advertisements for a published product.

Focusing on the steps indicated in this chapter, test developers can draw on the accumulated history of ability tests, as well as the promise of the "new rules of measurement" emerging from the refinement of item response theory methods (Embretson & Hershberger, 1999). There is certainly no shortage of options when it comes to defining the purpose for a new test, planning the research and psychometrics for that instrument, and attending to the pragmatics and usefulness of its final published form. Fortunately, the test design and test development journey is a well-charted one, as demonstrated by this and the other chapters of this handbook.

REFERENCES

American Educational Research Association (AERA), American Psychological Association (APA), & National Council on Measurement in Education (NCME). (1999). *Standards for educational and psychological testing* (3rd ed.). Washington, DC: American Educational Research Association.

Bagnato, S. J., Neisworth, J. T., & Munson, S. M. (1989). *Linking developmental assessment and early intervention. Curriculum-based prescriptions*. Rockville, MD: Aspen.

Bayley, N. (1993). *Bayley Scales of Infant Development* (2nd ed.). San Antonio, TX: Harcourt Assessment.

Bennett, G. K., Seashore, H. G., & Wesman, A. G. (1984). *Differential Aptitude Tests: Technical supplement*. San Antonio, TX: Harcourt Assessment.

Berk, R. A. (Ed.). (1984). *A guide to criterion-referenced test construction*. Baltimore, MD: The Johns Hopkins University Press.

Binet, A., & Simon, T. (1916). *The development of intelligence in children* (Trans. E. Kite). Baltimore, MD: Williams & Wilkins.

Braden, J. P., & Elliott, S. N. (2003). Accommodations on the Stanford-Binet Intelligence Scales, Fifth Edition. In G. H. Roid (Ed.), *Interpretive manual: Expanded guide for the interpretation of SB5 test results* (pp. 135–143). Itasca, IL: Riverside.

Buros Institute. (2003). *Fifteenth mental measurements yearbook*. Lincoln, NE: Author.

Bruininks, R. H. (2000). *Bruininks-Oseretsky Test of Motor Proficiency*. Circle Pines, MN: American Guidance Service.

Campbell, D. T., & Fiske, D. W. (1959). Convergent and discriminant validation by the multitrait-multimethod matrix. *Psychological Bulletin, 56,* 81–105.

Collins, L. M., & Sayer, A. G. (Eds.). (2001). *New methods for the analysis of change*. Washington, DC: American Psychological Association.

Carroll, J. B. (1993). *Human cognitive abilities*. New York: Cambridge University Press.

Cronbach, L. J. (1970). *Essentials of psychological testing* (3rd ed.). New York: Harper & Row.

Cronbach, L. J., & Gleser, G. C. (1965). *Psychological tests and personnel decisions*. Urbana: University of Illinois Press.

Cronbach, L. J., & Meehl, P. E. (1955). Construct validity in psychological tests. *Psychological Bulletin, 52,* 281–302.

Elliott, S. N., Braden, J. P., & White, J. L. (2001) *Assessing one and all: Educational accountability for students with disabilities*. Reston, VA: Council for Exceptional Children.

Embretson, S. E. (1996). The new rules of measurement. *Psychological Assessment, 8,* 341–349.

Embretson, S. E., & Hershberger, S. (Eds.). (1999). *The new rules of measurement: What every psychologist and educator should know*. Mahwah, NJ: Lawrence Erlbaum Associates.

Embretson, S. E., & Reise, S. P. (2000). *Item response theory for psychologists*. Mahwah, NJ: Lawrence Erlbaum Associates.

Flanagan, D. P., & Ortiz, S. O. (2001). *Essentials of cross-battery assessment*. New York: Wiley.

Goldstein, F. C., & Levin, H. S. (1984). Intellectual and academic outcome following closed head injury in children and adolescents. *Developmental Neuropsychology, 1,* 195–214.

Gorsuch, R. L. (1983). *Factor analysis*. Hillsdale, NJ: Lawrence Erlbaum Associates.

Grimm, L. G., & Yarnold, P. R. (2000). *Reading and understanding multivariate statistics*. Washington, DC: American Psychological Association.

Haladyna, T. M. (2004). *Developing and validating multiple-choice test items* (3rd ed.). Mahwah, NJ: Lawrence Erlbaum Associates.

Hambleton, R. K., & Swaminathan, H. (1985). *Item response theory*. Boston: Kluwer.

Harcourt Assessment. (1997). *Wechsler Adult Intelligence Scale—Third Edition (WAIS-III) and Wechsler Memory Scale—Third Edition (WMS-III) technical manual*. San Antonio, TX: Harcourt Assessment.

Harcourt Assessment. (2003). *Wechsler Intelligence Scale for Children—Fourth Edition (WISC-IV)*. San Antonio, TX: Harcourt Assessment.

Holland, P. W., & Wainer, H. (Eds.). (1993). *Differential item functioning*. Hillsdale, NJ: Lawrence Erlbaum Associates.

Kaufman, A. S., & Kaufman, N. L. (2004). *Kaufman Assessment Battery for Children, Second Edition* (K-ABC-II). Circle Pines, MN: American Guidance Service.

Larson, G. E. (1994). Armed Services Vocational Aptitude Battery. In R. J. Sternberg (Ed.). *Encyclopedia of human intelligence*. New York: Macmillan.

Lezak, M. D. (1995). *Neuropsychological assessment* (3rd ed.). New York: Oxford University Press.

Lincacre, J. M., & Wright, B. D. (2000). *WINSTEPS v. 3.00: Rasch item analysis computer program manual*. Chicago: MESA.

Lohman, D. F. (1993, October). Teaching and testing to develop fluid abilities. *Educational Researcher,* 12–23.

Lord, F. M. (1980). *Applications of item response theory to practical testing problems*. Hilsdale, NJ: Lawrence Erlbaum Associates.

Madsen, D. H., Pomplun, M., Carson, A. D., & Roid, G. H. (2004). *Criterion- versus norm-referenced measurement of intelligence with the SB5*. Paper presented at the National Association of School Psychologists annual meetings, Dallas, TX, April. (Available from Riverside Publishing, 425 Spring Lake Drive, Itasca, IL 60143.)

McGrew, K. S., & Woodcock, R. W. (2001). *Woodcock-Johnson III technical manual*. Itasca, IL: Riverside.

Messick, S. (1980). Test validity and the ethics of assessment. *American Psychologist, 35,* 1012–1027.

Messick, S. (1989). Validity. In R. L. Linn (Ed.), *Educational measurement* (3rd ed., pp. 13–103). New York: MacMillan.

Messick, S. (1995). Validity of psychological assessment. *American Psychologist, 50,* 741–749.

Miller, L. J., & Roid, G. H. (1994). *Toddler and Infant Motor Evaluation (TIME)*. San Antonio, TX: Harcourt Assessment.
Rasch, G. (1980). *Probabilistic models for some intelligence and attainment tests*. Chicago: University of Chicago Press.
Roid, G. H. (2003). *Stanford-Binet Intelligence Scales, Fifth Edition technical manual*. Itasca, IL: Riverside.
Roid, G. H., & Haladyna, T. M. (1982). *A technology for test item writing*. Orlando, FL: Academic Press.
Roid, G. H., & Miller, L. J. (1997). *Leiter International Performance Scale—Revised*. Wood Dale, IL: Stoelting.
Roid, G. H., & Sampers, J. (2004). *Merrill-Palmer Revised Scales of Development (M-P-R) manual*. Wood Dale, IL: Stoelting.
Ruf, D. (2003). *Use of SB5 in the assessment of high abilities* [Assessment Service Bulletin Number 3]. Itasca, IL: Riverside.
Terman, L. M. (1916). *The measurement of intelligence: An explanation of and a complete guide for the use of the Stanford revision and extension of the Binet-Simon Scale*. Boston: Houghton-Mifflin.
Thissen, D., Chen, W-H., & Bock, R. D. (2002). *MILTILOG-7: Analysis of multiple-category response data.* [Computer software]. St. Paul, MN: Assessment Systems Corporation.
Thompson, R. J., Goldstein, R. F., Oehler, J. M., Gustafson, K. E., Catlett, A. T., & Brazy, J. E. (1994). Developmental outcome of very low birth weight infants as a function of biological risk and psychosocial risk. *Developmental and Behavioral Pediatrics, 15*(4), 232–238.
Thurlow, M. L., Elliott, J. L., & Ysseldyke, J. E. (1998). *Testing students with disabilities: Practical strategies for complying with district and state requirements*. Thousand Oaks, CA: Corwin Press.
van der Linden, W., & Glas, C. A. W. (2001). *Computerized adaptive testing*. Boston: Kluwer.
van der Linden, W., & Hambleton, R. K. (1997). *Modern item response theory*. New York: Springer-Verlag.
Wainer, H. (Ed.) (2000). *Computerized adaptive testing: A primer* (2nd ed.). Mahwah, NJ: Lawrence Erlbaum Associates.
Wainer, H., & Lewis, C. (1990). Toward a psychometrics for testlets. *Journal of Educational Measurement, 27,* 1–14.
Woodcock, R. W., & Dahl, M. N. (1971). *A common scale for the measurement of person ability and test item difficulty.* (AGS Paper No. 10). Circle Pines, MN: American Guidance Service.
Woodcock, R. W., & Johnson, M. B. (1989). *Woodcock-Johnson—Revised Tests of Cognitive Ability*. Itasca, IL: Riverside.
Woodcock, R. W., McGrew, K. S., & Mather, N. (2001). *Woodcock-Johnson III Tests of Cognitive Abilities*. Itasca, IL: Riverside.
Zimowski, M., Muraki, E., Mislevy, R. J., & Bock, R. D. (2003). *BILOG-MG 3.0 item response theory analysis* [Computer software]. St. Paul, MN: Assessment Systems Corporation.

24

Designing Computerized Adaptive Tests

Tim Davey
Mary J. Pitoniak
Educational Testing Service

This chapter focuses on computerized adaptive tests (CATs) that provide continuous scores through the use of individual items or sets of items that are naturally and inextricably linked. This focus excludes tests used for other purposes (e.g., to make classification decisions) and tests in which larger sets of unrelated items are used (e.g., in a multistage design). This chapter is written with the practitioner in mind and with an emphasis on identifying and discussing the decisions that must be made and the considerations that should be taken into account when designing and implementing a CAT. However, this discussion is necessarily preceded by a description of the psychometric methods and procedures that have been developed for administering and scoring adaptive tests. The chapter concludes with what may well be the most practical question of all: Under what conditions and circumstances is adaptive testing best employed? It is strongly argued that CAT is a good and viable choice only under very particular conditions. Indeed, many if not most of the operational problems that have occurred and been attributed to CAT are the result of it having been used under inappropriate circumstances. The intent is to provide practitioners with the information needed to realistically judge alternatives.

Computer-based tests take many forms, with designs that range from simple to quite elaborate. At the simple end of the spectrum are *linear* tests that use the computer only as means of administering what is in most respects identical to a conventional paper-and-pencil test. These tests present each examinee the same predetermined set of items in the same predetermined order, just like a conventional test. The computer merely replaces paper as the medium for displaying questions and collecting answers.

Somewhat more complicated designs assemble a different test for each examinee, but do not attempt to fit these tests to each examinee's unique measurement needs. The computer is used here to first assemble each test, often with regard to detailed specifications. Test delivery and scoring then usually follows the same procedures employed by linear tests.

Computerized adaptive testing (CAT) introduces still another level of complexity. Under CAT, different tests are again assembled for different examinees. However, with CAT each test is specifically matched to the needs of each examinee, with the goal of optimizing measurement. This is done by assembling the test as the examinee works, using information gained early in the test to influence the construction of the remainder. Every examinee's test is therefore built sequentially, with each item selected contingent on performance on the portion of the test administered so far.

Important distinctions can be drawn even within the class of adaptive test designs. For example, some CAT variants select items individually, with a decision as to what to administer next being made following each response. Other designs select items in blocks or sets, with decisions made only after each group of items is answered. Some versions of this design are called *multilevel* or *multistage* tests (Jodoin, 2003; Luecht & Nungester, 1998).

Different adaptive test designs have also evolved to best suit different measurement purposes or goals. One sort of adaptive test tries to precisely locate each examinee along a continuous performance scale; a second variety attempts only to classify examinees into two or more broad categories. Examples of the latter type of test include computerized classification testing (Kalohn & Spray, 2000), adaptive mastery testing (Kingsbury & Zara, 1999), and computerized mastery testing (Sheehan & Lewis, 1992).

The range of variation among adaptive test designs requires this chapter to narrow its focus to present more than a superficial overview. We thus concentrate on adaptive tests that provide continuous scores rather than classification decisions. Luecht (chap. 25, this volume) discusses the alternative case, where the test is designed to make accurate classification decisions.

We also focus on designs that work at the level of individual items as opposed to larger blocks. The exception to this is the allowance of groups or sets composed of items that are naturally and inextricably linked. An example is a text passage or other stimulus material to which several items are attached and upon which they collectively draw.

This chapter is written with the practitioner in mind and with an emphasis on identifying and discussing the decisions that must be made and the considerations that should be taken into account when designing and implementing a CAT. However, this discussion is necessarily preceded by a description of the psychometric methods and procedures that have been developed for administering and scoring adaptive tests. The information presented here is needed to set the context for the subsequent discussion of more practical issues. Technical detail is avoided to the extent possible.

A related matter concerns the extensive reliance of adaptive testing on Item Response Theory (IRT), a latent model whose full description lies outside the scope of this chapter. Although familiarity with IRT is not a prerequisite for what follows, it is likely to enhance understanding. The interested reader is therefore directed to any of a number of good references on the subject (e.g., Hambleton, Swaminathan, & Rogers, 1991; see also Embretson & Reise, 2000).

The discussion of decisions and issues concludes with what may well be the most practical question of all: Under what conditions and circumstances is adaptive testing best employed? It is strongly argued that CAT is a good and viable choice only under very particular conditions. Indeed, many if not most of the operational problems that have occurred and been attributed to CAT are the result of it having been used under inappropriate circumstances (Davey & Nering, 2002). The intent is to provide practitioners with the information needed to realistically judge alternatives. As observed by Parshall, Spray, Kalohn, and Davey (2002), some testing programs have turned to computer administration and CAT more because they could, rather than because they should.

OVERVIEW OF THE CAT ADMINISTRATION PROCESS

The process of administering an adaptive test consists of two basic steps: item selection and score estimation. Both are repeated each time an item is presented and answered. The first step determines the most appropriate item to administer given what is currently known about the examinee's performance level. The second step uses the response or responses (correct or

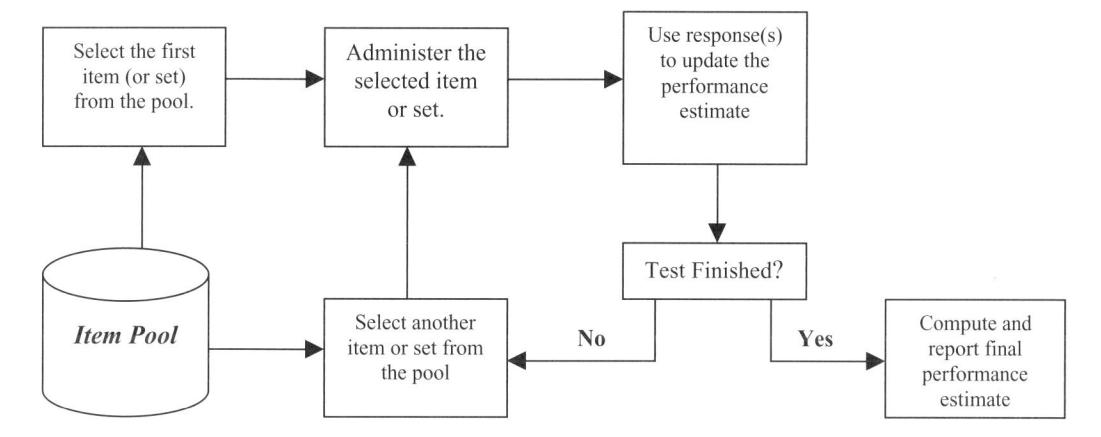

FIG. 24.1. CAT administration process.

incorrect) to the item or items just presented to refine the score or performance estimate so that the next item presented can be more appropriate still. Because answers to earlier questions determine which questions are asked later, the nature of an adaptive test successively changes as the examinee's performance level is gradually revealed.

This process is diagrammed in Figure 24.1, beginning with the selection of the first item from the *pool*, a collection of items large enough that any single examinee sees only a small fraction. More will be said later about the item pool, the size, structure, and character of which are critical to the inner workings of a CAT.

The first item or set is presented and answered, with the answer or answers then used to derive a preliminary estimate of the examinee's performance level. This estimate, although necessarily poor, is then used to determine which item or set is best administered next. The response or responses to that item or set refine the performance estimate and the process continues.

Items are selected with regard to at least three considerations.[1] The first is to optimize test efficiency by measuring examinees to appropriate levels of precision with as few items as possible. Because different researchers have applied different definitions to terms like *efficiency*, *appropriate*, and *precision*, a variety of selection procedures with different ideas regarding optimality have been developed. Some of the more important and commonly used item selection methods are briefly reviewed in this chapter.

The second consideration in item selection is that each examinee's test be properly balanced in terms of item substance or content. The intent is to have adaptive tests follow the same sort of content-driven test assembly process that has been used with conventional tests for decades. The substantive meaning of conventional test scores has long been dictated by creating test specifications that spell out the sort of items a test includes and in what proportions they are included. These specifications are often termed *constraints* because they restrict the set of possible combinations of items chosen to comprise a test. Where competing methods for achieving content balance differ is in the mechanism used to satisfy these constraints. Proper development of test assembly specifications has important practical consequences and is thus a recurring theme in this chapter.

The third item selection consideration is to protect certain items from overexposure and to encourage the use of less popular items. Without protection, some items are administered to a large proportion of examinees, whereas others are used rarely or not at all. Items used too

---

[1]For convenience, the distinction between *items* and *sets* is dropped and the use of *item* is considered as encompassing *sets* as well.

frequently can threaten test security because they may become known to examinees; items administered too seldom are a waste of resources (Davey & Nering, 2002; Mills & Steffen, 2000). Several item selection methods are briefly reviewed in this chapter.

Once an item is administered and answered, the response is used to refine an ongoing estimate of the examinee's proficiency. This estimate is necessarily rough early on, but improves as the test continues. Proficiency is estimated according to the item response model assumed to underlie test administration. A variety of different estimation methods are available, each of which carries a combination of both appealing and unappealing properties; these procedures are reviewed within the chapter.

CAT CONCEPTS AND METHODS

Researchers have developed and proposed a host of procedures and options for implementing each of the basic tasks needed to assemble and score an adaptive test. Methods have proliferated largely because none can be recommended as ideal for all testing programs and under all circumstances. Instead, the procedures that are best depend on the unique characteristics of a given testing program. Test content, item formats, examinee population, and even the subjective values of the test's owners and score users are all relevant considerations. These considerations are therefore outlined before specific procedures and test administration options are described.

The first topic covered is the central role played by test specifications, which are the foundation upon which tests are constructed. Proper test specifications completely dictate the substantive characteristics of a test, and it is impossible for a CAT to perform well unless sufficient attention has been paid to its underpinnings. The importance of test specifications is therefore a theme returned to frequently.

Guidelines for assembling the item pools from which adaptive tests are drawn are presented next. Pool size, composition, construction, and maintenance are among the topics covered. This section closes with a brief description of some of the more promising alternatives for item selection and test scoring.

Test Specifications

All tests, both conventional and adaptive, are properly developed and assembled according to test specifications, which are rules that dictate each test form's substantive properties in some detail.[2] The *Standards for Educational and Psychological Testing* (American Educational Research Association [AERA], American Psychological Association [APA], & National Council on Measurement in Education [NCME], 1999; hereafter referred to as the *Standards*), note that test specifications include the content covered by the test, proposed number of items, format(s) of items, desired psychometric properties of items, and item and section arrangement (Standard 3.3).[3] Item content pertains to the substance (e.g. knowledge, skills, attitudes, etc.) that an item measures, whereas type and format define the way that examinees are presented information, interact with that information, and render a response.

Test specifications are usually based on a taxonomy that positions each item within the substantive domain that the test measures. For example, the taxonomy for a high school–level math

---

[2]*Test form* is used throughout to denote the particular combination of items administered to any examinee. With conventional tests, large numbers of examinees are administered the same form. In contrast, adaptive forms are individually tailored and so are virtually unique to each examinee.

[3]Useful guidelines for the development of computer-based tests can also be found in Association of Test Publishers (2002).

test may include branches for arithmetic, algebra, geometry, and trigonometry items. Beneath each of these major classes, increasingly specific distinctions among items may be made at several additional levels. For example, algebra items might be classified as elementary or intermediate. Going further, an intermediate algebra item might be specified as dealing with exponents.

Specifications often dictate the number of items that each test form is to contain from each branch of the item taxonomy. The math test in our example might specify 15 items from the algebra branch, 10 from geometry, and 5 from trigonometry. Beyond this, several approaches can be taken. One approach is to follow the item taxonomy and dictate the composition of the test at greater levels of detail. For example, the 15 algebra items may be specified as including 9 intermediate and 6 elementary items, with the 9 intermediate items including 2 with exponents.

Lower level specifications might also be dealt with by what can be viewed as similar to "randomization" in sampling or experimental design. Rather than dictating the exact composition of each form, the specifications might instead stipulate only that lower levels of the taxonomy are sampled in a representative way. So, rather than insisting that each form contain exactly two exponent items, the specifications might restrict the number of such items to no more than two. The idea is to prevent exponents or any other specific area of knowledge from becoming too large a component of any form.

As detailed below, test specifications serve two equally important functions. The first is to ensure that that the test measures the appropriate construct. One source of evidence in this regard is that based on test content (AERA, APA, & NCME, 1999). Whether or not the content of a test is appropriate largely calls for judgment on the part of subject matter experts (SMEs). For example, high school mathematics teachers may conclude that a proper test simply must include items that use the quadratic equation. The required content is such an important component of the domain being measured that reasonable judgment dictates its inclusion. A collection of such judgments results in a set of assembly specifications.

The second purpose of test specifications is to ensure that different test forms constructed at different times or for different examinees each measure the same substantive composite, or combination of skills, knowledge, or attitudes. Forms that measure the same composite are usually termed *substantively parallel*. Parallelism is a necessary but far from sufficient condition for scores to be directly comparable across examinees who were tested with different forms.

Although it is often assumed that test specifications developed to ensure consistency of content also produce substantively parallel forms, this is not necessarily the case. The difference is that consistency of content is a subjective property, whereas parallelism is objective and can in theory be observed. Tests that are judged or appear to be measuring the same skills may not in fact do so. This is discussed further when the assembly procedures for conventional and adaptive tests are contrasted.

Item Types and Formats

An item's type and format describe how it looks and functions from the examinee's perspective. Although the standard multiple-choice item has long been a staple of conventional tests, a wide variety of lesser known alternatives have been developed for paper administration (Anastasi, 1988; Haladyna, 2004). The idea of experimenting with different ways of measuring a construct is not a new one. However, the added capabilities that the computer provides test developers have led to both increased interest and added variety. First and foremost, the computer allows for a true interaction between examinee and item. Whereas paper is a passive and static medium, the computer can present items and information in a dynamic and reactive way. The computer also permits the convenient display of sound and motion in addition to text and graphics. Although a number of conventional tests have included sound and video, doing so has always been inconvenient and limiting. For example, conventional tests of listening skills have had proctors play recordings for rooms full of examinees. However, this approach is prone to technical difficulties and requires examinees to be tested at the same pace and be ready for the recorded information at the same time. In contrast, the computer can reliably deliver recorded information on an individualized basis.

Recent years have seen many new item types developed to take advantage of these and other capabilities that computerized administration offers. Several reviews have been written cataloging item types developed for use with computer-based testing. Parshall, Davey, and Pashley (2000) provided an overview of several dimensions along which innovative item types may be classified and described: item format, response action, media inclusion, and level of interactivity. Zenisky and Sireci (2002) also described and provided numerous examples of novel item formats. Sireci and Zenisky (chap. 14, this volume) provide a review of validity evidence for different item types in computer-based testing. Huff and Sireci (2001) also discussed validity issues related to item formats. The reader is referred to these sources for extensive information about item types and formats.

Three considerations regarding items are important from the perspective of adaptive testing. First, a CAT must be based on items that can be immediately, and presumably electronically, scored. Because subsequent items are selected based on the observed performance on preceding items, it is necessary that items be scored in real time, as the test proceeds. Items that need to be scored by human raters are thus ruled out of CAT administration. Fortunately, technology has begun to enable electronic scoring of items that even recently required human raters. For example, a number of systems already in operational use are able to score open-ended writing samples (Burstein, 2003; Burstein, Chodorow, & Leacock, 2004; Burstein & Marcu, 2003). Other systems under development or already in use are able to assess the content of short, open-ended responses (Leacock & Chodorow, 2003), or even evaluate performance on complex, open-ended items like physician–patient interactions (Clauser & Schuwirth, 2002).

A second consideration is that CAT should work most effectively and efficiently when based on items that are discrete and independent of one another rather than grouped into units that share a common stimulus. In theory at least, the more item selection decisions that can be made, and the more often the examinee's proficiency estimate can be refined, the better. Proficiency estimates can be quite poor and unstable early in a test. Having an examinee embark on an inappropriately easy or difficult four- or five-item unit on the basis of a misleading proficiency estimate may contribute little measurement information.

A third, but less important, consideration is that the use of lengthy and complex items may contradict one goal often associated with CAT—that of obtaining a precise ability estimate across a wide range of content within a relatively short amount of time. Elaborate and time-consuming interactive items are better suited to simpler computer-based test designs than they are to adaptive testing (Parshall et al., 2002).

Item Pools

The pool is the collection of items from which adaptive tests are drawn. For a CAT to work effectively, the pool must be more than a random collection of items that have been haphazardly thrown together. It should be assembled carefully, much like an expanded version of a test form, and with regard to the same or analogous criteria. The two basic characteristics of an item pool are its size and its composition.

Pool Size

The commonly cited but not entirely congruent rules of thumb maintain that an item pool should contain the equivalent of anywhere from 5 to 10 conventional test forms (Parshall et al.,

2002; Stocking, 1994). However, the reality is a bit more complicated. An item pool should be sized with regard to a number of considerations. The first is the level of detail of the test specifications. The more detailed the test assembly rules, the larger the item pool must be to adequately support selecting tests that meet all rules. As an analogy, a store that sells a wide variety of merchandise must keep a larger inventory on hand to make sure that the shelves stay stocked.

The examinee population should also be a factor in determining pool size. A population that spans a very wide range of proficiency likely needs a larger pool than a population that is more homogenous. A sufficient number of items should be available at each level of proficiency and it takes more items to effectively cover a wider range of proficiency levels.

For similar reasons, a properly sized item pool also weighs the desired level of test precision versus the desired test length. Short and precise tests are possible only if there is a tight fit between item difficulty and an examinee's level of proficiency. Closely targeting each level of proficiency requires a larger pool just as does properly targeting more widely dispersed levels of proficiency.

A fourth consideration dictating pool size is test security. This is discussed in more detail when the issue of item exposure is examined. However, the simple version is that the smaller the item pool, the more often each item needs to be administered. If having the same items appear frequently constitutes a security concern, then larger pools are needed to distribute item use more widely (Way, Steffen, & Anderson, 2002).

None of these considerations lead naturally to hard and fast rules from which an appropriate pool size can be computed. Instead, an appropriate size must be discovered by trial and error, ideally in a simulation environment, as described later in the chapter. Simulating the administration of thousands of tests from pools of various sizes allows the test developer to judge the impact of each of these factors. Unfortunately, these judgments are specific to a particular set of content specifications, a particular examinee population, and particular choices of test length and precision. There is no simple and general equation.

Pool Composition

Item pools should be assembled with regard to the same standards and concerns as conventional test forms. Assembly therefore starts with the test specifications that dictate the number of items of each sort that each test should contain. The pool ideally ensures that a ready supply of items of each sort is available at all points of the test for examinees at all proficiency levels. Because the course of an adaptive test is often difficult to predict, this is easier said than done. However, a reasonable starting point is to construct a pool that mirrors the test specifications in terms of balance. Content areas and item types that are well represented on each test should be equally well represented in the pool. Within each item category, the items available should also ideally span a range of difficulty. This may not be possible because some content areas or item types might not permit easy (or difficult) items to be written.

Item Selection and Test Scoring Procedures

Item selection methods are the heart of the adaptive testing process. These methods determine which items each examinee is administered and in which order. Although most of the machinery that underlies CAT labors in obscurity beyond the view of examinees, the work (or at least the outcome) of item selection is all too visible. The impressions of both examinees and score users are driven primarily by the items that they see.

A complete and detailed description of all of the test administration and scoring procedures that have been proposed is beyond our current scope. Furthermore, it would likely be outdated before it appeared in print. Instead, we point out some of the more important and commonly implemented procedures and identify some trends in their development.

Early CAT procedures focused almost exclusively on optimizing test efficiency, the goal being to measure examinees as reliably as possible with as short a test as possible (Lord, 1980). The prospect of combining increased precision with decreased testing time was believed to be the most compelling advantage of adaptive testing.

However, as adaptive testing went from being researched to being operationally implemented, other test characteristics attracted attention. Item exposure rates became a concern when it was realized that certain questions were administered to virtually every examinee whereas others went entirely unused (Sympson & Hetter, 1985). Similarly, control of test content became an issue when it was noticed that tests differed across examinees not just in their level of difficulty, but also in the composite of traits that they measured (Stocking & Swanson, 1993).

The solution to these and other problems was to broaden the range of factors that were considered when items were selected. As noted, newer item selection methods now take item content and test security considerations into account as well as striving for precise and efficient measurement. Although methods for meeting each of these three considerations are often described and discussed independently, we emphasize the extent to which they interact. An ideal item selection procedure seamlessly integrates all three factors into the decision process.

Measurement Considerations

The measurement precision of adaptive tests has typically been characterized by either test information or by the standard errors of the proficiency estimates that serve as scores. Test information is an important concept of the IRT models that underlie CAT item selection and scoring (Lord, 1980). Most simply put, the information function indicates a test's strength at each value along the proficiency range. Information is high where the test is effectively distinguishing examinees. Information can also be viewed as a generalization of the classical measure of test reliability in that it recognizes that test precision varies along the proficiency scale. Information is directly related to the standard errors of examinee score estimates. However, standard errors of measurement can now be made conditional on proficiency level as well.

Test information is computed by summing the similarly defined item information functions across the items in a given test form. The item information function is interpreted in the same way as test information, but is specific to each item. Item information indicates both an item's measurement strength and where along the proficiency scale that strength is greater or lesser. A more informative, stronger item is one that classical test theory would identify as more highly discriminating. Item information is thus related to but more refined than the classical correlation between item score and total test score.

Like test information, item information recognizes that an item's strength differs across the proficiency scale. This recognition both reveals the potential of adaptive testing and provides the means of realizing that potential. An examinee is most effectively and efficiently measured by assembling a test composed of items that measure strongly at that examinee's level of proficiency. Although this principle is simple in theory, it is complicated in practice by an inconvenient paradox. If we knew an examinee's proficiency, we could build an ideal test. Of course, if we knew an examinee's proficiency, we would not need to administer that test. The solution is to proceed iteratively, using each item administered to refine a proficiency estimate and then using that proficiency estimate to refine the selection of subsequent items.

This solution is implemented in slightly different ways by the number of item selection procedures that have been developed and proposed. One of the oldest and most commonly implemented methods is termed *maximum information* (Weiss, 1974). The theory behind maximum information item selection is simple: select items that provide maximum information at the examinee's proficiency level. Items that provide information elsewhere are wasted, just like the too-difficult and too-easy items that limit the efficiency of conventional tests. The ideal test is composed of those pool items that are most informative at the examinee's true proficiency. However, because the examinee's true proficiency is unknown, items are selected to be maximally informative at each of the series of increasingly better proficiency estimates obtained as the test proceeds. This process is less than completely efficient because proficiency estimates change continuously and sometimes dramatically during testing. Items selected to be maximally informative at estimated proficiency values may end up supplying little or no information at the estimate that holds at the end of the test (and that is presumably much closer to "truth").

Maximum information item selection is easily applied. Following each response, proficiency estimate is updated based on all items answered to that point. All unused items remaining in the pool are then ranked by the amount of information they provide at the current estimate, and the top item on this list is selected for administration. As detailed below, an exposure control procedure may enter at this point to determine whether the selected item is actually administered. If the selected item is not administered, attention moves to the next highest item on the list. This continues until an item is administered and answered. A new proficiency estimate is then computed and the cycle begins again.

One drawback of maximum information is that it is very strongly drawn to highly discriminating items. These items are selected virtually to the exclusion of all others unless an effective exposure control procedure intervenes. Without exposure control, it is common for a very small proportion of the item pool to account for the vast majority of item administrations. It was in fact this problem that led to the development of exposure control procedures.

Matched difficulty is an even simpler item selection procedure that draws from the pool the item whose IRT difficulty parameter comes closest to matching the examinee's current proficiency estimate. Aside from this detail, the general operation of the adaptive test proceeds just as it does under maximum information. Because selection is based only on difficulty, item discrimination is not considered. However, it is this apparent oversight that has led to the recent revival of the procedure (Ban, Wang, & Yi, 1999). Because discrimination is not considered, selection is not drawn to a handful of highly informative items. Instead, matched difficulty uses items at much more balanced rates than does maximum information. Even so, it is advisable to implement some additional form of exposure control as a safeguard.

In theory, the trade-off for balanced exposure rates is a decrease in efficiency compared to maximum information selection. However, maximum information selection usually must be tempered by a strong exposure control procedure, which can also dramatically lower test efficiency. Comparing maximum information and matched difficulty is then a matter of determining which method of balancing exposure rates degrades efficiency the least. More is said about this when item exposure control methods are discussed in detail.

Two other methods for item selection also bear mentioning. The first of these can be termed *stratified discrimination* in that the method begins by stratifying the item pool according to item discrimination (Chang & Ying, 1999). Less informative (less discriminating) items are placed in the top stratum whereas more informative items are placed at the bottom. At each point of the test, items are selected from only one of the strata. The "active" stratum changes as the test proceeds, with early items being drawn from the top, or least discriminating, stratum. Selection is made from more discriminating strata toward the middle of the test and from the most discriminating stratum by the end. Within each stratum, items are selected by matched difficulty.

This approach offers two advantages. First, like matched difficulty, stratified discrimination generally leads naturally to more balanced rates of item use. Second, it makes sense to begin a test with less discriminating items and reserve more discriminating items until later. Early in a test we have only the roughest guess as to the examinee's level of proficiency. The problem with administering highly discriminating items at this point is that such items tend to discriminate well only over a narrow proficiency range. They are like a tightly focused spotlight that shines intensely but casts little light outside of a narrow beam. Less discriminating items are more like floodlights that illuminate a wide area but not as brightly. The idea is to use the floodlights early on to search out and roughly locate the examinee, then switch to spotlights to inspect things more closely.

Still another alternative is called *specific information* item selection. This method doles out discriminating items not by chance or according to some fixed schedule, but rather according to need (Davey & Fan, 2000). Simply put, discriminating items are reserved for examinees who, for a variety of reasons, are best served by them. To determine which examinees need discriminating items and when in the course of the test these items are needed, it is first necessary to define what constitutes normal progress through the test. *Progress,* in this context, is the rate at which a proficiency estimate becomes precise or, equivalently, the rate at which test information is accumulated as the test proceeds. Normal progress for a particular examinee is characterized by information accumulating at a rate typical of other examinees at the same proficiency level. This can be represented by a series of intermediate information values or targets that indicate how much information should have been accumulated after each item is administered. Each examinee's progress is monitored by continually comparing the amount of information actually accumulated to that required at each point throughout the test. Examinees who are making adequate progress receive moderately discriminating items to maintain that pace. Examinees who are behind schedule with respect to the target are brought back in line by more highly discriminating items. Examinees ahead of pace are administered less discriminating items.

Content Considerations

Tests chosen solely on the basis of maximizing precision are unlikely to automatically meet the test specifications that define a test's substantive properties. Content must therefore be made a consideration of the item selection process. This has most commonly been done by formalizing test specifications as a network of constraints imposed on item selection (Stocking & Swanson, 1993; van der Linden & Reese, 1998). Combinatorial optimization methods or heuristics are then used to solve the resulting problem by selecting items that jointly satisfy all constraints. The way this works in practice varies across specific procedures, but the general idea is to encourage the administration of items from content domains that have, so far in the test, been underrepresented. If, midway through a test, no items from a particular domain have been administered, pressure to do so steadily increases as the test continues.

Heuristic approaches assign a value or utility to both the measurement and content properties of an item. As described, measurement utility is usually related to the information the item provides at the current proficiency estimate. Content utility is measured by the extent to which administering an item would bring the current content "balance" of the test in line with specifications. Utility is thus high for items from so-far underrepresented content categories and low for items from overrepresented categories. The measurement and content utilities are then combined for each item in some way, yielding a total utility for each pool item. Selection then focuses on those items with greatest overall utility.

Measurement and content utilities are usually combined as a weighted sum. Varying the weights attached to the measurement or content components allows priority to be given to either measurement strength and efficiency or to exactly and repeatedly satisfying all test construction rules. Weights are generally "tuned" for a given situation through a simulation process that is described in a subsequent section.

Constraints can also be solved by *integer programming* methods, which are a set of mathematical algorithms designed for constrained optimization problems. CAT item selection is just such a problem, where the objective is to maximize test precision under the constraint that selected tests conform to test construction rules. Van der Linden described a procedure for item selection called *shadow testing* (van der Linden, 2000; van der Linden & Reese, 1998). At each choice point, this procedure selects not just the next item for administration, but rather all of the items needed to fill out the remainder of the test. This is done such that the completed test, were it administered, would satisfy all test construction rules while maximizing measurement precision at the current proficiency estimate. In fact, only one of the selected items is actually administered, with this item chosen either randomly or to maximize information at the current proficiency estimate. The proficiency estimate is then updated taking the new response into account and the process continues.

The benefit of selecting a complete test rather than a single item at each choice point is that it provides a means of looking ahead and ensuring that a solution to the test construction rules is always available. Algorithms that lack this foresight run the risk of "painting themselves into a corner" and ending up in a situation where it is necessary to break a test specification or construction rule.

In practice, little difference is found between heuristic and integer programming approaches to item selection (Robin, van der Linden, Eignor, Steffen, & Stocking, 2004). This is because both are solving the same basic problem: maximizing test precision subject to test construction rules or constraints. The integer programming solution is guaranteed to select a test that meets specifications when it is possible to do so. The heuristic approach occasionally produces a test that fails to satisfy all specifications but is more easily and flexibly implemented.

Exposure Control

The third factor in item selection is motivated mainly by test security. The individualized nature of CATs often leads to their being delivered "on demand" rather than on a small number of fixed administration dates, as has long been the norm with large-scale standardized tests. Practical and logistical considerations usually require that the same items be used repeatedly over an extended period (Davey & Nering, 2002). The concern is that repeated exposure over time leads to items becoming known to examinees, who then no longer respond as the underlying IRT model assumes. Scores that are artificially biased upward may then result.

This problem is exacerbated by the common CAT tendency to administer items with distinctly unbalanced rates. This is because most item selection procedures "prefer" items with certain characteristics. This preference may hinge on item content, item measurement properties, item pool characteristics, or some interaction of these factors. Essentially, items "compete" with one another for the attention of the selection procedure and this competition inevitably produces winners and losers.

The impact of unbalanced item exposure rates on test security is twofold. First, the more frequently an item is administered, the more likely it is to become known to examinees. Second, the popular items that are most likely to be known to examinees are those that an examinee is most likely to be administered. The role of exposure control is therefore to enhance test security by restricting the administration of the most frequently selected items and forcing administration of less commonly selected items.

Most exposure control procedures work by imposing an oversight and review process on item selection. Items are selected in the usual way according to content and measurement properties and then submitted to exposure control for approval. If the exposure control procedure determines that the selected item is not likely to be overused, it approves the item being administered. However, if the selected item is of the sort that is frequently chosen, exposure control often prohibits its use and forces a new selection. Items selected but not administered are set aside either permanently or until there is no choice but to use them. Although most exposure control procedures take the same general approach, they differ in how the decision to administer or set aside the selected item is made.

Sympson and Hetter (1985) were among the first to address the problem of exposure control and devised a solution that has proven to be the model for most subsequent development. Their solution assigned an *exposure control parameter* to each item. This parameter takes a value between 0 and 1, and dictates how often the question is administered if selected. For example, an item with an exposure parameter of 0.25 is administered only 25% of the time it is selected. An item with an exposure parameter of 1 is administered every time it is selected. Properly set, exposure parameters can precisely control not how often an item is selected, but rather how often it is actually exposed to examinees.

More recent developments in exposure control have largely followed this same strategy, differing mainly in how the exposure parameters are derived. For example, it was soon recognized that although Sympson and Hetter's method was effective in controlling the use of middle difficulty items, it was less effective for very easy or very difficult items. These items are generally selected for administration only to extreme examinees. Because such examinees are rare, extreme items are unlikely to be frequently selected. Exposure parameters for these items reflect this by allowing them to be administered every time selected. This can, for example, allow the tests of very able examinees to overlap substantially. Able examinees testing at different times could therefore easily share information with and aid one another.

One solution is to condition exposure control parameters on the proficiency of the examinee being tested. A number of procedures for doing so have been proposed (Stocking & Lewis, 1995a, 1995b; Thomasson, 1995). These procedures assign each item not a single exposure parameter but rather a series of parameters that differ across proficiency levels. A difficult item is rarely selected other than for able examinees, where it is an overwhelmingly popular choice. There is therefore little concern about it being exposed too often to moderate- and low-proficiency examinees. The item's exposure parameters across this proficiency range can be then be left near unity, allowing it to be always administered as a welcome change of pace on those rare occasions when it is selected. However, hard items must be protected against overexposure to high-performing examinees. The exposure parameters in this proficiency range are then set to restrict administration to only a small fraction of the occasions the item is selected. Exposure control parameters are set by trial and error, through a series of simulations that try to predict what happens when a test and an item pool are in operational use.

Proficiency Estimation and Test Scoring

An adaptive test uses proficiency estimates for two distinct purposes. The first is to guide item selection during the test. These estimates, termed *interim,* are updated periodically or continuously as the test proceeds and are used to identify those items that are most appropriately administered. Interim estimates are internal to the test's functioning and are usually unknown to the examinee. The second use of proficiency estimation is to produce the score seen by the examinee and/or others when the test is finished. Aptly enough, these estimates are termed *final*. Because the requirements of interim and final proficiency estimates are surprisingly different, it may well be the case that different estimation procedures are best used to obtain them.

Early in a test, interim estimates are based on few responses and so are subject to considerable instability, potentially swinging wildly from one extreme to the other as items are answered correctly or incorrectly. Although each of these different estimates represents the current best guess of where the examinee's proficiency will eventually fall at the conclusion of the test, some guesses are better than others for selecting subsequent items. For example, because most examinee proficiencies are centered around zero, an estimate biased toward zero generally leads to the administration of more informative items than does an estimate biased away from zero. In general, an interim estimate needs to be computable from even a single response, should be relatively stable even for short tests, and is ideally biased toward rather than away from average proficiency values.

Final proficiency estimation presents a very different set of circumstances. The test is complete and therefore generally long and informative enough that small-sample performance is no longer an issue. Final proficiency estimates are nearly always computable and relatively stable. However, there are other requirements. The final estimate should be as precise as possible or, equivalently, have minimal standard error. This standard error should also be known and computable. A final estimate should also distinguish among examinees to the greatest extent possible, with examinees who perform differently being scored differently.

Common choices for proficiency estimation include maximum likelihood, one of several Bayesian estimators, or one of a class of more exotic, robust methods. Maximum likelihood estimation was proposed very early in the developmental history of CAT (Birnbaum, 1968) and remains a popular choice for operational implementations. The *maximum likelihood estimate* (MLE) is determined by finding the maximum value of the *likelihood function,* which traces the probability of the observed item responses across the proficiency scale. The MLE is then the proficiency value most likely to have produced the observed response pattern. MLEs are unstable for short tests and can be unbounded (that is, they may take on values of $\pm\infty$; Yen, Burket, & Sykes, 1991). The estimate must be set to arbitrary values in these cases. The MLE has relatively minor bias toward extreme values, and multiple maxima are occasionally present (Lord, 1983; Samejima, 1993a, 1993b). Despite these shortcomings, the MLE has optimal properties that are realized as test length increases. Hence, the MLE is best used as a final estimate; it is much less suited for interim use.

Bayes mean (EAP) and Bayes mode (MAP) estimates are both quite stable and always computable (bounded). Bayes estimates are obtained by finding the mean or mode of a modified likelihood function that incorporates prior information or belief about examinees' proficiencies. Bayes estimates are biased toward central values if prior distributions are properly specified. Multiple modes are nonexistent, again assuming that a reasonable prior is set. Because of their stability with short tests, Bayes estimates are well suited for interim use. However, their bias recommends against their being used as final estimates.

Both maximum likelihood and Bayes estimates make strong assumptions about how examinees respond to test items. In practice, these assumptions are never entirely valid, and the theoretically optimal properties enjoyed by MLEs and Bayes estimates may not be realized. Accordingly, a number of alternative estimators have been developed based on the statistical theory of robustness. These include the biweight (Mosteller & Tukey, 1977) and several types of m-estimators (Jones, 1982). Robust estimators can be used in either interim or final circumstances.

Summary

This section introduced the ideas and some of the methods that underlie adaptive testing. This introduction was necessarily brief, with the reader interested in greater detail referred to a number of good resources. The books by Wainer et al. (2000), Parshall et al. (2002), Sands, Waters, & McBride (1997) and van der Linden & Glas (2000) each provide substantial detail at a very accessible level.

Most of the ideas described are extensions and refinements of those that have long been in use with conventional tests. For example, it is well recognized that the quality and usefulness of a conventional test depends strongly on the thought and care given to developing specifications that properly detail the content and format of the items that comprise the test. Good specifications are an even greater priority for adaptive tests, a fact that continues to be stressed and illustrated in the following sections. Both item pools and automated test assembly procedures have roots in conventional testing. Many conventional tests are assembled, either individually or in parallel batches, from established item banks that often contain many more items than needed to populate the forms being assembled. The important differences are that conventional forms are assembled to best serve an average examinee rather than any specific individual and that automated test assembly procedures usually produce only the rough draft of a conventional form. The final draft of a conventional form usually emerges following careful review by an experienced test developer. The absence of this review in CAT is offered below as but one of the strong arguments for the importance of solid test specifications.

IMPLEMENTING AN ADAPTIVE TEST

This section reviews some of the many choices and decisions that must be made to implement an adaptive testing program. Identifying the numerous factors that must be considered when making these decisions is emphasized. Although the presentation is linear, it quickly becomes apparent that most of these matters interact with one another. Decisions made in one area invariably affect the choices that must be made in another area, and some of the more important connections are highlighted.

We begin by examining a set of particularly sticky issues that surround the development of test specifications. This is followed by a discussion of the importance of finding the proper compromise between the conflicting priorities of short test length, precise measurement, and high test security. A short section then sketches some of the considerations in choosing item selection and test scoring procedures. The difficulties inherent in assembling, calibrating, and scaling the large cohorts of items from which pools are assembled are then briefly analyzed.

The second half of this section describes a simulation process that is recommended for informing test development decisions and evaluating their consequences. Simulations have been found to usefully predict how a test design is likely to fare operationally. A *test design* is the end product of all the decisions and choices that characterize a program in essential detail. Test designs therefore incorporate test specifications, choices for test length and precision, the selected test administration and scoring procedures, and decisions regarding item pool size and composition. A complete test design goes even further, specifying item pretest and pool replacement plans. Simulations can be used both to compare competing test designs and to determine whether a given design is likely to be successful. It is also shown that simulations are not only useful in the initial design of a program, but remain a necessary part of ongoing operational activities like item pool development and the setting of exposure control parameters.

Developing Test Specifications

The important role played by specifications for tests of all sorts was discussed previously. This section builds on that discussion and stresses the particular importance of good specifications with adaptive tests. This added importance is the result of three fundamental differences between conventional and adaptive tests. The first is that CAT item selection procedures bear complete responsibility for assembling proper test forms. There is no possibility for human review. The second is that a CAT administers each examinee a test form that is essentially unique. Because any sort of conventional equating is impossible, scores are comparable only to the extent that the forms are substantively parallel and the underlying IRT model is properly fit. Third, adaptive tests are invariably scored by IRT proficiency estimates. Some characteristics of these estimates have important and surprising implications for test specifications. Because of the increased significance of carefully crafted test specifications in the CAT format, several questions that may arise related to their functioning will now be addressed.

Can Test Specifications Be Trusted to Assemble Proper Forms?

Although computerized algorithms that have much in common with those used for CAT item selection are often used to assemble conventional tests, computer-assembled tests are generally subjected to extensive human review prior to being administered. This is because the specifications that govern automated assembly are not thought to encompass all the considerations that a human test developer brings to bear. The belief is that a human test developer knows something that the computer does not, and thus can identify problems that have escaped a test assembly algorithm.

Consider, as a practical example, a science test that an algorithm has built and that has been found to meet all test specifications. However, the reviewer notes that there is one item on the ecology of streams, another on ocean currents, and a third on lake-effect snow. The reviewer might well decide that there is simply too much water represented on this test form. The problem is that unless "water" is specifically coded as an item characteristic and controlled by the test specifications, there is no way for the computerized algorithm to have known or recognized what the reviewer realized.

The test developer can make any of several decisions at this point. The first is to conclude that the presence of three water-themed items neither materially affects the trait that the test is measuring nor is likely to be disturbing or surprising to examinees. It might be decided that water is irrelevant to what the test measures and its absence or presence does not affect the content of the test form. The form can therefore be safely administered without changes.

A second possible conclusion is that examinees would find the surplus of water unusual, but that it would not affect their performance or alter the meaning of their score. In this case, the test form might be changed for purely cosmetic reasons. Replacing one or more of the water items would not impact the substance of the test or what it measures.

Finally, it might be concluded that having too many water items is indeed a substantive problem. It might be believed that the presence of these items does impact scores and score interpretation, and that some examinees, perhaps those with greater knowledge of or experience with watery matters, benefit whereas other examinees are disadvantaged. This can certainly happen when subject matter that is intended to be peripheral to the trait being measured by a test becomes important by being inadvertently overrepresented. It would therefore be necessary to manually revise the test form and replace some of the water items with questions that have a drier context.

A surplus of water-themed items might be an idiosyncratic problem that never happens again. Should it prove persistent, it might be decided to explicitly code the mention of water in an item and control the number of such items through an additional test assembly rule. However, the decision to add test specifications must be carefully considered because each additional rule makes test assembly more difficult. More detailed specifications may also require that very large pools of items be available to support assembly. The line is a fine one; more relaxed specifications make it more likely that forms assembled by computer are judged inadequate by human reviewers, whereas more detailed specifications may constrain selection so severely that the test has little freedom to adapt to the examinee.

Insufficiently detailed specifications can lead to a range of problems of increasing severity. At the mildest end, specifications may permit the administration of tests that are unusual in some respect or that appear to be measuring something unintended. These are the kinds of forms that, on review, a test developer might change for cosmetic reasons. Administering these forms may result in little more than occasional examinee inquiries or complaints.

In more serious cases, the testing program may lose credibility among SMEs who recognize that some or many of the tests delivered do not provide evidence of validity based on test content. These deficient forms are those that a reviewer might change for content as well as cosmetic reasons.

Specifications are rarely detailed enough to deal directly with what might be termed item *enemies*. These are pairs or clusters of items that test developers would generally prohibit from appearing together on the same form. Items can be judged as enemies if they are likely to cue one another, or if they are simply too similar or redundant. Enemies are typically handled in a somewhat ad hoc manner. For example, once an item has been administered, all of its enemies might be marked as ineligible for selection later in the test.

Do Test Specifications Guarantee That Different Tests Measure the Same Trait?

At the extreme, test specifications may be so loose or poorly defined that they fail to guarantee that different forms of the same test measure the same trait. That a test accurately measures what it measures is not enough. Alternate forms of the same test must also all measure the same thing. Although form-to-form variation can be a serious problem for a conventional testing program, its effects are greatly magnified with CAT because of the number of forms that a CAT delivers. If alternate forms of a conventional test measure slightly different traits, at least the large examinee cohorts who test under the same form can be directly compared. Comparisons become difficult only between examinees who tested under different forms. With CAT virtually every examinee takes a unique test form, meaning that all scores can be less than completely comparable with one another. This sort of problem is most easily identified by computing a test–retest reliability coefficient from a sample of examinees who are each tested on two occasions spanning a short interval. This more direct estimate of test reliability should agree substantially with internal or model-based estimates based on test information and is preferred by the *Standards* (Standard 2.16; AERA, APA, & NCME, 1999).

There is also the opportunity to equate slightly misaligned forms of a conventional test. Although equating is neither intended to nor entirely effective at adjusting away extensive substantive variation across test forms, it can mitigate minor variation to some degree. CAT lacks any similar mechanism for adjusting away minor form-to-form substantive variations. Instead, CATs rely entirely on the quality and fit of the underlying IRT model to make scores comparable. IRT fit is likely to be poor if a test measures a different trait for each examinee.

Even highly detailed specifications do not ensure substantively parallel test forms. This is because forms are parallel only if the test specifications are based on and truly balance the substantive factors that influence examinee performance. Whereas a SME's ideas of proper specifications might serve to produce forms that appear to provide evidence of validity based on test content (AERA, APA, & NCME, 1999) there is no guarantee that these forms are substantively parallel. Most test specifications are based on the substantive taxonomy that organizes and drives item development. Although this framework is useful for that purpose, it does not always accurately describe the way examinees respond to items. Evidence based on response processes (AERA, APA, & NCME, 1999) should also be sought when possible.

For these reasons, adaptive test developers must have a very clear understanding of the dimensional structure of the construct being measured. The *Standards* (AERA, APA, & NCME, 1999) refer to this as evidence based on internal structure. The interaction of this structure with the examinee population must also be carefully considered, because the observed dimensionality of a test depends as strongly on the examinees as it does on the items. A test that appears distinctly multidimensional in one population can look strongly unidimensional in another. Extremely homogeneous examinee populations can make almost any test look unidimensional.

Test developers must then build their understanding of the test's dimensional structure into the specifications that govern forms assembly. Again, this is far easier said than done. Testing programs transitioning from conventional paper-and-pencil administration to CAT have a considerable advantage over programs that are being introduced as adaptive. The value of experience with a construct and an examinee population cannot be overstated. There is also great benefit to having years of operational data to analyze from a dimensional perspective.

How Does Item Response Theory Scoring Impact Test Specifications?

The fact that adaptive tests are usually scored by IRT proficiency estimates can complicate the preceding discussion in very subtle ways. Test specifications generally indicate the numbers of items of each content classification that comprise a proper test. These numbers are taken as proxies for the weight or importance of the influence of each content area or item type on total scores. Important content areas or item types exert more influence on test scores by being proportionally heavily represented in each test form. This works reasonably well, at least in theory, when all items contribute equally to total scores. This is largely the case with traditional number-right or formula scoring schemes, where correct answers count for 1 point and wrong answers count as 0 or a small but constant negative value (Wainer & Thissen, 2001).

Unfortunately, items generally do not contribute equally to IRT proficiency estimates. The exception is the one-parameter or Rasch model, where proficiency estimates are one-to-one transformations of corresponding number-right scores. Items exert equal influence on scores under the Rasch model as a direct consequence of that model's assumption that items are all equally discriminating. More general IRT models (such as the two- and three-parameter logistic models) allow discrimination, and so proportional influence, to vary across items. The logic in doing so relates to item discrimination being a measure of the "strength" with which an item measures proficiency. Stronger, more discriminating items then influence scoring more than weaker, less discriminating items. Examples can be readily devised of content areas or item types exerting influence on total scores far out of proportion to their representation in the test specifications. A handful of very discriminating items can easily outweigh the contribution of a much larger number of weak items.

A partial solution is to consider the typical strength of the items in a content area or of a certain type when test specifications are developed, adjusting the relative proportion of the test devoted to each area accordingly. Substantively important areas that are generally populated with weaker items are then weighted even more heavily in the specifications than their sheer importance dictates. Similarly, less important domains in which stronger items are the norm are downweighted in the specifications still further. The idea is to properly weight or balance not the numbers of items in each area, but rather the influence that they exert.

A more comprehensive, if difficult to implement, solution is to develop adaptive test specifications that dictate not numbers of items but instead their direct influence on measurement. This could be implemented in a number of ways, depending on how *influence* is defined and measured. For example, rather than dictating the number of items each content area is to contribute to a test, specifications could instead require each area to contribute a certain amount of measurement information (Davey & Thomas, 1996). Because information varies both across items and across the proficiency scale, this could result in different numbers of items from each content area being administered to different examinees. Although the number of items varies, their proportional influence is held constant. Much more work is needed in this area, which has so far largely escaped researchers' attention.

Test Precision and Length

Adaptive tests attempt to strike a delicate balance between several attractive but conflicting test properties. Short test length, high score precision, and efficient use of available item resources are all appealing features. Unfortunately, attempts to achieve any one of these goals often work against achieving the others. Shortening test length lessens test precision. Raising test precision leads to inefficient item use. Everything interacts with everything else, and the way that the knots are tangled depends on the characteristics of a testing program and the things that program most values.

It is useful to distinguish between two aspects of adaptive test precision, both of which can be controlled by test developers only to a rough extent. The first is the general level or degree of precision, with some tests being required to be more precise than others. For example, a test that certifies neurosurgeons should probably be more certain in its results than a test that determines whether a grade school child needs extra help learning fractions. Test *reliability* has long been the most common measure of test precision (Lord & Novick, 1968).

The second consideration of test precision is to recognize that it can vary across proficiency levels. Some of this variability is intentional and the result of a test's construction. For example, a test used to identify minimally competent examinees is assembled differently from one used to identify scholarship candidates. One provides better measurement of low-scoring examinees and the other is stronger across the upper score range. Differences in precision across score ranges are largely ignored by indices like test reliability that are averaged across score levels. However, the IRT index of precision, test information, is specific to or conditional on score level. This allows the precision target of an adaptive test to explicitly recognize that some score ranges need to be better measured than others.

Test precision targets should be based, first and foremost, on how a test's scores are used. Although uniformly high precision is hard to argue against in principle, it does not come free of charge. For example, misguided attempts to maximize test precision can jeopardize validity based on test content by valuing each item's measurement properties more highly than its content properties. High precision, particularly coupled with short test length, can also jeopardize test security by requiring a small number of very strong items to be administered repeatedly. Each testing program must strike its own compromise among the three conflicting goals of high test precision, short test length, and high security. This compromise is shaped by practical limitations, the purposes of a test, and the values of its developers and sponsors as much as it is by statistical and psychometric considerations. In general, the following statements are true:

- Short tests can be highly precise only at the expense of unbalanced item use.
- Short tests can become more balanced in their rates of item use (i.e., more secure) only at the expense of lessened test precision.
- Tests can balance item use and retain precision only by becoming longer.

It is recommended that test developers experiment with a variety of test lengths and exposure control settings to find the proper compromise that produces adequate precision without excessive test length of severely unbalanced item use rates. A simulation procedure is suggested for carrying out this evaluation.

CATs may be of either fixed or variable length. With fixed-length CATs, all examinees receive tests of the same length. For a fixed-length test, the desired level of precision must first be determined based on the usual considerations of how scores will be used. Test length is then gauged accordingly to provide that level of precision. This can be complicated because a CAT is very likely to measure different examinees with very different levels of precision. Where on the proficiency scale an examinee is located, the strength of the item pool at that level of proficiency, and even the consistency with which an examinee responds all influence precision. This last is particularly disconcerting, in that it points out that some examinees are just more easily measured than others. Examinees who respond predictably (as the underlying IRT model expects them to) are more easily measured than examinees who respond in unexpected ways. Predictable examinees can be well targeted from early in a test and presented a series of highly discriminating items. Examinees who respond in unexpected ways are more difficult to target and less likely to receive informative tests.

Variable-length testing was at least in part motivated by the inconsistency and unpredictability inherent in the measurement quality of fixed-length tests. With a variable-length test, examinees are tested until a specified level of precision is reached. Different examinees may therefore take different numbers of items, which may or may not be desirable, or acceptable, given a testing program's circumstances. One certain complication is it can be difficult to fairly administer a variable-length test under fixed time limits. Although this can be addressed by imposing time limits that are generous enough to allow even the longest test to be completed without undue pressure, examinees administered longer tests may then be more affected by fatigue than those given shorter tests.

A second problem is subtler and concerns a possible interaction between test length and bias in proficiency estimates (Parshall et al., 2002). Proficiency estimates may be underestimated for low-performing examinees who receive shorter tests and for high-performing examinees who take longer tests. In contrast, estimates may be overestimated for lower proficiency examinees who receive longer tests and higher proficiency examinees who take shorter tests. However, these effects are likely to be small and diminish as test length and precision increase.

Choosing Item Selection and Test Scoring Procedures

It was noted previously that test developers can choose from a wide variety of item selection and test scoring methodologies and that research has so far shown none of these to be uniformly superior to all others. What works best depends on the particular circumstances of a given testing program, its examinees, and the values of its sponsors and developers. The case made more broadly that all CAT design decisions are interconnected can also be made specifically in the area of item selection and scoring. It is difficult or impossible to consider item selection in isolation of test scoring and vice versa. Procedures should be evaluated and chosen as complete "packages" rather than as individual components. A test administration and scoring package requires decisions in the following areas:

1. **Item selection procedures:** These decisions specify how measurement, content, and exposure considerations combine to produce an item selection decision. Special cases such as the selection of the first item or how ties are broken when two or more items are equally ideal under the defined rules must also be handled.
2. **Test scoring procedures:** Decisions in this area should distinguish between interim and final scoring. Bayes and robust scoring procedures are well suited to interim scoring, whereas maximum likelihood scoring is best reserved for final scoring. A special case that must be resolved here is how examinees who fail to finish their tests are scored.
3. **Test stopping rules:** Tests can end under any of three conditions: a designated number of items have been administered, a designated time limit has been reached, or a specified precision target has been achieved. Test-stopping rules determine which of these conditions are applicable and how they are applied.

Again, the importance of evaluating item selection and scoring procedures jointly rather than individually cannot be stressed more strongly. An item selection procedure may work exceptionally well when paired with one interim scoring procedure but poorly when paired with another. For example, maximum information item selection is much more sensitive to the characteristics of interim proficiency estimates than are other selection procedures that are less driven by item discrimination. So to be fairly evaluated, maximum information selection needs to be paired with an appropriate interim scoring procedure. Similarly, maximum likelihood final proficiency estimates may be more dependent than alternative "robust" scoring procedures on the characteristics of the tests that have been selected by the item selection procedures. Maximum likelihood scoring may therefore dominate robust estimators in some contexts but not in others. All of these dependencies demand collective evaluation.

Item Banks, Item Pools, Item Calibration, and Pretesting

Perhaps the most important decisions facing CAT test developers deal with managing items and their associated data. An *item bank* is the collection of all items that are available to a testing program. Establishing an initial item bank, choosing an IRT model and tying all items to its scale, assembling item pools, and designing a data collection plan for continuously replenishing the item supply are all critical and time-consuming tasks. Each of these is discussed in turn.

Establishing an Item Bank

Most operational adaptive tests have enjoyed the benefit of transitioning from an existing paper-and-pencil program of long standing. A large supply of appropriate items is therefore readily available to stock the initial item bank. Although moving items from paper to computer is not without complications, it is far simpler and less costly than generating a bank from scratch.

That said, one advantage to generating an entirely new bank is the ability to allow the CAT test specifications to guide development. Banks transitioning from paper need to be evaluated to determine which items remain suitable for computerized administration and whether additional items are needed.

Parshall et al. (2002) identified several criteria for reviewing an existing item bank prior to it being used to support a CAT. The first of these was the item's continued relevance to the CAT test specifications. Conventional test specifications should be applied to CAT only with caution, and to the extent that specifications need to change, existing items may or may not remain appropriate.

A second concern is the use of items that may have been developed some time ago. Older items need to be reviewed to determine whether their content remains relevant. This is particularly true in fast-changing technical fields. Finally, items need extensive review to identify pairs or clusters of item enemies that should not appear together on the same CAT form.

Few rules of thumb can be offered for determining how large an item bank must be to adequately support a given testing program. Some programs can survive using only a single item pool, in which case the bank needs only to be large enough to spawn that one pool. However, test security concerns may require high-stakes programs to assemble and use multiple item pools, and demand banks holding thousands of items.

Calibrating and Scaling an Item Bank

Adaptive testing is highly dependent on IRT. Although IRT serves a number of purposes with CAT, its most important responsibility is to permit examinees who have taken entirely different tests to be comparably scored. At least two things must be true for this to be possible.

First, all items administered during an adaptive test must have been properly calibrated by an IRT model. Second, all item calibrations must have been linked to the same underlying proficiency scale. Satisfying both of these conditions requires that substantial data samples of the proper sort be available for each item being considered for bank membership. Data for the initial bank need to have been collected and calibrated prior to the testing program becoming operational. Most large-scale programs also carry on continuous item development and pretesting activities during operational testing to enlarge or replenish the item bank.

A number of IRT models can be considered for use. The choice depends first on the types of items being administered. For example, some IRT models are restricted to items that are scored only as right or wrong whereas other models permit more continuous or partial-credit scoring. A second consideration often taken into account is the size of the data samples available for calibration. Simpler IRT models can be successfully applied to smaller samples, whereas more complex models require larger samples. However, although small available sample sizes may require the use of a simpler IRT model, they do not justify it. Simpler models make stronger assumptions that are more likely to be violated. The resulting poor model fit can threaten the comparability of examinee scores.

Once the proper IRT model is selected and data are identified or collected, calibrations can begin. The primary issues to consider are the source and design of the data used to calibrate the initial item bank. Most testing programs end up in one of two situations. The first is to use an existing conventional test not only as a source of the initial item bank, but also as a source of calibration data. Absent an existing data source, the alternative is to engage in a large item pretesting and data collection effort. This can take place via either a paper-based or computerized test administration. The advantage of a special pretesting effort is that it allows the data collection design to be specified to ensure that all items can be jointly calibrated to a common scale. It is noted below that this is not necessarily the case with existing conventional data. The drawback to special pretesting is that examinee motivation may be suspect if no importance attaches to their efforts. This can lead to invalid calibrations.

Calibrations based on paper data can be troubling. Items may look and function very differently on computer than they did on paper. Long reading passages may require scrolling or paging on screen, or figures may lack sufficient detail when displayed. Sets of items that share a common passage or stimulus also raise concerns. Even if the passage can be presented on the screen in its entirety, it is unlikely that all of the attached items can be displayed alongside it. All such differences in appearance can translate into differences in function and examinee performance. In contrast, items that fit comfortably on a single screen, require relatively little reading, and lack figures may translate without change.

The differences between conventional paper administration and eventual use in a CAT go well beyond appearance. For example, examinees often highlight words or annotate figures in their test booklets, something impossible or clumsy in a CAT. Items on a paper form also appear in a fixed context, meaning that their position in the test and among their surrounding items is constant across examinees. Once part of a CAT, an item can appear in any position and with any surrounding items. To the extent that context and position affects paper calibrations, they improperly predict item performance in a CAT. A common example is the last few items on a paper form that many examinees struggled to finish under a tight time limit. The data on these items, and hence their calibrations, likely suggest that these items are much more difficult then they are.

The structure of existing data may be another source of concern. Even if each of a series of conventional forms can be successfully calibrated, it may not be possible to link the individual calibrations together to create a common proficiency scale. Linking of separate calibrations is analogous to test equating and makes the same requirements on data: individual calibrations must share common items or be based on common or randomly equivalent examinees. An arbitrarily chosen set of conventional test forms may or may not satisfy any of these conditions. In many cases initial calibrations must be stitched together like a patchwork quilt to form a common proficiency scale. The difficulties in doing so should be kept in mind when existing items and data are being considered for inclusion in an initial bank or when data collection on newly developed items is being planned.

Despite these challenges, it is possible to use existing paper data as the basis of initial bank calibrations, provided test developers recognize the potential for difficulty and work cautiously. However, the initial item bank is usually insufficient to support a program indefinitely. This is because security concerns often require that heavily used items be given lengthy vacations or retired from the bank altogether. Banks may therefore continually lose their most effective members as highly discriminating (and hence heavily used) items are removed either temporarily or permanently. Additional items must be developed both to augment a bank that was initially too small and to make good losses owing to retirement.

Prior to operational use, new items must be pretested, calibrated, and linked to the common scale. Pretest data on newly created items may be obtained either through a freestanding pretest or by pretesting within or alongside operational tests. Freestanding pretests are subject to the same caveats applied to special data collections. Examinees must be reasonably motivated and there must be a way of getting the new item calibrations onto the common scale. Including some number of items that are already calibrated on scale alongside the new items is a common linking design.

Pretesting alongside operational testing has so far been the preferred approach for large-scale programs. This is both to address concerns regarding examinee motivation and to avoid the effort and expense of special pretest data collections. An ideal design for collecting item pretest data has the following features:

1. **The calibration sample is representative of the entire examinee population.** Although IRT is sometimes purported as providing "person-free item measurement," such is never observed in practice. Because the location and scale of item parameter estimates are indeterminate, calibrations are indeed affected by the characteristics of the examinee sample.[4] It is permissible for calibration samples to differ in the mean or variance of their proficiency distributions. These differences are easily corrected for by properly linking newly calibrated items to the current scale. However, scale linking cannot correct a flawed pretest sampling design.

2. **Calibration samples are sufficiently large.** Although there is published research regarding the examinee sample sizes required to support calibrations (see Jones, Smith, & Talley, chap. 22, this volume), these studies might be read as providing only general guidelines. In practice, the required sample size depends heavily both on the data collection design and on the particular calibration methods. Weaker data collection designs (sparser response matrices, less representative examinee samples, etc.) require larger samples and stronger designs require smaller samples.

3. **Pretest items are not easily identifiable.** If pretest items are clearly identifiable, there is no guarantee that examinees who recognized that the items do not contribute to scores respond to the best of their ability. Pretest items then appear to be more difficult than they actually are. It is therefore important that pretest items be properly disguised. Examinees need to know that some of the items they are administered do not count toward their score, but they should be very uncertain where these items are located.

---

[4]Only the location is indeterminate under the one-parameter or Rasch model.

4. **Pretest items do not interfere with operational measurement.** By definition, the performance characteristics of pretest items are unknown. This is why these items cannot and should not contribute to scoring. Although most new items function properly, a handful may negatively affect an examinee's performance on surrounding items. For example, an item may be exceptionally difficult and so require an exceptionally long time to answer. Time lost here can certainly affect overall performance. It is therefore best that pretest items be isolated from operational items. The challenge is to do so without making the pretest section easily identifiable.

A choice must be made on the placement of the pretest items in relation to the operational items (items that contribute to the examinee's score). One approach is to place the pretest items within a separate section. Generally, examinees are told that a portion of their test does not count toward their score, but are not told where the pretest items are located. Because the pretest section is isolated from the operational test, it is less likely to affect the performance that counts, thereby satisfying condition (4). However, despite efforts to camouflage the pretest section, it remains possible that some examinees could spot it for what it is, violating condition (3). Their resulting unmotivated performance may affect item calibration.

An alternative is to more completely disguise pretest items by embedding them within or appended to operational items in a single section. Although embedding decreases the possibility of examinees identifying pretest items as such, it sharply increases the possibility of interference with operational performance. Appending items to the end of an operational section theoretically reduces their impact, but still runs the risks of affecting an examinee's timing and pacing. It also increases the chances of a block of pretest items being spotted as what it is. Furthermore, relegating pretest items to the end of a test when examinees are fatigued and pressed for time makes it more likely that calibrations misestimate item difficulty.[5]

Regardless of the method used, it is critical to carefully consider the amount of operational pretesting that needs to be done to keep a CAT pool large enough to support continued testing. Parshall et al. (2002) provided several guidelines for calculating how many items are needed to make the CAT self-sustaining. First, it must be decided how much of each examinee's total test can be devoted to pretesting. A ceiling of one fourth the testing time is suggested; exceeding that amount is seen as unfair to the examinee, because any time allotted to pretest items cannot be used for operational items. Second, an estimate should be made of the proportion of the item pool that the average test length represents. For example, a fixed test length of 40 items represents one fifth of an item pool containing 200 items. Third, the number of examinee responses required to obtain a reliable estimate of an item's parameters should be calculated. For a testing program using the Rasch model, approximately 100 to 300 responses may be needed. If the three-parameter logistic model is being used, more responses are required; 700 to 1,000 per item are preferable. Fourth, it should be assumed that anywhere from 5 to 20% of the pretest items will be deemed unusable operationally.

The information obtained through these four steps should be considered in combination with the number of examinees to be tested each year to determine how many usable new items can be expected to result from the operational pretesting process. The number of operational items that can be retired from the bank follows directly from that calculation; items cannot be retired if they are not being replaced, at least not without progressive weakening of the

---

[5]Item difficulty could be either over- or underestimated, depending on circumstances. Although hurried responses almost certainly lead to difficulty being overestimated, the more interesting case is when examinees fail to reach the pretest items. Scoring unreached items as incorrect, like rushed responses, leads to difficulty being overestimated. However, to the extent that speed of responding and proficiency are related, coding the unreached items as simply absent from the calibration can lead to difficulty being underestimated.

bank over time. Parshall et al. (2002) noted that if security concerns require items to be retired more quickly than the operational pretesting efforts allow, supplemental pretesting might be required.

Ironically, the pursuit of both short and reliable tests can lead to increased pretest requirements. Very efficient tests must make frequent use of highly discriminating items, which quickly become known to examinees and so must be retired from use. Unfortunately, it may be necessary to pretest 10 items to find a suitable replacement for each retired item that discriminated at the 90th percentile. The irony is that any time savings afforded by a highly efficient operational test may be more than offset by the increased pretesting time required to maintain a stable item bank.

Evaluating Test Designs and Item Pools Through Simulation

Simulations have long been used to evaluate adaptive testing procedures. Although real examinees are full of surprises that any simulation process will fail to anticipate, simulation results have been found to usefully predict how a proposed test design will work when implemented. Simulations are recommended for two different purposes. The first is to inform and evaluate test design decisions. Test developers should probably produce a range of test designs, each based on different assumptions and expectations, and then use simulations to determine which is likely to work best. The second use of simulations is as part of the ongoing operational process of pool assembly. However, the nuts and bolts of the simulation procedures are the same in both cases.

CAT simulations are based on the IRT model that is assumed to underlie item and examinee performance. This model can calculate the probability of an examinee at a given proficiency level correctly answering a given calibrated item. These probabilities allow item responses to be generated for each examinee by a stochastic process.

A simulation begins by first generating an examinee's proficiency value. These values can be drawn randomly from distributions that resemble those of the operational examinee population or set to values spaced along the proficiency range.[6] Once assigned proficiencies, simulated examinees can work through their adaptive tests much like real examinees would. Items are chosen according to specified selection procedures and test assembly rules, proficiencies are estimated given the examinee's simulated responses, and final scores can be assigned. One of the great benefits of simulations is that final scores can be compared to the "true" proficiency that an examinee was assigned, permitting the precision of the test to be directly determined.

Simulation sample sizes should be as large as is practical. Exceptions include simulations designed to model the impact of operational testing on item pools and banks, or the effectiveness of IRT calibration procedures. Samples in these cases should resemble those that are observed operationally.

Evaluating Item Pools Through Simulation

There are few rules available to guide pool assembly. Building a pool is often an iterative process of trial and error. Simulations that predict how a given pool will perform operationally aid this process. Various configurations are explored until performance is deemed acceptable. A successful pool is one that allows tests that conform to all specifications to be easily and

---

[6]Simulations based on randomly generated proficiency values allow item use rates, score distributions, and other observed test characteristics to be predicted. Spaced proficiency values facilitate estimation of conditional properties such as the bias or standard errors of test score estimates.

routinely selected and administered. Furthermore, these tests measure examinees with appropriate levels of precision and avoid excessive reuse of popular items. These are empirical questions that can be answered by simulating test results from a prospective pool. Pools that fail this evaluation must be modified to correct the observed problems. For example, it may be found that a certain test specification cannot consistently be met unless more items from a given content area are added to the pool. A pool may also be unable to meet test precision targets until it is strengthened with additional highly discriminating items. The cycle of adjustments and evaluations continues until a successful pool results.

Evaluating Test Designs

Simulations accurately predict operational results only to the extent that they accurately reflect a testing program's circumstances. Simulations must therefore incorporate all of those that make a testing program unique. Some of these things are external to the test, such as the characteristics of the examinee population and the ways test scores are used. The remaining factors follow from the test design, and thus include content specifications and test assembly rules, test length, item selection and scoring procedures, and item pool characteristics. An ideal simulation models new item development, pretesting, and calibration activities, and predicts the results of several years of operational testing. The consequences of some test design decisions may not be immediately apparent but instead reveal themselves over time.

Although the simulation process is fairly straightforward from a technical perspective, evaluation of results is less so. Early comparisons of adaptive testing procedures were made with regard to a narrow set of criteria. Foremost among these was test precision or its close associate, test efficiency. In a simulation, test reliability or one of its surrogates, for example, test information or the conditional standard errors of proficiency estimates, usually defines precision. *Efficiency* is simply test precision divided by test length. Precision and efficiency were highly prized because these were believed to be the principal "values added" of adaptive testing. However, in recent years it has been realized that other test features are of equal or greater importance (Davey & Fan, 2000; Davey & Parshall, 1995). As such, the following list goes well beyond the more traditional criteria.

1. **Efficiency and precision:** Most test designs attempt to attain a specified level of precision or reliability. This target may be either carried over from an existing conventional test or devised based on how test scores are used. Two things generally vary across competing test designs. The first is the test length needed to attain the specified precision level. Test designs capable of meeting precision requirements with shorter test lengths are more efficient. Test designs may also vary in the extent that they are able to meet the specified precision target. Some test designs are likely to be more flexible than others in meeting specific targets.
2. **Test consistency:** Test designs may differ in the extent to which each examinee is measured to the precision target. In many cases, exceeding the precision target is almost as undesirable as falling short. Measuring some examinees more precisely than necessary wastes resources (in the form of item exposures) that could be used more productively with later examinees.
3. **Test sustainability:** This broad and vitally important criterion has so far rarely been considered. Essentially, *sustainability* refers to the ease with which a test design can be operationally maintained over time. At least three factors are important here.
    a. What level of ongoing item development and pretesting is needed to sustain the testing program over time? More sustainable test designs require less item development and pretesting to maintain item bank quality at stable levels.

b. How balanced is item pool use? More sustainable test designs use items more effectively by balancing use. With balanced item use, every item appears with roughly equal frequency. When item use is poorly balanced, a few items appear very often and a large number are rarely or never used. Unbalanced item use affects sustainability by making a small number of exceptional items carry much of the burden. These items quickly reach the retirement threshold and must be replaced. However, a large number of new items must be pretested to find the few that are exceptional enough to adequately replace those being retired from use. Under a more balanced test design more commonplace items are used often enough to reach retirement. Fewer new items need to be pretested to replace these more typical items.

c. How easy are item pools to develop? Test designs that facilitate item pool development are more easily sustained over time. Several factors influence the ease or difficulty of pool development, with some of these factors more easily quantified than others. One factor concerns the conditions that a pool must meet to be effective. Presumably, pools required to meet fewer and weaker conditions are easier to develop. However, the extent to which pools parallel the structure of the bank is also important. Pools representative of the item bank are likely easier to develop than pools that sample the bank more selectively. Finally, pools that operate in ways that are more predictable are easier to develop than pools that function unpredictably. Minor changes to item pools should result in equally minor changes in the way a pool functions.

Test sustainability is best evaluated through simulations that predict the effects of several years of operational test administration. Each test design starts with an initial item bank and then works through several years of operational testing. Pools are built, tests administered, item use tracked, frequently administered items retired, and new items pretested and entered into the bank. Comparing the bank at the end of this cycle with that at the outset reveals whether the design and all its assumptions (item development requirements, pretest volumes, pool specifications, pool development, item retirement limits, etc.) are able to keep the bank stable and the testing program thereby sustainable. Working backward, the test design settings and assumptions necessary for stability can be determined.

4. **Robustness:** Examinees occasionally respond to test items in unexpected ways. Carelessness, speededness, item preexposure, unusual educational backgrounds, and a host of other factors are potential causes. Both conventional and adaptive tests are likely to poorly measure examinees who respond idiosyncratically. However, some CAT test designs may cope better than others. A series of simulations is conducted to evaluate each test design in this regard. Each simulation of generates data according to one of several identified nonstandard response models. The evaluation determines how successful each test design is in recovering true proficiency values despite the presence of unusual or aberrant responding. A second aspect of robustness is the ability of a test design to recognize when something has gone awry. An ideal test design incorporates quality control diagnostics that identify unusual tests and examinees as such.

5. **Conformity:** A *conforming test* meets all the requirements imposed upon it. Conforming tests therefore both comply with all content specifications and measure to specified levels of precision. A better test design is one capable of delivering a higher proportion of conforming tests.

6. **Level of control afforded:** A better test design affords test developers more complete and convenient control over test characteristics and outcomes. For example, developers should be able to specify how precisely a test measures, how precision varies across score ranges, and how item usage rates are balanced.

Fairly Comparing Test Designs

The interactions and conflicts between test length, test precision, and item use balance can make it hard to fairly compare test designs. For example, a design can appear to be more efficient (shorter and/or more precise) by using items in a very unbalanced way. Requiring all designs to be sustainable is one means of putting each on a common footing. An efficient design therefore gets full credit for efficiency only if it is not attained at the expense of unbalanced item use and the increased need for item replacement associated with such use. Similarly, a design that perfectly balances item use might require long operational tests or be unable to meet precision requirements. It is only in the context of a full, sustainable operational design that testing procedures can be fairly compared.

Conducting simulations in which multiple factors are evaluated also provides information needed to comply with Standard 3.12, which calls for documentation of the rationale and supporting evidence for CAT administration procedures, including those for item selection and exposure, scoring, and stopping rules (AERA, APA, & NCME, 1999). Results of the simulations will also provide support for claims that scores produced by alternate sets of items, as is done in CAT, are interchangeable (Standard 4.10).

CONSIDERATIONS IN ADOPTING COMPUTERIZED ADAPTIVE TESTS

We conclude by addressing what might be the most important practical question of all: under what conditions is adaptive testing likely to offer significant advantages over conventional designs? Although CAT can be very appropriate and effective in some cases, the stakes attached to an examination, the expected number of examinees to be tested, and whether testing takes place continuously or periodically are some of the practical matters that dictate whether CAT makes sense or offers advantages in a particular context. This section reviews some of the characteristics of CATs that should be considered when deciding whether a test should be administered adaptively.

Changed Measurement

Standardized tests are often criticized as artificial, measuring performance in ways divorced from real-world behaviors. At least some of this criticism is a product of the constraints that paper-based administration imposes on test developers. Paper is restricted to displaying static text and graphics, offers no real means of interacting with the examinee, and sharply limits the ways in which examinees can respond. As noted, computers can free test developers from these restrictions. They can present sound and motion, interact dynamically with examinees, and accept responses through a variety of modes. A CAT, like any test administered on computer, can therefore be a richer, more realistic experience that allows more direct measurement of the traits in question.

Improved Measurement Precision and Efficiency

A conventional test is like an off-the-rack suit in that both fit the average individual reasonably well but misfit at the extremes. Conventional tests are designed to effectively measure examinees who fall at the middle of the performance range. This is sensible; most examinees are clustered around midrange performance levels. Extreme performance at either the high or low end is relatively rare. The consequence is that a conventional test generally contains only a few items that are truly appropriate for examinees that fall outside middle score ranges. Measurement of extreme examinees is then both poor and inefficient. Adaptive testing solves these problems by selecting items that target each examinee's observed level of performance. The result is much greater efficiency, which can be used to increase measurement precision, decrease test length, or both.

Increased Operational Convenience

CATs can offer various conveniences to both examinees and test sponsors. For example, CATs are often administered continuously rather than on only a small number of fixed occasions. This can allow examinees to test when they want to rather than when the test sponsor allows them to. CATs are generally able to provide examinees with a score report immediately upon conclusion of the test, a feature that may or may not be available with simpler computerized testing designs. Immediate scoring is particularly important when coupled with flexible scheduling. It allows examinees to meet tight application deadlines, move directly to employment, or simply decide that their performance was substandard and register to retest.

Computerized administration can also be more convenient for the test sponsor. Conventional paper-and-pencil tests often require a human proctor to distribute test booklets and answer sheets, keep track of time limits, and collect materials after the test ends. Administering a CAT can be as simple as parking an examinee in front of a computer. Although proctors are still required for highly secure administration, the computer can collect demographic data, orient the examinee to the testing process, administer and time the test, and produce a score report at the conclusion. Different examinees can sit side by side taking different tests with different time limits for different purposes. With conventional administration, these two examinees would likely need to be tested at different times or in different places.

Cost

It is currently much more expensive to test on computer than it is with paper and pencil (Clauser & Schuwirth, 2002; Parshall et al., 2002; Vale, 1995). This is because of factors at play in both the test development and test administration processes. Test development costs can be higher for CAT because of the large item pools needed to effectively test examinees across a wide ability range. For test administration, it is certainly true that CAT can trim costs in some areas. For example, test materials do not need to be printed and shipped to the test site, and then shipped back for scoring. Rather, all of this information can be transferred electronically in both directions. However, at present these small savings are more than offset by much higher administration costs. As Parshall et al. noted, the economies of scale work against a CAT because providing one more empty chair in a school or other testing venue for a paper-and-pencil administration is, and will likely continue to be, easier and cheaper than reserving one more computer station.

Stakes and Security

Increased security has sometimes been touted as an advantage of CAT. It is probably true that that electronic files can be stored and shipped more securely than can test booklets and answer sheets. Moreover, it is certainly true that CAT largely eliminates the problem of examinees copying responses from neighboring examinees. These advantages have in fact allowed test sponsors to conclude that CATs can remain secure despite being continuously administered.

However, continuous CAT administration can introduce new, and possibly more pernicious, security risks (Mills & Steffen, 2000). These risks are most likely to be exploited when the stakes attached to test performance are highest.

Examinee Volume

Adaptive tests are most appropriate for programs that serve large numbers of examinees. First, such programs are better able to bear the added expense of developing and administering a CAT. Small programs may lack the financial resources, the large established bank of items, and the examinee samples needed to pretest additional items. If the number of examinees to be tested is small, then the expense of developing and administering a CAT may be too great. A testing program that administers tests to a large number of examinees is likely to have item pools of sufficient breadth and depth to support CAT administrations; a low-volume testing program is not. The pretesting needed to maintain a CAT pool sufficient to support future administrations may also be difficult to accomplish with low examinee volume. CAT programs, particularly those that are continuously administered, can have a voracious appetite for items, all of which need to be pretested and IRT calibrated prior to operational use. This can impose such a burden that with even very large CAT programs, it is not unusual for 25% or more of each examinee's test session to be given over to item pretesting (Mills & Steffen, 2000). These cost and practical issues may cast doubt on the reasonableness of implementing a CAT with a low-stakes test; examinees may not be willing to pay the higher costs usually incurred with a CAT (or any computer-based test) as opposed to a paper-and-pencil test.

Properly weighing all of these factors may well lead to the conclusion that computer-based testing and CAT are either inappropriate or impractical for a particular testing program. For example, it might be discovered that three or four test administrations per year offer examinees almost the same utility as (much more expensive) continuous testing. Vale (1995) noted that "time savings translate into dollar savings only when the time has value. Time typically has great value when a candidate must pass a test to get a license to practice a profession" (p. 293). Scheduling efficiencies may not be worth the cost of CAT if, for example, an examinee can practice his or her profession with a provisional license.

The purpose of the test is a factor that should be considered when deciding between types of computer-based tests. For example, for a licensure test in which the agency seeks to determine which examinees have sufficient knowledge to practice and which do not, a CAT is not the best choice. A form of computer-based testing designed for classification is best suited for that type of application (see Luecht, chap. 25, this volume). In contrast, CAT is the best choice for a test that used to distinguish among examinees at all points on the score scale.

Examinees' perceptions of the test, particularly a CAT, should also be taken into consideration. A CAT does not generally allow item review; some examinees find such a feature disconcerting. Whether or not that factor should be allowed to determine the testing design is a decision to be made by the testing program.

The types of items to be administered may also play a role in deciding between a CAT and another type of computer-based test. Although computer administration is attractive in its ability to support novel item types, some of them may be better suited for a linear form of computer-based testing than for CAT. Complex item types may be difficult to incorporate into a CAT design. In addition, if they require a fair amount of time and provide correspondingly little information to be taken into account in determining the examinee's ability level, one of the usual goals of CAT—shortening the testing time—is not likely to be achieved.

REFERENCES

American Educational Research Association (AERA), American Psychological Association (APA), & National Council on Measurement in Education (NCME). (1999). *Standards for educational and psychological testing* (3rd ed.). Washington, DC: American Educational Research Association.

Anastasi, A. (1988). *Psychological testing* (6th ed.). New York: Macmillan.

Association of Test Publishers. (2002). *Guidelines for computer-based testing.* Washington, DC: Author.

Ban, J., Wang, T., & Yi, Q. (1999, June). *Comparison of a-stratification, maximum information and matched difficulty methods in adaptive testing.* Paper presented at the annual meeting of the Psychometric Society, Lawrence, KS.

Birnbaum, A. (1968). Some latent trait models and their use in inferring an examinee's ability. In F. M. Lord and M. R. Novick (Eds.), *Statistical theories of mental test scores* (chaps. 17–20). Reading, MA: Addison-Wesley.

Burstein, J. (2003). The *e-rater*® scoring engine: Automated essay scoring with natural language processing. In M. D. Shermis & J. Burstein (Eds.), *Automated essay scoring: A cross-disciplinary perspective.* Mahwah, NJ: Lawrence Erlbaum Associates.

Burstein, J., Chodorow, M., & Leacock, C. (2004). Automated essay evaluation: The Criterion online writing service. *AI Magazine, 25*(3), 27–36.

Burstein, J., & Marcu, D. (2003). Automated evaluation of discourse structure in student essays. In M. D. Shermis & J. Burstein (Eds.), *Automated essay scoring: A cross-disciplinary perspective* (pp. 209–229). Mahwah, NJ: Lawrence Erlbaum Associates.

Chang, H.-H., & Ying, Z. (1999). α-Stratified multistage computerized adaptive testing. *Applied Psychological Measurement, 23,* 211–222.

Clauser, B. E., & Schuwirth, L. W. T. (2002). The use of computers in assessments. In G. Norman, C. van der Vleuten, & D. Newble (Eds.), *The international handbook for research in medical education* (pp. 757–791). Boston: Kluwer.

Davey, T. C., & Fan, M. (2000, April). *Specific information item selection for adaptive testing.* Paper presented at the annual meeting of the National Council for Measurement in Education, New Orleans, LA.

Davey, T., & Nering, M. (2002). Controlling item exposure and maintaining item security. In C. N. Mills, M. T. Potenza, J. J. Fremer, & W. C. Ward (Eds.), *Computer-based testing: Building the foundation for future assessments* (pp. 165–191). Mahwah, NJ: Lawrence Erlbaum Associates.

Davey, T. C., & Parshall, C. G. (1995, April). *New algorithms for item selection and exposure control with computerized adaptive testing.* Paper presented at the annual meeting of the American Educational Research Association, San Francisco.

Davey, T., & Thomas, L. (1996, April). *Constructing adaptive tests to parallel conventional programs.* Paper presented at the annual meeting of the American Educational Research Association, New York.

Embretson, S. E. & Reise, S. P. (2000). *Item response theory for psychologists.* Mahwah, NJ: Lawrence Erlbaum Associates.

Haladyna, T. (2004). *Developing and validating multiple-choice test items.* Mahwah, NJ: Lawrence Erlbaum Associates.

Hambleton, R. K., Swaminathan, H. R., & Rogers, J. (1991). *Fundamentals of item response theory.* Thousand Oaks, CA: Sage.

Huff, K. L., & Sireci, S. G. (2001). Validity issues in computer-based testing. *Educational Measurement: Issues and Practice, 20*(3), 16–25.

Jodoin, M. G. (2003). *Psychometric properties of several computer-based test designs with ideal and constrained item pools.* Unpublished doctoral dissertation, University of Massachusetts, Amherst.

Jones, D. H. (1982). *Tools of robustness for item response theory* (ETS RR-82-41). Princeton, NJ: Educational Testing Service.

Kalohn, J. C., & Spray, J. A. (2000, April). *Test security and item exposure control for computer-based examinations: Performance of a computerized classification test for professional certification.* Paper presented at the annual meeting of the National Council on Measurement in Education, New Orleans, LA.

Kingsbury, G. G., & Zara, A. R. (1999, April). *A comparison of conventional and adaptive testing procedures for making single-point decisions.* Paper presented at the annual meeting of the National Council on Measurement in Education, Montreal, Quebec, Canada.

Leacock, C., & Chodorow, M. (2003). C-rater: Scoring of short-answer questions. *Computers and the Humanities, 37*(4), 389–405.

Lord, F. M. (1980). *Applications of item response theory to practical testing problems.* Hillsdale, NJ: Lawrence Erlbaum Associates.

Lord, F. M. (1983). Unbiased estimators of ability parameters, of their variance, and of their parallel-forms reliability. *Psychometrika, 48,* 233–245.

Lord, F. M., & Novick, M. (1968). *Statistical theories of mental test scores.* Reading, MA: Addison Wesley.

Luecht, R. M., & Nungester, R. (1998). Some practical examples of computer-adaptive sequential testing. *Journal of Educational Measurement, 35,* 239–249.

Mills, C. N., & Steffen, M. (2000). The GRE computer adaptive test: Operational issues. In W. J. van der Linden & C. A. W. Glas (Eds.), *Computerized adaptive testing: Theory and practice* (pp. 75–99). Norwell, MA: Kluwer.

Mosteller, F., & Tukey, J. (1977). *Data analysis and regression.* Reading, MA: Addison-Wesley.

Parshall, C. G., Davey, T., & Pashley, P. J. (2000). Innovative item types for computerized testing. In W. J. van der Linden & C. A. W. Glas (Eds.), *Computerized adaptive testing: Theory and practice* (pp. 129–148). Norwell, MA: Kluwer.

Parshall, C. G., Spray, J. A., Kalohn, J. C., & Davey, T. (2002). *Practical considerations in computer-based testing.* New York: Springer-Verlag.

Robin, F., van der Linden, W. J., Eignor, D. R., Steffen, M., & Stocking, M. L. (2004). *A comparison of two procedures for constrained adaptive test construction* (ETS RR-04-39). Princeton, NJ: Educational Testing Service.

Samejima, F. (1993a). An approximation for the bias function of the maximum likelihood estimate of a latent variable for the general case where the item responses are discrete. *Psychometrika, 58,* 119–138.

Samejima, F. (1993b). The bias function of the maximum likelihood estimate of ability for the dichotomous response level. *Psychometrika, 58,* 195–209.

Sands, W. A., Waters, B. K., & McBride, J. R. (Eds.). (1997). *Computerized adaptive testing: From inquiry to operation.* Washington, DC: American Psychology Association.

Sheehan, K., & Lewis, C. (1992). Computerized mastery testing with nonequivalent testlets. *Applied Psychological Measurement, 16,* 65–76.

Stocking, M. L. (1994). *Three practical issues for modern adaptive testing item pools* (ETS RR-94-5). Princeton, NJ: Educational Testing Service.

Stocking, M. L., & Lewis, C. (1995a). *A new method of controlling item exposure in computerized adaptive testing* (ETS RR-95-25). Princeton, NJ: Educational Testing Service.

Stocking, M. L., & Lewis, C. (1995b). *Controlling item exposure conditional on ability in computerized adaptive testing* (ETS RR-95-24). Princeton, NJ: Educational Testing Service.

Stocking, M. L., & Swanson, L. (1993). A method for severely constrained item selection in adaptive testing. *Applied Psychological Measurement, 17,* 277–292.

Sympson, J. B., & Hetter, R. D. (1985). *Controlling item-exposure rates in computerized adaptive testing.* Proceedings of the 27th annual meeting of the Military Testing Association (pp. 973–977). San Diego: Navy Personnel Research and Development Center.

Thomasson, G. L. (1995, June). *New item exposure control algorithms for computerized adaptive testing.* Paper presented at the annual meeting of the Psychometric Society, Minneapolis, MN.

Vale, C. D. (1995). Computerized testing in licensure. In J. C. Impara (Ed.), *Licensure testing: Purposes, procedures, and practices* (pp. 291–320). Lincoln, NE: Buros Institute of Mental Measurements.

van der Linden, W. J. (2000). Constrained adaptive testing with shadow tests. In W. J. van der Linden & C. A. W. Glas (Eds.), *Computerized adaptive testing: Theory and practice* (pp. 27–52). Boston: Kluwer.

van der Linden, W. J. & Glas, C. A. W. (2000). *Computerized adaptive testing: Theory and practice* (pp. 27–52). Boston: Kluwer.

van der Linden, W. J., & Reese, L. M. (1998). A model for optimal constrained adaptive testing. *Applied Psychological Measurement, 22,* 259–270.

Wainer, H., Dorans, N., Flaughter, R. Green, B., Mislevy, R., Steinberg, L., & Thissen, D. (2000). *Computerized adaptive testing: A primer* (2nd ed.). Hillsdale, NJ: Lawrence Erlbaum Associates.

Wainer, H., & Thissen, D. (2001). True score theory: The traditional method. In D. Thissen & H. Wainer (Eds.), *Test scoring* (pp. 23–72). Mahwah, NJ: Lawrence Erlbaum Associates.

Way, W. D., Steffen, M. & Anderson, G. S. (2002). Developing, maintaining, and renewing the item inventory to support CBT. In C. N. Mills, M. T. Potenza, J. J. Fremer & W. C. Ward (Eds.), *Computer-based testing: Building the foundation for future assessments* (pp. 143–164). Mahwah, NJ: Lawrence Erlbaum Associates.

Weiss, D. J. (1974). *Strategies of adaptive ability measurement* (RR 74-5Z). Minneapolis: Psychometric Methods Program, Department of Psychology, University of Minnesota.

Yen, W. M., Burket, G. R., & Sykes, R. C. (1991). Nonunique solutions to the likelihood equation for the three-parameter logistic model, *Psychometrika, 56,* 39–54.

Zenisky, A. L., & Sireci, S. G. (2002). Technological innovations in large-scale assessment. *Applied Measurement in Education, 15,* 337–362.

25

Designing Tests for Pass–Fail Decisions Using Item Response Theory

Richard M. Luecht
University of North Carolina at Greensboro

This chapter reviews some applications of common Item Response Theory (IRT) models to test design and test construction for mastery tests that involve pass–fail decisions. The chapter specifically focuses on IRT item and test information functions and uses of targeted test information designs that maximize the reliability of mastery or competence-based decisions. The chapter introduces automated test assembly (ATA) methods as a recommended strategy for test developers to consider. ATA employs computerized item-selection algorithms that achieve parallel measurement precision across test forms while simultaneously meeting all relevant content and other test constrains. The use of ATA is extended to multistage test designs that combine mastery testing with potentially adaptive-diagnostic testing capabilities for failing examinees. A discussion of item banking and inventory management is included. Finally, some general recommendations are provided for test development practitioners.

Many examinations are used to make a simple pass–fail decision. These have historically been called *criterion-referenced tests, mastery tests,* and other names. In this chapter, I generically refer to these types of examinations as *mastery tests*. At a somewhat abstract level, mastery testing is fairly straightforward. A test form is constructed to assess one or more knowledge and skill domains by some prescribed item selection process. A score scale is established for the test form and a standard is set denoting the passing score on the scale. Test takers who exceed the cut score are assumed to have met the established threshold of skills and knowledge—that is, they are "competent." In addition to ignoring many important standard-setting issues, as well as glossing over a multitude of technical psychometric considerations, this abstracted view of mastery testing overlooks many important and sometimes complex issues specifically related to test design, item banking, and test assembly.

This chapter addresses these test development issues. An overview of item response theory (IRT) applicable to mastery testing contexts is presented, focusing on test information. Second, using a computer simulation, how IRT test information relates to decision accuracy for mastery tests is discussed. A discussion of automated test assembly and the use of IRT target test information functions follows. The need for test development inventory control models for creating and maintaining item banks capable of supporting large-scale test production is addressed. A discussion of some of the common mastery test design models from the perspective of using absolute and relative test information functions is next. Finally, recommendations for test developers are presented.

ITEM RESPONSE THEORY ITEM AND TEST CHARACTERISTIC AND TEST INFORMATION FUNCTIONS

There are many practical advantages in using IRT over classical test theory (Hambleton & Swaminathan, 1985; Lord, 1980). One advantage is that items and examinees can be calibrated to a common measurement scale and both item and test characteristics can be interpreted relative to specific points or regions of the underlying proficiency scale. For example, IRT allows estimates of the measurement precision a particular item, a test form, or even the entire item bank at specific proficiency levels. This notion of conditional test information provides test developers a powerful way to manipulate the amount of measurement precision allocated to particular regions of the proficiency scale. For mastery testing, this capability to control the location and amount of precision near the pass–fail cut score is extremely important for optimizing the accuracy of mastery decisions.

One of the most popular and general IRT models is the three-parameter logistic (3PL) model. The 3PL model is appropriate for dichotomously scored items (e.g., selected-response questions) and is characterized by a mathematical function,

$$P_i(\theta) \equiv P_i = c_i + \frac{(1 - c_i)}{1 + exp\,[-Da_i(\theta - b_i)]} \tag{25.1}$$

where $P_i(\theta)$ is the probability of getting item i correct for examinees having proficiency scores denoted as θ. D is a scaling constant often set to $D = 1.7$ when the logistic function in Equation 25.1 needs to approximate a cumulative normal probability function, where θ is distributed with a mean of zero and variance of one.[1] It is common to call this probability function a *response function*. The item parameters, a_i, b_i, and c_i, determine the shape of a particular item response function across the θ scale. Figure 25.1 depicts the item response functions for three items. When plotted, these are called *item characteristic curves* (ICCs). The item parameters used to generate the ICCs are displayed in the legend of the plot.

Each ICC shows the probability of correctly answering a dichotomously scored item (e.g., a selected-response item scored right or wrong). The response probability, $P_i(\theta)$, changes as a function of the item characteristics and the examinee's proficiency. For example, the probability of an examinee having a proficiency score of $\theta = 1.0$ correctly answering item 1, represented by the dash-dot line (−·−), is 0.60. In contrast, the same examinee is expected to answer item 2, represented by the dashed line (—) with near certainty; that is, the probability of getting item 2 correct for an examinee with a proficiency score of $\theta = 1.0$ is 0.985. An ICC therefore presents a conditional indication of the item's difficulty for examinees at a specific level of proficiency. As the proficiency goes up, so does the probability of getting the item correct.

As noted, item parameters control the shape of an ICC. The IRT location parameter, denoted b, shifts each curve left or right and is an indicator of the relative item difficulty of the item

---

[1] When "normal ogive" scaling is used (i.e., $D = 1.7$), and assuming that θ is normally distributed, we can treat θ as a z-score. For example, we can state that the 20th percentile is $\theta = -0.84$, which corresponds to the 20th percentile for unit normal z-scores. Normal ogive scaling therefore facilitates basic interpretations of θ for practitioners familiar with z-scores and the normal curve.

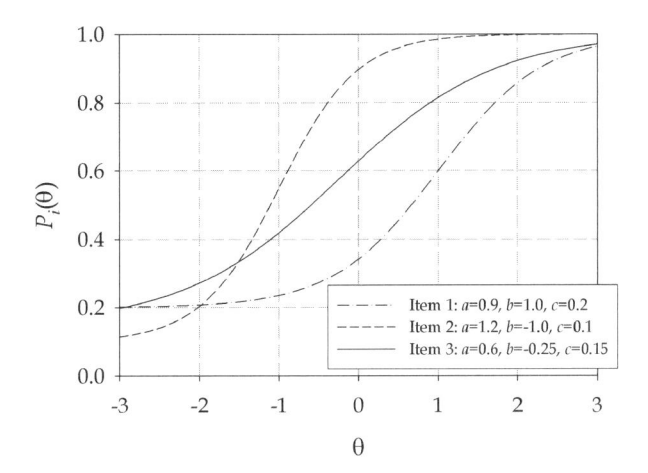

FIG. 25.1. 3PL ICCs for three items: Discrimination parameters, $\mathbf{a} = \{0.9, 1.2, 0.6\}$; difficulty parameters, $\mathbf{b} = \{-1.0, -0.25, 1.0\}$; and lower asymptote parameters, $\mathbf{c} = \{0.2, 0.15, 0.1\}$.

on the θ metric. For example, the ICC for item 1, where $b = 1.0$, is shifted furthest to the right and is therefore more difficult than the other two items. Item 2 is the easier item because $b = -1.0$. The probability associated with scores equal to the b-parameter (i.e., $\theta = b$) is $(1 + c)/2$.

The a-parameter, often called the *discrimination parameter*, specifies the slope or steepness of each ICC. In Figure 25.1, the slopes of the ICCs correspond to the ordering of the three item discrimination parameters ($a_3 < a_1 < a_2$). Item 3 has the flattest slope and is least discriminating. The ICC for item 2 has the steepest slope and is most discriminating. Finally, the c parameter denotes the lower asymptote of the response function. This parameter is associated with noise in the response patterns at the lowest proficiency levels (e.g., noise from random guessing on difficult items by lower proficiency test takers). For example, $c_i = 0.1$ for item 2, indicating that this item has the lowest apparent asymptote and, by implication, suggests that there is less random noise in the response patterns of examinees in the lower regions of the score scale for item 2 than for the other two items.

Other IRT models can also be employed in mastery testing. The two-parameter logistic (2PL) model fixes the lower asymptote parameters at zero or some other constant for all items (i.e., $c_i = c$ for all items, $i = 1, \ldots, n$). The one-parameter (1PL) or Rasch model (Rasch, 1960) fixes the lower asymptote parameters at zero and also constrains the slope parameter to be constant (i.e., $a_i = a$ for all items, $i = 1, \ldots, n$), usually with $a = 1.0$. The 1PL response function is shown in Equation 25.2. Again, the constant D can be set to 1.7 to approximate a cumulative normal density or to 1.0 for logistic scaling.

$$P_i(\theta) \equiv P_i = \frac{1}{1 + exp\left[-D(\theta - b_i)\right]} \quad (25.2)$$

Figure 25.2 shows the ICCs for three items using the 1PL model. The b-parameters are displayed in the legend of the plot. It should be immediately clear that the ICCs for the 1PL model are all shaped the same but differ in item difficulty (location). Under the 1PL (and 2PL) model(s) the b-parameter corresponds to the value of θ at which an examinee has a 0.50 probability of getting the item correct (i.e., $P_i = 0.50$ when $\theta = b_i$).

Forcing the ICCs to have a fixed shape and differ only in location implies that the 1PL model usually demonstrates worse fit to empirical response data than the 2PL and 3PL models. In

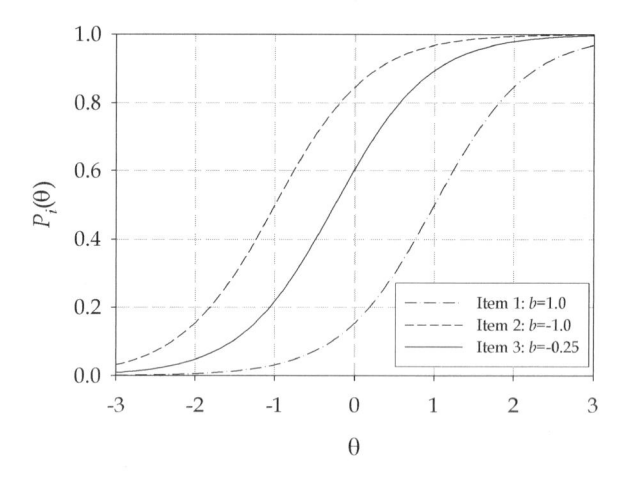

FIG. 25.2. 1PL ICCs for three items with difficulty parameters **b** = {1.0, −1.0, −0.25}.

general, adding parameters to any statistical model improves its fit to real data. Conversely, any time we introduce constraints on the parameters in an IRT model (e.g., setting $a_i = a = 1.0$, or $c_i = c = 0.0$) the capability of finessing the shape of the probability function to fit nuances in the item response data is limited. However, fit should never be the sole criteria in selecting an IRT model; in fact, there is a long-standing debate as to what ought to be the appropriate criterion and how this issue should be investigated. What is very clear to many testing practitioners is that there is an inevitable trade off between model fit and estimation stability. The 3PL is acknowledged to fit most multiple-choice (and other types of selected-response) data better than the 1PL or 2PL. Yet, attempting to estimate stable 3PL parameters from smaller samples can be extremely challenging, resulting in (possibly) serious problems when attempting to maintain the stability of the item bank metrics and passing scores over time.[2]

The item parameters must be estimated from scored response data. That is, the item responses for a sizeable sample of examinees taking one or more test forms need to be scored—dichotomously in the case of the 1PL, 2PL, and 3PL—and then analyzed by specialized computer software that computes estimates of the a-, b-, and c-parameters for each item. As noted, this analysis process is called *calibration*. There are a number of very good IRT calibration software packages; two of the more popular packages are BILOG-MG (Zimowski, Muraki, Mislevy, & Bock, 2003) for the 1PL, 2PL, and 3PL models, and WINSTEPS (Linacre, 2004) for the Rasch 1PL model. Additional equating steps may be required to link the item parameter estimates to a common scale (e.g., Hambleton & Swaminathan, 1985; Kolen & Brennan, 1995). Once the item parameters are estimated and linked a common scale, they can be banked in a database for subsequent use in test construction and scoring.

From a test construction perspective, one of the most important IRT developments is the *information function* (Birnbaum, 1968; Hambleton and Swaminathan, 1985; Lord, 1980). An item information function (IIF) indicates the contribution of each item to score precision within particular regions of the θ scale. The information functions directly influence the accuracy of mastery decisions. Consequently, manipulating the information functions via good test design and appropriate test assembly practices, can to a large extent control the accuracy of the decisions we make in mastery testing.

---

[2]Estimation problems with the 3PL include nonconvergence of the numerical estimation solutions from ill-conditioned likelihood functions, empirical underidentification of the model parameters leading to large error covariances for the parameter estimates, and complications in equating or linking 3PL metrics over time when the c-parameters vary across calibration samples.

25. IRT-BASED MASTERY TESTING 579

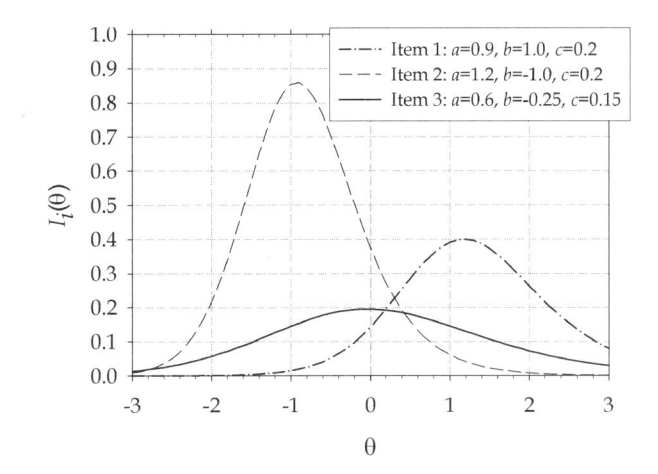

FIG. 25.3. 3PL IIFs for three items: discrimination parameters, **a** = {0.9, 1.2, 0.6}; difficulty parameters, **b** = {−1.0, −0.25, 1.0}; and lower asymptote parameters **c** = {0.2, 0.15, 0.1}.

The 3PL IIF can be expressed as

$$I_i(\theta) \equiv I_i = \frac{D^2 a_i^2 Q_i (P_i - c_i)^2}{P_i (1 - c_i)^2}, \tag{25.3}$$

where $Q_i = 1 - P_i$ (the complement of the probability, P_i). The b-parameter influences the location of the maximum information that an item provides. The a-parameter influences the amount of information for an item. The c-parameter has some influence on the amount of information.

Figure 25.3 shows the 3PL item information functions for the three items displayed Figure 25.1 as ICCs. The maximum information that an item provides is proportional to the a-parameter. Item 2 has the largest a-parameter ($a_2 = 1.2$) and provides the most information, as indicated by the height of the IIF at its peak, $I_2^{max} = 0.86$. In contrast, the maximum information for the other two items is substantially less ($I_1^{max} = 0.40$ and $I_3^{max} = 0.19$) because those items have smaller a-parameters.

Although the amount of information an item provides is largely a function of the a-parameters, the location of maximum item information is directly related to the item difficulty, b. The point on the θ scale where the IIF attains its maximum value can be computed as

$$\theta_{max} = b_i + \frac{1}{Da_i} \ln\left(\frac{1 + \sqrt{1 + 8c_i}}{2}\right) \tag{25.4}$$

where $\ln$ denotes the natural logarithm function. Using this formula, the location values of maximum information for the IIFs shown in Figure 25.3 are easily determined as: $\theta_{max(Item\ 1)} = 1.17$, $\theta_{max(Item\ 2)} = -0.92$, and $\theta_{max(Item\ 3)} = -0.04$. Note that when c is zero, $\theta_{max} = b$.

To avoid having to generate a plot to identify the peak of an IIF, we can instead conveniently compute that quantity using

$$I_i(\theta_{max}) = I_i^{max} = \frac{D^2 a_i^2}{8(1 - c_i)^2}\left[1 - 20c_i - 8c_i^2 + (1 + 8c_i)^{3/2}\right] \tag{25.5}$$

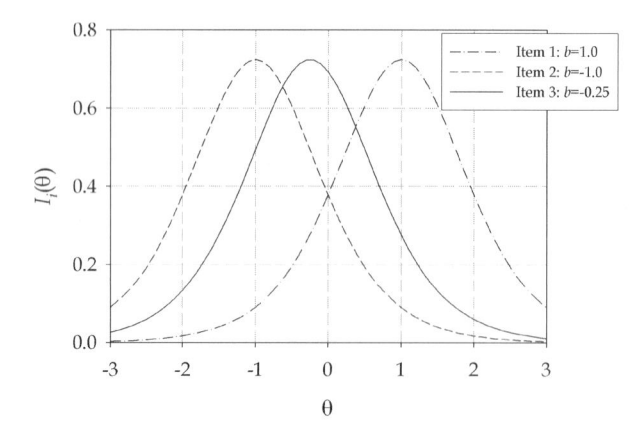

FIG. 25.4. 1PL IIFs for three items with difficulty parameters **b** = {1.0, −1.0, −0.25}.

(Lord, 1980, p. 152). This equation can be used to confirm that the peaks of the information curves in Figure 25.2 are, indeed, $I_1^{max} = 0.40$, $I_2^{max} = 0.86$, and $I_3^{max} = 0.19$, as noted.

Under the 1PL model, the item information functions all have the same shape (Figure 25.4). These IIFs correspond to the three 1PL item characteristic curves shown in Figure 25.2. For the 1PL model, the maximum amount of item information can be shown to be exactly 0.25 when $D = 1.0$. When $D = 1.7$ (for normal ogive scaling), the maximum item information equals 0.7225 for all items—a value that can be visually confirmed in Figure 25.4. For the 2PL model—or more generally, when $c = 0$, Equation 25.5 simplifies to $I_i^{max} = 0.25 D^2 a_i^2$. For both the 1PL and 2PL models, the item difficulty is the point of maximum information—that is, $\theta_{max} = b$.

Although the item information functions are important in their own right, they take on even greater utility when considered in aggregate for a test, test section, or testlet.[3] The item information functions can be conveniently summed at any value of θ to compute the test information function (TIF). That is,

$$I(\theta) = \sum_i I_i = \sum_i \frac{D^2 a_i^2 Q_i (P_i - c_i)^2}{P_i (1 - c_i)^2}. \qquad (25.6)$$

The TIF, denoted $I(\theta)$, is inversely proportional to the error variance of the sampling distribution for the estimates of θ. This relationship can be expressed as

$$V(\hat{\theta} | \theta) = I(\theta)^{-1} = \frac{1}{\sum_i I_i}. \qquad (25.7)$$

Furthermore, taking the square root of Equation 25.7 provides the standard deviation of the sampling errors of estimate or standard error. These standard errors are highly useful in quantifying uncertainty about the accuracy of proficiency score estimates—especially score estimates in the region of the pass–fail cut score.

---

[3]*Testlet* has been popularized for computer-based tests as a collection of items that are always administered as intact units. Each test may have multiple testlets. Testlets may share a common stimulus or merely be presented as intact units to facilitate data management, scoring, and so on.

TABLE 25.1
Descriptive Summary of 3PL Item Parameters for Three 25-Item Tests (see Figure 25.5)

	Test 1			Test 2			Test 3		
	a	b	c	a	b	c	a	b	c
Mean	0.93	0.01	0.14	0.50	−0.84	0.17	0.92	−0.88	0.18
SD	0.42	0.76	0.07	0.12	0.24	0.01	0.24	0.23	0.01
Minimum	0.39	−1.25	0.03	0.31	−1.32	0.16	0.62	−1.35	0.15
Maximum	1.84	1.81	0.26	0.77	−0.52	0.20	1.50	−0.43	0.20

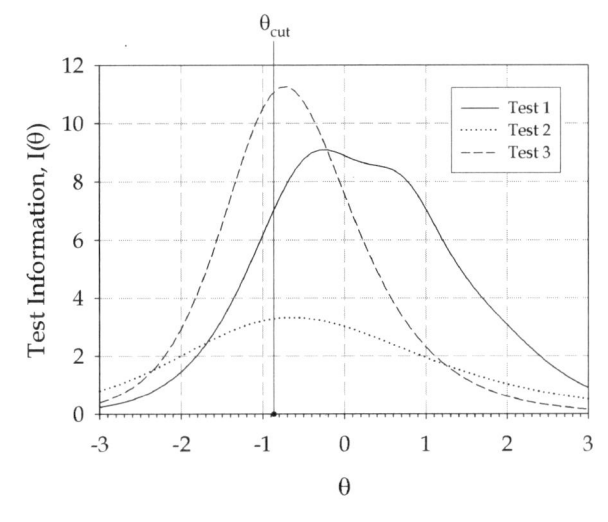

FIG. 25.5. TIFs for three 25-item tests (3PL parameters; see Table 25.1).

Figure 25.5 shows the test information functions for three tests: Test 1, Test 2, and Test 3. Each test is composed of exactly 25 items. The descriptive item statistics for the 3PL item parameters are summarized in Table 25.1.

Because this chapter deals with mastery tests, it seems useful to discuss the test information functions for these three tests with respect to a specific passing score. Therefore, consider a pass–fail cut score at the 20th percentile of the examinee population (i.e., 80% of the examinee population is expected to pass the examination). Assuming that θ is normally distributed with a mean of zero and variance of one, and without speculating as to how the cut score might have been determined, we can therefore use $\theta_{cut} = -0.84$ as the cut score, which is indicated by the vertical line in Figure 25.5 (also see footnote 1).

Test 3 (the dashed line) depicts a TIF that seems reasonable for a mastery test with a cut score of $\theta_{cut} = -0.84$. That is, the Test 3 test information function is peaked near to the cut score and has a reasonably high amount of information. The corresponding standard error is approximately 0.30 at the cut score. Table 25.1 confirms that the mean of the a-parameters is reasonably high with a small standard deviation. The item difficulties for Test 3 are homogeneous and centered near the cut score. In contrast, the peak of the TIF for Test 2 (the dotted line) is also near to the cut score, but the amount of information is relatively low. The value of the TIF at the cut score is $I(-0.84) = 3.3$ and the corresponding standard error is

0.55. As Table 25.1 shows, the *b*-parameters are tightly clustered near the cut score (the mean item difficulty is −0.84 with a standard deviation of 0.25 indicating fairly homogeneous items), but the 25 items are not very discriminating, on average. We therefore conclude that, although the items for Test 2 are fairly well targeted in difficulty, they lack adequate discrimination.

The peak of the Test 1 curve (the solid line) indicates that this test is most informative nearer to the population average, where $\mu(\theta) = 0.0$, and decreases in information in the region of the cut score. However, Test 1 is still a "better" test—information wise—than Test 2 in the region of the cut score. The average item discrimination for Test 1 is almost identical to that of Test 3 (see Table 25.1), but the Test 1 items are more heterogeneous in terms of both item discrimination and difficulty. The mean item difficulty for the 25 items is zero, which shifts the peak of the information away from the cut score and nearer to the population mean. We therefore could argue that Test 1 is somewhat harder than it needs to be for purposes of making accurate pass–fail decisions.

Now consider three 25-item tests composed of 1PL parameter estimates. The *b*-parameters are summarized in Table 25.2 and the corresponding test information functions are displayed in Figure 25.6.

For purposes of discussion, we again consider a cut score of $\theta_{cut} = -0.84$. Test 3 clearly provides the most information in the region of the cut score. Tests 1 and 2 have about the same amount of test information at their respective peaks, but within different regions of the scale. Test 1 is most informative near $\theta = 0.0$; Test 2 is most informative near the cut score.

TABLE 25.2
Descriptive Summary of 1PL *b*-Parameters for Three 25-Item Tests (see Figure 25.6)

	Test 1	Test 2	Test 3
Mean	0.01	−0.84	−0.88
SD	0.76	0.90	0.23
Minimum	−1.25	−2.77	−1.35
Maximum	1.81	0.84	−0.43

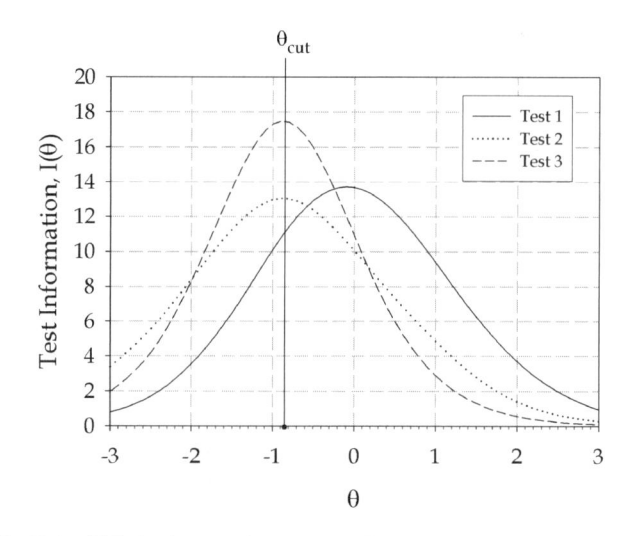

FIG. 25.6. TIFs for three 25-item tests (1PL parameters; see Table 25.2).

Test 2 has approximately the same average item difficulty as Test 3, but the standard deviation of the b-parameters for Test 2 is noticeably larger (see Table 25.2). The consequence of the greater variance of the b-parameters for Test 2 is that the test information is spread out more and correspondingly reduced at the cut score.

IRT calibration programs like BILOG-MG (Zimowski et al., 2003) and WINSTEPS (Linacre, 2004) provide item and test information function plots to facilitate an evaluation of particular items, a test form, or even an item bank. IRT functions can also be computed and plotted in spreadsheet programs such as Microsoft Excel.

TEST INFORMATION AND DECISION ACCURACY

When constructing achievement tests and group tests, it is fairly straightforward to determine the maximum amount of error we are willing to tolerate within different regions of the proficiency scale and then convert the standard errors or error variances to a test specification for some minimum amount of information (e.g., Kelderman, 1987; Luecht, 1992; van der Linden, 1998). But for mastery tests, we need to shift our focus to the amount of information needed near the cut score and how that information translates into improved decision accuracy. Unfortunately, is more difficult to determine how a particular value of the error variance, standard error, or test information function specifically translates into improvements in decision accuracy.[4] Changes in test length and different characteristics of the test items yield different amounts of test information at different points of the proficiency scale. The location of the mastery cut score and characteristics of the examinee population and can also impact decision accuracy.

I designed a computer simulation to demonstrate how test length and various item characteristics—more generally, changes in test information functions at various cut scores—impact decision accuracy for mastery tests[5]. This simulation addressed two issues: (1) the characteristics of the item pool and (2) the location of the mastery cut score. To address the first issue, three very large item pools were generated: (i) an *easy* item pool (mean item difficulty, $\mu_b = -0.50$, $\sigma_b = 1.0$); (ii) a *moderate difficulty* item pool ($\mu_b = 0.0$, $\sigma_b = 1.0$); (iii) and a *difficult* item pool ($\mu_b = 0.50$, $\sigma_b = 1.0$). Each item pool was composed of randomly generated 3PL item parameters.[6] The item discrimination parameters were sampled from a distribution with $\mu_a = 0.65$ and $\sigma_b = 0.4$, regardless of the average difficulty of each item pool. The mean level of discrimination, perhaps seeming a bit low for educational achievement testing or certain types of group tests, corresponds approximately to what many professional certification and licensure agencies report as the average discrimination on their mastery tests. The c-parameters are fixed at 0.15 for all of the items in all of the item pools. The second issue involving the location of the cut point was managed by evaluating decision accuracy relative to three cut scores: at the 20th percentile of a normal distribution ($\theta_{cut} = -0.84$); at the mean ($\theta_{cut} = 0.0$); and at the 70th percentile ($\theta_{cut} = 0.52$).

The computer simulation proceeds as follows. First, a test form is created by randomly choosing a test length, k, where $5 \leq k \leq 150$ items. This allows test length to be included as a random factor in the design. Second, k item a-parameters and b-parameters are sampled from one of the three item pools. Third, each test form is "administered" by the simulation

---

[4]Wilcox (1976) demonstrated how the binomial error model could be used to for very homogeneous items. Convenient analytical methods to predict the change in decision accuracy as a function of changes in test information for heterogeneous tests are not readily available.

[5]The author wrote all of the computer software for these simulations. The software was compiled using double-precision real numbers for all calculations. Normal deviates were computed using the Box-Mueller algorithm.

[6]A normal distribution, $b \sim (\mu_b, \sigma_b^2)$, was used for sampling the b-parameters. A log-normal distribution, $ln(a) \sim (\mu_a, \sigma_a^2)$, was used for sampling the a-parameters.

		Estimated Proficiencies	
		$\hat{\theta} \geq \theta_{cut}$	$\hat{\theta} < \theta_{cut}$
True	$\theta \geq \theta_{cut}$	Correct Pass	False Negative
Proficiencies	$\theta < \theta_{cut}$	False Positive	Correct Fail

FIG. 25.7. A two-by-two Table of possible classification decisions.

software to 1,000 normally distributed examinees ($\mu_\theta = 0, \sigma_\theta = 1.0$). Dichotomous responses are generated for each simulated examinee to all k items a particular test form. The simulated k item responses are then scored—that is, a score, $\hat{\theta}$, was estimated for each examinee—using the 3PL item parameters.[7] Finally, decision accuracy was determined by comparing each simulated examinee's true proficiency, θ, and estimated score, $\hat{\theta}$, to the established cut score ($-0.84, 0.0,$ or 0.52). The four possible classification decision outcomes are depicted in Figure 25.7.

Correct-pass decisions occur when both the examinee's true proficiency and estimated score are greater than or equal to the cut score. Conversely, *correct-fail decisions* occur when both the true proficiency score and estimated score are below the cut score. *False-negative errors* result when examinees who should pass, based on their true competency, fail to attain the passing score on a particular test form. *False-positive errors* occur when examinees who should not pass, based on their true competency, pass an examination by chance. There are obviously many policy issues to resolve when evaluating false-negative and false-positive errors (e.g., costs, consequences). It is even possible to develop weighting mechanisms to reflect differential policies about decision errors. For example, false-positive errors are usually considered to be more serious than false-negative errors when issuing a medical license because they represent greater dangers to the public (i.e., granting an incompetent individual a license to practice medicine). For our present purposes, however, we consider these two types of errors to be equally serious.

The simulation was repeated for 1,000 randomly selected test forms selected from each of the three item pools. In turn, each test form was "administered" to one thousand examinees. Table 25.3 summarizes the distributions of item statistics for the three thousand test forms. The mean a-parameters for the test forms stayed close to $\mu_a = 0.65$, on average, as intended. As noted, $\mu_a = 0.65$ is a reasonable value to use for mastery testing simulations. The means of the test-form mean b-parameters, $-0.52, 0.03,$ and 0.47, reflect the average difficulties of each item pool; that is, $\mu_{b(Easy)} = -0.50$, $\mu_{b(Moderate)} = 0.0$, and $\mu_{b(Difficult)} = 0.50$. The test lengths ranged from 5 to 150 items for each of the three item pools, with mean test lengths of 75 to 78 items.

Although not reported here, the sampling distributions for the 3,000 samples ($N = 1,000$ per test form) closely approximated the unit normal distribution (i.e., $\theta \sim [0, 1]$). Table 25.4 summarizes the amount of test information for the test forms at the three cut scores and the corresponding standard errors of estimate. Decisions accuracy is also summarized in this table, where the frequencies are computed per 1,000 examinees. Note that as the cut score increases, the number of false-negative errors also increased, on average. The number of false-positive errors remained relatively constant, averaging about 47.5 incorrect passing decisions per 1,000 examinees.

---

[7]Expected a posteriori scores (Bock & Aitkin, 1981; Mislevy, 1986) were computed for each examinee, using the generating item parameters. Employing estimated item parameters for IRT scoring, based on calibrations of independent samples of simulated examinees, might have provided a closer approximation to reality. However, I decided not to address calibration and linking issues in this simulation, given the large number of test forms involved.

TABLE 25.3
Descriptive Summary of Item Parameters for the Simulation Conditions (1,000 Tests Generated Per Condition)

	Easy Pool ($\theta_{cut} = -0.84$)		Moderate Pool ($\theta_{cut} = 0.0$)		Difficult Pool ($\theta_{cut} = 0.52$)	
	Mean	SD	Mean	SD	Mean	SD
a-Parameters						
Mean	0.65	0.31	0.66	0.32	0.66	0.31
SD	0.38	0.21	0.37	0.23	0.38	0.22
b-Parameters						
Mean	−0.52	1.02	0.03	1.04	0.47	1.48
SD	0.76	0.45	0.73	0.46	0.74	0.44
Test length						
Items (*n*)	75.47	42.17	77.80	41.96	74.86	42.89

TABLE 25.4
Descriptive Summary of Test Information, Standard Errors, and Classification Decision Accuracy/Errors

	Easy Pool ($\theta_{cut} = -0.84$)		Moderate Pool ($\theta_{cut} = 0.0$)		Difficult Pool ($\theta_{cut} = 0.52$)	
Outcome Data	Mean	SD	Mean	SD	Mean	SD
Test information SE						
$I(\theta_{cut})$	13.62	13.18	14.72	13.97	12.06	12.97
$SE(\theta_{cut})$	0.46	0.64	0.40	0.34	0.56	1.18
Classification decisions						
Correct passing	772.64	17.66	441.24	38.51	225.22	51.43
Correc failing	143.46	35.13	446.70	36.74	654.86	29.94
False negatives	36.02	13.01	58.97	36.26	78.32	51.39
False positives	47.87	33.86	53.10	33.95	41.60	26.52

No attempt was made to justify false-positive errors as being more important than false-negative errors. Therefore, a total decision accuracy frequency was computed as the simple sum of the correct passing decisions and the correct failing decisions (or, conversely, as 1,000 minus the sum of the false-positive and false-negative errors). Table 25.5 reports the correlations between this total decision accuracy frequency and the five test characteristics varied in this study: (1) the test length; (2) the mean of the *a*-parameters for each test form; (3) the standard deviation of the *a*-parameters; (4) the mean of the *b*-parameters for each test form; and (5) the standard deviation of the *b*-parameters. The correlation sets are arrayed left to right by item pool difficulty (i.e., easy to difficult across columns). It should be noted that all of the intercorrelations

TABLE 25.5
Correlations Between Test Form Characteristics and Total Classification Accuracy
(Correlations are Between the Row Variables and Total Classification Accuracy)

	Easy ($\theta_{cut} = -0.84$)	Moderate ($\theta_{cut} = 0.0$)	Difficulty ($\theta_{cut} = 0.52$)
Mean a-parameters	0.359	0.358	0.291
SD a-parameters	0.195	0.151	0.089
Mean b-parameters	−0.279	−0.099	−0.077
SD b-parameters	0.007	−0.018	0.023
Test length	0.611	0.588	0.546

among the five test characteristics were near zero (i.e., none exceeded 0.08), implying that the zero-order correlations in Table 25.5 can be directly interpreted. Positive correlations indicate that the associated test characteristics are associated with improved classification accuracy. Negative correlations indicate that increases in the associated test characteristics tend to increase the number of decision errors.

Some interesting trends are evident from the patterns of correlations. Quite predictably, increasing test length always increases decision accuracy, regardless of the difficulty of the item pool and corresponding location of the cut score. When the cut score is at the 20th percentile, both the mean and standard deviation of the a-parameters appear to substantially influence decision accuracy, if the item pool is easy. As the item pool gets more difficult and the cut score moves toward the upper end of the proficiency scale, the a-parameters have slightly less influence on decision accuracy. Interestingly, increasing the mean item difficulty for the test forms decreases decision accuracy at $\theta_{cut} = -0.84$. This result admonishes test developers against making a test too difficult when the cut score is in the lower tail of the score distribution.

The empirical total decision accuracy frequency (per 1,000 simulated examinees) is plotted as a function of the test information at the cut score, for each of the three item pools, where the easy, moderate, and difficult item pools respectively correspond to cut scores set at the 20th, 50th, and 70th percentiles of a normal distribution. A LOWESS smoothing function (Cleveland & Devlin, 1988) provides an excellent fit to the data points and was used as a type of empirical receiver-operator characteristic (ROC) function, similar to a power curve. The use of ROC function plots originated in signal detection theory (e.g., Coombs, Dawes, & Tversky, 1970). Each ROC is a plot of the true-positive rate against the false-positive rate. The ROCs can be simultaneously plotted for the different possible cut points of a particular diagnostic (detection) test or for different diagnostic tests. The plot demonstrates tradeoff between sensitivity and specificity; that is, any increase in sensitivity is accompanied by a decrease in specificity. More rapid growth in the curve indicates a more accurate test (or higher power to detect a difference). As the curve approaches the 45-degree diagonal of the ROC space, the test is considered to be less accurate.

Figure 25.8 displays the three decision accuracy curves for the easy, moderate, and difficult item pools. Interpreting these graphs is straightforward. For example, suppose that we were to decide that 90% decision accuracy is a reasonable goal. If the cut point for our mastery test is near the 20th percentile and our item pool, on average, has mean difficulty parameter estimates near to that cut score, then we can achieve that target level of accuracy by building tests that have information values near to 5 or 6. However, suppose that we instead adopt a more stringent policy of considering no more than 5% error to be acceptable (i.e., a target of

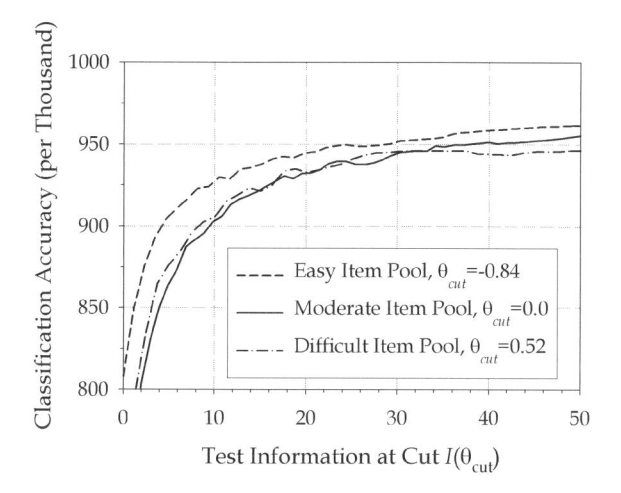

FIG. 25.8. Classification accuracy (correct classifications per 1,000 examinees) as a function of test information for three item pools (easy, moderate, and difficult).

95% accuracy). If we have our cut score set near the 20th percentile and have a fairly easy item pool, we need an information peak near to $I(\theta_{cut} = -0.84) = 24$ to maintain an average error rate of about 5% across test forms. If the cut score is located at the mean of the population or above the mean, even with a corresponding shift in mean item pool difficulty, we can see that we would require peak information of 30 or more near the cut score. In practice, having small item pools that lack adequate discrimination or creating item pools that are too difficult or too easy with respect to maximizing test information in the region of the cut score may make it virtually impossible to even achieve a 5% accuracy rate because of the mismatch between the average difficulty of the items and the location of the cut score.

What should be very clear from this simulation is that controlling the location and amount of the IRT information provided by a test should be a key consideration in test design and assembly. In turn, maintaining the requisite supply of information to meet present and future test development demands becomes an item banking and inventory control matter.

TEST INFORMATION TARGETING AND AUTOMATED TEST ASSEMBLY

IRT test information functions are powerful mechanisms for designing and building mastery tests. The basic idea is to establish a "target" that designates a prescribed amount of test information in the region of the established cut score for building test forms. We can than select items to meet that target.

There are two possible qualifications of *target* within the context of designing mastery testing: absolute targets and relative targets. An *absolute target* is an explicit TIF curve to be met. An absolute target can be a single point or may be indicated by a discrete set of values meant to represent an entire TIF curve. For example, in the previous section, a target test information value at the cut score, $I(\theta_{cut} = -0.84) = 24$, helped to achieve an average decision accuracy rate of 95% for test forms selected from a relatively easy item pool. With an absolute target, the goal in test assembly is to select the items for all future test forms to match the established TIF curve. The absolute target is conceptually similar to having an engineering specification for manufacturing test forms; it ensures consistently built tests that yield a prescribed amount of test information where it is needed.

A special case of an absolute target is a *minimum absolute* target. With a minimum absolute target, the goal is to select items for each test form to at least provide some minimum prescribed amount of test information needed. There are other strategies that researchers have advocated for generating absolute target information functions, ranging from using the TIF from an existing test form as the target (or the average TIF from several test forms) to various methods of weighting the information demands within various regions of the θ scale (Kelderman, 1987; Luecht, 1992; Luecht & Burgin, 2003; van der Linden, 1998).

The second interpretation is that the target is the maximum possible value of the test information function in the region of the cut score. In this latter case, we establish a *relative target* to do the best we can to produce one or more maximally informative mastery tests using the items we have on hand, recognizing that the actual test-form TIFs may change as the characteristics of the item bank change over time.[8] It is desirable to ensure that all of the test forms yield a similar amount of information, especially in the region of the cut score. That is, we want avoid selecting the most informative items from the item pool for only a small number of test forms.[9] The automated test assembly example discussed in the next section demonstrates this complication.

Target information functions are increasingly being used for test construction as part of a sophisticated technology known as *automated test assembly* (ATA). ATA uses mathematical programming algorithms and heuristics to solve one or more basic supply-and-demand problems (van der Linden & Boekkooi-Timminga, 1989; Armstrong & Jones, 1992; Armstrong, Jones, Li, & Wu, 1996; Luecht, 1998; Luecht & Hirsch, 1992; Swanson & Stocking, 1993; van der Linden, 1998; van der Linden & Adema, 1998). The item pool is the *supply*. The test information target(s) and associated constraints are the *demands*. The basic ATA challenge is to select the items that meet all of the test specification demands, and in all likelihood, to build multiple test forms. Most ATA algorithms and heuristics can incorporate absolute or relative targets, along with potentially large numbers of nonstatistical test specifications such as content constraints, cognitive requirements, and so on. Although specialized ATA computer software is required to implement ATA, both commercial and public domain computer programs are increasingly becoming available.

It is important to understand that all of the items in an item pool must be calibrated to a common θ metric to properly implement ATA. That is, we need (stable) IRT item parameter estimates for every item in the item pool.[10] Furthermore, those items need to be calibrated or otherwise linked to a common bank scale. Techniques for calibrating items on a bank scale are discussed by Hambleton and Swaminathan (1985) and Kolen and Brennan (1995). The items must also be coded for content and any other attributes used in test construction. Some testing programs have relatively few content coding schemes; others use elaborate taxonomies that may code each item on 20 or more different sets of attributes.

In ATA using IRT, the test specifications are made up of two types: (1) IRT test information targets (formally converted into quantities called *objective functions* to be maximized or minimized) and (2) constraints. Constraints can reflect exact counts such as the test length or the

---

[8] These two perspectives on targeting have been synthesized using mathematical programming (van der Linden, 1998). That is, an *objective function* can be designed to correspond to the amount of test information to be maximized or, the objective function can be expressed as a distance between an established target TIF and the test form TIF to be minimized.

[9] The same problem is faced for computerized adaptive testing (CAT). By choosing the maximally informative items, we tend to overuse the best items for most examinees. If we restrict the use of an item once some number of examinees are administered that item, the tests almost certainly degrade in precision over time. In CAT, exposure controls are typically implemented to manage this tradeoff between maximizing test information.

[10] ATA can be used to content balance tryout sections containing experimental items that may not have item statistics available. However, the ATA application discussed here, using IRT, assumes that every item in the item pool has IRT statistics available.

TABLE 25.6
Descriptive Summary of the Item Pool for ATA

	Item Counts		a-Parameters		b-Parameters		c-Parameters	
		(%)	Mean	(SD)	Mean	(SD)	Mean	(SD)
A	157	(35.4)	0.67	(0.26)	−0.32	(0.89)	0.17	(0.12)
B	175	(39.5)	0.72	(0.24)	−0.22	(0.80)	0.17	(0.10)
C	27	(6.1)	0.67	(0.19)	−0.50	(1.08)	0.19	(0.11)
D	84	(19.0)	0.81	(0.26)	−0.01	(0.72)	0.18	(0.10)
All	443	(100.0)	0.72	(0.25)	−0.23	(0.84)	0.18	(0.11)

number of items having pictorial content. Constraints can also be represented as an acceptable range of frequencies for items having some attribute (e.g., 5 to 15 items coded as "geometry items"). Virtually any countable or otherwise quantifiable attribute can be constrained in ATA. Examples include word counts, average readability, and so on. The problem is specified for the ATA software as the target(s) and constraints. The software then chooses the items to meet the target, subject to also satisfying all of the constraints.

A relatively simple example illustrates how ATA works in an IRT context. Suppose that we want to build four 60-item test forms that have parallel statistical characteristics. There are four content areas for this test labeled A, B, C, and D. The test specifications call for exactly 21 items from content area A, 24 items from content area B, 4 items from content area C, and 11 items from content area D. The item pool is composed of 443 items from a certification examination and all of the items were calibrated to a common scale, using the 3PL model. Table 25.6 presents summary statistics for the for the item pool.

The first ATA build is an absolute test information target (Target A) to correspond to a 60-item test that essentially matches the average item characteristics in the item pool (see the "All" row in Table 25.6). An ATA heuristic called the normalized weighted absolute deviation heuristic (NWADH) (Luecht, 1998, 2000) is used to sequentially build the four test forms.[11] Each test form is required to meet the exact distribution of content described. No item overlap is allowed across forms. The test information functions for Target A (the solid, heavy line) and the four test forms (labeled A1, A2, A3, and A4) are plotted in Figure 25.9.

Obviously, the TIFs for the four test forms closely match the target. The ATA build is successful; there are four nearly parallel test forms. Further, the item statistics, although not reported here, also closely correspond to the average characteristics of the item pool.

To better appreciate the practical utility of ATA, consider that four 60-item content-balanced test forms, each meeting the same absolute target for difficulty and test information, are constructed in less than 3 seconds on a personal computer with a Pentium IV processor. Although this particular ATA build might be "too easy"—that is, Target A mirrors the characteristics of the item pool and the content of the item pool is proportional to the requirements for each 60-item test form, there is a very important message here. ATA should be easy! The more closely we construct item pools to match the demands for test forms, the fewer complications we encounter in ATA. Although ATA algorithms and heuristics can indeed solve problems

---

[11] A DOS-based software program called CASTISEL (Luecht, 1998) implements the NWADH as was used for these ATA builds.

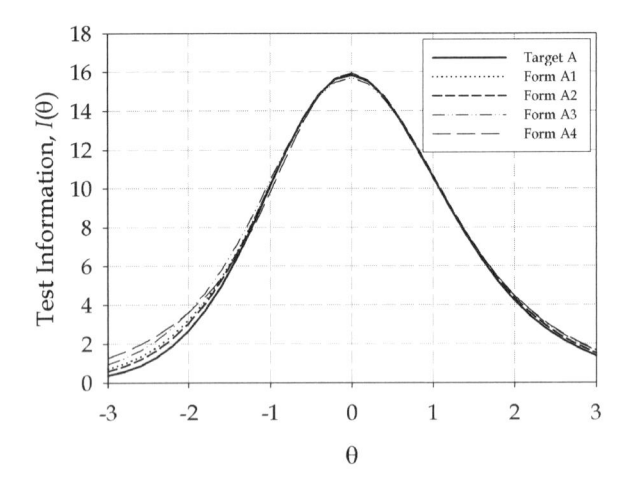

FIG. 25.9. Four forms sequentially built to match Target A.

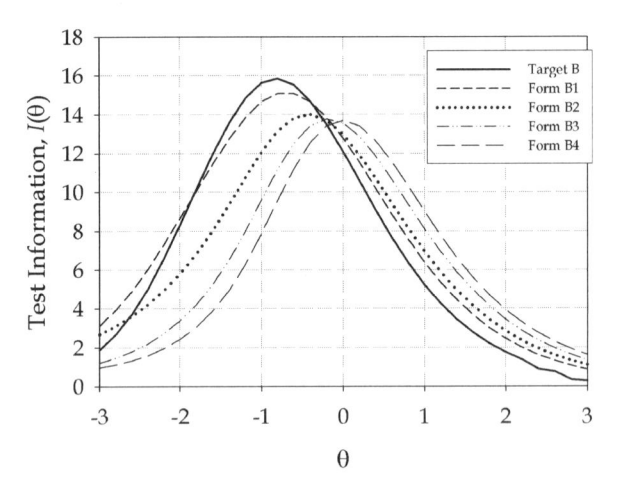

FIG. 25.10. Four forms sequentially built to match Target B.

with severely competing demands (e.g., Luecht, 1998, 2000; Swanson & Stocking, 1993), the bigger question is, "Why would a test developer want to do that?" That is, why create an item pool with particular supply characteristics and then demand something else?

It is relatively easy to show the impact of introducing competition between the statistical characteristics of the item pool (the supply) and test specifications (the demands). Consider building four more test forms from the same item pool, but now use a new target TIF shifted to the left. Target B vis designed to request peak information near to $\theta = -0.8$. The NWADH was again employed in a sequential ATA build and the resulting TIFs for forms B1, B2, B3, and B4 are shown in Figure 25.10.

Because of the sequential ATA build, Form B1 (the first test form selected) comes close to Target B, but Forms B2, B3, and B4 systematically deviate from the target. The NWADH could easily be modified to simultaneously build the four forms to be more parallel, thus avoiding the obvious degradation in the solutions under a sequential build, but it is unlikely that any of the forms would match Target B and satisfy the content constraints. If these test forms must meet Target B, the best solution is to effectively design the item pool to achieve that goal.

ITEM POOL INVENTORY MANAGEMENT

The ATA examples in the previous section clearly demonstrate the need to continually evaluate the test information in the item pool in conjunction with the target requirements. When absolute targets are employed, the supply must be proportional to the demands. The TIF for the item pool should at least have the same shape, with the peak located near the same point of the θ scale as the target. The amount of information provided by the item pool in the region of the cut score should be equal to or greater than the target TIF times the number of nonoverlapping test forms needed over some prescribed time frame. It is further recommended to routinely carry out these evaluations of test information functions by major content areas.

By incorporating targeted test information into the consideration of item production needs, test developers can avoid the problem of writing strictly to content demands. Item writing needs to focus more than just on content coverage. IRT provides a concrete way of evaluating the degree to which future statistical test characteristic demands can be met. Although the field of psychometrics cannot yet prescribe how test developers can write items to achieve particular IRT characteristics, it is possible to employ a more principled approaches to item writing, ideally resulting in systematic improvements in the manufacturing processes that are used to create item pools. First, item modeling and item cloning techniques can be used to create items that predictably mimic the characteristics of the highest demand items. Second, by routinely pilot testing and calibrating new items, and evaluating their statistical properties relative to the test specifications, it ought to be possible to reduce item-writing efforts in areas where items are too abundant or aberrant insofar as not meeting the targets. Irvine and Kyllonen (2002) and Haladyna (2004) are excellent resources on modern item writing practices. van der Linden (2005) has further suggested the use of mathematical programming techniques to develop item production and inventory control models that attempt to optimally match item writers or classes of item writers to specific item writing demands. (Also see Boekkooi-Timminga [1990] and Veldkamp & van der Linden [2000].)

ALTERNATIVE TEST DESIGNS FOR MASTERY TESTS

The discussion and examples thus far have focused exclusively on fixed-length test forms. There are other test designs employed in mastery testing, including item-level computerized mastery testing (iCMT), linear-on-the-fly testing (LOTF), testlet-based computerized mastery testing (tb-CMT), and computer-adaptive multistage testing (ca-MST). By incorporating the concepts of absolute or relative test information targets, we can easily show the extensions of ATA to these other test designs.

An iCMT assembles the tests in real time. The tests can be either fixed or variable length. When variable-length tests are used, a decision rule must be implemented. The sequential probability ratio test (SPRT; see Spray & Reckase, 1996) is typically used to end the test, based on the statistical likelihood of classifying an examinee as below some lower bound or above some upper bound. Each item is selected using a relative target of maximizing the test information at the cut score.[12] It should be obvious that if the items are selected to maximize $I(\theta_{cut})$, iCMT produces the same test unless constraints are placed on the amount of times particular items can be selected. At the same time, if reuse is overly constrained (e.g., if no item reuse is allowed), the quality of the test forms is incrementally worse, similar to the problem demonstrated in the previous section for Target B. To overcome this dilemma, various

---
[12]Kingsbury and Weiss (1983) introduced an adaptive variant of iCMT that uses a relative target at the examinees provisional proficiency estimate.

randomization schemes can be introduced into the iCMT assembly process in the form of item exposure controls (e.g., Stocking & Lewis, 2000). These item exposure controls mitigate the tendency of the ATA algorithm to always choose the best (same) items in terms of the information provided at the cut score.

A LOTF, in principle, generates a unique test form for each examinee (Folk & Smith, 2002). Test assembly can be performed in real time or a large number of test forms can be preassembled and randomly assigned to the examinees. Using ATA, we can see that LOTF is merely a special case of multiple fixed-form test construction, using an absolute target TIF. Future test development needs can be modeled using the target TIF and the number of expected (nonoverlapping) test forms.

A tb-CMT uses preconstructed, statistically parallel, content-balanced testlets (Lewis & Sheehan, 1990; Vos & Glas, 2000). As noted, *testlet* refers to a small number of items administered as an intact unit. For tb-CMT, multiple testlets are constructed using ATA, with a common, absolute target TIF. The content may vary across the testlets or all testlets may proportionally represent the content for the entire test. These testlets can be randomly administered to the examinees in a sequence of stages. Either a fixed number of testlets can be administered to every examinee, or the tb-CMT test delivery software may administer a variable-length test, using a statistically based stopping rule such as the SPRT or a criterion based on a loss function that quantifies that risk of making errors in passing or failing the examinees (see Lewis & Sheehan, 1990). Relative targeting can also be used of tb-CMT. For relative targeting, some number of nonoverlapping testlets must be chosen by ATA to be maximally informative in the region of the cut score, with additional constraints placed on the amount of variability in test information allowed among the testlets (e.g., van der Linden & Reese, 1998). With relative targets, the quality of the testlets may change over time; however, this approach uses ATA to construct the best possible mastery tests, given the item pool on hand at within each test construction window.

For ca-MST, the ATA software must build multiple testlets using different absolute target TIFs and possibly different content (Luecht, 2000; Luecht & Nungester, 1998). Once constructed, the testlets are prepackaged in self-administering sets called *panels*. Figure 25.11 presents a 1-2-2 ca-MST panel design for a mastery test. There are five testlets (A to E) administered in three stages. Each testlet can be constructed to meet a separate absolute target TIF as noted in Figure 25.11. Furthermore, each testlet slot can have its own, distinct content specifications (i.e., constraint sets for ATA). Different content specifications can even be used across stages or for different routes. Given the TIFs and content specifications, multiple panels can be constructed using ATA, and packaged for delivery by computer.

These types of ca-MST designs also have important implications for diagnostic testing in the mastery testing context. In addition to making the critical pass–fail decision, ca-MST panels can be flexibly designed to adaptively improve the accuracy of diagnostic score profiles for clearly failing candidates. For example, using a 1-2-2 panel design like the one shown in Figure 25.11, testlets with diagnostically richer test content and potentially different TIF-by-content allocations can be administered in the easier route to Stage 3 (testlets A+B+D) to maximize the accuracy of a score profile (Luecht, 1997).

SOME RECOMMENDED TEST DEVELOPMENT STRATEGIES

This section highlights some test design recommendations for test developers. These recommendations build on the previous sections.

First, it perhaps goes without saying, but using IRT demands having access to reasonably stable pretest response data to properly calibrate the items and to establish a bank scale for

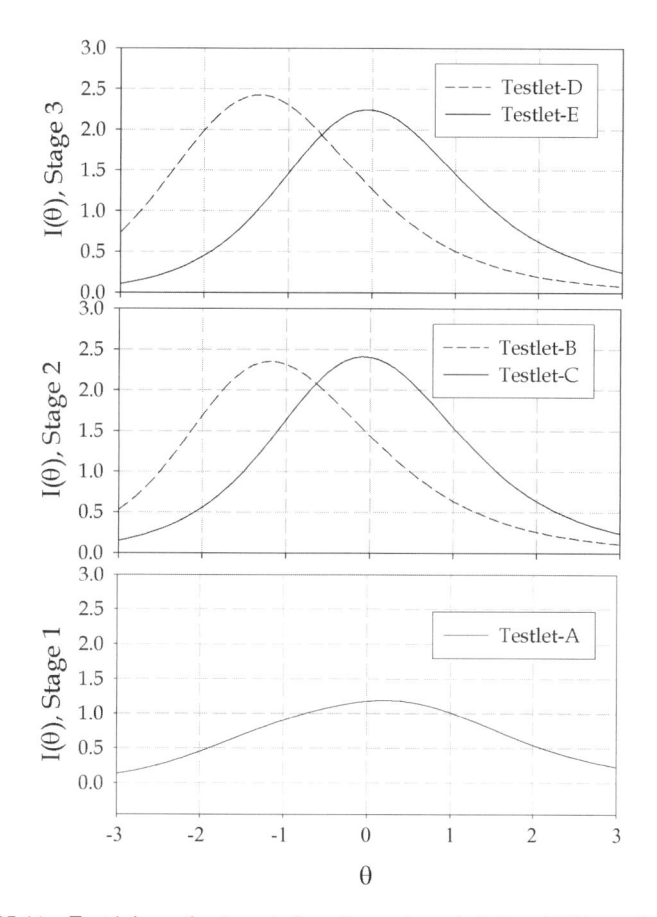

FIG. 25.11. Test information targets for a three-stage 1–2–2 ca-MST panel design.

subsequent use in test development. Stated another way, without response data, IRT cannot be used.[13] An embedded pretest design can be easily implemented for pilot testing small blocks of items along with operational (scored) items. That is, create unscored pretest slots on every operational test form to gather motivated examinee response data for purposes of calibrating the items.

Second, choose an IRT model and calibration software that works for the type of data and sample sizes likely to be encountered during ongoing experimental pretesting of the items. The 3PL model should not be the only model considered. It is true that the 3PL typically fits selected-response data better than the 2PL or 1PL models; however, that model can require 1,000 or more responses per item to estimate stable parameters. The 1PL is robust and entirely usable with 300 (and sometimes fewer) responses, making it an ideal choice for smaller testing programs or programs that need to pretest large numbers of items. Regardless of the choice of model, calibrate all items to a common metric.

Third, be clear about where the examinees are located and where critical decisions are needed along the calibrated (bank) score scale. For example, compute and review IRT distributions of proficiency scores for samples of previous test takers. Locate the cut score on the θ metric. This

---

[13] There has been some research done using regression modeling to predict item statistics (e.g., Mislevy, Sheehan, & Wingersky, 1993). However, those approaches have typically been recommended to supplement, not replace, item pretesting.

can be done using normative data (e.g., the percentile associated with the pass–fail cut score for a representative sample from the population) or by directly mapping a cut score to the θ metric. It is relatively straightforward to use the test characteristic curve to map a percent-correct or number-correct cut score for a calibrated test to the θ metric, following an empirical standard setting study (Kane, 1987; Luecht, 1993, 1995; van der Linden, 1982).

Fourth, explore the test information functions for the current item bank. Plot the test information curves for all items belonging to the primary content areas to evaluate where the item bank has the most and least information. Consider location of the peak IRT test information in the bank, by content area, relative to the cut score. Some changes in item writing may be warranted if the peaks of the test information curves are located well away from the cut score. Closely scrutinize the items for content areas that have test information curves substantially higher than the cut score. As the simulation study demonstrated, making a test more difficult than needed can lead to greater decision errors in a mastery context than making the test easier than needed.

Fifth, if moving toward computer-based testing, select a test design and delivery model (e.g., fixed forms, tb-CMT, or ca-MST) that works for the size and nature of items in your current item bank. Once a model is selected, use a test information targeting strategy to (a) ensure maximum information in the region of the cut score; (b) lead to consistently reliable test forms over time and (versus just once); and (c) adequately use a majority of items in the bank. The latter point should not be taken lightly. If the height of the test information target is too high and narrow, large portions of the item bank may be wasted—a costly strategy—and the items that are chosen may be at risk of overexposure. Test information targeting should be viewed as more of an engineering design discipline than an art form intended to assure the production of high-quality tests over time.

Sixth, to the extent feasible, adopt a credible method of ATA to produce test forms. When only one or two test forms are generated every year, test committees composed of subject-matter experts may seem like a reasonable alternative to ATA. However, in the long run, ATA usually proves to be far faster than manual test construction and does a better job of producing both content-parallel and statistically parallel test forms. There is an initial implementation period that involves training staff to use the ATA software, coding all of the items in the item bank, developing software to interface with the item bank data base, designing feasible test information targets, and working with subject matter experts to create a feasible system of test constraints. However, the long-term efficiencies and benefits in terms of test validity, reliability are usually well worth the investment.

Finally, develop an inventory management plan that explicitly ties item writing demands to the content and test information needs specified by ATA. Infeasibility problems in test assembly usually occur for one reason—there are not sufficient items in the item bank to meet the explicit demands of test production. Obviously, if the test is supposed to maximize information in the region of the cut score, more items are needed there than elsewhere along the score scale. Once the inventory management system properly identifies the demands, item modeling and other principled item writing techniques may hold promise to create items with the appropriate content and at the requisite level of difficulty.

SUMMARY

To say that IRT has revolutionized test development is an understatement. IRT item and test characteristic and information functions provide practitioners with some very powerful statistical tools to view the precision of existing test forms and to design the statistical specifications for new test forms. Simply stated, by appropriately using targeted test information, test developers can put measurement precision where it is needed most.

The ability to use targeted test information is critical in mastery testing because decisions are typically isolated to a specific pass–fail cut score. As the computer simulation study presented in this chapter demonstrated, amassing test information in region of the cut score directly impacts decision accuracy. By using a combination of analytical techniques and IRT-based computer simulations like the one discussed here, a testing program can determine the amount of test information needed near the cut score for their own item pools.

This chapter further demonstrated how easy it is to achieve parallel measurement precision across test forms by using ATA to match a target TIF while simultaneously meeting all relevant content and other test constrains. The practice of using targeted test information and ATA can also be extended to multistage test designs that combine mastery testing with potentially adaptive-diagnostic testing capabilities for failing examinees.

REFERENCES

Armstrong, R. D., & Jones, D. H. (1992). Polynomial algorithms for item matching. *Applied Psychological Measurement, 16*, 271–288.

Armstrong, R. D., Jones, D. H., Li, X., & Wu, I. L. (1996). A study of a network flow algorithm and a noncorrecting algorithm for test assembly. *Applied Psychological Measurement, 20*, 89–98.

Birnbaum, A. (1968). Some latent trait models and their use in inferring an examinee's ability. In F. M. Lord & M. R. Novick (Eds.), *Statistical theories of mental test scores*. Reading, MA: Addison-Wesley.

Bock, R. D., & Aitkin, M. (1981). Marginal maximum likelihood estimation of item parameters: An application of the EM-algorithm. *Psychometrika, 46*, 443–459.

Boekkooi-Timminga, E. (1990). Parallel test construction for IRT-based item banks. *Journal of Educational Statistics, 15*, 129–145.

Cleveland, W. S., & Devlin, S. (1988). Locally weighted regression analysis by local fitting. *Journal of the American Statistical Association, 83*, 596–640.

Coombs, C., Dawes, R. M., & Tversky, A. (1970) *Mathematical psychology*. Englewood Cliffs, NJ: Prentice-Hall.

Folk, V. G., & Smith, R. L. (2002). Models for delivery of CBTs. In C. N. Mills, M. T. Potenza, J. J. Fremer, & W. C. Ward (Eds.), *Computer-based testing: building the foundation for future assessments* (pp. 41–66). Mahwah, NJ: Lawrence Erlbaum and Associates.

Haladyna, T. M. (2004). *Developing and validating multiple-choice tet items* (3rd ed.). Mahwah, NJ: Lawrence Erlbaum Associates.

Hambleton, R. K., & Swaminathan, H. (1985). *Item response theory: Principles and applications*. Boston: Kluwer-Nijhoff.

Irvine, S. H., & Kyllonen, P. C. (Eds.). (2002). *Item generation for test development*. Mahwah, NJ: Lawrence Erlbaum Associates.

Kane, M. T. (1987). On the use of IRT models with judgmental standard setting procedures. *Journal of Educational Measurement, 24*, 333–345.

Kelderman, H. (1987). A procedure to assess target information functions. In van der Linden (Ed.), *IRT-based test construction* [research report 87-2]. Enschede, The Netherlands: University of Twente, Department of Educational Measurement and Data Analysis.

Kingsbury, G. G., & Weiss, D. J. (1983). A comparison of IRT-based adaptive mastery testing and a sequential mastery testing procedure. In D. J. Weiss (Ed.), *New Horizons in testing: Latent trait theory and computerized adaptive testing* (pp. 257–283). New York: Academic Press.

Kolen, M. J., & Brennan, R. L. (1995). *Test equating: methods and practices*. New York: Springer-Verlag.

Lewis, C., & Sheehan, K. (1990). Using Bayesian decision theory to design a computer mastery test. *Applied Psychological Measurement, 14*, 367–382.

Linacre, J. M. (2004). *WINSTEPS Version 3.54*. [computer program]. Chicago: Author.

Lord, F. M. (1980). *Applications of item response theory to practical testing problems*. Mahwah, NJ: Lawrence Erlbaum Associates.

Luecht, R. M. (April, 1992). *Generating target information functions and item specifications in test design*. Paper presented at the Annual Meeting of the National Council on Measurement in Education, San Francisco, CA.

Luecht, R. M. (1993). *Using IRT to improve the standard-setting process for dichotomous and polytomous items.* Paper presented at the Annual Meeting of the National Council on Measurement in Education, Atlanta, GA.

Luecht, R. M. (1995). *Some technical insights into response-based standard setting for dichotomous and polytomous items.* Paper presented at the Annual Meeting of the National Council on Measurement in Education, San Francisco, CA.

Luecht, R. M. (1997, April). *An adaptive sequential paradigm for managing multidimensional content.* Paper presented at the Annual Meeting of the American Educational Research Association, Chicago, IL.

Luecht, R. M. (1998). Computer-assisted test assembly using optimization heuristics. *Applied Psychological Measurement, 22,* 224–236.

Luecht, R. M. (2000, April). *Implementing the computer-adaptive sequential testing (CAST) framework to mass produce high quality computer-adaptive and mastery tests.* Paper presented at the Annual Meeting of the National Council on Measurement in Education, New Orleans, LA.

Luecht, R. M., & Burgin, W. (April, 2003). *Matching test design to decisions: Test specifications and use of automated test assembly for adaptive multi-stage testlets.* Paper to be presented at the Annual Meeting of the National Council on Measurement in Education, Chicago, IL.

Luecht, R. M., & Hirsch, T. M. (1992). Computerized test construction using an average growth approximation of target information functions. *Applied Psychological Measurement, 16,* 41–52.

Luecht, R. M., & Nungester, R. (1998). Some practical examples of computer-adaptive sequential testing. *Journal of Educational Measurement, 35*(3), 229–249.

Mislevy, R. J. (1986). Bayes modal estimation in item response models. *Psychometrika, 51,* 177–195.

Mislevy, R. J., Sheehan, K. M., & Wingersky, M. (1993). How to equate tests with little or no data. *Journal of Educational Measurement, 30,* 55–78.

Rasch, G. (1960). *Probabilistic models for some intelligence and attainment tests.* Copenhagen: Danish Institute for Educational Research.

Spray, J. A., & Reckase, M. D. (1996). Comparison of SPRT and sequential Bayes procedures for classifying examinees into two categories using a computerized test. *Journal of Educational and Behavioral Statistics, 21,* 405–414.

Stocking, M. L., & Lewis, C. (2000). Methods of controlling item exposure CAT. In W. van der Linden & C. A.W. Glas (Eds.), *Computerized adaptive testing* (pp. 163–182). Dordrecht: Kluwer.

Swanson, L., & Stocking, M. L. (1993). A model and heuristic for solving very large item selection problems. *Applied Psychological Measurement, 17,* 151–166.

van der Linden, W. J. (1982). A latent trait method for determining intrajudge inconsistency in the Angoff and Nedelsky techniques of standard setting. *Journal of Educational Measurement, 19,* 295–308.

van der Linden, W. J. (1998). Optimal assembly of psychological and educational tests. *Applied Psychological Measurement, 22,* 195–211.

van der Linden, W. J. (2005). *Linear models for optimal test design.* New York: Springer.

van der Linden, W. J., & Adema, J. (1998). Simultaneous assembly of multiple test forms. *Journal of Educational Measurement, 35,* 185–198.

van der Linden, W. J., & Boekkooi-Timminga, E. (1989). A maximin model for test design with practical test constraints. *Psychometrika, 54,* 237–247.

van der Linden, W. J., & Reese, L. M. (1998). A model for optimal constrained adaptive testing. *Applied Psychological Measurements, 22,* 259–270.

Veldkamp, B. P., & van der Linden, W. J. (2000). Designing item pools for computerized adaptive testing. In W. van der Linden & C. A. W. Glas (Eds.), *Computerized adaptive testing* (pp. 149–162.) Dordrecht: Kluwer.

Vos, H. J. & Glas, C. A. W. (2000). Testlet-based adaptive mastery testing. In W. van der Linden & C. A. W. Glas (Eds.), *Computerized adaptive testing* (pp. 289–309). Dordrecht: Kluwer.

Wilcox, R. (1976). A note on the length and passing score of a mastery test. *Journal of Educational Statistics, 1,* 359–364.

Zimowski, M. F., Muraki, E., Mislevy, R. J., & Bock, R. D. (2003). *BILOG-MG 3* [computer program]. Chicago: Scientific Software International.

V
Test Production and Administration

26

Test Production Effects on Validity

Dan Campion
Sherri Miller
ACT

Assembling and readying a test for administration require close attention to test validity. A typographical error can ruin an item or even a whole test. This chapter describes the steps in assembling and producing a test so that the test content conforms to the developer's intentions and to the best publishing practices. The chapter begins by asking test developers to view their entire development process from a publisher's point of view, focusing on the final product test takers receive and highlighting the importance of advance planning and clear communication. The chapter's next section discusses test formats for paper-and-pencil tests and computer-based tests, emphasizing the factors of legibility, readability, and reproducibility. The chapter concludes by offering guidelines for procedures and quality control to ensure that tests are error free. Because testing programs differ widely and technological changes affect the production process frequently, the chapter often offers guiding principles and questions rather than specific prescriptions. However, detailed examples, specific pointers, and recommended approaches are provided across the entire range of practical questions that arise in test assembly and production.

ADOPTING A PUBLISHING PERSPECTIVE

Testing means publishing. Eventually, the results of the processes described in previous chapters must be translated into products (tests) for audiences (examinees). Ancillary publications—such as guidelines for item writers, test preparation guides for students, administration manuals for proctors, and reports for test users and the public—may also be required. So every testing program encompasses a publishing function and must handle or delegate an array of planning, scheduling, manufacturing, and distribution details. That is, a test developer or agency must build its own publishing wing or else carefully choose a test publisher willing and equipped to faithfully carry out the developer's intentions. This chapter describes what is required to turn assessment plans into published products—more specifically, into error-free tests that maintain test validity. We hope that the chapter helps test developers and agencies to decide whether, and how, to build in-house publishing capabilities. We hope also that it helps test publishers—both those within a testing agency and those working under commission—to collaborate successfully with the development teams who brought the tests along to the point at which they are ready for production.

Although our topic is test production—the steps in getting the test assembled and ready for administration—we want to emphasize that producing valid tests requires developers to consider the final published product throughout the test development process. We have observed that, although measurement professionals are generally skilled at estimation, their estimates of the publishing steps it takes to implement their ideas can often be perilously low. Brilliant test designs fail if the developers neglect to plan the material, formatting, labor, time, budget, and other resources required to translate their design into physical objects like test booklets, on-screen displays, and audiocassettes tailored to the validity requirements of the test and the needs of test takers. Therefore, a brief review of the steps in test development as a whole is warranted. Allowing for exceptions, the test development cycle is easily sketched.

Start-Up Phase

1. Determine purpose(s) and use(s).
2. Develop preliminary time-and-task schedules and testing schedules; review and refine during the cycle.
3. Develop/design the construct and the test specifications.
4. Budget resources (e.g., estimate needed staffing and costs).
5. Estimate item needs.
6. Prepare item-writer guides.
7. Identify item writers.

Pretest Phase

1. Acquire items.
2. Word process and edit items.
3. Internally review items for content and fairness.
4. Revise items.
5. Externally review items for content and fairness.
6. Revise items.
7. Rereview/rerevise items as necessary.
8. Format items for publication.
9. Finalize scoring keys/rubrics.
10. Manufacture test booklets/CD-ROMS.
11. Identify pretest population and administer pretest.
12. Analyze statistical results; resolve miskeys and other flaws.
13. Identify pool of statistically passing items.
14. Organize item bank.

Operational Phase

1. Qualitatively evaluate and sort items in pool.
2. Construct test forms/active pool based on test content and statistical specifications.
3. Internally review and check forms/active pool versus test specifications.
4. Revise forms/active pool as necessary.
5. Document keys and match to specs.
6. Internally review forms/active pool for content and fairness.
7. Revise forms/active pool.

8. Externally review forms/active pool for content and fairness.
9. Rereview/rerevise as necessary.
10. Construct test battery forms (paper-and-pencil tests only).
11. Internally review test battery forms for balance and cluing.
12. Format test battery forms/active pool for publication.
13. Finalize scoring keys/rubrics.
14. Manufacture test battery form booklets/CD-ROMS.
15. Conduct scaling/equating/norming study as required by program.
16. Analyze results of study; resolve problems.
17. Administer operational test battery forms/active pool.
18. Score test battery form/computer-based test.
19. Analyze results (e.g., reliability, differential item functioning [DIF] analyses); resolve problems.
20. Prepare and send score reports.
21. Respond to item challenges, if any.
22. Organize item bank and database.

We recommend this sketch as a rough outline for a how-to exercise for test developers: Adapt the sketch to your own needs and think backward through the process, considering the practical needs and challenges to be met. This exercise, whether undertaken at the beginning of a new program or a review of an ongoing one, reveals hazards and highlights opportunities. It will help you avert mishaps and gain efficiency and economy. The exercise can be as simple or elaborate as you care to make it or circumstances require. You might, for instance, make one pass through the outline focusing on quality control (QC), another pass focusing on staff requirements, and so forth. Details count. It is important to carefully define each task and to clearly identify who is responsible for each task. Unassigned activities do not get done, and vague assignments get fuzzy results.

A young editor starting out at a venerable encyclopedia publisher years ago was startled one day when told by an old hand that the first decision the company's leaders made regarding a new edition of the reference book set was to specify the size of the wooden bookshelf. It seemed an amusing misplacement of priorities to the young editor at the time, but later came to appear wise, and now looks inevitable. Publishing is ultimately a manufacturing process, and everything follows from the artifact produced. If the encyclopedia makers did not place their order early for the right quantity of timber, they and their customers would not have had a place to house their volumes of knowledge. By analogy, a test maker needs to identify lots of critical dimensions early in the process and keep them in view throughout production.

For instance, a test developer needs to ensure that test preparation materials approximate actual tests (American Educational Research Association [AERA], American Psychological Association [APA], & National Council on Measurement in Education [NCME], 1999, Standards 8.1 and 8.2). Test reviewers must see the test materials in final format or a reasonable approximation thereof (Standard 3.6). The operational test should look exactly like the pretest (e.g., stimulus and items are on facing pages). Or perhaps the operational test format can vary from the pretest format within certain limits of tolerance (e.g., there are page-turning effects, but they are minimal) that need to be monitored. Are the appropriate computer hardware and software available to ensure these product characteristics? Are there adequate staff, time, and equipment to get such jobs done? Unlike the encyclopedia publisher, a developer does not need to design a bookshelf (unless the examinees are exceptionally unlucky), but the dimensions of things like test booklets and answer sheets do need to be specified. Working backward through the test development outline, list features already decided upon—either by test developer or client—and features yet to be stipulated. List questions about the best methods and processes to achieve the intended products. And identify what you can least afford to have go wrong. These lists inform planning. Some lists can become agenda items for discussion with colleagues, vendors, and clients. Other lists can become checklists for use in QC.

Why are such lists not ready-made? Because test programs differ and technology changes quickly. Benchmarks (pointers for test formats and QC) and mileposts (procedural steps) can, however, guide list making to suit specific testing program and technological resources. Accordingly, the next major section of this chapter discusses test format and the final major section discusses procedures and QC. These sections' content should be considered not only in the context of test production (making the artifact), but also in the larger context of test development (conceiving and designing the test). As with the encyclopedia publisher, what seems superficially as if it should be the last decision reached may well turn out to be the decision to make first.

TEST FORMAT

General Considerations

Tests are utilitarian objects. Their form should follow from their function. A test's format should help test takers to do their best work without interference. Although complicated documents, tests must be presented simply if they are to be valid and fair. Examinees should not be hampered by confusing directions, unwieldy layouts, busy typefaces, or mazelike illustrations—unless the ability being tested is skill in dealing with needless obstacles. Making the complex simple is the art and craft of designing test formats. This same idea applies to both paper-and-pencil tests (PPTs) and computer-based tests (CBTs). There is no reason the results should lack aesthetic value.

For a guiding principle use Thoreau's "Simplify, simplify," or better yet, "Simplify." But of course the devil is in the details, and simplification is itself a complicated process. Fortunately, design guidelines older than Gutenberg and as recent as the latest edition of *The Chicago Manual of Style* (2003) help. The main ideas are to use familiar formats and sturdy fonts, minimize page-turning and scrolling, make the presentation as intuitive as possible, and clearly state all directions. Examinees then know what to expect, can easily read the test, navigate it conveniently, and get through the exercise with the least fuss.

Good test design is inclusive. In accord with the school of thinking known as "universal design," assessments should be "designed and developed from the beginning to allow participation of the widest possible range of students, and to result in valid inferences about performance for all students who participate in the assessment" (Thompson, Johnstone, & Thurlow, 2002, p. 5). Designing tests from the beginning to accommodate the needs of virtually all students makes for fair tests, as advocated by the *Standards for Educational and Psychological Testing* (AERA, APA, & NCME, 1999, pp. 74–75). It also is the most practical and convenient approach for all concerned, from test makers to test takers. The definition of *universal design* speaks as well to efficiency and economy as it does to fairness: "the design of products and environments to be usable by all people, to the greatest extent possible, without the need for adaptation or specialized design" (The Center for Universal Design, 1997, p. 1).

As advocates of universal design acknowledge, however, "the concept of universally designed assessments is still a work in progress" (Thompson et al., 1997, n.p.). And as its practitioners acknowledge, "the Principles of Universal Design address only universally usable design, while the practice of design involves more than consideration for usability. Designers must also incorporate other considerations such as economic, engineering, cultural, gender, and environmental concerns in their design processes" (The Center for Universal Design, 1997, p. 3). This chapter forms common cause with the "work in progress" of universal design, and in those few cases where departures from current universal design guidelines are recommended, other motivating considerations are offered.

Test design and assembly should be preceded by careful consideration of how the test will be administered operationally. Will the means of presentation be entirely print, entirely computerized, or will both means be used? Will there be large-print editions? Audiocassette or audio compact disc versions? Reader scripts? A Braille edition? Will there be artwork? If so, will it need to be rendered in raised-line drawing format for use with the audio and Braille editions? Taking the range of formats into account ahead of time reduces or obviates the need to retrofit for alternative editions. However, it may not always be possible to foretell all the editions. That is why it is best to design tests for maximum flexibility to meet the widest range of needs. For example, if a test is to have a Braille edition, the original test design should avoid these design features: graphs or pictures irrelevant to the construct, vertical or diagonal text, keys and legends positioned left of or below a figure or item, items that depend on reading graphics for which no textual description is supplied, and purely decorative design features (Thompson et al., 1997, p. 12). In general (except for the occasional graph that requires some labels to be diagonal to avoid crowding), these design features are best avoided for all readers. Good design for one audience is likely to be good design for all.

In considering the variant editions, "the size of the bookcase," that is, how much space is available to fill, becomes an important factor. In each format, will there be a problem in fitting the test on the page or the computer screen? For instance, a large table or graph that runs across two pages in a regular-type booklet will not fit in a large-type booklet or on screen in such a way as to all be visible at once. Large, finely detailed artwork that fits on one page in a regular-type booklet may not translate well into large-type editions or on screen—or may require page turning or scrolling. In evaluating the space available in each format, economy of means in graphics is best: effective "design strategies are transparent and self-effacing in character" (Tufte, 1990, p. 33). Testing program guidelines should specify maximum dimensions for tables and artwork.

The same idea holds true for text. For instance, if a reading test passage fits on one page in a regular-type printed booklet, does it also fit on one page in other formats, including on screen? If not, is test validity or comparability compromised, or does the testing protocol compensate for the difference, such as by giving examinees extra time to navigate? Or, to take another example, if a mathematics test booklet has blank space for examinees to do scratch work on the same page as a test item, is there equivalent space in other editions, and provision for doing scratch work while taking the computer-based version? Thinking across platforms helps to prevent a testing program from falling between them.

Of course it is imperative to provide clear instructions to test takers (Standards 3.20 and 5.5). If there are several editions of the test, The directions need to be as nearly identical as feasible. Deciding when examinees are to read overall test and subtest directions—in the testing time allotted, or before timing begins—helps to determine which pages/screens the directions appear on. Similarly, formatting with respect to numbering of items and lettering of alternative responses to multiple-choice items should be identical or parallel. Answer documents should be made as nearly equivalent as possible for PPTs and their computer-based counterparts. Designing with foresight helps to make alternative versions resemble one another as closely as can be achieved and prevents mishaps like answer sheets that do not match their corresponding test booklets in numbering or lettering. Just as important as clear and consistent instructions is avoiding of gratuitous variation in item presentation. Across editions, there should be standard format and terminology. For example, in multiple-choice mathematics and science tests, where numerals frequently are offered as answer choices, the numerals should be aligned and spaced consistently, and data tables and graphs should be labeled and identified consistently.

Beside considering the operational versions of a test, developers must gauge how closely an operational test must resemble antecedent pilot test, field test, and pretest. Must these versions all be identical? Or can it be shown that, for example, changing a page layout or resizing an illustration between tryout and operational testing does not affect item performance? It is important to establish criteria for such judgments well in advance of pretesting, because designs are still malleable at early stages. It is important to consider *page-turning effects* (changes in item performance associated with altered page breaks). Pretesting four-page test units and assuming that dropping failed items and cutting the units to two pages for the operational test will work requires that the pretest item statistics hold up well under operational conditions and that prediction equations predict. Undertaking studies to show that item performance remains stable or falls within acceptable limits when four pages are cut down to two is necessary unless page breaks are kept the same (in this case, either by limiting unit length to two pages or by using blank space to pad the operational test to four pages).

With general test formatting considerations defined and at least provisional decisions made, the details particular to PPTs and to CBTs can be considered; they are treated in the following two subsections. But first, test formatting and production across versions and platforms needs addressing. In a new testing program, there is an opportunity to engineer efficiencies into the system. In an existing testing program, efficiency may be increased.

The main question is whether or not an item bank is used. Smaller testing programs may not need one, but a computerized library of items and associated databases has become a virtual necessity in large-scale testing programs. Although design and maintenance of an item bank is a large topic (see Vale, chap. 11, this volume), only a small but important part is of concern here: in what formats must materials be entered into the item bank, and in what formats can they be withdrawn? It would be ideal if an item bank were flexible enough to accept materials from many kinds of software, and to output in many formats—or, alternatively, that there were, say, one standard text and graphic program that would "do it all." Changes in technology open new possibilities and foreclose on old methods frequently, but at the time of this writing no item bank was a clear pane of glass, and no software program a clear beam of light.

It is likely that an existing item bank needs test materials in one or another of the widely used word processing programs, such as Microsoft Word or WordPerfect, and graphics programs, such as CorelDraw or Lotus Freelance. Whatever the set of programs is, having test authors submit materials in those programs "upstream" and using them consistently in the course of item editing makes for a smooth process. Adding features and software—for example, to add mathematical symbols and graphics, or even to customize some formats and type—may be necessary. All these must be tested and troubleshot in the item bank to ensure they are accepted, stored, and output satisfactorily (both accurately and swiftly). Similarly, the test developer needs to check on such features as line breaks—are they preserved in the item bank? Do they need to be? Where text line numbers are used, as in some reading tests, the developer needs either to ensure that line breaks are the same or that there are QC steps to adjust line numbers. Customized word processing software may help to mesh with the item bank's database software.

Some item banks may be equipped to output camera-ready copy or digital files suitable for use in producing printed test booklets and for display on screen for CBTs. However, this is often not the case; the item bank generates word processing files similar or identical to the files entered into the item bank, and these generally are not suitable for print production or direct display on screen. The intervening step of a desktop publishing system generally is required.

In a small testing program that has no item bank or a very small one, the entire editorial production of tests can be handled in a desktop publishing environment. That is, in-house writers and editors can input the tests directly in one or another of the proprietary software packages, such as QuarkXPress or Adobe InDesign, which are available for both PC and Macintosh operating systems. However, larger testing programs that use large item banks often must forgo this direct approach. They may, however, export files from the item bank into a desktop publishing system. Such a system assembles text, graphics, and formats into pages of formatted, publication-ready material. *Publication-ready* means ready to be released to a printing company or for CBT production. Printing companies ordinarily have their own production steps: (1) prepress work, in which camera-ready copy is photographed, or digital files are "preflighted" for proper raster image processing and page imposition, and the printing plates are made; (2) presswork, in which the booklets are actually printed; and (3) postpress work, or collating, folding, binding, and bundling for storage or delivery. Similarly, CBT producers need to check and perhaps make adjustments to the digital files, format them for display on screen, and test all functions and systems.

It is important, whether an item bank is in use or not, to plan and maintain a postproduction storage and retrieval system that archives the materials—camera-ready copy, film negatives, digital files, or a combination of these—that were actually used to produce the finished product. Absent such a system, much costly work must be redone when the occasion for reprints arises. When proper provisions are made, the well-organized archive makes economical and timely reprinting possible.

Two major (and many minor) revolutions have taken place in print production since 1970. Years ago, a sheaf of copy was given to a Linotype operator, who set the type on a big pipe organ–like machine that dealt out hot lead type (a "hot-type" environment). Tabular material was set monotype: metal type set by individual letters and digits in a tray and bound with string. Pages could be printed directly from these forms of type, or reproduced photographically to make a printing plate. Next came "cold type," in which computers were used to produce camera-ready copy that was photographed, and the negative film was used to make printing plates. More recently, the printing industry has moved to "disk-to-plate" production, in which the photographic step is replaced by the use of a computer-driven thermal laser to etch the printing plate. (Both film and laser methods are currently in use, as are variants like disk-to-film and other processes. The choice of method is often made ad hoc, based on factors including print quantity, schedule, cost, and required quality.) Each revolution has brought improvements, but each has entailed risks and required equal or even expanded effort in planning and QC. This brief digression into history is important because further revolutions will occur, and the developer can expect to encounter trade-offs between advantages (such as better, more reliable print quality) and liabilities (such as increased complication). Given the complexity, variety, and frequent updating of hardware and software, and the potential for misunderstandings and mismatched assumptions, it is essential that test developers communicate clearly with printers and CBT programmers about compatibility issues, how files are converted, which software versions are in use, and so forth. Processing text or graphics before defining what the printer and programmer need is ill advised.

Certainly, advance planning is important. Costs and time-and-task schedules should be developed early, shared with staff and vendors, and monitored regularly. The "bookcase" analogy applies: It is pointless to design a 64-page test if your budget will pay for only 40 pages. If a test is being prepared in June and July to be administered in October, the printer must have press time available in August or September to allow time for shipping to test centers.

In keeping with Standard 5.7, test security must be maintained for all versions throughout test assembly and production. Letters of agreement or contracts are signed with all item writers, testing staff, suppliers, vendors, transportation companies, delivery services, and anyone else involved in the generation, storage, and transmission of the tests, stipulating that test materials and administration information are to be kept confidential. Such agreements or contracts must include provisions for all media (e.g., paper, film, disks, CD-ROMS, tape backups, audio recordings) and for the secure disposal of unused and damaged test materials, test materials spoiled in manufacture, and dated materials.

Paper-and-Pencil Tests

Test booklet covers need to tell a lot, and they are a good place to begin a discussion of the format of PPT booklets. The covers must address at least these five audiences, each for a different purpose: test takers, test developers, test supervisors, printing plant staff, and fulfillment (warehouse, distribution, and delivery) staff. The way to think about each aspect of the test-booklet-as-artifact is to identify the audiences and purposes and address each in turn.

Test takers come first. They need the name of the test and general directions for taking it. These should probably go on the outside front cover (OFC), although sometimes directions on the outside back cover (OBC) are acceptable or preferable. If examinees are not to open the booklet until the supervisor says so, the directions must include this information prominently. If examinees are to use an answer sheet or other sort of answer document, that needs to be said, together with explicit instructions for giving answers. (The answer document should match, to the extent possible, the fonts and design cues on the booklet covers.) The directions need to state whether examinees are to write in the test booklet. And if examinees are required to identify themselves in writing on the booklet, space must be provided and clearly labeled to receive printed name, signature, identification number, and any other information needed.

To meet their responsibilities under Standard 5.5 to give test takers clear instructions, test developers need to verify that the test directions are correct and complete. Developers also may need to identify the test by form code number and administration date or year, and add these in print to the cover. To thwart cheating (Standard 5.6), test developers may need to print "scrambled" forms (equivalent forms with units or items rearranged). These scrambled forms need to be distinguished on their covers, such as by use of a different form code number.

Test supervisors need to verify that each examinee has the appropriate test booklet. Again, form code numbers assist in this checking; use of a second color to distinguish variants may also be helpful. Such notices as "Return to [Testing Agency] immediately after testing" may need to be included.

Printing plant staff need to verify that the right covers are applied to the right content. The safeguards mentioned may suffice, but in some cases an additional reference code may be required on the OFC or OBC. If the test protocol demands that the booklets be spiraled and serial numbered, then the cover design must leave room for the serial number to be applied, and the printer must be given instructions for serialization.

The staff who fulfill orders for the test booklets need to consult the code numbers and serial numbers. In some cases, an additional inventory code number is needed to facilitate storage, order picking, and verification of delivery. (Such inventory code numbers may sometimes be applied to packaging materials rather than to the booklets themselves.)

There may be a need for additional material on the covers. For instance, if the test is to be copyrighted, the copyright notice may need to appear on the OFC if there is no room inside or if an inside notice could distract examinees' attention from items.

In sum, test booklet covers are not the simple, one-purpose documents they may at first appear to be. And all the various messages they convey need to be encompassed in as simple and unified a format as the designer (whether that is you or a professional designer you have the resources to retain) can devise.

Type Specifications

In meeting such challenges, the designer drafts *type specifications* (type specs), which are instructions for the typography and layout of all the pages in the test booklet. (Answer sheets, answer documents, or answer folders generally are scannable documents that require a specialized designer. "Generic" answer sheets are available from suppliers. If the developer plans to use one of these, giving a copy to the booklet designer is important so that the booklet design is compatible. If working with a designer to customize an answer sheet, clearly identify who is responsible for document compatibility.) The test booklet type specs need to meet the best practices in the publishing industry and satisfy the particular needs of test takers, while balancing a hypothetical ideal design against constraints imposed by testing conditions and budgets. Finding the optimal solutions requires good communication between a knowledgeable designer and test developers who are familiar with the curriculum, instruction, and instructional materials used in the area being tested. Their joint task is to craft type specs that maximize these three key factors:

1. **Legibility:** how easily readers can recognize the letters and words and decipher the text;
2. **Readability:** not what "readability formulas" attempt to measure, but rather how inviting and understandable the page looks; and
3. **Reproducibility:** how well the material looks in the final product, given the chosen printing process, paper, and ink.

The test developer's role is to provide the designer with context: to describe what counts for test validity (e.g., to say what size type is typical at the grade level tested). The designer's role is to weigh the options given the context, advise the developer about practical and technical consequences of design decisions, and craft the final type specs. The key point for everyone to bear in mind is that all elements of design work together. Changing just one element incautiously can make a whole design unravel.

Probably the first decision is to specify the dimensions of the text booklet. In the United States and Canada, the typical *trim size* (length and width of a test booklet page) is $8\frac{1}{2}$ by 11 inches (22 by 28 cm) for sheet-fed presses and $8\frac{3}{8}$ by $10\frac{7}{18}$ inches (21.3 by 27.6 cm) for web (roll-fed) presses. In most other countries, the typical trim size is that of International Organization for Standardization (ISO) size A4 paper: 21 by 29.7 cm (8.3 by 11.7 inches). The dimensions of the *type page* (the region inside the four margins) need to be specified, as do the dimensions of the margins themselves, and if text is set in multiple columns the column width and the intercolumn width. These measurements are expressed in terms of *points* and *picas*, traditional measures of type; a pica is approximately $\frac{1}{6}$ inch (.42 cm) and comprises 12 points.

Paper and ink come next. Almost all test booklets are printed in black ink on white or, preferably, off-white paper. Coated, glossy, and bright white papers produce eyestrain and should be avoided. The object is to have good, but not painfully stark, contrast between type and paper. A good 45- or 50-pound uncoated stock works for most booklets; 60-pound (lined for writing) does better for booklets in which students write short answers or essays. The paper should have medium to high opacity. Adding colored inks throughout a booklet increases printing costs and for that reason alone generally is avoided. If use of color is an option, do not have important distinctions depend on discriminating green from red, because readers with color-deficient vision have trouble distinguishing these colors (Tufte, 1990, p. 93, 2001, p. 183).

In considering the type itself, bear in mind that decisions about all typographic features, though separated for discussion, are interrelated.

All the typefaces type sizes, and required features of each font (e.g., italic, boldface, small caps) must be included in the type specs. Doing an early inventory, including all mathematical and scientific characters and related software, greatly helps planning and fosters accurate results. Be sure to include specs not only for *body type* (for running text) but also for *display type* (for titles, headings, subheads, and such directions as "TURN THE PAGE"), *rules* (straight lines to divide columns, surround tables, etc.), *folios* (page numbers), and any other type (e.g., for code numbers, copyright notice).

In choosing typefaces, there is wide consensus that serif type faces are best for running text, a mixture of serif and sans serif for display type. (*Serifs* are the small cross-strokes at the ends of letters.) It is probably safe to say that over the past 50 years about 95% of book, newspaper, and magazine text has been published in serif typefaces like Times Roman, Bookman, and Baskerville. Experts disagree about whether serif or sans serif is inherently easier to read, but the question is moot because serif is so prevalent, and what readers learn with and grow accustomed to decides what is easiest for them to read. Most experts agree that a whole page of sans serif text looks dull gray on the page, whereas serif invites a reader in. Moreover, serif type invariably distinguishes between similar characters such as the uppercase letter I and the lowercase letter el; among sans serif faces, Tahoma does, but Arial and Helvetica do not. For body type, the authors prefer Times Roman (or its variant Times New Roman). Times Roman is a sturdy font familiar to most readers and designed not only with legibility but also deadlines, varying grades of paper, and harried pressrooms in mind. Times has proved to be a reliable workhorse in many different applications. Arial, Helvetica, and Tahoma are good display typefaces. Occasional heads, and important guide words like "STOP," can—and for emphasis should—be set all caps. Running text never should.

What size type is appropriate for your test? Most readers do well with 10-, 11-, or 12-point type. For very young readers and those just learning to read, about 14-point type is preferred. In large-print tests for readers with visual impairments, 18-point type is appropriate.

Legibility and readability are affected by the amount of space between lines of type, known as *leading* (from its origin in the era of lead type). Leading is expressed as the number of points measured "base-to-base" (B/B) between each *baseline* (the line determined by the bottoms of capital letters). For example, the notation "10/11" (read "ten-on-eleven") represents 10-point type set on 11 points leading (11 points B/B). The minimum leading is the same point size as the type, e.g., 12/12. For maximum legibility across a page, leading adds 20 to 30% space between lines, as in 10/12 or 12/14. However, such generous leading decreases the number of lines per page, which has disadvantages in cost to the maker and convenience to the reader. The need for extra leading can be reduced or eliminated by such means as introducing an extra line of leading between paragraphs and shortening the length of typeset lines.

For most readers, optimal line length is about 24 picas (about 4 inches or 10.2 cm). Wider lines tend to tire the eye and make it hard to find the beginning of the next line. Given a page width of $8^1/_2$ or $8^3/_8$ inches (22 or 21.3 cm) with a type page width (allowing for left and right margins) of about 45 picas (a little over 7 inches or 17.8 cm), only one column of text set at the optimal measure fits, leaving a great deal of blank space. This design is seldom appropriate for tests because it forces examinees to turn many pages, which is both disruptive to the individual's train of thought and annoying to other test takers. Moreover, it may forbid placing related material on facing pages for reference. It also drives up the number of pages, which increases costs and, consequently, test fees. The solution in test design—as in the design of reference books and periodicals—is to set type in two columns each about 20 picas (about $3^1/_2$ inches or 9 cm) wide, separated by about 2 picas of blank space. Such a page strikes a reasonable and familiar balance among needs and has been widely adopted in large-scale tests. It has the advantage that it converts column-for-page into large-print format.

Should the columns be set *justified* (both left and right margins aligned) or *ragged right* (the left margin aligned, but the right margin staggered)? Designers have disagreed—with some vigor, it must be said—about which way is kinder to readers. Martin Jamison (1998) has written a spirited and sensible history of the issue. We have in our own files confident recommendations of ragged right that are set justified, and forceful arguments for justified that are set ragged right.

The suggested guidelines for universally designed large-scale assessments published in 2002, and widely reproduced since (e.g., Johnstone, 2003), recommend ragged right

(Thompson et al., 2002, p. 19). We believe that the evidence cited is insufficient to support that recommendation. Most of the cited studies involved few subjects (e.g., Gregory & Poulton, 1970, $N = 86$; Muncer, Gorman, Gorman, & Bibel, 1986, $N = 56$; Thompson, 1991, $N = 40$; Zachrisson, 1965, $N = 48$). Hartley (1985) acknowledges there is little empirical support for preferring ragged right (p. 31). Studies attempted to measure as many as seven design features simultaneously (Grise, Beattie, & Algozzine, 1982), used typewritten (not typeset) text read by readers in the unnatural position of resting their heads on chin rests (Zachrisson), used a very narrow (5.5 cm [$2^3/_{16}$ inches]; 13 picas) column width (Gregory & Poulton), or had other features that limit or disallow generalization. And in fact these studies' authors are cautious in interpreting their results. In that for centuries almost all well-crafted books have been set justified, the extraordinary claim that ragged right is better seems to us to lack sufficient foundation.

Indeed, a 1974 review of research on the legibility of children's books reported that—except for young children learning to read—research had shown no reason to prefer justified or ragged right (Watts & Nisbet, 1974, pp. 56–57). However, the authors acknowledged reservations about overhasty conclusions in view of "the complexity of the factors operating" (p. 57). These factors are *word spacing* (the space between words), *letterspacing* (the space between letters), hyphenation, and the overall management of blank space on the page. Karen Schriver thoughtfully deals with these factors in her *Dynamics in Document Design* (1997), in a section titled "To Justify or Not to Justify? May Be the Wrong Question." Although Thompson, Johnston, and Thurlow cite Shriver in support of ragged right, she says this:

> The results across the research literature are inconsistent.... When justified texts are formatted using word spacing that has been adjusted so there is relatively equal horizontal space between the words, then the difference between justified and ragged right disappears. We can conclude that quarreling over the issue of justifying the text or not is probably the wrong concern. The right concern is how to achieve a text without rivers and excessive hyphenation. (pp. 269–270)

Rivers are "paths running vertically through the text that connect the blank spaces between words on adjacent lines" (p. 270). Avoiding that distracting feature, excessive hyphenation, and such problems as *close* (crowded) and *open* (loose) lines are matters expertly addressed by James Felici in his *Complete Manual of Typography* (2003), in a chapter titled "Controlling Hyphenation and Justification." He points out that ragged right has its own set of problems (e.g., "wild rag" with "rogue lines" that disrupt reading). It is clear from his exposition that both justified and ragged right often are set ill, hampering the reader, but when set well help the reader. What counts is the skill of the typesetter, not the choice of one or the other way of managing the right-hand margin. Inept typesetting—whether done by a person or by software lazily left on factory defaults—botches the job and impedes readers' progress in either format. If a typesetter knows his or her craft, text is legible and readable in the chosen format. The test developer's concern should be to select either ragged right or justified text based on such factors as the grade level and content area of the test. Justified text has the advantage of allowing more words per page. It also offers greater ecological validity for most tests because it is the format encountered in typical reading situations.

Type specs should include all the default settings for such things as indentions for paragraphs, block quotations, item stems and responses, and so forth. It is wise to allow exceptions to solve unusual fit problems. Mathematical and scientific tests have many special typographical requirements. The developer and designer should decide whether the default settings in such math programs as MathType, for instance, are satisfactory and, if not, what to do about it. For instance, a developer may wish to customize the size of superscripts and subscripts, fractions, mixed numbers, and roots, or to adjust the leading for item stems that contain overbars, vector symbols, and arc symbols.

Graphics and tables also require attention in type specs. For instance, such features may be held to one column in width or allowed the full width of the type page. Symbols and labels for graphics must be clear, and preferably should match the typeface of running text. Keys and legends should be placed to the right of or above figures for ease of reading. Although black-and-white line drawings should be used as much as possible for simplicity's sake, figures may include shading to aid representation of three dimensions and to assist in differentiating adjoining regions, as on a map. Graphic *fills* (patterns, like diagonal lines, and dots) should be used sparingly, because they pose visual challenges to some readers and do not invariably print well. If fills are used, it is good practice to troubleshoot them all the way through print production to verify that they will come off press as intended. If camera-ready copy is used, type specs should include the mechanical requirements (to be decided by the production staff and printer). If digital graphic files are to be used, it is good practice to list all the required file formats (e.g., EPS files, bitmap files) in the specifications, along with all fonts and settings that should be loaded onto the computers used in editorial and print production.

Page Layout

Page layout is as important as typography. Test takers must be able to get their bearings, distinguish directions from text and items, find their way around test units under timed conditions, and tell when to turn the page and when not to. Layouts must above all be designed to anticipate and meet these needs. Layouts should also help test administrators (e.g., by letting proctors verify that examinees are turned to the proper page). Layouts can help to maintain test security and QC (e.g., by labeling each page with a test code for easy identification). And finally, good layouts can limit printing complications and costs.

Booklet covers were discussed earlier. For inside pages, we offer the following guidelines.

Tests may begin *verso* (on a left-hand and therefore even-numbered page) or *recto* (on a right-hand and therefore odd-numbered page). In many cases, having all tests begin verso works best; the first test page is the inside front cover, which saves space, and layout of related material on facing pages is made easier. As much as possible, stimulus and items should appear on the same or facing pages. This keeps page turning in the testing room to a minimum and allows examinees to make comparisons with all related information in view.

Save space whenever possible, without compromising clarity. Space in test booklets is very valuable. With most bindings, booklet page counts can be adjusted only in four-page or eight-page increments because the printing press or other manufacturing equipment so requires. Often all test forms must have the same number of pages because binding or serial-numbering machines so require or because of shipping or sorting demands. It is a foolish economy to sacrifice legibility or readability crassly. But to ignore the real costs of extra pages—especially when pages are blank padding for uniform page counts—is wasteful and expensive.

Build in "you are here" features. Test numbers or simple identifying symbols at the tops of text pages can help test takers to stay on track and help test proctors to verify that examinees are on the proper test. Each test heading should clearly and prominently display how many questions are on the test and how much time is allowed. Directions for page turning (like GO ON or STOP) should appear at the bottom of every test page and be prominent. Folios should appear unobtrusively and should not be expressed on the outside covers or on any blank inside pages. Putting unobtrusive code numbers at the bottom of every page aids in manufacturing (by guiding the printer and bindery staff) and in test security (by identifying the source in event of theft, loss, or unauthorized photocopying).

Items should be easy to locate and easy to distinguish from stimuli. Bold type for item numbers and option letters helps. The typography and layout of the answer sheet must be taken into account. The answer sheet and test must match in number of subtests, test numbering, item numbering, number of options, option lettering, and so on. It is often helpful to alternate option letters (e.g., odd-numbered items lettered A, B, C, D, E; even-numbered items lettered F, J, H, J, K) to help test takers keep their place. Of course, if you are using a generic answer sheet, you must reverse-design your booklet to match the sheet, and explain to test takers any discrepancy.

When the stimulus comprises different kinds of material (e.g., text, figures, and tables), the page layout should relate the elements logically. Whenever possible, avoid odd-shaped or large tables and graphs; they usually create page-fit problems. In fitting text, the developer may want to specify that all columns align at the bottom of the type page; but if that arrangement creates large gaps of blank space, specifying short columns on some pages or letting column depth vary helps.

Avoid *bad breaks*, unsightly or misleading arrangements of type. There are several varieties: *Widows* are very short lines at the end of paragraphs. They can be tolerated within a column, but not at the top of a page or column. An *orphan* is the first line of a paragraph at the end of a column or page. An introductory line at the end of a column, or a subhead alone or with only a single line of text beneath it, is another bad break. All these can be corrected by using extra leading between paragraphs to force lines forward or backward, or by rerunning lines to "pick up" short lines. Incorrect hyphenation (which software does not always detect and sometimes actually creates) is yet another type of bad break, which can be made right by adjusting word spacing or letterspacing in the affected line and lines adjacent. You may wish, especially in mathematical and scientific tests, to stipulate that numerals and the units or nouns they modify should not break at line ends (e.g., 20 / miles; 15.6 / kilometers; 22 / percent). Generally, mathematical and chemical equations should be set on their own line rather than broken between lines; when equations must be broken, they should break only after an equals sign.

Printing Specifications

Printing specs instruct the printer how to proceed with a job. Writing them requires collaboration to ensure all needs and dates are met. The specs should run a page or two, covering all the essentials but not obscuring them with microscopic detail:

Title: may need codes and dates appended
Quantity: expressed as numerals and words
Finished size: generally same as trim size
Page count: usually a multiple of 4; "self-cover" if the same paper is used for covers and inside pages
Materials furnished: specifies keylines; mechanicals; camera-ready copy; PDF files; negatives from previous printing
Artwork ready: date when the artwork—i.e., copy—is to be delivered to the printer; typically 4 to 6 weeks before delivery date
Proofs: specifies what sort of printer's proofs the printer provides for proofreading: bluelines (or "blues") for proofs made from film negatives, or digital proofs for proofs printed from digital files; specifies how many working days are allowed for review
Ink: specifies "1 color: black" or "*x* colors" and lists them by name and by Pantone Matching System (PMS) number; specifies whether text prints on 1 or 2 sides of a sheet
Paper: specifies grade and characteristics required, e.g., "white groundwood, uncoated, 50 pound; opacity is essential"
Binding/Finishing: specifies method and dimension, e.g., *saddlestitch* or *saddlewire* (both terms meaning "staple through the fold") along 11-inch (28 cm) dimension
Additional information: specifies spiraling, serial numbering, and sealing information—e.g., "collate 15 versions; after collating, serial number booklets on the outside front cover in the upper right corner (four digits), serial number range: 1001 to 7001"; specifies security

policy and requirements; specifies packaging, e.g., "tie in bundles of 30" or "box in 100s, label carton with inventory code number"; specifies date of secure return of disks or camera copy from printer to client

Folded and gathered sheets (F and Gs): specifies when printed sheets, if required, will be delivered for QC

Collated and stapled samples (CSTs): specifies when printed sample booklets will be delivered for QC

Cost: specifies cost—unless there is a separate billing document for this

Date: specifies date specifications were approved

Job number: specifies the client and/or the printer job number

Contact: specifies the client and/or the printer contact person

Delivery date: specifies day when finished booklets are to be delivered to client

Computer-Based Tests

The rapidity of change in computer technology requires an emphasis on principles rather than on specific formats in this section. There are many types of CBTs at present, including computer-adaptive tests (CATs) and computer-administered tests that are not adaptive. Some CBTs are Web-based, while others are based instead on locally networked computers. All these types require that hardware and software requirements be specified early in planning, to ensure consistent results during production and a uniform look (and sound) and functionality when examinees test.

What should the test look like? The criteria for on-screen display are familiar: legibility, readability, and reproducibility. Most of what was said about PPTs applies here. But instead of designing a page, the developer needs to design a graphical user interface. In doing so, all persons involved should use the same parlance. Use of the same edition of a standard reference like *The Microsoft Manual of Style for Technical Publications* helps everyone to understand one another.

Among the first steps in the recursive process of designing a CBT is the specification of a "writer" (a word processor for text and markup language, e.g., Word rich text format [RTF] files) and a "reader" (a software program that converts the files for display on screen together with the interactive functions required). Both the writer and the reader need to be chosen while keeping the final appearance on screen in mind. That appearance largely depends on monitor screen size, screen resolution, and font size (Bridgeman, Lennon, & Jackenthal, 2002).

Suppose a developer specifies that all test takers (except those testing with accommodations) test with the same size monitor—say, 15 or 17 inch (38 or 43 cm). The developer needs to decide how to divide up the screen, such as by splitting it with stimulus to the left and questions to the right. The developer also needs to specify the number and dimensions of windows on screen, because they determine the depth and width (in inches and in pixels) available for text and graphics. These dimensions should be considered in light of the size and required crispness of images and text. At present, the achievable crispness on typical screens is about two thirds to three quarters of that of type on paper. Screen resolution must be specified bearing in mind that the resolution affects the size of type on screen (e.g., 12-point type appears smaller at 1024×768 than at 640×480 pixels). Hence font size must be specified in tandem with resolution, so that there is high enough resolution to get crisp images for illustrations and the type is optimally legible. Fourteen-point type at 1024×768 resolution is a reasonably good combination for CBTs. The developer also wants to allow examinees to keep material in view and scroll or page the text as little as possible.

As to choice of typeface, there is at the time of this writing a wide preference for sans serif fonts—exactly the opposite as for paper. Sans serif is thought to be more legible and more readable on screen because serifs tend to blur. This may change as technology evolves. It is widely felt that setting on screen text ragged right creates a more legible result than setting text justified. The sans serif faces Arial and Tahoma are reasonable choices for running text on screen (the latter having the advantage of better distinguishing between certain characters, e.g. I versus el). Display fonts can also be sans serif, but serif faces can be used for variety. It is important to specify which character sets are required (e.g., italic, bold, bold italic), which special characters must be included (e.g., en dashes, em dashes), and what options are needed for kerning (adjusting space between selected characters). Specifying a soft, pale background color creates proper contrast.

Mathematics on screen requires particular attention. A program like MathType is essential for most math tests—and the developer or designer may need to customize things like fences (parentheses, brackets, braces) and prime symbols, fractions, mixed numbers, spacing, leading, and alignment for a particular on-screen application.

If a test contains graphics, it is necessary to specify the number of screen colors and the proper software (e.g., Photoshop) to create and display the files (e.g., GIF files for color and motion; JPEG files for photos). Building a function that allows examinees to enlarge the graphics, or to move them, may be required. As with PPTs, it is desirable to avoid "busy" graphics having elaborate designs and avoid using color schemes, especially red–green, to distinguish important information (unless the colors are identified by word labels for examinees with impaired color perception). Similarly, if the test has a sound component, the developer needs to specify software to generate WAV files and to specify guidelines for avoiding unnecessarily complicated sound content.

In making all these specifications, observing the criterion of reproducibility is essential. Is the test overdesigned for the testing population, which may not have the technical resources the design specifications require? Can the developer be confident of compliance all along the line with the software specifications? With hardware specifications for monitor size and resolution, processor speed, RAM, hard drive capacity, refresh rate, and Web connection speed?

How should the test work? The functionality of a test—the interplay between events like reading an item on screen and reacting to it by using the mouse or keyboard—is developed in a process called *storyboarding*, a detailed outline of every interactive element of a CBT. It must allow for both valid and invalid examinee responses and must follow the sequence of events from a welcome page through examinee identification; tutorials in mouse/keyboard navigation; test directions; help, clock, and intermission functions; the test; and score-reporting pages. The storyboard must include all the specifications for what appears on screen and aurally, including the test materials themselves; all surrounding and embedded functions such as windows and hotspots, highlights, and hyperlinks; and the scoring and score-reporting functions. Storyboarding demands empathy with the test taker. How fast or slow should the screen scroll? Would tabs or buttons that "turn pages" of text work better than scroll bars that navigate continuously through text? Or perhaps both means should be provided? Can examinees refer back to the directions during testing? Are "you-are-here" markers like "Question 21 of 40" and "*X* minutes remain" built in?

PROCEDURES AND QUALITY CONTROL

Typical Procedure

In assembling a test, *procedures* (the steps to follow) and *quality control* (the definition and application of standards to ensure quality) must be integrated. Each developer, in documenting its test production process, may treat procedures and QC together, in one narrative, or may find it more convenient to separate procedures from QC guidelines, as is done in this discussion. The former treatment has the advantage of continuity (which often makes it the safer practice), but at the cost of length and repetition. The latter method sacrifices linearity to brevity. Both numbered lists and flow charts are helpful. The authors chose, arbitrarily, to use a list for the PPT example and a chart for the CBT example.

Paper-and-Pencil Tests

The following is one possible sequence of steps for assembling a PPT test battery form. The sequence fills in portions of the earlier sketch. Assembling a stand-alone pretest is a subset of or a variation on these steps; if pretesting is done by distributing pretest items in an operational test battery form, then additional steps (e.g., an added cluing check) are needed. The following list offers one model of the "who, what, and when" of test production. The authors think it important to include who and when because procedures are not abstractions outside time and human interaction, although sometimes they are written—and thus go unfulfilled—as if they were. The abbreviations are D for development staff; B, item bank staff; P, desktop publishing staff; A, test administration staff; C, consultants; and V, vendors.

1. Review item statistics and perform key check (D; date).
2. Conduct item content and editorial review to verify validity, classification (D; date).
3. Initially construct subtests per test specifications and qualitative judgments about topic variety, diversity, and so on (D; date).
4. Review initial subtests for cluing, editorial mix and quality; prepare for item bank by assigning item numbers and foil letters; send paper copy to item bank (D; date).
5. Generate subtests and answer keys (B; date).
6. Proofread/correct as necessary (D, B; dates).
7. Review subtests per fairness, content, and editorial policies (D, C; dates).
8. Replace items as necessary/proofread (D, B; dates).
9. Final review subtests: match specs, order items from easiest to hardest, adjust key positions, perform overall check; mark up for typesetter; send paper and electronic copy to desktop publishing (D; date).
10. Typeset and format (P; date).
11. Proofread keylines (D; date).
12. Correct/proofread (P, D; dates).
13. Have surrogate test takers "take" subtests and write item explanations (C, D; dates).
14. Proofread keysheets, cross-checking with item explanations (D; date).
15. Assemble test battery forms per test specifications; balance topics; do cluing checks across subtests (D; date).
16. Verify keysheets for scoring (D; date).
17. Designate test battery forms by code number (D; date).
18. Compile final match-specs reports (D; date).
19. Typeset test battery form folios, codes, and covers (P; date).
20. Do final QC of test battery forms for release to printer (D, A, P; dates).
21. Send PDF files to printer (P; date).
22. RIP files and make digital proofs (V; date).
23. Proofread digital proofs against final keylines (D, P; dates).
24. Make plates from the electronic file used to make the digital proofs and print F and Gs or CSTs (V; date).
25. Check F and Gs or CSTs against final keylines (D, P; dates).
26. Receive and inspect printed samples (D, P, A; dates).

27. Distribute tests (*A*, *V*; dates).
28. Administer test (*A*; date).
29. Process answer sheets (*A*, *V*; dates).
30. Do preliminary item analysis, QC for miskeys (*D*; date).
31. Perform live scoring and reporting (*D*, *A*, *V*; dates).
32. Do technical analysis (e.g., DIF, completion rate). (*D*; date).

Concurrent with procedures like these, additional procedures are required for document control (e.g., archive materials for reprints), stock control (e.g., alert system when quantity is depleted), and inspection (e.g., are booklets mildewing on the shelf?). Records of all transactions should be filed in a way the developer prescribes, so that decisions can be traced. Electronic files (including backups) are essential, but leaving a paper trail is highly advisable. Clear security procedures are necessary, including rules for disposal (shredding) of all secure paper and electronic media. Procedures must include sign-off checklists for recording the approvals of the responsible persons and the date of approval.

Computer-Based Tests

The developer has specified the hardware and software requirements, completed the preliminary and detailed designing phases, developed codes for the items, and pilot tested the systems of a CBT. To prepare for beta testing, and for subsequent test administration, maintenance, and enhancement, procedures to guide the process are necessary. Many of these procedures resemble those listed for PPTs, which are not repeated here. Computer-specific procedures develop from the circumstances of a particular CBT. Software idiosyncrasies need workarounds, and these add new procedures. Owing to incessant technological change, procedures frequently need revision. In fact, one recent proposal for university-wide CBTs uses a "Catherine Wheel"—a disk with pinwheel spirals spinning outward from its hub—as a model for the "evolutionary development of [the] system" and the quality assurance thereof (Zakrzewski & Steven, 2003, pp. 609–611). That seems a useful way of looking at a modest-scale CBT program. The model offered here is more prosaic, the simple flow chart in Figure 26.1.

For large-scale CBTs, flow charts more complicated than subway maps have been designed. Figure 26.1 illustrates, using the same abbreviations used in the previous section, the basics, which include the three kinds of QC after items have been banked: (a) How do things look? (b) How do things function? (c) Are the psychometric features in order? Because CBT "procedures" are in these areas hardwired to "QC," several QC issues are discussed here.

Most of the typographic features of text and graphics should be present in "Item entry"; hotspots and other CBT features are added in the item bank. The QC on screen at the banking stage focuses on the rendering of all these features before the tests are put into the application. After the tests are in the application, the QC turns its focus to the keyboard and mouse functions (but does not ignore the on-screen look). At both these QC stages, all computers must be set up alike. A complete list of the specifications and settings is necessary; every user should verify that all needed fonts are loaded and that settings are correct before beginning QC. Problems encountered here should be shared with test administrators in the field so that similar glitches—for example, Web browsers altering the size of type—can be averted in testing sessions.

Every user should have instructions on how to manage the CBT files (e.g., how to download revised versions). Version control during CBT QC is crucial. There should be a formal system for thoroughly documenting and reporting problems (e.g., by means of incident reports that identify the version, describe the problem, and include corrections marked on screen shots) and for verifying and documenting corrections, complete with checklists to record persons responsible and dates (perhaps even time of day). Similarly, final approvals must be documented. And

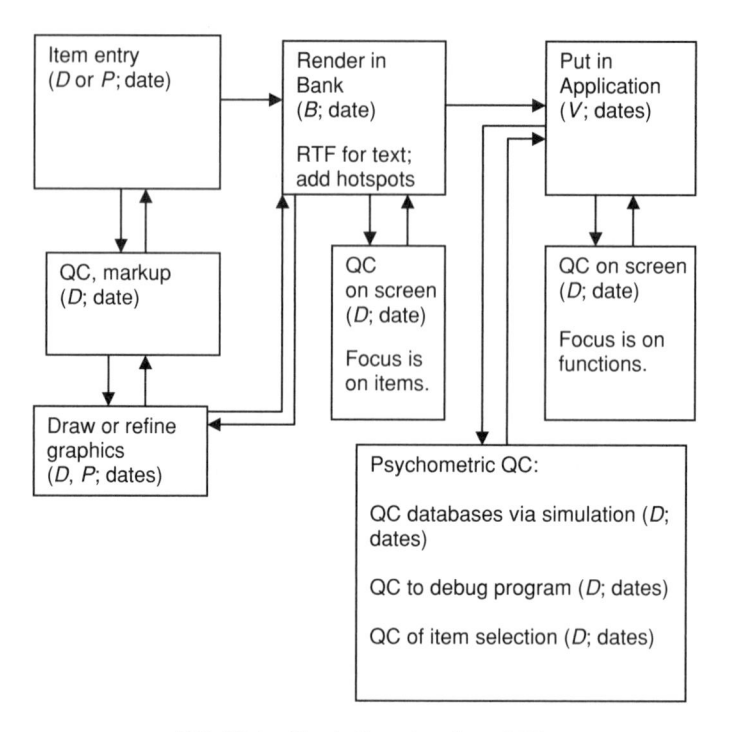

FIG. 26.1. Simple flow chart for a CAT.

people should check all critical features, even those that the computer has been programmed to check (e.g., number of items in a test). Such redundancy is essential.

CATs need special care in "Psychometric QC." For example, item selection must be managed and monitored for conformity with test specifications for both item pools and individual test sessions (see Davey & Pitoniak, chap. 24, this volume). Similarly, CBTs must be balanced for fairness, diversity, topics, and tone. Whether a design allows for coded-item sorting on the fly by computer, or item sorting by human judgment to monitor the contents of the item pool, the developer needs to set written procedures to establish the flow and to resolve problems. And it is essential, under Standard 3.12, to control item exposure, so item exposure rates need to be monitored, compared with exposure criteria rates, and adjusted as required.

Quality Control

"To appreciate the importance of error-free tests, you ... have to keep in mind that test materials are among the most closely scrutinized written materials in existence" (Estes, 1989, p. 3). If proofreaders of "closely scrutinized" documents do not catch an error, the odds are that the audience will spot it—as readers of Psalm 119:161 did, when an edition of the Bible was published reading, "Printers [instead of 'Princes'] have persecuted me without a cause" ("Thou Shalt Be Diligent," 2004). In what follows, emphasis is on the "who, how, where, and why" of test production, focusing on producing error-free tests.

QC should not be attempted in isolation. QC staff need to see the big picture. Making a table like Table 26.1 helps show QC staff why their work is critical and where it fits into the development system. QC staff should know as much about the system in general, and production methods in particular, as possible. A tour of the printing plant, for instance, can reveal previously unused capabilities and unsuspected risks.

TABLE 26.1
The Role of QC in the Test Development System

		Type of QC	
Purpose of QC	Item	Test, subtest	Test battery, CAT
Fairness	Passages and items are free of language, roles, situations, and contexts offensive or demeaning to any population group; do not privilege or penalize any group; contain no elements extraneous to the construct; are grade-level appropriate; are interesting; and avoid giving emotional distress to examinees.	Passages and items are balanced in multicultural and gender representation. The combination of passages and items does not privilege or penalize any group.	Tests are balanced in multicultural and gender representation. The combination of materials in the tests does not privilege or penalize any group.
Content accuracy	Passages and items match test construct/specs. Items avoid test-wise cluing.	Selection matches specs. There is no interitem cluing or overlap. There is a good mix of topics and items.	Selection matches specs. There is no intertest cluing. There is a good mix of topics and items.
Editorial	Passages and items meet word-length specs; meet test quality criteria; employ bias-free writing; meet adaptation policy; are factually accurate; conform to source; are scribally correct; conform to house style; and meet design, typographic, format, and layout specs.	Selection conforms to source documents. Selection has been formatted correctly. Selection contains no gratuitous variations in style. Test directions are clear and correct.	Selection conforms to source documents. Selection has been formatted correctly. Selection contains no gratuitous variations in style. Manufactured tests meet all quality criteria.
Key verification	Keyed responses are correct. Item rationales are valid.	Keysheets are correct. Item justifications are valid.	Keysheets are correct and are cross-checked with source documents. Item justifications are valid. Materials for responding to item challenges have been accurately filed.

Within the larger domain of test development, QC should itself be systematized. Guidelines should be explicit and consistent. Checklists should be used to map out and record QC work. And staff should be familiarized with the work and what can go wrong. In short, plan QC. But do not just plan QC. No one can plan for everything. QC includes fending off what the novelist Peter De Vries called "the unexpected that lies in ambush for all intellectual endeavor" (1976, p. 7). After all, most QC failures—and editors and proofreaders are great collectors of news clippings about costly typos, botched operations, and other handmade disasters—occurred while QC plans were in place. Somebody (A) Fell asleep at the switch; (B) Did not verify; (C) Neglected to notify; or (D) None of the above. Sometimes the authority, guideline, or standard itself is wrong; editors also avidly collect lists of mistakes they find in dictionaries, style books, QC manuals, and handbooks. So it is sometimes good practice to defamiliarize a task (e.g., by subdividing it or by performing, it in reverse), or to have someone unfamiliar with a project do an extra read-through of proofs to catch any mistakes or anomalies others may have missed.

As much as on plans, you must rely on persons. It follows that accountability is as critical as system. There must be clear lines of responsibility for who is to do what, and when. Having the right people in the right jobs is important. QC work demands orderliness, caution, and patience, but a sense of the game or hunt (as in "hunting for errors") helps.

Accountability has no force and system has no strength without reporting and documentation. QC findings must be circulated so as to effect corrections; offer feedback to editors, content staff, and item writers; and suggest enhancements for the future. Checklists help to meet these purposes. In doing so, they embody the core of QC: system, accountability, and reporting and documentation (Estes, 1989, p. 3).

After tests have gone through the content review, editorial review, and cluing and other checks, they enter production. QC staff should be equipped with the following resources.

1. Standard reference works designated as the authorities for the project; in the United States, these are typically the current editions of *Merriam-Webster's Collegiate Dictionary, Webster's Dictionary of English Usage, The Chicago Manual of Style,* and *The Publication Manual of the American Psychological Association.* The proofreaders' shelves should also hold standard reference works such as the current edition of *The Gregg Reference Manual* (Sabin, 2004), several guides like *Guidelines for Bias-Free Writing* (Schwartz et al., 1995), a hefty dictionary like *Webster's Third New International Dictionary,* and some classics like Evans and Evans' *Dictionary of Contemporary American Usage* (1957).
2. A copy of the security policy.
3. Sample pages and keysheets from previous editions, if available.
4. A glossary of terms key to the project.
5. Type and printing specifications.
6. A list of proofreader's marks.
7. A style sheet for the project (to bar gratuitous variation in wording and style for such things as numerals, abbreviations, and capitalization).
8. A list of known trouble spots (e.g., matching graphics to text), known software glitches, and typographic features that do not automatically convert among the text processors in use.
9. A copy of the acknowledgments, fair use, and permissions policies.
10. Checklists and routing procedures.

So equipped, editors can begin preparing copy for typesetting and formatting. Typically, an editor marks up a paper copy with whatever instructions are necessary for the desktop publisher to proceed and attaches a cover sheet or transmittal form identifying the test and designating it *Secure* or *Confidential*. Often, a colored ink or pencil lead is used to make the markup stand out. (Distinguishing colors may be used for different categories of changes, or to identify the source; e.g., red for editorial, blue for typesetter). All markup must be clear, as must file photocopies (so make sure all colors used reproduce). A checklist should identify all materials (e.g., test directions) that need to accompany test copy. The most mundane features need careful attention: Are test titles, number of minutes, number of items correct? Should it be "answer sheet," "answer folder," or "answer document"? Should directions say "circles," "ovals," or "spaces" on the answer document? Do the foil letters match the answer document? Are facing pages required; if so, are they marked up correctly? Is the page count within specifications? Do all booklets in the series need the same number of pages?

In marking copy, standard proofreader's marks are used. Comments and queries not intended to be set in type are circled. Sticky notes may be useful to flag pages, but they can fall off and be lost; thus, all markup is done directly on copy. Copy should not be stapled, and it should be on one side of the paper only. Blank pages should be indicated by a blank sheet marked with the useful oxymoron "Page [xx] prints blank." Any accompanying sample materials not intended to be set in type must be clearly marked "Not Copy."

Typically, electronic copy is provided to the typesetter or formatter along with paper copy. Find out which typographic features input in the copy file are rendered perfectly by the desktop system. Ordinarily, no features (e.g., italic, bold) that carry over should be marked up (to keep copy clean for typesetter and proofreaders). Features that are not rendered must be marked up. Requests for special page layouts must be marked up, as must requests to resize graphics or ensure their positions next to or above each other. If text lines are numbered for reference and the lines are rerun, all items containing line references should be marked so the typesetter can adjust the references and proofreaders can check them. When typeset material (*proof*) is securely returned, the following QC guidelines apply.

1. Check everything. Nothing on the page (or computer screen) should be ignored. When in doubt, query. Complacency invites error, and it is easy to overlook the obvious.
2. Use computer QC aids, but do not depend on them. Spelling and grammar checkers are useful redundancies but are not to be trusted to catch or prevent errors, for reasons that many popular verses of the "Eye halve a spelling chequer" sort attest.
3. In correcting an error, do not create a new one. Making a change in copy can easily create a new error, in both markup and typesetting.
4. Assume there is an error. The ballplayer who assumes the ball is coming his or her way is prepared to make the catch.
5. Always verify that you have the correct source document. Given the pace and variety of editorial work, it is easy to pull the wrong source document from a file. Given the complexity of computer systems and the necessity of keeping predecessors and variants on file, it is easy to save or retrieve the wrong version. Superseded paper copy should be marked with the date and the words "Dead Copy" to prevent later proofreaders from mistaking it for live copy.
6. Vary QC reading style to the task. For example, a read-through for sense requires attentive normal reading. Proofreading to verify conformity between two documents requires attentive comparison; normal reading actually interferes with comparison.
7. Search for one type of error at a time. Divided attention invites errors. Whenever possible, split the QC task and make multiple passes through the copy.
8. Do not let up at late production steps. The closer to the final product, the more conducive the climate can be to missing mistakes. QC must be maintained or intensified when a project is close to going on press or on screen.

Each step in the editorial production process entails its own QC requirements. The level of QC cannot be prescribed generically but must be determined in local context. For instance, "copy" produced early in production (conversion of item writer files; item banking versions) may need to be treated like "proof" if much retyping or reformatting was done. After copy has been typeset and formatted by desktop publishing, there is ordinarily a "preliminary" proof stage for a format check and, possibly, a proofreading. The next stage is "final proof," when the desktop files have been readied for release to the printer or CBT programmer. Ordinarily, this stage requires close proofreading. The next stage is "printer's proofs" for print jobs (or on-screen renderings for CBTs). Printer's proofs may be *bluelines* (so called for their pale blue image on pale yellow photosensitive paper), which are photographic prints of the film negatives the printer uses to make the printing plates; or they may be *digital proofs*, which are printouts from the electronic files the printer uses to make the printing plates. Bluelines are WYSIWYG (what you see is what you get), but, unfortunately, digital proofs often are not as clear (especially for graphics) as the printed image because the "proofer"—the printer used to make them—usually is not capable of fine detail. Printer's proofs ordinarily require close proofreading if they are for the first printing of a job. Subsequent printings from the same negatives may not need as close a proofreading, but subsequent printings from digital files need care to protect against problems from corrupted files. It is best to communicate with publications staff and vendors to determine the appropriate level of QC. Again, if corrections are made at the printer's proof stage (or on-screen renderings for CBTs), consultation is necessary to decide what method and level of QC is needed for the corrections.

After all the proof stages of print jobs are completed and proofs have been approved, the presses roll. For print jobs printed from negatives, the printer ordinarily delivers *printed samples* (CSTs) randomly selected from the print run. These ordinarily are inspected for mechanical problems on press (ink spots, smearing) but do not need proofreading. For large print jobs from digital files, the printer may deliver F and Gs first, for a QC check before the pages are collated and bound; F and Gs may need proofreading to guard against problems in computerized platemaking. CSTs are checked later.

There are various ways of parsing out levels of QC. The authors recommend *proofreading, reading-through, reviewing,* and *inspecting.*

Proofreading is the process of verifying that a proof (target document) conforms to copy (a source document). Proofreaders are responsible for detecting and marking for correction all errors in text and artwork, including errors in typography and format.

Two-person (read-aloud) proofreading is used to check that nothing has been inadvertently left out or introduced. All features are read aloud, including punctuation. The reader pauses to allow the listener to sight-proofread graphics and other visual features (or the sight proofreading is done later). The more experienced proofreader's eyes should be on the target document. It is good to have content area staff participate. Fine details cannot be ignored. For example, software does not infallibly convert. We have seen degree symbols rendered correctly in one item and erroneously rendered as Greek letters in a nearby item. Large problems—entire pages of gibberish—are easily caught. Smaller problems are insidious and must be watched for closely. Some proofreaders find that placing a blank sheet or file card beneath the line being read helps them concentrate.

One-person (sight) proofreading is used to verify format, line breaks, graphics, alignments, spelling, and other visual features. It may be *close* (word by word or even letter by letter), or *line by line* (to match for completeness and sequence), depending on the particular requirements. When a change has been made on a page, the whole page should be read to make sure no accidental changes (e.g., loss of typographic commands; lines carried to the next page) were made. The proofreader should use a pica ruler or leading gauge to verify that type specs have been met. The authors recommend the QC be done by checklist, like this one for graphics:

1. Artwork is matched to proper item?
2. Artwork complies with page layout specs?
3. Artwork meets purpose in size and detail?
4. Artwork elements are all present and correct?
5. Artwork is free of unnecessary elements?
6. All proportions, perspectives, relations, angles, slopes, scales, and other features are correct?

7. Labels, arrows, all other symbols are correct?
8. Legends, key, titles, etc. are correct?
9. Legends, key, titles, etc. all match?
10. Text references to artwork all are correct?

There are also several kinds of *reading-through*. In a *read-through for sense*, the reader looks for any mistakes, contradictions, infelicities, sources of bias, or other faults that might perplex or offend a test taker. The reader does not deliberately look for typos, though of course marks any that are found. A read-through for sense may detect inconsistencies that result from constructing an operational test from materials pretested at different times or inconsistently copyedited. The developer then has to decide whether the inconsistencies are serious enough to warrant action such as item replacement.

In a *read-through for typos*, the reader looks for misspellings and similar mistakes. In doing so, he or she must try not to read for sense. Similar read-throughs can be done to detect bad breaks at the ends of lines, widows and orphans, and so on.

Reviewing refers to running through a checklist like this one to make sure a proof (or CBT rendering on screen) conforms to all specifications:

1. Scan for broken type, fuzzy images, stray marks.
2. Scan for typos.
3. Scan for wrong fonts.
4. Check top of every page for test identifiers.
5. Check page numbering.
6. Check on-page code numbers.
7. Check end-of-page and end-of-test directions.
8. Check name of test.
9. Check number of minutes and number of items.
10. Check test directions.
11. Check consecutive numbering of items.
12. Check appropriate lettering of foils.
13. Check each section begins on correct folio.
14. Check end-of-test-battery directions.
15. Check survey questions.
16. Check all math and science symbols.
17. Check all line reference numbers.
18. Check examinee identification block.
19. Check for facing pages where required.
20. Check that each subtest begins verso.

For CBTs, a *functional review* consists of working through a checklist of keyboard and mouse actions to troubleshoot the functionality of the CBT. Functional review needs to troubleshoot provisions for examinee errors as well as examinee successes (e.g., what happens when an examinee inputs his or her name where an ID number belongs?).

For PPTs, *inspecting* means turning the pages of printed sample booklets to spot any manufacturing defects (e.g., inking too heavy or too light; pages out of order, duplicated, or omitted; defects in the paper; or printer's marks showing on the page). For CBTs, *inspecting* means running through a test session in a test center, to ascertain whether all screens and functions are working properly on equipment in the field.

In all QC involving reading on screen, schedules must be arranged and equipment provided to prevent eyestrain to those doing the work.

What QC level is appropriate at given stages of proof? That is a question to discuss with staff members and vendors and to revisit when there are changes to software, hardware, or other factors. Two 2-person proofreadings are necessary for operational tests at the keyline stage, and one 2-person proofreading and one 1-person proofreading are necessary at the stage of blueline/digital proof or on-screen rendering. At least two separate 1-person proofreadings should be given to corrected pages at any stage. And every stage should see proof checked against one or more checklists for conformity with specifications; this holds even for reprints. The question sometimes arises why such QC checks are necessary for reprints from negatives previously used. The answer is that negatives can degrade over time in storage. It pays to play it safe.

And who will QC the QCers? You want error-free tests, so a QC error rate of zero is the standard. But perfection is statistically unlikely. The authors believe that judicious use of the guidelines offered here allows many published products to indeed be flawless, because multiple QC methods were applied in succession. But individual QC steps unavoidably let mistakes through. Remarkably little empirical work is available on this subject, so it is difficult to say what an expectable rate of error might be, or even if it makes sense to hypothesize such a rate, given that circumstances and texts vary widely. How much error is tolerable at particular QC steps is a matter of the developer's best judgment, based on experience for the testing program.

Someday, despite everyone's best efforts, an error may appear in an operational test. In that event, the developer needs to identify how the mistake happened and make a plan to prevent a recurrence. Cases of downright negligence or deliberate sabotage are, fortunately, extremely rare. There is every likelihood that an improbable combination of circumstances conspired against success, and that the plan consists of blocking the small gaps that let the mistake through. In advance of a mishap, there needs to be a contingency plan identifying who is to be notified and who is responsible for making a policy decision about remedies and public announcements.

When all production steps are concluded and it is time to register for copyright, *Circular 64: Copyright Registration for Secure Tests* (United States Copyright Office, 2002) gives full details on how to do so.

In many ways, a testing program *is* the test booklet or other document you publish (Estes, p. 2). It is certain that test validity depends on accurate rendition of the test content and design. We hope this discussion of "test production effects on validity" helps to effect the test developer's intentions.

ACKNOWLEDGMENT

We thank Wayne Patience for his careful review of and valuable comments on this chapter.

REFERENCES

American Educational Research Association (AERA), American Psychological Association (APA), & National Council on Measurement in Education (NCME). (1999). *Standards for educational and psychological testing* (rev. ed.). Washington, DC: American Educational Research Association.

Bridgeman, B., Lennon, M. L., & Jackenthal, A. (2002, April). *Effects of screen size, screen resolution, and display rate on computer-based test performance*. Paper presented at the annual meeting of the National Council on Measurement in Education, New Orleans. Retrieved July 9, 2004, from http://www.ets.org/research/dload/AERA2002-bri2.pdf

The Center for Universal Design. (1997). *The principles of universal design* (version 2.0). Raleigh: North Carolina State University.

De Vries, P. (1976). *I hear America swinging*. Boston: Little, Brown.

Estes, C. (1989, October). *Proofreading seminar*. Paper presented at ACT, Iowa City, IA.

Evans, B., & Evans, C. (1957). *A dictionary of contemporary American usage*. New York: Random House.

Felici, J. (2003). *The complete manual of typography: A guide to setting perfect type*. Berkeley, CA: Peachpit Press, for Adobe Press.

Gregory, M., & Poulton, E. C. (1970). Even versus uneven right-hand margins and the rate of comprehension in reading. *Ergonomics, 13*(4), 427–434.

Grise, P., Beattie, S., & Algozzine, B. (1982). Assessment of minimum competency in fifth grade learning disabled students: Test modifications make a difference. *Journal of Educational Research, 76,* 35–40.

Hartley, J. (1985). *Designing instructional text* (2nd ed.). London: Kogan Page.

Jamison, M. (1998, January). The changeable course of typographic justification [electronic version]. *Journal of Scholarly Publishing, 29*(2), 71–86.

Johnstone, D. J. (2003). *Improving validity of large-scale tests: Universal design and student performance* (technical report 37). Minneapolis: University of Minnesota, National Center on Educational Outcomes. Retrieved June 26, 2004, from http://education.umn.edu/NCEO/OnlinePubs/Technical37.htm

Merriam-Webster's collegiate dictionary (11th ed.). (2003). Springfield, MA: Merriam-Webster.

Microsoft manual of style for technical publications (3rd ed.). (2003). Redmond, WA: Microsoft Press.

Muncer, S. J., Gorman, B. S., Gorman, S., & Bibel, D. (1986). Right is wrong: An examination of the effect of right justification on reading. *British Journal of Educational Technology, 6*(1), 75–85.

Publication manual of the American Psychological Association (5th ed.). (2001). Washington, DC: American Psychological Association.

Sabin, W. (2004). *The Gregg reference manual: A manual of style, grammar, usage, and formatting* (10th ed.). Boston: McGraw-Hill/Irwin.

Schwartz, M., & The task force on bias-free language of the Association of American University Presses. (1995). *Guidelines for bias-free writing*. Bloomington: Indiana University Press.

Shriver, K. A. (1997). *Dynamics in document design*. New York: John Wiley & Sons.

Thompson, D. R. (1991). *Reading print media: The effects of justification and column rule on memory*. Paper presented at the Southwest Symposium, Southwest Education Council for Journalism and Mass Communication, Corpus Christi, TX. (ERIC Document Reproduction Service No. ED337749)

Thompson, S., Johnston, C. J., & Thurlow, M. L. (2002). *Universal design applied to large scale assessments* (Synthesis Report 44). Minneapolis: University of Minnesota, National Center on Educational Outcomes.

Thou shalt be diligent, Bible proofreaders believe. (2004, May 23). *The Sunday World-Herald* [Omaha, NE], p. A6.

Tufte, E. R. (1990). *Envisioning information*. Cheshire, CT: Graphics Press.

Tufte, E. R. (2001). *The visual display of quantitative information* (2nd ed.). Cheshire, CT: Graphics Press.

United States Copyright Office. (2002, June). *Copyright registration for secure tests* (Circular 64). Retrieved July 19, 2004, from http://www.copyright.gov/circs/circ64.pdf

University of Chicago Press Staff. (2003). *The Chicago manual of style* (15th ed.). Chicago: University of Chicago Press.

Watts, L., & Nisbet, J. (1974). *Legibility in children's books: A review of research*. Windsor, Berkshire, England: NFER.

Webster's dictionary of English usage (Rev. ed.). (1994). Springfield, MA: Merriam-Webster.

Webster's third new international dictionary, unabridged. (2002). Springfield, MA: Merriam-Webster.

Zachrisson, B. (1965). *Studies in the legibility of printed text*. Stockholm: Almqvist & Wiksell.

Zakrzewski, S., & Steven, C. (2003). Computer-based assessment: quality assurance issues, the hub of the wheel [electronic version]. *Assessment & Evaluation in Higher Education, 28*(6), 609–623.

27

Test Administration

Rose C. McCallin
Colorado Department of Regulatory Agencies

Test administration practices may (a) threaten the intended score interpretations for which a test was chosen, (b) provide evidence that strengthens a particular inference about a trait the test aims to measure, or (c) lead to data that supports alternate hypotheses about a construct of interest. This chapter examines the importance of planning for and conducting standardized administrations of tests to increase the validity of test score interpretations and uses. The chapter discusses how test administration threats to the validity of score interpretations can be avoided by following the test administration standards promulgated by the *Standards for Educational and Psychological Testing* (American Educational Research Association [AERA], American Psychological Association [APA], and National Council on Measurement in Education [NCME], 1999).

The chapter is divided into four parts (1) Test Administration Threats to Validity; (2) Test Administration Standards and Efforts that Enhance Standardization; (3) Accumulating Validity Evidence and Auditing Test Administration Practices; and (4) Test Administration: Some Visions and Practical Considerations. The first part of the chapter examines the construct irrelevancy of miscreant administration that systematically increases or decreases test scores for a group of test takers or an individual examinee. The role of standardization in test administration follows, along with a discussion about how standardization can reduce validity threats. Five job aids are offered to promote effective administration. The third part of the chapter explores test administration opportunities to collect validity evidence and recommends independent auditing mechanisms that can lead to improvements in test programs. The chapter concludes with some ideas about how test developers can encourage effective test administrations. Information is provided to help test programs design and implement a validity research agenda that leads to effective test administrations and the ongoing identification and elimination of validity threats.

This chapter examines the importance of planning for and conducting standardized administrations of tests to increase the validity of test score interpretations and uses. The chapter discusses how test administration threats to the validity of score interpretations can be avoided by focusing on key test administration standards promulgated by the *Standards for Educational and Psychological Testing* (American Educational Research Association [AERA], American Psychological Association [APA], & National Council on Measurement in Education [NCME],

1999). The chapter is divided into the following four parts:

1. Test Administration Threats to Validity
2. Test Administration Standards and Efforts that Enhance Standardization
3. Accumulating Validity Evidence and Auditing Test Administration Practices
4. Test Administration: Some Visions and Practical Considerations

Part 1 acknowledges the evolving conceptualizations of validity as a unitary concept. Two main threats to validity, construct underrepresentation and construct-irrelevant variance (CIV), are examined with reference to whether test administration practices (a) narrow the meaning of test scores or (b) systematically contribute extraneous information to test scores. The section focuses primarily on the construct irrelevancy of miscreant administration that systematically increases or decreases test scores for a group of test takers or an individual examinee.

Part 2 presents key test administration standards within the *Standards* (AERA, APA, & NCME, 1999) and discusses how they can help to minimize CIV threats to the validity of test score interpretations. The section also discusses how to select and train test administrators so that they know how to meet the standardization requirements for each test they administer. Five job aids are introduced in Part 2, one for each key function within a test administration program.

Part 3 of the chapter discusses the opportunities that each administration of a test provides in the ongoing accumulation and evaluation of evidence that supports or refutes current validity arguments. The author also calls for a need to revisit the development of independent auditing programs. Part 4 reflects on some ways that test administration has evolved with innovations in society. Current and future test administration initiatives are provided, along with the five job aids that are included as appendices to the chapter.

TEST ADMINISTRATION THREATS TO VALIDITY

Validity is "the degree to which evidence and theory support the interpretations of test scores entailed by proposed uses of tests" (AERA, APA, & NCME, 1999, p. 9). This chapter treats validity as a unified concept (Messick, 1989). Although differences of opinion remain among validity theorists, this chapter like others (e.g., Haladyna, chap. 32, this volume; Kane, chap. 7, this volume; Linn, chap. 2, this volume) is consistent with modern validity theory as described in the recent *Standards:*

> Evolving conceptualizations of the concept of validity no longer speak of different types of validity but speak instead of different lines of validity evidence, all in the service of providing information relevant to a specific intended interpretation of test scores. Thus, many lines of evidence can contribute to an understanding of the construct meaning of test scores. (AERA, APA, & NCME, 1999, p. 5)

Validation is the process of developing sound arguments for and against proposed test uses and interpretations (AERA, APA, & NCME, 1999; Cronbach, 1988; Haertel, 1999; Kane, 1992, 2001, 2002, chap. 7, this volume). Plausible rival hypotheses can be formulated by considering "whether a test measures less or more than its proposed construct" (AERA, APA, & NCME, 1999, p. 10). Effective validation involves examining evidence regarding propositions about the plausibility of coherent validity arguments (Cronbach, 1988; Haertel, 1999; Haladyna, chap. 32, this volume; Kane, chap. 7, this volume; Linn, chap. 2, this volume). Embracing the scientific ideal requires a balanced approach in the validation process so that efforts strive to understand and disclose all evidence about tests and testing practices.

Validity as a unified concept means that an argument for a particular interpretation of a test score is only as strong as the weakest evidence used to support the implied inference (Crooks, Kane, & Cohen, 1996; Kane, chap. 7, this volume; Kane, Crooks, & Cohen, 1999). Haertel (1999, p. 5) summed it up well when he said, "Massive evidence in support of one proposition really doesn't buy us much if evidence for some other key proposition is lacking."

Figure 27.1 provides a context for two types of test administration threats to the validity of score interpretations: practices that introduce systematic error (CIV) and those that narrow the meaning of test scores (construct underrepresentation). Figure 27.1 acknowledges "validity as the most fundamental consideration in developing and evaluating tests" (AERA, APA, & NCME, 1999, p. 9). The sources of validity evidence in Figure 27.1 are complex and depend on the propositions in validity arguments. The propositions may lead to evidence that supports the validity arguments or may require revisions to some assumptions.

Validity Threats and Embracing the Scientific Ideal

Haladyna and Downing (2004, p. 18) identify at least five major threats to validity: construct underrepresentation, faulty logic underlying causal inferences about scores, test score interpretations and uses that may have negative consequences, test scores that lack reproducibility, and CIV. The *Standards* focus on construct underrepresentation and CIV threats to validity by proposing and evaluating alternate hypotheses that can lead to information about whether a test measures less or more than its proposed construct (AERA, APA, & NCME, 1999, p. 10).

Test developers have both economic and practical disincentives when it comes to identifying, understanding, and disclosing threats to the validity of score interpretations of their testing programs (Haertel, 1999). The point can be made, however, that the costs of acknowledging weaknesses of tests and testing practices are never as high as the costs of decisions based on test scores that

- Fail to capture important aspects of a construct; or
- Are affected by processes that are extraneous to the intended construct.

The *Standards* make clear that "nearly all tests leave out elements that some potential users believe should be measured and include some elements that potential users consider inappropriate" (AERA, APA, & NCME, 1999, p. 10). Measurement professionals know that, in practice, there is no test that yields observed scores that are free from errors of measurement. The profession's record in educating test consumers about the imprecision of test scores, however, can stand to improve considerably (Popham, 2003). Test developers, in particular, have the responsibility to educate test users about the limitations associated with using test scores from a single measure to inform decisions (e.g., see AERA, APA, & NCME, 1999, Standard 13.7, pp. 146–147). This chapter aims to further this cause by instilling among test developers the importance of educating test administrators about how they can recognize and minimize construct underrepresentation and construct-irrelevant threats to the validity of test score interpretations.

Test Administration and Construct Underrepresentation Threats to Validity

At first glance, it may appear that construct underrepresentation threats to validity primarily arise because test developers neglected to include in the test important aspects of the intended construct. There are instances, however, in which the test administrator, the testing system,

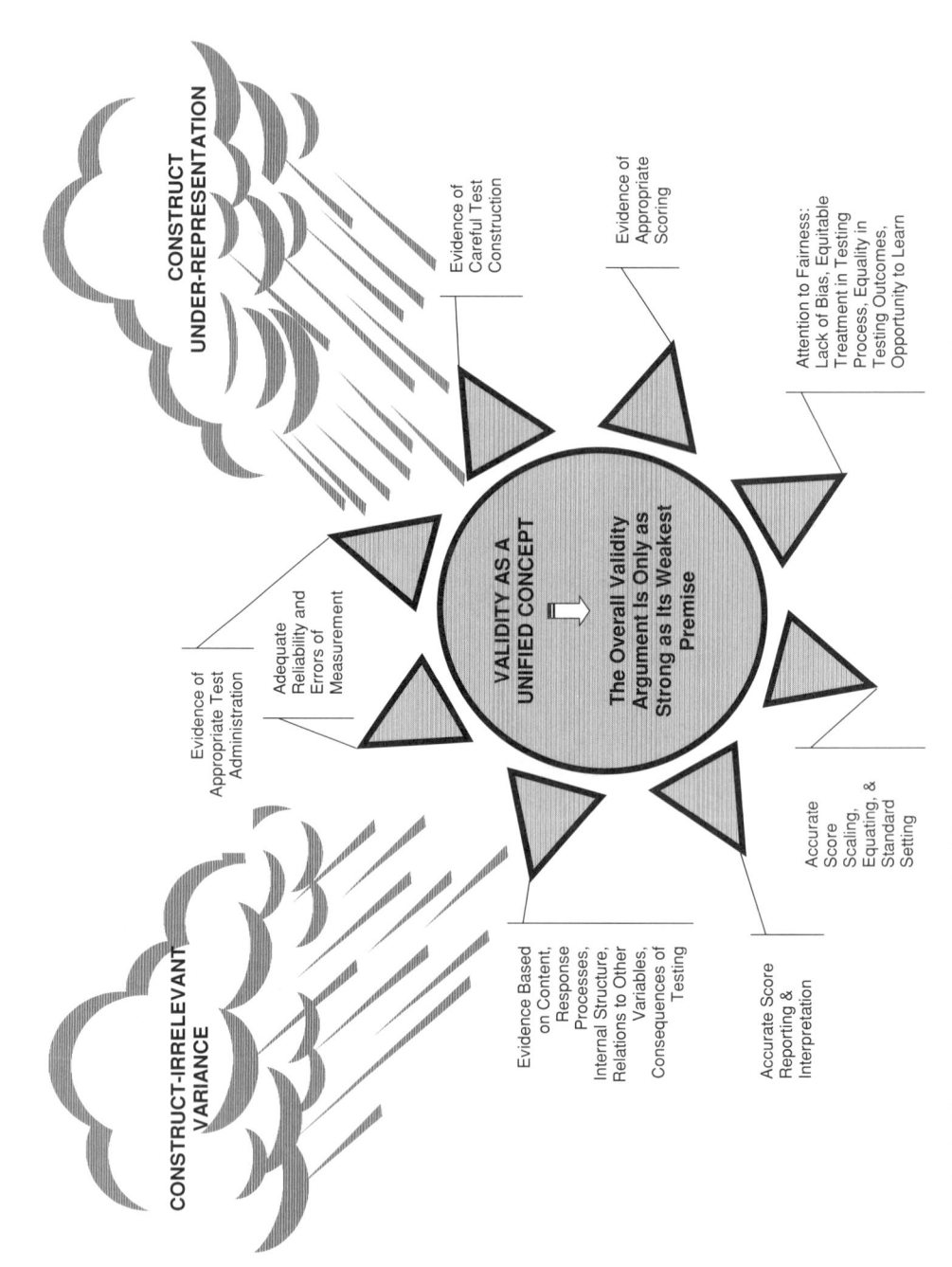

FIG. 27.1. Validity arguments, sources of validity evidence, and test administration threats to the validity of score interpretations.

and the overall testing process can lead to narrowed meanings of test scores (Kane, chap. 7, this volume; Kane, Crooks, & Cohen, 1999).

For example, consider a performance test that requires test administrators to elicit behaviors that sample the intended construct. The test administrators then rate test taker performance on the behaviors they elicited. The validity of the score interpretations can be compromised if the procedures used to elicit test taker behaviors do not yield a representative and relevant sample of performance in the intended construct (AERA, APA, & NCME, 1999, Standard 3.15, p. 46). Scores that are limited in the extent to which they represent the intended construct threaten the validity of the interpretation of a test taker's performance. This holds true even if it can be shown that test administrators follow the scoring rubrics correctly. This observation relates to the discussion about the overall strength of the validity argument. The accurate scoring of behaviors that do not capture important aspects of the intended construct does little to render valid interpretations of the narrowed scores.

In another example, consider the standardization that is possible when computers instead of humans are used to administer tests and record and score examinee responses. The consistency in the delivery of computer-based tests postulates in theory that every test taker will receive a generally comparable testing experience. The standardization across computer-delivered test events and test sites leads to the assumption that administrations are consistent, regardless of the model used by the test program (e.g., linear or adaptive testing). Test programs that utilize technology to automate, standardize, or maximize the efficiency of the measurement process, however, still are not exempt from construct underrepresentation threats to validity. Tests that are administered adaptively by computer require large banks of calibrated items that meet both the test specifications and the item information functions to estimate efficiently test taker standing in the intended construct. Construct underrepresentation owing to item banks that are insufficient in depth or breadth of homogeneous items may threaten the validity of a test taker's estimated ability on a posited unidimensional latent trait.

A third example involves the inappropriate omission of certain tasks within a performance measure to accommodate a test taker with a qualified disability (AERA, APA, & NCME, 1999, Standard 10.5, pp. 106–107; Thurlow, Thompson, & Lazarus, chap. 28, this volume). The resulting score cannot be interpreted validly with respect to the intended construct unless the omitted items were replaced with items that (a) cover the intended construct in the same way as the original items, (b) lead to estimates of performance that are essentially equivalent to those measured by the original items, and (c) lend to reasonable accommodations that do not alter materially the measurement of the intended construct.

Construct underrepresentation also may threaten the validity of score interpretations if test takers overinterpret the information provided in score reports. Depending on the purposes of a testing program, some programs may provide failing test takers diagnostic feedback about their criterion referenced performance in the content areas that comprise the intended construct. The information usually is provided to help identify areas that require further study before a retest attempt. The presentation of the diagnostic information should take into account and communicate at some level the precision of the measurement that underlies the estimated performance in each content area of the intended construct (AERA, APA, & NCME, 1999, Standard 1.10, pp. 19–20; Ryan, chap. 29, this volume). Even when the feedback is presented to reflect the diagnostic purpose of the information (e.g., graphically along a strength–weakness continuum that does not reflect categorical-level or interval-level measurement), there still are individuals who may use the information inappropriately. Some examinees may compute numerical scores by content area and then sum their scores to determine how close they came to the pass–fail cut point or other level of proficiency. This inappropriate use of the diagnostic feedback inevitably leads to misinterpretations of test results because "data are extrapolated beyond the range of available data or are interpolated without sufficient data points" (AERA, APA, &

NCME, 1999, Standard 4.1, p. 54; Ryan, chap. 29, this volume). The construct underrepresentation that threatens the validity of the interpretations based on inappropriately converted test scores is only one facet within the larger area of score interpretations, scaling, equating, and standard setting (see AERA, APA, & NCME, 1999, pp. 49–60; Cizek, chap. 10, this volume; Ryan, chap. 29, this volume). The communication and interpretation of information presented in score reports is acknowledged in this chapter because test administrators often are associated with onsite scoring and score reporting activities. Test takers may ask for assistance in interpreting their score reports when onsite test administration staff issue these reports. Test administrators typically are not trained to assume these responsibilities, which have their own set of complexities (AERA, APA, & NCME, 1999, Standard 13.14, p. 148).

Test Administration and Construct-Irrelevant Variance Threats to Validity

No matter how carefully a test is administered, the obtained (observed) scores of a group of test takers are a function of random error, systematic error that is attributable to CIV, and a "true" score (Haladyna, chap. 32, this volume; Haladyna & Downing, 2004, pp. 18–19; Lord & Novick, 1968, pp. 43–44). Random error (a) has an expected value of zero across a set of test scores; (b) is not correlated with true and observed scores; and (c) may affect an examinee's score in either a positive or negative direction.

In contrast to random error, CIV error is constant error that systematically influences scores for groups of test takers or for a specific individual (Haladyna & Downing, 2004, p. 18). CIV error may systematically over- or underestimate true scores by introducing components in scores that are not part of the intended construct (AERA, APA, & NCME, 1999, p. 10; Haladyna, chap. 32, this volume; Haladyna & Downing, 2004, p. 18).

Random and systematic errors affect the valid interpretation of test scores. Random errors reduce the consistency of the test scores, thus limiting the confidence that can be placed in them. Systematic errors cause scores to be inaccurate, by introducing construct-irrelevant easiness or construct-irrelevant difficulty to test scores for a group of test takers or a specific individual (Haladyna, chap. 32, this volume; Haladyna & Downing, 2004, p. 18). Because random error is unpredictable, uncorrelated with true and observed scores, and expected to sum to zero (see Lord & Novick, 1968, pp. 37–38), it makes sense to focus test administration efforts on activities aimed at identifying and minimizing CIV error variance, which systematically increases or decrease test scores for a group of test takers or individual examinees.

Construct-Irrelevant Variance and Test Delivery Formats

It can be challenging to identify systematic error that is attributable to the ways a test is administered, regardless of the delivery format (e.g., paper-based tests, computer-delivered tests). Dedicated test sites, designed specifically for computer-delivered tests, generally offer environments that do not vary markedly across sites or administrations of a test. Many computer-delivered test programs also offer frequent opportunities to test throughout the year. The ability to test often allows the testing program to manage the demand for testing opportunities. This in turn eliminates the need to test large numbers of test takers at the same time for a given program. Testing small numbers of examinees can help to control for CIV error variance associated with large scale test administrations (e.g., environmental distractions; variability across test sites). The opportunity to test frequently, however, requires adequate item banks. Insufficient item banks can lead to other sources of CIV error variance (e.g., overexposure of certain items and test score drift).

Merely using the computer to deliver tests also may introduce CIV threats to the validity of test score interpretations. Examples include tests that require a level of computer proficiency or familiarity with the test delivery software. If the test itself does not aim to measure these dimensions, then a systematic source of irrelevant error may be present in the test scores of those who do not possess proficiency in using the testing system (AERA, APA, & NCME, 1999, Standard 13.18, p. 149; Huff & Sireci, 2001; Sireci & Zenisky, chap. 14, this volume). Finally, computer-delivered test vendors base test costs partly on examinee volume and seat time. If the test developer reduces testing time to control costs, a "speededness" element of CIV may be introduced in the test scores that otherwise is not intended to be a component of the measurement construct (Haladyna & Downing, 2004; Huff & Sireci, 2001). Additional discussion about CIV and speededness is provided in the next section.

Compare the computer-delivered testing model to programs that offer tests only a few times per year. If the program has large numbers of examinees, it may be difficult to find suitable test sites that offer essentially equivalent test environments. Many programs that administer tests infrequently during the year also are likely to deliver tests in a paper-based format.

Paper-based test administrations rely primarily on humans to ensure standardized conditions. The likelihood for nonstandard test administrations increases when humans are timing the test, reading instructions to test takers, and overseeing the answer sheets, which serve as the basis for subsequent interpretations of test taker performance. These are only a few examples of the sources of systematic error that may surface in a paper-based test administration environment.

Any decision to offer tests electronically needs to consider the additional costs that accompany computer-based test delivery. Costs may include (a) increased numbers of quality items in item banks and (b) substantial investments in computing, communications, and other technology-related infrastructure (see Impara & Foster, chap. 5, this volume). The costs associated with developing more test items that also can facilitate the efficiencies of adaptive testing can be daunting even if the test administration is outsourced to a vendor specializing in the secure, electronic delivery and scoring of computerized tests (see Trent & Roeber, chap. 3, this volume). Other chapters examine extensively item development issues associated with increasing in size and quality the item banks for a test program (see Baranowski, chap. 15, this volume; Downing, chap. 1, this volume; Hambleton & Jirka, chap. 18, this volume).

Test Administration Construct-Irrelevant Variance That Affects Groups of Test Takers

Table 27.1 provides some examples of test administration-related CIV that generally affect test takers within the test session in which they occur. It can be argued that sources of CIV may impact examinees differently within a group. Some test takers may be more sensitive to the source of CIV than others. The level in which scores in a group contain systematic error owing to a particular CIV source may differ. The important distinction here is that the sources of CIV presented in Table 27.1 are pervasive and constant in the test administration. These types of group-specific CIV are not internal sources of systematic error that examinees bring to the testing process. Instead, they occur during the test session and are systematic errors that are constant across all members of a particular group (Haladyna & Downing, 2004).

Test administrations that alter time limits specified by the test developer can impact the validity of interpretations of a group of scores. The sources of CIV from alterations in timing are problematic for tests that are speeded as well as for power tests (i.e., tests on which most examinees are expected to complete all items). Research about test accommodations that alter testing time generally indicates that increasing test time on tests benefits all examinees, both those with and without disabilities (see Pitoniak & Royer, 2001). Although experimental

TABLE 27.1
Construct-Irrelevant Variance Threats to Validity that Affect Groups of Test Takers

Types CIV Threats	Examples
Altering test administration requirements	• Changing time limits. • Modifying test instructions so that examinee responses do not have same meaning as those in the validation studies. • Offering different delivery formats that change measurement of the construct. • Variations that occur to increase test scores without concurrent improvements in performance in the intended construct (e.g., giving hints or answers to groups of examinees; altering examinee responses; cleaning up answer sheets for some but not all test sessions).
Variability across test sites	• Testing conditions are not equivalent or comparable from one site to the next site (i.e., threats to fairness). • Inadvertent posting of instructional aids in classrooms. • Equipment in test administration differs in important aspects from: site to site, the learning/training environments, and/or equipment used in the validation studies.
Interruptions during test sessions	• Requiring test takers to relocate after testing has started. • Power outages need to evacuate site during session. • Disturbances or other distractions during testing.
Differences in the time of day at which the test is administered	• Administering tests at times in which examinees are not likely to perform optimally.
Changing scoring practices in the middle of a test session	• Examiner drift in applying scoring criteria to rate performance on skills tests. • Requiring examiners to recalibrate their ratings as they are administering a performance test.
Sources of systematic irrelevant variance due to technological variables	• Inadequate bandwidth, hardware, and/or other technical problems that that influence the integrity of test scores.

studies are problematic in disabilities research (see Thurlow, Thompson, & Lazarus, chap. 28, this volume), studies outside of the disability arena show that extra time can benefit examinee performance on measures thought to be power tests (Lane, Stone, Ankenmann, & Liu, 1995). Lane et al. (1995) found evidence of speededness on two items in a constructed-response mathematics performance test that was intended to be a power test. This finding points out the possibility that power tests may contain some items that are in fact speeded. When speed of processing is an aspect that is present within a test, then alterations in test administration time can impact the validity of the score interpretations for examinee groups that receive non-equivalent test time.

The sources of group-level CIV from test administration practices ultimately impact scores in one of two ways: test taker scores are either higher or lower than they would be if the sources of CIV were eliminated. For example, test administrators who cannot or do not read the test instructions properly can (a) confuse the group of examinees so they do not know what is expected and (b) miscommunicate expectations about response marking, how to change answers properly, or if guessing or omitting responses to items benefits or disadvantages test taker scores. Most of these examples introduce sources of CIV that can make a test more difficult.

Sometimes test administrators change the entire delivery of the test so that the test no longer measures the intended construct. An obvious example involves an administration in which the teacher reads test items to the class when the purpose of the test is to measure reading ability. If intentional, this behavior constitutes dishonest test practices (e.g., see Popham, 2003). The increased emphasis in high-stakes testing and pressures to improve student test scores reinforces the need for more research about alterations in test administrations and sources of CIV that impacts groups of test takers (Haladyna & Downing, 2004, p. 20). This example also underscores why it makes sense to employ independent test administrators without conflicts of interest as a way to minimize sources of group-level CIV.

At some point in time, virtually all test takers experience test environments that are not conducive to effective test performance. Test sites that are not comparable with one another sometimes can be advantageous to groups (e.g., a teacher forgets to remove instructional aids posted in a classroom that relate to the test content). These events rarely surface in test taker complaints about test experiences. Yet the benefits of such aids may be reflected consistently in group-level scores for months or years (Banks, 1996). The systematic error associated with being able to reference otherwise prohibited instructional aids during a test administration is virtually impossible to detect and eliminate from test scores.

Test takers usually are motivated to identify events that may cause them to score lower than they would have scored under reasonably normal conditions. Complaints from groups of test takers can indicate a weak link within the test administration process. Sources of CIV that are identifiable, however, do not necessarily mean that adjustments to reduce or eliminate their impact are likely to be successful. Many of the group-specific CIV sources in Table 27.1 can be managed by

- Identifying potential sources of CIV and working to prevent these threats from arising in the first place;
- Determining the effect size for the source of CIV in group test scores via ANOVA or linear regression (e.g., see Haladyna & Downing, 2004, p. 19; Hicks, 1982, pp. 129–159);
- Adjusting group scores to reduce or eliminate sources of CIV whenever possible (see Haladyna & Downing, 2004, p. 19); and
- Bringing the information that is uncovered about sources of CIV full circle: Training test administrators about sources of CIV that were detected from a test session they administered and showing them how to minimize the reoccurrence of these errors in the future.

Test Administration Construct-Irrelevant Variance That Affects Individual Examinees

Person-specific CIV is systematic error that can overestimate or underestimate an individual examinee's score (AERA, APA, & NCME, 1999, pp. 10–11; Haladyna, chap. 32, this volume; Haladyna & Downing, 2004). Some sources of CIV that are internal to test takers and generally can be attributed to test administration practices are presented in Table 27.2.

The information in Table 27.2 focuses on sources of CIV that are related to test administration activities. There are many other ways in which sources of CIV impact the validity of an individual's test score, but are not due to test administration practices (see Haladyna & Downing, 2004, pp. 23–25). The various sources of CIV listed in Table 27.2 lend some insight about the seriousness of person-specific sources of CIV. In the area of cheating, test takers who have prior access to test items threaten any attempts to measure and interpret validly scores about their standing in the intended construct (Cizek, 1999; Haladyna & Downing, 2004; Impara & Foster, chap. 5, this volume). Considerable attention in the literature about test preparation indicates that both ethical and questionable test preparation and coaching practices can contribute sources of CIV to test scores (e.g., Haladyna & Downing, 2004; Haladyna,

TABLE 27.2
Construct-Irrelevant Variance Threats to Validity that Affect the Individual Examinee

Types of CIV Threats	Examples
Prior exposure to test items	• Compromises in test security that lead to test form/item exposure.
Test anxiety that influences cognitive functioning	• Pressure to do well on test causes emotional reactions.
	• Test administrator hovers over examinee or causes unwarranted suspicion in test environment.
	• Test administrator creates hostile climate for test taker.
Test administrator practices that elicit test wiseness	• Some examinees get inadvertent clues from test administrator.
Level of examinee motivation	• Examinee underperforms on test to rebel against administration/policies/program/authority.
Examinee fatigue (cognitive, emotional, physical)	• Test administrator contributes to examinee fatigue.
Examinee misunderstands test instructions	• Test administrator does not ensure that examinee understands the test instructions.
Examinee does not know how to navigate testing system	• Test taker becomes anxious to an extent that impacts performance.
	• Examinee records responses incorrectly so does not get credit for right answers.
	• Examinee does not finish test owing to lack of proficiency in using testing system.

Nolen, & Haas, 1991; Mehrens & Kaminski, 1989; Popham, 1991, 2003). Crocker (2003, chap. 6, this volume) discusses ethical approaches to test preparation and test administration and examines test taker rights and responsibilities in more depth. The *Standards* note that valid interpretations of test scores "assume that a test taker has earned fairly a particular score or pass/fail decision" (AERA, APA, & NCME, 1999, p. 85).

The *Standards* pay considerable attention to test taker rights and responsibilities and the information that examinees deserve before and during testing sessions (e.g., impact of guessing effects, time limits) (AERA, APA, & NCME, 1999, Standard 8.2, pp. 86–87). Providing all examinees with information about a test session also may help to reduce some sources of CIV associated with test anxiety. The opportunity for test takers to take some practice items before the actual test session is important too so that they know what is expected of them (see Crocker, chap. 6, this volume).

Providing test takers with tutorials to acquaint them with computer interfaces for electronically delivered tests is increasing in practice as evidence accumulates about sources of CIV associated with computerized test delivery and the use of other media in testing (AERA, APA, & NCME, 1999, Standard 13.18, p. 149; Huff & Sireci, 2001; Sireci & Zenisky, chap. 14, this volume). In addition, test administrators need to be proficient in using the testing systems.

TEST ADMINISTRATION STANDARDS AND EFFORTS THAT ENHANCE STANDARDIZATION

The examples given in Tables 27.1 and 27.2 underscore the principle that the valid interpretation of test scores relies on the expectation that every test administration has been conducted under the same, standardized conditions of measurement. Standardization is crucial in test administrations because it reduces the opportunities for sources of CIV, especially CIV that is external to test takers.

Standardization is an environment in which the test taker instructions, the test settings, and the scoring procedures follow the same detailed procedures (AERA, APA, & NCME, 1999, p. 61). Standardization that leads to comparable measurement for all examinees is the key to obtaining data that can be (a) interpreted properly, (b) compared appropriately, and (c) used according to the principle that every test taker is assessed in a fair manner.

The *Standards* acknowledge that although tests may differ in their degree of standardization (e.g., use of parallel test forms and/or testlets within forms; tailoring instructions so examinees can understand what is required of them), the goal of standardization across all administrations of a test is "to provide accurate and comparable measurement for everyone, and unfair advantage to no one" (AERA, APA, & NCME, 1999, p. 61). Test administrators must consider that any compromises in standardization are likely to reduce the validity of score interpretations.

"The usefulness and interpretability of test scores require that the test be administered and scored according to the developer's instructions" (AERA, APA, & NCME, 1999, p. 61). As many other chapters in this book discuss, the test administration requirements typically are specified as test developers attend to item format and response demands, time restrictions, the characteristics of test takers, and the scoring demands (AERA, APA, & NCME, 1999, Standard 3.3, p. 43). Although professional judgment plays an important role in developing test specifications (AERA, APA, & NCME, 1999, p. 43), the activities to codify the scoring requirements, prepare the test taker instructions, and conduct the validation research all lead to the formulation of the test administration requirements (see Becker & Pomplun, chap. 30, this volume; Downing, chap. 1, this volume; Linn, chap. 2, this volume; Roid, chap. 23, this volume; Raymond & Neustel, chap. 9, this volume; Wendler & Walker, chap. 20, this volume).

Table 27.3 lists the predominant test administration standards relevant to ensuring fairness and comparability in test administration activities. The examples of group-specific and person-specific sources of CIV, discussed in the first part of this chapter, are carried forward and synthesized in Table 27.3. The key test administration standards (AERA, APA, & NCME, 1999), the sources of CIV threats, and the examples given in Table 27.3 provide a context for understanding the ways in which each standard helps to minimize sources of test administration-related CIV.

Efforts That Enhance Standardization

Selecting Appropriate Test Administrators

Hiring the right people to be test administrators is an important test administration requirement. Attention to this step seems obvious, yet in practice the lack of wisdom in this regard can be astonishing (e.g., using teachers as test administrators in high-stakes testing programs because the teachers are convenient and do not appear as a direct cost to the testing program).

According to the *Standards,* the test user (i.e., entity that selects and uses a test) has numerous responsibilities to the test publisher, the test takers, parents and guardians, policy makers, the general public, and others who may be impacted by the tests they select, administer, score, and use to make decisions (AERA, APA, & NCME, 1999, pp. 111–118). No matter how well the test developer performs his or her responsibilities, the proper use of standardized measures and interpretations of scores ultimately are the responsibility of the test user (AERA, APA, & NCME, 1999, p. 111). The test user is responsible for knowing the test purposes, administration requirements, population of test takers, and how to interpret and use properly validity information (AERA, APA, & NCME, 1999, Standard 11.11 p. 113).

The test user has specific due diligence requirements in the selection and training of test administrators. First, all test administrators need to be screened for conflicts of interest and for

TABLE 27.3
Test Administrator Standards and Standardization Requirements

Standard	Brief Description of Text	Page(s)	Main CIV Threat(s) (Primary Entity Affected)
3.19	• Present directions with sufficient clarity so others can replicate administration conditions.	46–47	• Examinee misunderstands instructions (individual)
3.20	• Instructions to test takers should contain sufficient detail so they can respond to tasks in the manner intended by test developer.		
5.1	• Test administrators should follow standardized procedures for administration.	63	• Altering test administration (group)
5.2	• Document modifications or disruptions of standardized test administration procedures or scoring.	63	• Altering test administration (group) • Testing interruptions (group) • Changing scoring in middle of session (group) • Technology issues (group)
5.4	• Testing environment should furnish reasonable comfort with minimal distractions.	63	• Variability across test sites (group) • Testing interruptions (group) • Test anxiety (individual) • Examinee motivation (individual) • Examinee fatigue (individual)
5.6	• Reasonable efforts should be made to ensure the integrity of test scores.	64	• Altering test administration (group) • Inadvertent posting of instructional aids in classroom (group) • Time of day differences (group) • Technological issues (group) • Problems using testing software (individual) • Prior exposure (individual) • Eliciting test-wiseness (individual)
5.7	• Test users are responsible for the security of test materials at all times.	64	• Prior exposure (individual)
5.9	• Test scoring that involves human judgment requires adequate scoring rubrics, monitoring for score drift, and documentation.	64–65	• Changing scoring in middle of test session (group)
6.11	• If a test permits more than one method of administration, the test developer must document score interchangeability (e.g., response marking methods that are interchangeable).	70	• Examinee records responses incorrectly (individual)
8.6	• Test data: Protect from improper disclosure; confidentiality requirement extends to electronic transmittal methods.	88	• Technological issues (group)
13.18	• Tests administered and scored using multimedia or computers	149	• Examine lack of proficiency in using testing system (individual)

criminal records that may lead a reasonable person to question an individual's fitness to serve in any test administration capacity. Employers increasingly are checking criminal records of job applicants to prevent business theft among other things ("watch it!" 2004). Test administrators obviously should not be the same individuals who may be held accountable for the quality of examinee performance on tests they administer.

The security agreements test administration staff agree to uphold may vary in emphasis depending on the specific test administration functions each individual performs. In general, all test security agreements should cover the following areas:

- Communicate that test content is both copyrighted and nondisclosed in perpetuity (or for a period of time in which each test item is considered "active" in the item bank);
- Require the potential administrator to attest that he or she (a) does not have any conflicts of interest, (b) will not engage in activities that a reasonable person would deem as copyright infringement and/or a conflict of interest for a certain period of time (the window of time may depend on how often the test item banks are revised), and (c) will disclose to the test user and the test owner any present or future employment that may be viewed by a reasonable person as being a conflict of interest; and
- Communicate the legal and financial consequences of any activities in which administrator involvement leads to compromises in item security or infringes on copyright protections.

Test developers can seek injunctive relief (a writ ordered by a court of equity that requires an individual to do or to refrain from doing a specified act) against individuals who may be offering test preparation services or engaging in activities that constitute copyright infringement. Still this offers little consolation when it comes to rebuilding the item banks and reestablishing the integrity of a testing program. Impara and Foster (chap. 5, this volume) provide additional details about test development security issues.

Other considerations in the selection of appropriate test administration staff include (a) ensuring that administrators can read the test instructions reasonably well so test takers can understand what is required of them; (b) making sure that test administrators have the requisite technological skills to conduct the test administration activities; and (c) ensuring that administrators have the capability to perform the physical and cognitive demands required of the test administration activities, including but not limited to skills in multitasking, conflict resolution, and documenting testing irregularities.

Test Administrator Training

Test developers have many opportunities (if not responsibilities) to ensure that test administrators follow the standardization requirements to increase the validity of score interpretations (AERA, APA, & NCME, 1999, Standard 3.19, pp. 46–47). Test administration training materials should be designed so that test administrators (a) understand what they need to do to uphold security and standardization requirements; (b) receive instruction and feedback about their performance; and (c) apply the necessary concepts and principles to appropriate test settings before the actual test administration. Adequate test administrator training efforts do not consist of crash courses the day of the test. Proper training and guided learning opportunities for testing staff offer some of the best investments possible when it comes to managing the risks associated with sources of CIV. Investments in test administrator training have substantial returns in relation to their costs. Proper training and guided learning opportunities also are essentially risk-free investments, provided that proper security measures are taken at all times. Compare these returns to those that ignore training altogether. Why depend on chance or luck that test administrators will perform as required? Test administrators are one of the most important factors that lead to the proper identification and reporting of administration anomalies that may call into question the inferences that can be made from the test scores.

Test Administration Job Aids

Five separate but related "job aids" are included in the appendices to this chapter. The five job aids are relevant primarily to paper-based test administrations because this delivery format carries a greater probability for risk exposures from to lapses in standardization and other test administration sources of CIV threats to validity. In addition, the majority of high-stakes test programs still use paper-based test administrations.

Four of the five job aids focus on the primary responsibilities and deliverables required of the key test administration functions associated mainly with paper-based test administrations. The fifth job aid serves as a guide for handling common test administration emergencies. The job aids cover the following entities:

- Appendix A: Test Owner & Test User
- Appendix B: Test User/Lead Test Administrator
- Appendix C: Test Proctor
- Appendix D: Site Coordinator
- Appendix E: Responding to Emergencies

Job aids support work processes by serving as guides to help direct or enlighten performance (Rossett & Gautier-Downes, 1991). Job aids do not take the place of training, instruction or the tools that are needed to perform a particular work function. The key idea associated with the value of a job aid is that knowing how and when to use one is possible only after the individual has received the requisite instruction, practice, and feedback that lead to the acquisition of job skills. Job aids are like the "code book" that an electrician uses in the field to handle a wide variety of tasks in accordance with state and local ordinances.

Each of the five job aids are synchronized to allow an approximate, coordinated timeframe for planning and conducting a test administration program. Appendix A is targeted to the test owner or developer and the test user. Most of the time and activities presented in Appendix A are aimed at developing the administrative framework and the critical elements that provide the foundation for a test administration program. Note that this job aid and the four other job aids are not "proctor manuals" nor do they constitute the instructional materials needed to train adequately the test administrators. Proctor manuals, test administrator training materials, and the technical test documents are considered part of the *Test Development and Revision* and *Supporting Documentation for Tests* work that is created in concert with the test development activities and the validity studies (see AERA, APA, & NCME, 1999, pp. 37–48, 67–70; also Becker & Pomplun, chap. 30, this volume; Downing, chap. 1, this volume; Haladyna, chap. 32, this volume).

Appendix A contains the important test administration elements that test takers need well before the test is administered. This information, usually published in a candidate handbook, should be available at least 6 months before the first test scheduling date (which may be 8 or more months before the first test administration date). The candidate handbook is like a university or college catalog in that it sets the rules, regulations, content specifications, and testing requirements that generally are in effect at the time a test candidate sits for the test. The candidate handbook is included as part of Appendix A because it communicates to test takers the expectations regarding test administration practices, procedures, and requirements.

Appendix B focuses on the "Test User/Lead Test Administrator" function within the test administration team. These functions are somewhat analogous to the "lead coach and the quarterback" staff of a football team. Most of Appendix B is devoted to creating the game plan for each test administration. The many items under "Security" link to standardization and test administrator training requirements. Appendix C provides guidance for the "Test Proctor" administration function. Many of the elements in Appendix C cover the actual test day activities, which commonly are associated with test administration. Appendix D is devoted to "Site Coordinator" functions. The planning, security, and many factors that contribute to standardization are covered in this job aid. Appendix E is relevant to responding (vs. reacting) to "Testing Emergencies." The job aid addresses a variety of issues including (a) theft, (b) fraud, (c) cheating, (d) site evacuation, (e) inclement weather, and (f) threats to the security of item banks. The job aids in the appendices offer a variety of ways and ideas to reduce risk exposures that can lead to sources of CIV.

Standardization is one of the most important factors in administering tests properly so that testing conditions are comparable for all examinees. Standardization is a necessary (but not sufficient) condition that enables the valid interpretation of test scores. Test administration practices may be considered synonymous with notions of both standardization and fairness when (AERA, APA, & NCME, 1999):

- The adequacy of the physical test site takes into consideration variables such as accessibility, comfort, lighting, privacy, space, and environments that are reasonably free from distractions;
- Test site personnel are unbiased and knowledgeable about the test procedures so that all candidates receive comparable measurement opportunities;
- Security policies and procedures strive to prevent fraudulent behaviors;
- Test materials and equipment offer all candidates comparable opportunities to demonstrate their knowledge, skills, and abilities; and
- Test administrations are comparable in the timing requirements and offer clear, easy-to-understand directions.

Finally, in cases that warrant nonstandard test administrations, the reasonableness of the accommodations or modifications should be judged as to whether they alter the meaning of the test scores or violate the principles of fairness that aim to ensure that every test taker is assessed in an equitable way (see Abedi, chap. 17, this volume; Thurlow, Thompson, & Lazarus, chap. 28, this volume).

ACCUMULATING VALIDITY EVIDENCE AND AUDITING TEST ADMINISTRATION PRACTICES

The quest for the ongoing accumulation of validity evidence and the evaluation of validity, both evidence that supports and that which refutes current validity arguments, is not a new idea (Cronbach, 1988). The need for independent auditing systems to monitor the quality of standardized testing practices, which play a significant role both in the validity of test score interpretations and in the ongoing collection of validity evidence, also is not a new idea (e.g., Downing & Haladyna, 1996; Madaus, 1992). The testing profession has made relatively little progress on either frontier to date. There are many disincentives associated with embracing the scientific ideal, as Haertel (1999, p. 6) described well:

> Undertaking studies that no one is asking for, that no one else is doing, that might call our work into question, and that might be used against us in court is, to say the least, unappealing.

Haladyna et al. (1991, pp. 5–6) noted that test administration practices constitute a major source of test score pollution (e.g., unequal handling of checking answer sheets for completion and marking errors; deviations in reading test directions or increasing testing time; differences in following the mandated procedures; undetected instances of cheating). Haladyna et al. (1991, p. 6) indicated that "many are aware of the problem of test score pollution and the external conditions that lead to polluting practices." Banks (1996) echoed this concern when she questioned the degree to which assumptions about standardized test conditions are valid, noting that teacher (test administrator) complacency or ignorance combined with complex, burdensome test administration procedures leads to misadministrations of tests more frequently than is acknowledged.

It has been about 15 years since Madaus (1992) examined various models for test auditing and proposed an independent auditing mechanism that could provide test users guidelines for validation studies designed to test disconfirming hypotheses. Likewise, a decade has passed since Downing and Haladyna (1996) questioned whether high-stakes testing programs should be subject to external review. Recent accounts indicate that test administration practices continue to be problematic (Popham, 2003). In addition, a review by Haladyna and Downing (2004) suggests research still is sparse about test administration sources of systematic errors associated with CIV.

Downing and Haladyna (1996) reviewed and suggested some possible models for external, independent evaluations. They also posed a number of questions related to test administration and test score validation in their proposed external evaluation models for high-stakes test programs (Downing & Haladyna, 1996). One question particularly relevant to the issues raised in this chapter is this: "Are variations in [test] administration[,] factors in test results?" (Downing & Haladyna, 1996, p. 9).

In some instances in which test administration practices lead to sources of CIV, the test takers and even the administrators may be able to assist in identifying the nature of these errors. Efforts to obtain systematically feedback about the quality of the test administration activities, however, can be met with suspicion by both test takers and test administrators. Test takers may be reluctant to offer information about sources of CIV if they believe their responses to a structured survey may be linked to their test data. Test administrators may withhold information about sources of CIV if they think they may be blamed or punished. Assuming these hurdles can be resolved, the timely collection of test taker opinions offers some promise in helping researchers uncover otherwise hidden sources of CIV threats to the validity of test score interpretations.

The dual needs for ongoing evaluations of test administration practices and the accumulation of validity evidence remain critical responsibilities that transcend all aspects of test development. Although the test user is expected to collect and thoroughly research all sources of information about possible test administration irregularities (AERA 1999, APA, & NCME, Standard 8.11, p. 89), it seems clear that ongoing programs to evaluate testing practices have yet to fully emerge. This may be a function to some degree that outside of litigation, there are few incentives for implementing ongoing programs that lead to enforcing proper testing practices. As Madaus (1992, p. 27) observed, "the demands of test validation often clash with the commercial nature of applied testing."

The emphasis on high-stakes testing appears to be increasing (Elementary and Secondary Education Act—No Child Left Behind, 2002). It is imperative to revisit today the work of Downing and Haladyna (1996) and others (e.g., Madaus, 1992) to identify plausible models to that can promote ongoing validation studies. This includes regular, systematic research that examines how well testing practices adhere to the standardization requirements that lead to fairness and comparability across testing events. Accordingly, the principles that deserve to be revisited include the following (Downing & Haladyna, 1996, p. 10):

- Identify the testing programs that appear to demonstrate the greatest need for external evaluation;
- Select and recruit evaluators who are independent (no conflicts of interest), have adequate psychometric training and experience, and who know the *Standards* and how to apply them (AREA, APA, & NCME, 1999);
- Reference multiple sources of information about the testing program;
- Document results and report recommendations for improvements to testing programs to appropriate responsible parties; and
- Require follow-up and release to the public, efforts made by the testing program in response to the evaluation recommendations.

It is important that audit reports can be released to the public. Audit findings that are made public carry far more weight than an evaluation that remains undisclosed.

Requiring high-stakes testing programs to undergo periodic independent reviews is a significant responsibility the testing profession has only begun to explore. These suggestions provide guidance about how to build audit mechanisms. The real challenge remains in convincing (1) more commercial test developers and (2) the policy makers who promulgate testing for accountability and instructional reform to each embrace the opportunities that are possible for ongoing constructive improvements in testing programs.

SOME VISIONS AND PRACTICAL CONSIDERATIONS

It is fitting at this juncture to reflect on the chapter's focus on test administration-related sources of CIV and standardization and how these notions relate to the fascination in America over the past 100 years to measure systematically aspects about social life. In *The First Measured Century,* the authors acknowledge the ideas this chapter and the measurement profession as a whole, convey regularly when it comes to interpreting validly the outcomes of measurement activities:

> Of course, measurement in the social sciences does not yield certitude. The measurers, the social scientists, the politicians, the advocates, and the activists often disagree about what the data really mean. But, on balance, the explosion of numerical investigation has indeed offered great value: an imperfect measure of accountability, an imperfect way of problem-solving, and an imperfect way of seeing that many things we thought were so, weren't. (Wattenberg, Caplow, & Hicks, 2001, p. xiii)

The U.S. Department of Labor *Report on the American Workforce 2001* (available from http://www.bls.gov/opub/rtaw/rtawhome.htm) indicates that the American workforce is much better off now than in 1900 (p. 3). The *Report* attributes today's workforce improvements to a confluence of factors, including but not limited to technology, capital, demography, education, immigration, and government intervention (U.S. Department of Labor, 2001). Technological developments pervade virtually every work place improvement discussed in the *Report*. Technology and capital, however, go hand-in-hand: As technological improvements make their way through the economy, new technology requires large amounts of capital to make its way into the workplace (U.S. Department of Labor, 2001, p. 5).

The past century saw many strides in the measurement arena, including improvements in theories, methods, and services. Technology also is pervasive in many of these testing improvements. The diffusion of technology to improve instruction, learning, and testing in the public elementary and secondary schools in this country, however, appears largely to be a vision yet to be realized. The promises of interactive learning environments, in which testing and instruction are embedded in courseware, have not established significant roots in the school system as envisioned in the 1980s. Bunderson, Inouye, and Olsen (1989) wrote that the diffusion of information processing technology would revolutionize the ways in which computerized tests were being administered and utilized for educationally relevant institutional or individual purposes. Bunderson et al. (1989) proposed teaching and measurement systems, with theoretical underpinnings in the expert knowledge model, in which learner control under stipulated conditions would meld together instructional and testing events. Likewise, Bennett (1998) observed that large-scale, high-stakes test programs may no longer "survive" to the extent that formative tests embedded within instruction could provide the information needed for summative decision making.

High-stakes test programs, however, are not likely to disappear from the testing horizon. There are too many decisions that require the efficient information that these tests provide (e.g., selection, diagnostic, licensing, and promotion, to name a few). Instructional courseware that embeds formative tests to inform learning has a place on the testing horizon as well. Test developers can capitalize on this instructional technology by exploiting its features to offer the customized learning guidance and support that is so necessary for test administrator training efforts. It is not for lack of innovation in hardware and software that the demand for quality instructional courseware that makes possible embedded learning guidance is relatively nonexistent in the nation's primary and secondary educational institutions. One needs to look no further than the advertisements in the Sunday paper to see the latest simulation games on the market to know these applications are possible. As the *Report on the American Workforce 2001* indicates, it takes capital to diffuse technology throughout the workforce (U.S. Department of Labor, 2001, p. 5). Although the requisite capital for instructional innovations of this nature does not appear to be in abundance within our nation's schools, it seems timely for test developers to invest some of their capital in the development of interactive courseware that can be used to train/retrain in meaningful ways test administration staff. Such training can establish the core cognitive and skill structures in memory that each test administrator needs to possess before he or she can facilitate in expert ways the collection of quality item response data. Since these data are at the heart of the test developer's investments in the test program, investments in test administration training courseware can offer significant bargains with respect to present and future validity returns. Proper training, combined with job aids like those provided in the appendices to this chapter, can lead to real progress in minimizing the potential for sources of CIV related to test administration practices.

Quality test development also requires test developers to design and implement a validity research agenda for each test program. Figure 27.1 offers some ways to think about how an integrated validity research agenda may be envisioned. For example, in the area of test administration threats to validity, evidence about "equitable treatment in the testing process" may include designing and implementing a program to determine systematically how well examinees are receiving adequate opportunities (a) to demonstrate their abilities (AERA, APA, & NCME, 1999, Standard 7.12, p. 84) and (b) to acquire familiarity with the test format and the test system interface (AERA, APA, & NCME, 1999, Standard 13.18, p. 149). If evidence indicates that examinees are experiencing problems with the testing interface, then the test developer needs to determine how to eliminate this threat to the validity of test score interpretations. The test developer also needs to determine if test scores should be cancelled due to this validity threat, and if so, make arrangements to retest examinees on an equivalent form of the test under corrected testing conditions. This kind of honesty and opportunity to cure responsibly life's imperfect moments in testing, models for all, educational and business practices that foster the very integrity test developers expect of their customers.

ACKNOWLEDGMENT

The author acknowledges with gratitude the assistance of Steven M. Downing and Thomas M. Haladyna, the editors, as well as Norman Hertz, Kara Schmitt, and Edythe McClatchy Pahl, who reviewed earlier versions of this manuscript and made suggestions that led to significant improvements.

APPENDIX A: TEST OWNER AND TEST USER RESPONSIBILITIES AND DELIVERABLES

SECURITY

Twelve to 15 Months Before Dates of Scheduled Tests

- ☑ Identity potential lead test administrators, test proctors, site coordinators, and test accommodations proctors within each geographic area in which tests are to be administered.
- ☑ Develop test security, conflict of interest, and employment disclosure forms.
- ☑ Develop background security check form.
- ☑ Develop agreement to serve form.
- ☑ Develop selection confirmation form.
- ☑ Develop manuals for lead test administrator, test proctors, site coordinators, and test accommodations staff.
- ☑ Develop all transmittal forms to ensure test materials tracking.
- ☑ Contract with armored security services (if applicable).
- ☑ Contract with armed security guard/loss prevention firm (if applicable).
- ☑ Contract with private carrier and provide for insurance coverage.
- ☑ Contract with test sites, bar code scanner, and other vendors to lease equipment, if applicable.

CANDIDATE HANDBOOK

Nine to 12 Months Before Dates of Scheduled Tests

- ☑ Develop and distribute proctor manuals and candidate handbook, to include:
  - ☑ Application materials and process.
  - ☑ Test specifications, sample test items, scoring criteria, and results reporting.
  - ☑ Testing policies.
    - ☑ Frequency of tests, costs, and retesting.
    - ☑ Describe testing process and intended use of test results.
    - ☑ Information about test taker confidentiality and video recording of candidate during test session, if applicable.
    - ☑ Information about test taker rights, appeals, and informed consent.
    - ☑ Impersonation, fraud, and cheating.
    - ☑ Admittance requirements (identification, admission tickets, late arrivals, prohibited items, etc.).
  - ☑ Develop tutorials for CBT interface practice, if applicable.

HIRE TEST SITE ADMINISTRATION STAFF

Six to 9 Months Before Dates of Scheduled Tests

- ☑ Contact potential staff and invite individuals to apply for positions for which they have been identified (e.g., lead test administrator, test proctor, site coordinator, test accommodation proctor).
- ☑ Send application materials, including background security check form and test security, conflict of interest, and employment disclosure forms.
- ☑ Perform background checks on applicants.
- ☑ Notify successful applicants and send agreement to serve form.
- ☑ Obtain completed materials and send selection confirmation form with W-9 form.
- ☑ Provide lead test administrator list of hires and alternates and contact information.

TRAINING AND MANUALS

Three to 6 Months Before Dates of Scheduled Tests

- ☑ Distribute lead test administrator manual.
- ☑ Schedule and conduct lead test administrator training.

One to 3 Months before Dates of Scheduled Tests

- ☑ Distribute proctor, site coordinator, and test accommodations manuals.
- ☑ Schedule and conduct proctor, site coordinator, and test accommodations staff training (require lead test administrators to attend).

TEST MATERIALS AND STAFF AVAILABILITY

One Week Before Scheduled Exam and Test Day

- ☑ Coordinate armored security, security guards, bar code scanner, and other leased equipment vendors with lead test administrators.
- ☑ Distribute test materials and transmittal/tracking forms.
- ☑ Provide contact information for test day.

APPENDIX B: TEST USER/LEAD TEST ADMINISTRATOR ROLES AND RESPONSIBILITIES

SECURITY

Six to 9 Months Before Dates of Scheduled Tests

- ☑ Receive list and contact information for selected test proctors, site coordinator, test accommodations staff, alternates.
- ☑ Review candidate handbook.
- ☑ Contact test proctors and site coordinator: Review test security, conflict of interest, and employment disclosure agreements.

- ☑ Contact armored security, loss prevention firms to confirm services, if applicable.
- ☑ Contact test sites, private carrier, and equipment providers to confirm arrangements and schedule site inspections.

Three to 6 Months Before Dates of Scheduled Tests

- ☑ Receive and review lead administrator manual.
- ☑ Attend training; complete test taker tutorials, if applicable.
- ☑ Initial site inspections (Final inspections done by site coordinator).
  - ☑ Secure storage vaults—no ceiling panels; cement floors, cement and vertical bar locking file cabinets, reinforced doors.
  - ☑ Restricted access.
  - ☑ Acceptable locks on doors and windows.
  - ☑ 24/7 security monitoring and alarms.
  - ☑ Industrial cross-cut shredders, if applicable.
  - ☑ Make sure staff wear ID badges.
  - ☑ Slow scan cameras, electronic fingerprinting equipment, if applicable.
  - ☑ CBT: Secured server, file encryption, restricted access to test CRT/LCD monitors, locking doors.
  - ☑ Accessible restrooms.
  - ☑ Lighting, ventilation, heating, air conditioning, noise.
  - ☑ Acceptable tables and chairs.
  - ☑ Private rooms for ADA and security.

One to 3 Months Before Dates of Scheduled Tests

- ☑ Review manuals and attend training for test proctors, site coordinators, and ADA accommodations staff.

TEST MATERIALS RECEIPT

One Week Before Scheduled Test Date

- ☑ Sign for shipments and store in secure lockup.
- ☑ Two proctors present when open to verify security and counts.
- ☑ Scan bar codes, complete, sign, and fax test transmittal forms, reconcile disparities.
- ☑ Store in secure vaults—notify secure transportation service provider that will deliver to sites afternoon before test date.

SITE SET-UP

One Day Before Dates of Scheduled Tests

- ☑ Ensure test check-in and check-out areas and rooms set up properly, special equipment delivered and in working order.
- ☑ Post signage, give staff ID badges.
- ☑ Check that proper rosters, test materials, answer sheets, seating charts and seats ID'd.
- ☑ Review security requirements with all staff.

TEST ADMINISTRATION

Day of Scheduled Tests

- ☑ Security staff, proctors, site coordinators present at least 1 hour before check-in—alternates available.
- ☑ Review procedures, security requirements, methods to contact.
- ☑ Staff in assigned rooms and ready to perform duties.
- ☑ Equipment working: Slow scan video cameras and signage that video taping (if applicable), bar code scanners.
- ☑ Candidates admitted and checked-out one at a time and according to ID requirements; check for prohibited items.
- ☑ Monitor halls and rest rooms—ensure test takers have passes.
- ☑ Follow standardization requirements.

MATERIALS ACCOUNTING AND SHIPPING

End of Test Day

- ☑ Count all materials, scan bar codes, and complete transmittal sheets.
- ☑ Use packing sheets for each deliverable; submit time sheets; ship all back same day.
- ☑ Leave site only after accounting for all items.

APPENDIX C: TEST PROCTOR ROLES AND RESPONSIBILITIES

SECURITY

Six to 9 Months Before Dates of Scheduled Tests

- ☑ Confirm security, conflict of interest, & employment agreements with lead test administrator.
- ☑ Review candidate handbook.

One to 3 Months Before Dates of Scheduled Tests

- ☑ Receive and review test proctor manual.
- ☑ Attend training, complete proctor tutorials, if applicable.

TEST MATERIALS CONFIRMATION AND PACKING

One Week Before Scheduled Test Date

- ☑ Assist lead test administrator in verifying identification numbers and count of test materials, scan bar codes.
- ☑ Collate test materials, answer sheets, rosters, seating charts, seat ID cards, signage, entry/exit passes, ID badges, time sheets, reimbursement forms, packing materials for each test site—involves two proctors to check work of each other; seal boxes for each site when verified.

- ☑ Store labeled, sealed boxes in secure vaults—ensure boxes addressed properly for secure transportation services provider to deliver to test site day before test date.
- ☑ Visit assigned test site/make a "dry run" to site so know location and traffic.

SITE PREPARATION

One Day Before Dates of Scheduled Tests

- ☑ Inspect tables and chairs; determine if OK and arranged properly—if not, contact site coordinator.
- ☑ Confirm or set-up check-in and check-out stations.
- ☑ Affix seat ID cards to tables/desks.
- ☑ Familiarize self with test facility (e.g., secure storage, rest room location, special testing room, etc.).
- ☑ Sign-in boxes from secure delivery staff in afternoon and open immediately to verify proper materials delivered to site—lock-up.
- ☑ Review security requirements.

TEST ADMINISTRATION

Day of Scheduled Tests

- ☑ On site 1 hour before check-in—log-out test materials for rooms assigned.
- ☑ Obtain ID badge.
- ☑ Review procedures, security requirements, methods to contact lead test administrator.
- ☑ Check-in-process.
  - ☑ Equipment working: Slow scan video cameras, if applicable.
  - ☑ Proper signage posted to inform that taping candidate.
  - ☑ Admit one at a time: check two forms of ID (one with picture), check signatures, admittance letters, and for prohibited items.
  - ☑ Test begins.
    - ☑ Close door—do not admit late candidates.
    - ☑ Distribute pencils and answer sheets/CBT: log into system and confirm correct test.
    - ☑ Read instructions and wait until complete answer sheet basic/information. CBT: complete tutorial for interface familiarity.
    - ☑ Begin testing—set timing clock and monitor candidates.
    - ☑ Irregularities: two proctors must witness and independently document.
    - ☑ Monitors in halls and rest rooms—make sure test takers have passes.
    - ☑ Test administered according to standardization requirements.
    - ☑ Test ends: Check-out one at a time; examinees remain seated—log each out (time, signatures) and issue exit pass.

MATERIALS ACCOUNTING AND SHIPPING

End of Test Day

- ☑ Count all materials, scan bar codes, and complete reimbursement forms.
- ☑ Use packing sheets for each deliverable, ship all back same day.
- ☑ Leave after logged out and dismissed by lead test administrator.

APPENDIX D: SITE COORDINATOR ROLES AND RESPONSIBILITIES

SECURITY

Six to 9 Months Before Dates of Scheduled Tests

- Confirm and security, conflict of interest, employment agreement with lead test administrator.
- Review candidate handbook.
- Coordinate with lead test coordinator about sites procured by test user/test owner.

Three to 6 Months Before Dates of Scheduled Tests

- Receive and review initial site inspection report conducted by lead test administrator.

One to 3 Months Before Dates of Scheduled Tests

- Receive and review site coordinator manual.
- Attend training, complete test taker tutorials, if applicable.
- Conduct site inspections.
  - Secure storage vaults—no ceiling panels; cement floors; cement and vertical bar locking file cabinets, and reinforced doors.
  - Restricted access and site staff wear ID.
  - Acceptable locks on doors and windows.
  - 24/7 security monitoring and alarms.
  - Emergency equipment (fire extinguishers, safety manuals, evacuation maps and plans).
  - Space for leased equipment (industrial cross-cut shredders, etc.).
  - Confirm site hours of operation.
  - Slow scan cameras, electronic fingerprinting equipment, if applicable.
  - CBT: Secured server, file encryption, restricted access to CRT/LCD test monitors, locking doors.
  - Accessible restrooms.
  - Lighting, ventilation, temperature, and noise.
  - Acceptable tables and chairs.
  - Private rooms for ADA and meet security requirements.
  - Safe locations, easy to locate, clean.
  - Standardization of sites.
  - In-house staff on-site during test, if needed.
- Prepare and submit report of site conditions to lead test administrator.

SITE PREPARATION

One Week Before Dates of Scheduled Tests

- Inspect tables and chairs; determine if OK—if not, arrange for acceptable furniture.
- Meet with site set-up staff and go over requirements.
- Confirm that shredders, other required equipment scheduled for delivery on day before test date.

Two Days Before Scheduled Test Dates

- ☑ Monitor set-up of rooms, check-in and check-out stations, and facility agreements.
- ☑ Confirm secure storage ready for deliveries.

One Day Before Scheduled Test Dates

- ☑ Meet with lead test administration and test proctors to make sure arrangements acceptable.
- ☑ Assist in receipt, verification, and storage of materials shipments.
- ☑ Affix seat ID cards to tables/desks.
- ☑ Post signage (outside facility) and within facility.
- ☑ Verify that required equipment is in place and working properly.
- ☑ Confirm security requirements OK.

TEST ADMINISTRATION

Day of Scheduled Tests

- ☑ On site 2 hours before check-in—log-out test materials for rooms assigned; obtain ID badge.
- ☑ Monitor halls and facility.
- ☑ Review procedures, security requirements, and methods for all staff to contact you.
- ☑ Provide on-site support for all test site issues.

MATERIALS ACCOUNTING AND SHIPPING

End of Test Day

- ☑ Assist with materials shipment activities and complete reimbursement forms.
- ☑ Ensure equipment pick up that day.
- ☑ Leave after logged out and dismissed by lead test administrator.

APPENDIX E: RESPONDING TO EMERGENCIES

THEFT, FRAUD, AND CHEATING

Potential Theft

- ☑ Missing test booklets
  - ☑ Notify lead test administrator immediately.
  - ☑ Identify point in time when last accounted for test booklet and determine test booklet ID number.
  - ☑ If test session is still in progress and no one has left test session, announce to test takers that someone has received two test booklets. Ask them to check their materials. This process typically is successful in helping to locate a missing test booklet.
  - ☑ If test session is over and test takers have been checked out, determine missing test ID number. Identify when last knew test booklet was on site. Look at test taker seating charts and rosters to identify if test booklet was ever logged out to a test taker. If not, try to determine its whereabouts.

- In all cases, prepare written explanation of incident on irregularity report form. Include information about who discovered booklet was missing, circumstances under which discovery was made, time of discovery, what was done to try and locate test booklet, test booklet ID number, sign report (proctor and lead test administrator).
- Details will help test owner and test user to determine if responses from test sessions that used test form should be scored or cancelled, if statistical analyses can detect unusual response data, etc.
- Check for missing test booklet pages during check out; if discovered afterward, ID booklet and examinee that was assigned booklet; file irregularity report.

Potential Fraud

- Impersonation
    - Check two forms of identification (one ID should be an official government-issued ID with a picture and signature).
    - Compare official ID with picture to candidate; check if signatures match; check admissions ticket.
    - Get sample of examinee signature.
    - If application form required picture ID, bring these forms to test sessions and compare pictures and signatures.
    - Consult with another proctor and lead test administrator if suspect impersonation. Complete irregularity report.

Potential Cheating

- Suspect cheating
    - Have another proctor verify behavior.
    - Relocate suspected test takers.
    - Note on seating chart and roster.
    - File irregularity report.

TEST SITE EMERGENCIES

Site Evacuation

- Safety of human life takes precedence.
    - Instruct examinees to put answer sheets and other test materials inside test booklets.
    - Leave room in single-file, putting test materials into secure bin that can be locked and carried out with unused test materials by test proctors (if practical).
    - Windows and doors should be shut and locked upon exit.
    - Call lead test administrator; file irregularities report, notify test owner/test user/contact person.
    - Cancel test sessions or resume.

Power Outages

- Test takers and staff remain seated.
- Receive directions from lead test administrator.
- If evacuation is planned, follow above procedure.

INCLEMENT WEATHER

Late Arrivals—Cancel or Reschedule Test Sessions

- ☑ Lead test administrator interface with test owner/test user—proceed as directed.

FINAL NOTE: ITEM BANK EXPOSURE

Never Use Entire Item Bank for Test Session

- ☑ Test owner should build item banks so the entire bank is never at risk for total exposure in any test session.

REFERENCES

American Educational Research Association (AERA), American Psychological Association (APA), & National Council on Measurement in Education (NCME). (1999). *Standards for educational and psychological tests*. Washington, DC: American Educational Research Association.

Banks, K. E. (1996). Current issues in test administration. In J. O'Reilly, & Glidden, H. G. (Eds.), *National Association of Test Directors 1996 Symposia: Vol. 12*. (pp. 1–6).

Bennett, R. E. (1998). *Reinventing assessment: Speculations on the future of large-scale testing*. Princeton, NJ: Policy Information Center, Educational Testing Service.

Bunderson, C. V., Inouye, D. K., & Olsen, J. B. (1989). The four generations of computerized educational measurement. In R. L. Linn (Ed.), *Educational measurement* (3rd ed.), (pp. 367–407). New York: American Council on Education & MacMillan.

Cizek, G. J. (1999). *Cheating on tests: How to do it, detect it, and prevent it*. Mahwah, NJ: Lawrence Erlbaum Associates.

Crocker, L. (2003). Teaching for the test: Validity, fairness, and moral action. *Educational Measurement: Issues and Practice, 22*(3), 5–11.

Cronbach, L. J. (1988). Five perspectives on validity argument. In H. Wainer & H. I. Braun (Eds.), *Test validity* (pp. 3–17). Hillsdale, NJ: Lawrence Erlbaum Associates.

Crooks, T. J., Kane, M. T., & Cohen, A. S. (1996). Threats to the valid use of assessment. *Assessment in Education, 3*(3), 265–285.

Downing, S. M., & Haladyna, T. M. (1996). A model for evaluating high-stakes testing programs: Why the fox should not guard the chicken coop. *Educational Measurement: Issues and Practice, 15*(1), 5–12.

Haertel, E. H. (1999). Validity arguments for high-stakes testing: In search of the evidence. *Educational Measurement: Issues and Practice, 18*(4), 5–9.

Haladyna, T. M., & Downing, S. M. (2004). Construct irrelevant variance in high stakes testing. *Educational Measurement: Issues and Practice, 23*(1), 17–27.

Haladyna, T. M., Nolen, S. B., & Haas, N. S. (1991). Raising standardized achievement test scores and the origins of test score pollution. *Educational Researcher, 20*(5), 2–7.

Hicks, C. R. (1982). *Fundamental concepts in the design of experiments* (3rd ed.). New York: Holt, Rinehart & Winston, Inc.

Huff, K. L., & Sireci, S. G. (2001). Validity issues in computer-based testing. *Educational Measurement: Issues and Practice, 20*(3), 16–25.

Kane, M. T. (1992). An argument-based approach to validity. *Psychological Bulletin, 112*, 527–535.

Kane, M. T. (2001). Current concerns in validity theory. *Journal of Educational Measurement, 38*(4), 319–342.

Kane, M. T. (2002). Validating high-stakes testing programs. *Educational Measurement: Issues and Practice, 21*(1), 31–41.

Kane, M. T., Crooks, T. J., & Cohen, A. S. (1999). Validating measures of performance. *Educational Measurement: Issues and Practice, 18*(2), 5–17.

Lane, S., Stone, C. A., Ankenmann, R. D., & Liu, M. (1995). Examination of the assumptions and properties of the graded item response model: An example using a mathematics performance assessment. *Applied Measurement in Education, 8*(4), 313–340.

Lord, F. M., & Novick, M. R. (1968). *Statistical theories of mental test scores*. Reading, MA: Addison Welsey.

Madaus, G. F. (1992). An independent auditing mechanism for testing. *Educational Measurement: Issues and Practices, 11*(1), 26–31.

Mehrens, W. A., & Kaminski, J. (1989). Methods for improving standardized test scores: Fruitful, fruitless, or fraudulent? *Educational Measurement: Issues and Practice, 8,* 14–22.

Messick, S. (1989). Validity. In R. L. Linn (Ed.), *Educational measurement* (3rd ed., pp. 13–103.) New York: American Council on Education & MacMillan.

No Child Left Behind Act. Public Law No. 107-110, 115 Stat. 1425, 2002.

Pitoniak, M. J., & Royer, J. M. (2001). Testing accommodations for examinees with disabilities: A review of psychometric, legal, and social policy issues. *Review of Educational Research, 71*(1), 53–104.

Popham, W. J. (1991). Appropriateness of teachers' test-preparation practices. *Educational Measurement: Issues and Practice, 10*(4), 12–16.

Popham, W. J. (2003). Seeking redemption for our psychometric sins. *Educational Measurement: Issues and Practice, 22*(1), 45–48.

Rossett, A., & Gautier-Downes, J. (1991). *A handbook of job aids.* San Francisco: Pfeiffer & Company.

U.S. Department of Labor. (2001). *Report on the American Workforce 2001.* Retrieved December 6, 2004, from http://www.bls.gov/opub/rtaw/rtawhome.htm.

Watch it! Background checks popular. (2004, November 28). *Sunday Gazette-Mail: The Denver Post,* p. G-1.

Wattenberg, B. J., Caplow, T., & Hicks, L. (2001). *The first measured century: An illustrated guide to trends in america, 1900–2000.* Washington, DC: American Enterprise Institute for Public Policy Research.

28

Considerations for the Administration of Tests to Special Needs Students: Accommodations, Modifications, and More

Martha L. Thurlow
Sandra J. Thompson
Sheryl S. Lazarus
University of Minnesota

This chapter provides an overview of important considerations for the administration of tests to examinees with special needs. The growing participation of individuals with disabilities and English language learners in testing—at the K–12 level, the postsecondary level, and for credentialing—has implications for the design, development, and administration of tests. The definition and role of accommodations and modifications are discussed as well as innovative approaches to the design of assessments that reduce the need for accommodations. The chapter includes a detailed discussion of how accommodations may be used to provide special needs populations with access to tests as well as a discussion of the major challenges that surround the use of accommodations and modifications—policy variations, research without clear implications, and implementation issues. The chapter concludes with a discussion of the potential of universally designed assessments, which are designed from the beginning to be accessible to the broadest group of examinees.

The demographic makeup of the United States has changed dramatically over the past two decades. K–12 schools and institutions of higher education are serving students who are increasingly diverse in cultural background, socioeconomic status, and disability status. Federal laws now require that state assessments used for school accountability include students who previously had been underserved both instructionally and in the assessment of their achievement. These students include English language learners (ELLs) and students with disabilities. Access to K–12 and postsecondary education and now the opportunity for equitable access to large-scale tests and other assessments is a significant step forward for students with special needs. With this advance, test designers face new issues and challenges as they develop assessments appropriate for a broader group of examinees than in the past.

In addressing considerations for the administration of tests to special needs students, this chapter covers a range of assessments for which the testing policies for these students vary considerably. Changes in the testing situation known as *accommodations* and *modifications* are among the most controversial of the administration considerations for special needs students.

As Zieky (chap. 16, this volume) notes "the topic of when and how to provide accommodations is complicated, has become highly politicized, and is subject to a great deal of litigation." Not only are there significant differences in policies and practices for individuals with disabilities and ELLs, but there are also dramatic differences in policies and practices for preschool and K–12 assessments versus those for the postsecondary level, which include assessments designed for entrance or placement (for institutions of higher education, graduate schools, or military programs, for example) and those used to verify attainment of skills (as in credentialing or certification examinations). A chapter devoted to special needs individuals that covers all of these must necessarily be broad. To the extent possible, this broad coverage is made meaningful by providing specific examples. Hopefully, this makes the information more concrete and understandable.

Two scenarios exemplify some best practice in testing today for special needs students and provide the basis for the discussion in this chapter. Both of the scenarios deal with students with disabilities, where the law, policies, and practices are generally more defined than they are for ELLs. These illustrate jumping off points for considerations about both students with disabilities and English language learners–and for thinking about other types of tests, including, for example, graduation tests, advanced placement tests, and the host of tests that exist outside of the K–12 education system.

Scenario 1

It is the day of the state math test. Ten-year-old Jason arrives at school rested and confident of his ability to demonstrate his knowledge and skills on the test. Prior to today he and his teacher discussed how he would be using the same accommodations on the test that he usually uses in his classroom. He knows that the test questions are presented on a compact disc (CD) as well as in the written test booklet, and that he is using a calculator and graph paper. He also knows that he will circle his answers directly in the test booklet, rather than use the scannable bubble sheet. The accommodations that he uses for both instruction and assessment are based on what his Individualized Education Program (IEP) team had decided that he needed. He knows that this IEP team includes his special education teacher, his general education teacher, his parents, the school psychologist, and his principal.

When he arrives in the testing room, the CD player and headphones (that he usually uses in class) are in the study carrel, along with pencils, graph paper, and the calculator (that he also usually uses in class). He is greeted by the test administrator who goes through the practice questions with him to make sure all of his equipment is working properly and that he is confident of his ability to progress from one question to the next. While he is taking the test, the test administrator stops by periodically to make sure everything continues to work properly. After he finishes and hands in the test, he leaves the room and the test administrator carefully transfers his answers to a bubble sheet. The transfer is checked by another test administrator before handing it in. The test administrators have signed a nondisclosure form and understand the importance of test security.

Scenario 2

Ann is nearing completion of her undergraduate degree. When she entered the university, she was required to provide documentation from a licensed professional in her state that she had a disability even though she had received special education services in high school. Throughout her years at college, the Office of Disability Services on her campus helped her to understand all the procedures that she needed to follow to get accommodations and the other supports that she needed to meaningfully participate in her classes.

Today Ann is taking the examination required by her state as part of the credentialing process for teachers. A few months ago, she submitted a request for test accommodations to the testing company. The request included a certificate of eligibility that contained information about the nature of her disability, her functional limitations, her relevant medical history, and a list of test instruments—including the relevant subtest scores—used to document her disability, and the specific accommodations requested.

Ann enters the test room. She explains that she has a disability and that her registration forms indicate that she needs to use several accommodations to access the test. The test administrator checks Ann's ID and looks through the papers lying on the table. He confirms that his records indicate that Ann has extended test time and additional rest breaks. A few minutes later, he gives Ann her test materials and explains the test and the accommodation procedures. He also asks if there are any questions.

Ann begins the test. The test is difficult, but Ann carefully reads each question and marks her responses on the bubble sheet. Ann feels confident of her ability to answer the questions even though she tires quickly. After completing a segment of the test, Ann is able to take a short rest break. After taking several additional short breaks, Ann completes the test and gives the materials to the test administrator.

OVERVIEW

Ten years ago, a chapter on this topic probably would not have been in this book. It is with almost breakneck speed that the assessment community has had to realize that today's test takers also include a significant number of individuals with disabilities and a significant number of individuals whose first language is not English. The growing participation of these individuals in testing has implications for the design, development, and administration of tests. No person involved in testing today can afford not to know about these test takers, how they participate in testing, and the implications of their participation.

We refer to accommodations, modifications, and "more" in the title to this chapter because changes in the testing situation (a broad definition of *accommodations* or *modifications*) are what many consider to be the defining feature of the assessment participation of special needs individuals. In fact, the "more" in our title is very important—it is about what it takes to make a successful and valid assessment of special needs students. Validity for special needs students (as part of the testing population), in turn, increases the validity for the entire testing population.

It is important for readers to realize that the students in K–12 schools today are being given access to improved assessment systems in ways that did not exist even a few years ago. Students with disabilities and ELLs are receiving accommodations in unprecedented numbers. Federal dollars have been devoted to research on the assessment of these students (especially on accommodations and modifications) and considerable effort has gone into technical assistance on the topic. Legal requirements, as well as political realities, have led to the demise of the "old view" of standardized assessment that could ignore special needs populations. As students who have received accommodated assessments move up in grade and into postsecondary education, they carry their expectations for accommodations with them. Individuals who work on postsecondary and credentialing examinations cannot ignore the growing population of individuals with disabilities who are taking their examinations, nor can they ignore ELLs. All in the assessment community must know about these learners, about the role of accommodations and modifications in their participation in assessments, and about ways to improve assessments so that in the future there may be less need for accommodations and modifications and more accurate measurement of participating individuals with special disability or language needs.

The purpose of this chapter is to provide the reader with a general understanding of three topics that support considerations for the administration of tests to special needs students: (1) the characteristics of individuals with disabilities and ELLs in the United States; (2) the definition, role, and function of accommodations and modifications in testing, and (3) an alternative approach to improving assessment conditions for special needs test takers.

The chapter first discusses accommodations and modifications—what they are, the laws that apply to them, and their changing role. Major challenges surrounding accommodations and modifications are highlighted, including policy variations, research without clear implications, and implementation issues. An alternative approach that highlights what has been referred to as *universally designed* assessments (e.g., the design of challenging assessments from the beginning for the broadest range of students) is presented.

When writing for the *Bar Examiner*, Thurlow, Elliott, Erickson, and Ysseldyke (1997) argued that test developers who fail to consider the needs of all test takers, including those with special needs, when constructing assessment instruments:

> will find the issues surrounding accommodations far more difficult to resolve than those developers who have kept these individuals in mind during the entire development process. The selection of test items, presentation modes, and response options are all decision points that should take into account the needs of examinees with [special needs]. (p. 17)

This statement was published the year when the federal special education law first required that all students with disabilities participate in state and district assessments, a law that marked the beginning of some impressive changes in special education and assessment as we know it today. The statement proved to be an accurate forecast of future assessment issues. No assessment today can avoid the impact of participation of individuals with disabilities and ELLs. And, although some still may not believe it, assessments have in many ways improved because of the participation of these individuals.

SPECIAL POPULATIONS

Nearly 6 million children with disabilities between the ages of 6 and 21 receive special education services in the United States. About 12% of all students enrolled in K–12 schools are students with disabilities. The primary disability of almost half of these students is a learning disability; another 19% have speech or language impairments. Students receiving special education services have IEPs that address their needs related to any of fourteen disability categories that are diverse in nature: autism, deafness, blindness, developmental delay, emotional disturbance, hearing impairments, mental retardation, multiple disabilities, orthopedic impairments, other health impairments, specific learning disabilities, speech and language impairments, traumatic brain injury, and visual impairments. Only about one tenth of all students with disabilities have significant cognitive impairments such as significant mental retardation or traumatic brain injury (U.S. Department of Education, 2002c). This national picture belies the variability that exists from state to state in the prevalence of disabilities. For example, in the most recent child count data available from the U.S. Department of Education (2002b), the percentage of a state's student population that was identified as having learning disabilities ranged from 2.2% of students in Kentucky to 6.7% of students in Massachusetts. Variability within states has been noted as well. Donovan and Cross (2002) summarized the variations and their causes as follows:

> These [state] differences occur due to idiosyncratic state funding mechanisms, variations in state classification criteria for the various disabilities, and other local, poorly understood influences....
> Although less well documented, in-state variability in the prevalence of different categories of disabilities also exists. Some of the variations may reflect different levels of performance in urban

and suburban districts (Gottlieb et al., 1994, 1999), while others may be explained by the degree of rigor in applying state classification criteria in decisions about eligibility. Some of the intrastate variations are likely to reflect real differences in district student populations, while others cannot be easily explained. (p. 223)

An increasing number of students in the United States has disabilities for which they do not receive special education services, but for which they receive accommodations under provisions of an accommodation plan (Section 504 of the Rehabilitation Act of 1973). These students include those with physical disabilities who are in wheelchairs, for example, or who have health impairments such as asthma, which may require special accommodations but not necessarily special education services. Students with attention deficit hyperactivity disorder also sometimes receive accommodations through 504 accommodation plans.

About 3.5 million students in the United States (or about 6% of all students) have *limited English proficiency*, the term used in federal law; however, most leaders in the field now refer to these students as ELLs. More than 60% of all ELLs live in California, Texas, and Florida. Several states have very few ELLs; fewer than 1,000 ELLs live in either Vermont or West Virginia. Across the country, the percentages of ELLs represented by the top five non-English languages are Spanish (79.0%), Vietnamese (2.0%), Hmong (1.6%), Chinese (1.0%), and Korean (1.0%; National Clearinghouse for English Language Acquisition, 2004).

Almost 8% of all ELLs also have an identified disability that qualifies them to receive special education services (Hopstock & Stephenson, 2003). Some states appear to be more aware that students may have both a disability and be an ELL because the percentage of ELLs also receiving special education services in a state ranges from less than 0.1% to more than 17%.

There currently also is great variation among states in the percentage of students with special needs who participate in state assessments. For example, during the 2001 to 2002 school year, 97% of middle school students with disabilities in Kansas participated in the general assessment, but only 47% participated in Texas and 30% in West Virginia (Thurlow, Wiley, & Bielinski, 2003). Even greater variability was reported in a special report by *Education Week* (Ansell, 2004), with participation rates for 2002 to 2003 ranging from 40 to 100% of students with disabilities participating in the state assessment. This type of inconsistency is being addressed currently through federal education laws (e.g., Individuals with Disabilities Education Act [IDEA]; *No Child Left Behind* [NCLB]) that require the participation of all students in statewide assessments—all includes students with disabilities, ELLs, and ELLs with disabilities.

ACCOMMODATIONS AND MODIFICATIONS IN ASSESSMENTS

Definition of Terms

The words *accommodation* and *modification* are used to indicate that changes are made to what is considered the "standardized" test condition. For example, a person taking a test in a separate room with a scribe to write answers may appear to be taking a different test than a typical examinee. Jason in Scenario 1, using a CD player and headphones, certainly does not appear to be taking the same test as a typical 10-year-old test taker in his school. Despite the fact that students using accommodations or modifications may look like they are taking different tests, one of the most viable ways to actually attain greater comparability in testing for students with special needs—including students with disabilities and ELLs—is through the use of accommodations. *Accommodations* are tools and procedures that provide equitable

TABLE 28.1
Examples of Accommodations

Presentation
- Visual presentation accommodations include: large print, magnification devices, and sign language
- Tactile Presentation accommodations include: Braille, Nemeth code, and tactile graphics
- Auditory presentation accommodations include: human reader, audio tape or compact disk, and audio amplification devices
- Multi-modal presentation accommodations include: screen readers, video, and talking materials and equipment

Response
- Response accommodations include: scribe, word processor, electronic text-to-speech conversion, Brailler, tape recorder, and response in test booklet rather than separate answer sheet
- Materials or devices used to solve or organize responses include calculation devices, spelling and grammar checking devices, and visual/graphic organizers

Timing and Scheduling
- Timing/scheduling accommodations include: extended time, multiple or frequent breaks, change schedule or order of subtests

Setting
- Reduce distractions to the student or reduce distractions the student may cause to other students
- Change location to increase physical access or to use special equipment

Linguistic
- Simplified English, written native language translation of English test items, native language test version, oral interpretation of test items in the native language bilingual dictionary or glossary, and response of student in the native language

Other
- Special test preparation
- On-task/focusing prompts
- Any accommodation that a student needs that does not fit under the existing categories

---

instructional and assessment access for students with disabilities and ELLs in the areas of presentation, response, timing, scheduling, setting, and linguistics. According to Tindal and Fuchs (1999) a test change is considered an accommodation if it does not alter the construct being measured, is based on individual need, and is effective for students who need the change and not effective for others. This last point is being adjusted as research evidence accumulates to indicate that some accommodations may clarify constructs for all students, not just those with disabilities or ELLs (see Sireci, Li, & Scarpati, 2003).

In most states, accommodations policies organize the accommodations into categories similar to the following groupings: presentation accommodations, response accommodations, setting accommodations, and timing or scheduling accommodations. Within each of these categories, there is a long list of test changes, often with specific conditions under which they are allowed (or not allowed), under which scores are aggregated (or not aggregated), or under which scores are reported (or not reported) (Thurlow, Lazarus, Thompson, & Morse, 2005). Another accommodation category—linguistic accommodations and linguistic support accommodations—is currently emerging with the recognition of the need for, and appropriateness of, accommodations for ELLs (Rivera, Collum, Shafer, & Sia, 2004).

Table 28.1 lists examples of accommodations by category. The specific accommodations that have been included within a category have changed over time as people have figured out the specific functions of the accommodations. Thus, as you look at the information in Table 28.1, it may seem inconsistent with a list that you have seen in your state. The information in Table 28.1 reflects the most recent views about how to categorize accommodations in state policies (Clapper, Morse, Lazarus, Thompson, & Thurlow, 2005) and who benefits from the use of the accommodations.

Changes in the way tests are administered or taken may change the construct being measured and these changes are commonly referred to as *modifications, adaptations, alternates, nonstandard accommodations, nonallowable accommodations,* or *nonapproved accommodations* (Thurlow & Wiener, 2000). In some states and on some tests there may be consequences if modifications are used, but they are varied and sometimes difficult to understand. Common consequences include "flagged" test scores, scores that do not count, and in some cases, scores that count for some purposes but not others.

Hollenbeck, Rozek-Tedesco, Tindal, and Glasgrow (2000) specified four attributes that must be present for a test alteration to be considered an accommodation:

- **Unchanged constructs:** test alternations must not alter the constructs being measured.
- **Individual need:** the test alteration must be based on individual need and, thus, not chosen haphazardly.
- **Differential effects:** test alteration must be differential in effect by student or group.
- **Sameness of inference:** test alternations must generate similar inferences between accommodated and standard scores.

In the literature, most definitions of accommodations have focused on one of three key aspects of accommodations. One aspect is the *nature* of the changes—changes in the procedures or materials used in assessment. A second aspect is in the *purpose*—to achieve equitable testing, or a "level playing field." The third aspect is the *goal*—to ensure that the same construct is assessed. In early definitions and discussions about accommodations, the emphasis tended to be given to the nature of the changes. Later definitions emphasized that the purpose of accommodations was to ensure that all students had a level playing field. Now, with the increase in emphasis on including cognitive and learning principles in assessment development and research, the field is shifting its attention to designing accommodations in terms of ensuring a valid measure of the target construct. These nuanced differences in the definition of accommodations are important to keep in mind as we address the considerations for the administration of tests to special needs students.

WHAT LAWS SAY ABOUT ACCOMMODATIONS

Federal education policy related to assessments has been almost silent on the topic of accommodations, with only general references in law and in regulations. What the law has been clear about is that students with disabilities are to be included in state assessments for accountability. In 1994 the *Improving America's Schools Act* set this expectation. Then the reauthorization of IDEA in 1997 clarified that this expectation applied to students with disabilities, which prior to then had been the group assumed to be exempted from the requirements (Yell, 1998). More recently, NCLB clarified that *all* students are to be included in school accountability systems. It requires that schools, districts, and states show that all subgroups of students, including students with disabilities and ELLs, make progress toward closing the achievement gap (U.S. Department of Education, 2002a). Accommodations were viewed as a logical part of ensuring the assessment participation of students with disabilities. With the reauthorization of IDEA in 2004, direct attention was given to assessment accommodations, with new requirements that states develop guidelines for the provision of appropriate assessment accommodations and that they report the number of students using accommodations during assessments.

It has not been obvious from law that accommodations are viewed as a way to ensure assessment participation or the valid assessment of ELLs. Nevertheless, state policies and guidelines are creating a clear expectation that accommodations are, at least to some extent, an aspect of the appropriate assessment of ELLs as well as students with disabilities (see U.S. Department of Education, 2002b).

Although these laws assume the importance of "accommodations," they are unclear in the terms that they use. IDEA 97 used *accommodation* and *modification* as essentially equivalent terms, which was inconsistent with general usage in the field where *accommodations* were considered to be changes that allowed comparable inferences to be reached and *modifications* to be changes that altered the nature of the inference that could be reached. In a similar manner, NCLB uses *accommodations* and *adaptations* as essentially equivalent terms. With IDEA's reauthorization in 2004, the use of *modification* was dropped, suggesting a recognition of the distinction in meaning.

IDEA and NCLB apply only to K–12 schools. Federal laws that apply to institutions of higher education (e.g., Section 504 of the Rehabilitation Act of 1973; Americans with Disabilities Act of 1990 [ADA]) are less clear about their application to services for individuals with disabilities. In contrast to typical practice in the K–12 educational system, individuals with disabilities in higher education "become the entity or person wholly responsible for initiating, leading, managing, and following through with a process of determining assistance that might be provided by the postsecondary institution" (Stodden, Jones, & Chang, 2003, p. 35).

Despite the necessity of initiation of action by a person with disabilities, both Section 504 and ADA help provide equitable access and prevent discrimination for students with disabilities in postsecondary education. Section 504 applies to colleges that receive any federal financial assistance. ADA applies to either the public or private sector and focuses on employment and the provision of services by government entities such as public universities. Its goal is to provide individuals with disabilities protection against discrimination. Both laws provide individuals with "reasonable accommodations."

According to Grossman (2001), "by instructing colleges to distinguish carefully between what is essential and what is tangential, the courts have used Section 504 and the ADA to create equal educational opportunity for the disability community without lowering academic standards" (p. 3). In the assessment arena, the importance of making distinctions between what is essential and what is tangential or between what is relevant and what is irrelevant is increasingly being brought to the forefront of critical considerations. The ease with which these distinctions can be made has been brought into question for many assessments. Nevertheless, interpretation of the law is a continuing effort, as evident in continued court cases over whether specific accommodations are "reasonable" and whether they change the requirements of the job, the academic requirements for a course, or the difficulty of a test.

CHANGING ROLE OF ACCOMMODATIONS

The purpose of accommodations in testing has varied from simply enabling students with disabilities and English language learners to have access to a test, to allowing for valid measurement of students' knowledge and skills. According to Ryan and DeMark (2002), "Validity is the central issue in evaluating the appropriateness of all forms of assessment and must remain the critical criterion guiding assessment development, applications, and the use of assessment results" (p. 67). However, there is a great deal of controversy about the "fairness" of many test accommodations, about which students should have access to accommodations, and about how accommodation decisions are made. The nature of the controversy is somewhat different within the K–12 system compared to the postsecondary system.

According to Heubert and Hauser (1999), "fairness, like validity, cannot be properly addressed as an afterthought once the test has been developed, administered, and used. It must be confronted throughout the interconnected phases of the testing process, from test design and development to administration, scoring, interpretation, and use" (p. 81). See Zieky (chap. 16, this volume) for a detailed discussion of fairness and the role of fairness reviews in the test development process. The *Standards for Educational and Psychological Testing* (American Educational Research Association [AERA], American Psychological Association [APA], & National Counsil on Measurement in Education [NCME], 1999) also address this need by requiring that

> all examinees be given a comparable opportunity to demonstrate their standing on the construct(s) the test is intended to measure. Just treatment also includes such factors as appropriate testing conditions and equal opportunity to become familiar with the test format, practice materials, and so forth. Fairness also requires that all examinees be afforded appropriate testing conditions. (p. 74)

Haladyna and Downing (2004) define *construct-irrelevant variance* (CIV) as "error variance that results from systematic error" (p. 18). CIV refers to a change in a test score that is unrelated (or immaterial) to the construct being measured. The systematic error differs from random error because it is person or group specific. For example, if the purpose of a test item on a mathematics test is to measure problem-solving skills, but the test item includes difficult vocabulary words, then students with greater vocabulary skills may be more likely to correctly answer the item than other students—and thus a systematic error is introduced. Linn (2002) summarized the purpose of assessment accommodations as "removing disadvantages due to disabilities that are irrelevant to the construct the test is intended to measure without giving unfair advantage to those being accommodated" (p. 36). Haladyna and Downing (2004) concluded:

> Federal law requires that students with disabilities be included in assessments, but the law does not explain which accommodations are acceptable or specify the criteria for accommodation. If such accommodations are carried out uniformly in all school districts and states, then differences in performance will not be due to this source of CIV. (p. 24)

Despite these reasoned arguments, there continues to be disagreement on what constitutes appropriate testing conditions, what is fair, and what makes for comparable opportunity to demonstrate relevant knowledge and skills. Furthermore, it is not always clear which alterations in testing procedures or materials are relevant to the construct—at least there seem to be differences in the opinions of experts (Bielinski, Sheinker, & Ysseldyke, 2003). The hope that there will be consistent policies or implementation of policies is probably just that—still a hope. Indeed, the appropriateness of specific changes often depends on the construct targeted for measurement. Thus, it is essential that test developers and administrators know the current status of practice, including all the flaws, so that these considerations can be incorporated in ways that support the best measurement of diverse student populations.

MAJOR CHALLENGES SURROUNDING ACCOMMODATIONS

There are three major challenges that currently surround the use of accommodations and modifications in assessments. One challenge relates to the policies that apply to the use of accommodations and modifications, or more specifically, the variability in these policies. Second, research designed to provide evidence of which accommodation produces valid scores has been mired in complexities that have resulted in few conclusive statements or implications. Finally, implementation issues continue to escalate and these involve both decision-making problems and logistical struggles. These are touched on only briefly in this chapter, but they are at the heart of issues that surround accommodations and at the impetus for the "more"— alternatives to providing accommodations and modifications.

Accommodation Policy Variations

Policies vary both for the K–12 state and district assessments that involve all students and for the postsecondary assessments that are more selective. The National Center on Educational Outcomes (NCEO) has tracked state accommodation policies for many years and there is a wealth of information on the NCEO Web site (www.nceo.info) for those readers interested in delving more deeply into the topic. Only a broad sweep view is presented here and focuses primarily on K–12 assessments. Postsecondary institutions and the developers of standardized assessments at the postsecondary level have generated their own policies and procedures for considering and implementing accommodations requests.

All states now have accommodation policies for their K–12 assessments (Thurlow et al., 2005), and over 80% of states keep track of the use of accommodations during state accountability assessments (Thompson & Thurlow, 2003). However, there continues to be only limited consensus on what constitutes an "appropriate" or "acceptable" accommodation as states struggle with decisions about how to score and report the use of accommodations that some consider "nonstandard" or "nonscorable."

In the postsecondary world, test results play important roles, such as in admissions decisions by institutions of higher education and credentialing decisions made by various professional licensing associations. Several lawsuits have been brought against states and testing companies when an individual was denied access to needed accommodations or when an individual's score was flagged because the student used assessment accommodations (Center on Education Policy, 2002; Disability Rights Advocates, 2001). Some of the major companies that develop post-K–12 tests, where most flagging occurred, no longer flag scores (Educational Testing Service [ETS], 2002). Companies have also recently developed accommodation policies that clearly define which accommodations are permitted, how the accommodations should be implemented, and who qualifies to use an accommodation (ACT, 2002).

Accommodation policies are important to discuss because they drive much of what is demanded of test developers (e.g., what accommodations must be considered? will the test be made available in Braille?) and what happens in the administration of the assessment (e.g., whether there is a need to plan for multiple human readers of a test or many tape players that students can use to regulate the tape recorded reading of the test). There has been much change in states' accommodations policies since they were first examined in the early 1990s (Thurlow, Ysseldyke, & Silverstein, 1995), and most recently one of the greatest changes has been that states seem to be honing in on the need to clarify the purpose of the test and the construct being tested, rather than just the goal of providing the student with access to the testing situation. The following is a brief description of the categories that are being used in the most recent conceptualization of accommodations categories by the National Center on Educational Outcomes (Clapper et al., 2005):

- **Presentation accommodations** allow students to access instruction and assessments in ways that do not require them to visually read standard print. These alternate modes of access include visual, tactile, auditory, and a combination of visual and auditory accommodations. Students who benefit the most from presentation accommodations are those with *print disabilities*, defined as difficulty or inability to visually read standard print because of a physical, sensory, or cognitive disability.

- **Response accommodations** allow students to complete assignments, tests, and activities in different ways or to solve or organize problems using some type of assistive device or organizer. These include accommodations that allow flexibility in how students represent problems for themselves, such as allowing enough space for students to write in test booklets in ways that allow for representing ideas with pictures, graphics, or mechanisms that aid their memory. Response accommodations can benefit students with physical, sensory, or learning disabilities (including difficulties with memory, sequencing, directionality, alignment, and organization).
- **Timing and scheduling accommodations** change the allowable length of time to complete assignments, tests, and activities, and may also change the way the time is organized. Timing accommodations give students the time and the breaks they need to complete assignments, tests, or activities. Timing accommodations are most helpful for students who need more time than generally allowed to complete assignments, tests, and activities. Extra time may be needed to process written text (e.g., a student with a learning disability who processes information slowly), to write (e.g., a student with limited dexterity as a result of arthritis), or to use other accommodations or equipment (e.g., audio tape, scribe, assistive technology). Scheduling changes may include the specific time of day, day of the week, or number of days over which a test or part of a test is administered. These accommodations often meet the needs created by medication schedules or fatigue created by the use of other accommodations (e.g., use of large print by person with very limited vision).
- **Setting accommodations** change the location in which a student receives instruction or participates in an assessment, or the conditions of an instructional or assessment setting. Students may be allowed to sit in a different location from the majority of students to reduce distractions to themselves or others, or to increase physical access or access to special equipment. Some students may need changes in the conditions of an instructional setting. Changes in instructional and assessment locations can benefit students who are easily distracted in large group settings and who concentrate best in a small group or individual setting. Changes in location also benefit students who receive accommodations (e.g., reader, scribe, frequent breaks) that might distract other students. Students with physical disabilities might need a more accessible location, specific room conditions, or special equipment.
- **Linguistic accommodations** lessen the language load of a test. They include accommodations that simplify or clarify the English language used on the test as well as those that provide support in the native language. Linguistic accommodations typically do not change the content of an assessment. Rather, they help to make the content more understandable. Students who are identified as ELLs or ELLs with disabilities are most likely to benefit from linguistic accommodations. According to the National Center on Educational Outcomes (Clapper et al., 2005) educators should not rely just on a specialist's knowledge about second language acquisition, but should also involve the student when deciding on linguistic accommodations to offer on a test. For example, some ELLs may speak their native language but not read or write it. Others may read and write their native language, but still may not have had any academic content instruction in that language (e.g., because of a lack of teachers who speak or write that language), so these students would be unfamiliar with the academic vocabulary in their native langauge.

Despite the description of accommodations presented, there are many inconsistencies across states in accommodation policies. What is allowed in one state may be prohibited in another. Although not as common now, for many years this situation could be found for the same standardized tests used in two states. Current inconsistencies in accommodation policies from state to state are creating great challenges for the National Assessment of Educational Progress (NAEP). Varying participation rates in NAEP seem to be related to differences in state and NAEP accommodation policies (Government Accountability Office, 2005; Robelen, 2003). These are important challenges because NAEP has been placed in the role of an external standard that can be used to assess variations in the rigor of state accountability assessments. Also, as students move from state to state, they are likely to encounter situations in which accommodations that they use—and were allowed in the state they moved from—are not allowed in their new state. This issue begs for solutions—more thoughtful test development, more careful specification of the constructs being measured, and more thoughtful considerations of how scores can be reported when accommodations are used that are considered to invalidate a score (Haladyna & Downing, 2004).

Although accommodation policies, especially in the K–12 system, have been studied for many years, it is only relatively recently that we have had information on the use of accommodations (Thurlow, 2001). These data indicate that not only is there considerable variability from state to state in the percentages of students with disabilities using accommodations—accommodation use by students with disabilities ranged from 8 to 82% (see also Thompson & Thurlow, 1999)—but that there also is a disconnect between the accommodations most frequently permitted in state policies and those that are most frequently used. Thurlow and Bolt (2001) documented that the accommodations most frequently permitted in state policies for statewide assessments were Braille; computer or machine; dictated response; extended time; interpreter; large print; mark answer in booklet; read aloud; read, reread, or explain directions; and test breaks as needed. In a survey of special education teachers in four states, Lazarus, Thompson, and Thurlow (2005) also found that some of the accommodations frequently mentioned in state policies are not the most commonly provided accommodations. Only 2% of the teachers indicated that Braille was a frequently provided accommodation at their school. Fewer than 10% of the teachers indicated that either large print or the use of a scribe were frequently provided accommodations. About 16% of the teachers indicated that writing in the test booklet was used often. According to the Lazarus et al. (2005) study, the eight most frequently provided accommodations were (1) extended/extra time; (2) small group/individual administration; (3) test items read aloud; (4) directions read aloud; (5) alternate setting; (6) clarification of directions; (7) preferential seating; and (8) breaks as needed.

Research Findings Without Clear Implications

Many studies have analyzed the impact of the use of various accommodations by students with disabilities and ELLs on the validity and reliability of scores from assessments. The results of these studies have been synthesized in several literature reviews and meta-analyses (Abedi, chap. 17, this volume; Abedi, Hofsteter & Lord, 2004; Rivera et al., 2004; Sireci et al., 2003; Thompson, Blount, & Thurlow, 2002; Tindal, 2003). The research includes policy studies, evaluation studies, and experimental comparisons.

Examples of studies focused on accommodations for students with disabilities include a comparison of computer mode versus handwritten mode story compositions for a statewide writing test (Hollenbeck, Tindal, Harniss, & Almond, 1999); and responding by giving dictated responses (Koretz, 1997; Koretz & Hamilton, 1999); and extended time (e.g., Fuchs, Fuchs, Eaton, Hamlett, & Karns, 2000). Examples of studies focused on accommodations for ELLs include an investigation of oral and written administration of math tests in English and Spanish (Kopriva, 1994); use of extended time (Hafner, 1999); responding in written form or in native language (Abedi, Lord, Hofstetter, & Baker, 2000); and use of dictionaries (Albus, Thurlow, Liu, & Bielinski, 2005). To date, there has been no research specifically on accommodations for students who are ELLs and who also have a disability.

Research indicates that poorly designed test items are more difficult than nonflawed tests items and that lower achieving students are more likely to have difficulty with a poorly designed test item than other students (Downing, 2005; Haladyna & Downing, 2004.) Recent work on universally designed assessments similarly has concluded that changing characteristics of test items that do not change the construct measured can produce significantly higher levels of performance in generally low-performing students, including those with disabilities and those who are ELLs (Johnstone, 2003; also see Abedi, chap. 17, this volume).

Research to validate accommodations is growing, but this research is difficult to conduct and rarely provides conclusive evidence about the effects of accommodations on validity (Bielinski, Thurlow, Ysseldyke, Friedebach, & Friedebach, 2001; Bolt & Thurlow, 2004; Elliott, Kratochwill, & McKevitt, 2001; Koretz, & Hamilton, 2000; Thompson et al., 2002; Tindal & Fuchs, 1999). Both test designers and policy makers grapple with decisions about the role of accommodations and which accommodations invalidate assessment scores. For example, the repeated revisions in state accommodation policies since the early 1990s is just one indicator of the controversy surrounding the need to provide accommodations that enable students with disabilities to participate and show their knowledge and skills in assessments (Thurlow et al., 2005). Likewise, institutions of higher education and credentialing agencies have used different approaches to determine how and for whom accommodations should be provided, generally reverting to a restrictive, documentation-based approach to accommodation provision. According to Stage and Milne (1996), "although much research evidence is based on studies of younger, pre-college students, many authors have pointed out that attitudinal barriers and organizational structures within universities may impede the attainment of [students with disabilities'] educational goals" (p. 429).

Tindal (2003) suggests that much of the past research has lacked consistency and effectiveness and that it is difficult to generalize the results because most of the research presents the results of a single study that analyzed a unique population. Many of the studies also had methodological issues related to the measurement of the effectiveness of accommodation use. For example, some accommodations may improve the performance of all student subgroups (e.g., students with disabilities, ELLs, and general education students) rather than only improving the performance of students with disabilities and having no impact on the performance of the general education population. Other methodological issues included lack of control groups, reliance on correlational studies, and reliance on post hoc analyses without external criterion measures.

NCEO summarized the results of 46 empirical research studies on accommodations published from 1999 through 2001 (Thompson et al., 2002). Computer administration, oral presentation, and extended time accommodations showed a positive effect on student test scores in at least four studies. However, there were a number of additional studies included in the review that found no significant effects on scores through the use of these accommodations.

In an extensive review of the accommodation literature, Sireci et al. (2003) concluded that several challenges related to the use of accommodations still need to be solved. Research is needed to provide policy makers, test designers, and educators with clear guidance about how to determine which accommodations are appropriate for which individual students. Once this issue has been clarified, better studies of test score validity can be conducted that examine the extent to which the use of an accommodation increases the scores of students who need them to access the assessment, as well as how the use of accommodations can make the measurement comparable for both students with disabilities and for students without disabilities (Thompson et al., 2002).

Many stakeholders (including policy makers, professional associations, educators, and the general public) have opinions about what the potential impact of accommodations might be on test validity, student access, and student opportunity to access future educational and career opportunities. For example, a number of years ago the National Council of Teachers of English (NCTE)

> challenged the validity of indirect measures of writing, such as tests of grammar, writing mechanics, and editing tests. NCTE insisted that the valid measurement of students' writing ability requires the assessment of actual samples of students' writing performance evaluated against standards or rubrics defining critical characteristics of grade-level expectations for written work. (Ryan & DeMark, 2002, p. 68)

This has implications for accommodations. If the writing test was a test where students were required to edit a paragraph and make corrections, then it could not be presented in a "read-aloud" format. But, the NCTE concerns suggest that what actually constitutes a valid measure of writing must be considered first. If it is the assessment of actual student writing performance, what implications does that have for accommodations? Is spelling being assessed? If not, can students use a dictionary or a spell-check on a computer? These critical questions have not always been asked when large-scale tests were designed, or when states and other entities have developed accommodation policies for students with special needs. Difficulty answering these questions usually is related to the lack of a clear and specific definition of the construct being measured.

Similarly, the National Council of Teachers of Mathematics believes that mathematical ability should refer to "rich, comprehensive, and integrated forms of mathematical reasoning and communication and not merely to a set of discrete skills" (Ryan & DeMark, 2002, p. 68). This has important implications for accommodations, especially the use of a calculator on mathematics assessments. How "communication" is defined is equally important; does it involve only words expressed in a certain way (e.g., in writing) or is it a braoder concept (such as picture drawing or verbal expression)?

Those involved in test design, decision making, and administration must begin to more clearly define the constructs assessed, particularly with regard to test specifications. Test designers need to consider the different types of skills and knowledge that different individual test items are designed to measure. It is important to consider what constructs each item (and the overall assessment) is intended to measure and what constitutes construct-irrelevant variance (CIV). When this is done, it is easier to determine which accommodations affect the construct and which do not. Several states have done this in the area of mathematics by determining that a calculator cannot be used for items that assess computation, but that it can be used for general problem solving (Thurlow et al., 2005). Other states have determined that reading decoding skills are to be tested in the elementary grades, but not at later grades.

According to Tindal (2003), emphasis should be placed "on the meaning of the construct (and the accommodations) and not just the score" (p. 4). For example, if a test contains a reading passage and the decoding of print is not the construct being measured, then perhaps a variety of modes of print interaction could be permitted, including not only visual (such as on the printed page or on a computer screen), but also tactile (feeling print, such as Braille) or auditory (such as listening to printed messages, as on the radio or TV), or even multimodal (using any combination of modalities, as in assistive reading and viewing programs—digital talking news).

It is a common belief that accommodations can eliminate barriers that are irrelevant to the construct being assessed. Unfortunately, we often do not know for sure whether the barriers are truly irrelevant or whether they result in a change in what the test is trying to measure (Thurlow, Elliott, & Ysseldyke, 2003). As an example of this complex issue, consider the fact that any test that employs language (i.e., virtually all tests in an educational setting) is, in part, a measure of language skills (AERA, APA, & NCME, 1999).

Reading the test to the student is one of the most controversial accommodations in the K–12 educational system. An example of this is the case of a student who became blind in high school. Reading the test to the student initially was considered to produce an invalid score. A lawsuit, however, raised questions about whether decoding printed text is a skill that is still measured in high school. Even at the elementary school level, is decoding perhaps a skill measured for some items, but not others? An important accommodation question is whether a student with a reading disability (as a result of a learning or sensory impairment) could receive points for some items for which decoding is not a tested skill, but not receive points for items for which decoding is a tested skill. Some states are laying out their blueprints and test specifications in such a way that they clarify that decoding is measured in the early grades, but not in high school (Thompson, Johnstone, Thurlow, & Clapper, 2004). In many of these states, the read-aloud accommodation, for example, is not allowed in the elementary school grades, but is allowed in high school.

Research on the effects of accommodations is guided ultimately by the need for accessible measures that are generally considered to be fair. Fairness implies that the score of an examinee was not affected by a contruct-irrelevant factor and that "examinees of equal standing with respect to the construct the test is intended to measure should on average earn the same test score, irrespective of group membership" (AERA, APA, & NCME, 1999, p. 74). The *Standards for Educational and Psychological Tests* refer to this as *fairness*, with this definition:

> Fairness requires that all examinees be afforded appropriate testing conditions.... In some cases, aspects of the testing process that pose no particular challenge for most examinees may prevent specific groups or individuals from accurately demonstrating their standing with respect to the construct of interest. In some instances, greater comparability may sometimes be attained if standardized procedures are modified. (AERA, APA, & NCME, 1999, p. 75)

Implementation Issues

For students in the K–12 system, the process of making decisions about accommodations and then ensuring that those decisions are carried out is a major challenge. For students with disabilities, IEP teams are responsible for determining appropriate accommodations for instruction and for assessments, and these are recorded on each student's IEP. Research on these decisions has documented the difficulty in making the decisions and in carrying them out (DeStefano, Shriner, & Lloyd, 2001; Rhode Island Department of Education, 2003). Although these implementation difficulties can be improved through training, as demonstrated by Shriner and DeStefano (2003) and through data-based decision-making systems (Fuchs & Fuchs, 2001), there continues to be a lack of state training on accommodations so that the information gets to the districts, to the schools, and to the IEP teams (Langley & Olsen, 2003).

Information on the decision-making process and whether it is carried out is less clear for ELLs because in most states decisions about accommodations are made by the student's teacher (i.e., only a few states have groups of decision makers who determine accommodations for ELLs). There is less often a formal record of the decision, and thus it becomes more difficult to track whether the decision is carried into the assessment setting.

The provision of an appropriate decision-making strategy and adequate training to IEP teams and those who make the decisions for English language learners, as well as solutions to many logistical problems that surround the provision of accommodations in the K–12 assessment situation are essential for moving toward better assessments. The issues in postsecondary assessment are much more controlled, and thus without the implementation issues that surround accommodations in K–12. Nevertheless, the implementation issues that surround accommodations in postsecondary education may be greater if needed accommodations are being denied to individuals who require them to demonstrate their knowledge and skills, without compromising the constructs that the assessment is designed to measure.

UNIVERSALLY DESIGNED ASSESSMENTS—THE "MORE" OF ASSESSMENTS

New technology is changing the manner in which accommodations are administered and the manner in which the examinee records his or her responses. There is a need for well-designed tests that minimize the need for accommodations. Assessments that are designed up front to permit the participation of the widest range of students and minimize the need for accommodations without compromising the reliability or validity of assessment are becoming more common in the field of education. Test developers have begun to recognize that a well-designed assessment is a better measure for all students, including those students with disabilities and those who are learning English. According to Thompson, Johnstone, and Thurlow (2002), well-designed tests that are inclusive of all students have several key elements:

- Precisely defined constructs;
- Accessible, nonbiased items;
- Amendable to accommodations;
- Simple, clear, and intuitive instructions and procedures;
- Maximum readability and comprehensibility; and
- Maximum legibility.

The essential idea behind universally designed assessments is that they are to ensure that the assessment measures what is really intended—the relevant constructs—rather than construct irrelevant information. The purpose of universally designed assessments is to eliminate (or at least reduce) these factors, because CIV tends to incorrectly increase or decrease a test score. Early on, those thinking about accommodations realized that it was possible that reliance on accommodations could perhaps be lessened if something was done to improve the assessments themselves. Butler and Stevens (1997) contemplated this in relation to ELLs and argued that "the process of determining whether accommodations are effective, efforts to clarify test tasks—for example, prompts, questions, and directions to make them more accessible to English language learners—might in fact actually clarify and improve test content for all students" (p. 25).

Research on how to develop universally designed assessments and whether they indeed make a difference for students with disabilities and ELLs has begun to produce results. Thompson, Johnstone, and Miller (2005) used a think-aloud process with students with disabilities to determine how students approached multiple choice and constructed-response math items to determine what they saw and how they worked through the items, and where the stumbling blocks in design were for these students. Cognitive lab procedures using reflexive think aloud techniques have been used with ELLs and non-ELLs (Winter, 2003; Winter, Kopriva, Chen, & Wiley, 2004). Johnstone (2003) compared traditionally designed items with items that he, a trained community advisory committee, and a subject matter expert redesigned using universal design principles. He found a moderate effect size favoring universally designed items. Abedi and his colleagues (e.g., Abedi, chap.17, this volume; Abedi, Hofstetter, Baker, & Lord, 2001; Abedi & Lord, 2001) have focused on the linguistic complexity of test items in assessments as a significant source of measurement error for ELLs. Test development companies now are touting their assessments as being universally designed. Whether this is just a change in the face design or true universal design in which developers have grappled with the construct-relevant and construct-irrelevant issues remains to be seen. Universal design, however, appears to be guiding current assessment discussion.

This discussion of universal design is often wrapped up with discussions of computer-based testing. Although they are clearly not one in the same, and transferring a test onto a computer can actually create many access problems for students (Thompson, Quenemoen, & Thurlow, 2005), there are many benefits that can be achieved from placing assessments on computers and online, with accommodations built in so that students who need them may have access to them.

CONSIDERATIONS AND IMPLICATIONS FOR ADMINISTRATION

Considerations for the administration of tests to special needs students have been sprinkled throughout this chapter as we have discussed the challenges that surround accommodations and the innovative approaches to the design of assessments that are now being undertaken. There are several summary considerations for administration that are important to keep in mind.

First, there continues to be a need for additional work in the area of accommodations and modifications. Some of the work that needs to be done is research, but it has become clear that research is not going to answer all the questions that we have about accommodations. In particular, research is not likely to answer some of the critical implementation questions that exist. Because accommodations are supposed to be effective only when they meet an individual student's needs, the complications of conducting research are immense. Traditional randomized experimental designs are very difficult to conduct, especially because they require that groups of students be exposed to the same accommodation or package of accommodations. Another useful activity is continued work on what is appropriate. It is important to gain consensus among experts about what are appropriate test administration procedures rather than waiting for the research to provide definitive answers.

Because experimental research is not going to provide all the answers, it is also essential for test developers to be trained in the concepts of standards and assessments, alignment of assessments with standards, and the principles behind accommodations. In addition, test developers and administrators should be familiar with the concepts of universal design and should be aware of the ways in which students participate in the assessment system, be it in the general assessment without accommodations, the general or alternate assessment with accommodations, or in the alternate assessment. The students participating in assessments should be asked to participate in interviews or surveys so that more information is obtained about them and their experiences.

Even if additional research definitively determines how accommodations should be used to produce valid test scores, accommodations will never be used to their fullest potential unless students with disabilities understand the role of accommodations. Once students move beyond elementary school, some students with disabilities become concerned about "being different" from the other students and refuse to use needed accommodations. Students need to fully understand the consequences of this choice. There is an additional need to educate students with disabilities about how to self-advocate for needed accommodations. There also needs to be a dialogue between students and educators about which accommodations a particular student is willing to use. Students who are trained in how to self-advocate can greatly increase the likelihood that documented accommodations are provided on test day (Thompson, Lazarus, Thurlow, & Clapper, 2005).

The need for students to advocate also suggests another need. Communication between the K–12 and postsecondary systems requires continued improvement. Although there is some evidence that postsecondary education and testing systems are attending to what has been happening in the K–12 system, it has not always been the case that this occurred equally in both directions. Much more collaboration across systems is needed. It can only make the assessment process better for students, and perhaps improve the assessment process in both the K–12 and the postsecondary systems.

Finally, there is still much to learn about improving the assessments that we give to students. The authors believe that requiring the participation of students with disabilities and ELLs in large-scale assessments is helping us to think more carefully than we might have had these requirements not been in place. Making decisions about how to design and administer tests for students with special needs clarifies the essential role that access plays in achieving valid assessment results. By increasing access for these students, validity is increased, and thus comparability across students—with and without disabilities, or with and without limited English skills—is increased.

ACKNOWLEDGMENTS

The preparation of this manuscript was supported, in part, by a cooperative agreement (H326G000001) between the U.S. Department of Education, Office of Special Education Programs and the University of Minnesota (National Center on Educational Outcomes). Opinions expressed herein are those of the authors, however, and do not necessarily reflect those of the U.S. Department of Education or Offices within it.

The authors acknowledge the timely and thoughtful reviews and comments provided by Robert Doljanac, Research Associate, Institute on Community Integration, University of Minnesota, and by Phoebe Winter, Consultant in Educational and Psychological Assessment Design, Statistical Analysis, and Educational Research and Evaluation. Their insights and suggestions, as well as those of the book's editors, were much appreciated.

REFERENCES

Abedi, J., Hofstetter, C., Baker, E., & Lord, C. (2001). *NAEP math performance and test accommodations: Interactions with student language background* (CSE Technical Report 536). Los Angeles: University of California, CRESST.

Abedi, J., Hofstetter, C., & Lord, C. (2004). Assessment accommodations for English language learners: Implications for policy based research. *Review of Educational Research, 74*(1), 1–28.

Abedi, J., & Lord, C. (2001). The language factor in mathematics tests. *Applied Measurement in Education, 14*, 219–234.

Abedi, J., Lord, C., Hofstetter, C., & Baker, E. (2000). Impact of accommodation strategies on English language learners test performance. *Educational Measurement: Issues and Practice, 19*(3), 16–26.

ACT. (2002). *ACT policy for documentation to support requests for testing accommodations on the ACT assessment*. Retrieved January 3, 2002 from http://www.act.org/aap/disabpolicy.html.

Albus, D., Thurlow, M., & Liu, K., & Bielinski, J. (2005). The effect of a simplified English language dictionary on the reading test performance of limited English proficient students. *Journal of Educational Research, 98*(4), 245–254.

American Educational Research Association (AERA), American Psychological Association (APA), & National Council on Measurement in Education (NCME). (1999). *Standards for educational and psychological tests*. Washington, DC: American Educational Research Association.

Ansell, S. E. (2004, January 8). Put to the test. *Education Week, 23*(17), 75–79.

Bielinski, J., Sheinker, A., & Ysseldyke, J. (2003). *Varied opinions on how to report accommodated test scores: Findings based on CTB/McGraw-Hill's framework for classifying accommodations* (Synthesis Report 49). Minneapolis: University of Minnesota, National Center on Educational Outcomes.

Bielinski, J., Thurlow, M., Ysseldyke, J., Friedebach, J., & Friedebach, M. (2001). *Read-aloud accommodation: Effects on multiple-choice reading and math items* (Technical Report 31). Minneapolis: University of Minnesota, National Center on Educational Outcomes.

Bolt, S. E., & Thurlow, M. L. (2004). Five of the most frequently allowed testing accommodations in state policy. *Remedial and Special Education, 25*(3), 141–152.

Butler, F. A., & Stevens, R. (1997). *Accommodation strategies for English language learners on large-scale assessments: student characteristics and other considerations.* Los Angeles: Center for the Study of Evaluation, Standards and Student Testing.

Center on Education Policy. (2002). *State high school exit exams: A baseline report.* Washington, DC: Author.

Clapper, A., Morse, A., Lazarus, S., Thompson, S., & Thurlow, M. (2005). *2003 state policies on assessment participation and accommodations* (Synthesis Report 56). Minneapolis: University of Minnesota, National Center on Educational Outcomes.

DeStefano, L., Shriner, J. G., & Lloyd, C. A. (2001). Teacher decision making in participation of students with disabilities in large-scale assessment. *Exceptional Children, 68*(1), 7–22.

Disability Rights Advocates. (2001). *Do no harm—High stakes testing and students with learning disabilities.* Oakland, CA: Author.

Donovan, M. S., & Cross, C. R. (Eds.). (2002). *Minority students in special and gifted education.* Washington, DC: National Academy Press.

Downing, S. M. (2005). The effects of violating standard item writing principles on tests and students: The consequences of using flawed test items on achievement examinations in medical education. *Advances in Health Sciences Education, 10,* 133–143.

Educational Testing Service (ETS). (2002). *Educational Testing Service agrees with disability groups to stop "flagging" on graduate admissions test.* Retrieved January 4, 2004 from http://www.ets.org/aboutets/news/01020701/html.

Elliott, S., Kratochwill, R., & McKevitt, B. (2001). Experimental analysis of the effects of testing accommodations on the scores of students with and without disabilities. *Journal of School Psychology, 39,* 3–24.

Fuchs, L. S., & Fuchs, D. (2001). Helping teachers formulate sound test accommodation decisions for students with learning disabilities. *Learning Disabilities Research and Practice, 16*(3), 174–181.

Fuchs, L. S., Fuchs, D., Eaton, S. B., Hamlett, C., & Karns, K. (2000). Supplementing teacher judgments about test accommodations with objective data sources. *School Psychology Review, 29*(1), 65–85.

Gottlieb, J., Alter, M, & Gottlieb, B. W. (1999). General education placement for special education students in urban schools. In M. J. Coutinho & A.C. Repp (Eds.), *Inclusion: The integration of students with disabilities.* Belmont, CA: Wadsworth.

Gottlieb, J., Alter, M., Gottlieb, B. W., & Wishner, J. (1994). Special education in urban American: It's not justifiable for many. *The Journal of Special Education, 25,* 155–167.

Government Accountability Office (GAO). (2005). No Child Left Behind Act: Most students with disabilities participated in statewide assessments, but inclusion options could be improved (GAO-05-618). Washington, DC: Author.

Grossman, P. D. (2001). Making accommodations: The legal world of students with disabilities. *Academe: Bulletin of the American Association of University Professors, 87,* 41–46.

Hafner, A. (1999, June). *Assessment accommodations that provide valid inferences for LEP students.* Paper presented at the annual conference of the Council of Chief State School Officers, Salt Lake City, UT.

Haladyna, T. M., & Downing, S. M. (2004). Construct-irrelevant variance in high-stakes testing. *Educational Measurement: Issues and Practice, 23*(1), 17–27.

Heubert, J., & Hauser, R. (Eds.). (1999). *High stakes: Testing for tracking, promotion, and graduation.* Washington, DC. National Academy Press.

Hollenbeck, K., Rozek-Tedesco, M., Tindal, G., & Glasgrow, A. (2000). An exploratory study of student-paced versus teacher-paced accommodations for large-scale math tests. *Journal of Special Education Technology, 15*(2), 27–36.

Hollenbeck, K., Tindal, G., Harniss, M., & Almond, P. (1999). *The effect of using computers as an accommodation in a statewide writing test.* Eugene: University of Oregon, BRT.

Hopstock, P. J., & Stephenson, T. G. (2003). *Descriptive study of services to LEP students and LEP students with disabilities* [Special Topic Report 2]. Washington, DC: U.S. Department of Education, Office of Special Education Programs. Retrieved July 1, 2004 from http://www.ncela.gwu.edu/resabout/research/descriptivestudyfiles/

Johnstone, C. J. (2003). *Improving validity of large-scale tests: Universal design and student performance* [Technical Report 37]. Minneapolis: University of Minnesota, National Center on Educational Outcomes.

Kopriva, R. (1994). *Validity issues in performance assessment for low, mid and high achieving ESL and English only elementary students* [Technical Report]. Sacramento: California Department of Education.

Koretz, D. (1997). *The assessment of students with disabilities in Kentucky* [CSE Technical Report No. 431]. Los Angeles, CA: Center for Research on Standards and Student Testing.

Koretz, D., & Hamilton, L. (1999). *Assessing students with disabilities in Kentucky: The effects of accommodations, format, and subject* [Technical Report No. 498]. Los Angeles, CA: Center for Research on Standards and Student Testing. (ERIC Document Reproduction Service No. ED 440 148.)

Koretz, D., & Hamilton, L. (2000). Assessment of students with disabilities in Kentucky: Inclusion, student performance, and validity. *Educational Evaluation and Policy Analysis, 22*(3), 255–272.

Langley, J., & Olsen, K. (2003). *Training district and state personnel on accommodations: A study of state practices, challenges and resources.* Washington, DC: Council of Chief State School Officers.

Lazarus, S., Thompson, S., & Thurlow, M. (2005). *How students access accommodations in assessment and instruction: Results of a survey of special education teachers* (Issue Brief). College Park: University of Maryland, Educational Policy Reform Research Institute.

Linn, R. L. (2002). Validation of the uses and interpretations of results of state assessment and accountability systems. In G. Tindal & M. Haladyna (Eds.), *Large-scale assessment programs for all students.* Mahwah, NJ: Lawrence Erlbaum Associates.

National Clearinghouse on English Language Acquisition. (2004). *Language backgrounds of limited English proficient (LEP) students in the U.S. and outlying areas, 2000–2001 (sorted by estimated rank).* Retrieved July 10, 2004 from http://ncela.gwu.edu/stats/toplanguages/rank.xls.

Rhode Island Department of Education. (2003). *Rhode Island assessment accommodation study: Research summary.* Minneapolis: University of Minnesota, National Center on Educational Outcomes. Retrieved July 10, 2004 from http://education.umn.edu/NCEO/TopicAreas/Accommodations/RhodeIsland/htm.

Rivera, C., Collum, E., Shafer, L., & Sia, J. K. (2004). *Analysis of state assessment policies regarding the accommodation of English language learners, SY 2000–2001.* Arlington, VA: George Washington University, Center for Equity and Excellence in Education.

Robelen, E. W. (2003, November 26). NAEP board seeks consistency on special-needs students. *Education Week, 23*(13), 18.

Ryan, J. M., & DeMark, S. (2002). Variation in achievement scores related to gender, item format, and content area tested. In G. Tindal and M. Haladyna (Eds.), *Large-scale assessment programs for all students.* Mahwah, NJ: Lawrence Erlbaum Associates.

Shriner, J. G., & DeStefhano, L. (2003). Participation and accommodation in state assessment: The role of individualized education programs. *Exceptional Children, 69*(2), 147–161.

Sireci, S. G., Li, S., & Scarpati, S. (2003). *The effects of test accommodation on test performance: A review of the literature* [Research Report 485]. Amherst, MA: Center for Educational Assessment.

Stage, F. K., & Milne, N. V. (1996). Invisible scholars: Students with learning disabilities. *Journal of Higher Education, 67*(4), 426–445.

Stodden, R., Jones, M., & Chang, K. (2003). *Services, supports and accommodations for individuals with disabilities: An analysis across secondary education, postsecondary education and employment.* Manoa: University of Hawaii at Manoa, Center on Disability Studies. Retrieved June 20, 2004 from http://www.rrtc.hawaii.edu/producet/phases/phase3.asp.

Thompson, S. J., Blount, A., & Thurlow, M. L. (2002). *A summary of research on the effects of test accommodations: 1999 through 2001* [Technical Report 34]. Minneapolis: University of Minnesota, National Center on Educational Outcomes.

Thompson, S. J., Johnstone, C. J., & Miller, N. (2005). *Universally designing assessments using a "think aloud" analysis* [Technical Report 43]. Minneapolis: University of Minnesota, National Center on Educational Outcomes.

Thompson, S. J., Johnstone, C. J., & Thurlow, M. L. (2002). *Universal design applied to large scale assessments* [Synthesis Report 44]. Minneapolis: University of Minnesota, National Center on Educational Outcomes.

Thompson, S. J., Johnstone, C. J., Thurlow, M. L., & Clapper, A. (2004). *State literacy standards, practice, and testing: Exploring accessibility* [Technical Report 38]. Minneapolis: University of Minnesota, National Center on Educational Outcomes.

Thompson, S. J., Lazarus, S. S., Thurlow, M. L., & Clapper, A. (2005). *The role of accommodations in educational accountability systems* [Topical Review 8]. College Park: University of Maryland, Educational Policy Reform Research Institute.

Thompson, S. J., Quenemoen, R. F., & Thurlow, M. L. (2005). Factors to consider in the design of inclusive online assessments. In M. Hricko, S. Howell, & D. Williams (Eds.), *Online assessment and measurement: Foundations and challenges.* Hershey, PA: Idea Group.

Thompson, S. J., & Thurlow, M. L. (1999). *1999 state special education outcomes: A report on state activities at the end of the century.* Minneapolis: University of Minnesota, National Center on Educational Outcomes.

Thompson, S. J., & Thurlow, M. L. (2003). *2003 state special education outcomes: Marching on.* Minneapolis: University of Minnesota, National Center on Educational Outcomes.

Thurlow, M. L. (2001). *Use of accommodations in state assessments: What databases tell us about differential levels of use and how to document the use of accommodations* [Technical Report 30]. Minneapolis: University of Minnesota, National Center on Educational Outcomes.

Thurlow, M. L., & Bolt, S. (2001). *Empirical support for accommodations most often allowed in state policy* [Synthesis Report 41]. Minneapolis: University of Minnesota, National Center on Educational Outcomes.

Thurlow, M. L., Elliott, J. L., Erickson, R. N., & Ysseldyke, J. E. (1997). Learning disabilities and accommodations: Best practice for bar exams. *The Bar Examiner, 66*(4), 17–30.

Thurlow, M. L., Elliott, J. L., & Ysseldyke, J. E. (2003). *Testing students with disabilities: Practical strategies for complying with district and state requirements* (2nd ed.). Thousand Oaks, CA: Corwin.

Thurlow, M. L., Lazarus, S. S., Thompson, S. J., & Morse, A. B. (2005). State policies on assessment participation and accommodations for students with disabilities. *The Journal of Special Education, 38*(4) 232–240.

Thurlow, M. L., & Wiener, D. (2000). *Non-approved accommodations: Recommendations for use and reporting* [Policy Directions No. 11]. Minneapolis: University of Minnesota, National Center on Educational Outcomes.

Thurlow, M., Wiley, H. I., & Bielinski, J. (2003). *Going public: What 2000–2001 reports tell us about the performance of students with disabilities* [Technical Report 35]. Minneapolis: University of Minnesota, National Center on Educational Outcomes.

Thurlow, M. L., Ysseldyke, J. E., & Silverstein, B. (1995). Testing accommodations for students with disabilities. *Remedial and Special Education, 16*(5), 260–270.

Tindal, G. (2003, August). *Test accommodations research: Decision-making outcomes, and designs.* Paper presented at the Validity and Accommodations: Psychometric and Policy Perspectives Conference, College Park, MD.

Tindal, G., & Fuchs, L. S. (1999). *A summary of research on test changes: An empirical basis for defining accommodations.* Lexington: University of Kentucky, Mid-South Research Resource Center.

U.S. Department of Education. (2002a). *No Child Left Behind.* Retrieved June 24, 2004 from http://www.ed.gov/nclb/landing.jhtml?src=pb.

U.S. Department of Education. (2002b). *No Child Left Behind: A desktop reference.* Washington, DC: Office of Elementary and Secondary Education.

U.S. Department of Education (2002c). *Twenty-fourth annual report to Congress on the implementation of the Individuals with Disabilities Education Act.* Washington, DC: Author. Retrieved July 1, 2004 from http://www.Ed.gov/about/offices/list/osers/osep/research.html.

Winter, P. C. (2003). *Construct validity: What are we really measuring?* Presentation at the annual National Conference on Large-Scale Assessments, San Diego.

Winter, P. C., Kopriva, R. J., Chen, C., & Wiley, D. E. (2004). *Exploring student and item factors that affect assessment validity: Results from a large-scale cognitive lab.* Paper presented at the annual meeting of the National Council on Measurement in Education, San Diego.

Yell, M. L. (1998). *The law and special education.* Upper Saddle River, NJ: Prentice-Hall.

VI

Post-test Activities

29

Practices, Issues, and Trends in Student Test Score Reporting

Joseph M. Ryan
Arizona State University

The chapter begins with an introduction that includes a discussion of portions of the *Standards of Educational and Psychological Testing* (American Educational Research Association [AERA], American Psychological Association [APA], National Council on Measurement in Education [NCME], 1999) relevant to the design and valid use of test score reports. The introduction presents a basic framework for score reports that explicates the typical content and format consideration that go into designing a score report and provides examples illustrating some fundamental approaches. The second major section describes what is currently known about score reports and their impact and efficacy in communicating assessment results and supporting valid interpretations of test scores. This includes a summary review of the literature of score reporting from numerous informative and comprehensive sources. This section contains several recommendations for score reporting. The third section reports on a study of score reporting features and formats that used a series of focus groups to first identify some key features of score reports and then to have educators evaluate score reports developed to reflect these features. The final section of the chapter summarizes the major findings, offers brief lists of key guidelines, and examines several broader issues related to score reports and their valid interpretation.

A *score report* is a form of communication. Like all forms of communication, score reports have a sender, message, medium, intent, and audience. The *sender* of score reports for a large-scale assessment program is the sponsoring agency or institution generally working through a contractor (see Trent and Roeber, chap. 3, this volume). The *message* deals with the content of the score report and the *medium* is the score report format. This chapter explores the message and the medium of score reports in detail, summarizes what has been learned about the benefits and disadvantages of including or excluding certain content, and examines the impact of various formats on the effectiveness of communicating to various audiences.

The value of various score reports reflects the match between the report, the intended audience, and anticipated use. Score reports are prepared for students, their parents, teachers, principals, governing boards, other public bodies, and the public at large. A score report appropriate and helpful for one group could be substantially off target for a different audience. Broadly speaking, assessment programs and the score reports they employ are designed for two major intents or purposes. First, score reports serve an instructional purpose to inform various audiences about students' learning, the efficacy of instruction, and the impact and value of curriculum. A second fundamental purpose is to provide information for various local, state, and national accountability programs. Score reports must be evaluated relative to these different purposes, even though they sometimes overlap considerably.

Two aspects of score reporting are not addressed in this chapter. First, the technical and format particulars of web-based and other types of electronic score report delivery systems are not reviewed. The chapter's major findings apply, for the most part, to both print and electronically presented score report information. There are additional issues related to the use of web-based and other electronically presented report information, however, that go beyond the scope of this review. Electronically presented score reports have numerous advantages over paper approaches. The omission of discussion specific to electronically delivered score report information and formats reflects a matter of focus and emphasis on issues common to paper and electronic presentation of score reports. Second, the chapter does not examine the wide range of interpretative guides and materials that often accompany score reports. These are important aids to interpreting score reports and may, when properly used, have a useful impact of the value of score reports. Goodman and Hambleton (2004) provide a valuable review of these materials with numerous illustrations and examples.

TEST SCORE REPORTING AND THE *STANDARDS FOR EDUCATIONAL AND PSYCHOLOGICAL TESTING*

The *Standards for Educational and Psychological Testing* (American Educational Research Association [AERA], American Psychological Association [APA], & National Council on Measurement in Education [NCME], 1999) address a wide range of issues and concerns related to all aspects of testing including test scoring and reporting of students' test performance. Central to all such issues is the concern about validity. According to the *Standards*,

> Validity refers to the degree to which evidence and theory support the interpretations of test scores entailed by proposed uses of tests.... It is the interpretations tests scores required by proposed uses that are evaluated, not the test itself. When test scores are used or interpreted in more than one way, each intended interpretation must be validated. (AERA, APA, & NCME, p. 9)

Because validity, by definition, focuses on the interpretation of test scores, then any feature of a score report that invites or encourages an interpretation that evidence or theory do not support has corrupted the validity of the assessment. To be sure, some misinterpretation is the responsibility of those receiving and using the test results. However, the inclusion of information that might lead to misinterpretation or the omission of information on a score report that mitigates against misinterpretations is the responsibility of those sponsoring the assessment.

Interpretation

The requirement that score report information support valid interpretation is seen in the following standards.

- **Standard 5.10:** When test score information is released to students, parents, legal representatives, teachers, clients, or the media, those responsible for testing programs should provide appropriate interpretations. The interpretations should describe in simple

language what the test covers, what scores mean, the precision of the scores, common misinterpretations of test scores, and how scores are used.
- **Standard 5.11:** When computer-prepared interpretations of test response protocols are reported, the sources, rationale, and empirical basis for these interpretations should be available, and their limitations should be described.
- **Standard 6.12:** Publishers and scoring services that offer computer-generated interpretations of test scores should provide a summary of the evidence supporting the interpretations given.
- **Standard 11.18:** When test results are released to the public or to policymakers, those responsible for the release should provide and explain any supplemental information that will minimize possible misinterpretations of the data.
- **Standard 12.9:** Professionals responsible for supervising group testing programs should ensure that the individuals who interpret the test scores are properly instructed in the appropriate methods for interpreting them.
- **Standard 12.15:** Those who use computer-generated interpretations of test data should evaluate the quality of the interpretations and, when possible, the relevance and appropriateness of the norms upon which the interpretations are based.
- **Standard 12.19:** The interpretation of test scores or patterns of test battery results should take cognizance of the many factors that may influence a particular testing outcome. Where appropriate, a description and analysis of the alternative hypotheses or explanations that may have contributed to the pattern of results should be included in the report.
- **Standard 12.20:** Except for some judicial or governmental referrals, or in some employment testing situations when the client is the employer, professionals should share test results and interpretations with the test taker. Such information should be expressed in language that the test taker, or when appropriate the test taker's legal representative, can understand.
- **Standard 13.16:** In educational settings, whenever a test score is reported, the date of test administration should be reported. This information and the age of any norms used for interpretation should be considered by test users in making inferences.

These nine standards have in common the clear message that the valid interpretation and use of test results is the responsibility of those who develop and administer the assessments and who produce the score reports and interpretive materials. Responsibility for valid interpretation and use is shared, of course, with various audiences to whom the test results are presented.

Data in Groups

In many circumstances, scores are reported for students who have been assigned to various groups. In some instances, the groups reflect shared demographic characteristics of the students; in other cases groups may be based on organizational or administrative units. The *Standards* explicitly address reporting students' test results in groups in the following three standards. Standard 8.8 is especially relevant to reporting students' test results in performance or achievement levels or categories, a common approach that many educators believe is useful.

- **Standard 5.12:** When group-level information is obtained by aggregating the results of partial tests taken by individuals, validity and reliability should be reported for the level of aggregation at which results are reported. Scores should not be reported for individuals unless the validity, comparability, and reliability of such scores have been established.
- **Standard 7.8:** When scores are disaggregated and publicly reported for groups identified by characteristics such as gender, ethnicity, age, language proficiency, or disability,

cautionary statements should be included whenever credible research reports that test scores may not have comparable meaning across these different groups.
- **Standard 8.8:** When score reporting includes assigning individuals to categories, the categories should be chosen carefully and described precisely. The least stigmatizing labels, consistent with accurate representation, should always be assigned.

Timeliness

There are two standards related to the timeliness for reporting test results.

- **Standard 11.6:** Unless the circumstances clearly require that the test results be withheld, the test user is obligated to provide a timely report of the results that is understandable to the test taker and others entitled to receive this information.
- **Standard 11.17:** In situations where the public is entitled to receive a summary of test results, test users should formulate a policy regarding timely release of the results and apply that policy consistently over time.

Gain Scores

Change scores or gain scores are addressed in Standard 13.17.

- **Standard 13.17:** When change or gain scores are used, such scores should be defined and their technical qualities should be reported.

Change or gain scores have not commonly been reported in statewide testing programs although current requirements for reporting adequate yearly progress amount to asking about gains in attainment. There is a commonly reported set of scores that are similar to change or gain scores and to which Standard 13.17 should be applied. Many testing programs report students' performance on subdomains or strands. In mathematics, for example, these commonly include subscores such as number sense and numeration, geometry, and measurement. Scores on these subdomains are often presented in a way that invites and encourages comparisons between a student's performance on the different strands. Such comparisons amount to interpreting difference scores on correlated and sometimes highly correlated scales. Standard 13.17 suggests that the valid interpretation of these differences demands that the technical qualities of the differences be reported. Such information might include the reliability and standard errors of the pairwise differences for all pairs of subscales or subdomains. This topic is examined again later in this chapter.

Following this introduction, the chapter presents a basic framework for score reports. The framework explicates the typical content and format consideration that go into designing a score report and provides examples illustrating a few fundamental approaches. The second major section describes what we currently know about score reports and their impact and efficacy in communicating assessment results and supporting valid interpretations. This includes a summary review of the literature of score reporting from Goodman and Hambleton (2004), and a summary of several recent informative studies by Forte Fast and Tucker (2001), National Education Goals Panel (NEGP) (1998), and finally a review of the study by Goodman and Hambleton (2004). The third section reports on a study of score reporting features and formats conducted by Ryan (2003). The final section of the chapter presents a listing of suggestions for designing score reports and four general guidelines for score reporting.

BASIC INFORMATION IN SCORE REPORTS

Score reports can be developed for a wide range of audiences and purposes, and numerous features of score reports can be considered. Nevertheless, there are certain common features of all score reports. A framework of eight key characteristics of score reports is presented here to provide a common understanding of basic terms and concepts used throughout this chapter. These are standard features found in virtually all score reports and should be con-

TABLE 29.1
Score Reporting Framework With Features, Options, and Notes

Reporting Feature	Options and Notes
Report audience	Student, parent, teacher, principal, district administrator, and state official.
	Reports are prepared for various audiences and what is contained in the report and how the information is presented generally varies depending on the audience and users of the reports.
Scale or metric for reporting	Raw score, percentage correct, scale scores, percentiles, stanines, grade equivalent, and normal curve equivalent.
	The scale or scales in which scores are reported can add clarity or confusion to the score report. It is often simpler to report raw scores or percent correct scores, but these scales do not provide comparability across strands on a single test or between two different tests.
Reference for interpretation	Norm referenced, standards referenced (achievement levels), or both.
	Test results can be interpreted in reference to some normative information, such as percentiles or by reporting how students in the school, district, and state perform on the test. In most states, test scores are reported in terms of content and/or performance standards. Reporting students' tests scores in terms of performance achievement levels is proving to be a popular approach.
Assessment unit	Item, strand (e.g., subscale or subdomain), total test.
	Educators' interest for more instructionally useful information often leads to the request for information about how students perform on individual items or on subsets of items such as content strands. Strand-level information is commonly reported but has technical limitations that will be examined later in this chapter.
Reporting unit	Student, classroom, school, district, state, nation.
	Score reports are routinely provided for individual students and for different aggregations of students from classrooms to the entire nation. Certain features of all reports are the same, but each level of report requires different information and approaches.
Error of measurement	For each unit, metric, and test level combination.
	The precision with which test scores are measured is often reported for performance at the total test level. However, the standard error of measurement is not always presented when strand-level achievement is reported. The errors of measurement for interpretations suggested by a score report should be reported. Charts and tables that invite comparing students' achievement across strands should report the standard errors of the differences.
Mode of presentation	Numeric, graphic, narrative.
	Test results can be presented numerically, graphically or in descriptive narrative form. The best approach for different audiences is not always the same and the use of multiple modes of presentation with some built-in redundancy is often seen in score reports.
Reporting medium	Print, web based (static), web based (interactive).
	Test results have been traditionally presented in printed hard copy form. This practice will likely continue for some time but electronic versions supplied via the Internet or on CDs are quite common.

TABLE 29.2
Example of Basic Information in a Student Report

Strand	Number of Items	Number Correct	Percent Correct
Number relationships	11	10	91
Geometry	6	4	67
Algebra	7	4	57
Measurement	10	4	40
Total	34	22	65

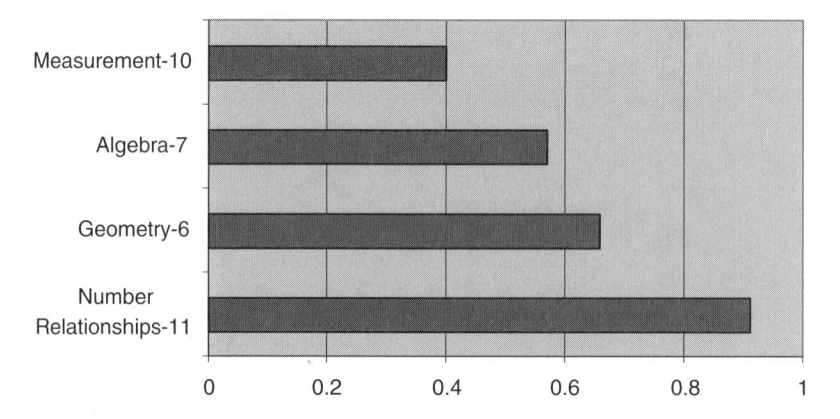

FIG. 29.1. Bar chart illustration of subscale reporting format.

sidered when developing any score report. This framework was developed from a review of numerous score reports from state and commercial assessment programs and the review of examples from various studies to be mentioned later in this chapter. These basic characteristics of score reports that need to be considered in designing a reporting system and are shown in Table 29.1.

Most of the features and various combinations of these features are familiar to educators and others who use score reports. A simple example of basic information that might be contained on a student report is displayed in Table 29.2 with a hypothetical example of a 34-item test composed of four strands or subscales (the terms *strands*, *subscales*, and *subdomains* are used interchangeably in this chapter).

The information in Table 29.2, although commonly reported, is not especially meaningful by itself. The relative difficulty of the subscales is not clear because the raw score metric does not provide a scale on which the strand difficulties have been equated. Standardized scale scores at the strand level equated across all strands would provide a reporting metric on which students' performance can be meaningfully compared. Because there is no indication of the error of measurement or the standard errors of the means in this table, there is no way to determine whether the differential performance on the strands exceeds chance. In addition, there are no normative or achievement level connections that could be used in interpreting these scores. The results shown in Table 29.2 can be shown graphically as in the bar chart in Figure 29.1.

Subscale	Basic	Proficient	Advanced
Number Relationships			▓
Geometry		▓	
Algebra		▓	
Measurement	▓		

FIG. 29.2. Illustration of interpreting subscale performance at cut score; the shaded area shows students' achievement level.

TABLE 29.3
Illustration of Interpreting Subscale Performance at Cut Score

Subscale	Points Possible	Raw Score Below Proficient	Proficient Level Sore Band	Raw Score Above Proficient
Number relationships	11		(5–6)	10
Geometry	6		(2–3)	4
Algebra	7		(2–3)	4
Measurement	10	4	(5–6)	

The actual information in the bar chart is not different than the information in the table format. Valid inferences about a student's relative strengths and weaknesses across the strands could be made if the scales for the strands were equated. Graphical displays such as shown in Figure 29.1 are often more easily understood by more audiences than tables of numbers.

A student's performance relative to achievement level categories is shown in Figure 29.2. Such a display implicitly assumes some form of comparable equated scales across the strands. The usefulness of the information in Figure 29.2 is increased if the figure includes information about where in the achievement level a student is located and if the errors of measurement or classification consistency are provided.

An interesting variation on the basic raw score table (Table 29.2) and the achievement level referenced table (Figure 29.2) is shown in Table 29.3. This type of table has been used by one state to enhance the interpretation of students' strand-level performance. In this table, raw scores at the strand level are referenced to performance that is expected of students at the *proficient* cut score set on the total test.

The cut score for the proficient level on the total test is interpolated to the strand level. The strand-interpolated cut score is truncated and 1 score point is added to form a band designed to show where students at the proficient level on the total test are expected to perform on the strand. A confidence interval could also be formed by adding and subtracting one or more standard errors of measurement around the interpolated cut score. Students are reported as having a "weakness" or "strength" on the strand depending on whether they have scored above or below the proficient level band. The raw score on each subscale is also reported. This approach has the added meaning of referencing an achievement level, and any achievement level (e.g., below basic, basic, proficient, advanced, or accelerated). In this approach, all items are on the same scale, but the set of items on the different subscales are not necessarily equally difficult; for example, the geometry subscale may be more difficult than the measurement subscale. The lack of comparability in difficulty across subscales is compensated for in the interpolation process and is revealed by the fact that the proficient level band can have different raw score

	Basic	Proficient	Advanced
Subscale	Scale Score 200 --500		
Number Relationships			--X--
Geometry		-----X-----	
Algebra		-----X------	
Measurement	---X---		

FIG. 29.3. Subscale performance referencing achievement levels and with errors of measurement.

values even for subscales with the same number of items. This report, by itself, does not give an indication of the errors of measurement for the individual subscales or the differences between the subscales.

Many score reports attempt to reflect students' performance at the strand level in terms of achievement levels defined on the total test score and also show the subscale errors of measurement. A basic version of this format is shown in Figure 29.3.

This figure shows a student's performance at the strand level in terms of the scale score metric and in terms of the overall achievement levels of basic, proficient, and advanced. The X on each line represents the students' strand score and the dashes to the left and right of the X represent the 95% confidence interval around the score. The slightly wider intervals around geometry and algebra indicate larger errors of measurement, suggesting that these subscales might be shorter than the number relationships and measurement subscales.

These features of score reports for individual students can be carried through to reports for groups of students such as classrooms, schools and school, districts. Many of the same features are incorporated into group reports with the reporting value generally being a group mean, group standard error, or a group percentage when classification categories are employed.

Research on Test Score Reporting and Interpretation

Previous research on score reporting and test interpretation is modest in scope and detail compared to research on other topics that the measurement and psychometric communities have explored. Such research as exists, however, presents a fairly consistent picture of the ineffectiveness of score reports to communicate meaningful information to various stakeholder groups.

A valuable recent resource for educators interested in the score reports and test interpretation is provided by Goodman and Hambleton (2004) in "Student Test Score Reports and Interpretive Guides: Review of Current Practices and Suggestions for Future Research." Much of the research review below is taken from this work and the Goodman and Hambleton study is reviewed in detail as well.

The review of the research related to score reports begins with a summary of the literature review as presented by Goodman and Hambleton (2004). This research summary is followed by a discussion of three studies that include a state-level case, a national panel review, and the study by Goodman and Hambleton (2004). There is considerable consistency in the findings concerning score reports across these four sources.

Research Review Summary and Trends

The major finding of this review is that many users of assessment data have difficulty interpreting and understanding results presented in large-scale assessment reports. This general conclusion is based on Hambleton (2002), Hambleton and Slater (1997), Impara, Divine, Bruce,

Liverman, and Gay (1991), Jaeger (1998), the NEGP (1998), the National Research Council (NRC, 2001), and Wainer, Hambleton, and Meara (1999), as cited in Goodman and Hambleton (2004).

This conclusion is based on research reviews that focused substantially on the National Assessment of Educational Progress (NAEP) score reporting approaches and formats which present group-based results. Goodman and Hambleton assert, however, that "...many findings and principles that have emerged from this research are relevant to student-level score reports..." (2004, p. 149). The results of this work clearly apply to the general issues of providing informative and useful score reports for individual students and other levels of score reporting. Among the problems seen in score reports as critiqued in this literature are the following (Goodman & Hambleton, 2004, p. 149):

- Reports assumed an inappropriately high level of statistical knowledge.
- Statistical jargon confused and even intimidated some users.
- Technical terms, symbols, and concepts were required to understand the message underlying even simple data.
- Technical symbols were misunderstood or ignored by many users of the reports.
- Too much information made it difficult for readers to find and extract what they really wanted to know.
- The inclusions of overly dense displays were challenging to those reading the reports.
- Graphical alternatives to textual and tabular formats were not used often enough.
- Increased clutter or perceptual inaccuracies sometimes occurred when displays were redesigned for easy access (e.g., using three-dimensional bar and pie charts).
- Reports lacked descriptive information (e.g., definitions and concrete examples) that would have helped provide meaning to the assessment results.

Goodman and Hambleton also report a set of general principles that they have extracted from recent literature of score reporting that they cite in their work and this includes Hambleton (2002), Hambleton and Slater (1997), Jaeger (1998), NRC (2001), Snodgrass and Salzman (2002), Wainer (1997a), Wainer et al. (1999), and Ysseldyke and Nelson (2002). The literature cited by Goodman and Hambleton relating to the visual display of quantitative information include Tufte (1983, 1990), Tukey (1990), Wainer (1990, 1992, 1997b), and Wainer and Thissen (1981). The principles seen in the literature include the following (Goodman & Hambleton, 2004, p. 150):

- Making the report readable, concise, and visually attractive;
- Keeping the presentation clear, simple, and uncluttered;
- Not trying to do too much with a data display (i.e., displays should be designed to satisfy a small number of preestablished purposes);
- Including text to support and improve the interpretation of charts and tables;
- Minimizing the use of statistical jargon;
- Including a glossary of key terms;
- Using bar charts to facilitate comparisons;
- Grouping data in meaningful ways;
- Using boxes or graphics to highlight main findings;
- Avoiding the use of decimals;
- Using color in a purposeful manner (given the potential for misuse, however, the general use of color was not universally recommended);
- Piloting the reports with members of the intended audience; and
- Creating specially designed reports for different audiences.

A State-Level Case Study

Forte Fast and Tucker (2001) describe a very useful and informative four-stage process for reviewing and redesigning the reporting system for the Connecticut Mastery Test program that could be applied in any number of settings. Stage one involved a review of the state's existing state assessment reports and state and federal reporting requirements. Stage two extended the study to a review of assessment reports from other states. A very effective stage three involved a series of focus group meetings held around the state that included parents, teachers, and administrators. In stage four, information from all sources was used to redesign the student, classroom, school, district, and state reports.

In the focus groups, Forte Fast and Tucker (2001) reported the comments of different groups who were asked to respond to different score reports. This approach is, in itself, an important model because it shows that the expectations and needs of different groups must be considered when examining the effectiveness of different score reports. In this study, parents and teachers reviewed individual student reports; teachers and administrators reviewed classroom-level summaries and diagnostic reports; and school and district administrators reviewed school, district, and statewide reports.

The comments offered by different stakeholder groups examining different reports provide ideas and suggestions for designing test reporting documents and systems more responsive to the needs of the respective intended audiences. One important outcome of the study demonstrated the value of asking intended audiences about the reports that they were most likely to use. The groups in this study had specific suggestions about the reports intended for their use. More generally, the results of this study, looking across the various levels of reporting, reflect the need for assessment program designers to consider issues within the following broad categories of assessment report features:

- format features (e.g., type face, font size, bold, use of color, general layout);
- graphical displays;
- numeric displays;
- normative information;
- detail and specificity (especially about strengths and weaknesses);
- support materials;
- glossary of terms;
- directions to supplementary information; and
- easily reproduced materials.

National Review Panel

The NEGP (1998) provided suggestions about how states could more effectively communicate with parents about state standards and state assessment programs and how state score reports could be enhanced (Goodman & Hambleton, 2004). The NEGP report provides a number of useful suggestions about how schools could work more effectively with parents. Of special interest is the use of a focus group employed in the NEGP study in much the same way as the focus groups in the Fort Fast and Tucker (2001) project. The NEGP focus group was composed of 11 parents from across the United States and was used to gather information about what parents like and dislike about various score reports. In the focus group, parents were asked to review and comment on six individual student reports produced by commercial test publishers. The results of this study, as described in Goodman and Hambleton (2004), show the following. In general, parents involved in the study:

- appreciated explanations of what the scores on the test meant;
- liked to be able to tell at a glance how their child performed;

- liked to see subtest scores and descriptions of the skills assessed by the test; and
- appreciated learning what could be done to improve a student's score.

Parents did not like reports that:

- were too technical (e.g., containing statistical jargon and complex definitions);
- did not give recommendations on what they should do with the test results; and
- used small fonts that made parts of the reports difficult to read.

This study provided results that are informative and consistent with other research on score reporting. Of particular importance, again, is the use of a parent focus group as the basic data collection procedures. It seems increasingly clear that there is considerable value in asking stakeholder groups to review drafts and prototypes of score reports that will eventually be used to supply them test result information and on the basis of which they may be expected to take action.

A Review and Analysis of State, Commercial, and Canadian Province Score Reports

Goodman and Hambleton (2004) presented a study that examined the score reports from 11 states, three testing companies, and two Canadian province-wide assessments. The study focused on score reports for individual students and began with an iterative content analysis to review, analyze, and summarize each of the student reports. A category coding system was created to address the key features of the score reports taken as a group.

The synopsis of the major findings of the Goodman and Hambleton study follow the general outline of their report. The information presented below is taken directly from their report with minor rephrasing and reorganization.

Features That Make Score Reports More Readable

The review of the score reports show that certain features of the reports seem to make them more readable, and include the following:

- using headings and other devices, such as boxes, lines, white space, and perhaps color to organize reports;
- using a highlights section that provides readers with an overall summary of results;
- using graphical displays to draw readers' attention to major results showing how students performed overall or on major components of the test; and
- designing reports for specific audiences to meet the different needs of different groups.

Personalized Score Reports

Several score reports examined by Goodman and Hambleton employed the strategy of personalizing reports by using the student's first name in several places in the report. This seems to be a useful score report feature, but it does require an accurate name file that can be sorted and matched with a report data file. The results should look like more than just a name dropped into a fixed space by accommodating names of different lengths.

Features That Appear to Add Meaning for Intended Users of Student Score Reports

A major point of studying score reports is to develop reports that are understandable to those who read and use them. The score reports reviewed show a number of design features that make reports more meaningful to students, parents and teachers. Goodman and Hambleton report the following:

- describing the skills and knowledge assessed by the test;
- describing the expected levels of performance on the test through well-defined performance levels;
- describing the skills and knowledge a student possesses or does not yet possess through use of performance levels or diagnostic information such as subdomain results and descriptions of specific strengths or weaknesses of particular students;
- reporting the results of relevant comparison groups (e.g., other students in the school, district, and state; and,
- reporting results in multiple ways (e.g., using numbers, graphics, and narrative text).

Reporting Results in Relation to Performance Levels

Following the approach that evolved with the NAEP program and are embedded in the *No Child Left Behind* act, state assessment programs have performance standards that define various achievement levels. The findings of Goodman and Hambleton show that there are several important features of score reports that present the results of students' performance in relation to the performance levels, including the following:

- providing a general description of the performance levels;
- displaying results graphically with accompanying text;
- presenting some form of normative information such as the percent of students at different performance levels for a school, district or the state;
- showing or reporting how close a student is in achieving different performance levels; and
- providing information about errors of measurement when reporting students' performance levels.

All of these features are seen as providing more meaningful information about students' performance in relation to various performance levels. The concern about information regarding precision or standard errors of measurement is of particular interest. There are several aspects of the performance level reporting approach in which precision is relevant. Certainly, knowing the standard errors of measurement for the measurement instruments and for any subset of items such as a subdomain or strand is critical. In addition, precision in the classification of students might also be reported. The classification consistency for a single test administration can be estimated using the procedures of Huynh (1976, 1978). Finally, if students are assigned to achievement levels for different content strands for the purposes of identifying strengths and weaknesses, then the reliability or precision of the differences in strand level performance should be investigated and reported.

Reporting Diagnostic Information—Subdomain (Strand) Scores

State assessment programs are generally established for two purposes: instructional support and accountability. The instructional support function suggests that assessment programs provide diagnostically useful information to teachers and other educators that can be used to review and revise school programs. The diagnostic information from state assessments takes the form of subdomain or strand-level information. In mathematics, for example, common subdomains or strands include numbers and operations, geometry, algebra, measurement, patterns and functions, and data analysis and probability.

Goodman and Hambleton found that most large-scale assessment programs provide strand-level information in the form of raw scores, percent-correct scores, or percentile scores. Another common metric for reporting strand-level performance is the use of scale scores. Additional meaning can be added to students' strand-level information by reporting some form of comparative information, such as district or state performance on the strands.

Providing information about the precision of the measurement at the strand level is an often neglected but critical feature essential in interpreting the results. The reliability of strand-level performance is examined in detail later in this chapter. Reporting performance on the strands is often the basis for developing a profile of strengths and weakness for a student, for example, the student is stronger in certain strands and weaker in others. Such interpretations invite inferences about differences in strand-level performance and in such cases the precision of the differences should become a matter of concern.

Limitations and Weaknesses of Score Reports

In their summary, Goodman and Hambleton observe that although many features of the score reports they studied seem useful and others are promising, certain weaknesses or potential weaknesses were noted, including the following:

- Excessive amounts of information (e.g., multiple types of comparable scores) were included in some reports and essential pieces of information (e.g., the purpose of the test, information about how the results will be and should be used) were not provided in others.
- In many instances, information regarding the precision of test scores is not provided, making the results appear more accurate than they are.
- Although not widespread, statistical jargon such as *standard errors, NCE scores*, and *Lexile scores* were present in more than a few reports.
- Key terms, including the critical performance levels, were not always defined in the reports or interpretive guides, leaving the interpretations up to users, many of whom may be unaware of the proper interpretations to be made.
- Efforts to report a large amount of information in a small physical space resulted in reports and interpretive guides that appeared dense and cluttered. Small font size was a common cause of concern across many reports and guides.

General Recommendations for Score Reporting

Based on their review, Goodman and Hambleton offered the following recommendations for designing score reports.

- Score reports should be clear, concise, and visually attractive.
- Score reports should include easy-to-read text that supports and improves the interpretation of charts and tables.
- Care should be taken to not try to do too much with a data display (i.e., displays should be designed to satisfy a small number of preestablished purposes).
- Devices such as boxes and graphics should be used to highlight main findings.
- Data should be grouped in meaningful ways.
- Small fonts, footnotes, and statistical jargon should be avoided.
- Key terms should be defined, preferably within a glossary.
- Reports should be piloted with members of the intended audience.
- Consideration should be given to the creation of specially designed reports that cater to the particular needs of different users.

Discussion and Conclusions

There is no simple summary of features and formats that make score reports informative and meaningful for various stakeholder groups. The Goodman and Hambleton summary, and the research literature summary they provide, contain the listing of about every score report feature that has been identified as affecting score report interpretation. These summaries of score report strengths and weaknesses and the general principles for score report design should be used at the planning, development, and pilot testing stages when score reports are being conceptualized, designed, and first drafted.

The review of score reporting literature and practice reveals the use of focus groups to evaluate various score reports designed for different audiences. The use of parent, teacher, and community focus groups to pilot test score report is recommended as a valuable step in developing informative and useful score reports. It seems reasonable to recommend field testing score reports with their intended audiences in much the same way that test items and tests are thoroughly reviewed and field tested before being used.

Finally, it is important to be clear that this review of score reporting literature and practices does not address the actual use of score reports. The review reports what researchers and practitioners thought and said about various score reports, not how users of the reports interpreted the data or what practitioners actually did with them. A different line of research might involve researchers visiting schools and school district offices to observe and interview students, teachers, district personnel, and parents. The purpose of such research would be to describe how the information in various score reports was interpreted and actually used in schools and school districts.

THE SOUTH CAROLINA/SERVE STUDY OF SCORE REPORTING FORMATS

A study of score reporting formats was conducted in a collaborative project that included the South Carolina Department of Education's Office of Assessment, SERVE, and this chapter's author. The study was supported with a grant from the National Science Foundation. In this study, a three-stage process was used to collect information about what educators wanted to see in score reports provided in the state assessment program. The first stage employed a focus group that was inductive in nature and asked participants to respond to two very broad, open-ended questions. In stage two, the results of this first focus group were synthesized with guidelines suggested by the review of the measurement literature and by models for score reporting from other settings. The synthesis led to the construction of six prototype score report formats. The third stage employed a focus group that was deductive in nature and asked participants to respond to specific questions about the six prototype report formats.

What Are Educators Looking for in Score Reports?

Focus Group 1

Participants in the first focus group were selected by state department administrators and staff to include educators representing different types of schools, regions of the state, constituencies, and educational perspectives. The fourteen participants were very experienced with the state assessment program, Palmetto Achievement Challenge Tests (PACT), and included teachers, district and state curriculum coordinators, and district and state research and assessment directors and specialists. After an orientation to the session and the study, participants were asked to consider and discuss the following questions:

- What information from PACT assessments reported at the district, school, and classroom levels would be most helpful in developing curriculum and planning instruction?
- What should PACT assessment reports contain and look like to be most useful at the school and district levels?

These questions were intentionally open ended to encourage participants to offer their own ideas rather than asking them to react or respond to ideas or suggestions from the Department of Education or the researcher.

Discussion Procedures

Participants discussed the focus questions in two subgroups arranged to be representative of the group as a whole. The conversations in both subgroups were lively and all members of the groups participated actively. Certain common themes emerged quite clearly and quickly in both subgroups. Participants recorded ideas, issues, or suggestions on a response form supplied for this purpose. After participants made their individual notes, they shared their comments and common themes and issues were identified and recorded.

Major Findings

Two major substantive themes emerged from a review of the participant's comments. The participants saw a need for greater specificity in reporting students' performance and the need for more meaningful substantive descriptions of what scores and achievement levels indicate students know and can do.

Six Prototype Score Reports and Their Evaluation

The results of the first focus group indicated the need for more specificity in reporting students' performance and more meaningful substantive descriptions of scores and achievement levels. These findings were synthesized with guidelines from a review of the measurement literature, with examples of score reporting from other settings and with an understanding of the local program and its history. This synthesis led to the development of six prototype score reports. These were not complete and final versions of score reports but presented format and content elements that could be incorporated into an operational score report. Versions of these score report components were prepared using archival data from the state assessment program and a second focus group was convened to evaluate the six prototype score reports.

Participants and Procedures

The second focus group session with South Carolina educators was used to review and evaluate the prototype score reporting strategies and formats. The membership of the first focus group was expanded to 21 participants for this second session and included educators with backgrounds similar to those in this first group. A set of explanatory materials was developed for each score reporting strategy and format. These materials contained a description of each strategy the researcher used to explain the strategy to focus group participants. An example of each reporting format was also provided to the participants.

Participants were charged with the specific tasks of reviewing the six approaches to score reporting. Participants were asked to review each of the six prototypes and discuss and answer the following questions for each approach:

- Will a school or school district find this information helpful?
- How could a school or school district use this information?
- Could this information be modified to be more informative or useful?
- How can this information be best presented?
- Might there be any problems in how this information is used?

The researcher presented each of the six score reporting strategies and an example of the report format. Participants were invited to ask questions and discuss the material. Participants reviewed each reporting strategy and format individually and wrote comments and suggestions about the strategy on the comment sheet provided. They then discussed each strategy and format in one of three subgroups and recorded the common observations on flip charts. These flip chart results were transcribed as the primary data for the evaluation. The whole group then reconvened to review and discuss the major findings of each subgroup as recorded on the flip charts and in individuals' notes.

In addition to the qualitative focus group data, quantitative ratings were collected to determine the focus group's evaluation of the usefulness of the six reporting strategies and formats. Each participant rated the strategies at two times in the review process—after the facilitator had described all of the procedures but before any group discussion, and then again at the end of the entire focus group process. Participants applied the rating scale from two perspectives for each score reporting strategy. The first ratings were completed from the perspective of a classroom teacher and the second ratings were from the perspective of a district administrator. The details of the quantitative rating scale and the results are presented after the results of the focus group are presented.

Item Content Objective Mapping

The first reporting format examined was a graphical mapping of items referred to in the study as an *item content objective map*. Such figures are also known as *item maps* or *variable maps* (Wright & Stone, 1979; Wright & Masters, 1982). An example of an item content objective map is shown in Figure 29.4. The strategy presents a rectangular graphical display in which the vertical axis represents the measurement scale reported in the scale–score metric. The achievement level at each cut score is shown on the vertical scale. The scale is divided into four groups, namely *below basic, basic, proficient*, and *advanced*. The horizontal axis is used to locate the strands as nominal categorical variables. At each strand location, the items that measure that strand are shown by locating the items' positions on the vertical scale-score difficulty dimension and providing a brief (one- or two-word) description.

Focus Group Evaluation. The comments of the focus group to this approach were mixed, with many of the same participants providing comments about pros, cons, and ways to improve the item mapping approach. The positive comments recorded by the participants on their worksheets and subgroup summary forms in response to the item content objective mapping strategy include such comments as, "Provides a ranking of scores from easy to difficult with specific reference to the cut points"; "Could be valuable for determinations of staff development priorities"; "I like this because it tells you a lot about how the test works. Even if the questions change every year it gives you something to go on..."; "Provides a content-based context for assessment interpretation"; and "The concept of associating scale score performance with strands/content." The major substantive value seems to be that the assessment results are connected or embedded into the curriculum as represented by the strands and the item-level

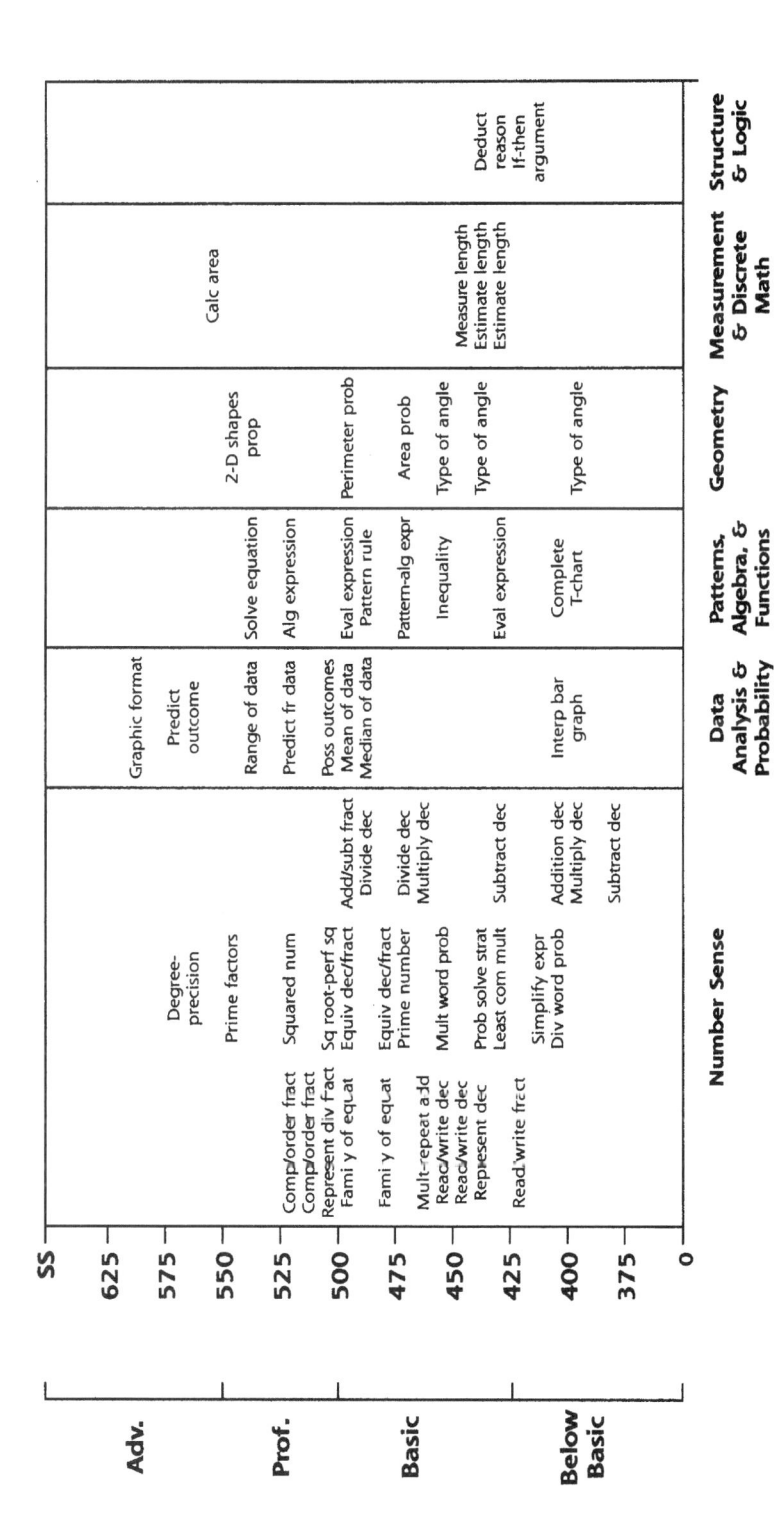

SS	Number Sense	Data Analysis & Probability	Patterns, Algebra, & Functions	Geometry	Measurement & Discrete Math	Structure & Logic
625						
Adv. 575	Degree-precision					
550	Prime factors	Graphic format				
525	Squared num	Predict outcome			Calc area	
Prof. 500	Sq root-perf sq Equiv dec/fract	Range of data Predict fr data	Solve equation Alg expression			
475	Add/subt fract Divide dec	Poss outcomes Mean of data Median of data	Eval expression Pattern rule	2-D shapes prop		
450	Equiv dec/fract Prime number		Pattern-alg expr	Perimeter prob		
Basic 425	Divide dec Multiply dec		Inequality	Area prob Type of angle		
	Mult-repeat add Read/write dec		Eval expression	Type of angle	Measure length Estimate length Estimate length	
400	Represent dec					
Below Basic 375	Read/write fract	Subtract dec	Complete T-chart	Type of angle		Deduct reason If-then argument
	Simplify expr Div word prob	Interp bar graph				
	Addition dec Multiply dec					
0	Subtract dec					

FIG. 29.4. Example of item content objective map.

codes and the descriptors. The connection between the cut scores, scale scores, and content is also seen as a useful aspect of this score reporting approach.

Focus group participants expressed a number of concerns in evaluating the item content objective mapping strategy. Participants were concerned with the ability of teachers, parents, and others to correctly interpret graphically presented information. The group discussed the strategy of plotting on the vertical axis items based on their difficulty and students based on ability such that students had a 0.50 probability of answering an item correctly if they were on the same level as the item on the graph. A number of participants familiar with the NAEP achievement levels approach felt that a higher response probability would be more appropriate. Finally, the item map used in the focus group was based on a single field test form and not all content standards are represented on each form. The group was concerned that the omission of some standards on a particular map might lead educators to ignore instructional attention to eligible content standards because they happened not to be represented on one particular test.

Focus group participants had a number of suggestions about how the item map approach could be improved. The group suggested developing more complete narrative descriptors and training exercises to accompany the item map approach. They saw the need for an additional cut line subdividing the below basic category. The group discussed the suggestion of a high-tech version of the item map with item map score reports available electronically on the web. Such maps could have an interface with several databases that could be accessed by clicking on the items on the map elements. The interface could provide such information as elaborated definitions of the content standard with examples, sample items that could be used to assess the standard, curricular and instructional resource materials, and connections to other useful web-based materials.

The response of the focus group participants to the use of an item content objective mapping approach for reporting assessment results can be characterized as "shows promise, has some potential, but needs work." The value of such an approach seems to lie primarily in the way it integrates assessment results with content standards. Concerns about this approach seemed to focus around three questions.

First, what aggregation of items should be mapped? The map reviewed by the focus group represented a single test form, but several test forms or an entire bank of items could be plotted on the map. Second, what response probability should be used in plotting the items? A response probability of 0.50 was used in this study but in other applications a response probability of 0.67 or even higher is often used. The response probability of 0.50 seems appropriate for information provided to teachers for the purpose of informing instructional decisions. In contrast, a response probability of 0.67 or higher would align students' scores with content objectives for which additional instruction might not be necessary because the students had already shown a level of attainment (0.67 or higher) that suggests content mastery. A response probability of 0.67 or higher seems appropriate for information provided to educators, parents, and other stake holders for the purpose of accountability and program auditing. A third question raised in the focus group discussion was what types of interpretative materials and professional development opportunities would be needed to help users of the reports in the assessment system interpret the information correctly? However useful the item content objective mapping approach may or may not be, materials and training support for any new reporting system were seen as essential.

Achievement Performance Level Narrative

The *achievement performance level narrative* approach involves developing a narrative that describes the content and content demands at each achievement level. This approach is

> **Third Grade Mathematics Achievement Level Descriptions**
>
> *Below Basic*
> Third-grade students scoring at the "Below Basic" level are able to estimate and perform basic operations with whole numbers. They can identify simple number sentences and expressions, simple patterns, and common two-and three-dimensional geometric figures and geometric properties. The student at the "Below Basic" level can read tables and answer questions based on data contained in the tables as long as the questions require no more than simple computations.
>
> Students scoring at the "Below Basic" level tend to be unable to solve multi-step problems and problems involving division. They tend to be weak in measurement. They also tend to have difficulty reading and interpreting scales and working with pictorial representations.
>
> **Basic**
> Third-grade students scoring at the "Basic" level are able to answer problems requiring more than one-step or operation, alternate between two different types of patterns, and apply straightforward concepts of probability. Their performance differs from the performance of students scoring at the "Below Basic" levels in the amount of data that can be handled, the number of steps required by the problem, the nature of the mathematics vocabulary, and the degree of reasoning required.
>
> Student scoring at the "Basic" level do not appear adept with measurement concepts such as reading and interpreting scales. They also have difficulty working with pictorial representations, fractions, and division.
>
> **Proficient**
> Third-grade students scoring at the "Proficient" level are able to interpret and translate pictorial representations. They exhibit an understanding of the concepts of fractions and division. They can apply straightforward measurement concepts. When units of a scale are marked, they are able to read and interpret scales. Students scoring at the "Proficient" level are able to translate language into numerical concepts.
>
> Students scoring at the "Proficient" level tend to have difficulty problem solving when required to use spatial sense.
>
> **Advanced**
> Third-grade students scoring at the "Advanced" level make connections among mathematic ideas and communicate their mathematical thinking and reasoning coherently and clearly. They have stronger spatial sense than other students. They are more tenacious than students at other levels in approaching problems that appear longer and/or more complex. They are able to tackle problems requiring approaches that are not commonly used.

FIG. 29.5. Example of an achievement level performance narrative for Grade 3 Mathematics.

most widely known through its use in the NAEP. Narrative descriptions are developed by first placing each item from a test into one of the four achievement level categories based on the item's difficulty. There is considerable discussion in the psychometric community about exactly which items should be considered exemplars and included as part of the narrative for the respective achievement levels (see Zwick, Senturk, Wang, & Loomis, 2001.)

In the South Carolina/SERVE study, items were reviewed from all test forms that had been given in the current assessment program in Grade 3 Mathematics and Grade 8 English/Language Arts. Performance level descriptions were based on items if students at the cut score for the performance level had approximately a 0.67 probability of answering the items correctly. The operational range for the response probability turned out to be 0.60 to 0.75 to identify a sufficient number of items. In addition, narratives were developed only if two or more items measuring a content objective were available so that no part of the achievement level description actually described the content of a single item. A content panel looked at items with lower and higher response probabilities for the strands and objectives in order to get a better sense of the substantive features involved. The staff of the Office of Assessment prepared the item data, and state department content experts prepared the achievement level descriptions. The achievement levels descriptions for Grade 3 Mathematics and Grade 8 English/Language Arts are shown in Figures 29.5 and 29.6 respectively.

> **Eighth Grade English/Language Arts Achievement Level Descriptions**
>
> **Below Basic**
> Eighth-grade students scoring at the "Below Basic" level are able to skim and locate obvious details using key words or phrases in passages that are of high interest to them. When the passage provides a stated main idea, the student at the "Below Basic" level is able to identify that main idea, and he or she is able to draw simple conclusions about the passage when the text provides obvious support for those conclusions.
>
> Eighth-grade students scoring at the "Below Basic" level tend to be unable to locate details in longer, denser passages. They tend to be unable to handle poetry, and they are unable to combine reading strategies in order to draw higher-level conclusions about the text they read.
>
> **Basic**
> Eighth-grade students scoring at the "Basic" level are able to locate details in longer passages and make simple inferences from informational and literary text that is of high interest. They are able to paraphrase the main idea, and they are able to provide literal interpretations in reading informational and literary text. Students scoring at the "Basic" level are able to combine strategies (e.g. locate details to make an inference) while reading, and they are able to recognize the literary elements (e.g., simile and point of view) first introduced during elementary school.
>
> Eighth-grade students scoring at the "Basic" level tend to have difficulty providing literal interpretations for poetry. They tend to have difficulty analyzing literary elements and figurative language that is introduced in middle school. They also tend to have difficulty in going beyond the text to answer constructed response questions or supporting their response with details.
>
> **Proficient**
> Eighth-grade students scoring at the "Proficient" level are able to make distinctions among and analyze details to make more complex inferences regarding the longer, denser informational, literary, and poetic text that they read. Eighth grade students scoring at the "Proficient" level are able to understand and analyze both literal and figurative language, and they are adept at interpreting and drawing conclusions in poetry. They are able to go beyond the text to answer constructed response to questions and tend to support their responses with details.
>
> Eighth-grade students scoring at the "Proficient" level tend to have trouble evaluating reading material, and their written responses, while accurate, tend not to be insightful and creative.
>
> **Advanced**
> Eighth-grade students scoring at the "Advanced" level are able to make fine distinctions among many details to make more complex inferences regarding the longer, denser informational, literary, and poetic text that they read. They are able to understand, analyze, and evaluate both literal and figurative language, and they are adept at interpreting and drawing conclusions in poetry. In addition, advanced students are able to provide detailed, complete, insightful, and creative answers to constructed questions relating to written text.

FIG. 29.6. Example of an achievement level performance narrative for Grade 8 English/Langusge Arts.

Focus Group Evaluation. The written comments in response to the achievement level descriptions were clearly and consistently quite positive, as were the oral comments during the discussion. The participants felt very strongly that this approach would be useful, informative, and helpful for teachers and principles, and especially helpful in communicating with parents and other members of the community. Focus group participants offered such comments as "Good communication tool for parent conferences"; "In general this is the most useful document for me as a principal"; and "Yes teachers will find useful. Teachers could use these narratives in talking with parents. Principals could use this in conjunction with test scores to focus on possible curriculum alignment and implementation in collaborative planning."

Concerns about this approach focused on the desire to have the descriptions more specific and more explicitly tied to the state content objectives. The group also observed that these narrative descriptions would only be as rich and detailed as the items on a test or in an item bank. Learning outcomes for which there were relatively few operational items would not be well described in the narrative.

The focus group participants were quite positive about the narrative description of achievement performance but, nevertheless, had a number of suggestions for improving this approach. The most frequent suggestion was to take the narrative and present it in bullet form. The description of Proficient Level for Grade 3 Mathematics in bullet form is shown below.

Third grade students scoring in the proficient level:

- are able to interpret and translate pictorial representations;
- exhibit an understanding of the concepts of fractions and division;
- can apply straightforward measurement concepts;
- are able to read and interpret scales when units of a scale are marked;
- are able to translate language into numerical concepts; and
- tend to have difficulty problem solving when required to use spatial sense.

The focus group members discussed the value of connecting instructionally related materials to each achievement level so that teachers and others could use the information in a diagnostic-prescriptive fashion. The group recognized that not all objectives would be represented in the description and referred to such objectives as showing "no pattern." They suggested providing a list of objectives that were tested but not represented in the narrative.

Strand Achievement Levels for Individual Students

The initial focus group that responded to general open-ended questions suggested that educators would find score reports useful if they showed students' achievement at the strand level in terms of the achievement level classifications of below basic (BB), basic (B), proficient (P), and advanced (A). Such an approach provides a finer level of detail that is often thought to have more diagnostic value than classifying students based on total test performance. All standardized tests designed for norm-referenced interpretations are reported at a level of detail finer than the total test score and educators seem accustomed to having such information.

Developing strand-level achievement reports involves interpolating cut scores from the total test level to each strand. In this study, the interpolation was done using the one-parameter Item Response Theory (IRT) model. The probability of a correct response to each item measuring a content strand was calculated using the IRT ability (θ) at the respective cut scores. With the one-parameter IRT model, the sum of these probabilities is the expected raw score on the strand for students at the cut score being evaluated. Students who take this test have an observed raw score on each strand and this observed strand-level score is compared to the expected strand-level cut scores to classify the student.

Several features of this approach were carefully explained to the focus group for their consideration before they began their discussion and evaluation of this procedure. Generally, the expected strand cut scores are not integers so the interpolated values are rounded to the nearest integer value and the rounding of the strand-level cut scores introduces some error. For some strands it is not possible to attain a level of "advanced" because there were not a sufficient number of items at the advanced level on that strand. Great care must be used when interpreting students' achievement levels on the strands.

The reliability of the strand scores is low and the standard error of measurement is large for the strands because of the relatively small number of items used on each strand. In many cases, the differences across strand scores for students are not statistically significant except when the lowest scores on one strand are compared to highest scores on another. Students' achievement level classification on the total test is not a simple sum or average of students' achievement levels classifications on the strands. Students with the same achievement level

Student ID	Total Test Level	Strand 1 Number & Operations Level	Strand 2 Algebra Level	Strand 3 Geometry Level	Strand 4 Measurement Level	Strand 6 Data Analysis & Probability Level
XXXXXX	BB	B	B	BB	BB	BB
XXXXXX	BB	BB	BB	BB	BB	BB
XXXXXX	B	B	B	B	BB	BB
XXXXXX	BB	BB	BB	BB	BB	BB
XXXXXX	BB	BB	BB	B	BB	BB
XXXXXX	B	B	B	P	BB	BB
XXXXXX	BB	BB	BB	BB	BB	BB

BB = Below Basic ; B = Basic ; P = Proficient

FIG. 29.7. Example of a strand achievement level report for individual students for Grade 3 Mathematics.

based on the total test could have different profiles of achievement level classifications on the strands. An example of the strand achievement level report that the focus group members examined is shown in Figure 29.7.

Focus Group Evaluation. There were some positive responses to reporting students' achievement level classification at the strand level. Several focus group participants felt that this kind of information might be appropriate for teachers, useful for schools, and informative for parents. These positive comments were offered despite the qualifications about reliability and the likelihood that some differences in classifications would be based on strand scores that were not significantly different. There were several other suggestions about the value of this approach, but these were generally qualified based on the technical shortcomings of the strand-level scores.

The focus group participants expressed a number of concerns about reporting individual student's achievement levels for each strand. The concerns focused on (1) its value or lack of value for teachers making instructional decisions; (2) the general nature of the information as being broad, misleading, and perhaps confusing; and (3) the lack of reliability in the classifications at the strand level. Comments like, "Too much room for bad decisions on this one"; "Too much room for misinterpretation"; and "Misleading information" were common.

Focus group participants had some mixed thoughts about the use of strand-level classifications but generally seemed to express reservation about this approach. The concerns expressed by the focus group reflected concerns about the reliability of the strand-level reports and these concerns may have been influenced by the facilitator comments during the exposition to the group on this method.

The concern about strand-level achievement reports generally relates to the lack of reliability at the strand level. The strands are relatively short and, therefore, likely to lack the reliability recommended for making inferences about students (AERA, APA, & NCME, 1999). The reliability of the strands was explored in detail in a follow-up study and the following brief summary of the results is quite revealing (see Ryan [2003] for details). Reporting students' performance on different content strands is done to allow comparisons of student achievement across strands. This approach is designed to support inferences that students are doing better or less well on some strands compared to others. It is critical to note that the inference that needs to be supported is an inference about differences between strands scores, not just inferences about scores on a strand.

The reliability estimates of the five strands in Grade 3 mathematics range from 0.44 for the 5-item data analysis and probability strand to 0.83 for the 10 items measuring number and operations. These strands are highly correlated and the reliability of the difference between these two strands is only 0.24. The 10 pairwise reliabilities for the differences between the 5 strands range from −0.06 (measurement compared to data analysis and probability) to a high of 0.35 (number and operations compared to geometry). Many of the reliabilities of the differences are numerically close to zero. Inferences about differential performance across strands are based on these pairwise difference and the reliabilities of these differences seem too low to allow for valid inferences about differential performance. In general, only the lowest one or two scores on one strand are significantly different from the highest one or two scores on another strand and for some of the shorter strands, no scores are different between strands.

The standard errors of the pairwise strand differences were used to construct confidence intervals around the differences. For example, the standard error for the difference between data analysis and probability and numbers and operations is 1.32 (in logits). A 95% confidence interval was constructed and the differences scores of the 44,000 students used in the study were examined. Only 8.8% of the students had differences in their performance (based on the common logit scale) on these two strands that exceeded the 95% confidence interval. Thus, only for these students are claims about differences in performance between these two strands supported by the reliability of the data. Any assertions about differences in strand performance for the remaining 91.2% of the students are unsupported.

The situation is even further complicated by recognizing the inappropriateness of using a 95% confidence interval to examine each pair of differences across a set of 10 pairwise comparisons. (With 5 strands, there are 10 paired comparisons.) If one wants an error rate of 0.05 across the set of the 10 paired comparisons, than the 0.05 testwise error rate must be adjusted to .005 (0.05/10 = .005) for each of the 10 paired comparisons. Using 0.005 to construct the confidence interval and examining the differential performance of the 44,000 students shows that the range of the differences does not exceed chance level for any student. Thus, the differences in students' performance on the data analysis and probability and numbers and operations strands cannot be significant for any students if the family-wise error rate of 0.05 is maintained. Very similar results as those summarized for Grade 3 Mathematics were found for Grade 8 Language Arts.

Strand Achievement Levels for Groups

Reporting strand achievement levels for groups of students is similar to the previously described approach applied to individual students except that data are aggregated by groups such as classroom, schools, districts, and state. A summary table is constructed showing the percentage of students in the below basic, basic, proficient, and advanced levels for each strand. Some of the same cautions as described for the individual approach apply to the group-based approach. The group-based statistics (proportions) are more stable; they reflect aggregates of students and the errors of measurement are likely random and balance out. In this study, it was not possible to attain a level of advanced for algebra because there was not a sufficient number of items at the advanced level for that strand. The example of this format reviewed by the focus group is shown in Figure 29.8.

Focus Group Evaluation. The response of the focus group to reporting strand performance of groups of students for various achievement levels was mixed. Positive sentiments suggest a value in examining relative strengths and weaknesses in students' learning for the

STRAND LEVEL INTERPRETATION OF ACHIEVEMENT LEVELS FOR GROUPS, SUCH AS SCHOOLS, SCHOOL DISTRICTS, AND THE STATE					
	1	2	3	4	5
Achievement Level	Total Test	Number & Operations	Algebra	Geometry	Measurement	Data Analysis & Probability
	%	%	%	%	%	%
Advanced	5.90	8.12	*	8.89	15.93	7.64
Proficient	13.44	11.43	27.13	13.89	13.92	18.77
Basic	34.12	41.02	23.90	32.93	16.48	26.10
Below Basic	46.55	39.43	48.97	44.29	53.68	47.49

*There were no Algebra items of sufficient difficulty to allow students to demonstrate advanced status on the strand.

FIG. 29.8. Example of strand achievement level performance report for Grade 3 Mathematics.

different strands. This was seen as useful because it helps to identify instructional weaknesses that occur across classrooms. Focus group participants thought this reporting format could provide a reliable picture of students' general strengths and weaknesses, and thus inform decisions about instruction and curriculum, as long as sufficiently large groups were involved.

The approach was seen as appropriate for relatively large schools but not for classrooms or even for a grade level in a small school. For large groups of students, aggregated across instructional units such as schools or grades, the diagnostic value was seen as limited because it would not be clear which particular students in a group showing a deficiency in a particular strand might be most in need of assistance.

The comments of the group indicate that the information at the strand level is still too broad to provide teachers and others with specific information about strengths and weaknesses, even for a large group. In addition, the comments suggest a belief that the approach is viable in terms of reliability for only relatively larger aggregations of students such as school districts, possibly schools, and grade levels in large schools.

Item- and Strand-Level Reporting of Differences Between Observed and Expected Group Performance

South Carolina once used item-level reporting showing the proportion of students in a school, district, and the state who answered each item correctly. A variation of this type of item-level reporting was developed for review in this study because of the state history with item reporting and because of the first focus group's request for as much specificity as possible. The approach compared how a group of students did on each item compared to their predicted or expected performance.

This reporting approach employs a group's mean IRT ability (based on mean raw score) and the IRT difficulty values of the items based on statewide data. The IRT-based probability of a correct response, given an item's difficulty and the group's mean ability, was used as an estimate of the proportion of students in a group expected to answer an item correctly. The observed proportion answering correctly was calculated from the actual response data and the difference between the observed and expected proportions was calculated. The differences were reported by item within strand and means for each strand were also reported. In this analysis, each group is, in effect, acting as its own control.

Part of the example of a district-level report used in the focus group discussion was based on information generated from this strategy (Figure 29.9). The items in the example were

Strand	Item#	Item Description	District's Observed Percent Correct	District's District's Percent Correct	Difference from Expected
Strand 1: Number and Operation	D1 - 08		42	36	6
	D1 - 15		76	78	−2
	D1 - 01		51	52	−1
	D1 - 09		72	70	2
	D1 - 07		28	24	4
	D1 - 06		55	52	3
	D1 - 05		34	25	9
	D1 - 03		69	69	0
	D1 - 02		90	95	−5
Mean			**57**	**55**	**2**
Strand 2: Algebra	D1 - 16		93	94	−1
	D1 - 04		58	59	−1
	D1 - 11		74	75	−1
	D1 - 12		72	75	−3
	D1 - 13		76	78	−2
	D1 - 14		66	64	2
	D1 - 10		55	55	0
Mean			**71**	**71**	**−1**

FIG. 29.9. Portion of sample report for the observed, expected, and differences of strand and item performance strategy for a district.

not listed in the order on the test but were grouped by strand. The level of detail in the item descriptions turned out to be of great interest to the focus group but was left blank in the example.

Focus Group Evaluation. The first comment by a participant during the open discussion of this reporting format was this: "This is a formula for mediocrity." Although a bit harsh, it expresses the concern that a school or district might have item-level performance in line with expectations but the performance could still be quite low. The possibility that such "on-level" performance might lead to complacency was clearly a major concern of the group. In addition, some expressed concern that the information would be too difficult to explain and subject to misinterpretation. The group suggested that the addition of a column reporting the percent of students statewide who answered each item correctly could provide a normative comparison. With the inclusion of statewide data, a district could see that students might be achieving as expected but were still performing below the state level. The importance of careful descriptions of what is being measured by each item and strand emerged again as being valued by the participants. Numerous suggestions and comments were made indicating that the value of this approach would be related to the clarity and detail with which the item descriptions were written.

Observed, Expected, and Differences in Strand/Item Performance at the Achievement Level Cut Scores

The reporting approach just described involves comparing a group's performance on the item to the performance that would be expected based on their overall average score on the test. The final approach reviewed is similar except that it compares a group's performance on the items to the performance expected by students at each cut score. The IRT ability at each cut score and the IRT item difficulties were combined in the IRT model to estimate the probability that students with ability at the level of each cut score would correctly answer each item on the test. This probability was used as an estimate of the proportion of students at each cut score expected to answer the items correctly. The proportion of students at each cut score expected to answer the item correctly was then compared to the observed proportion of students in a district who actually answered the items correctly. The differences between these expected and observed proportions are the proportions of district students who did more or less well than students at the respective cut scores. A portion of the example of this type of score report used in the focus group is shown as Figure 29.10.

This strategy can be interpreted as reporting how well a district is doing on each item relative to students at each achievement level cut score. This tells districts how far they have to go to reach each standard or how far above each standard their students perform. To facilitate interpretation, the items are ordered by strand and strand-level means are reported. The level of detail in the item descriptions is critical and, at the minimum, the objective that each item measures should be identified.

Focus Group Evaluation. The focus group's evaluation of this approach was generally positive, but accompanied by many questions and some misgivings. The questions and many suggestions offered all dealt with the nature and level of detail in the item descriptions. As seen with other score reporting approaches, the group was using the level of detail and substantive nature of the descriptions as a critical evaluative criterion. The greater the details and substance, the more the group said they would like the approach. Several participants suggested that the item formats be identified, at least indicating if the item employed a constructed or selected-response format. In general, the focus group saw this approach as useful for school districts and large schools. Concerns about the complexity of this report, the difficulty involved in explaining it properly, and the possibility of misinterpretation were expressed.

Rating of the Reporting Strategies

In addition to the qualitative aspects of the focus group evaluation, participants in the second focus group were asked to rate each of the six reporting formats in terms of its usefulness at the school and district levels. They completed the rating scale twice, once after the facilitator had described all of the procedures but before any group discussion and sharing took place, and then again at the end of the entire focus group process.

Participants applied the rating scale from two perspectives for each score reporting strategy. The first ratings were completed from the perspective of a classroom teacher and the second ratings were from the perspective of a district administrator. In completing the rating, participants were directed to consider the following questions:

- Will a school or school district find this information helpful?
- How could a school or school district use this information?
- Could this information be modified to be more informative or useful?
- How can this information be best presented?
- Might there be any problems in how this information is used?

Participants rated all of the item mapping/score reporting strategies on a scale of 1 through 4, where:

1 = No use to educators
2 = Limited use to educators
3 = Considerable use to educators
4 = Very useful to educators

Strand	Item#	Item Description	District Observed Percent Correct	State Expected Percent at Basic	State Expected Percent at Proficient	State Expected Percent at Advanced	District Percent Above/Below at Basic	District Percent Above/Below at Proficient	District Percent Above/Below at Advanced
Strand 1: Number & Operations	D1-08		42	41	71	85	1	-29	-43
	D1-15		76	81	94	97	-5	-18	-21
	D1-01		51	58	83	92	-7	-32	-41
	D1-09		72	75	91	96	-3	-19	-24
	D1-07		28	27	57	75	1	-29	-47
	D1-06		55	58	83	92	-3	-28	-37
	D1-05		34	14	30	39	20	4	-5
	D1-03		69	74	91	96	-5	-22	-27
	D1-02		90	94	98	99	-4	-8	-9
Mean			**57**	**58**	**78**	**86**	**-1**	**-20**	**-28**
Strand 2 Algebra	D1-16		93	47	49	50	46	44	43
	D1-04		58	65	87	94	-7	-29	-36
	D1-11		74	79	93	97	-5	-19	-23
	D1-12		72	79	93	97	-7	-21	-25
	D1-13		76	81	94	97	-5	-18	-21
	D1-14		66	70	89	95	-4	-23	-29
	D1-10		55	61	85	93	-6	-30	-38
Mean			**71**	**69**	**84**	**89**	**2**	**-14**	**-18**

FIG. 29.10. Portion of sample report based on the observed, expected, and differences in the strand and item performance strategy at the cut scores.

Item Mapping/Reporting Strategy	Classroom Teacher				District Administrator/Coord.			
	N	L	C	V	N	L	C	V
1. Graphical Mapping	1	2	3	4	1	2	3	4
2. Narrative Description	1	2	3	4	1	2	3	4
3. Strand Level—Individual	1	2	3	4	1	2	3	4
4. Strand Level—Groups	1	2	3	4	1	2	3	4
5. Observed vs. Expected, Same Group	1	2	3	4	1	2	3	4
6. Observed vs. Expected at Cut Scores	1	2	3	4	1	2	3	4

FIG. 29.11. Focus group form for rating score reporting formats.

TABLE 29.4
Mean Ratings of the Reporting Strategies

Reporting Strategy	Before Discussions		After Discussions		Overall Mean (Rank)
	Teacher/School	District	Teacher/School	District	
1. Item Content Objective Mapping	3.00	2.94	2.82	2.94	2.93 (2)
2. Achievement Level Narrative	3.25	3.00	3.12	3.00	3.09 (1)
3. Strand Level—Individual	2.13	1.87	1.41	1.47	1.72 (6)
4. Strand Level—Groups	2.44	3.13	1.93	2.75	2.56 (4)
5. Observed, Expected—Same Group	2.13	2.67	2.19	2.47	2.37 (5)
6. Observed, Expected—Cut Scores	2.27	3.00	2.87	3.19	2.83 (3)
Mean	2.54	2.77	2.39	2.64	

The focus group members were asked to complete the form first from the perspective of the classroom or classroom teacher and then again from the perspective of a school district administrator or coordinator. The rating response portion of the form that was used is shown below in Figure 29.11.

Rating Scale Results. The mean ratings for the six reporting formats are shown in Table 29.4. These data provide a different way to examine the focus groups' opinions about the six score reporting formats. Statistical tests of difference were intentionally not performed to avoid overinterpretation of the results based on a purposefully selected volunteer sample. Results of the ratings include the following findings.

- **Strategy 2,** the achievement performance level narrative approach received the highest mean rating overall and this reporting strategy was generally rated higher than the other strategies before and after discussion.
- **Strategy 1,** the item content objective mapping approach, received the next highest ratings.
- **Strategy 6** was rated as being considerably more useful to educators than Strategy 5. Strategy 6 involves reporting the differences between how group of students did on each item (observed performance) and the expected performance for students at the achievement level cut scores. Strategy 5 involves the observed and expected performance of the same group with no comparison to other groups.
- The mean of **Strategy 6** increased from the first to the second rating whereas, in general, the ratings declined after the focus group discussions.

- **Strategy 3,** the strand achievement levels approach for individual students, was rated as having no use or limited use to educators.

DISCUSSION AND CONCLUSIONS

The purpose of this chapter was to review and evaluate various approaches to score reporting that can be used to present students' test scores in ways that are as informative and helpful to students, parents, and educators as possible. This project studied the features and formats of score reports that increase their value to educators for identifying students' strengths and weakness and for supporting accountability programs. The chapter included a review of assessment reporting research literature and practices. This review was followed by a presentation of the South Carolina/SERVE field-based study of score reporting formats. A brief summary and discussion of the major findings of this chapter is presented below, followed by a discussion of several other related issues.

The Review of Score Report Research and Practices

The review of assessment reporting research and practices revealed that many educators have difficulty interpreting score reports from large scale assessment programs. The review identified a wide range of features in score reports that can be manipulated to make score reports more informative and user friendly. This summary examines two features of score reports: basic content and format, language, and display features.

Basic Content of a Score Report

In general, the score reports should be related as closely and explicitly as possible to the content standards the assessment is designed to examine. It is valuable to report at the finest level of detail or smallest assessment unit for which reliable information can be presented. The finest level of detail is the test item, then content clusters such as strands (e.g., subscales or subdomains), and then the total test.

Whereas it is essential to report results in relation to content standards, it is critical to present results in relation to performance standards as well. There are a variety of procedures for reporting scores in relation to performance cut scores and performance levels. The important feature is that a reader has a way to know where the score is located relative to performance level cut score or interval.

Many practitioners found some form of normative information useful in understanding assessment results. Locating students in achievement levels and reporting percentages of students at these levels for a school, district, or state serves this purpose. Traditional norm-referenced reporting such as percentiles can also be considered. The reliability or precisions of all score results should be reported. Reliability is related to the level of reporting and as the level of reporting becomes smaller (e.g., moves from groups to individuals, from total test to strands and items) the reliability of individual scores becomes lower. Thus, at the smaller levels of reporting, it is increasingly unwise and misleading to report individual scores and more appropriate to report scores of groups of students. Performance-referenced reporting should included information about the precision or reliability of the classification. In summary, a score report should:

- be related to content standards as clearly and explicitly and as possible;
- be reported in relation to performance standards;

- include some form of normative information;
- be reported at the finest level of detail for which reliable information can be provided; and
- include information about precision for all scores presented.

Score Report Format, Language, and Display Features

The physical format of score reports is critical and it is difficult to summarize the wide variety of specific suggestions about the format of score reports that emerged from the reviews in this study. The general or overall look of the reports is an essential feature. The ease with which a reader can find the most important information and the actual print elements seem to influence readers' response to score reports. In regard to general format features, score reports should:

- be clean, as simple as possible, and uncluttered;
- highlight important results in some way, (e.g., boxes, boldface type); and
- use print features such as font size, style, and spacing that make it as easy as possible for the reader to understand the report.

Score reports are a unique reading material for most adults because they often include numbers, tables of numbers, graphs, charts, and narrative elements. The reviews offer a number of suggestions for the use of numeric and visual presented information. A summary of some of the key recommendations includes:

- avoiding jargon unfamiliar to the intended audience;
- avoiding statistical terms;
- providing an explanation or glossary for any measurement terms used;
- using simple and clear graphs, charts, and tables; and
- using text to explain graphs, charts and tables.

The South Carolina/SERVE Study of Score Report Features and Formats

The South Carolina/SERVE study was conducted to design, develop, and evaluate different types of score reports as part of this project. Field-based educators offered guidance on critical features that score reports might contain. Six reporting formats were developed that reflected this advice and the information from the reviews of research and practice. Educators reviewed the six score reporting formats and qualitative and quantitative evaluation information were collected. The results of the study show considerable consistency with the guidelines and principles found in the review of the score reporting research and practices. The six reporting formats are:

1. Item content objective mapping;
2. Achievement performance level narrative;
3. Strand achievement level for individual students;
4. Strand achievement level for groups;
5. Item strand level reporting of differences between observed and expected group performance; and

6. Observed, expected, and differences in strand/item performance at the achievement level cut scores.

A brief summary of the evaluation of each of the six reporting formats is presented to show the connection between the guidelines and principles from the review of score reporting research and practice and the issues raised by the educators reviewing these score report formats. The strategies and summaries are presented in order from most to least useful as evaluated by the focus group participants, which is consistent with the rating scale results.

Strategy 2—Achievement Performance Level Narrative

The evaluation data show that educators found the narrative descriptions of achievement levels the most useful reporting format they reviewed. This score reporting format has several features identified in the reviews of research and practices. First, it is content referenced and, in fact, content referenced at a fairly fine level of detail. The descriptions are based on a review of items that measure specific learning objectives, the finest level of content classification in the assessment program. Second, the achievement levels provide a normative interpretation; they are ordered categories. Third, the achievement levels are presented in purely verbal format with no tables, charts, or graphs. Interestingly, the reviewers recommended that the narrative format be deconstructed and the results be presented in the form of key bullets, an approach that highlights the key results and present the information more clearly and concisely.

Strategy 1—Item Content Objective Map

The focus group reviewers saw the graphical mapping of content objectives as having value and potential. This format is also content referenced in that the plot symbols used are words or phrases that reflect the content being measured. The reviewers recommend that the plot symbols contain more detailed descriptions of the content. The map has a normative feature in that the location of the achievement levels is also shown on the graph. The reviewers express concern that the graphical format might be difficult for teachers to understand, requiring interpretive guides and professional development activities. The review of research and practice suggests that graphs should be simple and concise and the graph used in this approach to score reporting is neither.

Strategy 4—Strand Achievement Levels for Groups

The review of the strategy of reporting strand achievement levels for groups was mixed but generally positive. The group saw some value in these strategy but expressed concerns. Reporting strand-level achievement for groups of students was seen as useful for some general purposes. The strands reflect the content and the levels represent performances and are, in some sense, normative information. There did not seem to be enough specificity in this approach to be useful to classroom teachers because it does not specifically identify individual students' areas of weaknesses.

Strategy 6—Observed, Expected, and Differences in the Strand and Item Performance at the Achievement Level Cut Scores

The review of this score reporting strategy was mixed but generally positive. Reporting the item level performance of a school or school district compared to how students at the achievement level cut scores were expected to perform appealed to members of the focus group. The potential value of this approach was connected to how much detail was used in describing the item and strand content. This approach has several features suggested as beneficial in the review of research and practices. The item and strand descriptions reference the content; performance is reported at the finest level of detail, namely the test item; and the performance achievement levels are used, which offers a normative feature to the report. The physical format of the report, however, leaves much to be desired. It is busy, cluttered, and complex and needs supporting materials and explanation. If the information in the strategy could be presented in a more straightforward fashion, this approach to score reporting might be seen as more useful.

Strategy 3—Strand Achievement Levels for Individuals

The review of this score reporting strategy was mixed but mostly negative. Participants liked the idea of a score report providing information about students' performance on each strand in relation to the achievement levels. Such an approach provides content- and performance-related information for each student. The major concern about reporting achievement-level performance for individual students on each strand was the unreliability of the scores at the stand level. A detailed analysis of strand level results showed than over 96% of the pairwise differences in students' performance on the strands were not significantly different from random variation. Thus, inferences about students' strengths and weakness based on comparing performance on the strands is misleading in all but a very few cases.

Strategy 5—Item- and Strand-Level Reporting of Differences Between Group Observed and Expected Performance

The evaluation data from the practitioners indicated clearly that this reporting strategy did not provide useful information. Item-level data were viewed as a positive feature of a score report. However, developing expectation for a group based on its own overall level of achievement was seen as dangerously misleading because a school or district could meet its expectation and, if the expectation was for modest achievement, school leaders could have a false sense achievement because they had accomplished what was expected of them.

OTHER SCORE REPORTING CONSIDERATIONS

Use of Focus Groups

The use of focus groups to evaluate various score reports designed for different audiences is reported in the review of research and practices and proved to be very informative in the South Carolina/SERVE study. Using parent, teacher, and community focus groups to pilot test score report is strongly recommended. No matter how carefully one might attend to the guidelines and suggestions offered in the review of research and practice, having the people that the report is designed to inform evaluate the usefulness of the report is an invaluable step in developing informative and effective score reports.

Interpretive Guides and Other Materials

This review does not consider interpretive guides and other forms of support materials. The design, development, and distribution of print and web-based supplementary resources is also an important part of a comprehensive reporting system and the interested reader can examine Goodman and Hambleton (2004) for a review of these materials.

The Actual Use of Score Reports

As mentioned, it is important to note that this review of score reporting research and practices, as well as the South Carolina/SERVE study conducted as part of this project, does not address the question of how teachers, principals, parents, and others actually use score reports. The review reports what researchers and practitioners thought and said about various score reports, not what practitioners actually did with them. A different line of research might involve researchers visiting schools and school district offices to observe and interview students, teachers, district personnel, and parents. The purpose of this line of research would be to describe how the information in various score reports is actually used in schools and school districts.

The Standards for Educational and Psychological Testing

The development and dissemination of score reports should be informed and guided by the *Standards for Educational and Psychological Testing* (AERA, APA, & NCME, 1999). Score reports and reporting procedures are addressed explicitly in a number of *Standards* reviewed in this chapter. Central to all considerations is developing score reports that support and encourage valid interpretations of test results and minimize score report features that might invite incorrect interpretations that corrupt the validity of the assessment program.

ACKNOWLEDGMENT

The research reported in this Chapter was supported by The National Science Foundation Award No. REC–99787977, through SERVE, and also with the support of the Office of Assessment, South Carolina Department of Education. The author wishes to acknowledge the careful critique and very helpful advice of the editors of this volume as well as the assistance of Dr. Sharon Osborn Popp and Ms. Lauren D'Amico in reviewing and preparing this chapter.

REFERENCES

American Educational Research Association (AERA), American Psychological Association (APA), & National Council on Measurement in Education (NCME). (1999). *Standards for educational and psychological testing.* Washington, DC: American Educational Research Association.

Forte Fast, E. & Tucker, C. (2001, April) *Redesign of the student assessment reporting system in Connecticut*. Paper presented at the annual meeting of the American Educational Research Association, Seattle, WA.

Goodman, D. P., & Hambleton, R. K. (2004). Student test score reports and interpretive guides: Review of current practices and suggestions for future research. *Applied Measurement in Education, 17*(2), 145–221

Hambleton, R. K. (2002). How can we make NAEP and state test score reporting scales and reports more understandable? In R. W. Lissitz & W. D. Schafer (Eds.), *Assessment in educational reform* (pp. 192–205). Boston: Allyn & Bacon.

Hambleton, R. K., & Slater, S. (1997). *Are NAEP executive summary reports understandable to policy makers and educators?* [CSE Technical Report 430]. Los Angeles, CA: National Center for Research on Evaluation, Standards, and Student Teaching.

Impara, J. C., Divine, K. P., Bruce, F. A., Liverman, M. R., & Gay, A. (1991). Does interpretive test score information help teachers? *Educational Measurement: Issues and Practice, 10*(4), 16–18.

Huynh, H. (1976). On the reliability of decisions in domain referenced testing. *Journal of Educational Measurement, 13*, 253–264.

Huynh, H, (1978). Reliability of multiple classifications. *Psychometrika, 43*, 317–325.

Jaeger, R. (1998). *Reporting the results of the National Assessment of Educational Progress* [NVS NAEP Validity Studies]. Washington, DC: American Institutes for Research.

National Education Goals Panel (NEGP). (1998). *Talking about tests: An idea book for state leaders.* Washington, DC: U.S. Government Printing Office.

National Research Council (NRC). (2001). *NAEP reporting practices: Investigating district-level and market-basket reporting.* Washington, DC: National Academy Press.

Ryan, J. M. (2003). *An analysis of item mapping and test reporting strategies: Final report.* Retrieved October, 2003 from www.serve.org/Assessment/assessment-publicationh1.php.

Snodgrass, D., & Salzman, J. A. (2002, April). *Creating the Rosetta stone: Deciphering the language of accountability to improve student performance.* Paper presented at the meeting of the American Educational Research Association, New Orleans, LA.

Tufte, E. R. (1983). *The visual display of quantitative information.* Cheshire, CT: Graphics Press.

Tufte, E. R. (1990). *Envisioning information.* Cheshire, CT: Graphics Press.

Tukey, J. W. (1990). Data-based graphics: Visual display in the decades to come. *Statistical Science, 5*(3), 327–339.

Wainer, H. (1990). Graphical visions from William Playfair to John Tukey. *Statistical Science, 5*(3), 340–346.

Wainer, H. (1992). Understanding graphs and tables. *Educational Researcher, 21*(1), 14–23.

Wainer, H. (1997a). Improving tabular displays: With NAEP tables as examples and inspirations. *Journal of Educational and Behavioral Statistics, 22*(1), 1–30.

Wainer, H. (1997b). *Visual revelations: Graphical tales of fate and deception from Napoleon Bonaparte to Ross Perot.* New York: Copernicus Books.

Wainer, H., Hambleton, R. K., & Meara, K. (1999). Alternative displays for communicating NAEP results: A redesign and validity study. *Journal of Educational Measurement, 36*(4), 301–335.

Wainer, H., & Thissen, D. (1981). Graphical data analysis. In M. R. Rosenzweig & L. W. Porter (Eds.), *Annual review of psychology* (pp. 191–241). Palo Alto, CA: Annual Reviews.

Wright, B. D., & Masters, G. N. (1982). *Rating scale analysis.* Chicago: MESA Press.

Wright, B. D. & Stone, M. (1979). *Best test design.* Chicago: MESA Press.

Ysseldyke, J., & Nelson, J. R. (2002). Reporting results of student performance on large-scale assessments. In G. Tindal & T. M. Haladyna (Eds.), *Large-scale assessment programs for all students* (pp. 467–480). Mahwah, NJ: Lawrence Erlbaum Associates.

Zwick, R., Senturk, D., Wang, J., & Loomis, S. C. (2001). An investigation of alternative methods for item mapping in the National Assessment of Educational Progress. *Educational Measurement: Issues and Practice, 20*(2), 15–25.

30

Technical Reporting and Documentation

Douglas F. Becker
Mark R. Pomplun
Handbook of Test Development

Complete and thorough documentation of the test development process can be viewed as the foundation necessary for valid interpretation and use of test scores. This chapter looks at technical documentation requirements for testing programs with a focus on the *Standards for Educational and Psychological Testing* and the *Code of Fair Testing Practices in Education*. A general outline for documentation is offered and discussed.

There is little doubt that the *Standards for Educational and Psychological Testing* (American Educational Research Association [AERA], American Psychological Association [APA], National Council on Measurement in Education [NCME], 1999) and the *Code of Fair Testing Practices in Education* (Joint Committee on Testing Practices, 2003) are influential documents in guiding the efforts of test developers and psychometricians. And although these documents are not intended to be necessarily mandatory, exhaustive, or definitive, their prescriptive nature has largely been embraced by test publishers, state testing authorities, and other organizations involved in testing and measurement. The *Standards for Educational and Psychological Testing (Standards)*, alone, provide a corpus around which much of this book has been focused and Linn (chap. 2, this volume) provides an excellent history and overview of the *Standards* and their importance relative to test development. The guidelines set forth by the *Standards* and the *Code of Fair Testing Practices in Education (Code)* cast a framework for technical reporting and documentation that ultimately becomes the backbone of any testing program.

This chapter addresses technical reporting and documentation as critically important activities associated with sound test development. Whether addressing assessments administered to a group or an individual, paper-and-pencil, computer-based, or computerized adaptive tests, complete and thorough documentation becomes the primary source of important information. Technical manuals, reports, user's guides, and test manuals provide an opportunity for an accurate accounting of all the relevant evidence necessary to support and defend a test, including careful test construction, adequate score reliability, appropriate test administration and scoring, accurate scaling, equating and standard setting, and careful attention to examinee fairness issues. When all is said and done, however, the quality and integrity of a testing program can be reduced to a body of validity evidence gathered for the instrument. "Ultimately, the validity of an intended interpretation of test scores relies on all the available evidence relevant to the technical quality of a testing system" (AERA, APA, & NCME, 1999, p. 17). In short, it is necessary to document, document, document.

Currently, the *Standards* provide guidelines for documentation. At least 76 of the 92 standards covered in the first four chapters of the *Standards* address some level of documentation. Fifteen standards, additionally, are provided in Chapter 6, "Supporting Documentation for Tests." These standards cover a broad range of topics including, but not limited to, the availability and interpretability (of documentation), rationale for the test, specification of target populations, reliability and validation, and computer-generated score reports. As indicated in the opening of that section, "The provision of supporting documents for tests is the primary means by which test developers, publishers, and distributors communicate with test users" (p. 67). Table 30.1 provides excerpts from Haladyna's (2002) brief discussion of the guidelines for supporting documentation found in Chapter 6 of the *Standards*.

In addition to the *Standards*, many testing organizations have, as well, embraced the *Code of Fair Testing Practices in Education*, a statement of the obligations to test takers of those who develop, administer, or use educational tests and test data. The development of the *Code* was sponsored by a joint committee of the American Association for Counseling and Development, Association for Measurement and Evaluation in Counseling and Development, AERA, APA, American Speech–Language–Hearing Association, and NCME to advance, in the public interest, the quality of testing practices.

The *Code* sets forth fairness criteria in four areas: developing and selecting appropriate tests; interpreting scores; striving for fairness to test takers of different races, gender, ethnic backgrounds, or handicapping conditions; and providing information to test takers about tests and about test takers' rights. It is intended to be consistent with the relevant parts of the *Standards*. The *Code* is not meant to add new principles over and above those in the *Standards* or to change their meaning. Rather, it is intended to represent the spirit of selected portions of the *Standards* in a way that is relevant and meaningful to developers and users of tests, as well as to test takers and their parents or guardians. States, districts, schools, organizations, and individual professionals are encouraged to commit themselves to fairness in testing and safeguarding the rights of test takers. The *Code* is intended to assist in carrying out such commitments.

Test developers do not have to go too far into the *Code* before they are presented with clear directives to "provide evidence," "provide clear descriptions," and "provide information." Table 30.2, which contains material adapted from the *Code*, illustrates this point.

It is clear from both the *Standards* and the *Code* that the responsibility of documentation for test developers extends well beyond simply the development phase of a test. Careful and thorough documentation must address all aspects of an assessment program, from item and test development, through test administration and scoring, and finally through reporting and interpretation of test results. Although the focus of this book is clearly on test development, mention of these other areas must be made when addressing technical reporting and documentation.

Documentation of the actual test development procedures, however, can be viewed as foundation work. It is needed to provide evidence of validity for accountability, to adhere to the *Standards* and to respond to legal threats to the testing program (Haladyna, 2002). The documentation of the development of the curriculum, test blueprint, item development, item review, field testing, item statistics, bias reviews, construction of final test forms, and equating specifically provide content evidence of validity and form the foundation for appropriate score use and interpretation. The audiences for the documentation include the public, legislators, school board members, media, courts, and testing specialists (Haladyna, 2002). The importance of supporting documentation for test development was demonstrated by the

TABLE 30.1
Technical Standards on Documentation

Standard	Comment
6.1. Test documents should be made available to those interested in this information.	This basic standard justifies supporting documentation.
6.2. Documents should be complete, accurate, and clearly written for their intended audiences.	This standard applies universally to all supporting documents.
6.3. The rationale for the test and the intended interpretations and uses should be clearly stated. Evidence should support these interpretations and uses. When misuse is possible, cautions should be specified.	This standard identifies the important idea that validation must occur for each intended interpretation and use, and those who identify new interpretations and uses to test scores are responsible for providing validity evidence supporting that new interpretation or use.
6.4. Provide test specifications and a description of the population to be tested.	This shows the content of the test and identifies the population to be tested, so validity evidence applies to that content and that population.
6.5. Technical data including descriptive statistics should be provided in a technical report.	This standard identifies one of the values of the technical report.
6.6. When a test reflects a course, specific training, curriculum, textbook, or packaged instructions, the supporting documentation should identify and describe these materials.	In most instances, this is a state's content standard, but it might also refer to a training curriculum, job analysis, or specific reference materials for each test item in the item bank.
6.9. Studies should be cited that provide validity evidence.	In many instances, research provides important guidelines and support for certain testing practices (see Haladyna, chap 32, this volume).
6.10. Materials should be presented that help to interpret test results.	This standard addresses the importance of documentation and publications that explain test results, showing proper, validated interpretations and uses of test scores.
6.11. If administration methods vary, then evidence should be presented for the interchangeability of results.	This standard refers to paper-and-pencil and various forms of computerized administration.
6.12. Computer-generated scores and score interpretations should be clearly explained.	The transition to computer-generated scoring needs to be well supported to assure test takers and the public of its equivalence with traditional paper-and-pencil testing.

Adapted from Haladyna, T. M. (2002). Supporting documentation: Assuring More Valid Test Score Interpretations and Uses. In Tindal, G. & Haladyna, T. M. (Eds.), *Large-scale assessments for all students: Validity, technical adequacy, and implementation*. Mahwah, NJ: Lawrence Erlbaum Associates, Inc.

GI Forum et al. v. Texas Education Agency et al. (1999) court case. Essentially, the federal court upheld the validity of the Texas graduation test based on extensive evidence of content validity (Phillips, 2002).

Documentation of the test development process provides a basis for validating test score interpretation and use. As Haladyna (2002) states, "Supporting documentation is a continuous process of planning, collecting, organizing, and archiving information that satisfies this need to know about the validity of test score interpretation and use" (p. 89). For test developers, documentation reveals the processes used to create the items and test. The interaction of items and samples in test development events forms the basis for validity of test score interpretation and use.

TABLE 30.2
Excerpts From the Code of Fair Testing Practices for Education

---

A. Developing and Selecting Appropriate Tests
Test developers: Test developers should provide the information and supporting evidence that test users need to select appropriate tests.
- A-1. Provide evidence of what the test measures, the recommended uses, the intended test takers, and the strengths and limitations of the test, including the level of precision of the test scores.
- A-2. Describe how the content and skills to be tested were selected and how the tests were developed.
- A-3. Communicate information about a test's characteristics at a level of detail appropriate to the intended test users.
- A-4. Provide guidance on the levels of skills, knowledge, and training necessary for appropriate review, selection, and administration of tests.
- A-5. Provide evidence that the technical quality, including reliability and validity, of the test meets its intended purposes.

B. Administering and Scoring Tests
Test developers: Test developers should explain how to administer and score tests correctly and fairly.
- B-1. Provide clear descriptions of detailed procedures for administering tests in a standardized manner.
- B-2. Provide guidelines on reasonable procedures for assessing persons with disabilities who need special accommodations or those with diverse linguistic backgrounds.
- B-3. Provide information to test takers or test users on test question formats and procedures for answering test questions, including information on the use of any needed materials and equipment.
- B-4. Establish and implement procedures to ensure the security of testing materials during all phases of test development, administration, scoring, and reporting.
- B-5. Provide procedures, materials, and guidelines for scoring the tests and for monitoring the accuracy of the scoring process. If scoring the test is the responsibility of the test developer, provide adequate training for scorers.

C. Reporting and Interpreting Test Results
Test developers: Test developers should report test results accurately and provide information to help test users interpret test results correctly.
- C-1. Provide information to support recommended interpretations of the results, including the nature of the content, norms or comparison groups, and other technical evidence. Advise test users of the benefits and limitations of test results and their interpretation. Warn against assigning greater precision than is warranted.
- C-2. Provide guidance regarding the interpretations of results for tests administered with modifications. Inform test users of potential problems in interpreting test results when tests or test administration procedures are modified.
- C-3. Specify appropriate uses of test results and warn test users of potential misuses.
- C-4. When test developers set standards, provide the rationale, procedures, and evidence for setting performance standards or passing scores. Avoid using stigmatizing labels.
- C-5. Encourage test users to base decisions about test takers on multiple sources of appropriate information, not on a single test score.
- C-6. Provide information to enable test users to accurately interpret and report test results for groups of test takers, including information about who were and who were not included in the different groups being compared, and information about factors that might influence the interpretation of results.

Adapted from Joint Committee on Testing Practices. (1988). *Code of fair testing practices in education.* Washington, DC: Author.

GENERAL APPROACH

It is broadly accepted that validity is an attribute of information derived from tests that describes the extent to which the inferences made from results are supported by the methods used to develop the instrument and the implementation of the program in which it is used. Generally speaking, assessment information is not considered valid or invalid in any absolute sense, but rather valid in relation to a particular purpose or invalid in relation to another. And valid score

TABLE 30.3
General Outline for Technical Documentation

Overview and Purpose of the assessment
   Philosophical basis for the assessment
   Population served by the assessment
Description of the assessment
   Test development procedures
      Test specifications
      Selection of item writers
      Item construction
      Review of items
      Item tryouts
      Item analysis of tryout units
      Assembly of forms
      Content and fairness review of test forms
      Postoperational review
   Scoring procedures
Technical characteristics
   Sampling
   Item- and test-level statistics
   Scaling and equating data
   Reliability and measurement error
Validity evidence
   Content validity argument
   Comparisons of different groups
   Statistical relationships
   Test preparation
   Retests
   Decision-based statistics
   Differential prediction/impact
   Setting cut scores
   Other evidence
Score reporting and research services
   Score reports
   Research and reporting services
References

interpretations can only occur provided there are clear descriptions of the purposes of testing and by effective reporting of results.

Many outstanding examples of technical documentation currently exist. Two such examples are the *ACT Assessment Technical Manual* (ACT, Inc., 1997) and the *Guide to Research and Development* for the *Iowa Tests of Basic Skills* and the *Iowa Tests of Educational Development* (Riverside Publishing, 2003). Table 30.3 provides a general outline that has served as a basis for some of the better examples of technical documentation.

Overview and Purpose of the Assessment

The first section of the documentation should provide a context for the information that follows. In particular, the section should provide an overview as well as the purpose(s) of the testing program (e.g., minimum competency, high school graduation, or accountability). The history of the testing program with an emphasis on changes in the past year needs to be supplied. This is consistent with Standard 6.13. This history preferably should include the policy decisions, the decision makers or stakeholders in the assessment program, and the contractors who completed the work.

Validity must be judged in relation to purpose. Different purposes may call for tests built to different specifications. Thus, for example, a test intended to determine whether students have reached a particular performance standard in a local district is not likely to have much validity for measuring differences in progress toward individually determined goals. Similarly, a testing program designed primarily to answer accountability questions may not be the best program for stimulating differential instruction and creative teaching. Therefore, the purpose of the assessment, including the philosophical basis for the assessment and the intended population to be served, should be clearly articulated in this opening section.

Description of the Assessment

The second component of a thorough technical document should include a clear description of the tests including development and scoring procedures. Included in this section should be an overview of the test specifications or blueprint (Standard 6.4). For large-scale tests, this blueprint frequently includes content by process cells. For example, mathematics content areas could include patterns and algebra, spatial and geometry, and number sense. Process strands might include reasoning, communication, and problem solving. Test specifications could also include the number of items, item types, and score points for each content by process cell. (See Raymond and Neustel, chap. 9, this volume, and Webb, chap. 8, this volume, for more information on test specifications.) For individual ability tests, test specifications are more likely to describe the cognitive components for each subtest that were manipulated across various ages to measure a particular construct.

Other aspects of the test development procedures that should be covered include training, writing, reviewing, and selecting the items for the forms. This description should also include a short summary of the operational or final form items including events such as pilots, tryouts, and operational testing. In addition to describing how the content and skills to be tested were selected and how the tests were developed, information about a test's characteristics at a level of detail appropriate to the intended test users should be clearly communicated. Evidence on the performance of test takers of diverse subgroups is provided, describing efforts to obtain sample sizes that are adequate for subgroup analyses in an effort to help ensure that differences in performance are related to the skills being assessed and not related to other factors.

Scoring procedures should be well documented also. A clear description of standardized scoring procedures not only helps to ensure accurate scoring and reporting, but also an awareness, if not understanding, of the effort that goes into deriving a score from an assessment. Particularly when scoring involves a human rater component, documentation should address those efforts designed to ensure that every test prompt is scored according to the same standardized criteria and that the criteria do not change as raters progress through their task.

Technical Characteristics

The actual technical characteristics of an assessment (item- and test-level statistics, scaling and equating data, and reliability/measurement error) comprise the next important aspect of the documentation process. Enough information should be provided so that a qualified user or reviewer of the documentation can evaluate the appropriateness and technical adequacy of the test. The documentation of the technical characteristics of a test should communicate this important information completely, accurately, and with clarity. As with most aspects of technical reporting and documentation, test developers and publishers need to decide when this information is made available and how this information is best communicated to various user groups. Whatever the form, sufficient information should be provided to allow test users and those affected by the test use to make necessary judgments about the test or resulting scores, to reduce the potential for misunderstanding or misuse of test scores.

The test development documentation should provide a rationale or argument supporting appropriate and inappropriate score interpretations. This rationale should include a description of the test taker samples in the development events (Standard 6.4), how these samples contributed to the accessibility of the tests for all students, and how appropriate and inappropriate score interpretations result from modifications, accommodations, and alternative assessments. The samples determine for which populations the scores are appropriate given the desired interpretation. Simple examples include the need for a representative sample for normative scores or the inclusion of special education students in the sample if the test scores serve as accountability measures for these students.

This section should describe the sampling design used in each development event. Although the operational events are usually full census, sampling designs are frequently used in the pilots and field tests or tryout events. Samples are either purposeful, with a sampling design and targets by sample cells, or voluntary with only sample sizes as targets. Even though pilots employ small samples, the inclusion of diverse populations in "cognitive lab" pilots can provide early direction for decisions on the need for accommodations, modifications, and alternate assessments.

When sampling designs dictate the participation of specific groups of students, descriptive statistics should document the percentages that declined invitations and the characteristics of the resulting sample. When census testing is conducted, the percent of the population who participated should be reported. If the percent of participation is below 90%, then some explanation may be needed. Even if the sampling design rests on volunteer participation, samples should be described in terms of gender, race/ethnicity, public versus private schools, and urban versus rural areas. National and state population statistics for the target sample are useful to facilitate judgments of the representativeness of the sample for each event.

The participation of groups traditionally excluded from large-scale testing such as students with disabilities and English-language learners should be reported. Any changes to increase accessibility of the form for all students should also be documented. For example, changing vocabulary, including more pictures and graphs, using slightly larger print, and simplifying language are methods to increase the accessibility of the operational form for all students. The participation of student groups traditionally excluded from the standard administration group, including any formal studies of score validity, should provide a rationale for the development of an operational assessment that includes as many students as possible. In individual ability testing, a common practice is conducting studies and reporting scores for diverse populations such as English-language learners and students with disabilities (Roid, 2003). These studies demonstrate convergent and divergent validity by the pattern of scores and their comparison with groups of matched students from the regular test administration group.

Consistent with Standard 10.3, results from the participation of students with severe disabilities could direct the development of alternate assessments such as portfolios. The participation of all students in the development events starts the process of alternate assessment development (Standards 10.4 and 10.7). This process includes (a) deciding that accommodations are not sufficient for all students, (b) study of the operational construct or content area to determine areas of problematic measurement, and (c) field testing to support validity (Helwig, 2002). The field testing needs to include a standard for comparing the results, establishing concurrent evidence, providing structural data, and determining the generalizability across groups.

As a result, the nature of participation for these groups needs documentation. One view of a continuum of participation is operational form without accommodations, operational form with accommodations, nonstandard or modified operational form, and alternate assessment. Because of the differences across states in how these terms are defined, the documentation should clearly define and distinguish each change to the test. When tests are translated, the methods used, empirical and logical evidence, and reliability and validity of the translated scores need supporting documentation.

The documentation should be clear as to where on this continuum scores are comparable and eligible for aggregation versus where scores should not be aggregated. Most experts agree that this point hinges on the nature of the accommodations, with some not changing the construct measured and others needing study. The lack of consensus between test publishers and test takers about which accommodations change the construct was demonstrated by the College Board decision in 2003 to reverse their earlier practice of flagging scores for students who required extended testing time. Consistent with Standards 6.3 and 10.7, cautions should be plainly made against common misuses and inappropriate interpretations of scores from these different versions of the operational form. If scores are not comparable across all groups, validity evidence for the noncomparable subgroups needs to be provided (Standard 9.2). Guidelines for these decisions are available from publishers (CTB/McGraw Hill, 2001) as well as research organizations (Thurlow, House, Boys, Scott, & Ysseldyke, 2000).

Another area where documentation for test developers is important is score scale considerations. If not described elsewhere, types of scores, scaling model, software programs, linking plans and procedures, within and across grade scales, and characteristics of the scales should be documented. Although the use of IRT provides item and ability scores on the same scale, testing programs that use classical measurement models have item scales that differ from score scales. For example, at the Educational Testing Service, some programs have items linked to a delta scale. If the item and score scales are different, then the item scale should be described and documented.

The *Standards* provide a broad framework of what technical information should be documented and reported; however, considerable discretion is typically exercised within this framework. The criteria presented in Table 30.4 are intended as an example of how the framework might be practically implemented. Not all assessments use the same kinds of measurement procedures, and this should not be seen as an attempt to prescribe methodology. Rather, there are fundamental aspects of the technical documentation process that should be included in nearly all technical manuals and reports for large-scale testing. The list of suggested technical criteria, shown on the following page, is provided for illustrative purposes.

Validity Evidence

As discussed previously, the procedures used to develop and revise test materials and interpretive information lay the foundation for test validity. Meaningful evidence related to inferences based on test scores, not to mention desirable consequences of those inferences, can only provide test scores with apparent and perhaps temporary social utility unless the test development process itself yields meaningful test materials. Content quality is thus the essence of arguments for test validity (Linn, Baker, & Dunbar, 1991).

As Kane so clearly illustrates (chap. 7, this volume), "To validate a proposed interpretation or use of test scores is to evaluate the claims being based on the test scores. The specific mix of evidence needed for validation depends on the inferences being drawn and the assumptions being made." The types of statistical data that might be considered as evidence of test validity include reliability coefficients, difficulty indices of individual test items, indices of the discriminating power of the items, indices of differential item functioning (DIF), and correlations with other measures such as course grades, scores on other tests of the same type, or experimental measures of the same content or skills.

TABLE 30.4
Technical Criteria

Test and item-level information
   n, mean, median, interquartile range
   Standard deviation
   Raw score frequency distribution, cumulative frequency
   Statistical tables (given sufficient n) for raw, scale, and theta scores for:
      Achievement-level groups
         NCLB groups (e.g., LEP, Special Education, gender, etc.)
      Achievement-level-by-NCLB group
   p-values, item means, item-test correlations
   DIF analyses for NCLB groups, including sample size
   IRT results
      IRT model specified for all items
      IRT item parameters for all items
      Item fit statistics
      Test information curves

Test equating and scaling results
   Description of horizontal equating methods
   Description of vertical scaling methods
   Delta plots for adjacent years for anchor items, if applicable
   Identification of item format for anchor items, if applicable
   Description (and formulas) of score conversion to scale
   Descriptions of rounding procedures

Reliability and measurement error information
   Hand scoring reliability
   Rater effects
   Reliability and validity of individual and group scores

All of these types of evidence reflect on the validity of the interpretation or use of the test score, but they do not guarantee validity. They do not prove that the test really measures what it purports to measure. They certainly cannot reveal whether the things being measured are those that ought to be measured. A high reliability coefficient, for example, shows that the test is measuring something consistently but does not indicate what that "something" is. Of two tests with the same title, the one with the higher reliability may actually be the less valid for a particular purpose. For instance, one can build a highly reliable mathematics test by including only items dealing with simple computation, but this is not a valid test of problem-solving skills and should not be so identified. Similarly, a poor test may show the same distribution of item difficulties as a good test, or it may show a higher average index of discrimination than a more valid test.

This is not meant to imply that well-designed validation studies are of little or no value. Rather, published tests should be supported by an ongoing program of research. It should be recognized, however, that rational judgment plays an important part in evaluating the validity of test score interpretations with respect to both content and process standards and in interpreting statistical evidence from well-designed validity studies.

Scorer Agreement and Interrater Reliability

The accurate assignment of scores to open-ended and performance assessments is of paramount concern with any assessment program that calls for student-generated work and certainly affects the validity of scores obtained from an assessment. Such accuracy does not happen, however, without planning and hard work. For example, the consistent and accurate scoring of student generated work requires the selection of only the best and most consistent readers. These readers are then trained in the consistent and accurate scoring of all student work via the scoring rubrics. Once the readers are trained, they must qualify with live student papers before they are allowed to score. Once selected, there are validation sets (live student papers with known scores) that are used to ensure that the readers have remained consistent and have not "drifted" away from the task at hand. In addition, each student response is read by at least two readers and any disagreement between readings goes to a team leader for resolution. At the end of each scoring day, the percentage of agreement, distribution of scores, and number of resolutions needed are generated. These data are investigated for potential problems associated with any of the scoring rubrics, training or readers. Upon the completion of scoring, the agreement indices (i.e., the percentage agreement and other agreement statistics depending upon final number of score points per rubric) should be documented. In addition, the correlation between first and second reading should be obtained and presented as well as the frequency of blank, invalid, off-topic, and resolved scores. All of this should be carefully documented.

Setting Cut Scores

The theory and practice of setting performance standards, or cut scores, has evolved dramatically in recent decades. Cizek's significant contribution in this area, *Setting Performance Standards: Concepts, Methods, and Perspectives* (2001), assembles much of what is now known about setting performance standards into a single, user-friendly volume. His treatment of the subject in this volume (chap. 10) provides a condensed and digestible overview of standard setting for the test developer. Camilli, Cizek, and Lugg (2001) note in their chapter that although standard-setting procedures can vary greatly, they all have roughly equivalent internal systems of rules and procedures: "The fact that such rules or procedures were designed and followed is essential validity evidence; failure to do so may be viewed as prima facie evidence (or testimony) against the validity of a passing score" (p. 471). Such a statement simply underscores the importance of thorough and accurate technical reporting and documentation. Standards 4.19, 4.20, and 4.21 all speak to issues around setting cut scores and highlight that the rationale and procedures should be clearly documented.

Computer-Based Testing Issues

The use of computers to deliver tests raises additional documentation issues. Unique documentation concerns for computerized tests include test security, delivery of items, item pools, item calibrations, and score comparability. For fairness and validity issues, and to be consistent with Standard 5.7, developers need to document the security of test materials. Two areas of security concerns, especially for computer-adaptive tests, are the distribution channel for the item pool and overexposure of the items in the pool (Way, 1998). Specific to test developers, security procedures should be documented during the test development process, including access to item banking software, and access to locations where items are authored and prepared for computer delivery. During the publishing phase, security is also needed at the point of test publication, usually by limiting use to a single computer or network server. In addition, security procedures should be documented for the transmission of computerized testing item pools from a central location to the remote test administration centers including password protections, encryption and fragmentation of transmitted data, and documentation of all data transmission. Documentation of security in the test administration center is also necessary, including checking and monitoring of examinees and maintaining the security of the administration software.

The other security concern that affects test validity is overexposure of items in the pool. For computer-adaptive tests, test developers should report item exposure rates, average item overlap, and the size of the item pool. Readers can then compare these to recommended values (Way, 1998). Also related to item exposure are item pool policies. Test developers should report how often item pools are changed as well as how they are changed. This documentation includes descriptive statistics from regular monitoring of item performance to ensure the stability of the item parameters on which computer delivery is based. Documentation should also reflect how often this monitoring results in the recalibration or removal of items in the pool.

If test items are generated by computer software, documentation should provide a clear description of the process and should reference the research performed to support the validity of the item generation program. If items are delivered adaptively, documentation should describe how items are selected for administration, the first and subsequent, and stopping rules if appropriate. If the pool was initially calibrated from a paper-and-pencil format, this should be documented. Item retirement should also be addressed. If constructed-response items are scored by computer, then the test developer should provide documentation describing the software program used to perform the scoring, including the development of the scoring rubric, and reference research studies that support the reliability and validity of the scoring program (Standard 6.12). Last, consistent with Standards 4.11 and 6.11, when comparability is claimed with paper-and-pencil forms, studies should be described and referenced supporting the score comparability.

Score Reporting and Research Services

With the *No Child Left Behind* (NCLB) mandate that states are required to "produce individual student interpretive, descriptive, and diagnostic reports...that allow parents, teachers, and principals to understand...information regarding achievement on...standards...in an understandable and uniform format, and to the extent practicable, in a language that parents can understand" (NCLB, 2001, §1111 [b] [3] [C] [xii]), score reports are receiving more interest and scrutiny than ever before. However, Impara, Divine, Bruce, Liverman, and Gay (1991) found that many teachers misunderstood information commonly displayed on score reports. More recently, Goodman and Hambleton (2004) found that "many users of assessment data have difficulty interpreting and understanding results presented in large-scale assessment reports" (p. 149). These studies, coupled with the NCLB mandate, show the importance of documentation of the procedures and implementation of score reporting practices.

The documentation should include description of the scores reported, their metric, how they were calculated, and the source of any criterion or normative information important for their interpretation. For example, currently many reports contain information about the relationship of scores to performance levels. These levels need clear definitions and appropriate text and figures on reports to clarify interpretation.

In addition, appropriate uses of scores for individual students and groups of student need to be described (Standard 5.10). The appropriate uses should also include cautions about common inappropriate uses of scores. These cautions could include warnings about the uses of extreme scores, interpretation of scores, and the use and interpretation of subscores for objectives or standards. Discussion of these issues should clearly distinguish between the reporting unit (student, class, school, etc.) and aggregated group versus individual scores (Standard 5.12). In addition, appropriate use of aggregate scores for program evaluation and accountability goals needs discussion. Consequences resulting from these uses of the scores should also be studied and documented (Standard 13.1).

The rationale for the layout and design of the reports is also important. Goodman and Hambleton (2004) recommended that reports be piloted with focus groups. Description is needed of the focus groups, if any, that helped to make final layout and design decisions. The relationship of the focus group(s) and the target audience(s) for the reports should be explained. In addition, the rationale for decisions about common problems of reports such as excessive information, technical jargon, reliability and error reporting devices (Standard 13.14), and the combination of figures and graphs with text should be discussed. Other important issues that need documentation include the use of accommodation flags and interpretation of score profiles.

To allow proper interpretation of scores, documentation needs to clearly explain how scores for performance items were calculated, including the number of raters, how scores from different raters were used to calculate the final score, how significant score discrepancies were resolved, and how discrepancy rater scores were used in the final score. Any weighting of constructed-response scores in relation to multiple-choice scores needs documentation. If not explained elsewhere, this documentation should state how omitted items and items not reached were scored; should clarify how blank constructed-response items were scored; and should include any additional rubrics for zero scores. Last, the process and development of rubrics for alternative assessments needs documentation. Other issues that need to be documented are the reporting mediums (print, CD, web), how any of the scores offered by each differ, and the security attached to each medium (Standard 5.13).

SUMMARY

This chapter reviewed technical documentation requirements for testing programs. The chapter focused on the use of the *Standards for Educational and Psychological Testing* and the *Code of Fair Testing Practices in Education* as guidelines for test development documentation. Careful and thorough documentation must occur throughout all aspects of an assessment program, from test development, through test administration and scoring, and finally through reporting and interpretation of test results.

Documentation of test development procedures can be viewed as the foundation for accountability validity, to adhere to the *Standards*, and to respond to legal threats to the testing program. Documentation of the test development process provides the basis for validating test score interpretation and use. The interaction of items and samples in test development events forms the basis for validity of test score interpretation and use.

A general outline for documentation was provided and included the purpose of the assessment, description of the assessment, test development procedures, scoring procedures, technical characteristics, validity evidence, and score reporting. Technical information should include test and item-level information, test equating and scaling results, and reliability and measurement error information.

The test development documentation should support the rationale or argument supporting appropriate and inappropriate score interpretations. To support this rationale, documentation should include a description of the test taker samples in the development events, how these samples contributed to the accessibility of the tests for all students, and how appropriate and inappropriate score interpretations result from modifications, accommodations, and alternative assessments. Depending on the nature of the testing program, documentation may need to include interrater information, how cut scores were set, and information on computer-based testing concerns. All programs need to not only document score reporting information, but also need to document program efforts to ensure that users understand appropriate and inappropriate interpretation and uses of the scores. Because the quality and integrity of a testing program ultimately rest on the body of validity evidence gathered for the instrument, test developers need to document, document, and document.

REFERENCES

ACT, Inc. (1997). *ACT assessment technical manual.* Iowa City, IA: Author.

American Educational Research Association (AERA), American Psychological Association (APA), & National Council on Measurement in Education (NCME). (1985). *Standards for educational and psychological testing.* Washington, DC: American Psychological Association.

CTB/McGraw-Hill. (2001). *Guidelines for inclusive test administration.* Monterey, CA: Author.

Camilli, G., Cizek, G. J., & Lugg, C. A. (2001). Psychometric theory and the validation of performance standards: History and future perspectives. In G. J. Cizek (Ed.), *Setting performance standards: Concepts, methods, and perspectives.* Mahwah, NJ: Lawrence Erlbaum Associates.

Cizek, G. J. (Ed.). (2001). *Setting performance standards: Concepts, methods, and perspectives.* Mahwah, NJ: Lawrence Erlbaum Associates.

GI Forum et al. v. Texas Education Agency et al. 87 F. Supp. 2d 667, 142 Ed. Law Rep. 907 (W.D. TX 1999).

Goodman, D. P., & Hambleton, R. K. (2004). Student test score reports and interpretative guides: Review of current practices and suggestions for future research. *Applied Measurement in Education, 17*(2), 145–220.

Haladyna, T. M. (2002). Supporting documentation: Assuring more valid test score interpretations and uses. In G. Tindal & T. M. Haladyna (Eds.), *Large-scale assessment programs for all students: Validity, technical adequacy and implementation.* Mahwah, NJ: Lawrence Erlbaum Associates.

Helwig, R. (2002). A methodology for creating an alternative assessment system using modified measures. In G. Tindal & T. M. Haladyna (Eds.), *Large-scale assessment programs for all students: Validity, technical adequacy and implementation.* Mahwah, NJ: Lawrence Erlbaum Associates.

Impara, J. C., Divine, K. P., Bruce, F. A., Liverman, M. R., & Gay, A. (1991). Does interpretative test score information help teachers? *Educational Measurement: Issues and Practices, 10*(4), 16–18.

Joint Committee on Testing Practices. (1988). *Code of fair testing practices in education.* Washington, DC: Author.

Linn, R. L., Baker, E. L., & Dunbar, S. B. (1991). Complex, performance-based assessments: Expectations and validation criteria. *Educational Researcher, 20*(8), 15–21.

No Child Left Behind Act (NCLB) of 2001. (2002). Pub. L. No. 107-110, §_1111, 115 Stat. 1449–1452.

Phillips, S. E. (2002). Legal issues affecting special populations in large-scale testing programs. In G. Tindal & T. M. Haladyna (Eds.), *Large-scale assessment programs for all students: Validity, technical adequacy and implementation.* Mahwah, NJ: Lawrence Erlbaum Associates.

Riverside Publishing. (2003). *Guide to research and development for the Iowa Tests of Basic Skills.* Itasca, IL: Author.

Roid, G. H. (2003). *Stanford-Binet Intelligence Scales, fifth edition, technical manual.* Itasca, IL: Riverside Publishing.

Thurlow, M., House, A., Boys, C., Scott, D., & Ysseldyke, J. (2000). *State participation and accommodation policies for students with disabilities: 1999 update* [Synthesis Report 33]. Minneapolis: University of Minnesota, National Center on Educational Outcomes.

Way. W. D. (1998). Protecting the integrity of computerized testing item pools. *Educational Measurement: Issues and Practice, 17*(4), 17–27.

31

Evaluating Tests

Chad W. Buckendahl and Barbara S. Plake
Buros Center for Testing/University of Nebraska–Lincoln

This chapter describes professional standards and guidelines for evaluating tests and testing programs. A brief history of efforts to independently evaluate tests is also included. The primary focus of the chapter is to provide developers, practitioners, and consumers with strategies for evaluating tests and testing programs for which they may be familiar or responsible. The strategies described here can be applied to both commercially available tests and proprietary tests and testing programs. These strategies are important because validation research is a continuous process.

Evaluating the technical quality of tests and testing programs has been a consideration within the professional testing community for many years. Professional organizations have promulgated standards and guidelines that describe the characteristics of expectations for validity in tests and testing programs. Monitoring the quality of these instruments and programs, though, has generally relied on self-regulating efforts to ensure that the aspects of the program reflect those professionally adopted standards. Certifying one's own work as representing high quality without independent verification has prompted individuals and organizations to ask for greater assurance of the validity of these tests and testing programs.

This chapter begins by briefly describing some of the professional standards and guidelines that have been developed and revised over the past 50 years representing the professional testing community's expectations for tests and testing programs. Because Linn (chap. 2, this volume) focuses specifically on these standards and discusses them in greater depth, this topic is only briefly addressed here. Next, the characteristics of an independent monitoring agency are described. This discussion is then followed by information about individuals and organizations that have promoted independence in test quality monitoring. The remaining sections focus on operational strategies for evaluating both commercially available and proprietary tests and testing programs.

PROFESSIONAL STANDARDS

Organizations involved with testing have long considered expectations for appropriate practices to be consistent with the work in their field. The American Psychological Association (APA) published *Technical Recommendations for Psychological Tests and Diagnostic Techniques* (APA, 1954) as an initial effort to define the characteristics for acceptable development, analysis, and interpretation of tests and their results. Because these recommendations focused exclusively on the wide range of psychological tests that were being used, there was a need to characterize similar expectations for tests in education. In response to this need, the American Educational Research Association (AERA) and the National Council on Measurements used in Education (later National Council on Measurement in Education [NCME]) a year later published *Technical Recommendations for Achievement Tests* (AERA & NCME, 1955) to address these quality issues in the context of education.

Two decades after these separate standards were published, these organizations combined efforts to jointly publish the *Standards for Educational and Psychological Tests* (APA, AERA, & NCME, 1974) that included a broader scope for tests and testing programs. This joint effort was revised to reflect current research and practice in 1985 and 1999.

In addition to these organizations, others have produced standards that focus on tests for a specific purpose or delivered to examinees in a specific mode. For example, the American Federation of Teachers (AFT), National Education Association (NEA), and NCME jointly produced standards for what classroom teachers should know about assessment (AFT, NEA, & NCME, 1990). In a similar vein, the American Association of School Administrators (AASA), the National Association of Elementary School Principals (NAESP), the National Association of Secondary School Principals (NASSP), and the NCME jointly published a document containing standards for what educational administrators need to know about assessment (AASA, NAESP, NASSP, & NCME, 1997).

Beyond some of the educational examples, the Society for Industrial and Organizational Psychology (SIOP) promotes the *Principles for Validation and Use of Personnel Selection Procedures* (SIOP, 2003) that focus on testing within an employment setting. And in terms of delivery strategies, the Association of Test Publishers (ATP) produced the *Guidelines for Computer-Based Testing and the Internet* (ATP, 2001) to address the growing interest and use in testing that occurs electronically. The International Test Commission (ITC) has also devoted efforts to articulate standards for testing. These include *Guidelines for Test Adaptation* (ITC, 2001) and draft *Guidelines for Computerized Testing* (ITC, 2004).

There are a number of professional standards and guidelines that recommend certain professional practices for test development, interpretation, and use. Within education, professional organizations, including AERA, APA, and NCME, have generally served as the broadest supporters of quality testing. However, as with most professional standards, they remain voluntary and may not be enforceable within the profession. The next section discusses individuals and organizations that have promoted varying levels of independent monitoring for tests and testing programs.

INDEPENDENT EVALUATION

When purchasing a product such as a television, camera, or computer, many consumers gather information about the variety of brands available based on the intended usage, repair history, or cost. This information may have come from the product developer or it may have come from an independent agency. Most consumers have more confidence in the information provided about these products from an independent, objective agency. It is important for consumers to recognize that a product developer has at least a biased perspective, if not a conflict of interest, in the kinds of information they might provide in product manuals or marketing materials about the quality of their products.

The challenge of evaluating information for consumer products was one of the reasons the Consumers Union was created in 1936. The organization publishes *Consumer Reports* to provide independent opinions on various characteristics of commercially available products. A primary benefit to consumers is that information is available and derived from a source that is independent of the manufacturers of the products that have an obvious vested interest in selling their products. Avoiding a conflict of interest in creating and then evaluating a product has also been a concern within testing. A key distinction, though, between the efforts of the Consumers Union and evaluating testing programs is that test reviewers are asked to rely on information provided by the test developers. There is an assumption of the veracity of the information provided in a testing program's technical manuals and supporting documentation.

As an advocate for defining expectations for test quality, Giles M. Ruch (1925) assigned responsibility to test authors, publishers, and users for appropriate use and interpretation for the educational and psychological tests. He described the "minimum essentials" that he believed were necessary for potential users to evaluate the quality of a test they might select. These essentials required evidence of validity, reliability, administration, scoring, norms, and cost. Although discussed separately by Ruch, these elements represent characteristics of our more contemporary perception of construct validity and continue to be appropriate today. Kane (chap. 7, this volume) offers a comprehensive discussion of this more current validity theory.

Ruch's concerns were recognized and then extended to an independent entity by Oscar K. Buros through his publication of the first volume in the *Mental Measurements Yearbook* (MMY) (1938) series. Buros was concerned that test scores were being marketed or used for purposes for which they were not designed or intended. His strategy to address these concerns was to conduct and publish critically candid reviews about the technical quality of commercially available tests. Publishing these reviews provided a common, independent source that potential users could access to evaluate the variety of tests that they may be considering. The MMY series continues to be published today in book form and electronically by the Buros Institute of Mental Measurements at the University of Nebraska—Lincoln. Subsequent yearbooks have carried on the historical service of independently reviewing the technical quality of new or revised versions of commercially available tests.

As an alternative to the MMY, the *Test Critiques* series was created in 1984 to provide reviews of technical quality for well-known educational and psychological tests (Keyser & Sweetland, 1984–1994). Originally published by Test Corporation of America and later by PRO-ED, the series produced volumes from 1984 to 1994. The intent was to provide an additional source of information about the psychometric characteristics of these tests for potential users. However, because the series was housed within a test publisher, there may have been an appearance of a conflict of interest to potential consumers.

The MMY series and *Test Critiques* references have a notable limitation in their scope: they focus on tests that are commercially available and have technical information that can meet certain review criteria. Consequently, they do not address the array of tests that are being used in a proprietary setting. Many tests used for admissions, certification, education, licensure, and personnel selection purposes are not commercially available and therefore may not meet the criteria for inclusion in these volumes. This is problematic because the scores from these proprietary programs may be used for high-stakes purposes. These purposes may include scholarship eligibility, entry into a profession, or employment eligibility. In these instances, who evaluates the evidence that supports the use of the test scores for these purposes? More important, to what extent is the evaluating agency free from conflicts of interest that could undermine a reviewer's potential objectivity? Individuals and organizations have provided us with some models for consideration.

Madaus (1992) recommended an independent agency for monitoring tests and testing programs with the intent of protecting consumers from possible conflicts of interest. He uses the Food and Drug Administration as an example of a governmental model and the aforementioned Consumers Union as a private agency that represents consumers' interests (Madaus, 1992). The concept of consumer protection is reiterated by Downing and Haladyna (1996), where they also propose a model for independently evaluating testing programs that begins with the testing company or agency itself rather than a regulatory agency. Both articles cite Educational Testing Service's (ETS; 1984) audit program as an example of how a testing program might be systematically evaluated. However, concerns about independence of the evaluators in this model from the programs being evaluated cannot be dismissed.

There has been a renewed interest in the level of independence of agencies that certify their own work as representing high quality. Much of this interest has risen, in part, from the problems experienced by the energy company Enron beginning in the fall of 2002. In simple terms, Enron was a publicly traded company where it was alleged that it used the same firm for both accounting and auditing services. When problems were discovered in the financial records, there were questions about the relationship between the two divisions of the company that conducted the work. The concerns were not limited to accounting. Within this same time period, other organizations were beset by criticisms that questioned the independence of the members of their boards of directors. Some decisions made by board members may have improperly benefited individual members of the boards rather than the shareholders they were asked to represent. These concerns extend to the testing community. Without a mechanism within the profession to monitor quality, we are left to rely on external arbiters of quality that may not be knowledgeable about the requirements for technical quality in the profession (see Mehrens & Popham, 1992; Pyburn, 1990).

ACCREDITATION

The professional organizations—the AERA, APA, ATP, ITC, NCME, and SIOP—have promulgated expectations for good practice within testing, but do not have the authority to enforce them. Thus, interpretation and compliance with these standards rests on the individuals or organizations that develop, publish, or use tests. Because this may not be sufficient to ensure quality, some agencies have undertaken systematic efforts to monitor the quality of these proprietary tests and testing programs. Each of these is briefly described here.

The National Commission for Certifying Agencies (NCCA) is a separate accrediting arm of the National Organization for Competency Assurance (NOCA), a group that has members from a variety of credentialing settings. The accrediting body is intended to monitor a participating organizations' compliance with the NCCA standards (NCCA, 2003) through its accreditation program. The accrediting function serves to verify that members are complying with the NCCA standards to which they have jointly agreed to adhere. The accrediting model utilizes an evaluation of the different dimensions of the purpose, resources, responsibility to stakeholders, assessment instruments, recertification, and maintenance procedures in the program. If the processes meet the expectations outlined in the standards, a program becomes accredited for a certain period of time (generally 5 years), during which they agree to build tests in accordance to the accredited process. The continuous monitoring of quality during the accreditation period requires annual reporting to verify that the test developer is following the processes and procedures that were initially determined to meet the NCCA standards.

These standards were recently updated (NCCA, 2003). Any substantive changes to practices are also included in these reports. The evaluators used for reviewing the test development processes are generally members of NOCA, but do not work for the company or agency that they are reviewing. A peer review process like this allows for a level of external independence, but may be worrisome to the organization being reviewed because individuals from competing organizations who are reviewing the materials may unintentionally discover information during the course of their review that could benefit their own organization. Protecting the integrity of what may be proprietary practices may discourage an organization from opening their practices to an external review. It is also possible that persons from a competing organization may not be unbiased in their evaluations.

The Buros Institute for Assessment Consultation and Outreach (BIACO) developed an accreditation program in 2000 to respond to a need that emerged within different sectors of the proprietary testing community. BIACO developed a set of standards for proprietary tests within the information technology certification field. These were later revised to reflect proprietary tests within all content areas (BIACO, 2002). The standards included expectations for test development, maintenance, administration, scoring, and security. Combining elements of the AERA, APA, and NCME *Standards* (1999) and the ATP *Guidelines* (2001), the delivery mode for the testing program was also included as a consideration. An added feature of BIACO's standards was the inclusion of security expectations that could impact the validity of score interpretations.

Operationally, BIACO's model for accreditation includes two stages. The first stage focuses on the processes that an organization uses to develop and maintain their testing program(s). However, because acceptable processes do not necessarily ensure quality results, the second stage of the accreditation model examines the individual tests that result from the accredited processes. This stage serves as a mechanism for continuous quality monitoring during the accreditation. As with NCCA, BIACO's accreditation generally lasts for 5 years, but may be shorter depending on the pace at which the agency's content domain or procedures change.

The American National Standards Institute (ANSI) also recently developed an accreditation program that focuses on certifying agencies. As part of the International Standards Organization (ISO), ANSI is well known for standards they have developed within industrial settings. Because of ISO's international scope, ANSI's program may appeal to organizations that seek reciprocal acceptance of certain credentials. The accreditation model is similar to NCCA in that industry peers may review the processes that participating organizations submit. The ANSI standards focus on the management processes associated with testing programs that certify individuals. Although there are psychometric elements of the review, these focus on the processes that an organization may use. Continuous monitoring under this accreditation model is accomplished through annual reporting of information about the program.

Thus far, we have discussed where expectations for quality testing practice are found, the need for independence in evaluating quality, and described individuals and organizations that have developed different models for accomplishing this objective. The next step, then, is to discuss the specific elements that should be reviewed in a testing program. We also describe how these review elements may differ for commercially available and proprietary testing programs in the subsequent sections.

COMMERCIALLY AVAILABLE TESTS

The AERA, APA, and NCME (1999) *Standards* has a chapter on "Supporting Documentation for Tests" that serves as a broad guide for test publishers and users. Haladyna (2002) expands on these expectations for different user groups and offers recommendations for how to organize and present this documentation. Although the *Standards* are generally applicable to all tests, historically they have been seen as most relevant to commercially available tests. The objective of the recommended documentation is to provide test users with the information they need to make informed decisions about the nature and quality of test scores and to allow users to determine the appropriateness of the test for the intended purposes. The *Standards* described in this chapter can be categorized into three general areas: purpose, test development, and technical information.

Purpose

It is essential that test users have a clear understanding of the intended uses of the test. This importance is reinforced by the number of *Standards* (AERA, APA, & NCME, 1999) that refer to the intended use or interpretation of test scores. For example, Standards 1.1, 1.2, 1.3, 1.4, 3.2, 3.6, 3.7, 3.26, 3.27, 4.1, 4.3, 4.4, 4.9, 4.10, 5.12, 6.3, 6.4, 6.9, and 6.15 relate specifically to information or documentation about the purpose or intended uses for test-scores.[1] In this section of documentation, test producers should detail the purpose of the test, including the intended audience or population. If the purpose of the test is to provide information about a psychological diagnosis, it is imperative that the documentation clearly specify the age range of the test takers. For example, a test may be designed to identify depression symptoms in adults; if so, it should be documented that the test questions and reading level are appropriate for measuring the trait in that population. In addition, information should be given about known appropriate uses and any known inappropriate uses of test scores. It is important for test users to know who is qualified to administer and interpret test results. In some cases, specialized training is needed to properly administer a test, especially a test that is individually administered. In some cases, special training is not required to administer or score the test, but training may be required for test interpretation.

Test Development

Scores on a test are the result of test takers' performance on the tasks, items, or prompts that comprise the instrument. Therefore, central to the use of test scores is the appropriateness of the test content. In many cases, the test is designed to provide scores that are consistent with a psychological or educational theory. Therefore, the basis for this theory is needed to inform test consumers what serves as the underlying foundation for the development of the test.

Once the theoretical or empirical framework supporting the development of the test is described, the documentation should identify who developed the test items and how they are qualified to do this work. The qualification of persons engaged in the development of the questions, as well as those who reviewed the questions, should be documented. Pilot and field testing strategies should be specified as well as any decision rules for inclusion or exclusion of questions during the test design, development, and revision process. The populations used for pilot testing should be specified and shown to be comparable to the intended population for the test.

Technical Information

A substantial part of the documentation should be devoted to technical information. This includes procedures used for scaling and norming. If norm-referenced score interpretations are supported, then detailed information must be provided on the norm group, including the time period, age, gender, race, and ethnicity of participants and demographic information about the participants. This information should be compared to the intended population for the test and is often compared to the most current census data.

---

[1] Each of the topics discussed in this section relates to expectations articulated in the *Standards* (AERA, APA, & NCME, 1999). For readability, references to specific standards are omitted in the text, but are included in Appendix A with its respective topic.

Evidence should be presented about the generalizability of the scores. For example, if the test intends to measure a stable characteristic, then information about short- and long-term test–retest reliability is of interest. If the score is intended to represent a homogeneous content area, then measures of internal consistency and reliability should be provided. In general, the more and varied evidence that is presented to support the intended purposes of the test, the more confidence test users have in the utility of test results.

Validity evidence must be documented. The analyses needed to support uses of scores vary as a function of those intended uses. If the intended use of the scores is to document that students in elementary school are making adequate progress in a given mathematics domain (perhaps as specified by a mathematics teachers' association), then it is critical that the alignment of the test content to this prescribed mathematics domain be supported. Collateral evidence could indicate that the students their teachers judge as being successful in the mathematics curriculum are also students who perform well on the test.

For a test that is designed to diagnose a psychological condition such as depression, it is essential that evidence is provided that verifies that patients who have been diagnosed with depression are identified as such by their test scores, and persons who are not clinically depressed do not produce test scores that would indicate they have that condition. As with reliability evidence, many and varied pieces of appropriate evidence increase the confidence that the test scores do in fact measure what the test intends and the test scores can be used effectively for the intended purposes.

The purpose of documentation for commercially available tests is to provide test users and reviewers with the information they need to make sound judgments about the nature, quality, and utility of the test and whether or not it is appropriate for its intended uses. Therefore, this documentation must provide clear information about the intended uses. Once the intended uses are specified, all of the remaining documentation follows in support of these intended uses. Test development must be consistent with the underlying theory that supports the intended uses. Pilot testing, tryouts, and revisions of test items during the test development process must all be consistent with the intended uses and population. Likewise, any norm group must be congruent with the intended population. The kinds and variety of validity evidence are dictated by the intended purposes of the test. If the documentation provides this information, test users and reviewers have the information they need to make informed decisions about the validity of the test for their purposes.

PROPRIETARY TESTS

Evaluating proprietary tests relies on strategies and expectations that are similar to those of the commercially available tests with some notable additions. Because central agencies are generally responsible for producing, administering, scoring, reporting, and maintaining proprietary testing programs, there may be less transparency to examinees or potential users about the technical quality of these programs. Technical manuals documenting this technical quality may not be available outside the company that developed the test, making it difficult to verify whether or not the testing program meets accepted professional standards. In general, technical manuals that document the following types of technical quality evidence are recommended to organize and present this information.

Organizational Characteristics

Some initial evaluative questions about the quality of a testing program involve characteristics of the individuals or the organization that is developing the test. It is important that the individuals who are responsible for these processes are knowledgeable about both psychometric

Purpose

The purpose or intended use of the scores from a test represents the guiding principle behind reviewing any testing program and is the primary validity question. This question is central to a proprietary testing setting because the program may exist for one or multiple purposes. For example, the scores from a state's student testing program may be intended to support curriculum decisions, instructional programs, and accountability needs. The validity framework for this testing program is likely to be different than the one developed for a licensure testing program that focuses on distinguishing candidates who are at least minimally qualified to enter a profession from those who are not qualified and may present a danger to the public. Testing programs should be explicit in describing the intended use(s) of the scores from their tests. More important, these programs should also specify the limitations of their test scores and discourage reasonably foreseeable misuses. Communicating this information should be consistent in both the technical information and marketing materials that are used by the testing program.

Test Development

Specific development processes are generally unique to a given testing program and are related to its purpose. However, there are common elements that should be evident in any testing program. An early stage in the test development process is to define the knowledge, skills, abilities, and judgments that are expected for the program's examinees and related to the purpose of the test. This content specification may be accomplished through agreed upon content standards developed by national learned societies (e.g., education) or through a national practice analysis[2] (e.g., licensure, certification). Documentation that describes the process and results of these activities should be available and should reference published materials that potential examinees can access. As part of this documentation of the content specification processes, the test developer should describe the qualifications of the subject matter experts (SME) and also describe the extent to which they participated in the process. To evaluate whether the SMEs were appropriate, an evaluator needs to know who these individuals were and what they did during the development processes.

Because a test only samples from a larger content domain, the next step is to evaluate the link between the content specifications and the test specifications or blueprint. There should be a clear, documented link between content and test. A related aspect is to determine the strategy to weight the components of the test to match the content specifications. The content on the test should be representative of the specifications from the broader content domain.

In developing the items or tasks for the test, there should be evidence that the items link to the test specifications and were developed using acceptable strategies. There should also be documented processes for reviewing items for clarity, content accuracy, and format. An item piloting and revision process and results should also be described in documented materials. Schedules for item revision and redevelopment that are unique to the purpose of the test should also be included. If alternate forms of the test are developed, these should be evaluated for content equivalence to ensure that the content specifications are linked to each form of the

---

[2]This activity may also be characterized as a *job, task,* or *occupational analysis.*

test. It is also important to ensure that if alternate forms of the test are developed, they can be supported under the current frequency of administration and the size of the item bank from which test forms are developed.

In addition to alternate forms of the test that may be developed, translated versions of the test may also be created to be administered in a language other than the one in which it was originally developed. If translations of test forms are created, the documentation for the test should include information about the other language(s) into which the test has been translated as well as the methodologies for translating or adapting the forms.

Although many times considered later in the development process, understanding how scores will eventually be used is important to discuss at an early stage. Definitions of performance that correspond to the classification(s) or decision(s) that will be made with the scores are called *performance level descriptors*. Although they can be used to guide development, they are also critical to the standard-setting processes described in the next section. These performance level descriptors should be developed to be consistent with the number of decisions that are intended. For example, many educational testing programs seek to classify student performance into four levels (e.g., below basic, basic, proficient, and advanced). Performance level descriptors for each of these levels are needed to define the characteristics of students at each level. The number of descriptors necessary to define these levels is greater than the number needed to define a minimally competent candidate for a licensure test because the number of decision points is greater in the educational example.

Reliability

Assessing the characteristics of the scores that result from administering the tests represents a next evaluative step. One of these critical score characteristics is reliability. Crooks, Kane, and Cohen (1996) and Kane (chap. 7, this volume) argue that any validity argument is only as strong as its weakest link. Thus, without adequate reliability evidence, other validity evidence may not be meaningful. Reliability may be demonstrated using a variety of methods, but should be appropriate given the type of test items or tasks, the criticality of the decision, and the important sources of measurement error. It is also important to evaluate the extent to which inferences about scores are justifiable. For example, an educational test that provides diagnostic subtest scores for informing curriculum and instruction should demonstrate that the reliability of the scores produced by these subtests are sufficient to support the level of inference that is desired. A supplemental analysis that examines the decision consistency is also important to demonstrate that the decisions that result from the test support assertions about examinee performance.

As a follow-up to the global indices that may be reported for reliability, item analyses should be conducted to examine how well these items are performing in terms of item difficulty and discrimination (Livingston, chap. 19, this volume). Additional item analyses might include differential item functioning, which serves as an empirical check for bias and item drift or item exposure analyses to evaluate whether the items are continuing to function as expected. Items should be retained if they possess acceptable characteristics and contribute to the decisions that flow from the scores. They should be revised or replaced in the item bank if they do not.

For adaptive tests, there may be additional characteristics to evaluate. The item selection algorithm that selects items should include the necessary constraints to ensure content representation of the desired content domain. If a stopping rule is employed, the rules or procedures for ensuring that decisions about examinee performance are consistent should also be included. Additional considerations to control item exposure, sampling from the broader item pool, and transforming raw scores to scale scores may also factor into the selected model.

Standard Setting

The procedures and results for setting the cut score for the test should be described in addition to the qualifications of the panelists who participate in the process. In general, a systematic strategy that considers both the operational definition of performance and the difficulty of the test should be used rather than a norm-referenced, arbitrary, or capricious decision. There are a variety of methods for establishing cut scores that rely on test-based or examinee-based judgmental methods in addition to some empirical methods. See Cizek (chap. 10, this volume) for a discussion of some of these standard-setting methodologies. The policy decision that results from the standard-setting activities may be included as it relates to the defensibility of the cut score. If alternate forms of the test are used, the equating strategies that the testing program uses should also be included in the documentation to provide evidence of how decisions from different forms are equivalent.

Administration

Similar to the commercially available tests, there are characteristics of administering proprietary tests that may impact the validity of the scores (Campion & Miller, chap. 26, this volume; McCallin, chap. 27, this volume). When evaluating these tests, information about the administration characteristics should be contained within an examinee manual, handbook, or detailed set of directions. The types of information this manual should contain include a description of the administration procedures, how, and when the test is administered. Depending on the type of testing program, it may also be important to evaluate how sites are selected, the training procedures for examiners, and how these are monitored. Strategies for verifying an examinee's identity or accommodations that may be allowable would also be examined here. The administration manual may also describe the review and retake policies that are part of the program and the conditions under which these may occur as they may impact security concerns.

Security

The validity of inferences made about scores may also be impacted by the level of security a proprietary program maintains. Information about a testing program's security procedures should be documented in a manual. In the manual, procedures should be described that address the physical security protocols for developing the test, the test answer key, printing the tests, examination sites, and inventory of materials. With the wide use of electronic storage, additional security questions related to item bank access, item or task replenishment, and the confidentiality of examinee information are important to consider. A related security concern focuses on methods for fraud detection. Although discussed in more depth by Impara and Foster (chap. 5, this volume), ensuring that examinees have equal opportunities to demonstrate performance is critical to making valid inferences about their performance.

SUMMARY

As highlighted in this chapter, there is a range of standards and guidelines for evaluating tests and testing programs that are promoted by professional organizations. Types of evidence that both commercially available and proprietary testing programs should provide to document the quality of their program were discussed. This information is essential for potential users to evaluate the purpose of the test, appropriate uses, and the supporting validity evidence. There are public and professional interests that are served through continuous evaluation and improvement. The independent auditing of an industry that is so critical to society offers needed protection to the public. Ensuring the credibility of tests and testing programs through external verification enhances the reputation of our profession.

Because of the number of standards that are available to guide practice, it may be difficult for organizations and users to know where to focus their quality control efforts. The authors recommend that organizations utilize both internal and independent, external strategies for quality control. An internal approach might include ensuring that qualified individuals within an organization follow and document practices based on professional standards. This approach requires that the organization have test development processes that are documented and followed by individuals in the organization. Internal quality control evidence is an important component of the test development process. It also serves as the basis for any external evaluation of quality.

In contrast, an external approach might include an independent, technical advisory committee or an independent agency that evaluates the procedures and practices of the organization against appropriate professional standards. The extent to which an external quality control strategy is employed is a function of the purpose and intended use of the test scores. Although measures of both internal and external quality control are important to document the validity of a program, critical decisions based on test scores suggest a greater need for independent, external support. This support may be very important for testing programs that have been or may be challenged.

ACKNOWLEDGMENT

The authors are grateful to Jeffrey K. Smith for providing substantive and editorial suggestions for improving the quality of this chapter.

APPENDIX A: SUGGESTED OUTLINE FOR A TECHNICAL MANUAL FOR A TESTING PROGRAM[3]

I. Organizational characteristics
   a. Qualifications of staff (*Standards pp. 1–2*)
   b. Relationship with other program aspects (e.g., training, textbooks, etc.)
II. Purpose
   a. Scope and use of scores; inappropriate uses (Standards 1.1, 1.2, 1.3, 1.4, 3.2, 3.6, 8.1, 11.1, 11.2, 11.5, 11.16, 11.24, 13.2, 13.3, 13.7, 13.12, 14.14)
   b. Validation framework (Standards 1.1, 1.2, 1.3, 1.4, 1.5, 1.6, 1.13, 1.14, 1.22, 1.23, 1.24, 14.1)
III. Test development
   a. Defining knowledge, skills, abilities, judgments (i.e. content specification) (Standards 1.6, 1.7, 1.8, 3.1, 3.3, 3.5, 3.9, 3.11, 3.15, 14.6, 14.8, 14.10, 14.11, 14.14)
   b. SME qualifications and participation (Standards 1.7, 3.5, 3.6, 14.9)
   c. Test specifications (blueprint)(Standards 3.2, 3.3, 3.4, 3.5, 3.7, 3.11, 3.14, 3.15, 3.16, 3.17, 4.16, 6.4, 7.9)
   d. Item/task development
      i. Evidence that items/tasks link to test specifications (Standards 1.8, 1.11, 1.12, 3.2, 3.3)
      ii. Item/task review procedures and results (Standards 3.5, 3.11, 3.25, 3.26)

---

[3]References in this section relate to the *Standards for Educational and Psychological Testing* (AERA, APA, & NCME, 1999).

  iii. Pilot testing procedures and results (Standards 3.7, 3.8)
  iv. Decision rules for determining item quality (Standards 3.6, 3.7, 3.8, 3.9)
  v. Schedule for item/task redevelopment (Standards 3.25, 3.26)
 Test forms
  i. Characteristics of alternate forms (Standard 3.16)
  ii. Schedule for alternate form implementation (Standards 3.25, 3.26)
 e. Test adaptations
  i. Characteristics of adaptations (Standards 3.16, 4.14, 4.15, 4.16)
  ii. Language/cultural adaptation methods (Standards 3.16, 5.3, 9.7)

IV. Psychometric properties
 a. Reliability
  i. Score reliability procedures and results (Standards 2.1, 2.2, 2.3, 2.4, 2.5, 2.6, 2.7, 2.8, 2.9, 2.10, 2.11, 2.12, 2.13, 2.14, 2.15, 2.16, 2.17, 2.18, 2.19, 2.20, 3.3, 3.19, 3.23, 5.12, 9.1, 9.7, 9.9, 11.1, 11.2, 11.19, 12.13, 13.8, 13.12, 14.15, 15.6)
  ii. Decision consistency reliability procedures and results (Standards 2.14, 2.15, 14.15)
 b. Item analyses
  i. Item analysis procedures and results (Standards 3.7, 3.9, 3.10, 3.12)
  ii. DIF analysis procedures and results (Standard 7.3)
 c. Adaptive tests
  i. Item selection algorithm including constraints, stopping rule (Standard 2.16)
  ii. Score transformation procedures and results (Standard 5.1)
 d. Passing scores
  i. Procedures and results for setting passing (cut) score(s) (Standards 2.14, 2.15, 4.4, 4.11, 4.19, 4.20, 4.21, 6.5, 6.12, 13.6, 14.17)
  ii. Qualifications of passing score panelists (Standards 1.7, 3.5, 4.19, 4.21)
 e. Equating
  i. Procedures and results for equating test forms (Standards 4.11, 4.12, 4.13)

V. Administration
 a. Registration procedures (Standards 8.2, 12.10, 15.10)
 b. Administration procedures and location (Standards 3.9, 3.20, 5.4, 5.5, 8.1, 12.8, 12.12, 13.10)
 c. Accommodation procedures (Standards 2.18, 3.21, 9.3, 9.11, 10.1, 10.8, 11.16)
 d. Score reporting and interpretation (Standards 1.10, 1.12, 2.11, 2.17, 3.4, 5.8, 5.9, 5.10, 6.5, 6.12, 7.8, 8.8, 11.6, 11.17, 11.18, 12.9, 12.15, 12.20, 13.12, 13.13, 13.14, 13.19, 15.11, 15.12)
 e. Examinee appeal and retake policies (Standards 8.13, 11.12)

VI. Security
 a. Internal security procedures
  i. Item/task development (Standards 11.8, 11.9)
  ii. Item/task exposure and replenishment (Standards 4.17, 6.4)
  iii. Test key (Standards 11.8, 11.9)
 b. Administration security procedures
  i. Verification of examinee identity (Standards 3.20, 5.6, 12.8, 12.12, 13.10)
  ii. Test sites (Standards 5.4, 5.5, 5.6)
  iii. Printed/electronic materials access (Standards 5.7, 11.9, 12.11)
 c. Fraud detection (Standards 5.6, 5.7, 11.7, 12.11, 13.11)
 d. Confidentiality of examinee information (Standards 8.2, 8.6, 12.11)

APPENDIX B: WEB SITES FOR ORGANIZATIONS REFERENCED IN THIS CHAPTER

American Association of School Administrators (AASA): www.aasa.org
American Educational Research Association (AERA): www.aera.net
American Federation of Teachers (AFT): www.aft.org
American National Standards Institute (ANSI): www.ansi.org
American Psychological Association (APA): www.apa.org
Association of Test Publishers (ATP): www.testpublishers.org
Buros Center for Testing: www.unl.edu/buros
Consumers Union (CU): www.consumersunion.org
Educational Testing Service (ETS): www.ets.org
Food and Drug Administration (FDA): www.fda.gov
International Standards Organization (ISO): www.iso.org
International Test Commission (ITC): www.intestcom.org
National Association of Elementary School Principals (NAESP): www.naesp.org
National Association of Secondary School Principals (NASSP): www.nassp.org
National Commission for Certifying Agencies (NCCA): www.noca.org/ncca/ncca.htm
National Council on Measurement in Education (NCME): www.ncme.org
National Education Association (NEA): www.nea.org
National Organization for Competency Assurance (NOCA): www.noca.org
PRO-ED: www.proedinc.com
Society for Industrial and Organizational Psychologists (SIOP): www.siop.org

REFERENCES

American Association of School Administrators (AASA), National Association of Elementary School Principals (NAESP), National Association of Secondary School Principals (NASSP), & National Council on Measurement in Education (NCME). (1997). *Competency standards in student assessment for educational administrators.* Washington, DC: Author.

American Educational Research Association (AERA), American Psychological Association (APA), & National Council on Measurement in Education (NCME). (1999). *Standards for educational and psychological testing.* Washington, DC: Author.

American Educational Research Association, Committee on Test Standards, & National Council on Measurements Used in Education. (1955). *Technical recommendations for achievement tests.* Washington, DC: Author.

American Federation of Teachers, National Education Association, and National Council on Measurement in Education (1990). Standards for teacher competence in educational assessment of students. *Educational Measurement: Issues and Practice, 9* (3), 30 32.

American Psychological Association (APA). (1954). *Technical recommendations for psychological tests and diagnostic techniques.* Washington, DC: Author.

American Psychological Association, American Educational Research Association, National Council on Measurement in Education. (1974). *Standard for educational and psychological tests.* Washington, DC: American Psychological Association.

Association of Test Publishers (ATP). (2001). *Guidelines for computer-based testing.* Washington, DC: Author.

Buros, O. K. (1938). *Mental measurements yearbook.* Highland Park, NJ: Gryphon.

Buros Institute for Assessment Consultation and Outreach (BIACO). (2002). *Standards for proprietary testing programs.* Lincoln, NE: Author.

Crooks, T. J., Kane, M. T., & Cohen, A. S. (1996). Threats to valid uses of assessments. *Assessment in Education, 3*(3), 265–285.

Downing, S. M., & Haladyna, T. M. (1996). A model for evaluating high-stakes testing programs: Why the fox should not guard the chicken coop. *Educational Measurement: Issues and Practice, 15*(1), 5–12.

Educational Testing Service (ETS). (1984). *The ETS audit program.* Princeton, NJ: Author.

Haladyna, T. M. (2002). Supporting documentation: Assuring more valid test score interpretations and uses. In G. Tindal & T. Haladyna (Eds.), *Large-scale assessment programs for all students: Development, implementation, and analysis* (pp. 89–198). Mahwah, NJ: Lawrence Erlbaum Associates.

International Test Commission (ITC). (2001). *ITC test adaptation guidelines.* Retrieved July 12, 2004 from http://www.intestcom.org/test_adapt.htm.

International Test Commission (ITC). (2004). *International guidelines on computer-based and internet delivered tests* (v. 0.5). Retrieved July 12, 2004 from http://www.intestcom.org/itc_projects.htm.

Keyser, D. J., & Sweetland, R. C. (Eds.) (1984–1994). *Test critiques Vol. I–X.* Kansas City, MO: Test Corporation of America and Austin, TX: PRO-ED.

Madaus, G. F. (1992). An independent auditing mechanism for testing. *Educational Measurement: Issues and Practice, 11*(1), 26–31.

Mehrens, W. A., & Popham, W. J. (1992). How to evaluate the legal defensibility of high-stakes tests. *Applied Measurement in Education, 5,* 265–283.

National Commission for Certifying Agencies (NCCA). (2003). *Standards for the accreditation of certification programs.* Washington, DC: National Organization for Competency Assurance.

Pyburn, K. M. (1990). Legal challenges to licensing examinations. *Educational Measurement: Issues and Practice, 9*(4), 5–14.

Ruch, G. M. (1925). Minimum essentials in reporting data on standard tests. *Journal of Educational Research, 12,* 349–358.

Society for Industrial and Organizational Psychology. (2003). *Principles for the validation and use of personnel selection procedures.* College Park, MD: Author.

32

Roles and Importance of Validity Studies in Test Development

Thomas M. Haladyna
Arizona State University West

The validation of any test score interpretation or use requires a logical argument about appropriateness of that interpretation or use and evidence that supports the argument. This evidence may take one of two forms: procedural or empirical. The mix of evidence is used to make an evaluative judgment about validity. This chapter addresses studies that provide empirical validity evidence. A simple taxonomy is presented that shows different sources of empirical validity evidence arising from studies. We have a body of evidence supporting valid interpretation or use, and we have a body of evidence that threatens validity. Two sources of this opposing evidence are construct-irrelevant variance and construct underrepresentation. This validity evidence is usually test program specific. However, we also have a body of evidence that applies more generally to more than one testing program. This too supports or threatens validity. Testing program sponsors and their staffs are encouraged to plan and complete validity studies that provide specific validity evidence, and, when possible, also complete studies that address problems that provide new validity evidence or expose threats to validity and propose ways to reduce or eliminate these threats.

The planning, designing, creating, and administering of any testing program for any purpose are highly dependent on a body of knowledge that comes from research and experience. The chapters in this volume share the experiences of test developers and provide a body of knowledge about test development. This volume also provides a substantial body of research to support concepts, principles, and procedures that these test developers advocate. Downing (chap. 1, this volume) offers a 12-step planning process toward the end of creating a testing program. An important aspect of that process involves validation (Kane, chap. 7, this volume), Linn (chap. 2, this volume) shows why the *Standards for Educational and Psychological Testing* (American Educational Research Association [AERA], American Psychological Association [APA], & National Council on Measurement in Education [NCME], 1999) are so important for test developers.

This chapter shows how research is a vital, ongoing process in the establishment, continuance, and most important, validation of any testing program. Without research, a testing program will have difficulty generating sufficient evidence to validate its intended test score interpretations and uses. Research can also generate validity evidence that may weaken or invalidate a particular test score interpretation or use. By discovering a threat to validity, test developers can take action to reduce or eliminate each threat. Finally, research can introduce or illuminate new concepts, principles, or procedures that improve test development and scoring and, by that, promote more valid test score interpretations.

This chapter begins with a brief definition of *validity*. Although validity has been discussed often and extensively, its definition provides a good context for the ideas presented in this chapter. A basis for this chapter comes directly from the unified view of validity popularized in an influential essay by Messick (1989) and embodied in the *Standards* (AERA, APA, & NCME, 1999). Next, *validity study* is broadly defined. After that, a context is provided that includes types of testing programs for which validity studies are useful. Then, a typology of validity studies is presented. Examples are given that show the variety and importance of these studies in building high-quality testing programs and validating test score interpretations and uses. At the end of this chapter, recommendations are offered to sponsors of testing programs regarding the kinds of validity studies that should be done.

VALIDITY

The most important concern for any test is the validity of its score interpretations or uses. Kane (1992) and Messick (1989, 1995a, 1995b), among others, discuss the requirements for validity. Generally, *validity* entails an argument or proposition that a specific test score interpretation or use is valid. *Validation* is the process of developing this argument and assembling validity evidence to support the argument. As Messick (1995a) notes, validation is an ongoing process and validity evolves during this process. In this context, validity is judged in degrees and never in absolute terms.

Messick (1989, 1995a, 1995b) also argued that validity evidence comes from different sources. The degree of validity is a matter of professional judgment based on a consideration of the logic of the validity argument and the validity evidence, which comes in procedural and empirical forms (Downing & Haladyna, 1996, 1997). Examples of procedural validity evidence involve activities described and supported in the *Standards* (AERA, APA, & NCME, 1999). In this volume, authors have recommended ways to identify and define content, develop test items, validate test item performance, design tests, achieve comparability among test forms in test design, and set standards. A complementary source of validity evidence is empirical, and is the topic in this chapter.

An important point about validation is that validity evidence can be positive or negative. The positive instance supports an argument supporting the test interpretation or use, and the negative instance provides support for the counterargument that the interpretation or use is not valid. Thus, negative evidence weakens the validity argument (Cronbach, 1987). Cronbach noted in his retrospective essay on construct validity:

> Despite many statements calling for focus on rival hypotheses, most of those who undertake CV [sic: construct validity] have remained confirmationist. Falsification, obviously, is something we prefer to do unto the constructions of others. (1989, p. 153)

Although, research is seldom aimed at uncovering negative validity evidence in a testing program, it benefits all testing programs for a sponsor of a testing program to devote some resource to "looking for trouble before it finds you." Crooks, Kane, and Cohen (1996) argue that eight linked stages of test development exist, and any threat to validity in this chain weakens the overall judgment about validity. The discovery of negative validity evidence in this chain of test development activities can motivate improvements in a testing program by reducing or eliminating each threat to validity.

Most large-scale testing programs engage in research programs that provide empirical evidence to support the valid interpretation and use of each test. These testing programs often contribute beyond simply providing validity evidence for their testing program. Researchers uncover new procedures, introduce new concepts, or expose situations or conditions that might invalidate a test score interpretation or use.

For example, the *Stanford-Binet Intelligence Test* (Roid, 2003) is generally accepted as a highly valid measure of general intelligence. We have many studies that provide a variety of evidence concerning the validity of test score interpretations and uses of the *Stanford-Binet* (consult the technical manual or contact their publisher for further information on these studies: http://www.nelson.com/nelson/contact/default.html). Moreover, the field of intelligence testing has been one of the most heavily researched in the history of psychology. Bias in intelligence testing has been on ongoing concern of researchers (Jensen, 1980). Thus, the validity of most intelligence tests rests on both test-specific and general forms of research supporting test score interpretations and uses.

The *Scholastic Assessment Test* (SAT-I) sponsored by the College Entrance Examination Board also has a long history of development that has been well validated thanks to many studies. Like the *Stanford-Binet*, validity studies have been conducted since the introduction of the earlier SAT in 1926 to the present. Consult their Web page for a list of validity studies that contribute to the argument that these scores are helpful in making college admissions decisions (http://www.collegeboard.com/splash). This long-term commitment to validity is one reason why this test has enjoyed such widespread success despite continued attacks from critics (Crouse & Trusheim, 1988; Owen, 1985), who created logical arguments and cited research to challenge the validity of interpretations and uses of this test's scores.

The *Standards* (AERA, APA, & NCME, 1999) provide an excellent source of information about validity evidence that might be assembled to validate a test score interpretation or use. Linn (chap. 2, this volume) emphasizes the importance of the *Standards* in test development. Other sources concerning the nature and types of validity evidence that might be used in validation include Haladyna (2002a) and Downing and Haladyna (1996, 1997).

Contexts for Validity Study

All testing programs have common types of validity evidence that should be included. Among these studies are reliability, comparability, equating, and item quality. As we know, testing programs can measure single or multiple constructs and have different purposes. These different purposes lead to the need for unique types of validity evidence. Three major types of testing programs are discussed for illustrative purposes. Other types of testing programs exist that also are part of this context, and these other testing programs may also require unique types of validity evidence. The overriding principle of this section applies to these other types of testing programs as well: Validity evidence is likely to vary according to the types of constructs measured and the particular uses of the test scores we intend.

Large Scale Achievement Tests

Many test programs measure scholastic or academic achievement in a well-established domain of knowledge and skills. Most school district and state elementary- and secondary-level achievement tests fall in this category. Most professional training programs have end-of-training proficiency tests. Nationally known achievement tests also fall in this category, including the *Stanford Achievement Test,* the *Iowa Test of Basic Skills,* and the *TerraNova*. All have a basis in scholastic curricula. The intended interpretation of these tests is to describe achievement of each student or group of students for various purposes, including curriculum analysis and evaluation, instructional evaluation, school or school district evaluation, individual student growth, diagnosis of learning problems for each student or any group of students, and, even, promotion and graduation.

Credentialing Tests

Many testing programs are dedicated to measuring professional knowledge and skills. This type of testing program is used for credentialing, specifically for certification and licensing. A credentialing test is often conceived to be a sample of professional knowledge and skills that are identified through the process of practice analysis (also known as *job analysis*, *role delineation*, or *task analysis* (see Raymond, & Neustel, chap. 9, this volume). The kind of interpretation intended in these tests is a candidate's status in a well-defined domain of professional knowledge or skills. A second type of credentialing test involves some indicator of how the professional person performs in their profession. For a physician, a simulated patient examination might be used. For a dentist, there is a live-patient examination as the terminal criterion before licensing; for other professions, there are internships, where the candidate for a credential is observed practicing their profession. A comprehensive source of information about this type of testing program can be found in Impara (1995).

Admissions Tests

Tests have been designed exclusively for informing admissions decisions. The two best-known admissions tests are the newly revised SAT and the American College Test (ACT) Assessment. These tests emphasize the measurement of student learning in a rigorous high school curriculum. Both tests are intended to measure student advantage. The Graduate Record Examination (GRE) is widely used to identify talented students for graduate programs. Many professions have a highly selective admissions test in such fields as medicine, dentistry, law, and business, for example. These tests usually measure verbal, quantitative, and analytical abilities typically associated with intelligence. Regardless of whether the construct is mainly achievement or mainly intelligence, each of these admission tests is used for the purpose of informing admissions decisions. The objective of validity research is to know how well admission test results predict future scholastic achievement.

The Importance of Context

Depending on which type of test is being developing, the research agenda for validity studies differs. The agenda for curriculum-based achievement tests may focus on content definition as described by Webb (chap. 8, this volume), item development, and ways in which test scores might be compromised, especially in a high-stakes settings (Haladyna & Downing, 2004). The agenda for a credentialing test may include studies of the defining of content through the practice (Raymond & Neustel, chap. 9, this volume), dimensionality, the quality of test items in reference to the practice analysis (Downing, chap. 12, this volume), and the comparability of test forms. The research agenda for admissions tests might focus less on content but emphasize predictability and look for sources that contaminate the interpretation of test scores, such as extensive coaching or test preparation. The main idea is that the type of testing program usually leads to a unique research agenda that focuses on types of validity evidence and problems that are confronted in that type of testing program.

Defining a Validity Study

Validity study is used here to identify any inquiry where the outcome provides information that affects the judgment of validity of a test score interpretation or use. Quantitative studies can be descriptive or experimental, but a broader interpretation of *validity study* is intended here, and includes reviews of research, qualitative studies, archival information, news reports, anecdotal reports, and other information that informs those who make judgments about validity. Because validation involves a judgment after the evaluator considers the mix of validity evidence, using all sources of information makes for a more informed judgment. Any validation rests on the adequacy of the validity evidence considered in the context of this logical argument being made for a test score interpretation or use. The validity study is a main source of validity evidence.

Validity studies contribute to broad categories of validity evidence (Messick, 1995a, 1995b), which he identifies as content, substantive, structural, generalizability, external, and consequential. These categories provide a basis for different types of validity studies. The value of these categories is to sharpen our thinking and appreciation for the breadth of evidence assembled to support a test score interpretation or use. Messick describes *validation* as a process of integrating these sources of evidence to strengthen the argument for an interpretation or use and to dispel rivaling hypotheses that may weaken validity.

This broad definition of a validity study features two major categories of validity studies. The first is vital to any judgment about validity in that testing program. The second is less direct but nonetheless contributes important information that affects the judgment of validity. This first type includes all studies that are specific to a testing program. Three subcategories exist for this first type of study. The first subcategory includes ordinary, routine studies associated with all or most testing programs. These studies are intended to support validity, but can also provide information about weak links in the chain of reasoning supporting validity.

The second subcategory includes studies of construct-irrelevant variance (CIV) and construct underrepresentation. These studies are likely to provide negative validity evidence countering the first type of validity studies that are test program specific. The third category includes studies that address specific problems that arise in the course of test development, scoring, or reporting. These problems may involve CIV or construct underrepresentation, but can also relate to other categories of validity evidence.

The third subcategory includes studies that arise when a problem presents itself that requires immediate attention. Some problems are unexpected changes in passing rates, sudden shifts in annual trend analyses, a severe security problem resulting in compromised items, and changes in test administration (from paper and pencil to computerized testing) that may affect performance. The number and range of such problems are enormous.

The second category of validity study includes all studies that apply to more than one testing program. These studies are also very diverse but contribute to the well-documented practices of test development. This handbook exemplifies these kinds of studies. What emerge from these studies are concepts, principles, and procedures bearing on better ways to develop tests and score tests results. In a very important way, these studies increase validity by providing guidance in important phases of test development and scoring. The balance of this chapter discusses each type of validity study and, where appropriate, examples are drawn from research literature or other sources.

VALIDITY STUDIES SPECIFIC TO A TESTING PROGRAM

Subcategory 1: Studies That Provide Validity Evidence in Support of the Claim for a Test Score Interpretation or Use

The majority of validity studies conducted within any testing program includes very routine studies. The purpose of this type of study is to provide validity evidence that supports a specific interpretation or use of a test score. The need for documentation is well established and justified in the *Standards* (AERA, APA, & NCME, 1999, chap. 6) and Haladyna (2002b). The annual technical report is one of the best opportunities to publicly display this validity evidence. Test sponsors are increasingly becoming more sophisticated about research as evidence and the need for documentation of this research. Test sponsor Web pages can be used to display this evidence to the public. What are some of the categories of studies that fall into this first subcategory?

Content-Related Validity Evidence

For an achievement test, a content analysis is recommended (Webb, chap. 8, this volume). The resulting research report shows that the content has been defined and explicated in a satisfactory way so that the basis for the test is well grounded in some curriculum. As Webb and others have shown, this initial and important phase in test development is increasing in scientific rigor as is demanded by the increase in high-stakes test score use. Nichols and Sugrue (1999) argue that many modern achievement tests are very likely to underrepresent the intended construct because test development is centered on knowledge-and-skill constructs as opposed to constructs representing cognitively complex abilities (Lohman, 1993; Sternberg, 1998). The *Standards* (AERA, APA, & NCME, 1999) are very clear about this need. For instance, on page 45 of the *Standards*, standard 3.11 states that "test developers should document the extent to which the content domain of a test represents the defined domain and test specifications."

For a professional credentialing examination, a practice analysis is recommended (Raymond & Neustel, chap. 9, this volume). Like the content analysis for achievement tests, practice analysis is more widely accepted and a necessary initial step in test development for a credentialing testing programs. The *Standards* (AERA, APA, & NCME, 1999) are also very clear about this need (see chap. 14, and in particular standards 14.8, 14.9, 14.10, 14.11, and 14.14). These standards address procedures and studies that comprise important content-related validity evidence.

Validity Evidence for Item Quality

Item development is a long-term, laborious process that provides the item bank used in any testing program. Documentation of procedures is a vital element in validation (Haladyna, 2002b). Although the process is not thought of as empirically driven research, the procedures followed provide a type of qualitative evidence of the adequacy of item development (Downing & Haladyna 1996). There are some empirical features to item development that arise, as noted by Livingston (chap. 19, this volume) involving item analysis. This handbook is dedicated to providing concepts, principles, and procedures that are universally adopted and widely used because of their positive effect on validity. Haladyna (2004) argues that validity can also apply to item response interpretation and use just as we do for the validity of a test score interpretation or use. From the item and item response perspectives, procedures and empirical studies are part of the mix of evidence used to validate item responses. This validity evidence may not appear in a technical report for security reasons, but the process and summary statistics provide a tangible result of a validity study attesting to the quality of a testing program's test items.

Validity Evidence for Comparability and Equating

Equating for scale comparability is a major concern in testing programs where equivalence between parallel forms and trend data is needed across time. In some instances, vertical scaling is done to measure performance through developmental phases of learning. The studies that are undertaken here are technically complex, but their accuracy is vital to validity.

Documentation of such procedures and results assure the test sponsors and the public about comparability of scores for different test forms and trends over time. When unusual or unexpected trends or differences occur, one of the suspected causes is error in the equating procedures or bad sampling. Research is the key to unlocking the answers to these problems. For example, standard 4.10 from the *Standards* (AERA, APA, & NCME, 1999, p. 57) justify a specific technical study regarding score equivalence of equated test forms. Both the rationale and evidence for equivalence should be presented. Standards 4.11 through 4.13 deal with specific aspects of equating. This topic also addresses comparability of test scores for diverse learners who may need accommodations. These persons may have disabilities requiring an Individual Education Plan, limited English proficiency, or inadequate exposure to instruction or training.

Validity Evidence Concerning the Setting of Standards

Standard setting is another type of study that has high-stakes consequences on examinees and the public. Studies should be well done and documented. These studies may seem routine yet provide another important piece of validity evidence. Cizek (chap. 10, this volume) provides background on these procedures and their importance to validity. An edited volume by Cizek (1999) is an authoritative source on the collective wisdom on standard setting. When a standard is set, the process should be treated as a study and be reported as such. The report constitutes an important piece of validity evidence.

Descriptive Statistics

Descriptive statistics of test performance of examinees and information concerning demographic variables are an ordinary type of research that answer basic questions about test performance. An important aspect of this kind of report is the description of the sample of examinees and its match to the intended population. Another important aspect is the study of trends over test dates to look for aberrations, such as abrupt and unexpected changes in passing rates. Although descriptive statistics involving demographics and item and test performance may seem routine, such studies are essential. For example, Standard 3.8 argues that for a field test of items, the characteristics of the sample should be known and compared to the characteristics of the population. For studies involving prediction and other criterion-related or group difference studies, description of the sample is important. It also follows that descriptive and inferential statistical procedures are done adequately, and the report of such studies is open for scrutiny.

Reliability and Standard Errors

One of the most basic and essential type of validity evidence is reliability. Indeed, an entire chapter of the prestigious *Educational Measurement* (Linn, 1989) is devoted to this topic, and other works authoritatively deal with this topic. Chapter 2 of the *Standards* (AERA, APA, & NCME, 1999) is devoted to reliability. Brennan (2001) provides a definitive book on generalizability theory and analyses dealing with many sources of errors of measurement. Generalizability studies are often recommended and done for testing programs where subjective judgments are made using rating scales. These studies are also useful for objectively scored tests. Both reliability and standard errors of measurement should be reported. In instances where subjective scoring is done, rater consistency and rater effects should be studied and reported. In some instances, where formats are objective and subjective, stratified coefficient α should be used.

Criterion-Related Validity Studies

Studies where a criterion is predicted using a test score, and other predictors, such as with admissions test, are very common. Such studies may involve bivariate or multivariate techniques and have threats to validity that arise from sampling, missing data, using linear techniques when data is not linearly distributed, restriction of range, low reliability, and exclusion of subgroups from the sample representing the population. These kinds of studies are important in admissions testing as well as in employment and credentialing testing. This type of study is essential to the validity claim for any testing program where prediction or correlation to a criterion is done. If examinees are classified into categories or pass–fail decisions are made, it is expected that a decision consistency index be reported and conditional standard errors should be reported (AERA, APA, & NCME, 1999).

Consequential

Standard 1.24 states that some factor existing in a test or the way it is reported, interpreted, or used may in some way contribute to unintended consequences. These outcomes should be studied and evaluated. A good example is the onset of high-stakes testing in our schools. If teachers and school leaders are accountable, one way to obtain higher test scores is to narrow the focus of the curriculum in the school to exactly to the content tested. Such a strategy is educationally unsound and undesirable. Evidence of such negative consequences works against valid test score interpretation or use. For instance, Nolen, Haladyna, and Haas (1992) reported on extensive inappropriate test preparation practices in one state. Smith (1991) echoed these findings in a qualitative study. She reported on the negative consequences of this pressure to perform. High-stakes accountability may cause some educators to corrupt test scores. Study of the consequences of testing and test policies is an emerging field in testing (Mehrens, 1998).

The categories of empirical studies described are not comprehensive of the realm of all such studies of this first subcategory of type 1 studies. These subcategory 1 studies are necessary to support validity. Test sponsors should be cognizant of the importance of these studies and ensure that the annual technical report contains documentation of these studies and their results as bearing on validity. The public should have access to such information, and posting technical reports and validity studies of this type on Web pages are an important and easy way to provide the public with access to information that supports validity in a testing program. However, data should never be released if they compromise security. Publishing item-level statistics or releasing items may jeopardize the validity of a testing program. As these studies represent fundamental validity evidence, type 1 studies should always be done and reported in a technical report.

Subcategory 2: Studies That Threaten a Test Score Interpretation of Use

It is noteworthy to point out that all studies described in subcategory 1 are intended to support validity, but may actually produce evidence against the argument for validity. In this second subcategory of validity studies germane to a specific testing program, studies are actually intended to explore the possibility that a testing program has threats to validity.

Construct-Irrelevant Variance

As noted, CIV is a threat to validity (Messick, 1984, 1989). Simply stated, CIV is systematic, constant error that is part of a test score. This error may increase or decrease test scores for some subsample of the sample being tested. Some examinees obtain higher or lower scores than other examinees because of some construct-irrelevant factor. We never know how much random error is contained in any specific test score, but it is possible to uncover sources of this systematic error and estimate its seriousness.

Lord and Novick (1968) formulated CIV in theoretical terms as a second type of error as distinguished from random error. Thorndike (1920) referred to this type of error as *constant*. Although Lord and Novick did not use the term CIV, it is clear from their discussion what was intended. The formula for an observed score is:

$$y = t + e_1 + e_2 \tag{32.1}$$

where y is the observed score, t is the true score, e_1 is random error that is involved with reliability and e_2 is random error that is involved with CIV. Consider rater severity in any performance test that is subjectively scored. For the variable rater, e_2 should be zero. Unfortunately, there is abundant, documented evidence that e_2 is positive for some examinees and negative for others. If rater severity is high, the effect of this kind of error alone can have consequences on whether some student passes or fails a high-stakes test (Haladyna, 2004).

Haladyna and Downing (2004) propose a typology of sources of CIV, and cite examples of each source. They also obtain further documentation from news reports and archival information. Published research on CIV is not as extensive as it should be. It is hard to motivate test development and test analyst personnel to establish a research agenda that looks for negative validity evidence that may undermine what they are trying to accomplish with validation. Often, research on CIV comes from critics of testing policies and testing programs. One source of information about CIV in general comes from the National Center for Fair and Open Testing (http://www.fairtest.org/). Their mission simply stated is: The National Center for Fair & Open Testing (FairTest) works to end the misuses and flaws of standardized testing and to ensure that evaluation of students, teachers and schools is fair, open, valid and educationally beneficial." Although the Center's mission is laudable and it provides much accurate information about sources of CIV in standardized testing, this organization also has policies and a point of view about educational testing that may affect their objectivity on matters calling for professional judgment. As with any source of information, one should check other sources for convergent evidence or authenticate findings in some other way.

Another source of negative evidence comes from essays or books that mix research with conclusions. One example is *The Case Against Standardized Testing* by Alfie Kohn (2000). Information obtained from these sources, like any others sources, needs to be evaluated for their truth. Nonetheless, the search for CIV has to include all sources of information to obtain the most complete evaluation of this important threat to validity.

Three examples are given here of studies of CIV. Each represents a different approach, but each increases our understanding about how CIV can undermine our best efforts to validate a testing program.

In high-stakes performance testing that is subjectively scored, rater effects include a set of tendencies on the part of raters that weaken validity. Myford and Wolfe (2003) provide one of the most comprehensive reviews of rater effects in performance testing. This report reflects a long-term effort to collect and summarize the literature bearing on CIV introduced by raters in subjective scoring of performance tests. This kind of research exemplifies the role that research reviews play in influencing test development or scoring. In this instance, their work informs the argument for or against adjusting test scores when sources of CIV are detected that are attributed to raters.

Another example comes from a study by Bishop and Frisbie (1999) involving the *Iowa Test of Basic Skills*. They wondered if some items that were on the third grade test form and were also presented on the fourth grade test form would compromise validity due to exposure of the items. They conducted an experimental study with overlapping and nonoverlapping items on these two test forms. There was no evidence that exposure at an earlier grade led to higher performance at the next grade for the same items. Thus, this study provided some evidence that this threat to CIV might not be serious.

A third example comes from the National Center for Fair and Open Testing's *FairTest Examiner* (2001). They report a scoring error on a national graduate admissions test that affected about 3% of all persons taking the test. They argued that the error may have cost some students the chance of being admitted to a graduate program. Another report from the same issue shows that scores were inflated owing to a scoring error on the Minnesota state achievement test (http://www.childrenfirstamerica.org/DailyNews/04Mar/0309041.htm). Scoring errors in testing seem to be epidemic. The consequences of such errors are difficult to ascertain or even if these errors were corrected. Studies should be done and publicly reported by test sponsors when the test score interpretation or use affects or informs the public. But such reports are very rare in the literature; they are more common in the newspapers and on the Web. These two examples did not come from reports in refereed journals. Usually, such reports of CIV come from a variety of other sources. In both instances, an annual technical report where data are tracked over years may reveal aberrations in trends that signal such scoring errors and other sources of CIV.

The discussion and three examples show that CIV is a significant threat to validity. Every testing program should identify which of the threats are most imminent and then plan research to identify the threat and evaluate its seriousness. Subsequently, each source of CIV should be reduced or eliminated if it threatens validity.

Construct Underrepresentation

Messick (1989) coined the phrase *construct underrepresentation* to signify another type of threat to validity where the measure of a construct may not be faithful or accurate to the definition. A useful, related concept is *fidelity*, the logical correspondence between measure and construct definition, which he attributed to Loevinger (1957). Messick (1995a, 1995b) identified content and substantive aspects of construct validation that seem to be associated with construct underrepresentation.

One example comes from the measurement of writing, a complex cognitive ability. The test with highest fidelity to the construct of writing involves performance. The writing performance test elicits a sample that is subjectively scored using a holistic rating scale or a set of analytic trait rating scales (rubrics). There are also multiple-choice tests of writing skills, such as spelling, punctuation, grammar, and capitalization. These multiple-choice test scores have a high correlation with writing performance measures, but these multiple-choice test scores do not have high fidelity with the construct of writing. We could develop a curriculum that emphasizes the learning of writing skills without affecting writing itself. If we used a test of writing skills to make an inference about someone's writing ability, we would be underrepresenting the construct. Writing skills are one part of writing ability. A multiple-choice test of writing skills underrepresents the construct of writing ability.

Studies that provide content-related validity evidence are rare but increasing. Webb (chap. 8, this volume) and Raymond and Neustel (chap. 9, this volume) update the science of construct definition and content analysis for two types of tests, achievement and credentialing. As the science of construct explication grows, there will be more studies concerning content. These studies are necessarily subcategory 1 in the typology in this chapter, but other types of studies contribute to our understanding of construct underrepresentation.

A test sponsor and developer faces an omnipresent dilemma that the test they are developing is either unidimensional or multidimensional. Tate (2002, 2004) argues that many achievement and credentialing tests are multidimensional, because our content analysis or practice analysis, test specifications, and item development all emphasize topics that relate to a general domain of achievement. These topics, even if highly correlated, constitute a basis for multidimensionality. Tate also argues that studies of dimensionality are vital to understanding the nature of the construct being measured. At a more practical level, can subscores be responsibly and validly interpreted and reported or used for high-stakes purposes or program evaluation? This is particularly problematic when a unidimensional scaling method is used, which seems to argue that a single total score is a sufficient statistic for a construct being measuring. The multidimensional perspective argues that a construct is made up of separable, distinctive traits that may be highly intercorrelated.

Walker and Beretvas (2003) provide one example of a study of dimensionality as affecting validity of test score interpretations and use. They discuss the dilemma of using unidimensional scaling models for multidimensional data and the effects on score interpretations and other factors, some of which may constitute CIV. They point out that previous research was done with simulated data, and their study involved real data. They concluded that when unidimensional models are used for multidimensional data, incorrect inferences can be made about students when a set of performance standards is used. Their more complex multidimensional model classified 10% of fourth graders and 16% of seventh graders when compared to a simpler, unidimensional model. They also concluded that the casual assumption of unidimensionality may lead to increased measurement error, particularly in reporting subscores. Ryan (chap. 29, this volume) presents a scholarly analysis of this problem and argues that the reliability of subscores can be severely limited with many tests.

An important step in test development is selecting the appropriate item format once content has been established and test specifications are being created. A decision in this process is the choice of item formats. DeMars (1998) completed a study that examined the hypothesis about the achievement construct measured as a function of different item constructed-response and selected-response item formats. She also evaluated the interaction of gender with these formats. She found that gender did not interact with the type of item format, and differences in content as a function of item formats did not materialize. There is a considerable, growing literature on this issue, and it continues to hold high interest for many test researchers (Haladyna, 2004; Rodriguez, 2002). There seems to be a persistent suspicion that item formats may dictate the type of content measured and cognitive demand elicited. Studies of item format capabilities and interactions of selected variables, such as gender, with item formats continue to explore the potential for this type of construct underrepresentation.

Studies of construct underrepresentation, like studies of CIV, are important to ensure that threats to validity are being anticipated and an active research program is defending against these threats. It is imperative that test developers and test sponsors think about a research agenda that not only includes the vital type 1 studies but also includes type 2 and type 3 studies that may identify factors that jeopardize validity.

Subcategory 3: Studies That Address Other Problems That Threaten Test Score Interpretation or Use

Invariably, a test developer or test analyst identifies a problem or potential problem that in some way undermines the validity of a test score interpretation or use. This problem is likely to be related to CIV or construct underrepresentation. A study is undertaken to identify the problem, estimate its severity, and recommend remedial action. Testing program personnel should aggressively seek to identify these problems and plan studies to address their resolution.

A very practical problem in test development is how to obtain test specification weights from a job analysis for a credentialing examination. Spray and Huang (2000) studied this problem and reviewed the scant literature. They propose a method that involves the use of item response theory. They propose four independent techniques for obtaining test specifications, and they provide a research agenda for future study of this problem. This kind of research fills a gap in the technology of test development in the important step of transforming a job or practice analysis into test specifications. Raymond and Neustel (chap. 9, this volume) discuss the job/practice analysis more extensively and provides more background on this particular problem. Webb (chap. 8, this volume) discusses methods for creating test specifications from content analysis for educational achievement tests.

Buckendahl, Smith, Impara, and Plake (2002) provide another good example of research on a problem for a specific testing program. They compared two methods for setting cut scores on an educational achievement test for seventh grade mathematics. They reviewed the literature and point out the need for more studies on the issue of choosing a standard-setting method. This kind of research answers a very practical question about the validity competing standard-setting methods.

A third example involves computer-based test administration. Bridgeman, Lennon, and Jackenthal (2003) designed an experimental study to determine if screen size, resolution, and display rate affected student performance on a computer-based test. This study was designed to evaluate a CIV threat to validity in the GRE and the Test of English as a Foreign Language. They found no differences for mathematics scores but verbal scores seemed slightly influenced by higher resolution screens. Thus, their finding sends a warning to the test developers that the type of monitor used may affect student performance in a construct-irrelevant way.

These three examples show how testing program staff identify problems that threaten validity and how they use research to study and, hopefully, dispel the threat. It seems natural that all testing programs experience problems that empirical study may resolve. As part of an annual review of any testing program, it seems natural to plan some studies of pressing problems and keep a contingency fund for future, unexpected problems, so that research can be done when the problem surfaces. Immediate action can curtail threats to validity that lead to serious negative consequences.

Validity Studies That Apply to More Than One Testing Program

The majority of studies appearing in such journals as *Applied Measurement in Education, Educational Assessment, Educational and Psychological Measurement, Journal of Applied Measurement*, and the *Journal of Educational Measurement* often introduce concepts, principles, or procedures or address problems of general nature that apply to a wider array of testing programs. Papers presented at annual meetings of the AERA and the NCME also provide some of this literature. In fact, the mission of such journals is to advance the science in test development and scoring that indirectly benefits validity. This fifth type of validity study is the most indirect of the set of five presented in Table 32.1, but test developers and analysts conduct work based on experiences and the concepts, principles, and procedures that they think lead to better tests that give us more valid test score interpretations and uses. In this section four studies are presented that fall in this category.

A Study That Introduces a Concept

Automated item generation has been a long-standing interest among test developers (Haladyna, 2004; Irvine & Kyllonen, 2001; Roid & Haladyna, 1982). Recently, researchers have been interested in item design concepts that advance the science of item development. Enright, Morley, and Sheehan (2002) studied the effects of systematic item variation on item statistics. The concept they introduced advances our capability to design test items of predictable

TABLE 32.1
Types of Validity Studies

Validity Studies Specific to a Testing Program	
1. Studies that provide validity evidence in support of the claim for a test score interpretation or use.	Practice analysis (Raymond & Neustel, chap. 9, this volume), content analysis (Webb, chap. 8, this volume), item analysis, standard setting, equating for comparability, reliability.
2. Studies that threaten a test score interpretation or use	2a. CIV: Cheating, scoring errors, student anxiety, fatigue, motivation, nonresponse, unethical test preparation, inappropriate test administration, and rater severity.
	2b. Studies of dimensionality, item format/content interactions, cognitive demand of test items.
3. Studies that address other problems that threaten test score interpretation or use.	Unexpected results for one test year, drop in reliability, drift in item parameters over time, changing of a test edition involving renorming, redesign of a published test, possible security problem.
Validity Studies That Apply to More Than One Testing Program	
Studies that lead to the establishment of concepts, principles, or procedures that guide, inform, or improve test development or scoring.	These studies are diverse in nature but contribute to the well-documented practices found in test development and scoring. This volume contains hundreds of references to such studies. The use of the concepts, principles, and procedures emerging from these studies contributes to validity.

statistical quality much faster than the traditional method where item writers write each item. As research continues in this field, future studies will inform us about how to rapidly produce items using the concept they proposed. The establishment of this concept leads to principles and procedures that improve test development and scoring.

A Study That Introduces a Principle

A *principle* is a guideline or rule that is followed to obtain the most valid result in test development and scoring. A good example of this comes from the problem of nonresponse in testing and how to score student response strings when we have omitted or not-reached responses. De Ayala, Plake, and Impara (2001) provide an interesting analysis of this problem and cite earlier comments and research to the extent that notreached items should be ignored and not scored as incorrect. The logical explanation for omitted responses may favor scoring each omit as incorrect or giving some neutral value. These researchers compared a variety of scoring procedures and reached a conclusion about an optimal procedure. Interestingly, the principles espoused in this study also led to a recommended procedure.

A Study That Introduces a Procedure

Computerized adaptive testing (CAT) has been long championed as a more efficient way of testing, but threats to validity exist. If students copy from other test takers or use compromised items, test results are likely to contain CIV that contaminates test score interpretations and weakens validity. Meijer (2002) studied the detection of aberrant response patterns with CAT. He presented the problem and a theory for its solution, and then he analyzed data to show how some item response patterns may be aberrant. He compared three methods and made a recommendation. This kind of research impressively works on a problem to improve test scoring that results in a recommended procedure for detecting outlier performance.

A Study of a Pervasive Problem

An example of a pervasive problem affecting the validity of an achievement test score interpretation is the study of the role of transfer in performance assessment. Because performance testing tends to produce less-than-desirable reliability estimates, and the sampling of complex problems may not be sufficient for the domain of possible problems, performance testing has not become extensive in state achievement testing. Parkes (2001) presents an analysis of this problem and proposes a research agenda that seeks to answer essential questions about the validity of performance test scores. The proposed set of future studies continues the recent practice of marrying cognitive learning theory and psychometrics. This line of research may lead to the improvement of performance testing and realization of its promise to reform elementary and secondary education more in the line of construct-centered teaching and student assessments.

These four examples show how research conducted each year contributes to a growing literature that influences test development and scoring. Testing organizations such as ACT, California Test Bureau–McGraw-Hill, ETS, Harcourt Educational Measurement, and Riverside Publishing have researchers whose articles often appear in journals or are reported at conferences. Faculty and graduate students from colleges and universities also produce a considerable amount of this kind of research. Credentialing boards and federal, state, and local educational agencies also have researchers who report this kind of research. The federal government often supports such research. Without this press for new concepts, principles, and procedures, and the solution of problems affecting many testing programs, the technology for testing could not advance. Fortunately, our technology for test development and scoring has advanced very rapidly.

RECOMMENDATIONS FOR PRACTICE

As shown in this chapter, validity studies have many important functions in a testing program.

1. All testing programs should complete subcategory 1 validity studies and document each one in a technical report. Access should be provided to specific study reports. As these studies constitute essential validity evidence, it is unconscionable that a testing program would not engage in validation research of this nature. It is a good idea to also link this evidence to the *Standards* (AERA, APA, & NCME, 1999), as Linn (chap. 2, this volume) urges.
2. All testing programs should engage in subcategory 2 studies. CIV and construct underrepresentation are serious threats to validity in virtually any testing program. A research agenda should be created that addresses these threats in rank-order of severity. The search and eventual elimination or reduction of each threat can only strengthen the argument for validity.
3. All testing programs face unique problems that call for research that falls in subcategory 3. Often, these problems arise suddenly and require immediate attention. It is difficult to plan for studies that address suddenly arising problems, but it is good policy to have a contingency fund for such eventualities. As these problems arise, research can identify the severity of the problem and possibly offer a solution. Testing organizations may have staff for these kinds of studies or may want to outsource this work.
4. Many researchers in the area of testing identify and pursue programs of study that in some way increase validity, either by introducing new concepts, principles, or procedures, or addressing problems that generally affect many testing programs. The majority of

published journal articles in the field of educational measurement fall into this category. This research is often the result of thoughtful leadership by sponsors of testing programs. Given resources available in every testing program, such research should be encouraged because it benefits the community of test developers and analysts worldwide.

SUMMARY AND CONCLUSION

This chapter defined *validity study* very broadly and argued that validity studies are crucial to validation. Two types of validity studies were described: one specific for a testing program and the other general and applicable to many testing programs. Both types contribute to improving validity. Examples of each were provided. Test sponsors and test development staff are strongly urged to consider doing validity studies that are germane to their testing program and support any research that may have value to the field of testing.

A problem that exists in test development is a lack of connectedness among these validity studies. Reviews of research that tie together disparate research are very helpful. But in general, these kinds of studies are often disconnected. Ideally, there is need for a unified theory that includes a prevailing statistical theory of test scores, and a commonly accepted technology for developing tests and scoring test results. This handbook represents our best attempt at developing this technology. Future editions of this handbook will be better, largely because of the efforts of contributors such as those found in these chapters but also due to the continuance of validity studies described in this chapter.

ACKNOWLEDGMENTS

The author gratefully acknowledges reviews of this chapter by Steve Downing and Michael Kane and their suggestions for improvements. For those aspects of this chapter that seem worthwhile, credit goes to the author; for those aspects that seem weak or poorly written, blame should go to them.

REFERENCES

American Educational Research Association (AERA), American Psychological Association (APA), & National Council on Measurement in Education (NCME). (1999). *Standards for educational and psychological testing*. Washington, DC: American Educational Research Association.

Bishop, N. S., & Frisbie, D. A. (1999). The effect of test item familiarization on achievement test scores. *Applied Measurement in Education, 12*(4), 327–341.

Bridgeman, B., Lennon, M. L., & Jackenthal, A. (2003). Effects of screen size, screen resolution, and display rate on computer-based test performance. *Applied Measurement in Education, 16*, 191–205.

Brennan, R. L. (2001). *Generalizability theory*. New York: Springer-Verlag.

Buckendahl, C. W., Smith, R. W., Impara, J. C., & Plake, B. S. (2002). A comparison of Angoff and bookmark standard setting methods. *Journal of Educational Measurement, 39*(3), 253–263.

Cizek, G. J. (1999). *Cheating on tests: How to do it, detect it, and prevent it*. Mahwah, NJ: Lawrence Erlbaum Associates.

Cronbach, L. J. (1987). Five perspectives of the validity argument. In H. Wainer & H. I. Braun (Eds.), *Test validity*. Hillsdale, NJ: Lawrence Erlbaum Associates.

Cronbach, L. J. (1989). Construct validation after thirty years. In R. E. Linn (Ed.), *Intelligence: Measurement, theory, and public policy* (pp. 147–171). Urbana: University of Illinois Press.

Crooks. T. J., Kane, M. T., & Cohen, A. S. (1996). Threats to valid use of assessments. *Assessment in Education, 3*(3), 265–285.

Crouse, J., & Trusheim, D. (1988). *The case against the SAT*. Chicago: The University of Chicago Press.

De Ayala, R., Plake, B. S., & Impara, J. C. (2001). The impact of omitted responses on the accuracy of ability estimation in item response theory. *Journal of Educational Measurement, 38*(3), 213–234.

DeMars, C. E. (1998). Gender differences in mathematics and science on a high school proficiency exam: The role of response format. *Applied Measurement in Education, 11*(3), 279–299.

Downing, S. M., & Haladyna, T. M. (1996). Model for evaluating high-stakes testing programs: Why the fox should not guard the chicken coop. *Educational Measurement: Issues and Practice, 15,* 5–12.

Downing, S. M., & Haladyna, T. M. (1997). Test item development: Validity evidence from quality assurance procedures. *Applied Measurement in Education, 10,* 61–82.

Enright, M. K., Morley, M., & Sheehan, K. M. (2002). Items by design: The impact of systematic feature variation on item statistical characteristics, *Applied Measurement in Education, 15*(1), 49–74.

Haladyna, T. M. (2002a). Epilogue: Theory and research improve large-scale testing. In G. Tindal & T. Haladyna (Eds.), *Large-scale assessment programs for all students: Development, implementation, and analysis* (pp. 483–497). Mahwah, NJ: Lawrence Erlbaum Associates.

Haladyna, T. M. (2002b). Supporting documentation: Assuring more valid test score interpretations and uses. In G. Tindal & T. M. Haladyna (Eds.) *Large-scale assessment for all students: Validity, technical adequacy, and implementation* (pp. 89–108). Mahwah, NJ: Lawrence Erlbaum Associates.

Haladyna, T. M. (2004). *Developing and validating multiple-choice test items* (3rd ed). Mahwah, NJ: Lawrence Erlbaum Associates.

Haladyna, T. M., & Downing, S. M. (2004). Construct-irrelevant variance in high-stakes testing. *Educational Measurement: Issues and Practice, 23*(1), 17–27.

Impara, J. C. (Ed.). (1995). *Licensure testing: Purposes, procedures, and practices. Buros-Nebraska series on measurement and testing.* Lincoln, NE: Buros Institute of Mental Measurements.

Irvine, S. H., & Kyllonen, P. C. (Eds.). (2001). *Item generation for test development.* Mahwah, NJ: Lawrence Erlbaum Associates.

Jensen, A. R. (1980) *Bias in mental testing.* New York: The Free Press.

Kane, M. T. (1992). An argument-based approach to validity. *Psychological Bulletin, 112,* 527–535.

Kohn, A. (2000). *The case against standardized testing: Raising test scores, ruining the schools.* Portsmouth, NH: Heineman.

Linn, R. L. (Ed.). (1989). *Educational measurement* (3rd ed.). New York: American Council on Education & MacMillan.

Lohman, D. F. (1993). Teaching and testing to develop fluid abilities. *Educational Researcher, 22,* 12–23.

Loevinger, J. (1957). Objective tests as instruments of psychological theory. *Psychological Reports, 3,* 635–694.

Lord, F. M., & Novick, M. R. (1968). *Statistical theories of mental test scores.* Reading, MA: Addison-Wesley.

Mehrens, W. (1998). Consequences of assessment: What is evidence? *Education Policy Analysis Archives, 6*(13). Retrieved July 25, 2005 from http://epaa.asu.edu/epaa/v6n13.html.

Meijer, R. (2002). Outlier detection in high-stakes certification testing. *Journal of Educational Measurement, 11*(4), 301–310.

Messick, S. (1984). The psychology of educational measurement. *Journal of Educational Measurement, 21,* 215–237.

Messick, S. (1989). Validity. In R. L. Linn (Ed.), *Educational measurement* (3rd ed., pp. 13–104). New York: American Council on Education and Macmillan.

Messick, S. (1995a). Validity of psychological assessment: Validation of inferences from persons' responses and performances as scientific inquiry into score meaning. *American Psychologist, 50,* 741–749.

Messick, S. (1995b). Standards of validity and the validity of standards in performance assessment.*Educational Measurement: Issues and Practice, 14*(4), 5–8.

Myford, C., & Wolfe, E. W. (2003). Detecting and measuring rater effects using the many-faceted Rasch model. *Journal of Applied Measurement, 4,* 386–422.

Nichols, P., & Sugrue, B. (1999). The lack of fidelity between cognitively complex constructs and conventional test development practices. *Educational Measurement: Issues and Practice, 18*(2), 18–29.

National Center for Fair and Open Testing. (2001, Summer). More errors plague testing. *FairTest Examiner, 15*(3), 6–7.

Nolen, S. B., Haladyna, T. M., & Haas, N. S. (1992). Uses and abuses of achievement test scores. *Educational Measurement: Issues and Practices, 11,* 9–15.

Owen, D. (1985). *None of the above: Behind the myth of scholastic aptitude.* Boston: Houghton Mifflin.

Parkes, J. (2001). The role of transfer in the variability of performance assessment scores. *Educational Assessment, 7*(2), 143–163.

Rodriguez, M. (2002). Choosing an item format. In G. Tindal & T. M. Haladyna (Eds). *Large-scale assessment programs for all students: Validity, technical adequacy, and implementation* (pp. 213–231). Mahwah, NJ: Lawrence Erlbaum Associates.

Roid, G. H. (2003). *Stanford-Binet intelligence test* (5th ed.). Scarborough, ON, CA: Nelson Thompson Learning.

Roid, G. H., & Haladyna, T. M. (1982). *Toward a technology of test-item writing.* New York: Academic Press.

Smith, M. L. (1991). Put to the test: The effects of external testing on teachers. *Educational Researcher, 20,* 8–11.
Spray, J. A., & Huang, C. (2000). Obtaining test blueprint weights from job analysis surveys. *Journal of Educational Measurement, 37*(3), 187–201.
Sternberg, R. J. (1998). Abilities are forms of developing expertise. *Educational Researcher, 27*(3), 11–20.
Tate, R. (2002). Test dimensionality. In G. Tindal & T. M Haladyna (Eds.), *Large-scale assessment programs for all student: Validity, technical adequacy, and implementation* (pp. 180–211).Mahwah, NJ: Lawrence Erlbaum Associates.
Tate, R. (2004). Implications of multidimensionality for total score and subscore performance. *Applied Measurement in Education, 17*(2), 89–112.
Thorndike, E. L. (1920). A constant error in psychological ratings. *Journal of Applied Psychology, 4,* 25–29.
Walker, C. M., & Beretvas, S. N. (2003). Comparing multidimensional and unidimensional proficiency classifications: Multidimensional IRT as a diagnostic aid. *Journal of Educational Measurement, 40*(3), 255–275.

VII
Epilogue

Epilogue

Cynthia Board Schmeiser
ACT

After reading this *Handbook of Test Development*, one has to be stunned with the significant progress we have made in test development over the past 40 years, particularly in the last 20. What this handbook makes startlingly clear are the great strides that have been made in bringing a more scientific approach to a profession that was largely based on opinion and intuition forty years ago. The substantive recommendations for practitioners are substantially based on research that has been conducted rather than conveying what has become the "common law" of test development conveyed through advice and opinion through its history.

The purpose of the *Handbook* as stated by Downing and Haladyna is to serve as a:

> ...systematic and comprehensive source of information about developing tests of knowledge, skills, and ability. The Handbook presents the state-of-the-art of developing tests in the twenty-first century.

In my opinion, the handbook has achieved this purpose and more. The handbook not only provides a comprehensive treatment of the major considerations in the test development process, but addresses the new issues in test development that have come with applications of technology in testing, both those in support of the test development process (e.g., computerized testing) and those against (e.g., use of technology to breach test security). More importantly, all of the contributors to the *Handbook* based the content of their chapters on the *Standards for Educational and Psychological Testing,* which serve as the foundation for sound test development practice.

Although the handbook is intended to be a comprehensive summary of state-of-the-art test development practice, nearly all of the chapters go beyond current practice by suggesting implications for the future. I cannot help but reflect on some of the visions that these chapters created for me. Permit me to share some of the dreams and hopes that were evoked by the handbook.

In the last 20 years, the standards-based reform movement in education has had an enormous impact on curriculum, instruction, and assessment. The use of assessment results for evaluative purposes has grown and become legislatively formalized. Expectations of growth and improvement in achievement and performance are now commonplace. But against this backdrop of accountability and expectations for improvement are what I consider to be real implications for test development and the expectations that are likely to be placed upon it in the near future.

We all know that true reform will never be accomplished through testing alone. The large-scale tests being developed and used today for accountability purposes measure the status of achievement and progress over time. One wonders, however, whether we, as test development professionals, need to focus more on the design of tests that are directly connected to instruction as a fundamental component of test design so that they not only provide more detailed information about student knowledge, skills, and abilities, but provide their results in terms of empirically supported instructional interventions. The current methodologies for doing this are, in my opinion, clumsy at best, but with the foundation summarized in this handbook, we have the ways and means to do this.

A new idea? Not at all. Diagnostic testing has been with our profession for a long time, but we have not made the advancements in test development practice to advance more dynamic assessment practices that are well articulated with instruction early in the test design stage. We need test design to be predicated on the need to report fine gradations of information that are directly connected to next instructional steps which are empirically documented as appropriate. This leads me to wonder whether we, as test developers, need to think more about scientific applications of test development within the context of current issues in education. I think we do.

Just as we want to evaluate the outcomes of instruction by assessment and use those results to improve instruction, we should also demand of ourselves increased vigilance in evaluating the decisions we make in the test design stage and use this information to improve test and item pool design and development. For example, the item usage patterns in a computer adaptive testing pool can be used to evaluate how well the item selection and item exposure algorithms are working vis à vis the test blueprint and also inform the next round of item development. Similarly, the effectiveness of particular item formats in assessing certain types of tasks should be evaluated as to what they are measuring and how well and should be used to inform the test blueprints. All decisions made in test design and development should be evaluated routinely to determine if they are ultimately consistent with the intended purposes and uses of the test results.

Although the handbook does not focus in depth on the technology of item writing, I would offer a word of caution. Although great advances have been made in item-generation technologies in the past decade, I think it is important that we not sacrifice the art of test development that comes from the creative ideas for test items from the minds of educator–practitioners who are immersed in the educational process on a daily basis for the efficiencies that accrue to test developers when technology is used to generate items. We need to find the proper balance between the artful creativity that comes from our most experienced educators with the science of item writing.

At the same time, we must not lose sight of the need to uphold the highest ethical standards of our profession as we practice test development. More and more, the day-to-day demands on test development raise issues that press the ethical principles of all of us. Although it was not within the intended scope of the handbook to address these pressures directly, we must not lose sight of the need to maintain the highest standards of our profession in our behavior as well as in our methodologies.

All of this is to say that there is no doubt that this handbook will serve as a valuable resource to all of us, not only those who are studying to enter our profession, but for those of us who practice test development on a daily basis. I urge all of us to continue to strive to make what we do matter to those we serve—those about whom we make inferences on the basis of test results—the examinees. We should embrace as our goal the design of tests that provide results that give guidance to each and every examinee about what they should do next after receiving their results, whether to strengthen specific weaknesses in knowledges, skills, or abilities, or to continue to push attainment to the next level. We must never sacrifice what is right for the examinees we serve for test development practices that make it easier on us as test developers.

Although trite but true, we have come a long way as evidenced by the fine work of those who contributed to this *Handbook on Test Development*, but there is much left to do.

Author Index

A

Abedi, J., 29, 380, 381, 382, 383, 385, 386, 387, 389, 664, 668
Accountability Works, Inc., 39
Ackerman, T. A., 333, 511
Adams, M. J., 385, 386, 387, 390
Adema, J., 511, 588
Albus, D., 664
Alexander, C., 71
Algina, J., 379, 495, 498, 506, 508, 519
Algozzine, B., 609
Allalouf, A., 115, 118
Allen, M. J., 379
Allen, N. L., 470, 478
Almond, P., 449, 450, 664
Almond, R. G., 61, 82
American Association of School Administrators (AASA), 726
American Board of Physical Medicine and Rehabilitation, 203
American College Testing (ACT), Inc., 662, 715
American Educational Research Association (AERA), American Psychological Association (APA), & National Council on Measurement in Education (NCME), x, 4, 7, 10, 20, 22, 23, 27, 28, 29, 30, 31, 32, 33, 34, 35, 36, 37, 45, 116, 117, 118, 119, 123, 124, 125, 131, 156, 157, 176, 181, 189, 190, 201, 205, 206, 227, 228, 233, 238, 303, 305, 312, 314, 321, 326, 340, 344, 354, 355, 360, 361, 364, 373, 378, 379, 446, 470, 484, 488, 489, 490, 491, 492, 493, 497, 508, 509, 514, 518, 531, 532, 534, 537, 539, 546, 547, 558, 569, 601, 602, 625, 626, 627, 629, 630, 631, 633, 661, 666, 667, 678, 698, 709, 711, 712, 726, 729, 730, 739, 740, 741, 744, 745, 746, 752
American Educational Research Association (AERA) & National Council on Measurement Used in Education, 27, 726
American Federation of Teachers (AFT), 726

American Medical Association Manual of Style, 350
American Psychological Association (APA), 27, 726
American Psychological Association (APA), American Educational Research Association (AERA), & National Council on Measurement in Education (NCME), 27, 726
Anastasi, A., 450, 547
Anderson, G. S., 549
Anderson, S., 355
Andrich, D., 196
Angoff, W. H., 19, 133, 231, 239, 242, 360, 453, 464, 470, 474, 477, 503
Ankenmann, R. D., 632
Ansell, S. E., 657
Armstrong, R. D., 588
Ash, R. A., 205, 211
Association of Test Publishers (ATP), 726
Attali, Y., 13

B

Bachman, L. F., 68
Bacon, T. P., 495, 506, 511
Baddeley, A. D., 385, 388
Bagnato, S. J., 536,
Baker, E. L., 310, 380, 381, 382, 664, 668, 718
Baker, F. B., 511
Baker, R. L., 121
Baldwin, L. E., 385
Ban, J., 551
Banks, K. W., 633
Bar-Hillel, F. B., 120, 261, 262
Barmish, B. R., 511
Barnard, Y. F., 213
Barnes, L. L. B., 495, 501
Barrows, H. S., 206
Barton, K., 372
Bateson, D. J., 116

761

Baugh, J., 386
Baxter, G., 66
Bay, L., 251
Bayley, N., 528
Beaton, A. E., 470
Beattie, S., 609
Becker, D. F., 292
Beguin, A. A., 479
Bejar, I. I., 80, 338, 404
Bennett, G. K., 528
Bennett, R. E., 176, 211, 305, 310, 331, 335, 337, 341, 345
Ben-Shakar, G., 115, 118
Beretvas, S. N., 749
Bergstrom, B. A., 262
Berk, R. A., 360, 530
Bertrand, R., 293
Betebenner, D. W., 120
Beuk, C. H., 254, 256
Bever, T., 389
Bhola, D. S., 31
Bibel, D., 609
Biber, D., 388
Bielinski, J., 657, 661, 664, 665
Biggs, J. B., 68
Binet, A., 540
Birnbaum, A., 555, 578
Bishop, C. H., 116, 202, 747
Bloom, B. S., 166, 192, 203, 288
Blount, A., 664
Board, C., 353, 403
Bock, R. D., 512, 531, 578
Boekkooi-Timminga, E., 511, 588, 591
Bolt, S. E., 665
Bond, L., 116, 117, 310, 362
Bonnur, K., 121
Booch, G., 79, 264, 268
Bordage, G., 293
Bormuth, J. R., 299, 306, 385
Botel, M., 386
Boulet, J. R., 17
Bourque, L. B., 194
Bourque, M. L., 401
Boys, C., 718
Braden, J. P., 539
Bradley, N., 264
Brand, S., 63
Brandt, S., 345
Braswell, J., 330, 337
Braun, H. I., 462
Breese, J. S., 61
Brennan, R. L., 8, 13, 20, 109, 110, 142, 145, 205, 289, 312, 379, 458, 463, 469, 470, 471, 475, 476, 477, 478, 480, 495, 496, 510, 515, 516, 517, 518, 519, 520, 578, 588, 745
Bresnock, A. E., 354
Breyer, F. J., 509
Bridgeman, B., 612, 750
Bridgeman, P., 140, 141

Brossell, G., 310, 311
Brown, J. D., 311
Brown, L. M., 355
Bruce, F. A., 684, 721
Bruinks, R. H., 528
Buckendahl, C. W., 31, 247, 750
Bunch, M., 248
Burgin, W., 588
Burket, G. R., 555
Buros Institute for Assessment Consultation and Outreach (BIACO), 729
Buros Institute, 538
Burstein, J., 290, 548
Butler, F. A., 668
Butterfield, E., 140, 146

C

California Test Bureau (CTB)/McGraw-Hill, 470, 484, 718
Camilli, G., 720
Campbell, D. T., 532
Campion, M. A., 185, 192, 211
Cannell, J. J., 121
Cantor, J. A., 349, 350, 351
Capell, F. J., 310
Carey, P., 333
Carlson, A. B., 503, 504
Carpenter, J., 404
Carpenter, P. A., 386
Carr, P., 310
Carretier, H., 293
Carroll, J. B., 388, 391, 527, 528, 532
Carson, A. D., 537
Carter, K., 120
Case, S. M., 293, 297, 357
Castellon-Wellington, M., 381
Celce-Murcia, M., 386, 387, 388
Center for Universal Design, 318, 602
Center on Education Policy, 662
Chai, S., 215, 217, 218
Chalifour, C. L., 405
Chall, J. S., 385
Chang, H.-H., 551
Chang, K., 660
Chason, W. M., 501
Chen, C., 668
Chen, W.-H., 512, 531
Chia, M., 478
Chodorow, M., 548
Choppin, B. H., 261
Chou, C. P., 310
Cisco Systems, 65
Cizek, G. J., 19, 116, 121, 206, 226, 228, 239, 248, 400, 408, 633, 720, 745
Clapper, A., 659, 662, 663, 667, 669
Clauser, B. E., 143, 338, 548, 570
Cleary, T. A., 362

Cleveland, W. S., 586
Clyman, S. G., 338
Code of Fair Testing Practices in Education, 319
Cohen, A. S., 133, 135, 479, 511, 520, 627, 629, 733, 740
Cohen, J. A., 508
Cole, N. S., 360, 361, 362, 371, 372
College Board, 447
Collins, A. M., 68
Collins, L. M., 535
Collis, K. F., 68
Colliver, J. A., 206
Collum, E., 658
Colton, D., 183, 190, 194
Conrad, S. H., 495
Cook, L. L., 205, 453, 463, 501, 518
Cooke, N. J., 213
Coombs, C., 586
Cornelius, E. T., 182
Corrigan, B., 195
Cortina, J. M., 382
Council of Chief State School Officers (CCSSO), 40, 306
Crandall, J., 333, 335, 336, 386
Crehan, K., 353
Crist, M. K., 61
Crocker, L., 116, 122, 125, 379, 495, 498, 499, 506, 519
Cronbach, L. J., 133, 134, 135, 136, 138, 142, 145, 147, 148, 150, 151, 157, 305, 306, 379, 527, 530, 626, 740
Crooks, T. J., 133, 134, 627, 629, 733, 740
Cross, C. R., 656
Crouse, J., 741
Cummins, D. D., 380, 387
Cureton, E. E., 133

D

D'Costa, A., 192, 194, 202, 203
Dahl, M. N., 536
Dale, E., 386
Darlington, R. B., 362
Davey, T., 112, 226, 332, 399, 544, 546, 548, 552, 553, 559, 567
Davies, P., 388
Dawes, R. M., 195, 586
Dawson-Saunders, B., 355
De Champlain, A., 495, 496, 502
De Corte, E., 380
De Gruijter, D. N. M., 501
De Vries, P., 617
De Win, L., 380
Deane, P., 296
DeAyala, R., 751
DeCecco, J. P., 166
Delaney-Klinger, K. D., 192
Delgado, A. R., 352
DeMark, S., 660, 666

DeMars, C. E., 479, 749
Desimone, L. A., 184, 194
DeStefano, L., 667
deVillers, J., 389
deVillers, P., 389
Devlin, S., 586
Devore, R., 338
Diamond, L., 402
Dillman, D. A., 194
Dinero, T. E., 501
Disability Rights Advocates, 662
Divgi, D. R., 501
Divine, K. P., 684, 721
Dodd, B. G., 343
Donoghue, J. R., 496, 507
Donovan, M. S., 656
Dorans, N. J., 109, 320, 373, 441, 454, 458, 461, 462, 463, 464
Dornic, S., 378
Downing, S. M., 10, 11, 12, 14, 17, 18, 19, 23, 44, 91, 94, 95, 97, 98, 99, 101, 242, 243, 287, 289, 290, 291, 292, 293, 296, 299, 306, 330, 342, 349, 350, 352, 353, 366, 378, 379, 445, 627, 630, 631, 633, 661, 664, 665, 728, 740, 741, 742, 744, 747
Drasgow, F., 495
Dubose, P., 518
Dudycha, A. L., 404
Dunbar, S. B., 310, 718
Duran, R. P., 380, 382, 383
Dym, C. L., 63
Dynamics in Document Design, 609

E

Eaton, S. B., 664
Ebel, R. L., 19, 116, 133, 291, 293, 306
Educational Testing Service (ETS), 354, 363, 365, 366, 367, 368, 369, 370, 662, 728
Edwards, D. S., 182
Eignor, D. R., 336, 553
Eisner, E., 145
Elliot, R., 362
Elliot, S., 656, 666
Elliott, J. L., 539
Elliott, S. N., 539
Elstein, A. S., 206
Embretson, S. E., 68, 138, 478, 528, 536, 537, 544
Engelhart, M. D., 288
Enright, M. K., 407, 750
Equal Employment Opportunity Commission (EEOC), 183
Erickson, R. N., 656
Erwin, T. D., 314
Escobar, F., 382
Estes, C., 183, 190, 194, 616, 618
Evans, B., 618
Evans, C., 618
Evans, J., 333

F

Fagerlund, K. A., 192
Fair Test Examiner, 748
Fan, M., 552, 567
Fan, X., 453
Farish, S. J., 493, 495, 506, 511
Farmer, E., 401
Fast, E., 680, 686
Federal Information Processing Standard (FIPS), 276
Feldhusen, J. F., 445
Feldt, L. S., 145, 499, 510
Felici, J., 609
Ferrara, P., 192
Fielder, E. P., 194
Figueroa, R. A., 378
Finegan, E., 386
Fink, A., 194
Fisher, T. L., 404
Fiske, D. W., 532
Fitzgerald, 335, 336
Fitzpatrick, C., 343
Fitzpatrick, R., 142
Fitzpatrick, S. J., 182
Fivars, G., 182
Flanagan, D. P., 533
Flanagan, J. C., 182
Fleishman, E. A., 182, 188, 192, 202, 204, 215
Flockton, L., 134
Folk, V. G., 592
Forster, K. I., 386, 495, 511
Forte Fast, E., 680
Fowles, M. E., 102, 103, 314
Frampton, D., 20
Francis, W. N., 385, 388, 391
Frank, L. A., 355
Frary, R. B., 350, 352
Fraser, C., 495, 502
Fraser, S. L., 195, 197
Freedle, R., 406, 418
Freeman, G. G., 386
Friedebach, J., 665
Friedebach, M., 665
Friedman, L., 182
Frisbie, D. A., 291, 292, 747
Fuchs, D., 658, 664, 665, 667
Fuchs, L. S., 658, 664, 665, 667
Furst, E. J., 288

G

Gael, S., 183, 186
Gagne, R. M., 166
Gamma, E., 61, 71
Garcia, P., 406
Gardner, K. M., 61, 71
Gathercole, S. E., 385, 388
Gay, A., 685, 721
Gershon, R. C., 262

Gessaroli, M. E., 495, 502
Gibbons, R., 502
Gifford, J., 401
Gitomer, D. H., 69, 312
Glas, C. A., 531, 538, 555, 592
Glasgrow, A., 659
Gleser, G. C., 142, 379, 530
Golan, S., 121
Goldman, R. P., 61
Goldstein, F. C., 536
Goodenough, F., 151
Goodman, D. P., 20, 206, 678, 680, 684, 685, 686, 687, 708, 721
Gorman, B. S., 609
Gorman, S., 609
Gorsuch, R. L., 534
Government Accountability Office, 664
Granowsky, A., 386
Graue, M. E., 121
Graves, P. E., 354
Gray, G. T., 353
Greaud, V., 340
Green, B. F., 305, 340
Green, D. R., 246, 247, 354, 360
Green, K., 405
Greene, J., 4, 201, 202, 461, 493, 494, 495, 496, 510, 511
Greeno, J. G., 68, 380
Gregory, M., 609
Grimm, L. G., 534
Grise, P., 609
Gronlund, N. E., 306, 378
Gross, L. J., 352
Grossman, P. D., 660
Guille, R., 355
Guion, R., 149
Gulliksen, H., 464
Gupta, N. C., 499

H

Haas, N. S., 121, 746
Habbick, T., 343
Haertel, E. H., 310, 471, 501, 509, 626, 627
Hafner, A., 664
Haiman, J., 387, 389
Hakel, M. D., 182
Haladyna, T. M., 10, 11, 14, 17, 18, 23, 44, 91, 94, 95, 97, 98, 99, 101, 104, 118, 176, 206, 266, 287, 288, 289, 290, 291, 292, 293, 296, 297, 299, 305, 306, 330, 342, 349, 350, 351, 352, 353, 366, 378, 380, 445, 503, 533, 547, 591, 627, 630, 631, 633, 661, 664, 665, 712, 713, 728, 729, 740, 741, 742, 744, 747, 749, 750
Halliday, M. A. K., 386
Hambleton, R. K., 15, 16, 17, 20, 120, 181, 206, 228, 237, 242, 243, 253, 262, 309, 343, 354, 400, 401, 408, 409, 416, 453, 478, 499, 500, 501, 507, 508, 536, 537, 544, 576, 578, 588, 678, 680, 684, 685, 686, 687, 708, 721

Hamel, L., 79
Hamilton, L., 116, 162, 664
Hamlett, C., 664
Hansen, E. G., 381
Hanson, B. A., 478, 479, 516, 517
Harcourt Assessment (also known as Harcourt Educational Measurement), 470, 481, 528, 529
Hargrove, T. Y., 115
Harniss, M., 664
Harris, D. J., 463, 470, 477, 483
Hartley, J., 609
Harvey, R. J., 181, 182, 183, 186, 189, 190, 191
Harwell, M. R., 495
Haug, C. A., 381, 479
Hauser, R., 661
Heim, A. W., 291
Heller, J. I., 380
Helm, R., 61
Helwig, R., 717
Henderson, 470
Henryson, S., 495
Henzel, T. R., 203, 296
Herman, J. L., 121
Hershberger, S., 528
Hetter, R., 550, 554
Heubert, J., 661
Hicks, C. R., 633
Hilgers, T., 311
Hill, I. K., 203
Hill, W. H., 288
Hirsch, T. M., 511, 588
Hiscox, M. D., 261
Hoffman, B., 293
Hofstee, W. K. B., 19
Hofstetter, C., 380, 381, 382, 664, 668
Holland, P. W., 320, 373, 441, 461, 462, 537
Hollenbeck, K., 659, 664
Holzman, G. B., 296
Hoover, H. D., 320, 455, 470, 478, 517
Hopstock, P. J., 657
Hoskens, M., 478, 479
House, A., 718
Huang, C-Y., 10, 191, 195, 196, 749
Hudson, S., 314
Hudson, T., 380
Huff, K. L., 339, 548, 631
Hughes, G. L., 190, 213, 215
Hullin, C. L., 495, 496
Hunt, K. W., 386
Huot, B., 314
Huynh, H., 471, 472, 509

I

Imbens-Bailey, A., 381
Impara, J. C., 19, 31, 242, 247, 406, 684, 721, 742, 750, 751
IMS Global Learning Consortium, 262, 263, 265, 268, 278

International Test Commission (ITC), 45, 726
Irvine, S. H., 591, 750
Isham, S. P., 496, 507
Ishikawa, S., 71

J

Jackenthal, A., 612, 750
Jacobs, A. M., 182
Jacobs, V. S., 385
Jacobson, I., 79
Jaeger, R. M., 237, 238, 248, 249
Jameson, J., 336, 406
Jamison, M., 608
Janowski, J. E., 495
Jarjoura, D., 205
Jeanneret, P. R., 182
Jensen, A. R., 741
Jodoin, M. G., 341, 544
Johnson, M. B., 537
Johnson, R., 61
Johnstone, C. J., 318, 372
Johnstone, D. J., 608, 665, 667, 668
Joint Committee on Testing Practices, 117, 118, 711
Jones, D. H., 489, 555, 588
Jones, M. G., 115
Jones, M., 660
Jones, P. E., 495, 497, 506, 511
Jones, P. L., 386
Joseph, M. J., 196
Joreskog, K. G., 502
Jozefowicz, R. F., 11, 299
Just, M., 386

K

Kahl, S., 57, 251
Kahneman, D., 453
Kalohn, J. C., 206, 544
Kaminski, J., 117, 121
Kane, M. T., 133, 135, 136, 137, 139, 141, 142, 144, 145, 146, 147, 170, 181, 183, 188, 189, 190, 192, 194, 195, 196, 197, 199, 210, 226, 230, 515, 594, 626, 627, 629, 733, 740
Karkee, T., 479
Karns, K., 664
Kaufman, A. S., 533
Kaufman, N. L., 533
Keates, J. A., 499
Kehoe, J., 351, 352, 353, 354, 355
Kelderman, H., 583, 588
Keller, L. A., 353
Keyser, D. J., 727
Khaliq, S. N., 343
Kiely, G., 297
Kilminster, S., 20
Kim, S., 479, 520
Kim-Boscardin, C., 381

King, J., 386
Kingsbury, C., 183, 190, 194
Kingsbury, G. G., 544, 591
Kingston, N. M., 251, 253
Kintsch, W., 380
Kiplinger, V. L., 381
Kirsch, I., 336
Klare, G. R., 385
Klein, S. P., 162, 205
Knapp, J., 186, 187
Knapp, L., 186, 187
Kohn, A., 747
Kolen, M. J., 13, 20, 150, 205, 289, 455, 458, 463, 469, 470, 471, 475, 476, 477, 478, 479, 480, 495, 496, 515, 516, 517, 519, 520, 518, 578, 588
Kong, A., 352
Konitzer, R., 61
Koons, H., 248
Kopriva, R., 664, 668
Koretz, D., 116, 372, 664
Kostin, I., 406, 418
Kramer, G. A., 206
Krathwohl, D. R., 288
Kromrey, J. D., 495, 501, 506, 511, 518
Kruglov, L., 402, 504
Krypsin, W. J., 445
Kubiak, A., 458
Kucera, H., 385, 388, 391
Kulik, C. C., 121
Kulik, J. A., 121
Kupin, J., 330, 337
Kyllonen, P. C., 591, 750

L

LaDuca, A., 182, 185, 191, 203, 296
LaFloch, K. C., 184, 194
LaHart, C., 305, 331
Landy, F. J., 192, 213, 215
Lane, S., 632
Langley, J., 667
Larsen, S. C., 386
Larsen-Freeman, D., 386, 387, 388
Larson, C., 182
Larson, G. E., 528
Lazarus, S. S., 381, 658, 659, 664, 669
Leacock, C., 548
Leary, L. F., 109
Lee, O. K., 478
Lehmann, I. J., 12
Lemann, N., 118
Lemke, J. L., 387, 389
Lennon, M. L., 612, 750
Lennon, R. T., 510
Leon, S., 380
Leung, S. W., 187
Levine, E. L., 182, 189, 190, 198, 202, 211
Levine, H. S., 536
Lewis, C., 437, 478, 479, 509, 537, 544, 554, 592

Lewis, D. M., 246, 247
Lezak, M. D., 533
Li, H. H., 502
Li, X., 588, 658
Lieska, N. G., 19, 242, 243
Linacre, J. M., 495, 535, 536, 578, 583
Lindquist, E. F., 304
Linn, R. L., 116, 117, 118, 120, 121, 135, 151, 230, 306, 310, 324, 362, 378, 379, 447, 661, 718, 745
Lissak, R. I., 495
Lissitz, R. W., 471, 472
Liu, J., 454
Liu, K., 632, 664
Liverman, M. R., 721
Livingston, S. A., 231, 248, 249, 250, 437, 455, 509, 519, 520
Lloyd, C. A., 667
Loevinger, J., 141, 144, 151, 748
Lohman, D. F., 148, 535, 744
Lomax, R. G., 121
Loo, R., 495
Loomis, S., 401
Lord, F. M., 29, 296, 380, 381, 382, 385, 386, 453, 456, 460, 461, 462, 495, 496, 499, 500, 528, 550, 555, 560, 576, 578, 580, 664, 668, 747
Lorge, I.., 402, 504
Loyd, B. H., 478
Luecht, R. M., 511, 512, 544, 583, 588, 589, 590, 592, 594
Lugg, C. A., 720
Lukas, J. F., 449

M

MacDonald, R. P., 386, 453
MacGinitie, W. H., 385
MacRury, K., 320
Madaus, G. F., 121, 728
Madsen, D. H., 537
Maihoff, N. A., 381
Malouf, D. B., 339
Marcu, D., 548
Marelli, A. E., 350, 351, 354
Margolis, M. J., 338
Markman, A. B., 63
Markwell, S. J., 206
Marsella, J., 311
Marshall, J. L., 509
Martin, J. R., 386
Martin, J. T., 340
Martinez, M. E., 305, 330
Marzano, R. J., 166
Masters, G. N., 478, 499, 500, 503, 505
Mather, N., 533
Mayfield, M. S., 192
McBride, J. R., 262, 340, 476, 555
McCaffrey, D., 116
McCann, S. J. H., 109
McCormick, E. J., 182, 185

McDonald, R. P., 495, 498, 500, 502, 511
McGrew, K. S., 533, 537
McGuire, C., 182
McKinley, D.W., 17
McShane, F., 192
McShane, T. D., 352
Mecham, R. C., 182
Meehl, P. E., 134, 140, 151, 527, 530
Mehrens, W. A., 12, 117, 124, 125, 728, 746
Meijer, R., 751
Melican, G. J., 458
Mental Measurements Yearbook (MMY), 727
Merriam-Websters Collegiate Dictionary, 618
Messick, S., 23, 62, 74, 92, 118, 135, 141, 142, 148, 151, 170, 173, 176, 204, 205, 206, 287, 289, 304, 330, 374, 378, 383, 447, 449, 450, 472, 488, 489, 490, 491, 531, 532, 626, 740, 743, 746, 748
Mestre, J. P., 387
Michael, W. B., 352
Microsoft Corporation, 335
Microsoft Manual of Style for Technical Publications, 612
Miller, G. E., 182, 202
Miller, N., 668
Miller, L. J., 528, 530, 532, 537
Millman, J., 4, 16, 201, 202, 203, 305, 461, 493, 494, 495, 496, 510, 511
Mills, C. N., 546, 571
Mills, L., 355
Milne, N. V., 665
Mirocha, J., 380
Mislevy, R. J., 61, 66, 72, 79, 82, 381, 401, 406, 449, 462, 496, 512, 531, 578, 593
Mitzel, H. C., 246, 247
Miyoshi, J., 381
Moore, M., 339
Morgeson, F. P., 185, 192, 211
Morley, M., 336, 407, 750
Morris, P., 310
Morrison, E. J., 142
Morse, A. B., 658, 659
Moshinsky, A., 406
Moss, P., 133, 310
Mosteller, F., 352, 555
M-Tech, 276
Mueller, D. J., 353
Muncer, S. J., 609
Munson, S. M., 536
Muraki, E., 478, 512, 531, 578
Murphy, E., 309
Murray-Ward, M., 262
Myford, C., 747

N

Nanda, H., 142, 379
National Assessment Governing Board (NAGB), 30, 163, 166

National Assessment of Educational Progress (NAEP), 163
National Association of Elementary School Principals (NAESP), 726
National Association of Secondary School Principals (NASSP), 726
National Center for Fair & Open Testing, 293
National Commission for Certifying Agencies (NCCA), 728
National Conference of Examiners for Engineering and Surveying, 202, 203
National Council of Architectural Registration Boards, 202
National Council of Teachers of Mathematics, 157, 172
National Council on Measurement in Education (NCME), 737
National Education Association (NEA), 27, 726
National Education Goals Panel (NEGP), 680
National Organization for Competency Assurance (NOCA), 728
National Research Council (NRC), 69, 162, 166, 157, 159, 160, 165, 172
Nedelsky, L., 231, 243, 245
Neely, D. L., 109
Neisworth, J. T., 536
Nering, M., 112, 399, 546, 553
Nevo, B., 495, 496, 506, 507, 511
Newble, M., 20
Newman, F. M., 134, 182, 187, 189, 190, 215
Nielsen, D., 140
Nisbet, J., 609
Nitko, A. J., 306, 469, 472
No Child Left Behind (NCLB), 394, 469, 657, 721
Norcini, J. J., 19, 20, 355
Novick, M. R., 362, 499, 508, 560, 747
Nungester, R., 544, 592

O

Octo Barnett, G., 352
Ohlsson, S., 148
Olbrei, I., 386
Olsen, K., 667
Orlando, M., 500
Orr, E. W., 386
Ortiz, S. O., 533
Osterlind, S. J., 201, 202, 203, 305, 306, 318
Owen, D., 741

P

PADI Research Group, 71
Page, G., 293
Palmer, A. S., 68
Park, K., 333
Parker, R. M., 386
Parkes, J., 752

Parshall, C. G., 266, 332, 493, 495, 501, 507, 518, 544, 548, 555, 561, 562, 565, 566, 567, 570
Pashley, P. J., 266, 332, 548
Patz, R. J., 246, 247, 478
Pauley, A., 387
Pearlman, M., 205, 511
Perchonock, E., 386
Perlman, C., 470
Petersen, N. S., 205, 453, 455, 463, 464, 470, 474, 477, 517, 518
Philips, S. E., 713
Pitoniak, M. J., 631
Plake, B. S., 19, 242, 243, 247, 253, 406, 750, 751
Plummer, J., 380
Pomplun, M., 537
Popham, W. J., 116, 117, 120, 121, 124, 125, 162, 201, 306, 627, 633, 728
Popper, K. R., 136
Porter, T., 31, 133
Powers, D. E., 117, 118, 102, 103, 405
Pownall, M. T., 355
Prekeges, J. L., 203
Prien, E. P., 213, 215
Publication Manual of the American Psychological Association, 350, 618
Pulton, E. C., 609
Pyburn, K. M., 728

Q

Quaintance, M. K., 182, 188, 192, 202, 204, 215
Quardt, D., 337
Quellmalz, E., 310
Quenemoen, R. F., 669
Quereshi, M. Y., 404
QuestionMark, 113

R

Rabinowitz, S., 345
Rachor, R. E., 353
Raible, M. D., 19, 242, 243
Rajaratnam, N., 142, 379
Rakel, R., 197
Ramsey, P., 360
Rasch, G., 478, 499, 528, 535, 577
Ravitch, D., 364, 365, 367, 368
Raymond, M. R., 10, 181, 183, 185, 186, 189, 190, 191, 192, 194, 195, 196, 204, 209, 210, 215, 217, 220, 233
Reckase, M. D., 234, 591
Ree, M. J., 340
Reese, L. M., 552, 553, 592
Reeves, D. B., 125
Reid, J. B., 233
Reise, S. P., 478, 528, 536, 537, 544
Reshetar, R. A., 355
Resnick, L.B., 31, 68

Reusser, K., 380
Rhode Island Department of Education, 667
Rhodes, N. C., 386
Rice Jr., W. K., 470
Richardson, M., 140
Richman, B., 388
Riley, M. S., 380
Rivera, C., 658, 664
Riverside Publishing, 715
Rizavi, S., 400, 401, 507
Robelen, E. W., 664
Roberts, T., 20
Robin, F., 553
Roccas, S., 406
Rock, D. A., 117, 305, 310, 331, 337
Rodriguez, M. C., 10, 11, 94, 95, 289, 290, 291, 292, 296, 306, 350, 445, 749
Rogers, H. J., 416, 453, 478
Rogers, J., 354, 500, 544
Rogers, W. T., 116
Roid, G. H., 296, 299, 445, 528, 529, 530, 532, 533, 534, 535, 536, 537, 538, 539, 741, 750
Rosenfeld, M., 187, 192, 194
Ross, L. P., 338
Rothery, A., 387
Rothman, R., 31
Rottenberg, C., 116, 121
Royer, J. M., 631
Rozeboom, W., 135, 151
Rozek-Tedesco, M., 659
Ruch, G. M., 727
Rudner, L., 262, 495, 501, 502, 506
Ruf, D., 531
Rumbaugh, J., 79
Rupp, A. A., 406
Rush, A., 61
Ryan, J. J., 117
Ryan, J. M., 660, 666, 680

S

Sabin, W., 618
Sackett, P. R., 310
Salomon, G., 206
Salvia, J., 379
Samejima, F., 478, 555
Sampers, J., 528, 532, 535, 537
Sanchez, J. I., 189, 190, 195, 197, 198
Sandberg, J. A. C., 213
Sanders, N. M., 121
Sanders, P. F., 511
Sandoval, J., 383
Sands, W. A., 262, 555
Sarnacki, R. E., 116
Savin, H. B., 386
Sawyer, N. S., 203
Sax, G., 352
Sayer, A. G. 535

Scarpati, S., 658
Schachter, P., 387
Schaefer, L., 204
Schmeiser, C. B., 4, 117, 118, 122, 353
Schmitt, A. P., 320
Schneider, C., 471
Schnike, D., 215
Schrader, W. B., 453
Schrock, T. J., 353
Schulz, E. M., 470, 478
Schum, D. A., 61, 62, 63
Schuwirth, L. W., 350, 548, 570
Schwartz, M., 618
Scott, D., 718
Scott, W., 133
Scruggs, T. E., 121
Seashore, H. G., 528
Sebrechts, M. M., 335, 341, 345
Seddon, G. M., 206
Shafer, L., 658
Shavelson, R. J., 142, 166, 379
Shea, J. A., 19, 20
Shealy, R. T., 440
Sheehan, K. M., 296, 401, 406, 407, 592, 593, 544, 750
Sheinker, A., 661
Shen, L., 478
Shepard, L. A., 121, 132, 133, 135, 136, 141, 145, 361, 362, 363
Shimberg, B., 181, 192
Shin, S.-H., 470
Shindoll, R. R., 266, 296
Shriner, J. G., 667
Shriver, K. A., 609
Shuard, H., 387
Shulman, L. S., 206
Shyu, C.-Y., 470
Sia, J. K., 658
Siegler, R. S., 68
Silverstein, B., 662
Silverstein, M., 71
Simon, H. A., 63, 85
Simon, T., 540
Sireci, S. G., 105, 106, 332, 339, 343, 353, 400, 401, 495, 507, 548, 658, 664, 665
Slater, S., 503, 684
Slattery, J. B., 31
Slaughter, R. C., 182, 215
Slobin, D. I., 386
Smith, M. L., 115, 116, 121, 181, 247
Smith, R. L., 503, 504, 592
Smith, R. W., 495, 502, 506, 511, 512, 746, 750
Snow, R. E., 148
Society for Industrial and Organization Psychology (SIOP), 726
Solano-Flores, G., 166
Sorbom, D., 502
Spandel, V., 314
Spanos, G., 386, 387, 389

Sprafka, S. A., 206
Spray, J. A., 10, 191, 195, 196, 215, 217, 218, 591, 544, 749
Springston, F. J., 109
Stage, F. K., 665
Staples, W. I., 296
Stecher, B. M., 116, 120, 121
Steffen, M., 499, 546, 549, 553, 571
Steinberg, L. S., 61, 69, 82, 440, 450
Stephenson, T. G., 657
Sternberg, R. J., 744
Steven, C., 615
Stevens, R., 668
Stiggins, R. J., 306, 314
Stocking, M. L., 78, 205, 496, 511, 549, 550, 553, 554, 588, 590, 592
Stodden, R., 660
Stone, C. A., 632
Stone, M. H., 495, 499, 505, 511
Stout, W., 440, 502
Strunk, W., 350
Subkoviak, M. J., 165, 495, 496, 509
Surgue, B., 744
Swaminathan, H., 262, 400, 401, 416, 417, 453, 478, 500, 507, 508, 509, 536, 544, 544, 576, 578, 588
Swanson, D. B., 293, 297
Swanson, E., 350
Swanson, L., 78, 205, 511, 550, 552, 588, 590
Sweeney, K., 251
Sweetland, R. C., 727
Swineford, F., 495
Swinton, S. S., 118
Syder, F. H., 387
Sykes, R. C., 555
Sympson, J. B., 340, 550, 554

T

Tamassia, C., 333
Tanenbaum, A. S., 273, 277
Tang, K. L., 502
Tangen, K., 140
Taranath, S. N., 182, 196
Tate, R., 748
Taylor, C., 336, 342
Taylor, D. D., 203
Teegarden, B., 61
Templeton, B., 296
Tennant, A., 495
Terman, L. M., 540
Texas Education Agency, 713
Thayer, D. T., 373, 437
Thayn, K. S., 495, 506
Thissen, D., 16, 17, 297, 312, 330, 341, 440, 496, 500, 512, 531, 559
Thomas, L., 559
Thommason, G., 554

Thompson, D. R., 609, 658, 659, 662, 664, 665, 667, 668, 669
Thompson, R. J., 535
Thompson, S. J., 318, 339, 372, 381
Thompson, S., 602, 603, 609
Thorndike, R. L., 306, 361, 402, 504, 747
Thornton, R. F., 192
Thou shall be diligent, Bible proofreaders believe, 616
Thuenissen, T. J. J. M., 511
Thurlow, M. L., 318, 339, 372, 381, 539, 656, 657, 658, 659, 662, 664, 665, 666, 667, 668, 669, 718
Thurstone, L. L., 451
Tillers, P., 61, 63
Tindal, G., 658, 659, 664, 665, 666
Tong, Y., 470, 477
Toulmin, S. E., 62, 70
Traub, R. E., 320, 501
Trenholme, B., 386
Tretiak, R., 385
Trevisan, M. S., 352
Trusheim, D., 741
Tsai, T., 516
Tucker, C., 680
Tufte, E. R., 603, 607
Tukey, J., 555
Turner, R., 333
Tversky, A., 453, 586

U

Umer, J., 262
Unicode Consortium, 273
United States Copyright Office, 622
United States Department of Education, 156, 172, 656, 659, 660
University of Chicago Press Staff, 350, 602

V

Vale, C. D., 520, 570, 571
van der Linden, W. J., 15, 16, 262, 499, 511, 531, 536, 537, 538, 552, 553, 555, 583, 588, 591, 592, 594
van der Vleuten, C. P. M., 350
van de Vijver, F. J. R., 501
VanLehn, K., 71
vanSomeron, M.W., 213
Veal, L., 314
Veldkamp, B. P., 591
Verschaffel, L., 380
Verschoor, A. J., 511
Violato, C., 353
Vlissides, J., 61
von Davier, A. A., 462
Vos, H. J., 592
Vranek, J. B., 31
Vu, N. V., 206
Vukmirovic, Z., 471

W

Wainer, H., 16, 17, 292, 297, 312, 330, 341, 440, 496, 501, 531, 537, 555, 559
Wakin, M., 382
Walker, C. M., 749
Walker, G., 333, 335, 336
Walker, M. E., 453
Wang, M. D., 386
Wang, N., 215, 218
Wang, T., 551
Wang, X., 312, 385
Ward, W.C., 176, 262, 305, 331
Waters, B. K., 262, 555
Watts, K. P., 291
Watts, L., 609
Way, W. D., 549, 720, 721
Webb, N. L., 142, 157, 162, 163, 166, 206
Webb, N. M., 379
Webster's Dictionary of English Usage, 618
Webster's Third New International Dictionary, Unabridged, 618
Weimer, R., 380
Weiss, D. J., 340, 550, 591
Weiten, W., 353
Welch, C., 4, 320
Wellman, R. P., 61
Wells, P. C., 203
Wendler, C. LW, 445
Wertsch, J. V., 160
Wesman, A. G., 528
Whelan, G. P., 17
White, E. B., 350
White, E. M., 314
White, J. L., 539
White, K. P., 121, 204, 354
Whitely, S. E., 495, 511
Whitney, D. R., 353, 402
Wightman, L., 205
Wigmore, J. H., 62, 71
Wilcox, R., 583
Wiley, A., 353
Wiley, D. E., 657
Wilkinson, T., 20
Williams, C. O., 194
Willingham, W. W., 371, 372
Willoughby, T. L., 404
Wilson, D., 502
Wilson, W. L., 115, 125, 181, 190, 191
Wingersky, M., 593
Winter, P. C., 668
Wise, L. L., 476
Wise, S. L., 495, 501
Witt, E. A., 215
Wolfe, E. W., 747
Wood, R., 157, 502
Woodcock, R. W., 533, 536, 537
World-Wide Web Consortium, 79

Wright, B. D., 470, 495, 499, 500, 501, 503, 505, 511, 535, 536
Wu, I. L., 588

X

Xing, D., 400, 401, 507

Y

Yao, L., 478, 479
Yarnold, P. R., 534
Yell, M. L., 659
Yen, W. M., 379, 478, 479, 555
Yi, Q., 501, 551
Ying, Z., 551
Young, M. J., 265, 273
Youtz, C., 352
Ysseldyke, J., 379, 539, 656, 661, 662, 665, 666, 718

Z

Zachisson, B., 609
Zakrzewski, S., 615
Zara, A. R., 544
Zenisky, A. L., 105, 106, 332, 548
Zieky, M. J., 19, 231, 237, 248, 249, 250, 361, 374, 455, 496, 507
Zimowski, M., 512, 531, 536, 578, 583
Zipf, G. K., 385
Zwick, R., 118

Subject Index

A

Abilities, 527–528
Ability test, 527–542
    Planning, 529–532
    Pragmatics, 538–540
    Psychometrics, 534–538
    Research, 532–534
Achievement tests, 7, 487
    Large-scale tests, 446
    Small-scale tests, 487, 493–494,
Accommodations/modifications, 539, 653–673
    Changing role, 660–661
    Considerations for administration, 669–670
    Definitions, 657–659
    Implementation issues, 667–668
    Law, 659–660
    Policy variations, 662–664
    Validity research, 664–667
American College Testing Program (ACT), 117
Americans with Disabilities Act (ADA), 5, 16
Architectural Registration Exam, 107

B

Braindump, 104

C

Candidate handbook, 643–644
Certification examinations, 8
Certified Public Accountants Examination, 107, 338–339
Cheating (see fraud), 91–94
Classical test theory, 498–500
Code of Fair Testing Practices in Education, 118, 319, 711–714
Cognitive processes, 30
Computer-based tests, 111–112, 612–613, 615–616, 720–721
Computerized adaptive testing (CAT), 543–573
    Administration, 544–546
    Conceptual assessment framework, 75–77
    Considerations for using, 569–571
    Exposure control in CAT, 553–554
    Implementing, 556–569
    Methods, 546–556
Construct under representation, 173, 330, 627–630, 743, 748–749
Constructed-response item (Also Performance item), 32, 303–327
    Authentic, 107
    Definitions of, 305
    Development of, 309–310
    Field testing, 321–323
    General strategies for combating fraud, 102–104
    Prompt development, 306–307, 311
    Protocols, 47
    Reviews, 314–321
    Rubric development, 33, 312–314
        Analytical, 316–317
        Holistic, 315
    Scoring, 16–18, 33–34, 507–508, 719–720
    Technical considerations, 312
    Test assembly, 321–325
    Topic selection, 310–312
Constructed-response item formats, 304–305, 448–450
    Completion, 106–107, 337
    Complex problem-solving item, 117
    Computer-based essay, 338
    Corrections and substitutions, 337
    Formulating hypotheses, 337–338
    Graphical modeling, 337, 338
    Problem-solving vignette, 338–339
    Short answer and fill-in blanks items, 104

773

Construct-irrelevant variance (CIV) (also, bias, contaminants, nuisance variable, extraneous variable, systematic error), 5, 12, 14, 17, 18, 29, 47, 92, 93, 104, 124, 144, 289, 330–331, 339, 342, 345, 363, 366–367, 374, 377–380, 383–384, 393, 630–634, 640–641, 662, 743, 746–748

Content identification, 7–8, 155–180, 447–448, 552–553
- Adequacy of coverage of content domain, 31
- Alignment, 163–171
- Attributes, 171–175
- Content coverage, 29–30
- Content definition, 7–8, 28–29
- Content model, 133–134
- Content specifications, 157–160
- Curricular alignment, 31, 117
- Delineation of the construct or domain to be measured, 28–29
- Learning expectations, 161–162
- Other content attributes in content specifications, 171–175
- State-adopted content, 31
- Test specifications, 175–179

Content-related validity evidence, 31, 139–142, 149–150, 447–448, 744
- Construct model, 134
- Content model, 133–135
- Criterion model, 133
- Curricular alignment, 31, 117
- Evolving role, 132–135
- Standardized measures, 146–147
- Target scores, 147–148
- Universe scores, 147–148

Contracting for testing services, 39–59
- Context description, 57–58
- Criteria used in evaluating proposals, 53
- Describe all requirements of request for proposal, 46–47
- Determine adequacy of funding, 44
- Evaluating proposals, 46, 52–56
- Identify potential vendors, 51–52
- Management plan and progress reporting, 51
- Negotiating requirements and costs, 46
- Negotiating the contract, 56–58
- Negotiation strategies, RFPs, 56–57
- Performance/bid bonds and penalty/liquidated damage clauses, 46
- Planning, 40–43
- Procurement process, 44–45
- Project schedule, 50
- Request for Proposals (RFP), 43–52
- Subcontracting work, 45
- Technical proposal, 54

Council of Chief State School Officers, 39
Criterion-referenced scale score, 36, 575

D

Data forensics, 92
Decision theory, 229–238, 501–502, 583–587

False-negative decision, 230
False-positive decision, 230
Dimensionality, 502, 534, 558–559
Differential item functioning (DIF), 35, 320, 373–374, 423, 439
Documentation (see technical reporting)

E

Education Leaders Council, 39
Educational Measurement, 4
English language learners (ELLs), 377, 380–382, 653, 654, 657
Equating, 18, 514–517
- Choosing a method, 461–464, 475–476, 480, 519–520
- Common item design, 13, 410–411, 472–474, 518
- Common person design, 474–475, 517–518
- Data collection, 517
- Embedded items, 459–460
- Equipercentile design, 519–520
- Equivalent groups design, 476
- Hieronymous scaling, 477
- Item response theory scaling, 478–480
- Linear design, 520
- Over time, 515–516
- Thurstone absolute scaling, 477–478
- True-score equating design, 520

Equity, inclusiveness, and fairness, 172–173
Evaluating tests, 725–738
- Accreditation, 728–729
- Commercially available tests, 729–731
- Independent evaluation, 726–728
- Professional standards, 726
- Proprietary tests, 731–734

Evidence-centered assessment design, 61–90, 449–450
- Conceptual assessment framework, 75–76
- Construct-centered approach, 62
- Domain analysis, 67–70
- Domain modeling, 70–75
- Evidence, 77–85
- Knowledge representations, 63, 66
- Layers, 66–85
- Open System Interconnection reference model, 65
- Student model, 77
- Task model, 78

F

Fairness review, 319–320, 359–376
- Guidelines, 364–370
- History, 360–361
- Meanings, 361–363
- Procedures, 370–371

FairTest, 293
Field testing (item tryout), 32, 48, 321–323, 459–460, 461

Fraud, 91–114
    Computer-based test, 105–107, 111–112
    Item development strategies for combating, 94–102, 113–114
    Multiple versions and multiple forms, 108–111
    Performance test, 102–105
    Piracy of items, 93–94
    Randomly-ordered response choices, 108
    Test assembly strategies, 105–107
    Types, 93–94

G

Graduate Management Admissions Council, 103
Graduate Management Admissions Test, 117
Graduate Record Examination, 117, 341

H

How students learn, 159–160

I

Innovative computer-based item formats, 329–347
    Future of, 344–345
    Practical issues, 342–344
    Research, 339–342
Intellectual property and test security, 121–122
Item, 263–268, 387, 528–529
    Development, 10–12, 31–32, 47
    Editing, 32, 349–350, 353–355
    Estimated cost, 22, 275
    Exposure, 553–554
    Review, 32
    Selection, 35
    Strategies to combat fraud, 94–113
Item analysis, 18, 34–35, 399–420, 421–441, 537
    Factors affecting, 437–438
    Graphical procedures, 424–427
    Judgmental procedures, 400–401
        Anchor-based, 411
        Item-mapping, 411
    Research, 408–415
Item banking, 21–22, 261–284, 548–549, 562–567
    Bankers, 271–277
    Evaluation, 591
    History, 261–263
    Inventory, 457–458
    Organization, 268–271
    Software, 284–285
Item calibration, 469, 496–497, 562–566, 577–579, 591
    With no item response data, 503–505
    With sample sizes up to 100, 505–506
    With sample sizes from 100 to 200, 506–507
    With sample sizes more than 200, 508

Item difficulty, 422, 431–432, 451
    Anchor-based method, 399–420
    Item-mapping method, 411
    Judgmental estimation, 401–407
        Review of research, 401–408
Item discrimination, 422–423, 432–436, 451, 577–583
    At a point, 434–435
    Biserial, 433–434
    Delta index, 450
    Factors affecting estimation, 437–439
    Item response curves, 421, 423–424, 427–432, 440–441
    Point-biserial, 433–434
Item formats, 32, 331–332, 448–450, 547–548
    Complex problem solving, 107
    Computer-based items, 105–106, 329–347
    Traditional vs. innovative, 330–331
Item generation, technology of, 296–297
    Item forms, 533
    Item modeling, 296
    Item shells, 296
    Item variants/clones, 112–113
Item information function, 456, 579–581
Item response theory, 421, 499–501, 559–560, 576–583
Item tryouts (see field testing)
Item-writer training, 11–12, 308–309
Item-writing guidelines, 33, 294, 350–353

J

Job analysis (Also practice analysis, task analysis), 7, 181–220, 400–401
    Data analysis of ratings, 194–201
    Task inventory questionnaires, 183–194
    Methods, 182–194
    Test specifications, 201–208
    Transforming ratings to test specifications, 208–220

K

Key balance of options, 13

L

Language issues in tests, 377–394
    Language as source of construct-irrelevant variance (CIV), 383–384
    Theoretical framework, 377–384
    Linguistic features of test that produce CIV, 385–393
Large-scale testing, 445–467, 741
    Considerations, 446–450
    Maintenance, 460–466
    Operational, 456–460
    Psychometrics, 450–456
Law School Admission Test, 117

Linguistic modification of a test, 387–390, 393
    Complexity, 377, 378
    Comprehension, 385–393
    Features of test items, 385–387
    Modifying language features of items, 380–382
    Practical implications, 384–385

M

Medical College Admissions Test, 117
Multiple-choice item (See selected-response item)
Multiple-choice item formats (See selected-response item formats)

N

National Assessment of Educational Progress, 30, 401
National Board of Medical Examiners, 338
National Council of Architectural Registration Boards, 338
National Council on Measurement in Education, xii, 27, 100, 101
National Research Council, 69
National Science Foundation, 66
No Child Left Behind Act of 2001, 120, 156, 172, 361
Norm-referenced scale score, 35–36

P

Performance items (see Constructed-response items)
Practice analysis (see Job analysis)
Pretesting (see Field testing)
    Properties, 267–268
    Purpose, 227–228

Q

Quality control, 14–15, 49

R

Reliability, 36–37, 733
    Test length, 560–561
    Pass/fail, 508–509
    Interrater agreement (reliability), 719–720
Responsibilities of test users in school settings, 121–124
Reviewing test items, 314–321, 353–354

S

Scaling, 35–36, 463–464, 466
    Growth, change, 471, 535–537
    Models, 534–535

Score reports, 20–21, 37, 677–710, 721–722
    Basic information, 681–690
    Content, 705–706
    Determining the scale to report, 454–455
    Format, 706–708
    Research, 684–689
    South Carolina study, 690–705
Security issues, 14, 15, 49, 94–113, 460, 570–571, 643, 648–649
Selected-response item, 32, 288–299, 448–450
    Anatomy of, 295
    Difficulty of development, 292–293
    Flawed items, 34–35, 290
    General strategies, 95–103
    Guessing, 291
    Number of options, 291–292
    Principles of effective item writing, 11, 294, 350–353
    Reviews, 353–355, 359–376
    Strengths and limitations, 289–291
Selected-response item formats, 10, 293–296
    Extended multiple-choice, 333
    Drag-and-connect, 335
    Drag-and-drop item, 106
    Extended matching items, 297–299
    Formulating hypotheses, 337–338
    Inserting text, 336–337
    Item set, (Also known as testlet and context-dependent item set), 297
    Multiple selection, 333–334
    Multiple-choice, 293, 295–296
    Multiple true/false item, 101
    Ordering information, 335
    Problem solving vignette, 338–339
    Scoring, 451–454, 554–555, 561–562
    Select and classify, 335–336
    Specifying relationships, 334–335
Small-scale testing, 487–525
    Gathering pretest data, 493–496
    Modeling items and tests, 496–509
    Assembling parallel forms, 509–514
Special need populations, 653–673
    Accommodations and modifications, 657–659
    Changing role of accommodation, 660–661
    Challenges for accommodation, 661–668
    Definition, 656–657
    Laws, 659–660
    Universally designed tests, 668–669
Standard setting, 18–20, 226–227, 720
    Angoff method, 239–242
    Beuk method, 254–255
    Body of work method, 250–253
    Bookmark method, 246–248
    Borderline examinee, definition, 19
    Borderline group method, 20, 250
    Common considerations, 229–238
    Contrasting groups method, 19, 248–249
    Cut score (Passing score), 18–20, 225–256, 253–254
    Hofstee method, 255–256
    Nedelsky method, 243–246

Relative and absolute standard-setting methods, 19
Standard-setting standards, 228–229
Yes/No method, 242–243
Standardization, 15, 634–635, 639
Standardized measures of observable attributes, 146–147
Standards for Educational and Psychological Testing, x, 5, 7, 10, 16, 20, 23, 27–38, 45, 62, 115, 117, 118–119, 121–123, 126, 131, 156, 157, 175–176, 181, 189, 190, 201, 205, 206, 227–229, 238, 287, 303, 305, 312, 314, 321, 326, 340, 344, 354, 355, 360, 361, 375, 377, 378, 446, 447, 470, 488–492, 558, 602, 625–626, 634–639, 661, 667, 678–680, 709, 711–713, 722, 726, 729, 739, 744

T

Technical reporting, 22–23, 711–723
Description of the testing program, 716
Technical characteristics, 716–718
Technical requirements, 49–50
Validity evidence, 718–719
Test administration, 15–16, 34, 625–652
Accommodations/modifications, 539, 669–670
Computerized adaptive, 543–546
Linear, 543
Multilevel/multistage, 544
Threats to validity, 626–634
Training, 637–638
Test construction 3, 278–282, 323–325
Test design and assembly, 12–14, 146–147, 460–461, 537–538
Alternatives, 591–592
Automated test assembly, 587–590
Computerized adaptive tests, 549–554, 561–562
Evaluating test designs, 567–569
Parallel forms (alternate forms), 112–113, 509–514
Target population, 447
Test creation, 278–282
Using test specifications, 510
Vertical scales, 472–476
Test development, 3, 5
Item banking, 21–22
Planning, 4–6
Test content, 7–8
Test specifications, 9–10
Item development, 10–12
Technical report, 22–23
Test design, 12–14, 35–36
Test production, 14–15
Test administration, 15–16
Test scoring, 16–18
Twelve steps for effective, 5
Reporting test results, 20–21
Setting passing (cut) scores, 18–20
Test information function, 455–456, 550–552, 583–587, 587–591
Test of English as a Foreign Language, 342

Test preparation, 115, 116, 122–124
Coaching, 116
College admission testing, 117–120
K-12 testing, 120–121
Research directions for test preparation, 124–126
Test production, 14–15, 599–623
Perspective, 599–602
Format, 602–613
Production, 614–616
Quality control, 616–622
Test specifications, 9–10, 175–179, 201–205, 546–547, 556–559
Cognitive processes, 30–31
Content, 29–30
Documentation of test specifications, 31
Effects of item response theory on test specifications, 559–560
Evaluation of test specifications, 31
Nature and use, 201–208
Practice analysis to test specifications, 208–220
Test standards sources, 27–28, 117, 714, 726
Test study guides, 116
Test wiseness, 116
Twelve steps of effective test development, 5

U

United States Army Alpha Test, 293
Universally designed assessments, 318–319, 656, 668–669

V

Validation, 143–146, 626
Validity, 28, 131–132, 488–489, 490–492, 626–627, 678–680, 715–716, 739–740, 740–741
Argument, 62, 135–136, 147
Evaluating the proposed interpretive argument, 138–139
Developing and evaluating an interpretive argument, 136–139
Developing the test and the interpretive argument, 137–138
Falsify the validity argument, 136
Extrapolations from the universe scores to target scores, 147–148
Generalization inference, 144–145
Inferences from universe scores to target scores, 142
Scoring inference, 143–144
Target domains, 140–141
Measurement procedures and universe of generalization, 141–142
Validity threats, 626–634, 743
Validity research, 532–534, 664–667, 721–722, 740
Validity study, 740
Contexts, 741–743
Types, 743–752

Validity evidence, 132–135, 639–641, 718–719
　Comparability and scaling, 744–745
　Content-related, 139–142, 149–150, 744
　Consequential, 746
　Construct-irrelevant variance, 746–748
　Construct underrepresentation, 748–749
　Criterion-related, 746
　Documentation, 711–723, 718–719
　Item quality, 744
　Negative validity evidence, 136
　Reliability, 745
　Standard setting, 745
Vertical scaling, 469–485
　Advice for developing, 482–484
　Choosing a method, 480
　Evaluating results, 480–482
　Grade to grade growth, 471
　Growth, 471
　Test content and domain definition, 471

LB3051 .H31987 2006
Handbook of test development